THE HISTORY AND ANTIQUITIES OF THE PARISH OF DARLINGTON

By
W. Hylton Dyer Longstaffe, F.S.A.

With a new Introduction by
Robert Wood

REPUBLISHED PATRICK & SHOTTON 1973
First Published 1854

Republished 1973 by Patrick & Shotton
17 Norton Road
Stockton-on-Tees

ISBN 0 903169 06 1

Printed in Great Britain by
The Scolar Press Limited, Menston, Yorkshire

INTRODUCTION

by ROBERT WOOD

I have for Longstaffe's 'History and Antiquities of Darlington' the same cherished affection as I used to have for the country store of long ago, and for the same reason. In neither were the valuable and useful contents set out to the best advantage, but those who searched diligently enough found all they required and much more than they ever dreamed existed. The unknown and unsuspected treasures brought to light so often distracted the thoughts and delighted the minds of the discoverers that all sense of time was lost, and it frequently required sharp reminders from friends arriving on the scene to bring back the absent-minded pursuers of serendipity blinking into the sunlight.

There is enough meat in this one volume to form the basis of a small library of local history. Too much, in fact, for Longstaffe confesses in his Preface 'I have been compelled at a greatly increased cost of production and occupation of time to crowd as many facts into every page as my type will allow, to avoid remarks, and allow the reader to form his own conclusions.' The author had intended his book to be of a 'light, sketchy and amusing character', but as his researches turned up more and more material he came to realise that the first history written of any place should be a 'magazine of evidences' to which popular writers could turn for facts to bear out their generalities. In other words, his book became a repository of all sorts of scraps of information concerning Darlington, its history, its people, its folklore, and all the multifarious activities which make an ancient town a living organism. What it lacks is any attempt to range these facts to show the development of the various aspects of Darlington life through the ages.

That remark is in no sense a criticism of Longstaffe or his book. Looking back on the local historians who emerged in the first surge of national awakening which marked the early years of the reign of the young Queen Victoria, one is amazed at the youth and enormous industry of the people concerned.

Longstaffe was just 21 years old when the first part of his History was published in 1848. Ord was 33 when he began his History of Cleveland in 1843, yet in each case the books of these two young men appear to be the work of mature minds. They possessed the happy combination of youthful industry and enthusiasm coupled with the sound judgement of men of experience, and as a result produced books which still stand unsurpassed in their particular fields of local history.

It is a remarkable fact that Longstaffe spent only five years of his long life as a resident of Darlington. He was born on 2nd September 1826, at Norton, near Stockton, the eldest of a family of nine. His father was a surgeon who died whilst our author was attending Norton Grammar School, and his son fondly remembered him as a man full of curious information, an illuminator of armorials, a sketcher of flowers, and a careful and meticulous etcher of anatomies. His family tree was closely intertwined with the Hyltons of Durham, the Hiltons of Darlington, and the Gibsons and Lynns of Stranton, near West Hartlepool, so he was deeply immersed in the intimate relationships of many of the eminent families and the local history of south-east Durham.

He left school on the death of his father and was employed in an office at York, but in a short time moved to Thirsk, where he spent three years before coming to Darlington in 1845 as a clerk to Mr. J. S. Peacock, the attorney. He impressed his employer so much with his interest in local history that he, in turn, introduced him to his father-in-law, Francis Mewburn, the Borough Bailiff of Darlington, who had collected an enormous amount of local memoranda which had been of great assistance in the compilation of Brockett's 'Glossary of North Country Words', Ord's 'Cleveland', and Surtees' 'History of Durham'.

Mewburn in his turn introduced this youth of 19 to the leading families of the district and they, attracted by his youthful enthusiasm for history, gave him access to their archives, both private and public. As a result his knowledge of local history increased by leaps and bounds, and in February 1846 he gave a lecture to a crowded audience crammed into the Assembly Room of the Sun Inn on the 'Annals and Characteristics of Darlington'. The interest this lecture evinced and the enthusiasm it aroused among influential people induced him to write his book on the history of Darlington, which, as was usual at that period, first appeared in parts. The periodical it appeared in was The Darlington and Stockton Times and the first part was published in August 1848 when the author was not yet 22 years old. The final portion appeared in 1854.

The book is loosely arranged in six divisions, which are rather oddly named. The first is 'Situation, Name and Waters', the next 'Regal, Noble and Military', which is sub-divided into six chapters; the third is 'Ecclesiastical', the fourth 'Domestic', the fifth 'Transit and Agriculture', and the sixth 'Families and Pedigrees'. Within each of these divisions the text is embellished with copious notes to clarify and extend various details. The whole work is a mine of antiquarian lore set down simply and in many cases without comment.

In 1850 Longstaffe moved to Gateshead and in the following year became the articled pupil of Mr. Kell, Solicitor. He was admitted to full practice in 1857, and in the course of time became a partner and later the owner of the business. He married Margaret, the daughter of Thomas Abbott of Darlington.

When he moved to Gateshead he became a member of the Newcastle Antiquarian Society and in 1855 joined the Surtees Society. He was a founder member of the Northumberland and Durham Archaeological Society. In all these societies his outstanding abilities as an antiquarian and historian were soon recognised and his writings gained for him the eminence he deserved.

He was a welcome guest at Blackwell Hall, the residence of the Allans, whenever he returned to Darlington, and when Mr. R. H. Allan died in 1879 he left his old friend a personal bequest of £500, with a promise of £1,000 more if he agreed to finish Surtees' monumental 'History of Durham', but this he never did.

Longstaffe died on the 4th February 1898, at Gateshead, and was buried in the Old Cemetery, Jesmond Road, Newcastle. He had been living in seclusion for the last few years of his life, and perhaps this is why contemporary newspapers had little to say of the passing of a man who had spent half a century making notable contributions to our knowledge and appreciation of the history and architecture of the North Counry and the characteristics of its citizens.

His 'History of Darlington' may be a difficult book for the reader to get into, and the student may find the rich veins of local lore and legend hard to work, but they must not complain. Here in one volume is practically all that could be dug out of manuscripts and books, indentures and charters, in 1850, concerning Darlington. Longstaffe rifled libraries of books and stacks of deed boxes and archives to extract the rich ore he included in this one volume. All that his readers have to do is to search this book, and although it may take time to find the information they want, they will be amply rewarded.

Darlington has reason to be immensely grateful to the young clerk whose enthusiasm collected together and put down on paper this glorious miscellany of Darlington history. It would not be accurate to describe it as a glowing tapestry depicting Darlington's development through the ages. Perhaps a more fitting and more homely description of it would be 'a many-hued patchwork quilt in which are brought together the colourful fragments of the long story of "Darnton-i-the-dirt" '!

12th January 1973 ROBERT WOOD

W Hylton Longstaffe del. 1849. Cave & Son York

S. CUTHBERT'S COLLEGIATE CHURCH IN DARLINGTON.

This plate is presented by Robert Henry Allan,

of Blackwell Hall, Esqr. J.P., F.S.A.

High Sheriff of the County of Durham.

THE

HISTORY AND ANTIQUITIES

OF

THE PARISH OF

DARLINGTON,

IN THE BISHOPRICK.

BY

W. Hylton Dyer Longstaffe, Esq., F.S.A.

"Enquire, I pray thee, of the former age, and prepare thyself to the search of their fathers: for we are of yesterday, and know nothing.—Shall not they teach thee, and tell thee, and utter words out of their heart."—(*Job*, viii.)

DARLINGTON:
THE PROPRIETORS OF THE DARLINGTON AND STOCKTON TIMES.
LONDON:
J. HENRY PARKER, 377, STRAND; AND J. B. NICHOLS AND SON,
25, PARLIAMENT-STREET.
NEWCASTLE: G. B. RICHARDSON, CLAYTON-STREET-WEST.
1854.

TO

Robert Henry Allan, Esq., F. S. A., D. L.,

OF BLACKWELL HALL,

IN THE PARISH OF DARLINGTON, AND OF BARTON,

IN RICHMONDSHIRE,

ONE OF HER MAJESTY'S JUSTICES OF THE PEACE FOR THE COUNTY OF DURHAM,

AND NORTH RIDING OF YORKSHIRE,

THIS VOLUME,

DEVOTED TO THE HISTORY OF THE PARISH IN WHICH HE IS

THE MOST EXTENSIVE LANDOWNER,

AND THE VERY GROUNDWORK OF WHICH HAS BEEN FURNISHED BY HIS

LARGE COLLECTION OF ARCHIVES,

IS,

FROM FEELINGS OF THE DEEPEST GRATITUDE

FOR HIS UNIFORM GENEROSITY,

DEDICATED.

PREFACE.

In presenting my patrons the conclusion of my labours, I have to apologise for that delay in their appearance which is so often and unavoidably the case in topographical works. It has greatly added to my facilities for the pictorial illustration and elaboration of my materials, but it is a grief to me when I reflect upon the number of those subscribers who looked upon my pursuits with the eye of kindness, and who are now beyond the sphere in which I could have laid their results before them. Death has laid his cold touch on some I looked up to, with the reverence due to the aristocracy of talent. Sir Robert Peel, Sir Cuthbert Sharp, and Colonel William Havelock, K. H., giants all in diverse walks, are silent and in stillness. My dear friends and fellows in the quiet walks of letters, Thomas Eastoe Abbott, William Rymer, and John Wilkinson, have died in the fulness of faith and hope. And the gentlemanly and landless scion of the great house of Ogle, who, almost all unheeded, came to Darlington to die, and with whom I forgot canker and care, lies low in the cemetery of St. Cuthbert. Yet I have left me many to reprove or congratulate me with a loving voice. "There is but one society on earth—the noble living and the noble dead."

Had not the materials alluded to in my dedication, and referred to in almost every page, been laid before me, my book would have been a lifeless skeleton; and had it not received the pictorial illustrations which have proceeded from the same hand, its appearance would have been comparatively melancholy. I have, as I conceive, consulted the feelings of the valuable friend I thus dimly refer to, by thanking him in a less ostentatious place, and in the text itself. I have pursued the same course with almost all other kindly helps. The references tell their own tale. If my memory is not equal to my wishes, I rely on forgiveness from the injured. I have however, reserved this place to state that the archives of His Grace the Duke of Cleveland and Edward Pease, Esq., in addition to those at Blackwell Hall, Clervaux Castle, the Bodleian Library, the Dean and Chapter's Library at Durham, and the Auditor's office, with the Halmot Rolls, the Parochial Registers and accounts, and the Borough Books, have, in the most handsome manner been placed at my service, and I have thankfully used them as far as my limited means and time permitted. It would be most ungrateful not to add that the courtesy of their custodiers has ever been exercised to me; and that in addition to the above records, those of Newcastle have been fully as open to me, through the able agency of Mr G. Bouchier Richardson, who grudged his friend no amount of labour, where his excellent abstracts were likely to elucidate a subject.

In the composition of this history, I soon found that if the value of my book was to depend on its authority as a book of reference, and a faithful record of the mouldering MSS. I have had before me, it could not be of the light, sketchy, and amusing character I once chalked out. I saw that the first history of every place is necessarily a magazine of evidences, to which the more popular writer can at every turn allude, to bear out his generalities. New matter has started up at every turn, and in my very pleasure at its occurrence, has harassed me in the alteration of my plans; and I have been compelled, at a greatly increased cost of production and occupation of time, to crowd as many facts into every page as my type would allow, to avoid remarks, and allow the reader to form his own conclusions.

It is the charm of Archæology that the field of enquiry is never exhausted. This work does not form an exception to the rule. It is necessarily imperfect. Nay, it is doubtless inaccurate in some particulars. Though no document has been tampered with, and I have spared no pains in sifting evidence, information is sometimes unintentionally based on false or exaggerated premises, and tradition is notoriously a corrupt source of history. But where no contemporaneous written proof exists, the experienced reader will be on his guard. I have related traditions sans colour, and sans alteration; friendship has been broken with me for my zeal on this very point; and I can safely put forth my book as an honest enquiry after, if not an absolute arrival at, truth.

LIST OF SUBSCRIBERS.

The names of Subscribers who have died since the commencement of the Work are printed in Italics.

His Grace the Duke of Cleveland, K. G., 12 copies, 2 large paper.
Right Hon. Sir Robert Peel, Bart., M. P., large paper.
Sir Cuthbert Sharp, Knt., F. S. A., Newcastle-upon-Tyne.
Lieut-Col. Wm. Havelock, K. H., 14th Light Dragoons.
Lieut-Col. H. Havelock, C. B., 53rd Regiment of Foot.
The Archæological Institute of Great Britain and Ireland.
The Literary and Philosophical Society of Newcastle-upon-Tyne.
The Society of Antiquaries, Newcastle-upon-Tyne.
The Darlington Mechanics' Institution.
The Stockton Subscription Library.
Robert Henry Allan, Esq., F. S. A., Blackwell Hall, 12 copies, 6 on large paper.
Miss Allan, Harewood Grove, Darlington.
William Allan, Esq., Blackwell Grange, large paper.
George Allison, Esq., Darlington.
William Aldam, Esq., Doncaster.
Rev. William Atthill, Horsford, St. Faith's, Norwich, large paper.
Thos. Eastoe Abbott, Esq., Rose Villa, Darlington.
Freville Lambton Burne, Esq.
Mrs. Anstey, Norton, near Stockton-upon-Tees.
The Rev. Dr. Bandinell, Bodleian Library, Oxford, large paper.
William Backhouse, Esq., Darlington.
John Church Backhouse, Esq., Blackwell, large paper.
Edmund Backhouse, Esq., Middleton Tyas, large paper.
Sir John Bernard Burke, Ulster King of Arms.
Henry Belcher, Esq., Whitby.
Wm. Bewick, Esq., Haughton-le-Skerne, near Darlington.
Thomas Bowes, Esq., Darlington.
Mrs. Barclay, Blackwell.
Mr. John Bewick, Eldon Cottage, Bermondsey.
Mr. Matthew Bell, jun., Richmond.
Thomas Bouch, Esq., C. E., 1, Hanover Street, Edinburgh.
W. G. J. Barker, Esq., Harmby, near Leyburn.
Augustus F. Bellasis, Esq., St. John's Wood, London.

Thomas Bell, Esq., Newcastle-upon-Tyne, large paper.
W. R. Bell, Esq., Norton Grammar School, near Stockton.
Mr. John Buckton, Darlington, large paper.
Mr. A. C. Birchall, Darlington.
Mr. Thomas Blyth, Darlington.
Henry Brady, Esq., Gateshead.
W. H. Brockett, Esq., Gateshead.
Francis Bennett, Esq., Gateshead.
Rev. Dr. Collingwood Bruce, F.S.A., Newcastle-upon-Tyne.
W. C. Copperthwaite, Esq., F. S. S., Borough Bailiff of Malton.
Mr. G. J. Crossley, Manchester.
Mr. T. A. Cockin, London.
Mrs. Cudworth, Coniscliffe Lane, Darlington, 2 copies.
Captain Collyer, large paper.
Henry Chaytor, Esq., Croft, large paper.
Captain Colling, Redhall, Haughton-le-Skerne.
Mr. W. W. Child, Bank, Stockton.
Mrs. Dunn, Hurworth, large paper.
H. C. Dakeyne, Esq., 34, Hamilton Terrace, St. John's Wood, London.
Joseph Dodds, Esq., Stockton-upon-Tees.
Mr. James Dees, C. E., Esk Meals, Ravenglass, Cumberland.
Mr. Thomas Dobson, jun,, Darlington.
Mr. Hugh Dunn, Darlington.
J. Dean, Esq., Staindrop.
Edwin Eddison, Esq., Leeds.
Mr. Geo. Elwin, Old Hall, Darlington.
John Fenwick, Esq., F.S.A., Newcastle-upon-Tyne, large and small paper.
Mr. Fossick, Darlington.
Mr. Joseph Forster, land agent, Durham.
Mr. Joseph Forster, Harewood Hill, Darlington.
Mr. James Ferguson, Helmsley Blackmoor.
Robert Fothergill, Esq., Bedale.
W. S. Grey, Esq., Barrister at Law, Norton, large paper.
Wm. Grey, Esq., Norton, near Stockton.
John Grey, Esq., Stockton.
Mr. David Grey, Bank Top, Darlington.
Matthew Gaunt, Esq., Barrister at Law, Leek, Staffordshire.
Matthew Gaunt, Esq., Alderman of Leeds, Yorkshire.
Francis Gibson, Esq., Saffron Walden, two copies, one on large paper.
Mr. Oswald Gilkes, Darlington.
John Hogg, Esq., Barrister at Law, Norton.
The Rev. A. J. Howell, Incumbent of Darlington.
William Harker, Esq., Theakstone Villa, Bedale.
John Harris, Esq., C. E., Darlington, two copies, one on large paper.
Richard Hollon, Esq., York.
Thomas Horner, Esq., Darlington.
Mr. John Harrison, High Row, Darlington.
Mr. Robert Heslop, Darlington.
Richard Hodgkinson, Esq., Pennerley Lodge, Beaulieu, Southampton.
Joseph Hill, Esq., Stockton.
Timothy Hutton, Esq., Clifton Castle, Bedale.
William Hepple, Esq., Bishop Auckland.
John Hodgson Hinde, Esq., Acton House, Felton, Northumberland.
Henry Ingledew, Esq., Newcastle-upon-Tyne.

Miss Ianson, West Terrace, Darlington.
T. Hayes Jackson, Esq., Darlington.
Henry Robt. Allan Johnson, Esq., Bishopwearmouth, large paper.
R. H. Keenlyside, Esq., M.D., Stockton.
Mr. William Kitching, Darlington.
Mr. John Kay, Darlington, large paper.
William Kell, Esq., F. S. A., Gateshead.
The Rev. R. W. Lloyd, Wilnecote, Tamworth.
Mrs. Livick, Darlington.
John Bailey Langhorne, Esq., Richmond, large paper.
Francis Mewburn, Esq., Borough Bailiff of Darlington.
M. M. Milburn, Esq., Sowerby, near Thirsk.
Mrs. Milbank, Blackwell.
The Rev. E. J. Midgley, Medomsley, Gateshead, two large paper copies.
George Milner, Esq., F. S. A., Hull.
John Moore, Esq., Sunderland.
John Middleton, Esq., Architect, Darlington.
Mr. Thomas Mac Nay, Darlington.
Mr. Thomas Maclachlan, Darlington.
Mr. George Mason, C. E., Darlington.
W. Crawford Newby, Esq., Stockton.
Charles Wallace Ogle, Esq., Hundons.
Henry Ornsby, Esq., Darlington.
Mr. John Ord, Newtown, Darlington.
Mr. John Robert Ord, High Terrace, Darlington.
Mr. Richard Ord, Stockton.
Mr. William Oliver, Darlington.
Edward Pease, Esq., Darlington, 5 copies, 1 large.
Mrs. Pease, Feethams, Darlington.
Joseph Pease, Esq., South End, Darlington, 3 copies, 1 large.
John Pease, Esq., East Mount, Darlington, 2 copies.
Henry Pease, Esq., Pierremont, Darlington, 2 copies.
John Beaumont Pease, Esq., North Lodge, Darlington.
James Pallister, Esq., Little Burdon, 2 copies, 1 on large paper.
The Rev. J. C. Plumer, Elstree, Herefordshire.
George Peirson, Esq., Marske, Cleveland.
Nathaniel Plews, Esq., Darlington, large paper.
Henry Peckitt, Esq., Carlton Husthwaite, near Thirsk.
J. S. Peacock, Esq., Darlington, large paper.
W. H. Peacock, Esq., Barnsley, large paper.
Thomas Peters, Esq., York.
Mr. M. Potts, jun., Darlington.
Mrs. Quelch, Bowburn, near Durham.
William Rymer, Esq., Darlington.
Thomas Richardson, Esq., Ayton, near Stokesley.
Thomas Richmond, Esq., Stockton.
S. W. Rix, Esq., Beccles.
The Rev. Thomas Robson, Grammar School, Darlington.
Mr. W. Robson, High Row, Darlington.
Mr. James Readman, Stockton.
Mr. Robert Robson, Sunderland, large paper.
Mr. Jervis Robinson, Blackfriars Road, London.
Mr. William Richardson, Darlington.
The Rev. J. Raine, Crook Hall, large paper.

H. Pascoe Smith, Esq., Hall Garth, near Darlington, two copies.
G. J. Scurfield, Esq., Hurworth, near Darlington, large paper.
Mr. Joseph Stephenson, C. E., Darlington.
Henry Stapylton, Esq., Judge of the County Courts, Durham.
A. T. Steavenson, Esq., Darlington.
Mr. Joseph Sams, Darlington and London.
Mr. T. C. Sheppard, Darlington.
Mr. Storey, St. Cuthbert's Schools, Darlington.
Jonathan Thompson, Esq., Stubbing Court, Chesterfield.
The Rev. W. S. Temple, Leamington.
John Thompson, Esq., Wooler.
Mrs. J. Brough Taylor, St. Thomas' Street, Newcastle.
Mrs. Todhunter, Harewood Hill, Darlington.
Messrs. R. Thompson and Co., Darlington, ten copies.
Mr. Edwin S. Thompson, London, large paper.
Nicholas Trant, Esq., Bedale.
George Taylor, Esq., High Bailiff of the County Courts, Durham.
The Rev. Geo. Thompson, Wisbeach, large paper.
Robert Wise, Esq., Highfield House, Malton.
T. G. Wright, Esq., M. D., Wakefield.
H. R. E. Wright, Esq., Stockton.
Albert Way, Esq., F. S. A., Wonham Manor, Reigate.
O. B. Wooler, Esq., Darlington.
The Rev. R. H. Williamson, jun., Lamesley.
Mr. John Wilkinson, Darlington; two copies, one on large paper.
Mr. G. J. Wilson, Darlington.
Mr. Thomas Watson, Darlington.
J. R. Wilson, Esq., Stockton.
Thomas Wilson, Esq., Fell House, Gateshead.

DIRECTIONS TO THE BINDER.

The Binder will place the separately-printed Illustrations in the following order :—

Immediately after the termination of the divisions paged in Arabic numerals, he will place the pedigrees (which are unpaged) as they now stand in Part IV. To follow them he will transfer Division VI (which is paged in Roman numerals) from Part III. The Roman numerals then follow consecutively to the end of the Index.

The Title, Preface, and List of Subscribers, to commence the volume, will be found at the conclusion of Part IV.

DARLINGTON;

ITS ANNALS AND CHARACTERISTICS.

DIVISION I.

SITUATION, NAME, AND WATERS.

THE RIVER TEES, after dashing for some distance through rocks vast and wild, receives the "rosy flow" of the Greta, and meandering through fields and green plantations, with ever and anon a peaceful village or stately mansion on its banks, arrives at a point of soft and delicate beauty. The Skerne, a sluggish, but withal, in some parts, a pretty stream, rushes through a single arch into the larger course, on a shelving bed of red sandstone, and gliding through a deeply-recessed and noble bridge, of enormous Gothic arches, with some opposition loses its colour, and becomes one and the same with the Tees. At the confluence, it constitutes a boundary between two parishes, Darlington and Hurworth. The former is an irregular district, boundering the Tees for some distance, and skirted by the parishes of Coniscliffe, Heighington, Haughton-le-Skerne, and Hurworth, in the palatinate, and by Cleasby and Croft in Yorkshire. It is divided into four townships: Darlington, Archdeacon Newton, Blackwell, and Cockerton; that of Darlington being subdivided into the constableries of Darlington Borough, Bondgate, Priestgate or Prebend-row, and Oxen-le-field.

ETYMOLOGY OF THESE NAMES.

Lambarde, in his Dictionary, p. 91, mentions "DARNTON, Dearungtun, *antiquitus*, and Dearington," as "a market towne in the byshoprike of Durham, which one Styr, by lycence of Kinge Etheldred, gave to Aldhune,

Byshop of Durham, imediately after that he came to sattle the sea at Durham." Allan adds, " Darningtun, Derlyngton, Darneton, Darrhton, and Darlington (as the name of this town is variously spelt or written), ... Query, if any derivation from the Saxons." (*Allan MSS.*)

Not to mention the popular joke of the name of Darlington having arisen from the circumstance of there having been originally only three farm-houses on the site, called *Dar*, *Ling*, and *Ton*, the derivations given are amusingly numerous. Behold ! *cum notis :*

1. *Deor* or *deorling*, *dilectus*, and *tun* or *ton*, *villa*, the chosen town, built on holy land, and the favourite place of the prelates.—*Hutchinson.*

2. " I have somewhere seen that the Skerne was called the *Dare*, and *Dare-inge-tun* would very well represent the actual site of the place, amidst the deep rich inges or meadows of the Skerne." *Surtees.*—4 Edw. VI. Demise to Lawrence Thornell, Gent., of the Low Parke of Darlington and the *Medowes on the Skerne.*—" The These, beyng past Ramforth, it runneth betwene Persore and Cliffe, and in the way to Croftes Bridge taketh in the *Skerne*, a pretye water which riseth above Trimdon, and goeth by Fishburne, Bradbury, Preston, and *Darlington : and finally meeting with the Cocke becke, it falleth into the These beneath Stapleton, before it come to Croftes bridge.* . . . . . Leland, writing of the These, repeateth the names of sundry riuerets, whereof in the former Treatize I have made no mencion at all, notwithstanding that some of their courses may be touched in the same, as the Thurisgill, whose heade is not farre from the Spittle that I do reade of in Stanmoore ; the Grettey commeth by Barningham and Mortham, and falleth into the These above Croftes bridge. *The Dare or Dere runneth by Darlington, and likewise into the These above the aforesayd bridge.*" *Harrison's Description of England, prefixed to Hollinshed's Chronicles*, edit. 1577, pp. 30, 68.—37 Eliz. A close of Nun-Stainton Manor *on the Skerne* is described as *Darlyng-close.*

3. The same derivation, substituting the Cockerbeck as identical with the Dare. " Now, in the winter months, this stream, from being swollen, and rushing directly at right angles into the Skerne (which is then also much enlarged), overflows its banks, and causes a separate stream to run parallel with the Skerne for a considerable distance, causing, however (though much improved of late), a quantity of wet and marshy ground ; this gives rise to the *ing*, which is the Danish for a low and wet ground ; therefore, the name signifies the town on the Ings of the Dare, the letter (*l*) being merely interposed for euphony " (*Darlington and Stockton Times*, No. 1).—" The These, a river that beareth and feedeth an excellent salmon . . . . in the waie to Croftsbridge taketh in the Skerne, a pretie water, which riseth above Trimdon, and goeth by Fishburne, Bradburie, Preston, Braforton, Skirmingham, the Burdons, Haughton, and *Darlington*, and there finallie meeting with *Cocke-becke or Dare*, it falleth in the These beneath Stapleton, before it come to Croftsbridge, and (as it should seeme) is the same which Leland calleth Gretteie or Grettie." Such is Hutchinson's quotation of Hollinshed, from some apparently later edition, very different from that of 1577 now before me. It seems to be an awkward attempt by a stranger to this country to incorporate Leland's description with Harrison's; and the Cockerbeck as little fulfils the former description of the Dare as the Skerne corresponds with the Greta. It does not flow into the Tees, as the Dare of 1577 did ; nor could it be said to run by Darlington. As to *Ing*, it seems originally to have meant an *in* or *inclosure*, as distinguished from the common field (*Brockett's Glossary*), and is used for any low flat ground. Ihre says *Œng* is a flat meadow between a town and a river, on which the market or fair is held, which is an exact description of the Ings on which the great fortnight fair for cattle is held at Wakefield.

4. *Dare*, water, *ing*, a meadow, *ton*, a town, *the Town on the watery meadows*, " from the quantity of water which formerly overflowed the banks of the Skerne, covering

many acres of ground for upwards of a mile." (E. S. Thompson, in *Darlington and Stockton Times*, 1847.) Leland's Dare was, however, clearly a river.

5. *Dar*, water, *ling*, diminutive (gosling, &c.) and *ton*, *the town on the small stream.* (Same paper. "Veritas.") But the *l* is modern.

6. *The town of Deorn's son. Ing*, in Saxon, being equivalent to *son* in modern times. J. R.

It may already have been surmised that I incline to Surtees's opinion; and this I do in consequence of the very clear identification in the Hollinshed of 1577 of the Dare and Skerne. In the earliest records, however, the name occurs as *Dearningtun, Dernington, Dernigntune*, forms correctly contracted in *Darnton* and *Dernton.* Now, Derne, in names of rivers, has a tendency to change into Dare. Thus, on the Severn, Harrison mentions *Dour* or *Dourn*-steir-fall, *Darnt*, which runneth to *Darington* (a common spelling also of our Darlington), and into the sea at Darntmouth, and the Darne in the West Riding of Yorkshire (now *Derne*), which cometh to *Darton* (another orthography of my subject place) ward, to *Derfielde*, &c. The word which, in its form Darnt or Dernt, Harrison in describing a stream of the name which falls into the Thames, makes identical with *Darwent*, is very common in names of rivers; witness the secluded Derness which flows into the Wear. In all probability the Skerne or Dare was anciently the Derne. It may have connection with water, or with *derne, dearnenga*, Sax: secret, dark, hidden, or it may be to point out the sluggishness of the water, and be identical with the northern *Terne* or *Derne*, a standing pool.

Helbecke, in Westmoreland, so called "bycause it commeth from the *derne* and *elinge* mountaines by a town of the same denomination." *Harrison.* Bailey gives *Ellinge* (*alleine*, alone, *Teut.*) as solitary, lonely, &c.; and truly *many* of the Westmoreland streams are *derne* and *elinge.*

"The Terne riseth *in a mere* nere unto *Terne Mere* in Staffordshire." *Harrison.*

"Flass Hall stands *low and sequestered*, within a reach of the *Derness*," &c. *Surtees.*

In a cliff on Hartside, Northumberland, is a strong cavernous fissure called *Darney Hall*, probably, says Hodgson, from the *water*, which in some parts of the fissure can be ascertained to be in it by the splashing noise made at its bottom by throwing stones into it. [Qu. from *Derne*, hidden, and *ey* or *ea*, water.]

Parson and White's Directory mentions that Darlington is "said to have derived its name from the lingering stream of the old *Dar* or *Der*, which evidently formed *a pool and morass* from opposite the church to the mill-holme."

A Darlington, in Devonshire, occurs 1 Edw. I. (*Inq. p. m.*) and a Darlington in Nott, 4 Edw. III. (*Abb. Rot. orig.*) Darrington, near Pontefract, oddly has Stapleton and Smeaton near it, like our Darlington.

Bondgate.—"*Unde* Framwellgate? It is, at any rate, a corrupt orthography, and has nothing to do with a *well.* Leland, I observe, calls it *Framagate*, and mentions a street of the same name at Kendal. Now, will you have my conjecture? for a fool's bolt, they say, is soon shot. It should be written *Framengate* (as it is in one place by Leland), and was, originally, a street set apart for the habitation of foreigners, or persons not entitled to the franchise of the city: from *Frem* or *Fremd, alienus, extraneus.* It was certainly a custom, in ancient times, for people of the same description to reside together, as the Jews do in most places to this day; and hence your *Bondgate in Darlington*, Auckland, &c. You may overturn this fine system if you can." (*Ritson to Mr Harrison*, 1797). It is merely necessary to add, for the information of strangers, that Bondgate in Darlington includes those portions of the town not enjoying the franchise of the Borough and Prebend-row. In Hatfield's Survey (about 1380), *Cokyrton-gate* occurs as the name of the street now bearing the appellation of Bondgate in particular.

PREBEND ROW, or PRIESTGATE. This little district takes its name from its including the possessions of the Prebendary of Darlington, in the collegiate church. *Row* is Ræwa, Saxon. "*Row* and *Raw*," observes Mr Hodgson, in his History of Northumberland, "are akin to the French *rue;* but in the upland part of the northern counties were formerly chiefly confined to those lines of dwelling-houses which lay along the fell sides, and had between them and the beck, or river of the dale, the inclosed ground, of which the houses were the several messuages."

As to *gate* in Priestgate and other streets, the word has no reference to fortifications, but simply means a way or road. In many northern villages the public road passing through is still called the *towngate;* and we have the expressions, "Gang your *gate*" (go your way); "What *gate* are ye ganging?" "How many *gates* (journies) have ye taken?" "To go *agatewards*" (to accompany a short way). The word is Saxon. Families of the names of Wood and Wright were living at *Darnton Yatts*, parish of Haughton, in the last century.

OXENHALE, OXENHALL, OXEN-LE-FIELD, or OXENEYFIELD. A very proper name for a detached portion of Darlington township, locally situated in that of Blackwell, and containing the famous Hell-Kettles. *Ea* is water. In its singular number it occurs in *Heaton* on the *Ewsburn; Eaton*, Water-*ea*ton (pleonastic), the river *Ey*molt, &c. In its plural, in the rivers *Ex, Ax, Esk, Ouse* (on which is *Ox*borough), in *Jesmond* (originally *Jesmouth*, the mouth of the *Ewsburn*, the *j* being nothing but the Saxon particle *ge*, so long retained in our language, sometimes also pronounced hard, as in Gosbeck), *Ouse*-mere (part of Ulleswater), and a long string of places, deriving from the various forms of the word. Egglescliffe sometimes occurs as *Ex*cliff and *Aix*cliffe. Brewster remarks, that wherever "aix" occurs in names of towns in France, it implies the presence of waters, particularly mineral waters. *Oxen-le-Field* is the *field of waters; Oxenhale*, the low place of waters. There is an Oxenfield in Lancashire, near Winander-meer, and an Oxenhall in Gloucestershire. Oxney Island, in Kent, is surrounded by the river Rother. The name extended to the township of Blackwell. In Hatfield's Survey, it is stated, under "Blackwell," that Peter Thomesson, in right of his wife, held half an acre and half a rood in *Oxenhal-flat*, 16*d.*

COCKERTON, from the Cockerbeck.

ARCHDEACON NEWTON. "The new town," where the *Archdeacon* of Durham has a manor.

Blackwell. *Black* is often applied to water, as in Blackmere, Blackburn, from the blackness of the Derwent on which it stands, &c. ; but the word is of very extensive meaning. In such names as *Black* Banks (in this township), *Black Blakehope*, &c., it evidently means *bleak*, the former being part of Blackwell-moor ; but *blake*, in the western parts of the north of England, includes all the shades of *terra di sienna*, from dark-coloured gold to the brown of mahogany. It is yellow, tinged with red, but free from any blue. But in the Saxon *blacian* or *blæcan*, which mean to blacken, to grow pale, to bleach, all warmth is taken out, and the hue becomes chilled with blue or black shades (*Hodgson*). A wound in the North is said to be *blakening* when it puts on an appearance of healing. As to *well*, in this case it probably has reference to the sweeping turn of the river ; *wellen*, in German, signifying *to turn*. Thus the Latins have *volvo*, and *wel* implies waves, which are continually coming and going. If it refers to water, it is simply the old word, *elle*, water, aspirated by *w*, in the same manner as it is by *h* in *Holl*and, *Hull*, &c. There were certainly some wells at Blackwell, famous enough to give names to fields.

LOCAL FAMILIES NAMED AFTER THE TOWNSHIPS.

Residence or birth at Darlington, of course gave name to families. A great number of ecclesiastics were named after it, some of which will hereafter occur. In an early Denton charter among the witnesses occur "Ricardo de Holynsede ; Bernardo filio et hærede de Derlyngton." A local race of the name occurs in the first register, and the plague of 1597 carried off Robert Darnton, or Darlington, his wife, William Darnton or Darlington, and . . . . Darnton. The name straggles on among the registers and lists of freeholders, till 1622, when John Darlington, son and heir of Robert, lately deceased, was admitted to his father's burgage, in Blackwellgate, and excused the payment of his relief on account of poverty. John Darnton, par. Winston, was married by license to Jane Richardson, par. Haughton, in 1665, and William Darnton, *a stranger*, was buried here in 1727-8. The name occurs again in full vigour at that period, and continues to this day in the town. A family of Darnton has been settled in Leeds for between 200 and 300 years past, of which race Darnton Lupton, and John Darnton Luccock, were respectively mayors of that town in 1845 and 1846. But the name occurs elsewhere in the West Riding, and its owners may be sprung from Darrington.

1568. John Docketh, clark curat, in Whitworth, leaves "to *Annes Darneton* a gemer lambe, and Alleson Pickering, my seruands, a gemer lamb."

There were some very respectable booksellers of the name in Darlington. Vesey and Darnton occur in 1762, and Thomas Darnton and William

Darnton separately occur in 1779. The latter was printer and seller of some Pastoral Poems, by J. Richardson, Yarm, in that year. The poems are full of Damons and Chloes, and are tiresome enough, but the printing is bold and good. In 1776, one of these Darntons occurs in partnership with one Smith, as printer of a sketch of the life of Bishop Trevor, but the tract was, in fact, one of George Allan's, and the following passage from his son's lively paper, in Nichols's Literary Anecdotes, will sufficiently explain the circumstance. "Being thus set up, as above, with a regular apparatus, he hired a devil, a poor fellow that occasioned him more trouble than if he had done all the drudgery himself; but he believed the man to be honest, and as he was friendless, so far from dismissing him without remuneration, he enabled him to enter into partnership with a bookseller in Darlington; and on finishing the Legend of St. Cuthbert, he permitted George Smith to be placed in the title as the printer, with a view to gain him some credit in his profession. [*Darlington: Printed by George Smith,* 1777.] This partnership did not last long; but, during its continuance, my father very kindly corrected the press, even of every common handbill that went from the office; and though he did not condescend to correct ballads, the printing of which was the chief part of the business, a copy was always brought to him. He had a bundle of these performances, which I am not able to find; but I recollect it contained a vast display of ribaldry and typographical error, which were equally amusing. After Smith's failure, he was again retained for the private press; but he was the perpetual cause of trouble and anxiety, for my father never went into the printing-room without being irritated by the dirty manner in which the forms were kept, and the filthy state of the types when distributed. Besides this, more time was lost in correcting repeated proofs, than he could well bear; and the fellow becoming shamefully addicted to cock-fighting, a vice very prevalent in this county, which my father, if possible, held in greater abhorrence than drunkenness, he was dismissed. He was, however, never totally abandoned by him; and is now living at Darlington, obtaining occasional employment, having some relief from the parish, and sometimes partaking of a share of my bounty. The amusement was carried on afterwards by the assistance of a relation, whose time was his own; and the correction of the press was latterly the only part my father performed." Many of my older readers will recollect the good for nothing retainer to the Allans, Geordie Smith, and both old and young may still picture the last of his partner's family, that "ancient lady" Miss Darnton, who so long was bookseller and sole newspaper agent for the town, in the shop now Mr. Charge, the sadler's, next to the Fleece. Her success made her rather saucy, and a gentleman told me once, that when a blushing modest youth, he cautiously went into her shop to ask for Shakspeare's Works, the answer he got was "Why, I think you're like one of Shakspeare's characters yourself," which made him blush still more, nor did he ever discover what sort of character was alluded to.

The following coats are given by Burke, under the name of *Darlington:* 1. Az. guttee ar. or a fesse or, three crosses crosslet gu. *Crest,* a winged pillar. 2. The same arms, adding in chief a leopard's face of the second. 3. Az. guttee ar. on a fesse between three leopards' heads or, as many crosses crosslet gu. The arms given for *Darling,* of London, are nearly similar, Az. guttee ar. on a fesse of the last three crosses crosslet fitchee gu. In the seal of John de Derlyngtone, Canon in Lanchester Collegiate Church and Prebendary of the Prebend of Esh, 1380, he displays a shield bearing a plain cross, charged with five objects like eagles displayed, and surrounded by the legend,

" * Sigillu' : ioh'is : de : derlyngtone :"

Qu. if not the arms of Duresme. Ar. on a cross gu. 5 fleur-de-lis or. The seal is engraved in Surtees.

In a collection of armorial bearings begun by Geo. Allan, and continued by Mr. Edw. Robson, there is a description in the hand of the latter of a coat for "*Darlington town,*" without any authority quoted, viz., six lioncels rampant or, 3, 2 and 1. The heading of the Darlington Mercury in 1773, however, only displays the arms of the see. The old seal of the Grammar School presented a rebus, a rude D and a *tun,* and the same idea occurs in Fountains Abbey, in those parts which were built by John Darneton, abbot from 1478 to 1494. In the Nine Altars' Chapel, on a keystone of one of the older lights, is the bust of an angel holding a *tun,* with the word *dern* inscribed on its breast; above this is a large bird, a scroll, containing another allusion *B'n'd' fontes d'no* (O *fountains,* bless the Lord). Above the large window, over the western door, is a niche, supported by the figure of a bird, holding a crosier, and perched on a *tun,* from whence issues a label inscribed *dern,* and the date 1494. In both cases, if, says Walbran, in his capital little Guide to Ripon, &c., the bird represents a *thrush,* there was exhibited a second rebus for the founder *Thurstan,* but if an eagle, it may, as the symbol of St. *John,* signify only the christian name ot Darneton.

ARCHDEACON NEWTON. *Hugo de Newton* held a burgage in *le Chares* (Post House Wynd) by fealty, and three suits at the Borough Court. Richard Northman, son of Dionisia Orre, nephew and heir. 10 Hatfield.

BLACKWELL. In 8 Bury, *Ralph Blacwell* held a messuage and five score acres in Blackwell, by homage, fealty, and 24s. Richard, his son and heir, aged 22. 5 Hatfield, *Richard Blacwell,* jointly with Sibil, his wife, a messuage and five ox-gangs, by 23s. 8d., value 40s. Ralph, son and heir, aged twenty-six weeks. At the time of Hatfield's Survey, (about 1380) this property (which shows that twenty acres went to the ox-gang at Blackwell) is holden by John Middleton, *in right of his wife,* by the description of one messuage and five ox-gangs, which were once *John of Blackwell's,* and were granted by charter to hold by knight's service, and the 16th part multure [at Blackwell Mill] *et cooperabit* molas supra le Louthre,* 23s. 8d. rent.

* Surtees, sub tit. Blackwell.

The same John holds a parcel of tillage called *Gromball*, containing 16 acr. and 3 roods, and 2 parcels of tillage called *Lynholme* * and *Elstantoftes;* and one tenement called *Le Castle Hill*, with the herbage of *Bathley*, containing four acres of meadow and pasture: also, the same John holds one plot or parcel, which is built upon, and half an ox-gang; a toft, with a croft of half a rood, 12d., and the toft which was once *William of Oxenhall's*, with a croft of one acre, by charter, 2d. The family long continued at Blackwell.

1575. June 31. John Myddleton of Blackwell, to be buried in Darneton churche Eldest son John Myddleton; son Robert xx*l*. over his porc'on—daughters Ellen and Jane x*l*. over their porc'ons—to the poore xs.—to the repayre of Darneton Church iiis. iiiid.—to James Whyte of London, my brother-in-lawe, and Anne his wyfe, to eyther a ryall—to Mr. Hall xiis.—Francis Wyclyffe a goulde ryall, trusting he will be frendly to my children—my wife Elizabeth, Mr. Frauncis Wyclyffe, and Mr. Harrison to see my will performed. Witness, James Thorneton, clerke, Leonard Dodsworth, John Harrison. Proved 7 Oct. 1575.

5 Dec. 21 Eliz. Elizabeth, widow of John Middleton, held half a close called *Stick-bitch*, when she died, 29 June, 17 Eliz. John, son and heir, aged 18. (Stick-a-bitch is a farm between Darlington and Croft. At Hatfield's Survey Emma Morrell held three acres at *Spyklyt*. *Qu. Stickabitch?)*

Thomas, son of John Midleton of Blackwell Feildhouse, bap. Oct. 21, 1631.—Same day, Elizabeth Midleton, wife of the said John, bur.—John Midleton, senior, of Blackwell, bur. Feb. 29, 1631-2.—Katherine Midleton, widow, of Blackwell, bur. Sep. 26, 1632.—John Middleton of Blackwell, gent., bur. Dec. 30, 1659.—William Middleton of Blackwell, the elder, bur. 20 July, 1671.—Mr. John Middleton of Cleseby, bur. 22 April, 1686.—William, *s*. William Middleton of Blackwell, bap. 24 July, 1656.—Thomas, &c., 24 April, 1663.—*(Darlington Par. Reg.)*

1633. Ralph Blackwell, adm. to *Tresham* (Stressholmes.)—*(Halmot Court Books, Blackwell.)*

1642. John Middleton demises to Thomas Swinburne, executor to James Bellasis, Esq., deceased, all right in a close called *Tresham* and some townland.—*(Ib.)*

22 Cha. I. Eleanor Winteringhton, next of kin, *(consang.)* and heiress of Ralph Blackwell, adm. to premises at Cockerton. Ralph is called her *uncle* in the body of the admittance.—(Ralph Blackwell of Cockerton, bur. 2 Dec., 1644.—*Par. Reg.)*

The name is found straggling previously both in Darlington and Haughton Registers. Most of the property of the Blackwells and Middletons eventually came to the Allans.

OXENHALE. Under Boldon book, William held Oxenhall under certain services, and the same tenure is recited in the inquest on Nicholas de Oxenhale, who died seized of the manor in 1337, leaving Richard his son and heir. The local name occurs no more, and the manor passed to the Nevilles.

* Elizabeth, wife of Francis Wardel, of Linnam-House, near Blackwell, buried 20th December, 1695.

SITUATION AND CHARACTER OF SCENERY.

When Raumer visited England in 1835, Richmond and Darlington, as well as Durham and the vale of the Wear, reminded him of the countries on the Elbe and the valley of the Elbe between Pillnitz and Dresden. The nearest mountains swell in but a distant view, "clad in colours of the air," no castles proudly tower in the skies, the vallies are not confined by steep rocks, and there is an utter want of romance about the scenes near Darlington, but then all this leads to a quietness of beauty which is on no account to be overlooked. The calm of mind produced by the silent shade of numberless varieties of trees, and by the sweet river side scenes, which as Howitt remarks, abound, and yet are so little observed by travellers in the north-eastern counties of England, arises from a more pleasing, though less nervous tone of admiration, than that caused by the rugged elegance of more broken country. There is a rich and comfortable appearance about the hidden vale of Tees, and the ideas produced on my mind on my first approach to Darlington, on a pedestrian excursion in 1842, when I left Stapleton and gazed on the various dyes of the woods of Baydale, have not yet departed, although now writing, immediately after a morning's walk, on this cold 22nd day of December. The snugness of the woody bounds of Grange, the sullen and half-congealed Tees, the waning moon and stars, and the crisp line formed by the leafless trees against the gradually reddening grey of the East, rising from a bosom of the hoar frost's silver, gave an effect to the appearance of Blackwell, which in no way yielded to its autumnal dress. The day scene from Woodside, and the unveiling of the West, near the Nunnery, are two delicate morsels for any one who finds

> Books in running brooks,
> Sermons in stones, and good in every thing.

But I leave all details for my rural chapters, my distant readers will gather an inkling of what I want to be at, and picture a soft, fertile, and extensive valley. Fill ye up the scene with one or two rivers on their journey to the deep, a steeple on a height, a spire in a hollow, with pleasant seats and warm plantations; such are the suburbs of Darlington. The old part of the town stands on a steepish declivity, facing the East, with the Skerne slowly wandering

> Like human life, to endless sleep,

at its foot. It is a very central station, is on the course of the great line of road from London to Berwick, one of the eight grand thoroughfares set out in Harrison's Description of England, prefixed to Hollinshed, and in his instructions, "How a man may journey from any notable towne in England, to the citie of London, or from London to any notable towne in the Realme," it occurs in the way from Barwike to Yorke, thus:

From Durham to Darington, xiij. mile.
From Darington to Northalerton, xiiij. mile.

In our days, these distances would stand as 18 and 16 miles. Darlington is distant 12 miles from Stockton, 16 from Barnard-castle, 12 from Richmond, 32 from Newcastle ($39\frac{3}{4}$ by rail), 48 from York (45 by rail), and 241 from the metropolis. Dibdin in his Tour (ii. 247), says that "Upon the whole the county of DURHAM all through, cannot boast, I think, a large aggregate of riches. DARLINGTON would be nothing if it were not a post town. HARTLEPOOL is a poor inconsiderable fishing town; and if it were not for the clerical revenue and patronage of DURHAM, I should think that SUNDERLAND might buy the whole county." The present state of affairs shows how very little Dibdin knew of the resources of Darlington, when he says that it would be nothing without its posting. It is true that the new mode of transit has brought great wealth to some of its inhabitants, but independently of that, its markets and manufactures have ever made it a place of some consequence. In Leland's time it was "the best market-town in the Bishoprick, saving Duresme," and in later times "the most noted town in England for the linen manufacture, especially Hugabacks,"* nay more, if we adopt another writer's zealous assertion, for such manufactures it was "the most noted place *in the whole world!*"†

THE WATERS OF THE PARISH OF DARLINGTON.

The parish is watered by three rivers, the Tees, the Skerne, and the Cockerbeck. The first of these eccentrically winds from Tees Cottage to Blackwell and thence to Croft bridge, near which, as before mentioned, it receives the sluggish Skerne. The Cockerbeck flowing from Walworth, on its arrival at the Darlington territories, divides in times of flood, and causes a large portion of the parish to become an island, one branch assuming the name of Baydale Beck,‡ and falling into the Tees near Tees Cottage, the other retaining its name and meandering along until it runs into the Skerne, at right angles, at the head of Northgate.

ANNALS OF THE WATERS.

And, first, their victims claim our notice. A long and dreary list might be presented to my readers, were I to include all that have been chronicled,

* John Dyer's MSS.

† Universal Magazine, 1749, "from an ingenious correspondent, who subscribes himself *Conyers*."

‡ This beck only carries off the waste or overflowing waters of the Cockerbeck; its head being on a higher level than the bed of the larger brook.

but knowing how harrowing it is to have the memorials of their deaths dragged before eyes but newly tearless, I have confined the melancholy catalogue to the earlier entries of the register and one or two of the more remarkable of the modern records.

1608. May 23.—Agnes Thompson, a servant of John Watson, drowned in Tees, and buried.

1613. July 3.—John Horner, who was drowned, the son of Robert Horner of Darlington, buried.

1620. May.—An infant drowned in the river of Skerne, buried.

June 1.—Barbary Rutter, dau. of Ralph Rutter of Blackwell, drowned and buried.

1621-2. March 1.—Henry Wetherelt of Aldbrough, drowned in Tees, buried.

— 15.—A certain old woman called *Old Agnes*, drowned in Skerne, buried.

1623-4. January 18.—Agnes Thompson of Blackwell, drowned under the mill wheel, buried.

1624. Oct. 12.—Katherine Lawsonn, wife of Lancelot Lawsonn of Gainforde, drowned in Tees, buried.

1624-5. March 10.—Bartholomew Langestraffe and Margaret Langstraffe, *sons (filii!)* of John Langstraffe of Blackwell, drowned, buried.

1626. March 25.—Thomas Dent of Midleton a rawe, drowned in the river of Skerne, buried.

1628. June 6.—Margaret Simpson of Ovington, drowned in Tees, buried.

1638. July 22.—William Allanson of Darlington, drowned in the river of Skerne, buried.

1639-40. March 11.—Thomas Branson, of Darlington, drowned in the river of Skerne, buried.

1641. Oct. 12.—Cuthbert Birde of Midleton tires, drowned in Tees, buried.

1652. April 8.—Isabell Sympson, the daugter of Anthony Sympson of Blackwell, who was supposed to be slaine, bap.

1652. April 20.—Anthonye Sympson of Blackwell, was Burried when he was found in Blackwell mill damme, and had not been sene for 18 weeke.

1652-3. Feb. 26.—Francis Sympson, late wife of Anthnie Sympson of Blackwell, buried.

1653. Dec.—Henry Firbanke of Forcet, in the countie of Yorke, who was found lying drowned in Blackwell Holme, buried.

Blackwell Holme is the low ground lying South of the new road leading down to Blackwell bridge, under Holme Wood. It is probable that the unfortunate man was crossing the horse ford which was close to the place where the bridge now stands (the ferry being lower down, opposite Stapleton), and that his body was swept round the bold curve of the river into the Holme and left there. A holme signifies land overgrown with natural trees in the vicinity of water (as the Holmes at Thirsk) no matter whether flat or steep. In the latter character are the Holme Bank and the High Holmes near Hill House.

Blackwell Holme, which sometime belonged to Raby Vane, by marriage with the daughter of Archdeacon Sayer, is copyhold, and appears to have formed part of the vast district called Baydales, as in 1640 mention is made of "*Badell banke in Blackwell field alias Blackwel Holme*," and in 1644,

"*Blackwell Holme within Badell alias Badell Flatt.*"* At present, Baydale Banks and Baydale Bank Bottom are names in Mr. R. H. Allan's freehold estate of Baydales. Both it and Blackwell Holme were the estates of George Allan, Esq., M.P., but Blackwell Holme was subsequently sold to the Bowers of Welham. In draining the morass of Baydale bottoms, numbers of gnarled oaks were found, either fallen from the banks above, or swept to that position by the river. They were huge patriarchs of the forest, black as ebony, but sound at the heart withal.

1653-4. March 2.—A stranger was buried who was found drowned in Skearne about Glassen-Sikes.

Glassensikes is the name of certain closes of which (with Windmill Hill) Christopher Barnes (Borough Bailiff) died seised in 1630-1, and which were purchased from the family of Bowes of Thornton Hall, by Miss Allan. The Allans sold a portion of them piecemeal, but the lots were subsequently bought up and reunited by the late Jonathan Backhouse, Esq. This territory is watered by a small runner of the same name which flows past the new parsonage house and Harewood Grove, crosses under the Croft road (being formerly an open stell upon it) and joins the Skerne at the place to which it gives name. The word is probably composed of GLASSENE, blue or grey, and SIKE, the old legal term for anything less than a *beck*, which in its turn is anything less than a *river*. The former word is still used for blue or grey in Wales, and the following extract from the valuable notes to the *Lays of the Deer Forest, &c.*, by the Stuarts is too appropriate to be omitted. After remarking that grey was anciently the badge of the churl and peasant, they observe that there was another cause for which it was peculiarly disagreeable to the Highlanders when first introduced among them.

"Among them grey was to their imagination what black is to their neighbours, a personification of sombre, superstitious and ghostly ideas, and hence associated with phantoms and demons. Thus, an apparition is called *an Riochd*—the grey or wan; the spectre foreboding death, *am bodach glas*—the grey carl; a phantom in the shape of a goat, *an Glastig* or *Glasdidh*†—the grey; and as in the South, the great enemy is named familiarly "the *black* gentleman," so in the Highlands he is called Mac-an-*Riochda*—'the son of the *Grey*.' In the ideas of the old wives and children of the last century, all these personifications, except one, were as nearly as possible those of the modern dubh-ghall deer-stalker in his hodden grey—wanting only the *Jim Crow, ruffian*, or *crush hat*, enormities which had not then completed the masquerade of Death and Satan.

"It is easy to trace the origin of this association. The ancient Caledonian hell, like that of Scandinavia, was a frozen and glassy region, an island named *Ifrinn*, far away among the '*wan* waters' of the Northern ocean, and inclosed in everlasting ice, and snow, and fog. In this dim region the appearance of the evil spirits, like that of mortals in similar circumstances, was believed to be wan and shadowy, like men seen through a frosty mist."

* Halmot Court Books.

† "It has pleased a writer of the Cockney school of Highlanders to convert this word into *Glaslig*, which, we take leave to observe, is unknown in the Highlands, and did not exist before the year 1841."

Sir Walter Scott, in his "Lady of the Lake," alludes to the same superstition:

> "His dazzled eyes
> Beheld the river-demon rise;
> The mountain-mist took form and limb,
> Of noontide-hag or goblin grim;"

and adds, in a note, that "the *noontide-hag*, called in Gaelic *Glas-lich*, a tall, emaciated, gigantic female figure, is supposed, in particular, to haunt the district of Knoidart."

Now, though I by no means intend to assert that the glassene gentleman or lady (for I am unable to define the ghost's gender) haunting Glassensikes is seen at noonday,* I will maintain that Glassensikes has goblins as grim as any river-dæmons of Scottish land. Headless gentlemen, who disappeared in flame, headless ladies, white cats, white rabbits, white dogs, black dogs; "shapes that walk at dead of night, and clank their chains;"† in fact, all the characteristics of the Northern Barguest were to be seen in full perfection at Glassensikes. It is true that these awful visions occasionally resolved themselves into a pony, shackled in an adjoining field, or Stamper's white dog, or a pair of sweethearts "under the cold moon," (Qy: Did poets ever hear of persons walking above the moon, be she hot or be she chill?) but still a vast amount of *credible* evidence exists about the fallen glories of the night-roaming ghost of Glassensikes. The Glassensikes witnesses are not all thoughtless, and superstitious men. An old gentleman of Darlington was, at the witching hour of midnight, returning from Oxeneyfield. It was a bright moonlight night, and the glories of the firmament led him, as he says, to possess a more contemplative turn of mind than he ever felt before or since. In such a frame he thought that if nothing was to be seen in the day, nothing could well haunt Glassensikes by night, and in firm faith, but without any wish to exercise an idle curiosity, he determined to look to it very narrowly, and satisfy himself as to the fallacy of the popular notion. Accordingly, when he came to the place where the road to Harewood Hill now turns off, he looked back, and was greatly surprised to see a large animal's head popped through the stile at the commencement of the footpath, leading by the present Woodside to Blackwell. Next came a body. Lastly, came a tail. Now my hero, having at first no idea that the unwelcome visitant was a ghost, was afraid that it would fly at him, for it bounced into the middle of the road and stared intently at him, whereupon he looked at it for some minutes, not knowing well what to do, and beginning to be somewhat amazed, for it was much larger than a Newfoundland dog, and unlike any dog he had ever seen, though well acquainted with all the canine specimens in the

* There is a noontide ghost not very far off, however,—of whom hereafter.

† What does Grose mean by saying that "dragging chains is not the fashion of English ghosts; chains and black vestments being chiefly the accoutrements of foreign spectres, seen in arbitrary governments: dead or alive, English spirits are free?" for in the North, the chain-dragging is one of the grand characteristics of unhouselled spirits.

neighbourhood; moreover it was as black as a hound of hell. He thought it best to win the affections of so savage a brute, so cracked his fingers invitingly at it, and practised various other little arts for some time. The dog, however, was quite immovable, still staring ferociously, and as a near approach to it did not seem desirable, he turned his back and came to Darlington, as mystified about the reality of the Glassensikes ghost as ever. Of late years, this harmless sprite has seemingly become disgusted with the increased traffic past its wonted dwelling, and has become a very well-behaved domestic creature. The stream, however, loves to make new ghosts, and by its stagnant nature does every thing in its power to obtain them.

The headless man who vanished in flame, was, of course, the many-named imp, ycleped Robin Goodfellow, Hobgoblin, Mad Crisp, Will-the-Wispe,* Will-with-a-wisp, Will-a'-Wisp, Will-and-the-wisp, William-with-a-wispe, Will-o'-the-wisp, Kitty-with-a-wisp, Kit-with-the-canstick (candlestick), Jack-with-a-lanthorn, Jack-w'-a-lanthorns, Fire-drake, Brenning-drake, Dicke-a-Tuesday, Ignis fatuus, or Foolish Fire (because, says Blount, it only feareth fools), Elf-fire, Gyl-burnt-Tayle, Gillion-a-burnt-taile, Sylham lamps (being very frequent at Sylham in Suffolk), Sylens (Reginald Scot), Death-fires, Wat (seen in Buckinghamshire prisons), Mab (*mab-led* or *mob-led* in Warwickshire, signifies being led astray by a Will-o'-the-Wispe) with all the varieties of Puck. When seen on ship masts it is styled a complaisance, St. Helen's fire, St. Helmes fires, the Fires of St. Peter and St. Paul, St. Herme's fire and St. Ermyn; in classic times Helen, and when two lights occurred, Castor and Pollux. The phenomenon is a forerunner of death in popular fancy, at sea it is a weather symbol, and in superstitious times the Romanist clergy persuaded the people that the lights were souls come out of Purgatory all in flame, to move them to give money, to say mass for them, each man thinking they might be some relations' souls.†

The grand settlement of the Ignis fatuus (a natural marvel never yet satisfactorily explained) was in the little square field, now surrounded by roads. It revelled in its bogginess, the hedge near the Blackwell-lane was lit up by unearthly flames, and a woeful wight was unable to return from Blackwell on one occasion, in consequence of a great *gulph of fire* there. I am given to understand that the Will-o'-Wisp has been seen even since Harewood Hill was built, and the field improved. I am not sure that the headless man of Prescott's stile (somewhat further up the bank, and hard by a little plantation of Nordykes, where the footpath to Blackwell turns out of the field into the lane) has quite disappeared from the ken of earthly eyes. I know not what the Prescotts did, but surely some dark deeds crossed their annals, or else their old deserted mansion at Blackwell, and their stile leading to it, would not have become the haunted spots they have.

Lady ghosts are favourite accompaniments of water in the North. Both my former residences, Norton and Thirsk, had white ladies near them, on

* A torch composed of a twist of straw.

† Ellis's Brand, 1842, iii. 218.

melancholy streams ; indeed, in the latter case, the runner took a name from the circumstance, and is called the White-lass-beck. Like the Glassensikes spirit, the White-lass is rather protean in her notions, turning into a white dog, and an ugly animal which comes rattling into the town with a tremendous clitter-my-clatter, and is there styled a barguest. Occasionally, too, she turns into a genuine lady of flesh and blood, tumbling over a stile. The Norton goblins are equally eccentric. Two gentlemen (one, a very dear friend of mine, *et est mihi sœpe vocandus,* now deceased) saw near a water an exquisitely beautiful white heifer turn into *a roll of Irish linen,* and then, when it vanished, one of them beheld a fair white damsel. The Thirsk maid was murdered ; and, some years ago, when a skeleton was dug up in a gravel pit near the beck, it was at once said to be that of the poor girl.

Glassensikes has a rival in a streamlet running across a most uncanny-looking little glen between Darlington and Haughton, near Throstle Nest, where the maiden, the cat, and other shapes, gathered around the luckless traveller. But though they have not builders to blame for intrusion, they have fallen into the pet, and are now heard of even less than their cousins of the glassene sike.

So much *de albis puellis :* on, on with the records of death.

1714. May 14.—Joyce Habbs of Blackwell, drown'd in the Teaze, bur.

1721. Dec 19.—William Hall, servant to Christopher Wardel of Blackwell, drown'd i'th' Tees, buried.

1722. July 10.—The corpse of one supposed to have been a man cast up by the Tees near Blackwell, buried.

1722. Dec. 31.—Robert Luck of Darlington, bricklayer, buried, he was drown'd in the Tees at Nesham.

1724. April 1.—John Longstaff of Darlington, drown'd in the Mill-pott, buried.

1725. July 1.—Mr. John Child of Blackwell, (who was drown'd in that part of the Tees call'd *Consclif Caldron* or *Hob's hole* on ye 2d of June), buried.

Here are more ghostly associations. Hob is a name for many spirits of very varying characters. There was a *Hob Hedeless* (Headless) who infested the road between Hurworth and Neasham, but could not cross the running stream of the Kent, a little stream flowing into the Tees at the latter place. He was exorcised and laid under a large stone, formerly on the road side, for ninety-nine years and a day, on which stone, if any luckless personage sat, he would be glued there for ever. When the road was altered the stone was fearlessly removed. In the Coniscliffe case, Hob was probably one of the kelpies or evil spirits of the waters, who, as in Wensleydale, generally appeared as a horse.

Kelpies of Scotland sat by the lake sides and lured women and children to their subaqueous haunts, there to be immediately devoured, or swelled the water beyond its usual limits, to overwhelm the hapless traveller. The later name for the goblin of the Tees is **Peg-Powler**, who is useful in keeping children from going too near the river.* Some of my readers will doubtless have a faint recollection of being awfully alarmed in their youthful days, least when they chanced to be alone on the margin of the stream, "Peg Powler, with her green hair," should issue forth and snatch them into her watery chambers. The parental threat, "Peg-Powler will get you," is synonymous with "the Boggly-bo will get you," which I well remember being frightened with by servants. The Bogle, however, like the Shelly-coat of the Scottish waters, and the brags and barguests of Durham is, I think, more plaguing than fatal. But who was BO, whose name is so terrific to children, and a test of manhood when addressed to a goose? Warton gives him a Scandinavian origin, and describes him as a mighty cleaver of skulls; while Chalmers has provided him with a Welsh pedigree.† Great must have been his fame. The name of Marlborough, who has been dead little more than a century, is no longer terrific to the children of France; Richard of the Lion's heart has ceased to be a bugbear to the sons of the crescent; but BO, tremendous BO, still rules with iron sway the scions of the oaken-souled sea-kings of the nursing soil whence those transitory heroes sprung.

The legend of Peg-Powler bears much resemblance to the Irish superstition "embalmed in the affecting wail of the mother for her son, seduced by the daughters of the waters to drown in their coral caves," and to the ideas attached to the Chippeway lake Minsisagaigoming, or "the dwelling place of the mysterious spirit," who, as a beautiful lady or an old woman, took away to the spirit-land those whom he loved. A benevolent spirit resided in *Hob-hole*, a natural cavern in Runswick Bay, Yorkshire, formed like the *fairy coves* at Hartlepool, and the recesses near Sunderland, by the constant action of the tide. Hob was supposed to cure the hooping-cough; and an impious and idolatrous charm, till late years, was considered efficacious. The patient was carried into the cave, and the parent, with a loud voice, invoked its deity,

Hob-hole Hob!
My bairn's getten 't kink-cough,
Tak't off, tak't off.‡

1730. June 22.—William, son of William Groves, of Darlington (drown'd by accident), bur.

1730. June 25.—Elizabeth Lee, of West Auckland, a young woman (drowned), bur.

1734. December 15.—Anna, wife of Leonard Lakenby, of Darlington, unfortunately drowned.

1735. December 25.—Phillis, wife of Wm. Herd, of Darlington, accidentally drowned.

1737—8. March 23.—John Nateby, of Blackwell, farmer, unfortunately drowned in

* Her Pegship does not, however, confine herself to the running waters. Neighbouring ponds are also honoured by her presence.

† Rambles in Northumberland. The author assumes that Sir Walter Scott's *barguest* of Durham and Newcastle is a mistake for *bo*guest. I know nothing about these two particular instances, but all the spirits of a similar name which have occurred to me in Yorkshire were certainly called *bar*guests; and the likeness to the words brag, and the German barg geist, satisfies me that this pronunciation is correct.

‡ Ord's Cleveland, 303.

the Tees, upon the 30th of January last, and not taken up till 21st of this instant, buried.

1746. April 8.—John Thompson, of Darlington, flax dresser, who had drowned himself, buried.

1751. August 5.—Ann Jackson, a servant-maid, who was drowned at Blackwell, buried.

1762. November 9.—William Leighton, of the parish of Shotley, in Northumberland, stonemason, who was drowned in the river Teese, about Winston, and carried by the force of the stream down to Blackwell, and there thrown out, buried.

1773. August 27.—James Teasdale, a labouring man, from Durham, and who was unfortunately drown'd in the river Tees, buried.

1794. March 9.—Jane Patterson, of Bedale, who was drowned in the river Tees, nigh Blackwell, buried.

1796. February 17.—Lewis Hammond, cabinet-maker, an itinerant, drowned in the mill-dam, buried.

1798. Joanna Husband, of Darlington, spinster, daughter of Edward Husband, glover.—March 14th, This poor woman was missed. Buried April 10, aged forty-two. Drowned in the mill-dam.

1804. Martin Brown of Darlington, batchelor, aged 22 years, drowned in the Skerne, December 25, buried 27.

1818. February.—An infant drowned in the Skern, found near Skern-House, about the age of one month, buried.

This is the first of a series of records of similar outrages on humanity. Three children were found in one week in the sullen mill-dam.

1825. May 2.—John Newton, Barton, found drowned at Blackwell, aged 47, buried.

1832. Nov. 5.—George Stout (drowned at Neesham Ford), Darlington, aged 42, buried.

In the churchyard is the following inscription: "Sacred to the memory of John Morton, of Liverpool, who was unfortunately drowned whilst bathing in the Tees, the 10th of July, 1838, aged 27 years."

January 5, 1840. Sunday afternoon. As Mr. John Chisman of Blackwell mill, and Mr. Rutter were walking on the shore of the river Skerne, about three hundred yards from the mill, on the way to Darlington, they observed something in the water like a flannel petticoat; a fork was procured and a substance raised which proved to be the body of a female. It was carefully removed, with further assistance, to a granary at the mill, where an inquest was held before William Trotter, Esq., coroner for Darlington Ward, on the following day and, by adjournment, on the day succeeding. The evidence went to show that the deceased was a young woman named Susan Dagley, a native of Coventry, who had worked at Messrs. Pease's mill for about nine months, and was missed from her lodging at Priestgate, in Darlington, about five weeks previous, since which period every effort for her discovery had been unsuccessful. Thomas Brownrigg, a fellow lodger, had been taken into custody on the suspicion arising from the circumstance that, on the night of Friday, the 29th of November, about half-past seven in the evening, she threw her tea-tin on the table of her lodgings and went out without speaking a word to any one. Brownrigg, who lodged in the same house, went out about seven and returned at half-past nine o'clock the same evening when he said to another lodger, named Woodhams, "Woodhams, have you seen anything of Susan?" And before he had time to reply he asked the same question of the old woman, Jane Scott, who kept the lodging-house. On the Sunday, Brownrigg told Woodhams he had been seeking all over for her; and a female named Margery Newton deposed that about seven that morning she saw Brownrigg coming up from the water in a stooping position. Mr. Arthur Strother had examined the body and found the arms and hips to be very much bruised, the lungs healthy, the brain much gorged with blood, no appearance of pregnancy, and considered that the murder must have been committed before the body was thrown into the water. The deposition of Brownrigg went to account for the use he made of his time on the night in question, the particulars of which coincided with the statements which two or three other witnesses made as to the times when they saw him. Verdict of "Wilful murder against some person or persons unknown."*

1844. August 2. A boy, of Blackwell, named Fenwick, about 11 years old, while crossing the Tees, was carried away by a flood, which came down suddenly in consequence of the late rains. It is singular that in the same month in 1845, an inquest was held on the body of his brother Joseph, aged 10, who had been an inmate of the Victoria Asylum, Newcastle, and was, at the time of his death, on a visit to his friends. Although blind, he could go about and had strayed on the high road at the time the Richmond omnibus and Cook's circus carriages were passing each other. He was knocked down by the omnibus horses, and run over before it could be stopped, it being on the declivity of the hill leading down to Blackwell bridge.

Whit-Tuesday, 1846. A youth 13 years old, son of Mr. Wm. Nicholson, comber, of this town, while bathing a little above Tees Cottage, got out of his depth and was drowned, though the most strenuous efforts were made by his fellows to save him, (one of whom nearly experienced the same fate). "The river Tees is exceedingly unsafe for inexperienced people to bathe in: the bottom, being chiefly of a sandy nature, is by the frequent floods continually shifting, and it is not an unfrequent thing for a person unacquainted with the water to slip from a place not knee-deep into a hole eight or ten feet in depth."†

1846. November 26. Great excitement pervaded the town this day on the intelligence being received that the conductor of the mail cart from the York and Newcastle Railway Station was drowned in the Skerne, and the bags lost. The poor man whose name was Henry Nesbit, but who was better known by the cognomen of *Harry Boots*, set off from the station as usual, with the night mail bags, but not arriving at the King's Head Inn, inquiries were made, and one of the omnibus drivers said he had seen some-

* Richardson's Local Historian's Table Book. † Durham *Advertiser*.

thing like a cart upside down in the Mill-pot. The cart and horse were found, but poor Harry was not discovered till the morning of the 27th, the body having been moving about in the Mill-pot the whole of the previous day, as the place where it was found had been dragged previously without success. The river was considerably swollen, and it would appear that the deceased must have attempted the narrow and dangerous passage called the Mill Bank; where there is no railing, and slipped off the bounding wall into the water. The mail-bags were found in a tolerable condition by Mr. Gent, of Polam, a considerable distance from the stream. "Harry Boots" was buried with much respect, and is commemorated by a tombstone in the churchyard.

Many of the melancholy accidents I have mentioned were doubtless in the time of

FLOODS,

which rapidly rush down the Tees and Skerne. In February, 1753, the former rose in some parts fifteen feet above high water mark, washing the turnpike house at Croft down, whereby £50 of the road money was lost in the water. In a letter* dated from Redmarshall, in March, Mr. Johnson writes to Dr. Birch, that "it drowned almost entirely all the village of Neesham, having destroyed every house except one, to which all the people resorted, and by good luck saved their lives, though with the loss of all their cattle, and stacks of hay and corn." "The great flood," however, was *par eminence*, that of November, 1771, which caused most disastrous consequences on the Tyne, Wear, and Tees.† The water passed through Gainford, and carried away about seven yards of the churchyard, with the coffins and corpses; some of them stopped at Mr. Hill's ground at Blackwell. The Castle-hill at Blackwell‡ was washed away. The water was above six feet high in William Allison's house at Oxenhall Field; it spoiled the corn stacks, drowned two of his fat oxen, a mare and a foal, and [another ?] with foal, of the Traveller's breed, with a four years' old one of the same sort, very valuable; a draught horse, and a ram that cost him ten guineas, and spoiled all the household property below stairs; 'twas as high as the centre of his clock pointer. He saved his stallion, which was in a stable built on purpose for him, that stood on the highest ground, though he was up to the rump in water. The family at Slip Inn abandoned the house, and escaped with much difficulty to William Jolly's; had they stayed three minutes longer they had been drowned. At Croft, the flood was in the church, and the

* Bibliotheca Topographica Britan.

† See Richardson's Local Historian's Table Book, sub 1771,—Brewster's Stockton, and a small reprint of the accounts of the terrible inundations of 1771 and 1815, published by Charnley, of Newcastle, in 1818, from which the following remarks are taken.

‡ This expression must be taken *cum grano salis*. The flood, doubtless, was very destructive to this venerable remain, but its utter desolation has been in very gradual progress, and a remnant still remains.—W. H. L.

gates carried away. There a man and a wife forced to the house top, clung by the rigging tree a long time, but at last the old woman, being no longer able to bear herself up, took leave of her husband and dropped, but he out of lasting affection, replied, "no, my dear, as we have lived forty years happily together, so let us die in peace and love," and instantly leaving his hold, resigned himself to the Will of Providence. It happened, however, that the upper floor of the house was left standing, and they were happily saved thereon, the water having subsided.

In this flood, the Tees rose twenty feet higher than the oldest man living could remember, and as the quantity of water in it and the Tyne and Wear, appeared so much more than the apparent quantity of rain which had fallen, incessantly, but not heavily, on two previous days, many conjectured that a water-spout must have broken near the sources, which are very near to each other. At Barnard-castle the water ejected a dyer from his cellars, just as a few tammies in the kettle were receiving their last process. After the torrent had subsided, he visited his kettle in great anxiety, when, removing the sand and mud at the top, his goods were found to have attained a colour beyond his most sanguine expectations. They were sent to London, and gave such satisfaction, that orders were forwarded for a further supply of the same shade, but the dyer, not being again assisted by the genius of the river, failed in every attempt to produce it.

Great damage was also done at Darlington and along the banks of the Tees, by the floods of December, 1815. On February 2, 1822, a most tempestuous wind, with heavy rain, was the precursor of more heavy floods in the north. The Tees began to rise at nine o'clock on Saturday evening, and the road from Croft Bridge to Darlington was impassable. On Sunday morning the water was seven feet deep in the main street of Stockton, and the mail passed through Hurworth. The water stood fifteen feet on Croft Bridge. Another severe flood happened in July, 1828, and in October, 1829, the Tees rose to a height not exceeded within the memory of the oldest inhabitant of Barnard-castle, sweeping away the new bridge, then building at Whorlton, to the ruin of the unfortunate builders. The Tees was also very high in August, 1832.*

This river is frequently frozen, notwithstanding the tides and rapid current. In 1780 it was frozen eight weeks, and in 1784, when the ice was eight and a half inches in thickness, a sheep was roasted upon the river at Portrack.

One of the most remarkable

CHARACTERISTICS OF THE TEES,

is its fancy for winding in eccentric curves. From this circumstance, indeed, it derives its name, the Celtic *Taoi,* signifying winding. We have

* Sykes's Local Records, edit. 1833.

more rivers than one of this name in Her Majesty's dominions, and the Thiess, a large river, flows into the Danube. In "the winding Tay," we have the word in nearly its original form, and a pleonasm strikingly expressive of the propriety of its appropriation. Dyer fell into the same venial error when he talks about "the shady dales of *winding Towy*, Merlin's fabled haunt," Towy being only a modification of Tay. Every one recollects the Tajo (pronounced Tayo) flowing past Lisbon; there is a Tava flowing into the Danube, and another river of the same name in Moravia; nay, there is even a Tay *in China!*

The following popular sayings connected with the Tees may amuse:

An otter in the Wear,
You may find but once a year;
An otter in the Tees,
You may find at your ease.

The Tyne, the Tees, the Till, the Tarset and the Tweed,
The Alne, the Blyth, the Font, the Tarret and the Read.

The Tees, the Tyne, and Tweed, the Tarret and the Till,
The Team, the Font, and Pont, the Tippal and the Dill.*

Escaped the Tees and was drowned in the Tyne.

So the Welsh say "To escape Cluyd and be drowned in Conway," in general proverbial speech, "out of the frying-pan into the fire," and "out of God's blessing into the warm sun." Here are two more locals of the same meaning.

Out o'Bisho'brig† into Yorkshire.

"Tute‡ *again*"—made the lad leave Yorkshire,
And when he gat into Bisho'brigg he was *nivver* dune.§

The Tees has, however, been celebrated in more polished numbers. It is introduced by "the gentle Spenser" into his "Marriage of the Thames and Medway," thus:

Then came the bride, the loving Medway came,
Her gentle lockes adowne her back did flowe
Unto her waste, with flowers bescattered,
The which ambrosial odours forthe did throwe
To all about, and all her shoulders spred
As a new-spring; and likewise on her head
A chapelet of sundrie flowres she wore:
On her two pretty handmaids did attend,
One cal'd the Theise, the other cal'd the Crane;
Which on her waited, things amisse to mend,
And both behinde upheld her spredding traine.

* The principal Northumbrian rivers.

† Bishopric—*par eminence*—of Durham.

‡ Do it.

§ This and the preceeding ancient saws are from my friend Mr M. Aislabie Denham, of Piercebridge's extensive collection of popular sayings of the five Northern counties. May they successfully increase and at length see the light of the world!

Mason exclaims,

> Rejoice! as if the thundering Tees himself
> Reigned there amid his cataracts sublime.

However, near Darlington, the poet's idea is not realized. This noble stream "that beareth and feedeth an excellent salmon" has passed the terrible grandeur of its falls; flown by the castle of the Baliols, which "standeth stately" on its crags; and reached the vale where sloping banks and shady groves hang over it with rapture, and where, rolling amidst laughing meads in all the majesty of pride, it was first cheered by early civilization, as shown by the minute distribution of parishes, and gave name to the gallant race, who, first taking the salmon as their ensign, showed their deep reverence for the waters of their home "super Teysam." How Father Tees meanders! by the rich woods of Baydale; by Castle Hill and the sweep of Blackwell Holme; through the time-worn arcade of Croft; jutting round Rock Cliff; kindly saluting Hurworth and Neasham; hurrying south to embrace the soft lawns of Sockburn; and then dashing back again, entranced by the luxuriant walks of Dinsdale; really one might almost suppose he was seeking some fair streamlet to woo and win, remembering his sweet union with the Greta:

> Where issuing from her darksome bed,
> She caught the morning's eastern red,
> And through the softening vale below
> Rolled her bright waves, in rosy flow,
> All blushing to her bridal bed
> Like some fair maid in convent bred.

"After Derlington," says Camden,* the Tees has no towns of more note on its banks, but washes the edges of green fields and country villages with its winding stream, and at length throws itself at a wide mouth into the sea." Yarm is, however, described as *bigger and better built than Darlington* by him,† to which character we need only apply De Foe's remark on it; "*it has seen much better days,*" as it now merely contains 1500 inhabitants, while Darlington has nearly 11,000.

The Tees abounds with fishes of the salmon kind, consisting in popular diction, of sparling, brandling, trout, salmon-trout or scurves, summer-cock, and salmon. The convent of Durham occasionally procured their fresh water fish from the Tees.

> 1508. To Edward Smyth for sparling and place apud Teass......
> 1539-40. For 300 sparlinge from Teys against Christmas, 12*d.*‡

The fishery of salmon is now, of course, confined to certain periods. The

* Gough's edit. † Britannia, ii, 943. ‡ Bursar's books.

fence days fixed by the North Riding and Durham Sessions, in 1848, are Sept. 17, and Feb. 14, the fish being taken in summer. Near Dinsdale are the celebrated Fish-locks, for intercepting them in their migrations. This opposition to the natural disposition of the salmon, to go some thirty miles further up the river in spawning season, is exceedingly destructive to the race, and projects have been set on foot to procure its abolition, but they have always failed.

Among the various other fish inhabiting the *brave river called Teeze,** some belonged to the Bishop, by virtue of his regal privileges.

That the Bpp has the royaltyes of the river of Tease, as Whales, Sturgeon, Purposes, or the like, taken on that side the river next the county of Durham, within the manor of Stockton, and all wracks of the sea, but know not what they are worth :—not 5*l.* per ann.—*Survey of Stockton Manor, taken when the Parliament sold the possessions of the see.*

At this day "not one shilling" possibly would be a more correct return. Whales we have none, the porpoises uselessly gambol near the sandbanks at the river's mouth, and a sturgeon is a rarity. A remarkably large one, caught below Yarm, was exhibited alive at Darlington, in 1848 ; it measured 7 *ft.* 5 *in.* in length, and weighed about 8½ *st.* In former days this "Royal Fish" would very probably have grieved the pious soul of good old Cosin. The charges of catching and curing five sturgeon at his manor of Howden, in 1662, what with dill and rosemary, eleven gallons of white wine at 2*s.* 8*d.* the gallon, 16½ gallons of vinegar at 1*s.* 8*d.* the gallon, and one thing and another, came to 5*l.* 17*s.* 1*d.*, which the Bishop reasonably thought rather a costly matter, as the fish were chiefly given away to my Lord Clarendon, my Lady Gerard, &c. So he desired his Howden steward *to catch no more sturgeons,* and sharply adds "you need not have item'd *me* for your *dill and rosemary.*" For the first assizes after this prelate's consecration, held at Durham, Aug. 12, 1661, when all men's hearts were full of joy at the restoration, we have the following charges :

For a fatt oxe, bought of Wm. Man, of Peircebridge, 11*l.* 5*s.* 0*d.*
To the carrier, for bringing *a case of sturgeon fro' Darenton,* 4*s.* 10*d.*

Truly might Mr. Arden exclaim, "We are prepared to receive the Judges *nobly,*" and doubtless Mr. Neile was equally true in asserting, "We eat and drink *abominably.*"

* Brewster's Stockton, edit. 1796, p. 22.

THE SKERNE

Is almost as amusing as the Tees in its twistings, as the low grounds adjoining the foot road from Darlington to Haughton, and near Blackwell Mill (where the ancient course conducts the waste water), may well testify, but in all other respects it widely differs, being a small, still, sluggish stream, flowing through cars and marshes. From the Well-springs to the north of Trimdon, rises Hurworth-Burn, which runs east for nearly two miles, then turns south, crosses the Hartlepool road, and at the distance of half a mile to the south-west, sinks entirely, and disappears in a swallow-hole in the limestone rock. Near this spot the South Skerne rises and meets the North Skerne near Nunstainton. The latter has its source in the marsh which separates Thrislington from Ferry-hill wood, and is soon augmented by powerful feeders from the limestone rock skirting the morass. At Ferry-hill the Convent of Durham had a swanpool, but the silver swans have long ceased to oar their way across their loch, and the swannery is now occupied by railroads and station-houses.* A flat of marshy land, peat bottoming on clay, extends along the whole upper course of the Skerne, and has been much fertilized by draining, retaining its verdure in the most parching drought. At Mainsforth the peat lies uniformly about eleven feet deep, below that is blue clay of great depth ; nearer the edge of the level the peat borders on limestone, through which constant springs, which never vary in winter or summer, burst with great force. The roots of the trees which have been planted on these grounds have run almost entirely along the surface, never venturing to plunge a fibre into the wet peat. The roots of the willow in particular (of large growth), are one complete mass of fibres closely interwoven, and as regularly spread on the surface of the peat as if levelled by a carpenter's plane. The Scotch fir has reached fifty feet in height, with a girth of six or seven feet, the root meanwhile, not striking two feet below the turf.

This little water of Skerne contains twelve species of fish : 1, roach ; 2, dace ; 3, chub ; 4, gudgeon ; 5, minnow ; 6, miller's thumb ; 7, stickleback ; 8, trout, *rare ;* 9, pike ; 10, barbut or eelpout ; 11, eel ; 12, lamprey (*petromyzon branchialis*).

Of these the barbut, *gadius lota,* is not of very common occurrence ; it is an inhabitant of still lazy streams like the Skerne, where it frequents the deepest pools or hollows under bridges ; it is seldom caught by an angle, nor is more than one usually found in any one pool. It is not uncommon in the Wiske, near Northallerton. The whole skin seems like shagreen, or marked with the impression of small pin-heads. A barbut taken in the Skerne, near Hardwick-mill, June 21, 1811, measured sixteen inches, and

* Raine, in the Glossary to the Durham Household Book. Surtees Society.

weighed 14¼ ounces The stomach contained a minnow and some weed. The Saxon fisherman in Elfric's Dialogues, names among his fishes eels and *eelpouts.* The latter name seems now to be confined to the north. Both Plott and Morton mention this fish as of very rare occurrence, the latter saying that in Northamptonshire it is found only in the Nen. Plott states that only four had been taken in Staffordshire, in his memory, and gives a good description of the fish from a specimen twenty inches long, taken in Faseley Dam, in the Tame, Aug. 1654, and presented to Colonel Comberford, of Comberford,* "who caused it to be drawn to the life and placed in his hall." These general remarks are culled from Surtees, who feared the *Nymphœa Alba*, the beautiful white water lily, was extirpated, he certainly remembered seeing it in the Skerne, near Mordon, and mentions it as being preserved in ponds at Mainsforth. The yellow still exists.

The Isle, a gloomy residence of the L'Isles and Tempests, is completely insulated by the Skerne and small streams, and is always liable to be inundated. The capabilities of the Skerne, for such amusement, have been tested in a costly manner by the Railway Company, who, from their piling bills, must have become well satisfied with the truth of the old adage,

When Roseberry Topping wears a hat,
Morden-Carrs will suffer for that.†

The Scotch have a similar saw anent a stream, with a similar name.

When Cairnsmuir puts on his hat
Palmuir and *Skyreburn* laugh at that.

The Skerne, in records, is frequently the Skyren. The following odd compound of Law-Latin and English, is too curious to be omitted.

Carta Ricardi Prioris, de manerio de Woodham, concesso Thome de Whitworth per divisas.

Omnibus, &c., Ricardus, Prior Dunelm. et ejusd. loci conventus. Noveritis nos dedisse, &c. dilecto et fideli nostro Thome de Whitworth, pro homagio et fideli servicio suo, manerium de Wodum, cum omnibus suis pertin. per metas et divisas subscriptas, viz. "*a fforth versus Aclemore quod ducit a Windleston usque Derlyngton*, per petras ex parte orientali vie, ascendendo usque *Dissyngtrelawe* et a dicto Lawe usque parvum *kerre* per unam petram jacentem juxta dictum kerre, et sic tunc ultra viam ex parte

* A truly honourable race, who I find stuck close to their hall of Comberford, from the days of Stephen, till their extinction in the male line in 1671, and who little need the marvellous proof of their antiquity, in possessing a sort of banshee, in the shape or rather sound of three knocks heard in the hall before the decease of any of the family, though the party might be at never so great a distance. One branch was represented by the Ensors of Wilnecote, par. Tamworth, the ancestors of Sarah Ensor, "whose grandmother was a Shakspear, descended from a brother of everybody's Shakspear" according to the assertion of her husband, John Dyer, the gentle author of Grongar Hill.

† Denham's MSS.

occidentali usque Wyndlilston *Stotfald,* per petras ex parte orientalidi cti Stotfald et a dicto Stotfald usque Holmeslawe et a dicto Lawe usque magnam petram, et a dicta petra usque *blakdobb* juxta unam semitam que ducit a Wyndleston usque Wodom. Et a dicta semita usque ad antiquam fossam per unam petram et unam *sike* quod extendit usque rivulum versus Chilton more ex parte occidentali le Reshefforthe, et sic per dictum rivulum descendendo usque Staynton-Milne per unum sike usque *Skerne.* et sic per aquam de *Skyren* usque *Wodomburn-mouthe,* et sic per Wodomburn equaliter ascendendo usque *predictum fforthe, quod ducit a Wyndilston usque Derlyngton retro,*habendum, &c.

The monks had also a fish-pool at Ferry Hill, and as late as 1631, a lease of Cleves Cross farm mentions the *Eel-ark,* a device it is presumed to take eels, still so abundant. In 1364-5, the Bursar paid "the expenses of a chaplain for two days at Ketton, about the fishing against the feast of S. Cuthbert, in March, 4*s.* 3*d.*" The fishery was probably for eels in this instance. The Skerne was also famous for its pikes.*

Small as this rivulet is, it is extremely important in a commercial point of view. Its water is so famous for bleaching linen, that great quantities have been sent hither for that purpose from Scotland,† besides the vast manufactured stock at Darlington. In 1810, in the course of thirteen miles adjacent, the Skerne turned twelve mills ; seven for corn, two for spinning linen yarn, one for woollen, one fulling mill, and one for grinding optical glasses. The *sike* running past Favordale joins it at Coatham Mundeville.

There is a remarkable pentagonal field to the N.E. of Newton Ketton, in which four considerable rivulets arise, and during a great part of the year water may be seen running in four different directions, occasionally in great quantities. The first runs from its S.E. corner to Byersgill, Stainton, Bishopton, Thorp and Blakeston, and passing between Norton and Billingham, flows into the Tees near Portrack. The second springs from the south fence only a few yards from the first, and falls into the Skerne, below Ketton County Bridge. The third proceeds from the S.W. corner, and penetrating the gloomy gill of Lovesome Hill, augments the Skerne near the factory of Coatham Mundeville. The fourth rises in the N.W. corner, and gliding past Preston Lodge, through the Earl of Eldon's estates, mixes with the waters of Morden Carrs, before Ricnall Grange, after passing beneath the Clarence and York and Newcastle Railways. Pity that such a singular close does not exist in the east, there it would have established the fame of some geographical speculator, and fixed the site of Eden at once.

* Gough's Camden.

† Luckombe's Gazeteer, 1790.

THE COCKERBECK OR COCKE-BECK.

Flows from Walworth and joins the Skerne in Northgate. Many rivers bear similar names. Thus we have in Cumberland,

The *Cocker* and the Calder,
The Dutton and the Derwent,
The Eden and the Ellen,
The Eamont and the Esk,
The Greta and the Gelt,
The Leven and the Liddal,
The Irving and the Irt,
The Mite and Peteril,
The Waver and Wampool.*

Camden takes the etymology of cockney from the Thames, which he says was of old time called Cockney. A wicked writer in the Literary Gazette,† says, "There was formerly a little brook by Turnmill-street, called Cockney. Perhaps the ducking bath of the noisy Cyprians on the cucking-stool? May not *cockney* and also *cucking-stool* be from the term *coquean?* If so, certainly a most unenviable derivation." In our case, I sincerely hope the cucking-stool (*alias* ducking-stool) in the town was amply sufficient for all our "scolding queans" without any *Cuck-her-becks* being called into requisition. All joke aside, we may presume a cocke-boat is from the same source, whatever it may be, as Cocke-beck.

As before stated, Badle-beck in time of floods carries off the waste water of the Cocker-beck. It has its own resources in other seasons, in the shape of various gutters intersecting the low lands near, and which, with the main channel, form a pool at the roadside, near Moudon Bridge, which may perhaps, properly be called the head of Badle-beck. In the hot days of summer, however, in spite of all its gutters, pools, springs, and drains, it is almost if not completely dry. At the bridge near Badle-beck Inn, it forms a very pretty little gill.

THE HELL-KETTLES.

—— Then I do bid adieu
To Bernard's battelled towers, and seriously pursue
My course to Neptune's Court; but as forthwith I runne,
The Skern, a dainty nymph, saluting Darlington,
Comes in to give me ayd, and being prowd and ranke,
Shee chanc'd to looke aside, and spieth neere her banke,

* Denham's MSS.

† 1846, p. 426.

(That from their lothsome brimms do breath a sulpherous sweat)
Hell-Kettles rightly cald, that with the very sight,
This water-nymph, my Skerne, is put in such affright,
That with unusuall speed she on her course doth hast,
And rashly runnes herselfe into my widened waste.
Drayton's Polyolbion, 29*th song, Tees loquitur.*

An article in the Newcastle Magazine, for 1826, fancifully endeavoured to discover Homer's Hell in New Zealand ! but our Hells at home are quite as perplexing as those of Grecian bards. Spiritually, Hell is the place of the doomed; temporally, it is the same, but in the one case it is the receptacle of those who steal, in the other, the stronghold of the stolen. Don't you recollect, good reader, the man who

—— had, as well
As the bold Trojan knight, seen *Hell:*
Not with a counterfeited pass
Of golden bough, but true *gold lace.**

And the note explaining that tailors call that place *hell* where they put all they steal? Again, Hell spiritual is sometimes Paradise; so, in a minor way, is Hell temporal:

BARLEY-BREAK, OR LAST IN HELL.

We two are last in Hell: what may we fear
To be tormented, or kept prisoners here:
Alas! if kissing be of plagues the worst,
We'll wish, in Hell we had been last and first.

A verse from Herrick's Hesperides, alluding to a pleasant forfeit in the old game of Barley-break, in which three couples played. One went to each end of the ground, and ran across, when the couple in the middle (or Hell) caught, if they could, one of the running couples and placed them in Hell instead. In names of places the word is equally various in its signification. It may mean a hill, or a hole, or water, and as a place may be seated on a hill by the side of water, or *vice versa,* and if by water, in nine cases out of ten, must be low also, in the same proportion it is almost impossible to state the origin of a name with *Hell* in its composition. The confusion is made still worse by the word being often corrupted into *hill,* as in Hylton (anciently Heltun) by the Wear; Hellegate afterwards Hylgate, now Water-row, in Morpeth, leading from the Wansbeck; Hilton, near Staindrop, formerly Helton (on a hill); Hilton Beacon, in Westmoreland, formerly Helton Bacon (under a hill), &c. Again, *helle* is still used as a verb, "to pour out in a rapid manner," hence probably Helvellyn, a cascade on the Glaamæn,

* Hudibras.

in Norway, and Helvellyn, in Cumberland, down which a cataract rushes. Lastly, it means solitary, lonely, as in Hellebeck.

I have referred to this latter word in p. 3. Thoresby, in his Diary for 1694, thus mentions it. "On the left nothing but a ghastly precipice to the Fell-foot, which, I think, may as well be called Hell-foot, as those riverets (which Camden mentions, p. 727) Hell-becks, because creeping in waste, solitary, and unsightly places, amongst the mountains upon the borders of Lancashire."

Hodgson, in his Northumberland, decidedly says that the name of our Hell-Kettles means *water*-kettles (being in Oxen-le-field, the Field of Waters), in illustration of which I throw together half a dozen names in the parish.

North and South *Helmer* Arm, the names of two closes of the Wharton land between Darlington and Haughton, in 1771. Helmer, Elmer, or Aylmer, is a pleonastic expression, signifying *the lake of waters.*

Elstantoftes, at Blackwell, see p. 8.

Elesbankes, at Darlington, mentioned in Hatfield's Survey, and probably on the Skerne.

Ellyngmedowe, wherein the Punder, of Darlington, had half an acre at the same period.

Le Elling, a copyhold close in Bondgate, to which Jane Sober, widow of William Sober, was adm. in 1621.*

Ellvis, in Darneton, a copyhold parcel of land mentioned, 1642.†

19 Feb. 42 Eliz. Wm. *Helcoat* held one ox-gang in Cockerton, late Edward Perkinson's, by knight's service, leaving Michael his son and heir, who alienated to Marshall, Smith, and Lewlin. Pardon to John Marshall for 20 acr. of land, 20 of meadow, and 20 of pasture, from Michael Helcoates, 9 Jac. 1611. John Smith, 10 acr. of meadow, from Helcoates, 26 July, 44 Eliz. Anthony Gilpyn had pardon for acquiring the same from John Smith, 20 Aug. 1628. 14 Feb. 42 Eliz. Richard Lewlin *d.* seized of lands purchased of Michael Helcotes, held by the 40th part of a knight's fee. Henry, his son and heir, aged 6 years. John Marshall *d.* seised of 20 acr. of meadow, as much of pasture and as much of arable, 1634, leaving Robert his *s.* and *h.* æt. 38.‡ Francis Helcott and Helenor Todd, married 1594-5, Jan. 26. *Par. Reg.*

10 Skirlaw, John Tesedale died, seized of lands in the Westfield of Darlington, in a certain place called *Hell,* which in Bishop Langley's time, were the possession of the Eures (Inq. p. m. Rad. Eure, 17 Langley) and Hutchinson thinks it not unreasonable that the Hell-Kettles took their name from being situate in this land, but I scarcely think it can be identified with the territory of Oxen-le-field, which lies nearly due south of the town. The Punder held half an acre in the Westfield, at Hatfield's Survey.

Another writer derives the name from the British *hal,* an alkali (whence *halen,* salt) and *kiddle,* or *kidle,* a dam: Hal-Kiddles, salt pits.§ But the most elaborate idea is that in Hutchinson.

"Most of our lime works, marle-pits, and allum-pits are wrought much deeper than six yards ; water standing in hollows, from whence marle has been gotten, will taste

* Halmot Court Bks.

† Ibid.—I Geo. 1, Wm. Davison and Eliza ux. to George Allen, merchant. *Elvis* alias *Ellings* alias *Le Ings.*

‡ Surtees. § Beauties of England and Wales.

pungent on the tongue, and curdle milk and soap [as that of these pools does]: we know of no allum being wrought here, though it abounds in Cleveland, not many miles distant, but the use of marle was very early, and it is probable these were marle-pits: they resemble the workings in other counties, where marling is still practised. Marle was known to the Romans, and by them exported hence to foreign countries; we have statues mentioned by our antiquaries, dedicated to *Nehallennia* or the *new moon*, particularly some inscribed by *Negociator Cretarius Britannicianus*, a dealer in *marle, chalk*, or *fuller's earth*, to the British territories; and these being called *Nehallennia's Kettles*, or of NIE-HEL, in the old German tongue, from the trader's dedication, might be corrupted to, or called Hell's Kettles, and the monastic writers, to efface the memory of the old superstition, might devise the miraculous account."

And yet, after all these solemn devices for a name, I verily believe that the earthquake origin, is, in the main, true, though it may be handed to us in an exaggerated form, and that the name has merely a reference to the infernal character of the production and water of these marvellous kettles. Such was the popular idea of it in Harrison's time, as appears from the following singular passage:

"What the foolish people dreame of the Hell-Kettles, it is not worthy the rehersall, yet to the ende the lewde opinion conceyved of them maye growe into contempt, I will say thus much also of those pits. Ther are certeine pittes or rather three litle poles, a myle from Darlington, and a quarter of a myle distant from the These bankes, *which the people call the Kettes of Hell, or the Devil's Ketteles, as if he shoulde seethe soules of sinfull men and women in them: they adde also that the spirites have oft beene harde to crye and yell about them*, wyth other like talke, savouring altogether of pagane infidelitye. The truth is, (and of this opinion also was Cuthbert Tunstall, Byshop of Durham) that the colemines in those places are kindled, or if there be no coles, there may a mine of some other unctuous matter be set on fire, which beyng here and there consumed, the earth falleth in, and so doth leave a pitte. In deede the water is nowe and then warme as they saye, and beside that it is not cleere, the people suppose them to be an hundred faddame deepe, the byggest of them also hath an issue into the These. But ynough of these woonders least I doe seeme to be touched in thys description, and thus much of the Hel-Kettles."—Harrison in Hollinshed, 1577, i. 94.

Certes, the idea of the spirits being boiled is most horrible!

The kettles next morning were boiling and foaming,
A groan in their deeps was full ghastily booming,
A sulphureous stench was ymixt in the air,
And the carles they were cowed and said many a prayer.

But the days when the peasants could boil their pottage in the Hell-Kettles have long fleeted, and travellers by rail may not say like those by road of 1634,* "The three admired deepe pitts, called Hell Kettles, we left *boyling* by Darlington."*

* A Relation of a short Survey, begun at the city of Norwich, on Monday, August 11th, 1634, and ending at the same place. By a captain, a lieutenant, and an ancient; all three of the Military Company in Norwich.

Neither do authors write thus:

> In the country hereabouts (*in hujus agro*, in a field belonging to this place, G.) are three pits of a surprising depth, commonly called Hell-Kettles, from the water heated in them by the compression (*Antiperistasis*, Reverberation, G.) of the air [!]*

And notwithstanding Daniel De Foe says so decisively "As to the Hell-Kettles, so much talked up for a wonder, which are to be seen as we ride from the Tees to Darlington, I had already seen so little of wonder in such country tales, that I was not hastily deluded again. 'Tis evident they are nothing but coal pits filled with water by the River Tees,"---we do not find that coal or other† mineral has been dug thereabouts, and certainly pits of 114 and 75 feet diameter bear no very great resemblance to coal pits drowned. Besides the depth, notwithstanding the superstitions and the proverb

As Deep as the Hell Kettles,‡

occasionally applied to convey the idea of an *unfathomable* mystery, is very moderate. Dr. Jabez Kay wrote to Bishop Gibson :---" The name of bottomless pits made me provide myself with a line above 200 fathoms long, and a lead weight proportionable. But much smaller preparations would have served. For the deepest of them took but fifteen fathom or thirty yards of our line." According to the measurement of Mr. Grose and Mr. Allan, however, October 18, 1774, the figures stand thus:

Diameter of the three larger kettles about	. . .	38 yards.
Ditto smallest about	. . . .	28 ditto.

Depth of the four kettles respectively, 19½, 17, 14, and 5½ feet.

Another class of popular ideas includes a number of floating traditions of passages from the kettles to the Skerne and Tees having been discovered. One legend connects itself with some eastern diver, or " man of colour" who dived and passed from one of the pools to the Skerne, but the story is more common of a goose or duck, which found its way into the Tees. In Leland's time there lived a prudent wary man, ycleped Anthony Bellasyse, a doctor in civil law, master in Chancery, and one of the council of the North, who was younger brother of Richard Bellasyse, Esq., and laid the foundations of the Newburgh House of Bellasyse, by obtaining a grant of the scite of the abbey there, which he settled on his nephew. Of this worthy, Leland notes§ in this wise, " Mr. Doctor Bellazis tolde me that a dukke, markid after the

* Gough's Camden. An old translation of Camden has it thus :—" In this Townefield are three pitts of a wonderful depth, the common people tearme them Hell-Kettles, because the water in them by the Antiperistasis or reverberation of the cold air striking thereupon waxeth hote."

† I have somewhere seen the Hell-Kettles supposed to be lime-pits.

‡ Denham MSS. § Itin. vi. 24.

fascion of dukkes of the Bishopricke of Duresme, was put into one of the pooles called Hel Ketelles, betwixt Darlington and Tese bank, and after was found at [Crofte] Bridge, upon Tese thereby, wher Gervalx* duelleth, and that be it the people had a certain conjecture, that there was *specus subterr.* betwixt the ij places." Surtees† shrewdly remarks that nothing is more natural than that the duck should leave the sulphureous brackish pool in which she was placed, and *walk* across two or three green fields, to the Tees. Camden attributes this discovery to Bishop Cuthbert Tunstall, and calls the animal he had marked a *goose.* Gibson makes a sad mistake when he says that the tradition has ceased in the neighbourhood.

The fact is, that any subterranean passage is impossible, and the legend ridiculous. The opening of such would be visible in a river, though it is not in the kettles, and the latter would rise in floods to the same level with the stream. But there they are, sable, solemn, still, sulphureous. Floods and droughts come and go with their effects on the Tees and Skerne, but the Hell-Kettles rest the same evermore. They are, in reality, fast flowing springs. Three of them are joined by a surface channel, and the water is carried away by a stell or streamlet which supplies the neighbouring farms with water, and runs into the Skerne, the fourth and smallest pool is detached and close to the road. The water is drunk by the cattle, and does not seem to be at all injurious to them, but the pike and eels frequenting the kettles, always eat soft and watery, as if out of season, being in truth, natural prisoners, where a freeborn fish would certainly fret away all his fatness.‡ Surtees mentions the following plants as growing at Hell-Kettles, *Hippuris Vulgaris,* mare's tail; *Chara hispida; Utricularia Vulgaris,* common hooded milfoil; *Schœnus mariscus,* prickly bog-rush; *Potamogeton pectinatum,* fennel-leaved pondweed; *Lemna trisulca,* ivy-leaved duckweed; and *carex stricta.* The ponds are much choaked with vegetation.

The chronicles of Henry II's. reign§ are full of "uncouth wonders," and the year 1178 must have been a most marvellous one.

* Clervaux of Croft. † Vol. i. 202. ‡ Gordon's Guide to Croft, &c., 1834.

§ I do not think the following has been added to any of our county histories, though it forms a capital gloss on the grant by this king to Bishop Flambard, of a market at Norton, on the Lord's Day, and is extremely curious in a literary point of view, to boot:—In Brompton's Chronicle, it is related that as Henry was passing through Wales, on his return from Ireland, in the Spring of 1172, he stopped at Cardiff Castle, on a Sunday, to hear mass; after which, as he was mounting his horse to be off again, there was presented before him a somewhat singular apparition, a man with red hair and a *round tonsure,* a distinction which would seem to imply that there were still in Wales some priests of the olden church who held out against Romish innovations, and retained the ancient national crescent-shaped tonsure. He was lean and tall, attired in a white tunic, and barefoot. This individual began in the *Teutonic* tongue, "Gode olde Kinge," and delivered a command from Christ, as he said, and his mother, from John the Baptist, and from Peter, that he should suffer no traffic or servile works to be done throughout his dominions on the Sabbath-day, except only such as pertained to the use of food; which command, if he observed, whatever he might undertake, he should easily accomplish. Although only the three first words are chronicled in what the writer calls Teutonic (i. e. Saxon or English) there can

"This yeare," says old Hollinshed, "on the Sunday before the nativitie of S. John Baptist, being the eighteenth of June. after the setting of the sunne, there appeared a marvellous sighte in the aire vnto certaine persons that beheld the same. For whereas the newe moone shone foorth very faire, with his horns towardes the east, straighte wayes the upper horne was devided into two, out of the middes of whiche devision, a brenning brand sprang up, casting from it a farre off coales and sparkes, as it had bin of fire. The body of the moone in the meane time that was beneath, seemed to wrast and writh in resemblance like to an adder or snake that had bin beaten, and anone after it came to the olde state agayne. This chanced above a dosen times, and at length from horne to horne it became halfe blacke.*

In September following, the moone beyng about seven and twentith dayes olde, at sixe of the clocke, the sunne was eclipsed, not universally, but particularly, for the body thereof appeared as it wer horned, shoting the hornes towards the west, as the moone doth, being twentie dayes olde. The residue of the compasse of it, was covered with a blacke roundell, whiche comming downe by little and little, threw about the horned brightnesse that remained, til both the hornes came to hang down on eyther side to the earthwards, and as the blacke roundell went by little and little forwardes, the hornes at length were turned towards the west, and so the blacknes passing away, the sunne received hir brightnesse againe. In the meane time, the aire being ful of cloudes of divers coulours, as red, yellow, greene, and pale, holp the peoples sight with more ease to discerne the maner of it. (A strange eclips of the sunne, *in the margin.*) The K. thys yeare held his Christmas at Winchester, at whiche time, newes came abroade of a great wonder that hadde chaunced at a place called *Oxenhale, within the Lordship of Derlington*, in which place a part of the earth lifted it selfe up on height in apparance like to a mighty Tower, and so it remained from nine of the clocke in the morning, till the even tyde, and then it fell downe with an horrible noise, so that all suche as were neighbours thereabout, were put in great feare. That peece of earth with the fall, was swallowed up, leaving a greate deepe pitte in the place, as *was* to be seene many yeares after."†

It does not seem to have struck the chronicler that the pit still remained in the shape of Hell-Kettles, nor does he account for its disappearance. The event is more minutely detailed in Brompton's Chronicle.‡

be no doubt that the rest, though recorded in Latin, was in the same, and it appears that the king understood English, though he might not be able to speak it, for he, speaking in *French*, desired his attendant soldier to ask the rustic if he had dreamed all this. The soldier (who must have spoken both languages) made the enquiry accordingly, in *English*, when the man replied to the king *in the same language as before*. "Whether I have dreamed it or no, mark this day; for, unless thou shalt do what I have told thee, and amend thy life, thou shalt within a year's time hear such news as thou shalt mourn to the day of thy death." Then he vanished, and calamities thickened on the perverse king. His profane market at Norton waned and fell, and like the heap at Oxenhale, the place of the Market Cross is marked by a large pool, called *Cross Dyke*, which, as *dyke* is applied to any thing formed by digging, may have been artificially caused. Some years ago I remember its being perfectly dry in a hot summer, but was too young to observe whether any remains of the Cross foundations existed.

* Gerua. Dors. *in margine.*

† An. Reg. 25. Rog. Houe. 1179. *in margine*, i. e. the year 1179 began at the Christmas in mention. Roger Hoveden wrote at the end of 12th and beginning of the 13th centuries.

‡ Brompton was abbot of Jorevale or Jerveaux, in Yorkshire, and Selden has shewn that the book was by no means written by him, but merely procured for the house while he presided. The chronicle begins with St. Augustine's mission, and ends in 1199, though the author (who wrote it in or after 1328) intimates at the commencement his design of bringing it down to the time of Edward I. It is compiled from earlier authorities, some of which we do not now possess.

1179. About Christmas, a wonderful and unheard of event fell out at Oxenhale, viz., that in the very domain of Lord Hugh, Bishop of Durham, the ground rose up on high with such vehemence, that it was equal to the highest tops of the mountains, and towered above the lofty pinnacles of the churches; and at that height remained from the ninth hour of the day even to sunset. But at sunset it fell with so horrible a crash, that it terrified all who saw that heap, and heard the noise of its fall, whence many died from that fear; for the earth swallowed it up, and caused in the same place a very deep pit.*

Camden, quoting a nearly similar passage from the Chronicles† of Tynemouth, says that the earthquake origin of Hell-Kettles was at his time adopted by "the wiser sort and men of better judgment." Lord Lyttleton‡ observes that in the account "only one pit is mentioned, and naturally the falling in of an heap of soil so raised would form but one. This hill probably was puffed up by subterraneous fires, like that in the Lucrine Lake, now called Monte-novo; but what has filled up the chasm caused by its sinking, or divided it into different cavities, it is not easy to say." Gordon adds that "as modern philosophy has ascertained that sulphur and water are active agents in the production both of earthquakes and volcanoes, it seems highly probable that the water of the spring having found its way into the bed of sulphur, which impregnates the Spas at Croft and Dinsdale, excited the volcanic action described by the chronicler; then as soon as the pent up vapours got vent, the ground would, of course, sink down, and the spring having thus gained the surface, would produce the hollows which subsist to this day. In fact we learn from Sir William Hamilton's account of the great earthquake in Calabria, in 1783, that circular hollows filled with water were produced in the plain of Rosarno, during that awful convulsion of nature." When roads were bad and communication slow, events would become much altered in their transmission from mouth to mouth, before they reached the chronicler's ears, and if the phenomenon was of irregular extent, and caused more hills and pits than one, the largest would probably only be recorded. Allowing that there is a difficulty in the identification, is there not a much greater one in answering the question, "If Hell-Kettles are not the vestiges of the earthquake, where was the deep pit, and what has blotted its trace from Oxen-le-field?" In Cheshire, A.D. 165.., "a quantity of earth foundered and fell down a vast depth,"§ and near Leeming a similar occurrence took place about a century ago. The ground gave way and a deep pond appeared. Men with

* Ann. 1179. Infra vero idem natale Domini contigit apud Oxenhale quoddam mirabile a seculo inauditum, exilicet, quod in ipsa Domini Hugonis Episcopi Dunelmensis cultura, terra se in altum ita vehementer elavit quod summis montium cacuminibus abæquaretur, et quod super alta templorum pinnacula, emineret, et illa altitudo ab hora diei nona usque ad occasum solis permansit. Sole vero occidente, eum tam horribili strepitu cecidit, quod omnes cumulum illum videntes, et strepitum casus illius audientes perterruit; unde multi timore illo obierunt; nam tellus eum absorbuit, et puteum profundissimum ibidem fecit.

† They mention the "deep pit" as being "to be seene for a testimony unto this day."

‡ Life of King Henry II. Appendix, p. 24. 4to. edit.

§ Aubrey's Wiltshire, Roy. Soc. p. 106.

teams were employed to fill it up, and had almost succeeded, when one day, on their return from dinner all had disappeared, and the hole was as deep as ever. It is said to be unfathomable, is nearly full of water, and now surrounded by a strong hedge to prevent accidents. A man is reported to have sunk with the earth, and the field is called **The Earthquake Field**.* By the way, some fifty years ago, a gentleman lodging at Jamie Trenholme's, in Blackwellgate, leaped into one of the Hell-Kettles, and was drowned.

Thrice happy associates, who keep up the sport,
To the field haste away, to HELL-KETTLES resort;
And crown, boys, and crown all confusion's dear joys,
With rancour, and malice, and nonsense, and noise.
Derry down, &c.

And whilst you are drinking from Cocitus' cup,
And Lucifer laughs as you quaff the toast up,
The muse who hangs loitering upon your dull heel,
Will further descriptions and characters steal.
Derry down, &c.

Such are the two last stanzas of "NIMROD'S GARLAND: OR, DARLINGTON CHACE," a desperately personal tract from George Allan's press, a piece of no incident, and whose allusions are too local to be very interesting. It was succeeded by "A Tail-piece to the Darlington Chase," and "The Dismal Lamentations of a Monopolist of Game, some time since mournfully sung on the banks of the Don; at present applied by Christopher Fungus, Esq., to himself and his brother, Nimrod Fungus, Esq., and bellowed out with greater pathos on the banks of the Tees, to the tune of "Babes in the Wood." *Mutato nomine, de te Fabula narratur.* London: Printed in Blackwall Close, 1783. Licensed and entered according to order." This latter is not without spirit, but in the present excitement on the game question, may not be exactly suitable to the pages of a book for all readers, though withal highly amusing.

H [i] ll had a great ox—sheep I've in store,
Hare or mutton, our dinner's the same;
Our servants will not think of neck-beef,
When their bellies are filled with GAME.

An odd tract was published by M. Darnton, in 1791, entitled "HELL-KETTLES, WITH THE ORIGIN OF DARLINGTON: A DRAMATIC PASTORAL," prefaced by a short and rather important description of the place. Then comes an apology from the author in lines of a peculiar construction:

His work, devoid of rhetorical charms,
But aims at narrative—not stage alarms.

* Ex inf. Nicholai Trant de Bedale, Chirurg.

The Dramatis Personæ are, Minerva; Sylvia, a shepherdess; Arcadius, a shepherd betrothed to Sylvia, and the Genius of Darlington. Sylvia, in a grove, pensive and terrified at the convulsions of nature, is approached by Arcadius, who, in horror asks if his hapless absence has "forced hesperion drops from those adorable luminaries," whereupon she gives an account of the direful presages which had happened near the confluence of the Dare and Tisa, and the tremendous sounds which "reechoed from the *neighbouring* mountains."* Arcadius informs her that these things were pronounced at Acley's sacred grove, and is interrupted by Minerva, who calms their fears and explains in a way not very relevant to the catastrophe, how the Naiads, Neptune, Sol, and Vulcan, would combine to bless Deira. The Genius of Darlington sings about Mercury visiting "the sweet banks of the Dare," and with Ceres, Pan, Bacchus, and Silenus, forming a mart at Darlington, which Jove approves:

Old Cuthbert, whose miracles fill the dull page
 Of monastic transcribers from Rome;
His bones claim the merit our pains to assuage,
 His veiled courtesy softens our doom.
Appalled by this pretext, the son of great Ulph,
 Adds the town to his patron's domains,
In hopes of avoiding Charybdis' feigned gulph
 And the torment of Chimera's flames.

Grave Leland in after-times prancing this way,
 The archives of famed Albion to trace,
'Tis meet, said the Sire, to my Prince to convey
 A picture so apt for his grace:
He noted the Temple, the Palace, and Mart,
 With the soft-flowing stream of old Dar:
All Phœnix-like risen, not harmed by the smart
 Of frenzy, disaster, and jar.

The happy association of the stately Cuthbert, with Bacchus and Silenus, the idea of Styr son of Ulphus having ever dreamed of Charybdis and Chimera, and the gallant contempt of vulgar chronology, displayed in the genius of 1179 recalling Leland and bluff Hal in his narration, all are as refreshing in these iron days as a cucumber in summer, and exhibit a vigour of conception well deserving of a guerdon from the *Pastoral* Aid Society. There is, after all, something curious, considering how Darlington has caused railways to spread over the globe, in Minerva's bouncing prophecy of a time when "this fertile district shall be the luminary of agricultural science; distant empires shall profit by her instructions; and the Scythian deserts be ameliorated with her implements."

One note more as to marle-pits. I have just been to Hell-Kettles, tasted

* Where are they?

all their waters, and could not distinguish any pungency whatever, they were slightly favoured with iron,* and by no means unpleasant to the taste. A dog drank them readily, and completely nullified the popular notion that the canine species will not venture to swim across these pits of Avernus. The water of the large pool was beautifully clear round the margin, discovering a bed lined with vegetation of an exquisite green, indeed it merits the appellation of a very pretty little mere, the two conjoined were darker, and the smallest quite muddy. There was something about all these pits, nevertheless, unearthly and solemn, producing an effect upon the mind, peculiar and lasting. A friend adds one more origin for them, viz., that they were workings for iron stone. Poor old chroniclers, what liars we modern sceptics would make you!

WELLS.

In 1545 when Henry VIII. granted the messuage in Darlington which had belonged to the Priory of Mountgrace to Thomas Whytehed (nearly related to the last Prior and first Dean of Durham), in free socage, it is described as "all the messuage formerly in the tenure of Rich. Aleynson, now of Christopher Hogge and Agnes his wife in Darlington otherwise Darneton *upon the well*."† This was, doubtless, the spring which gave name to Tubwell Row, more anciently *le well rawe, juxta Tubbwell*,‡ and which was, like the well in Skinnergate, of sufficient consequence to need annual overseers. The overseers of *le Tubbwell* and *Skinnergaite Well* (two for each) occur from 1612 when the Borough books commence, and cease during the hiatus (1633-1710) in them, for in 1760 the overseers of the Highways were amerced for not repairing the Tubwell. It is now covered by a pump.

1612. The Jurors lay a paine that none shall wash cloathes, fish, or such like things at the Tubwell to putrifie the same upon paine of 6s 8d.

1621. A paine none shall washe any clothes, fyshe, or scower any skeles§ tubbes or other vessels, but at or below *the litle well at the tubwell* upon paine of 3s. 4d. (*Borough Books.*)

The well in Hundegate ‖ is mentioned in the charter by which Bishop Beke gave to the Church of Darlington a messuage as a vicarage house, near the gate of his mansion, with one venell ¶ which formerly led to the well, by

* The presence of iron is very visible near them, and a spring strongly impregnated with it originates a stell in a neighbouring field.

† Surtees. ‡ Borough Books, 1612.

§ A skele is a small round tub of wood, with an upright handle of the same material, rising at one side instead of an arched one across of iron. ‖ Fontem de Hundegate.

¶ Narrow Passage. A venell, called Hundgate Well, is mentioned as a boundary in 1507.

the taking in of which the messuage was enlarged. This was in 1309. In 1621 the daughter of Mrs. Hearyn and the wife of Henry Shawe were amerced for abusing the well in Hungate.*

In the Nessfield estate, close to the Skerne, is the Drop-well, covered by a brick arch by the Allans and of very tardy flow, which, accompanied by a group of cattle in the summer, constitutes a happy picture. Between Darlington and Haughton also, near the foot-path from Northgate is the Rock-well, which springs from rock seemingly formed of small stones united by a limey substance. This, with its canopy of trees, is also a beautiful little scene, but it has been much injured in latter years by a wholesale plunder of part of the rock, to the great regret of all lovers of nature's elegance.

16 Jas. I. Surrender of a close in Cockerton, called Capsay-hill, bounded on the S. by Cole-street, and on the W. by *Capsay well* close.—(*Halmot Books.*)

1642. Thomas, Lord Faulconbridg Baron of Yaram, nephew and heir of James Bellasis, Esq. deceased, adm. to Grasse Inn Moore, Kilnegarth, Kay Close, Cheisley, East and West Myers, *Well leezes*, Annat Thorne, *Annat well*, and Huntersheile field, in Blackwell, which belonged to his uncle, James. In the next court, James's widow, Isabella, adm. to some of the Towne land, Blackwell, and his executor, Thomas Swinborne, to all the closes specified above. (*Halmot Books.*) James Bellasis lived at Owton, and in Stranton church is a costly monument to him, displaying his effigy as rising from the tomb and throwing off a winding sheet, with a long epitaph in the usual fulsome style of the period.

One of the springs in the Baydales estate flows down a grim little glen called Grimsley Gill (a most appropriate cognomen), and uniting with a larger runner which proceeds from another spring rising in the middle of a field and is never dry, finds its way to the Tees.

BRIDGES.

In some old charter at Durham I remember mention being made of a ford at Darlington, but a Bridge existed here in very early times. In 1343, Cecilia Underwood† leaves "*ponti ultra aquam de Skyrryn* 13*s.* 4*d.* Item ponti de Halghton 6*s.* 8*d.* Item qui vocatur Walkebrigg 2*s.* Item pontibus inter villam de Norton et Herdewyk 3*s.*" Leland says, "Darington Bridge of stone is, as I remembre, of three arches," but, in after times, it possessed nine goodly arches, which are very conspicuous in Bailey's print of 1760, and which Defoe, in 1727, mentions as "a high stone bridge over little or no water." In fact at that time and until a very recent period the river was wide and shallow and formed a vast morass along its banks on the eastern side. At the October sessions, 1751, a view and report were ordered of

* In 1666, land called Houndwells is mentioned in Haughton. Hutch. iii. 181.

† Of whom hereafter.

S. Wilkinson del. 1760. J. Bailey sc. 1776, Cave & Sons, York resc. 1849.

South East Aspect of Darlington in 1760.

This Plate is presented by

Rob.t Henry Allan

Haughton and Burdon* Bridges, and also the road at the N.E. end of Darlington Bridge; and in April, 1752, the report of Tho. Davison, Geo. Allan, W. Sutton, John Emerson, and Henry Thorpe, justices, who, with the county surveyor, had viewed the premises, certified:

"That the said Bridges and road are very insufficient and Dangerous in the winter season for Carts, Carriages, and Persons passing on horseback along the same, by reason of the Deepness of the said Road and the overflowing of the River Skearn upon the same, and at the said bridges (even in very small floods) whereby not only carriages but also laden horses are frequently stopt for several days together; and we do also certify that the said Bridges and Road have been, time immemorialy, used for Carts and Carriages, and (as it appears to us) have been constantly Repaired and Amended by the County of Durham; and we do also certify that it will (in our opinion) be absolutely necessary, and for the Publick good, to enlarge the said Bridges and Road, viz., by Building another large Arch at the East End of Burdon Bridge sufficient for Carriages, and to raise the road at each end of the said Bridge; also, by taking down and widening the Arch of the Bridge at Haughton, and raising the Road at the East End thereof; also, by raising the Road at the North-East End of Darlington Bridge with a Battlement or Flank Wall on the side thereof, so as to make the same sufficient, and fit for Carts and Carriages to pass along the same with safety."

The estimate in 1753 of John Hunter for building the proposed wall, for "10 cundels to take off the springs in that part of the road," for levelling the road to the height of the wall and paving a "causey" in front of the houses was £50 7*s*. The wall was to be 1 yard high and 12 yards distant from the houses.

In 1767 Messrs. R. and W. Nelson, of Melsonby, contracted to build a new bridge for £860, of Gatherley Moor stone. In this estimate, the parapet was to be of brick, but in 1768 Counsel moved that at an extra cost of £140 (making the total cost £1000) a stone parapet should be erected by Nelsons on the ground of the insecurity of a 140 yards line of brick which would be a perpetual charge to the county "as it was in the old Bridge where repaired with bricks." Six out of ten magistrates consented.†

This bridge is a plain one of 3 arches, much too narrow (especially in the footpaths) for the traffic upon it as an approach from the Railway station, and shamefully encroached upon by ugly sheds, &c., built upon the parapet walls. It stands at the foot of Tubwell Row (which is called Briggate by Hutchinson) by the side of the scite of the old nine-arched bridge, which, after all, had a very gallant effect.

The Skerne is also crossed by iron bridges at the feet of Priestgate and Workhouse lane, and by sundry smaller bridges communicating with Northgate, none of which deserve mention. Those by which the two railways pass over it are, however, fine structures, that on the York and Newcastle line is

* In 1430 Bishop Langley granted indulgences to all those who should give alms and monies for making a bridge between Halghton and Burdon.

† Papers penès R. H. Allan, Esq.

indeed a most elegant object near the Drop-well, consisting of light elliptical arches on lofty piers. Between the town and the Tees, the Skerne runs under Nought or Snipe Bridge and Oxenfield Bridge; the latter being almost at its estuary, over it the Croft road passes. Snipe bridge is of brick, very narrow, and apparently built upon the remains of a wider one of stone. It has two arches, the Skerne running through one, and a little sike flowing by the territory of Humble-sykes, through the other, joining the Skerne under a willow's shade just after. Snipe House is close by, and the place has a degree of beauty about it.

1649. That Francis Goundry, pinder, of Darnton, shall scoore and dresse the stell nere Darnton Bridge before Whit Sonday. (*Halmot Books.*)

1592. The Dean and Chapter of Durham bestowed out of their funds for repairing highways and bridges, "To the highway between Cottom and Darlington £1 10*s*. To *Skerne Oxen bridge* £1." £20 a-year was spent by the Chapter for this purpose, upon their foundation.

1710. John Dent, of *Nought bridge*, par. Darlington occurs. (*Borough Books.*) Nought (neat) is a general word for cattle. We have a Nought Fair.

The Cockerbeck after leaving the head of Badle-beck (which is crossed by Moudon Bridge, near Moudon House, and the Barnard-castle road) flows under a good stone bridge (near which is Stepping-stone Close), and another in Northgate, which has recently been widened, and near which John, the son of Robert Hutchinson, of Thurslington Hall, a young man, was slain by a fall from his horse in 1713. (*Par. Reg.*)

1620. Bridgend house and Bridgend close, Cockerton, occur. (*Halmot Books.*)

1627. Christopher Skepper adm. to Cockerton Briggs Close (*Halmot Books.*) This fellow was son of Christopher Skepper, of Durham, who was clerk of the Halmot Court, steward of Darlington Borough Court, 1612, and "the 13th son of his father." He died 1623. Young Kit was a "prodigal," and when he was admitted to his father's lands, by order of Mr Justice Hutton, in 1625, it was only on giving security to pay his father's debts, for which he was then imprisoned, and to keep harmless his two brothers, William and Moses. The latter was clerk of the Halmot Courts, and Christopher Sherwood, Rector of Bishopwearmouth, preached his funeral sermon (1641), from the odd text, "Moses my servant is dead." (*Mickleton's MSS.*) There are Skepper's Closes in the Hill Close House estate, which are leasehold of the Bishop, an unusual tenure here. Chr. Skepper was amerced in 1621 for keeping undersitters in his house. (*Borough Books.*

*** 1619. A paine of 39*s*. that Richard Patteson shall, before the feast of St. John Baptist next, eyther joyne with Hurwoorth and make a bridge betwixte the Lordshipp of Hurwoorth and the grounde belonging the Borrough of Darlington in the usuall way on Brankin Moore, or otherwise avoyde his cowegaite before that tyme of the said moore for ever hereafter, for which charge he hadd the said cowegait formerlie graunted. (*Borough Books.*) A small runner divides the townships of Hurworth and Darlington.

Formerly the coaches from Richmond, &c., came round by Croft, but, in 1832 the foundation-stone of a bridge of Gatherley-moor freestone was laid. It consists of 3 light elliptical arches, the centre one being 78 feet and the two side arches each 63 feet span, and was designed by Mr. Green, of Newcastle. A Toll is exacted on both horse and foot passengers. On Dec. 16, 1833, the Tees rose with great rapidity to an unusual height, and, as a labourer was attempting to secure some timber* at the new bridge, it was swept away with the man upon it, and carried down the stream. On arriving at Croft Bridge, the dangerous situation of the man was observed by a gentleman on horseback, who immediately galloped to Hurworth, and gave the alarm ; and, on the timber arriving at that place, the man was removed by a boat, in a state of great agitation, and safely landed ashore.

Croft bridge is one of the noblest bridges of ancient date that we have in the North. It has 6 large arches and 1 smaller arch on the Southern side, each of which is boldly ribbed, and the widening of the bridge instead of deteriorating from their beauty has added greatly to their richness, the new part being similar to the old, though the bounding line is very visible on close inspection. The North Riding of Yorkshire repairs 95 yards 2 inches, and Durham 53 yards and 2 inches.

The blue boundary stone is on the pier of the 3rd arch from the Durham side, and is inscribed :—" DUN.) CONTRIBVAT NORTH RID. COM. EBOR. ET COM. DUNEL. STATV. APVD SESS. VTRQ^{e} GEN. PAC. AN. DO. 1673." In former times, however, the metes and bounds on a Tees bridge when thieves " took Darnton Trod" were matters of life and death as much as of *£. s. d.* now, a circumstance seized by Surtees in his excellent ballad founded on the fact of James Manfield, of Wycliff, *gentilman*, claiming sanctuary at St. Cuthbert's door in 1485, for having, with others, assaulted and slain the Rector of Wycliff with a Wallych bill (Welsh bill or axe.)

He twirled till he wakened brother John ;
" O ho," the friar cried,
" We set lyght by these mad pranks on the Tees,
If they keep the southern side.

" But hadst thou done so *in Darnton Ward,*
At the Blue-stone of the Brigg.
By'r Lady, thou had far'd as hard
As Dallaval did for his pigge.†

" Ho, penancer ! here's a jolly fellow
Has slain a Tees-water priest."
" Gramercy," quoth he, " if the 'vowson be ours,
The damage will be with the least.

* The wreck of a jetty swept down by the flood. The labourer's name was Jeffrey Butterfield.

† I have heard it oft told, that one morning of old, Seaton Delaval Hall was a Tynemouth monk's stall. This fat monk he did prig the roast head of a pig, just about to be eaten by the gay lord of Seaton, who whacked him so sore that he eat little more, and died, as they say, in a year and a day. But the prior and each monk, put the knight in a funk, and made him give lands to add to their sands, and cut on a cross, now scarce worth a toss, their own rhyme on the guilt he had done with his hilt. Now, thus ran that note on the rascal he smote—

O horrid dede ! To kill a man for a pig's hede.

"These rascals are neither streight, nor strict ;
They keep not St. Cuthbert's rule ;
He that follows not Benedict
I count him for a fule.

*** 1598. Bishop Matthew writes to Archbishop Hutton informing him that the pledges lately delivered by Sir Robert Kerr, Warden of the Middle marches of the Scottish border, were to be conveyed to York, and be received at Alnwick by Mr. Wm. Fenwick, from whom the Sheriff of Durham was to receive them at Gateshead and deliver them to the Sheriff of Yorkshire at Croft Bridge, "*being the usuall place betwene that countie and this to deliver and receave all maner of prisoners.*" However, the event was that the Under-Sheriff of Durham received them "at the Blewe Stone upon Tine brigg" and conducted them all the way to York.* The prior circumstances are curious. Sir Robert Carey, deputy-warden of the East marches of England, wrote to Kerr to fix a day to take order for quieting the Borders till his return from London. Kerr made Carey's man drunk, left him and came to an English village, broke up a house, took a poor fellow whom he murdered, went home to bed, and sent the messenger next day with the appointment. On the day fixed Carey left Kerr in the lurch and rode to London, and on his return sought redress in vain. The Scotch Borderers, glad of the quarrel, stole in all directions, Carey often caught them and coolly hanged them, and says "All this while we were but in *jest.*" At last Kerr's favourite Geordie Bourne was taken, and though on the representation of the Borderers, who feared Kerr's fury, Carey suspended his execution and posts were sent to Kerr that he might make terms, yet Carey on hearing from the thief's own lips what a villain he had been, in the meantime executed him, and Kerr's coming was a second time a mere hoax. A Commission of the two kingdoms now sat and found many malefactors guilty on both sides who were to be delivered as pledges till satisfaction for the thefts was made. Kerr failing in bringing his prisoners yielded himself and actually chose Carey for his guardian. The two became good friends. Kerr was delivered to the Archbishop but his pledges were got and he set at liberty. Carey thenceforth obtained justice at his hands, and the friendship so curiously formed was lasting.

There are some good old bridges, too, at Barnard-castle, Piersebridge, and Yarm on the Tees. Formerly a great number of travellers crossed at Neasham Ferry and drank a naulum with Charon† there, who, when I crossed a year or two ago, was represented by a sort of Flibbertigibbet of importance and impertinence the most comical that could well be imagined.

Dear Reader, did you ever see the soldier on Darnton Bridge, who, when you approached, gave a jump on the wall and dashed headlong to the waters below with a gurgle and splash ? If you have not, others have, that is all.

* Hutton Correspondence, Surtees Society, 137. 139.
† Tour of Thomas Kirk, of Cookridge, co. York, 1677. Richardson's reprints, No. 25.

[*Arch in the Old Hall, Darlington.*]

DIVISION II.

REGAL, NOBLE, AND MILITARY.

Chapter I. Annals from the Earliest Period to the Death of Richard III.

A little rule, a little sway,
A sun-beam in a winter's day,
Is all the proud and mighty have
Between the cradle and the grave.—*Grongar Hill.*

LET me on entering upon this field of labour, trespass somewhat on my ecclesiastical division, and drag from thence the possible cause of Darlington's standing higher than its neighbours. In 893 the Lindisfarne clerks thought it high time to look about them, for they began to understand "that the

Danes would not (like the Devill) be affrighted away with holy water, and saw by the bad successe of other monasteries, that it was not safe trusting to the protection of a Saint."* So, forthwith wandering

———————from Holy Ile,
O'er northern mountain, marsh, and moor,
From sea to sea, from shore to shore,
Seven years Saint Cuthbert's corpse they bore.

"While these things were going on," says Prior Wessington,† "Saint Cuthbert ceased not from performing miracles; for which reason, in those parts, at a distance from the eastern coast *(in partibus occidentalibus)*, where the said Bishop and Abbot for a while sojourned, through fear of the Danes, many churches and chapels were afterwards built in honor of Saint Cuthbert —the names of which are elsewhere contained."‡ The Prior here refers to a list of these churches which he had compiled and placed over the choir door of his Church of Durham. Of course among them is *Ecclesia Collegiata de Darlington.*§ The Bishop and clergy would rest here on their way from Westmoreland, Cutherston|| (Cuthbert's Town), and Barton, to Cleveland. They selected their places of safety with great judgment, and we cannot wonder that the hidden pastures on the verge of the Derne should tempt their sojourn. Barton is, I think, popularly noted for its two bridges and two churches, St. Mary's and St. Cuthbert's, and concerning these latter an odd legend is kept up respecting two sisters, whose hatred of each other was so intense, that they would not worship their Creator under the same roof; so instead of building none at all, as would now be the case, they built *two* churches. Of course I do not guarantee the occurrence of any truth at all in so unlikely a story.

The wanderers after visiting Cowton (Cudton, the town of Cuthbert, as spelt in Domesday) and divers places in Cleveland, arrived at Craike, (a lonely hill there, surrounded by deep forests, so thick, that according to old tradition, a squirrel could hop from thence to York from bough to bough.)

They probably passed through Sessay, a little detached parish of Allertonshire, whose church is dedicated to St. Cuthbert, though not mentioned in the

* Hegge's Legend, &c.

† MS. D. and C. Lib. B. III. 30. The assertion is amply borne out by tradition.

‡ Raine's St. Cuthbert, 44.

§ Sanderson's transcript.

|| "Cotherston, where they christen calves, hopple lops, and kneeband spiders." Some hot-headed fanatics of the 17th century actually did perform the profane rite alluded to, in contempt of baptism, but I do not know whether Cotherston was pre-eminently famed for such doings. The latter characteristics of Cotherston are inexplicable. On the south side of the road, near Doe Park (Ledger Hall) stands the pedestal or socket of what has been probably a cross; it resembles a trough, and here it was where they christened calves as they say. Others state that it was for resting coffins upon. This reminds me of a rude trough near Borrowby, co. York, where Roman Catholic funerals stop in their procession to the auld kirk-yard of Leek.

list. The old church of Sessay has been pulled down and a new one erected; it was a miserably Italianised structure, but had points of interest. Zigzag mouldings built up here and there testified its Norman origin, and the stained glass was curious. On entering, you saw in the West window, first and foremost, a bird composedly playing the bagpipes, and the arms of England and France. Then in the North windows was a chest or coffin containing bones of ghastly hue (relics?) a noble Tudor crown, and the rebus of Thomas Magnus, an *Agnus** Dei with M thereupon† and his motto above, As God wyll. But who was this *great* man whose brasses alone kept their place in the midst of blue flags marked with the matrices of others? The inscription under his noble figure tells you that he was "Archideacon of thest Rydyng in the Metropolitan Chyrche of Yorke and parson of this Chyrche whiche Dyed the xxviijo day of August Anno domini Mºcccccº l." but the villagers will tell you something more. They will tell you how "Master Thomas Magnus" was found an infant in a basket on the morning of St. Thomas's day, and brought up jointly among the inhabitants of Sessay where he was found—how the Saint's day furnished a Christian name for the embryo parson, and his bringing up a surname, Thomas Amang us—how being a steady youth, he was noticed by the respectable family of Dawnie (ancestors of Lord Downe, present owner) and was engaged as a servant to one of the young gentlemen, which afforded him an opportunity of obtaining some learning—how he improved his abilities and rose to high preferment, and then growing ashamed of his style changed it to Thomas Magnus or Thomas the Great—how pious a man he was, (for all effigies in churches are said by peasants to have represented good men)—but not how he imagined that according to his motto "As God will," when God had decreed the disgrace of Wolsey it was proper for all good men to shun and insult him, and how he excused himself from receiving the Cardinal at his official residence, *as his house was too poor for such a guest!* Magnus was Rector of Bedale also, and according to Camden, (who places his finding at Newark, and doubtless he would know the truth from "our fathers,") he was a most dreadful pluralist.

"Schollers pride hath wrought alterations in some names which have been sweetned in sound, by drawing them to the Latine *Analogie*. As that notable non-resident in our fathers time, Doctor Magnus, who being a foundling at Newarke upon Trent, where hee erected a grammar schoole, was called by the people *T. Among us*, for that hee was famous among them. But he profiting in learning, turned *Among us*, into *Magnus*, and was famous by that name, not only here, but also in forraine places, where hee was Ambassadour."‡ Camden's Remaines, Ed. 1637, p. 146.

* "Doctor quam *magnus!* gravis his, his mitis ut *agnus*."

† The herbage is full of columbines, and the corner brasses of the tombstone bear columbines and lambs alternately. Query, if the former does not allude to his origin?

The Columbine, in tawny often taken,
Is then ascribed to such as are forsaken.
Browne's Britannia's Pastorals, 1613, b. i. song 2.

‡ He was at Flodden Field.

Wherever it be localized, the legend is probably quite true. Names for foundlings were often manufactured in like manner, thus Cuthbert Godsend was christened 17 Feb., 1565, at St. Nicholas, Durham. But such a name in a Darlington case was far too humble for our worthies of 1601 to register, so Godsend was latinized, and the following stately entry inserted:

Thomas a deo missus, puer egenus, sepultus.

in plain English:—Thomas Godsend (sent by God) a destitute boy, buried.

To return to Saint Cuthbert, whose travelling propensities were of a disgustingly modern stamp (not to speak of his trip down the Tweed from Melrose to Tilmouth in a stone coffin*), as much so as those *teetotal* feasts of his votaries at Blencogo in Cumberland, where nothing was drunk save the beverage furnished by the Naiad of *Helly* (Holy) *Well* nigh **St. Cuthbert's Stane.** Another of his wells exists at Scorton near Richmond, and is called **Cuddy Kell.** It is said that it is good for cutaneous diseases and rheumatism, and that there was a monastery or church to the Saint near the spot, though no vestiges remain, being probably a site chosen as his resting place. As to Darlington, it may be matter of conjecture whether, as we gather from "ould wrytynges very pythye and pytyfull for to reade," that women were excluded from all churches and cemeteries where St. Cuthbert's body had rested,† the Western bays of the church nave might possibly serve as a Lady Chapel, in the same way as the Western chapel or Galilee of Durham, built by the same "joly byshop," Hugh Pudsey. They were never pewed, and there is some tradition about a carved oak screen which divided them from the remainder of the church. *Sed quære,* how could fair maidens enter this suppositious chapel of theirs without treading the cemetry with their unhallowed feet? I am afraid my suggestion must fall through.

The monks on returning from Craike, settled at Chester-le-Street, but the Danes ejecting them again in 995, they briefly sojourned at Ripon, and finally settled at Durham. All this I have introduced here, simply because here we have our first recorded event at Darlington, and perhaps one reason for Styr's gift of Darlington to the church.

The earliest direct occurrence of the name of Darlington is found between 1003 and 1016, when four magnates met at the fair city of York. These were Ethelred the unready king, Archbishop Wulstan, Bishop Aldhune of Durham, and Styr, son of Ulphus, *civis dives,* who had obtained licence from the hapless monarch, that he might give Dearningtun with its dependencies to Saint Cuthbert; and now before the king, archbishop, and bishop, with many others of the chief personages of the realm, the donation was solemnized

* This legend I slur over, because it is probable that it emanated from the fertile brain of Master Lambe, Vicar of Norham, whose song of the Laidley worm was printed by Hutchinson, as "a song 500 years old, made by the old mountain Bard, Duncan Frasier, living on Cheviot A. D. 1270, from an ancient MS."

† Richardson's Table Bk. Leg. Div. ii, 344.

with a heavy curse on all who should violate the patrimony of the Saint.* In those good old days, grants were made in some worshipful presence, and at some solemn tide or assembly, and in the absence of charters a visible token was frequently added to witness the fact before all men for ever, like Jacob's pillar, round which his brethren cast an heap of stones.† Witness the gallant horn of Ulphus, who in Canute's time was prince of Deira (in which division of Northumbria Darlington generally seems to have been situate) still to be seen in the metropolitical cathedral of the province. As this worthy was very probably the father of Styr, I give Camden's account of the transaction. "By reason," says he, "of the difference which was like to rise between his sons about the sharing of his lands and lordships after his death, he resolved to make them all alike; and thereupon coming to York with that horn wherewith he was used to drink, filled it with wine, and kneeling devoutly before the altar of God and Saint Peter, prince of the Apostles, drank the wine, and by that ceremony enfeoffed this church with all his lands and revenues." Nor did the offering of tokens cease with the general usage of written documents. Bishop Flambard, dying and sorrowful, made restitution to the convent of Durham of the lands he had withheld from them by a charter, but not content with that, the conscience stricken prelate commanded his attendants to carry him to the high altar, resting upon which he publicly lamented his transgressions, and offered a ring on the altar in restitution of all things. A gold ring was frequently placed in the wax seal, and I now look at a deed of as late a date as 1628, whereby John Oswolde, sen. of Darlington, yeoman, settles all his effects on his 3 daughters "as yet of tender years," to which as a seal a perforated half groat of James I. is attached and sewed to the pendant slip of parchment.‡

Styr, then, with a swinging long curse on all possible future violators ot the church's privileges, which was a very necessary part of the ceremony,

> "Terras Cuthberti qui non spoliare verentur
> Esse queant certi quod morte mala morientur."§

gave to St. Cuthbert, Dearningtun or Darlington with its appendages,|| together with lands in Coniscliffe, Cockerton, Haughton, Normanby, and Seaton, and by this grant it is presumed the manors of the Bishops in this town arose.

"These," says Hegge, "were the beginnings of the church of Durham, where Aldwinus (the last Bishopp of Chester and the first of Durham) first ascended the episcopall chayre, anno Dom. 996, in the reigne of King Ethelred, who (whiles St Dunstan was baptizing him,) * * * * at which St. Dunstan sware by God, and his mother, that he would prove a lazie fellow.

* Simeon iii. 4. † Genesis xxxi, 45.

‡ This document is the property of R. H. Allan, Esq.

§ Engraved on a beam in Trinity College, Oxford. Hegge's Legend of St. Cuthbert, edit. I. B. Taylor, p. 31.

|| "Illis diebus quidam nomine Stir filius Alfi, tempore Ethelredi Regis, contulit S. Cuthberto Derlington cum suis appendiciis."—Lel. Coll. i. 425.

"However, to maintaine the lazines of the Monks of Durham, he gave St. Cuthbert Darlington, with the appurtnances: where, afterwards, Hugh Pudsay built both a mannour and a church. To these possessions, Snaculfus, one of the nobilitie, added Bridbyrig (Bradbury) Mordun, and Socceburge (Sockburn). So ready was the devotion of those times to give all to the church and to become poor, to be made rich in the world to come, as if, forsooth, the monks were only the men that must be happie in both worlds."*

It has been mentioned that Coniscliffe was a locality where Styr gave lands,† and it may be that his father Ulphus was the son of Thoraldus and identical with Ulphus,‡ from whom the Greystocks professed to descend. Certainly they long held the manor of Coniscliffe, having a manor house at Nether or Low Consicliffe, described in the 15th century§ as "the site of the manor house, 12 messuages, value 20*s.*; a close called the Hallgarth 6 acr., value 20*s.*" &c. The present Hallgarth is a field facing the traveller on passing down the town street full of mounds and foundations. In 1292 Lord John of Greystock had "within Cunoisclyve *Gallows* and Ingfangenethef, chattels of felons condemned in the court of the same franchise, &c. But whatever might be his origin, Styr is known as the father of Sigen, who was the third wife of Uchtred, Earl of Northumbria. Uchtred had been formerly married to Ecgfrida, daughter of Aldhune the Bishop, but, tiring of her, he sent her back to her father; she married, secondly, Kilvert, a Yorkshire thane, who also sent her back; at last she became a nun, and was buried in the cemetery of Durham. Aldhune had gilded his daughter with Barmton, Skerningham, and Elton, but they were returned to the church on her repudiation by Uchtred. Sigen is stated to have been given by her father to the earl as a bribe for killing his great enemy, Turebrand;‖ but, after marrying a third wife, Elgiva, daughter of King Ethelred, Uchtred was himself treacherously slain by a rich and noble Dane, of that name, after submitting to Canute, who is said to have winked at the plot. His son Aldred (by Ecgfrida) slew Turebrand Hold, the murderer, but was himself murdered by Carle, Turebrand's son, in a wood called Risewood, and was succeeded by Eadulph, his half-brother, son of Sigen, who made sad depredations on the Welch, and gave great displeasure to Hardicanute. He submitted to that monarch, but was slain immediately afterwards by Siward who "reigned in his stead."

1041.—In this year also Hardicanute betrayed Eadulf, the earl, while under his protection: and he became thus a belier of his "wed."—*Anglo Saxon Chronicle.*

* Taylor's edit. I have left Ethelred's offence to the reader's imagination. Hegge gives the credit of the subject's generosity to the monarch it seems.

† According to the Red Book of Durham, these lands were given by Snaculph, son of Cykell, who also gave Sockburn, &c., as above.

‡ The name has survived the wreck of ages. Henry Hix Ulph, of West Ham, Essex, has just crossed my eye in a newspaper.

§ Inq. p.m. Joh. Graystock, mil. 30 Langley.

‖ Simeon Dun. 80. The whole history of the Northumbrian earls is full of difficulties. I have referred to Hodgson's Northumberland, on the subject throughout.

The hapless earl's son, Osulph, was in after years made Earl, north of the Tyne, by Earl Morcar, but being deprived of his office by the Conqueror, and succeeded by Copsi, he collected around him a band of desperadoes in the like circumstances, with whom he beset a house where Copsi was at a feast, and pursuing him to a church, whither he fled for sanctuary, they fired it, and he was slain by his expelled predecessor at the gate. In the following autumn Osulph himself received a mortal wound by the spear of a robber whom he imprudently attacked. The blood of Styr however still flowed, but in a more quiet channel. Gospatric, Sigen's younger son, who never attained to the honor of the earldom, had a son Uethred, lord of Raby in the time of the Confessor and Conqueror, who had two sons, Dolfin the progenitor of the Fitz-Meldreds and gallant Nevilles, and Eadulf, surnamed Rus, who seems to have inherited all the fiery disposition of his race.

Here followeth the Bishop's Tragedy, or a narration of a bishop being slain in woeful wise by wicked men who took rede too short.

It appears that on the death of Earl Waltheof, son of Siward, who was beheaded 1075, more that the king might get his riches than for anything else, Walcher,* the first Norman bishop, bought the earldom of Northumberland in the same manner as Hugh Pudsey did in after days. The offices of Earl of Northumberland and Earl Palatine of Durham, were distinct. The latter was a perpetual right, the former a granted one for life only. The people viewed Walcher's exercise of the spiritual and temporal powers united with very little reverence, and his severities under the usurper made the union still more detestable. Liulph, a Saxon nobleman who had married Aldgitha, a granddaughter of Uchtred, was in great favour with the Bishop, and his estates suffering dreadfully from the oppression of his deputy and kinsman Gilbert, he complained to the prelate of his officer's misdeeds. The latter in resentment beset the Saxon's house in the night-time and put him and the greatest part of his family to death. The popular odium was increased to perfect madness at this event, and the bishop's useless anger against the offence, the perpetrators being allowed to go at large ; and at his council held at Gateshead, it brought forth fruit. Nothing could save him, all his promises, all his threats were in vain, and under the leadership of Liulph's kinsman, Eadulf Rus, the mob gathered round the doomed assembly with the watchword **Short rede, good rede, slea ye the bishoppe**† The few guards and the hated Gilbert at once met their fate, but the bishop's end was solemn and dignified. The church to which he had retreated was fired and all who rushed out were instantly slain. The last of the assembly was the venerable prelate. The fire urged him to the enemy's sword ; the enemy drove him back to the flames. But the time was none for irresolution. The

* Pronounced Walker, as the word is in fact spelt in Hollinshed.

† That is, the shortest advice is the best.

fire blazed upon him on every hand. Short was his prayer to Heaven, he advanced to the howling multitude. With one hand he made a fruitless signal to command silence; with the other he sanctified himself with the sign of the cross; and, folding himself in his robe, he veiled his face, and was instantly pierced to the heart with a lance, when his awful remains were inhumanly mangled with many a sword. The hand that held the lance is said to have been that of Eadulf, the hand by which Eadulf was soon after slain was that of a woman. He was buried at Jedburgh, but his body was cast out by the command of Turgot, when prior of Durham, and left to rot upon the earth*; while the Bishop rested in his own chapter-house. He had gone with but few guards, it seems, in spite of a prediction by one Eardulf, who *rose from the dead* at Ravensworth for the express purpose. At his funeral he started up, and after his friends were recovered from their fright by a proper quantity of holy water, he told them all that he had seen, during a trance of 12 hours.† He had seen many of his old acquaintances blessed in flower-covered mansions, but, oh, as to the torments he witnessed for the incorrigibles then alive, and especially for the murderers of Walcher, let me breathe them not.

You might almost smell brimstone, his flames were so blue.

And so much for the blood-stained descendants of Styr the donor of Derningtun. Few and evil were the days of the earls of Northumbria, yet fancy loves to linger round some of their memories; as that of Oslac, hoary-haired and prudent hero, driven in 975 over the rolling t ide—over the gannet's bath —over the water's throng—over the whale's domain—of home bereaved; and Siward the noble giant (albeit his grandfather was a [lover disguised as a ?] bear), who lives in Shakspere's rhythm, founded on a popular anecdote,

Siward. Had he his hurts before?
Rosse. Ay, on the front.
Siward. Why, then, God's soldier be he!
Had I as many sons as I have hairs
I would not wish them to a fairer death.

and who rose from his death bed and once more buckled on his armour, saying "That it became not a valiant man to die lying like a beast," and therewith gave up the ghost.

In one of the English versions of the popular romance of Horn, the hero's father is called Hatheolf, and he ruled over all England north of the Humber. Horn's companions were "eight knave childer," whom the king intrusted to the care of his steward Arlaund, who was "to lern hem to ride." Meanwhile

* Hutch. vol. i.

† If this were the whole time elapsed since his death, how quickly was the poor man to be hurried to his long home.

the Danes invaded the northern counties of England, and had collected their plunder ready to be borne to their ships in Cleveland :

> Alle her pray to schip thai bere,
> In Clifland bi Tese side.

King Hathelof thereupon assembled his army on "Alerton More", hastened to attack the invaders while they were still in Cleveland ; and gained a complete victory over them.

> Whoso goth or rideth ther-bi,
> Yete may men se ther bones ly
> Bi Seynt Sibiles kirke.

After this success the King hunted on "Blakeowe more," and having given a feast at Pickering, he went to York, and there met Arlaund with Horn, and caused his subjects to swear fealty to the latter as his successor. Nine months afterwards came three kings out of Ireland :—

> Out of Yrland com Kings thre;
> Ther names can y telle the
> Wele withouten les.
> Ferwele and Winwald wern ther to,
> Malkan king was on of tho,
> Proude in ich a pres :
> Al Westmerland stroyed thay.
> The word com on a Whissonday
> To king Hatheolf at his des.

He met the Irish on "Staynes more," when two of the three kings were slain, but Hatheolf fell by the hand of the remaining one Malkan, after having been overpowered by the multitude of his assailants, who withdrew to their own country, but "an earl of Northumberland," taking occasion of the death king, and of the minority of his son, seized upon his kingdom, and Arlaund fled with Horn to the court of Honlac, a king who reigned "fer southe in Inglond." Here his intercourse with the king's only daughter, Rimneld, was discovered by Wigard and Wikele, and he was obliged to fly, under the name of Godebounde, to Wales. He there met a knight in a forest who conducted him to King "Elydan" who held a court at "Snowedoune." Here he obtained favour, and Elydan's son "Tinlawe," a king in Ireland, having sent to request aid against the same Irish who had invaded Horn's own country, he accompanied the messengers back with a favorable answer. The king of Wales with his men were however detained by contrary winds ; Horn and the two sons of the Irish king, with their army, were obliged to fight against superior numbers ; the two princes were taken and put to death and Horn wounded, but he had slain Malkan, and his death was followed by the defeat of the invaders. Finlak's daughter, Acula, tended Horn's wounds, and became deeply enamoured of him. She declared to him her love, but he was faithful to Rimneld, and, the seven years he had made the term of his absence being passed, with a hundred knights he set out, rescued her from King "Moging," who would have married her, slew Wigard, and compelled Wikele to confess his treason. He then returned to Northumberland to recover his hereditary possessions which it appears had been usurped by *Thorobrond*. Here the poem ends abruptly by a defect in the MS. It agrees in general plot with the French and older English versions, but the names and places are in it so essentially English that it appears to have been formed on a more ancient model, and may be the last form of a purely Saxon legend.* The names of Hatheolf and Thorobrond in this curious old romance bear a strong resemblance to those of Waltheof (father of Styr's son-in-law), and Turebrand in real history, yet the incidents seem to refer to a date before the Danes gained any regular settlement in Northumbria.

In 1086 Robert de Molbray was earl of Northumberland but was devested for rebellion in 1095. Henry, prince of Scotland, of the blood of Waltheof the last, was created earl by Stephen in 1138, and by a charter he apprises his barons and men of the monks of Durham (shewing that the church of Durham was still considered to be within the jurisdiction of the earldom), of all their possessions being "in his own hand and in his own protection and in his peace," and he charges them to hold such in peace and preserve them from all harm. His son Malcolm, afterwards King, succeeded, but Henry II in 1157 wrenched from him the restitution of Northumberland, Cumberland, and Westmoreland, and though William the Lion was proclaimed Earl, by Duncan earl of Fife and others, the inheritance had for ever gone from Scotland. Simon de St. Liz. III. also of the blood of the old Earls then succeeded. Hugh Pudsey bought the earldom in 1192 for life, and in 1377 Henry Piercy was created Earl of Northumberland; but all the ancient jurisdiction seems well nigh to have passed away.

Yet never, in its palmist days, had the earldom seen a more gallant race than that which now gained its faded honours, and whose crescent badge graces the initial on my first page. The Percys—heroes of chronicle, romance, and song—were no mean successors of the warlike sons of Waltheof, and they seem almost to have succeeded to their bloody fate. The first earl of Northumberland and his brother the earl of Worcester, both served with honour in the French wars of Edward III: both long enjoyed the favour of his weak successor and were by him elevated to their earldoms; both deserted his falling fortunes and combined to place the domineering Bolingbroke on the throne; and both, unable to bear the rod they had given, endeavoured by open war to depose him, and perished.† Follow to "the Hotspur of the North; he that kills me some six or seven dozen of Scots at a breakfast,

* Wright's Essays on "Mediæval English Literature," &c. i. 123.

† W. E. Surtees, in "Richardson's Table Book." Leg. Div ii. 287.

washes his hands and says to his wife,—'*Fye upon this quiet life! I want work*,' "*—to his death field of Shrewsbury, amidst the conflicting cries of "St. George" and "Esperance, Percy"†—and to the second earl, slain for the Red Rose at St. Albans—to his sons, Thomas, slain in the same cause at Northampton, Ralph, who fell at Hedgely Moor with the proud boast "I have saved the bird in my bosom" (his loyalty), and Richard, slain for Lancaster at Towton—to the third Earl who met with the same fate—to the fourth Earl slain at his own manor-house of Cocklodge, near Thirsk, in upholding the seventh Harry's oppressions—to his grandson Sir Thomas, beguiled by those who raised the cry "Thousands for a Percy!" to a traitor's death at Tyburn—to the seventh Earl, betrayed by a Douglas (the name so oft opposed to Percy), and beheaded in the Pavement at York—to the eighth Earl, who shot himself in the Tower—to the scion of the race involved in Gunpowder Plot—to the betrothed of Elizabeth Percy, sole heiress of her house, Thomas Thynne, assassinated in 1682;—nay, do even more, look at that bold and bad man who for a time had possession of the dignity, John Dudley; look back to the older earls of Northumberland, and say if ever title had been more luckless to its possessors and their families. Out of eight earls of the Percy race in two centuries, only two died in their beds. Craik notes also the reluctance of Percy blood to flow in other than female veins to the present day as a remarkable fact.

If at any time more male births have taken place than have barely sufficed to keep up the descent of the title from father to son, they have usually proved unproductive. Indeed, this has been uniformly the case, with one exception, for more than three centuries, to go no further back. The seventh Earl of Northumberland, who succeeded to the title in 1537, left only four daughters. His brother, the eighth Earl besides three daughters, had eight sons, but all of them died either unmarried or without issue. The ninth Earl left two sons and two daughters; out of the sons only the eldest had issue. The tenth Earl had six daughters and only one son; and that son who became the eleventh Earl, left only one child, a daughter. That daughter, the second heiress of her house, besides six daughters, had seven sons; but of them all only the eldest had issue; and he again left only a daughter, once more and for the third time to transfer the stream of descent to a new channel. Her eldest son, the second Duke, left two sons; but the elder of the two, who became the third Duke, died without issue; and the present Duke, who is the younger, has no family. Of the second son of the first Duke, however, who succeeded his father as Baron Louvaine, and was afterwards created Earl of Beverley, the posterity in both sexes is very numerous.‡—*Romance of the Peerage.*

One more odd circumstance, if it were true, is disclosed in the proceedings relating to the claim of James Percy, the trunk maker, to the Earldom of

* Shakspere. Henry IV.

† The family motto is *Esperance en Dieu*, sometimes slightly varied.

‡ Some remarkable instances of this tendency occur to me. The estates of George Strong esq., of Sutton by Brough, co. Leic. descended through no less than five successive heiresses viz. those of Strong, Ensor, Dyer, Gaunt, and Franks. In like manner the manor of the monastery of Guisborough at Stranton, passed successively through the heiresses of Gibson, Kitchen, Weemes, and Hylton, and even after this female heirship had ceased, for two successions only one weakly son in each carried down the honours of the family.

Northumberland, in 1680, wherein he says, "when you came first to me, I shewed you a mold like a half-moon upon my body, (born into the world with it,) as hath been the like on some of the Percys formerly. Now search William Percy, and see if God hath marked him so; surely God did foresee the troubles, although the law takes no notice; but God makes a true decision, even as he has pleased to make Esau hairy and Jacob smooth." The parliament viewed this divine signature (as James called it) with much less respect, and he lost the Earldom.

The origin of the name Algernon in the family, it seems, is to be found in the circumstance that William de Percy who came over with the Conqueror, was amongst his contemporaries surnamed *Alsgernons, or William with the Whiskers.*

And the Percys of romance, what rhymes have they created, what lofty and soaring though simple stanzas. How "Chevy Chase," and the "Battle of Otterburne" warm the chilliest soul; how the sorrows of the "Nut-Brown Maid," and the "Fair Flower of Northumberland" melt the roughest heart! The former of these two ballads is supposed to relate to Lady Margaret Percy the daughter of the fifth earl, and her husband Henry Clifford, who is said to have lived the life of an outlaw before he succeeded as eleventh Baron Clifford, and is printed by Percy; the latter narrates the dismal deceit practised by a false knight of Scotland whom the "Fair Flower" released from captivity in cells of her father the good Earl of Northumberland. It is a choice production of the hatred formerly shown to the Scotch on the Borders, and may be found in Richardson's Table Book.*

All you, fair maidens! be warned by me,
 (Follow my love, come over the strand!)
Scots never were true, nor ever will be,
 To Lord, nor Lady, nor fair England.

The days when such words of feud were sung, are happily passed away, and let *me* pass from the gallant Earls of Northumberland, into whose association Squire Styr has so lengthily led me, by throwing together a note or two about their lands in Darlington.

1617. The Earl of Northumberland, a freeholder in the Borough.

1627. Rowland Place, Esq. adm. to a burgage of arable land lately pertaining to the Earl of Northumberland. The old Percys occur no more.

1722. Sir Hugh Smithson of Stanwick, co. York, Barronett, leases to William Chipsis of Darlington, yeo. *Vazie Close*, containing 3 acres at Blackwellgate end. ("The corner close between Blackwell and Coniscliffe laines.") The close probably belonged to the Coniscliffe family of Vasey, a visitation family of 1615 (no arms entered, though the family afterwards assumed those of the old Lords de Vesci), and of whom John Vasie, gen. was a freeholder in the Borough in 1617. In his inventory 1642, are mentioned "one bugle horn, 10*s.*; his armour, 7*l.* 10*s.*; and 12 London drinking-glasses, 7*s.*"

* Leg. Div. i. 25.

He was son of Christopher. In 1638 John Kelsey was adm. to a burgage in Mathergarthes between the burgage of George Jackson of Bedall on the South, and a burgage formerly Xpofer Vasye's on the North, and being *le nienth rigg a le Sowth Dike.* (Vazie Close is now occupied by new streets.)

1817. Hugh, Duke of Northumberland, settled to uses all that close or parcel of ground situate in Darlington, containing or reputed to be two burgages as it lyeth and adjoineth on a street called *Bathgate*; and all those two closes or parcels of ground commonly called *Vassey's Closes* lying at *Blackwell-gate* and in Darlington; and all manner of pasture Gates in a Moor called *Brankin Moor* to the same belonging. And all those several closes or parcels of ground within the precincts and territories of Darlington; commonly called *Batthall* alias *Bathell Field*, *Turner Close*, and *Baidell closes*, theretofore purchased of *Henry Garth, gent.* (These fields are situate on Baydale Beck at its junction with the Tees.)

1773. July 2. The Duke and Dutchess of Northumberland arrived in this town, in their way to Alnwick, on which account a man, generally known by the name of Signior Pecketto, saluted them, as usual, with his patereroes; the last he fired unluckily burst, and there being a number of spectators, some of the splinters flew among them and shattered the hand of one boy, and tore the leg of another in a shocking manner, and many others were slightly wounded.—*Darlington Mercury.*

This seems no improper place to glance at the princely estate of the bishops of Durham, who will henceforth appear more as sovereigns than prelates. A work confined to one parish of their domains seems no fitting field for any dissertations as to whether the Palatine jurisdiction began before the conquest or after, or in what particulars it differed from the privileges of the earls of Northumbria. It is however extremely probable that though the office of the latter was not abolished, it was considerably modified as to Durham, and the Palatine powers then given to, or by tacit permission assumed by, Walcher and continued by his successors. At all events from that period we constantly find the maxim true that *Quicquid Rex habet extra, Episcopus habet intra.*

Solum Dunelmense stola judicat et ense.

"The vicinity of Scotland, then an active and vigilant enemy, and, not less, the insecure state of the Northern province, always restless under the severity of the Norman yoke, demanded that at such a distance from the seat of Government a power should exist capable of acting on emergency with vigour and promptitude; and the motives are apparent which would incline the Monarch to select for this important trust an enlightened ecclesiastic, appointed by and attached to the Crown; in preference to a hereditary noble, less easily conciliated, and already possessing a dangerous share of local influence. Owning henceforth within the limits of the Palatinate, no earthly superior, the successive prelates of Durham continued for four centuries to exercise every right attached to a distinct and independent sovereignty. Of this royalty, the limits were at all times co-extensive with the bounds of the Palatinate."*

By this extraordinary franchise, the bishops levied taxes, made truces with their enemies, raised troops within the liberty, impressed ships for war, sate in judgment of life and death, and held execution of life and limb. They created Barons, who formed their council or parliament: the greater part of the lands within the liberty were held of the bishops in capite, as lords paramount; they coined money, built churches, instituted corporations by charter, and granted fairs and markets; they had all manner of royal jurisdiction, both civil and military; they were lord high admirals of the sea and waters, that lie within or adjoining the palatinate; had vice-admirals and courts of admiralty, judges to determine according to the maritime laws, registers, examiners, officers of beaconage, &c., &c.†

The barons of the bishopric seem to have been generally the Prior, Hylton of Hylton,‡ Conyers of Sockburn, Bulmer of Brancepeth, Surtees of Dinsdale, Hansard of Evenwood, Lumley of Lumley, Fitz-Marmaduke of Ravensworth, and "two of the county of Lincoln," but varied at different periods. Some of these families, such as Conyers, Hylton, and Bulmer, had a prescriptive right to supporters of their arms. John Fitz-Marmaduke (who dying in 1311 in Scotland, was boiled in a hugh cauldron, and his bones transported at leisure across the border) although apparently only a baron of the bishopric, subscribed in 1300 the memorable letter of the English barons to Pope Boniface, asserting the independence of the English crown, and renouncing his interference in the dispute with Scotland. His daughter was styled Countess of Ravenshelm. These barons§ constituted a *Chamber of Peers* at Durham, under the presidency of the Bishop, who was by no means an arbitary Sovereign, his power being considerably limited by his barons who were consulted, or interfered of their own accord in matters of importance. Thus: when Bishop Beaumont had solicited vexatious bulls and instruments to annoy the Monks, at one time procuring the sole and arbitary appointment to the Priorate, at another a fourth of the annual revenues of the church to defray the expences of the Scottish war; the Council prevented the Bishop from putting these oppressive instruments into force.

Having thus given to the reader the necessary information respecting the singular sovereignty exercised by the bishop and his barons over Darlington and the remainder of the Palatinate for many generations, I shall proceed to

* Surtees, i. xvi. It will be remembered that the Scotch royal race claimed the Northumbrian jurisdiction by descent. The Conqueror also erected Chester into a Palatinate, as being on th hostile borders of Wales.

† Sharpe's Hartlepool, 12.

‡ Qui baroniam Hilton tenuer. de episc. Dur. The Hyltons were however more than once summoned to Parliament, perhaps as barons of the realm. John Hylton, Esq., "the last of the barons" of the bishopric, (for though the function was lost, popular courtesy always gave the old title) died in 1746.

§ Amongst the charters of Pudsey, another baron is mentioned. "Habeat, &c. sicut aliquis Baronum nostrorum."—Carta facta Will. fil. Will. fil. regis Stephani de terra de Parva Halcton.—Geoffrey d'Escolland was a baron of the bishopric in Flambard's time.

give the remainder of this chapter in a chronological form, noticing all the way the successions of Bishops for purposes of reference, as many documents are dated according to the years of the pontificate of the bishop, rather than the reign of the monarch.

1018. Died, Aldhune, first bishop of Durham, in whose episcopate Darlington had been given to the church by Styr. He seems to have been married, at all events he had a good-for-nothing daughter, sent home by two husbands as before mentioned. After his death the See remained vacant for three years; at last while the ecclesiastics were sitting in chapter, a joking priest called

EADMUND

jestingly exclaimed, "why cannot you make me a bishop?" a careless speech which was instantly considered to be produced by divine impulse, and St. Cuthbert from his shrine confirmed the idea; "or perchance a Monke his good friend, that lay hid under it: for I do not read that St. Cuthbert ever drank in his pottage that (by the proverb) he should speak in his grave."* Eadmund however sorely lamented his jest, yet he proved himself a very proper man to be a Bishop. He was succeeded by

EADRED

in 1041. This fellow had by some means seized the treasures of the church and therewith bought the nomination of Hardicanute, however in a few months he died, and again undue influence of the crown was used in procuring the appointment of

EGELRIC,

a monk of Peterborough, in 1042, who abdicated in favour of his brother

EGELWIN.

1069. Robert Cumin, whom William had placed over Northumbria, having provoked the people of Durham by his cruelties, they rose up and slew him and his seven hundred guards. William immediately marched North. A detachment met with a fog at Northallerton, which with divers

* Hegge.

tales of the people* anent St. Cuthbert, drove them back. But the Conqueror cared not a whit for the Saint, and pressing forward, caused the monks to flee with his body to Lindisfarne. For 60 miles between York and Durham, he destroyed houses, villages, monasteries, churches and all, reducing the tract to a horrible desert. A dreadful famine followed, and mortality unheard of. Men were glad to eat horses, cats, dogs, and at last even human carcases. The lands lay untilled for nine years infested by robbers and beasts of prey, and the poor remnant of the inhabitants spared from the sword died in the fields, overwhelmed with want and misery.†

1070. Scarcely had the last plague passed ere another came. Malcolm, king of Scotland, made an inroad through Cumberland (then in his hands) and carrying dreadful devastation down the course of the crystal Tees, penetrated into Cleveland and burnt and destroyed everything in his march. At Hunderthwaite, opposite Eggleston, the people of Teesdale made a stand and were routed with great slaughter. Meanwhile Gospatric, the earl of Northumberland, invaded Cumberland, and returning with many spoils, shut himself up in Bambrough castle, and by sallies from thence, weakened and annoyed Malcolm's forces on their return by the eastern coast. Enraged by these sufferings the Scottish king committed most horrid cruelties upon the people,‡ and carried such multitudes into captivity, that for many years after scarce a cottage in Scotland was destitute of English slaves.§

1071. Egelwin, borne down with the miseries of his country and church, fled with considerable treasure for Cologne, but by adverse winds was driven into Scotland. He afterwards joined Morcar in the Isle of Ely, was taken prisoner, and died a miserable death of famine and a broken heart.

Such was the end of the last Saxon bishop of Durham. From this time a much greater splendour attaches to the history of the Prelates, in consequence of the palatine jurisdiction becoming apparent. Shorn as it was by Henry VIII. of its attributes, it still preserved a wonderful degree of state in later times. In 1682 Pepys writes to Mr. Hewer, that he and Mr. Legg had "made a step to Durham, where the Bishop seems to live more like a

* "God having pitie upon them," (the inhabitants.) *Stowe.*

† Bad as the tyrant's conduct might be, I really think, from subsequent events, that the accounts are exaggerated. Hollinshed's language is more elegant than the majority of old chronicles :—"The goodly cities with theyr towers and steeples set up on a stately height, and reaching as it were into the aire: the beautifull fields and pastures, watered with the course of sweete and pleasant rivers, if a straunger shoulde then have behelde and also knowen before they were thus defaced, hee woulde surely have lamented.——The King's army comming into the countrey that lyeth betwixt the Rivers Theise and Tyne, found nothing but voyde fieldes and bare walles, the people with their goodes and cattell being fled and withdrawen into the Wooddes and Mountaynes."

‡ Ford, l. v. c. 18.

§ The tradition that Ulnaby, Carlebury, Walworth, &c., were burned on an incursion of the Scots perhaps refers to this raid. The old Norman chapel of Walworth remains as a barn, with a piscina, in Chapel-Garth, and the foundations of the old village are distinctly visible.

prince of this, than a preacher of the other world." And the Bishops would appear to have flourished in *bodily* estate in their prosperity. I have heard in Darlington, lads puffing off their "Herrings, fine herrings!" in this style "Now, mistress! here's harrings wiv bellies like bishops,'" but how far is it below that glorious old Newcastle cry:—"'Ere's yer caller herrin'! 'Ere's yer caller fresh herrin! 'Ere's 'resh heerin, resh heerin! Fower a penny; fower a penny; fower a penny, caller heerin! * * * * * * * * 'Ere's yer caller ware, wi' bellies as big as Bishops'! Fresh heerin! fresh heerin!!"

WALCHER

who succeeded to the see, was invited over by the king in 1072 to take this episcopacy.

1072. The clergy of Durham having returned from Lindisfarne, the Conqueror on his return from a Scottish expedition, wherein he had forced Malcolm to propose terms of accommodation, determined to "see the incorruptible Saint so magnified. And never were the Monks so afraid to have their imposture discovered, for now they had not leisure to cheat the spectators, with a living Monk, instead of dead St. Cuthbert, but made so many delays and entreaties to the contrary, that the king in a fever of anger was strook with such an heat, that hastening out of the church, and taking his horse, the Monks (in their historie) make him never stay his course till he passed over the Teese, and out of the presincts of the bishoprick, where he received his former temper."*

> "The King, I fear, is poisoned by a Monk."
>
> *Shakspere.*

1080. May 14. Walcher was murdered in the manner before described, and the palatinate again felt the effects of William's displeasure administered by his brother Odo. After a vacancy of six months the king, on Nov. 9, nominated to the Bishopric

WILLIAM DE CARILEPHO,

a Norman Abbot and chief Justiciary of England, who was consecrated Jan. 3. His removal of the secular priests from his cathedral will be found under the Collegiate Church. He died Jan. 6, 1095, and after a vacancy† of more than three years the see was filled by

* Hegge.

† During which the king "transferred into his treasurie 300*l.* by yeere forth of the Bishopricke." *Stowe.*

RALPH FLAMBARD,

a most obsequious exactor of the Red-haired king, consecrated June 5, 1099. On Henry's accession he was thrown into prison for his enormities. However he was afterwards restored and his palatine franchise confirmed. His death happened on Sep. 5, 1128.

GALFRID RUFUS,

Chancellor of England, was consecrated Aug. 6, 1133, the see having been vacant for nearly five years.

1138. David of Scotland having penetrated into England as far as Northallerton, was routed on Cowton Moor (Battle of the Standard.)

The river Tees full oft did sigh,
As she rolled her winding flood,
That ever her silver tide so clear
Should be swelled with human blood.

The English were led by the venerable archbishop Thurstan, and were greatly assisted by another veteran, Walter de Gaunt, of great repute in arms, whose father was nephew to the Conqueror's Queen.

" Now tell me yon hosts," the king he cried,
" And thou shalt have gold and fee—
And who is yon chief that rides along
With his locks so aged grey ?"

" Oh, that is Sir Walter de Gaunt you see,
And he hath been grey full long,
But many's the troop that he doth lead,
And they are stout and strong."*

The Gaunts, or Gants, sometime Earls of Lincoln, held Hundmanby in Yorkshire, and their name is still kept up among the populace.

Gilbert Gant
Left Hundmanby moor
To Hundmanby poor,
That they might never want.

* The Battle of Cuton Moor, a modern ballad in Evans's coll.

Such is the rhyme formerly sung round the market cross there on every Shrove Tuesday, in everlasting remembrance of the good donor. Query if not "Gilbert the Good" who died 1241.* But his days were evil.

> Gilbert de Gant—
> And in those days good women were scant,
> Some said they were few and some said they were many ;
> But in the days of Robert Coultas
> One was sold at the Market Cross for a penny.

Or, according to another version, which doubtless the ladies of Hundmanby would prefer to sing,

> Gilbert Gant—
> And in them days good men were scant,
> Some said they was scarce and some said they was many ;
> But when Robert Coultas was a Lord
> There was one sold for a penny.

These odd and rather amusing remnants of olden verse are I think unpublished, and were lately gathered by Matthew Gaunt, esq., of Leek, from the lips of Hundmanby seniors.

1139. Peace was restored by the cession of the earldom of Northumberland to Henry, prince of Scotland, who however was to have no jurisdiction over the palatinate. This seems to prove the non-existence of the franchise of the Bishoprick in early times, else why was it now so expressly reserved ?

1140. May 6. Died, Bishop Rufus. At his death a Scotch priest called William Cumin usurped the see, and actually forged Apostolic letters. However the ecclesiastics would not elect him, and in obedience to genuine orders from the Pope, escaped to York and chose

WILLIAM DE ST. BARBARA,

Dean of York, March 14, 1143. The intruder's nephew attempted in vain to convert into a fortress the church of Merrington,† and Roger Conyers who had protected his lawful prelate in his fortress of Bishopton, by some means

* In Heckington Church windows, Lincolnshire, was for years preserved the simple but appropriate sentence " *The Lord love De Gaunt.*"

† It was not unusual to make church towers serve as fortresses. Bedale Tower has a fire-place, portcullis groove, and even a *forica* of stone throughout. There is a strange tale about a fire-placed room in Middleham Steeple connected with a dean who is said to have lived there to avoid arrest.

had the address to bring the usurper to become prostrate at his feet. St. Barbara was enthroned Oct 18, 1144. Cumin had made Durham a perfect "Hell upon Earth," and used every cruelty. Some of his prisoners were suspended across ropes, with heavy weights attached to their neck and feet, others were repeatedly plunged into the frozen bed of the river; of others the naked feet, protruded through an aperture of the wall, were exposed to all the severity of the night, in fact his genius would have done honour to an Inquisitor-General himself. Barbara died 1152, Nov. 14, and was succeeded by the magnificent

HUGH DE PUDSEY,

Elected Feb. 1152, consecrated 20 Dec. 1153, and with the monks who had chosen him, soundly whipped, naked, at the church of Beverley, for not having consulted the Archbishop. The good men soon regretted their choice and sufferings, for Pudsey was haughty, austere, and reserved. He was nephew to King Stephen.

1164. This is given* as the *circiter* date of the erection of the Manor-house or Hall of the Bishops at Darlington by Hugh Pudsey, and the architecture of the Chapel would seem to confirm the truth of the appropriation. See a full description of this building hereafter.

Pudsey's Bible in four vols., folio, remains in the Dean and Chapter's Library, and is one of the finest MSS. there. The illuminations exhibit every variety of the Norman style of architecture. The books have, however, suffered sorely from Dr. Dobson's Lady or nurse, who on rainy days amused his child in the library and cut out the "bonny shows" for it to play with.

1183. Pudsey caused a general survey to be made of all the ancient demesne and villenage lands of his bishopric, in the manner and form of Doomsday-book. This is called Boldon-Buke, probably either from being compiled at "Canny Bowdon," or from the other manors being regulated according to Boldon Manor, which is the first in the record. I quote the entries relating to Darlington parish from the Record Commissioners' edition, taken from the very accurate transcript in the Bodleian Library. The variations in the copies kept at Durham are given in brackets.

Derlington. In Derlington there are forty-eight oxgangs, which the villains hold as well of the old villenage† as of the new, and render for each oxgang 5*s*. and are to mow the whole of the Bishop's meadow and win and lead his hay, and to have a corrody‡

* Hutchinson. i. 181.

† "Tam de veteri villenagio quam de novo quas villani tenent." Surtees says "which the tenants in villenage hold as well under the old as the new bailiwick."

‡ An allowance for maintenance.

once; to enclose the plantation* and the court; and to perform the accustomed services at the mill; and for each oxgang to lead one wain of Wodelade† and carry loads in the Bishop's journies; and besides to fetch three loads annually of wine, herrings and salt.

Twelve farmers hold as many oxgangs and render rent as the villains, but do not work, nor go on the Bishop's embassies. [and they go on the Bishop's embassies.]

Osbet Bate [Kate] holds two oxgangs and renders rent 32*d.* [22*d.* Surtees] and goes on the Bishop's embassies. [wanting in some copies.]

The son [sons] of Wibert holds two oxgangs for which William [Gilbert] used to render 8*s.* and now renders for the same, with an increase of four acres, 10*s.* and goes on embassies.

Odo holds a toft and sows thirty-three acres of tillage (unless they be barren) [where the beech grove‡ was] and renders 10*s.* only [without services] and in another part 26½ acres for which he renders 10*s.* until Robert son of William de Moubray, who is his ward, attains his age.

Gaufloie [Galfrid Joie] twenty acres by 40*d.* and goes on the Bishop's embassies.

(Engeliamus, son of Robert Marescall, six acres by 12*d.*) [Lambert holds six acres.]

The smith holds eight acres (by furnishing the iron-work for the ploughs of Little Halton, and the small iron-work within the court of Derlington) [at the will of the bishop.]

(Four cottagers render 18*d.* for their tofts) [four cottagers render 3*s.* and help in making mullions§ of hay, and carry fruit and work at the mill for their tofts.||]

The Punder holds nine acres and has traves** like other Punders, and renders five score hens and five hundred eggs.

(The Borough renders 5*l.*

The Dyer of cloths half a mark) [The Borough, the Dyers, and the farm-rents render thirty marks.††]

The Mills of Derlington, Haluton and Ketton, render thirty marks.

Blakewell. In Blakewell there are forty-six [forty-seven] oxgangs which the villains hold, and render, and do service in all points as the villains of Derlington.

Five farmers hold four oxgangs, and render and do service like the farmers of Derlington.

Thomas, the son of Robert, holds an oxgang and renders 40*d.*

Four acres which were of John Russey [Rufus] render 16*d.*

Adam, son of Ralph de Stapelton, holds four oxgangs and one parcel of tillage of sixteen acres and three roods, and renders 5*s.* 4*d.*, and shall be overseer of the keepers of the portion land‡‡ and goes on the Bishop's embassies. The same Adam renders for the herbage of Batella 32*d.*

* "*Virgultum.*" "The limits of the court, from whence the term, "*The verge of the court*" seems to be derived." *Hutch.*

† That is, laden with wood for fuel at the Hall and other purposes.

‡ Ubi fagina fuit.

§ Hay Ricks.

|| A Toft is a piece of ground whereon a house stood or stands. The Tofts at Piersebridge constitute a field at the entrance of the village on the river, and the small Roman brass coins found there are called *Toft Pennies.* A Croft is a piece of ground attached to the Toft.

** A trave or thrave of Corn is twenty-four bundles or sheaves. *Hutch.* iii. 217.

†† Ten marks. *Surtees.*

‡‡ Surtees has it "and he shall look to the performance of the Bishop's autumn tillage." The original is "et erit sup' p'cac' custod'." *Porcacio*, a certain portion, one long ridge or *rig*, from *porca*, a rig of land rising like a hog's back. Thus we have the Four Rigs in Bondgate, and see p. 55.

(Seven Cottagers render 3*s.* 10*d.*) [Ten Cottagers render 5*s.* and assist in making mullions of hay, and carry fruit, and work at the mill.]

Robert Blund for a little parcel of land near the Tees 6*d.*

Hugh the Punder for one acre, 12*d.* and one toft of the waste.

COKERTON In Cokerton there are forty-seven oxgangs which the villains hold, and render and do service in all points as the villains of Derlington.

Four farmers hold three and a half oxgangs and render and do service like the farmers of Derlington.

Six cottagers render 3*s.* 10*d.* and do service in all points as those of Blakewell.

OXENHALE. William holds Oxenhale, viz.: one carucate and three [two] portions of tillage within the territory of Derlington, which Osbert de Seleby used to hold under fee-farm in exchange for two carucates of the land of Ketton, which his father and himself used to hold in drengage* and which he for himself and his heirs quit-claimed to the bishop and his successors for ever. He ought also to have a horse-mill and is quit of multure, he and his land, and of service at the mill, and renders 60*s.* per annum, besides doing the fourth part of one drenge, viz.: he ploughs four acres, and sows with the Bishop's seed, harrows, and tills four portions in autumn, viz. three with all his men, and all his household, except the housewife, and the fourth with one man from every house except his own proper house, which shall be free. He keeps a dog and horse for the fourth part of the year, carries wine with a wain of four oxen and performs *utvarr'* when it shall be laid on the bishopric.

William of Oxenhale evidently held the chief rank among the tenants in the Parish. As to *utvarr'*† or *outward* as Hatfield's survey has it, Hutchinson (who calls it *Vaware*) imagines that it "related to the chace, and implied an out-watch at the extremities of the chace, it being usual to make a kind of circumvallation, if the term may be allowed, or circle of watchmen, to prevent the game from escaping the bounds: it is still practised in some of the Northern counties, where the lords have a boon-hunt; of which an instance is in Martindale, in Cumberland, a chace belonging to the Hasell family." "Such a custom," adds Surtees, "was certainly common from India to these Islands; but the text rather seems to imply some service of only occasional occurrence. May not *outward* refer to the more serious operations of war, and intend the keeping watch or scouting on the advance of an enemy."

The expression "the Borough, the Dyers and the farm-rents" (*furm'*) has also been very differently construed. Surtees thinks it a most curious conclusion that the tolls of this ancient and prescriptive borough were farmed out and on lease, while Hutchinson says "The *ferme*, or *firma*, our best law expositors define to be a royal tribute, for the sovereign's entertainment for one night on his journies, and it was the badge of a royal borough or vill.

* Spelman says that those who hold under this servile tenure, were tenants *in capite*, and were such as at the Conquest, being put out of their estates were afterwards restored. The nature of the services in this country may be seen by the description of those performed by William for his fourth of a drenge at Oxenhale.

† The term recurs as *wt ware'* in the drenge tenure of Robert Fitz Melred (lord of Raby) at Wessawe.

In Doomsday-book *Comes meriton tempore Regis Edwardi reddebat firmam unius noctis,* it is also named in King Edgar's charter to Ely." It may be remarked that under Durham, in Boldon Buke, it is stated that "*Erat autem Civitas ad firmam.*"

The Bishop evidently at the date of the record kept at least an occasional household here, and the tenants in villenage were charged with the carriage of wood and wine, to which are added two rather uncommon items, herrings and salt, the first probably from Hartlepool, the other from Seaton or the old salt-works at the Tees-mouth. Indeed with the beeves and mutton which the deep meadows of the Skerne would furnish to salt for winter store, there would be little else to lead for the hospitality of the house. A provision is also inserted for the transport of such articles of use or luxury as the bishop might require when he moved from manor to manor.*

These extracts from Boldon Buke would not be complete without the following, under the head of LITTLE HALUGHTON, which was then in demense in the lord's hand. Pudsey afterwards granted it to the grandson of Stephen. (p. 56)

Adam de Seleby holds at farm the demesne of this place with a stock of two ploughs and two harrows, and with the land sown *sicut in cirograffo* contained ; with the Grange and fold yard (*curia clausa*) and renders eight marks. And he finds a litter for the Lord Bishop in his journies at Derlington.

And besides he has the custody of the house and court of the Lord Bishop at Derlington and those things that are brought thither, at his own cost, in consideration of a certain parcel of tillage called Hacdale, which he holds in the fields of Derlington opposite the Hall on the E. side of it, across the water.

(The pasture with the sheep is in the hands of the Bishop, but Adam, if he will, may have in the same pasture one hundred sheep during the term for which he shall hold the the said farm.)

1189. While Richard I. was preparing for his crusade, the bishop caught the military mania and took the vow also, making most splendid preparations at the expence of his grievously taxed people. He rued in time, but the king had heard of all this, and was graciously pleased to wish to borrow the money raised and now useless. This brought about a bargain for the purchase of the earldom, wapentake, and manor of Sadberge, to be annexed to the see of Durham for ever, together with the earldom of Northumberland for life, for which the prelate was to pay 11,000*l.* Henceforward the mitre of Durham was graced with an earl's coronet, and the sword accompanied the pastoral staff. The young king at his investiture of the vain man could not help laughing merrily at the inconsistent characters he was joining, saying "Am not I cunning, and my craftsmaster, that can make a young Earl of an old Bishop?" But this prelate was fit to be an earl, for the world (as one of that age said of him) *was not* CRUCIFIXUS *to him, but* INFIXUS *in him.*†

* Surtees.

† Camden's Remaines.

Hollinshed says that Richard "sold to hym the manor of Seggesfielde or Sadberge, with the wapentake belonging to the same, and also found means to perswade him to buy *his owne province*, which he did, giving to the King an inestimable summe of money, and was thereupon created an Erle by the King for the same: whereupon he was entitled both Bishoppe and Earle of Durham,* whereat the Kyng woulde jest afterwards and say, what a cunning craftsman am I, that have made a newe Earle of an olde Bishoppe." One thousand marks more procured the appointment of chief justiciary of all England and regent north of the Humber, while similar means obtained a dispensation of his vow from the Holy see, "which fayleth no man that is surcharged with white or red mettall, and would be eased." The regent of the North was however soon sorely handled, for Longchamp instead of allowing him to act in conjunction with him very coolly shut the prince-bishop up in the Tower.

1194. On Richard's return our bishop did not fare much better. Hugh had furnished 2000*lbs.* of silver towards his sovereign's ransom, and had even resigned his earldom on the king's coolness being manifest, but the latter learned that the bishop had only remitted a small portion of the sums he had extorted from his vassals on pretence of raising the ransom, on which account he devised repeated occasions to impose various fines and penalties on the embezzler; and this he did with greater severity, as the Bishop did not in any way conceal his riches, and among all his mischances and troubles ceased not from the building of our church at *Dernington*† nor from other religious works. Soon after, William of Scotland being in treaty for the restitution of Northumberland, for a sum of money, the bishop outbid him, and set out for London with the money (2000 marks), but died at Howden, (having eaten at Craike too many good things at supper), Mar. 3. He made restitution to the monks of all lands he had illegally dispossessed them of, adding the vill of Newton, which he purchased and confirmed to them by charter, and left the 2000 marks to the king he had promised him. St. Godrick the holy saint of Finchale, had told him he should be seven years blind before his death, this the Bishop believed in a literal sense, and deferring his repentance till the time of his blindness, "dyed unprovided for death. But if good deeds be satisfactorie, then dyed he not in debt for his sinnes." If one may judge from the silly bargains he made, he was indeed blind. Throughout his life his ambition was unbounded, and the only reflections which can fill the mind on viewing the magnificent temple and the once handsome mansion which he erected at Darlington are those which point alike to his other works, and mark them all as monuments raised by pride to his memory, inscribed with

* Stowe repeats this statement. Durham was therefore still in some respects included in the earldom of Northumberland.

† Sic. Gaufridus de Coldingham. Surtees Society.

the perpetuation of the vile extortions and grievous oppressions he committed on his distressed province.* Still he was a great man in his way.

PHILIP DE POICTEU,

a native of Aquitaine, was elected 30 Dec. 1195: consecrated 12 May, 1197. His quarrels with the monks exceeded all those of his predecessors in violence, and give one a queer idea of episcopacy. He beset the cathedral with troops; commanding fire and smoke to be put to the windows and doors, and exhibiting the most supreme contempt for St. Cuthbert, with a tumultuous mob interrupted the convent in the holy offices of his festival, breaking in upon the altar, laying impious hands on the sacred furniture and dragging forth the prior and monks ministering there. He died 22 April, 1208, and the see was vacant for nine years and a half.

RICHARD DE MARISCO,

Chancellor of England, consecrated 2 July, 1217. One of his seals represents him standing on an insulated piece of ground, surrounded by bulrushes growing out of the water---DE MARISCO.

Two confirmatory charters of this Bishop, or possibly one of him and one of his successor, relate to Bishop Philip's grant of Mayland, Satley, to Bartholomew de Mariscis under the tenure of *a pair of gilt spurs*, to be presented to the bishop on St. Cuthbert's feast in September. One of these charters is dated "at Deryngton, 6 May, the first year of our episcopacy."†

He died 1 May, 1226, after a stormy reign spent in disputes with the monks: however one of them made him an odd epitaph of a dozen lines all ending in *itis*. He was found dead in bed at Peterborough Abbey after having daintily refreshed himself with costly meats, in going with a "great rowt of men of lawe" towards London, in maintenance of "his most filthy quarrell he picked against religious persons."‡

RICHARD POOR

Had the Royal assent 22 July, 1228; died 15 Apr. 1237.

* I have adopted almost the very words of Hutchinson, I can devise none more effective. But let us give the prelate his due. He redeemed the plate of the church which, with that of other fanes, was called into requisition for the king's ransom. Richard was not very scrupulous about sacrilege, and the punishment attendant on that sin overtook him at Chaluz.

Christe, Tui *chalicis* prædo fit præda *Chalucis*:
Œre brevi rejicis qui tulit *æra* crucis.

† Surtees. ‡ Stowe.

During his episcopacy, Peter de Brus, Lord of Skelton, whilst guardian of Hartness during the minority of the fifth Robert de Brus, opposed the prelatical claim to the wreck of the sea, in his ward's lordship, and caused his servants to carry away a wrecked boat, for which they were fined 50*s.* by the Justices of Sadberge, and it seems that a burgess of Hartlepool named Gerard de Seton had on the occasion of the dispute been favourable to the prelate's claims. Peter, upon the fine being inflicted, sent one of his servants called Hugh de Haubgere and many others, who took the unfortunate burgess and lodged him in the dungeons of Skelton. The Bishop was not to be outdone. He pronounced all the pains and perils of excommunication by name against those who seized his supporter in the liberty between the Tyne and Tees, and compelled the mighty baron to disgorge his prey and allow poor Gerard to go quietly back to his own fire-side. And now came his revenge.

For the capture &c. Peter de Brus was fined 20*l.* by the Bishop's justices. However, William, Earl of Albemarle, and John de Lacy, Earl of Lincoln, came to the Bishop at Derlyngton, where they remained three days for the express purpose of endeavouring to bring about a reconciliation ; and at their instance the Bishop relaxed in his demand of the fine, and the quarrel was brought to an amicable conclusion, upon condition that henceforth the bishop should have the wreck of the sea without contradiction.

After this there was a dispute about another vessel wrecked, but the Bailiffs of the Bishop seized it, and the Justices of Sadberge ordered that from its mast should be made a wooden cross as a memorial, which in Bp. Kellawe's time, nearly a century afterwards, was yet standing in a place called Blakelawe, on the high road [*alta strata*] between Sadberge and Hetrepol, and from its yard was made a candlelabrum, upon which were placed the wax and candles in the church of Sadberge.*

"Three times tell an Ave-bead,
And thrice a Paternoster say,
Then kiss with me the holy reed,
So shall we safely wend our way."

Sadbury Cross is now the name of a field between Sadberge and Long-Newton, and a floating tradition states that in the time of the plague, all the trade of Sadberge was transacted at this place. There is a similar legend about Marske Cross in Cleveland, whither, it is said, the market of Guisbrough was removed, when the pestilence had well nigh depopulated the town.

* Bp. Kellawe's register.

NICHOLAS DE FARNEHAM,

Elected 11 June, 1237 ; resigned 8 April, 1240. Before his election there was a repetition of the disgusting cont estbetween the convent and the crown which had distinguished many former elections. Whilst the Monks were pressing for the confirmation of their Prior, Melsonby, whom they had elected, one of them exclaimed, " Sire, it is no great matter of favour that we ask ; " "And if ye want no favour," retorted the angry Monarch, "none shall ye have."

WALTER DE KIRKHAM.

Elected 21 Apr.; consecrated 5 Dec. 1259 ; died 9 Aug. 1260. On the reverse of his seal he is seen praying to St. Cuthbert in this unscriptural verse.

Presul	Cuthberte,	regnem	super	ethera	per	te.
Bishop	Cuthbert,	may I reign	above	the skies	by	thee.

which is very different from Bishop de Insula's harmless superscription

Signum Cuthberti signat secreta Roberti.

In Kirkham's time, the Durham monks were for long interdicted for opposing the Pope's exactions. "Oh, (sayeth Matthew Paris) if in that their tribulation they might have had fellows, and in their constant doings aiders, how happily had the Church of England triumphed over her tormentors and oppressors."*

1260. Henry III. was obliged this year to interfere with Kirkham's official, Roger de Siton, (master of Sherburn hospital). He had cited forty of the Burgesses of Newcastle to appear before him *at Derlington* on uncertain business, and with the Archdeacon of Northumberland, had made it a practice to enforce them to appear at his courts and visitations, from day to day at distant places out of their borough, contrary to custom ; and to inquire into matters† against their will. From the expence and loss of time attending this grievance, the merchants and artificers were so injured and worn out that some of them were actually reduced to the miserable necessity of begging. The King, on application, issued two severe writs to the offenders and to the Bishop himself, commanding them at once to desist from their usurpations against his crown and dignity.‡ Seyton or Siton however rose to

* Hollinshed.

† They considered themselves liable to sift causes of Matrimony and Testament only.

‡ Claus. 44 Hen. III., p. i. m. 12. Prynne ii. 826., a book extremely scarce, the greatest part of the impression being burnt in the Great Fire. *Allan MSS.*

be a Judge of the Common Pleas in 1268, and in 1274 he was bound with Hugh de Derlington, Prior of Durham, for the executors of Bishop Stichill to pay his debts to the King.

ROBERT DE STICHILL,

Elected 30 Sep., 1260 ; consecrated 13 Feb., 1261 ; died 4 Aug. 1274. His seneschal Geoffrey Russell founded, in 1274, a chantry in the chapel of St. Mary Magdalene, at Cotum Amundeville upon Scyrn, par. Haughton, for a chaplain to pray for the souls of Tho. de Amundeville, Ralph his father, and Clare his mother. This chapel is utterly demolished, but the cemetery was used for interment long after the reformation, as appears by entries in Haughton register.

ROBERT DE INSULA, (ENGLISH, HALIELAND) ALIAS, DE COQUINA,

Elected 24 Sep., 1274 ; died June, 1283. The bishop was of very humble origin, which he never hid. To his mother he gave an honourable establishment, and once when he went to see her, he asked "And how fares my sweet mother ?" "Never worse," quoth she. "And what ails thee, or troubles thee ? hast thou not men, and women, and attendants sufficient ?" "Yea," quoth she, "and more than enough ; I say to one 'Go,' and he runs ; to another, 'Come hither, fellow,' and the varlet falls down on his knees ; and in short all things go on so abominably smooth, that my heart is bursting for something to spite me, and pick a quarrel withal."

1278. October. The charter of appropriation of the church at (Bishop) Middleham to Finchale Abbey by this bishop, is dated at Derlington.

ANTHONY BEKE.

Elected 9 July, 1283 ; consecrated 9 Jan. 1283 ; died 1310, March 3. In his time the court of Durham exhibited all the appendages of Royalty ; nobles addressed the Palatine sovereign kneeling, and instead of menial servants, knights waited in his presence chamber, and at his table, bareheaded and standing. He gave 40*s.** for as many fresh herrings ; and hearing one say "this cloth is so dear that even Bishop Anthony would not venture to

* The price even now would be exorbitant, but the reader must remember the much greater value of money at that time to arrive at the proper idea of the bishop's magnificence. 40*s.* would perhaps now be about 80*l.* !

pay for it;" he immediately ordered it to be bought and cut up into horse cloths.*

In this bishop's episcopacy begins the series of prelatical coins of Durham, which have been fully described by Mark Noble, in his Dissertations on the subject, in which he was ably assisted by Geo. Allan, (as acknowledged in his preface) and had access to the cabinets of that gentleman, Mr. Barker, and John Scott Hylton, Esq., from which he took some of his specimens. Several other types might now be added. A very curious penny of Bishop Sherwood with S on Richard III's bust is given in the Pictorial History of England. Mr. M. A. Denham has a penny struck in the reign of Henry IV., V., or VI., on which is a roundel (not an annulet) and a mullet at the sides of the king's bust. My father had one of Hatfield, with the pastoral staff turned to the left; and in my own possession is a curious one of Beaumont, found at South Kilvington, near Thirsk, in which the mint mark is a lion rampant with *two* fleur de lis at one side of it only. Many more varieties might be raked up.†

Surtees in one place‡ makes this bishop builder of the episcopal palace at Darlington. I am not even aware of any material alterations made by him in it, and the historian was possibly confounding him with the other proud prelate, Hugh Pudsey, for the moment. I believe however that Beke paled the enclosed park belonging to the manor.§

Anthony was a staunch member of the church *militant*, but sometimes went further than his talents warranted. At the battle of Falkirk against the Scots, he received a severe rebuke from Lord Ralph Basset, of Drayton, "My Lord Bishop, you may go and say mass, which better becometh you, than to teach us what we have to do, for we will do that which belongeth to the order of war."‖

Indeed Beke lived in a degree of splendour and military pomp inferior to none but his sovereign. When Edward came down to Newcastle in 1296, with an army of 30,000 foot and 4000 heavy armed horsemen, he was accompanied by the forces of the bishop consisting of 1000 foot and 500 horse. In the war with Scotland he had with him twenty-six standards of his own family or principality, and his ordinary suit comprised 140 knights.¶ St. Cuthbert's banner floated over this princely array, and a monk of Durham was the standard-bearer. At the battle of Falkirk, Beke had in his company thirty-two banners.**

1291. On the 16 April, Edward I. dated a summons at Derlyngton to fifty-seven of his military tenants of the northern counties, among whom are named John de Baliol, Robert de Brus, William de Vesey, Hugh de Lovall,

* Graystones, c. 14.

† Thomas Lincolne of Derlyngton, bondsman in 1490 for George Strayll, mintmaster of Bp. Sherwood.

‡ Vol. i. p. cix. § Hutch. iii. 188. ‖ Hollinshed.

¶ Graystanes. ** Scala Chronica.

the lady de Ros, Margaret de Ros, and William de Heron, who were to accompany him with horse and arms, and all the service they owed him, at Norham, for six weeks, reckoning from Easter ; and the sheriffs of the northern counties received orders to give notice to all within their districts, who owed the king military service, to give the same attendance.* At the assembly convened at Norham, the bishop of Durham addressed the states of Scotland, informing them that Edward's purpose in coming to the borders was to maintain the tranquillity of that kingdom and to do impartial justice to the claimants of the crown, in the character of supreme lord of Scotland, and that he gave them three weeks to deliberate on the matter. At the close of that time his title was recognised, and in 1292 he gave judgment for Baliol.

While Beke was employed in the service of his sovereign, the Archbishop of York renewed the claims of his predecessors to jurisdiction over the bishoprick. He sent to Durham his notary-public and clerks by the pope's authority with official letters of citation, who were immediately placed in close durance by the bishop's officers, and Beke sent word that they were to be detained in defiance of all admonitions to enlarge them. The archbishop thundered a sentence of interdict against him, and issued his precept (May, 1292) to the prior of Boulton to excommunicate the bishop in his own churches of Alverton, Derlington, and other places, which the prior obeyed, and the case came before parliament.† The archbishop found himself in a much more awkward predicament than his predecessor, who fled from Durham on a one-eared palfrey in an attempt at visitation ; for his high offences in presuming to enforce the release by ecclesiastical censures, instead of the king's process, and to excommunicate any person in the king's service or attending on his person, were adjudged by the parliament as worthy of being punished not only then but in all succeeding ages, by imprisonment of the ecclesiastics who should be guilty thereof, and by heavy fines and ransoms. Accordingly notwithstanding his pall, the archbishop found himself in the same sorry case as his officials, being committed to the Tower and obliged to find sureties for the payment of the large sum of four thousand marks to the king.‡

* Rymer, v. ii. fo. 525.

† Placita Parl. 21. Edw. I. 1292.

‡ In Bp. Beaumont's time, whenever the archbishop came to Allertonshire to visit, the bishop of Durham opposed him with *an armed force.* A compromise was come to in 1330 when the church at Leak was appropriated for the maintenance of the bishop's table, with the reserve of an annual pension to himself, and another to the chapter of York. Leak Church stands lonely amidst green fields near a solitary Hall. A north Chapel is screened off by a rich parclose of the 14th century retaining its original paintings of birds and flowers, and in the south chapel (to which is attached the *Cross Keys* farm of some £150 per annum, appropriated to the repair of Five Sisters window at York) are two magnificently carved stall ends dated 1519. On an ancient bell, said to come from Rievaulx, is the humble legend, + O : PATER : AELREDE : GRENDALE : MISERI : MISERERE. "O Father, commiserate the miserable Aelred Grendale."

1293. An inquisition was taken touching the bishop's liberties before Hugh de Cressingham and his fellow justices, at Newcastle-upon-Tyne, under the statute *de quo warranto*. The bishop and those holding liberties in his palatinate, had neglected to justify their title, on the statutory proclamation, on which default the liberties were seized into the king's hands, until they should answer. However the bishop having pleaded in parliament various matters, as well in error as otherwise, had full restitution. The record, among other matters, states that he had three coroners in the three wards of Durham, and others at Sadberge, Bedlington, and Norham, and that he had fairs and markets at Durham, Derlington, and Norham. The full palatine powers are recapitulated. An inspeximus of this record was obtained in the time of bishop Langley, 1409.*

1302. Mar. 5. Edward I. dates at Derlyngton an instrument addressed to the pope, appointing ambassadors and proctors to treat with him. *Rymer's Fœdera.* 30 *Edw. I.*

In the latter part of Edward's reign the Bishop fell sadly from his high estate. His barons led a dissention against him for compelling the people of the palatinate to go out of its limits in warfare, which as *hali-werke* folks (holding by the service of defending St. Cuthbert's patrimony) they were not bound to do, while the pope pronounced his suspension for not answering a charge of illegally interfering in the election of a prior. He went with a splendid parade to Rome in consequence, and came back with honour; but a worse enemy was at home. Edward had long been jealous of his potent subject, and seized the circumstance of his leaving England without licence, with other matters of offence, as an excuse for depriving him of his bishoprick. He was restored, and again† deprived; but Edward's own hour-glass was now run out, and in his successor's time the prelate emerged from disgrace with the distinguished dignities of Count palatine and Bishop of Durham, Earl of Sadberge, King of Man, (so created by the new king) and Patriarch of Jerusalem (a title conferred by a new pope of 1305). He was the first bishop buried within the walls of the cathedral; respect for St. Cuthbert having deterred his predecessors from suffering a body to come there. But Beke resembled Cuthbert in no small degree, for his continence was so singular that he never looked a woman full in the face, and alone among the bishops present, dared to touch the remains of St. William of York on their translation, bold in his conscious chastity. He never took more than one sleep, saying that it did not become a man to turn himself in bed, and he was perpetually riding from one manor to another, or hunting or hawking.

* Rymer, viii. 572.

† The borough of Derlington is expressly mentioned in the bishop's petition to Parliament 35 Edw. I., 1307, for the restoration of the temporalities in consequence of the inconvenience from his not being able to hold Court-Baron, &c. Referred to the king's Justices.

RICHARD KELLAWE,

Elected 31 Mar., 1311 ; consecrated 20 May ; died 9 Oct., 1316.

1316. In Edw. II.'s wars with Scotland, the Scots often ravaged the Palatinate, and this year they entered the bishoprick by the mountainous passes of the Western frontier, and, avoiding Barnard-Castle, rolled like a destructive flood down the vales of the Wear and Tees, then united their forces, and wasted the country round Durham. The country was exhausted with miseries ; famine* and pestilence followed war, and the marches of the two kingdoms were reduced to a state of destitution which had not been felt since the days of the Norman tyrant. A new invasion followed the next year, and three seasons of sterility had carried distress to the highest pitch. All this had arisen from Bannockburn, for after that event Bruce and Douglas had ravaged the palatinate, exacted tribute, and retreated by the course of the Tees and Swale, leaving their marks of destruction behind them. Their way was plain in after years.†

LEWIS BEAUMONT.

Leave of election 19 Oct., 1317 ; consecrated 26 March, 1318.

The Raid of the Bishop.

Bishop Lewis Beaumont was a near relation of the Queen of England, through whose interest he became Bishop of Durham. During the election the Earls of Lancaster, Hereford, and Pembroke waited within the church the event of the conclave ; Henry Beaumont, his brother, was also there. Some of the savage nobility threatened that if a monk were elected they would slap his shaven crown ! Notwithstanding, the electors preserved their purity and elected their aged prior, but the tears of Edward's queen prevailed on her wavering consort to refuse confirmation, and to write letters to the pope who obeyed the injunction, and bestowed the see on the heartless wretch for whom it was asked. Beaumont proposing to be installed on the feast of St. Cuthbert, in September, 1317, began his progress to the north, attended by a splendid retinue, accompanied by his brother, Henry Beaumont, and two cardinals from Rome. At Darlington the bishop was met by a messenger

* The descriptions of the famine are so horrible as to be scarcely credible. The poor stole fat dogs to eat. *Those dogs became fat by feeding on the beasts and cattle that died.* Some others in hidden places did mitigate their hunger with the flesh of their own children. The thieves that were in prison did pluck in pieces those that were newly brought in, and greedily devoured them half alive !

† Surtees.

from Durham to warn him that the road was in possession of marauders, but the high rank and sacred dignity of Lewis and his companions seemed to place danger at defiance, and the friendly information was not only treated with great contempt, but the most improper motives were attributed to the Prior who sent it, the bishop and his brother saying that he wished to impede the consecration. They turned their backs on the convenient Hall of Darlington and wended on.* A few hours verified the prediction. At Rushyford a desperate band waited the arrival of the party, and the Bishop and his companions were speedily enveloped in a cloud of light horsemen under the command of Gilbert Middleton, a Northumbrian gentleman. After rifling the whole party, Middleton restored the cardinals' horses, and suffered them to proceed. The Bishop, however, and his brother, were carried off to Mitford Castle,† and thrown into prison.

The capture of Bishop Beaumont, (says Surtees,) took place where between Woodham and Ferryhill, the road crosses a small sullen rivulet, in a low and sequestered spot, well calculated for surprize, and the prevention of escape. In Rymer's Fœdera, it is said to have taken place at *Aile,* (qu. *Acle,* i. e. Aycliffe,) where the passage over the Skerne would be equally convenient.

The outlaws at first intended to spare the cardinals, and their immediate attendants; but when one after another cried out, "and I belong to the cardinals," they began to think they would have but little pay for their trouble, and, wise in their generation, they took the summary resolution of rifling the whole party.

Hollinshed says, that Sir Gilbert Middleton "being offended y[t] Master Lewes Beamont was preferred unto the bishops sea of Durham, and Henrie Stanforde put from it, that was first elected, and after displaced by the King's sute made unto the Pope, tooke the sayd Lewes Beamont and his brother Henrie on Winglesdon Moore, nere unto Darington,‡ leading the Bishop to Morpath, and his brother the Lorde Beaumont unto the Castell of Mitford, &c., and that the knight was so advaunced in pride therewith, that he proclamed himselfe Duke of Northumberlande, and joyning in friendshippe with Robert Bruce, cruelly destroyed the countie of Richmond."

Gilbert de Middleton was a kinsman of Adam de Swinburne, sheriff of Northumberland, whom the King had used harshly in some Border matters. Sharing in his wrong, he flew to arms, and assembling a large collection of desperate adventurers, took all the Northumberland castles, save Alnwick, Bamburgh, and Norham, and carried fire and terror through Cleveland. But the Loyalists assembling, his army began to forsake him, and he shut himself up in his castle of Mitford, when he was taken, through the treachery of his followers. On his trial, in 1318, the King gave sentence, that he should be dragged through the city of London to the gallows, and there alive hung up, and alive taken down, and beheaded: his head sent to the city of London: and as his heart had had the audacity to excogitate the horrible felonies he had done against God, the holy church, and his liege lord, they were ordered to be burnt under the gallows, his body to be quartered, and one part sent to Newcastle, another to York, the third to

* Ad vadum Cirporum inter Feri et Wodom. *Graystanes.*

† Hutchinson. But see Hollinshed.

‡ "When they came neere unto the towne of Derlington, certayne robbers breaking out of a valley, Gilbert Middleton and Walter Selby beeing their captaynes, sodaynelie sette upon the familie of the Cardinalles and of Lodowike on Wigelseden Moore, &c. *Stowe,* who also states that the two Beaumonts were conveyed to different castles. Windlestone moor is meant.

Bristol, and the fourth to Dover. Many forfeitures succeeded. The wars of Scotland had reduced Northumberland from prosperity to a desert, and the inhabitants were left without subsistence, save the plunder they could get in Scotland, and their ill-paid wages, as soldiers. When therefore, the sheriff, for representing their hardships, was disgraced by imprisonment, can it be wondered at that they should turn the weapons their weak and cruel lord had put into their hands, against himself, and liege subjects.* War will always turn against its originator, and, after all, poor Middleton has been overloaded with guilt. Of Sir Ralph Fitz Robert, who assumed the name of Greystock, says Dugdale, "he besieged Gilbert de Middleton, and divers others with him, in the castle of Mitford, for certain traitrous actions done by them, in Northumberland; and that not long after, being in Gateshead, at breakfast, he was, through the contrivance of the same Gilbert and his party, there poisoned, 3rd July, an. 1323, 17 Edward II, and buried in the Abbey of Newminster,† near the high altar." The fact is, Middleton was executed five years before, in 1318, by the most undeniable evidence. His seal is engraved in Surtees, plate x. 22. It is attached to a receipt for money levied under a pretence of protecting the Palatinate at that period.

The treasures of the church were lavished for Lewis's redemption, and the captives were liberated. Beaumont was consecrated at Westminster on the 26th of March, 1318. The monks must have been shocked and surprised at the strange mixture of levity and ignorance which this new bishop exhibited during the solemnity. Unable to pronounce the word *metropolitice* in the official instrument, he cried out in his native French, "Let us suppose it read." Proceeding further, *in ænigmate* stopped him altogether, when he exclaimed, "By St. Louis, it is not courteous to introduce such words." Lewis's conduct towards the convent to whose liberality he was so deeply indebted,‡ was marked by a most capricious exercise of power. In vain the monks attempted to conciliate his favour by gifts or by attention. "You do nothing for me," said he, "nor will I do anything for you; you may pray for my death, for whilst I live you shall have no favour from me." His private expenses were enormous. He died in September, 1333, and was buried at Durham, before the high altar, in the place where his gravestone has been lately found, consisting of two immense slabs weighing about six tons. It is believed that in point of magnitude and weight they have no equal in England; consisting of two slabs of north country blue marble, and not characterized by the ancrinites which are found in the marble of the Wear near Stanhope. They were probably procured from the bed of the Tees near Barnard-Castle.

1317. Sir Gosseline Deinvile and his brother Robert, with two hundred men in the habit of Friars, did many notable robberies, they spoiled the bishop of Durham's palaces, leaving nothing in them but bare walls, for the which they were after hanged at York. *Stowe.*

1318. The Scots penetrated into Yorkshire, sacking Northallerton, Ripon, &c, and spread destruction over the whole country, and in 1369, while the

* See Abbr. Placit. 332, and Hodgson's Northumberland.

† Near Morpeth.

‡ Even the habits, plate, and jewels of the church had to be sold for the purpose.

king was beseiging Berwick, came by the Western march and discomfited the English at Myton upon Swale.

1321. "After the Epiphanie, when the truce fayled betwixt the two realmes of England and Scotland, an army of Scots entred England, and came into the Bishoprike of Durham. The Earle of Murrey stayed *at Darington*, but James Dowglas and the Steward of Scotland went forth to waste the country, the one towards Hartilpoole and Cleveland, and the other towards Richmont: but they of the countie of Richmont (as before they had done) gave a great summe of money to save their countrie from inuasion.

"The Scottes that time remayned within Englande by the space of fiftene dayes or more. The Knightes and Gentlemen of the north partes, came vnto the Earle of Lancaster that lay the same tyme at Pomfret, offering to goe foorth with him to giue the enimies battaile, if hee would assyst them: But the Earle seemed that he had no lust to fyght in defence of hys Prince, that sought to oppresse hym wrongfully, (as he took it) and therefore he dissembled the matter, and so the Scots returned at their pleasure without encounter." *Hollinshed.*

Before this the Pope had cursed Robert le Brus; and he, James Douglas, and Thomas Randulf, Earl of Murray, were accursed throughout England every day at mass three times. This "put the king and the realme to great cost and charge," and yet Robert le Brus and co. cared not a whit for their cursings.

1322. While the English forces were assembling at Newcastle, Robert Bruce passing them "came with a great power of Scottes into Yorkeshir, and king Edward being at York, and hering of this came to Blakehoumore with such pour as he could sodenly gather, and toke a hylle bi Bylaund Abbay for his fortresse, wher the king and his cumpany were discomfitid, and the Count of Richmont taken, and the Lord Sully, a baron of France, and many others; and the King's self scarcely escapid to Rivalles Abbay." (*Leland, Coll.* I. 550., II. 474.) The royal plate, jewels, and privy seal were seized, and Ripon and Beverley plundered. A truce for thirteen years was concluded in 1323, and the Commissioners swore to its observance *on the souls of Bruce and of Edward.** Some write that on their return from the expedition of 1322, the Scots spoiled Northallerton and the other towns on their route.†

ROBERT DE GRAYSTANES,

the Historian, was elected by the monks, and even consecrated on 14 Nov., 1333, but the temporalities were denied him and he was forced to succumb to the King's tutor,

RICHARD DE BURY,

who had been provided by the pope, and to whom the temporalities were restored, 7 Dec., 1333; died 1345.

* Rymer, iii. 1001-2, 1021-2. † Fabian.

Bury's love of books was so violent, that, as he says himself, it put him in a kind of rapture and made him neglect all other business. From his work *Philobiblos*, a treatise for the management of the splendid library, which he founded for the students at Oxford, he was called *Philobiblos* himself, a lover of books. He frequently corresponded with Petrarch.

It is said of this munificent man that when he travelled from Durham to Newcastle, he gave twelve marks in charity, between Durham and Stockton eight marks, between Durham and Auckland five marks, and from Durham to Middleham 100*s*.*

1327. Edward III. preparing to invade Scotland, the Scotch invaded England and penetrated as far as Stanhope Park. They sent ambassadors to Edward at York to treat for peace, but not succeeding, and observing that the English soldiers were "cloathed all in coates and hoodes embroidred with flowers and branches verye seemely, and used to nourishe theyr beardes," they affixed in derision this rhyme on the cathedral doors "towarde Stangate."

Long beardes, hartelesse,
Paynted hoodes, wytlesse,
Gaye coates, gracelesse,
Make Englande thriftlesse.†

Edward, according to lord Hailes, left York on the tenth of July, halted at Topcliffe the eleventh and twelfth, and reached Durham on the thirteenth. According to Froissart, he left York in the morning and reached Durham at night, which is rather a forcing on reason of a forced march. The Scotch, to Edward's great annoyance, retreated without a battle, and he lay on the tenth of August at Durham again, disbanding at York on the fifteenth.

"At this tyme Archibald Duglas toke great Prayes in the Bishopriche of Duresme, and encounterid with a band of Englisch Men *at Darlington*, and killid many of them Shortely after the Scottes by covine fledde clere away from Stanhop Park in the Night. Wherefore the yong king Edward *wept tendrely*, and returnid to York." (*Scala Chronica in Leland's Coll.*)

Peace was concluded in 1328, and the heir of Scotland married to Edward's sister Jane, called *Joan of the Tower*, and by the Scots *Joan make peace*. But clouds soon overspread the glowing prospect.

1333. Apr. 1. Edward marched north and was again at Durham. He entered Scotland in aid of Edward Baliol, bore down all opposition, and closed the campaign by the bloody victory of Halidon Hill. During his sojourn in Durham, his queen Philippa, after supping with the king in the priory, retired to rest. St. Cuthbert was no respecter of persons, and though the poor queen was not doomed to penance, like two women from Newcastle who "by instigation of the devil and attempt temerarious," attempted to see the saint's shrine, yet she was compelled by the monks to quit her husband's bed

* Stowe. † Hollinshed, edit. 1577.

and make for the castle in all haste, clad only in her nether garments.* Edward entered Scotland in aid of Edward Baliol, bore down all opposition, and closed the campaign by the bloody victory of Halidon Hill, at which Archibald Douglas, the governor of Scotland in the absence of king David, was slain, to the great consolation of Darlington, I trow.

1336. June 18. King Edward III. granted a licence to John Gros, of Berwick, to assign property to Tynemouth Priory. This document is dated at Darlington.† Two days after we find him at Newcastle, on his road to Scotland to suppress the revolt against Baliol. All however was in vain, and the indomitable spirit of that country wearied Edward out.

1338. Mar. 26. Letters Patent "pro Roberto de Artoys, de annuitate," are dated by the king at Derlyngton. *(Rymer's Fœdera.)* This was in his northern journey connected with the seige of Dunbar.

1342-3 Feb. 20. The bishop *by common counsel and consent of the whole community of his liberty*, having made composition for a truce with Scotland, by promising payment of one hundred and sixty marks, and 8*l*. 13*s*. 4*d*. for expenses of ambassadors, &c., orders by precept of his day that John Randolf should raise the proportion payable by Darlington Ward by taxation.‡ On the sixth of February preceeding, Bury appointed Robert Brackenbury, grandfather of the celebrated lieutenant of the Tower, and thirty others to array all the defensible men in Darlington Ward to oppose the Scots.

THOMAS HATFIELD.

Elected 8 May, 1345; died 8 May, 1381.

1346. In the king's great expedition to France this year, which ended in the glorious contest of Cressy, he was accompanied by Master William Killesby, clerk, who is named by Stowe as one of those leading a great army of soldiers well appointed, at the embarkment at Portsmouth. This churchman was more than once employed in warlike affairs. Edward was also accompanied in his luckless Flanders trip of 1340 by "two chapleynes that were his Secretaries, Sir William Killesby, and Sir Philip Weston;" and again Hollinshed writes that his Secretary, Sir William Killesby, stirred him to take displeasure against the archbishop of Canterbury John Stratford, who was accused of preventing the king in his late campaign being furnished with money, by not looking after the collectors, and charging the king with oppression while he had the rule of the realm in his hands under the king. The prelate was a man of spirit, excommunicated all who did violence to the clergy or their goods, a sentence which struck at Edward himself; and wrote a letter to the king full of the highest claims for ecclesiastical superiority over

* Raine's St. Cuthbert, 37.

† Pat. 9 Edw. III. p. 1. m. 7, vel 8. Tanner's Not. Mon.

‡ Rot. Bury, sched. 13.

kings. This was not a likely way of obtaining the pardon of Edward, who omitted his name in summoning parliament. Stratford appeared in full vestments, demanded entrance as the highest peer, and after two days rejection forced the king to give way.

Killesby was in Brittany in 1345 in an army on behalf of the duke of that country, who however soon died, and he returned to England.*

Both Killesby and Weston held prebendal stalls in Darlington church,† and appear to have been in high favour with the king. In 1343 royal letters issued, extending special protection for William de Kildesby of all his preferments, he having, by the king's licence, gone into foreign parts, and "by reason of laudable obedience to us by the said William bestowed," that king now extended his gracious favour to him, and prevented any man from injuring him in his possessions. These were of no small value, for besides the "prebend in the church of Derlyngton," he held five other prebends, one hospital, one church, one free-chapel, and six other chapels dependant.‡ So much for the purity of the church at that time.

Philip de Weston was admitted Dean of York in 1347, both by the king's and archbishop's letters on his behalf. When he died is not known, but the next dean occurring is cardinal Talyrandos de Petagoricis, whom, Mr. Willis says, the pope thrust into the deanery, and outed Weston. The same author adds that he enjoyed it till 1366, when he died. *(Drake's Eboracum.)*

The collegiate church must have been well stocked with these king-caressed ecclesiastics, who doubtless looked after their spiritual charges in very slight fashion, for, in 1343, Weston was made a commissioner to treat with the Flemish in company with Master John Waweyn, who as Canon of Derlyngton learned in both§ laws," often occurs with John de Montgomery knt. in public instruments in 1336, being called by the king his "trusty proctors and ambassadors."||

As to the titles of *Sir* and *Master*, given to the three prebendaries, take a note from Percy's Reliques :—

"The title of Sir was not formerly peculiar to knights, it was given to Priests, and sometimes to very inferior personages.

Dr. Johnson thinks this title was applied to such as had taken the degree of A.B. in the universities, who are still styled *Domini*, "Sirs," to distinguish them from undergraduates, who have no prefix, and from Masters of Arts, who are styled *Magistri*, 'Masters.'"

General usage in early times gave the title of *Domnus* to an ecclesiastical superior, reserving *Dominus* for our Lord. Cælestem *Dominum*, terrestrem dicito *domnum*.

1346. During the king's invasion of France, David of Scotland rushed down on our fair vales with an immense army. In this campaign he "appointed to preserve foure tounes onely from burning, to witte, Hexham, Corbridge, Darington, and Durham, to the ende he might in them lay up such

* Hollinshed.

† Allan's Collectanea Dunelmensia.

‡ Rymer's Fœdera, sub 17 Edw. III.

§ Civil and canon.

|| Rymer's Fœdera.

store of vitayles, as he should provide abrode in the Countrey, wherewith to susteyne his army during the time of his abyding in those parties." * I do not however trace him further South than the entrancing seat of Beaupaire. The end of this border raid came to pass at Redhills or Neville's Cross, near Durham on October 17, where, by the assistance of St. Cuthbert's Corporax cloth, the Scots were totally routed, their king taken, and the Black Rood of Scotland,† miraculously delivered to one of his predecessors, transported to the church of Durham. Neville's Cross had existed on the spot long before, but a new and very fair cross of stone was now erected by Lord Ralph Neville "one of the most excellent and chief persons" at the battle. In 1639, "in the night time, the same was broken down, and defaced by some lewd, and contemptuous wicked persons, thereto encouraged (as it seemed) by some who loved Christ the worse for the Cross sake."‡ As for the previous cross on the spot, take the following hint from Raine. §

"A cross was the usual boundary or march stone between Lord and Lord, and most especially where three Lords might have met and shaken hands with each other from their respective estates. The Nevilles were owners of Brancepeth, and in all probability the old cross might have taken its name from the fact, that it stood upon the precise spot at which a man who was bound to my Lord Neville, of Brancepeth, would quit the great and much frequented ecclesiastical way between Durham and Bearpark. The cross of the Nevilles, I dare say the very saltire of their shield, would remind a young Lumley, or a Hilton, of the place to which he was going, and would prompt him to spur on his steed till he had reached the side of the Prior of Durham, in whose suite he had ascended the hill, and wish him solace at Beaurepaire, gently bidding him farewell."

When *cross* occurs in names of fields, I believe it almost always has reference to ancient metes and bounds. Sandhutton Cross, at the junction of the townships of Thirsk and Sandhutton, still stands. There are boundary crosses at Borrowby in the same country on the Cross-Keys farm ; and here we have *Cross-Woods*, the first two fields in Blackwell township, boundering Glassensikes, and *Lamb-Cross Hill*,‖ the field at this side of Prescott's stile, where a cross would be useful, either as a bound between it and the territory of Nor-

* Hollinshed.

† There is no man that could tell of what matter this crosse was made, whether of metall, stone, or of tree. *Hollinshed*.

‡ The Rites, &c., of the church of Durham, collected out of ancient MSS. about the time of the suppression, published by J. Davies, of Kidwelly, 1672. An extremely scarce little 12mo. of 164 pp. A degree of peculiarity attaches to it, in having *two* dedications to the same man, James Mickleton, esq. dated respectively Sep. 4 and Oct. 4, 1671, (I speak only from my own copy) in differing language, but to the same effect. Mickleton is mentioned as collector of the subject matter, and is well known as an earnest Durham antiquary. He died in 1695, leaving his MSS. for four years to Sir Robert Eden, Bart., Abraham Hilton, gent., and John Spearman, and afterwards as to certain of his MSS. to the same persons, or their nominee, to be printed.

§ St. Cuthbert, 106.

‖ Does this refer to a cross with the Agnus-Dei fairly sculptured thereon, or to the soft sward on which the lambkins capered ?

dykes, or if we take the North side of the close, as between Blackwell and Darlington townships. Then there is *Croce-flatt* or *Crosse-flatt*, an estate of the very Nevilles just spoken of, and situate in Clay Row, which was sold by Henry, father of the last Earl of Westmoreland, to the Stories, from whom it passed through the Collings and Crosbys, to the Allans.* It was a custom to erect crosses where churches first burst on the view. Crosse-flatt and Lamb-cross-Hill would both be very proper places for such mementos, where the traveller from Yarm or from Richmond, on the brow from whence the tapering spire of the collegiate church was delight to the eye, would pray and praise.

In the conveyance from Francis Storye, of Mortham, (Morton) co. Durham, gent., and Henry his son and heir, of Harleshawe, co. York, gent., to Francis Foster for 120*l.* of Crosse flatt, sixteen acres, [called one close in 7 James I.] it is described as "a parcell of the lait landes of Henry, lait Earle of Westmerland, and by him sold to Cuthberte Storye, lait father of the said Frauncis and laid fourth by partition of the said townshipp of Darlington, in leue of a part of the said Earle's landes," and in the feoffment accompanying, as bounded by W. Four Riggs, belonging to the Glebe of Darlington ; S. The King's street. (i. e. the road to Yarm.) † In 1731 it contained twenty-six acres, seven perches, and the whole North side of the Bank Top colony is built upon it. It is in the township of Bondgate, but is freehold.

The head of the family was Gilbert de Neville, an admiral‡ in the fleet of the Conqueror, in 1066. His grandson Geoffrey married Emma, daughter and heiress of Bertram de Bulmer, and obtained Brancepeth and Sheriff-Hutton lordships. His son Henry dying 1227, s. p. his daughter Isabel succeeded to the estates, and marrying Robert Fitz-Melred, lord of Raby, her son Geoffrey assumed the Neville surname, and from him all the later Nevilles sprung.

Geoffrey was the father of Robert, whose son, Robert the younger, died in his father's life-time. He had married Mary, daughter and eventually sole heiress of the great Baron Ranulph Fitz-Ribald, of Middleham, but the union was hapless. Mary of Middleham, said to have been fair and gentle, wept over the early grave of her husband, who died the victim of a savage revenge ;§ she survived on her own inheritance, and dying in 1320, lies buried at Coverham Abbey, founded by her ancestors. Her only son Ralph Neville succeeded his grandfather as lord of Raby, and was an indolent man, sometimes showing gleams of gallant bearing, but generally fonder of the society of the canons of Coverham than of living in his paternal homes. It is to be hoped that the character of the monks is not to be judged by the deeds of their devotee, for Kellawe obliged him, when long past the period of his

* Included in the Grange estates sold.

† Archives penes R. H. Allan, esq.

‡ The old Neville coat was "Or, fretty Gu. on a canton Sa. *an ancient ship*."

§ " Robertus iste de Neville membra, manibus irati viri cujusdam cujus uxorem ingenuam violaverat, apud Craven perdidit."

youth, to do penance for a deplorable delinquency.* Mary Fitz-Ranulph deeming her son none of the most competent to manage this world's wealth, settled her manors of Middleham and Coverdale on her grandson Robert, **The Peacock of the North**.

He, *in superbiis*, "for despite who might rule most," assaulted and slew Richard Fitz-Marmaduke, son of the boiled baron,† on Elvet bridge, as he was riding to open the County Courts, but, next year, in leading a disorderly band to plunder the Scottish march, was slain himself at Bewyck Park, leaving a brother Ralph to gain the glories of Neville's Cross.

In 1651, the manor of Winston was held of Raby by one broad arrow feathered with *peacock feathers*. At Middleham in a house opposite the castle, a sculpture of a pheasant or peacock is built in. Above the North door of Staindrop church also, is a sculpture far more like a bird than a lion, as it has been designated. It is therefore probable that the proud by-name of Robert might originate in a badge, like Richard III.'s "bloody boar of York."

The reader must not imagine that the phrase "I'll nevel thee," or "give thee a nevelling" scattered over the north, has any relation to this family, uproarious as some of its members were. *Nevel* simply means to beat violently with the fist or nief. The word is still used.

> "She'll deal her *Neaves* about her, I hear tell
> She's timerous to please, and varra Fell,
> First thing that comes to hand she'll let it flee,
> Neans yable to abide her Crueltie ;
> She'll Nawpe and *Nevel* them without a cause."
> *A Yorkshire Dialogue*. 1697.

And it is classical English :—

> Give me your *nief*; Monsieur Mustard-seed !
> *Midsummer Night's Dream.*

In 1290,‡ or in Hugh de Derlyngton's previous priorate, according to Dugdale, had arisen a dispute between Ralph Neville and the prior of Durham. The Nevilles, in respect of the honour of Raby, annually offered a stag, and Ralph claimed that he and his company should be feasted by the prior on the occasion. Imagination easily pictures the woe of the brethren, how the prior would explain that the noble's numerous train would sadly reduce both stag and usual larder, and how a portly brother would solemnly demonstrate,

* Citacio Domini Ranulfi de Neville, publicata tam in ecclesia de Stayndrop, quam in manerio suo de Raby xvii Octr. anno 3 pontif. pro incestu et adulteriis cum Anastasia, filia sua, uxore Domini Walteri de Fauconberg.

† See page 56.

‡ Graystanes.

like Toby Heyrick* of later days, the impossibility of the fat spinning round. The upshot was that the Prior declined to accept the stag when laid at the shrine of the abstemious Cuthbert. Long were the faces of the hungry retainers, bitter were their words, and most awful were their nevellings of the sonsy monks at the altar. Up rose the courage of the latter, and down came the huge candles they were carrying on the offenders, with such good will that they beat a retreat, leaving the stag. The succeeding Ralph (of Neville's cross) claimed in 1331 the privilege with an aggravation, for he wanted not only a dinner, but to stop all day and demolish a breakfast next morning. However on the prior's remonstrances and submission for that once, the Neville brought but few with him, more for an honour than a burden, and shortly after dinner left, saying, "What doth a breakfast signify to me? Nothing." The stag was brought in with winding of horns, and a very old rhyme, the lament for Robert, father of Mary of Middleham's spouse, runs:

> Wel, qwa sal thir hornes blau,
> Haly Rod thi day?
> Nou is he dede and lies law
> Was wont to blaw thaim ay.†

The hero of the fight left a son John, Lord Neville, who inherited all his father's talents, and filled the highest offices of the state.‡ His two brothers stand in curious juxtaposition—one was archbishop of York, the other a chief leader of the Lollards! He died in 1388, being seized of a messuage and nine acres at Blackwell held by fealty only, and of a messuage in Cockerton, and four oxgangs.§ This John Neville and John Fairfax, clerk, acquired moreover the manor of Oxenhale from John, son of Roger de Belgrave, before 1378, which, under Hatfield's survey, was held by Lord Neville in drengage by the old service of Boldon Buke, and the estate descended to the last Earl.

His son and successor, Ralph, raised his family honours to the highest pitch of magnificence, and by his second marriage with Joan, legitimized daughter of John of Gaunt, became brother-in-law to his sovereign. Engaged as he was in all the events of the day, his character stands forth in unmistakable colours. Staunch in loyalty, he used means none the most scrupulous. He prevented his former associate Northumberland joining his son Hotspur

* Vicar Toby of Gainford, who actually once wrote a note declining to partake of a haunch of venison, apologising, as a reason, that he understood *four* were invited: and as Mr.—was one of them, he was sure there would not be *fat for more than two!*

† Graystanes. See further in Hutchinson, ii. 84.

‡ Licence to castellate Raby, 1379. It was the age of such works. Witness Hylton and Lumley. Darlington is distinctly seen from Raby Tower.

§ Inq. p. m. John Nevyll, Chivaler, 1 Skirlaw.

at the fight of Shrewsbury, and in the second insurrection in the north he dispersed the insurgents on Shipton Moor, by an artifice of more dubious character, sending their leaders, whom he had paltered with, to the scaffold.

Ralph received his title from the deserted king in 1397, when "the Lord of Westmerland, named Dan Raby Nevell," * was made Earl of Westmoreland. With Henry he was in highest favour, sometimes putting in an old rhyme to assist his arguments, such as

Who so wyll Fraunce wynne, must with Scotland fyrst beginne.†

He died full of years and honours in 1426, being buried under a magnificent tomb of alabaster, in his own collegiate church of Staindrop.

From the earl's first bed sprung the Earls of Westmoreland, from his second, the princely line of Warwick and of Salisbury, (whose blood mingled with that of Plantagenet), the lords of Fauconberg, Latimer,‡ and Abergavenny,§ and Bishop Robert Neville of Durham.

The Earl died seized of the Manors of Oxenale, val. 20*l.*, and Blakwell; one messuage and three oxgangs in Cockerton, val. 13*s.* 4*d.*; seven messuages, twelve cottages, twenty-four burgages, four oxgangs, six acres of land, and six acres of meadow in Derlington, and one close and one Dove-cote, val. 40*s.*

A tenement in Cockerton (then in possession of the Garths) is described as *Nevil's house* in 1683. *Surtees.*

Pardon from Bp. Nevill (a° 5) to his nephew Ralph (2nd earl) for lands at Darlington, formerly acquired without license, by Ralph, Earl of Westmoreland, deceased, from Sir Thomas Gray, knt.

Robert the adulterer and Robert the Peacock had well nigh passed out of remembrance, and the fate attendant upon the lords of Neville, of seeing their first-born die in their lifetime, seemed to slumber, but it suddenly revived, and for three generations the earldom never passed from father to son. John,

* Stowe. *Dan* is the exact and proper rendering of *Dominus*. Hollinshed prints *Dauraby*, and Leland calls him *Da Raby*. Hutch. iii. 264.

† Hollinshed.

‡ The last Neville, lord Latimer, in a direct line, John, who died in 1577, is buried under a gallant effigy in Well Church, near Masham, the table on which it rests being covered with incised names. These, from the dignity of the persons thus commemorating themselves, seem to be marks of honour paid to the deceased rather than mere emblems of a foolish passion for defacing monuments with initials and shoemarks; and to have been done at much the same time, probably by a party of gentlemen visiting the church together. Here are some :—"CHARLES FAIRFAX—MARMADUKE DANBY : JULY : 9 : 1618 : —TH : DANBIE. 1618. GRATIAS. DEO.—WILL. LVMLEY—IO : IERTON—WILIAM : WANDESFORD—JOHN : COLE : 1618 :—RO : FRANCKLIN. 1618." Some appear to be facsimiles of signatures. Here too rests Dorothy Vere, predecessor of Queen Catherine Parr in the bed of the lord Latimer; and here is a slab which might vie with Bp. Beaumont's, 12 ft. 1 in. by 4 ft. 8 in., formerly covered by brass.

§ The brazen shield of Richard, son of the first lord Abergavenny, torn from his tomb and affixed to the font at Staindrop, still retains the deep gules of the Neville quartering.

the great earl's gallant son, who discomfited fifty Frenchmen with thirteen English, died in his father's lifetime, leaving a son, Ralph, to succeed to the earldom and a diminished estate; for Middleham, and many a fair lordship were rent away for the descendants of Joan of Lancaster. His only son, John, died without issue, and he himself in 1484, being memorialized by wooden effigies of himself and wife at Brancepeth, on which the Lancastrian collar of SS, has given way to the white rose and sun with the silver boar of Richard. His nephew, Ralph, was third earl, whose only son, Ralph, perished like his predecessors in early prime, and was buried in the southern chapel of Brancepeth, "whereupon the erle took much thoght and dyed at Horneby Castle, in Richmontshire, and there is buryed in the paroche chirche." The lost heir had left a son, Ralph, who became fourth earl, and died in 1549, leaving Henry, the fifth earl, who died in 1563, and was buried in Staindrop Church, under a handsome but debased wooden altar tomb. He was succeeded by his son Charles, of whom, alas! I have mournful things to relate anon.

Perhaps this most ancient and historic race had been somewhat shorn of its glory before the fifth earl sold Croce flatt. The second earl had granted a burgage in le Welrawe (situated between two burgages which he retained) to Thomas Bichborne, who rendered 3*s*. 4*d*. per ann. to him in respect of it, before 23 Henry VI.*

The fifth Earl also sold lands in Blackwell, in 1563, to Edward Perkinson, of Beaumond Hill. The race was in rapid decline, and during the Rising of the North the queen instructed Sussex to state that " one of the earles has already so spoyled his owne patrimonie, as he will not let to spoile and consume all other men's that he may cume by."

Raskelf (pronounced Rascal) seems to have been a sort of appendage for younger scions of the Nevilles,

Rascal Town with roguish people
A bursten bell† and wooden church steeple.

Popular Rhyme.

And what a steeple! Four hugh trunks of oak run up the corners from top to bottom. It is an addition to the original structure, the old west window forming the Tower arch. On one of the bells is the odd legend, (S. F.) R. W. REMEMBER THY END AND FLIE R. D. 1593—GOD SAVE THIS *NAVEL* A. H. (S.F.), and in a window is a decayed effigy, in stained glass, of a Neville (14th cent.) resting on a pillow marked with the saltire.

At Heighington church are three unnoticed but very interesting bells.† The two first are dedicated to St. Peter and St. Paul, as fancied securities against tempests. The inscriptions are in ornamented gothic capitals, and read thus:—First, " † PURGATOS. NOS. IUNGITOS. AULE. CELI. PAULE." Second, " † TU. PETRE. PULSATUS. PERUERSOS. MITIGA. FLATUS." The third has a figure of the virgin

* Archives penes R. H. Allan, esq.

† *Var.* a drunken parson.

† On Bedale bell is a curious rhyming legend:
"+ IOU : EGO : CUM : FIAM : CRUCE : CUSTOS : LAUDO : MARIAM :
DIGNA : DEI : LAUDE : MATER : DIGNISSIMA : GAUDE."

and child, well executed ; and the arms of Neville and.........(three annulets), with this rhyming invocation to the virgin, in black letter, " + *O. mater. dia. me. sana. bona. maria.*"

1348. The Bishop issued his mandate to Rob. de Brackenbury and others, to levy on Darlington Ward its proportion of four hundred marks, with the *consent of the nobles, headmen, and all the commonalty* of his royal liberty of Durham, in compensation of the expense he had sustained in his preparations for its defence.* The instrument is remarkable, it issues with the assent of a collective legislative body, in the same language as the king's mandates, issued with the assent of parliament, (*magnates proceres et tota communitas.*)

Circa 1380. A general survey of the bishop's lands was made, after the fashion of Boldon Buke, called Hatfield's Survey, but in addition to the demesne and villenage lands, containing a record of the freeholders paying rents.

By this survey Darlington comprised,

Thirty-nine free tenants, who hold fifty-seven parcels of ground and messuages by divers several rents, payable at the four usual terms.

The tenants hold amongst them certain lands, viz. : Calfhouse, Swatergate, Elesbankes, Sadbergate, Cockyrtongate, Bathelgate, Duresmgate, Prestgate, and Huraworthgate, by ancient custom, as it is said, from which the lord receives nothing, notwithstanding that these are parcels of the lord's ancient and proper waste.

Fourteen tenants hold ten oxgangs of the demesne under twenty shillings rent per oxgang.

There is a plot of ground in the occupation of the Vicar of Derlyngton, worth, as it is said, twelve-pence per annum.

There is a place within the enclosure of the manor, with a curtilage on which a house is built, in which the Janitor dwells, worth per ann. as is said, three shillings and fourpence.

Ralph of Eseby holds two messuages and two oxgangs, and pays for each oxgang five shillings. [the services exactly as those of the tenants in villenage under Boldon Book ;] in all ten shillings.

Thirteen other bond tenants hold twenty messuages and thirty oxgangs on the same terms. [of the services of the bonds nothing is said here, *quia postea in Villa de Cokirton*]

The tenants jointly hold the common forge ; four-pence rent at the four terms.

For toll of ale from the tenants in villenage, twelve-pence ; for toll of ale from the burgesses of Derlyngton, two shillings.

William de Hoton and John de Teesdale hold the whole fishery by metes and bounds in the field, and pay two shillings.

The same tenants pay for the office of Punder fifty-three shillings and four-pence, to which office appertain nine acres of land and meadow, viz. : in Besfield, three acres ; in Dodmersfield, half-an-acre : in the Westfield, half-an-acre, within the verge (*virgultum*) of the manor, half-an-acre of meadow at the end of Ellyngmedowe, half-an-acre in Polinpole, one acre of meadow, and one acre of arable.

For the toll of the market place and market of Derlyngton, with the profits of the Mills of Derlyngton, Blakwell and Holughton and the suit of the tenants of Queshowe, the bakehouse, the assise of bread and ale, the profits of the Borough Court with the Dye-house, there is rendered four score and ten pounds.†

* Randal's MSS.

† Allan. 94*l*. Surtees.

The aforesaid bond tenants among them render yearly at Christmas thirty-five hens; the same tenants render yearly for Wodsilver* at the aforesaid festival two shillings.

Twenty-seven tenants hold various messuages, tenements, cottages, with divers acres under the name of Exchequer-lands.

All the tenants of Exchequer-land perform among them the services of four cottagers, viz.: in making hayricks, and they carry fruit, and work at the mill whenever it is declared what cottagers ought to do those services.

† Ingelram Gentill and his partners hold the borough of Derlyngton with the profits of the mills and the Dye-house, and other profits pertaining to the borough, rendering yearly four score and thirteen pounds and six shillings.

Oxenhale. Lord de Neville ‡ holds the manor of Oxenhall rendering yearly at the four usual terms sixty shillings. Also for services at Martinmas 6*s*. 8*d*. viz. for the ploughing of four acres of land, and he harrows four acres of land sown with the Bishop's seed, and tills four portions in autumn, viz. three with all his men and his whole family except the housewife, and the fourth with one man from every house except his own proper house, and keeps a dog and horse for a quarter of a year, and carries wine with a wain of four oxen, and performs *Outeward* in the Bishopric when imposed, as much as pertains to the fourth part of one Drenge, rendering yearly at the terms aforesaid, in all 66*s*. 8*d*.

Blakwell. *Free-tenants.* John Middleton holds by right of his wife, one messuage, and five oxgangs of land by charter, formerly of John de Blakwell, by knight's service and multure (one sixteenth) *et cooperabit molas supra le Louthre*, rendering 23*s*. 8*d*.

The same John holds a certain parcel of tillage called Gromball, containing 16 acres 3 roods, rendering ....

The same John holds there two parcels of tillage, called Lynholm and Ellestantoftes containing 16 acres by estimation, rendering ....

The same John holds one tenement called le Castelhill, with the herbage of Bathley, containing 4 acres of meadow and pasture, rendering ....

The same John holds one place built on, and half an oxgang of land, rendering ......

The same John holds one toft with one croft, containing half a rood of land, rendering yearly at the usual terms 12*d*.

The same John holds one toft, formerly William de Oxenhall's, with one croft, containing one acre, rendering by charter 2*d*.

William Strygate, chaplain, holds one acre at Ellestontoft by knight's service, rendering 4*d*.

Emma Morrell holds three acres at Spykbyt by knight's service, rendering 14*d*.

Peter Thomesson, in right of his wife, holds half-an-acre and half a rood, lying in Oxenhalflat, rendering 16*d*.

Four other tenants hold certain lands by knight's service, and pay............

Bond-lands. John Verty holds one oxgang, rendering yearly at the four usual terms and is bound to mow the whole meadow of the Bishop, and make and lead the hay, and to have a corrody once, and to enclose the verge and court, and to do the works which he is accustomed to do at the mill, and to lead one wain (*quadrig.*) of Wodlade, and to carry loads in the journies of the Bishop; and besides three loads yearly, to fetch wine, herrings, and salt; rendering yearly at the four usual terms 5*s*.

* Money paid for the liberty of cutting and gathering wood ?

† This is evidently an addition to the original survey. *Surtees.*

‡ His ancestor, Fitz-Melred, under Boldon Buke held a carucate at Quosshur (Whessoe) by similar services. Surtees remarks that the involutions of the feudal systems frequently present the spectacle of a gallant noble holding by a servile tenure under a much meaner lord than the Bishop of Durham.

Nineteen other tenants hold twenty-four messuages, and thirty-nine oxgangs and a half, on the same terms. The same bond-tenants hold amongst them five oxgangs, which was once bond-land, rendering at the Feast of the Purification of the blessed Mary as it is said, ten quarters of wheat, and five quarters of barley, and fifteen of oats. [For the services of the bond lands nothing is said, *quia postea in villa de Cokerton.*]

Cottagers. John Pothow and Peter Thomesson hold one cottage, make hay-ricks, carry fruit and work at the mill, rendering yearly at the four usual terms 21*d.*: four other cottages are held by doing the same services, and rendering yearly a rent of ......

Exchequer-lands. Twenty-five tenants hold certain tofts and crofts, tenements and lands by the name of Exchequer Lands, free of all service (*sine operibus*), only paying divers annual rents.

All the tenants of the Exchequer answer for services and cottages as above, till it be seen on which tenements those services should be charged.

The bond-tenants hold an acre of land called Punderland, rendering yearly at the same terms 2*s.* 6*d.*

The same bond-tenants pay for the office of Punder yearly 10*s.*

The same tenants pay at the festival of the Nativity of St. John for Wodlades 11*s.* 9*d.*

The same bond-tenants hold among them the toll of ale, rendering yearly 3*s.*

.... hold among them a pasture called Rathel, rendering yearly 10*s.* 8*d.*

All the tenants of the vill hold a tenement, once Roger Stapilton's, rendering yearly 8*d.*

From the township for an increment of one toft, yearly, at the usual terms, 18*d.*

From the aforesaid vill for a pasture called le Longdraght, a yearly rent at the usual terms of 16*s.*

From the aforesaid vill for Wodsilver at Martinmas, one hen; at Christmas, 2*s.*, thirty-two hens.

There is there a water-mill, and it is in the hands of the tenants of the vill of Derlyngton with the farm rent.

COKIRTON. *Free-Tenants.* John Morton holds a messuage and four oxgangs, by knight's service, and 20*s.*, and one parcel, once of Margaret Ralph, rendering yearly 12*d.*

Geoffrey Kellaw holds a messuage and oxgang, and renders one hen and a farthing at Michaelmas.

John Dowe holds one tenement, which he acquired from John Morton, 12*d.*

Cottagers. John Dow holds a cottage and garden containing an acre of meadow-land; rendering 3*s.* 4*d.* yearly, and shall drive cattle (*fugavit animalia*), to the lord's manor-house when required; and he cleans the houses within the manor-place of Derlyngton against the coming of the lord or his officers. Three others hold cottages on the same terms.

All the tenants of the cottages make hay-ricks, carry fruit, and work at the mill.

Bond-lands. John Cornforth holds two messuages and two oxgangs, rendering yearly for each oxgang 5*s.* at the four usual terms, and is bound to mow the whole meadow of the Bishop, and to make hay and lead it, and to have a corrody once, and to enclose the verge and court, and to lead a wain of Wodlades, and to carry loads in the Bishop's journies, and three loads yearly besides, bringing wine, herrings and salt; and to do the works he is accustomed to do at the mill, rendering at the terms aforesaid 10*s.*

Eighteen other bond-tenants hold thirty-seven oxgangs and twenty-nine messuages by the same conditions.

The same bond-tenants render yearly at the Feast of St. John for Wodlades 11*s.*10*d.*

The same tenants for the office of Punder, yearly, 10*s.*

The same tenants for the toll of ale there, yearly, 2*s.*

All the tenants there are bound to answer for the rent of a plot near the gate, (*juxta portam*) formerly in the tenure of Stephen the Punder.

The same tenants for an increment of a croft, and a croft formerly Ralph Fitz-Ralph's 2*s*.

Bond-services. From the bond-services of Bondgate, Blakwell, and Cockirton, viz., for five score and thirteen oxgangs for each 15*d*. and more, in the whole 2*s*. 4*d*. at Michaelmas, as is said, whence a total sum of.........

Bond-lands at Penyferme. Eleven tenants hold eight oxgangs, rendering 18*s*. 9*d*. an oxgang, at the four usual terms.

Exchequer-lands. Thirteen tenants hold nine tenements and other parcels under a yearly rent.

All the tenants of Exchequer-land, except those who are charged as above with services, perform amongst them such services as pertain to two cottages, until it be shown from whom those individual services are due.

Little Haughton occurs thus,

Free-tenants. William Walworth, chivaler, a messuage and oxgang 6*s*.

Bond-tenants. William Donkan pays, inter alia, one hen to the Punder of Derlyngton. Six others hold six messuages and oxgangs by the same rents and services.

Demesne-lands. Hugh de Westwyk, chaplain, holds half the manor of Haughton called *Rewmond*, for £6 13*s*. 8*d*. The other half is in the hands of the Bishop, and the Bailiff of Darlington reckons for it in his account. The said manor contains eight carucates and *each carucate is six score acres, worth a groat (!) an acre*, and nine acres of meadow in *Halekeld-holm*, which used to be sold (i. e. the hay ?) for 46*s*. 8*d*, are in the hands of the Bailiff of Derlington, who accounts for them.

JOHN FORDHAM

Was provided by the pope, 9 Sep., 1381. He encouraged Richard II. in all his indiscretions, and was by coercion of the barons, banished by the king in 1388, from this see, to acquire that of Ely.

1384. Dec. 16. King Richard II. by charter, reciting that the bishop and his predecessors held the manor and wapentake of Sadberge, and the manors and towns of Derlyngton, &c., &c., confirms the possession of them and all the privileges of the liberty of the county palatine.

WALTER SKIRLAW

Was appointed by the pope the same day that Fordham was removed. He died in 1405.

He was said to be the son of a sieve-maker, to which origin his arms were supposed to allude ; Argent, six wands in true-love proper. He built a strong tower to Howden church, whence cometh the rhyme

Bishop Skirlaw indeed was good to his people,
He built them a school-house and heightened the steeple.

Surtees says that his arms are on the front of Hylton castle, and remarks

"The mitres of Cosin and of Crewe (in spite of Pope's sarcasm) deservedly continue to decorate our churches, but what must be the merits of that future Prelate whose bearings shall grace the halls and gateways of our lay Rectors?" I doubt the fact. The saltire of Neville in an adjoining shield is moulded in the same style (a mannerism of the age), and I imagine the plain cross so ornamented is simply that of Vesci. The mouldings do not interlace at all.

CARDINAL THOMAS LANGLEY

Elected 7 May, 1406; died 20 Nov., 1437.

1407. By the interest the cardinal possessed at court (being chancellor) he obtained a royal charter from Henry IV., confirming all the liberties and privileges granted to the bishops by the several potentates, from the establishment of the see. Darlington manor is mentioned in the inspeximus of Richard II.'s charter.

ROBERT NEVILLE

Son of the great earl by Joan Beaufort, translated from Salisbury 1437, died 9 July, 1457. His doings for Darlington will be noticed under the Collegiate Church.

LAWRENCE BOOTH

Consecrated Sep., 1457; translated to York 1476. He was a staunch Lancastrian, having been chaplain to Queen Margaret, but after the chivalry of the red rose had died *die Dominica in ramis Palmarum** at Towton, and a short disgrace and suspension from his temporalities, he adopted the flower of pallid hue.

WILLIAM DUDLEY

Elected Sep., 1476; died Nov., 1483; after seeing the blood of Edward IV. set aside, and Richard, duke of Gloucester, one of his justices in the first year of his pontificate, placed in their seat.

JOHN SHERWOOD

Elected Jan., 1484-5; died 12 Jan., 1493. He walked on one hand of

* So in the Inquisitions of the fallen. The battle was fought on Palm Sunday.

Richard at his coronation, forgetful of many favours conferred by the late monarch, and for some reason had not the temporalities restored till within sixteen days of that bloody battle in which the crown was torn from the house of Plantagenet and placed on the brow of Tudor. Richard loved the stately inheritance of Anne of Warwick, and abode at times in the Baliol's walls. It would be convenient to him to have a resting-place at the spot where he would leave the high road, and wander along the Tees, to that favoured seat; and this leads me to the following Inquisition.

An Inquisition upon the death of Richard, late King of England. An Inquisition indented, taken at Auckland in the county of Durham, on Thursday, the 15th day of June in the 2nd year of the pontificate of John, &c., before Thomas Fenton, esq., eschaetor of the said Bishop in the county of Durham, by virtue of his office, upon the oaths of Roger Conyers, knt., Thomas Lumley, esq., John Eshe, esq., Robert Dalton, esq., Thomas Surtays, esq., Thomas Lambton, esq., Alexander Fetherstonhalgh, esq., Thomas Posseley esq., John Claxton, esq., Robert Pollerd, esq., Robert Walker, Thomas Delvas, John Southorn, Thomas Coundon, jurors: who upon their oath say,

That Richard, late King of England, *de facto* but not *de jure*, at a Parliament holden at Westminster the......day of......in the......year of the reign of King Henry VII., *was attainted of high treason*,* and by the authority of the same Parliament it was ordered and appointed that the said Richard, late King of England, and all others who have any estate in lands or tenements in fee simple, or in fee tail, to the use of him, Richard late King of England, shall forfeit them by authority of Parliament aforesaid; and that the said Richard, late King of England, was so seized in possession as of fee on the day on which he died, of one capital messuage, forty acres of land and thirty acres of land with their appurtenances in Derlyngton, late Henry Elstofle's, which are held of the said Lord Bishop in chief by military service, and by service of rendering him the Lord Bishop yearly, at his Exchequer at Durham, at the usual terms there 21*s*. 8*d*., and of doing suit in the county of Durham *de quindena in quindenam*, and are worth yearly in all proceeds beyond reprizes 100*s*. And the said Jurors say that the said Richard, late King of England, did not hold other or more lands or tenements in possession or reversion, nor any other person for his use in the county of Durham.† And that he died the 18th‡ day of August last past. In witness whereof the Jurors aforesaid have to this Inquisition interchangeably placed their seals the day and place aforesaid.§

At this distance of time I am unable to trace this property of the last of the Plantagenets, nor do I know the history of *Kings house*, in right of which Edward Whitehead stood constable of Bondgate in 1696.‖ The old rhyme

* A high flight of Parliament (saith Buck, the apologetic historian of Richard) to attaint a King of High Treason.

† Barnard Castle was not considered within the palatinate at this period, and did not escheat to the bishop.

‡ The battle was however fought on the 22nd.

§ The original latin is given in Surtees, i. clxvi.

‖ A Booke of remembrance, or an inrolment of memorable things belonging to Bondgate in Darlington. The constables and other officers were chosen in respect of lands, alternately liable to furnish them. The book has belonged to the greeves, and contains lists of officers, beginning 1638-9. It will be hereafter referred to as *Bondgate Book*. The following information is valuable:—"30 acres is an axgang at Sedgefield, 16 acres at Hurworth, and 20 in Yorkeshire."

Jacke of Norffolke be not too bolde
For Dikon thy master is boughte and solde

would at first thought lead us to *Dickon-kists,* (which with Town-end fields and Thorney Beck closes constituted an estate of the balival family of Barnes) as possibly memorializing Richard, but I believe that they took their name from the family of Dickons, descendants of Ralph Dykone, Rector of Haughton-le-Skerne in 15...

Sic transit gloria mundi:—the stream of Lethe has flowed on and washed away all traditions connected with Richard in the North. The very site of his capital messuage and land at Darlington is unknown, and at Middleham itself the Nevilles are seldom named. The memory of their glory has passed away like a morning cloud, save with the few who shew a cherished match in their pedigree, and claim to be descended of their blood. The great Plantagenet is forgotten in that place he loved so well and cherished so truly. Gentle Lady Anne is never named in what was once her heritage. But of their son, the flower that perished so timelessly one slight memento yet remains in a small ruinous apartment of the castle named

The Prince's Chamber.

Chapter II. The Tudors.

"Thou rememberest
Since once I sat upon a promontory,
And heard a mermaid, on a dolphin's back
Uttering such dulcet and harmonious breath,
That the rude sea grew civil at her song ;
And certain stars shot madly from their spheres,
To hear the sea-maid's musick."
Midsummer Night's Dream.

THE White Rose had ceased to bloom, but its fragrance was remembered. The Hawthorn never gained the affections of the people of the North Countrie, who during the whole period of the Tudor dynasty remained in an almost perpetual commotion.

Richard was greatly beloved in the North. He seems to have had the welfare of his neighbours at heart, and his foundation of the colleges of Middleham and Barnard-Castle give but little countenance to the ogre-like character generally attributed to him. When the people of Thirsk rose against his exactions, and slew the earl of Northumberland in attempting to enforce them, it was affirmed "that the Northern men bare against this earl continual grudge ever since the death of King Richard, whom they entirely favoured."* This feeling died out, but another soon rose. There was no part of the north where the "first pale and struggling ray of the reformation broke with more unwelcome lustre," and Sadler stated in 1569 that "there be not in all this countrey, ten gentillmen that do favour and allowe of her majesties procedings in the cause of religion."

The state of religion had been low indeed. The farce of St. Cuthbert's incorruptibility and power had been implicitly believed, and the relic lists of the Church of Durham catalogued with the most ludicrous items.

According to an enumeration of 1383, the monks possessed a pix of crystal, containing the milk of St. Mary the Virgin ; portions of the sepulchre and chemise of St. Mary the Virgin, and part of the rock upon which St. Mary the Mother of our Lord *mulgebat lac suum* ; a portion of the bones of St. Alkmund, of St. Exuperius the martyr, *of the Annunciation of St. Mary*, &c. &c. in a bag of cloth of gold ; a piece of the breast of St. Gracian the Virgin and Martyr, sc. *inter mamillas* ; two claws of a Griffin ; three Griffin's eggs ;† Manna from the Virgin Mary's grave ; a portion of the bread the Lord blessed ; a piece of the identical tree under which were the three angels with Abraham ; a stone, said to be *bread turned into stone* ; portion of the stone with which St. Stephen was stoned ; a piece of wood of the prison of St. John the Baptist ; a piece of the *throne*

* Hollinshed.

† St. Cuthbert's followers were fond of such things. In the British Museum is a horn inscribed ✝ GRYPHI VNGVIS DIVO CVTHBERTO DVNELMENSI SACER. This Griffin's claw is in fact the horn of the Egyptian Ibex !

where Jesus sat with his disciples; a piece of the *stone* upon which the Lord *wrote* when his disciples questioned him of the law; and a piece of the TWELVE THRONES OF THE APOSTLES ! *

But though they thus enslaved the populace, the Durham ecclesiastics themselves had assumed a tone of independence, and had manfully resisted the exactions of the pope, who had besides the British senate to contend with, an alarming spirit of opposition having risen which threatened a total exclusion of his supremacy. His fears were lightened by Edward III.'s application to him for the election of his secretary, Hatfield, to the see of Durham in apposition to his own acts against Romish interference; the request was as balm to his wounded spirit, and he piously exclaimed " Truly, if the king of England had made interest for an ass he should have been gratified."

In a temporal point of view, the Reformation worked badly enough. Poverty pervaded the kingdom, poor-laws crept in, and estates increased by sacrilege fell to pieces. The profligate waste attendant on the new movement alarmed and disgusted the old nobility. The distress of the poor on the dissolution of monasteries, the evident unconcern of government for proper spiritual arrangements, the hurt done to the pride of the magnates by the abolition of many long cherished privileges of the palatinate, and the piety of the last popish bishop, had deep effect on the haly-werke folks. Tunstall's zeal was amusing. He bought up Tindal's New Testament to burn in Cheapside. Tindal was delighted, as the edition was faulty, and he too poor as yet to issue a new one. The next year he sent an amended cargo from Antwerp, with the laughable information that the greatest encouragement he had had was from Tunstall. Our prelate however became afterwards very moderate in his opinions and acts, submitting to changes which he could not assent to. He was deprived† in Edward VI.'s reign, restored in Mary's, and again deprived in Elizabeth's, ending his blameless life in privacy. His diocese had escaped persecution, through his refusal to bring any man's blood upon his head; and the disgrace of shedding blood in it for religion was reserved for the pontificate of a protestant bishop and the reign of a protestant queen. The ancient faith all the while "lay like lees at the bottom of men's hearts; and if the vessel was ever so little stirred came to the top." The arrival of the Queen of Scots also created universal interest and added to the motives inspiring the discontented spirits appearing in the annals to which I now return.

1487. Lambert Simnel's rebellion took place, in which the Plantagenet bias of the people seems apparent. Henry personally conducted a severe inquisition in the northern parts, and by virtue of a royal writ, the bishop Sherwood (himself in no great favour) issued a commission to enquire *de*

* See the whole list in Raine's St. Cuthbert.

† Because Dudley was entranced with his revenues. The bishoprick was dissolved and the usual fate of sacrilege followed. Edward died in his youthful bloom, and Dudley perished on the scaffold.

insurrectionibus infra regiam libertatem Dunelm. He died in 1493 at Rome. His errand was perhaps rebellious, for his effects were sequestered by the crown.

RICHARD FOX,

Translated from Bath and Wells, Dec. 1494; translated to Winchester, Oct. 1502. He was a warrior and councillor for Henry VII. to whom he was executor, but his fortunes waned in the succeeding reign before the aspiring Wolsey.

1502. Margaret, eldest daughter of king Henry VII., passed through Darlington. In Leland's Collectanea is an account styled "The Fyancelles of Margaret, eldest daughter of King Henry VII., to James [IV.], king of Scotland: together with her departure from England, journey into Scotland, her reception and marriage there, and the great feasts held on that account. Written by John Younge, Somerset Herald, who attended the Princess on her journey." This worthy says,

"The xixth day of the said monneth (July), the quene departed from Allerton, in fayr aray and noble companyd, and Syr James Straungwysch, knight, scheryffe for the said lordschyp, for the said bishop, mett hyr welle accompanyd.

After sche drew to Darneton to hyr bed, and three mylle from the said place cam to hyr the Lord Lomley and hys son, accompanyd of many gentylmen and others welle apoynted, ther folks arayed with their liveray and well monted, to the nombre of xxiiij. horsys.

"At the village of Nesham she was mett by Syr Rawf Bowes and Syr William Aylton [Hylton], welle apoynted, with a fayr company arayed in their liverays, to the nombre of xl. horsys, well apoynted and well horst.

"In the saide place of Nesham was the saide quene receyved with the abbasse and religyouses, with the crosse without the gatt, and the bischop of Durham gaffe hyr the sayd crosse for to kisse. At two mylle ny to the said towne of Darneton, mett the quene, Syr William Boummer, scheryffe of the lordship of Durham. In company with hym was Syr William Ewers, and many other folks of honor of that contre, in fayr order, well apoynted of liverays and horst; to the nombre of six score horsys.

"By the said company was sche conveyed to Darnton. And at the gatt of the church of the said place, war revested the vicayr and folks of the church, wer doing as sche had done on the dayes before, sche was led to the manayer of the said byschop of Durham for that nyght.

"The xxth day of the said monneth the quene departed from Darnton in fayr aray, and with the precedente company went to the town of Durham," &c. The account says that at Durham "sche was well cheryscht, and hyr costs borne by the said bischop."

Fox, who more than once occurs as prime mover in courtly pageants, had taken part in the ceremonies at York. A great feast was given to the princess at Durham, on the 23rd July, the anniversary of his installation.

It is related of Margaret's affianced that having taken arms against his father, he imposed on himself the penance of continually wearing an iron chain about his waist. Some amusingly pompous stanzas on the marriage occur in Evans's Ballads :---

O fair, fairest of every fair,
Princess most pleasant and preclare,
The lustiest alive that be,
Welcome to Scotland to be queen.

Young tender plant of pulchritude,
Descended of imperial blood,
Fresh fragrant flower of fairhood sheen,
Welcome to Scotland to be queen.

Sweet lusty *imp* of beauty clear,
Most mighty king's daughter dear,
Born of a princess most serene,
Welcome of Scotland to be queen.

Welcome the rose both red and white,
Welcome the flower of our delight,
Our spirit rejoicing from the spleen,
Welcome of Scotland to be queen.

The princess's mode of travelling may interest. She rode on a "faire palfrey, but after her was conveyed by two footmen, one varey riche litere,* borne by two faire coursers varey nobly drest, in wich litere the sayd qwene was borne in the *intryng of the good townes,* or otherways to her good playsur."

WILLIAM SEVER,

Translated from Carlisle, Oct., 1502 ; died 1505.

CARDINAL CHRISTOPHER BAINBRIGG,

A native of Hilton Beacon, near Appleby, received restitution Nov., 1507 ; translated to York 1508. He was poisoned at Rome in 1514, by his house-steward whom he had struck in a fit of passion. "A servant will not be corrected by words." *Prov.* xxix. 19. "A Bishop must be no striker." 1 *Tim.* iii. 3. So Fuller pleads both for and against him.

THOMAS RUTHALL,

Nominated Apr. 1509 ; died in London Feb. 1522-3, of chagrin, having de-

* When Queene Elizabethe came to the Crowne
A Coach in England then was scarcely knowne :
Then 'twas as rare to see one, as to spye
A tradesman that had never told a lye.
Taylor, the Water Poet.

livered, by mistake, the inventory of his own private fortune (instead of a survey he had compiled of the royal revenues) to Wolsey, who with malicious satisfaction placed the record before his sovereign, observing that though he would be disappointed of the expected information, he would know where to apply for assistance.

CARDINAL THOMAS WOLSEY,

the cause of Ruthall's death, succeeded, and sat on the Durham throne from April, 1523, to April, 1529, never once visiting his diocese. I once more light upon the name of

CUTHBERT TUNSTALL,

Translated from London 1529.

Leland says he was born at Hacforth, in Richmontshire, and was "base sunne to Tunstal, as I hard, by one of the Coniers daughters." Some doubt is thrown upon the statement,* but even if true, his mother was not the only erring maid of the gentle blood of Conyers. Agnes Conyers was excommunicated Feb. 18, and published 12 March, 1608-9.† On May 24, 1609, "the infant of Agnes Conyers illegitimately begotten" was buried at Darlington.

Reginald Tunstall, chaplain, was presented by his namesake (perhaps relative), to the prebend of Newton, p. m. Tho. Hall, cler. in 1540.

1536. The people of the north, from causes already hinted at, readily joined company with many a noble and many a clerk, and rose in the *Pilgrimage of Grace* under Robert Aske,‡ but listening to offers, appointed deputies to treat with Henry. In answer to their demand that the liberty of the church of Durham should have old customs by act of parliament, he plainly said that "they were brutes and inexpert folks," and gave a general pardon, which amused and dispersed them. But the ejected clergy induced the leaders again to rise in arms in 1537, when they were taken and put to death, the abbots of Fountains, Jervaux, and Rievaulx, and the prior of Bridlington being in the number. Lady Bulmer was *burned* for rebellion. The first families of the bishopric had been concerned, the heir of Lumley

* See Surtees. Leland was however a contemporary.

† Darlington par. reg. fly-leaf.

‡ Forth shall come a *worme*, an *Aske* with one eye,
He shall be the chiefe of the mainye:
He shall gather of chivalrie a full faire flocke
Half capon and half cocke,
The chicken shall the capon slay
And after that shall be no *May*.

These rhymes, Wilfred Holme says, were recited in the host as an ambiguous prophecy of their expedition. They may be part of the absurd, but ancient prophecies of Merlin, revived in every popular movement. Was Aske really defective in sight? and does the last line allude to some intended destruction of all successors to the *hawthorn* badge of the seventh Henry?

was executed, and the general fear and *tykell* feeling of the good folks of Darlington is most graphically drawn in the following curious letter from Sir Ralph Sadler, dated at Newcastle 28 Jan., 1537-8.*

Forasmuch as I wrote unto your lordeship from Yorke, the success of my jorney thither, it may please you also, semblably, to hear what state I have founde the countrey in betwixt Yorke and Newcastell, which, as I wrote unto your lordeship in my last lettres, was reported unto me at Yorke to be very wilde. Nevertheles, to declare the treweth as farre as I coulde perceyve throughout all the bishopricke as I rode, I saw the people to be in very good quyetnes ; and none of the honest sorte, that had any thinge to lose, desiring the contrary, except such as having nothing of their owne, wolde be glad to have such a worlde as whereby they might have opportunytye to robbe and spoyle them that have ; and that generally is the opynyon of all men in these parts ; for undoubtedly the honest sorte of men throughout all this contrey do gretely desyre quyttness ; and yet there hath ben som stirrying in the bishopricke ; and, not passing ii or iii dayes before my comyng, musters made in Cliveland uppon the hilles, which was by means of dyvers billes and scrowes sett uppon posts and church-dores thoroughly out the bishopricke, and tost and scatered abrode in the contrey by some sedyteous persons, which do nothing else but go up and downe to devise mischief and devision ; and by such meanes it was put into the hedds of the people, that my Lord of Norff. cam down with a grete armye and power to do execucion, and to hang and draw from Doncaster to Berwyke, in all places northwarde, notwithstanding the kinges pardon ; and so the people throughout all the northe be brought in worse case then the Lincolnshire men : which tales and ymaginacions beyng so sowen amongst the people, did in such wyse styrre and incense them, that surely, as I am informed, had not Mr. Bowes com home when he did, it had ben very lyke to have made a new insurrection. Undoubtedly he hath well don his parte, as I have lerned of divers, in stayeing off the contrey throughout the hole bishopricke ; and now they have taken such order, that whatsoever falsehods or reports, billes, lettres, or scrowes, shall be sowen abrode, they shal gyve no light credit unto them, but rather do their devoyres to apprehende the devysors and reporters of the same, and so the people be in good staye and quyetness in all places of the bishopricke ; and fully determined, as Mr Bowes told me, to make no more assemblies, but to rest uppon my Lord of Norff. comyng. Syr, I saw no likelihood of any lyghtnes or desyre of devision amongst the people throughout the hole bishopricke, which is a gret countrey, savyng in one towne, which is called *Daryngton;* and there I noted and perceyved the people to be very fykell. My chance was to come into the towne in the evenyng about vi of the clocke, or somewhat afore ; and when I alyghted at my lodging, I think there was not passing iii or iiii persons standing about the inne doore, assuring your lordeshipp, that I was scant ascended up a payr of steres into my chaumber, but there was about xxx or xl persons assembled in the strete afore my chamber wyndows, with clubbs and batts, and there they cam roonyng out of all quarters of the strete, and stode together on a plompe [i.e. in a body], whispering and rownding together ; whereuppon I called unto me myn host, who seemed to be an honest man, and I asked him, what the people meant to assemble so together ? he answered me, That when they saw or harde of any comying out of the south, they used always so to gather togither to here newes. I told him it was ill suffered of them that were the heddes of the toune to let them make such unlawfull assemblies together in the strete ; and that it was a very ill example, and harde to judge what inconveniencys might followe, or what attemptats they wold enterprise when such a nomber of light felowes were assembled. He answered me by his faith, that the hedds of the towne could not

* Cotton MSS. Caligula ii. 344. Sadler, ii. 597.

rule them, ne durst, for their lyves, speke any fowle words to them; and, quod he, ye shall see that I shall cause them to scatter abrode, and every man to go to his home by and by. Mary, quod I, if ye do well, ye shoulde set som of them by the heles. No, quod he, God defende; for so myght we bryng a thousand in our toppes within an hower; but, quod he, ye shall see me order them well ynough with fayre wordes; and thereuppon he went to the rowte in the strete, as they stode whispering togither, and, with his cappe in his hands, prayed them to leve their whispering, and every man to go home; and there come they all about him, and asked him who I was? whense I cam? and whither I wold? Myn hoste told them, that I was the Kyng's servante, and going from his highnes in ambassade into Scotland: Whereunto one of them replyed, and sayed, That could not be true, for the Kyng of Scotts was in Fraunce. Nevertheles, in fine, myn host so pacyfyed them, that every man went his way; but moche ado he had, as he told me, to persuade them to beleve that I went into Scotland; and they all, with one voyce, asked, When my Lorde of Norff. wold com, and with what company? And so myn host cam to me, as a messenger from them, to know the trewth; and I sent them worde that he wolde be at Danncaster at Candlemas even; and that he brought no more with him but his owne household servants; which pleased them wonderous well; and so every man departed, and I harde no more of them. I assure your lordship the people be very tykell, and, methinketh, in a marvellous straunge case and perplexity; for they stare and loke for things, and fayne wolde have they cannot tell what. So as, in my poure opynyon, it requyreth a gret diligence and circumspection for the edefyeing and establishing of them; which aperteyning to the office of a prynce and kyng, it becometh not me to talke of; not doubting but our most gracious Prynce and Sovereign Lorde, with the mature advysement of his Most Honourable Counsaile, will so provyde for the same as shall apperteyne.

This letter was written on proceeding on a reconnoitreing embassy to Scotland during the absence of James V. in France. Surtees remarks that Sir Rafe was both stout and sage, yet mine host proved the wiser man. The duke of Norfolk had acted with great rigour in the executions after the second outbreak, till the king's free pardon closed the butchery.

These impolitic outbreaks hastened the destruction of the religious houses, and it was thought expedient to curtail the dangerous powers of the counts palatine of Durham. The bishop was deprived of his choicest regalia; prevented from screening any offenders by a clause taking pardons of treasons and felonies away from him; various processes were to be thenceforth in the king's name, and his justices acquired jurisdiction in the franchise. The glory was departed. Henceforth I shall cease my bishop headings, for the shadow of royalty alone remained. The Durham house of peers occurs no more.

1538. About this year that famous antiquary John Leland began his peregrinations, under a commission from Henry VIII., to bring our monuments "out of deadly darkness to lively light." The fruits of this enterprize, which lasted some seven years, he presented to the king as a new year's gift, in the thirty-seventh year of his reign.

Almost every page of this delightful old author evinces his deep appreciation of beauty. The "exceding pleasaunt ground" of Sockburn a little beneath whose "maner place is a great were for fisch" did not escape his penetrating eye. He had crossed the "*trajec-*

tus over Tese" there, and come to Neasham, "and then a v. miles to Darington by pure good corne. Darington Bridge of stone is, as I remember, of three arches, it is the best market town in the Bisshoprick, saving Duresme. There is an exceeding long and fair altare stone *de vario marmore, hoc est, nigro albis maculis distincto,* at the high altare in the collegiate paroche church of Darington. There is a Dene longging to this college and . . . . . prebendaries. The Bisshop of Duresme hath a praty palace in this toune. From Darlington to Acheland eight good miles by resonable good corne and pasture." His descriptions are always to the point, nothing could give a better idea of magnificence than the statement that "Raby is the largest castel of logginges in al the North Cuntery," though its grandeur had already declined under the late Nevilles; "the great Chaumber was exceding large, but now it is fals rofid and devided into two or three partes" and a *petigre* in coloured glass had given way to plain. He recounts "the Quikke market of Darlington standing betwixt Teese and Were." "Hugo de Puteaco, as the Dene of Duresme tolde me, made the howse that the Byshops of Duresme have at Darlengton," and from an old book at Durham he found that Stire gave with St. Cuthbert, Darington, two carucates in Lumley.

On May 5, 1543, Sir Ralph Sadler writes to the council that the earl of Angus prayed him "to write to your grace, that it might please the same to send so much money to Berwick to Mr. Shelley, to be paid to mine appointment, as should be sufficient to pay his wages and his brother's; for that, he thinketh, it would be noted, if he should send his servant so far within England as to Darlington for money, whereof might grow some bruit and suspicion, which he would be glad to avoid." This was during Sir Ralph's embassy, to arrange the marriage between the young queen of Scots and prince Edward, when Angus was in the pay of England.

On the 30 Oct., 1543, Sadler writes that lord Somervail having been appointed to repair to Henry VIII. with the minds of the lords of Scotland, Sir George Douglas (brother to Angus), had said to him "that he will accompany the said lord Somervail to Darlington, because himself will speak with my lord of Suffolk, both touching such things as the said lord Somervail hath in charge, as also for the Border matters, wherein he complaineth much of the damage done daily to such as," he saith, "be the king's majesty's friends." In the correspondence between the council and Sir Ralph Evers orders are given not to spare the friends of Sir George Douglas in the incursions, as he was suspected to be a false friend. Sir Ralph's next dispatch, Nov. 6, shows that Somervail had been taken by the opposite party: "But sir George Douglas hath sent me word, 'that he will forthwith repair to Darlington to my lord of Suffolk, to advertise him of all such things as the said lord Somervail had in charge, to the intent he may signify the same to the king's highness.'" On the eighth he says "I am advised sir George Douglas was at Berwick on Tuesday last; and therefore I think, or this time, he is with your lordships." Sir George had been in England before, he and the earl of Glencairn promised in May "they will ride it in eight days," *i. e.*, to London, and he was again dispatched in June to the king. The French interest completely outweighed Henry's, had it not, Mary's flames might have never burned, Elizabeth's axe never been lifted, Lady Jane have pursued her classics in comfort, and Mary of Scotland never lost her head.

1553. "John Darington, yeoman of the close carre of the roobes," had four yards of black cloth at Edward VI.'s funeral. *Archæologia.*

Another local name occurs, that of Wm. Brackenburye, gent., rider, surveyor of the stable. A gleam of interest is thrown over the family from its connection with the stout lieutenant of the Tower, who is represented by Shakspere as a passive adversary to the princes' murder, and who had the posthumous honour of being connected with the master for whom he died on Bosworth field, as the only other person forfeited who held Palatine lands. An entail saved Selaby. The great grand nephew of the lieutenant appears in all the ceremonies of the maiden queen, and was perhaps in Shakspere's eye when he characterized the Lieutenant with all courtly deference. Thus, when Richard praises, without saying wherefore, Jane Shore's cherry lip and pretty foot, with ludicrous gravity he answers " With that, my Lord, myself have nought to do."

Selaby finally passed to the Vanes, and is in the language of Surtees, one of the most sparkling gems in the Cleveland coronet, one of the loveliest emerald spots in the Vane's domain. It was for many years the residence of the Hon. Frederic Vane, second son of the first Earl of Darlington, and owes many beauties to his simple and elegant taste.

1617-8. Wm. Brakenburie of Cockerton, bur.—1618. Ann, *d.* of Thomas Brakenburie of Cockerton, bap.—1644. Dorithy, *d.* of Matthew Breckenburie of Newton, bap.—1698-9. Dorothy Brackenbury of Newton, bur.

1560-1. Elected, JAMES PILKINGTON, S. T. P., the first protestant bishop of Durham, a Calvinistic exile. The queen having heard that he gave his daughter a £10,000 portion, as much as Henry VIII. had bequeathed *her*, scotched the see of £1000 a-year and settled it on her garrison at Berwick.* Elizabeth, as is well known, detested marriage in ecclesiastics. The bishop stood stoutly for his church's possessions, but he himself so wasted them that an action was brought against his executors for delapidation, a previously unknown occurrence. He converted the college bells of Auckland, which he *brust in peaces,* to his own use, made a bowling-alley and archery gallery where divine service was before celebrated, and took away a very fair steeple-head from Stockton manor, &c.,† He misliked the surplice and the square cap, "because the head is not square," though he generally pressed non-resistance to trivial matters of form in this dark province where "the priests went with swords and daggers, and such coarse apparel as they could get." His obsequies were in accordance with his life.

" He died at Auckland the 23d. of January, 1579; presently after whose death one being appoynted to bowell him, who shewing himself unskillful therein, leaving unfinyshed that work, whereof *one Williams of Darneton* being sent for, for that purpose, soddenly putting his hand into the dead body unawares, hurt hymself upon the said knyfe, not knowing of the same. He was streightway after buryed in the parish church of St. Andrew Auckland without any solempnitie, for that he did not like nor allowe of such ceremonies. But he was afterwards, by the appointment of some that were in authority, taken up agayn, for that they were given to understand that he was not so

* Strype. † Hunter's MSS.

honorably buryed as became such a Bysshop to be, by reason whereof his body was taken up agayn, and was carryed to Durham upon a very tempestuous day, and there lyeth buried in the quire of the cathedrall church of Duresme, under a marble *tunne* taken out of ye Colledg of Auckland, being ye *tunne (Ita.)* of one Tompson, once Deane of ye said Colledg, and from thence carryed to Durham; and in cariage a corner of the said stone did burst, notwithstanding it was set together again, and so lyeth erected above ye said Busshop." *Hunter's MSS.*

The grandson of his brother Leonard the Prebendary, also named Leonard, was baptized at Merrington in 1614, and lived at Darlington, dying in 1674, his inventory being dated March *id. an.* His dau. Alice was baptized here 1640, May 30, and his wife Alice was bur. May 4 following. He must have married again, four more children occurring:—William, bap. 1643, bur. 1644-5; Leonard bap. 1645-6; Elizabeth, 1647-8; and Dorothy, 1652.

1569. The Rising of the North. The dissatisfaction of the people at the change of religion, and their attachment for the feudal lords, had long prepared them for a general rise, which was hurried on by the arrival of the beautiful Mary of Scotland, and the fears for the safety of her imprudent suitor the Duke of Norfolk. On the first alarm, Elizabeth summoned the Percy and the Neville chiefs to court, where perhaps, (as their talents were but indifferent) a mere temporary restraint awaited them, they were, however, practised upon by Romish emissaries who persuaded them that their lives were in danger. On the night of the day on which Thomas Percy, Earl of Northumberland, K. G., received the queen's letters in his manor-house at Topcliffe, certain conspirators perceiving him to be wavering, caused a servant to bustle in and knock at his chamber door, willing him in haste to shift for himself for his enemies had beset him, whereupon he arose, and conveyed himself to his keeper's house: in the same instant they caused the bells of the town to be rung backward, and so raised as many as they could.* There is an old post and pan house, with a striking gable end, at Thorpfield at the junction of the Thirsk and Topcliffe townships, which is perhaps the keeper's house alluded to. At all events it is on the road to Brancepeth, and contains a mantelpiece finely carved with the full insignia of the unfortunate earl surrounded with the garter. Motto, Esperance Dieu. The next afternoon he departed to Brancepeth where he met Charles Neville, Earl of Westmoreland and confederates in similar fears. From thence they issued some professedly loyal proclamations, commanding the queen's subjects, in her highness' name, to repair to them for the security of her person.

The rebellion had at first been slighted, but the queen's party soon began to assemble, though in number few in the bishopric. William Hilton,† esq., (afterwards knighted in 1570 at Carlisle by Sussex) furnished 100 horse

* Hollinshed. Sharp's Memorials of the Rebellion. These two works, with Stowe, are consulted throughout. The dates are uniformly from the Bowes MSS. in Sharp. Stowe and Hollinshed vary materially.

† Connected in more ways than one with the Bowes family by intermarriages. Baker, p. 570, says that the Queen repaid the sums of money borrowed, "which won her no less love than if she had given it."

and lent the queen 50*l.* on her privy seal. Christopher Addy, gent., who had been coroner of Darlington ward under Tunstall and some other gentlemen did the like.

On November 13, Sussex, the president of the north, wrote to Sir George Bowes from York, that he heard that sixty of the earl's horsemen were to lodge at Darnton, and pay *one penny a meal, and one penny day and night for hay.* The council at York also wrote to the queen that they had ordered 2500 footmen to be at Darneton on the 21st. Sussex despatched letters from her majesty to the rebel noblemen once more demanding their appearance, and backed them himself, promising that their friends would stand firmly with them, but they were too far advanced to submit. On the 15th Bowes wrote to Sussex that he had requested his party to assemble at Barnard Castell; that people armed and well mounted, came daily northwards over Teyse, as of Sunday last, in the afternoon, came over at Croft and Newsam (Neasham), where he had continual watch, within eight persons of one hundred, well horsed and like to have privy coats, but not warlike weaponed, except some daggers; and that the rebel army diminished rather than increased, they riding at night southwards and coming again of the day northwards, to make shews. "For any rate, at a pennye the meal, or a pennye leverage, Darneton, I have sent to knowe; but there was, nor ys noo suche, neither any lyenge there, save th' Erle of Northumberland's fawkener, with hys hawks." A most hurried* letter to Sussex followed, informing him of the acts of the rebels at Durham. They entered the Minster, tore the Bible and other books, and the same night returned to Brancepeth. Their proceedings are amusing enough, and to shew the sad havoc made among the solid books provided by our reformers, take the proceedings at Sedgefield. Richard Fleitham of that place, husbandman, deposed,

"That passing throwgh the towne streit he mett with Brian Headlham to whom, when this examinate tolde that he went down to Roland Hixson house, the said Brian wylled hym to bydd Hixson send up the church books, and he might born the books byfore he went to Darlington, which messaidge this examinate dyd to the said in his bedd; but what the said Roland and other dyd with the books, or at the borning of them, he cannott depose; howbeyt yeisterday this examinate hard Isabell Gulling and Margarett Snawdon told this examinate and John Johnson at the crosse, that Roland Hixson, seinge the flames of the books fleinge up, said, '*Lowe, wher the Homilies flees to the devyll.*' "

Hixson, who was churchwarden, denied all this, and stated that "when one old booke of the clark's was in burninge, this deponent said alowd, "*See wher the byble bornes;*" which word he spoke to the intent that the byble should not be cauld for, which is yett safe therebye. Margaret Snawdon deposed that she saw Roland when "lyfting up the leaves of them with his staff, he said, '*Se the dyvell domines*† *fle into the allyment:*' "‡ and another witness flatly says that Roland was the cause of all the

* So hurried, that Bowes actually directed it in mistake to the rebel earl of Westmoreland, as president of the North council.

† Apparently a slang term for the Homilies. ‡ Element—here the air.

mischief in Sedgefield Church, " and yett wold cover his doing by setting his faulte of Brian Headlham and others."

We find under the head of Brancepeth the deposition of Henry Rutter, of Durham, concerning the baptism of his child, who said, that he " was at home in Elvet, wher he dwellith, at the birth of his child articulate,* which was borne upon a tewsday, the morrow after the Earles rose, and at that present tyme this examinate was sent for to John Byers, to wait upon his lorde and master, the Earl of Westmerland, and to be with his lordship the morrow next after, being Weddensday, at *Darlington*." During his absence it appears that his child was christened by the curate at Brancepeth, by my Lady Westmoreland's commandment, after Popish fashion.†

November 16. " This night,‡ in the evening, both the earls, with a great band of horsemen, did ride forth, and was seen pass southwards, towards Darneton, and, as the *brutte* (report) goeth, meaneth to pass to Rychmonde, which town is greatly misliked, and upon good cause. We have a marvellous lack of armour, but specially of weapon; and can not tell how to supply it, either for these [at Barnard-castle] nor for those footmen appointed to be in readiness at Darneton on the 21st of this month."§ *Bowes.*

On this day, the rebels were at Darlington, and sent horsemen to gather as many recruits as possible. The proclamations of the earls all accuse the queen's counsellors of seeking to destroy the ancient nobility and true religion. The Darlington proclamation assumes more characteristic importance from its having been penned by Thomas Jenny, at the dictation of Marmaduke Blakiston, and by the command of Westmoreland.

Thomas, Earl of Northumberland, and Charles, Earl of Westmoreland, the Queen's most true and lawful subjects, and to all her highness' people, sendeth greeting:— Whereas, divers *new set up* nobles about the Queen's Majesty, have and do daily, not only go about to overthrow and put down the *ancient* nobility of this realm, but also have misused the Queen's Majesty's own person, and also have by the space of twelve years now past, set up, and maintained a new found religion and heresy, contrary to God's word. For the amending and redressing whereof, divers foreign powers do purpose shortly to invade these realms, which will be to our utter destruction, if we do not ourselves speedily forfend the same. Wherefore we are now constrained at this time to go about to amend and redress it ourselves, which if we should not do and foreigners enter upon us we should be all made slaves and bondsmen to them. These are therefore to will and to require you, and every of you, being above the age of 16 years and not 60, as your duty towards God doth bind you, for the setting forth of his true catholic religion, and as you tender the common wealth of your country; to come and resort unto us with all speed, with all such armour and furniture, as you, or any of you, have. This fail you not herein, as you will answer the contrary at your perils. God save the Queen.—*MSS. Harl.* 6990,44.

" And at Darnton," writes Bowes on the 17th, " they offer great wage to such as will serve them; and hath not only stayed the people in many parts

* That is, named in the article now answered.

† Durham Eccl. proc. Sur. Soc. p. 177.

‡ "Last night" appears to be meant.

§ The orthography is here modernised, a liberty I shall sometimes adopt when the pronunciation is not affected. Obsolete words and names are given as in the original.

of Richmondshire from assembling to me, and the commissioners hither, but hath in the bishopric called all the people in Darneton together, and this day they make their musters there, and appoint captains to such number of footmen as they have levied. They have constrained, by force, sundry to follow them ; as the people of Bishopton, tenants of John Conyers,* my son-in-law, being ready to come forwards to serve the Queen's Majesty under him here, they not only forced them to go with them, but compelled the rest of the town, armed and unarmed, to go to Darneton ; and hourly advertisement cometh, of their constraining men to serve them. And the fear is so increased, that in manner no man dare travel."

He further reports that "masse was yesterday at Darnton ; and John Swinburn, *with a staffe*, drove before him the poor folks, to hasten them to hear the same." Stow states that "they had holi-water, but no masse for want of vestments." Hollinshed,† however, (a bitter enemy, it must be owned), says that at Darington they "had masse, which the earles and the rest heard with such lewde devotion as they had," and in another edition quoted by Drake in his Eboracum that "they lewdly heard mass, and besprinkled all their army with Holy Water." The earls now declared that their object was to determine "to whom of mere right the true succession of the crown appertaineth."

From Darlington the earls marched on the night of the 16th to Richmond. Bowes on the 20th recounts their movements :—"On Tuesdaye, to Darington,‡ there they sente for the sundrie precepts : proclamations most wicked. Wednesdaie, to Richmond, where they altered the manner of their proclamation, whiche is suche, if they be suche as the copies delivered, purporte, that it would grieve any honest hearte to heare it."

The rebels proceeded to Clifford Moor, where they mustered about 5600 men, their greatest number. The city of York had become active, and on the 18th November John Lutton, esq. at Mace, "was directed to conduct one hundred men to Darnton, at the citie charge ;—to have 40s. towards his chardge, and further allowans at his home comyng." This order was revoked ; and Mr. Dawson, with one other honest person, was to conduct them to Darneton. Yorkshire was more loyal than Durham, and from some cause or other undetermined, the earls turned their backs upon it and returned to the bishopric. On the 29th, Bowes says,

"They have a greate number of fatt cattell that they have spoyled in theyr joyrneye, which they dryve to Derneton warde ; and, as I am informed, meanethe to bestowe abowte Stocton, where they have fogge and haye, greate plentye, of the Byshoppe of

* Of Sockburn, who married Sir George's daughter, Agnes. He actively supported his father-in-law.

† Edit. 1577.

‡ In 1573, in answer to certain queries by Lord Burghley concerning the rebellion, Sir George laments that two proclamations of the Earls had been stolen from his house at Cowton. "The one proclamed at Darneton, which was but simple : and the other proclamed at Ripon, which was the most effectuall thing they did."

Durham's and myne, and corne enewffe, of the Deanes and others harde by them ; and the beste contrethe of corne joynethe to thoyse parts, of thys rever of Tees, of bothe syds ; as of the one, Byllingham, Norton, and such lyke ; and of the other syde, Cleveland, where Xpofer Nevell nowe ys. - - - They everye day come and offer scrymyshinge and beareth in oure scoute and scewryers ; but we take noo layrom, but kepethe close* - - - The general brewte here ys, they wyll besege me ; but I am in noo feare. And there footman ys fallen in there marche towards Darneton, which seamethe they rather wyll imploye them abowte Hartlepoyle, rather [than] to hasserde thys place."

Hartlepool however being secured, a long seige of Barnard Castle followed. Bowes gallantly defended it, but was obliged to surrender honorably (partly owing to the numerous desertions to the rebels).

From a list of the levies assembled at Barnard Castle, who required pay I find that there were musters of horsemen at Darneton on Nov. 24, and of footmen on the 26th. 41 light horsemen entered there had 16*d.* per day, each, 98 foot soldiers 8*d.* Their captain, Rauff Tailboys, Esq., of Thornton Hall, had 8*s.*, his lieutenant 4s., ensign bearer 12*d.*, sergeant 12*d.*, drummer 12*d.*

Bowes, marching out of the castle under a composition, proceeded to Sessay, where he met the Earl of Sussex, Lieutenant-General in the North, with an army of some 5,000 men, and was made Marshall of the conjoined forces, which marched by Croftbridge, Darlington† and Aycliffe, to Durham. But a more formidable muster was behind.

" They (the rebels) were not onely pursued by the Erle of Sussex and other with him, hauing a power with them of 7,000 men, being almost at theyr heeles, but also by the Earle of Warwike, and the Lorde Clynton, high Admyrall of Englande wyth a farre greater armie of 12,000 men raysed by the Queenes Maiesties Commission out of the South and middle parties of the realme.- - The coming forward of these forces, caused the rebels so much to quaile in courage, that they durst not abyde to trie the matter with dint of sworde. For whereas the Erle of Warwike, and the Lord Admyrall, being aduanced forwarde to *Darington*, ment the next day to haue sent Robert Glouer then Portculeys, and now Somerset Herault (who in this journey attended on the Lorde Admyrall, as Norrey king of Armes did vpon the Earle of Warwike) unto the rebels, vpon such message as for the time and state of things was thought conuenient, the same night aduertisements came from the Erle of Sussex vnto the Erle of Warwik, and

* " Coward, a coward, of Barney Castell
Dare not come out to fight a battell."
Popular rhyme still current.

† "The xiith day, I intende to be at Darneton." *Sussex to Sir W. Cecil.* 8 *Dec.* On the 17th, Hunsdon, Sir Ralph Sadler and Sussex met at Croft-Bridge, consulted, marched forward, and hearing that the rebels, understanding of their appointment to be at Darneton, had fled, stayed their footmen at Darneton until they might see whether it should be necessary to draw them on to Duresme, or that they might *casse* (dismiss) a great part of them for diminishing of charges. On that day, Sussex wrote to Cecil from " Smyton four miles from Darneton," at 2, a.m., the confederates to the council from "Arclif (Aycliffe) between Darneton and Duresme," and the Earl of Rutland to Cecil "from Eghinton (Heighington), betwene Durham and Darnton." On the 18th, T. Sutton writes from Darlington,—" The rebells fled yesternight from Durham to Hexham, accompanied with their horsemen ; only having discharged all their fotmen, and willed them to provide for themselves."

to the Lorde Admirall, that the two Earles of Northumberlande, and Westmerlande, were fledde, as the truth was they were in deede, first from Durham, whither the sayde Glouer should haue bene sent vnto them, and now vpon the Earle of Sussex his comming vnto Exham, they shrank quite away, and fled into Scotlande, without bidding their companie farewell."—*(Hollinshed.)*

The puissant army of Warwick marched on to Durham though the rebellion was completely at an end.

The Countess of Northumberland was left on foot at the house of a borderer :—" He is weil kend, Johne of the Syide—a greatar thief did never ryide"—" a cottage not to be compared to any dog-kennel in England." However he kept faith and the Countess escaped to Flanders. Her luckless husband was betrayed by Hector Graham, of Harelaw to the Regent Murray, whose successor Morton sold him to Lord Hunsdon to expiate his errors on the scaffold. To TAKE HECTOR'S CLOAK has become proverbial for betraying a friend, and the villain somehow fell suddenly from affluence into unaccountable poverty. I annex a few of Sir John Forster's charges in the conveying of Percy to York and in his return with his company—

For three post horses from Durham to Darnton..........................	3*s.* 10*d.*
For the charges at Darnton, on Wednesday at night and Thursdaye morning...	19*l.* 18*s.*
For three post horses from Darnton to Toplef............................	5*s.* 2*d.*
On Sunday night at Darnton *(on his return)*............................	11*l.* 10*s.*

Westmoreland housed at Carr of Ferniherst's, where Sir Robert Constable a Yorkshire gentleman and relation of the Earls visited him, " *Hector of Tharlowes hedd was wished to have been eaten amongs us at supper.*" Constable told the exile of the miseries of his house and followers till *the tears overhayled his cheks abundantly ;* the villain professes to have not been able to forbear weeping to see him so suddenly fall to repentance, and yet was all the time trying to allure him to ruin in England. He came with missives to the Countess who remained at Brancepeth. He kissed her lord's ring, and gave it to her. She was passing joyful, and told him in the simplicity of her heart of her counsel to her lord to throw himself at the mercy of the Queen. Constable had " talked with many but never with her like," and yet notwithstanding the impression this excellent lady made on him, he wiled from her every secret and transmitted them to Sadler with jewel tokens delivered for her lord and his hosts. AS TO THE SHIP IS ANCHOR AND CABLE, SO TO THY FRIEND BE THOU, CONSTABLE.*

The Earl was of a very amorous bent. The beautiful ballad by Surtees suggested by an old tower on the brook in Langleydale (which is said to have been the residence of his mistress) is well known.† Constable hints at a jealousy of the Lord of Ferniherst about Westmoreland and his "new wanton lady." At an age little suited for such an enterprize and in exile, he was wooing Richardot's daughter most attentively for his second spouse, but her father required more pension from Spain before consent. He was in some warlike business abroad, but contumely was showered upon the hapless wanderers and he closed his day alone and in obscurity. His Countess and daughters received an allowance from the queen, and the latter became very notorious in harbouring seminary priests.

* A quaint scrap under a ship (Constable's crest), in Knight's MSS. Caius Coll. Camb.

† The first verse of the Lamentation of John Musgrave, a robber, was probably in Surtees's remembrance.

Down Plumpton Park as I did pass,
I heard a bird sing in a glen :
The chiefest of her song it was,
Farewell the flower of serving-men.

1569-70. Jan. 1. Among the prisoners remaining in the gaol at Durham in Bowes's custody, was Cuthbert Storye, of Darlington, *having inheritance*, and he was still there on the 26th. During their durance vile, the gentlemen paid 6*s*. 8*d*. and the "meaner sort" 3*s*. 4*d*. weekly for their meat and drink.

On the 15 May, the bill of attainder was passed. Among the attainted are Thomas Norton, John Gower, Cuthbert Wytham, and Thomas Jenny, gent., the penner of the Darlington proclamation, who finally escaped to Flanders.

"To the secretaryship, indeed, I drew them ther last proclamation, which I did at Dorrington, being comanded thereto by the Earl of Westmerland, who tooke me by the arme, and said, sence you are amongst us, we will make you do the thing we will; and therupon comanded one M. Blaxton* to give me instruction, and I penned it accordingly; and then was the first that ever I knew what they intended in taking up armes."—*State Paper*, *Jenny's examination.*

Jan. 8. Sussex sent a note to Cecil of 300 and odd persons to be "exequuted by marciall lawe," in this county, in which occur "of townesmen of Darneton, 16." In this town forty-one were appointed to be slain, composed of "prisoners here, two, constables, twenty-three, of the towne and not yet taken, sixteen." In fact at Darneton were to be executed "all the constables of Darneton warde,—the townesmen of Darneton." Well might the Bishop lament that "the cuntre is in grete mysere," for "few innocent are left to trie the giltie."†

About 481 joined in Darlington Ward, of whom ninety-nine were executed. The seat of the rebellion was essentially in this ward. The names of the "meaner sorte" executed, possess little interest, but "*Hobby that God sent us*, at Darlington," is an exception.‡

Sir Geo. Bowes to the Earl of Sussex.

My humble duty, &c. The executions are done, or will this day, and to morrow be done through all the Byshopricke, according to your L. direction, saving in a part of Darneton Ward, where as yet I command; although I have both by day and night caused to search their towns, but they be wholly fled, the names of which towns I send your lordship in a billet here inclosed; which be of the worst doers of the whole country, and lieth, for most part, of the street. But I hope that upon my going from Darneton they will draw home, upon whose coming I have taken such order, that I will send of my horsemen suddenly; and hopeth by that means, to get them, thinking very convenient that they should have the harder justice for their evil dealing. I have taken such order with these that dealeth with the goods of those executed, that they should deal favorably with the wives and children, so as they might only not have cause to complain, but be satisfied; and, so far as I know, so they are: for in all Darneton, by this composition, I caused [to] make for me an agreement with the wives, cometh but to

* Marmaduke Blakiston, younger son of Tho. B. of Blakiston, esq., "a principal wrytor of things."

† Sadler, ii. 95.

‡ Bowes MSS. to which through Sharp I am so much indebted.

8*l*. for where I find them, and hath many children I take nothing at all. And for the more favouring of them, I have committed the doing hereof to the worshipful neighbours, with instructions to favour the poor, and to deal favorably with all. I have newly taken order for receipt of prisoners to be received from the Lord Scrope, but my servants waited all a day and night before I got them word what to do: and I humbly desire to know whether I shall stay these prisoners at Barnard Castle or to bring them to Richmond, where I fear there will be very strait room, for I hear it is very full; and this day, by ten of the clock, by God's grace, I will be there. But sure time is convenient to be somewhat prolonged, for in this course I find the constables, in sundry places, hath accused these that did least, and excused the greatest offenders; and many of themselves that denied before your Lordship to be with the Earls, both was with the rebels in all their journies, and strained the rest to the same by hard words, which I have sought for, but cannot get; for which cause I mean not from henceforth, to deliver any of the constables before the justice be ended, and then, if they be clear to let them pass. I use even that course your Lordship did, and execute none that hath not both been of the first journey and in some of the second journies, accompanied with the rebels. And, thus ready to set towards Richmond, I humbly take my leave. From Darneton, the 8th of January, by eight of the clock in the morning, 1569.

Jan. 9. In a list of names of such as the Earl of Warwick and the Lord Admiral had received into their protection are the names of *Hen. Killinghall*, and *John Corneforth*, [of the Blackwell family ?]

The Yorkshire executions (200) followed those of the Bishoprick, and Sussex who seems to have been thoroughly disgusted, writes to Cecil from Darnton, "I was first a lieutenant, I was after little better than a marshall; I had then nothing left to me but to direct *hanging matters*." The Queen hurried the executions on. Bowes appears to have been more contented with his lot than Sussex, for on hanging one Harrison in his own orchard, tradition ascribes to him the savage expression "that the best fruit a tree could bear, was a dead traitor," and his conscience, if popular fancies about a certain room at Streatlam be true, will not suffer his unquiet ghost to rest. The Queen's command was that none who had freeholds or were noted wealthy should be executed, they *purchasing* their lives.

The following extract will show how Darlington headed the melancholy catalogue of places most deeply involved:—

	Joined.	Executed.
Broughe of Darneton	55	10
Bondgayte in Darneton	28	6
Cockerton	14	3
Blackewell	18	4
Haughton	4	1
Sedgefield...	19	5
Billingham	22	5
Wolveston	19	4
Hart	17	4
Norton*		
Byshopton	16	4
Farye on the Hyll	15	5

* Left blank. *Bowes MSS.*

	Joined.	Executed.
Eglyston	16	
Wolsyngham	16	4
Ingleton	13	3
Staynedroppe	44	7
Rabye	27	5
Forest of Langleye	19	4
Saynt Elen Awkeland	12	2
Cockefeilde	15	3
Pearsbrige	13	2
Lyndsecke	11	
Aykecliffe	21	3

None of the other townships exceed 10 in their numbers.

After the Rebellion was quietly over, there seems to have been a sale of horses at the usual Whitsuntide fair at Darlington by the Council's command. In the dispute about the will of Sir Robert Brandling of Newcastle, (1568-9) Henry Brandling said that Christopher Chaytor refused on the Friday that Sir Robert died "about Whitsondaye" to make his will, for that "he must ryde that night towardes *Darlington,* for markyn of horses there to be sold in the fair, by the Conselles commandmente; and promised to comme to hym agayne within a week after."*

A revengeful inroad to Scotland followed the putting down of the rebellion, in which one Captain Darrington had the command of fifty horsemen.

In 26 Eliz. we find *John Trollop*, a pardoned rebel, presenting before "John Awbrey and the rest of the Queen's Commissioners of concealed lands, then sitting at *Derlington*," the messuage called Thornley, as "concelement," and obtaining a grant of the estate under 10*s*. crown-rent for ever. The estate had been given to Ralph Bowes, Esq., who seems soon to have come to an understanding with the forfeited family, and granted the patent to the use of John Trollop. Trollop died in extreme age in 1611, after constant troubles about his lands with the crown, and is oddly said in the Kelloe register to have been *buried by himselfe*.† His father was perhaps the happier man, pleasantly stating in his will that God had given him "an honeste parte in this world, which is a good wyfe, who haithe been and is *not onlie moche comfortable to me, but also moche profitable*."

Cuthbert Witham attainted, was son of William Witham,‡ of Darlington, whose grandfather Thomas lived at Brittonby, near this place, and married Inet co-heiress of Wanton of Cliffe. In 1535 William Witham as bailiff of Derlyngton returned 16*l*. town-rents to the bishop and received as fee 100*s*.§

Cuthbert Storie, of Darlington, appears not only to have been pardoned but to have kept his lands.|| Some were however alienated before. In 1586 he was a picker and stealer and was made to disgorge the stones and planks which he had taken away from a bridge over the mill dam at the North end of Norgait, and which was ordered to be re-constructed with a Landstaith four yards wide for the ease of the people at the costs of Bondgate.¶

Thomas Norton, of Skerningham, was arrained at Westminster, 6 April, 1570, and confessed his treason. He was brother of the patriarchal rebel Richard Norton, who

* Eccl. Proc. Sur. Soc. 123. † I. e. in his own porch.
‡ Thoresby's Duc. Leod. § Valor Ecclesiasticus.
|| Terr. Cuthberti Storey attinct. Redd. tene. in Darneton 40*l*. 6*s*. *Sadler's State Papers*, ii. 200. ¶ Mill papers. R. H. Allan, esq.

bore a cross with a streamer before the army, and whose descendant Maior or Maulger Norton, of Clowbeck, co. Ebor. bought a burgage in Blackwellgate of George Fetherstonhaugh, of Thornaby-upon-Tees, in 1623. The whole tribe of the "wicked people" of Norton Conyers were infected with disloyalty. Thomas married Elizabeth, coh. of Eshe, and *jure uxoris* possessed Skerningham. He was "an offender in the rebellyon in the tyme of King Henry VIIIth,"* and for this second offence was drawn, hanged, beheaded, and quartered at Tyburn in presence of his nephew Christopher, who immediately after suffered the same fate, very repentant.† The latter stated that "by the way betwixt Dorham and Darnton cam Mr. Agramont Ratlef, and T. Geny, [and] Blaxton, which comfortyd the coman sorte; and the next day in the monyng, came about 1000 fotmen and horsemen to the Earlls. Thayt day thaye to Rychemond, to store [stir] Rychmondshire, wheare the Earll of Northomerland staid that nygt, and Westmerland com backe to Darnton againe. They ij aponted to meet at Alarton, the next day, as they did." I do not enter here into the sorrows of the main branch of Norton, not even daring to be captivated with EXALTED EMILY—MAID OF THE BLASTED FAMILY, but I may state one curious fact. In the brazen shields in the Norton porch at Wath Church the family arms are carefully erased, the impalement of Ward remaining perfect; and in a window, the quarterings all gleam upon the chancel floor, save the paternal coat. It is totally destroyed.

In 1573 the Queen granted Skerningham manor to Ralph Taylboys, Esq., who purchased in trust for the ancient family, and in 1597 Robert Tailbois, of Thornton, reconveyed to Thomas the son of the slain. He did not long possess it. In 1606, he with Dorothy his wife, Elizabeth Taylboys his mother, and Elizabeth his only child, granted all his bonny lands away and retired to the neighbouring town of Darlington, worn down probably with pecuniary incumbrances he had been unable to shake off. He was buried in our churchyard on Apr. 29, 1615, as "Thomas Norton, gentleman, of Darlington, and late of Skirmingham."‡

John Gower, of Richmond, gent., was pardoned at the warm intercession of Sussex, as he *simply* was led to this his first fault. His mother was about to be re-married to Cottrell, Sussex's secretary, besides, the land was scarce 50*l.* per ann., one-half whereof was settled on her.

Sussex begged for him to be allowed to compound, but the land was all confiscated, and according to Sadler, ii. 193, was worth some 135*l.*, of which his Darlington tenements were set down at 20*l.* Ralph Gower his father had purchased Bennet's lands in Darlington, which the Queen granted to Robert Bowes, Esq.§ Bennet *Hall*, Bennet Field, and Dowcroft, occur together a century afterwards.

Robert Claxton, of Burnhall, was pardoned at the earnest request of the Bowes family, with whom he was connected by marriage. He had a son Anthony, a brother Anthony who died an infant, and an uncle Anthony. In 1602, Anthony Claxton married Margaret Newton at Darlington. George Claxton of the Hulam family alienated property in Hungait next the Deanry in 1564-5 to the Hodgsons, who sold it with Kilnegarth, in Hungaite, to Bulmer Prescote in 1626. In 1624 Richard Potter was ordered to hinder none from carrying water from the lane in Hungaite at his kilne side, and was fined for *harbouringe roguishe people in his kilne.*||

* Surtess, i. Appendix.

† Their heads were set on London Bridge and their quarters upon the gates of the city. Thomas in saying his prayers in Latin, prayed the preacher not to molest his conscience. He at last consented to say the Lord's prayer and belief in English, and desired the audience and all the saints in heaven to pray for him as well then as after his death.

‡ A Mr. John Norton sometimes said to be of Skerningham, sometimes of Lasenby, and sometimes of Ravens Hall, par. Lamesley, was executed for harbouring Thomas Palliser, a seminary priest, at Durham, 1600. His wife, Margaret, supposed to be pregnant, was reprieved and afterwards pardoned. The story may relate to John son of old Richard Norton, and Margaret Readshaw his second wife, though he would be 76 years old.

§ Mickleton, xxxiii., 101. || Borough Books.

John Claxton, of Darlington, gent., in 1563-4 desires to be buried at Hurworth, near his wife, leaves to his son George the care of John, Margaret, and Mary Claxton, whose grandfather was Edmund Hogeson, and to his mother an old angel. He was a legatee of John Claxton, of Chester le Street, gent., cousin of Sir John of Nettlesworth, the son of Robert Claxton, of Old Parke, another rebel of 1569, who was saved from execution by Leicester. The Claxtons were zealously attached to the Nevilles in all their branches.*

Henry Killinghall, esq., of Middleton St. George, (see p. 110) possessed the Greets and Nicholson Hill† in the field of Nessfield. His grandfather Robert had settled lands in Derlyngton on his widow, which were greatly increased by his father John by purchase from John Lord Lumley and Jane his wife. John in 1572 left 10*s.* to the poor of Darlington, mentions his leased *cole pittes* at Wyndleston and Ryton ; leaves to his loving sister Anne Parkinson‡ his *thre chistes* in his chamber that he laid in at Mydleton ; his standishe ; and his estate at Kerleburie to use at her discretion to her *contentacion* and to the profit of his children if she should think meet : and Trasfourthe Hill and his purchased lands at Darlington to his son Henry. Then he disposes of his horses, giving his " nephe Henrye Parkinson a baye colte, Raphe Jameson baye farralas horse, Robert Bankes my horse cauld *lumpe in the houghe* (a curious name alluding to deformity), and Thomas Brystowe my graye ga'son horse."§ William, John's elder brother, from whom he derived, charged estates in 1521 " for the sustentacon of an honest preste which I will shall syng for the sowles of me, myn auncestors and heires in the parishe churche of Midilton George by the space of seven yeres next after my death perceyving yerly for his salary vij markes."‖ Henry had a son Francis who was proceeded against in 1636 for a clandestine marriage with Margery his pretended wife. " Margery Killinghall, of Darlington, buried 1644-5 " is perhaps identical with her or her husband's sister Margery. She occurs on the flyleaf of the register among some recusants.¶

The Nevilles.—The claims of the expiring line of Weardale were never advanced, but the younger line of Latimer petitioned for the lands and honours of Westmoreland, and Edmond Neville reminds James I. of his assurance that " if you were King of England, I was Earle of Westmoreland without exception ; the credit of which message was warranted by a letter from my *Lord of Darlington* (*Dirleton?* quoth Surtees) assuring further, that now my fortunes shall rise with yours ; and irrevocably ratified by your sacred Majestie in your postscript, written with your royal hand, which was never yet known to retract what it deliberately set downe, in the words, ' I shall now with grace promise you to your right, and satisfy you to your expectation '; which letters was likewise styled to *the Earl of Westmoreland.*" James not only broke his word, but Edmund was actually cited for having assumed the title with which the king had accosted him. The Judges decided that the earldom was forfeited, and that Edmund had no title to the honours of that earl who fell "*for his service and affection to the King's mother.*" An empty honour at Eastham in Essex records him as " Lord Lattimer, Earl of

* Sharp's Memorials of the Rebellion.

† These freehold lands (except 5a. 3r. 30p. and the old farm-stead on the top of the hill, sold to John Pease, esq.) as well as Nessfield, are now the properties of R. H. Allan, esq., a descendant of Henry Killinghall, and of the Sobers, of Nessfield.

‡ He married Anne, daughter of Richard Perkinson of Beamond Hill. *Standishe* signifies an inkstand. § Archives penes R. H. Allan, esq.—Query. *Garson*, a youth, here applied to a young horse. *Farralas* is still used in the sense of *barren.*

‖ Original will, penes R. H. Allan, esq. There is a curious endorsement in his "awne hand wrytyng" whereby he " by gud delyberation and for speciall cause" cancels a legacy of 160*l.* out of West Hartburn.

¶ Middleton George. 1611. Spiritual Court Proceedings against Wm. Kyllyngall, esq., who "entertayneth in his house as kitchin wench a woman that hath had two basterds at a birth (as if that made the matter worse !), it is not pretended he is suspected with her, but he owes 8*s.* 4*d.* sessement, and *licks the churchwarden with his staffe when he calls for it.*" Mr. K. answered that "he acted out of Charitie, and struck the churchwarden lightlie with a small gold-headed cane which he useth to walk with ordinarily." *Surtees MSS.*

Westmerland, lineally descended from the honorable blood of kings and princes, and the seventh Earle of Westmerland of the name of Nevills." The barony of Latimer however fell into abeyance among the daughters of John, who died in 1577.

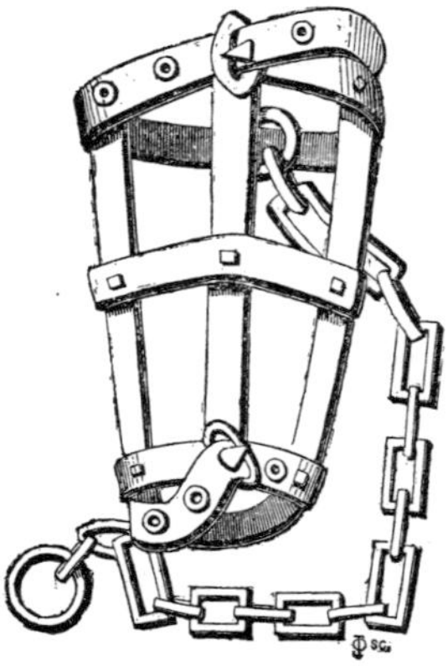

It would be endless to give any idea of the memorials of the Nevilles. Their saltire occurs everywhere. John Clervaux is proudly recorded at Croft as "nephew to Ralph Nevil the first Earl of Westmoreland," and by the same connexion his son Richard as "of the blood of Edward IV. and Richard III. in the third generation." His monument (date 1490) is bespangled with a singular badge, of which I give a cut, apparently a muzzle of some sort. The deceased was Esquire of the body of Henry VI. and his arms are surrounded by the SS. ornament. A race of the name occur as small resident burgesses in Skinnergate, in the 17th century.

The Chaytors, representatives of the main line of Clervaux, also, held burgages in Skinnergate (south of the Grammar School property), Blackwellgate, and Hungate, " as more fully may appear by an old book called le Terrier containing all deeds and evidences of lands," to which William Chaitor was admitted in 1612, but being under age, the Bailiff and Steward granted him leave to claim admission again when of full age.

1662. " The 6th day of Oc'ber a very sad accedent befell Mr. Henrie Chaiter of Gaineford *as he was coming from Darlington* in soe much that he fell from his horse and was suddenly slaine, from which Good Lord deliver us, and was buried nobly by his friends and neighbours the 8th day of the foresaid mounth, together with his funeral sermon, the subject of which was the 22 of Revelations and the 12th verse.—Et ecce venio cito : Et merces mea mecum est : Etc : &c." *Gainford Par. Reg.*

Among the widely extended possessions of the unfortunate Neville which were confiscated, were some at Blackwell.* His predecessor Henry had, as we have seen, granted certain lands there to Edward Perkinson, of Beaumond Hill, who died in 1567 seised of 1 messuage, 5 cottages, 100 acres meadow, 40 pasture. Henry was his heir, but he devised part of Blackwell to his second son Cuthbert, then under age, who was afterwards a gentleman living at Darlington, and buried there in 1618. The Parkinsons were tinged with disaffection, and Sadler mentions Mr. Perkinson, of Beamond-hill, as being reported " to have saved the Earl in the rebellion time."

In 1609 Bartholomew Garnett, gent., died seised of lands in Blackwell, sometime Perkinson's, held by knight's service and 24*s.* 10*d.* rent. Robert was his son and heir. I have little doubt that this rent is identical with the 23*s.* 8*d.* or 24*s.*† rent formerly paid by the Middletons for the messuage and five oxgangs they had heired from the Blackwells, and which were also held by knight's service. The manor of Blackwell held by Ralph the great Earl probably consisted of all their freehold‡ (including Castle Hill) as well as the small estate held by John Nevyll, Chivaler, in 1388, by fealty only. Lang-drafts also, which was Exchequer Land, eventually joined the freehold.§

* Hutch. iii. † Vide p. 7. ‡ They only held copyholds in later times.

§ 1622. Partition of Blackwell Commons. To George Parkinson in leiwe and consideracon of the six and half oxg. of freehold land and to such other persons as shall have right to the said freehold, these grounds, Badell banck, Langdraught, Cald, Rell, and Dowdie bancks, with all other grounds lyeing under the banck from the holme towards Consclyffe, belonging to the Towneshipp of Blackwell, alsoe eight acres in the southend of Snipe abutting upon Brankinmoor neer Skerne, and alsoe the residue of Brankinmoor (not otherwise assigned) as part of the said freehold land, also the eatage of the loaning in Brankinmoor. There are something like manorial rights to freehold wastes recognized here, no quantity is prescribed, as in the cases of the other assignees.

Robert Garnet before 1631 conveyed a moiety of a capital messuage and six oxgangs, late his father Bartholomew's to Matthew Bracken gent. The entirety passed to George Parkinson, of Haghouse, gent., in 1638, being held by knight's service.

The Parkinsons now probably possessed the whole of the Neville property, for previously to this a messuage and farmehold late occupied by Robert Garnett had come into their hands, which Margerie Parkinson, of Woodrington,* co. Northum., widow of the suspected rebel Henry Parkinson, gent., (who had sold Beaumond Hill) conveyed in 1615 to George Parkinson, of Haghouse. The deed was produced in 1617 in evidence on behalf of Margerie and George against *Anthony Nevell* and Mathew Bracken complainants. I do not know the relationship of the man thus mixed up with a portion of the Neville manor to its lords, but he lived in gentle state near their green fields. In 1615 he occurs as of Blackwell in the sheriff's list of all the Knightes, Esquires, and Gentlemen resident in the Bishoprick, and in 18 Jac. 1. no heirs appearing at the Halmot Court on three callings, Timothy Comyn, gent., and Wm. Hall, draper, were adm. by the Bishop's special mandate to a close called France formerly Anthony Nevell's. In 1622 half of France and some of the Towneland, viz., Mayland, were demised by Matt. Bracken, survivor of Anth. Nevell, deceased. In 22 Jac. 1. the heir had turned up, for Charles Nevill, s. and h. of Anthony was adm. to the other half of Franc a parcel

* She was daughter of Sir John Widdrington, or Woodrington, knt. I take it that the entry "1592. June 1. James Witherington, son of Isacke Witherington, baptized :" in our register, refers to a child of her brother Isaac who had issue Robert and Elizabeth, both living in 1625, and that the connection with the neighbouring family of Parkinson, brought him here. In the inventory of his nephew Roger Widdrington of Harbottle, 1641, are some items which show that the deceased must have had a splendid taste for jewellery, for he had 3 watches in his pocket, 10 bloodstones, 2 silver seals, one gold tooth-pick, one gold signet on his finger, and 103*l.* in his purse. A trunk sent away in danger of the Scotts, contained of gold and silver imbroidered gloves iij pare; of plaine gloves vi paire; of wrought purses with gold and silver ii; table booke of silver i; *set of silver counters, viz.*, 38 *with a silver box* i; silver boxes ii; red silk and silver points viii; bracelets of currall and curralline ii; black cheane i; black braceletts ii; gold and silver thred of pearles ii; silver bell i; silver hatband i; hot-water celler of plush i; black bonelace ;— jewelles, in one box, corsanits with dimond i, pearle braceletts i, co... in gold i, gold crosses ii, gold rings ix, aggat beads, xv silver bodkins, corrall one peece, box with spirit of rosemarie, plushe petticote, colour reed, with silver lace i, scarlet waistcote with silver lace i, brode reed scarfe with silver and gold lace i, hollon smocks iij, night vails laced i. These are only some of the articles but they show the magnificence of Roger and his spouse.

To give an idea of what the counters would be like, I will briefly describe some similar articles of silver, kindly put into my hands by O. B. Wooler, esq., of Darlington. They are of the size of half a crown, very thin, and engraven on one side with figures of street vendors, on the other with birds and flowers, being contained in a silver box flowered, and containing in the inside of the lid a fine embossed head of Charles I. The numbers range to thirty-six but some are lost, the remainder are all curious as giving the cries of the time.

"*Lanthorne and a whole candell light.—Haue you any chaires to mend.—Codlinges hot, hot codlinges.—By a cocke or a gelding, (A woman with a toy windmill and horses' heads for children, on sticks.)—Band strings or hankercher buttons.—Mussels, lilley white mussels.—Macarell, new macarell.—Haue you any work for a Tinker.—What kichin stuffe haue you maids.—Sum broken Breade and meate.—White vnions, white St. Thomas vnions.—Worke for cooper, worke for cooper.—Chimney sweepe.—I haue fresh cheese and creame.—I haue ripe hartichokes Mistris.—Buy my dish of great smelts.—Ells or yeards by yeard or Ells.—Buy a bresh, buy a bresh.—Buy a screene or straw hatt.—Fine oranges fine lemons.—Small cole a penny a peake.—New flownders new.—Buy a steele or a tinder-box.—What ould iron or sowrdes or rapiers.—Haue you any cornes on your feet or toos, (a man with a staff, on his breast a tablet whereon are divers corns extracted, armed with most awfully long roots.)—New bookes newly printed and newly com forth.—What ragges, what ould ragges.*"

in Badell Bancke, &c., and in 1631, he (called "gentleman") sold to Wm. Corneforth, two oxgangs in Blackwell. So ceased the name of Neville there*. France is now the name of a six-and-a-half acre close belonging to R. H. Allan, esq., adjoining his estate called Far Howdens farm, and in 1526† I find mention made of Fraunce-howse, which was perhaps the residence of the last Neville of Blackwell. As to *Badell Bancke*, it was a general name for all the banks overhanging the deep amphitheatre of the Tees from Blackwell Holme to Badle Beck.‡

The Garnetts were perhaps nearly related to Anthony Garnett, Lord of Egglescliffe, who died in 1631, and whose grandfather James was "of Blasterfield in Westmerland."§ In 1626 Anthony son of Robert Garnett, of Blackwell, gent., deceased, was apprenticed to George Farnaby, Merchant Adventurer and Boothman of Newcastle-upon-Tyne, for ten years, and was in 1627 set over to Jane Garnett. In 1658 this Anthony, then a free brother of the community, petitioned that part of his arrears paid in might be restored, in regard his poll money was doubled and he absent in Yorkshire when warned to several courts and for absence fined. He hsd 30*s*. restored.|| In 1642, George Garnett¶ was a copyholder at Blackwell.

In 1666 John Garnett, Lord of Egglescliffe (son of Anthony) entered his pedigree at Darneton. Three years afterwards, Alice "the onely daughter and child of Mr. John Garnett" was laid beneath the sod, and the next year (1670) the childless father, who had been captain of horse in the Regiment of Col. Geo. Heron, and deeply engaged in the service of Charles I., sold his fair manor and retired to Darlington, where he only survived four years, being buried there 2 March, 1674-5. By his will he left 50*l*. to the poor of his former home. His wife Alice, daughter of Chr. Place, of Dinsdale, Esq., and widow of Michael Pemberton, Esq., of Aislaby, a major in the service of Charles I., was buried at Darlington in 1685.

The Parkinsons of Hagghouse, near Durham, were evidently one of the many branches of the Beaumond Hill race. The Seal of George the purchaser exhibits the usual coat Gules, on a chevron between three ostrich *feathers* arg. as many pellets, a mullet of six points for difference.** The Perkinsons were in fact originally *Fetherstonhaughs*, one of that family called *Perkin* having a son *Perkinson*.†† In 14 Cha. I. George Parkinson and his son and heir Edward mortgaged the property bought from Margerie (rate 8*l*. per cent.) to Tobye Ewbancke, of Stainthropp, gent.,‡‡ who must have acquired the whole estate in fee, holding 12 oxg. in Blackwell in 1679.

* Is Nevelson a decadence of Neville or Nevell? Isabella Nevelson, d. of Nicholas Nevelson of Langton, par. Gainford, bap. 1643.—*Darlington P. R.*

† Bishops Rolls. ‡ Vide p. 11. § Visit. 1615. || Merchts. Bks. N. C.

¶ Son of Robert, he had a son John, adm. to *Blackholme*, Badell Bankes in Blackwell field, some Bord Land beyond *le Markstones*, &c. He also possessed Stresham Closes and Garth Ends (now part of Mr R. H. Allan's Southern Estate), and had a son George who sold to the Sayers. Bord Land is land appropriated by the lord of a manor for the support of his board or table.

** Rickatson deeds penes R. H. Allan, esq., from whose valuable collections of title deeds the whole evidence on the Blackwell freeholds are taken, except where otherwise expressed. †† Visit. 1575. John Fetherstonhaugh confirmed the narration.

‡‡ Toby's first wife, Elizabeth, was widow of Richard Stobert. In her will she makes her father-in-law, Stephen Hegge and mother Anne Hegg, guardians to her daughter Ann Stobert. Stephen Hegge and Ann Walthorn were married at Darlington, 27 October, 1596. Robert Hegge, the author of the Legend of St. Cuthbert, "replete with good sense and refined wit," (who had a brother, Stephen, a parson, bur. at Whitworth in 1662), was born in 1599 at Durham, his parents being Stephen Hegge, notary-public, and Anne, dau. of Robert Swyft, a prebendary. When Mr. Taylor was preparing his edition of the Legend, Surtees found the entry of their burials in the Cathedral, but not of their son's, and was much annoyed. "What a beast Hegg must have been not to be buried there too, or what a brute the Sacristan must have been to omit his register!" He died in 1629.

The lingering of the Blackwell freehold in the blood of its ancient owners is curious. The present possessor, R. H. Allan, Esq., descends directly from the great earl through the Greys of Heton and Chillingham, whose coat also formed the most cherished quartering of the Ewbankes, as appears from the seal of Henry Ewbanke affixed to a Blackwell deed of 1670.

Tobye, who removed to Eggleston, fell into difficulties, and in 1658 Leonard Scott, of Hull, gent., obtained a judgment against him for 600*l.* debt and 21*s.* costs. In 29 Cha. II , a messuage, garden, orchard, and four closes called *Long Draught*, *Broad feild* or *Lamb flatt*, *Castle hill*, and *Castle bancke*, were extended as a *moiety* of his possessions at Blackwell, and delivered to Scott till payment.

In 1668, old Toby (then of Stainthropp again) and his son and heir Henry conveyed the property mortgaged by Parkinson in 14 Cha. I. to John Tempest, Esq., and others as Trustees to secure annuities, viz., 70*l.* to himself, 50*l.* to his wife Mary,* 30*l.* to Mary Storye, widow, 10*l.* to Toby the younger, and 20*l.* to Roger Bainbrigg. The property passed through different hands to Francis Forster, of Durham, in mortgage. In a fine of 1675 it is described as 4 mess. 1. orch. 40 acr. of land, 230 acr. mead, 230 acr. past. in Blackwell and *Blackwell Home.*† In 1684, the heir Henry Ewbanck, of Winsor, co. Berks, esq., sold *Blackwell Freehold Farme* (Robert Garnett, and Chr. Talbott,‡ Esq., named among the former occupiers) to Wm. Richardson, of London, gent.,§ who had acquired Scott's interest, and now received all the usual privileges of a manor ; "Court Leet and Court Barron, perquisits and profitts of courts, goods and chattells of felons, fugitives, persons outlawed and putt in exigent, and felons of themselves, deodands, waifs,escrays and all other royalties." Serjeant John Jefferson and *Doctor Isaac Basire*‖ of Durham, released their legal estates. In 1688, Forster's dau. and h. Elizabeth and her husband the hon. Charles Mountague, Esq., (Collins' Peerage ii. 292) also released on payment of mortgage money. Richardson was a major.

Blackwell Freehold Farm was settled by Richardson on his daughter Martha, who married Richard Booth, of York, gent., and in 1721 the two settled a messuage and garth on the backside thereof and the parcels called the *Long Draughts*, the *Middle holm*, the *Farr holm*, the *Banks*, *Dowdoe*, and *Castle* otherwise *Castle Hill.* Booth left these possessions to his daughter Ann and her husband Wm. Staines. She in her widowhood at Stockton sold to Chr. Denton, of Gray's Inn, Esq., from whom it descended to his sister Elizabeth who married Thomas Hill, Esq., of Manfield. In 1803 the Hills sold this estate, as well as Blackwell Holme, to George Allan, Esq., M.P., from whom the late John Allan, Esq., purchased Blackwell Hall (which he enlarged) and the Home Garth (near it) with Castle Hill in 1808, and the rest of the freeholds including the tithes were sold to him by Mr. G. Allan's representatives in 1833. In addition to which, some

* Generally called Margaret, and queried as "? Dor. or Mary" in the Grey pedigree in Raine's North Durham. In Surtees's Ewbanke ped. *Mary* is properly given. She was the daughter of Henry Grey, esq., fourth son of Sir Ralph Grey of Chillingham, knt. (descended from Sir Thomas Grey, of Heton, knt., who married Alice, daughter of Ralph Neville, K.G. first Earl of Westmoreland by the Lady Margaret Stafford), by Mary, daughter of Sir John Widdrington, of Widdrington, knt., and was married at Grindon, co. Durham, 31 Jan. 1613. Her sister Isabel Grey also was married at Grindon, 8 June, 1612, to John Pemberton, of Aislaby, esq. The Pembertons who were seated at Stanhope in 1400, are now represented by the Allans, who are of course entitled to the Grey quartering.

† In 1684 called *Blackwell Holme*

‡ Chr. Talbott, or *Taubart*, often held public offices for Blackwell and Bondgate between 1660 and 1700.

§ In 1685 the freeholders of Blackwell were Wm. Richardson, gent., in London ; Whayre Fawcett, gent., [the heir of John Cornforth] ; Thomas Garthorne (sold to Peter Hutchinson who lives at Cornforth.)

‖ The great royalist, who fled the kingdom to propagate the doctrine of the Church of England among the Greeks and the Arabians. He was prebendary of the 7th stall. See his life by the Rev. W. N. Darnell, Rector of Stanhope.

copyhold closes formerly called Well-Garth, Gill-Garth, Grimsley-Gill and Dockes, with two closes in Darlington township called Darnton close* and Ravensnab, (the latter added by the present owner) now form the Northern estate ; while the Southern or Hall portion has been augmented by copyholds chiefly derived from Watson,† Vane and Arden, the two latter families taking from Sayer and Prescott. Almost the whole of the houses (including the old deserted mansion of the Prescotts, popularly styled " *The Old Manor House*") in the village, were bought by the late Mr. John Allan, whose purchases in the township of Blackwell amounted to £34,300.‡

The old manor of Blackwell having thus become consolidated, no subowners were left to do suit and service, the manorial customs tacitly expired, and in " these piping times of peace " the military service is excused to its lords. Not so, however, the rent of 24*s.* 10*d.* which is still duly and truly exacted by my Lord of Durham's officers.

⁂ Cuthbert Waistell,§ of Baydale, near Darlington, married Anne Bunny (bap. 1690) of the ancient family of Bunny of Newsham. Her brother Edmund was at the summer assizes, 1708, defendant in some cause relative to lands there, against Edward and Sarah Wren, plaintiffs, in which after he had obtained a verdict he was shot dead in his return on the spot of ground between the rivers Wear and Browney.|| The money and watch on his person were untouched and the mystery was never explained. His brother George Bunny's daughter Mary married John Burton, of Darlington.

The Neville estate is full of entrancing nooks and shady dells, from which glances of the Tees and all its rich banks and fertile flats may be obtained. The Seat-house, " bosomed high in tufted trees," is placed on the brow of a hill in a most choice station, rising over the river, and commanding the deep meadows and green levels of the Tees which form an amphitheatre of three or four miles hemmed in by rising wooded grounds. From various portions of the domain---from Castle Hill---from Baydale wood and Ravensnab, the views are " beautiful exceedingly." A rare combination of wood and water, hill and dale, characterises the scenery, and the *coup d' œil*, is at once rich, varied, and romantic.

In consequence of the irruptions of the "thundering Tees," which here makes a singularly sudden and rapid sweep, that portion of the freehold called Castle Hill, is much reduced in quantity. In the memory of old men now living, its ample brow was decked with the cotter's dwelling and his sunny garden, all of which have fallen, one by one, into the dark remorseless stream below! The formation of a strong embankment, together with a formidable jetty or pier composed of Barton stone, recently erected at much ex-

* The corner field opposite Salutation. In 1703 it was called Scot's Close or Bedall Bank, and the road leading past it was styled the *coal street* from Cockerton to Blackwell.

† John Watson, a Stockton merchant, derived partly in 13 Geo. I. from John Middleton, whose messuage abutted on a tenement late of Wm. Cornforth on the E. now also the Allans'.

‡ The freeholds in the whole territory are :—The Hall and pleasure grounds formerly Home Garth, 4a.—Long Draughts, 68a.—West Holm, 10a. 2r. 4p.—West Bottom, 3r. 18p.—East Holm, (subdivided) 18a. 1r. 13p.—East Bottom, 2r. 14p.—Chilton field, 20a. 1r. 20p.—Twelve acres, 11a. 1r. 20p.—Low Cow Pasture, 20a. 2r. 10p.—Baydale bank, 8a. 1r. 1p.—Baydale bank Bottom, 5a. 9r. 34p.—Crooks, 1a. 2r. 21p.—Dowdy bank, 3a. 3r. 10p.—Dowdy Bank Bottom (subdivided), 7a. 2r. 34p.—Castle *alias* Castle Hill, 1a. 5p.—Darnton Close, 4a. 2r. 3p.—External Lands (adjoining the river Tees), 20a. 18p.—Gravel Beds, 7a. 24p.—Total freehold, 214a. 9p.

§ Mr. Geo. Wastell was constable of Blackwell in 1681 " for freehold."

|| Between Browney Bridge and Sunderland Bridge.

penseby the present proprietor, has, at last, when all other appliances failed, effectually secured this venerable remain from further demolition.*

Battela in Boldon Buke is considered by Hutchinson to be identical with Battle-law, or hill, and in Hatfield's survey Castle Hill and the herbage of Bathleygo together. It is remarkable that at Kendal opposite the Castle is *Castle-law-hill*, and immediately below it is a spot called *Battle place*.† In Wolsey's time the councillors to my Lord of Duresme ordered that the inhabitants and husbandmen of Bondgate should have to farm a ground called the *Battelfeld*. The subject will occur under Bathele Hospital and Badlefeld Chapel, and as it is said that "**When Julius Caesar was a king, Bowes Castle was a famous thing**,"‡ perhaps I had better leave Blackwell Battle and Castle to a like misty antiquity. One might easily multiply instances of similar titles given to places without even a tradition of blood, indeed at present such places are the chosen resorts of fairy elves. What would Tower Hill (or *Castellarium* as Ralph Surteys calls it in an early charter) at Middleton be without the sweet little folks who wash their clothes in the Tees, or Pudding-pie-hill§ near Thirsk without the philanthropic race who furnish puddings and pies and vouchsafe subterranean music on Pancake Tuesday to the giddy little votaries who run round and round the hill first, stick their knives in, and apply their buzzing heads to hear those glad strains. Blackwell anyhow is a lovesome vill, but the innocent thraldom of fairy land notions will clothe its verdant mounds and fragrant flowers with a more abundant elegance.

When the sun is westward flying,
Cloudless tints of crimson dying,
Fitful lovers farewells sighing,
Kine by hedgerows idly lying ;—
When through the wood-lined vale of Tees
Sweeps a mild and whispering breeze,
That brings to Crooks and Grimsley Gill
The freshness of each pebbly rill,
And scatters scents from blossomed leas
On hawthorn bounds and *wedded trees* ;||—
When mists of murky eve are thrown
Where stately stood the altar-stone,
And sweetly chimed the sanctus-bell
In Baydale's fair and free chappelle ;—

* See page 19. † Beauties of England and Wales.

‡ Denham's MSS. There was a *Battellawe* at Hawthorne in 11 Jas. I. *Badayle* is an archaism for Battle. See Halliwell's Dict. § Said to have had a watch tower to Thirsk Castle.

|| In one part of the estate, behind the old Tithebarn, an ash and a sycamore spring from one hugh trunk : so closely did they *cuddle* when young. What would the good Miss Allan have said to them ! She, like the maiden queen, had no appreciation for ends and determinations put to virgin estates in her household, and invariably dismissed any offending members of her miniature court. One poor fellow's affection was too mighty for him, and he rushed into the matrimonial Charybdis. A gentle hint to depart of course followed, but the love-stricken victim never left Grange. He shot himself there, and hence, perhaps, originated many a thrilling tale of ghastly complexion, which used to be told of that pleasant place.

When homeward peasants tread the path
Through pastures green to Blackwell Wath ; *—
Castle Hill and Neville's dell
Brighten under elfish spell,
Voices ring around the well,†
Light as murmured hum of bees ;—
And with echo soft and long
Midst the wild and gleesome throng
Sinks to sleep the gentle song
Of the maiden sprite of Tees.‡

The manor of Oxen-le-field was also among the possessions of the lady-loving lord, as well as some burgage property in Tubwell adjoining other that had been granted off under a yearly rent, and in Northgate.

By letters patent, 1574, the Queen granted to Thomas Brickwell and Andrew Palmer, the messuage called Oxnetfield Grange, to hold of the Crown by the 40th part of a knight's fee. A free-rent of 3*l.* 6*s.* 8*d.* was due from the premises to the Bishop of Durham. In 1602. Palmer released to Brickwell, who in the same year sold to William Bore. Before 1700, Oxneyfield was purchased by the Milbankes, and is still parcel of the entailed estate.

A lease of Oxen-le-field had been granted to Henry the 5th Earl in the decadence of the family. The truth is that he got the fortune of his step-daughter Margaret Gascoigne (daughter of Sir Henry Gascoigne, of Sedbury in Richmondshire, by Margaret Cholmley afterwards the Earl's second wife) and gave her the lease in its stead. The editors of Spelman's Sacrilege of course attribute the misfortunes of the later Nevilles to their possessing certain dissolved monasteries, and it seems that the Deanery of Darlington may be added to them. The lady's wardrobe is interesting.

" An Invitory of all the goods and cattells wich were Margaret Gascoigne's, single-woman, within the bishopbrick of Durham, lait deceased, at the whyt friers in London, praised by Thomas Lacy, gentilman, Anno Domini, 1567, the xxiiij. of March.

" First, one lesse of grang called *Oxnold Feld night Dallington*, maid by the Right honorable Henry lait Erle of Westmerland, to hir in recompenc of hir child's porcon wich he had remaining in his hands of the yerely value of lx*l.*, the rents paid and all other paments discharged. Item the said erle did by his last will and testament geve and bequith vnto hir all that his interest and lease for terme of yeres wich he had in the *deanrye of Darlington* of yerly value the rents paid, &c., of xl*l.* She nether aught any debts nor yet gave any legaces.- -First a goune of chaungable taffatie laid one with gold laic 66*s.* 8*d.* A goune of silk grogram laid one with silke laic 46s. 8*d.* One old goune of moccado 26*s.* 8*d.* Two kirtells wherof one of changable taffatie th' other of grogram 30*s.* Two peticotts thone of skerlet th' other of stamell 35*s.* Two frenche hodes with lytle billiment of gold 66*s.* 8*d.* Other necessary apparell 26*s.* 8*d.* Summa of the apparell 14*l.* 18*s.* 4*d.*"§

A survey was taken 14 June, 1570, of the Lordship of Raby by Commissioners. They reported the Castle as being " tenne myles from Darneton," a " marvelouse huge house---*yet ys there no order or proporcion in the buylding thereof---lyke a monstrouse old Abbey*, and will soone decay, yf it be

* The old ford. The friendly ferry was but a few paces further on. † In Well-garth.

‡ Peg Powler was no *malicious* naiad slow-gliding on the silvery stream. I believe her pilferings were solely prompted by excessive affection for the "bonny bairns" she bore away.

§ Surtees Soc. Wills and Inventories.

not continually repayred, yt standyth so open---upon the greate waste called *Feuds Fell* and Weredale."*

1632. Feb. 12. Contract between the citizens of London and Sir Hen. Vane for lands within the Lordship of Raby, viz., Raby, Bolam, the Carrs in Staindrop, Langleydale, Langleydale forest, three parts of Strickley parks with the mill there, *Darlington*, Langton, Somerhouse, Houghton, Stillington, and Pethraw, all of the yearly rent of 166*l*. 3*s*. 6*d*., and lands in the Lordship of Barnardcastle, rent 116*l*. 16*s*. 3*d*., the two lordships sold together at the rate of 35 years' purchase for 9904*l*. 11*s*. 3*d*.†

1577. Richard Barnes, Bishop. He soon wrote to Lord Burleigh about his *stubborn churlish* flock, who shewed but *Jack of Napes charity* in their hearts, and who slandered him "*according to the Northern guise*, which is never to be ashamed however they bely and deface him whom they hate,‡ yea though it be before the honorablest." He calls the church of Durham an *Augie Stabulum*, "whose stinke is grievous in the nose of God and men." The crown soon demanded more than the discharge of his duties, and extorted leases every year.

In 1578 the watermills of Darlington and Blackwell were granted to the queen for forty years, rent 22*l*. She granted them to William Appleton. Barnes's second wife Fridesmunda, was sprung *ex illustri ac generosa Giffardorum familia*, and was related to the Darlington family of that name. Hutchinson gives her epitaph at St. Andrew's Auckland, as being in brass, partly on the verge of a stone in which a female figure is inlaid, and partly above and near the figure. The effigy is that of an ecclesiastic, and the inscriptions are all on an oblong brass on another stone. The Bishop died in 1587. His dau. Elizabeth *m*. Robert *s*. of Ralph Talboys of Thornton Hall, esq., and his son Timothy Barnes, gent. lived there in 1594 when he acquired Hunden Closes in Bondgate, late of John Barnes, of Haughton, clerk. His daughter Fridesmunda was born at Auckland in 1616. In 1621-2 he filled public offices here, in 1623 he recovered in the Borough Court from Tho. Atkinson *one goulde ringe inamled* or 19*s*., and in 1624 was surety for *Robert* Barnes. The Rector of Haughton-le-Skerne was an unscrupulous chancellor for his brother the bishop and a bitter enemy to Barnard Gilpin; he acquired lands from Henry Killinghall, gent., in 29 Eliz. He had two daughters of whom Margery (eventually sole heiress) *m*. Wm. Lambton, of Stainton, esq., who left two daus. and cohs., viz. Anne, *m*. to Nich. Chaytor, esq., and Margaret, *m*. to John Killinghall, esq.

1594. Before giving a narration of a martyrdom in Darlington, it must be observed that it was not *professedly* for religion that the poor man suffered, but for *high treason*, a circumstance which drags it into this division of my book. The severities against Papists and Puritans in Elizabeth's reign are startling. It is true that the seminary priests were generally downright rebels, plotting and corresponding with the enemy continually; it is also true that all dissenters were very aggravating in their conduct. "Roaring in time of divine service in the queer" was not a solemn way of diffusing opinions at Bishopwearmouth; the "slacke comers to church" at Whitburne were also "common scouldes," and the Harrisons of Barnard-Castle did wrong

* Gyll's MSS. quoted by Allan. † Allan MSS. R. H. A.

‡ This is in fact rather a compliment than the reverse. We were not backbiters.

in "pipeing and dancing in divine service-time on the Sabaoth," however much they might hold the Protestant observance of that sacred day strict and puritanical. However, the poor folks of Rome were sorely tormented. If they did not go once a month to church,* they were imprisoned, if then they did not conform, they were banished, and if they returned, the penalty was *death.* Priests made by Roman authority were forbid under pain of death to come into England, and from 1577 to 1603, one hundred and twenty-four priests, and fifty-seven laymen and women for harbouring them, suffered the extreme penalty.

I have given an instance or two in the foregoing sentences of recusant buffoonery from Surtees's MS. notes out of the Spiritual Court books. My readers will thank me for a few more extracts of odd cases.

Gateshead. 1677. Rich. Wilson for enclosing a burial place for *Secretaries* (*Sectaries*) —*Bp. Wearmouth.* 1613. Grace Burdon for denying the clark's wages—she laid the blame on her son Tho. Burdon who had the money, and I suppose spent it.—Alice Colin of the same place "*confest* that she is an *outrageous scolde* and a *disquieter* of the neighbourhood whereby *much* disquietnes doeth arise," absolved on admonition.—*Whorlton.* Sad complaints against Alice Lawson *an outragious papist* for pulling forth Rauff Heighley's servant out of his stall in church time, and interrupting Alison Heighley in her stall in the chappell.—*Sedgefield.* John Atkinson for brawling in church and drawing his dirke or dagge before he left the same upon Geo. Brabin.—*Cockfield.* offic. contra Will. Lodge p. suspic. ad. cum Margar. Lodge. Appeared and cleared himself saying that she was "a very decrepite *ugly old woman,*" and that he had not the least suspicion, &c., but thought the information came of the malice of Kitty Stevenson, late servant of Widow Lodge, detected for stealing "*a pare of lether britches belonging the said widow* and some *other* plough geare."—1615. Offic. contra Edw. Blackett, *gent.*, on a similar charge. Lyonel Fargeson, a piper of Wolsingham, deposed, that "about nine yeares since he married Isabel Sympson, having then a child of two yeares old called Mary Blacket, born at the house of the said Edward Blackett at Hoppeland, and which he promised to maintain, and to give the said Isabel *two-pence* a week, but hath *never given nothing* save 10*s.* 6*d.* in money in all nine years ; a grote at another time and *an ould pair of britches not worth a boon*, three shillings, &c., &c.

In 1523, Ralph Swalwell was chaplain of St. James's Chantry in the Bishop's Palace at Darlington, and the family in after years was evidently a suspected one. In 1570 Thomas Swalwell, Curate at Ebchester, Medomsley and Brancepeth successively, was accused of having upheld confession, "abusinge the example of the tene leapers, whome Christ commaundyd upon there clensinge to shew themselves to the prest," but he denied that and other charges.† Poor George is said to have been born at Darlington, the place of his execution. He was ordained in 1577, became reader or curate at Houghton-le-Spring, and was presented by the Master and Brethren of Sherburn to the vicarage of Kelloe, but Bp. Barnes refused institution, claiming the presentation himself. The remainder of his life will be found in the following extract from *Challoner's Missionary Priests.*

* At the last sermon preached by Archbp. Hutton at York, the Popish recusants who were present in obedience to orders, were so obstreperous that they were obliged *to be gagged.*

† Sur. Soc. Dur. Eccl. Proc.

George Swallowell* was born in the bishopric of Durham, and brought up in the protestant religion; and for some time officiated in the double capacity of reader and of schoolmaster at Houghton-le-Spring, in the same bishopric. Going one day to visit a catholic gentleman imprisoned for his recusancy, and falling in discourse on the subject of religion, he was so closely pressed by the gentleman upon the article of his mission, and that of his prelates, that he was forced, by way of a last slip, to shelter himself under the queen's spiritual supremacy, and to derive their commissions from her authority. The gentleman exposed to him the absurdity of making a woman, whom St. Paul did not allow to speak in the church, the head of the church, and the fountain of ecclesiastical jurisdiction; and treated so well both this and other points of controversy, that Mr. Swallowell, who was none of those who are resolved to be rebels to the light, yielded to the strength of his arguments. And not content privately to embrace the truth, he, not long after, publicly professed from the pulpit, *that he had hitherto been in an error, but was now convinced that they had no true mission in their church, and therefore he would no longer officiate there.*

Upon this he was apprehended, and committed to Durham gaol, and, after a year's imprisonment, was brought to the bar, at the same time with Mr. Bost and Mr. Ingram, and stood between them, At first, through fear of that cruel death to which he was condemned, he yielded to go to the church and to conform to what the judges required of him. Whereupon Mr. Bost, looking at him, said, *George Swallowell, what hast thou done?* At these words of the confessor of Christ, he was struck with a great damp and confession, and desired the judge and the lord president (who at that time was the earl of Huntingdon) *for God's sake to let him have his word again.* To which the judge replied, *Swallowell, look well what thou doest; for, although thou be condemned, yet the queen is merciful.* But still he craved to have his desire granted. Then the judge answered, *If thou be so earnest, thou shalt have thy word again, say what thou wilt.* Then presently he recalled what he had formerly yielded unto, and courageously said, *that in that faith wherein those two priests did die, he would also die; and that the same faith which they professed, he did also profess.* With that Mr. Bost looked at him again, and said, *Hold thee there, Swallowell, and my soul for thine:* and with these words he laid his hand upon his head. Then the lord president said, *Away with Bost, for he is reconciling him.* Upon this his judgment was pronounced, which was, to be hanged, drawn, and quartered at Darlington.

Upon the day designed for execution he was brought two miles off the place on foot, and then was put into a cart, where he lay on his back with his hands and eyes up to heaven, and so was drawn to the gallows. To terrify him the more they led him by two great fires, the one made for burning his bowels, the other for boiling his quarters; and withal, four ministers attended him to strive to bring him over to their way of thinking; but he would not give ear to them or stay with them, but went presently to the ladder, and there fell down upon his knees and continued for some time in prayer; then making the sign of the cross, he went up the ladder, and having leave of the sheriff to speak, he said, *I renounce all heresy:* and spoke some other words which were not well heard by the people; with which the sheriff being offended, struck him with his rod, and told him that if he had no more to say he should go up farther, for the rope should be put about his neck, which being done, Mr. Swallowell desired if there were any catholics there they would say three *paters*, three *aves*, and the *creed* for him: and so making the sign of the cross upon himself, he was turned off the ladder. After he had hung awhile they cut the rope and let him fall; and the hangman, who was but a boy, drew him along by the rope yet alive, and there dismembered and bowelled him,

* From a manuscript in my hands, and from bishop Yepez's History of the Persecution, l. 5, c. 5, who had his informations from letters sent over from England, two months after Mr. Swallowell's execution. *Challoner.*

and cast his bowels into the fire. At the taking out of his heart, he lifted up his left hand to his head, which the hangman laid down again ; and when the heart was cast into the fire, the same hand laid itself over the open body. Then the hangman cut off his head and held it up saying, " Behold the head of a traitor ! " His quarters, after they were boiled in the cauldron, were buried in the baker's dunghill.

He suffered at Darlington, *vulgo* Darnton, July 26, 1594.*

Bost suffered at Dryburn,† and Ingram at Newcastle.

1589. Matthew Hutton, Bishop. His son, Timothy Hutton of Marske, died in 1629, "*anno ultimæ patientiæ sanctorum,*"‡ having charged his son *always to keep a Levite in his house.*

Timothy Hutton of Blackwell, *m.* Margaret Corneforth (qu. dau. of Cuthbert Cornforth of Blackwell, and bap. 1598.) in 1621, and had issue Elenor, bap. 1622, Anne 1623-4, (bur. 1634) Christofer 1629, and Robert 1634. *Par. Reg.*

Robert Hutton, S. T. P., Rector of Haughton-le-Skerne, desires in 1619 to be buried " in the Quyer at Haughton, neere his wyfe's stalle, under the blewe stone in the east side of the churche." Anne, the daughter of this reverend man *(venerabilis viri)*, *m.* John Vaux, or Wausse a gentleman of Darlington, who proceeded in 1616 against Rowland Vasie for unjust detention of a book called *Jo. Vigo*, damage 20*s.* and obtained an order for the redelivery of it to Richard Packering (formerly steward of the Borough Court), at Darnton, at or before Great Monday next after Martinmas. Vasie next courted Vaux for unjust recovery of *Jo. Vigo,* damage 25*s.*, the latter made default and lost. *(Condemnatur.)*

1595. Toby Mathew succeeded as Bishop ; ripe in learning, eloquence, and wit. He said that he could as well not *be*, as not *be merry*, and when he left Durham for York, that it was for *lack of grace*, for according to a homely Northern proverb, *York has the highest rack, but Durham the deeper manger.*

1597. Sep. 21. Captain Slouch buried. (He died of the plague.) *Par. Reg.*

1599. John Evered, a soldier on travel *(miles peregrinus)*, who died in Blackwell, buried. *Par. Reg.*

* A little variation occurs in a Brussels printed Church Hist. of England from 1500 to 1688, of 1732, where it is said that " Boast observing Swalwell to be somewhat intimidated during his trial, and that his answers insinuated something of conforming, clapped him on the back, saying, " *George, take courage, my Soul for thine, all will be well, take courage.*" Upon this Swalwell recovered himself from the consternation he lay under, and went through the remainder of his trial with great resolution ; the Jury brought him in guilty of death for being proselyted to the Church of Rome. He was attended to the place of execution by four ministers of the Church of England, whose assistance he refused with a great deal of good manners ; he kneeled down at the foot of the ladder, and made a public profession of the Roman Catholick faith. He suffered at Darlington 26 July, 1594, and his body was thrown *into a hole near the Gallows.*

† Near Durham. When turned off the ladder, he was instantly cut down, and standing on his feet was butchered alive. At the taking out of his heart he said aloud, " Jesus, Jesus, Jesus, forgive thee." Toby Mathew, his college friend, exclaimed " It was pity so much worth should have died that day."

‡ Monument, Richmond.

Chapter III. The Stuarts.

Darnton has a bonny, bonny church,
With a broach upon the steeple:
But Darnton is a mucky, mucky town,
And mair sham on the people.*

So says this rude old rhyme now, so said King Jamie, and Defoe a century ago considered that Darlington had "nothing remarkable but dirt, and a high stone bridge over little or no water." And though any condemnations did not come well from the mouth of that royal oddity, whose skin was so soft and irritable that he could not bear to wash it, who was always tumbling into fluids impure while hunting in most clumsy wise, and whose tongue was so large that he could not drink without bespattering the bystanders; yet it must be owned that a town whose streets were only *lately paved* in 1749,† and were described in 1790‡ as being very dirty in winter *not being paved*, had a very good title to the terms "Dirty Darnton," and "Darnton i't' dirt."§

In olden times, however, people put up with much more than they do now. Each house had a dunghill on its *fore front*. As late as 1710 it was ordered "that every one keep their dunghill in winter well shuffled up, and that the same be carried away before Whitsuntide," and though in 1621 the householders were to keep and cause to be sweeped the street clean before their doors, and cause the mire and dung to be carried away, the injunction was but little regarded. The old orders occur again for a grand removal before Whitsun even, or as in 1631 before Midsummer. Nor were they the

* Denham's MSS. The same saying with change of name is afloat respecting Chester-le-street. Broach is a Northern word for any spire; in Leicestershire and other districts it signifies a spire springing from the tower without any intermediate parapet. In Yorkshire it is *broitch*, as "Wakefield broitch." Darlington broach is very famous as a landmark. "Aye, I got in seet o' Darnton broach." From Roseberry Topping

"Fair Darlington's tall spire, emerging, gleams."

I always think of a good roast goose on seeing it, for *broche* is a spit, a spire being pointed like one.

† Universal Magazine. ‡ Luckombe's Gazetteer.

§ "The weavers are all out o' wark
For the mills are all at a stand,
The combers are all out o' wark tee
And there's nut a bit wark to be fand:
Sae wee'll all to Stinking Shildon,
For it's ower wi' Darnton-in't-Dirt,
Sae wee'll all to Stinking Shildon,
And the Deevil tak Darnton -in't-Dirt.
[Var: And Dirty Darnton may gang to the Deevil.]

A verse from a modern song.

smaller streets only which were so treated. The Market Place and the King's Street (any thoroughfare), are the places named in the orders.*

It was in April, 1617, that James I. proceeded to have another look at his ancient lands. The usual order does not occur till May, so he would have full advantage of all dunghills, sandholes, and other nuisances. A minute and very general tradition represents the king arriving at the old Mudhouse in Tubwell-Row. This fabric, which is still remembered, was where Watson the saddler's shop now stands, and its rough material was tastefully beautified with cows' horns intermixed here and there. Within were "the wainscotted room," and "the little wainscotted room," in the latter of which the king slept on his journey to Scotland, the event being commemorated by a panel which I cannot follow the fate of, but some of the other woodwork is in the hands of Mr. Wm. Kitching. Unless the monarch was very closely boxed up in travelling, I do not see why he should be unaware of the dirt and designation of Darlington, but perhaps he was in the humour for one of those quaint flights of subacid humour for which he was so famous; however he opened his window and popped out his head to enquire "where he had got to?" "Darnton" was the reply. *"Darnton!---Humph!---I think it's Darnton i't' Dirt,"* exclaimed James, with the success attendant on all royal wits, and ever since the byname has been perpetuated. Doubtless the dunghills were much worse favoured objects than the beatific lands of wealth he surveyed from the high place on which he sat above Houghton-le-side, at his first arrival, and which still delights in the name of Legs Cross.

Two inns only are mentioned at this period, the Bull Inn (next the Bull-Wynd, where the Bulmer crest is still ascendant), and the Crown, in the Well Rawe, bought by Rowland Burdon of the heir of Margery Lassells in 1629.* Was not the latter the very house where James abode? His grandson was memorialized on the sign of the Royal Oak on the High Row, where the king in the oak and a fat Roundhead or two beneath were fairly pourtrayed. The house so adorned was thatched like many other houses in the same row, in the memory of seniors yet alive.

I should like to know what James would have said to the dismal deeps of Cat-kill Lonnin. A visit there could not but have been gratifying to the Royal crusader against witchcraft, and the awkward huntsman. It is the lane which intersects Newtown and leads from the great North road at Travellers' Rest to Sadberge and Yarm, being formerly much used by waggons and carts in conveying lime and coals to the farms further South, and to many parts of Cleveland. But the roads of Great Stainton are improved and railroads are still better, so the lane at Newtown is seldom used, and in most parts is in a wretched state. It is called Sadberge, Broom, or Cat-kill Lane or Lonnin. The Broom has now disappeared, with the exception of a single plant which sprang from the ground where much soil had been removed, and perhaps had remained there as a seed for centuries. As for the name of Cat-kill, a friend well recollects a nursery tale when he was young, reciting that during some night in the year (it was either Halloween or April fool een or some other een), all the cats in the neighbourhood for many miles round held their meeting and bivouacked in a particular place in the lane, holding annual consultations, devising future schemes, planning, plotting and contriving, mewing and squalling. There were black cats, white cats, grey cats, yellow cats, and not a few tortoise-shell cats; and the story goes on to say how they dispersed prior to day break, and how the most dreadful noises and horrifying screams caused by their disagreeing and fighting were heard. For the latter amusement was not to be wondered at, seeing that so many outrageous and belligerent creatures were congregated together; and in proof of all this marvellous narration's correctness, if any person visited the place next morning, there laid before him the ground quite saturated with grimalkin gore—nay more, to remove every doubt as to assassination and slaughter having been the order of the night, six, eight, or ten bleeding male or female tabbies were sure to be found, laid grim, gelid, and ghastly, where the infernal conflict had been lost and won.*

And yet this place of horrid deed is in summer very fair. There grows the witches-vervain (fit denizen of such a spot), the veronica, the valerian, the elegant and varied eglantine, the wiling woodbine, the creeping bryony, the fragrant thyme. The wild strawberry furnishes fruit plentiful, large, delicious, and the blackberries, bumblekites or brambles, are so abundant that their votaries readily come five and six miles for them. Many a basket is annually taken thence to Darlington and there sold for mickle profit, and in the season it is very usual for parties to call with their baskets or tins at Newtown to enquire the nearest road to the far famed Cat-kill. But in winter, woe be to the luckless traverser of that miry way.

At the end of Cat-kill Lonnin, where four roads meet near Stainton, is Patie's Nook, a place of ghastly grey renown. Patie's beer-house was a place of no very good associations in any way. One market-day, at Darlington, two farmers, Pringle and Race, fell out sadly, and Pringle threatened " Before the sun rise to-morrow, I will be revenged of you." Race passed through Haughton, Pringle after him, and that was the last time that he was seen alive. Two butchers intended to halt at Patie's Nook at midnight, but looking in first, they saw two men by a glimmering light; one supported a dead man's body bleeding from ear to ear, the other held a basin to catch his blood. The butchers fled in horror. It was conjectured that Pringle and Patie burnt poor Race's body in an oven, but no evidence was procured; the murderers escaped, and the vile den has wholly passed away.

James had a namesake who became Bishop James in 1606, and who was fairly scolded to death at Durham by King James, so roundly that he retired to Auckland and died of a violent fit of stone and strangury, brought on by perfect vexation three days afterwards. The cause was, perhaps, the bishop's contest with his citizens relative to privileges and representation, or his neglect in the Darnton journey in not brewing any ale for the king, till within five days of his visit to Durham.

The two James's had met before, when the king on his first arrival was feasted by the Lord of Lumley, whose pedigree was expatiated on by the future bishop (some relation of the family) without sparing him a single ancestor credible or incredible, till the Scotchman wearied with the eternal blazon, exclaimed " Oh! mon, gang na further; let me digest the knowledge I ha gained, for, by my saul, I did na ken Adam's name was Lumley." The expression was cutting, and came as ill from the monarch's mouth as his Darlington one did. Thoresby was delighted in 1703 at seeing at good Mr. Parker's the pedigree of *King James from Adam*, probably something like the marvellous genealogy of his ancestors in the Anglo Saxon Chronicle, which deduces Ethelwulf from Woden and 34 other barbarous old fellows to Sceaf, "that is the son of Noah, he was

* It is probable the idea is founded on fact. It is well known that a moaning cat has often drawn together crowds of pussies, whose "horrid sympathies" ended in a frightful massacre of each other. See Bewick's Quadrupeds.

born in Noah's ark ;" and from Noah to "Adam the first man, and our Father, that is, Christ. Amen."

John Lumley, gent., of Archdeacon Newton (second cousin of Henry Blakiston, of the same place) who was buried at Darlington in 1638, was son of Roger Lumley, "that dyed in the jayle," and was "buried in the queer" of S. Mary-le-Bow, Durham, in 1606, of the Asselhouses or Axwell branch. *Cassandray* Lumley, a daughter of John Lumley, was bap. 1639, and a lower family of the name runs throughout the registers. *Lovil Lumley* was a weaver in 1716.

1617. RICHARD NEILE, Bishop. One of the most unprincipled flatterers of James I.

1620. Sep. "Symon Gifford, of Darnton parish, gent., for not shoeing one private corslett," and other parties upon a muster for Darlington ward (Aug. 11.), having "contemptuously by their defaults hindered, and in a sort frustrated that his Majesty's service," the Bishop orders Mr. Fra. Wrenn, of Heighington, and John Dowthwaite, high constable in Darnton Ward, to summon the offenders before him. *J. B. Taylor's MSS.*

1627-8. GEORGE MONTEIGNE, Bishop.

1628. JOHN HOWSON, Bishop.

1632. THOMAS MORTON, S. T. P., a man after the fashion of Tunstall, succeeded to the bishoprick. The Darlington ringers received "for ringing at my Lo. Bpp's. [Howson] first coming" 2*s.* 6*d.*,* but they got a penny more for a very equivocal compliment to the new-made bishop in this year, "To ringers at my Lo. Bpp's. going out of the countrey 2*s.* 7*d.*"

I add a few more bellringing charges, of a very turncoat spirit. 1632. For ryngynge for the kynge, 2*s.* 3*d.* 1651. Payd the ringers when Worcester defeate was, 5*s.* 1660. To the ringers upon proclaiminge the Kinge, and for a sacke of cooles, 8*s.* 3*d.* 1668. For taking down the great bell, 1*l.* 10. ; for hanging her up, in all, and wages, 10*s.* 1678. July 8. Paid the ringers at the Duke of Monmouth his return 5*s.* [after his campaign against the Scotch Covenanters and the victory of Bothwellbrig.] 1684. Feb. 16. To ringers when king James II. was proclaimed 10*s.* 1688. To the ringers on thanksgiving day for the young Prinse† in money, ale, and coles, 7*s.* 4*d.* 14 Feb. For tarr-barrell, coles, and ringing a peele 2*s.* 6*d.* 1689. Ringing for King William's victory . . . . 1690. For coales, tar-barrells, and ringing on the victory in Ireland, 6*s.* 4*d.* 1767. To a half-hour glass for the bell ringers 1*s.* 1790. John Longhorn, he declining being any longer a bell-ringer, 3*s.* 1795. Bell-ringers, Prince William of Gloucester, past through Darlington in a coach, 9*s.* Do. on the Duke of York going to and returning from Newcastle (*good,* in pencil) 18*s.* 1800. Mar. Bell-

* Par. Bks. 1630.

† The Pretender, introduced by Swift in lines on the prayer prepared by the bishops of Chester, Peterbrough, and Durham (Nathaniel Crew.)

> Two Toms and Nat. in council were sat
> To rig up a new thanksgiving,
> With a dainty fine prayer, for the birth of an heir,
> That's neither dead nor living.

ringers, on a victory, but name forgot, 9*s.* 1808. Fancy ringing nights and mornings, 5*l.* 5*s.* 1818. Bell-ringers, (Queen's funeral day), *very hard day*, 2*l.* 4*s.* 1819. Bell-ringers on Prince Leopold passing, 16*s.* 1827. Sep. Bell-ringers, Marquis of Cleveland, 18*s.* Do., Duke of Wellington, 1*l.* 1*s.* 1832. Bell-ringers, on Earl Grey passing through Darlington, 12*s.* I, of course, do not give a tithe of state ringings. In 1832, were two or three Reform Bill ringings.

They were evil times that I enter upon. The register and parish books show this.

1637. June 29. Hugh Spencer, servant of Henry Ellstobb of Darlington, who died a violent death, buried at Armitage* heade. 1638. December 17. Beatrix Harrison of Darlington, who died a violent death, buried p. Blackwell lane. 1639-40. January 17. Jane, wife of John Sigswicke of Darlington, who died a violent death, buried. A great many Scotch and soldiers occur. 1640. Aug. 26. John, a soldier, whose surname was unknown, soldier, buried. 1643-4. Feb. 12. Patricious Davison, soldier, buried. 1649-50. *Obedience*, dau. of Henry Paris, soldier, was buried. Puritanical names are excessively rare in the Darlington registers. *Faith* Robinson had placed faith in Cuthbert Stricklin before her final act of faith, on July 28, 1633, when she married him, for their son was baptized in November following. 1655. Henry Casson, liewtenant to Captain Hargrave, and Dorothie Perkins, of Darlington, marryed att Henknowle, by Francis Wren, esq. 1658-9. Jan. 15. Christopher Allinson, a trouper, whome was under the comand of Maigor Ginkins, drowned besides Ketton Bridg, was buried.

1635. To a souldier which came to the church on a Sunday, 6*d.* 1648. To three companies of Irish, 1*s.* 1649. To a gentlewoman that came from Ireland with a passe, 6*d.* 1650. To three companyes of Irish travellers, 1*s.* These were, probably, persons who fled from the horrors of the Irish rebellion.

In "a taxation upon the county of Durham towards 2000*li.* to a ship to be sent out a°. 1636," occur the items;—The tithes of Newton, Blackwell, and Cockerton, value 70*l.*; Darnton Deanery, with the tithes and glebe there, 200*l.*; William Bower, of Oxnetfield, 100*l.*; Peter Boubanke, of Darlington, 150*l.*; Thomas Long, of Blackwell, 50*l.*; Cuthbert Robinson, of Cockerton, 50*l.*; William Middleton, of Blackwell, 50*l.*;† all in the division of Mr Richard Cornforth. Many other obnoxious orders for ship money occur on the county.

1639. Much alarm was caused by the Spanish Armada being prepared in great strength this year. Sir Robert Dudley, Sir Griffin Markeham, and Sir Guy Stanley were colonels in it, "*also there is one Nevil, who termeth himself Earl of Westmerland, who hath a great command.*" ‡ Whatever were its intentions, it was totally defeated by the Dutch.

* I have no other record than the name about the hermit's lowly dwelling place. Edward Robinson, of *Hermitage vulgo Banck Top*, was bur. 1712. It adjoined the Horsemill on the E. See under MILLS.

† Randall's MSS. The ecclesiastical revenues were taxed at 2 per cent. the personal estates at 13*s.* 4*d.* per cent.

‡ Rushworth. Who was this Neville? The luckless lord of 1569 died in 1601. And where are all the Raby records? From Collectanea Curiosa (ii. 218) it seems that the Lord Bar-

1639. Among the gentry of the bishopric charged with the equipment of light horse for the service of Charles I., is his unfortunate northern expedition, " in which the *solemn league and covenant* first reared its hydra head," occurs, " Mr. Francis Forster, of Darlington, a horse."

See the Forster pedigree in Surtees, making Francis the son of Christopher* (will 1580) by Mald d. and coh. of Geo. Fennye† of Darlington, potecarye, who, by will, mentions his daughter Mald Forster, her children Francis, Margaret, Jennet, Christofer. But this George Fenney and his wife Margery, settle their burgage on le well rawe, (subject to rent to Charles, Earl of Westmoreland,) in 4 Eliz., on *Cuthbert* Foster and Matilda their daughter *in liberum maritagium*, and Cuthbert sold it with *quoddam pannum e crinibus confectum, anglice a kilne haire*, to the Jeffraisons who sold to the Giffards. There seem to have been two Fosters of the name of Francis,‡ one of whom (who *m.* Elizabeth, dau. of Richard Heighington of Graystones, gent.) bought Nicholson's Hill and Croceflat,§ sold by his son Richard of Morton and Darlington, who (with a younger son, Mr Thomas Foster of Darlington, papist,||) had a s. and h. Francis, of West Hartburn, (the Killinghall *manor* or *Forster House*, which passed to the Rev. W. Addison Fountaine) and he had a son John. " Here lies the body of Margaret Foster, wife of John Foster of West Hartburne, gentleman, and daughter of Thomas Askue [of Dinsdale, Yorks.], gentleman. She was buried the sixteenth day of March, and in the year 1694." *M. I. Sockburn.*

Jane Foster, *illeg. d.* of John Foster and *Vile Rogerson* of Darlington, bap. 1633

nard had them not, and that Mr. Carte could no where find them. They were missing so early as 1616 when the commissioners after minute enquiries in the neighbourhood, were content to learn from *viva voce* testimony the metes and bounds of the long lands which had passed in one race for so many centuries. Did they follow the unfortunate earl across the sea in *kistes*, or were they destroyed by the powers that *were ?*

* A Christopher Foster occurs here in 31 Hen. 8. The name is almost invariably Foster rather than Forster.

† *Daughter Eliz. Bellamye*, her children Cuthbert, Thomas, Margaret, and Elizabeth—dau. Alice—nephew Christofer Ilee, 4*l.* per ann. out of Clarybutts (see Ile)—nephew Robert Ilee a house in Darlington—*brother Christofer Fenny* a goulde ringe. Was not this George the brother of James Fenny, *potticarie*, of Newcastle ? who, by will, (1560 ?) leaves to " my *brother George's* doughter Janne one silver sawlte with a cover doble gilte beinge my lesser salte and syxe silver spones of the maydenheddes; *my said brother his daughter, Elizabethe Fennye*, one playne pece of silver contening xiiij unc'; *his dowghter Mawde Fenne* fyve poundes towarde her marriage; *brother Xpofer Fenee.*" *Surt. Soc. Wills.*

‡ Margery d. Francis Foster bap. 1593-4 (*m.* Mr John Wilkinson of Barton, and had issue Francis Wilkinson of Monkend, near Croft.—Marmaduke Gill, merchant, who dyed at Mr. Francis Wilkinson's of Darlington, bur. 12 May, 1654. Timothy Wormely, the son of Henry Wormely of Rickell, esq., who dyed att Mr. Francis Wilkinson's house, bur. 18 Aug., 1654. *Dar. Par. Reg.)* Richard Foster and Jennet Robinson, 1593, (she *d.* a widow, 1638). The wife of Francis Foster bur. 3 September, 1597 (plague). Robert Foster, bur. 1598. Jennet, d. Francis bp., 1601. Christopher s. do. bp. 1603, bur. 1606. George do. bp. 12 May, 1605, bur. 1605-6. (Francis Foster of Darlington, and Elizabeth Heighington of Graystones, 19 May, 1605, *Haughton.)* Cicily w. Francis Foster of D. bur. 26 Apr., 1606. Richard s. Francis, bap. 15 Mar., 1609-10. George do. 1612-3. (Three infants bur 1611, 1615, 1616.)

§ Also lands at Middleton, High Moore, and Swyneflatt from Ralph Hedworth, gent. Marmaduke Surtees granted them in 1566 in trust for John, son of Richard Hedworth of Whickham and Ann his wife, granddaughter of Marmaduke. Anne Hedworth, widow, and Ralph, her son, and Eleanor, his wife, alienated in 1612 and 1619 to Place and Forster. Ralph Hedworth of Darlington, gent., bur. 1627; Elinor, widow, 1628. (Nicholson's Hill was sold lately by R. H. Allan, esq., to John Pease, esq.)

|| By a second marriage. Elizabeth, his first wife, was burried in 1634-5, when her dau. Margaret was bap.

(He was s. of Christopher, mentioned in Geo. Fennye's will, and bur. 1618, and was bap. 1614). Mary, wife of Robert Foster, buried with her infant, 1667. John s. of John Foster of East Witton, in Wensadaill, a stranger, *pro cujus educatione manucaptor est Guilielmus Clarke*, bap. 1615. (Undertakers for the bringing up of every *filius nullius* and stranger's child, seem to have been compelled to enter into an obligation deposited with the churchwardens. The Register is full of such minutes. Chargeability to the parish was thus sought to be guarded against.)

Francis Foster was a disclaimer in 1615, but in 1649, Richard, his son, conveys the Greets, and Nicholson Hill, parcel of Nesfield, sometymes of Henry Killinghall, esq., *with the seate or pewe in the churche belonginge the premises*, and uses a seal with the Yorkshire Fosters' coat, *a chevron between* 3 *bugle-horns*, while his son Francis, on the same document, oddly seals *with the raguly bend and garbs of Killinghall*, having perhaps picked up such a seal on the premises. Richard also used the device of the pelican and her young.

As to Simon Gifford,* the contemptuous subject of 1620, and purchaser of Forster's Neville property, he lived in a *cheefe house* in Priestgate, and Prebend Row, (forming the angle), having bought part of the Prebendal passessions in 1619, of Darley and Crompton. He sprung from a very ancient family of Staffordsh. and Bucks, and displays a gallant shield in the Durham visitation of 1615, Gifford (Gu. 3 lions passant in pale ar.) quartering Kirkstowe, Vaulx, Winslow, and Nunsegle. His father was John Gifford, *priest*, and his eldest brother was Robert Gifford,† of Darlington, whose only son (by Jane, d. of John Prestland, of Sounde, Chesh.,) John was bur. in 1591-2. In 1604, Elizabeth Jenyson, of Walworth, widow, bequeathed "to Mr. Gyfford, of Darneton, a booke, being a conference betwixt Doctor Whitguifte and Mr. Cartwright, and 40*s*., and to his wief sixe silver spoones with apostles' heads, ‡ and to his brother Simon Gyfford 40*s*." Simon was the fourth son, and *m.* 1. Meriol, d. of John Middleton, of Blackwell, in 1604, she *d.* in 1630, and he *m.* 2. Dorothy Anderson in 1637-8, (Mrs. *Dorothery Gefforth*, bur. 1675.) who was, probably, sister (and bap., 1584, at St. Nich., N.C.) of Roger Anderson,§ who *m.* Jane Bower, of Oxenlefield, children of Francis Anderson, alderman, of Newcastle. By Meriol he had issue, 1, *Colonel John Gyfford*, of Coulovolye, co. Cork, bap. 1604-5, conveyed the Prebend-row property to his bro. Robert, in 19 Cha. II. 2, 3, *Roger*, *Nicholas*, *d. inf.* 4, *William*, bap. 1609, living 1615. 5, *Elizabeth*, bap. 1616-7 *m.* Nicholas Swinborne,‖ clerke, 1639. 6, *Frances*,

* Giffard in the registers. The G is soft. *Gefforth* or *Jefford* was the popular pronunciation.

† In the register of his son's burial, the word *m'ri (magistri)* is inserted above his name, an unusual title in the early registers here.

‡ It was the custom to decorate the *knoppes* of spoons with saints, angels, apostles, scallop shells, lions, our Lady, or maiden's heads. Spoons so decorated were, and plain ones still are customarily given in many places at christenings or on paying the first visit to a lady *in stramine*.

§ Mr. John Anderson, the son of Sir Henry Anderson, knight, of Long Cowton, in Yorkshire, bur. 1668. See a Naboth sort of story in the Star Chamber record (8 Car. 1.), given by Rushworth, about Sir Henry Anderson coveting to gain the rectory of East Cowton from one Bacon, who refused to sell it. Maultus, a factotum of Anderson's, met Bacon in East Cowton, bidding him get out of the town, like a skip jack fellow as he was, or else he should be beaten out, and afterwards picking another quarrel, took hold of his horse bridle and struck him on the breast with a staff in the presence of Sir Henry, who, after one Green had also beaten poor Bacon about the neck and shoulders with a pitchfork, said that he was not cudgelled half enough. The knight and his son Henry, Green and Maultus were committed to the fleet and heavily fined, besides paying 100*l*. to the stricken Bacon. These Andersons came from Newcastle also.

Susanna Manors, the wife of Henry Manors, gentleman, who was tabled with Mr. Anderson, was buried, 1654. *Par. Reg.*

‖ *Roger Swinburne et Linskell sepult.* 26 *Feb.*, 1590-1. The latter name is also spelt *Linscale*. The mode of registry is curious.

bap. 1619. Both these lasses are remembered in the will of Dame Elizabeth Freville, (dau. of Eliz. Jenison above,) in 1631. 7, ROBERT, master and mariner, Kingston-upon-Hull, bap. 1628-9, succeeded to the Neville burgage, and died before 1669. His son ROBERT, merchant, Hull, joined his mother, Ann, in selling the whole Prebend-row and Tubwell-row properties to the Boulbys (Pierremont, the seat of Hen. Pease, esq., is built on part of *Boulbys' Lands)* in 1688.

In 21 Jas. there was a decree in the Durham chancery against Simon *Jefford*, for "the newe erecting of a horse milne within his burgage, and hawking and grinding of corne of the burgesses, &c., within the Borough, and the coppyholders, &c., within Bondgate and Cockerton."

1640. Aug. 28. The victory of Newburn (where the Scotch artillery so frightened the English army that Sir Thomas Fairfax, one of their commanders, did not stick to own that till he passed the Tees, his legs trembled under him, *) having, in fact, given Leslie's morose army of Scottish covenanters, with their blue ribbons, in profane allusion to Numb. xv. 38, possession of Northumberland and the bishopric, where their extortions were excessive, the bishop fled to Stockton castle, and Dr. Belcanqual, the dean, (who as *runaway Doctor Balcanki* has become proverbial,) was still more hasty in his flight, having written the king's large declaration against the Scots. Strafford received intelligence of the defeat at Darlington, "14 miles south of Durham, and about 26 miles from Newcastle, and as far from York." He had purposed to have been with the army before any engagement; but now endeavouring to make the best he could of an ill business, he sent a messenger to the army, requiring the chief officers to ralley all scattered forces and to keep close in a body and march into Yorkshire. The same day the king advanced to Northallerton towards the army, "being ten miles short of Darlington," anticipating a personal encounter with the Scots, but on the sad news reaching his ear he hastened back to York. On the 30th, the earl issued the following order, in pursuance whereof the majority of the country people drove their cattle and sheep into Yorkshire, and removed most of their families thither also.†

"The Earl of Strafford, Lord Lieutenant-General of his Majesties army, to all Sheriffs, Constables of the Peace, High Constables, and other his Majesties officers:—Whereas his Majesties army is now marching from Newcastle to Darlington, and the villages thereunto adjacent. These are specially to require you, and the rest of the High Constables, to use your utmost diligence in causing to be brought hither, by four a clock this afternoon at the farthest, all such quantities of butter, bread, cheese, and milk, as you can possibly furnish, for the victualling of his Majesties said army, which, being brought hither by the several owners, I shall take special care to see them justly satisfied the price of their commodities; it being his Majesties gracious intention there shall be no burthern nor oppression to his Majesties good and loving subjects. These are likewise farther to require you, that with the assistance of the Justice of Peace adjoyning, you give order for the taking away of all the *upper milstones* in all the mills in that your ward, and to bury or otherwise to break them, that the said mills may not be of any use to the army of the Scotch rebels. You are likewise to require all his Ma-

* Burnet. † Rushworth, ii. 1239, 1240.

jesties subjects to remove all their cattle and other goods, as soon as possibly they can, out of their countrey into places more remote and of greater safety for them, until the return of his Majesty, which will be very shortly, by the help of God, that his good subjects may be powerfully secured from the fears and dangers threatned by the said rebels. Given under my Hand and Seal, at Darlington, Aug. 30, 1640.—STRAFFORD.

A grievous tax of 350*l.* a-day on the county, by the Scots, followed, with hay and straw *ad libitum,* (sans recompense). By the Ripon treaty it was agreed that the Tees should be the bounds of both armies, and that 850*l.* a-day was to be levied out of Northumberland and Durham, Westmoreland and Cumberland,* which burden continued till August, 1641, when the Scotch received 60,000*l.* for disbanding, and government stood indebted to the palatinate in 25,663*l.* 13*s.* 10*d.* in balance.

1640. A royalist broadside is preserved in the Bodleian library, and is published in Richardson's Table Book, Leg Div. i. 199 entititled "GOOD NEWES FROM THE NORTH. Truly relating how about a hundred of the Scottish rebels, intending to plunder the house of M. Pudsie, (at Stapleton in the Bishoprick of Durham), were set upon by a troupe of our horsemen, under the conduct of that truly valorous gentleman Lieutenant Smith, lieutenant to the noble Sir John Digby; thirty-nine of them (wherof some were men of quality) are taken prisoners, the rest all slaine except four or five which fled, wherof two are drowned. The names of them is inserted in a list by it selfe. This was upon Friday about fore of the clock in the morning, the eighteenth day of this instant September, 1640."

The English troop are described by being "not far thence," *i. e.* from Stapleton, and Darlington, Piercebridge, or Blackwell is very probably the station meant, indeed they must have been as near, for the ballad says,

At foure o'th clock i'th morning,
(Let all the rest take warning,)
About a hundred of *these rebels came;*
To M. Pudsey's house, &c.

The English went

——— with all speed to Stapleton,
With all courage they rode on,
While Jockey was drinking his last carouse.

And yet a note at the end says, "At Stapelton, three miles beyond Peace bridge, *wee met with the Scots at* 4 *of the clocke in the* morning at Master Pudseys house in the bishoprick of Durham at breakfast." Those who fled "escaped by Croft bridge, where they say they made their randevous," and two, in their hurry to depart, were drowned as some alledged. On the list of thirty-eight prisoners are "*Sir Archibald Douglasse,* Sergent Maior to Collonel," "*Ja. Ogley* (Ogle), Sergeant to the said Mayor," and "Allen Duckdell, a dutch boy, wounded."

The moral is that as the pitcher may go so often to the well that it may come home broken at the last, so Archibald Douglas may take great preys in 1327, and his namesake be taken in 1640, and that it is well to get your business done before beginning to eat and drink a solid Friday's breakfast.

* Rushworth.

1642. Prince Rupert landed at Newcastle "with armes and ammunition, and, as it is said with money ; such speed hee made thence to his majestie, as his neck had like to have suffered a prejudice *neere Darneton.* The passage at Tinmouth, wotwithstanding the supposed guard of shipping is very easie, the parliament is farre off, and sees not the connivance." *Speciall Passages, &c.*

In November, the Earl of Newcastle (afterwards Marquis) formed the four Northern counties into a Royalist association. Of it the "Fairfax correspondence" says :---

"It is now more than time to provide against this Northern storm. Sir Christopher Wray, Captain Hotham, and Captain Hatcher, with their three troops of horse, and four companies of foot, advance towards the bishopric of Durham—*venienti occurre morbo.* At *Darnton* they have the first advantage, which, by lighting upon a troop of the enemy which resisted little, gave good fleshing to their soldiers. For, besides the routing of it, it struck such a terror through the bishopric of Durham, that itself could not be confident of its security.

Here was the Danish Ambassador met with, whose errands might have merited a worse entertainment than a fair dismissal; but his comrade, Colonel Cochrane, escaped not so well; whose interception (to some well known) was not of the least consequence. From Darnton they proceed to Percie Brigg, a place fortified by the bishopric forces, to make their pass by into Yorkshire. Here they fell upon their works, and not without success neither. Here was the first man of note slain on either side, since this storm begun. Colonel Thomas Howard, with . . . . men of his; and not one lost, nor above three wounded, on the other side.

"But this was a hold too tenable to be forced. From hence our friends take the courage to invite the encountering of my Lord of Newcastle, and press it as a thing feasible. Brave resolutions had need of other judgments ; for, had we had forces enough to encounter them, yet had we without any coercion opened the pass to the Yorkists, to have fallen upon our best friends in the western parts of Yorkshire, which, yet for the satisfaction of those who desired it, was not altogether declined; but how difficult a thing it would be to regain it, after an encounter of equal hazard, every man may safely judge."

The Marquis, Dec. 1, forced the passage, "with great cannon," after a sharp conflict, with a small party of Fairfax's horse, under Hotham, on his march to York.

Blackwell seems to have had a sad time of it. In April, 1646, "by reason of the inordinate multitude of Scotch soldiers who have disturbed the town of Blackwell, the tenants there, who owe suit to this court, dare not come forth from their houses," and are excused. *(Halmot Bks.)* The following extracts from the township books will give an idea of the heavy burdens of our ancestors.

1656. The sesses at Blackwell were "at pound" 2*s*. for repaire of bridges, 14*s*. for the armie and navie, and 4*s*. for other disbursements, among which I find,

For a laime souldier at Jane Harrison al night, 4*d*. For four baggage horses to Allerton, 2*s*. 8*d*. To a souldier going to his colours, 2*d*. Fixing of a common muskitt, 6d.

1657. Aug. 14. To a man that had losse by Dunkirkes, 4*d*. Dec. 29. To a man and wife that had great losse by Dunkirkes, 1*s*. Jan. 9. To a souldier and his wife 2*d*. To two men with a passe from Colo. Wren, 4*d*.

1658. Among the sesses of Blackwell is one of "3*s.* *at li.* for procuring knightes and burgesses."*

For a lame souldier his nightes lodging, 2*d.*—for carriing him to Dar'n on horsbacc, 2*d.*

1659. To a lame souldier with a passe, 4*d.*—for six baggage horses to Allerton, 2*s.*, they receiving 1*s.* a peece ther per hire—for five horses to Durham, who received 1*s.* hire ther a peece, 3*s.* 4*d.*—for three horses to Durham more than state wages, 3*s.*, and for a boy to helpe bacc with horses, 6*d.*—for the constables charges going with them 2*s.*

November the 23*th.* 37 of Capt. Bircle his draggoons quartered in Blackwell for five dayes, at 16*d.* per diem for man and horse.

December the 3*th.* A parte of Capt. Backhouse his horse quartered in Blackwell for twenty dayes, at 20*d.* per diem for man and horse.

December the 24th. Capt. Palmer with ensigne and 70 of his men quartered in Blackwell, one day.

(These lusty fellows, with Lamber's armie, swallowed up a sesse of 45*l.* being 15*s.* per oxgang. Captn. Hoyles and his man with 71 of his footmen belonging to General Lamber, were quartered in Blackwell on the 21st. and received 8*d.* a day.)

1659-60. Jan. 7. 98 baggage horses and 60 men belonging *General Monkes*† were at Blackwell for two nights and a day cast after 8*d.* a man and 6*d.* a horse more than they paid. On the 10th, 108 foot under Colo. Emerson arrived for three days, at the rate of 4*d.* a day for a man, and 40 men and one horse for other three days. On the 19th 39 baggage horses and 20 men stayed one night. 2*d.* per horse, 4*d.* per man, and on Feb. 18, 51 of Capt. Hardstaffe's men were quartered two days at 8*d.* per day, to the total cost of Blackwell township of 18*l.* 0*s.* 8*d.*

1644. April. Several matters of minor warfare took place in the early part of this year between the royalists of the north and Leslie's army, which came to the assistance of parliament. The disasters of the former in Yorkshire dragged the gallant marquis of Newcastle away. He marched on the 13th from Durham to Auckland, and from thence, the next day, to Barnard-castle and Piercebridge. At the same time Leslie broke up his camp at Quarrington and moved to Ferry Hill, and next day to Darlington, where his horse came up with the rear of the marquis's army, and made some prisoners. The marquis entered York on the 19th, and on the 20th Leslie joined Fairfax at Tadcaster. The fatal fray of Marston Moor completed the king's ruin in the north.

1646. The act of Parliament passed for abolishing episcopacy, and another soon followed for the sale of bishops' lands.

A valuation of the temporalities of the bishoprics was taken in 1647, when the sale of episcopal lands commenced. All the residences and manors of the Bishop of Durham are returned. The present rents and profits of Darlington yearly were 262*l.* 5*s.* 1*d.* and the improvements above per annum, 306*l.* 13*s.* 4*d.*—*(Rawlinson's MSS.)*

1651-2. The style of the borough court was "The Court Barron of the Right hon. Sir John Wollaston, knt, John Fookes, James Bunce, William Gibb, Samuell Addy, Tho. Arnold, Chr. Packe, John Bellamye, Edw. Hooker, Thos Noell, Ric. Gilde, Wm. Hobson, Fra. Ash, Jno. Babington, Law. Bromfeild, Alex. Jaaces, Ric. Veiner, Ste.

* The palatinate was admitted to the previously unknown privilege of parliamentary representation during Cromwell's usurpation.

† Why was such an out-of-the-way place as Blackwell chosen in such important marches? See the histories for the effects of Monk's proceedure.

Eswicke, Rob. Meede, and James Storye.* John Middleton, gent., baliffe; and George Dale, gent, Seneschall." In 1657 it was "of the Right Worll. Stephen Eswicke, esq., alderman of the city of London." George Kirby, gent., filled Dale's place. In the same year May 5, Richard Hilton occurs in his stead.

1645. The Court Halmot of our Lord Charles, now king, &c., (the temporalities of the bishoprick being in the hands of the said king by virtue of orders of Parliament.—23 Cha. 1., of John Wollaston, knt., and the other trustees as above.—1652, of the Right Worshipfull Steven Estwick, Esquire, lord of the mannor of Darlington, &c.—1659, of the Right Hon. Robert Lord Tichburne and three others aldermen of the city of London.

1647. April 11. Buried,† George Rickatson of Darlington, gent., a recusant, and consequently a sufferer.

He married, firstly, Alice . . . . . bur. 1623, Aug.; and, secondly, in the succeeding January, Jennet, the widow of Robert Warde, (who had a son Chr. Warde,) and sued, in 1624, for money lent to John Guye, deceased, by Warde, andfor the detention of one clothbayte, damage 3*s.* 8*d.*, for one yarde of sage culloured broade baze sold by Warde to Guye, and one yearde and a halfe of cotton 3*s.* 6*d.*‡

He was steward for the borough from 1617 to 1633 or later, with a slight hiatus in 1626-7 when Richard Mathew, gent., occurs on the change of bishops. In 1625 he and the bailiff, Thomas Barnes, *were both fined in their own court* for overstint on Brankin Moor. The jurors were in truth independent to a fault. In open court, in 1622, Thomas Sober "stubbornlie refused to serve of the lordes jurie saying he could not serve for he had other business to goe aboute," and the following year Richard Wood attended and said he would not serve, Of course, both were fined. The bailiff, Barnes, refused to accept the verdict of the jurors in 1629, and the steward would not hazard the responsibiliy of taking it, so that court was useless. The suitors were little better. Henry Shawe, a defeated plaintiff, was fined in 1622 for saying in court that the jurors "hadd not donne justice betwixt him, Eastgate and Beecroft," and in 1625 John Chambers, jun., for exclaiming *youe will do the devill; I caire not a pinne for your fyninge,* "meaning if he were fyned for his misdemeanor."

Rickatson was probably a backslider, for he served as churchwarden in 1623. He compounded as "George Rixon of Darneton, a convicted recusant" in 1632 with the Recusancy Commissioners at York, by a lease to be made to him of his majesty's *two-thirds* of his lands for 41 years if the same should so long be forfeited by reason of his recusancy, rent 40*s.* All actions, debts, and forfeitures were stopped and remitted for 20*l.*, and the rent was paid till 164.., when the property passed away.

A gentlemanly race of Huttons were settled at Walworth, Cockerton, and Woodham. In 1551, Ralph Hutton of Walwoorth, gent., settles property in Sunderland, Woodham, and Darlington on himself, rem., as to Sunderland and half of Darlington on George his s. and h.; and Woodham and the other half of Darlington on Robert, his younger son, for life, rem. to George. By his will, the same year, this Raff Hooton bequeaths "my soull to Almightie God my Creator and redemor, and to our blessed ladye Saynt Marye,

* These were the parliamentary trustees.

† From an affidavit with the Beckfield deeds, R. H. Allan, esq. The registers were very carelessly kept, and his name does not occur.

‡ Borough Books. The Wards were a gentlemanly family, abounding at Hurworth, Dinsdale, and Darlington. Robert Ward *m.* Janet Roukwood at Darlington, 1595. Robert Ward, borough bailiff 1606, a disclaimer 1615. 1627, Robert Ward of Over Dinsdale, co. Ebor. yeo., settles a third of various borough lands, some ner *Clararubutts*, to uses. Isabel Ward of Darlington, *an old maid*, bur. 1695.

and to all the hollye companye of hevon ; my bodye to be buryed in the parishe churche at Heighington, with my mortuarye due and accustumed." Having three rings of gold not equal in value he gives them to his daughters according to ages, the best to the elder. His heir received the rich portion of " a silver salt with silver spoones and a silver pece." Some burgages in Derlington (not settled) were destined for Robert for life, on paying thereout 20*l.* to his sisters ; if he refused, George the reversioner had the offer, and if this hard-hearted wretch also declined property saddled with so vast an incumbrance (which after all was no joke in those days), parental fondness directed it to be sold, and the money divided among the daughters. Had George left male issue it is evident the younger son would have had to make the best of his bequests while he lived ; however, events turned out favourably for him. The testator left him executor, and appointed his " welbeloved *cosinges* and frendes Roberte Tempest of Holmset,* John Hooton of Hunwike, William Smythe of Eshe, Edwarde Perkynson of Beamont-hill, Francys Perkynson the yonger, and Nycholas Yonge of Heighington supervisors. Then follows one of those legacies, so common in old wills, to a superior. " To my landslord, Mr. William Askughe, knight, and to my ladye his wyfe, and to Mr. William Askughe there eldest son to everye of them *one old ryall for a token to the entente to be good to my children.*" The policy of remembering the heir of a declining feudal lord is self-evident.

George removed to Sunderland, where his sister Mary had married one Biggins, and granted to her and her two sons, Christofer and Henry, his Sunderland lands, and to *Henrye*† and John Biggins, two *other* of her sons, his Darneton moiety. His brother Robert sorrowed to see it go out of the name, and George in his will of 1618, after reciting the grants, and that " my brother Robert seemeth discontented and threatneth sutes whereby my bondes for performance of said grantes may be endangered to the great greafe and troble amongst freinds," offers him a bait of the moiety of all Darneton landes not yet disposed of, and all Woodham, on condition of his confirming the grants, a proposal too good to be slighted. He also gives his niece Margaret Foster 4*l.* *per ann.* out of these lands " not yett passed awaye." He had previously granted a lease of half of them to his sister Margaret Huton, of Sadberge, for thirteen years after his death.

The moiety granted to the Bigginses had been the inheritance of Robert Millott, esq.‡ and was composed of lands in Cockerton and Bondgate. They sold them to George Rickatson, of Darlington, yeoman, formerly when of Thornton in Cleaveland a lessee of the property under George Hutton. A dispute soon arose with George Parkinson of Hagghouse, trustee § for Robert Hutton. Arbitrators in 1624 insisted that " the said parties shall be lovers and freinds," and the moieties of *Hutton's Lands* were set out. Robert and his son Thomas, then gentlemen of Cockerton,|| received property in Hungait, Brankinmoore, Symson's feild and adjoining Cockerton, the Banckeclose, Winterfeild nigh Stooperdaill, Stooperdaill and Kelley Meadowes. Rickatson took the decayed fruntstead and garth next Mr. Thomas Barnes his house, the Beckfeild and Elley hill " being sommer ground frome the gait neere Norgait bridge unto the gait adjoyning

* He was attainted with his son Michael for the Rebellion of 1569, and fled. His cousin Grace married *Cuthbert Hutton of Hutton-John*, in Cumberland, esq. Cuddy's family bore cushions in their shield as well as the archbishop's people of Lancashire, but their crest was two *eagles' heads* erased in saltire enfiled with a coronet. The Huttons of Walworth, and the Bigginses always sealed with the figure of a bird of uncertain genus, neither on shield nor wreath. The Hunwick Huttons bore *an eagle displayed*, with an ostrich's head between two ostrich wings expanded, holding a horseshoe as a crest.

† Had she *two* sons of that name ?

‡ Hutton, then of Durham, bought the property in 1574 of Thomas Melott of Whitell, par. Chester, esq.

§ Robert married Anne Parkinson at Witton Gilbert in 1597,and settled his lands on George and on Wm. Parkinson of Northfolk, co. York, gent., as trustees in 21 Jac.

|| Robert Hutton of Cockerton, gent. bur. 1633 ; Thomas of do. 1630 ; Jane of do. widow 1644-5.

upon Grainge Close Loaninge."* Hutton went to Woodham, and his descendants long held the property there.

One may almost trace the decay of the wearied victim of Protestant persecution. His elaborate signature, the key to his identity in various capacities gives way to a rude mark *Geo. R.* in 1641, and in the following year, he with his son and heir William, an apothecary of Westminster, sells to Wm. Priscott for 445*l.*, two parts of one cottage in Darlington, found by inquisition and certified into his Majesty's Court of Exchequer, and three little crofts not so found,† and Beckfeild and Elley-hill; 100*l* was to be retained till a discharge was obtained from the Exchequer, but in 1646, for 20*l.* allowed out of the purchase money, Rickatson was released from further trouble and Prescott agreed to discharge himself.

Rickatson's fellow officer, Barnes, lost his estates in another way. The following singular document will explain itself.

"xvijmo: die Aprilis 1646. Dunelm.—Whereas Bulmer Priscott late of Darlington, deceased, was indebted to mr. Thomas Barnes of Darlington aforesaid, likewise deceased, as by a bond thereof may appeare, and whereas the said Thomas Barnes and William Barnes, his sonne, were both of them delinquentes against the state so that by ordinance of Parliament the said debt is nowe become due to the state, and upon payment thereof to the estate, the said Bulmer Priscott and his executors and administrators by the said ordinance of Parliament is to be discharged of the said bond and all penaltyes touching the same. And whereas William Priscott, sonne of the said Bulmer Priscott, hath this day payed and satisfyed to this Committee or such as they have appoynted for that purpose the aforesaid summe and debt of Twenty pounds. It is therefore thought fitt, and so ordered by the said Committee, That the said William Priscott and Margarett Priscott his mother, and the executors and administrators of the said Bulmer Priscott shall from henceforth stand and be clearely freed and discharged off and from all penaltyes, payments, forfeitures, and losses touching the said bond, or by reason of any clause or condic'on therein conteyned. Given at Durham the day and yeare above said, RICHARD LILBURNE.—GEO: LILBURNE:—GEO: GREY.—JO: HALL:—G: VANE:—CHR: FULTHORPE. —FRAN: WREN.—CL: FULTHORPE.

Aprill the xvij° 1646.—Received of William Priscott of Darneton, the some of fowerteene pounds, fower shillings, three-pence, in part of twenty pounds oweing by his father Bulmer Priscott, late deceased, to William Barnes delinquent, I say received for the use of the Commonwealth the some of xiiij*li.* iiij*s.* iij*d.* JO. MIDDLETON."

1649. Sep. 27. William Barnes having paid his full fine, the Commissioners for compounding, freed his estates from sequestration. The next day he was in trouble again, and gave a bond for payment of 388*l.* by instalments of 50*l.* which was paid by 1654-5 and the estates freed again. His estates in 1650 let for 148*l.* 6*s.* 8*d.* and stood in the book of rates at 80*l.*; among them occur Glassin sikes,‡ Winmill hills, Hendons,

* Title deeds, R. H. Allan esq.

† Rickatson made sure of a cottage and three little crofts (not found) by passing them to Prescott, who in 1642 settled them on the recusant's daughter Elizabeth and her heirs, rem. Meriott wife of Mat. Cooper and Margaret Rickatson his daughters and heirs, rem. Wm. his son. The roundheads were extremely harsh to the popish recusants, as well as to the members of the national church, yet Prescott, the buyer up of recusants' and delinquents' lands, evidently acted kindly to them on the sly. Matthew and Meriott had loved not wisely, but too well. Their illegitimate son, Christopher Rickatson, alias Cooper, was bap. 23 Mar. 1641.

‡ The statement in page 12 is not quite correct. The moiety of a moiety of a moiety of an oxgang passed from Robert Bowes [of Bondgate] and Margaret [Gregorie] his wife in 1642 to the Turners who bought the other moiety from the Gregories and sold to John Theobalds, 22 Cha. II., who held a field called Polam, "parcel of the office of the pinder in

[Heddons] behind Cockerton, and Thornbeck hill. *Wastell's house* and some other property were sold by him in 1654 to Wm. Priscott, grosier, for *525l. and for one white faced coult.* Micklemyres, an estate of Richard Oswold of *Neither* (Low) *Consley*, was doubly sequestered : first, in respect of John Wytham of Cliffe, a recusant who had lent money on it ; and second, in 1644, of William Barnes who had a lease of it. Oswold sold it to Prescott, and the land was freed from sequestration in 1653,* no trust appearing for Wytham, and Barnes's lease having run out.

1648. Nov. 4. A soldier *under the command of General Cromwale* buried. *(Par. Reg.)* Cromwell at the time was moving rapidly about in these parts, quelling the royalists. He had a meeting with the gentlemen of the four Northern counties, who agreed upon a petition to the Parliament for justice against delinquents, and for a Commission to be sent down to try such as they should apprehend.†

1650. The Parliament caused the King's Arms to be defaced and expunged out of all places of public worship, and courts of Judicature, throughout their Dominions‡: "to make the giddy people forget the Garlick and Onyons of Egypt *they much hankered after.*"

Accordingly we find in the Darlington Church Accounts the entry in 1650, "For defacing the King's Armes 1*s.*" This proved a dear job in the end, for in 1660 occurs "To John Deniss for y[e] drawinge y[e] King's Armes, 1*l.* 18*s.* 6*d.*

1653. An address to Cromwell and his council was presented from "many honest people" of the county of Durham, expressing their gratification at his goodness in performing his engagements "to God and this poor nation," and their adherence to him and his government, but it is signed by only one person of really ancient and considerable family, John Brakenbury. It contains the Darlington names of Jo. Middleton§ and William Priscott. The former

Darlington," (the Polinpole of Hatfield's Survey) and the two moieties as Polam Hill, alias Glassensikes. In 1712 John Theobalds of Brafferton, gent. sold the latter property to the Warwickes of Whitwell in the Whyns, par. Catterick, who parted in 1727 to Robert Hylton, Surgeon. Hylton sold to Lawrence Brockett of Hilton, par. Staindrop, and joined in conveying to the Wensleys three closes called Glassen-sikes, alias Heads Closes, from whom James Allan, esq., purchased in 1754 as Polam Hill alias Glazensykes. Polam had passed to the Lambtons before 1790. I do not know the history of the Barnes portion of Glassensikes. *Title Deeds. R. H. A.* 1675, For lying the stippin stones at Glassinsik 2*d.* *Bondgate Books.*

* Title deeds, R. H. Allan, esq., in the old fashion, being enclosed in a little box covered with leather and lined with black letter scraps. I have seen more than one of these.

† Memorials of the English affairs, &c. (1682).

‡ Britain's Triumphs, a coeval publication.

§ The numerous Johns of this family are rather confusing. JOHN (I.) who *d.* 1575 (see p. 8) left a son JOHN (II.) aged 18 in 21 Eliz. and buried 1631-2 as *senior.* JOHN (III.) who lived at Blackwell-feild-house, occurring as *junior* till his father's death, must have been an extraordinary character. He married five times, and from Thomas, his child by his fourth wife being baptized 21 *Oct.* 1631, we may well imagine of his third wife *bur.* 23 *Mar.* 1630-1, that in popular but expressive dialect he *brust* her heart. I give his wives as they stand. 1. Agnes Lightfote, *m.* 1607, *bur.* 13 Mar. 1610-1 as Anne. (Agnes and Anne were identical in those days). 2. Anne . . . . . *bur.* 27 Feb. 1625-6. 3. Elinor Marshall, *m.* 27 June 1626 (only four months after her predecessor's death) *bur.* 23 Mar. 1630-1. 4. Eliz. Gouldsbrough *m.* by licence 8 June 1631. I have already hinted at the sin attendant on in 1657 was appointed one of the perpetual visitors of Oliver's college at Durham, which, after some show of success, sunk *in silentio* at the Restoration.

Bishop Morton after many troubles, died in 1659, and it is pleasing to observe old Sir Henry Vane, the arch-enemy of Bishops, assisting him to a comfortable income.

1656. May. "The Commissioners for the county of Durham for securing the peace of the Commonwealth," were sitting at Darlington, decimating estates and playing havoc among delinquents.*

Then were the days when sword-slipers abounded and the craft passed from father to son. Anton Eastgatte, of Darlington, Well Row, Sword-sliper, bur. 1662. Anthony Eastgate, of Darlington, Sword-sliper, bur. 1682. A sword-sliper was properly the maker of scabbards, but the word was of much larger acceptation. "*Sword-sleiper*, a dresser or maker of swords; so used in the North of England; and a cutler with them deals onely in knives." *Blount.*

I throw together a few military entries here. 1707-8. A serjeant who travelling through this towne was seized with sickness and died, buried.—1712-3. Robert, son of Dorothy Taylor, a stranger, (and as shee says) wife to John Taylor a lame soldier, bap. —1720-1. William, son of Wm. Hammerton, who pretended to be married but could not make it appear, a dragoon in Captain Morgan's troop of Evans's Regiment, bap.—

this marriage, and the Christian may almost trace retribution in the fact that the christening of her child attended her own burial on Oct. 21 following. 5. Qu. Margaret Glover *m.* with lic. 10 Sep. 1632. The residence of the John Middleton she married is not recorded, and the draper *might* be meant; however, our hero certainly did marry once more, for he had more children,—the first, Jane, being *bap.* Nov. 10 following. This John Middleton of *Millfeild nighe Blackwell*, and John his son of Darlington, yeoman, were trustees for Simon Gifford (who *m.* the elder John's sister Meriol) respecting some Neville property in Welrawe. The younger John sealed with his initials as a merchant's mark and was doubtless the draper. Old John was *bur.* as of Blackwell Field-house, gent. in 1659. JOHN (IV.) was a draper at Darlington; the house at the corner of the Bull-wynd where the bull stands being described in 1666 as late in his possession. His republican and puritanical notions are at once discernable by the scriptural names abounding in his family, John, Nathaniel, Samuel, [William], Joshua, Sarah, Daniel, Deborah, Joseph. He is called *gent.* in the college appointment, and being borough bailiff for the usurpers of the see must have been a man of education and rank. Mrs. Elizabeth Middleton of Durham, widow, *bur.* here in 1689 was perhaps his relict. His eldest child, JOHN (V.) was *bap.* 28 Jul. 1633, occurs as *minimus natu* in attestations as distinct from his father who signed *junior* in 1649, and *d.* in 1659. His brother Joshua was a quaker and a freeholder in 1685. Nathaniel, (second son) was entered of Gray's Inn 1655, held property here, but resided as gent. at Durham; he married Thomasine d. of Richard Lee, of Durham, in 1655-6, and died 1692, leaving a son the famed "Lawyer Middleton," of Bee's diary, JOHN, (VI.) Barrister-at-law, recorder of Durham and Richmond, bailiff of Darlington 1688, who *m.* Anne *d.* of John Harrison, of Scarbrough, "Mrs. Cradock's cousen," 1685. He *d.* in Feb. 1702-3, she in Aug. following, leaving poor little JOHN (VII.) *bap* Sep. 1701, to shift for himself. And now for a bit of episcopal tenderness. His father being "eminent in his profession, and retained for the side against the bishop [Crewe the tory] on elections, held by lease for a footway, a piece of waiste for twenty-one years. Mr. M. died before the bishop nineteen years, and left a son two years old; the lease run to within three or four months. About a month before the Bishop died he refused to renew, and made Grey his secretary enter in his own name. Grey would not let the young gentleman have it under twenty-five years—as much as it would be worth if freehold." (*Gowland's MSS.*) The "young gentleman" was an esquire of Durham, and dying in 1745 ordered his estate to be sold and divided amongst his five sisters (all older than himself).

* Hutton Correspondence, Sur. Soc.

1722. *William, daughter* of Mr. James Ramsey, a Captain in Clayton's regiment, bap. —1729. Samuel Alcock, a dragoon in Capt. Ogle's* troop in Carpenter's regiment, bur. —1737-8. James Cunnengham of Darlington, an old soldier, bur.—1745. John, son of Dorothy Coates of Darlington, wife to Robert Coates, a private man in Col. Batterau's Regiment of foot, of which, the battalion he belongs to, is now, and has been a considerable time abroad, bap.—1750. A male child left in Skinnergate by one John Williams, a disbanded soldier, and afterwards called by the same name, bur.—1760. Alice, dau. of Marjory *Sanctus* (which must be translated *un*holy) wife of Nicholas Sanctus, a soldier in Gen. Offerril's Regiment and who has been abroad in America several years, bap.—1760. Francis, son of Thomas Walker, late of Darlington, Woolcomber, now a private man in the Durham Militia. N.B. This child is about two years old, and, through the parent's neglect, only now baptized, [with a sister Mary, evidently to save expense. The custom afterwards became general.]

In no place was the restoration of the king and bishops hailed with greater joy than in the north. Hope inspired the loyal lines, whose members had wasted their land and lives in the cause of the Stuarts, but they were woefully deceived, and nearly all the main gentry fell into the sere leaf of decay, borne down with sequestrations and incumbrances.

Among the petitioners for the restoration of the "primitive government of the church, for the good of their souls, and the county palatine, for the safeguard and governance of their estate," are the Killinghalls, Wm. Barnes, Edw. Suerties, (Elizabeth Barnes's mother-in-law, wife to John Bucke, of Sadberge, gent., who dyed in the house of Edward Sureties, in Darlington, was buried June 17, 1657,—Edward Sureties, of Darlington, Head Row, bur. 1663,) with numerous neighbouring gentry, such as Ralph Willie, of Croft bridge, who had compounded as a delinquent.

1660. John Cosin, S. T. P. Bishop.

* In "Joaks upon Joaks, or no joak like a true joak" are some comical humours of an earlier military Ogle. According to this history, John Ogle was "the younger son of a gentleman in Northamptonshire ; his fortune being small, he quickly spent it, but his sister, being mistress to the Duke of York, got him into the first troop of guards, under the command of the Duke of Monmouth." Of the tales here related, the following may serve as a sample :—"There being a general muster of life-guards in Hyde Park, and Ogle having lost his cloak at play, therefore he borrowed his ladyship's scarlet petticoat ; so, tying it up in a bundle, put it behind him, then mounted safe enough, as he thought. So away he went, but one of the rank perceiving the border, he gave the Duke of Monmouth some item of it, and fell into his rank again. The Duke, smiling to himself, said, '*Gentlemen, cloak all*' ; which they did, except Ogle, who, stammering and staring, saying, '*Cloak all, cloak all! what a——must we cloak for? It don't rain*' : but not cloaking, the Duke said, '*Mr. Ogle, why don't you obey the word of command? Cloak, sir!*' Said Ogle, '*Why, here then,*' and peeping his head out of the top of the petticoat, saying, '*I can't cloak, but I can petticoat with the best of you*'; which caused great laughter among the whole company."

In 1696, there was a sale of some property of Wm. Killinghall, esq., probably caused primarily by the civil wars. His steward states, that "Mr. Thomas Ogle bought all Mr. Killinghall's moiety of Stainton at 1650*l*., but *bafled* him out of 25*l*. *on account of a gentlewoman Mr. Ogle proposed as a match for Mr. Killinghall,* which if he had married the purchase was to be 1600*l*. onely, bnt [he] was to pay 1625*l*." Robert Colling, of Long Newton, who bought Haughton Field, also diddled him out of 10*l*., "by reason his money had laid ready some time; and Mr. Spearman calling in his 1600*l*. at this juncture wee were glad to comply with him and Mr. Ogle, by reason wee could not raise moneys any other way." Mr. Robert Hilton, of Stockton, bought a farm, &c. for 500*l*., and the lawyers were all growing fat out of the decaying squirarchy.—*Rent Rolls, R. H. A.*

[*Sockburn Church.*]

"It is time to acquaint you with a petty triumph at the river Tees, at my Lords' first approach to his County Palatine, which I believe exceeded not only the entries of all the present Bishops of England into their Bishopricks, but all their predecessors. My Lord having notice that the High Sheriff, accompanied with the whole of the gentry of the county and the militia-horse, expected his approach, took horse a little before his coming to the river side. As soone as he came in sight of the banks the trumpetts sounded, and the gentry, with the troops of horse, all in one body, judged to be about 1000, moved into the midst of the river, where, when my Lord came, the usual ceremony of delivering a great drawne faulchion was performed, after which the trumpetts sounded againe, and great acclamations of the people followed; which ended, they proceeded in order to Darlington."—*Miles Stapleton. Esq. to Sancroft (afterwards archbp. of Canterbury)*, 1661 *Aug*. 23.

"The confluence and alacritie of the gentry, clergy, and other people, was very great, and at my first entrance through the river of Tease, there was scarce any water to be seene for the multitude of horse and men that filled it, when the sword that killed the dragone was delivered to me with all the formality of trumpets, and gunshots, and acclamations that might be made. I am not much affected with such shews; but however, the cheerfulness of the county in the reception of their Bishop, is a good earnest given for better matters, which, by the grace and blessing of God, may in good time follow them."—*Cosin to Sancroft*, Aug. 22, 1661.

I do not wish my readers to be "*troubled with worms*," but let me mention that John Coniers, chivaler, as early as 1396 held by showing *one fawchon*, the manor of "*Sockburn, where Conyers, so trusty, a huge serpent did dish up, that had else eat the Bish-up, But now his old faulchion's grown rusty, grown rusty*." This formidable weapon consists of a huge broad blade, two feet five and a half inches long, fixed in a handle covered partly with ash. On the pommel are two shields :—1. The three lions of England. 2.

An eagle, displayed. The cross is engraved with the stiff, crisped foliage of the thirteenth century, in which dragons, with long leafy tails, form very prominent features. This sword is the title-deed to the estate. On the first entrance of every new bishop of Durham into his diocese, the lord of Sockburn, meeting him in the middle of Neasham ford, or Croft bridge, presents him with the falchion, addressing him with these words:—"My lord bishop, I here present you with the falchion wherewith the champion Conyers slew the worm, dragon, or fiery flying serpent, which destroyed man, woman, and child; in memory of which, the king then reigning, gave him the manor of Sockburn, to hold by this tenure, that, upon the first entrance of every bishop into the county, this falchion should be presented." The bishop returns it, wishing the lord of Sockburn health and long enjoyment of the manor.

The legendary tale is simply this, as described in Bowes' MSS.:—"In an ould manuscript which I have sene of the descent of Connyers, there is writ as followeth: Sir John Conyers, knight, slew that monstrous and poysonous vermine or wyverne, and aske or werme, which overthrew and devoured many people in fight, for that the sent of that poison was so strong that no person might abyde it, and by the providence of Almighty God this John Connyers, knight, overthrew the said monster and slew it. But, before he made this enterprise, having but one sonne, he went to the church of Sockburn in compleate armour, and offered up that his onely sonne to the Holy Ghost. That place where this great serpent laye was called Graystane; and, as it is written in the same manuscript, this John lieth buried in Sockburn church, in complete armour *before the Conquest*."

The grey stone is duly pointed out in a field near the church, as well as a trough, where, like the Laidley worm, the worm drank its milk, bathed itself, and returned to the river. The effigy is that of a fine knight of the 13th century, contemporary with the faulchion, his feet rest on a lion in mortal conflict with a winged *worm* or *ask*, and there is some tradition of the knight being covered with razors, (Lambton-like,) in the infernal fight, and that the horrid reptile is buried under the *grey stone*.

Barbara Conyers, widow, bur. 18 April, 1591. George Conyers, 15 Nov., 1596. William Conyers, of Darlington, *gent*, 14 Mar. 1666-7. George Conyers, a stranger, who *d.* at Cockerton, 2 April, 1667. Mr. William Conyers, of Elton turnpike, 4 Mar., 1749-40. Conyers Blenkinsop, of Darlington, weaver, 16 Mar., 1791. Frances, his widow, of Cockerton, 14 Mar., 1799, aged 82 years, (maiden name, Richardson, *m.* 1763). Catherine Flemming, a stranger, dau. of John F. and Eleanor, his wife, late Conyers, aged 1 year, 17 May, 1809. Conyers s. Conyers Blenkinsop, of Cockerton, weaver, bp. 1782. Wm. Conyers Smith, flaxdresser, and Mary Robson, spinster, both of this parish, *m.* 1807. David Conyers Burton, witness to a marriage, 1779. *Par. Reg.*

The Sockburn family held a burgage in Mathergarthes here, at the commencement of the 17th century. Rich. Conyers, *gent.* a freeholder, 1710. Thomas Conyers, of Oxan Feild House, bought a messuage in Tubwell Row, 1687.

Barbara Kennet, dau. Wm. Kennet, of Sockburn, knt., bur. 24 Jan., 1617-18. Sir William, who was of Sellendge, Kent, *m.* 2ndly, Catherine, dau. Sir John Conyers, and had a dau., Dorothy, bap. 1618, at Sockburn. The Darlington entry probably refers to a child by his former wife, Barbara Egleston, of Essex. The Kennetts, from the Plantagenet to Stuart, were "dancers, tilters, and very ancient courtiers."

Cosin restored the Bishops' manor house at Darlington from a state of complete dilapidation. Here is an account for part of the work.

Aprill 18th, 1668. Collected an assessment by order of a bye law of 3*s.* 6*d.* per Oxgan of all the towneland* of Bondgate in Darlington for paying for the leading of slates,

* 1647. Mem. By custom we find that the tenants of that copyhold land which is called Town-land, are to carry and lead to the manor-house of Darlington, for the use of the

stones, timber, and brick, for the bushop's hall and the toll-booth, which said assessment amounted unto *5l.* 17*s.* 10*d.* 33 oxgan : 3 foote and a half, as apperes at large per this booke. *

	£	s.	d.
Paied, to Mr. Lamb 34*s*., for what the neighbourhood of Bondgate did want, and fall short of ther proportion of draughts as to the aforesaid worke, I say	1	14	0
Pd. to John Longstaff, 10*s*., for leading 3 load of slates, for the bushop's hall, from Engleton, and hehad all the sallery besides, which was dew to us, as 2½*d*. per myle: flackett and wallett filled: and diners which we accompt as good as 4*s*. 4*d*. every load or draught, I say pd. him in money........	0	10	0
Pd. to Tho. Emerson, for leading 2 load of slates from Engleton...	0	6	8
Pd. to Antho. Elgy, for leading 3 load slates from Engleton.........	0	10	0
More for 3 *voages* † to Sedburge, for stones, and once to Brankin Moore, for brick, for bushop's hall........	0	6	8
Pd. the like sum to Chr. Hodgson, for the same worke.............	0	16	8

lord of the manor, wood, lime, and stone, not exceeding a tunnweight, in a wain, for the repair of the toll-booth of the Burrough of Darlington, and for the mills and bake-house in Darlington; and the tenants are to have 2½d. a mile, not exceeding 7 miles from the manor-house, nor going out of the county; and they are to have drink in their flaskets, meat in their wallets, and their dinner when they come home. Witnesses, George Bowbank, æt. 57; Ra. Collin, æt. 60; Robert Branson, æt. 60; William Maine, æt. 56; William Helcott, æt. 60.—*Halmot Court Books, Darlington Manor.*

A verdict of the Jurors of Blackwell, Cockerton, and Boundgate in Darlington, this seventh of October, 1667. Given unto Samuell Davison, esq. stuart of the Halmot Court, houlden the day and yeare aforesaid. First. Whereas ther was a returne made in the Halmot Court, houlden at Darlington, the 23rd of Aprill, 1633, the Coppihoulders was to have but 2*d*. a mile for the leading of wood, stone, and lime, we doe find it an absalute mistake in the Clarke that then was and we have proved it by som of the Jurors of that saide Jury and other witnessis, viz. John Sober, George Garnet, and Thomas Rowter, who was sworne that 2½*d*. a mile is the custommarie due for everie draught, which was alwayes paid or ought to be paid time out of miend; and that they are to have meat in ther wallets, beare in ther flackits, and dinners at ther returne; and that they are not to exceed or goe above seaven miles from the Manner house nor out of the County. Witnes, Thomas Dobson, greeve [of Blackwell]; jurors, George Garnett, Willm. Cornefourth, Cuth. Cornfourth, Willm. Midleton: John Lodge, greeve [of Cockerton]; jurors, John Dennis, Francis Blakey, Mathew Thompson, Edward Robinson: Willm. Priscott, greeve [of Bondgate]; jurors, Jo. Marshall, Rob. Nickleson, Rob. Corson, Ralph Collin. *Bondgate Book.*

In 1799, some accident having happened to the Tollbooth, the lessee of the Tolls, J. Wetherell, esq. of Field House, near Darlington, conceived he had a call on the Copyholders for repairs, and consulted Allan. The antiquary answered, that in Boldon Buke and Hatfield's survey no such service appeared, but that about 1652 and at some subsequent periods, he believed the lessee had claimed assistance, and accordingly inquests were taken at the Halmot Courts to the effect above stated, but that no evidence could be found of the performance of the custom, and that his father, though receiver of the tolls, never claimed it, in fact with the other copyholders, absolutely refused assistance to both Tollbooth and Mills. After hinting that by innovations, perversions, and unwarrantable exactions the lessees of both had forfeited any claim, Allan sensibly observes that were he lessee, he would neither fill the flacketts nor wallets of the copyholders, nor regale them with a good dinner, which would be far more expence than hiring workmen. The correspondence, owing to a report that he was assisting the lessee, was printed by Allan at the Grange press, and circulated among the copyholders.

* Referring to a list of the various owners. The *towne land* is there stated to be liable to repair the Tolbooth, Hall, and Mills. There occurs also a rental of the *Hall-land* 8 oxgangs. The book is the Bondgate book of remembrance.

† Voyages, journies. Still used: "We're ganging for a vage o' staanes."

	£	s.	d.
Pd. to Rob. Sober, for leading 2 load slates from Engleton*.........	0	6	8
More for 2 voages to Sedburge, and one for sand	0	3	7
Pd. to Mr. Daniell Gill, for Fetum farme rent for 3 yeres gon......	0	7	6
Pd. *for repaireing the church garth wall, which belongs to the copi-houlders adjoyneing on lady kirk stile well*.............................	0	15	5
Pd. when we agreed with Mr. Lamb, as the rest of Greeves did ...	0	0	8
Soe this accompt is right ballanced	*5l.*	*17s.*	*10d.*

p. me, Wm. Priscott, Greeve.

Bishop Cosin was not fortunate, the character of one of his daughters, Lady Burton, was marked at least with levity. He speaks of a rogueing letter which he had from Mr. Jo. Blakiston, (with whom he had more causes of quarrel than one,) boasting and triumphing of having ruined his daughter Burton in an ale-house in Westmoreland. His only surviving son, John, whom he solemnly laments in his last will as his *lost and only son* John Cosin, twice forsook the Protestant religion, having been perverted by the Jesuits and at last took orders in the church of Rome. He, in fact, left England under his maternal name of *(Christopher) Blakiston*,† and professed himself in a convent at Paris.‡ No threats or in treaties could persuade him to return, and his subsequent history is unknown.

Mr. Neile (undersheriff, and grandson of the bishop of that name) writes to Mr. Stapylton, in 1661-2, from London:—"I have several times bin with Mr. Cosens, he complains much of all the diskindnes of his father, and hath as fresh in his memory all the little petty things and the great ones betweene his sister and him, with all the circumstances of my Lord's taken his part, and is so full of that that he never talks of religion but only if it be put to him what religion he is of, as I have severall times done, then religion comes in at the tayle of all. There is noe body knows how to begin to worke upon anything, he is of the old humour, so violent and so passionate. This day Mr. Sandcroft was with him, but no hopes of anything, both for his passion and because he talks of going far beyond seas on Thursday at the farthest. - - - The Papists here allow him not a farthing; saith he hath lived ever since he came out of the north of what he brought with him," &c. - - - It appears that this obstinate, and, possibly, weak young man, refused the bishop's very moderate and proper offer to him, to maintain him, *in case he would go and live privately with his brother-in-law, Charles Gerard,* § *in the*

* Slates are not procured at Ingleton, and such entries probably mean then it was the depôt for the materials brought from Shipley and other places, above Barnard-castle.

† The bishop's wife was Frances, dau. of Marmaduke Blakiston, prebendary, of Newton Hall, younger son of John Blakiston, of Blakiston, near Norton. Curiously enough the lady's brother was *John Blakiston the regicide.*

‡ Cosin had been deemed a papist himself while prebendary of Durham, the puritans snapping at some "*cozening* devotions" with a *lewd* title page having I.H.S., &c., on it, and the turbulent Peter Smart carping at every decent ceremonial in the cathedral, and preservation of ancient art.

§ Charles Gerrard, esq., (brother to Sir Gilbert) married Frances, 3rd dau. of Cosin. He was the bishop's housekeeper of Darlington and bailiff of Cotham Mundeval. John *s.* Charles Gerard, [*Garratt erased*] gentellman, bap. 1662-3, [liv. 1671, *d.* before 1673, *s.p.*] ; Ratlife do. 1664 [*d.* before 1673] ; Charles s. Charles Gerrard, esq., of Darlington, 1665, [bur. 1666] ; (In 1673 Vere Gerard was sole child and heiress of the elder Charles); Charles Gerard, esq., bur. 15 April, 1665.—*Par. Reg.*

bishop's manor-house at Darlington, "till his mind be satisfied;" "but I never see man (adds Mr. Neile) so madd as Mr. Cosens when he was told it, *swearing the Inquisition would not be so ill as that, and death itselfe as good.*" Mr. Neile concludes a very long letter by some directions to Mr Stapylton how to send Mr. Cosens some clothes and immediate necessaries, "which he believes my lord will wink at, though he will shew him no countenance openly."

A few days after Mr. Neile writes that Mr. Cosin's journey ended "by com'ande from head and M. B. there, upon some report or other, for the present only to a more retyred lyfe here: he (Mr. Cosin) sayth he here *his man takes upon him to weare his clothes*, w[h] he thinkes, if may speake any thing, is to bould a tricke." In a subsequent letter M. B. is explained to be the head of a college abroad, of w[h] Mr Cosens had become a member, and whose orders he was bound to obey, to cross the seas and repair to head quarters when required. Mr. Cosin is afterwards represented as receiving small sums, sometimes with, and sometimes without the bishop's connivance, from his friends and relatives, and chiefly from his sister, *Lady Gerrard.**

Darlington, July 29th, 1662.—Sir,—I am come as farr as this place to meet the judge, who lay last night at Allerton, but is not come yett. We are prepared to entertaine him nobly at Durham Castle. - - - Pray will you go to the Woolsacke in the Poultre near the Compter, Mr Turford's shop, and there buy a gallon of his best oyle, and barrel of his Luca olives, if he has any fresh and very good come in: buy them in the same long and slender barrills they came in, and tell him the last oyle I had of him was none of his best. You may please to pay him out of my lord's money, and account it with me. If you can find any large good damaske prunes, which are not easily got, we want some for my lord, which pray gett for him. These things you may send any day from Billingsgate to Newcastle. Direct them to Mr. Jo. Blakiston's, at his house in Pilgrim-street, *but not towne-clerke,* Sir Jo. Marley giving him 300*l.* for it, to conclude all disputes, who intendes it for his sonne. Sam. Davison† says, his brother Cosin shall not

* Mary, Cosin's eldest daughter, married Sir Gilbert Gerard, knt. and bart. of Fiskerton, co. Linc.; Sheriff of Durham, 1660; Constable of Durham castle, and M.P. for Northallerton, 1678-9-80. He entailed the title on his issue by Mary (she being his second wife). He was son of Ratcliff Gerard, nephew to the Lord Gerard of Gerards Bromley, and, by Mary Cosin, had issue, Gilbert, aged 4, 1666, (2nd baronet; he had no issue, and the title became extinct, called *Gilbert Cosins Gerard)*; 2. Samuel ag. 2. (The bishop conveyed, in 1668, to his dau. Dame Mary, wife of Sir Gilbert Gerard, the manor of Great Chilton for her separate use. In 1697, Dame Elizabeth Gerard, relict and devisee of Sir Samuel Gerard, knt., of Brafferton, co. York, [who *d.* 1695,] and Thomas Owen alienated it.) 3. George, *b.* after 1671, mentioned by his brother Samuel in 1695; and two daughters, Charlotte and Mary, living 1671. Lady Gerrard re-married Mr Bassett, who became *entitled* to most of the bishop's estate, and, *for preventing disputes,* burnt eight or nine large chests of episcopal records, including the most ancient evidences of the see, at Helperby.

See in Pepys's correspondence, the lachrymose narration of Sir Sam. Morland in 1687, how, while "almost distracted for want of moneys," he was induced by a person whom he had relieved when starving, to marry "a very vertuous, pious, and sweet dispositioned lady, and an heiress who had 500*l.* per ann. in land of inheritance, and 4000*l.* in ready money, &c., &c.;" how he "really believed it a blessing from Heaven for his charity to that person;" how she immediately turned out to be "a coachman's daughter, not worth a shilling, and one who, about nine months since, was brought to bed of a bastard; how, with great difficulty, he got a sentence of divorce; how "Sir Gilbert Gerrard who had kept her ever since Christmas last and still kept her, and had hitherto fed lawyers to support her unjust cause, proceeded to get a certain proctor to enter an appeal against the sentence;" and how he asked sneaking Pepys to "*move the king to speak one word to my Lord Chancellor*" to put an end to his troubles.

Seal of Sir Gilbert Gerard in 1675. Quarterly, 1 and 4 [Arg.] a saltire, [gules] (a crescent for difference); 2 and 3 [azure] a lion rampant [ermine] ducally crowned [or], in the centre the bloody hand of the baronetage. *Crest.* A lion passant.

† Steward of the Halmot Court, and the third of Lady Burton's four husbands.

want. I have a great minde to send his truncke with his clothes, if you know whither I may direct it. If you see him, my service to him: tell him if he will but go to church with us, and doe as others doe amongst them, he may goe to heaven in good company without borrowing the keyes of the gates at Rome. My service to your wife. Your affectionatt, humble servantt, Edw. Arden.—For his hon'ble friend Mr. Myles Stapylton, at Mr. Hinde's house in the new buildings in Lothbury.

"We go, on Saterday, to Sunderland, my lord lies at Etterick's: [Walter Ettrick's, esq., first collector of customs at Sunderland, appointed by Government:] he preaches at Bpp. Wearmouth on Monday, he dines at Sir Tho. Davison's, and sees Stockton, and returnes to lie at Sir Tho. and next day to *Darlington* and so home."—*Mr. Arden to Mr. Stapylton*, 9 *Oct.*, 1662.

Cosin writes to Mr. Stapylton, 1667-8. Mar. 19. I recd. the draught of the lease for Bedbourne parke, &c.—You have mentioned my daughter, not as the relict of Charles Gerrard, but as the wife of T[homas] B[lakiston]* which I have not yet acknowledged, nor was it ever made knowne to mee that they were legally married and whensoever it shall be so made knowne I must professe beforehand that I am extreamly displeased with it, for I was most treacherously used above and for my part shall never owne it.

London, April 19*th*, 1670. *To Mr. Stapylton.*† If T. B. doth not purchase the moiety for one life from Cornefoorth at Darlington mills, hee is an ill manager of his business.‡ If he doth purchase it I will be content to renew it in three liues for nothing

* Thomas Blakiston, gent., sometime of Darlington, and bailiff of that town in 1669, afterwards of Durham, married Frances, widow of *Sir* Charles Gerard, *knt.*, (see Surtees,—but called *esq.*, only in his burial reg.) as above. She was buried in 1668-9, Mar. 10, at Darlington, as his wife. He died in 1710, and was buried in the cathedral, his only daughter Frances (bap. here in 1667), having died under age. George Goundrey to Thomas Blakiston, the office of the punder of Darlington, 1660. *(Halmot Bks.)* He was son of Henry Blakiston of the Gibside family, and had a cousin Roger, who, I suppose, was identical with Roger Blackeston, of Blackwell, gent., whose dau. Elizabeth was bap. 1661-2. An Blaikstone, of Blackwell, widow, bur. 1687. Thomas's great uncle, was Henry Blakiston, of Archdeacon Newton, gent., who *m.* Mary, d. of Henry Tonge, of Thickley and Denton, esq., in 1608-9. In those good old times when daughters stooped to the wisdom of their mothers most dutifully, we almost invariably find the bride at the house of her parent at her first maternal experience, accordingly, in 1609-10, *Mary Blaxton*, the d. of Henry, was christened at Denton, her step-grandmother *Tongue* and Ralph and Elizabeth Blaxston being sponsors; she *m.* Stephen Thompson, of Humbleton, co. York, in 1628. The succeeding children were Sir William Blakiston, of Archdeacon Newton, bp. 1613: (a distinguished loyalist, colonel in the service of Chas. I., knighted at Oxford, 1643, desperately wounded in the attack on Masseys quarters, Sep., 1644, administered to his father 1665; who *m.* Mary, d. of Sir Rich. Egerton, of Ridley, Chesh. bur. 1665 here, and had a dau. Mary, bap. 1631-2): *Henry*, bap. 1619-20, bur. at Heighington, 1623 : *Ralph*, bap. with his twin brother Henry, and bur. 1619, at Heighington. according to Surtees, but entered in the Darlington register: and *Penelope*, bur. at Heighington, 1617.

Henry, of course, accompanied his wife to Denton, *pro tem.* and resided there in 9 Jas. when William Morton, archdeacon of Durham, leased his manor of Archdeacon Newton to Thomas Liddell of Newcastle, merchant; Henry Blakiston of Denton, gent; and Anthony Byerley of Pycall, co. York, gent; rent, 21*l.* In 17 Jas. he again leased it to Ralph Blakiston of Gibside, esq., (created baronet in 1642, and nephew to Henry) for the lives of Henry's children, William and Mary, and Thomas Liddell of Newcastle, merchant. Henry's aunt Ann *m.* George Lumley of Axwell houses, and we find that John Lumley, her grandson, *d.* at Archdeacon Newton leaving his cousin Henry Blakiston, his sole executor, who acquired from his uncle William of Gibside, his "colemynes opened and not opened in the Snype, for 21 years," and 60*l.* and died in 1665, having apparently married a second wife Jane . . . . ., bur. 1659.

† From the original letter in the collections of the late J. Brough Taylor, esq.—The correspondence is gleaned from the extracts given by Surtees.

‡ I do not think that the negociation prospered, as John Cornforth, of Blackwell, gent., (see Charities) devises his moiety to his nephew Whayre Fawcett.

upon condition that if his daughter dyes that fine (which is worth 100*l.* or 80*l.* at least) shall be given to Fanny Hutton* or her mother. As for the other moiety it is allready settled upon Mr Charles Gerard's children who must likewise haue the leaze renewed gratis: but you say nothing of all the goods which my daughter left in the house and the half-yeere's rent at Bedbourne parke and other places which I think belonged to her children by Mr. Charles Gerard more than to her pretended new husband Mr. T. B. and his interloping daughter.† If he cannot agree with Cornefoorth to buy him out at his his owne charges for the benefit of this his daughter, I pray set your mind upon't and try what you and Mr. Kirby can doe to agree with him and buy out that one life which is lost that all the lease and the three liues may be renewed to Mr Charles Gerard's children for whom there is but a sorry provision hitherto made,—Jo. Duresme.

1670. Jan. 31. "You tell me Mr. Mathew‡ *is the Darlington*, and that you thought you had said so in your former letter, which, if you had, I should not have understood you no more than I doe now; nothing being added to the word *Darlington*, though I may guess at it, that you meaned *Darlington Steward*, but it seems you let your penne run too fast."

Cosin died in 1671-2, having left by will 5*l.* to the poor of Darlington.

The Gerrards or Jarratts would be left in a very incomplete state were I not to glance at the unearthly tread of *Lady Jarratt*, who still inhabits the old Manor House. It would be unpardonable to omit the veracious oral chronicles of her being murdered by some soldiery, and her leaving on a wall a ghastly impression of thumb and fingers in blood for ever, and far be it from me to attempt to philosophize on the fact that no scouring or white-washing could ever eradicate it. Yes, there were crimson spots on both wall and floor. And though workhouse arrangements have caused their destruction, poor Lady Jarratt's fate is still remembered. She has but one arm, for the other was cut and carried off by the ruthless warriors, that they might obtain a valuable ring thereon. Like the Silkies and cauld lads of the north, her ideas are composed of mischief and benevolence in equal proportions. Her grand sanctum is a supposed subterranean passage leading from the mansion to the church, which has been *(credat Judæus Apella!)* sometimes discovered but never dared to be explored, yet she is fond of perambulating in the midnight chill and the golden sunrise. She sits on the boundary wall and terrifies children on their road to toil on the opposite side of the stream at the factory which she mortally hates, making a house near it perfectly untenantable. Her musical tastes are not very refined, she jingles the pans of the establishment, and rattles the old pump handle when it is locked with great assiduity. These pranks accompany a very undesirable liking for maidens' bedsides, when "the bedclothes from the bed pulls she, and lays them naked all to view; twixt sleepe and wake, she does them take, and on the key-cold floor them throw;" and generally are perpetrated before births and deaths in the workhouse community. On these occasions she relents,

* The daughter of Lady Hutton, by her first husband Henry Burton, of the Gouldsbrough family. She married Cuthbert Sisson, apothecary.

† His daughter Frances, bap. in 1667.

‡ Richard Mathew, gen., occurs as steward of the borough in 1669.

and *makes coffee* for the sick, and in all her various appearances and offices within doors invariably makes a rustle-me-tustle with her stiff silk dress, but in the town she sinks into the very numerous community of white rabbits scampering about the market place in most gallant style. In fact she is Robin Goodfellow under another name. One thing more must be remembered, an old pair of spectacles tossing about the house in a mahogany case, are most stoutly affirmed by the master (rather fond of a joke, by the way) to be her Ladyship's. In truth, they are rather extraordinary, being large goggle glasses set in a *leather* frame, which has no legs, but is fixed by squeezing the nose, being elastic and capable of distention. The case seems modern.

Lady Jarratt is not the only Darlington sprite associated with coffee. A house in Tubwell Row used to be sorely infested by one who kept grinding away at a coffee mill continually. Its operations were at last traced to a wonderful door, the slightest opening of which hushed the noise, as it does in many a house besides. To show the public fervor for such superstitions, a large dog was once lying in the passage adjoining, from which a lad was most desperately *flayed* by seeing a ghost like a white calf with *eyes as big as saucers.*

1665. Aug. 12. John Glover, of Darlington, vintner, executes a bond for 40*l.* to Charles II. conditioned for paying to his Royal Highness James Duke of York 10*l.* on Mar. 25 next, and other 10*l.* on Sep. 29 following. The money was paid, and the bond rests among muniments relating to a burgage on the High Row bought by Peter Glover, *postmaister*, 3 Jas. I. of Toby and Henry Oswold.

The Glovers were one of the oldest families here, occurring as tanning skins in Skinnergate, and doubtless once made gloves in Glover's Wiend, where their property lay.

In 1615, the heralds disclaimed the coat* of Oswald Glover of Darneton, as a gentleman. His father was Christofer Glover, gaoler of Durham, under Tobie Mathew. Christofer built a house in Owengate, and died in Claypath, in Henry Wandles' house. His successor, in 1613, was Nic. Hodshon, *dictus Makeshift;* the next gaoler, Tho. Sonkey, built a house called *Sonkey's Folly*. This man's widow was *gaolotrix* till 1632, his daughter married Samuel Martin, clerk, *dictus Baggs*. John Peacock succeeded in 1632, his widow was also *gaoloress*, and remarried John Joplin, gaolor, *jure uxoris*, and who was hanged at York 1674-5. These from Mickleton, a goodly company truly. Christopher had the honour of holding the safe custody of the Lady Katherine Grey, one of Westmoreland's daughters, which buxom widow had been *judged*† for too great familiarities with a seminary priest, with the flesh mark in his face. She was to be kept forthcoming in his private house. Whether in this office of 1599 she corrupted him, I will not say, but one thing I know, that Christopher Glover, of Durham, caused Agnes Branson to be *judged* at Darlington, in 1605.‡ So much for the gaoler, now for the postmaster.

* John Glover, the postmaster of 1561, and his son seal bonds with "Ermine, a chief, charged with a label of five points."

† Censured in reputation. "Judge not, lest ye be judged."

‡ Branson House, the property of Wm. Bewick, esq., in Cockerton road, stands on the old estate of her family. Little Isabella, *notha*, died an infant. Robert Tailbois, of Thornton Hall, who died a prisoner in Durham Gaol, leaves "*to Christopher Glover, my keeper*, for my dyet in the gaole and for my other expences, after the rate of 10*s.* weekly since the sixth day of Februari, 1603; to my brother John Barnes, (he had married Bp. Barnes's

"John Glover, master of this ho'* and postmaster of Darnton," attests William Williamson, of Bushopaucland, gent's setting over to Peter Glover, tanner, of the wardship marriage and custody of the body and estate of George Marshall, son of a dead tanner, in 1591; and in 1596, George Bainbrigge, of Darneton, gent., conveys his *postshippe* of Darneton to Peter, (son of John ?)

In 1619, Toby Oswold† of Barmeston, co. Durham, gen., dolefully petitions " Sir Francis Verulam, the Lo: chancelor," against Peter. In 42 Eliz. he had possessed 1 cubbord with 3 great puter chargers 6*l.*; 1 counter or cubbord with a fourme 40*s.*; 1 long table, with a long-settle and a fourme 30*s.*; 1 other lesser seate 6*s.* 8*d.*; certain iron barrs and crakes 10*s.*; 1 standing bed steed 40*s.*; 1 long wrought table with a settle 40*s.*; 1 other standing bedd steed 20*s.*; 1 other bed steed 3*l.*; 1 beafe ledd 4*l.*; 1 cawell with a table 40*s.*; 16 firdales 20*s.*; total 25*l.* 6*s.* 8*d.*, in his burgage at Darneton. In 17 Eliz., he had let the burgage to Glover, "and your orater being then a young man, and being unwilling to sell the goods aforesaid," had allowed Glover the use of them till he should demand the same, and accordingly Glover received them as they stood in the hall, parlor, chamber over the hall, chamber over the mell doores, the little house behind the shopp, the kitchen, the loft, and the oxhouse, in the said burgage. After this Oswold sold the burgage to Glover, about 8 years before his petition, and demanded the goods or their value. But he, "not meaning nor intending to deale soe frindly and kindly with your orator as he deserved," refused to do so, and detained the goods, to the damage of 30*l.* to the orator. The latter then prays that as many of the witnesses were "old and decrepit," or did "remaine in remote severall places farre from the county of Durham," and could not conveniently be brought to any one place to give testimony by a tryall at the common law, and as he was persuaded that hee, the said Peter Glover, being a plaine dealing man, will truly confesse the receyving, &c.," the Lord Chancellor would issue a writt of subpœna, commanding Glover to answer the petition. An order was directed to John Lisle,‡ James Todd, Tymothy Barnes, and Robert Ward, gents., to appoint a day to receive defendant's answer.

dau. Eliz.) for my wyfe's dyet for three years at 30*l.* yearly," Proved, 1606.—Helen Tailbusse bur. 1591.—Elizabeth Tailbus, bur. 1597 (in the plague, she was, I fancy, the widow of the unfortunate Thomas Norton, sen., who re-married Anthony Taylboys). Margaret Tailbois, of Darlington, widow, bur. 1607.—*Par. Reg.*

Thornton Hall, on the road to Staindrop, is an interesting relic of the Tailbois family. It has much altered by the Salvin and Bowes races, but much of the projection, towards the road, is Perpendicular Gothic, being ornamented with right ugly nondescript animals near the top. In the upper story of this par tis a fine Jacobean ceiling with the arms and crest of Tailbois, and the devices of an anchor; fleur-de-lis, and escallop, in the pannelling. A still finer and older one is on the ground floor, intersected with beams carved with elaborate late Gothic tracery, and adorned with ciphers on the bosses and half way along the beams. The roof is evidently shortened, but the part remaining contains ciphers disposed as follows:—

R ∀ I Ⅎ A E ⊥ ∀ ˥ B	*Query*	R A I F A [N D I A N] E T A L B O I S [*date*]

evidently pointing out Raife Talboys, who *m.* 2. Jane Bertram. and *d.* 1591, as its constructor.

* The place where deeds are executed, is frequently set forth at that time. What would a modern lawyer say to such an attestation as that on a deed which "was sealed in the shoope of Francis Oswolde, betweene the howres of ix. and x. of the clook before noon, xvj. day of Februrij, 1571. ?" Glovers house was no doubt the later Post-house or Talbot Inn.

† 31 Eliz.; Francis Oswald settled the *Greets* on the marriage of his son John with Eliz. Glover.—John Oswald, a disclaimer, 1615.—1621-2, Cuthbert Smith and Elizabeth Oswold clandestinely married in the night, at Sedberge.—*Par Reg.* 18 Jas. I., presented that Ra. Nicholson prevented Rob. Oswold from placing his 'ladder, to mend said Robert's house. Ordered that he be allowed to let him do so. *Halmot Bks.* The Oswolds migrated to Coniscliffe.

‡ A lawyer, of Durham city, who sported a lion rampant on his seal the arms of De

Peter the *postmaister*, by will, Apr. 30, 1625, as a "yeoman, not sick in bodie, but *partly* infirme," leaves to his daughters, Jane, as yet unadvanced in marriage, 100*l.*, to be paid in 1½ year after her marriage; Margaret, (in the same predicament, she afterwards married John Middleton), 100*l.*, and Dorathie 100*l.*, to be paid her on the day of her marriage. This contingency happened very soon, as soon indeed as Peter became *fully* infirm, as appears from the two extraordinary entries, joining each other in the register. "1626, May 11, Charles Husband, [a lawyer, who wrote an exquisite hand,] and Dorothy Glover, married by licence.—12, Peter Glover, father of the said Dorothy, of Darlington, buried."—(Did the excitement kill the old man ?)—He leaves "to the poore people of the parish of Darlington, to be distributed at the church door 4*l.*—John Glover my son and heire, executor—my righte trustie, and dear beloved brother-in-law, John Ketlewell, and Jasper Ketlewell, supervisors; to either of them a Jacobus peece of gold, as a token and pledge of my love and last farewell, referringe every ambiguity (if any shall arise) in this my will, to be expounded construed and explained by my supervisors."

John *m.* Eliz. Stainsby, and had a son John, who was postmaster in 1651. He had male issue, John, vintner, (who was bound as in the text,) Peter, a clothmaker, of Holtbeck, co. York, Cuthbert a hotpresser, of London, and Benjamin, a mariner, of Newcastle. They sold the High Row property, (bounded on the South by Chairegate or Glover's Weand, and long after the posthouse*), to Robert Clifton, a sadler, of Cliffe, in 1681. The fixtures were in "the little chamber, the lad's chamber, Rob. Shippard's chamber, Elizabeth Harrison's chamber, the lord's chamber, the parlor, the hall or forehouse, the buttery," and included all things in the stables except "Nyne fardailes in the farr stable."

1669. "For lousing us from good behavor, 14*s.* 4*d.*" *Par. Bks.* The town had been bound over to its good behaviour, and was *loused* from the recognizance.

I throw together one or two more items.—1685. Paid at the visitation, for the proclamation concerning the rebells, prayer bookes and court fees, 7*s.* 6*d.* [Monmouth's Rebellion.] 1770. To Mary the daughter [of] Haward, a solgar, to cloth hir for sarvis, 10*s.*—1798. Calling a meeting on government account, 1*s.* 6*d.*—1800. Postage of a list of armoriall bearings pasting up at church, 1*s.* 0½*d.*

1674. The Hon. Nathaniel Crewe, Bishop. He afterwards became Lord Crewe of Stene, co. Northamp., and was a man made of courtly meanness, but *Crewe's charity* throws a veil over all. I have been told that he was the last bishop who resided at Darlington Manor House.

1677. In a return of Blackwell lands "at the full rack according to a warrant to us directed for the same purpose, and for raising the summe of 584,978*l.* 2*s.* 2½*d.* according

Insula. He occurs as bailiff of our borough court from 1606 to 1622 when he died, and was once sued therein by the grassmen for hirdwage on Brankin moor, 1*s.*, buys of the daughters of John Pape, deceased, in 1606, *Pichall*, two closes between Yarm lane and Turner's close, sometime of Wm. Pudsey, of Barford, esq., sells *Huntington's Close* to Thomas Barnes, in 1618.—Barbaria Lisle, widow of Darlington, bur. 1630.

* Sold by Hen. Burdon, *inholder*, in 1567 to Francis Oswold, merchant. The sign of a talbot springs forth in metal, and one windy day, the tongue being corroded flew off. Whereupon it passed into a popular joke that *the wind was once so strong at Darlington that it blew a dog's tongue out.* I have not mentioned this inn in p. 126, as the *sign* does not occur at the time there alluded to. It, however, was evidently the Posthouse from the 16th century downwards.

to act of parliament, for the speedy building of 30 ships of warre," Mr. Tobyas Ewbanck occurs as chief owner, rent 105*l.*

1678. Nov. 21. "Laid on a sesse of 9*d.* per oxgang at Blackwell, for the Trainband going to Durham. From other entries I find that the trainbands used to assemble at Bellasse Head and Hunwick Edge. The word militia first occurs in 1687, and is called *Mallitia* in 1691 in the Blackwell books.

1679. Blackwell township paid 6*s.* for the charge of leading one load of lime to the *Old Hall;* and 4*s.* towards the repairing of the *Tollbooth staires;* and in 1680, for leading slates and lime to the same buildings, 8*s.* per load.

1682-3. Jan. A company of troopers passing from Darlington to Durham are said to have assisted Mr. Brass to seize the probably insane Andrew Mills who as is well known, on Brass and his wife's absence on a Christmas visit murdered their three children at their residence near Ferryhill.

Tradition adds that the wretch's intention as to the youngest child was half frustrated by her entreaties and promises of bread, butter, and sugar, and some toys, but that in going of the room he met in the passage a hideous creature like a fierce wolf with red fiery eyes, its two legs were like those of a stag, its body resembled an eagle, and was supplied with two enormous wings; this apparition addressed Mills with a most unchristian croak, in the words

Go back, thou hateful wretch, resume thy cursed knife,
I long to view more blood, spare not the young one's life.

And the injunction was obeyed. It is said also that the old Brasses on their return heard the most dreadful howlings of dogs and screechings of owls, the horse bolted continually, and at last, at the place where *Andrew Mills's stob* afterwards stood, would not move a peg more. Andrew sprung from a thicket, and on enquiry told his horrid deed. The mother fell to the ground, and the troopers who were passing at the time helped to secure the murderer. Mary was conveyed to a place of safety, Dobbing again went on, and the hapless father arrived at his bloody home. There is a further supernatural story of Andrew's living several days on the stob or gallows from whence his agonised cries were heard for miles round; and of the people of Ferry Hill and the adjacent hamlets actually deserting their dwellings till life had departed from the poor wretch. A beautiful tale connects this surviving with the tenderness of a peasant girl beloved by Mills, who brought him milk every day, and fed him through the iron cage in which his tortured limbs were bound. He had persisted in his confession, that he had acted on the immediate suggestion of the devil who bid him *kill all! kill all!* The eldest girl struggled with him for some time, and he did not murder her till he had broken her arm, which she had placed as a bolt to secure the door of the inner chamber, where the younger children were sleeping. *Children* is not perhaps a proper expression, although used on their tomb, since the daughter who was about to be married was aged 20, the son 18, and the youngest daughter 11. Mills was 18 or 19. The stob was cut to pieces for charms.

1684. To Mr. Bell, with a letter from London with the names of the Royal family, 6*d.*---*Par. Bks.* This is a curious item; for it shows that the mercuries, diurnals, and intelligencers of the day, were not deemed sufficient for satisfactorily advertising public events to the minister and people.

1686-7. Charges for carts and carriages with baggage to Allerton and Auckland occur in the Blackwell books.

1688, July. "Articles to come 1*s.* 3*d.* Tarr barrell 1*s.* 6*d.* For new lock and stock 10*s.* 2*d.* *Blackwell Books.*

1688-9. 3 red coats for the trainband cost each 6*s.* 6*d.*

The following items occur in the parish books of St. Mary, in the South Bailey, Durham:—1688, Sep. 21. Six horses and two men to Darlington, 2*s.*—1689, April 2. A man and horse to Darlington with Capt. Delaval's company, 1*s.* 6*d.*—June 6. Two horses to Newcastle with General Ginkell, one with Capt. Delaval to Darlington, 11*s.* 6*d.* —Oct 6. Two horses to Darlington with the Princess Anne's dragoons, 7¼*d.*—Dec. 5. Twelve horses with the Danes to Darlington, 3*s.*

James II., while Duke of York, had, in 1660, married Anne, daughter of the celebrated Hyde, Earl of Clarendon, who, when a young barrister, married a female of obscure parentage, and there are some who assert that she was the daughter of a laundress at Darlington: this, however, is very uncertain, and the more probable opinion is that she was the daughter of a brewer, in a small town somewhere in the south of England. Whencesoever sprung, Hyde's humble favourite became grandmother of two reigning Queens of England, and, by her prudent, amiable, and exemplary conduct, secured the respect and admiration of the exalted circle in which she moved.*

1689. May. Blackwell raised 4*l.* 8*s.* 6*d.* for the first 3 months of their Majesties' supply of 70,000*l.* per month for 6 months.

1692-3. "Then proportioned the aid sess for their Majestyes K.W. and Q.M. for the year 93 for carrying on a *vigorous* warr against *Frances*, the towneshipp of Blackwall was cast that every 20*s.* in the book of rates to be 1*l.* 11*s.* 3*d.*—The sum to be raised quarterly is 9*l.* 2*s.* 7*d.*" This payment continued at least till 1696. Arthur Prescott was head owner, Major Richardson the next. The ardour of the rustics is quite refreshing.

1693. 4 April. "Laid on a sesse for the trainband being to meet at Darlington, on Friday next, being the 7th April, of 10*s.* per *li.*, for fixing armes with 2 musquetts stocks and 2 swords, scabards, and a sword and belt bought of Wm. Middleton, at 8*s.*; 12*d* a peece, Muster Master, beside there pay. Sesse raised, 2*li.* 2*s.* 3*d.*, q' how disposed on." *Blackwell Books. Trophe* money occurs as paid to the high constable, on May 3, this year.

1703. Thoresby, the Antiquary, sets down that on

"May 18. We passed the river Tees, in a fruitful country, which produces very large sheep; we stayed little in Darlington, hastening to Durham."

"May 20. We baited at Ferry-upon-the-Hill, which answers Kirk Merington (in the other road) as to its lofty situation, and got in good time to Darlington; viewing the town, where, by the encouragement of the late Queen Mary, is settled the linen manufacture; they make excellent huckaback and diaper, and some damask, &c. Went to transcribe what monuments I could find in the church; was pleased to find there several young persons met to sing psalms, which they performed very well, with great variety of tunes, &c., *but was concerned to see the adjoining house of the Bishop of Durham converted into a Quaker's workhouse.* There being a funeral, we had the happy opportunity of public prayers, which was comfortable. 21. The river Tees not being fordable by reason of the late rains, we went about by Croft bridge, where Sir William Chater has a seat, by which means we had the convenience of seeing the Hell-Kettles, the best

* Gordon's Guide to Croft, &c. I do not believe one word of the statement. I always understood that Hyde *m.* 1st. a daughter of Sir Geo. Ayloffe, who *d. s. p.*; and 2nd, Frances, dau. of Sir Thos. Aylesbury, who had with many other children, this daughter Anne.

W

account of which is in my late kind friend Dr. Jabez Cay's letter, inserted by Dr. Gibson in the new edition of the Britannia, p. 782."

Thoresby often passed through Darlington. At the age of 23 he came expecting to have met with Captain Widdrington here. This was on 6 April, 1680. On the 7th he was up early and went on to Durham where he found him, and thence to Newcastle, returning on the 8th. He and the Captain seem to have got rather too jolly occasionally in London, especially once "late on Saturday night at Captain Widdrington's, where was too great plenty of the strongest liquors, which afflicted me by their conquest of my friend, *which being partly on my account, I desire may be for my humiliation.*" On May 17, 1680, he was here again with his uncle, Michael Idle, and "carried pretty sister Abigail (her dear father's picture) along with me, and got safe to Darlington, 40 long miles, and yet she not at all weary." He passed through on his return from Newcastle on the 22nd following, "a most stormy rainy day." His father had died the preceding year, and the antiquary reigned in his stead as a merchant.

In September, 1681 and 1682, he was again in the town on his northern peregrinations.

A family of Thursbie, or Thoresby, occur at School Aycliffe and Brafferton as early as 1582. The following entries are from our own register. Ralph Thursbie, of Archdeacon Newton, buried at Heighington, 24 Aug., 1622. George Thersbey [a sadler], of Darlington, occurs 1690—1698. Thomas Thursby, attorney, and Jane Theobalds, spinster, married 4 June, 1705. Jane, wife of Mr. Thomas Thursby of Brafferton, attorney, buried 7 April, 1717. Affidavit that she was duly buried in woollen in obedience to the statute, made 12 April.

In Heighington churchyard is an ancient decorated coffin-lid bearing a cross, at the foot of which is a nondescript animal enclosed in a crocketted arch. There is a sword at the side, half the cross bar of which is cut off to make room for an inscription in ordinary Roman capitals :—IO : THVRSBIE . HIC . IACET.

The name is embalmed in the memory of John de Thoresby, archbishop of York, 1360, who was a diligent preacher and a positive reformer. "Hear God's law," said he, "taught in thy mother tongue, for that is better than to hear many masses."

In Thoresby's caustic remark about the workhouse is seen an evident prejudice against the Friends, although he was himself a dissenter. "1683. I cannot wholly omit my concern for some poor deluded quakers who were hurried down this street to York castle in greater numbers than was ever known in these parts. The Lord open the eyes of one party, and tender the hearts of the other. . . . 1702. With W. P. and another quaker about business ; found under a pretence of a holy simplicity, downright treachery, was tricked out of two guineas. Lord, pardon them ! "

Chapter IV. Annals from the Accession of George I. to the present time.

1721. William Talbot, Bishop. The abuses created in the palatinate by his son-in-law, Dr. Sayer and others, were crying enough to produce the famous Enquiry by Spearman in 1729. Amongst them was the corrupt granting and entering surrenders and copies of land as copyhold, which really were freehold, as in the case of the Pindar-close* at Darlington to John Theobalds, who afterwards mortgaged it to Mr. Warwick, as copyhold, yet again sold it as freehold to a third person, who, upon an ejectment brought, recovered it; and to make the fraud more colourable, the officer (Mr. Hutchinson) had entered a sham title in the paper-books, and contrived many surrenders from several persons, deriving in all appearance a plain title, and many persons successively interested for the space of 60 years, though not a word of truth or fact occurred in the series of that descent and title.

1730. Edward Chandler, Bishop.

It may be remembered to the honour of Bp. Chandler, that he never sold any of his patent offices, tho' he was offered several hundred pounds by Mr. R. R., an attorney at D——, for the clerkship of the Halmot Court, vacant on the death of Mr. John Mowbray, in 1735, which he nobly refused, and gave to his secretary, Mr. Whitaker, who was succeeded by Mr. Wyndham. On Mr. Ralph Trotter's surrender of the two patents as keeper of Birtley Wood and *housekeeper of the old palace at Darlington*, he granted the former to Mr. Christopher Johnson, his receiver, for three lives, and the latter for life, and also appointed him county clerk; which two last offices he still holds.—*Hutchinson*.

About the year 1730, Mr. Edward Walpole (afterwards Sir Edward, Knight of the Bath) returned from his travels on the continent, where the munificence of his father, the famous statesman, had enabled him to make a brilliant figure; and so very engaging was he found by the ladies, that he had no other appellation in Italy than that of "the handsome Englishman." It appears that at the time Mr. Walpole on his return lived in Pall Mall, there was opposite, and nearly facing Carlton House, a ready made linen warehouse, where gentlemen procured everything necessary for their wardrobes, such as gloves, &c. This shop was conducted by a very respectable female named Mrs. Rennie, assisted by several others, among whom was a pretty, interesting girl, named Mary Clement. Her father was at that time, or soon after, a postmaster at Darlington, a place of 40*l.* per annum, on which he supported a large family. This young woman had been bound apprentice to Mrs. Rennie, and employed in the usual duties of such a situation, which she discharged (as the old lady used to say) honestly and soberly. Her parents, however, from their extreme poverty, could supply her but very

* See p. 138, note, all the properties mentioned in which are treated in the transactions there stated as copyhold. Spearman must be received with caution.

sparingly with clothes or money. Mr. Walpole often passed a quarter of an hour in chat with the young women of the shop, and there was one of them, the attractive Mary Clement, who could make him forget the Italians and all the beauties of the English court. Mr. Walpole observed her wants, and had the address to make her little presents, in a way not to alarm the vigilance of her mistress, who exacted the strictest morality from the young persons under her care. Miss Clement was beautiful as an angel, with good, though uncultivated parts. Mrs. Rennie had begun to suspect that a connection was forming, which would not be to the honour of her apprentice. She apprised Mr. Clement of her suspicions, who immediately came up to town to carry her out of the vortex of temptation. The good old man met his daughter with tears; he told her his suspicion, and that he should carry her home, where, by living with sobriety and prudence, she might chance to be married to some decent tradesman. The girl, in appearance, acquiesced, and left the room shortly afterwards, as her parent imagined, to prepare for her return home, but she had other and far more ambitious plans. Whilst her father and mistress were discoursing in a little dark parlour behind the shop, the object of their cares slipped out, and without hat and cloak ran directly through Pall-Mall to Sir Edward's house,* at the top of it (that afterwards inhabited by Mrs. Keppel) where, the porter knowing her, she was admitted, although his master was absent. She went into the parlour, where the table was covered for dinner, and impatiently waited his return. The moment came; Sir Edward entered, and was heard to exclaim with great joy, "you here!" What explanations took place were, of course, in private; but the fair fugitive sat down that day at the head of his table, and never after left it. The fruits of this connection were Mrs. Keppel, the first; Maria afterwards Lady Waldegrave, and subsequently Duchess of Gloucester, the second; Lady Dysart (the wife of Lionel, fourth Earl of Dysart, died sans issue 1788), the third; and Colonel Walpole, the fourth; in the birth of whom, or soon after, the mother died. Never could fondness exceed that which Sir Edward always cherished for the mother of his children; nor was it confined to her or them alone, but extended itself to her relations,† for all of whom he in some way or other provided. His grief at her loss was proportioned to his affection: he constantly declined all overtures of marriage, and gave up his life to the education of his children. He had often been prompted to unite himself to Miss Clement by legal ties, but the threats of his father, Sir Robert, prevented his marriage; he avowing that if his son

* This incident is irreconcilable to a statement in some editions of this true romance, that Walpole was lodging at Mrs. Rennie's, and so became acquainted with Fair Mary of Darlington.

† Hammond Clement, esq. occurs in our registers as Ensign in Brigadier General Price's regiment of foot in 1747, and in 1759 as one of the Clerks to the Exchequer at London when his son *Edward* was buried. Captain Clement and Mr. John Clement, both of Darlington, received funeral papers and gloves at John Killinghall's funeral in 1762, and in 1781 John Clement was a banker here.

married Miss Clement, he would not only deprive him of his political interest, but exert it against him. It was, however, always said by those who had opportunity of knowing, that had Miss Clement survived Sir Robert, she would then have been Lady Walpole.

In the year 1758, her eldest daughter, Laura,* became the wife of the Hon. Frederick Keppel, brother to the Earl of Albermarle, and afterwards Bishop of Exeter. The Miss Walpoles now took a rank in society in which they had never before moved. The sisters of the Earl of Albemarle were their constant companions, and introduced them to persons of quality and fashion; they constantly appeared at the first routes and balls; and, in a word, were received every where but at court. The shade attending their birth shut them out from the drawing-room, till marriage (as in the case of Mrs. Keppel) had covered the defect, and given them the rank of another family. No one watched their progress upwards with more anxiety than the Earl of Waldegrave. This nobleman (one of the proudest in the kingdom) had long cherished a passion for Maria. The struggle between his passion and his pride was not a short one, and having conquered his own difficulties, it now only remained to attack those of the lady who had prepossessions; and Lord Waldegrave, though not young, was not disagreeable. The marriage took place in 1759. Her very amiable conduct through the whole life of her lord, added respect and esteem to the warmest admiration. About five years after their marriage, the small-pox attacked his lordship, and proved fatal. His lady found herself a young widow of rank and beauty. Had Lord Waldegrave possessed every advantage of youth and person, his death could not have been more sincerely regretted by his amiable relict. At length she emerged again into the world, and love and admiration everywhere followed her. She refused many offers; among others the Duke of Portland loudly proclaimed his discontent at her refusal. But the daughter of Mary Clement was destined to *royalty!* The Duke of Gloucester was not to be resisted, and two children, a prince and a princess (the late Duke of Gloucester and the Princess Sophia Matilda of Gloucester) were the fruits of their marriage, and hence it came within the bounds of *probability* that the descendants of the postmaster of Darlington might one day have swayed the British sceptre.†

1740. Immediately after a very severe winter the price of grain arose considerably, and a great scarcity was apprehended. There were great riots at Newcastle and at Stockton, where the mob rose when they saw some corn shipped.---"June 3. Our rioters still continue, and am much afraid will grow worse, and have a large reinforcement from the country; for there was a riot at Darlington yesterday, and they threaten to come to Stockton.---Nov. 30. A turbulent spirit is in every town in these parts, and some disturbances

* Occasionally given as Louisa.

† Flowers of Anecdote. Globe Newspaper, 7 Feb. 1845. Private information by favour of Mr. James Ferguson of Staindrop, and tradition.

have been at Darlington and Bernard-castle, and a little here."* In Aug., 1795, wheat was so scarce, that at Darlington and many other places it sold at a guinea per bushel, and oats at *5s.*†

1745. The loyalty of the Friends in Darlington was very remarkable at the time of the rebellion. On receiving intelligence that the Duke of Cumberland was coming from the south at a wintry time when the weather was severe, and by some means hearing that the soldiers were badly clothed, and lacking a sufficiency of creature-comforts, they in a most praiseworthy manner set to work and manufactured a great number of flannel waistcoats, which were ready for the poor men on their arrival at Darlington, and which, as the old lady‡ who remembered the Duke's march and gave this curious fact, remarked, might possibly be one cause of the Prince's defeat at Culloden. Less zealous were the farmers of Newtown, for they, ere the Duke approached Great Aycliffe, conveyed all their oxen and horses (which they considered might be of service to the forces, in carrying their carriages and luggage along the highway) and secreted them in a deep ravine and lonely, about a mile distant, and ycleped by foxhunters Byers Gill. There was, indeed, some excuse for this conduct, as many farmers in the neighbourhood had their beasts of burden taken away by compulsion along the road for many miles, without a recompense, some of which were never restored to the owners.

At that time lived one Gideon Gravett Phillips, esq., a Friend, a zealot in politics, and a liberal, upright man. An idea of his character may be formed from his obituary in the British Magazine for March, 1800 :---"Died at Darlington, in his 90th year, G. Phillips, esq., a quaker ; he has bequeathed the sum of 500*l.* to Mr. Combe the present lord-mayor for the city of London, and 100 guineas to Mr. Sheridan. At the late election of a lord-mayor Mr. Philips entered with the utmost zeal into the interests of Mr. Combe, and during the whole of the election was as warmly affected for the same, as if his own life and honour had been involved in the issue. He then resided at Darlington, and waited impatiently every day for the arrival of the papers to know the result. When the election terminated in that gentleman's favour, he was transported with joy, and put him down in his will for 500*l.* as a testimony of his approbation of his public character and conduct." This rural patriot lived in the house now Mr. J. H. Mowbray's, in Northgate, and when a body of the troops, marching north in 1745, were passing through and were quartered for the night on the private inhabitants as well as the inns, he received the eight or ten men allotted to him with great hospitality and plied them with ale and viands most vigorously, adding thereto a weighty

* Wm. Barker of Stockton's correspondence. Brewster, 152.

† MSS. of Robert Allan, esq. Sunniside.

‡ Mrs. Simpson, of Aycliffe. The same alacrity prevailed all over the north. See Sykes, i. 176. The Friends furnished 10,000 woollen waistcoats in four or five days at their own expense. They were made to double over the breast and belly, under the soldiers' own clothing.

breakfast before they departed. They, however, only marched to Durham and then returned, their services being too late.*

On the 25th September, there had been a muster of militia on Framwellgate Moor, to which Blackwell furnished a quota of six men at the expense of 19*l.* 17*s.* 8*d.*

On the 21st of October, the purveyors of General Wade's army arrived at Darlington and employed all the bakers in that town to get bread ready against the arrival of the army, then on its march to Newcastle.† St. George's Dragoons arrived shortly after,‡ and on the 31st General Wade's horse, Montague's horse, and St. George's dragoons were at Durham. Previous to the arrival of these and other forces his Majesty's Royal Hunters from Yorkshire had passed through, with the brave General Oglethorpe at their head; they made a most gallant appearance, being well equipped with martial accoutrements and mounted on fine horses, and arrived at Newcastle on the 25th October. "My father," says a venerable gentleman,§ "used to go behind where the Friends' meeting-house at present stands, to hear the fife for the first time in 1745. The Hessian soldiers were encamped there; they entered the fields from the Croft road, where my son Joseph Pease's gate now stands, and marched out *via* Cockerbeck to the north road and thus avoided the town altogether. I have a large dragoon's basket-headed sword found on the place of encampment." The unfortunate issue of Prince Charlie's daring need not be recapitulated. The Duke of Cumberland in his journey northward, had passed through Piercebridge, a short distance north of which his carriage broke down, but on his return he paid Darlington a visit in July 1746. Tradition says that he reported the road between Darlington and Croft as the worst he had ever travelled. R. H. Allan, esq. possesses a guinea of 1733, wrapped carefully in a paper and placed in a neat small bag of wash leather. The paper is rudely inscribed:---"*This is the Guine, which the Duke of Cumberland sent to John Dunn, (on his presenting him with a Bunch of Ripe Grape's: which grew at the Grainge) on his return to London from Scotland;*" and is endorsed, in James Allan's handwriting, "*Duke of Cumberland---John Dun Gr.*"

What is the meaning of a seal used by Francis Lowson, in 1751, on the deeds prepared by him; the bust of a flowing-haired cavalier in tartan, with a low hat and military belt; and at the sides P. C. ?||

Two Swiss soldiers of Hirtzel's regiment were buried here in December and January, 1745-6, and John Hess, a Dutch soldier, who died at Cockerton, papist, was buried 9th Jan. Blakeney's and Barrel's regiments are also mentioned about this time. In 1747 a child fathered upon — Mackane, esq. a captain in St. George's regiment of Dragoons, was bap.

* W. K. † Sykes. ‡ George Grey of Southwick's letter, Surtees, ii. 19.
§ Edward Pease, esq.
|| Deeds of the house late Tolson's, Northgate. Edward Pease, esq.

1750. JOSEPH BUTLER, Bishop, the celebrated author of the "Analogy." He had been presented to the rectory of Haughton-le-Skerne in 1722, where there was a necessity of rebuilding a great part of the parsonage-house, and Mr. Butler had neither money nor talents for that work, though he had expended 60*l.* which the executors of his predecessor, Richard Bellassyse, had paid him for delapidations, with a further sum in providing materials for it. Bishop Talbot very kindly gave him Stanhope Rectory instead, and the materials were taken by his successor, Thorpe, who partly repaired the present parsonage.

1752. RICHARD TREVOR, S. T. P., Bishop.

1761. The Hexham Riot of this year took place on the 9th of March, and had its origin in the opposition shewn by the inhabitants to the newly established regulations for raising the militia. A mob of at least 5000 persons assembled in the market-place of Hexham, where proceeding from outrage to outrage, they eventually shot an ensign belonging to the North-York militia (Mr. Joseph Hart, of Darlington), and a private soldier. The reluctant magistrates at last ordered the soldiers to fire, who immediately cleared the rabble. The man who shot Hart was instantly despatched. Twenty-four were left on the spot, eighteen of whom were dead and the rest dangerously wounded. Hart lingered till the morning of the 10th, and was buried at Hexham, with every honour, in the evening. On Aug. 17, Peter Patterson and Wm. Elder were attainted, and sentenced to be drawn, hung, cut down alive, disembowelled and their entrails burnt before their eyes, beheaded and quartered. Elder was pardoned, but Patterson was executed at Morpeth on October 5, when the rope breaking he unfortunately fell down before he was dead, and exclaimed more than once, "*Innocent blood is hard to spill.*" A new halter was procured, and after he had hung the time required by law, he was cut down and dismembered.* He was a tenant in Ogle barony, and had been unwillingly pressed into the rioters' service on their road from Hexham to Morpeth.

1770. April 18. On account of Mr. Wilkes's enlargement there were great rejoicings at Darlington, the bells were rung all the day, forty-five pieces of cannon were fired off, and in the evening there were bonfires and illuminations. An effigy was carried round the town and afterwards committed to the flames.†

1771. JOHN EGERTON, Bishop.

1772. June 4. Being the anniversary of his Majesty's birthday, the morning was ushered in by ringing of bells, &c., and in the evening there was a most brilliant assembly ;‡ a thing now quite unknown.

1773. " Last week as some workmen were digging for sand in Haughton church-yard, they found a human skeleton of a very extraordinary size ;

* Denham's MSS. Sykes's Local Records, i. 234 ; ii. 374. † Sykes.
‡ Darlington Pamphlet.

what is most remarkable some of the teeth in in its jaw were 2¼ in. long, and 1½ in. broad."*

A great number of skeletons have been found to the West of the church, especially in that part of the churchyard which is now applied to the useful formation of cottage gardens at a small rent. There are some *vestigia* of entrenchments near Red Hall, and a very general tradition of a great battle "once upon a time there," exists. Haughton church is a massive Norman remain high above the road, with a western door; an unusual feature in small country churches in this locality. There is a flag-memorial to one of the prioresses of Neasham under the tower, and part of a Saxon cross of knot-work is built into the chancel south wall. The church is most nobly fitted up with wood-work of Cosin's time, being a sort of imitation of Gothic-work, and very imposing it is.

1787. THOMAS THURLOW, D.D., Bishop.

1791. THE HON. SHUTE BARRINGTON, D.D., Bishop. At his entrance to the see he dined at Darlington, with his attendants, after receiving the Sockburn falchion from the hands of John Erasmus Blackett, esq., as substitute for Sir Edward Blackett, bart., lord of that manor.

1798. Aug. 30. The ladies presented Colours to the Darlington Volunteers (Sir Ralph Milbank, colonel), the event ending in the cultivation of their ancient acquaintance with a smoking surloin. A new song, "The Darlington Volunteers", was composed, of *very* refined expression, as one verse will show:---

Though base-hearted fellows, will merit deny,
Come forward, be firm, and all traitors defy;
For those who in darkness can thus love to dwell,
Will meet a reward, and a great one, in H—;
Then join hand and heart, to repel all our foes,
For we never can rest, till we give them a dose.
Fire away! fire away! may our brave volunteers,
Ne'er suffer the Frenchmen to put us in fears.†

1799. Sep. 5. On the news arriving of the Dutch fleet in the Texel having been surrendered to admiral Mitchell, the Darlington Volunteers met in the market-place of that town, and fired three fine vollies, and the town at night was brilliantly illuminated.‡

The Darlington Volunteers, like most other volunteers, fell into much ridicule, and three thundering broadsides from Simpkin in Darlington to his brother Simon in Wales, (in other words, from Dr. Peacock to the public at large) were the result. The scene opens with a general meeting, where Squire Noddy, with the resolutions framed by himself and his friend Natty, is foiled by Ruffhead; and one of the company wishing to know, supposed the French came, what were they to do, was called a fool for his pains, nay, Noddy disputed he had any brains. The second scene discovers Noddy reading an address to the town, which was as properly styled an address to the moon, declaring *inter alia* "that his guts had been plagued with intestine

* Darlington Mercury. † Original broadside. I merely give this *vulgarism* as a sign of the times. ‡ Sykes.

commotions, which at church and at meeting, disturbed his devotions," and concluding

——— with such a fine jingle
Of words, which he had so contrived to mingle,
That whether read backwards, or sideways, or straight ;
It was equally sensible, equally bright ;
Which, soon as the wooden committee had heard,
They the wonderful orator three times three cheered.
Then each gave him thanks in a bumper of wine,
And Natty declared, "*it wath vethy fine.*"

This letter ends with the melancholy black-balling of Natty as an officer, who sinks in anguish and is recovered by his friend Dr. Simper's phlebotomy. The third epistle is so good, that I give it nearly entire.

The Halnaby brewer, red-fac'd as a dragon,
Got a barrel of yeast, by the Newcastle waggon,
And in carrying it home to recruit his strong beer,
(The house, you know, always remark'd for good cheer),
The sun screening off by his coat like a wise man,
Was met in the street by a cunning Exciseman:
Who question'd him 'bout the contents of his cask:
The brewer, with an oath, said "he'd no right to ask,"
The gauger not liking the size of his fist,
Call'd in the military now to assist;
To the scene Captain Noddy, a file of men led,
With Corporal Nat and Barebones at their head;
The brewer, with such heroes, not liking to quarrel,
Very deliberately set down his barrel,
And soon as the screw put the bung into motion,
Each house in the Market-place felt the explosion;
But oh! had you seen our brave warriors then,
Here laid Captain Noddy, and there laid his men,
So besmeared with yeast from the foot to the head,
They look'd like Falstaff's men, all in buckram laid dead;
All our medical men were call'd on for assistance,
It was well that the Faculty were at no distance,
With cordials and lancets, mops, dishclouts, and soap,
Captain Nod was enabled one winker to ope,
And the first words he spoke to the folk who stood by,
Were, "*My friends, I'm resolved to conquer or die!*"
Ever since he has been with false notions impress'd
No one can convince him, the whole was but yeast.
To please him his friends in the delusion join—
To this day he believes he was blown from a mine.

While Barebones was blind, undergoing the drench,
He thought he was feather'd and tarr'd by the French;
He begg'd "that the monsieurs would spare but his life,
"For the sake of his little ones and his dear wife."
He confessed "that he had chang'd sides it was true,
"But his customers threaten'd, and what could he do,

" That his sentiments still remain'd fixt and the same,
" If *forc'd* to disguise them, *he* was not to blame."
He was going on thus, when he open'd his eyes.
(You may better conceive, than describe his surprise.)

Poor Natty got pretty well clear of the matter,
Tho' some half-crowns it cost him in lavendar water.

Now soon as these tidings had reached Sir Ralph,
And (tho' he'd lost his yeast), that our captain was safe,
He sent for our officers with him to dine,
To wash off the disgrace with a soaking of wine.
O what hurry and bustle was there to get ready
Their uniforms to meet Sir Ralph and his Lady.
And before these smart beaux could appear out, God bless em,
They had each to send for the drill sergeant to dress 'em,
But now they set forward in post-chaise and four,
(The colonel and lady had gone on before),
As soon as the squad reached Halnaby gates,
And the servants had once got a sight of their pates,
Away they all flew, and close bolted the doors,
Expecting not one was to live many hours.
Sir Ralph some other friends asked to meet 'em,
(With a more curious dish sure he never could treat 'em),
They were all in the drawing-room chasing the vapours,
And killing dull time with light-chat and the papers,
When in bolts the valet like one in despair,
So pale was his face and erect was his hair,
His mouth was wide open, and staring his eyes,
When he stammer'd out " Sir, here's the French in disguise !'
The confusion had now very general grown,
Such running and screaming both up stairs and down,
When the colonel luckily looking out saw
His bedizened brethren all waiting below,
The doors were unlock'd and in came such a corps,
(Captain Nod at their head) as was ne'er seen before,
The ladies arranged their dress and their features,
Not doubting a conquest 'mong five handsome creatures;
But with what contempt did each turn up her nose,
When she saw such Monmouth-street pegs hung with clothes,
They bow'd and they scrap'd moving both feet and head,
Look'd as tame as five lambs, but not one word was said.
When dinner was serv'd they laid siege to the dishes,
But still they remain'd as mute as five fishes.
Sir Ralph, to break silence, begg'd Noddy would join
His lady or him in a glass of good wine.
Noddy answer'd him straightway " *blown up by a mine!* "
This strange exclamation made the ladies all stare,
Expecting they all should be blown in the air,
But Noddy unmov'd, took his mutton and wine,
Tho' whenever he spoke, 'twas " *blown up by a mine!*"
The fears of the ladies being somewhat suppress'd
They endeavoured to get something out of the rest.
They address'd little Doctor—tho' before looking simple,
His face brighten'd up and he show'd off his dimple.

"Captain Simper," said one, "do permit me to ask,
"For if one don't know, 'tis an awkwardish task,
"How to fill a smelling-bottle without making a slop."
"*Maam,*" he answered, "*I oolways pat the battle in a cap.*"

This superfine lingo set all in a roar,
And not one of them ventured that day a word more.

To narrate the excitement in the town on the arrival of every post, and the rejoicings on the news of every victory, would be merely to write the history of every other town. The contents of the newspapers were duly proclaimed from *Bulmer's Stone* in Northgate by old Willy Bulmer, to a host of rustic counsellors assembled round him, and arrayed it with more consequence than even its marvellous revolving properties, for

In Darnton toune ther is a stane,
And most straunge is yt to tell,
That yt turnes nine times round aboute
When yt hears ye Clock strike twell.

Bulmer's stone stands in the front of some low cottages constituting Northgate House, and was only saved from the inhuman picks of some overseers who wanted to turn sextons, by being claimed as an appurtenance to those tenements, which were in a great measure built with round cobble stones. Like the many other rounded or water-worn fragments of the rocks at Shap Fell in Westmoreland, scattered over the North, it is called a *boulder stone,* as also from the use the weavers made of it to beat their linen yarn upon, a *battling stone.* A similar stone, used for a similar purpose, is on the brink of the Tees on the Yorkshire side at Piercebridge, and both have survived their occupation ; since "the times are changed ,and even we, seem changed with the times to be."

I have seen in a MS. letter the Boulder stone of Darlington classified with the black stone of Mecca, the *clach Dhu* or black stone of Scottish villages, and the smooth stones of the stream which the idolatrous people of God chose for their portion.* It may be so. Villages and towns oft-times arose around the Boulder stones, and legends almost invariably attach themselves to them, seeming the last lingerings of an old superstition which sprung from a natural feeling of reverence in men. They well knew that the finger of God had placed them there in some awful operation or disruption of nature, and congregated beside what gradually became an object of adoration.

This is not the place for any discussion as to the cause of boulders rolling up hill and down hill from their native cliffs to the places they now occupy, sometimes above and sometimes below their original level. It is, however, probable that they marched under the influence of glacial action, in whatever

* Isaiah, lvii. 6.

manner it might be developed. Further this deponent sayeth not, and leaves the stone alone. Si non vis jacere hunc lapidem, permitte jacere.

1826. William Van Mildert, Bishop, and last Count Palatine. For in our own time of restless and useless change, the legislature decreed that this blameless prelate should be *ultimus suorum*, and the fitting splendour of his obsequies, in 1836, were attended by a respect and a feeling which shone brightly in the cold mists of reform. *Verbum sap.*---" Yon kingless throne is now for ever bare ! "

1832. May 16. A large meeting was held in front of the Town Hall, when a petition to the Commons, praying them to address the king to recall Earl Grey to the nation, *and also to withhold all supplies to government of the public money*, until such a reform as would satisfy the country be granted, was unanimously agreed to. The speakers were Thos. Bowes, esq., Warren Maude, esq., Messrs. Sherwood, Mewburn, John Pease, Joseph Pease, sen., Nesham, Robinson, Coates, Hogarth, &c.*

1832. June 9. A meeting in the Town Hall resolved to express their satisfaction at the passing of the Reform Bill, by giving a dinner to the operatives of the town, and a committee was nominated to make the necessary arrangements. The following Tuesday was fixed upon, and many gentlemen and ladies purchased tickets which they distributed gratis. Three large oxen were bought, with a suitable proportion of bread, ale, and vegetables, besides a large supply of plum pudding, which was furnished by the liberality of private individuals and of the principal innkeepers, the latter of whom also undertook to cook. Every department was allotted to committees of three or four gentlemen. All the trades were marshalled under their respective banners by Mr. Geo. Elwin, and the order in which they were to march was fixed by ballot. The Darlington and West Auckland bands volunteered their services, and were provided with tickets for the dinner. The timber-merchants furnished deals, which were formed into tables, from 20 to 50 yards in length, in the market-place, and these were covered with cloth, furnished by the drapers. The tables were so arranged, that the elegant gas column in the square formed the centre, the spaces being wide enough to admit of the attendants freely passing each other, and the ale was in the shambles, under the charge of three gentlemen who were to distribute it to the tables. At 12 o'clock precisely the procession moved in the following order, from the Town Hall, amidst the thunders of thousands of voices: ---The National Flag, one hundred gentlemen, four abreast ; Earl Grey's Arms ; Lord Brougham's Arms ; the Darlington band ; an Emblematic Flag ; the Lodge of Odd Fellows, in full dress ; a banner ; the Woolcombers, with a sliver of blue and white wool across their breasts ; a banner ; the Coach-makers ; a banner ; the Coopers ; a banner ; the Worsted-weavers ; a banner ; the Linen-weavers ; a banner ; the Bricklayers ; a banner ; the

* Sykes.

Flax-dressers; a banner; the Shoemakers; a banner; the Carpenters; a banner; the Tanners, Curriers, Skinners, and Finishers, in their respective dresses and banners; a banner; the Bleachers; a banner; the Carpet-weavers, with a skein of blue, red, and white worsted yarn across their shoulder; a banner; the Sawyers; a banner; the Tailors; a banner; the Smiths; a banner; the Gardeners, with a triumphal arch and crown of ever-greens; a banner; the Painters; a banner; the Plumbers; a banner; the Shopmen; a banner; the Railway men. The procession marched round the town-boundaries and through the principal streets, the bands playing, bells ringing, guns firing in all directions, and colours waving from the windows, roofs, and chimneys. Multitudes from the neighbourhood flocked in to witness the magnificent spectacle. Upwards of 3000 men walked in the ranks, and so far as could be calculated, above 12,000 people were congregated on the occasion. The men of one tan-yard agreed to fine any one of themselves 5*s.* who should be intoxicated on that day. After perambulating the town, which occupied nearly two hours, the whole body was drawn up round the market-place. The bands which had continued playing incessantly during the march, ceased, and, with them, the acclamations of the people; for a minute there was a dead pause, all heads were uncovered, and at a given signal, three cheers from thousands rose to the skies. The various companies then filed off to the tables till all were stationed, that every man might know his own place. The people were then dismissed for an hour. At three o'clock the trades arrived and took their places at the tables, on which the attendants expeditiously placed the smoking viands, and the disused custom was revived of servant and master exchanging duties with each other. The delegates and committee were engaged in carving for and waiting on, the people; and at 4 o'clock they assembled at the work-house and dined together, thus concluding a day of rejoicing such as was never before witnessed in the North of England. The workmen of Messrs. Parker, of Haughton-le-Skerne, joined in the procession, carrying their banners, and returned to Haughton, where they were sumptuously regaled with plum-pudding and roast beef. The wives, sisters, and daughters of those who had dined in public, were regaled with tea and cakes in the open air, in various parts of the town, by the kind contributions of the ladies of Darlington. The following are selected from hundreds of mottoes that were emblazoned on the floating draperies of the trades' banners and other private flags:---The glorious triumph of 1832---May the Sun always shine on real Reformers, Earl Grey for ever---The Voice of the People is the Voice of God---Long live Earl Grey and all Reformers---The Day is ours---May the Sons of St. Crispin ever flourish with Reform---Let us rejoice, Reform is accomplished---The King, the People, and Reform---Reform is won, Victory is ours---Let the merry bells ring, Grey, Brougham, and the Bill---By Perseverance we have conquered---Truth and Justice have decided our Cause---Cleveland we adore---Durham we delight in---Long live Grey, Brougham, and their Colleagues, the Champions of Reform---A day of Liberty is worth an Eternity of Bondage --Success to the Town and Trade of Darlington---No Corn Laws---No Tithes---The righteous Man falleth seven times and riseth again---Let the King put away the wicked from before him, and his throne shall be established in Righteousness---England must be free as the Thoughts of Man---United we stand, divided we fall---Grey and Brougham---Victory follows the Brave---The glorious Triumph of Grey and Brougham---England expects every Man to do his Duty.*

1836. EDWARD MALTBY, bishop.

1847. Sep. 1. On his road to Wynyard Park on the occasion of the marriage of the Earl of Portarlington to Lady Alexandrina Vane, Sir Robert Peel was received in the Central Hall, at Darlington, by not less than from one thousand six hundred to two thousand persons. The borough bailiff, Francis Mewburn, esq., introduced the Right Honourable visitor, and Joseph Pease, esq., with an eloquent speech, presented him with the following address---

"To the Right Honourable Sir Robert Peel, bart., M.P.—We, the gentry, merchants, and inhabitants of the town of Darlington and its neighbourhood, in public meeting assembled, beg leave most respectfully to express to you, sir, the high satisfaction your arrival in this county has afforded us of addressing you, and giving utterance to our feelings of profound respect for, and admiration of, your distinguished talents, by which this country has, on many and important occasions, and under trying circumstances, been so signally benefitted.

"We contemplate with admiration the fidelity, zeal, and ability, with which you discharged the high duties of Prime Minister to our most gracious Queen, and your patient, persevering, and successful advocacy of an enlightened policy, calculated to develope the immense resources and advance the general well-being of this great country.

"To this tribute of our applause, respect, and gratitude, we add an expression of earnest desire that you may enjoy a long and uninterrupted life of health and happiness; and that whether in a more or less active sphere (as circumstances may require), you may still continue to give your Queen and your country the benefit of your services."

Sir Robert, on rising, was received with tremendous cheering, and proceeded to reply to the address :---

"Mr. Chief Bailiff, Mr. Pease, and gentlemen,—As my visit to this county has been influenced solely by considerations of private friendship, and as it necessarily will be of very limited duration, I did not expect that I should be called upon, to acknowledge any public demonstration of respect or approval, on account of the course which I have deemed it my duty to pursue as a minister of the crown, and as a member of the legislature. But I felt that I should make but an ill return for the kindness with which you were disposed to welcome my arrival in this ancient town, if I had shown any hesitation in receiving this address, in the manner which I was informed would be most satisfactory to those who have been parties to it. And perhaps I may be permitted to avail myself of this opportunity of returning to other parties, with whom I have not the same advantage of personal communication, my cordial acknowledgements for their willingness to confer on me similar honours, had it been in my power to accept them. (Hear and cheers.) I consider myself very fortunate that I am enabled, in your presence,

* Sykes.

personally to express to you the deep sense which I feel of the honour which has been conferred upon me. (Hear, and loud cheers.) I thank you for your assurance of confidence and esteem, and for the hearty good wishes which are conveyed in this address (renewed cheers). You do me justice in believing, that it has been my earnest desire to exert my influence or authority which I may have possessed for the advancement of the great objects referred to in this address—the developement of the national resources, and the promotion of the well-being and comfort of all classes of the community. (Loud and reiterated cheers.) By continuing to give my zealous support to all such measures as shall be calculated for the attainment of those important ends, I hope to be enabled to justify your confidence and to retain your favourable opinion (cheers). I now take leave of you, expressing my sincerest wishes for the prosperity of the town and neighbourhood of Darlington, and for the individual happiness and welfare of all whom I see around me." (Loud and long continued cheers.)

Thanks were then accorded to the distinguished guest for his visit, and to the Bailiff. Sir Robert afterwards slightly partook of a luncheon, and left for Wynyard in a carriage and four, amidst the hearty cheers of thousands.

This speech of the ex-minister created some sensation, and was freely remarked on in the prints of the day, therefore I have given it a preference over coronation rejoicings, and other petty events, which occurred in every other town in the kingdom.

These annals may properly be concluded by those of

PARLIAMENTARY REPRESENTATION.

Under the old palatine system, no knights were returned for this county to the general parliament, nor burgesses for the boroughs. In 1614, a few discontented gentlemen, who said "that they would humble the bishop and his courts together with all his clergy,"* attempted to obtain representatives for the county and city of Durham and borough of Barnard-castle, and in 1620-1, the modest number of fourteen members in all for the same districts, and for divers other boroughs in the county, which, as Surtees remarks, "might possibly be Darlington, Stockton, and Gateshead," were claimed very *un*reasonably, as the house reasonably considered. Hartlepool and Barnard-castle were picked out, the one being a port town, the other "the Prince his town," and the rest rejected "because of *pestering the house;* and because these *incorporated by the bishop, not by the king.*" Somehow all were thrown out. When the see was dissolved, the city and county each returned a member, on the restoration the privilege was swept away, but in 1666 a powerful attempt was made to regain representation, it being urged that the county since James I.'s time had paid the general taxes (from which border service had before exempted it) and ought to have members to vote in their impositions. Cosin stood out manfully for his palatine privileges, and in 1668 the bill was rejected, Mr. Vaughan declairng that if the commons had all their members there they would have no room for them. After his death, however, two for the county and two for the city were obtained (1673),

* Cosin in 1667.

which arrangement continued till 1832, when the county was divided in two, and Darlington became the political metropolis of the southern division, which returns two members.

A committee was formed in Darlington to secure the return of two liberal members for the new district, at the first election, and, subsequently, one of their number, Joseph Pease, jun., esq., (of the society of Friends), was nominated and was successful. The whole three candidates were, however, of liberal principles. They were

Joseph Pease, jun., esq., Darlington, who polled	2273
John Bowes, esq., Streatlam Castle, do.	2218
Robert Duncomb Shafto, esq., Whitworth, do.	1841

The novelty of the occasion brought in immense crowds on the chairing day, (Dec. 24), on which occasion the carriages and chairs provided for the two members, Pease and Bowes, were profusely decorated with ribbons and evergreens. They were returned without opposition in 1835 and 1837.

To the historian, any particular manifestation of popular opinion must ever be regarded as a sign of the times, and the progress of thought resulting in action. Such was the withdrawal of severe enactments against our fellow subjects attached to the church of Rome, and their admission to the Houses of Parliament. Such, under another phase, was the passing of the Reform Bill, the repeal of the Test and Corporation Acts, and, of a similar character, the decision of the constituency of South Durham. It was sanctioned and approved by the assembled Commons by unanimous vote, when Mr. Pease took his seat as the first quaker member of their powerful House. The manner in which his duties were performed constitutes no part of my history, but the circumstance is interesting as an illustration of the onward working of opinion and its local developement. His subsequent appearances at Court, the drawing rooms and levees of Royalty, and at the coronation of Her Majesty Queen Victoria in the court costume of the "earlier Friends," were incidents specially noticed in the public journals of the time, as marking a change of sentiment. May it not be termed a proof of the waning reign of prejudice, and an advance beyond toleration, to the free enjoyment of privileges vested in electors and the elected, worthy of our happy and envied constitution. And may it not be truly said that South Durham and Darlington bore a conspicuous place in the march of mind and civilization.

In 1841, Mr. Pease retired, but Mr. Bowes was again in the field, the candidates being

Lord Harry Vane, (brother to the present duke of Cleveland) liberal, who polled	2547
John Bowes, esq., liberal, who polled	2483
James Farrer, esq., Ingleborough, Yks., conservative, do. . . .	1739

The successful members were conducted through the town on horseback, in lieu of chairing, on June 12, and a violent thunderstorm effectually damped all incipient disturbances, about which much apprehension had been felt.

The proceedings at this election were marked throughout with riot. This was especially exemplified on Mr. Bowes's visit to Darlington, on the 28th June, for the purpose of addressing the electors. A more imposing spectacle has seldom been witnessed—the cavalcade, consisting principally of electors from Weardale, followed four and five abreast immediately in the rear of Mr. Bowes, who, with three of his friends, filled the first quadruple car. The following was the order of the procession:—Two gentlemen on horseback: the band playing "See the conquering hero comes:" the candidate and his friends: about three hundred horsemen, four abreast: a procession of carriages, filled with electors, succeeded by two hundred voters on horseback, each decorated with blue and white rosettes, &c., amid a large collection of banners. The procession paraded through the streets, and afterwards dispersed to the post houses. At 2 o'clock, Joseph Pease, esq., late M.P. for the division, appeared in front of the Sun inn, and introduced Mr. Bowes. The scene which ensued baffles all description. Stationed below the platform, were a few persons who commenced hooting, roaring, and bellowing, in such a manner as totally to prevent any below the platform hearing a single sentence delivered by Mr. Pease, who spoke, notwithstanding the tumult, for about twenty minutes. Mr. Bowes then followed, with a similar result for the space of half an hour, audible only to those close by him. After the speaking, the mob hovered about the market-place and on the High Row, with occasional outcries and the infliction of personal injury, until half-past 7 o'clock, when an altercation respecting a ribbon having taken place between two lads, they commenced fighting. The police interfered, and finding themselves, through their rashness, in an awkward dilemma, struck out, and one man, well known as a quiet inoffensive character, of the name of Robson, a butcher in Skinnergate, was unluckily struck by a police truncheon, and for sometime it was thought he was killed. A general attack was then made on the police who were obliged to fly in all directions, with loss of hats, truncheons, &c., two or three took refuge in the Town Hall, on which an attack was commenced and the windows smashed unremittingly, until past 11 o'clock, when their destruction being complete, a rush was made to the entrance door, which after some delay, was broken in, and had it not been for the scheming of some gentlemen in the news room at the south end of the building, who disguised the police, and smuggled them out by a private door, when the mob rushed in at the north end, they would doubtless have been massacred without mercy. The mob finding that they had escaped, tore up the bar railings, broke the forms and chairs, and committed every kind of outrage. They then formed in parties, and on their way home broke some windows in the upper story of Mr. D. Hampton's house, in the market-place, and made an attack on the Swiss Villa of T. E. Abbott, esq., Grange-road, and broke several windows.*

Mr. Bowes behaved in a truly honourable manner, in 1846, when he boldly published a letter to his constituents announcing a change in his views on agricultural protection, and his determination to support the commercial system of the government. A meeting was held at Darlington to express the approval of his supporters. He retired in 1847, having spent £30,000† in contesting this division. In July, of that year, Lord Harry Vane and Mr. Farrer were returned without opposition, and perambulated the town in four-horsed carriages without being chaired.

*** "Darlington, Posthouse, 10 September, 1789. Mr. Milbanke presents his most respectful compliments to the worthy freeholders of the town of Darlington, and will think himself greatly honoured to have the favour of their company at the Posthouse on Saturday Evening, *at half-past Six o'Clock to supper*."—The immaculate candidate was successful, but the election did not take place until 28th June, 1790.

* Richardson's Table Book.

† Statement of Mr. Mewburn on the hustings.

Chapter V. Title.

A recorded title derived from this town derives only from 1685, but "Lord Darlington" figures in two ballads of great antiquity. One is a mere adaptation of "Lord Barnard and Little Musgrave," though the *alias* hereabouts is *Barnabye* rather than Barnard. The other is common to both sides of the Border, and I am in doubt to which side it properly belongs. However, I give Darlington in Durham the benefit of the doubt, and present the reader with a version,* *cum notis* :---

Lord Darlington. An Ancient Ballad.

"O we were seven† brave sisters,
  Five of us died wi' child ;
And nane but you and I, Maisrey,
  So we'll gae maidens mild.‡"

"O haud your tongue now, Lady Margaret,
  Let a' your folly be ;
I'll gar you keep your true promise,
  To the lord§ ayont the sea.||"

* Given in Richardson's Table Book, by J. H. Dixon, esq., Tollington Park, Hornsey Middlesex, as "transcribed from a MS. copy, in possession of an antiquarian friend, collated with one printed in Buchan's Ancient Ballads and Songs ; Edinburgh, 1828." I have also had Buchan's reading before me, and have slightly altered Dixon's version. The incidents are precisely the same as those in "Fair Mabel of Wallington" given in the Table Book also, from Ritson, but the latter is a splendid ballad.

† An indefinite expression, as in scripture, so in ballads.

O we were sisters, sisters seven
We were the fairest under heaven.—*Cospatric.*

‡ The exact translation of *mitis*, which is of the titles given to the Virgin and is rendered *mild* in many versions of the ancient hymns, though *gentle* would now more properly express the meaning.

§ *Lad* in Buchan. If the locality is Scotch, Laird is probably meant, but if English, what shall we say ? The manors of Darlington are episcopal, Newton is archidiaconal, but the freehold ones of Oxen-le-field and Blackwell are free to Mr. Dixon's proposition, that the Lord of a manor is meant. Yet in the next verse a *baron* is evidently meant, as superior to a knight. It must be observed that although the names in ballads are generally taken from some actual families or places, yet the reciters often adopted them for their own fictions at the dictation of fancy, exactly as do modern novelists, and it may be that Lord Darlington is as much a fancy name as any of the Stanleys or Nevilles in later romance. It might however be a bye-name, and it is a coincidence that Adam *de Suatone* and Eve his wife granted property at Derlingtone, about 1320, to Wm. de Walleworde, who, with Olive his wife, granted "*manerium deDerlyngtone*," (which, as *manerium* was of extensive import, must have been a small freehold estate) to Richard Porter, and a burgage to his wife Agnes.

|| Supposing that Seaton Delaval was the lady's residence, no one in a Northumbrian village would now call Darlington *ayont* the sea, or a peasant there talk of bringing his bride *o'er* the sea from our borough, but when we call to mind how the interior of the northern counties was, in the feudal ages, infested with robbers, raiders, and marauders of all sorts, we may easily conceive that a Durham lover who, *a la* 'Johny Cope,' liked "to sleep in a hale skin," would prefer a sea voyage to Seaton Delaval, to a then more dangerous one by land. *Dixon.*

"O there is neither lord nor knight,
  My love shall ever won ;
Except it be Lord Darlington,
  And here he winna come.*"

But when the hour o' twall was past
  And near the hour o' ane ;
Lord Darlington came to the yetts,†
  Wi' thirty knights and ten.

It's he has wedded the Lady Margaret
  And brought her o'er the sea ;
And there was nane that lived on earth
  Sae happy as was she.

But when nine months were come and gane,
  Strong travailling took she ;
And ne'er a leech in a' the land ‡
  Could ease her maladie.

" Where will I get a little wee boy,
  Will won baith meat and fee ;
That will gae on to Seaton's yetts
  And bring my mother to me ? "

O ! out then spake the little foot page,
  And knelt on bended knee—
" O here am I, a little wee boy,
  That will won meat and fee ;
That will gae on to Seaton's yetts,
  And bring your mother to thee."

Then he is on to Seaton's yetts
  As fast as gang§ could he ;
Says " ye must come to Darlington,
  Your daughter for to see."

But when she came to Darlington town,
  Where there was little pride,||

* In Dixon's version the 2nd and 4th lines stand :—" My true lover e'er shall be"—"And he winna come here to me."

† Afterwards called Seaton's yetts. There are three Seatons on the northern coast, Seaton Carew, Seaton Delaval, and Monk Seaton. As the *yetts* must mean the outer *gates* of some large mansion, probably Seaton Delaval is the true locality, and the heroine was one of the family of Delaval. So Dixon, but Buchan says that the unfortunate lady the last [but one] of her sisters was of the house of Seaton, Aberdeenshire, which certainly was much further *ayont* the sea.

‡ " And nae physician in the land." *Buchan.*

§ I suspect it is here meant that the page took a land journey.

|| Whether this is any distinguishing mark of the present time it behoves me not to say. No very powerful family has ever resided there any time, and little else than a substantial council of burgesses and yeomen appear. The only place now in Scotland of the name is a modern portion of the inland manufacturing village of Stewarton, in Ayrshire. This suburb, originally called Templehouse and now Darlington, was fenced out by a Mr. Draus, who died in 1828, aged 49. A well-known author of Scotland informs me that in all his

The scobbs* were in the lady's mouth
The sharp sheer in her side.

Lord Darlington stood on the stair,
And gart the gowd rings flee ; †
" My halls and bowers, and a' shall gae waste
If my bonny love die for me."

" O haud your tongue, Lord Darlington,
Let a' your folly be ;
I bore the bird within my sides,
I'll suffer her to dee.

" He that marries a daughter o' mine
I wot he is a fule :
If he marries her at Candlemas tide
She'll be frae him at Yule.‡

" I had seven ance in companie,
This night I go my lane ; §
When I come to the salt water||
I wish that I may drown."

The other ballad was so imperfect that I had to supply the long blanks of my traditionary copy with verses a little altered from Percy's Lord Barnard and Little Musgrove. These are given in brackets.

Lord Darlington and Little Musgrove.

It was upon All-Hallows day
Of all the days in the year;

antiquarian dabblings, he never, to his recollection, fell on the name of Darlington connected with an actual place. In David Macpherson's accurate geographical index of Scotland, in which all the places mentioned in the old writers of Scotland are inserted, Darlington occurs in black letter, which is his manner of indicating places not in Scotland, and from the reference given to the situation in the accompanying map, our Darlington is at once seen to be the place meant. Still, under 1650, it is stated both in "Britain's Triumphs" and "Memorials of the English affairs," two publications of the 17th cent., that the English surprised a party of moss-troopers in *Darlington Castle*, which is associated with proceedings against Dalhousie and Roslin Castle, two places in Midlothian well known, from which one would expect to find Darlington within ten miles of Edinburgh. Yet the aforesaid courteous author, who resides in that ancient capital and is familiar with the district, never heard of such a place, and, as it does not occur on an inspection of Thomson's map of Edinburghshire, suspects that the English journalists have mistaken it for Dalkeith. Among my northern brethren be this Gordian knot. I am unable to trace the seal of "Lord Darlington, in yellow wax, ancient," mentioned in Fox's catalogue of the Allan Museum.

* Sores.

† " She kickt the table with her foot, she kickt it with her knee,
The silver plate into the fire so far she made it flee."
Fair Mabel of Wallington.

‡ The young ladies, according to Calvin's doctrine, had been predestinated ere they were born, to die in childbed, and nothing could have saved them, as the decree had gone forth. *Buchan.*

§ I. e. my way.

|| " And when I come to *Clyde's* water."—*Buchan.* This passage points out Darlington as lying south from Aberdeenshire, although the scent cannot be pursued further, our good town being on the east side of the island instead of the west.

Little Musgrove to church would go
  To see all the ladyes fair.

The first he met was clad in red,
  The second was all in green,
The third she was my Lord Darlington's* Lady
  The fairest that ever was seen.

[She cast an eye on Little Musgrove
  As bright as the summer's sun,
O then bethought him Little Musgrove
  This ladye's heart I have won.

Quoth she, " I have loved thee, Little Musgrove,
  Full long and many a day."
" So have I loved you, my lady fair,
  Yet word I never durst say."

" I have a bower at Oxenhall,†
  Full daintily bedight,
If thoult wend thither, my Little Musgrove,
  Thou shalt lie in my arms all night."

Quoth he, " I thank ye, ladye fair,
  This kindness ye shew to me;
And whether it be to my weal or woe,
  This night I will lie with thee."

All this beheard a little foot-page,
  By his ladye's coach as he ran:
Quoth he, " Though I am my ladye's page,
  Yet I'm my Lord Darlington's man.

Lord Darlington he shall know of this,
  Although I lose a limbe,
And where the briggs are broken down
  I'll lay me down and swim."

Like a harried man] sometimes he walked,
  [A mile] sometimes he ran,
Until he came to the broken brigg,
  Then he laid on his back and he swam.

["Asleep or awake, my Lord Darlington,
  As thou art a man of life,

* See the notes on this name in the last ballad.

† Bucklesford-Bury, in Percy. It is evident that in both versions the bower was an estate distinct from the injured husband's own lands. In mine the lady talks of her *father's* shepherd, and in Percy's Lord Barnard offers all Bucklesford-Bury to his page if he told true, an offer palpably absurd had it been his own ancient inheritance. To suit the Durham edition, I have taken Oxenhall as a fitting place. The reader may imagine that the lady was the heiress of the Oxenhalls, who became extinct circa 1340, and that Lord Darlington treated their estate as his own in expectancy of his father-in-law's death.—It will be observed that the lady reached the bower by a *coach* from the parish church, a circumstance which also pointed out Oxenhall as convenient for me.

Lo! this same night at Oxenhall,
Little Musgrove he lies with thy wife."

"If it be true, thou little foot-page,
This tale thou hast told to me,
Then all my lands at Oxenhall
I freely will give to thee.

But and it be a lie, thou little foot-page,
This tale thou hast told to me,
On the highest tree at Oxenhall
All hanged thou shalt be."

"Rise up, rise up, my merry men all,
And saddle me my good steed;
For this night must I to Oxenhall;
God wot, I had never more need."]

There was one of Lord Darlington's shepherds
That bore Musgrove good will,
He put his horn unto his mouth
And blew both loud and shrill.

And all the words that he did say
Were "Away, Musgrove, away!
For if Lord Darlington catch you here
With a sword he will you slay."

Little Musgrove he did arise
To hear what the horn did say,
["Methinks I hear Lord Darlington's horn
I would I were away."]

"Lie still, lie still, my Little Musgrove,
And keep me from the cold:
'Tis only one of my *father's* shepherds
Coming riding through the fold.

[Is not thy hawke upon the perch,
Thy horse eating corn and hay?
Is not a gay lady within thine arms:
And wouldst thou be away?"

By this Lord Darlington reached the door
And lighted upon a stone:
And he pulled out three silver keys,
And opened the doors each one.]

"How do you like my bed, Musgrove,
How do you like my sheet?
How do you like the fair ladye
That lies in your arms so sweet?"

"It is well I like your bed, my Lord,
And better I like your sheet,

And better I like the fair ladye
  That lies in my arms so sweet."

"Arise, arise, my little Musgrove,
  And put your clothing on :
It shall never be said in all my life,
  That I slew a naked man."

The very first blow Lord Darlington gave
  His wife got a deadly wound,
The very next blow Lord Darlington gave
  Musgrove lay dead on the ground.

"Make a grave both wide and deep
  To put this couple in :
And lay Lady Darlington on the right side*
  For she's come of a far better kin."

So merrily sung the nightingale,
  So sorrowful sung the sparrow;
Lord Darlington he has killed two to-day
  And he's to be hung to-morrow.

I add one more ballad, of exquisite sadness.

Prince Robert.

Published in Scott's Border Minstrelsy, from the recitation of Miss Christian Rutherford, sister to Sir Walter Scott's mother.

Prince Robert has wedded a gay ladye,
He has wedded her with a ring:
Prince Robert has wedded a gay ladye,
But he darna bring her hame.

" Your blessing, your blessing, my mother dear!
Your blessing now grant to me!"—
" Instead of a blessing ye sall have my curse,
And you'll get nae blessing frae me."—

She has called upon her waiting-maid,
To fill a glass of wine ;
She has call'd upon her fause steward,
To put rank poison in.

She has put it to her roudes† lip,
And to her roudes chin ;
She has put it to her fause fause mouth,
But the never a drap gaed in.

* " But lay my ladye o' the upper hande,
  For shee comes o' the better kin."—*Percy.*
The Musgroves were however a most excellent family of Cumberland, possessing "the Luck of Edenhall."

The concluding stanza has no likeness to Percy, and the punishment of hanging is improbable under the circumstances.

† Haggard.

He has put it to his bonny mouth,
And to his bonny chin,
He has put it to his cherry lip,
And sae fast the rank poison ran in.

"O ye hae poison'd your ae son, mother,
Youre ae son and your heir;
O ye hae poison'd your ae son, mother,
And sons you'll never hae mair.

"O where will I get a little boy,
That will win hose and shoon,
To rin sae fast to Darlinton,
And bid fair Eleanor come?"—

Then up and spake a little boy,
That wad win hose and shoon,—
"O I'll away to Darlinton,
And bid fair Eleanor come."—

O he has run to Darlinton,
And tirled at the pin;*
And wha was sae ready as Eleanor's sell
To let the bonny boy in.

"Youre gude mother has made ye a rare dinour,
She has made it baith good and fine;
Your gude mother has made ye a gay dinour,
And ye maun cum till her and dine."—

It's twenty lang miles to Sillertoun town,
The langest that ever were gane:
But the steed it was wight, and the lady was light,
And she cam linkin'† in.

But when she came to Sillertoun town,‡
And into Sillertoun ha',
The torches were burning, the ladies were mourning,
And they were weeping a'.

"O where is now my wedded lord,
And where now can he be?
O where is now my wedded lord?
For him I canna see."—

"Your wedded lord is dead," she says,
"And just gane to be laid in the clay:
Your wedded lord is dead," she says,
"And just gane to be buried the day.

* In the old method of latching doors there was a pin inside which was turned round to raise the latch. The expression here, I suppose, is synonymous with our "rattling a sneck."

† Riding briskly.

‡ Silton, near Northallerton, supposed to be the Seleton of the Saxons, is perhaps meant, but, as before mentioned, little dependence must be placed on ballad localities. Indeed Motherwell's editoin of Prince Robert, substitutes Sittengen's Rocks for Darlington.

"Ye'se get nane o' his gowd, ye'se get nane o' his gear,
Ye'se get nae thing frae me :
Ye'se no get an inch o' his gude braid land,
Though your heart suld burst in three."—

"I want nane o' his gowd, I want nane o' his gear,
I want nae land frae thee :
But I'll hae the rings that's on his finger,
For them he did promise to me."—

"Ye'se no get the rings that's on his finger,
Ye'se no get them frae me ;
Ye'e no get the rings that's on his finger,
An your heart suld burst in three."—

She's turn'd her back unto the wa',
And her face unto a rock ;
And there, before the mother's face,
Her very heart it broke.

The tane was buried in Marie's kirk,
The tother in Marie's quair ;*
And out o' the tane there sprang a birk,
And out o' the tother a brier.

And thae twa met, and thae twa plat,
The birk but and the brier ;
And by that ye may very weel ken
They were twa lovers dear.

I return to proven histories.

1685-6. Jan. 2. Catherine Sedley, daughter of Sir Charles of elegant and profligate memory, created by her royal paramour James II, Baroness of Darlington and Countess of Dorchester for life only.

"Sedley cursed the form that pleased a king," and excused his defection from James in the keenest irony, "I hate ingratitude, and as his majesty has done me the unlooked for honour of making *my* daughter a *countess*, I cannot do less in return than endeavour to make *his* daughter a *queen*." Catherine inherited much of her father's wit and all his indelicacy. She said of herself and colleagues (Lady Susan Bellasis and Miss Godfrey) "I wonder why he keeps us; it cannot be our beauty, for he must see that we have none ; and it cannot be our wit, for if *we* have any, *he* has not enough to find it out." Personal charms indeed she had none, with the exception of two brilliant eyes, the lustre of which, however, seemed fierce and unfeminine. Her form was lean but stately, her countenance haggard. Charles II. liked her conversation, and course repartees, but, laughing at her ugliness, said that the priests must have recommended her to his brother by way of penance. She laughed too, yet loved to adorn herself magnificently, and appeared in the theatre and the ring plastered, painted, clad in Brussels lace, glittering with diamonds, and affecting all the graces of eighteen.

Catharine had been the cause of much uneasiness to Mary Beatrice, of Modena, while

* The last two verses are common to many ballads, and are probably derived from some metrical romance, since we find the idea occur in the voluminous history of Sir Tristrem.

her husband was duke of York. On his accession to the throne, his mistress was pounced upon by Rochester and his party, as a medium for influencing him in opposition to to the queen's Catholic friends: seemingly pure and highminded cavaliers encouraged this vile design of tormenting a young queen, and even the countess of Rochester entered into it. Soon after James's accession the entreaties of his priests induced him to bid Catharine an eternal farewell, but she refused to leave Whitehall, and the amour was soon renewed by the instrumentality of Chiffinch. Catharine told her sovereign plainly what the Protestant lords only dared to hint, that his crown was at stake and that he was led to his ruin. In a fit of fondness, he determined to make her baroness of Darlington and countess of Dorchester; she saw all the peril of the step and declined the invidious honour; but he himself forced the patent into her hand. She at last accepted it on one condition, which was that he would give her a solemn promise that if he ever quitted her, he would himself announce his resolution to her and grant her a parting interview.

Day after day the queen's dishes were untasted, and tears rolled down her cheeks in the presence of the whole circle of courtiers. " Let me go," cried she to the king, " you have made your woman a countess; make her a queen! Put my crown on her head! Only let me hide myself in some convent where I may never see her more." - - - " You are ready to put your kingdom to hazard for the sake of your soul; and yet you are throwing away your soul for the sake of that creature!" - - - "Sir, is it possible that you would, for the sake of one passion, lose the merit of all your sacrifices?" The fact is that the king was alternately sinning and whipping himself, and Mary treasured up and at her death bequeathed to the convent of Chaillot, the scourge with which he had vigorously avenged her wrongs on his own shoulders. At last he was inveigled into a mourning multitude of Jesuits; the queen told him she was determined to witness no longer her own degradation, she would withdraw into a convent, and when sobs choked her voice, his majesty was instantly assailed like the tyrant in a Greek chorus, by the united remonstrances of the chorus, until he stated that he conferred the title to break off the connection more decently and promised to banish her. He implored Catharine to depart. He owned his promise, but added " I know too well the power which you have over me, I have not strength of mind to keep my resolution if I see you." He offered to convey her in all dignity to Flanders, and then threatened she should be sent by force. She answered that she was a martyr, a Protestant victim, that she was a free-born Englishwoman and would dwell where she pleased, while the Habeas Corpus Act and Magna Charta were laws; the king must remove her by force and then she would appeal to these laws of her country, and recover her liberty; " and Flanders," she cried " never! I have learned one thing from my friend the duchess of Mazarine, and that is never to trust myself in a country where there are convents;" and " I will not carry my shame among strangers." The king urged that it might be said " if she remained in England that she had still some power over his mind," she replied " that it was his majesty to whom the power appertained, yet she would be pulled to pieces by four horses before she would consent to be parted from him." At last the bribe of a large estate in Ireland prevailed on her to retire to that country, however she soon returned and again was intimate with James, but he was more cautious, the queen more forgiving, the mistress had no political influence, and is little more heard of, while Rochester reaped retribution, in disgrace.

Catherine had two children by the king (or Col. Graham the keeper of his privy purse) who owned them, 1. a son, who died young on the coronation day, and thus added to the many ill omens to the unhappy king on that event, and 2. Lady Catharine Darnley who was married 1. to the earl of Anglesey, and 2. to the Duke of Buckingham. She possessed some influence over her *brother* the Pretender, was extravagantly proud of her royal blood, and was in every respect a very spirited and extraordinary woman.

When Mary, the daughter of James, after the Revolution, as queen, turned her back on the Baroness of Darlington, the latter exclaimed " I beg your majesty to remember that if I broke one of the commandments *with* your father, you broke another *against* him. On that score we are both equal." After James's flight she married Sir David Collyer, first Earl of Portmore, by whom she had two sons, to whom she said "If any one calls you sons of a——you must bear it, for so you are; but if they call you bastards fight till you die, for you are Sir David's sons."*

1722. Apr. 10. Sophia Charlotte, Baroness of Kilmanseck, Countess of Platen and Countess of Leinster in Ireland, was created Baroness of Brentford and Countess of Darlington for life.

The women of the Meisenberg family for three generations engaged the amorous attentions of the house of Brunswick Luneburg. The Countess of Darlington's mother (daughter of Count Earl Philip von Meisenberg, and wife of M. [afterwards Count] Platen) was mistress to the old Elector of Hanover; she herself (and it seems almost incredible) to George I. his son, and her niece, the Countess of Yarmouth, to George II. Her mother had been too intimate also with the Count Konigsmark, and to stop the scandal had offered her daughter in marriage to him, but to his own murder and the melancholy imprisonment for life of the young queen of George I., he declined on scruples of conscience. These by no means afflicted George, who accepted the young Countess Platen as a mistress. She made a hasty match with a M. Kilmanseck to conceal her profligacy, and slipping her creditors, joined the Elector on his journey to England at a time when his other favourites hesitated to leave their own Hanover to reside in such a place. The king was pleased with her zeal, and she was for some time his reigning sultana. Honours were showered on the German demireps who made pretty pickings out of everything corrupt, and obtained the emoluments of various posts, the vacant ones being happily small, or else the degraded kingdom might have had the Countess of Darlington for Archbishop of Canterbury. One of the German ladies being abused by the mob, was said to have put her head out of the coach, and cried in bad English, "Good people, why you abuse us? We come for all your goods!" "Yes, and be d—d to you," answered a fellow, "and for all our chattels too."

"Lady Darlington," says Horace Walpole, "whom I saw at my mother's in my infancy, and whom I remember by being terrified by her enormous figure, was as corpulent and ample as the Duchess of Kendal was long and emaciated. Two fierce black eyes, large and rolling, beneath two lofty arched eyebrows; two acres of cheeks spread with crimson; an ocean of neck that overflowed, and was not distinguished from the lower part of her body; and no part restrained by stays—no wonder that a child dreaded such an ogress."

So unwieldy in bulk was this distinguished ornament of the court of St. James's, that the wits of the day bestowed on her the cognomen of "The Elephant and Castle." From another valuable authority we have a delineation a little less repulsive. "She had a greater vivacity in conversation," observes Lady Mary Wortley Montagu, "that ever I knew in a German of either sex. She loved reading, and had a taste for all polite learning. Her humour was easy and sociable. Her constitution inclined her to gallantry. She was well-bred and amusing in company. She knew both how to please and be pleased, and had experience enough to know it was hard to do either without money. Her unlimited expenses had left her with very little remaining, and she made what haste she could to take advantage of the opinion the English had of her power with the king, by receiving the presents that were made her from all quarters; and which she knew very well must cease, when it was known that the kings idleness carried him to her lodgings without either regard for her advice or affection for her person, which time and very bad paint had left her without any of the charms that once attracted

* Macauley and Lingard's Histories. Burnet's Own Time. Strickland's Queens of England. Suffolk Letters, &c.

him." The Pictorial History of England, iv. 383, makes a curious mistake, "The old lean mistress, the duchess of Kendal, stood firm for Walpole, but Carteret had secured the younger and thinner mistress, Madam Kilmanseg, now countess of Darlington, and her sister Madam Platen." This "thinner mistress" was "the Elephant and Castle," and she had no sister.*

No wonder the mob of London were highly diverted at their sovereign's tastes, and every sort of abuse was directed by the Jacobites against the court.†

"The ogress" had one daughter (Charlotte) by the king, who shared handsomely in the general plunder, and afterwards married Viscount Howe, by whom she had a son destined to raise the family to an enviable distinction. He was Admiral Lord Howe.

The countess of Darlington died some years before the Duchess of Kendal. Her arms are inserted in Allan's Illustrated Camden. Quarterly, 1 and 4, Az. three mullets ar. 2, or, a lion rampant gu. 3, vert, two fox's heads erased (Argent ?) facing each other. On an escutcheon of pretence Ar. three roses gu. Supporters, two lions rampant gu. crowned or, each charged with an escutcheon (arg. three roses gu.)

I gladly pass from these unpleasant characters to a gallant race of our English Aristocracy, and insert

The Pedigree of the family of Vane, Earls of Darlington and Dukes of Cleveland.

The early part of the Vane pedigree is much confused, but may be seen in the peerages. The family came from Monmouthshire to Kent. The first of the race connected with this county was

SIR HENRY VANE, a distinguished politician, Ambassador to various states, and Secretary of State to King Charles I., having been knighted by James I. in 1611. His dismissal from his offices and enmity to the Earl of Strafford (who, out of contempt to the Vanes, had been created Baron of Raby), with his consequent adherence to the Parliament, are matters of general history. He purchased Raby and Barnard Castle, and all the demesnes thereto belonging, from the crown (see p. 121). He entertained Charles I. at his castle at Raby in May, 1633, in his way to Scotland to be crowned; and he did the like in April, 1639, on the King's expedition to Scotland, when Sir Henry commanded a regiment of 1000 men. He died in 1654-5, aged 69, having *m.* Frances, d. and coh. of Tho. Darcy, of Tolshunt-Darcy, in co. Essex, esq., (she was bur. at Shipbourne, in Kent, 1663) by whom he had issue;

I. SIR HENRY, his successor.
II. Thomas. } *d. in f.*
III. John. }
IV. SIR GEORGE VANE, of Long Newton, knighted 1640, *m.* Elizabeth, the dau. and heiress of Sir Lyonel Maddison of Rogerly, co. Durham and Newcastle-upon-Tyne. He *d.* 1679, and was buried in Long Newton church, where there is a monument to him.

HIS HONOUR WONNE I'TH FIELD LIES HERE IN DUST,
HIS HONOUR GOT BY GRACE SHALL NEVER RUST;
THE FORMER FADES, THE LATTER SHALL FAILE NEVER,
FOR WHY, HE WAS S'R GEORGE ONCE, B'T ST. GEORGE EVER.

He was succeeded by his eldest son,

LIONEL, M.P. for the county of Durham, chosen 1698, 1700, 1701, who mar. Catherine, dau. and at length co-heir of Sir Geo. Fletcher. Bart., and was grandfather of

THE REV. HENRY VANE, D.D., Rector of Long Newton, and prebendary of Durham, created a Baronet in 1784, who mar. Frances, dau. of John Tempest, esq., and at length sole heiress of her brother John Tempest of Wynyard, and Old Durham, esq, and was succeeded by his only son and heir,

* Memoirs of Sophia Dorothea, Colburn, 1845, whence this sketch is chiefly derived

† Horace Walpole.

SIR HENRY VANE, Bart., who assumed the additional name of Tempest; he mar. 28th April, 1799, Anne Catherine, Countess of Antrim, and dying in 1813, was succeeded by his only dau. and heiress.

FRANCES ANNE EMILY, born 16 Jan., 1800, mar. 3 April, 1819, to Charles-William, present Marquis of Londonderry, who by royal licence assumed the name of Vane only.

v. Sir Walter Vane, of Shipbourne, a major-general under the Prince of Orange, killed at the battle of Seneffe in Germany, Aug. 1647. *d. s. p.*
vi. Charles Vane of Chopwell, Durham, *d. unm.*
vii. William. } *d. unm.*
viii. Edward. }
1. Margaret, *m.* Sir Tho. Penham.
2. Frances, *m.* Sir Robert Honeywood.
3. Anne, *m.* Sir Tho. Liddell of Ravensworth.
4. Elizabeth, *m.* Sir Fra. Vincent.
5. Catharine, *d. unm.* 1692.

SIR HENRY VANE (knighted by K. Char. I. 1640) "whose fame speaks trumpet-tongued to the hearts of Englishmen," is immortalized in Milton's beautiful sonnet, and no less so by Cromwell's celebrated ejaculation, "O Sir Harry Vane, Sir Harry Vane—the Lord deliver me from Sir Harry Vane." In Geneva he had imbibed many odd notions against the form of the government and the liturgy, inclining to the opinion of Origen that devils and all should be saved.* His subsequent attachment to the Parliament brought him strikingly out in the scene of politics, and Charles II. thinking that "certaynly he is too dangerous a man to lett live, if we can honestly put him out of the way,"† brought him to the block 14 June, 1662, when the drums struck up to prevent his being heard. While Treasurer to the Navy, (a place he held till the first wars between the English and Dutch) his fees amounted to little less than 30,000*l.* yearly; which he considering to be too much for a private subject, with rare honour gave up his patent (from Charles I. for life) to the then Parliament, desiring but 2000*l.* yearly for an agent he had bred up to the business, and the remainder to go to the public.‡ He was bur. at Shipbourne. His wife, Frances, dau. of Sir Chr. Wray, of Glentworth, Linc. Bart., *d.* in 1679 and was bur. at the same place, having had issue

i. Henry. }
ii. William. } *d. s. p.*
iii. Richard }
iv. Thomas, *m.* Frances, dr. of Sir Tho. Liddell; he was elected M.P. for the county of Durham, 21 June, 1675. He was attacked by the small-pox, and "was in a fever at Raby upon the day of his election, whereby he died the fourth day after, June 25th, in the morning." He died *s. p.*, aged 23, and was bur. at Staindrop.
v. CHRISTOPHER.
vi. Cecil. }
vii. Edward. } *d. inf.*
viii. Henry. }
1. Dorothy, *m.* Tho. Crispe of Essex, in 1679.
2. Frances, *m.* Edw. Kegwick, esq.
3. Mary, *m.* Sir James Tillie, of Pentillie Castle, Cornwall, knt. *d. s. p.* 1682, bur. at Shipbourne.
4. Anne. } *d. unm.*
5. Catherine. }
6. Albinia, *m.* Henry Forth, esq., an Alderman of London, and had issue Hen. Forth, esq., of Darlington, who *m.* Ann dr. of Richard Hilton, esq., and was bur. among the Hiltons at the entrance of Darlington Church in 1746. (See further in pedigree of HELTON, HYLTON, or HILTON hereafter.)

CHRISTOPHER VANE, created BARON BARNARD of Barnard Castle, 8 July, 1699, with remainder to heirs male. The title of Raby would have been preferred, but it was still in the male descendants of the unfortunate Strafford's younger brother. He succeeded his brother Thomas Vane as M. P. for the county of Durham 25 Oct., 1675, and was ousted in the elections of 1679 and 1680. He *d.* 28 Oct. 1723, aged 70, and was

* Surtees letters. J. B. T.

† Royal letter. Lansdown Collection, p. 125.

‡ Collins.

bur. at Shipbourne. He *m.* Elizabeth, eldest dau. of Gilbert Holles, Earl of Clare, and sister and co-heir to John, Duke of Newcastle, by whom he had issue

I. Henry. } *d. inf.*
II. Christopher. }
III. GILBERT.
IV. WILLIAM, chosen M.P. for this county in 1708, created Viscount Vane and Baron of Duncannon, co. Tyrone, in 1720, *d.* suddenly of an apoplexy, at his seat of Fairlawn, 20 May, 1734, aged 53, having three days before been elected M.P. for Kent, br. 5 June at Shipbourne. He *m.* Lucy, dr. and co-heiress of Wm. Jolliffe, esq., of Caverswell, Staffs. She *d.* 27 March, 1742, was bur. at Shipbourne, and had issue

I. Christopher, *d.* 1721, aged 17, bur. at Shipbourne.
II. John, *d.* at Naples, 5 Feb. 1723, aged 17, bur. at Shipbourne 17 Apr.
III. WILLIAM, *b.* 1714, succeeded as VISCOUNT VANE in 1734, mar. Frances, dau. of Francis Hawes, esq. and widow of Lord William Hamilton, *d.* 5 Apr. 1789 *s. p.* when the title became extinct, bur. at Shipbourne. An Act passed for the sale of his estates to pay his debts, and the tithes of Darlington which had been settled upon these Lords of Fairlawn, reverted thereupon to the main line by purchase.

1. Elizabeth. }
2. Albinia. } *d. inf.*
3. Mary. }
4. Grace, survived her father.

GILBERT VANE, BARON BARNARD, *d.* 1753, aged 75. *m.* Mary, dr. of Morgan Randyll, of Chilworth, Surrey, esq.; she *d.* at Newark, 4 Aug., 1728, aged 47, having had issue

I. HENRY.
II. Morgan, made Comptroller of the Stamp Office in 1732, *m.* Margaretta, dr. of Mr. Robert Knight, formerly Cashier to the South Sea Company, by whom there was a son, Morgan Vane. She *d.* at the Bath in May, 1739. He mar. secondly Anna Maria, dau. of — Fowler, esq., and thirdly to Mary, sister to John Woodyear, esq., by whom he had a dau. Mary Vane.
III. Thomas, *d.* 19 Feb. 1758.
IV. Gilbert, a Lieut.-Colonel in the Army, died unmarried in 1772.
V. Randal, died unmarried 1736.
VI. Charles, of Mount Ida, Norf., had an only dr. Henrietta, who *m.* Sir William Langham, Bart.

1. Anne, maid of honour to Queen Caroline; she *d.* at the Bath, unm. 11 Mar. 1735-6.
2. Elizabeth, *m.* Sir William Humble, Bart. She died 22 Feb. 1770.
3. Jane, *m.* Thomas Staunton, of Stockgrove, Bucks., esq., and had issue.

HENRY, 3rd BARON BARNARD, *b.* 1705, sometime (1747) M. P. for Durham and for Launceston and St. Maws, Cornwall, vice-treasurer of Ireland, &c., Lord Lieutenant and Vice-Admiral for Durham in 1754. In that year, (Apr. 3.) on the formation of the Duke of Newcastle's ministry he was created VISCOUNT BARNARD and EARL OF DARLINGTON, and filled high official employment. His character was variously represented in consequence of the hot state of party. Horace Walpole lashes him in his most bitter style, while the premier Duke panegyricised him in the Lords as "Harry Vane, who never said a false thing, or did a bad one." He *d.* 6 Mar. 1758. His wife was Grace Fitzroy, granddaughter of Charles II. by the beautiful Barbara Villiers, Duchess of Cleveland, and heiress to her brother the second Duke of Cleveland; she *d.* 1763, aged 66, having borne him issue

I. HENRY.
II. Frederick, of Sellaby, a man of the most elegant taste, M.P. for Durham, 1761, (an election which lasted nine days) *b.* 26 June, 1732, *d.* 1801. He *m.* Henrietta, sister of Sir Wm. Meredith, Bart., bur. 10 Mar., 1796, at Gainford, "above 70," and secondly on 7 Sep. 1797, at Gainford, Jane, eldest dr. of Arthur Lysaght, esq. of Bath, co. Somerset.
III. Raby Vane, owner, *jure uxoris*, of lands at Blackwell, &c., chosen M.P. for co. of Durham, 1758, *b.* 1736, *d.* 23 Oct. 1769, *m.* Elizabeth, dr. of George Sayer, D.D., Archdeacon of Durham. 17 Apr. 1768, Mar. The Hon. Raby Vane, esq., third brother to the Earl of Darlington, to Miss Eyres, of Lower Grosvenor Street, daughter to the late Bishop Eyres. *Lloyd's Evening Post, and Gent. Mag. of the day.* The marriage seems to have escaped Surtees (iv. 133) and the Peerages. His widow Elizabeth lived at Staindrop Hall, *d.* 28 May, 1789, aged 47, and by her own request was buried near the N.W. corner of Staindrop church-yard, where an altartomb perpetuates her memory.

1. Anna, *m.* first the Hon. Chas. Hope Weir, bro. of James, 3rd Earl of Hopetown, and secondly Brig.-Gen. the Hon. George Monson.
2. Mary, *m.* Ralph Carr, of Cocken, esq., *d. s. p.* 1781.
3. Henrietta, *d. unm.* 20 Jan. 1759.

HENRY VANE. 2ND EARL OF DARLINGTON, born in 1726, succeeded as Lord Lieut. and Vice-Admiral of the county in 1758. He was chosen M.P. for Durham, on his father being made a peer, in 1753, and was rechosen in 1754, Master of the Jewel Office and Governor of Carlisle, Alderman of Durham city, and Colonel of the Militia of Durham county, he *d.* 8 Sep. 1792, aged 65, being commemorated by a recumbent effigy and distant view of Raby on a mural monument of white marble, in Staindrop chancel. He is there called "a sincere and pious christian," who "stood forth in an age of increasing relaxation, a good and great example," and when, in 1775, George Colman, jun., in company with his father, (whose observation to a South Durham post-boy was "in phrase too classical for a north-country post-boy to understand; and the post-boy answered in a dialect quite incomprehensible to the translator of Terence") visited the Earl, who was an old acquaintance, he thought the first glimpse beneath his roof "presented a warmer picture of ancient hospitality than he had ever witnessed, or might perhaps ever see again." In like manner my grandsire, William Longstaffe, the worthy vicar of Kelloe (who *non obstante* his cloth, had been appointed a deputy-lieutenant under the Militia acts by this gallant old Earl in May, 1785) visited him in a tour of July following, and after a night's experience of Raby dining and dreaming, very sensibly notes his decided conviction, that the "most capacious and grand Gothic edifice" was indeed possessed of "comforts and conveniences, in a superior manner to any modern house he ever saw." All this hospitality has done anything but waned with the accession of a dukedom, and to have a proper idea of such splendour it must be remembered that the Nevilles themselves were at last borne down with the weight of doing everything in accordance with "Raby, the largest castel of logginges in al the North Cuntery." During this earl's time, in 1778, Mary Hildray died at Piercebridge, aged 107 years, all spent in single blessedness, and nearly 90 of which had seen her a tenant under the Raby family. His farm and farmyard were objects deserving the best attention, the farm included lands of the annual value of 1200*l.* wherein all the improvements in agriculture were practised. His lordship however retained one ancient usage, for on his farm the tillage lands were ploughed by between 20 and 30 teems of four oxen each. In the farmyard were close stands for upwards of 40 oxen, besides an open spacious fold with a cistern of water perpetually running; there were covered racks and pens for 800 sheep, and various other conveniences; the superintendence of all this being a treasure of enjoyment and health to the noble owner.

The Earl *m.* on the 10th March, 1757, Margaret, sister of James, the first Earl of Lonsdale, who *d.* at Langton Grange, deservedly lamented by all her poorer neighbours, on the 11th September, 1800. She had issue (with two daughters who *d. inf.*)

WILLIAM HARRY VANE, 3RD EARL OF DARLINGTON, Viscount and Baron Barnard, *b.* 27 July, 1766, Lord Lieutenant, Custos Rotulorum, and Vice-Admiral of Durham, Colonel of the Durham Militia, and sometime M.P. for Winchilsea, created a MARQUIS in 1827, and DUKE OF CLEVELAND and Baron Raby in 1833, elected K.G. in 1839, *d.* 29 Jan. 1842, aged 75, at his residence in St. James's Square, *bur.* in Staindrop Church where there is a recumbent effigy on an altar tomb to his memory. His grace *m.* first 19 Sep. 1787, Lady Katharine Powlett, 2nd dr. and coh. of Harry, sixth and last Duke of Bolton, and coh. of one moiety of the Barony of St. John of Basing, she d. 17 June, 1807; and secondly on the 27 July, 1813, Elizabeth, dr. of Robert Russell, esq. By his first lady only his grace had issue

I. HENRY.
II. William John Frederick, who assumed the name of Powlett, *b.* 3 Apr, 1792, sometime M.P. for this county, *m.* 3 July, 1815, Caroline, 5th dr. of William, Earl of Lonsdale, K.G., *b.* 17 Feb. 1792.
III. Harry George, *b.* 19 April, 1803. M.P. for South Durham.
1. Louisa-Catharine-Barbara, *b.* 4 Jan. 1791, *m.* 29 July, 1813, to Francis Forester, esq., brother to the late Lord Forester, and *d.* 8 Jan. 1821.
2. Caroline-Mary, *b.* 8 Feb. and *d.* 11 May, 1795.

3. Augusta-Henrietta, *b.* 26 Dec. 1796, *m.* 2 June, 1817, to Mark Milbanke, esq., of Thorpe Perrow, near Bedale, Yorks., M.P.
4. Laura, *m.* 24 Feb. 1823, to Lieut.-Col. William Henry Meyrick, of the 3rd Foot Guards.
5. Arabella, *b.* 2 June, 1801, *m.* 25 Apr., 1831, to The Hon. Richard Pepper Arden, of Pepper Hall, Yorkshire, now Lord Alvanly. (See Pedigree of Prescott hereafter.)

HENRY VANE, Second Duke and Marquis of Cleveland, K. G., Earl of Darlington, Viscount and Baron Barnard of Barnard Castle, and Baron Raby of Raby Castle, Col. in the Army and Col. of the Durham Militia, and sometime M.P. for the county of Durham, *b.* 16 Aug., 1788, succeeded to the title in 1842. He mar. 16 Nov., 1809, Sophia, eldest dau. of John, 4th Earl of Poulet, K.T., *b.* 16 March, 1785. On the occasion of his attaining his majority as Lord Barnard in 1809, an ox was roasted whole at Darlington and distributed with plenty of strong ale to the populace, and similar rejoicings occurred at other places. The skull of the ox roasted at Piersebridge is preserved in a butcher's shop there, the horns are gilded.

Insignia.

Arms. Quarterly. I. and IV., az. 3 sinister gauntlets or,* for Vane. II. and III. Quarterly, 1 and 4 quarterly France and England; 2 Scotland, 3 Ireland (being the arms of Charles II.) over all a baton sinister, compony ar. and az. for Fitzroy.

Crests. I. On a wreath, a dexter hand, couped above the wrist, erect in a gauntlet proper, bossed and rimmed or, brandishing a sword, also proper, for Vane. II. On a chapeau gu. turned-up ermine, a lion passant, guardant, or, crowned with a ducal coronet az. and gorged with a collar counter-compony ar. and az, for Fitzroy.

Supporters. Dexter, a griffin ar.; sinister, an antelope or, each gorged with a plain collar az. (formerly the griffin was worn charged with 3 gauntlets as in the arms, and the antelope with 3 martlets). These are the supporters of Vane, but those of Fitzroy have occasionally been adopted, viz. dexter, a lion guardant or, crowned and gorged as in the crest; sinister, a greyhound ar. collared as in the dexter.

Motto. Nec temere, nec timide.

*** I will here throw together an anecdote or two which occur to me, and which would confuse the stream of pedigree.

In 1714, the first Lord Barnard having taken some extraordinary displeasure against his son, on whom the castle of Raby was settled, got 200 workmen together of a sudden, and in a few days stripped it of its covering of lead, iron, glass, doors, boards, &c., to the value of 3000*l.* The Court of Chancery, however, no only granted an injunction to stay committing waste, but decreed that the castle should be repaired and put in the same condition it was in August 1714; for which purpose a commission issued to ascertain what ought to be done, and a master appointed to see it done, at the expense of Lord B.

The second Duke of Cleveland, brother to Grace Fitzroy, often resided at Raby, and in the hunting or sporting season, had also an occasional dormitory and refectory (both one room) in the house of one of the Raby tenants, at Piersebridge, which is still pointed out. He seems, judging from the popular traditions floating in South Durham, to have been a quiet, unoffending man, of the most unassuming simplicity. He doated upon the chase, and once when out on his favourite bent, his horse happened an accident, and he was compelled to mount a haystack to obtain as wide a scope of view as possible. The farmer's wife tenanting the adjacent farm bustled out and fiercely called him down. The peer's gentle explanation, "My good woman, I am the *Duke*," only added fresh fuel to the termagant's fire. "Why, I dinna care whether ye be *duke* or *drake*, ye shall come down." Another story has been bandied about in newspaper literature in fifty changes, but it is very generally localized in Darlington Ward. It seems that the

* There is a tradition that the original *arms* were a bloody hand, which was afterwards covered with a steel gauntlet. But does it not rather refer to the *crest?*

hot blood of Finch did not satisfactorily naturalize itself with the amiable duke, who used to hold his high-spirited wife's hanks of linen thread while she wound them, but often entangled them with his awkward handling. On one of these occasions she angrily exclaimed " you fool you," a taunt which even he could not tamely submit to, for he replied sharply " yes, I was a fool when I married you."

To pass to the Long-Newton members of the family of Vane. An old cartwright of Long-Newton, who made divers articles for one of them (Dr. Henry Vane, who was made a Bart. in 1782, I believe), being unable to write, used to make his bills out in a system of hieroglyphics, describing the items by rude drawings. In one of these precious documents there was a simple circle which puzzled the patrician most woefully, he recollected nothing of the sort being done for him, and in despair went to the old man to make enquiries. The latter however was more accustomed to invent hieroglyphics *pro tem.* than to read them when accomplished, and had completely forgotten the signification of the mystery. " Why," said he, scratching his head, " it's like a *cheese*, but what I nivver sould a cheese to your worship !—cheese—cheese—Oh ! I know what it is, it's a *grundstone*, and I've furgetten to put a pop int' middle on't."

In 1794, John Tempest, esq., of Wynyard, died. This benevolent gentleman had for upwards of forty years employed William Garthwaite, of Wolveston, as carpenter at the Hall, and afterwards as porter at the Lodge. Two or three days before he died, he asked the old man, if he could do anything to make him more comfortable, but he expressed himself to be quite content as he was. The squire died ; Madam Tempest his widow, requested nothing except the miniatures of her husband and son, and left Wynyard for Little Grove, near London. Harry Vane, of Long-Newton, was the heir to his uncle, but his long absence on the continent, his precarious health, and the total want of intelligence, rendered his existence extremely doubtful. One day his valet accidentally took up an English newspaper, and saw an advertisement requesting the immediate return of his master, and they both arrived at Wynyard with all possible expedition. At the entrance to the grounds they reined in their horses and were gently riding through, when, to their infinite surprise, a loud voice exclaimed " Come back ! " On looking round, a tall elderly man approached from the lodge, demanding where Harry had got authority to ride through without *his* leave ; a smile pervaded the baronet's features, which exasperated the old porter still more, and he fiercely cried " Thou's somebody's dirty lick-plate,* or thou never would come here in such an impudent manner ! " After amusing himself a little longer, the *lick-plate* threw off his disguise, and told the porter plainly who he was, for the porter had completely forgotten the young heir's features. The astonishment was now on the other side, but Sir Harry Vane Tempest (to give him his later title) told him good-naturedly to get his hat and stick and accompany him to the hall, talking over the events of his absence on the way. A visit to the lodge, to present the faithful creature with a guinea for a new wig, soon followed, and in his infirmity he was pensioned with his son and daughter at Darlington, and eventually was placed, through Sir Harry's influence, at Kirkleatham Hospital, where he died in 1818, aged 88.†

* A contemptuous epithet for an ill-bred person. I think I have seen somewhere, that the more menial servants in the houses of gentry-folks in olden times, were only allowed the privilege of licking the platters, after the superior servants had gobbled up the "cream of the dish."

† Ex inf. John Burlison, of Darlington, the hero's great grandson.

††† A lady in Darlington still performs the singular custom of presenting *three red roses* on Midsummer-day at Raby Castle, by which tenure she holds certain property near Cockfield (at Pethraw, I believe.)

[*View of the Manorhouse temp. Geo. Allan, archæol.*]

Chapter VI. Characteristics.

WE have but little left at Darlington in the way of remains of former glory. We may not say that this was a Roman station or Saxon fortress. Cade conjectured that the Roman road from York, came by Craike to Nesham and Sockburn where it crossed the Tees and ran on by Bishopton, Mainsforth, Old Durham, and Chester to Gateshead. On the other side Leeming Lane crosses at Piersbridge, which has become very famous for its Roman remains. "The direct road," says he, "from Darlington to Durham, I conjecture to have been a later work of some of the bishops; for, if you observe, when Canute came on penance here, he walked barefooted from Garmonsway" [to Durham].* In 1790, he wrote to Gough, that "a most valuable collection of Roman silver coins has, this year, been taken up out of the bed of the river Tees, near Darlington. I had about a dozen sent me for inspection; some of Trajan, Gordianus, Hadrian, Severus, Antoninus, Carausius, and others. Those that I saw were as perfect as if almost taken from the mint, but the treasure dispersed into divers hands." In later times a vast quantity of Roman 3rd. brass coins have been discovered in the Cockerbeck, between Mowdon bridge and Darlington, and in Baydalebeck, near the same bridge. The main deposit was adjoining the lands of William Allan, esq. I have seen an immense number in the hands of various owners. They are in the most perfect preservation, and are all of the Constantine family.†

* Correspondence. Nichols' Library Anecdotes.

† Those which have occurred to me are coins of the imperial ladies Helena and Flavia Maxima Fausta, of the two Constantines and Crispus. Many have on the exergue P.LON. no very rare characteristic, though an interesting one, it being considered to denote money struck at London. The rare reverse of Constantine II. VIRTUS EXERCIT. (a trophy between two captives), occurs among the London specimens. Mr. Sams has a fine collection of these Cockerton pieces.

Castle Hill has already been mentioned at sufficient length (p. 118), and the Tees has left it but little character ; it is opposite the seathouse of R. H. Allan, esq., whose labourers, in 1848, found in his grounds a singular leaden ornament with pellets in compartments.

The bishop's manor house at Darlington, is situate due south of the church. On entering the court-yard from the lane, opposite the porter's lodge is a small modern room, in which are two fine old oak chests, both of much the same age. One is beautifully inlaid in elegant panel-devices: the other is interesting as having the arms and crest of Eure (which appear to have been inlaid), and this inscription: "1575. R. E. THE. RIGHT.WORSHIPFVLL. RAVFE. EVRIE. THELDER. 1575."* Ralph Eurye, esq., was made borough bailiff in 1561, and the main branch of the Eures held lands at Darlington and Blackwell. The other chest is said to have been brought from Thornton Hall where it was *enchanted*, and stood for generations unopened, no one daring to meddle with it. Passing through the court-yard, we come to a doorway on the north of the building, which has been pointed ; indeed, the bounding label still remains. In a direct line with this is a neat little early English arch (see cut, page 43), the remnant of Pudsey's work, shut up in a sort of pantry. It was formerly the entrance of a long arched passage, leading to what is now a hen-house, supposed to have been a dungeon ; though why, it would be somewhat difficult to find out. This passage is now completely removed, and the hen-house so modernized as to retain little that appertaineth to "hoare antiquitie" save the massive stone walls. To this I ought to add that the floor has been raised, and the arch somewhat curtailed of its fair proportions. To the right of the space between the outer doorway and the arch is a large room of later architecture, apparently a hall. It is lighted by small, square, oblong lights ; and at the west end are two doorways, flat four-centered ; one leading into a closet, the other into the modern part of the workhouse. The wall-plate of the roof—also late florid—remains above these arches, showing the moulding of the ribs, which appear to have divided the roof into a series of square panels. The exterior roofs of the whole ancient part of the building are of good pitch, and are plain oak, as the workhouse-master informed me ; but the exact plan of the mansion cannot now be ascertained. One high square chimney retains an early corbel table, formed of minute arches. To the left of the entrance, and opposite the hall before described, is "the chapel" [St. James's], which is delineated in Allan's cut to the right. The whole of the exterior is roughcast. One may still see three Norman lights in the eastern gable (pointing out the date, 1160, as a probable one), and the sides had also small circular-headed lights of extremely deep splay. The chapel formerly opened out of the entrance passage by an enriched doorway, but the whole is now modernized. The foundation will be noticed in the Ecclesiastical Division. Up stairs, are the remains of what is

* The five is awkwardly made into three, and the date seems 1375; but the fraud is too palpable.

termed "the anquetting room," which has had traceried windows, one now forming a doorway. There is also a plain early stone fireplace.

In ancient times, we find the plot of ground on which the mansion stands called Hallgarth.

1311. Bishop Kellawe finding that persons had been treading the grass in the flat [*in fovea*] between the gate of his manor and the vicar's houses, in length from the gate aforesaid to the meadow called Fycton,* gives it to the vicar for life [in order that some honest person should have it, I suppose.] This bishop was a very exact and proper man, for in the next year, having heard that the nobles of England were gathering their forces, for the purpose of having a *grand tournament at Darlington*, he writes a peremptory mandate to his coroner of Sadberge, instructing him to prevent any such thing, for he would not have it in *his* liberty.† The flat abovementioned (now, I presume, the worthy workhouse master's fertile garden), is again mentioned in 1320, as *fossatum episcopi*, near a piece of meadow granted to Wm. s. Wm. de Walleworthe, by John s. Wm. s. Benedict de Derlington, who evidently took under a charter of 1290 from Bishop Beke to his father, of 4*a*. 3*r*. 4*p*. of land in the field of Derlingtone, *super Biscopflat*. In 1314 ? the same John granted to Wm. de Walleworde and Margery ux. *le Halleflat*. The excessively small parcels of ground conveyed in those early periods plainly shew the sad uncultivated state of the "fields." ‡

At the conclusion of the 13th century we find Stephen *de Buteleria* de Derlingtone, a seller, and Robert *Janitor*, a buyer, evidently officials of the bishop, the latter being probably father of Richard *Porter*, mentioned p. 171.

The custodiership of the Manor House is still a patent office, although the *locus in quo* has been sold. It accompanies the bailiwick of Coatham Mundeville and entitles its holder to 4 quarters of wheat from the bishop's tenants of Blackwell. 53*s*. 4*d*. is payable to him as bailiff of Coatham. The holders were generally lawyers.

The Manor House was bought by the township in 1806, for the purposes of a poor-house. It had been so used for some time before. A large pile of new buildings was erected to the south in 1808, the cost being partly deferred by the bequest of Mr. G. G. Phillips, (see p. 158), indicated on a slip of paper attached to his will "Town £100." Mr. George Elwin is workhouse-master, and everything is conducted in the most "apple-pie order."

POSTSCRIPT.

VISIT OF QUEEN VICTORIA. On the 28th of September, 1849, Darlington was once more in the route of a royal progress. Her present Majesty on her journey from Scotland to the Isle of Wight, most graciously consented to receive an address here. The Bank Top Station was repainted, and hung with evergreens and banners, platforms and terraces were prepared, floral crowns§ furnished, and all the petty splendour a rural town could muster was brought to bear on the event. At a public meeting, (Robert Henry Allan, esq., in the chair) the following address was decided upon, to be presented by the borough bailiff, such of the local nobility as could attend, the two members for the division, the magistrates of the district, the clergy and ministers of the town, together with Messrs. William Backhouse, Edmund Backhouse, Joseph Forster, Henry Hutchinson, John Kipling, Michael Middleton, Francis Mewburn, jun., Edward Kipling, James

* Qu., the modern Feethams, which, however, in 1631 was *Fetholmes*.

† Kellawe's Register. ‡ Charters. D. and C. Durham.

§ Mr. Marley, of Bank Top, furnished one, composed entirely of the richest dahlias.

Overend, Joseph Pease, J. B. Pease, Nathaniel Plews, Henry Pease, J. S. Peacock, and George Allison.

May it Please your Majesty. We, your Majesty's dutiful and loyal subjects, the Nobility, Magistrates, Clergy, Ministers, Gentry, Merchants, and other inhabitants of the town of Darlington and the neighbourhood, approach your Majesty with feelings of the most respectful and dutiful attachment to your august person and throne, and beg to offer the warmest and most cordial expression of our welcome on this your first Royal progress through the County of Durham.

We beg to express our grateful sense of the deep interest which your Majesty has ever been graciously pleased to evince in the welfare of your Majesty's subjects at large, and which has been so especially shown towards the inhabitants of Ireland by the late Royal visit to that country, which we fervently hope will strengthen the ties that attach them to your Majesty's throne and person.

We pray that your Majesty's reign may be long and prosperous,—characterized by that continued progress in social advancement which has rendered Great Britain so pre-eminent amongst surrounding nations.

We heartily desire that the remainder of your Majesty's journey may be safely accomplished, and that you, your Royal Consort, and Children, may possess every blessing which the Almighty can bestow, and every happiness which this world can afford.

Signed, on behalf of the Nobility, Magistrates, Clergy, Ministers, Gentry, Merchants, and other Inhabitants of the town of Darlington, and the Neighbourhood, in the County of Durham, in public meeting assembled.

FRA. MEWBURN, Chief Bailiff of Darlington.

On the day of presentation, the rain fell heavily, and but partially cleared up on the auspicious occasion. The enthusiasm of the many thousands assembled was however immense, and quiet and reverential withal. Nothing could be done with more decorum, and the appearance of so many magistrates and clergy in their vestments, as well as the plainer preachers of the Non-conformists, gave the precise spot of action more than common state. The shops were all closed and the bells of the churches of St. Cuthbert and St. John sent forth their merriest peals.

At 1·35 p.m. the Royal train appeared. The band struck up the Royal Anthem, and amidst deafening cheers the Queen entered the station. Her Majesty, as previously intimated, did not alight, but Sir George Grey having introduced the borough bailiff, he presented the address* to her Majesty, who received it in the most gracious manner. She also most benignly accepted a magnificent bouquet from Mr. John Harrison's Grange Road Gardens, and a large paper copy of all then published of this work. Captain Robson, of Heighington, formerly commander of the Royal Yacht, and Lord Harry Vane were both acknowledged by the Queen, who wore a light plaid shawl and white silk bonnet, trimmed in the simplest manner. Prince Albert and the Royal Children also won golden opinions by their condescension. One worthy old man was certain that "the little girl pulled the nosegay from her mother, sir, and smelt at it *very much*." The Marchioness of Douro alighted and remained a few minutes in the station. After remaining about fifteen minutes in the station, the train moved slowly through the crowded lines of spectators for York, amid repeated peals of cheers.

* I crouch in a note. It was on vellum, in the fullest decoration of medieval art I could combine with chastity of effect. In an initial letter hung the arms of England. In the copy of my work presented, I inserted a blank page containing a rich cross of foliage, which wreathed round four shields, 1 and 4, England; 2, Scotland; and 3, Ireland, "Humbly presented to her most gracious Majesty Queen Victoria, upon the occasion of her first royal progress through the county palatine of Durham, by her most dutiful subject the Author."

The day was completely a holiday, the shops were closed, and a glorious bonfire and heaps of noisy fireworks, with an illumination or two, made night cheerful.

POSTSCRIPT 2.

THE RISING OF THE NORTH. Among those who accompanied the Earl of Westmoreland "across the sea, and bid farewell to bower and green," was *Henry Sympson*, who returned in 1671 and confessed that he was *a native of Darlington*, 28 years of age; that he had served as a soldier under Captain Sanders, at Newhaven (Havre), who had married his aunt, and that when the town was given up he was suffering under the plague; that he now wanted to get a place at Newcastle or York as a hat maker; that his wife was a French woman, and her mother lived at Valencia; that he had heard the English, then at Lovyne, often "wishe that the Erle of Westmerland *had taken Sir George Bowes at the firste*, and kepte hyme stylle, for then they might have gone and taken York, and then all England wold have taken ther partes;" and that one Sherwood, a priest of Durham, sent home young Trollop, sick of the falling sickness. It seems from his account that the Earl of Westmoreland kept a good house at Louvain, having forty or fifty that came to meat with him.

*** Since writing the commencement of this division, I find that Kemble in his "Saxons in England" includes our Darlington, and Darlingscott, Worc., as sites of Saxon marks, which derived their name from the Deorlingas, a family, but I do not alter from my sentiments in p. 3. However, the subject is curious.

Land held in common was designated by the names Mark, and Shire. The smallest of these divisions, the Mark or March, was a plot marked out on which freemen settled for mutual profit and protection. The word denoted the territory, but especially applied to the woods, wastes, and boundary pastures, protecting the cultivated space,* and in which the Markmen had common rights. In a wider sense we have the Marches of Wales and Scotland, over which we had lords, like the Markgraves of Germany, with certain bounds to watch. The Marks increased with civilization and joined, the old boundaries became commons and were apportioned to the different parishes,† and at last

* In charters in the Treasury of the conclusion of the 13th cent. we find mention made of *Nesse* [Nessfield, a promotory or nose], a meadow called *Langsike*, the field of *Dedmire* [Dodmire], *le Crosflat*, *Rotherum* [a family of the name occur about 1590 here], *Hundon* and *Granhou*. All these small cultivated territories, and various others "in the field" were disposed of in the smallest quantities from two or three acres to half a rood, a circumstance bespeaking scarcity of good dry land; indeed a grant about 1313 of "the hay growing in the marshes of the field of Derlington," doubtless included the produce of an immense tract, such as it was.

† In Wolsey's time, for the appeasing of variancies betwixt the *burgesses* and inhabitants of the Burgh of Dernton, and the *husbandmen* and inhabitants of Bondgate in Dernton, concerning the common of pasture in Brankinmore and on the West-more in Bondgate with other pastures the burgesses claimed within Bondgate, it was ordered by Master Willyam Frankelyn, clerk, chaunceller of the Bysshoprick, Sir Willyam Bulmer the elder, knt., sheriff of the same, Sir Wm. Eure, knt., Sir Thomas Tempest, knt., steward of the Bisshoprick, Robert Bowes, esquier, *and other councillors to my Lord of Duresme*, that the inhabitants burgesses of the Burgh should have Brankinmoor with the inhabitants and tenants of Blackwell, and Hurworth; and the inhabitants and husbandmen of Bondgate the pasture called the West-more *and* Bondgate, and all other their pastures in Bondgate, and should have to farm a ground called the *Battelfeld*, with the pasture to the same belonging, paying as accustomed. Then follows an order 25th August, 1526, by Frankleyn, Bulmer, Eure, William Strangways, clerk, his Grace's surveyor, and John Bentley, *councellors of his Grace, within the bysshoprick of Duresme*, "that the inhabitants of the Burgh of Darnton shall have in severaltie, without interruption of the tenants of Blackwell and Hurworth, all their parcels of ground lying bebetwixt Fyrthfeild and Dodmerfield, and oone other parcell of ground lying upon a leche unto a stone brigge [see p. 40], and from thence unto Gawtmyre, and from thence extending unto the South side of Fraunce-howse; and that the inhabitants of Hurworth and Blackwell schall from henceforth use ne occupye eny comon within the precincts of the said ground assigned unto the Burgh of Dernton unto tyme that they shew a lawfull tytle why they ought to have comon, &c.; and that unto that tyme the inhabitants of the said Burgh schall have and use the said parcels, &c., in severaltie, and may enclose at their peril

even given in shares to private estates. The boundaries were generally a sike, as between Darlington and Hurworth: a *cross*, as between Darlington and Blackwell: an oak,* a hill, a stone,† and whatever it was, it was a marked and sacred emblem.‡

The markmen had a court or Markmoot, retained in the territorial jurisdiction of manor-lords, and frequently held, like the shire-moots, on a hill. The *Hill of the Sessions* at Sadberge as applied to a wapentake,§ and the *Castle Hill* at Blackwell to a freehold manor seem instances of these customs.

The borough of Darlington with its surrounding moors will give a tolerable idea of a mark on a small scale.

If Mr. Kemble's system is tenable, Cockerton would (as *ing* is not a necessary adjunct of a patromymic, being merely the genitive plural or generative case) be the seat of his Coceringas, who also settled at Cockerington, Linc. I am clear that unless rivers took their name from families, that my former opinions are correct, but Elstantofte at Blackwell smells strongly of the Saxon name *Helmstan.*

It is evident that parishes, manors, &c., took their origin from the Saxon marks, but streets took their names from bodies of men as well as topographical features. Glovers Wynd might perhaps refer to the property of the family of that name being situate in it, notwithstanding its proximity to Skinnergate, but the latter, with Bondgate, Priestgate, and Prebend Row were obviously the peculiar dwelling-places of the men their names refer to. Bull Wynd commemorates the Bulmers, the other ancient streets are named from their situation. What is Hundgate?

unto tyme the mater is otherways discussed. And all the inhabitaunts of the said Burgh shall from hensforth geve their attendance upon *my Lord's Grace his Scheriff and his Baylly of Derlyngton* for the tyme being, and thei ne ony of them *sehall not be reteyned to serve eny other*, upon peyne of forfeiture of the penaltie conteyned in the Statute of Reteynours; and also upon payn of forfeiting all such liberties and profits as they or eny of them claymeth or be entitled to have by reason of the said Burgh or otherwise."

The Blackwell commons were divided in 1612 and 1622 by a commission issued from Durham Chancery. The Commissioners set out for every oxgang 19 acres in the Townefeilds and one acre upon Brankinmoor. Sinckehill, Sinckebanck and broad Scoine in Stresham feild with a way through Blackwell nooke, *Walk mill* nooke, abutting on the Skerne on the E. and Briggie Loaning on the N., Snipe Sike, France Dike, Dowda, Wheatland gate, Sowrebancks, Brigghill and the Staggfold nooke occur, and may amuse the minute topographer and etymologist. A common passage was to be sett out and *doweld* [marked by *dowles* or *meres*] to Brankinmoor.

The portion of Brankinmoor occupied by the burgesses was divided into cattlegates separated by dikes. To order these, four grassmen were appointed each year, who sold the whins off the moor for the general benefit of the borough, but were frequently forestalled by roguish burgesses who "willfullie and obstinately" stole them for their own use. They had an officer called a Hirdman, who was not to be hired by the grassmen without consent of the bailiff and jury. A new Hird-house was ereeted in 1624. Ric. Johnson was fined in 1626 for depasturing horses in *le loaning vocat. Yarme loning.*

* In the freeholds of Blackwell are some ancient thorns, standing alone, and said by the rustics to mark the extent of the freehold portion. They are in the *Langdraughts*, and evidently boundered the *Exchequer Land.* See Hatfield's Survey.

† "Le Bordland and land extra lees markestones" mentioned at Blackwell in 1622.—*Halmot Bks.*

‡ 1612. John Liddell presented at the Barton Manor Courts, Yks.; because his wife having been warned by the overseers of the common works to come to repair the common ways, refused, and did not come; and for removing *quondam terminum* (Anglice, a *dowle, mere* or *marke*), between himself and John Gibson.

From the same rolls (penes R. H. Allan, esq., lord of two of the Barton manors) it appears that Richard Wycliffe of Darlington, gent., in right of his wife, widow of . . . . . Bettes, held Clowbecke house and Bettes' lands at Barton in 1517-8, and was dead before 1582. At Ingleby's court in 1479 the Abbot of St. Mary's, York, was declared contumacious in not rendering an ancient rent of a pound of pepper. *Conyers lonyng* and Castell Hilles are mentioned in 1589, and in 1599 there are persons amerced "for keping a goosse without a gander," and "for keping a skabbed mare."

§ Darlington Ward has occasionally been termed a wapentake. Collins, in his Peerage supposes the Stanhopes, Earles of Chesterfield, to have sprung from Stanhope in "Darlington-wapentake in the Bishoprick of Durham."

[*The Deanery. Temp. Geo. Allan, archæol.*]

DIVISION III.

ECCLESIASTICAL.

Chapter I. Papal.

SEVEN hundred years! The sun has risen and set, the trees have grown green and returned to golden, the bonny Tees congealed and thawed, but the church of God remained in all its beauty, like the pure expanse, to which its soaring spire directed the pilgrim's steps---seven hundred years, as near as may be. It is a long long time. More than twenty generations have worshipped there in their varying creeds and changing forms. Each of those races has passed into dust around it. Man of God! pass it not with light and listless heart.

Seven hundred years!---nay, I have gone back already in my tale for nearly a thousand.* I hurry on, and lead you to the times, nearly eight hundred years ago. The broach was not there, and probably a plain Saxon fabric occupied the site of Pudsey's glorious pile. But I may not look to the beautiful and its annals only.

After the first Norman Bishop, Walcher, William Carilepho succeeded, "who," says honest Hollinshed, "was the originall founder of the Universitie Colledge in Oxford, and by whose assistance, the Monkes gaping both for riches, ease, and possessions, founde the meanes to displace the secular Priestes of the Colledge of Durham, that they mighte get into theyr rooms as they did indeede soone after, to their great lucre and advantage." The change took place about 1084.

* See page 44.

This idea had been a favourite one with Walcher, and it is mentioned that the secular or ordinary clergy assisted the discontent which ended in his murder. At the eventual change, they were invited to become monks and remain, but only one accepted the offer. The bishop's acts were duly licensed by the pope, and a comfortable retreat and ample provision were made for the exiles in the churches of Auckland, Darlington, and Norton.* The foundation does not seem to have been perpetual. Auckland was re-founded in 1292, and Norton does not present prebendaries till 1227.

As to Darlington, this order of things had evidently died out, for Pudsey is said by Geoffrey of Coldingham to have decreed, that the order which was formerly in Durham should be *restored* in the church he was building at Dernington. This was not the only offence of Pudsey against the monks, since he encouraged a rival colony of exiles from Guisbrough in Durham itself, and very ill they bore the affront. I have already stated that the church here was building in the midst of the prelate's troubles in 1194, and I have but to add that four prebends were founded by him. The foundation charter cannot be found, but the constitution is fully set forth in the reforming ordinances of Bp. Neville, when the idleness and corruptions in the prebendaries had reached the maximum point. He curtailed the prebend of Darlington most woefully, founded a wealthy deanery by amalgamating its revenues with the vicarage, and the succession of deans and four prebendaries continued under that arrangement until the reformation. The sweeping changes then made, and the general status of the college at various periods, will be fully understood by the following documents and the accompanying notes.

In 1288, Pope Nicholas IV. granted the tenths to Edward I. for six years towards defraying the expence of an expedition to the Holy Land ; and that they might be collected to their full value, a taxation by the king's precept was begun in that year and finished in 1292. Another, called *Nova Taxatio*, as to some part of the province of York, was made in 1318, chiefly on account of the invasions of the Scots, by which the clergy of those border countries were rendered unable to pay the former tax.

Taxation of 1292.] Portions of Derlinton.—The portion of Andrew de Kirkenny, 16*l.* 13*s.* 4*d.* : Robert de Bele, 16*l.* 13*s.* 4*d.* : John de Metingham, 16*l.* 13*s.* 4*d.* : Walter de Langeton, 16*l.* 13*s.* 4*d.* : Vicar of the same, 6*l.* 23*s.* 4*d.* : [Total, 73*l.* 6*s.* 8d.]

New Taxation. 1318.] Portions of the church of Derlington. The portion of Roger de Waltham in the same, 9*l.* : Elias de Sordich, 9*l.* : Richard de Ayremynne, 9*l.* : Master John de Insula, 9*l.* : Vicar of the same, 1*l.* 4*s.* : total of the said portions, 37*l.* 4s.

Return. 1312.] The collectors of the tenth, yielded by the clergy to the bishop, gave the following account of the "Portions of Derlington."

* Some add Lanchester, Chester, Easington, and Heighington. "Prebendæ de Akeland Derlington et Northton institutæ a Guil. Episcopo, jussu Gregorii VII, Pont. Ro. ne deeset honestus clericis e Dunelmen. ecclesiæ expulsis victus."—*Lel. Collect.* i. 385. "Propter hoc creditur quod Prebendæ de Akelande, Derlington, Nortouna, et Ekington, factæ fuerunt tantum pro illis canonicis ut haberent unde viverent. Tam non sunt prebendæ in Ekington, et putant nunquam fuisse.—*Ib.* 332.

From the portion of Roger de Wiltham for the second term 12*s*. 8*d*. [struck out, "He shews an acquittance" added]. From the portion of Elias de Schordiche, for the second term 16*s*. 8*d*. From the portion of Master John de Insula for the second term 16*s*. 8*d*, from the time of Master W. de Ewell. From the portion of Sir Adam de Middleton for a whole year 33*s*. 4*d*.*

Muster. 1400.]—Henry IV. meditated a Scotch expedition, and musters were everywhere made to ascertain the strength of the kingdom, as well of clergy as of laity. The Durham church militant assembled on St. Giles's moor, when there were charged

The official of Durham because a prebendary of Derlington with 1 lancer and 1 archer. The vicar of Derlington with 1 lancer and 2 archers. Master Robert de Dalton, prebendary in Derlington, with 1 lancer and 1 archer (does not appear). Master William Hull, prebendary there, is charged otherwise as Rector of Stanhope, [in which capacity he appeared with 1 lancer, 1 hobler, and 3 archers]. John Maxfelde, prebendary there, with 1 lancer and 1 archer (does not appear).†

Bishop Neville's Ordinances.]—Bishop Neville materially altered the constitution of the collegiate church. In the preamble to his ordinance he states, that the church of St. Cuthbert, of Darlington, was graced with a number of prebendal stalls amply endowed; yet that none of the prebendaries either resided or provided a deputy, leaving the whole parochial cure charged on the Vicar, Master Richard Wytton, who was no longer able to support the burthern, his revenues being minished and brought low, as well by the pestilence which was rife among the people, as by other misfortunes and accidents; and moreover, on account of his exile revenues, *the name of Vicar was little honoured among the people.* On the petition therefore of the said Vicar, and in gracious consideration of the premises, the bishop instituted an inquisition into the revenues of the same church; the return to which writ of inquest stated,

"That there were four prebends in the church of Darlington, of which the first in order is named the Prebend of Darlington, the second of Cokerton, the third of Newton, the fourth of Blackwell.

"The prebendary of the prebend of Derlyngton has annexed to his prebend ten tenements within the vill of Derlyngton, then on lease as affirmed for 117*s*.; he has also two oxgangs of arable land, with the meadows pertaining to them, worth 26*s*. 8*d*. *per ann.*, and these are certain and settled, and form the *Corpus Prebendæ.* He receives also of uncertain matters the tithes of hay and grain of Derlyngton,‡ which he shall hold for three successive years, if he shall so long live; and during each of those three years he shall pay to the prebend of Cokerton 40*s*., to the prebend of Newton 40*s*., and to the prebend of Blackwell 4*l*.; and when the same three years are elapsed, the prebendary of Derlyngton is to transfer and betake himself, as to the perception of tithes, to the prebend of Blackwell, and to receive the tithes of hay and corn of Blackwell for three successive years; and for the next three of Newton; and for the next three of Cockerton; till having completed his cycle, he returns to Darlington." The prebendaries of Cokerton, Newton, and Blackwell succeeded each other in order, and each enjoyed the tithes of Darlington three years in twelve.

"The prebendary of Cokerton has for his *Corpus Prebendæ* two granaries leased for 26*s*. 8*d*., and two oxgangs of arable land, 26*s*. 8*d*. per ann.

"The prebendary of Newton has one new granary and three tenements leased for 30*s*. 6*d*., and two oxgangs 26*s*. 8d.

"The prebendary of Blakwell has one granary, two tenements, and a parcel of waste; sometime leased for 24*s*., and two oxgangs 26*s*. 8*d*.

"The prebend of Darlington with all its appurtenances is worth 18*l*. per ann.; the

* Treasury, D. and C. 8 Loc. 18. † The Three Historians. Surt. Soc. p. clxxxv.

‡ The Tithe-barn was in Feethams, in front of Mrs. Pease's house. Mr. Pease used to pay 10*s*. per annum for the site, but afterwards bought it of the late Duke of Cleveland.—E. P. The wheeling arrangement which follows is extremely curious and—inconvenient.

prebend of Cokerton 16*l.*; the prebend of Newton 12*l.*; and the prebend of Blakwell 20*l.*

"The said four prebendaries are only charged with the repairs of the chancel, and with the Royal Tenth when it shall happen, viz.: each of the above prebendaries is then charged with 18*s. ratione Prebendæ suæ.*"

And upon these premises, after mature advice, and with the consent of the prior and convent of Durham, bishop Neville ordained that the name of *Vicar* should cease and be changed into that of *Dean*;* and for the support of such decanal dignity he erected and established one additional prebend, to be perpetually held conjointly with the said deanery; which prebend was ordained to consist of the oblations, mortuaries, alterage, and offerings, which the vicar then held, *together with his ancient manse*;† "and further, whenever it shall happen that the prebend of Darlington shall become vacant by death, removal, or resignation, all the tithes of grain and hay whatsoever of the said prebend shall become integrally attached to the deanery; and the prebendary who shall be collated to the prebend of Darlington shall rest content with his two oxgangs of land, and his pension of 40*s.*; and after the said dean shall have held the tithes of Darlington three years, he shall then give up the said tithes, and, betaking himself to the next prebend, according to the cycle in the said collegiate chnrch established, shall receive the tithes of Newton, Cockerton, and Blackwell in succession, each for three years, and so return to Darlington." 8 Nov., 1439.—Confirmed by Pope Eugene IV. 6 id. Jan. 1441.‡

II. Another ordinance follows, 21 May, 1443, that every prebendary shall provide one officiating clerk, or shall in default pay five marks to the dean.

III. A third ordinance of the same prelate in 1451 on the petition of Roland Hardgyll, dean of Darlington, stating that it is inconvenient and prejudicial to the decanal hospitality to exchange his prebend in course, as well in the carriage of tithes as in the heaviness of the expences incurred, orders that in future the prebendaries of Darlington, Blackwell, Cockerton, and *Nor*ton, shall claim no pension from the prebendary occupying the tithes of Darlington, and that when the dean next goes in course to Darlington, he and his successors shall perpetually thereafter keep the said prebend, and remain there, leaving the other three prebendaries to their usual course of rotation.—(*Reg. Eccles. Dun. IV.* 77, 78.)

1501. *Nov.* 19. *Visitation of Darlington Collegiate Church.*]—Ralph Lepton, dean, does not reside, but is in the service of the bishop. Sir Wm. Wighteman, chaplain

* When the Dean of Darlington is named in documents of an earlier period, the ordinary *rural* dean is meant. Three instances of the bishop writing to this officer may be seen in Walbran's Gainford, pp. 65, 67, one of the epistles (1313) being addressed "*dilecto filio Decano christianitatis de Derlington,*" and enjoining that excommunication be pronounced in all churches of his deanery against some nonpayers of tithes to the convent of St. Mary at York, who had been excommunicated themselves in 1311, for nonpayment of their share of the expence of sending proctors of the clergy from this diocese to the Carlisle parliament.

† "To all, &c., Anthony [Beke] by divine permission bishop of Durham, greeting. Know ye that we, by the influence of divine grace, have granted, &c., to God and the blessed Mary the virgin, and to all saints, and to the church of St. Cuthbert of Derlington, and to Robert de Roveston, perpetual vicar of the same church, and all his successors for ever; All that messuage with the appurtenances in the town of Derlington, near the gate of our manor, which Adam de Stokeslay and Cecily his wife heretofore held of us, and one venel which heretofore led to the well of Hundegate, by [the taking in of] which the said messuage is enlarged and at one side is bounded by it. To hold, &c., Witnesses, Master William de S. Botulpho, now archdeacon of Durham, Sir [D'no] Thomas de Levesham, Sir Peter de Thoresby, Sir Guychard de Charron, John de Saundon, John de Skyrmyngham, Robert de Levingthorp, Wm. s. Benedict de Derlyngton, John de Blacwell, Peter the Clerk, Adam de Smeaton, and others." Confirmed by the Prior and Chapter 26 Mar. 1329.

‡ Reg. 3 Eccles. Dun. fo. 244.

priest of St. James there ; Sir Thomas Clerke, Sir Thomas Robinson, Sir Thomas Simpson, Sir Robert Dickson, Sir W. Knairsdale, and Tho. Tompson, chaplain, appeared. Richard Durham, John Duff, Tho. Tompson, and John Thompson, parishioners, say, that *the glass windows of the chancel are broken*, and that the proprietors* ought to sufficiently mend them before Christmas upon pain of 10*s*.†

Old Valor in Bishop Tunstall's Register, *p*. 1.]—The Deanery of Darlyngton 26*l*. per ann. In the church of Darlington ; the prebend of Prestgate 3*l*., of Newton 5*l*., of Cokerton 10*l*., of Blackwell 10*l*.

Valor in Randall's MSS.]—Darlington Collegiate Church. Deanery of Darlington 36*l*. 13*s*. 4*d*. Prebend of Cockerton 5*l*., of Blackwell 5*l*., of Newton 5*l*. 0*s*. 3*d*., of Rowe 1*l*. 13*s*. 4d., all in the patronage of the Bishop of Durham.

Valor Ecclesiasticus, 1535.]—The Deanery of the church of Derlington. Cuthbert Mersshall dean there. The aforesaid deanery is worth in the site of the mansion of the said dean there, and two oxgangs of arable land of the glebe of the same 26*s*. 8*d*.; tithes, oblations and other profits there 35*l*. 6*s*. 8d. Total value per annum 36*l*. 14*s*. 4*d*. - - - Rents paid, viz. monies yearly paid to the archdeacon of Durham for sinodals and procurations 2*s*., free farm rent to the Lord Bishop of Durham 3*s*., and for the salary of Robert Kelde, the chanters, and sacristan in the same church as by the foundation of his prebend in the hands of the said dean remaining 40*s*. Total per annum 5*s*. *(sic)* Sum of the reprises 5*s*. *ut supra*. - - - Salaries of chaplains, viz. monies yearly paid to two chaplains conducting the divine service celebrated daily in the said college, for the salary of each of them yearly 100*s*., besides which, the dean there and his successors for the time being are held and bound by the foundation of the same to sustain and support such honest chaplains there with meat and drink, salary, and other necessaries as becometh. Total per annum —. Clear value 36*l*. 8*s*. 4*d*. Tenth part thereof [the king's, for the computation of which the survey was made] 72*s*. 10*d*.

Prebends founded in the church of Derlyngton, viz. Prebends there, viz. Richard Manchester, prebendary of one prebend there per annum 100*s*., tenth part thereof 10*s*. - - - .... Hewes, prebendary of one prebend there per annum 100s., tenth part thereof 10*s*. - - - Thomas Hall, prebendary of one prebend there per annum 100*s*., tenth part thereof 10*s*. - - - Total value of the aforesaid prebends 15*l*. which is their clear value.

The Chantry of a certain free chapel called Badlefeld. Richard Manchester ; what pertains to the said Richard. The aforesaid chantry is worth in rents of a certain pasture and other fruits of the said chantry, yearly 40*s*., tenth part thereof 4*s*. - - - Thomas Chambre, perpetual chaplain, prebendary in the church of Derlyngton, of a certain prebend in Prestgate Derlington aforesaid. The aforesaid chantry‡ is worth in rents of certain cottages in Prestgate aforesaid, yearly, 33*s*. 4*d*. which is the clear value, tenth part thereof 3*s*. 4d.

The chantry of All Saints§ founded in the collegiate church of Derlington. Leo-

* The prebendaries. † MSS. D. and C. Durham.

‡ This is a curious arrangement. The revenues of the prebend of Priestgate or Row are applied in furnishing another chaplain to Badlefield. Chambre died in 1545, when Simon Binkes succeeded, and is called "chaplain." They also occur in the same order as prebendaries of Osmunderly church, Allertonshire. Chambre was Rector of Winston, and Binkes succeeded Wm. Carter, prebendary of Newton, as Rector of Redmershall. So they fared pretty respectably. Arrowsmith in his map attached to the Valor has mistaken the meaning of the record, he gives Prestgate as a chantry, and places the chantry of St. James at Hallgarth near Coatham Mundeville.

Richard Manchester, the other chaplain, was prebendary of Cockerton, and was succeeded by Robert Bushell, who also held both posts.

§ This chantry, which in Hunter's MSS. appears under the title of All-hallowes, has been hitherto inadvertently split in two, Robert Marshall's chantry (under which name it appears in the Grammar School charter) being considered as separate. A son of Robert nard Melmerby chantry priest of the same chantry. The aforesaid chantry is worth in rents of divers lands and tenements in divers towns and fields to the same chantry belonging 6*l.* 6*s.* 8*d.* - - - From thence in money annually paid for alms (at the yearly obit) for the souls of Robert Mershall and his parents for ever, and for the benefactors of the said chantry, as appears by computation 4*s.* (23*s.*)* (clear value 103*s.* 8*d.*) - - - From thence in reprises, viz., rents paid to our Lord the King for free rent out of lands in Thormondby, in the county of York, 5*s.*, and for ancient free rent paid to the Lord Bishop of Durham, for lands in the town and fields of Heighington, in the county of Durham, 3*s.*, and for free rent to the said Lord Bishop 4*d.*, and to the church of Derlington 4*d.*, and for the farm rent of a certain close in Thormondby aforesaid, possession of which is not allowed, and consequently no profit as yet comes therefrom, in all 8*s.* 8*d.* - - - Clear value 114*s.* (4*l.* 15*s.*) Tenth part, 11*s.* 5*d.*

The CHANTRY of the CHAPEL of ST. JAMES in the manor of the Lord Bishop of Durham in Halgarth there. Thomas Emerson chantry priest of the same. The said chantry is worth in money yearly received from the Lord Bishop of Durham in part of the salary 60s.,† and from the Lord Prior of Durham in money reckoned yearly 4 marks.‡ Total per annum 113*s.* 4*d.* which is the clear value. Tenth part, 11*s.* 4*d.*

Commission. 2 *Edw. VI.* (1548.)]—Thomas Hilton and Robert Brandlynge, knights ; Robert Mennell, serjaunte at law, and Henrye Whilreson, esquyres, were Commissioners for Duresme to survey all colledges, deanries, chauntries, stipendiarie priests, free chappells, &c. The return states as follows.

"The paryshe of Derlington havinge of howselinge people abowte———(*blank*).

Marescall is named in Boldon book. To give an idea of what allowance must be made in perusing these ancient accounts, I just note that in 1823 the possessions of this foundation produced £247 8 6 !

* The record here has been altered. The alterations are given in ( ).

† Two chantries are confounded here. The 60*s.* was paid by the Bishop in respect of his chapel of St. James attached to the Manor house. But the priest also held St. Mary's chantry in the church (for which the prior paid), and officiated at both places. In 1424 the Bishop collated Ralph Byrd, priest of the diocese of York, to the chantry in his manor of Derlington, stipend 60*s.* payable by his bailiff of Cotum Mundevyle, to which in augmentation the prior and chapter collated him also (by consent of the Bishop) to the chantry of St. Mary the virgin, in the church of Derlington, stipend 4 marks payable by the bursar.

‡ This was for ST. MARY'S CHANTRY, and in the reprises of the convent is again mentioned. "To Thomas Emerson and Thomas Caward, chantry priests in the churches of Derlyngton and Dedynsall, for their pensions issuing out of lands in Burdon, according to the foundation of Wm. Briton by charter, 106*s.* 8*d.*" - - - "To all, &c., Ralph [Kerneck, 1214-1233] the prior and the monks of Durham, greeting. Know, &c., that we ever will sustain two honest chaplains, of whom one shall receive 4 marks yearly and the other in like manner four, &c ; and of whom one shall celebrate divine service in the church of Derlyngton, and the other in the church of Dytensale for all the faithful, and for the souls of William Briton and Alice his wife, and all their ancestors and heirs. Moreover we will give to Agnes, the daughter of the same William whom he had by Matilda de Brafferton, and her heirs she shall conceive in lawful matrimony, one mark of silver in every year. But if it shall happen that the said Prior and Monks shall withdraw themselves from the aforesaid agreement, the vill of Burdun, with the mill and all other things, shall revert to the heirs of the said William Briton. The Chapter being witness." [*Reg. Eccles. Dunelm. pars* 1, *fo.* 107]. The salary was duly paid in 1531 by two instalments, and so in following years. - - - John Litster held two mess. in Northgate, rent 3*s.* 4*d.* to the altar of the blessed Mary in the church of Derlyngton of ancient grant. *Supervis. Hatfield pag.* 1. *Hunter's MSS.* - - - In the Treasury are two charters, one of the 13th cent. from R. the prior to Wm. Briton of all the vill of Burdon which he bought of Roger s. Roger de Burduna except two oxg. which Roger the father had *prius eleemosynariæ dederat*, rent two marks: the other of 1334, dated at Derlyngtone, John de Halughtone, chaplain, to Juliana dr. Wm. de Hackesby of property in Burdone, Derlyngtone and Bermeton, which he (John) had of the gift of John de Burdone s. Gilbert de Kettone, husband of said Juliana.

"The Chauntrey of All Seynts, *or the free scole** in the parishe church of Derlington. Thomas Rycherdson of the age of xxx yeres Incumbent. The yerely valewe iiij*l*. xix*s*. The repryses vj*s*. viij*d*. The remaine iiij*l*. xij*s*. iiij*d*. Stoke, &c., none.

"The Chauntry of Seint James, founded within the Bushope of Duresme Manor Place, Rawfe Cootes incumbent, having moreover a pencion of xl*s*. by yere paid by the King's Recevor of th' Augmentacon. The yerelie valewe with liij*s*. iiij*d*. of pencon paide owte of the courte of th' augmentacon and lx*s*. of pencon owte of the Excheker vj*l*.† Stocke, &c., none.

"The Deanrye and prebendes of Derlyngton in the parishe churche aforesayd. The incumbents ther Cutbert Marshall, dean and vicar, beinge a prebendary, William Carter prebendary, Symond Binks prebendary, the yerelie valewe liij*l*. vj*s*. viij*d*. Repryses that is to wytt in wages of iiij curats found by the dean xv*l*. v*s*. The Remaine xxxviij*l*. xx*d*. Stocke, &c., none.—Leade not mentioned.

"The yerelie obits within the churche aforeseyd. The yerelie valew v*s*. ij*d*. Stocke, &c., none.

"The rente perteyninge to the mayntenance of a lighte.‡—The yerely valew ij*s*.— Stocke, &c., none.

"Rente bequethed to the *afforseyd Grame Skole*. The yerly valewe iij*s*."

This survey is signed by Thomas Hilton,§ Robert Brandlyng and Thomas Eymis, before the signatures there being the following explanation.

"Memorandum. That the goodes and ornamentes perteyninge to the premysses be remayning moste parte according to the inventoryes therof taken by the former Commysyoners at the fyrste survey sithenns whiche tyme they have not bene otherwyse praysed or estemed, howbeyt they are synce by weringe or damaging very sore decayd from the goodness and valewe that they were then praysed to be of."

Royal Rents, temp. Edw. VI.]—In the Allan MSS. [*D. and C. Lib.*] there is an imperfect copy of the account of Tho. Collens, collector of the rents and firms here. From

* See Free School hereafter

† Here St. Mary's is again confounded with St. James's chantry.

‡ Thomas s. Jolanus de Morton held two burgages by 3 suits of court at the toll booth, and 8 pounds of wax to Darlington Church. Inq. 5 Bury.

§ This baron of Hylton was a striking character. He married the coheir of Clervaux, and his arms gleam behind a gallery in a window at Croft, but he had no children, although at the end of his life he might say, "if I survive—I'll marry five." Whether his wives tired of him and left this world in disgust, or he tired of them and *slew* them, like "brave Timothy! by wedlock three times bound—and thrice he snapt the chain the villain priest had bound," I dinna ken, but certain it is that he was a very sensibly changeable spirit, submitting to events he could not alter. In 1536 he joined the Pilgrimage of Grace, and went under St. Cuthbert's banner to Pomfret, to resist the king's encroachments on the ancient faith, but he bent like the willow, and obtained a pardon (and a lesson). He grew into favour with bluff Hal, and went along with his son's ministers in all the searching commissions of the time, notwithstanding which, Queen Mary appointed the quondam pilgrim and Protestant to be her Governor of Tynemouth, when he detained a Flanders ship laden with salt, took wares out of ships as passed him, "as he thought meet," and at last had directions from the privy council to forbear "to meddle with ships from countries in amity with the Queen." After all this, we find him on Elizabeth's accession wheeling round again and making an honest Protestant will without mention of a single saint, wherein he leaves a most gallant "gold chyne weing 33 ounces and half an ounce 100*l*." (*Inventory*) to accompany his whole lands to his heir, who was to be bound for both, that they should "discend from one to another, as is conteyned in my taile aforesaid." His brother William was a horrid wretch, if Dr. Bulleyn (whom he accused of poisoning Sir Thomas) is to be believed. Lady Hylton his brother's widow had redeemed his land, and lent him money, yet he sought her "shame, losse, yea, and bloode," and when he should have repaid her, "*then he gratifyed her, as he did mee.*"

it I gather that he accounted for 53*l.* 1*s.* 8*d.** rent, of the house and manse of the late Dean, and of two oxgangs of arable land of the glebe of the church, and of all tithes, &c., which to the late dean and perpetual vicar and prebendary *of the prebend of the altar* did belong; and of tithes, two oxgangs and two barns, of the Cockerton prebend; the same items including two orchards, of the Blackwall prebend; the same items including two gardens, of the Newton prebend; and the prebend of Rawe prebend; all which had been granted 2 Edw. VI. to Thomas Windsor, at that rent, charged with 2*s.* from the prebend of the altar to the archdeacon for the cure, and 3*s.* to the bishop, and the assigning a sufficient priest in aid of the Vicar, whose stipend the king had to pay. And for 66*s.* 8*d.* being 6*s.* 8*d* rent of one burgage in Derlington, and 60*s.* to the said chanters [St. James's, though not before mentioned] by the Bishop out of his charity and devotion. And for 46*s.* 8*d.* rent of lands and tenements in vill of Bondgate, mentions grant from Edw. VI. to John Perient, knt., and Tho. Reave, gent., for a competent sum, of the late free chapel of Batilfelde and all its lands, &c., in the fields of Batelfielde† on the West side of Derlington between the waste moore and Nether Cunscliffe. And for 7*s.* 2*d.* rent from lands and tenements [belonging] the *said*‡ obit, and the maintenance of one lamp and other lights there, viz. out of two burgages in Assendale§ in the tenure of Tho. Theughe 2*s.* 6*d.*; and one burgage in Derlington in the Dean's hands, 2*s.* 8*d.*; and one close called Midam Close in the tenure of Edmund Hodgson 2*s.*, sum, 7*s.* 2*d.* And for 25*s.* 4*d.*, rent of four cottages of the said chantery. And for 70*s.* rent of tenements of the said late chantery.||

Pensions payable to incumbents of Religious houses and chantries 1553, *as the same were issued out of the crown revenues from the receipt of the Abbey lands.*¶]—Darlington College, 1553. To Robert Bushell, prebendary of Cockerton, 1*l.* 10*s.*; Simon Binkes, prebendary of Prestgate, 1*l.* 13*s.* 4*d.*; John Hewis, prebendary of Blackwell, 1*l.* 13*s.* 4*d.*; Robert Warde, William Thompson, and Marmaduke Fayrebarne, each 3*l.*, 9*l.*; Anthony Wilde, 2*l.*; Thomas Richardson, minister [of All Saints chantry], 4*l.*; total, 19*l.* 16*s.* 8*d.* *Ex Reg. Tunstall. Ep. Dun. p.* 31. To Robert Bushell, incumbent of Battlefield Chapel, 2*l.* 6*s.* 8*d.*

* The values set down in the Valor of 1535 including Priestgate 1*l.* 13*s.* 4*d.* exactly make this sum.

† It is clear that this foundation was close beside Badlebeck Inn. See pp. 55, 119, and Bathele Hospital hereafter. It was in the patronage of the bishop and the chaplain or cantarist, had an annual sum paid him out of the Bishop's exchequer, *ab antiquo*. Cade had an odd idea that the ruins opposite Gainford were those of this chapel. Free chapels were places of religious worship exempt from all ordinary jurisdiction, save only that the incumbents were generally instituted by the bishop and inducted by the archdeacon of the place. Most of these chapels were built upon the manors and ancient demesnes of the crown, whilst in the king's hand, for the use of himself and his retinue when he came to reside there. And when the crown parted with those estates, the chapels went along with them, and their first freedom; but some lords having had free chapels in manors that do not appear to have been ancient demesne of the crown, such are thought to have been built and privileged by grants from the crown. All free chapels with the chantries were given to the king 1 Edw. VI. except some which are excepted in the acts, or such as are founded since. And by acts 26 Hen. VIII. and 1 Eliz. free chapels are charged with first fruits; but this the late Mr. Serjt. Hill conjectures must mean only such as were in the hands of subjects.

The king himself visits his free chapels and hospitals and not the ordinary: which office of visitation is executed for him by the chancellor.—*Burn's Eccl. Law.*

‡ It is evident that Allan's clerk, or whoever was his transcriber, has left out all the titles of the various accounts rendered. The 7*s.* corresponds with the revenue of the obits and light in the last document.

§ A local family of the name occurs at the commencement of the register.

|| These two items refer to All Saints chantry, corresponding to the £4 12 4 and 3s. in the last document.

¶ Willis's Hist. of Abbies, vol. ii. p. 73.

Stipend reserved at Dissolution.]—To the vicar of Darlington, 24 marks, 16*l.*; to the assistant curate, 12 marks, 8*l.*;—total, 24*l.* Deductions claimed at the Exchequer; poundage at 5*l. per cent.* 1*l.* 4*s.*; for two debentures at 3*s.* 8*d.* each, 7*s.* 4*d.*; for each debenture more 1*s.*, 2*s.*,—in all 1*l.* 13*s.* 4*d.* Remains de clare 22*l.* 6*s.* 8*d.*

The ultimate fate of the collegiate possessions may be shortly summed up. In 1626 the rents reserved by the crown were settled by Charles I. on his hapless consort, Henrietta, for life.* Of the property charged with those sums, the deanery including the tithes† and the glebe, passed to the Nevilles (see p. 120) and with their other property to the Vanes, who still hold it, and repair the chancel. The other prebendal possessions are briefly noticed below. The rector of Haughton receives portions of tithes from Darlington and Cockerton townships, but they are very inconsiderable.

5 Jas. Patent to Geo. Warde and Robert Morgan, gents., in consideration of the service of Thomas Viscount Fenton, captain of our guard; the portion of Robert Bushell, clerk, late prebendary of Cockerton, and the two barns belonging, rent 4*l.* 12*s.*; same of John Hewes, late prebendary of Blackwell, and two barns and two orchards, 4*l.* 12*s.*;—and the prebend called "Prebend Rawe," in burgage, in our borough of Darlington, alias Darneton, late received by Simon Binks 33*s.* 4*d.*, which were late parcel of the possessions of the late Deanery *or Rectory* of Darneton, alias Darlington, and came to Edw. VI. by Act of his first year for the dissolution of chantries, colleges, &c.: except two oxg. of the prebend of Cockerton, rent 8*s.*; and two oxg. of that of Blackwell, 8*s.*, granted to Gellius Meyrick and Henry Lindley. To hold of the manor of Estgreenwich in Kent, in free socage, subject to said rents. The tithes of Newton, late received by Wm. Carter, late prebendary, 4*l.* 12*s.*, were granted in 13 Jas. to Francis Morice and Robert Smith, two London gentlemen.

The Wards gradually purchased up all four prebends, Newton, Cockerton, Blackwell, and Row. The tithes of the first were sold by them to the Whelers, and a moiety were about 1823 conveyed to Lord Redesdale; the second were bought by the various landed proprietors concerned, in 1744; and the third by proprietors also, Chr. Hill paying 2200*l.* for a large portion in 1775; they are principally vested in the Allans. The prebend of Prebend's Row was bought by Sir John Lowther, of Lowther, bart., in 1661, consisting particularly of a messuage with Tenter Close and the Milne Close, three messuages (rent 3*s.* 4*d.* each) having been before granted to Simon Gifford, Wm. Hutchinson, and Alice Thady. In 1722 Lowther released his portion under the name of the King's Head, to Wm. Stevenson, innholder, who in 1726 released to Robert Bowes, of Thornton, esq., by the same name, including Long Close and Abrey Pickhalls.—The rents are still paid by that property and other burgages in Priestgate and Prebend Row.

The ecclesiastics probably had their own officers of defence, for Priestgate‡

* 36*l.* 13*s* 4*d.* out of the deanery of Darlington, and out of the tithes of wool, lambs, and calves in Darlington; 11*l.* 5*s.* 4*d.* out of the prebends of Cockerton, Blackwell, and Rawe, parcel of the deanery. Newton is omitted.

† "The tythes of this parish are *predial* and *mixed*, but no tythes are due to the minister. For the township of Darlington, Lord Darlington as impropriator has all tythes and mortuaries; and for the other townships, except Oxen-a-field, which pays a modus of 13*s.* 4*d.*, his lordship has only the mixed tythes: the predial tythes from such lands as are tythable, being the property of sundry laymen."—*Terrier.* The tithes have been commuted in all the townships.

‡ In 1313, Wm. de Barton (by charter in the Treasury) was bound to restore to John s. Wm. Benedict the charter of *Prestmenholme* at Derlington.

is a constabulary, and its inhabitants repair their own highways, and have overseers for the purpose. It is considered as part of the borough, though the bailiffs in former days had sad work with its tenants, who refused the title of burgesses and would do neither suit nor service. However, they cooled down. It is remarkable that this is the only part of the parish where women are by custom eligible to serve as constables, surely a remnant of St. Cuthbert's contemptuous opinions.

My readers may probably be interested in the amount of possessions the other religious houses acquired, during the long reign of papacy in England, at Darlington. They were the following.

Byland Abbey, Yorks. In a lease of Darlington tolls, &c., the Bishop covenants to allow out of the rents 4*s.* for the free rent of certain burgages in Darlington, then in the king's hands, and late belonging to the dissolved monasteries of Byland, Rievaulx, Mountgrace, and Firvax.*—Rob. Nevil, Bp. of Durham, in 1444, confirmed the grant of land at Darrington from Helewise wife of Geoffrey Fitz David to this house.†

Jorveaux Abbey, Yorks. Had possessions in Richmond, Derlyngton, and Alverton, rent 23*s.* 8*d.*‡ in 1535.

Mount Grace Priory, Yorks. Had possessions in Derlyngton, rent 10*s.* in 1535.‡

Easby Abbey, Yorks. Had "Lands and tenements in Darlington, 7*s.*" at the dissolution.§

Rievaulx Abbey. See above.

Staindrop Church. Some lands in Darlington were given for maintaining the lights in Staindrop church and for celebrating the obit of John Spicer.‖

Kepier Hospital. Bp. Pudsey gave thereto a toft in Darlington.¶ In 1535 the hospital held a free farm rent issuing out of a burgage in Derlington 3*s.*, having leased, I should think, the toft for a long term.‡

Neasham Priory. A licence occurs to the prioress to purchase premises here in 13 Neville. In 1535 the nuns held property here worth 5*s.* yearly,‡ which probably passed to the Lawsons with the other priory lands, as they occur as freeholders from 1617 of three burgages in Mathergarthes.

Let me now pass on to the church accessories, for it must be interesting to fill up the picture of the collegiate church and its officers.

Vestments given by Bishop Skirlaw, and named in his inventory 1406.]—"A set of vestments** of white silk, wrought with vine branches, leaves, and bunches of grapes, and little dragons, all *de blanco*,†† containing one chasuble and three copes with golden borders, having images of saints in tabernacles [canopied niches], and other two copes having borders of oversea gold cloth [*de panno aureo ultramarino*] and two tunics having running borders, with 3 albs, 2 amices, 2 stoles, and 3 maniples, with a frontal‡‡

* Allan MSS. Jervaux is meant. † Reg. de Byland.—Burton.
‡ Valor Eccles. See p. 37. § Clarkson's Richmond. ‖ Rot W. James No. 42.
¶ Hutchinson, ii. 384.

** *Vestimentum.* By which word, says Raine, is implied a complete set of robes as they were to be worn one above another on festivals. It is impossible to give any idea of the various garments without cuts, but I may refer to Raine's North Durham and St. Cuthbert, and any work on costume. The outer vestment or cope was always extremely fine, and was worn at Durham to a very late period. †† Embossed in white.

‡‡ The items which follow were for the altar. The curtains would project from the East wall at each end of the altar on iron rods, leaving sufficient room for an officiating priest between. See the Rites of Durham, &c.

having the salutation of the blessed virgin, and a plain subfrontal, and a pulvinar [cushion] of the same material. Item, two curtains of white tarterain* with upright embossed stripes of white [*palato blanco*] interlined with gold. Given to the church of Derlyngton." The testator appointed Alan de Newerk (our prebendary) an executor, and enriched all his collegiate churches from his own splendid vestry.

Plea of Oyer and Terminer, 27 *May*, 1509. 9 *Ruthall.*]—The Jurors on the second presentation found that John Watson, late of Warkworth, in the county of Northumberland, yeoman, did on the third day of March in the first year of Thomas Lord Bp., &c., at Derlyngton, in the county of Durham, about the hour of midnight, break and enter, with force and arms, into the church of Derlyngton, and into a certain house within the said church, called the *Tresor-howse*,† and did from thence feloniously steal, take, and carry away, thirteen silver zones,‡ parcel gilt, called *our Lady Jewells*, of the value of ten pounds ; one stagg of goulde, with a precious stone called a sapphire, set in it, ten marks ; one golden eagle, 13*s*. 4*d*. ; one silver tabernacle,§ parcel gilt, 13*s*. 4*d*. ; one jewel, called an *Agnus Dei*, with a broche of silver gilt, 6*s*. 8*d*. ; and one silver image, 6*s*. 8*d*. ; being the goods and chattels of the said church, and then in the custody of John Thomson and Willyam Stapelton, against the peace of the Lord Bishop, &c.||

Commission of 1553.]—Sir George Conyers and Sir Thomas Hylton, knights, and William Bellaces and Richard Vincent (the bearer of the certificate) esquires, were made Commissioners to receive all the "goods, plate, jewells, and redye money perteyning to all churches, chapels, guilds, fraternities, brotherhoods, and companies in the countie of the Byshopricke of Duresme, to the King's Highness' use." Indentures were taken for the safe custody of the remainder. They received "a vestment, two tynacles, and a cope of cloth of tyssue at Darneton," and left at "Darnetone, two challices, th'one gilt, th'other ungilt, with one paten weying xxxi unces ; foure bells in the stepell, a sance¶

* *Tartarino.*—A cloth brought from Tartary or of Tartarian work. *Ducange.*

† Perhaps identical with the present modernised vestry on the South of the choir ; and here arises a curious coincidence. On the 11th of February, 1846, the same place was again entered, and an attempt made to open into the safe, but failing, the thieves attempted, by breaking through one of the Sedilia, to enter the back of it. This intention was also fruitless. The thieves, whose ringleader was named Thomas *Watson*, were afterwards discovered, and though legal evidence was insufficient to bring home this particular robbery, he was convicted on another charge and transported. Robbery seems the fate of the valuables here, for on 1st April, 1774, the vestry was broken open, "and part of the communion plate stolen thereout, viz., a silver chalice and cover, that will hold about a wine pint, gilt with gold, but much tarnished, *on the cover either the years* 1517 *or* 1571 *is engraven*; a large plain silver salver, and a smaller one, the latter having gadrooned edges and bottom."—*(Reward Notice.)*

‡ The thirteen zones (a number in allusion to Christ and his apostles) had probably formed an offering for the use of the image of our Lady, at her chantry altar, on some high festival when it was the wont of the clergy to deck up their saints in "their better blue-breeches." Other items were also doubtless offerings, some might be gifts from the rich Mercatores of Darlington in the olden time, and others, such as the stag, [possibly in imitation of the living one yearly offered at the palatine church] from the old Raby lords of Blackwell and Oxenlefield.

§ The casket containing the smaller casket or pix, which held a portion of consecrated bread, for use at times elapsing between mass and mass in cases of emergency. See North Durham, 97.

|| Hunter's MSS.

¶ The Sanctus-bell, Sancte-bell, or Sacring-bell was used to call attention to the more solemn parts of the mass, as at the conclusion of the ordinary, when the words "*Sanctus, Sanctus, Sanctus, Deus Sabaoth*" were pronounced. It hung in the "Sancte-bell-cote," a turret on the exterior, to which a rope reached from the interior of the church ; but smaller hand-bells were also used [now almost universally], of which there were some at Darlington.

bell, two hand bells, iij lyttle sacring bells, a lyttyll bell that the clock smyteth one,* with a holy water fatt of stone." +

I annex one or two later notices of old horology at Darlington.

Die Sabbati. 20 Apr., 1594. Offic. against Robert Atkinson, William Bower, Robert Nicholson, Francis Oswald, Miles Grey, John Fawcett, Michael Jefferson, William Huetson, Geffrey Holume, Peter Collon, Lawrence Elgy, William Helcot, Lawrence Warde, John Dobson, Anthony Elgey, Lawrence Catherick, William Marshall, Robert Emerson, James Daile, John Atkinson, Richard Stockdale, Peter Glover, George Lassels, William Cornefourth, Richard Prescott, John Middleton, James Rokebie, Robert Branson, parishioners; Richard Stockdale and James Daile, churchwardens, and all the other parishioners, declared contumacious, for nonappearance; and the said churchwardens summoned to appear and shew what they had done touching the re-edifying of their clock in Darlington Church, heretofore commanded to be done by the Right Honorable Henry Earl of Huntingdon, Lord President of the North, and the Lord Bishop of Durham; which day the same Richard Stockdaile appeared, and alledged that assessment was already made, according to a particular then by him shewed to the Judge, and desired the Judge would ratify the same, &c.

1638. Paid John Davison making the Clock, 5*l.*—*Church Accounts.*

Richard Hogget, of Darlington, who rang the hour of eight *(qui pulsabat horam octavam)* bur. 10 Sep. 1638.

The following extract from a will of the period may not be out of place at this stage of my labours.

In the name of God Amen. Wednesday next before the feast of Saint Thomas the Apostle, A. D. 1343. I, Cecilia Underwod, wife of William, of Durham, merchant,—my soul to God and the blessed Mary and to all saints, and my body to be buried in the cemetery of Saint Cuthbert of Derlyngton—for my mortuary‡ the better cloth and the better beast happening to be my portion—to *my* high altar 10*s.*—to the fabric of the church of Derlyngton 10*s.*—[bridges, see p. 38]—to the priest officiating for my soul 10*l.*—for alms to the poor 20*s.*—to every priest officiating in the church of Derlyngton at the time of my decease 12*d.*—Peter the clerk§ 12*d.*—two other clerks 12*d.*—Cecilia de Barton 20*s.*—John Underwod|| and his children 20*l.*—John de Halghton, chaplain, 10*s.*—the children of John de Heworth 40*s.*—the children of Robert, son of the clerk, 40*s.*—Sir Adam de Exteldesham, chaplain, 6*s.* 8*d.*—Sir Richard de Manfeld, chaplain, 6*s.* 8*d.*—the children of Richard de Herwyk 40*s.*—Agnes dr. Richard de Herdewyk 20*s.*—Matilda dr. of Richard my son 40*s.*—the mother of the same Matilda 6*s.* 8*d.*—Cecily dr. of Wm. s. Wm.—for the expences to be incurred at my funeral 10*l.*—John de Heworth 20*s.*—Agnes de Blakeston 2*s.*—Alice Tynkeller 2*s.*—Thomas s. Wm. de Burdon 6*s.* 8*d.*—Cecily Broys¶ 6*s.* 8*d.*—John de Exham 12*d.*—Wm. de Thorp 40*d.*—Alice my granddaughter 6*s.* 8*d.*—John s. Alexander de Dunelm 13*s.* 4*d.*—Wm. de Morton 20*s.*—John Slauer 13*s.* 4*d.*—Amice de Thorp 6*s.* 8*d.*—Adam de Qwytebern 20*s.*—the clerks and widows praying for my soul and keeping watch round my body 10*s.*—Robert Carl'

* This is curious. We now choose the *large* bell.

\+ The stoup or bason standing at the entrance of the church, with the contents of which the congregation were sprinkled. It does not appear in this instance to have been fixed in the wall, but seemingly was a moveable chattel.

‡ The corpse-present to the church, usual at funerals.

§ Inq. p. m. 19 Hatfield, Peter son of Peter Clerkson: property here.

|| Inq. p. m. 9 Hatfield; Maude, widow of John Underwode, of property here: sister Emma Bruys coheir with Cecily of Thorpe.

¶ Inq. p. m. 9 Hatfield; John Bruys, of property here; dau. Emma coheir with his grandchild Cecily, dau. of Alice of Thorpe :- - - Charters appear from Walter of Shotton and his d. and h. Cecily of Thorpethewles.

13*s*. 4*d*.—John de Norton 6*s*. 8*d*.—John and Cecily children of John Underwod two chests which are in my chamber, together with 3 beds—Isabella, the wife of Robert Clerkeson my veil [*revale*] with a tunic—John Underwod my cloak (*clamidem*)—Sir Richard de Manfeld, chaplain, one bed convenient for him—William de Norton the cook 10*s*.—Robert called Brige 6*s*. 8*d*.—John of the Stable [*de Stabulo*] 40*d*.—residue to my son John and his children. Proved 21 Feb., 1343.

I now come to the incumbents.

VICARS.—*Peter*,* *Persona de Derlington*, occurs in the latter part of the 13th century as witness to a charter of Walter Bec, Baron of Eresby, father of the great Anthony Beke, granting Redmarshall property to Adam the carpenter of Darlington, whose son Richard again alienated. In 1320, Wm. de Wallewrde grants to William son of Peter the clerk (*Petri clerici*), of Derlingtone, three roods in exchange, and in 1329, Walter, son of William, son of Peter the clerk of Derlyngtone, grants to Wm. de Walleworthe and Olive his wife a wood in Granhou there.

Robert de Roveston, occurs perpetual vicar in 1309, in whose time Beke granted the vicarage-house.

Henry de Appilby in consequence of infirmity submitted his vicarage of Derlington, in 1341, to Kellawe to make arrangements, and because his seal was unknown to many people, he used the seal of the rural dean of Derlington. The bishop settled twelve marks yearly out of the fruits of the living upon him, and then by another instrument he resigned, to which John de Halgton put his seal.† The living was given to

Thomas de Rainham, who however resigned in 1343, and his successor‡ was

William de Welton, who perhaps resigned and reassumed, for in Dr. Hunter's MSS. he is stated to have succeeded in 1354 on the death of

Richard de Hadyngton, who occurs Vicar in 1344. Bishop Hatfield granted to John Verty, the valet of his kitchen, property in Northgate late of Richard de Hadyngton, vicar of Darlington.

William de Welton occurs again in 1354.

Robert de Hunmanby occurs Vicar July, 1360.§

William Hoton occurs July, 1398.|| Rector of Walkington in Howdenshire 1393, which he resigned for this living.¶

Richard Wytton occurs 1400.**

William Hesile occurs 1411. (see p. 208.)

William Huton occurs 1415.††

Stephen Austell occurs 27 Mar., 1416, and again as perpetual vicar in conjunction with Sir John Grismes, chaplain, 1 May, 1424.‡‡ He resigned in 1428, and was afterwards Dean of Lanchester, dying 27 Feb. 1461. Thurstan Ryston, rector of Stanhope, and Robert Poutheroun of Durham, chaplain, feoffed the churchwardens and parishioners of Lanchester, in 1462, of lands at Greencroft, on condition that they caused yearly *placebo* and *dirige* with mass to be solemnly celebrated in the church for the soul of Stephen Austell, late dean thereof, on his anniversary, viz. 27 Feb., and find a light

* Several Peters de Derlington occ. as priests in early times.
† Kellawe's Reg. ‡ Ibid.
§ Randal. From a copyhold bk., A. p. 277. || Ibid. B. 264. ¶ Hutchinson, iii.
** Hutch. List in Par. Reg. by Geo. Allan. †† Hutch. from Hunter's MSS.
‡‡ Randal, from Copyhold Bk., C. p. 168.

burning before the image of St. Catherine, where his body was buried. Under an arch in the side wall of the North aisle of that church is the recumbent effigy of an ecclesiastic with his hands elevated, clasping a chalice, well cut in Stanhope marble, which is believed to represent this ancient pastor of Darlington.*

Richard Wytton, vicar 1428, p. res. Austell, made DEAN in 1439 by Bp. Neville's ordinances, (see *ante*). In 1436, Jan. 1, occur *Richard Bicheburn*, vicar, Richard Penymaystr cl. and Tho. Tracy, chaplain† here, and in 1441, 13 Sep. Richard Bicheburn occurs as *Vicar*,‡ although the Deanery was then established and "Richard Wytton, Dean of Derlyngton" is mentioned as at the enthronement of Neville on 11 April that very year. That the word vicar should still accidentally be used, is very likely, and as Bitchburn and Witton-le-Wear are close together, I suspect that Wytton and Bicheburn are one person. Richard Witton, S. T. B., was chosen master of University College in 1426, and ceased 1440.§

DEANS.—*Richard Wytton*, first dean, 1439.

Sir‖ *Roland Hardgyll*, cl., confirmed 1451, occ. 11 Apr., 1455.

Sir Robert Symson, cl. occ. 14 Aug. 1466.¶

Ralph Lepton, in Decret. Bacc. occ. 9 Nov.. 1497, p. m. Symson, and 19 Nov., 1501. *Sir Thomas Clarke* occ. as parochial chaplain, 7 Jan., 1497, 25 May, 1499, and 19 Nov., 1501.** In 1507. the dean was present at the synod held in the Galilee on the bishoprick affairs, the see being vacant.†† *Sir Leonard Melmerbye*, occ. as curate 24 June, 1533.‡‡ He was chaplain of All Saints chantry in 1535.

Sir Robert Melmerby is placed among the deans by Hutchinson, as occurring on the above date 24 June, 1533. A Robert Melmorby occ. curate of Witton-le-Wear in 1558, and of Hamsterly in 1562.

Cuthbert Mershall, S. T. P. last dean, occ. 1535, 1547. He was vicar of Aycliffe, 1533, and Rector of Whitburn from 1525 to his death in 1549.—"Here lieth the body of Cuthbert Marshall, D.D., late archdeacon of Nottingham, prebendary of Ustwayte, canon residentiary of the metropolitan church of York, of whose soul God have mercy; the burial of whom was the xxvth day of January, in the year of our Lord God 1549."§§ I suppose he would be the same Sir Cuthbert Marshall, master of the grammar school of the Abbey of Durham, who in 1510 was called in to witness the statement of two claimants for sanctuary.‖‖

A list of the prebendaries would be useless and uninteresting, but besides the pluralists spoken of at p. 80, there were a few men holding Darlington honours, of importance enough to need a passing mention.

* Hutchinson.

† Randal, ex Inquis. Rot. (A) Nevil, No. 102. ‡ Randal.

§ Wood's Athenæ. ‖ *Dns* in orig. Perhaps *Dan* would be as correct a rendering in this and other instances. ¶ Hutchinson from Randal.

** Randal's MSS. Hutchinson gives him as a dean on the dates mentioned.

†† In Wolsey's time the dean of Auckland was very obstinate about the "prest money" required of the clergy for the King, and Frankelyn the temporal chancellor writes to the bishop that he had part of the offender's seditious speech, "which your grace shall see under a notarie signe subscribed with hands of Mr. Wardale your commissarie, Mr. Wytham *dean Darnton* and Mr. Folbury, master of your gramer scole at Duresme, whiche be right honest and substantiall men." The chancellor goes on to state with ludicrous gravity that the rebel's "act and dealyng was not farre discrepant from his own *nature and keynde* for his fadir grandsir and all other of his progenie *wer Scottishemen borne* and wheder he be so or not I stand in dowte."

‡‡ Randal, from Reg. Tunstal 12. §§ Drake's Eboracum.

‖‖ Sanctuarium Dunelmense, Surt. Soc. p. 59.

Thomas de Nevill was a prebendary here at the time of his death in 1362. He succeeded as master of Sherburn Hospital in 1339, and was prebendary in the churches of York and Howden as well as rector of Thorp Basset, co. York.

Henry de Ingelby who by his own account held five stalls and the valuable living of Haughton-le-Skerne, is interesting as the prebendary perpetuated by the Ingleby shield of arms on Darlington sedilia. He might well afford to subscribe a large quotum to the chancel repairs. He was second son of Sir Thomas Ingleby (one of the Justices of the court of Common Pleas, and founder of the family of Ingleby of Ripley, &c.), and his will was made and proved at York in 1375. "Henry de Ingelby, prebendary of the prebends of Southcave and Castre in the cathedral churches of York and Lincoln, of Oxton and Crophill in the church of Suthwell in the diocese of York, also prebendary in the Collegiate church of Derlington, and rector of the parish church of Halghton in the diocese of Durham, knowing that nothing is more certain than death, nor uncertain than its hour,—my soul to him who redeemed me by his most precious blood—my wretched body to be buried without worldly pomp in the cathedral church of York if I die at York or near it; if elsewhere, at the place of one of my benefices, then in the beneficial church of that place, before the high altar if convenient; but if at a place distant thirty miles from any of my benefices, then in the parish church there or in its cemetery—to the prioress and convent of Neceham five marks, [and to other religious houses and persons] to pray especially for the souls of Thomas de Ingilby my father and Edeline my mother, Sirs John de Ingilby, David de Wollour, and William de Dalton, and William de Benham, as well for the good estate of our Lord the King during life, and for his soul when he has departed this life, and for the souls of all the benefactors of my said friends as well as myself, and of all the faithful deceased,—to the chapter of York my iron chest which was Master Thomas de Nevell's, and stands in the revestry of the church of York."

Alan de Newark occurs in most of the Commissions of truce with Scotland in the latter part of the 14th cent., the clergy being then the only persons who in general were acquainted with the civic code, and high preferment usually rewarded their services in the legal way. Alan himself was amply remunerated as appears from his testament. He was *in utroque jure bacallarius,* and perpetually occurs as executor to his cotemporary clergy. John de Clyfford, the treasurer of York Cathedral, left him in 1393 one great cup, one great covered bowl of silver and 40*s*. His will, dated in the hall of his house at York in April, 1411, opens thus :—"In the name of our Lord Jhesus Christ, Amen. I, Alan de Newerk, clerk, in the diocese of York, knowing that in this vale of tears I have no abiding city, but seek another (oh! that by the infinite goodness of God it may be a happy one!), and seeing that dust as I am I shall return to dust, but when, where, or how is reserved to the divine knowledge only; that the transitory goods collected by me may in after times be of profit towards the recreation of the poor, the increase of religious training, the saving of mine and others' souls, and the praise of the divine majesty; do make and ordain my testament in this manner. I bequeath my soul to the infinite goodness of God and to the glorious Virgin Mary the mother of Jhesus Christ, to saint John the Evangelist and all saints of God, *by the intercession of whom I firmly trust to have eternal life,* and my body to be buried in the cathedral church of York, near the altar of saint John the Apostle and Evangelist, my master,* situate in the South transept [*in parte australi*] or elsewhere, if I die out of the province of York, as occasion as require." Leaves all his estate to charities to be named in codicils afterwards to be made. One of these was soon made. He names various establishments, benefices, and persons, to which he bequeaths sums that "they might pray for him to God." But I will only select a few passages. "I will that 10*l*. *be distributed among the poor and needy parishioners of the collegiate church of Derlington where I*

* I suppose it was at his altar that Newark officiated.

have a prebend—that on the day of my obit my executors shall dine with my friends to be invited by them, and feed fifty poor people, and have the fragments themselves—that one chaplain officiate at the altar of St. John the Evangelist in the church of York, for the souls of my bro. Thomas, my parents and of all those who hold of them, and my own soul for twenty years next ensuing my death, and shall have yearly 100*s*.—to have an obit in the church of York of 30*s*.—to the convent of St. Mary at York one gilt cup, having the form of a chalice, covered, on the top of which the image of a lion is fixed, and having the feet of lions—to William my kinsman one silver cup covered, figured at the bottom and on the cover—to Master William Newerk, my kinsman, the gilt silver cup which I have in daily use—to Lawrence Stafford, my clerk, one gown of *blacmedle* furred, and two hoods of black cloth *de lyre**—and to Peter Gell, my clerk, my gown *de blanco* furred, which has a hood." Proved 6 July, 1411. The testator was buried in the place he desired. "Orate pro anima Alani de Newark, curie Eborum quondam advocati, qui obiit xiii die mensis Junii an. Dom. 1412,† viam universe carnis est ingressus. Cujus anime, &c."

Nicholas Hulme occurs prebendary in 1427. He was rector of Redmarshall, and master of GreathamHospital, and along with the bishops of Norwich, and Coventry and Lechfeld, Richard Earl of Warwick, Richard Earl of Salisbury, &c., was one of Cardinal Langley's executors in 1439. The bishop left him "a gilt silver cup covered, chased *ad modum columbini** as it is intitled in my inventory." In 1436, John Palman, alias Coke [buried at Auckland] left him "i tabill," and in 1427 he is a legatee of one book of eleven chapters of Richard Ermet, in the will of John Newton the rector of Houghton-le-Spring, and master of Sherburn Hospital "a bad man." A beautiful brass in Greatham Chapel, with elegant blackletter raised on a cross-hatched ground reads:—"Orate pro a'i'abus Nicholai Hulme Joh'is Kelyng et Will'mi Estfelde clericor' quonda' huius hospitalis magistror' ac parentu' Fundatoru' suor' benefactoru' atq' om'i' fideliu' defu'ctor' quor' a'i'ab' p'piciet' deus AMEN."

William Tart, named a prebendary in 1414, (when he was appointed with the bishop's official, to hear a dispute), also occurs in Newton's will as a legatee of one silver cup with a cover.

Chapters frequently met in the church to determine knotty points, and inquisitions often taken therein. Thus the claims of Ralph Surtees against the convent to the patronage of Dinsdale rectory,‡ were defeated in 1240 "coram toto capitulo de Dernington---in ecclesia de Dernington." Thus in 1235, in the foundation of Stockton chapel it is stipulated that if the inhabitants were found "contumacious and rebellious" in performing their duties at the church of Norton, the vicar with the consent of the archdeacon of Durham, *and the chapter of Derlington*, might revoke the celebration of divine offices and ministration of the sacraments at Stockton altogether. Thus again in 1412 the archdeacon conducted an inquisition in this collegiate church as to the vacancy in the vicarage of Gainford ;§ and such instances might be enumerated with Inquisitions post mortem taken here *ad infinitum*.

* *Blacmedle* would be a black material mixed with another colour or fabric, and the hoods were plaited or had wreaths like the strings of a lyre. *Ad modum columbini* :—wreathing or twisting round the cap like the flower of that name.

† Drake. A mistake for 1411. The whole of the will and codicil in the latin may be seen in the Testamenta Eboracensia, Surtees Society.

‡ It had been granted to the church by charter made between 1174 and 1180, to which "Master Peter, canon of Der'ington," was witness.

§ Hunter's MSS. e Reg. Langley. The jury were, William Hesile, vicar of the church of Derlyngton ; Sir Richard Gardner, rector of the church of Dittensal ; Sirs John Uckarby,

I necessarily find in my ecclesiastical jottings, specimens of that "awful doom which canons tell shuts paradise, and opens hell." In 1311 Robert de Cokerton, a notary public, being excommunicated and remaining still in scorn of the sentence which was to restore good angels to him, was to be avoided by every man, &c., according to bishop Kellawe's injunction.* This was the bishop who prevented the tournament being held at Darlington, who spared not the great baron of Raby himself (p. 83) when caught in an unpardonable breach of morality; and here comes John de Alwent nearly as bad, having confessed before this ghostly prince that he had committed adultery with Agnes de Raby, and Annabella de Durham: and also *failed to prove that he had not* committed the like offence with Christiana Clergis, Annabella de Castle Barnard, and Emma le Aumbelour. The prelate mitigated the sentence somewhat in consequence of the station in life of the offender; nevertheless he was, clad only in linen, to be whipped round his parish church of Gainford on six several Sundays and festivals, and also round the market-place at Darlington on six several Mondays, during that part of the day when it should be most thronged. The vicar of Gainford was directed, under pain of the major excommunication, to monish publicly the said John to appear, and to see that he did appear on the succeeding Sunday in the churchyard and so forth, from the one day to the other, until the expiration of the term: and it was provided that, if he did not submit himself, he should be excommunicated throughout the whole archdeaconry of Durham, and shunned by his fellows as excommunicated until he should conform.† There is a still more laughable record of the same period preserved.‡ The then vicar of Darlington was walking through one of the streets when he fell in with a drunken man, who belaboured him so unmercifully that he was taken home, where he was confined for some time. The Ecclesiastical Court forthwith summoned the offender, but the summons was quite lost upon him, he did not appear, and being in contumacy, the pains of excommunication followed. These produced such feelings of alarm that he appeared in court and confessed his guilt, whereupon the sentence was reversed on his submitting to the following punishment. He was to stand at the Western portal of Darlington church, his only clothing the penance sheet; until the service was half over, when the congregation was to be edified by seeing one of the officials whack the barefooted sinner most soundly through the aisles with a whip of cord right stout and long. And as if that

William Smole, William Gseby, Thomas Norman, Thomas de Morton, and Thomas Langton, chaplains; and Thomas Zole, Adam Cor, John de Blackwell, Thomas Sharpe, William Werdall, and John Zole, laymen.

⁂ Acta capituli de Hextildesham apud Derlyngtone contra Johannem Johannis Feryman de Bubbewyth pauperem, presbyterum providendum de beneficio ecclesiastico in dioc. Dunelm. 1335.—*D. and C. Treasury. Catalogue No.* 2629.

* Kellawe's Reg. † Kellawe's Reg. Walbran's Gainford.

‡ The eminent antiquary who told the tale was unable to find the record at the moment again. I have no doubt but that my short version gives sufficiently the purport of it.

was not sufficient, the next day being market-day he was to be whacked through the street more soundly still. The following evidences of penance in protestant times will speak for themselves.

"Anno Domini 1608. Persons excommunicated. - - - Elinor Shaw, widow; Mary the wife of Francis Shaw, a stranger; Agnes wife of Thomas Robinson; Jane wife of John Wallis; Jennet Dent [bur. as "recusant" 8 Mar., 1636-7*]; Elizabeth Oswold wife of Henry Oswold; John Wetherell and his wife; Christofer Potter and his wife, strangers; John Dent; *Recusants*. - - - Jenet Coltard and Elinor Harrison; Isabella Harrison; *Excommunicated for fornication*. - - - Robert Husdons; Tho. Gowlande; Wm. Shaw; Ann Buswell; Jane Colthard; Scyth Smithson; Stephen Storie; Mark Shaw; Elizabeth Johnson; Margaret Lancaster; Richerd Dickeson; Margrett Thompson; Agnes Conyers [see p. 98]; *Dated February* 18, *Published March* 12, 1608. - - - Tho. Newton; Cuthbert Thornehill, absolved; Richard Johnson, absolved;† 9 *March*, 1610. - - - Margrett Stocdale; Raulph Maugeham; Frances Sayer; Isabell Salterston; Robert Husdons; Elizabeth Johnson; 1609, *Excommunicated at Durham*, 27 *April*, 1611, *Published* 5 *May*. - - - *(Darlington Par. Reg. fly leaf.)*

Die Jovis, 1625, Dec. 15, infra æde ven. viri Ri. Hunt S. T. P. Decano coram ipso Et ven. viris Joh. Cradock S. T. P. Canc. Dunelm et Jo. Lively, S. T. B.—"Offic. contra John Harperley de Stockton pro incest. cum Eliz. Wright sorore uxoris suæ. Wh day hour and place he being precognized appeared and confessed and was enjoined acknowledgment in penitential manner, in the churches of Norton and Stockton, wh he performed, and had also been ordered to perform the like penance *at the market crosses of Durham and Darneton* which he commuted and paid 6*l*. for ye same, and therefore desired that he might be no further proceeded against. Ordered to enter into recognizance in 40*l*. and sureties 20*l*. each, and to certify before 12 June next."—*(Brewster's Stockton.)*

1768. Sep. To washing the Pennance sheet,‡ 3*d*.—*Church Accounts*. [This is the last entry of the kind in the Darlington Books.]

* Fly-leaf of register.

† This and some other of the names are erased in another ink, probably on absolution. Some have crosses opposite.

‡ A ludicrous allusion to penance is made by Bishop Dodgson when describing his living of Elsdon in 1762. He says his richest farmers were Scotch dissenters, whose religion descended from father to son more as *a part of the personal estate*, rather than the result of reasoning or enthusiasm, and goes on to state that churchmen and presbyterians had a very good understanding, "for they not only intermarry with each other, but frequently do penance together in a white sheet, with a white wand, barefoot, in one of the coldest churches in England, and at the coldest season of the year: I dare not finish the description, for fear of bringing on a fit of the ague - - - If I was not assured by the best authority upon earth that the world was to be destroyed by fire, I should conclude that the day of destruction is at hand, but brought on us by means of an agent very opposite to that of heat. - - - The whole country is doing penance in a white sheet, for it began to snow on Sunday night, and the storm has continued ever since."

I add an extract or two more from this amusing divine's letters:—"My journey produced a great deal of pleasure till I reached Darlington, when I quitted the coach and began to fly, but my wings soon failed me, for the post horses which I hired at Durham were not able to move an inch further than the ninth mile stone. - - - A clog-maker combs out my wig *upon my Curate's head* by way of a block, and his wife powders it with a dredging box. The vestibule of the castle is a low stable, above it is the kitchen, in which are two little beds, joining to each other. The Curate and his wife lay in one and Margery the maid in the other. I lay in the parlour between two beds to keep me from being frozen to death. - - - I have lost the use of every thing but my reason, though my head is entrenched in three nightcaps, and my throat, which is very bad, is fortified with *a pair of stockings twisted in the form of a cravat*. As washing is very cheap I wear

A long list of ecclesiastics who took name* from this their birth-place might be furnished, but the only characters really interesting are the following:---

1258. *Hugo de Derlyngton* was elected sub-prior of Durham, and in 1285 he was made prior. During the wars of the barons, he conducted himself so prudently as to save the possessions of the church from depredation by either party. He contributed largely to the magnificence of his convent, and among various fine works† built the belfrey on the summit of the great tower of the cathedral, and enlarged the organ. Nor was his hospitality less notable. Whenever he came to his house, the poor people to whom his kitchen was ever open, danced before him. It is said of him that the common coinage of a penny was reduced to five mites, that he might distribute handfuls of that small money to a greater number of objects. When advanced in years and obliged to travel in a chariot, he constantly threw money from thence to the poor. Graystanes gives an instance of the prior's authority. "Bishop Stichill whilst he was resident in the castle at Durham, made it his custom to send wine to the convent. One day he ordered his brother to carry wine to the sub-prior's table, which on being presented gave offence to prior Hugo, who presided at the upper table, and thereupon he struck the table, and put an end to the dinner in the middle of the mess." In 1273 he resigned, and his successor, Richard Claxton, prior of Holy Island, was confirmed at Darlington. For some reason or other the new prior abdicated in 1285, when Hugo was recalled. He assented to the archbishop's jurisdiction during a vacancy of the see, and before his second resignation in 1290, was quite superannuated, yet so obstinate and resentful that when application was made for his removal, he sent to the bishop with the promise of large bribes if he would deny his assent, but the bishop at once hastened to Durham and Hugh was forced into a cession of his office. Graystanes gives the following graphic passage as to Hugh's second reign. After mentioning his removal of Richard

two shirts at a time, and for want of a wardrobe hang my great coat upon my own back, and generally keep on my boots in imitation of my namesake [Charles XII] of Sweden Indeed since the snow became two feet deep (as I wanted a chappin of yale from the public house) I made an offer of them to Margery the maid, *but her legs are too thick to make use of the offer*, and I am told that the greater part of my parishioners are not less substantial."—*Richardson's Table Book. Leg. Div.* 1. 232.

* "It was fashionable for the clergy," says Fuller, "especially if regulars, monks and, friars, to have their surnames (for syr-names they were not) or upper-names, because superadded to those given at the font, from the places of their nativity ; and therefore they are so good evidence to prove where they were born, as if we had the deposition of the midwife, and all the gossips present at their mother's labours. Hence it is that in such cases we seldom charge our margin with other authors, their surname being author enough to avow their births therein.

"Some impute this custom to the pride of the clergy, whose extraction generally was so obscure that they were ashamed of their parentage : an uncharitable opinion, to fix so foul a fault on so holy a function ; and most false, many in orders appearing of most honourable descent. Yet Richard bishop of London quitted Angervill, though his father Sir Richard Angervill was a knight of worth and worship, to be called of Bury, where he was born ; and William, bishop of Winchester, waived Pattin to wear Waynfleet, though he was eldest son to Richard Pattin, an esquire of great ancientry.

"Others say, that the clergy herein affected to be Levi-like, "who said to his father and mother, I have not seen him," (Deut. xxxiii, 9.), practising to be mimics Melchisedech, "without father, without mother, without descent," (Heb. vii, 3.), so as to render themselves independent of the world, without any coherence to carnal relations. Surely some were well minded herein, that as they might have no children, they would have no fathers beholding the place of their birth, as co-heir at least to their estates, to which many did plentifully pay for their nursing therein."

† See Hutchinson.

de Hoton from the priory of Lithum to Coldingham, when he was flourishing at the former place, he adds "for he hated him, because, while sub-prior in the days of prior Claxton on coming to Fynchall on St. John Baptist's day to visit the place and the brethren, as was the custom with the sub-prior, he asked to whom did Hugh the quondam prior confess ; when Hugh aforesaid answered, "I know, son, what I have to do, and to take care of my soul as well as you do yours." Therefore the enquiry was the spring of envy, and gave occasion for hatred. Whence when he was afterwards made prior, out of dislike of Richard de Hoton, who was a gracious youth, he sent monks to study at Oxford, and magnificently furnished sufficient expenses to them, I had rather it was the occasion of doing good, as an ill action. Hence came our redemption." Richard de Hoton was his successor, a fact which explains the prior's disinclination to resign.

1284. Died, JOHN DE DERLINGTON, who took the name of the place whereat he was was born, viz. Darlington in the bishopric, which may be justly proud of bearing so famous and learned a man and such a respecter of the Book of Books. He was bred a Dominican friar,* and a great clerk. Matthew Paris gives him the testimony that he was one "*qui literatura pollebat excellenter et consilio;*" and employing himself in acquiring a minute knowledge of the Scriptures, the fruit of his labours was "The Great" or "The English Concordance,"† which he finished about 1270, and was probably the first work of the kind ever attempted in this country. Henry III. made him his confessor (which argues his piety that so devout a prince used him in so conscientious an office), and in his time there arose a hot and high contest between the prior and convent of Trinity church, Dublin, who had elected William de la Corner, as archbishop, to that see, and the dean and chapter of St. Patricks, who had chosen Fromund le Brun the Pope's chaplain. Pope John XXI. cassated both elections and pitched on our Darlington as a good expedient for cutting the question short, and appointed him Archbishop, being in fact a person in whom king and pope met in some equal proportion, he being confessor to the one, and collector of Peter-pence (as also to his two successors Nicholas III. and Martin IV.) through all Ireland. Returning to England he sickened, died, and was buried in Preaching Friars, London.‡ He was the author of various works, amongst others "Disceptationes Scholasticæ," and Rudd in his catalogue of MSS. Dean and Chap. Lib. Durham, imagines him to be identical with the author of "Questiones XII librorum Metaphisice et IV librorum Ethicorum disputate a magistro Jo. de Ditenshale Anno Dni. M.CC. octogesimo tertio," in that collection. "For although they say he died in 1284, so small a difference might easily happen. That he was called Derlington perchance occurred (after he began to be notable) by his taking the name from the neighbouring town, so noted for its market, rather than from the ignoble vill [Dinsdale] in which he was born. Many instances of such changes might be adduced."

Sir Adam de Derlyngton occurs as a wealthy priest and landowner in the Cleveland district, in the 14th cent.§ He was Rector of Crathorne in 1348.

1346. *John de Derlington,* a canon of Guisburn, confirmed prior of that place.

1455. *Thomas Darlington,* a canon of Guisburn, in like manner confirmed.

John Blakewell, appointed Chaplain of Hilton chapel within Hilton castle, 1443, died before 1450.

1519. *Thomas Dernton,* alias Shepherd, was last Abbot of Eggleston, and received 13*l.* 6*s.* 8*d.* per ann. pension.||

* Hollinshed.—"*Ordinis Prœdicatorum.*" Leland's Coll. ii. 281.

† Ibid. ‡ Fuller, almost verbatim.

§ Brewster's Stockton. Inq. p. m. 18 Edw. III. Rot. Abbrev. temp. Edw. III., &c.

|| Whitaker's Richmondshire.

John Darneton, the Abbot of Fountains from 1478 to 1494, seems to have been an active and enterprising character, whose energetic building propensities caused the alterations detailed in Walbran's Guide to Ripon, &c.

THE COLLEGIATE CHURCH

ranks in importance among the Durham ecclesiastical edifices now in use, next to the Cathedral, and bears indisputable marks of the latter days of Bishop Pudsey. Hence it may be said to be in its general features a Transition rather than an Early English building, "and for elegant simplicity, may vie with any in the kingdom." It presents the solitary instance of a Durham church retaining its lofty roofs, which with the spire form a composition of no ordinary beauty.

The ground plan is much as Pudsey designed it, and comprehends a central tower, a choir with a small apartment attached on the South, now a vestry, but probably used formerly as the "Tresor-house," two transepts, a nave and two aisles, and until very lately a South porch. The Tower is peculiar, and measures two feet more from N. to S. than from E. to W. The general style is Early English but of varying character, the south transept appearing to be of later date than the other portions, which are quite of transitional detail. In the 14th century a serious settlement* of the building took place, the original stone roofs seem to have been supplanted by wooden ones ; the windows near the tower were blocked† and rood-lights inserted in two of them, while substantial corner supports were added ; the aisles were completely rebuilt though the doorways were retained ; the tower lights received decorated tracery ; and the roodloft, sedilia and piscina were furnished ; all this, by heraldic evidence, being in the time of Prebendary Ingleby who died in 1375. The fifteenth century witnessed the addition of the fine woodwork of the choir, the sixteenth the Easter sepulchre and the choir and vestry roofs, and the seventeenth the font cover and old pews in the North transept. With these preliminary remarks I shall proceed to give the details of this fine fabric, which belong to the period I have been chronicling.

ADMEASUREMENTS. (INTERIOR). Length of Choir, 33 ; Tower, 22 ; Nave, 72 ; total length of centre, 127 feet. Length of Aisles, 74 (the Western wall of these is two feet less in thickness than that of the Nave) ; breadth of transepts, 18 ; total length of wings, 92 feet. Length of each transept, 26 ; breadth of Tower, 24 ; total length across transepts, 76 feet. Breadth of Nave, 24 (to centre of pier) ; of each Aisle, 10 ; total breadth at West-end, 44 feet. Breadth of Chancel, 21 feet. Vestry, 16 by 12 feet. Nave composed of four compartments.

* This has twisted and shaken the whole of the church, especially the West-end, which is very much out of the perpendicular. It is attempted to be supported by long iron rods passing from the tower and bolted into the walls, but "it is to be regretted that an amount of money, which would have gone far towards rebuilding it, should have been spent in perpetuating a positive deformity."

† Billings's well-intentioned expression, "the blocking up of windows (as if the window-tax affected churches)," is not borne out by the fact. The Darlington folks have hurt their church enough, without being made answerable for *necessary* supports to the tower in the days of old.

Altar. The "exceeding long and fair altare stone *de vario marmore, hoc est, nigro albis maculis distincto* at the high altare" which Leland saw, has totally disappeared ; it probably came from the "faire quarre of blak marble spottid with white, in the very ripe of Tees," which he mentions as being "about a quarter of a mile beneth Ægleston [Priory]." There is nothing peculiar about the present arrangements. The two altar-books are inscribed "*Darlington Altar. J. H. S.*" on a good old binding which *on one side of each book only* has unluckily been supplanted by a new one of very inferior execution, with *I. H. S.* on, for show. Within is an Indian-ink drawing of a boy, pointing to a representation of one of the books inscribed "*This Book and its companion were the gift of Mr. John Cade, A.D. MDCCLXXI. For the use of the Altar in Darlington Church. S*[*amuel*] *W*[*ilkinson*] *Delin.*"

Arches. The tower rests on four superb obtuse arches of rectangular mouldings. They rise from clustered piers, of which the main pillars are of a pointed section, and each of them is furnished with two sub-pillars enclosed in rectangular formations. A large square block intervenes between the inner mouldings of the arch and the abacus. Some of the capitals are flowered, others moulded only, and both capitals and piers have been sorely cut and built upon, partly in the fourteenth century when the roodloft was constructed, and partly in later days. The S. W. cluster from which four arches spring in various directions, is still perfect and has a noble effect. Above these tower arches are four others opening into the roofs. Before the ceilings hid the latter they would appear to have been visible from below, and formed a sort of lantern, and must have had a very singular effect; they are plain chamfered. Each aisle opens into a transept by a single arch of fine detail. The Nave arches are curious. The three Westernmost are very wide and obtuse, of three orders chamfered, while the Easternmost is much narrower, of fine proportion and elegant mouldings. The same alteration takes place in the piers. Those under the plain arches are simple cylindrical and octagonal alternately, with corresponding responds at the W., but the more ornamented arch rests on a clustered respond and a beautiful pier, composed of four cylindrical and filleted shafts separated by pear shaped or pointed bowtells. Nevertheless they are coeval, for the clerestory does not alter, and one of the plainer arches partly rests upon the clustered pier. Owing to the settlement at the West end, the end arch is nearly circular, but throughout the church the prevailing feature of the whole of the architecture is endless variety and irregularity, though the general character is so admirably preserved that there is not the slightest appearance of incongruity.

Arch-buttresses. These are some masses of masonry inserted in the angles of the cross plan to support the tower. They cut off the angle and are supported by arches high above the ground, interrupting the plain early English strips which preceded them.

Aumbries. Small closets for various purposes. There is one in the Newel staircase at the S. W. corner of the S. transept, near the summit. It runs three feet into the thickness of the wall, and is wider than the entrance splay in the wall leading to it, which occupies 1 ft. 8 in. of the 3 feet.

Base-table. In the original work of the transepts and chancel, this is a simple slope into which the flat buttresses die.

Battlement. The South Aisle has a plain decorated parapet, and the vestry a debased one, the other parts of the church are furnished with battlements, which are all of comparatively late date.

Brasses, Sepulchral. Within the altar rails the mark of a figure and inscription on a veined marble slab. The like near the North stalls in the choir. Marks of two inscriptions in the North transept, on an enormous blue slab (which with the rest of this transept is elevated) bevelled at the S. edge. Next to it a slab with the mark of a chalice and inscription ; this style of brass is excessively rare in England, and the perfect one at Leeds is perhaps unique. It no doubt covered a chantry priest. Close to the North wall of this transept a slab which appears to have contained two full length figures canopied, with kneeling figures round, the matrix of one remains on a corner. Near the font the mark of an inscription. The like in South aisle just within the door. The like in the pavement of the destroyed South porch, in which also are the marks of two figures, inscription, and four corner pieces.

Buttresses. In the early English parts these are of very small projection, much resembling Norman ones. At the corners they form turret-like buildings of square form. The decorated buttresses are very irregular and more for use than show. See Arch-buttress.

Capitals. All fine. In the window and arcade shafts they are generally moulded with fine deep undercut members, but they also occur with the nailhead ornament inserted, and the crisp foliage of the period. The abacus is mostly round and overhangs in a very graceful manner, but in many instances (as in the pier capitals) it is of a square Norman character. In the South transepts the foliage introduced is of peculiar beauty. The pier capitals partially follow the form of the pier, but are in many instances square, and are only foliated in some instances. The unusual form of an Early English hexagonal capital occurs on several shafts in the North transept.

Chamfer, an arch moulding exceedingly abundant. In the North transept it springs in one instance from a fleur-de-lis ornament intervening between it and the capital of the supporting shaft.

Chantries. The North transept (see Brasses) has evidently been a chantry, probably that of All Saints, as I have observed that foundations to our lady are more usually on the Southern side of churches.

Coffin. A stone coffin dismantled of its lid lies near the choir door. Part of a coffinlid with cross flory was dug up in the churchyard a year or two ago but was suffered to be destroyed. The early stone in Barningham churchyard, Yorks., of which I present a cut

seems to be a coffinlid, and of Saxon date. It is nearly covered with grass and soil, but seems about three and a half or four inches thick. The coffinlids thus decorated served as monumental slabs, but in the Saxon period a sort of high *dos dane* monument appears to have been used, of which examples occur at Bedale.

Corbel-tables remain under the later battlements in the Nave and transepts, consisting of small blocks simply moulded and supporting the parapet.

Cross. There is no vestige of one, but there are the remains of two fine Saxon ones at

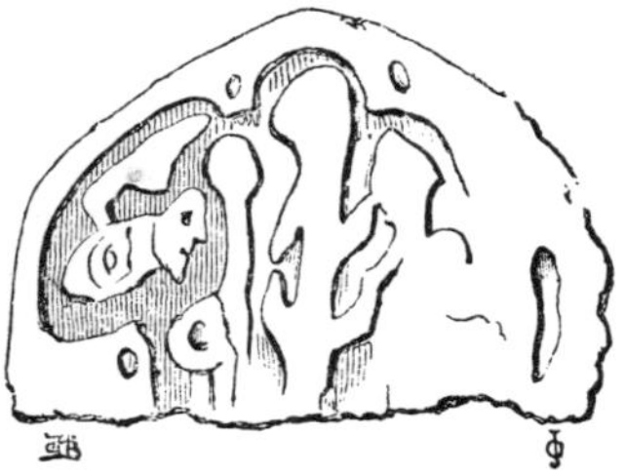

[*Details of Saxon tomb in Bedale Church, which has a tiled roof as below.*]

Aycliffe, five miles off, which are supposed to commemorate the two synods held there in 782 and 789. There are remains of the usual churchyard cross of Saxon date at Hauxwell, near Richmond, and at Bedale. Since writing p. 81, I find that as early as about 1313 the Walworths had family transactions respecting one rood on *le Crosflat*. See cuts over.

[*Part of Saxon tomb, found in Bedale Church, now penes W. Harker, Esq. Theakstone Villa.*]

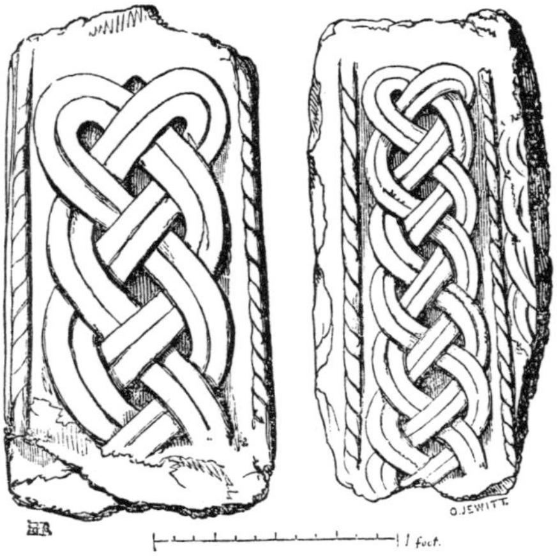

[*Part of Cross at Bedale.*]

Doorways. The Choir door is a plain square chamfered one in a buttress-like projection. The West door is grand in its simplicity. It is situate in a triangular headed projection of the wall. The capitals of three shafts (which have evidently been stolen for the marble) at each side alone remain, they support rectangular sets of deeply undercut roll mouldings, within which is a continuous bead moulding, sadly cut, to accommodate itself to a modern door. The North and South doors have chamfered mouldings and two shafts at each side; the latter has had a porch, but the former is placed in a projection which has a short piece of moulding at each side above the doorway. The outer door of the destroyed South porch was obtuse pointed, and is shown in Cade's print.

Dripstones generally run on in a string. Those of the Tower arches rest on shafts, and are adorned with an ornament like a nutmeg pared down to an hexagonal form. In the arcades of the South transept a cruciform flower, animals and human heads occur; the

latter are modern, being moulded partly from the physiognomy of a drunken man, and have nevertheless a good effect and a much more sensible expression than would be expected. The North door has moulded terminations, the South, rosettes. The decorated windows have masques.

[*Crosses at Aycliffe. See p.* 215.]

Effigy. There is but one monumental figure, of which I give a cut, (see next p.) but it must be nearly coeval with the fabric, being a female in the dress of the twelfth cent., holding a book (?) and supported by an angel. A fibula appears beneath the neck and an an *aulmoniere* is suspended from the girdle. Altogether the figure is much like that of Richard I's. queen, Berengaria. It now stands upright in the church near the Western door.

Font. Plainish circular shaft, on two steps of the same form ; the basin is octagonal lined with lead. It is coeval with the building, but is painted over. The fine late perpendicular cover (perhaps as late as Cosin's time) is also painted to imitate the material of which it is constructed—oak !

Galilee. See p. 46. The Glossary of Architecture says that " in some churches there are indications of the West end of the Nave having been parted off from the rest, either by a step in the floor, a division in the architecture, or some other line of demarcation : it was considered to be somewhat less sacred than the other portions of the building." At present the West bay only of our Nave is screened off as a porch, but this is quite a modern arrangement, and the screen was further eastward some few years ago. I am not even quite sure that the change of architecture at the commencement of the Easternmost arch of the Nave is without its meaning, for in Middleham church the mark of a screen of considerable height across the whole church at the same point is distinctly visible.

Material. " A hard grit-stone little injured by time." *Cade.* " The expence of the fabric before us was immense ; for the stone of which it is built, according to the opinion of judicious workmen, was brought above twelve miles, from the quarries of Cockfield-fell." —*Hutchinson.*

[*Cross at Hauxwell. See p.* 215.]

Newell-staircases. One at the S. W. of the South transept in a turret which changes from a square to an octagon. At the top this turret has small quatrefoil windows, and lower down plain slits ; it has a door into the churchyard and formerly had another into the church ; the staircase continues to the top of the turret, but at present is only used to attain the flat ceiling of the transept on which there is a passage beneath the old roof to the upper arches of the tower, which form the sides of a chamber for the bellringers. There is another newell-staircase in the roodloft.

Niches. A trefoiled one above the S. door, another at its W. side, and a third above the W. door, apparently for images.

Pinnacles. Those on the tower are modern, but at each side of the Western gable is an early example, with small pannels terminating in an octagonal spiret. At the summit of that on the S. is a mutilated sitting figure.

Piscina. In the *East* wall. The masonry is mainly original, but the blundering label and shields (one of which is charged with a mullet in bad imitation of Ingleby's estoile) are modern and of wood. There are two cinquefoiled recesses, the S. one has a basin divided into two parts, the North one runs deeper into the wall and is plain, having probably answered as a credence table. The two basins are apparently for the two uses of the piscina, the washing of the priest's hands and the rinsing of the chalice.

Roodloft. The Darlington example is perhaps unique. It is a massive stone gallery or platform, the whole width of the great chancel arch, some 13 feet in height and 7 in depth, having a wide ribbed archway in its centre, leading from the nave to the chancel. This arch is ribbed precisely like a bridge arch, and the whole now presents a bald effect ; but it appears that formerly it was ornamented heraldically, as Cade, in " Hell-Kettles" (which, since writing p. 36, I have found from a letter to Mr. Allan about offering it to Miss Darnton, was his production), laments " the destruction of the arms of benefactors to the fabric, cut in stone, and properly blazoned *over the entrance into the quire*, by a late reformer." The images of the rood were in allusion to St. John, xix. 26, "Christ on the cross saw his mother and the disciple whom he loved standing by." The sound of a door remains on tapping at the North end, and a portion of a winding staircase is still used as an access to the organ on the South. In the two blocked windows of the choir next to the choir arch are the remains of two small Decorated windows, (the South one with a trefoiled head, the North one having a cinquefoiled head and cinquefoiled transom) which served to throw light upon the Roodloft, which is also of Decorated date.

Roofs. Against the first piers from the West, on both sides of the Nave, there are clear evidences of the plan of vault adopted in the Aisles, consisting of portions of chamfered ribs, and in the North Aisle opposite these remains, an elegantly moulded corbel remains on the wall on which the ribbing fell. In the Nave where the two architectures join, a triply-shafted pillaret runs up the wall to the string beneath the clerestory, which latter part of the building has been so modernized as to leave no clue to what the shaft supported. Whatever was the contour of the Early English roofs, they have only left their moulding on the tower walls above the present line of leading, being supplanted by Decorated oaken roofs of five cants, there being no tie-beam or king-post. These remain in the Nave and Transepts,but are hidden by a modern plain pannelled ceiling, which extends to the Tower. The choir has a flattish Tudor roof as well as the Vestry. My own impression is, that the original roofs were vaulted arches, corresponding in shape and altitude to the upper arches of the tower, that the passage to the tower was from the newel staircase through the space between that arch and the apex of the weather moulding ; and that the weight of these roofs being blamed for the settlement in the fourteenth century, they were replaced by the canted ones which are of the later style of cant. It is remarkable that at one side only of the weather mouldings there is a hitch ; that of the South transept is shewn in my plate.

Sedilia. Three in gradation ascending to the East, consisting of trefoiled ogee arches : the compartments formed between the heads and the square outer moulding are also foiled, and contain shields, only one of which is charged and contains the estoile of Ingleby. The original depth of these seats cannot be ascertained, as the safe behind has interfered with them. The Sedilia were seats for the officials during certain parts of the mass.

Sepulchre. The Easter Sepulchre (at which were transacted some strange theatrical mysteries at Easter : see the Rites of Durham, &c.) consists of a Tudor-arched recess in the North wall of the Chancel under a square head embattled ; the spandrils formed by which are filled in with foliage, on which a colouring of green may still be dimly traced.

Spire. This feature of the church is part of the original design and is octagonal, each face being eight feet broad at the base At the angles are bold undercut bowtells, and some distance up, on the four cardinal fronts, are small trefoil lights with transoms of Decorated date. The height is 108 feet, 180 feet from the ground. It is supported partly on the main walls of the tower and partly on squinches in the corners.

On July 17, 1750, this beautiful spire, considered the highest and finest in the North of England, was rent and shaken from top to bottom. On the N. W. side of it, about three yards below the top, the stones were thrown quite out, so as to lay the inside open for a space near ten yards ; between which break and the bottom were several others, but none quite so large : the church also was much hurt and damaged. Several houses in the town were much shattered and laid open in many places ; some people were likewise struck down with the sulphureous blast, and lay senseless for several minutes, but none were killed. This storm occasioned fifteen yards of the spire to be taken down and rebuilt in 1752, and divine service could not be performed until the spire was taken down and the church repaired. The agreement with Robert Nelson of Melsonby, stone-cutter, and Robert Corney of Coatham, carpenter, stipulates that the spire should be rebuilt the same height as before, and that the fifteen yards required to be done accordingly should be performed for 105*l*. Unfortunately the mason omitted the moulding at the angles in the new part, and thus deprived it of much beauty. It is a coincidence that the only two spires of considerable elevation in the county, Chester and Darlington, should both have the same rhyme connected with them (p. 125), and have required rebuilding from the same cause.

Stalls. On each side of the choir are good panelled desks and miserere seats with carved elbows, fine florid. " Their oak bench ends, full five inches thick," says Billings, "are the most massive specimens we have ever met with. Their numerous edge mouldings would seem rather to belong to a large archway." The arms of Cardinal Langley fix them to a date about 1430, and the same insignia occur on the more numerous but less massive stalls at St. Andrews Auckland, at which church, and at Lanchester, the bishop had the first stall on the S. side ; the dean the first on the N., and at Durham the prior sat on the N. side in like manner. We may presume the same arrangement was followed at Darlington. The North stalls are imperfect, three of them having been demolished to make room for a great ugly pew at no distant period. There ought to be nine at each side, two being against the Roodloft. The desks and stands are handsomely panelled with bold tracery and the elbows and poppyheads are full of beautiful foliage, quiet angels, and comical heads with lolling tongues. The designs of the misereres, beginning at the W. stall of the N. set are these : 1, a little man with laced boots gathering or supporting flowers ; 2, a lion's head ; 3, the little man asleep, his boots *un*laced ; 4, a winged and clawed monster with a human head ; 5, (Easternmost of S. side) a human head ; 6, an eagle (a device which occurs in other parts) ; 7, an angel and open book ; 8, a winged monster having a lion's body and eagle's head ; 9, our said little man with one boot laced, the other unlaced, having a chain round the neck of a clawed monster whose leonic physiognomy seems to be smiling with amusement at the fierce strokes the little man gives with a ragged staff on his head (there is evidently a legend connected with this little man] ; 10, a human head ; 11, a crowned figure with two sceptres [whose face is much like that of the small man] between two griffins sejant gorged. This would be the bishop's seat. Five misereres are wanting besides those of the destroyed stalls. On the backs of some of the stalls are cuttings by the knives of some idle officials, " W," " Maria," in black letter, &c.

Steeple. A massy central tower of which the transept sides are two feet shorter than those of the Nave and chancel.

Strings. These occur in great abundance and of varied mouldings. One on the W. wall of the S. Transept terminates in an elegant rosette, and there is a very effective one

DARLINGTON COLLEGIATE CHURCH.

MISERERES.

W. Hylton Longstaffe, *del.* O. Jewitt, *sc.*

DARLINGTON COLLEGIATE CHURCH.

END AND MISERERE OF THE BISHOP'S STALL.

W. Hylton Longstaffe, *del.* O. Jewitt, *sc.*

on the W. front consisting of a zigzag formed of laurel-like leaves slanting in different directions.

TOOTH ORNAMENT. This occurs in one place only, the architrave of a small window in the W. side of the S. transept, which is generally of richer work than the rest of the building.

WINDOWS. These are the glory of Darlington Church. The West front is a very fine composition. Above the deeply recessed doorway in its shallow porch is an arcade of five rather obtuse arches with banded pillars, two of which are open as windows ; over these a triplet, the centre only open, in the gable. The East end, which in a late pamphlet of high authority is said to be "quite Norman," is in fact "quite modern" from a short distance off the ground, and has four plain semicircular lights. "The East end of the quire," says Cade, "being out of its perpendicular, by taking away the leaded conic roof (after the alienation of the college, temp. Edw. VI.) was repaired in the present humble manner by Lord Viscount Vane, the patron, in the year 1748 ; until that time, the stalls in the quire and architecture of the East end had a venerable appearance, being adorned with six large windows, and excellent Gothic work in stone and wainscot." Both Transept-ends have four lights disposed two and two ; in the N. one above these is a triplet of arches, the centre being pierced ; in the S. the gable is filled by a rose window consisting of a quatrefoil, the foils floriated. The other sides of the Transepts and choir have two sets of windows, pierced in fine internal arcades, of very varying detail in each arch. The nail head ornament occurs profusely, and the two centre lights of the lower set on each side of the choir are ornamented luxuriantly with a lozengy decoration of Norman contour, in which the lozenges at the angle of a rectangular moulding are filled up with a sort of four-leaved flower. In the small arches of the upper set near the Chancel arch in the N. Transept and Choir the peculiar feature of a smaller shaft, overtopping and resting upon the ordinary shaft, and supporting one member of the mouldings only, occurs. In the same Transept some of the lights have a different pitch of arch to that of the mouldings, the variation being remedied by the inelegant device of making the inner cylindrical moulding to grow broader towards its summit. The whole of the work in this part is of plainer character than in all other portions of the church. One of the arches in the choir arcades is semicircular. The South transept is peculiarly rich. The South side has two triplets with banded shafts, the centres blank, the sides pierced, in the lower range two rosettes of extreme chastity and elegance are introduced in the spandrils. On the E. the upper set has banded shafts and arches, with exquisite sunken trefoils and quatrefoils in the spandrils ; the lower range has a profusion of nail-head ornaments which extend to the trefoil and quatrefoil spandril panels, the shafts are plain. The W. window arcades are of the same rich character, and a rich rosette panel is introduced in a spandril, composed of four marigold-like flowers with five quatrefoiled flowers in the intervening spaces, the whole being surrounded with nail-heads. The clerestory of the Nave is ruined with plaster internally, and the plan is not apparent, but at the exterior it is a fine array of arches, disposed in triplets, the centre of each being pierced as a window. The aisle windows are square decorated, of prebendary Ingleby's time, and of much the same pattern as the sedilia, their heads are filled with ordinary and not very rich flowing tracery. The tower has a series of five Early English arches at each side filled with Decorated tracery, the centre one pierced as a belfry window.

My plate will exhibit the main features of this fine church, in which I have restored the shafts of the West Door, left out the circular plates in the West end, to which the supporting rods are fastened ; and as few headstones last a longer time than fifty or sixty years, I have not *entombed* and hurt the proportions of the work of Pudsey. In 1774, Cade published a S. W. view by Sam. Wilkinson, of very stiff execution. He gave it to his friend, Geo. Allan, whose son the M.P. presented it to Mr. Nichols, who placed it at the disposal of Surtees, for the use of his history, but it was not adopted.* The plate in Surtees is by Blore, it is effective, but all the arches are too sharp, and the tower too narrow. Billings, in his Architectural Antiquities of the County, has given beautiful N.W. and S. views of the exterior, a portion of the interior of the fine S. Transept, and smaller illustrations of portions of the zigzagged window of the choir and stall-work. The largest S.W. view is the latest, a lithograph from a drawing by Mr. Stephen Humble, of Dar-

* "I thank you for the handsome prints, in return for which I will send you my copper-plate of Darlington Church ; it may be useful in your family (as a private plate), but do not wish to put you under any restrictions."—*Cade to Allan*, 1788. The plate in Hutchinson is reduced from Cade's engraving.

lington; it includes a large portion of back ground, and is, with one or two exceptions, a correct likeness.

The Deanery in its former picturesque state is presented to my readers at the head of this chapter. Roughcast has been plentifully daubed thereon, and the mere outline of the building now remains to the S.W. of the church-yard.*

"The common seal of the said Collegiate Church," used by the church-wardens in 1507,† was a round one of the style of the thirteenth century. The Virgin and child are seated under a fine Early English canopy. ✠ SIGILLVM : COMMVNE : DE : DERNINGTVN.

* That Mr. Robert Crompton [of Skerne, co. York, and much mixed up with tithe dealings in the parish] shall within thirty days avoyde out of the Deanry the poor woomen dwelling there."—*Borough Books.*

† See the instrument under St. Paul's Rents hereafter.

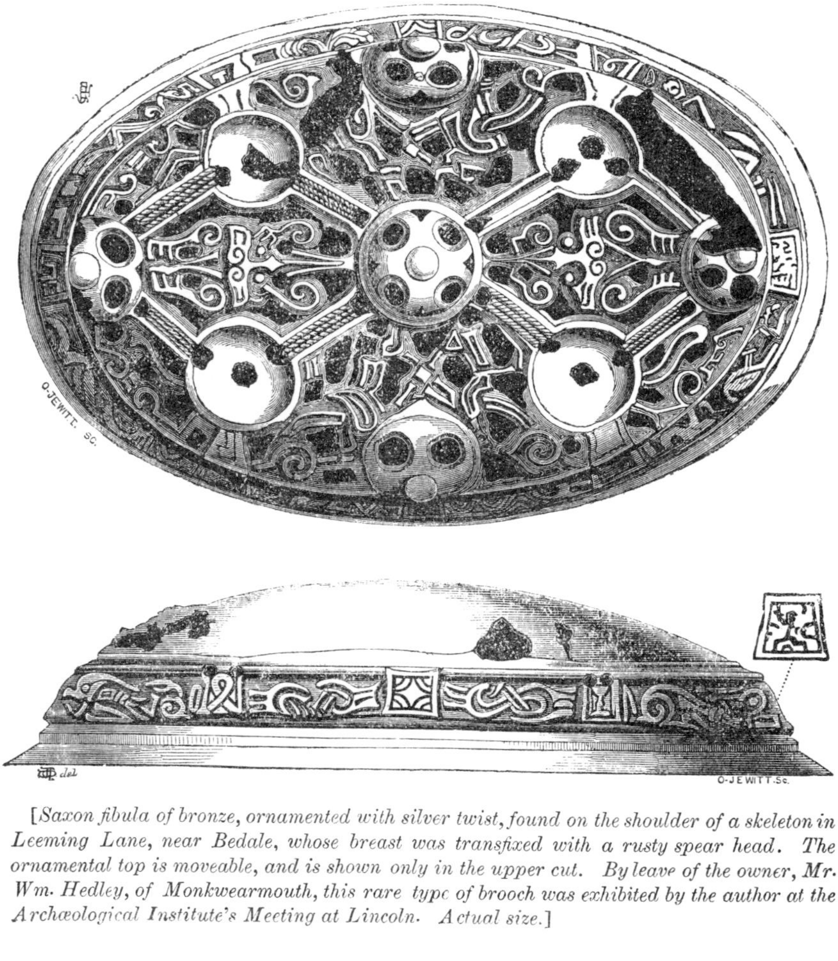

[*Saxon fibula of bronze, ornamented with silver twist, found on the shoulder of a skeleton in Leeming Lane, near Bedale, whose breast was transfixed with a rusty spear head. The ornamental top is moveable, and is shown only in the upper cut. By leave of the owner, Mr. Wm. Hedley, of Monkwearmouth, this rare type of brooch was exhibited by the author at the Archæological Institute's Meeting at Lincoln. Actual size.*]

Chapter II. Protestant.

I. The Church of England.

I RESUME the succession of Incumbents, who are now styled Perpetual Curates.

"*Sir John Clapham*, vicare of Darlington," occ. 1560.

Sir John Claxton, occ. 1561, 1565.

James Thornton, died 1571.

John Welshe, 1571, died of the plague in Darlington.*

John Woodfall, 1584. The Register commences June, 1590,† but it is remarkable that the first and second books are numbered 2 and 3.

Robert Gesford, 1601.

Robert Thomlinson, 1602, signs "Ro. Thomlinson, vicar," in the registers which were then first signed at the foot of each page by the incumbent and churchwardens. This practise continued till Clapperton's time. Margaret Thomlinson wife of Robert Thomlinson vicar of D. bur. 29 Jan., 1602-3. Robert Thomlinson and Alice Pape mar. 8 Sep., 1603 (the entry an autograph). Mrs. Alice Thomlinson had a house in the Head-rawe at Darlington, 1630. Alice Thomlinson of D. widow, bur. 8 Dec. 1644.

"A sermon preched by me Henrye umfray the first of Januarye beinge licensed by the Right Reverend farther in God Doctor Oerton [Overton] bishop of Caventre and Lechfeld anno Domini 1603." *Par. Reg. p.* 1.

I know not whether the wretch in the following entry from the Eryholme Register was a relative of our parson :—"1665. June 3. Richard Barnet and Martha Nesum of Dalton, mar. This Martha Nesum was the widow of John Nesum, who was barberously murdered by one Tomlinson, of Oxneyfield, cuming from Darlington. This Tomlinson was brother to Parson Heberon, of Croft, who he got to advance his Tythes."

Isaac Lowden (signs "*vicarius ibid.*," and "*Ecclesiæ Rector*") 1606. Bur. 3 Jan. 1611-2 as "minister of the word and vicar of this place."

Brian Grant, (*vicarius ibidem*) 1612. Bur. 26 Jan., 1621-2

Ralph Donkine, son of John Donkine, a clergyman on travel (*Clerici peregrini*) bap. 10 Dec., 1620. John [the father] undertaker for his bringing up. (See p. 131.)

* "He died of the plague at Darlington, A.D. 1597, there were buried in the month of August 89, and in September 136."—*Hutch.* This passage is obscure, but Welshe must have died at an earlier period, and is not among the registered victims of 1597.

† The Register is at first arranged in a way not very likely to tempt wary batchelors to enter the holy estate of matrimony, "The names of those baptized within the parish of Darlingtonn Anno Domini 1590."—"The names of those *buried and joined in matrimony* in the year aforesaid 1590." This arrangement has puzzled some stupid fellow who has altered the dates after 1590 till he came to 1596, when he found himself three years wrong, he having altered it to 1599, here he stopped, and so we now skip back from 1599 to 1597, from which year the dates are correct. With a little care and the guide of the queen's reign, we may detect the mistake all the way, but this is awkward in searches, and I should suggest the original year being restored in red ink. The years 1591 and 1592 begin with Feb. 1, the succeeding ones with March 25 as the practice was till 1752.

Robert Hope ("curate" and "minister") 1622; bur. as "vicar," 10 Feb., 1639-40. The following windy entry of the Cromwellian period perhaps alludes to his daughter Mary, bp. 1623-4.

1653. Dec. 4. The first publicac'on* was made in the parish Church of Darlington of a marriage intended Betweene Symon Willie the son of John and Margaret Willie of Thornton in the Beanes in the parish of North Otterington in the Countie of Yorke on the one p'tie and Mary Hope the daughter of Anne Hope Widdow in the parish of Darlington and no exceptions made.—11. The second publicac'on was made of the same persons and no exceptions against them.—18. The third publicac'on was made of the same parties and no exceptions came against them [" to hinder their p'ceedings in marriage" often added in other cases.]—21. The said parties was married in Yorkeshire. [In the Durham matches these words are usually added "By *Francis Wrenn* Esquier at Auckland one of the Justices of Peace for this Countie."]

George s. John Vincent, preacher (*concionatoris*) of D. bp. 20 June, 1636.

"The first day of November in the yeare of our lord god 1638 Thomas Ingmethorpe of Darlington, clerk, buried at Staindon."—*Par. Reg.* p. 1. He was born in Worcestershire, quitted Brazennose Coll. Oxon. without a degree; reputed a good Hebrew scholar, and appointed Master of Durham School, 1610; Rector of Stainton, 1594; deprived for "a reflecting sermon" against Ralph Tunstall, prebendary of the tenth stall. On his submission he was allowed to return to Stainton, where he taught ten or twelve boys till his decease.† A mercer of the same name d. at Darlington in Dec., 1650; and in Feb. following a Thomas Inglethorpe and Isabell Rymer are entered in our register as being married at Allerton. The name is very variously spelled. In 1648-9, Dr. Basire writes from Paris, "To my very loving friend, Mrs. Frances Basire, at Eaglescliffe, neare Yarum. Leave this with Mr. Ingmelthorp at Darlington in the County of Durham."

John Claypertonn ("minister") 1640. There was a John Clapperton, vicar of Woodhorn in Northumberland, whom Walker mentions as one that was driven from his living by the zealots during the Usurpation; and that his living was then valued at 120*l.* a year.‡ There is only one signature of Clayperton in the Darlington register, and it is in 1640. After April, 1645, there is a gap of half a year and the register becomes exceedingly imperfect.

1641. Sep. Nathaniel Warde, the loyalist vicar of Staindrop, (who becoming too militant was mortally wounded at Millum Castle seige in 1644) writes:—I heard only yesterday that all the clergy of Darlington district had been summoned by the magistrates to confirm by an oath that P. P. P. of the mob. They even say that the clergy, churchwardens, and overseers are compelled when they have taken the oath, to administer it to the rest of the parishioners, which when the mule breeds I will do."

John Rudd, minister, bur. 29 March, 1646-7.

A dreary gap occurs, and parish registrars§ were introduced during the time of the

* The late clerk of Coniscliffe, all smiles and crimson, used to vociferate the moment after the first banns of any couple were published, "God speed them weel!"

† Athen. i. 510.

‡ "Bishop Morton disposed of his spiritual preferments to none but his own chaplains, tried and found faithful. He however broke through this rule in favour of John Weemes and Anthony Maxton, two Scotchmen, for whom Charles I. asked and obtained prebendal stalls during his Northern progress in 163... The latter was also Rector of Wolsingham, and Clappurton, another Scot, obtained through the same royal recommodation the vicarage of ...."—*Surtees* i. xciv. n.

§ Christopher Wilkinson Book Anno Dom. 1651. (*erased*).—So this booke was Finished vp the said xxixth of September 1653 and a new Register Begun According to Act of Parliament, By me John Cooke The Chosen and Sworne Register for Darlington.—The suc-rebellion. Yet it is comfortable to think that in the worst of times, the people of Darlington had not forgotten their God and their church. In 1654, William Priscott (a Parliament man, by the way) paid to "the churchwardens for the use of the church," a heavy assessment of 20*s.* 5*d.* upon the land he had given 525*l.* and a colt for, and the services of a minister who preached "when we had not a ministere" were valued at 6*s.* worth of cheering sack.

John Darnton was an intruder during the Protectorate in Bedlington vicarage. "He was put in by sequestration."

Mr Coup of Darlington *clarecus* br. 24 Dec. 1659. In the Middleham registers the word *claricus* is used to designate a parish clerk in 1681.

George Bell,* was the first minister after the Restoration, 1661. He was father of George Bell, rector of Croft. The Rev. Mr. George Bell, minister of D. bur. 20 Mar. 1692-3. In the church accounts for 1691 is an item of 1*s.* 4*d.* "for a pint of brandy when Mr. George Bell, [the rector of Croft], preached here."

Christiana Melicensis filia Danielis Melicensis Magistri Artis Perigrinorum, bp. 3 Apr. 1665.

Mr James Tate, minister of Byshopton, br. 9 Jan. 1686-7. He lived at Darlington and occurs in the registers as minister of Sadbridge, Sadbiridge or Sadbury. He had numerous children.

George Thompson, D. D., 1693. He m., in 1701, Mrs. Jane Hodgson of Fieldhouse in this parish. "Here lieth the body of George Thomson D : D : Minister of Darlington and vicar of Coniscliffe who Departed this life March the 21st Ann. Dom. 1711 Ætat. 47. Here lieth the body of Jane the wife of George Thomson who departed this life the 29......[June, 1713."]—*Slab in Darlington Nave.*

Memorandum. That on Satterday the 24th of Aprill Anno Domini 1697 : The Hon. Robert Boothe Archdeacon of the Archdeaconry of Durham, with the Rev. Hammond Beaumont Official Visitted this church personally and then enjoyned, That the Sacrament of the Lords Supper be Administred Monthly, a Course of Catechizing throughout the whole year, duely performed, and Railles to the Communion Table Sett up, the performance of all which are to be certifyed at the next Michaelmas Visitac'on under the Minister and Churchwardens Hands. The said Catechizticall Lectures to be performed on every Sunday in the Afternoon, instead of a Sermon.—POSTH : SMITH, Register†

In 1705, a Brief was obtained for collecting throughout the kingdom alms for the reparation of Darlington Church. The Town received only 368*l.* 18*s.* 0*d.* out of 939*l.* 10*s.* 2*d.* the expenses of collection being 570*l.* 12*s.* 2*d.* !‡

John Hall, 1712, lived in the old Elizabethan brick house between Tubwell Row and the church-yard, now the Nag's Head,§ br. 2 Jan. 1727-8; his widow Barbara br. 1740-1. His son Thomas was "buried close before the Reading desk" in 1721.||

ceeding book was "Sould by William Hutcheson Bookeseller in Durham 1653."—Apr : the xxxth 1657. Bee it remembred that John Hodshon of Darlington gent. did this day take the oath for execution of the office of Parish Register within the parish of Darlington (being also duely) according to the forme of the Act of Parliament in this behalfe lately made and provided Before THO : LIDDELL . FRAN : WREN.—*Par. Reg.* Cook and Hodgson were schoolmasters. The registers begin to be in English in 1651. Up to Apr. 1645 they are beautifully kept, apparently by the clerk, certainly not by the clergyman. Then comes a gap of six months, and after that a very imperfect registry, for the new system was by no means an efficient one.

* The Latin was restored to the registers in 1664, but in Bell's time they are most shamefully kept, as many as six months together being totally wanting sometimes.

† Par. Reg. ‡ Allan's MSS. § Title deeds.

|| Hall and his two successors may truly be called "the three good registrars," and give a treat after the wretched productions of the idle parsons of Stuart days. Hall certifies

Cornelius Harrison, A.M., 1727, was son of John Harrison by Mary dr. of Cornelius Ford of Kings Norton.* Her sister Sarah was Dr. Johnson's mother, and the man of the Dictionary was therefore our parson's own cousin. "Next morning," says the sage in a letter to Mrs. Thrale, 12 Aug. 1773, on his tour to the Hebrides, "we changed our horses at Darlington, where Mr. Cornelius Harrison, a cousin-german of mine, was perpetual curate. He was the only one of my relations who ever rose in fortune above penury, or in character above neglect. The church is built crosswise, with a fine spire, and might invite a traveller to survey it; but I perhaps wanted vigour, and thought I wanted time."

Harrison had died in 1748 "universally lamented,"† and was buried in the South porch where a decaying brass remains. "To the memory of the Revd. Corns. Harrison, A. M., who departed this life Oct. 4th, 1748, aged 49. Likewise of Mary his wife who died Aug. 6th., 1798, aged 77. It is requested that this stone may never be removed." It is remarkable that the mural monument to his son Cornelius of Stubb House, esq., at Bowes, also states that "It is requested that the great stone below may never be disturbed." The marriage here, of "Mr. James Robson, of Ellerton in Yorkshire, to Miss Harrison, sister to Cornelius Harrison, esq., of Stubhouse; an accomplished young lady with a large fortune"‡ on 16 Oct., 1772, may be added to Dinsdale's pedigree.

Andrew Wood,§ A. M., 1748, master of St. John's Hospital, Barnard-Castle, rector of

that from 18 Oct. 1710, to 2 June, 1712, he found the register imperfect and empty, yet he contrived to fill up the vacuum very respectably.

* The whole connection may be seen in Dinsdale's Edwin and Emma, p. 48.

† "N.B. When hereafter in this Register I shall set after the name of any Person buried the letters r. a., I would be understood to mean that I received in due time an affidavit of that Person's having been buried in Woollen, according to Act of Parliament; and when I shall add after any name n. A. not., with any day of the month, I desire it may be understood that I received no affidavit, and notified the same in writing under my hand to the Church Wardens on the day specified. Sept. 20th, 1736. Cornelius Harrison."

In 30 Car. 2, it was enacted that the relations of the deceased should within eight days after interment bring an affidavit to the parson That the person was not put in or buried in any shirt, shift, sheet, or shroud made or mingled with flax, hemp, silk, hair, gold or silver, or any other than what is made of sheep's wool only, or in any coffin lined or faced with any cloth, stuff, or any thing made or mingled with any material but sheep's wool. And if no affidavit brought, the Parson was to certify to the Churchwardens or Overseers, and to enter burials and whether there was an affidavit in a Register. This Act was for the promotion of the Woollen manufacture, and was repealed 54 Geo. III. The Darlington entries are nearly all "n. A. not."

‡ Darlington Pamphlet.

§ The handwriting of Wood was truly beautiful, and the registers were painfully exact. "Memorandum. The Parchment of this Register being exceedingly bad to write upon, I have been in use to keep the Register of Baptisms first upon paper, and then at some leisure time (after preparing the parchment for receiving the ink) to transcribe it into this Parchment Book: And unfortunately before the said Transcript was made of the Baptisms from the 26th of June, 1767, to the 20th of March, 1768, both inclusive, the paper register containing the same was taken away or stolen out of one of the drawers under the Table in the vestry, where it was kept (in order that my Curate and I might equally, on all occasions, have access to it), and probably has been wantonly or mischievously destroyed. I have therefore taken all necessary pains to supply the said loss, so that I would fain hope there will be very few, if any, omissions or mistakes. Those who were baptized privately were chiefly supplied from the Curate's Pocket Book, wherein he entered the names and dates of those so baptized, at the time of the Baptisms; and the others were collected from the testimony of Parents, Sponsors, Midwives and Nurses, who were diligently examined with regard to the same. Note also, that if any observation occurs in this Parchment Register of Baptisms referring to a time posterior to the date of the Baptism of the child, such observation was made when the said paper Register was transcribed into this parchment one. See an example. Nov. 16, 1764 And. Wood, Curate." The example alluded

Gateshead, and Hedley in Surrey, and chaplain in ordinary to the King. He died of a fever, Thursday, 12 March 1772, and was buried in the choir of Gateshead church, where there is a mural monument in the South Aisle, inscribed "To the memory of Andrew Wood, M. A., Rector of this church. Born xxix May, MDCCXV; inducted ix Sept., MDCCLIX; interred, amidst the tears of his Parishioners, xv March, MDCCLXXII. This monument of their esteem, affection, and gratitude, was erected by the people of Gateshead."

Wood was one of the drawers up of the inscription for Noble's monument at Bolton-on-Swale. He was the constant correspondent of vicar Toby Heyrick of Gainford: and his residence was divided between Darlington and Gateshead. When at the former, he was always one of Toby's convivial guests. He was an uncommonly lively writer, as an epistolary correspondent; and was in his time the *primum mobile* and the very soul of festivity amongst the Maids of Honour and the chaplains at St. James's.* Mr. John Eden, of Gainford, one day invited Heyrick to dine with him; but, previous to the appointed time, requested him to call at his house, when he afforded him a preliminary gratification by the exhibition of a fine haunch of venison, that was acquiring a proper gusto in the larder. Toby paced round and round the joint, rejoicing in prospective at its forthcoming demolition: while Mr. Eden was discussing who should be invited, and hinted that Wood might be one. "Wood! No, no," said Toby, "Wood! No. He'l

to is this. 1764. Nov. 16. "Dorothy Daughter of James Robson of Darlington Breeches-Maker, and Mary English of Darlington (who at first alledged that they were married at Durham but since were married here in this church by Licence the 20th of December 1764) baptized."

"James Smith of this parish and Jane Garth of Saint Andrew Auckland spinster, married by licence &c. by T. H. Tidy, Curate of Gt. Stainton" 23 May 1764. "N.B. To supply Mr. Tidy's omission in the register of the above marriage, I observe, that the said James Smith is a clerk and my assistant Curate, and that the said Jane Garth is a spinster and a minor, and was married with the consent of Bowes Garth her natural and lawfull Father. AND. WOOD, Cur." Smith was afterwards minor canon of Durham and vicar of Ellingham co. Northum.

On another occasion, having left two pages blank by turning two leaves over at once, he notices the fact *six* times, covered six lines on one page with small crosses, and where he does not notice the error he wrote "Blank" *three times* on *every line* of the form, and then narrates with proper pride what he had done. In 1765, Allan writes to Ralph Bigland, esq Garter King of arms, thus:

"The 'Observations on Marriages, &c.,' [by Bigland himself] gave me inexpressible pleasure; and the more so as they in every respect agreed with my own sentiments. I have for a long time talked to the minister of our Parish, to make his entries in the same manner in the Register: and have offered voluntarily to be Public Register myself for the whole Parish, would he but give me leave. But what he alledges, is, that the public and late acts have prescribed a certain form, from which he dares not deviate. However, one may expressly follow that form; but surely additions can never do harm. One other part in regard to sealing Deeds, Wills, &c. with the person's own seal, has ever been a rule with me in the course of my profession, and which I ever will stick to; and so nice am I in this point, that when three or more seals are to be affixed to a Deed, and perhaps the party executing has none,—rather than there should be two alike, I frequently send to the shops for common penny seals." George has been busy with the registers, adding statistics and what not, and in one book "*Si quis Registrum hoc vel mutilare in ulla parte, vel nomen aliquod delere, addere, aut in falsum immutare, vel quovis alio modo violare audeat, pro sacrilegio habeatur a Domino.*"

* Geo. Allan the M.P. in Nichols's Lit. Anec. We once had an *Anthony* Wood here who was fined for digging a sand hole in the market place, 1626; and (to return to the eaters), *Nicholas* son of Thomas Wood of Darlington, was bp. in 1629, but I have no evidence that like his namesake of Kent he could at one meal demolish thirty dozen of pigeons. Catherine dr. of Mr. Wm. Wood of Darlington, M.D., br. 24 Ap. 1752. George Wood of D. gent. uncle to Andrew Wood minister, bur. 28 June 1769.

eat it all. We must not have him." Wood accordingly was not invited; but shortly after, he heard of the circumstance, and had not long to wait before he had an opportunity of paying Master Toby in his own coin. One Monday morning he espied him in Darlington market, purchasing a pair of soles, which he eyed with uncommon delight, and carefully deposited in the pocket of his upper coat. Wood being assured that, according to his usual custom, he would call at his house before he left the town, patiently waited his advent, for the consummation of his joke. On his arrival, he lavished every species of attention on him, and invited him to dinner. Toby, in the contemplation of the delicacy in his pocket, declined. Wood became still more urgent, and induced compliance at last, by the announcement that a remarkable fine pair of soles was to form part of the entertainment. So he stayed, and was delighted; and at length departed in peace to his vicarage at Gainford. He had not long been ensconced in his parlour, before he cried out, "Lucy, take those soles out of my coat pocket." Lucy forthwith duly searched the coat, but to no purpose, and reported the same. "Child you're mistaken," cried he; "go again." A "*non inventus*" was again returned to the inquisition; and his own personal investigation confirming the dread certainty that they had vanished, he very justly exclaimed; "Oh, that Wood, that Wood, he *has done me!*"*

"The Revd. Mr. Clark, Minister of Cliesby, Yorkshire," was bur. here 4 May, 1755.

Henry Hemington,† 1772. In the same year a subscription was opened for an afternoon lecture, and the Rev. Jos. Watkins, A.M., the sub-curate (who was much esteemed) commenced to preach two sermons accordingly in July. "Not only the opportunity this subscription will give servants and others in various situations to hear sermons, but the present prevailing taste for *novelty* in religion, makes it the more necessary."‡

The following monuments to the Sisson family occur in the church. On a slab in the nave:—"This stone sacred to the memory of Mr. Jonath'n Sisson of this town gent.,§ and Grace his wife was laid by their only son the Revd. Mr. Wm. Sisson Rectr. of Markshall in Essex, &c. He was the third son of Theodorus Sisson Esqr. of Kirkbarrow in the parish of Barton Westmr. and died Decr. . . . 1743 aged 78. And she

* Walbran's Gainford.

† "To the Churchwardens of the Parish of DARLINGTON in the County and Diocese of Durham.

WHEREAS it hath been represented unto me SAMUEL DICKENS, D.D., *archdeacon of Durham*, that it has become a Practice in your Parish, *to bring corpses to be buried at an unseasonable and improper Time*, to the great inconvenience of the minister and other officers whose Duty it is to attend and perform the Funeral Service at the Interment of the Deceased; And whereas the General Rule laid down by your minister (who has a Right in this case to prescribe such Rule,) is, *that in the Winter Season*, (to wit,) *from Michaelmas to Lady-day, every Corpse be brought to be buried by four o'Clock in the Afternoon: And in the Summer Season* (to wit,) *from Lady-day to Michaelmas, by seven o'Clock in the Afternoon.* These are to acquaint you, that I approve altogether of the said Rule, and moreover desire, that you will give Directions to the Clerk of your Parish, to signify this my approbation to the Parish in general, by publickly reading, or causeing to be read, this Letter addressed to you, in your church after Morning Service, upon the three following Sundays after it comes to your hands; in order that all the Inhabitants of your parish may hereby be duly apprized and admonished to bring their Corpses to be Buried at the times above stated and directed; and that they may likewise be made to understand, that the Minister will be justified in refusing to bury that day any Corpses that shall not be brought to the Place of Burial by the time appointed to bury in the Summer and Winter Seasons respectively. Given under my Hand at Durham this *Fourth* day of *December* in the year of our Lord 1776. SAMUEL DICKENS, Archdeacon of Durham.

‡ Darlington Pamphlet.

§ See Grammar School. "Mr. Jonathan Sisson late of Darlington, Grocer, bur. 12 Dec. 1743."

the Daughtr. of Mr. Francis Kaye Gent. died Febry. 10th. 1739-40, aged 79." - - - On mural monument, North aisle:—"Sacred to the memory of the Revd. William Sisson, A. M. who lies buried in this church; he was Rector of Marks Hall, and of the Donative church of Patswick in the County of Essex, Vicar of Norton in this County, and chaplain to the Garrison at Berwick-upon-Tweed; He departed this life January 27th 1773 aged 75."

William Gordon, A. M., 1784. Being non-resident, the Rev. James Topham officiated as sub-curate from 1792 to 1820. Against the vestry of Coniscliffe is a headstone inscribed, "In this place are sacredly deposited the mortal remains of The Revd. James Topham, vicar of Coniscliffe, who died July 12th, 1832, aged 76 years. In the year 1820 he was presented to this vicarage in the most handsome manner by the Hon. and Revd. Shute Barrington, Bishop of Durham, for his long and laborious services in the ministry of the large and populous town of Darlington, for the period of twenty-eight years. *Quiescat in Pace.*"*

John William Drage Merest, (vicar of Staindrop and Rector of Cockfield) 1831, p.m. Gordon. He resigned in 1846 for Wem in Shropshire.

The Rev. Wm. Nassau Leger, A. B., was assistant to the sub-curate during part of this ministry, and since his incumbency of St. Marys at the Tower, Ipswich, has printed some separate sermons, one of which on "The true faith," was preached in Norwich Cathedral.

Alexander James Howell, M.A., 1846. The Rev. Wm. Mark Wray is sub-curate. A parsonage house has lately been built in Coniscliffe Lane by the munificence of the lay-rector, the Duke of Cleveland, to whom Mr. Howell is domestic chaplain.

Darlington Curacy. The Duke of Cleveland Patron. Certified value 20*l* ---Proc. ep. 7*s*.---Lord Crewe's legacy 10*l.* per annum.---Real value about 300*l.* Not in charge. Subscribed augmentations 1720 and 1732, 200*l.* each time. Queen's Bounty thereupon 200*l.* each time. The whole 800*l.* laid out in lands, 1735.

The Pew book commences 1700. The front part of the gallery in the North Transept was erected in that year, and similar obnoxious erections gradually intruded themselves into the South Transept, both aisles and across the Nave.†

1763, Ordered [by the vestry] that no person shall bury in the church at a less sum than one guinea for the *layer-stall*,‡ for a grown person, and half a guinea for a child. By a child is meant one of ten years and under. There is to be no difference in the

* "Erected in memory of Lieut. William Topham, R. N., who died on board H.M.S. Vanguard on her passage from Athens to Malta, Octr. 1837, aged 41 years, and was buried at sea." - - - "In a vault near this stone are laid the remains of James Anthony Topham, late assistant surgeon in the 10th regiment of foot, and died Decr. 3d. 1841, aged 44 years." —*Darlington Churchyard.*

† There are some curious Jacobean pews in the North Transept, ornamented with beautiful iron scroll work hinges. Cade truly says that "the inside of the church is encumbered with very irregular seats and galleries which destroy the symmetry of the whole," and "at this time requires the assistance of some generous benefactors, towards beautifying and new modelling it upon a more improved and eligible plan."

‡ The layer-stall is the place of burial, the layer-stone the slab placed thereon. When burials were more customary in the church, they formed a handsome item of income to the church funds. In 1824, the church-wardens were directed in vestry to charge 10*l.* for every interment in the church, and only to allow lead coffins to be used for the purpose.

price upon the score of places. - - - That the Sexton shall make the graves four feet* deep for a grown person, and three feet for a child. And that the Churchwardens do provide proper iron rods, that the persons concerned may (if they please) measure the said depths.

1804. Faculty granted for resolution of vestry that the Churchwardens should immediately cause to be enclosed the middle and side Isles on the West-end of the church with folding doors, also *that the upper part of the said church should be enclosed for the purpose of making the said church more commodious and warm*,† and that the staircase leading to the West gallery should be removed, and placed against the North and South wall of the said church, and that pews should be erected and built in the vacant space where the staircase stood, and also other pews erected on vacant spaces at the West-end, and in the West gallery of the said church.

(In 1835 a number of pews were added at the West-end by the Churchwardens, and by them sold. The screen was removed back to range with the back part of the West gallery.)

A few extracts from the Terrier of 1806 shall follow :---

A person is appointed by the Churchwardens to toll a bell every morning during the summers half-year at five o'clock and during the winters at six.‡

Over its [the chancel's] entrance is a gallery erected for the blue coat boys, ab ve which is a picture with the device of a lion and unicorn rampant, and a crown placed betwixt them.§

(In 1709, a bookcase of theological books to the amount of some 21*l.* were given to the church, and are now in the vestry.)

There are four church-wardens for this parish, viz.: two for the townships of Darlington and Oxen-a-field, one for the townships of Archdeacon Newton and Cockerton, and one for the township of Blackwell. They are chosen in the vestry|| every Easter Tuesday out of those who profess the Protestants' persuasion. One of those for Darlington and Oxen-a-field is chosen first by the minister, the other by the parishioners, as are also the other two chosen by the parishioners of their respective townships.

The minister demands for every churching, 1*s.* 6*d.*—For every burial, 1*s.* 10*d.* (except from another parish, in that case 3*s.* 8*d.*, being double fees)—For every marriage by licence, 10*s.*, and for every ditto by banns, 5*s.*—The Easter offerings are collected every year at Easter, chiefly from the principal householders in the parish, who pay two-pence a head for themselves, and those of their families who are fourteen years of age and upwards. The whole of the surplice fees at this time amount to upwards of 53*l.*, which *(as no terrier is to be found)* we suppose to be substantiated by custom.

The clerk's demands, for every burial in this parish are 6*d.*—the sexton's, 1*s.* 8*d.* (1*s.* for tolling a bell,¶ and 8*d.* for making a grave); but if any person is brought here to be buried from some other parish they then demand double fees. Likewise, the clerk demands 2*s.* 6*d.* for a marriage by licence, and 1*s.* 6d. for a marriage by banns. The sexton, 1*s.* for a marriage by licence, and 6*d.* for one by banns. The clerk likewise demands 4*d.* every Easter of each principal householder in this parish. At that time the sexton procures what he can from each principal householder's benevolence. Each receives from his office about 30*l.* a year. The clerk is appointed by the minister, the sexton by the minister and churchwardens.

* Altered to 4ft. 6in. in 1831. Fee of 1*d.* per inch for additional depth to the sexton.

† Accordingly the screen was carried up to the roof, and the Western Bay completely blocked out.

‡ Discontinued.

§ There are now two paintings of the royal arms on the West screen. One dated 1733, the other quite modern.

|| See Grammar School Charter, *post.*

¶ Formerly the sexton at Darlington tolled the bell immediately after death, even if in the middle of the night.

Register Booke.*

BAPTISMS.† . . 1593, Mary dr. Richard *Bacchus* - - - 1594, Elizabeth *Boucher* dr. William Bouchar - - - 1594-5, Alice dr. William *Abram* - - - 1598, Dorothy baptized: *Avarilla* Lawson dr. of *Conan* of Blackwell.‡ - - - 1601, Elizabeth dr. *Manaash* Bolton, a traveller - - - 1603, Thomas Smith alias *Lonchishire*§ s. John Smith of D. - - - 1603-4, Richard Harrison, an orphan of Arch. Newton; *Christabella* dr. *Rinian* Englishe of Kirk Newton in Northumberland - - - 1607-8, Catherine dr. Thomas *Pharoah* of D. - - - 1608, William Allon illeg. s. William Allon and *one Joice* - - - 1614, An infant, a stranger, his father and mother being unknown - - - 1620, *Barbary Blackmantle* dr. John Blackmantle late of Bishopton - - - 1620-1, Thomas Tipladie, illeg. s. *Persie* Tipladie and Robert Tailor - - - 1629-30, Francis s. Leonard Emerson of Bondgait, bap. 17 Jan. but born the 6th of the month aforesaid.|| - - - 1631, Frances (daughter of no one¶ *erased)* whose father and mother were unknown - - - 1648, Jane, d. John Bradforth of D. (Memorandum. It is credibly informed that Jane should be Dorothy by the Godmother Alice Middleton the wife of Michael Middleton, *an insertion)* - - - 1652, William Liddell the sonne of Jane Lidle who was a traveller and was brought to bed at Cockerton: A child that was a travellers which lay at Luke Calverts in Skinnergate was bap., the name was Mary - - - 1662, *An A Lee*** dr. Frances A Lee of Cockerton - - - 1666. Bell s. Lawrence *Scrivener*, gent. of D. [evidently a lawyer] - - - 1678, Wm. s. Mr. William *Crescy* of D.††: George s. Geo. *Deminicus*, a stranger - - - 1702, A wandring beggers child baptized - - - 1708, Frances dr. Elizabeth Whitlock begotten by Robert Smith in adultery - - - 1710, *Peace* s. of *Praise* Wadman of D. Inn keeper [a *Patience* follows in 1715] - - - 1717, Hector s. John Ross a poor blind begger - - - 1718, Lucy the bastard d. of Anne Asquith and one *Old Thom:* Jane the wife of Robt. Lyddel of D. who had been educated from her infancie in the principles of Quakerism, aged 23 years or thereabouts - - - 1720, Sarah, dr. Christopher Gascoine of D. *a child of a year old or thereabouts:* Isabel d. of Mary Brunton. N.B. She was with child before married her present husband Thomas Brunton, as shee declar'd to me, by one Thoms. Martin of Durham, attorney - - - 1721, *Thamer* Cook a young woman of about 20 years of age, a Quaker - - - 1723, Samuel Hedley a Quaker aged 38 years or thereabouts - - - 1732, John, bastard son of Jane Macdonald of Blackwell, who refused to name the father - - - 1738, Judith, dr. Wm.

* On the fly-leaf are numerous loose entries, many relating to other parishes and recusants. "1625, collected and given upon a briefe for the poor of London, 5*s*. 21*d*. *ob*.

† A huge slice of christening cake is presented to the first person the procession may meet, in this neighbourhood, and the first time a child visits a neighbour or relation it is presented with a small quantity of salt, bread, and an egg; or, an egg, salt, and matches.

‡ Blackwell delighted greatly in Averillas. We find Averill Simpson (of a Blackwell family) bap. 1594; Avarilla *Roos*, dau. of Christofer of Blackwell, bap. 1598 (the entry preceeding Avarilla Lawson); Avarilla Branson of Blackwell bap. 1598-9; and Avarilla Langstaff of Blackwell bap. 1601; while Henry Parkinson of Whessoe had a wife Averilla bur. 1607-8.

Both the kindred races of Nesham and Brough Hall held freehold lands in Darlington in the 17th cent., and we find in one admittance a clear instance of the peculiar use of *cousin* or *consanguineus* for grandchild in the same way as *nephew* or *nepos* often expresses the same thing. Henry Lawson, esq.. *cousin* and nearest heir of Ralph Lawson, knt., deceased, viz. *son and heir of Roger*, *son and heir of the said Ralph* was postponed admittance till he brought forth the writings of his title.

§ "Given Lancasheare on his goeing away 12*d*. 1631."

|| The interval seems short, but it was evidently then thought far too long.

¶ *Filia nullius. Bastardus est filius nullius aut filius populi*, in law. "Comyn of ungentyl fadyr and gentyl moder, *spurius, a*, of fadyr gentylle and modyr ungentylle, *nothus, a*." *(Promp. Parv.)*

** Lee only in 1666. William Lea *(commonly called William a Lee)* of Morton, bur. 1649. *Haughton.*

†† O Phœbus, what a name!

Smelt of Cockerton, weaver, was baptized privately the 6th of this instant by the Rev. Mr. Brunton late curate of Manfield, of which thro' the neglect of the parents I was not informed till this day, (Mar. 24.) - - - 1739, Thomas bastard son of a stranger who lay-in at Elizabeth Neesham's at Cockerton, and *obstinately* refused to confess either her own name or the father's* - - - 1741, Anne, bastard dr. Martha K——, late servant at Bishop-Middleham, fathered upon *Mr. John Spearman* of the same place - - - 1743, Margaret dr. (supposed bastard) of John Stelling, joyner, and Margaret Story, both of D. and now under *sentence of excommunication* for cohabiting as man and wife, without any proof either of Storey's husband being dead, or of their being married [still under sentence in 1746] - - - 1750, Charles s. Roger Trueman and Grace Stephenson of D. who continue to live under *sentence of excommunication* for a cause assign'd July 24, 1748 in this register [there described as "clandestinely married......" *a line scratched out*] - - - 1751, James s. James Crawthorn and Margaret Bygate of Blackwell *who pretend to be married by one J. Walker*† - - - 1754, William s. David *Henireta* of London, shoe-maker: Dec. 26, Christopher s. James Catherick weaver. N.B. This child Christopher Catherick was born August the 9th 1748, as his father informs me; his mother I found was a Papist, and it was therefore probable that the child was before baptized by a Romish Priest, but his father being interrogated at the font, and answering that he did not know whether the child was already baptized or no, I baptized him according to the hypothetical form at the end of the office for private baptism. AND. WOOD, Curate. - - - 1766, John, supposed bastard s. of Margaret *Reason*, wife of John Reason (she living at D. and he *somewhere out of sight*) - - - 1769, Elizabeth dr. of Wilfred Lawrance late of D. house and sign painter (who, for a time, passed for a member of the church, and afterwards professed himself a quaker, and has long deserted his family) a girl of about 15 years of age, and is now in the workhouse of the poor of the township of D.: Ann, dr. Christopher B—— labourer and Margaret Taylor both of D. who gave out that they were married in Scotland. (N.B. They were refused marriage here in this church after the banns were asked out, upon the score of affinity; the said Margaret Taylor being, as is alledged, daughter of a sister by the half blood, of the said Christopher B—'s deceased wife) - - - 1773, Thomas Blackett of Mount-Pleasure,‡ brought up in the principles of the anabaptists, aged 23 years, and a schoolmaster.

MARRIAGES.§ 1594, *Gawain Ratcliff* and Agnes Richardson|| - - - 1620, Matthew Rimer and Elizabeth *Mauleverer* - - - 1683, *John Milton* and Margaret Newton. [They had several children.] - - - 1701, Richard Wood Bridler and Dorothy Hodgson spinster maried poor Darling'.¶ - - - 1713, Wm. Davison and Elizabeth Crawforth *both widowers* of D. - - - 1722, Michael *Gent* and Margaret *Dent* both of Cockerton - - - 1765, George *Bambrough* of this parish fell cutter and Elizabeth *Bambrough* of this par. spinster. Mark made by me for George Bambrough X *he being without both his hands.*—AND. WOOD, Cur. - - - 1794, Adam Yarker,** yeoman and Ann Mudd

* All our former clergy professed to adjudicate in such cases and peremptorily named the father in their registers. The ire of Dr. Johnson's cousin was evidently great on this contumacy.

† Of the Cuthbert Hilton school, no doubt. The couple were properly married the same year.

‡ Beyond Cockerton.

§ The running for the ribbon and firing of guns at these events seem extinct here, though well remembered.

|| Some cadets of the "radiant Ratcliffes" have embalmed their name in Ratcliffe Close at Blackwell. Thomas Radcliffe, gent., of Cockerton (whose sister and heiress Anne *m.* Leonard Dykes of Warthol Hall, Cumb., esq.) d. 1593, and a Thomas Ratcliffe of Darlington, gent., was living 1670.

¶ She was not a "poor darling," but both were poor and of Darlington.

** Better known as *Blind Adam.* He lived in Tubwell Row and died 1816, aged 57, having been blind from his birth. He possessed an extraordinary memory, especially applied to the registering the number of deaths, &c., which had occurred in the town for spinster, both of this parish - - - 1815, [A marriage entry even to the minister's signature.] J—— B—— [the bridegroom] desired me to write the above, but he and Miss F—— proceeded no further. This marriage was not solemnized. [The lady became reconciled and a proper entry occurs the month after].

BURIALS. 1591, A child of good man Blandes buryed : John Raynard child buryed* - - - 1593, A child of Elizabeth buried - - - 1594, Ray's wife *(Ray uxor)* - - - 1596, Willyam Turner wives mother - - - 1597, *Emmot* Tunstall widow : July. Here began the Plague. *(Hic incipiebat pestis)*† : December, Chippey buried. - - -

upwards of forty years. Without hesitating a moment, he could tell how many deaths had been in any given year or month, the exact day when the individual died, to whom they were related, &c. He was noted for the keeping of poultry, in which he greatly excelled ; his hens, owing to his superior management, laid their eggs in the winter season ; he knew them from each other, and could tell their name, colour, &c., as soon as he got them in his hand. Although he was descended from poor parents, and had but a small pittance called the blind's bounty, with the benevolence of a few charitable individuals, the profits arising from his poultry, &c., enabled him to realize 200*l*.

In 1804, died at Haughton-le-Skerne, Margaret Tate, aged 15. She "was born blind, she had no eyes, not even an aperture in the eye-lids."—*(Haughton Reg.)*

* The 's of the possessive case is still much omitted in the South Durham dialect.

† As the Penrith register truly states, there was "a *sore* plague in New Castle, Durrome, and Dernton in the yere of our lord God 1597." King's sermon at York in that year, says "The spring was unkind, &c., our July hath been like to February, our June even as April. God amend it in his mercy and stay this plague of waters." Hence probably arose the plague from the wet and inclement seasons and their attendant scarcity, but a contagious fever was prevalent in the North during all the latter years of Elizabeth. The exact nature of the Visitation of 1597 does not appear, though its very contagious nature seems evident from whole households being swept away, whilst in very neighbouring parishes where it had not found introduction, no unusual mortality occurs. Thus Darlington, Aycliffe, Merrington, Ferryhill, and Durham, adjacent to the great North road were severely visited, whilst Middleham and Sedgefield entirely escaped. The assizes of July 4 were deferred on account of the plague then raging at Newcastle, Durham, Darlington, &c. In that month twenty-seven burials occur in the Darlington registers, but the disease had probably been hovering on the town for some time, for in the February previous were fourteen burials, a number above the average. August is also headed "*Pestis*," and has eighty-nine burials registered. September has the awful number of one hundred and thirty-seven, and as if the fatal sword had cut off all the usual religious transactions of life, only one baptism. The first two days of October have thirteen burials, and then a fearsome gap exists till Nov. 30, when ordinary entries occur—the plague was stayed. During this horrible period the multitudes of entries cause them to be unusually brief, and they are arranged in double columns. "Jane Watson tom tylars maid : Widow Watson Tilars wife ; Emerson [the omission of the christian name occurs abundantly] ; Fetherston Hodgson maid ; Hunters servant ; Christofer Bland ; the wife of Christofer Bland ; a woman from the house of Christofer Bland ; a sister of Grace Painter ; the maternal aunt *(matertera)* of John Dobson ; Dandy Revill ; a waiting maid *(ancillula)* ; a man of Bondgate ; a woman of Bondgate ; *Ragmarian* [Marian, an old rag woman ?] ; Tomisia Groser ; Helen [the ?] *Pedlar* of Bongat ; Mabell." Could anything be shorter ? for the minister had ceased to put "buried" to the entries on the 12 Sep. The Darntons were completely swept out of the registers, and six Creathornes occur as buried. From another authority we learn that on the 17 Oct. "ther wer dead of the plague at Darlington 340." In Jan. and Feb. 1597-8 the plague ceased at Durham and Darlington, but broke out again the 15 Sep. the same year at the former place. "The Gate of Tongues unlocked, 1633" has "The Pestilence or Plague, *darting and casting botches, impostumes, and carbuncles or running sores*, suddenly and unawares waxeth strong, wasteth, destroyeth and killeth up great peoples and nations."

"1605. This yeare the plague was in Darneton, in Northallerton, and in Nesome," *(Eryholme Reg.)* there being buried in September, 20, and October, 22. In 1605-6. Richard Bowswell his wife and two daughters were all buried ; in the Aug. following there were 31 burials, two and three out of a family ; in September, 21 ; in October, 15 ; and even this last number was above the average. In April, 1623, were 17 burials. The great plague of 1636, so malignant at Barnard Castle [Sykes erroneously reads *Darlington*] that the Magdalene-tide fair was called down, does not appear in our registers ; but in 1644 and 1645 it prevailed in both towns. In Dec. here were 24 deaths ; Jan., 27 ; Feb., 49 ; March, 35 ; April, 18, the ordinary number bring seldom more than a dozen. The Hurworth Register states "1645. The Lord struck three and forty people here in this month of July, near all in this town, viz. Hurworth."

In 1757, 27 were buried in Sep., and 29 in Oct. In 1775, "the small pox very fatal these three months," viz. July, 30 ; Aug., 26 ; Sep., 19 burials. It was also very virulent in 1802. The diarrhœa and disentery have of late been fatal in summer-time, but the Asiatic Cholera has never yet desolated the town. Darlington was formerly famous for agues, which have been eradicated by the Skerne improvements.

- - - 1599-1600, A servant of Robert Sober by name *Crooked Will* - - - 1601, A poore child traveilling from towne to towne: A base gotten child born att Carnabyes of Blackwell - - - 1602, Margery a deaf woman of D.: A poore creple traveilling toward Scotland died att Cockerton and buried here: A man of Northumberland called Talour died at Jo. Scottes and here buried - - - 1602-3, Tristram Stainthropp, servant of Richard Stockdale of *Lowfe Hill*, Darlington - - - 1604-5, ... Laidman, a travelling woman of Stapleton, par. Croft - - - 1609, Margaret Douglasse, a traveller: William s. Xpofer Fawcett* of D. buried *apud Heriol*, 22 July - - - 1611-12, A certain woman a traveller, her name being unknown, a guest of John Bolton of Blackwell - - - 1614, Elizabeth, widow of D. - - - 1616-7, A poor woman, a traveller unknown, of Blackwell - - - 1620, Mary (her father and mother unknown) brought up with James Rokesbie of D. - - - 1621, An infant dead-born† illegitimate of Matthew Lorriman and Elizabeth Morton - - - 1622, A certain destitute woman a traveller - - - 1622-3, John Sigswicke a poor and destitute traveller - - - 1623, A certain woman, a destitute traveller, whose name was unknown: Laurence Cathericke *maximus natu*‡: George Willson (who a long time was blind) of Claie raw: A poor traveller unknown: A certain destitute woman a traveller, who died at Blackwell: A destitute boy, a traveller, whose name was unknown: A certain destitute woman, a traveller, found dead in a house of Blackwell: A poor man with a woman, travellers§ - - - 1624, June 6, Xpofer Simson of Thornabie, a traveller||. - - - 1625, Cicily Wilkinson of *Blackwell Bridge*

* A frequent name. Fawcetts Closes, part of Polam Hill farm penes R. H. Allan, esq.

† No "sunny-side" for it, the cold North part of the old church-garth would suffice for the unbaptized. In these parts few persons are interred on the back side of the church, from an old custom of reserving it for dead-born, unbaptized, suicides and excommunicated persons.

‡ Probably a grandfather, in superiority to *Senior* or *Major natu.*

§ A heavy year on travellers. The situation of Darlington on the Great North Road caused a great many chance rites.

|| The following inquest will be read with great interest, as illustrative of the singular hold a common superstition had on the *neighbours* of Blackwell. The old man was murdered late on Saturday, they found him, rode to Aldborough, brought the murderer who could only just have arrived, got the deputy coroner to the spot, held the inquest and funeral, all on Sunday. The defence of going to Darlington to buy more boots on Sunday morning, is an odd one. "Dunelm. Com. Inquisition, die Sabati 6th June, 1624, at Baydaill Bancke, within the territory of Blackwell, par. Darlington, upon sight of the body of Christopher Simpson, of Thornabie, co. York, labourer, found murdered there.

Whe find that Christopher Simpson, of Thornabie within the countye of Yorke, laborer, havinge, upon his occasions, traveled from Thornebye in Cleveland to Audborrowe in Richmondshire within the said countie, to Raph Simpson of the said towne of Audborrowe; and as it appereth by the confession of the said Raphe, beinge examined befor the deputie and us; [he having] before the deputie coroner and us of the jurie confessed, that Christopher Simpson, beinge his kinsman and frend, did upon Thursdaye last, beinge the third daye of June instant, come unto the house of the said Raph Simpson in Audborrowe; and after they had conferred together, they then did agree to goe unto the house of one John Metcalfe, of Gunnershield in Swaudaile, the next daye, wher the said Raph Simpson did buy of the said John Metcalfe a littell blacke mayre, and received of the said John tenne shillings in moneye; and then uppon Satterdaye they retorned into Richmond, and their Raph Simpson did buy a pair of bouts, and soe they retorned unto Audborrowe: and he saith his uncle (as he used to call him) did leve his baye mayre with him, beinge tyred, and that he did never see him after untill he cam to the place, beinge sent for wher he laye murthered.

And by the information of Francis Rawlinge of Audborrowe, and of Thomas Wilson of Manfeild feild House, in Yorkshire, given unto the deputie coroner Francis Raesbie, he [the said Francis Rawlinge] saith, that he did, upon Satterdaye in the eveninge, see Christopher Simpson passe by him on foote, and saluted him, and presently after Raph Simpson cam rydinge upon a littill blacke maire, and did leade a baye mayre in his hand after old Christopher: and Thomas Wilson he saith upon his information, that upon Satterdaye the fift day of June, laite in the eveninge, he and his wife havinge had an occation to walke into their grounds, which lye uppon the Hyghway side that leadeth from Manfield to Neather Countsclife, to see their goods, that he their espied too men cominge ridinge towards Countsclife; that they one did ryde upon a littell blacke, and the other upon a dunnish baye, and that he of the blacke did lead the waye to him of the baye, and openned the gaite unto him: and he stayinge and earnestly lookinge after him, too of his tennants did come from Manfield unto them, to whom he said, "What men weer those did passe by yowe even nowe?" whoe answered, that it was Raph Simpson of Audborrow and

Hill - - - 1625-6, Dorothy *Fenwicke* and her infant - - - 1626-7, A certain very poor servant commonly called *Agnes the traveller* [*vulgariter vocat' Agnes p'egr'*] - - - 1627 An infant whose name was unknown : [same day] the mother of the said infant - - - 1638-9, *Trothie* Kirby, a poor and destitute woman - - - 1655, Magdalene Parie, a stranger who dyed at Marie Shaws in Darlington - - - 1657, Francis Hall of Worsell, who died in D. by a fall from a horse - - - 1658, A boy, a stranger, which came from Hull - - - 1660, A *lade* which fell of a horse goeing to the colles, a stranger - - - 1662-3, John Stevens, a cripell whom died att Anton Scottes of D. - - - 1663, A lad which was slane in Carter thorne pitt - - - 1666, *Percevel Senex peregrinus* - - - 1669, Corney Cook of D.* - - - 1673-4, Elizabeth, wife of *eye* Watson - - - 1680, A traveler which was at Mrs. Heighingtons died and was buried - - - 1688, *Peter and Paull*, and whose sirname was Boyes, a Dutchman, dyed in Darlington - - - 1694, A poor man brought from one constable to another died at Darlington and was buried - - - 1696, *Funee* Langdale, a stranger papist - - - 1697, Jane Robinson, a poor passenger who dyed at Newton : a childe of George Thursby's of D., buried *unbaptized* - - - 1698, Mary Dunwell of D., *which received alms.*† - - - 1701, Sep., A poor woman, a traveller : John Fraser, a traveller : a poor man, a traveller : a wandering begger‡ - - - 1702-3,

an old man with him, and they passed towards Nether Countsclife ; and he with his wife and tennants went unto their owne house.

And Bartholmewe Harrison, of Neather Countsclife, beinge examined befor us the jurye, he saith, that he did meete Raph Simpson, upon Sunday morning before the sunne did arise, within twelve score of the place where Christopher laye murthered. But Raph being examined if that he had beene of that ground this day or not, he answered and said that he was not their ; but Harrison beinge called, he could not then denye but that he was their upon the ground, and said that he intended to have gone unto Darlington to have bought a paire of boots, and beinge within halfe a myle wanted money, as he saith, that would paye for a paire. And his pocketts beinge searched by the deputie coroner and Thomas Emmerson hye constable their was found in his pockett a corde maide of throumes [the warp ends of a weaver's web] which was bloody, and beinge demaunded to what end he had kept it, he answered that he did use to tye a wallet with it, and, being asked how the blood did com one it which was fresh and undried, he could not answer thereunto.

Likewise William Middleton of Blackwell beinge examined, he saith, that he having chardge of cariinge him to the gaole of Durham, he the said William saith that he wished him to confesse his fault and aske God forgeviness, to [which] Raph Simpson replyed and said, " Alas it would doe yow noe good that I should confesse it, and it would undoe and cast me awaye."

And lastlye, wee applyed the cord to the circle that was about the necke of the party murthered, and it did answer unto the cirkle ; *and wee caused the said Raph to handle the bodye ; and upon his handlinge and movinge, the body did bleed both at mouth, nose and eares.*

All these circumstances and profes considered, wee the jurye, whose names are underwritten, doe find and thinke that Raph Simpson, of Audborrowe within the countye of York, weaver, haith, by the instigation of the Devell or of somme secret malice, murdered and strangled Christopher Simpson, late of Thornabye in Cleveland within the countye of York, laborer, at and in a place of ground commonly called Baydayle Banckes Head, it being the fift day of June at night, this present year 1624. The names of us the juriors, FRANCIS CATHERICKE, JOHN MIDDLETON, WILLIAM X STAINSBY, THOMAS X GREGORY, THOMAS X MIDDLETON, ROBERT X LISTER, JOHN HODGSHON, JAMES JOHNSON, JOHN X HOOPER, ANTHONY X WREN, THOMAS X POTTER, ROBERTE X DOBSON, CHRISTOPHER X DUNWELL, ARTHUR X SWAINSTON."—*(Copied from the original in the Consistory Court at Durham by R. H. Allan, esq.)*

" The Baydayle Banckes Tragedy" has been the subject of more than one ballad, one of which thus opens :—

O Blackwell is a lovesome vill ! and Baydayle Bankes are bright !
The Sabbath breeze the crystal Tees with wavelets has bedight ;
Its oaks and elms are cool and thick, its meadows should be green,
But there are blades of deeper shades, a bloody red is seen.
" Come tell me, child, my Averil mild, why hairied thus you be ?"—
" Father ! there is a murthered man beneath yon greenwood tree."—
" Ho ! neighbours mine,—here Cornforth bold, and Middleton of might,
For there hath been a slaughter foul, at Baydayle Head last night."

* " 1668, To Jo. Cook and *Corney* at severall times in there sicknes," &c. *Church Accounts.*

† I have heard that some years ago nothing could be more opprobious a taunt in Darlington than the accusation of receiving parish relief.

‡ A pestilence surely must have afflicted the wandering tribes in September.

Mary Jaques, a poor* *fatherless and motherless* girle buried, Blackwell - - - 1706, John, a wandering beggar: *Mabell*† - - - 1708, Magdalene *Oar*, a wandering beggar - - - 1713, A certain stranger deaf and dumb‡ whose name unknown - - - 1713-4, Philis Unthank of D., widow, buried, found dead *and supposed to be torn with dogs or swine* - - - 1714, A certain young woman, a beggar, whose name was unknown - - - 1715, A certain poor woman called Margaret Brown who bore a child at Newton and died at Cockerton - - - 1716, Wm. Sourby, a poor servant who came to this market to be hired: John Lodge, heir of Rice-Carr§ house, who died very suddenly - - - 1716-7, John Anderson, a poor man brought to this town by a warrant - - - 1717, — son of George Tweedy of D., kill'd by the fall *on* an house: Mabil Scafe, a poor stranger who died at Coldsides: Eliz. dau. of one Wilfat *whose wife liv'd* on Tubwell Row: a certain poor stranger, said to come from Lumley, who died on childbearing: David Counsellar, commonly called *French Doctor* - - - 1719, John Powels of Arch-Deacon-Newton, who died suddenly as he was going to Cockerton: John Smith of D., glover, *who was killed by drinking Geneva:* John Pearson of D., who died in one of his fits - - - 1723, A man found dead at Blackwell-Moor: a certain poor stranger found almost dead in the way to Cunsc'iff: Margaret Blackett and Dorothy Brookbank, *sisters buried in one grave* - - - 1724 John Wilson of D., shoemaker (commonly called *Governor*‖) - - - 1725, William Gibson, a poor blind beggar: Mr. Edward Turner of Arch-deacon-Newton, *a Londoner:* Elizabeth Beck, widow (commonly called *Potter*) of D.: Catherine Kelloe of D., buried, a papist, no office perform'd - - - 1726, Samuel *Gramswhas*, who died suddenly at Thomas Hall's: Jane Cawell (commonly called *Scotch Jenny*¶) of D. - - - 1727, A certain poor man who fell down dead in the street: Alexander Rutherford, *a poor cobler belonging to Gateshead* - - - 1729, Henry Henderson *of Gateside*** *Fell, a poor cobler:* John Raven, a poor blind man of D.: Anne Denton of D., a poor *distracted* woman: a girl called Mary Simpson, *but supposed to be the daughter of Mr. Ralph Ashmole of Elwick Hall*†† - - - 1731, *Robert Roy*, a journey-man shoemaker, and Scotchman from Aberdeen: John, s. Joseph *Argent*, travelling pedlar - - - 1733, Thomas Craggs of Seaton (who shot himself at Blackwell): Mrs. Ann Woolrich, an old widow gentlewoman of D.‡‡ - - - 1734, Mary, d. James Smith of North Frodingham, *Mousetrap-maker* - - - 1737-8, Anne Flint, widow, a *very antient woman*, mother of Robert Flint, farmer, at Stick-a-bitch,§§ near D. - - - 1738, Stephen Luck of D.,

* At this period the word *poor* is perpetually placed after the entry.

† Nothing else, not even "buried."

‡ On New-years day, 1844, a little "*dummy*" who had been about Darlington for upwards of two years, frightened his wife (to whom he had been married only three months before) no small, by beginning to talk and shewing symptons of good hearing. He had professed to be deaf and dumb for years, and so guarded was he at all times, that when he had been put to bed drunk he never betrayed himself.

§ *Ryscar* in 1735-6. It is near Whessoe, opposite Honeypot.

‖ Nick-names are extraordinarily prevalent here. An old fortune-teller was called *Powder-Blue*, from her employing that substance in preference to the ordinary tea-leaves in her craft: and an aged servant of Mr. Richard Kitching, who died in 1848, was always *Jemmy Waddleduck*.

¶ "*To Scotch Jane 4d.*" *Ch. acc.* 1676.

** Was Gateshead famous for cobblers?

†† The Ashmalls were staunch Romanists; the last, Ferdinando, was a popish priest, and survived all his father's house, dying at the age of 104.

‡‡ Sister of Wm. Killinghall, esq., of Middleton-St.-George, whose will dated 1694, and widow of Philip Woolrich, esq.

§§ Stickbitche, afterwards Stick-a-bitch, is the name of a large district, formerly the Cornforths', between the road from Blackwell to Croft, and the Tees. Stick-a-bitch proper, which is now the property of Mrs. Colling, was bought by Johny Wardell or Weardale, the miser of Ketton, who flourished some eighty or ninety years ago, and was a well-known character at Barnard-castle and Richmond markets when there was no mart at Darlington for corn. The roads were bad and carts were little known, so Johny went in procession with six or eight horses laden with wheat, which he tied to the whins at the end of the town to save the expense of bait. On these occasions he was clad in a home-spun coat, manufactured by females on his farm, his feet were covered with rough shoes, and hoggers (large old stockings) covered his legs outwardly, and came to above his knees. His bricklayer, unfortunately killed by the falling of an arch of a cellar upon him at Cleasby - - - 1739, *Fredswith alias Priscilla* Hardy of D., widow - - - 1740-1, Robert Hill of D., *brought up to no business* - - - 1741, William Mason of D., a poor dumb man : a poor woman, whom they were carrying through the county as a vagrant, and of whom no more is known than that she was called in the warrant wife of John Robinson of Aberdeen - - - 1743, Hugh *Ewer*, a travelling painter, supposed to be of Edinburgh - - - 1744-5, Isabel Tindal of D., a poor blind woman - - - 1746, Joseph Baines, servant to John Hall of Whitehouse, near Sockburn, unfortunately kill'd by his cart - - - 1746-7, Jane Dent of D., an *ancient* woman out of the workhouse - - - 1749, John *Ryther*,* a stroller - - - 1750, Sarah, d. Wm. Leas, a strolling blind beggar - - - 1757, Alice Stephenson of D , (spinster, *erased*) single woman - - - 1758, William Robson senior of D., bricklayer, George Waters of D., carpenter, both kill'd by the fall of an arch in building a cellar for Mr. John Pease† - - - 1766, George Stedham (a convert to popery) of D., whitesmith - - - 1773, *Honour*, s. Wm. *Ptolomy* - - - 1799, Robert *Crosier* John *Mensforth* of D., s. Charles Mensforth gent., and his late wife Jane *Surtees*, aged 39 weeks 6 days: Samuel Gramshaw, &c., aged 16, scalded by falling into a furnace - - - 1801, Ann Pears of Cockerton, late Cauvill of Stenton, widow of David Pears, flaxdresser of D., aged 101 years‡ - - - 1804, T— R— of D. batchelor, *plebeian* - - - 1807, J— M— of D., founder of metal, aged 25, *suffocated by spirituous liquors* - - -

leathern smalls, having been worn by his grandfather and father, descended with other heirlooms to himself, and in the service of three generations had become so thickly frescoed with grease and dirt, that with the assistance of an old rusty nail, they served at market the purpose of a Roman wax tablet in the calculation of Johny's accounts. In this queer trim he appeared at Stick-a-bitch sale, when the vendors disputed his credit, but Johny assured them that whatever he bought he would pay for, and pulled an antique stocking from his pocket, which, to the astonishment of all, was weighty with old golden guineas. His ideas of another world were gross and earthly :—"*They may talk of heevens as they will, but gie me Ketton Greens* [a remarkably fertile field] *which grew seven crops of oats in seven years*." It was suggested to him that he was merely gathering money for his heirs to spend, but he contentedly replied : "*Beins, lads, if they hev as much plisshur in spending as I hev in getherin' it, een let them be deeing*." Yet though he professed to wink at future spendthrifts, he by no means approved of folly in his cotemporaries. He heard the hounds of neighbour Stephenson, of Brafferton, passing through his estates, "*Beins, lads, dee ye hear them yonder, they are crying esh and yak*" (ash and oak) ; he heard a new Lincolnshire pack of a louder and a differing tone, "*Beins, lads, dee but hear 'em, they roar out land and all ; land and all!*" and sure enough, Stephenson's folly kicked timber, land, and all away.—Wardell owned High Beaumond Hill, Aycliffe Wood, Chapel House opposite Gainford and Stickabitch, but Ketton was the Milbankes'. At their tenants' dinners, his toast was ever loyal to his landlord :—"*I'll gie ye a worthy and respectable gentleman, Mr. Sir Ralph Milbanke, esquire, knight and baron-knight*." Laugh not, Southrons, at immortal Johny; your own Twickenham register of 1705 records a baronet as a *barin night*. When farmers want a handful of straw to stop a sack-hole in carrying corn, the usual command is, "*Run away, lads, and bring me one o' Johny Wardell's clouts*," or, "*a Barney-Cassell wisp*." His daughter m. the son of Bryan Harrison of Barmpton, and their sons, I am told, were great men at bets, associated with George IV. and spirted Johny's estates through the air.

* It may be a failed decadent scion of the lordly house of Ryther of Harewood.

† A grocer, who came from Whitby. His family sprung from West Auckland.

‡ John Nichols, a labourer, died here in 1782, aged 107.—*(Gent. Mag.)* William Dixon, taylor, 1802, aged 100. Dorothy Pickney, late Blackett, widow of Jonathan Pickney, farmer, 1810, aged 102. Alice Turner, single woman, 1812, aged 100.—*(Par. Reg.)* John Yarrow, 1814, at Polam Farm, aged 110. He was a native of Mason Dinnington, in Northumberland ; was a servant to a farmer near North Shields in 1715 ; and remembered assisting at the plough when the constables went into the field and demanded the horses to convey military stores during the rebellion. He was able the preceding summer to cut turf in a field, as well as to attend to many domestic and rural occupations ; his diet chiefly consisted of bread, milk, and cheese.—(*Local Papers.*) Isabella Burnsides of Bondgate, 1817, aged 104. Mr. Benjamin Garnett, 1820, at Salutation, in this parish, aged 102.—(*Par. Reg.*) He never experienced one day's illness, and walked about till a few hours before his death, and had the use of his faculties to the last.—(*Local Papers.*) Jane Rutherford of Bondgate, 1820, aged 100. Esther Parkinson, 1832, aged 103. Elizabeth Brocket of Blackwell, 1833, aged 101.—(*Par. Reg.*) Mrs. Elizabeth Hurworth, 1842, aged 108. Mrs. Brown, 1848, aged 103.—(*Local Papers.*) In 1843, Serjeant Vickers's infant was christened here, its grandfather, grandmother, great grandfather and great grandmother being sponsors.

1705, Nov. 20. Tho. Whetstone was then buried, being turned of the age of 104 years, and born in the parish of Darnton.—*Eryholme Reg.*

1828, a person unknown, found dead in the township of Cockerton - - - 1833, Elizabeth *Stross, Strous, or Strowp*, Newcastle, aged 29: Peter *Medici*, Darlington, aged 13 months.

The Churchwardens' accounts commence in 1630.

1630. For the fountt Iron, 12*d.*: for soape to the belles, 2*d.*: for keeping the clocke and regester booke *to the clarke* 5*s.*: a locke to the *Awde-warpe* dore, 3*d.*: to a poor minister, 6*d.*: for fetching of a *slee dogg*, 6*d.** There was a child left at Cockerton the 16th of August, 1630, which was delivered to Roger Specke to keepe, and he had give' to buy close for the child, 2*s.*†: Michaell Rew for makeing the *crying wench* a coat, 6*d.*: to Renold Shawe and mother, when the mother *pretended* to take the child [which they kept for the parish] away, 12*d.*: to a poore child lying sick on the Armitage head, 6d.: to Mr. Goodwine‡ a distressed schooler, 2*s.* 6*d.*: received for *Rogue money* for the whole parish, 47*s.* 4*d.*§ - - - 1631. To a poore scholler, 12*d.*: to *Duke* Stapleton, 4*d.* [Marmaduke Stapleton lived at Blackwell]: to Susanna Liddall for putting her to be an apprintice at London, 3*s.* 4*d.*: given to an Irish gentleman that had fouer children *and had Earles Marshall*‖ *passe*, 12*d.*: to Hen. Auckland dureing imprisonment, 8*d.*: to Eliz. Jonson *for cureing Ann Spence scawld head*, 2*s.* 1*d.*, and *a pound of pick* [pitch] 3*d.*: to one John Browne of the city of Bristoll *being blind*, had by an accident of fire all his goods destroyed, 6*d.*: to Mrs. Kath. Russell, *a Scoth gentlewoman*, who had the kings majesties decretory passe and was great in distress, 1*s.*: to Mary Rigby of Havrat [Haverford] West in Pembrokeshire in Wailes, *who had the Earles of Pembroke passe president of Wailes* who had brunt with fire about the value 900*l.*, 1*s.*: to *Den* Dent, 2*d.*: to two distressed Irish gentlemen, 6*d.*: for mending all the tops of the hie windowes *which was cloven*: for xi yeards and iij quarters of fine Scotch cloath for a surplesse for Mr. Hopp, 17*s.* 7*d.*: for iij yeards of a Scotch cloath for a communion table cloth, 3*s.* 6*d.*: to *Mres Hope* for making table cloth and surplesse, 20*d.* ¶: for *French grening the borders of the pulpitt*,** and whittening the walls: for mending the communion taffity table cloth and silk for mending it, *being much torne in many peeces*, 2*s.* 6*d.*: *for getting rushes*†† *against Judges coming for struing in the church*, 16*d.*: to Wilfrey Lambe and carpenter's charges at their seccond coming, 4*s.*: for lying downe

* The use of sleuth or blood hounds was then much in vogue, and Denton in Northumberland and Chester-le-street appear to have been the places where the owners, and probably breeders of these animals lived. In 1592, James Watson, having escaped the clutches of the council of the North at York and fled northwards, was the cause of some charge to the Newcastle corporation, who sent men in all directions in the hope of obtaining tidings of the fugitive. They "paide for the chairges of three horses two days, and riding *to Darneton* and Sheiles to make enquirie for James Watson, commanded by Mr. Maior, 6*s.* 6*d*," and amusingly enough "for a sloohound and a man which led him, *to go make enquirie*" after him.

† At this period there were distinct overseers of the poor for the Borough and Bondgate, the assessments for both were delivered to the churchwardens and they were relieving officers.

‡ Perhaps the "poure scholler, being a churchman, and wanting means to travell withall" relieved at Chester-le-street the same year with 4*d.*

§ 1677, "Laid on a sesse of 2*d.* per oxgang for [reliefe of] prisoners in the King's Bench Marshalsey, house of correction at Durham, &c., commonly called Rogue Money."—*Blackwell Bks.*

‖ Both minister and churchwardens were saddled with charitable aids to itinerants, and noblemen granted passes in the manner of briefs.

¶ "Item, to Mris Hope upon Sct. Paules day for washing surplesses, 2*s.*" Both she and her successor Mrs. Bell received an annual sum for this office, which with the making gives us an agreeable idea of the plain useful parson's wives of those times. The said garments are called in the accounts *surpclothes, surplets*, &c.

** There are other charges for wood for the Pulpit cover, and for iron, lead, &c., for pulpit.

†† Generally *resshes*, and an annual affair till about 1660. 1634, To Francis Jobber for getting of flaggs 12*s.*, Item for leading of them 36*s.*, Item for dressing them and lieing them *and* the floore 2*l.* 6*s.* The reason of such heavy expenses does not appear.

and sowdering of vj webbs of leads which was torne up with *a violent and boysterous wind*, 4*s*. 2*d*. : for the great bell head yoake, being about xxvj inches square, and almost ij yeards long, and for brining of it *from Elme Parke* being sixtene myles, xv*s*. : for Quenes prayer, 4*d*. : to *Mr. Henry Barnes clarke of Bradley Burne forge* for new bel-clapper which weyeth v stones and iij lb. at ij ob. (½) p. lb., 15*s*. 2¼*d*. : given to Mr. Windfeild a preacher who preached three sermons, 3s. 4*d*. [An assessment follows, made by "*pound, poole,* and *gaits* of *Brankinmoore.*"] ["*Sic vale*" end these accounts.] - - - 1632. A new fine pulpit cloth of velvit, with a large silk fringe, which cost 20*s*. : Recd. of Charles Husband [the preceding warden] monye belongyng to the churche, 44*s*, *whearof ther was* 2*s. in farthynges* : for one *shatchell* [bag] to put the churche bookes in 12*d*. : for wrytyng a letter to the bell caster and sendyng yt to Durham, 20*d*. : to a poor preacher, 12*d*.*: spent at Raufe Hutton Court, 2*s*. 4*d*. : for dressing the churche loftes and the churche styll - - - 1633. Rec. for wine silver of all the parishe,† 31*s*. : to the bell founder for casting the greate bell anewe, 11*l*.‡ : spent the same night the bell was casten upon the bell founder and the woorkmen, 7*s*. : for a quart of secke to Mr. Arch-deacon [at his visitation] 12*d*, : for two flaggons and a bason, 33*s*. - - - 1634. To John Dennis for writinge of sentences in the church, 2*l*. 16*s*. 8*d*. : to the ringers upon the fift day of November, 3*s*. : for a sacke of coales and a tar barrell, 16*d*. [the first occurrence of such a custom, which became annual§]: for a pottle of secke to Mr. Chanclour and others, 2*s*. : our charges when we went to make oath upon the presentment *for recusantes goods and lands*, 4*s*. : George Langstraffe for *washing*‖ *the organs* and carring the greate bell tongue to Blackwell and bringing it back againe, 6*d*. : to a poore scholler, 6*d*. : a quart of secke for Mr. Vincent¶ - - - 1635. Por making the newe stalls, 9*l* 6*d*. : to three Irish people which weare in want, 6d. : to Charles Husband for one ell of his best blacke stuffe for making up the cushen, and one peniworth of threade, 2*s*. 7*d*: to Francis Emmerson for *three ounces and a halfe* of *silke fringe and buttons*, 10*s*. : John Bennet for loope lace and silke to the pulpit cloth and woorkmanshipp, 12*d*. : a quare of paper for writing, 4*d*. - - - 1636. Tow bookes for the fast, 2s. : an *houre glasse*** and a *standarde*, 2*s*. 2*d*. : a quart of wine to Mr. Bullocke in this towne, 12*d*. - - - 1637. George Langstafe for taking away the ould stalls, 6*d*. : to the ringers when the Bishop went by to London, 2*s*. 3*d*. : Mary Nicholson placead in first seat in the fourth stall from the font on the south alley because it was hir mother's, hir grandmother's, and hir great grandmother's, and paid for it 6*d*.†† - - - 1638. To the ringers when the buship of Durham caime from London. 2*s*. : one gallon of brunt wyne which

* The clergy were evidently on a miserably low footing throughout the 17th century.

† This money fell sadly short of the requirements, for twenty-two gallons at a cost of 2*l*. 18*s*. were consumed this year at the communions.

‡ Besides, the cost of 100*lbs*. of mettall at 8*d*.; 100*lbs*. at 7½*d*.; 75*lbs*. at 7*d*., and 24*lbs*. of pewther at 11*d*. came to 10*l*. 3*s*. 4*d*. The casters used to come from Durham and do there work here, probably to save carriage, a matter of great difficulty on the bad roads of the period.

§ Discontinued from 1653 to 1660.

‖ Misprinted *valuing* in Surtees. There is a tradition that our organs were purchased for Sedgefield church and carried thither, but the present instrument there is of much later date. After a long reign of fiddles and pitchpipes, a 500*l*. organ by Flight and Robson was procured for Darlington in 1820 by subscription. Mr. G. J. Crossley performs on this remarkably sweet instrument, which is placed on the roodscreen.

¶ See p. 222.

** For the pulpit. Gay's parson "spoke the hour-glass in her praise quite out." It would be placed in the *standarde* or frame.

†† On St. Paul's day the churchwardens let the stalls to persons wanting seats. They only let a single "room" or seat to each person, and a small fee was exacted. At the death of an individual, his representative had to be readmitted, and although hereditary claims were respected, they did not pass as a right. The members of several families would sit in one pew, and even where a family had erected a stall, seats to other parties were let by the wardens. The allottee sat till change or death. Before the century was out the assignment of pews were in vogue, and the expression "by consent of the churchwardens" gradually ceased

wee gave to Mr. Richinson and the rist of the woorkemen when they had done there woorke consarning the pillar and frame, 4*s.*; in *Inkelt* [coarse tape] for sirp clothes to Mr. Hope, 1*d.*; to a poure gentelman *which had bene a solger in the lowe cuntres*, 1*s.*: John Dennes for penting the dyell, 1*l.* 1*s.* 4*d.*: for penting the back of the pulpit, 4*d.*: given more to him [George Haton, the window mender] in regarde of the greate wynds which did great hurts, 4*s.* - - - 1639. Paid for John Sygsworth child when he was at the *Leager*, 5*s.*: paid for Mr. Clapperton when he came to the towne and when he went to Auckland to me lord, 20*d.*: for all our fower dinners and beere upon Easter tewes-day * 5*s.*: for a poore sicke soldyer at Will. Boyes house and for convaying him out of towne, 2*s*: for Mr. Thompson that preached the forenoon and afternoone for a quart of sack, 14*d.*†: for Mr. Scott at Bulmer Prescots when he preached, 20*d.*: to a poore minnister wife that was *robed*, 2*s.*: to a poore minnister that Mr. Clapperton sent, 1*s.*: for our *vaages* [see p. 144] to Auckland at severall tymes, 8*s.* - - - 1643. Paid old Elstoob besides the pore stocke and *bason*, 1*s.* 4*d.*: for one quart off wine when Mr. Doughty preached, 10*d.*: for one quart wine and one pinte sacke when an other gentleman preached which lay att Georg Stevesons, 1*s.* 8*d.* - - - 1646. To the ringers on the thankesgiveing day, 2*s.*: George Longstaff for keeping the clock and ringing at five a clock and eight, 13*s.* 4*d.* - - - 1648. To Irish women in May last, 1*s.* 6*d.*: to three companies of Irish, 1*s.*: for Mr. Couper‡ Bedrome for twelve weekes, 4*s.*: to a minister with a passe, 1*s.* - - - 1649. To a poore man travelling from *Lincolne to Richmond* with *one man to guide him* and three children, 6*d.*: for pounder *haver* [oats] for Howden, 1*s.* 5*d.* - - - 1650. Six quarts of sacke to the minister that preached when we had not a minister, 9*s.* - - - 1651. A quart of sacke to preaching ministers, 1*s.* 6*d.* - - - 1653. To Jo. Smith's son for setting of Jenet Wards legg, 5*s.*: to Geo. Pary *for carryinge him to the wells*,§ 2*s.*: to a poore distressed Irish woman and seven children, 1*s.* 6*d.*: for a primer to a poore boy, 4*d.*: for Edw. Holmes a poore scholler att the *petit school* for halfe a yeares teachinge, 3*s.* 3*d.*: to Widdow Ward for teaching three poore children three weeks, 9*d.* - - - 1654. To Mr. Johnson for preaching one sunday in sacke, 1*s.*: to a stranger that preached one sunday for a pinte of sacke, 1*s.*: to Alley Gibbon for keeping Ruddes woman, 4*s.*: for a new *bell* rope to John *Bell*, 10*s.*: to Willm Priscot for a quire of paper, 6*d.*: to the lasse which went to Newcastle, 7*s.* 6*d.* - - - 1655. My horsehire and my charges to Durham *to give in a presentment for recusants*, 2*s.* 6*d.*: George Langstraffe for carring the money which was collected for the protestants in France to a Justice, 6*d.*; John Woodmas for *water*‖ for Roger Jewet, 1*l.* 3*s.* 6*d.*: Ouswald Fawcit wife for her paynes and charges in curing Roger Jewet, 5*s.*: leyd out for an accidence for a poor boy, 6*d.* - - - 1656. Receaved of the arears of the sesse for the *Inkle Stock*, 2*l.* 13*s.* 4*d.*: for a pint of wyne and a pint of sack when Mr. Jesse preached, 1*s.* 6*d.*: a poore widow which had a lose by fyer, 1*s.*; to widow *Lumley* for hir releafe

* The day of election of wardens.

† Thompson took up his abode here. In 1644-5, 1*s.* 2*d.* was paid for the puritanical "directory" for him, and in 1646 and the following year or two, an annual charge of 3*s.* 4*d.* for his [very bad] keeping of the *regerstur* or *redgester*, in lieu of poor Henry Carter the clerk. In 1647 there was "more given to Mr. Thomson in regaird of his great necessitie, 6*s.* 8*d.*," and in the same year, after copious potations of "wine and beare" had been administered to this poor minister, and others that preached here, there was 5*s.* "more given to Mr. Thompson when he laid sicke."

‡ The *Coup* of the register (p. 223) and evidently a *very* poor minister, there being a number of items for his relief.

§ Were these the Croft wells, or some miraculous spa further off? "The sulphur well springing in a rich piece of ground cal'd the stinking pitts" at Croft was in fame for diseases of animals, about 1620, but was first made convenient for human votaries by Sir Wm. Chaytor, about 1670. After that a son of Mrs. Lodge, of Darlington, who had been blind several years by humours in his eyes, which had cost her in doctors about 10*l.*, after ten times bathing, became quite well. "Old Mr. Middleton, of Blackwell," was also cured of the gravel by it.—(*MS. penes Chaytor fam. Dated* 1714.)

‖ Was this the Croft water again? It was sold in flasks at the metropolis in 1713 at 1*s.* each. It will be observed that the sum paid by the wardens is a high one.

and for watching of hir *in hir distraction*, 2*s*. 6*d*. - - - 1657. Cloath to the pulpit *cod** 6*s*. 8*d*.: to the taylor for mending the cod and leather for the inner lineing to it, 1*s*. 6*d*. - - - 1658. A shett to Bridgwells lade to winde him in, 1*s*. 4*d*.: two pints of sacke and a pint of clarett sent to tow minesters which did preach heare, 2*s*. 5*d*.: for righting and macken up our acounts, 4*s*.: 1659. Reced. of Tho. Lackenby *for travelling on the lords day*, 2*s*.: of the brick man for his boy trangressin the lords day, 1*s*.: pd. with *Grate Dan*, son to Stockdayle when he was putte an aprentice, 20*s*.: Longstaff *for dressing the church after the Gaurds*† (kept, *erased*) *in it*, 2*s*. - - - 1660. To a distressed minester with a briefe, 6*d*.: for the booke of Common Prayer, 12*s*.: paid the ringers at the coronation day and bear, 7*s*.: given to the Docktor for his paines in offitiatinge the place and taking paines att severall times, 1*l*. - - - 1661. Recd. from Sir Wm. Blakestone against Christmas, 2*l*.: pd att seaverall times in beare when Mr. Steward preatched, 1*s*. 4*d*.: to an old man which had bene att the sessions being in wantt, 6*d*.: a pinte of sack when Mr. Bell preached, 1*s*.: a persons [parson's] wiffe in distresse, 1*s*.: for glazeing *the great winder*, 16*s*. 6*d*.: for *a foxe head* James Steed, 1*s*.‡: to Tho. *Clarvis* being sick att severall times, 2*s*. 1*d*.: for makeing the table cloth and *scouring the pewther*§ for the church, 6*d*.: pd. for officeiateing the place for preaching nighe four months, 6*l*. - - - 1662. To five souldiers that came with a passe to all churchwardens for releife, 1*s*: John Taylor *to help to heale his legg*, 6*d*.: for makeing a *clot* to the pulpit, 6*d*.: bringing two loads of stones to the font, 16*s*. 8*d*.: to the mayson for the stones and *setting up the font*, 2*l*. 18*s*. 8*d*.: for the *Letany seat*, 4*s*. 6*d*.: to a poore man *that had beene in Turky*, 4*d*. - - - 1663. For Leonard Pilkington charge to *ranspeth*|| and Ferryhill to enquire for workemen to make a *font cover*, 3*s*. 6*d*., Item, when Robert Bamlet and Bryan Heavysides came over, and *because of their deareness we could not agree with them*, they had for their charges 6*s*.: *whins to the church wall*, 1*s*.: a rope to the *watch worke of the clocke*, 8*s*. 6*d*.: wine to doctor Stewart when he preached, 2*s*.: John Cooke for wryting the returne of the *nonsolvents* before Mr. Gerard at Cockerton, 1*s*. 6*d*.: to Matthew Towley [the bell caster] for his charges *when he stayed till he was agreed with*, 15*s*.¶: for beere when Mr. Gerrard was present, 1*s*.: for carring the bells from the church doore to the forge, 3*s*. 6*d*. - - - 1664. For ringing on the kings birthday to Chr. Wood to *pay the ringers before Mr. Gerrard*, 9*s*: for a tarr barrell and coales then, 2*s*. 4*d*. - - - 1665. For the fast day booke, 2*s*. 6*d*.: for coales and a tarr barrel the third of June, 1*s*. 6*d*. - - - 1666. For mending the *great chist* and poor box, 3*s*. 6*d*.: for ringing one night when order [the school orders ?] came from my lord, 5*s*., for drink and candles that night, 10*d*.: one quart of sack bestowed on Mr. Jellett when he preached, 2*s*. 4*d*.: more bestowed on him at Ralph Collings when Mr. Bell was there, 1*s*. 8*d*.: Thomas Newbey Henry Richardson charges to Aukland to appear before my Lord upon Mr. Bells promotion, 5*s*. - - - 1667. For plaistering or *beamfilling* throughout the whole outside of the church, 13*s*. 4*d*. - - - 1669. For lousing us from good behavor, 14*s*. 4*d***

* In a former year called *cood*, i.e. a cushion.

† Before this entry turned up, a tradition of republican soldiers having quartered themselves in the church was familiar to me.

‡ A similar item occurs in 1675, 1686, 1688, &c. The Reynard breed were, like the wolves of Edgar's time, under a ban.

§ The very mediocre communion vessels of the day.

|| Where Cosin was fitting up the church with the most gorgeous oak work.

¶ A heavy sum, bespeaking potent potations to turn the *screw*. The wardens had previously buckled up their courage by "beere at our generall meeting when the worke for the bells was agreed upon."

** In the preceding year there was a civil war between the Darlington wardens, Thomas Blakiston and Robert Colthirst, two "gentlemen," and those for Cockerton and Blackwell, plain John Dennys the painter of the kings armes, and Wm. Cornforth the yeoman. Blakiston would only give credit to Cornforth for 1*l*. 16*s*. received from him for Blackwell collection, "but there was xxv*s*. more," says the yeoman, he having paid "to Mr. Thomas Blakiston at Jo. Hall's 36*s*. Item to him at Mr. Finleyes 25*s*. which is not acknowledg." The gentleman had evidently forgotten his transactions in his cups, and the dispute ran so high, that the two aristocrats would not enter their accounts; the countrymen had to petition the bishop and archdeacon against "Mr. Coultus and Mr. Blakiston our partners

- - - 1670. To Will. Bellwood with *young Clarfax*, 1*l.* 5*s.*: to the *lame dockter* for curing Duke Willson *of the evell*, 4*s.* 6*d.**: for a *bear* [bier] cover, 3*s.* 6*d.*: for a quart of wine for parson Raine, 1*s.*: collected upon a breefe for a fire in the towne of Wolsingham, 5*s.* 5*d.*: do. upon a peticion for one John Ridall of Northumberland, 3*s.* 3½*d.* - - - 1671. To Mr. Bell for burying *Tho. Clarfax*, 11*d.* - - - 1672. May 11th. To the ringers for ringing when the bishopp came from London, 4*s.* 6*d.*: for making one new cover for the *beere* and one new side and bars for the *bere*, 5*s.* - - - 1673. Given Jane Girlington *being necesesitated*, 1*s.* [she kept a pauper for the parish]: bestowed of Mr. Sissons *for curtiesies received*, 3*s.* 8*d.*: ringers upon proclameing the peace, 5*s.*: for a tar barrell and coales, 1*s.* 8*d.*: for *helpe* for Wharington lass *her heareing*, 1*s.* - - 1674. George Heddon *surveyor for Grainge Close:* James Cook for three pettecotes, 8*s.*: collected or gathered upon a breif about Oxford a very great losse by fire, amounting to the summe of 1700*li.* and upwardes, 8*s.* 5*d.* ob. one farthing. It was at Bisciter within ten miles of Oxford - - - 1675. Given a poore boye for carrying the certificate for freeing the poore from *hearth money*, [an old church due] 1*d.*: to three seamen that had lost their shipp they haveing a *strong* pass from the Justices of peace besides being objects of charity, 6*d.*: to a disstressed captaine, his wife and child, 1*s.*, haveing a certificate from as well severall justices in this countye as others and *goeing to the king*, being all night in towne; for a winding sheet for old Widdow Longstafe, 1*s.* 6*d.*; to two destressed men *that came out of the Indes*, 6*d.*: for a quart of clarrett when *Mr. Nevell* preached, 1*s.*: for two quarts of *clarret* for comunicants, 2*s.*: to two going *for the kings tutch*, 1*d.* - - - 1676. Wm. *Clervax* wynding sheet, 1*s.* 6*d.* - - - 1677. Recd. "from the old churchwardens 3*s.* 9*d.*, Item, of them *one copper shilling:* to John Dennis senior for writting the lords prayer and creed in capitall letrs draweing colloring of the frams and gild, 16*s.*: for drawing our presentments and attending the justices att *the petty sessions att Haughton*, 2*s.*: for a quarte of seck for the minister that came from Westmerland, 2*s.* 6*d.*: to Captan Humble Read which had a pas with the kings broade seal, 2*s.* 3*d.*: paid for *a quaker* that we had prisoner a night, to carry before Sir Henery Calverley, 1*s.*: two new prayer books for the publicke fast, 5*s.*: for goeing to *the private sessions att Haughton*, 1*s.*: for two *vages* to Durham att the visitations, 8*s.* - - - 1678. For paper when wee went about with St. Pauls breife, 1*d.*: given *the Arch Bpp. of Sames* [Samos] in Greece, haveing a comic'on from the king, 5*s.*†: Dorothy Apleby for keeping Tho. Marrshall's w—e and bastard, 7*s.* - - - 1680. For *sealeing where Thomas Stainsby brok downe*, 1*s.* 6*d.*: for making poore box: Hickson and Wright for *carring Isabell Monerd*‡ *from my dore*, 2*d.*: to a poore lame *shoulder* who had a pass, 6*d.*: for a coat for *Beedyrll*, 6*s.* 9*d.*: to Henry Walker kaptaine of a merchantt man who had a passe from Sir Ro: Claijton and Ld. Mayr of London, 2*s.* 6*d.*: to a gentelwon *who her husbond burnt in Iyrland*, 1*s.* - - - 1682. To two seawrecked gentlemen, 1*s.* 6*d.*: when *Mr. Peamont* preached, for a bottle of wine, 1*s.*§ - - - 1683. Mrs. Bell for exchangeing one of the communion flaggons, 1*s.* 8*d.*: Allowed Thom. Windall for the buryall of *Jack's* child, 2*s.* 8*d.* - - - 1684. To a pilot whose ship was cast away upon the Irish

not delivering the church booke church evidences and seale," and when they did get the *booke*, the writer could only say "I leave the rest for Mr. Blakston to enter," which he partly did. The consequence seems to have been a recognizance for the whole parish to keep the peace, but the wardens of 1669 went "to gitt the church booke," after various meetings "about the booke," and were *loused*.

* The *cure* was skin deep. "1672, Lanstafe for making *duck* Wilson grave, 4*d.*"

† Some more of these wandering Greeks and Armenians who "used their mitre for a beggar's cap," occur in other church accounts of the county.

‡ A troublesome woman. The same item occurs again, and one for her keep.

§ In the ensuing year of office, 1683-4, communion was celebrated at Pentecost, three bottles, two loaves; Midsummer, three bottles, two loaves; Michaelmas, two bottles, one loaf;—(Christmas?) one bottle, one loaf; Sunday before Easter, two bottles, two loaves: Good Friday, two bottles and one pint, two loaves; *Saturnday before Easter*, one bottle, one loaf; Easterday, seven bottles, five loaves; Sunday after Easter, five bottles, three loaves.

coast, 6*d.*: to the parsons order, given to a man *both deafe and dum* being sent from minister to minister to London, 6*d.* - - - 1685, To the ploomar in ale when wee first mett with him, 1*s.*: to an ould distressed minister, 6*d.* - - - 1686, Ralph Coats for making the clock, 13*l.*: to a captaine from France with a pass, 1*s.* - - - 1688, To a travilling schoolemaster with a strong passe, 1*s.*: to a disbanded officer in Ireland, 1*s.*: at the bone fire on kings birth-day, 1*s.* 6*d.*: to Mr. Ansells sonn whose father was taken prisoner by the Turks, towards his ransome, 4*s.*: spent at drawing up the certificate for reading dayly prayre and the new prayres for the king, 6*d.*: a load of coles and tarr-barrells on corronation day, 2*s.* 10*d.* - - - 1689, Receved *John Milton* child larestall, 1*s.* 8*d.*: ringing the 11th Aprill, 11*s.*: tarr-barrll and coals, 2*s.* - - - 1690, A botle of Hock to Parson *Tong** when he preached, 2*s.*: a botle of wine to Mr Batty, a Lancashire minester, when he preached, 1*s.* 6*d.*, more given him *being in destress*, 1*s.* - - - 1691, To the ringers for the victory of takeing Limerick, and a tar-barrell, 6*s.* 8*d.*: when the Dean of Durham preached here, spent in a treat with him, 3*s.* 6*d.*: to a parson wife goeing to London with a pass, 6*d.*: for a winding sheet for a pooer begger womans child, 1*s.* 2*d.*: for ringing for the victory at sea and ale to the ringers, 8*s.* 2*d.*: a strainger that preacht, a dozin of ale, 1*s.*: to the parson of Bppton when he preached, one dozin of ale, 1*s.*: to Thomas Lainge for keeping and *lyeing the plank at the Bridge end when the water is out, and takeing it upp and washing and* WRINING† *itt*, 1*s.* - - - 1692, Dec. 3, For a fox head, 1*s.*: Feb 22, to Widd. Tindal lying in, 1*s.*: March 3, to the same, 1*s.*: Apr. 7, to the ringers *when My Lord Lumbly was here*, 10*s.*: brief collected for the Christians in slavery in Turkey, 1*l.* 18*s.* 2*d.* - - - 1693, A collection made for Mr. Danll. Thwaites, minister, who preached twice that day. - - - 1694, To Henery Langstaffe for carrag of the bell, 1*l.* 1*s.*, for taking down the great bell, wages and ale, 10*s.*, for hanging *her* up, in ale and wages, 10*s.*: for prayer books when we got out of place, 5*s.*: for tolling the great bell the fifth of March, 1*s.* - - - 1767, To Robert Preston for burying the Human Bones found in Nelson's Garth‡ 4*d.* - - - 1768, To usual allowance for keeping this account 5*s.* - - - 1769, To Geo. Johnson for a Scutcheon to a lock to Vestry Box, 1*s.* - - - 1770, To Richard Robson for stopping Rat-holes in the church - - - 1772, Ordered that the churchwardens do attend Mrs. Eden and Miss Allan, and return them thanks in the name of the whole parish for their present (on Good Friday last) of two large silver flaggons for the use of the Communion Table in this church.§ - - - 1771, A bottle of wine for Mr. Addinson when

* Rector of Brancepeth for thirty years. See Tonge ped. in Surtees, iv., 4.

† It may be *wrming*; however, the word is written in a larger hand than the rest of the item, and I suspect that old Richard Hilton, the churchwarden, was perpetrating a joke.

‡ 4 July, 1767. As some workmen were digging in a field belonging to the town of Darlington, in order to lay the foundation of a house, they discovered the skeleton of a man. The bones were remarkably large, and by the position they were found in, it is imagined the body had been buried in the earth quite doubled.—*Gillespy's Coll.*

§ The flaggons cost 55*l.* 19*s.* 6*d.*, and their engraving 1*l.* 1*s.* On their sides, *I. H. S.* On their bottoms, *Vasum sacræ Mensæ Deo et Ecclesiæ S. Cuthberti in Darlington Humille offerunt Hanna Eden et Anna Allan, Anno Domini* 1772. The rest of the plate comprises a cup and two patens. On the side of the cup *I. H. S.*, encircled with, *Poculum Benedictionis, cui benedicimus, nonne Sanguinis Christi est?* On the rim of its lid, *Darlington Church*, 1775. *Donum Parochianorum de Darlington, A. D.* 1775. Under its bottom, *Hodgson Thornhill, Thomas Pickering, Gubernatores.* On the bottom of each plate *I. H. S.*, encircled with, *Panis quem frangimus, nonne Communio Corporis Christi est? quoniam unus est Panis, unum Corpus nos qui multi sumus, nam omnes ex uno illo Pane participamus.* On the outside of the bottom, *Donum Parochianorum de Darlington, A. D.* 1775. *Hodgson Thornhill, Thomas Pickering, Gubernatores.*

In a letter to J. Brough Taylor, esq., Surtees says in reference to some old Archdeacon's visitations of the commencement of the 17th cent., " There's another very odd story about a man at Darlington that could not take the communion, because he did not feel easy in his mind that he was in charity with all men, and after trying till another Sunday he said " he was not in charity nor noe man should make him in charitie with Franck Oswold and Will Hewatson, till they paid him his demands for otes and ended all matters, &c., and being advised, &c., he did groon outrageously and fell sick upont, and would not be any way persuaded.—Dismissed, as it seems they did not know what to do with him.——These preach, 2*s*.*; A *Hud* for Mr. Watkin when *maid* Master of Arts 1*l*. 17*s*. 3*d*.; Aug. 18, To calling down Cockerton feast,†2*d*.: - - - To Robert Hunter for teaching — Jackson *sum* of Len'd Jackson to play 50 tunes upon the Violin 1*l*. 1*s*.; to a new violin for him 18*s*. - - - 1772, To Postage of a letter and bill with *Lade Daw Dole*,‡ 6*d*.; seling and plaistering belfray 10*l*. 19*s*. - - - 1773, George Feetham cunstable attending to loke after the gamesters 1*s*. - - - 1778, Collected for Kirkburton inundation from house to house, 2*l*. 17*s*. 5*d*.; collected by the quakers for do. 4*s*. 6*d*. - - - 1783, To a strainger sick, 2*s*. - - - 1784, Mr. Downey for one of the Sentonces 1*l*.§ - - - 1791, For calling churchyard 2*d*. - - - 1791, Building Churchyard wall, 51*l*. 9*s*. - - - 1799,‖ Postage Birmingham letter with rules for soup society 1*s*. - - - 1800, Peid Wm. Askew constable for attending the churchwardens at the churchyard, town, and places adjacent, to prevent Sabath brecking, gameing, &c., the last year. Fifty-two Sundays at 6*d*. p. Sunday, 1*l*. 6*s*.; An umbrella¶ for Mr. Topham, 16*s*. - - - 1802, To Robert Walters for Lock to Stocks, 10*d*.** - - - 1803, Bellman for calls suppressing disorder on Easter Sunday, 1*s*.††; Nov. Vinegar for stoving the church 1*s*. 3*d*. - - - 1804, *Sope and Black Lead for momiments* - - - 1811, May 27, Summonsing four boys for transgression on Sundays and one put in Stocks; To paid for destroying vermin 4*d*. - - - 1814, *Allowance, &c. to Church Pillars*, 2*l*.; Removing Pillars and Walls building 1*l*. 16*s*. 4*d*. - - - 1818, George Ornsby Chaisehire to *sing* deeds [of extra burial ground] 1*l*. 16*s*. - - - 1819, Sand to clean church 6*s*. - - - 1826, June 27,‡‡ Constables attending Blackwell Feast 10*s*. - - - 1827, J. Spark watching churchyard 3*s*. - - - 1829, Tho. Todhunter's bill for Lamp posts in the Churchyard, *should have been paid by the Commissioners but refused*, 2*l*. 17*s*. 6*d*. - - - 1830, May 25, Wine and Biskets 7*s*. 8*d*., Glases at Mr. Piggs on account of the Bishop of Chester 2*s*.; Nov., Relief to a poor family on travel 2*s*. 9*d*.; Men getting up trees and gathering stones Churchyard 4*s*. 6*d*.; Men watching the trees in churchyard 2*s*.; John Rutherford for mending holes in several graves, 4*s*.§§

things really give one a very odd idea of the times and of the strange inquisitorial extent of the Spiritual Court, about the cleanly wight of the fireside at Darlington, and the workings of this other man's conscience, and Mr. Killinghall's kitchen wench, and some 'drunkerds and slacke comers to churche' at Bp. Midleham 1618.—My father remembered old Thompson, vicar of Middleham, fining absentees for 3 Sundays together one shilling."

The cleanly wight was one Wm. Johnson who "*(inter pocula)* in Willm. Hunsdens of Darlington his house *ligulas* [pointes] *suas laxabat et braccas suas dimittebat* before some gentlemen and others and there offered *alvum exonerare* by the fire, *which he partly effected before he could be stopped* in p'sence of all the company as is informed by the said William Hunsdens his wife greatly therwith offended." On the 20th Sep., 1600, he appeared, and having been gravely *admonished* by the archdeaconry official in the Spiritual Court, was so dismissed.

* Similar items for various preachers perpetually occur.

† A series of local feasts begin the last Sunday in July at Neasham, and proceed, I think, in the following order; Hurworth, Aldbrough, Stapleton and Blackwell, Cockerton, Haughton, Harrogate and Burdon, Sadberge and Coatham, Brafferton, Aycliffe. Duck-hunting, racing, drinking, banquetting and all sorts of secular sports are the order of the day, on the Sabbath and a day or two afterwards. Redworth hopping occurs as soon as the hay is won, when there is a run upon the fog.

‡ Lady Day Dole? Lady Calverley's charity.

§ There are some modern panels with sentences of scripture in different parts of the church.

‖ Sunday Schools are mentioned this year.

¶ For funerals. The said umbrella lasted seven years.

** The stocks, once the terror of Sunday sinners, repose from their labours in the sexton's closet in the church. "Jane Buttrey of Darlington, was seet in the *Stoxe* at Crofte, and was whipte out of the Towne the 8 day of Jan. 1672." *Croft Par. Reg.* "1657, For mending the iron of the stockes, 8*d*. 1685, To Rich. Fawcett which was arreare for stocks makeing, 1*s*. 6*d*."—*Blackwell Bks.*

†† In south Durham the brave take off the shoes of the fair, and demand a ransom, from twelve at noon on Easter Sunday to the same time on Monday, when the lasses whisk off the laddies' hats in similar fashion for twenty-four hours.

‡‡ This feast is much later in the year.

§§ About the time of the *Burkite* disclosures, an artist was travelling by the Courier coach from Newcastle to Darlington in company with his rather large and newly made packing case, which carried with it the strong rozeny smell of newly-dressed deal; there

- - - 1831, *Saxon's* [Sexton's] son for catching mice in the church 2*s*. - - - 1833, Feb. 12, Distributing bills on Church Robery 2*s*. - - - 1836, Removing stone coffin. 6*s*.

The cemetery of St. Cuthberts contains two acres and thirty-eight perches, exclusive of the church, and from 1798 to 1847, eight thousand four hundred and sixty-three persons were buried in it. The varying nature of its soil encourages decomposition, but it sadly wants closing for twenty years at least. The following inscriptions, with others scattered among the pedigrees, &c., occur in the church and churchyard.

North Transept.]—Here lieth the Body of *Hannah*, the wife of John *Scafe*, who died the 19th of January, 1766, in the 3...th year of her age much and deservedly lamented. Also *James* [?] their son who died May 16th, 1762, an infant.

South Transept.]—J. G.

In a vault, in the churchyard, lie the remains of *William Allison*, surgeon, who died Sepr. 6th, 1832, aged 70 years. And those of his widow, *Hannah Allison*, who died March 7th, 1833, aged 78 years. Also those of their grandchildren, the sons of W. J. Allison, of Ilford, Essex, viz. *John Allison*, who died Feby. 5th, 1820, aged 1 year and 4 months ; and *William Dixon Allison*, who died March 12th, 1820, aged 2 years and 5 months. Likewise, those of *Harriet Hodgshon*, the sister of Hannah Allison, and relict of the late Richd. Hodgshon, surgeon, of this place, who was buried June 2nd, 1837, aged 67 years.

Sacred to the memory of *Robert Botcherby*, who died July the 8th, 1838, aged 47 years. This tablet was erected by his affectionate wife.*

Chancel.]—Near this place lies the body of *John Trotter*, M. D.,† an honest and humane man, who during a residence of twenty-three years in Darlington practiced medicine with reputation and success. He departed this life Feb. 8th, 1784, aged 53.

[*John*] *Trotter*, M.D., 1784. [*On slab beneath last.*]

were also some hampers of "Newcastle salmon" and sundry old greasy traces on the coach. As evening deepened and all earthly scents grew powerful, the combined savours drew many a mysterious glance from the "outsiders," who commenced to whisper, then to speak to the guard, who mounting snuffed about with officious activity ; the upshot being that horror was depicted on every face. At last a clergyman stood up and pointing ominously to the suspected package asked the artist "Is that your box ?" "Yes." "There is a very offensive smell *from it*, Sir." And down he sat. It was needless to hint at the fish hampers, the *dead body* was in *that* box, and all shrunk from the *Resurrection-man*. When the coach stopped at the Cleaver, in Skinnergate, the supposed villain ordered great care in lowering his horrid charge, and the clergyman, whose suspicions were confirmed, demanded on behalf of the whole passengers that *the box* should be opened. The apple-faced host laughed outright ; "The luggage of a passenger I have known all my life shan't be touched." But the "whole coach" was peremptory, and the owner, to satisfy the inquisitive multitude, unlocked *the box*. As the lid turned on its hinges, a crack and a screach was heard ; all fell back in breathless anticipation of the horrid exhibition, many quitted the room, and a lady fainted away. They looked again, and the most divine face that human genius could pourtray burst upon them. It was the Madonna from the hand of Raphael ! rich in piety, innocence, and perfect beauty, which with great care the owner had brought from Italy. The clergyman apologized, the lady knelt (as a good Roman-Catholic should do), and all were enthralled by so wondrous a sight.

* Churchyard.]—"Erected in memory of *Eliza Botcherby*, daughter of Robert and Anna Botcherby, who died Feby. 10th, 1826, aged 10 months. Also of *Robert Clark Botcherby*, their son, who died June 5th, 1830, aged 18 months."

South Aisle.]—In memory of *Thomas Clark*, who lays interred on the South side of this churchyard, died September 18th, 1829, aged 75.

Sacred to the memory of *Robert Botcherby*, who died Jany. 15th, 1821, aged 76 years, and lies inter'd on the West side of this churchyard. Also of *Elizabeth Botcherby*, widow of the above Robert Botcherby, who died October 28th, 1835, aged 78 years.

† Father of John Trotter, esq., of Haughton-le-Skerne and Staindrop, who married the heiress of Dale, and had issue John Trotter, esq., M.D., Durham ; George Dale Trotter, esq., county treasurer ; William Trotter, esq., Bishop-Auckland ; Charles Trotter, esq., surgeon, Stockton, &c.

HERE lies interred the body of *James Raisbeck*, late alderman of Stockton, who departed this life April the 30th, 1778, aged 78 years.*

NAVE.]—To the memory of *Ralph Tunstall*, who died April the 21st, 1788, aged 80 years. He was an affectionate husband, a sincere friend, and a kind master. Also *Mary Tunstall*, widow of the above Ralph Tunstall, who died July the 8th, 1803, aged 88. *Thomasin Laurence* died 13th April, 1805, aged 82.

AT the Foot of this Pillar lies Jnterr'd *Charles Dalton Foord* son of Charles† and Mary Foord of London.

All those accomplishments he had acquir'd
For which a youth is valu'd and admir'd.
In Witt and Learning he supremely shone,
For at his age he was excell'd by none.
At Westminster he daily did improve,
And merited from all applause and love.
He much endur'd but was all patient mild,
A man in virtue tho' in vice a child.
Such was his life we doubt not but believe
A full reward he did at Death receive.

He died Decr. 29th, 1754, Aged 14.

ELIZABETH STEADMAN, died Feb. 12th, 1748, aged 18.

ROBT. STEADMAN, died Febry. 17th, 1749, aged 27. *Jane Steadman* died March 8th, 1750, ag . . . . Here lieth the . . . . of *Christopher* . . . . son of Iohn . . . . . . *Steadman* who . . . . . February the . . . . . . [*half covered by the Font*].

HERE lieth the body of *Michael Aiselby* who departed this life the 15th day of Ianuary 1762, aged 84 years.‡

HERE lyeth the body of *Robert Clifton*, grocer, son of John Clifton, attorney att law, of this town, who departed this life the 28th of May, 1734, aged 26 years.

SISTE viator, et respice paululum.
Si quid amica Mater, si Matrona modesta,
Si Uxor amantissima, si intacta Pudicitia
redolens Virtutem
Ad quod respicias, habeat.

* He was mayor of Stockton in 1736, 1742, 1746, and 1756, and mar. 1st. Jane Colling of Hurworth, of the family still seated there; and 2nd. at Darlington 24th July, 1759, Eliz. Hayton, of this parish, spinster, who was buried here 15th July, 1790. By his first wife he had issue Thomas, who died unm.; Anne, who m. Tho. Sheen of Newcastle, a descendant of Sheen of Surrey; and Jane, m. to Thomas Bone of the same place. Mr. Sheen's two daughters, Anne and Elizabeth, m. respectively the Rev. James Thomson (Vicar of Ormesby and perpetual curate of Eston, whose grandfather, James, was *cousin to Thomson the Poet*, and who himself was a "poetical parson," and published five or six vols. of poems and novels), and James Henzell of Newcastle. Both sisters had families: the fair portion of the former live at Norton and are old friends. They formed a trefoil, but my worthy brother-fancier of literature, Mr. W. R. Bell (the pedagogue of the ancient grammar school which rose on the site of the *Hermitage* at Norton), bit a leaf off. From James Raisbeck's brother Thomas, the later Raisbecks of Stockton descend.

† "Doorkeeper to the House of Lords."—*Par. Reg.*

‡ The Aslakbys (of Aislaby near Egglescliffe) held lands in Darlington. Sir Robert Danby of Thorpe Perrow near Bedale, knt., chief justice of the common pleas, held lands, &c. in Durham, Darlington, Gateshead, &c., in co. pal. *jure uxoris* Elizabeth daughter and co-heir of John Aslabye, esq, who had died 1432. Michael Aiselby was a great tanner who migrated from Barnard Castle, bought a tannery in Prebends Row in 1718, and rose to the rank of *gentleman*. He was a near relation to the Studley family which produced a Chancellor, and to the forefathers of my antiquarian friend Michael Aislabie Denham of Piersbridge. His large acquisitions produced the now rather old fashioned mansion of Monkend near Croft, and one of his three daughters, Margaret, was the wife of James Mewburn, esq. (of a Croft family), who lived *jure uxoris* at Monkend. The Aislabies were so fond of the name of Michael that one of them at Bowes having only daughters, and fearing that no son would ever arrive, ealled one of them *Michal.* The Pembertons, who acquired Aislaby by purchase only, were equally disposed to the name. Mother Shipton says: "When Egglescliffe sinks and Yarm swims, Aiselby will be the market town.'

Hic jacet *Anna Holmes* Uxor Francisci Holmes
In hoc Oppido Mercatoris :
Honestis nata Parentibus, honestis digna
Parentibus :
Multis flebilis occidit, Uxorio flebilior Marito
In cujus Memoriam hoc reposuit Marmor.
Obiit illa 27 : die Aprilis Anno Dom'i 1722
Ætat : 34.

. . . . c marmore etiamque requiescit *Franciscus Holmes* Vir integer fidelis, Et in omni Negotio Egregio, Obijt Die quarto Junij 1747 Ætatis Anno 59 : Filios Reliquit Duos Johannem In hoc Tumulo Conditum Et Franciscum Superstitem. Obijt *Iohannes* die 4o. Febru'ij 1747. Ætatis Anno 39.*

E. P.

HERE lieth the body of *Isabel* the wife of *Ralph Sanderson*, and daughter of John and . . . . . Elizabeth . . . . . who died January the 19th, 1723, Ætat. Suæ . . . .

W.

SOUTH AISLE.] . . . . ME . . . . . . *Colling*, died . . . . . . 1794, aged 85.

. . . . ughter of Io . . . . . . martha *Willso* . . . . dy'd 14 of febry. . . . 64, aged 1 ye . . .

SACRED to the memory of *William* . . . . *rgarth* lieutenant . . . . . . 97th regiment of . . . . died on the 27th . . . . . . 27 years.

To the memory of *James* the son of James and Ann *Wilson*, who died December 22nd 1791, aged 2 years.

IN memory of *Newby Lowson*, who died January 1st, 1781, aged 40 years. *Lucy*, daughter of Lucy and Newby *Lowson*, died March 4th, 1778, aged four years.

NORTH AISLE.]—J. B. . . . . . aged 76.

To the memory of *Iohn Cully Harrison* of Newton House in the county of York, Esquire, who died April XIII. A.D. MDCCC. aged XLII years : And also to that of his maternal relations Mr. *Thomas Burrell* of Darlington aged LXVIII ; and Mrs *Frances Burrell* aged LXXXI. This monument is inscribed by his affectionate relict D. Harrison.

IN memory of *Ralph Milbanke*, only son of the late Captain Ralph Milbanke, R.N., of Blackwell, first lieutenant of Her Majesty's ship Childers, who died at Hong Kong, in China, deeply and sincerely regretted by all who knew him, Augt. 28th, 1843, in the 34th year of his age.

IN THE CHURCHYARD.†]—IN memory of *Edward Charleton*, Northumberland, formerly major of the 5th reg. of foot, in which regt. he served ten years, and late major of the 11th regt. of foot, born Febry. 22nd, 1759, died May 22nd, 1839, aged 80 years. Who after a life of strict integrity and domestic virtue, departed this life with every hope, resting on the merits of a Divine Saviour, and saying to his beloved daughter "The same Saviour that supports me now will support you ;" words to her most precious and full of richest comfort.

THIS stone is erected to the memory of *David Johnston* of Allonby in Cumberland, and late acting foreman, for 8 years and 6 months, to Alfred Kitching of the Railway engine works, near this town ; by his fellow-workmen, as a tribute of their respect and

* The pith of this inscription is given on a mural monument :—"Sacred to the Memory of Mr. *Francis Holmes* of this Town Gent., *Ann* his wife, and *John* their son, who are Buried in the middle Isle of this Church. This monument was erected in the year 1776, by Francis Holmes as a Testimony of his Duty towards his Parents, and Affection towards his Brother."

† On a stone commemorating the family of Robert Robinson, innkeeper, 1766-1772, are the arms, crest and motto of the Masons' Company (as of London), with various mystic symbols. On another headstone are represented a skeleton creeping from under the cover of an altar tomb, two palm branches, a scull, a serpent biting its tail (eternity), two trumpets, under an eye enclosed in a half circle of clouds, and a very chubby cherub's head in clouds at each side of the last device.

esteem for his ability and exemplary conduct, which he exercised towards them in the discharge of his various duties. He died of consumption Jany. 29th, 1847, aged 35 years.

In Remembrance of *Wm. Burton*, Junr., student in medicine and surgery, who died of a fever the 29th of August 1804, before he had attain'd the 21st year of his age.

Peace to his ashes—to his memory Fame ;
Let these few lines intrinsic worth proclaim.
From Virtue's pleasing Paths he never rov'd,
Of man a lover, and by man belov'd.
Oh had he liv'd till learned age had run
The glorious Race his youth had but begun,
Then future myriads by Diseases torn,
Had thankful blest the day that He was born.*

Also his Brother *Joshua Burton* late a Capt' in the Navy died the 4th of Decr., 1810, aged 24 years, much respected.

⁎ 1755. The four old bells in Darlington church were recast by Lester of London, and two new ones added. They were hung and tuned by the ingenious Mr. James Harrison, from Barrow in Lincolnshire. Four of them were cast anew in 178 . . at the cost of 188*l*. 9*s*. 7½*d*. The weight of the six is 58cwt. 1qr. Harrison's curious piece of mechanism, which changed the tunes chimed every four hours, had baffled the skill of all our local mechanists for years and had fallen into complete disorder, when in 1843

* Here are a few more specimens of the muse unlearned :—

Discontented mother left to weep,
Dear Mother let me lie and sleep.

Her . . . . worth was only known to those
Who stood distracted while her eyes did close.

Hark : from the tombs a doleful sound,
My ears attend the cry,
" Ye living men, come view the ground,
Where you must shortly lie.
Princes, this clay must be your bed,
In spite of all your towers ;
The tall, the wise, the rev'rend head,
Must lie as low as ours."

My plant did flourish fair
Like to a rose in June,
But Death with his cold blast
Has cropt my tender bloom.

Weep not for her that's won the golden portal
With all her jewels crown'd nor stain'd nor dim :
All that she triumph'd in is now immortal,
Nor hush the seraph host's eternal hymn.

Those lovely buds so young and fair
Call'd hence by early doom,
Just came to show how sweet those flowers
In Paradise would bloom.

Remember Man, as thou goes by,
As thou art now, so once was I.
Repent in time, no time delay,
I in my prime was snatch'd away.

19 years I was a maid and 3 years was a wife,
The mother of 4 children and then departed life.

No marble marks thy couch of lowly sleep
But living *Statutes* there, are seen to weep,
Affliction's semblance, bends not o'er thy Tomb
Affliction's self ; deplores thy youthfull doom.

Farewell dear Grandmother dont fret for me
For long I have wished my dear mother to see
But now its pleased the Lord to take me away
And left my Brother a short time to stay.

The three last rhymes are on one stone, date 1846. The *Statute* one became quite popular, and in one instance is improved by reading " Statutes *their*."

A. Salvin Esq.r Architect. Cave & Son, York. Sc. 1849.

Trinity church: Darlington.

This plate is presented by Robert Henry Allan Esq.r F.S.A.

Mr. George Hoggart, a self-taught organ builder, put it into proper order and substituted some new tunes. The chimes play "God save the Queen," "Britons strike home," "Life let us cherish," "See the conquering hero," and the 4th Psalm tune, in rotation during the week till Sunday morning, when the barrel shifts to the psalm tune and resumes its place in twenty-four hours afterwards.

TRINITY CHURCH

stands on the road to Cockerton, and the foundation stone was laid by the new Bishop of Durham, Dr. Maltby, 4 Oct., 1836, when a silver trowel was presented to the Bishop by John Allan, esq., of Blackwell Hall. The style is Early English, the church consisting of one large Nave, two Aisles, and a porch tower on the South, in the second story of which is the vestry. The stair turret is crowned with a spiret, which in some situations has a rustic and extremely happy effect as contrasted with the thick surrounding foliage. The interior is light and convenient, but the flat ceiling detracts much from its beauty. There are 1010 sittings, 600 of which are to be free for ever. Some additional accommodation, by plain and good stalls, has recently been effected.

A good organ, built by our townsmen Geo. Hoggart and Sons, was added in 1844.

The district attached to this church comprises that part of the parish West of the following boundary. As to the township of Darlington, proceed South down the Great North Road, up Albion-street, down Commercial-street to Bondgate, cross to the end of Skinnergate and proceed down that street; the remaining boundary is formed by Coniscliffe Lane. It also contains the whole of the townships of Archdeacon Newton and Cockerton.

The incumbents have been,

Robert Hopper Williamson, Jun., son of the rector of Hurworth, resigned for Lamesley in 1847, when a silver salver was presented to him by his parishioners.

Thomas Webb Minton, 1847. For twenty years his zealous services in connection with St. Cuthbert's Church, had been gratefully felt by the parishioners, who, on his cessation from those offices, in consequence of the present curate being resident, presented him with a handsome coffee-pot, teapot, sugar basin, cream ewer, and purse of 100*l.* The income is about 180*l.* per annum.

The following monumental inscriptions occur:—

On a mural Gothic monument in the South Aisle, adorned with emblematic figures under rich canopies and surrounded by a bust in a niche.]—SACRED to the memory of *John Wood*, esquire, of Woodlands, who departed this life November the 25th, 1843, aged 57 years. "Blessed are the dead which die in the Lord, from henceforth: yea, saith the Spirit, that they may rest from their labours: and their works do follow them."—Revelation, c. 14, v. 13.*

* His loss was much felt. Among other charities, he had a soup kitchen at his own residence, in the winter months and at his own expense, whence the needy were bountifully supplied.

In the Churchyard.]—**Emily Mary Copley fourth daughter of Sir John Peniston Milbanke of Halnaby baronet born September seventh A'o D'i M'o dcccvi Wife of Edward Thomas Copley of Nether Hall near Doncaster Esquire died June first A'o D'i M'o dcccxxxxiv.***

SACRED to the memory of *William Rymer*, esq., solicitor, who died Dec. 28th, 1848, aged 53 years.—He looked for a City which hath foundations, whose Builder and maker is God.†

ST. JOHN'S CHURCH.

For some time a new town had been gradually arising on the East of the Skerne in Darlington, and at last an immense accession in the shape of a most populous colony, which gathered round the scene of its members' daily labours on the York, Newcastle, and Berwick Railway at Bank Top, rendered evident the need for forming a new church district, which, under Sir Robert Peel's Act, was accordingly effected, and made to include the whole of the parish East of the Skerne, with a population between three and four thousand. Until a church was built a warehouse belonging to the Railway Company was by them set apart for Divine worship. The church of St. John the Evangelist, now completed and open, affords accommodation for about six hundred and fifty persons. The Rev. George Brown is incumbent. John Middleton, esq., is the architect, and the style of the new building the Early English, somewhat late in the period. The plan consists of a chancel with vestry at North side, nave with North and South aisles (the latter with a porch), and a tower at the West end, which is intended to carry a spire 160 feet high. The tower opens to the nave by a lofty arch, beneath which is a stone screen for the support of an organ. Under the East window is a delicate reredos of seven trefoiled arches. The roofs are all open ; that of the nave is arched, and that of the chancel canted. There are open stalls throughout, with richly carved poppyheads. The reading-desk and pulpit are placed at opposite sides near the chancel arch ; the latter is richly arcaded and composed of Caen stone, being the gift of the architect. The stained glass in the great East window is arranged in circular and vesica-formed medallions, on which are presented Moses, the raising of the impotent man, St. Matthew, the Nativity, the celebrated symbol of the Trinity, the Saviour's

* This inscription is in relief round the sloping sides of a coffin-shaped stone, on the top of which is a decorated cross. A rich head-stone cross near is equally in the advance, but the first is the best. The rustic muse has scarcely obtained a footing here.

All you who come and see this stone,
Think how quickly I was gone :
Death does not always warning give,
Therefore prepare while you live.

† Mr. Rymer was a native of Malton, and being quite an enthusiast in the etymology of names of places, was to me a most agreeable companion. Although unable for some years to stir in his seat without assistance, and suffering great pain, he was ever quietly jocose, and his conversation had a vein of true religion which unobtrusively sunk deep into the hearts of his listeners. In all movements relative to the observance of the Sabbath and to the promotion of the cause of God, Mr. Rymer was foremost, and died in the full triumph of faith. His memory shall be blessed.—" Each honest neighbour shared his soul sincere, the orphan dropped a tear, and called him kind."

J. Middleton, Architect. W. Monkhouse, Lith. York.

Church of St John, Darlington.

the monogram I.H.S., St. John (the patron Saint), with his symbol the winged serpent in a chalice, the Last Supper, St. Mark, the Ascension, St. Luke, the Crucifixion. The side windows of the chancel and the clerestory lights are filled with various quarried patterns. The East windows of the aisles contain SS. Peter and Paul and foliage, the amount required for which was raised by the Misses Benson. There is a peal of six musical bells. The font was presented by Archdeacon Thorp, and is inscribed "The offering of Charles Thorp, D.D., Archdeacon, Anno Domini, 1848." The embroidered covering for the communion table was also presented by Mrs. Colling of Monkend, near Croft; and the tesselated pavement within the communion table by Herbert Minton, esq. It is of a very rich running aud circled pattern in blue, red and yellowish; the Evangelistic symbols, the angel of St. Matthew, the winged lion of St. Mark, the winged ox of St. Luke, and the eagle of St John being introduced. The remainder of the chancel is similarly adorned. The communion plate, costing 80*l.*, was munificently presented by Robert Henry Allan, esq., of Blackwell Hall; it consists of a paten, chalice, flagon, and offertory basin, all richly moulded and embossed with foliage and other decorations, in the same style as the church is built—the designs were furnished by the author. On the chalice is "*I. H. C.*," and on the basin, "*Deo Optimo Maximo hæc vasa eucharistica in usum ecclesiæ Sancti Johannis, Evangelistæ, dat dicat dedicat Robertus Henricus Allan, Armiger, Blackwellensis, Anno Domini MDCCCXLVIII.*" The latter also bears the quartered shield of Allan, Pemberton, Hindmarsh, Killinghall, Herdwyke, Lambton, and Dodsworth, impaling Gregson quartering Allgood, with crest on a cap of mail, and motto. The simple impalement of Allan and Gregson also occur on the other vessels. The foundation stone of this elegant edifice was laid by George Hudson, esq., M.P., then Lord Mayor of York, September 10th, 1847. The church has cost about 4000*l*, and it is a matter of regret that the building committee are responsible for a very large debt.

The incumbency is worth about 170*l.*

The Mother Church and Trinity Church have National Schools attached; the former in the Leadyard,* the latter in Commercial street.† A new school in connection with Trinity is now erecting in Union street. All three churches have Sunday schools, and there are branches of the Missionary and other societies connected with the church.

II. The Roman-Catholic Church.

In 1767 the Roman-Catholics in the parish were 84 (29 males, 55 females),‡

* Number of scholars, boys' day and Sunday school (Mr. J. A. Storey), 157; girls' ditto (Mrs. Dowell), 85. † Boys' day school, 160; Sunday, 130 (Mr. Horace St. Paul Armstrong); girls' day, 100; Sunday, 140 (Mrs. Wilson). These sliding numbers at Trinity school are curious.

‡ Randal's MSS. Some of the descriptions are curious. "Ann *Menel*, spinster, supposed to be brought up a papist and born at Craythorn, aged 30, Milliner. Mary w. Sam. Daine, brought up a papist; her husband a quaker! *Ave* Hayson, spinster, brought up a papist, *b.* at Byers Green in this co., servant maid. William *Bulmer*, brought up a papist, *b.* at

but about sixty years ago they had dwindled down to some twenty souls who "were accustomed to creep silently into a garret to avoid the insults of bigotry," and till 1824 were attended but once a month by a priest from Stockton. In 1827 (the chapel attached to the Witham mansion at Cliffe, seventeen miles off, having from untoward circumstances been sold and converted into a coach-house) the present chapel was opened, the old one being in a very bad state. It is behind Paradise Lane, and is built in the debased Gothic style, seventy by forty feet. Over the entrance are the Witham arms, and there are schools attached. The Very Rev. William Hogarth, D.D., Bishop of the Northern District, is incumbent, and the number of communicants now amount to nearly three hundred.

After the house of Carmelite or Teresian Nuns of the English nation (expelled at the reformation) had flourished for almost thirty years at Antwerp, a colony went forth from it to Lierre, in Belgium in 1648, consisting of ten sisters, with the mothers Margaret and Ursula, both of the Mostyn (of Wales) family. They continued there till the approach of the French army obliged them to fly, and at a very short notice they quitted their convent in 1794 for London. Under the patronage of Sir John Lawson, of Brough, they settled at St. Helen's Auckland, thence they removed, in 1804, to Cocken Hall, near Durham, where they remained till 1830, when they settled at Field House, between Blackwell and Cockerton, which was christened Carmel House, where some eighteen or twenty nuns under Madam Catherine Hargitt still reside, the Rev. Joseph Brown being confessor. He succeeded the Rev. James Roby, who died in 1841, aged 79, at Mount Carmel, he having been for more than fifty years the affectionate father of the community. He was one of the alumni of the English College at Douay. An extremely elegant Early English chapel is now erecting at the Nunnery, and it is just to remark that Mr. Priestman, of Darlington, a mason, with much taste for sculpture, is executing it in the most meritorious manner.

III. Protestant Nonconformity.

In 1645 the Parliament ordered four godly divines into the county, who were each paid 150*l.* yearly out of the possessions of the Dean and Chapter. Three were sent to the cathedral, and one to Barnard-Castle, viz. John Rogers,* a most virtuous man. At the Restoration he was ejected, aud presented by Lord Wharton to Croglin Rectory in Cumberland, from which he was again ejected by the black Bartholomew Act of Uniformity. A wandering life succeeded; but in 1672, the laws being mitigated, he licensed

Barnard Castle, weaver, aged 35. *Syth* Smith, widow, brought up a papist, *b.* at Catherick, co. York, aged 70, lives on her own, resided 1-12 [of a year]." Nearly all the families mentioned were of mixed creeds.

* The xviij of Aprill 1650 when Mr. Marsh and *Mr. Rogers* preached, their chardges and their Company at dinner, 4*s.*; 1659, for one pint sack bestowed on Mr. Rogers when he preached here, 1*s.* (same item for Mr. Marsh).—*Darlington Church Accounts.*

rooms and preached in Darlington and throughout Teesdale with great success. He was intimate with Sir Henry Vane, (who sometimes rode over from Raby to attend his labours), and died in 1688. He was succeeded by Mark Lisle,* and various other ministers† till 1797, when the Rev. Wm. Norris was sent here under the auspices of the Societas Evangelica (of Independent principles, and the Home Missionary Society of the day): he was succeeded in 1804 by the Rev. Wm. Graham,‡ whose Presbyterian bias caused a secession of the Independents in 1806, and in 1812 the present [Bethel] chapel was built for them in Union street by J. Ianson, esq., of London. It was enlarged in 1822 and will seat five hundred persons. School-rooms were built in 1832, but proving inefficient for the Sabbath school, new ones were opened in Kendrew street, in August, 1849, at a cost of 620*l.* (200*l.* of which was munificently contributed by J. C. Hopkins, esq.). Nearly three hundred children are taught in the school. The Rev. R. C. Pritchett, pastor.

The Society of Friends were located in early times at Darlington, and were subjected to some persecution.§ In 1776 its members in this parish numbered 160, average deaths per annum, 4. These statistics will be but little altered now. They first met at Cockerton, and their old burial place was, I believe, behind the Black Bull Inn at the angle of Blackwellgate and Grange road. They have now a handsome meeting-house (with a cemetery) in Skinnergate, and the Society has for some time been one of prevailing influence in the town.||

* Lyonel, s. Mr. Lisle a dissenting teacher, born 19 June, 1720 —*Startforth Reg.* *Shaftoe, daughter* of Mark Lisle formerly Dissenting Teacher at Darlington, bur. 1728-9. *Darlington.*

† A child of Andrew Hunter of D. *said to be* baptized by the Dissenting-Teacher, buried, but no burial office performed, 1722. Christopher Robinson of D. weaver, bur. but no office performed because a Presbyterian, 1723-4.—*Par. Reg.* About 1754, a Mr. Wood, a surgeon, preached in a room in Northgate; afterwards Mr. Carlisle, and then Mr. Tuff, married in 1772, to "Miss Polly Yellowley, a most accomplished young lady, with a handsome fortune." His character was but indifferent and the Presbyterian society broke up. John Nixon of D., gunsmith, died 1798 of an "apoplectic fit in the Presbyterian meeting-house."

‡ He published in 1809 "The grand Question considered, 'Am I in a state of grace?' with Miscellaneous gatherings" on various subjects, full of curious facts and odd opinions against instrumental music, &c.

§ County of Durham. The Information of William Thornaby of Richmond in the Count. Yorke, Whoe saith that upon the third day of July last being Sonday there was a meeting of Quakers that did meet at the house of Cuthburt Thomsons in Darnlinton and there did assemble themselves together and did hould a conventicle the said day contrary to the Act of Parlliamet which I shall prove by the oath of two witnesses as the said Act doth direct in that case made and provided. The names of those persons that did meet being foremerly:—Cuthburt Thomson aud his famely of Darlinton, his fines for suffering this meeting to be holden in his house, 20*l.*; John Craford and Margrett his wife of Blackwell, 1*l.* received and returned; Peter Gouldsbrough, same, 10*s.*; Lawrence Appelby, Darlington, 10*s.*, received Apr... ; Edward Fisher and Vrsselle his wife, of the same firste meeting——; James Wastell of Haughton ——; John Robinson of Cokerton and Ann his wife, 5*s.*, firrst meeting, 5*s.* Convicted these persons before Sir Francis Bowes, the 20th July, by the oath of these two witneses, Henery X Johnson his marke, Richard Parkin.

1 Sept., 35 Chas. II. Edward Boyes and Thomas Radclife, par. Darlington, come before Sir Robert Eden, Bartt., and Cuthbert Carr, Justices, and swear that Joshua Midleton mercer, Lawrence Apleby, William Dobson, Thos. Hodgson, Ursula Fisher, Anne King, Margarett Nixon, par. Darlington, and Christopher Hodgson, par. Hurworth, attended a Conventicle in Darlington on Sunday, 26 Augst., at the house of Robert Truman. Therefore we fine Midleton, Apleby, Dobson, Hodshon, King, and Apleby, 10*s.* each, they having been previously convicted. On Ursula Fisher and Margaret Nixon, 5*s.* each, being their first offence. On Robert Truman, 20*li.*, but by reason of his inability to pay the same, 10 on Tho. Hodshon and 10 on Ursula Fisher.

|| The late Mr. S Durham, a Friend, was travelling by stage coach to Darlington,

The followers of Wesley existed in Darlington from an early period of the history of Methodism, though it does not appear that he preached in Darlington before 1761, it being merely a road station on his route to and from Newcastle. But some of his coadjutors had preached in Darlington in a small thatched cottage with a mud floor in Clay Row, which stood on the site now occupied by the house of Mr. Middleton the currier. The hearers seldom numbered more than half a dozen, but on Wesley's visit, not half the congregation could obtain admittance, and he preached in the yard. The Wesleyans removed then into an obscure room in Northgate,* and in 1778 to a chapel built in Bondgate, still standing as the cabinet-maker's shop of Mr. Peverley.† On Sunday, 9 May, 1779, Wesley "preached in the Market Place, and all the people behaved well, but a party of the Queen's dragoons." His pulpit was a large stone (recently removed) at the church-gates, and, in reproving the rude soldiery, he reminded them of the tolerant principles of their master, George III., who at the time resisted the anti-Methodist feeling at court, and used his interference to secure the benefit of the Toleration Act as a protection to the Methodists from the continual violence of mobs. In 1786 the chapel was enlarged and side galleries erected, when Mr. Wesley re-opened it after the enlargement, and also preached in the "Raff-yard" (Commercial-street).‡ On another visit he stood on a hogshead at Mr. Pratt's door by the buildings which now bear his name.

when a gentleman near him avowed infidel sentiments and began to ridicule the sacred volume. "Friend," said Mr. S., "what dost thee find so ridiculous in the Bible?" "Oh!" said the infidel, "what man in his senses can believe that a stone from a sling could sink into a man's head and kill him." "Why," said Mr. S., "if Goliah's head was as soft as thine, there could have been no difficulty about it!"

The leading families of the Friends have made their fortunes with their own right hands, and have settled down in all the best and snuggest mansions near the town. They love ample gardens and green plantations, plain houses and high walls, and there is an air of the quintessence of comfort in their grounds. They are active in all works of public interest and improvement, and have always stood firm and active champions against war and slavery. To one of them, says Howitt, "Joseph Pease, sen., we owe the formation of a society,—that of British India,—which, if properly supported by the public, would confer more blessings on the population, both of this country and of the Indian peninsula, than it has ever yet been the privilege of human nature to work out."

⁂ Richard Lindley of Darlington, of the society of Friends, bequeathed 350*l*. to be placed at interest; 150*l*. was to be invested in government securities, and the dividends to be applied in the encouragement of a schoolmaster or schoolmasters of his own society; the remainder was secured in houses adjoining the Friends' Meeting-house, and the interest is divided among their poor members.

1773, May. "Died, in the Quakers' Almshouses in this town, Thomas Kipling, Woolcomber, aged 84, a sober, industrious, honest man, who left a widow, a few years older than himself. They were married near 59 years and supposed to be the oldest couple here. He lay near two years a prisoner in Durham gaol, at the suit of Mr. Hall, then Curate of this place, for his marriage fees, though they were married at the Quakers' Meeting."—*Darlington Mercury*.

* Subsequently the meeting-house of the Independents before a secession led to the erection of their present chapel. It is in a nameless passage South of the Post-office. "An old disciple" remembers, as a boy, joining in the derisive shout, common in those times, when "Michael Gingles," the original beadle of Methodism, carried the pulpit on his back from Clay Row to Northgate.

† It merely contained an end gallery, but the wonder of the age was, how it would ever be filled. The financial records of the Darlington society commence in the year 1778.

‡ He died in 1791, when Darlington had 183 members. Previously to 1805, Darlington was, in succession, an appendage to the Dales', the Yarm, and the Stockton circuits, but, in that year, became the head of a circuit which swallowed up two older circuit-towns, Yarm and Stockton, and included Hartlepool. Stockton is now a circuit-town with these towns attached.

The present chapel, a handsome Italian brick pile,* with stone dressings, stands in a recess on the South side of Bondgate, and was erected in 1812.†

The number of Wesleyans in Darlington in 1850 is 300, in the circuit (including twenty-four surrounding villages) 717. The ministers at present stationed here are the Rev. George Jackson, chairman of the Whitby and Darlington district, and the Rev. Luke H. Wiseman.

Wesley devoted much attention to what he called "the noblest institutions which have been seen in Europe for many centuries," Sunday Schools. They were adopted in the old Bondgate chapel soon after 1790, and removed to a large room in "Pratt's Buildings." In 1818 Thomas Pickering Robinson, esq. gave land in Skinnergate on which Sunday schools were built.‡ The first collection for missions occurs in 1799;§ there is a regular branch of the Wesleyan Missionary Society. The Darlington Benevolent and Strangers' Friend Society commenced in 1815, and employs visitors in visiting the sick poor of all denominations. The committee grant relief and the visitors administer it, adding seasonable religious instruction.||

In 1840, a handsome chapel was built in Paradise Row, by "the Wesleyan Methodist Association." It will seat from 700 to 800 persons, and has convenient vestries and spacious school rooms connected with it; in the latter of which a flourishing Sabbath school is conducted, consisting of upwards of 450 scholars. The premises were erected at a cost of about £2700.¶

* 64 by 52 feet, interior measurements. There is a gallery all round, and a semicircular apse at the West end containing communion arrangements and an orchestra above. Number of seats, about 1400. At the time of erection it was one of the largest Wesleyan chapels in the kingdom. Architect, Jenkins of London. Cost, above £4000. Class rooms, a large vestry, and two ministers' houses with small gardens, constitute the whole one of the most comfortable and complete religious establishments for miles round. A good organ by Nicholson of Rochdale (300*l*.) was added in 1840. Mr. Wm. Foggitt, gratuitous organist.

† Another chapel was built in Park-street, in 1831, for Darlington beyond Skerne; seats, 300. It has not been found so necessary as was anticipated, and is principally used as a Sunday school. A small chapel at Cockerton was built in 1823; seats, 150.

‡ Day schools under a separate trust were allowed, and a Lancasterian boys' day-school is kept below, and a Wesleyan girls' day-school of industry above. The girls are taught by a teacher from the Glasgow Training establishment. Number, upwards of 70. The Wesleyans occupy both rooms on the Sabbath. Children in these schools, upwards of 450; teachers, about 80; children admitted since their establishment, nearly 6000. Ten village schools in connection have upwards of 400 scholars.

§ The circuit included Stockton, Yarm, Hartlepool, Darlington, Bishop-Auckland, &c., and the collection was 2*l*. 12*s*. In 1848, the Darlington circuit, with its circumscribed bounds, produced 275*l*. 16*s*. 1*d*.

|| "The Wesleyans disclaim the designation of '*dissenters*,' that word conveying a distinctive idea on a principle of Ecclesiastical Polity, which they do not hold, i.e., the Scriptural unlawfulness of Establishments. Wesley commenced his labours as supplementary to those of the clergy, to rouse them to greater activity; and he intended his members to be embraced in their communion. Many of the most excellent churchmen have expressed their regret that his purposes and plans were not appreciated. His followers, therefore, became Nonconformists by fate, not by design; and they do not now, like some who have seceded from them, deny the Scriptural lawfulness of an Established Church, or join in the agitation for the separation of church and state. With Wesley, they wish such reforms as would give greater spiritual efficiency to the Established Church; but in all agitations their position is that of friendly neutrality. Wesley's motto was, 'The friends of all; the enemies of none.'"

¶ "The society worshipping in this chapel (known as the Wesleyan Methodist Association) withdrew from the Wesleyan Methodists in 1835, adopting a liberal form of church government, which they regard as being more fully in accordance with the principles of the New Testament. In matters of Christian doctrine, and modes of worship, there is no difference between them and the body from which they separated."

The Primitive Methodists have a chapel in Queen-street, built in 1821; and the Baptists have one in Archer-street.

There are schools connected with the various persuasions, and branches of many of their religious and moral societies.

*** I must now notice two eccentrics in religion.

In 1822, the notorious *Jonathan Martin* came into the employ of Mr. George Middleton, a tanner here, and then experienced some of his remarkable visions about Bonaparte's son reigning in England, &c. He spent his evenings in preaching and praying, and boasted in his autobiography, printed here in 1825, that through his labours in seven weeks, two hundred precious souls were set at liberty. He said that prayer-books had been the means of sending many to hell. In 1824, he had a coat and boots of seal skin with the hairy side outwards. After that he procured an ass, as useful in selling his publication and in imitation of our Saviour. He preached at the Market Cross to a society of Odd Fellows. Yet he was a good workman, lived a good deal among the Methodists, and took great care of his son whom he had placed with a Jewish pedlar, in in the idea that he was to assist in converting the Jews.

Almost every one that has frequented the markets of Darlington, Stockton, and other places in the county for the last fifty years, must recollect a middle sized, and fresh-looking man for his years, very plainly but decently dressed, who paraded the streets or visited the Inns, carrying under his arm a huge collection of ballads or pamphlets which he modestly offered to the persons he met with, crying "Buy a book, buy a book!" If one was bought for a penny, he was perfectly satisfied, and the gentlemen who had known him in better times would occasionally present him with a sixpence or shilling.

True it was that old George had once known better times. His father occupied a farm at Great Stainton, under the Pennyman family, his judgment being considered very superior in selecting cattle, and many came from a great distance to purchase his bulls and cows; nay, I believe that *Old Ben*—the Messrs. Collings' bull, from which descended most of their celebrated animals—was, when a calf, bought of Benjamin Ord, the father of our enthusiast, who was an only son, born in 1755, and a spoiled one. His attendance at school was very irregular, and frequently no coaxing could get him there for a single day in a whole week. Once in Stainton church during service, an older boy was experimenting on George's toe-nails, and by some means cut him to the quick: the agonised boy, sans reverence, roared out most lustily, for which he was deservedly reprimanded and his unlucky tormentor well whipped. Another day as he was sailing his ship in a deep well, a mischievous lad, called Jack Kemp, pushed him in head foremost and then ran off. He was saved from being drowned by a woman that was hay-making near, who drew him out by the legs, exclaiming, "*It's plain thou was't not born to be drowned, thou great booby.*" Again, he was standing near the filthy reservoir of a farmer's *middens*, when a gigantic fellow leapt upon his shoulders, George gave way, and both were engulphed, our hero undermost. He had on his Sunday garments and was hardly recognised by his play-fellows.

However, he contrived to live, and his father dying when he was young, and the Pennymans at that time requiring more rent, his mother engaged another farm at Cowpen near the sea. In his youth he had the vanity to suppose himself handsome, and fancied every young female that looked at him was in love with him. Yet he made a prudent choice in his first wife,* who, for the few years they lived together, made an amazing improvement in her husband, but unfortunately after five or six years she died in childbirth of twins, leaving them and other three children to the widower. He soon

* 1773. March. "Married at Hilton-Chapel, near Yarm, by the Rev. Mr. Peacock, Mr George Ord, an eminent farmer, to Miss Polly Preston of that place, a sprightly and well-accomplished young lady of 18 years of age, endowed with those perfections that promise the greatest felicity to the nuptial state."—*Darlington Mercury.*

got a much inferior helpmate; she was virtuous, careful and industrious enough, but then she gave in to all his whims and ways, and a dormant mental malady began to appear.

He left the Cowpen farm, took one of Sir John Eden at Preston-on-Tees, near Yarm, and having always been a humming, drumming, dreaming, musing fellow, now began to suppose himself superhuman and to see most absurd and chimerical visions. Every thing went wrong, his corn failed for want of cultivation, for want of attention his cattle died. He was now a vagabond, carrying his dreams, visions, and hymns, from one side of the island to the other, and twice he wrote, (without of course receiving any answer) to Mr. Pitt, representing that the nation was in the greatest danger, and could not be saved without his helping hand.

Although he could scarcely spell a word right, he was continually using his pen on hymns and spiritual plays of the most doggrel character. Sometimes he sung them at the Market crosses during the hirings of servants, or at other public meetings, and he commonly had a crowd of disorderly persons about him, some commiserating his situation, others casting dirt, stones, or vile potatoes in his face. He has been seen at Darlington near the Towns-house chanting his dismal rhymes, and the blood streaming from his nose, caused by some too well-directed aim; yet he never ceased his singing, and seemed to take no notice.

He wrote some of his sad and unconnected stuff to his worthy landlord Sir John, who for long had suffered him to remain, but wearied at length by his foolish conduct, he let the good farm to a more deserving tenant. George had a host of children by his second wife, who, with his elder ones, were reduced to ruin and distress. He was father, grandfather, and great grandfather to descendants almost innumerable, living in low employments; most of them he married off when they were little more than children; the old boy being a great stickler for matrimony.

He had once an interview with Johanna Southcote, but as two of a trade seldom agree, they came to cross purposes in their doctrines outrageously, for George considered *himself* the true Shiloh, and the vulgar prophetess was then destined to become *the mother of* Shiloh. In his writings he styled himself the chosen minister of God, the only true Branch, the Great I AM, the Messiah or Shiloh, the Prince of Peace, and many other names, and the good folks that knew him called him a second Solomon, Preacher George, the Antichrist, the Pope in disguise, the Ancient of Days, and sometimes the wandering Jew.

He traversed the three kingdoms: often when his finances were low he was conveyed in a pass cart from one township to another, and sometimes on his route homewards was farther from Preston-on-Tees at night than he had been in the morning. He declared most solemnly that he would never die, and was certainly, notwithstanding his age, very active; he rambled about in 1830 from house to house with great ease but was not so erect as formerly, he had lost his teeth, and his hair was white as snow. Still he was as amorous as ever, and the matrons and young lasses scampered off on his approach to avoid a divine salute, or a Sion kiss from the Ancient of days. Such damsels as submitted patiently to his tales of heavenly love and delight, were immediately registered in his Book of books, being destined afterwards to be seen hand in hand with him, singing and dancing in the air, and kicking with their feet the heads of those who were so stubborn as not to hearken to the charmer's voice.

The head of George's eldest son was full of perpendiculars, diameters, and wheels within wheels. He was under the firm impression that he had discovered the true perpetual motion, and was like his father very prolific.

The patriarch was, notwithstanding his predictions, gathered to his fathers. Both he and his son were buried at Seymour, in Cleveland, where a small property had been left them, the former to the very last resolutely maintaining his opinion that he was a true prophet.

Chapter III. Charities belonging to this Parish.

THE Free Grammar School, a mean building, stood Eastward of the Church on the Skerne, but in 1813 the site was added to the burial ground, and by agreement, the parish built another school of similar dimensions, to the South of the churchyard, to which an upper story was added in 1846. The notes appended to the following pith of the charter* will explain the whole foundation.

(1) " ELIZABETH,† &c., &c.,. Know ye that at the humble petition of our much beloved and faithful cousin, HENRY, Earl of WESTMERLAND,‡ and the Reverend Father in Christ, JAMES,§ Bishop of DURHAM, on behalf of our faithful liege subjects the inhabitants of the town of DARLYNGTON within the county palatine of Durham, to us, for a Grammar School there, to be erected and for ever established for the perpetual education, erudition, and instruction of boys and youth of that town,|| there to be trained, instructed and taught ; of our special grace, &c.; we will, grant, and ordain for us, our heirs and successors, that from henceforth there may and shall be a certain Grammar School in the said town of Darlyngton, which shall be called " *The Free Grammar School of Queen Elizabeth*," for the education, training, and instruction of boys and youth in Grammar,¶ to endure in future times for ever ; and that school, of one master** or

* The original Latin, with various other school papers, constitutes one of the Allan tracts. Hutchinson translated it in 1788 for James Allan, esq., and this reading was published by the town in 1818, and again in 1845 with an address on the school generally by T. E. Abbott, esq. In 1666 there was paid " to Mrs. Colthirst for the translating of the scholl patten into English, 13*s*." The husband of this blue-stocking was Rob. Colthirst, then Borough Bailiff; he was of Guisbrough in 1678, when he seals a law letter " for Mr. *Samuel Butler*, of Manchester, a haberdasher of hats, now at Yorke," with a fess between three *colts* passant; crest, a demi-lion rampant affrontee ; the insignia worn by Colthirst of Somersetshire : and was evidently of the family of Colthurst of Upleatham. See Ord's Cleveland, 350.

† The initial E of the charter contains the virgin queen in most gallant array. A good old full length portrait of the foundress, with the charter in her hand, was placed in the school by George Allan the antiquary, in remembrance of having received his first rudiments of literature there. The schools founded and sanctioned by Elizabeth are very numerous. She founded one at Yarm on the supplication of Tho. Conyers of that place, and by will 1589 he leaves his house and tenement at Darnton, &c., to Francis Nicholson, his wife's nephew, charged with 20*s*. yearly to the school of Yarome for ever. It is the property of James Johnson.

‡ Warden of the West Marches, and "a sensible and *well educated*, as well as a brave man" as appears from his letters.

§ Pilkington.

|| " Tho' the *town* of Darlington be only mentioned, yet the intention of the instituting such school is plain, that it is for the service of the *parish*, two of the Governors living always out of the township, and the twenty-four who chuse those governors, living many of them likewise out of the township ; yet such school is designed for the further instruction of those that can read, and not to teach children to read."—*Opinion of John Middleton, esq., of Durham, councellor at law*, 1688.

¶ This word is considered to imply the teaching of the dead languages, and they only are taught free.

** " 1631. Paid for fower burdens of Rushes and for dressing the Scholehouse at Mr. Richard Smelt entrance to the same, 16*d*. Item, for a bottle of wine and sugar for interteininge Mr. Smelt into the said Schoole house, 2*s*. 1638, For one quart of Clarit wyne when Mr. Robinson went to enter of the Skoule, 8*d*. 1666, For beare and tobaco bestowed on Mr. Bell and his schollers in the Rogation weeke, 1*s*. 10*d*. 1667, For ale and cakes in Rogation weeke for the schollars, 1*s*. 6*d*. 1669, Spent at Mr. Bells, 4*d*., for cakes to the scolers, 6*d*. 1677, To Margret Parkingson that the parson and scolars drunke when they went a proambulation att Cockerton, 2*s*." Other similar entries relating to the " beating the bounds" of the parish occur.

pedagogue, and one usher or sub-pedagogue,* for ever to continue and endure, we erect, ordain, create, found, and establish by these presents." (2) "The four wardens of Darlyngton, for the time being, shall be and shall be called Governors of the said Free

MASTERS.—Robert Hall, Scholl M'r of Derlington occ. 1559, 1571. Rob. Ovington, deprived by Rev. Hen. Dethicke, A.M., Surrogate, and Rev. Tho. Burton, offic. at Auckland chapel, witnesses having been examined, and churchwardens ordered to elect new master, 1579: Lewis Ambrose, occ. 1587: Rob. Hope, curate, lic. 1622: Tho. Hardy, 1630: Ric. Smelt. 1631: Rob. Clerke, lic. 1632: Ric. Birkbeck, lic. 9 Oct., 1634: [Matt. Phillipp, schoolmaster of Darlington, bur. 30 Apr., 1634, in the church]........Robinson, 1638: Ralph Johnson occ. 1652: John Cooke, 1653: John Hodshon, gen., 1657: Rev. Geo. Bell, curate, 1666: Isaac Richardson, occ. 1720. bur. 1723: Jonathan Sisson, 1723, bur. 1743: Rev. Tho. Marshall, discharged 1739, bur. 1740, "Curate of Barnard Castle and late Master of the Free School:" Rev. William Addison, formerly usher, app. 1739, resigned: Rev. Cuthbert Allen, of Hartforth, B.A., 1747, discharged 1748: Rev. Tho. Cooke, of Darlington, B.A, 1748, discharged 1750: Rev. Robt. Meetkirke, M.A., of Icklefield, Herts., M.A., 1750, resigned: Rev. Tho. Morland, 1755, d. 1807, ag. 78: Rev. Wm. Clementson, 1807, d. 1836. Rev. Geo. Wray, 1836, discharged 1840: Rev. Tho. Marshall, present master. The Rev. Thomas Robson, a native of Kirkby Thore, is the present usher. Robert Wilson, esq., was upwards of 14 years usher, and died 1836, aged 40. His successor was Hen. Wade, esq., a talented artist, who became master of Norton Grammar School, and now holds that of Wolsingham.

* 1738. Born at Ravensworth, near Richmond, Cuthbert Shaw, the son of a shoemaker, in low circumstances. After having, for some time, been usher in the Free Grammar school at Darlington, where he, in 1756, published his first poem, entitled "Liberty"; he became an actor, professing a handsome figure. But the speculation did not succeed, and he was reduced to *writing for bread.* He satired his contemporary poets, but his best work was his "Monody to the memory of Emma," his wife, who forfeited the countenance of her family, which was good, for his sake, and died in childbirth of an infant who did not long survive her. He instructed an infant son of the celebrated Philip Dormer Stanhope, Earl of Chesterfield, for some time; and George Lord Lyttleton, on reading the verses on a sorrow similar to that which inspired his own celebrated "Monody," desired Shaw's acquaintance, and distinguished him by praise, without assistance of a more tangible kind. Judging from the following lines in the Monody:—

> Come, Theban drug, the wretch's only aid,
> To my torn heart, its former peace restore, &c.

we should suppose the poet gave himself up to dissipated habits, opium, and intoxicating liquors. He died in 1771, in the prime of life, but sadly emaciated. Poor Shaw! Who speaks of him? Yet he expected immortality. In 1769 he wrote to George Allan, esq..—"Dear George,—I beg your pardon for having troubled you with a letter relative to Mr. Smart, [poor Christopher, the poet] whose pretensions, I am since informed, are merely visionary, and indeed from that and other circumstances, I am led to believe he still retains something of his former insanity. I have withdrawn myself from him for some weeks past. I hope, or at least am willing to flatter myself, your not answering my letter proceeds from the above frivolous application to you - - - The Monody is universally thought to be the best of the kind in any language; and I flatter myself you will be pleased to hear that it has procured me the regard of some of the most distinguished characters in the kingdom; among the rest I have the honour to be visited by Lord Lyttleton, a distinction he has not paid to any body since the days of Mr. Pope. Mr. Wilkes has sent me his acknowledgments in the most warm and sensible manner, and said if Lord T. came into administration, I have reason to flatter myself with something more substantial than fame. You now see plainly, that, though the malicious part of the world have regarded me as a vain pretender, so far from over-rating my abilities, I did not even dream of what I was capable of, on exerting myself. It is impossible to describe to you how desirous numbers of fortune and fashion shew themselves to cultivate my friendship. And must I yet solicit the continuance of yours in vain? You, who know me so firmly attached to you, that despight of all your unkindness, my heart will not suffer me to forget you." - - - "As to the essay you ask of me. I hope I have thought of something that will please you better. What think you of an Ode to Gratitude, inscribed to you as the projector and manager, and the rest of the subscribers. If this is agreeable to you, I will endeavour to delineate on it the manner of our studies, and way of living, going a hunting, &c., with Mr. Noble's character. I mean to make it a shilling pamphlet. I wait your answer on this head. I confess I could wish to be among the number of subscribers, but on my soul, the vast expense of physic and asses' milk which I am obliged constantly to use, have not left me a guinea to spare. I have something at heart which I must tell you. There is a ring (a most beautiful topaz set round with diamonds) which, when I was thought a dying man about two years ago, I had left you with some other matters. This ring, out of necessity, I was obliged to send—*you know where*—about eight months ago. I cannot bear it should be lost, as it was always intended for you, and had I not met with a late disappointment you should have had it, e'er this, without any demands on your pocket. I had five guineas, so you may easily imagine 'tis a ring of value. Therefore if you will be so kind as either trust me in this matter or send money to anybody else, that will be secret, I will give them the ticket, with directions where to get it. You are the only person in the world that has the least idea of my being at all straightened, otherwise I flatter myself there are many that would be proud to offer me their purses. But think not, my dear friend, I have endeavoured to be reconciled to you, to be troublesome; no, I would die sooner than have

Grammar School, and of the possessions, revenues, and goods of the said free school." (3) Nomination of "our beloved Marmaduke Fayr barne,* John Blackelock, John Dobson, and Stephen Camber, the present wardens of the said church of Darlyngton, to stand and be the first and present Governors," "the said office well and faithfully, to execute and hold, from the date of these presents, so long as they shall continue wardens of the same church." (4) The same Governors and their successors shall be "a body corporate and politic of themselves for ever by the name of Governors of the Free Grammar School of Queen Elizabeth, within the town of Darlyngton, within the county palatine of Durham, and of the possessions, revenues, and goods of the same free school." (5) They "shall have perpetual succession, and by that name may and shall be fit and capable persons in law to have, acquire, and receive to themselves and their successors, Governors, &c., manors, lands, tenements, possessions, revenues, and hereditaments, and also goods and chattels whatsoever of us, our heirs, and successors, or of any other person or persons whomsoever." (6) When "any one or more of the said four Governors for the time being shall die, or shall be removed from his office, then it may and shall be lawful for the four and twenty more substantial and discreet inhabitants of the said town,† or the major part of them, to appoint another fit person or other fit persons out of the inhabitants of the said town in the place or places of him or them so dying, or removed, as successors to the said office of Governors to elect and nominate, and so from time to time as often as the case shall happen."‡ (7) The Governors and their successors "for

harboured so despicable a thought, and to give you a proof of this, 'tis my resolution, if I live till summer, to retire somewhere into the country, where my small income will be more than equal to my necessities." - - - "The critical (who are a set of Scotchmen that I have trounced in the second edition of the Race) hate me past all endurance, and never commend me but when they are betrayed into praise, not knowing the author. I'll very shortly make scare-crows of 'em. They know I intend it, and are now trembling with apprehensions. My fame, dear George, is above their reach, and whilst I am happy in the friendship of those that are dear to me, ten thousand such squibs shall never hurt me." On Shaw's death, Doctor James Cowper, who had assisted him with both food and medicine in his greatest distress, wrote to Allan requesting that his poor relations at Darlington should be informed, as he had died intestate. "You must know that he is richer of late than formerly, by being concerned in some quack nostrums, of which he has had so good an income of late as to be able to set up his equipage, house, servants, &c., but by this, though he hurt himself, yet as the business he was engaged in continues to thrive, and by indentures now in my custody for the sake of doing justice to his legal executors, I observe that they run good for fifty years to come, to him, his executors and assignes; therefore it would be doing a charity to his poor relations to acquaint them of this affaire, and if they cannot come up directly, I believe a power of attorney to me to act for them and in their stead would be sufficient, for some time, least by delaying it his estate should be embazled by a number of people of bad character about him."

* Received a pension, 1553. P. 200. † Parish is meant.

‡ It would appear that previously it had not been considered necessary to fill up vacancies in the wardens. In 1631, the churchwardens delivered their accounts to "the minister, the fower and twentye, and the new elected churchwardens," and in 1668 paid their balance in hand "*after this accompt was by them and sundry of the xxiiij perused and examined.*" In 1651 "the churchwardens and the fower and twenty" agreed upon a rule as to foreigners and undersettlers, whose hosts were to appear before Mr. John Middleton, Baliffe, and give security to keep the parish harmless. In 1653, it was "unanimously *condiscended* unto and concluded upon" by the wardens "and the fower and twenty, according to the custome for letting thereof intrusted," that no person should let the school property without the consent of "the churchwardens *of the said towne* and fower and twenty aforesaid or the greater part of them to be agreed upon at a publique meeting in the church or elsewhere uppon publick notice." 1659, "Given to Widdow Richardson for to carry her son to London by the consent of the 24 that was at the church that time, 13*s*. 4*d*." 1663, Payd for beere at the conclusion of the sesse when the most part of the foure and twenty was present, 5*s*." In 1668, a churchrent in arrear was left to the xxiiij to consider of. In 1671, it was agreed "by the churchwardins and severall of the four and twenty that an assesment of twenty shillings per pound shalbe fourthwith leavied for flagging the church throughout the parrish." In 1675, the twenty-four consented to the wardens paying the balance due to a former overseer of the poor, and in 1682, to their giving Becke 1*s*. 6*d*. In 1683, Mary Bell, aged 12, was "by the consent of the 24, the churchwardens and overseers of the poore," put as an apprentice or servant to Cuthbert Corneforth," and her sister to Mr. Arthur Prescott in like manner. "The parish of Darlington has a select vestry of twenty-four. They are elected and proportioned as under: For the town and burrough of Darlington, 12; for the township of Blackwell, 6; for the townships of Cockerton and Arch-Deacon-Newton, 6."—(*Church Bks*. i. 515). In 1714, it was agreed by the twenty-four in vestry that in granting any future leases of the school property, public notice should be

ever hereafter shall have a common seal* to their acts aforesaid, and others in these our letters patent expressed and specified, or in any wise touching or concerning any part thereof, from time to time to be transacted and done, so often as to them shall seem expedient, and the case appear to require the same," and "by the name aforesaid, may plead and be impleaded, defend and be defended, answer and be answered for, in any courts or places, and before any Judges, and in any causes, actions, acts, suits, complaints, pleas, and demands, of what kind, nature, or condition soever the same shall be touching the premises or things hereinafter contained or any part thereof, or for any offences, trespasses, things, causes, or matters, by any person or persons done or committed or to be done or committed." (8) Grant that "the same Governors, and their successors, or the major part of them for the time being, for ever, may and shall have full power and authority, from time to time, of electing, nominating and appointing a pedagogue and usher to the said school, as often as to the same successors [*sic*, read *governors*] or their successors, or the major part of them, from circumstances them moving thereto shall seem [expedient]; and of removing the same pedagogue and usher, or either of them, from the same school, according to their sound discretions, and of placing or constituting others or other more fit, in their stead or steads, and of performing and doing every other thing which to the said free-school, or to the studies adopted in the same [*seu incumbentibus literis in eadem*] shall be necessary and expedient. (9) And that the same Governors and their successors, with the assent of the Earl of Westmerland and Bishop of Durham for the time being, from time to time do make and may have authority and be able to make good, fit, and salutary statutes, decrees, and orders in writing concerning and touching the management, order, government, and direction of the pedagogue and usher and scholars, of the said free school and each of them, for the time being, and the stipends and salaries of the same pedagogue and usher and all other matters whatsoever touching and concerning the said free school and the order, government, preservation, and disposition of the rents, revenues and goods appointed for the maintenance of the said school."† (10) Grant of "two messuages or tenements, and 24 acr. arable land, 8 acr. meadow, and 40 acr. pasture, in Heighington, then or late occupied by Nicholas Yonge or his assigns;‡ a burgage in le Well Rowe in Dar-

given in the church of the vestry meeting to contract with the tenants, the majority of the twenty-four to agree upon terms; and that accordingly the churchwardens should be chosen *out of* the twenty-four on Easter Tuesday, any one refusing to act as warden in his turn to quit, and another be elected in his stead by a majority of the twenty-four present and consent of the minister. It thus appears certain that by ancient custom whereof the memory of man runneth not to the contrary, the twenty-four of Darlington have full and *exclusive* power, as in the adjacent parish of Aycliffe, in all matters relative to the election of wardens, and the audit of their accounts, the levying of assessments and the management of church property. Indeed in 1794, the custom was so fully proved, that the Archdeacon refused to swear Harrington Lee as churchwarden for Darlington at his visitation, in consequence of the protest of Geo. Allan, the antiquary (worth all credit singly), that the "right of election was by antient custom *solely* vested in the twenty-four and *not in the parishioners*." As early as 1507, when the wardens (*see St. Paul's rents*) granted away church property, it was done "by and with the consent of the twenty-four *electors*."

* The present seal, made in 1748, contains an ugly figure of Queen Elizabeth. "COM. SIGILLUM. LIBRÆ. GRAMATICAL. SCHOL. REG. ELIZABETH. IN. VILLA. DE. DARLINGTON. 1567." [Should be 1563]. The ancient seal presented a royal image full horrible to behold amidst a few posies and a D and *tun*. "☓ SIGILLVM. LIBRE. SCHOLE. GRAM . . . . . EL'AB'I."

† "1666, For the drawing of the orders for the school and for getting them presented to my Lord, 10*s*." Some statutes were made in 1748 by the wardens by the assent of the Bishop, "the title of Earl of Westmorland named in the letters patent being then extinct.' They were printed by Allan with the charter. One of such statutes ordained that no master should be removed "unless some good and sufficient cause of complaint or misbehaviour, shall be exhibited in writing against such upper master and signed by us or our successors; and the same cause of complaint be first allowed of and declared by us or our successors for the time being, to be a sufficient cause to displace or remove such upper master." In 1840, the wardens removed Mr. Wray in their discretion, and it was decided in the Queen's Bench and Exchequer, that they had power so to do, and that the bye-law was invalid, as restraining and incompatible with the full powers of the charter, and that the master was removable without summons or proof of any charge. See the Law Reports, 1844.

‡ This farm contains 74a. 3p.—Rent in 1840, 143*l*. *Arkoles* (Hercules) Pickerin held it in 1638.

lyngton, then or late occupied by John Dobson or his assigns; another burgage in Well Rowe* then or late occupied by Robert Hall or his assigns;† a free and annual rent of 8*s*. 3*d*. out of a burgage in le Heade Rowe, then or late occupied by Thomas Thewe or his assigns; a similar rent of 4*s*. 3*d*. out of another burgage in le Heade Rowe, then or late occupied by Anthony Ashenden or his assigns;‡ and a close of land containing by estimation two oxgangs in the Town-fields and parish of Thornabye, co. York, then or late occupied by Ralph Burdon or his assigns;§ all lately parcel of the possessions of a late Chantry called *Roberte Marshalles Chauntery* late founded in the church of Darlyngton then dissolved: as fully as any late cantarist, chaplain, or any other governor and minister of the chantry, or any other person seized of the premises had enjoyed them; which premises lately amounted to the clear yearly value of 5*l*. 4*s*. 10*d*.;‖ to the said governors, to be holden "of us, our heirs, and successors as of our manor of Est Grenwiche, co. Kent, by fealty, in free socage only and not in capite, in lieu of all rents, services, &c." (11) Grant of all revenues of the premises from the feast of the annunciation 1 Edw. VI. "hitherto coming or growing, to have to the said Governors of our gift, without an account or any other thing for the same, to us, our heirs or successors, in any manner rendering."¶ (12) License for the governors or their successors to acquire from the crown or any other person, "any manors, messuages, lands, tenements, rectories, tithes, or other hereditaments whatsoever, within our realm of England, so as they do not exceed the clear yearly value of 10*l*. and are not held of us, our heirs or successors in capite," the statute of mortmain or any other thing to the contrary notwithstanding. (13) Grant that the Governors should have these letters patent under the Great Seal of England without any fine or fee "in our Hanaper, or otherwise to our use in any manner to be rendered."—Test. Westminster, 15 June, 5th year of reign. [1563] "By writ of privy seal and of the date aforesaid by authority of Parliament, PHYLLIPPES. Inrolled 20 Oct. 1567 by me, Willm. Clopton, Deput. Anth. Bone. Aud."

I give the remaining charities in chronological order.

1599. June 9. JOHN PAPE charged his burgage on the Head Rawe (now the property of Mr. John Thompson) with four horse loads of coals, and 3*s*. 4*d*. annually to the poor people of Darlington, the former to be paid at Christmas, and the latter to be bestowed in bread at Easter by the vicar and churchwardens; the aged poor and impo-

* The Tubwell Row property is on lease to the following parties. No. 3 in the report of the Commissioners of Charities to the Trustees of Mark Feetum from 1798 for 99 years, rent, 8*l*. 6*s*. No. 5, Wm. Walters from 1827 for 40 years, 45*l*. 10*s*. (it was 46*l*. but some outbuildings were annexed to No. 6.) No. 6, Messrs. R. Wilson and C. Watson from 1828 for 31 years, 15*l*. No. 7, Trustees of R. Smith, from 1801 for 99 years, 1*l*.

No. 4, Priestgate, Ann Haw, from 1797 for 99 years, 2*l*. 5*s*. There was also a piece of garden ground in Priestgate, let to Wm. Feetum, in 1801, for 99 years at 1*l*. per annum, for which the Commissioners stated that no rent was paid, the then master having sold his life interest for 4*l*. to Wm. Feetum, whose representatives now hold it.

There is also some ancient property in Skinnergate adjoining Dr. Peacock's property, held in 1840 by Rob. Wilson and Mary Rymer at a rent of 10*l*. 15*s*. per an. was formerly paid for a room belonging to it and occupied by the late Dr. but nothing had been received for 30 years previous to the report. (No. 8.)

† He was schoolmaster before the charter was obtained, in 1559, and occurs in 1567 as enrolling a deed in the Court Rolls of the Borough, under the title of "Clerk of the Court."

‡ These rents are paid by the owners of the Talbot Inn and the house adjoining.

§ Anciently called Cheavits farm—contains 27a. 2r. 10p. Rent, £25 10*s*. in 1840. Hutchinson says "There are four stints or beastgates in Brankin-Moor belonging to this school, and three were formerly let with the Tubwell-Row houses, and one with the Skinnergate house, and then rented at 8*s*. each, which, at this time, would be worth 40*s*. each. For a number of years by past, they have not been looked after, and are in a fair way of being lost. N.B. Charities are not barred by length of time, nor the statute of limitations."

‖ Revenue in 1840, £251 3*s*. 6*d*.

¶ The revenues of All Saints or Marshall's chantry had previously been supplied to the purposes of free education. See p. 199.

tent to be especially relieved. 3*s*. 4*d*. is paid in lieu of the coals,* and the like sum for bread at Easter is now added to the Christmas distribution.†

1616. CUTHBERT CORNEFORTH of Blackwell, bequeathed to the poors stock 4*l*. A bond for this sum was taken from Wm. and Tho. Cornforth his sons in 1644. The former borrowed 5*l*. more, and the latter had 10*l*. for ten months in 1659.

1630. The stock of the poor mounted to 20*l*, the yearly interest being 32*s*. 5*l*. of this sum was in the hands of the churchwardens, and the remainder out on bond for two sums, 8*l*. 12*s*. 10*d*., and 7*l*. 11*s*. 2*d*., the odd shillings being "consideracons for them." The 5*l*. was handed to Richard Wood in 1632.

1632-3. FRANCIS FORSTER, "for the great and good affection he bore unto the poor and aged people of Darnton," conveyed his two lesser houses, lately erected in Northgate, with liberty to go through his other house and garths for water to the Skearne, for the use of six poor men or women, impotent or too old and infirm to labour, born in Darlington or *resident there for three years*, to be nominated by his heirs and assigns with the assent of the churchwardens, or any two of them ; he and his heirs to repair the houses‡ or pay 20*s*. rent-charge out of the other house and garth. The cottages are occupied by two widows placed there by the churchwardens. The thatch was pulled off and tiles put on and other repairs to the amount of nearly 30*l*. done by Miss Russell, the owner of the adjoining property on the South, who sold it to Mr. John Smith Dyer.

1636. The poors stock amounted to 37*l*. consisting of the charities of *Mr. John Lisley*, Balyfe of Darlington, 4*l*., Corneforth, 4*l*., *William Johnson*, 10*l*., and *Robert Sober*, 10*l*.,§ "Maide upe sence by the churchwardens, 2*l*.: more, *William Tayler*, 5*l*.: more, *Richard Pickering*, 2*l*."

1636. Oct. 10. JAMES BELLASSES|| of Owton, co. Pal., esq., bequeaths his "messuage, burgage, tenements, and hereditaments that I lately bought of Ralph Wilson¶ in Darlington, with four beast gates in Bracken Moor," "that there shall be severall houses built of the front of the said tenement, for the erecting of which I have already made good provision of timber, bricke, and stone, and for the furthering and perfecting thereof I do bequeath 20*l*., and the same to be bestowed in the said work, thereby to place workmen for a lynning or wooling trade,** in such manner and sort as shall be most needfull and usefull for the towns of Blackwell and Darnton, and for the country next adjoining," and puts in trust "my well-beloved the Baliff, Burgesses, and the headmen *of the burrough* of Darlington in full power and authority from time to time, so often as need shall require, to order and dispose thereof, according to such uses as in my last will and testament is here set down and expressed."—"unto my nephew Sr. Wm. Bellasses, kt., one piece of plate left me by my uncle called *the nutt*, which I desire may be an heirlome to his house,"—"a tenement in Plumbton, co. Cumberland, called the Hallrigge, with another tenement thereunto adjoining called Clarke's tenement," and "my two

* On Christmas eve, 1670, the owner Widdow Priscott distributed "four lood of coals," and at Easter, in bread 3*s*. 4*d*. herself "in the presence of the churchwardens."

† The extreme minutiæ of these charities will be found in the copies of the foundations in the Church Account Book, i. 468.

‡ The item. "1688, For building foure rood of *Mud Wall* in the Alms house, 16*s*."—(*Church acc.*), can scarcely refer to this charity.

§ Bonds for this sum were taken from his son Edmund Sober in 1934 and 1652.

|| He died 1640. See p. 38.

¶ Called in 1655 "one house standing in Blackwellgate now in the occupacon of Raphe Wilson which he under pretence detaineth from the poore contrary to the will of James Bellase deceased," and which the wardens were ordered to obtain possession of. The property is in Skinnergate near Blackwellgate corner and is marked "Alms houses left by James Bellasses, esq., 1636." These tenements have for many years been occupied by three poor widows of the parish appointed by the churchwardens.

** Qu. if a manufactory of coarse tape was not established there. In 1656 the churchwardens received the arrears of the *Inkle mony* or *the sesse for the Inkle Stock*, and evidently made nothing by the speculation wherever its locality was, for in 1661 they paid "for takeing downe the Manchester lome 6*d*.," and in 1662 "received for the loome, of Michaell Middleton 1*l*. 9*s*."

tenements in Deaton."—"I bequeath the land in Howden and Blackwell in which Sr. Wm. Bellasses were nominated joynt purchaser bought of Robert Parkinson* and Francis Parkinson to be surrendered and made over to the Baliff, Burgesses, and headmen of the burrow of Darlington for the setting forward of a trade and to be joyned to my house at Darlington, and for such like uses as the house is given and provided for, desiring that my said nephew Sir Wm. Bellasses that he will make a surrender of the said lands in Blackwell and Howden to the said uses before-mentioned, which I hope he will do;† which if that my said nephew Sir Wm. Bellasses shall refuse, then my will is that the said Hallrigge, Clarke's tenement, and the two farms in Deaton shall be to the uses, limitation and purpose to be joined with the house at Darnton for the uses aforementioned.‡

1640-1. Feb. 26. HENRY HILTON, of Hilton, esq., Baron Hilton (i.e. Baron of the Bishoprick) by will devised the whole of his paternal estate for ninety-nine years to the City Chamber of London, charged with charities to some forty parishes, of which *Darleton* was to have 24*l.* annually, to be paid among the poor inhabitants, each individual to receive 40*s.*,§ and the parochial officers to return a true note of the names of the recipients to the next quarter sessions, at which it was to be filed in the sessions records.‖ His vanity and melancholy might now have occasioned serious doubts as to the sanity of his disposing mind. He had deserted the seat of his ancestors and buried himself in the seclusion of Billinghurst and Mitchel Grove in Sussex, accompanied only by one trusty kinsman, Mr. Nathaniel Hilton, the "faitheful and *painefull* pastor" of the former

* 12 Jas. I. Surr. from Robert Parkinson, gen., and Isabella ux. (examined apart from her husband) to Wm. Bellasses, esq., and James Bellasses, gen. of one oxgang *in the territories of Blackwell* and one cottage in Blackwell. "*This the Howdens.*" Poor Howdens contains four fields comprising about an oxgang (twenty acres), and is (like Blackwell Hill or Fidler's Close, the Northernmost close of the Grange grounds) improperly included in Darlington township. In the old church book the Lord's Rent is frequently paid to the Blackwell collector. 1665, Paid for Howdon part in leading stones to the bakehouse 3*d*., to Goundry for pinder *haver* [pinder's oats] 1*s.* 5*d.*

† He hoped in vain. In 1652 the parish agreed "by the consent of the churchwardens and the fower and twenty," to defend Howdens' tenant against Lord Falconbridge, who claimed the rent. No surrender was ever made to either the parish or the heir at law of Sir Wm., and the property had escheated to the Bishop as part of his copyhold manor of Bondgate; but in 1769 he ordered a grant to two persons to be nominated by the twenty-four, and James Allan and Newby Lowson, "nominated as trustees by the headmen and burgesses of the borough," were admitted in 1771. Allan survived, and the property remained vested in his family till 1830, when Mr. John Allan Wright surrendered it to other trustees. There is a road from Geneva House to it (see church accounts, ii. 139, and Vestry book for 1840), another from the Croft road bought in 1841, and a third, through the Polam Hall Grounds, belonging to Edmund Backhouse, esq.

‡ In 1683 and 1693 the land rent, joined with that of Poor Moor, was spent in apprenticing poor children, fitting them out with clothes and for ringing the 5 and 8 o'clock bell for the convenience of the linen and woollen trades no doubt. The funds were long spent in apprenticing, but in 1828 the inhabitants and headmen resolved that the charity should be managed by a committee of twenty-four (in which number are included five trustees, and the minister and churchwardens) who are to accouut to, and have vacancies filled up by the Vestry on Easter Tuesday; that the funds be lent to Linen and Woollen manufacturers whose capital does not exceed 300*l.*, in sums not less than 50*l.* and not more than 200*l.* at interest of one per cent., on two competent householders joining in security; that the sum borrowed be refunded on the manufacturer giving up his business, or being supposed to have realised the sum of 500*l.*; no term of loan to exceed seven years; surviving trustees to surrender on every vacancy to themselves and new trustees appointed by the Vestry, at the next court after the appointment.

In 1769, Poor Howdens land was let at Elizabeth Cade's, "for the benefit of trade *by Inch of Candle*:" a system of auction exploded by the sand-glass plan.

§ "1666, Given to severall poor people in their sickness and distress out of *Barranet* Hilton money, as by the paticuler may appear, 3*l.* 18*s.* 6*d.* 1682, Expended at Mr. Finly about *Barnt* Hilton money 6*d.*: Reced. *barnett* Hilton mony given to the poore: Received Bar' Hilton money 16*li.* and given to the poor *by consent of the neighbours.* 1688, Rec'd of Baron Hiltons Dole 16*li.* and disposed on according to the donor's will, as appeares by receipts." The parish books give much less sums as paid to each recipient than the 40*s.* so magnificently intended by the odd and perhaps super-vain testator, but no list occurs before 1693.

‖ "1678, Paid Mr. Crosby for fileing the accqt. for Hilton money, 1*s.* 1693, For entring [this charity] in the Court *Roweles*, 1*s.*

W Hylton Longstaffe, del

Stannard & Dixon, lith.

HYLTON CASTLE,

Co DURHAM.

West Front

A.D. 1728.

place. His heir at law during the term was to have 100*l.* annuity, and at its expiration to regain possession, *provided* the claimant should not profess to be the issue of the testator's own body. This proviso is repeated more than once with almost insane precaution, the Baron declaring "to his griefe, that if anie person shall pretend to be a child of my body begotten, which I hope noe body will be soe impudent and shameless ; I hereby calling God and man to witness that I have no child liveing of my body begotten, and if any such shall pretend so to be, I hereby declaire he or she so doing to be a very imposture."* The residue of his estate was to bind five children *of his kindred* to be apprentices, thereby to learn some honest trade to live in an honest vocation.

John, the heir, perilled the skeleton of an estate in the royal cause ; he would not give up his claims, and after the Restoration an amicable decree was obtained, the son of the gallant loyalist resumed his property, but the wasted revenue was unequal to the charges. Henry his successor complained that "hee and his wife and children have nothing to live on ;" and all the payments were at last reduced by one-third,† still leaving serious burdens, and ceased in 1739, in the last baron's time, at whose period the ancient part of the castle appeared in the state shown in my plate.

1641. Nov. 20. FRANCIS FORSTER, and Richard his son and heir, gentn., by Indenture (reciting that Christopher Forster, butcher, deceased, had by indenture, 1 Jan., 1605, demised to the said Francis a close joining on the N. upon the high road to Yarm for 1000 years) granted the same (now called Carlton close, about 2½ acr.) to the four churchwardens "of the Colegitt parish Church," and their successors, the profits to go to the use of the most poor, aged and impotent of the burrow and town of Darlington and Bondgate in Darlington, born there, or *resident for three years and by law not removable*, on the feast of St. John the Baptist and the 20th of December. Power for re-entry in case of default, and agreement that the churchwardens might demise the close *for one year but no longer* inserted.‡ The rents now form part of the Christmas distribution.

1642. Nov. THOMAS BARNES of Darlington, by his last will gave to the poor of Darlington 10*l.* for a stock. It was in the hands of his son Wm. Barnes in 1655.

1655. "Recd. of Lawrence Emerson 2*l.* which was given by *Raphe Blackwell* for the use of the poore."

1655. The churchwardens were ordered to call in the sums left by Barnes, Sober, and Corneforth.

1659. "Recd. of Mr. Glover for his rayles the use of the power, 1*s.*" The rails are in 1660 described as "att Norgatt end."

1659. APPRENTICES' FUND. The churchwardens and overseers of the poor of Darlington *township* from the POOR STOCK purchased§ of William Middleton of Blackwell,

* This strange proviso evidently points to some eating feeling of domestic disgust. His seclusion might be "upon some discontents between him and his wife, they having lived apart near 20 years," as well as "upon some discontents between him and his brother ;" neither of which were much to be wondered at if it be true that he made his charitable will "to merit pardon for 30 years, vicious life led with the Lady Jane Shelley, [his executrix]." When Guillim coolly wrote about the "great grandson of this generous gentleman" one can imagine the "melancholy baron" giving a twitch of agony in his coffin. He was buried in Old St. Pauls, but Lady Jane Shelley never expended the 1000*l.* left to make him a tomb like Dr. Donne's, according to Hilton's wishes. Ralph Spearman of Eachwick (the veritable Jonathan Oldbuck of Sir Walter) mentions an *on dit* that the Baron conceived displeasure at his next heir (Robert, who survived him only a few months) for refusing to come to his immediate presence till he had finished a game at cards.

† This parish joined in suit for the money in 1653 and 1680, in which last year it "paid Finley for Mr. Atrick [Ettrick] and Lady Hilton when they promised *Baronett* Hilton money." Some six parishes stuck out, and a decree for reducing the *dole* to 16*l.* was obtained by the then baron in 1691, but, before 1666, Darlington had compounded for 16*l.*, of which 1 . 15*s.* was apportioned to Blackwell. Mr. Ettrick's man was generally moneybearer. "1683, To Mr. Aterricks man 5*s.*, for a treat for him 2*s.* 10*d.*

It will be observed that the local meaning of baron was forgotten, and the burgesses of Darlington knowing that the family were not peers of the realm, thought that *baronet* must have been the baron's proper title.

‡ "1670. Dec. 24, to the poore, *Forsters daile.* 1*l.* 10*s.*"—*Ch. Acc.*

§ Churchwardens' account book 1767-1801, p. 65. being returns to the parliamentary inquiry of 1786 by Geo. Allan. "1659, Dece. 22th: pd. to *James* Midleton for : 6 : achers land on Blackwell moore for the use of the power of Darnton 15*l.*"

six acres of copyhold land upon Blackwell Moor, now called Poor Moor, which were surrendered by him accordingly, the rents to be applied for the placing out poor boys as apprentices. The property now comprehends three closes of nearly thirteen acres.

At the Vestry of 1828, this fund (erroneously styled *Middleton's Charity*) was ordered to be applied in giving a sum not less than 3*l.* nor more than 5*l.* to each apprentice, to be laid out in necessary expenses and clothing during his term at the discretion of the churchwardens and overseers; the boy not to be bound in the manner of a parish apprentice; and a statement by the said officers of their accounts to be laid before the Vestry for passing the ordinary churchwardens' accounts each year. These resolutions, as well as those concerning Bellasses' charity, were approved by the Charities' Commissioners, and were printed in 1830.

1675. Mar. 1. JOHN CORNFORTH, yeoman, Blackwell, gave by will 40*l.* to trustees, therewith to purchase land or put out for consideration, the profit to be distributed amongst the poor of Blackwell within the twelve days of Christmas. Whayre Fawcett (who married Jane, testator's sister) was compelled to pay this sum by the Bishop on inquisition of deceased's property, but it continued in his and his son's (Captain Whayre Fawcett) hands (the interest or *Cornforth dole* being distributed with Baron Hylton's dole,* every Christmas) till 1740, when "in regard great danger and difficulty had attended the putting out the said sums at interest," this and Prescott's legacy (together 60*l.*) were invested in a copyhold field, formerly the waste of the Lord called Stick Bitch, surrendered from Prescott Pepper, esq., to George Allan, jun., esq., and his sequels, in trust for the poor of Blackwell. The land in question is the orchard opposite the Nag's Head, between Darlington and Croft, and now lets for 12*l.* yearly, which is paid to Blackwell poor.

1671. Sober's 10*l.*, and 5*l.* left by the brother of Anthony Elgie (who held it) were out at use for the poor.

1686. May 22. THOMAS BARKER, of East Newbiggin, yeoman, charged his lands there with 20*s.* yearly to Darlington parish. The sum is paid by the Marquis of Londonderry's tenant, and forms part of the Christmas distribution.

1704. July 18. GEORGE BUCK, of Sadbury, gent., "being now attained to good old age, and not knowing how soon my summons may be to my last end," by will gave 100*l.* to be laid out in lands, three parts of the profits to be paid to the poor of Darlington parish, and the fourth part to the poor of Sadbury, to be paid yearly the first and second Sundays after the eleventh of November to the minister, and churchwardens, and overseers of the poor of the said parishes, to be by them distributed to the most indigent. This 100*l.* was laid out in the purchase of a copyhold close called Butt Close, alias Been Close, and an acre of waste land adjoining, and surrendered to Michael Hodgson, of Field House, and his heirs in trust. The property contains three parcels of about 3½ acres, and adjoins the South East end of Northgate bridge, and was surrendered that the premises should from time to time be surrendered as the said ministers, churchwardens, and overseers should appoint. The rents (after paying Sadberge its proportion) now form part of the Christmas distribution. There is still a "Buck" Inn at Sadberge.

1705. Feb. 2. ARTHUR PRESCOTT, gent., of Darlington, by will gave to trustees 40*l.* to be placed out at interest, one-half to be yearly distributed among the poor widows of Darlington, the other among the poor of Blackwell. The Darlington 20*l.* was in Mowbray's bank, which failed in 1814, but G. L. Hollingsworth, esq., one of the partners, paid the amount in 1827, and in 1828 it was invested in the purchase of 19*l.* 13*s.* 1*d.* new four per cents., and formed part of a sum standing in the names of Robert Botcherby and George Horner. The dividends form part of the Christmas distribution. For the Blackwell moiety see John Corneforth's charity.

1713. Apr. 19. DAME MARY CALVERLEY, by indenture, assigned to trustees 1000*l.* due

* Sax. *dœl*, a portion. Many charities are still called *doles* in Durham. The funeral dole is perhaps extinct. It was to procure rest to the soul of the deceased, that he might find his judge propitious, as we learn from Chrysostom's Homily xxxii. in Matt. cap. non.

to her on bond from Edward Pollen, and by indenture of even date they declared it to be in trust for such persons as she should appoint, and in default to lay out, after her decease, the principal, or so much as should come to their hands *in the purchase of lands and tenements*, and to apply the rents, (and interest until such purchase should be made) for the support of a charity school intended to be established at Darlington, for instructing poor children there in the principles of the Christian religion according to the Church of England, and for clothing them, and teaching them to read, write, and cast accounts, and buying them books, and putting them out apprentices to trades, and for the maintenance of a schoolmaster, under such regulations as the trustees should think proper. Vacancies in the trustees to be filled up by the survivors under hand and seal.

A subscription* was commenced in 1714 on the consideration that "profaneness and debauchery are greatly owing to a gross ignorance of the Christian religion," and in the following year Lady Calverley gave 150*l.* due from Mr. Kitt Pinckney to her. In 1719 Robert Noble of Darlington, apothecary, charged on the same house as his charity, 40*s.* yearly for the use of the BLUE COAT CHARITY SCHOOL, on condition that the several masters should be licenced by the bishop, be conformable to the liturgy as then established, and train up the boys in the principles and communion of the same, in default legacy to cease. The requirements have not been obeyed and the legacy is not received.

In 1722 Pollen's bond produced 650*l.*, and in 1729 the capital stock of the school amounting to 900*l.* (lent on bond to George Allan, sen.), it was thenceforth supported on the same, voluntary subscriptions having ceased. In 1750 George Allan (the son) accounted for 1280*l.*, and in 1800, 1392*l.* 9*s.* stock three per cent consols were transferred into the names of Samuel Forster, Jonathan Backhouse, and Stephen Buttery, which were afterwards changed to Jonathan Backhouse, junior, Samuel Forster, junior, and Thomas Buttery, being transferrees from the survivor of the first three.

There does not appear to have been any room appropriated to the school, and the scholars have been transferred to the master of the National School, who receives 18*l.* per annum for their tuition, his bill for school requisites, and 15*s.* for firing. The children receive an entire suit of clothing yearly, being in number twelve; they are named by the trustees and are called the *Blue coat boys*, though their peculiar dress is discontinued. The dividends amount to 41*l.* 15*s.* 4*d.*

1714. May 1. MATTHEW LAMB† gave to George Allan, of Darlington, merchant, and the churchwardens and their successors, heirs, and assigns, his yearly rent of 12*s.* of lawful *Britannish* money, charged on a burgage in Blackwellgate‡ and paid yearly on Good Friday; to be distributed at the discretion of George Allan, his heirs and assigns, and the churchwardens of Darlington to twelve of the poor and *needfullest* widows living in the town 1*s.* each, on Good Fryday. The amount is given accordingly at Christmas by the churchwardens.

1715. May 10. DAME MARY CALVERLY, widow of Sir John Calverly, by will directed the residue of a mortgage debt of 1500*l* upon Sir John Husband's estate at Ipsley, Warwicks. (after payment of legacies) to be invested at interest, or in the purchase of lands, the yearly dividends or rents to be paid amongst such poor people in any of the parishes between, and including Northallerton and Darlington, if an object required, as her executors and trustees should think fit. Up to the year 1821 the churchwardens received 10*l.* from her representatives, which they distributed to the poor of Darlington. Since that time nothing has been received An application was made in 1830 to Beilby Thompson, esq., of Escrick Park for the money since 1820, when Richard Thompson

* Papers. R. H. A.

† Steward of the Borough Court, 1710. His son William was deputy postmaster at Norwich, and becoming a defaulter in about 1000*l.*, extents were issued against his sureties John Raine, of Snowhall, and his father. The crown sold the latter's houses in the West Row (High Row) and the Sheep-market or East Row in 4 Geo. II.

‡ Formerly the Golden Lyon Inn.

(who had paid it) died, but his steward answered that the case had been fully investigated at York by the Commissioners of Charities, who decided against any claim upon him; that none of his estates were liable; and that he was not executor to his uncle Richard.

1719. May 20. ROBERT NOBLE, of Darlington, apothecary,* charged his burgage on the High Row with 20*s.* yearly to the churchwardens on the 29 Sep., who were to distribute the same from time to time to the poor of the town not receiving sess. The sum forms part of the Christmas distribution, being paid by Mr. Joseph Forster.

1720. May 20. CATHARINE CATHERICK, spinster, by will† charged her two copyhold messuages and orchard in Bondgate, in Darlington, with 52*s.* annually to the minister and churchwardens on the 1st. May and 1st November, to be laid out in 12*d.* worth of bread every Sunday, and distributed amongst the poor people of the town in their discretion most needful. The 2*l.* 12*s.* is paid annually in December, and bread to the amount of 4*s* 4*d.* given away on the last Sunday in every month in 1*d.* and 2*d.* loaves, to poor persons attending divine service, according to a list, the vacancies of which are filled up by the minister and churchwardens.

1791. Apr. 11. ELIZABETH WALKER, widow, by will proved at York, 1792, gave to the minister and churchwardens 50*l.* to be laid out on government security, and the interest divided on Christmas-day among twelve poor widows belonging to the town, as the minister and churchwardens should think fit. 58*l.* 3*s.* five per cent Loyalties, standing in the names of James Topham, Stephen Buttery, and Shaftoe Carr, were bought in 1800, and the dividends form part of the Christmas distribution.

1809. Jan. 1. SHAFTOE CARR, by will gave to the churchwardens of the township of Darlington 50*l.* to be invested at interest, which was to be distributed on St. Thomas's day yearly, among such poor people belonging to the township, as they should think fit. 50*l.* stock five per cents. was bought in 1819 in the names of Robert Botcherby and George Horner, reduced to 52*l.* 10*s.* new four per cents., the dividends augmenting the Christmas distributions.

1820. June 20. MRS. MARY PEASE, widow of Mr. Joseph Pease, of Darlington, woollen manufacturer, having purchased property in Chairgate, otherwise Glover's Weind, or Post House Weind, from Richard Scott and wife, and built thereon four alms-houses, by indenture of this date Scott's trustees convey the same, with a piece of ground used as a common road to the same and to dwelling-houses of Edward Pease the elder, and Joseph Pease the elder, and John Crawford, for a residue of a term of 980 years, to Edw. Pease, Jos. Pease, sen. (dead), John Pease, Jos. Pease, jun., John Beaumont Pease, Edward Pease, jun. (dead), Isaac Pease (dead), and Henry Pease, on trust to repair and insure the alms-houses, and permit four poor widows, aged sixty at least, of good moral character and not of the society of Quakers, to dwell therein, on paying 5*s.* a piece annually, these sums to be remitted in the discretion of the trustees, and to be used in repairing, insuring, and incidental trust charges, the surplus to accumulate in the funds or other security until, with compound interest, it should amount to 20*l.*, when the alms-houses should be rent free, and the interest be applied in trust charges, and the surplus divided among the alms-women, or accumulate until the next Christmas-day after the appointment of new trustees and then divided, so that the accumulation might always begin anew with new trustees. The trustees to fill up vacancies, and expulsion to follow marriage or gross impropriety in the alms women. No person to continue trustee after ceasing to be a member of the monthly meeting of Friends of Darlington district, and when the trustees are reduced to three, their powers to vest in the society of Friends at their monthly meetings, who were there to nominate as soon as convenient fit persons to make up the number of twelve to whom the premises were to be assigned.

* "Here lyeth the body of Mr. Robert Noble, of Darlington, apothecary, who died on the 15 of July in the 41 year of his age Anno Dom'i 1719." *Arms.* On a chief a lion passant (same as Noble of Reresbie, Leic.); impaling, a chevron between 3 covered cups.—*Entrance of Nave, Darlington Ch.*

† "To Elizabeth *Betessu* half a crown."

The 5*s.* rents have been occasionally demanded, but the cost of repairs, &c., have, it is believed, as yet prevented any investment. Four poor widows occupy the almshouses according to the donor's intentions.

The several charities distributed at Christmas* are usually augmented by a portion of the sacrament money, and some of the widows receive more in proportion, in respect of Elizabeth Walker's charity. The poor of the other townships of the parish, and occasionally persons of other parishes (if deserving), being resident in Darlington, receive a portion of the money thus distributed.†

There is another item of parochial revenue in the St. Paul's rents, being ancient rents reserved on church property ‡ leased in perpetuity, and paid on St. Paul's day, when much church business was formerly transacted.§ The

* 1660, Given to the poor att *Christs Tide*, 1*l.* 3*s.* 3*d.*

† Thomas Morton, of Darlington, left £3 to Gainford poor, before 1664, and in 1637-8 Edward Morton, of Morton Tinmoth, par. Gainford, was bur. here. In 1688, Mary Finley, of Darlington, widow, gave a third part of Broadgates (1*l.* 8*s.*) to Barnard Castle poor.

‡ I subjoin the pith of the original deed, from the wardens, of the burgage, afterwards the Kilnegarth in Hundgate. It seems the payment on St. Paul's day was an after arrangement for convenience. "Christ. *(xp'c.)* To all by whom this indented charter shall be seen or heard, John Thomson, John Gragrete, John Thomson, barker, and William Stapilton, wardens *(Iconomi*, literally *economists)*, or masters of the fabric of the collegiate church of Derlyngton, greeting. Know us the said wardens, or masters, by and with the consent of the four and twenty electors, to have given, &c., to Stephen Bland, of Derlyngton, our one messuage or burgage, in Hundgate, as it lies there between the burgage of the said Stephen, on the west, and the venell called Hundgate Welle, on the east. To have, &c., of us, the said masters, and our successors, the wardens or masters of the said church, for the time being, to the said Stephen Bland, his heirs and assigns, for ever. Paying and rendering to us and our said successors yearly 3*s.* 4*d.*, at the terms of Penticost and St. Martin, in winter, by equal portions. And if it happen that the said annual rent shall be in arrear and unpaid for half-a-year, no sufficient distress being found in the same messuage, then it shall be fully lawful for the said wardens, for the time being, the said messuage, &c., to re-enter, and peaceably re-have and hold, &c.. And the said Stephen Bland shall repair, sustain, build, and repair, the said messuage, in all necessaries and edifices, at the proper expenses of him and his heirs for ever. [Usual warranty.] In witness whereof, to this, our present indented charter, we have caused to be affixed the common seal of the said collegiate church. Dated on the feast of the conversion of St. Paul, A.D., 1507." *(Seal as in margin). Endorsed:*— "An auncient dead frome the churchewardens of Darnton to Stephen Bland, for a house in Hongaite.— Hond Gayt Hows." —*(Translated from orig. penes R. H. Allan, esq.)*

§ And, as usual, a drink perpetrated. A dinner was enjoyed by the minister and wardens, which costing some 6*s.* 8*d.* or 7*s.*, and "towlling the bell then" 2*d.*, left a very handsome assistance to the rates. In 1642, the puritans fed two ministers, two churchwardens, the clerk and sexton for 3*s.* 8*d.* only. But, *miserabile dictu*, the price of dinners and the number of feeders has so increased, and the rents by neglect diminished, that now the annual dinner cannot be kept up, and the rents accumulate for 3 or 4 years until a proper sum is raised. In 1763, the churchwardens were to "pay at the least 1 guinea for the public dinner on Easter Tuesday, and 6*s.* a-head more for every one of the company, which list in the notes is from the church accounts of 1630-1-2, with minutes of the later owners.*

Postscript.

P. 203 *and seq.*] I extract from a letter of an antiquary (dated " Spa, Belgique, Sep. 15, '49,) on some of the *cruciculæ* on these pages. " I think you will find *the zones of our lady* (p. 203) in the York Minster Inventory, in Dugdale, but what they were, I know not, save that they were doubtless *ex votos*, and hung around shrines, which seem to have been curiously bedizened with all manner of odds and ends, rings, beads, monilia, as for instance the stag, probably the hart couchant of Richard II., a badge so curiously shewn in his portrait at Wilton, in which all the attendant *angels* wear his livery of the hart, appended to their necks.

" Each altar required a bell, (pp. 203-4) and they took the host to the sick, with hand-bell and candle. I just now saw from my window the priest issue from the church, bearing a large silver ciborium, and preceded by his acolyte, who, in the hurry of the emergency, had slipped a rochet over the blue butchers-like smock-frock here worn by all the lower orders, and with lantern and bell scuffled away to some one *in extremis*. The distinction between sance bells and sacring bells is remarkable, the latter, I suppose, properly to be used at the elevation in the mass.†

exceed one-and-twenty. The same rule for St. Paul's day." "1768, Jan, 25. To Paul dinner, £1 1*s*.: Ministers and curates extraordinaries 5*s*.: Bell-ringers' drinks 5*s*. 6*d*.: and servants 2*s*. 6*d*." In 1830, the rents were thus applied:—" Feb. 24. 64 old men dined at Three Tuns, 1*s*. 6*d*., 4*l*. 16*s*. The above 64 old men averaged 66 years of age. Total amount of their ages, 4,224 years."

* Mris. Alice Tomlinson for her house on the Head rawe (John Thompson, also subject to Pape's charity) 12*d*. John Glover for his house (Talbot Inn) 12*s*. Bulmer Priscot for his kilnegarth in Hungaite (afterwards the Allans' residence, now R. Thompson's property) 3*s*. 4*d*. Mr. Tho. Barnes for a burgage in Skinergaite (in the Rose and Crown yard, Thomas Horner's in 1818) 8*d*. Henry Booth for John Glover's house in Skinergait (Punch Bowl yard ; Tho. Tutin 6*d*., John Dixon 8*d*., W. Dixon 1*s*. 2*d*., Miss Robinson 6*d*., Wm. Robinson of Haughton 6*d*.) 4*s*. Henry Elstobb for Renton's house in Skinnergate 18*d*. Ant. Renold for his house 18*d*. John Stephenson for a house in Skinnergayte 18*d*. (In 1818, 2 houses in Skinnergate, Rob. Walters and F. Priestman, paid 1*s*. 6*d*. each.) Tho. Garth for his house in Skinergait 3*s*. (Rose and Crown.) Ann Wilson widdow nere the well in Skinergaite for her house 3*s*. (Dr. Peacock.) Mris. Dorethie Hearing for her house 3*s*. 4d. (Ellerson's house in Blackwellgate.) John Vasey for his house and garth at Blackwellgait end 6*s*. (Vasey Close, lost by subdivision in building plots.) Mr. John Turner for his burgage next Bennet Hall (elsewhere Bennit field, Dove or Dow Crofts, late Dovers Crofts) 8*d*. Mr. John Cowton for his house at the church gaites 8*s*. 4*d*. (afterwards inhabited by parsons Hope and Bell.) Mr. Geo. Ricatson for the Lambe Flatt (alias Lampe Flat, now Lamb's Flats) 3*s*. More of Mr. Ricatson for house in the Weand 12*d*. (elsewhere *Vend*, now Woodhouse's house in Posthouse Wynd.) Wydow Rutter for one house in the Wend that was John Ward of Hurwourthe (*alias* in Chairegate) 12*d*. Mr. Bulmer Ile for his house in Ratten Rawe 6*s*. 8*d*. (Church Row, Miss Ness and Mr. Milburn each pay 3*s*. 4*d*.) Rob. Ile for his doore into the church yeard 6*d*. ("Mr. Robson's house the Flower Pot cou'd not get any thing for the door into the church yard this year shou'd be 6*d*.") John Middleton for Geo. Marshall's house in the borrow 6*s*. 8*d*. (Joint Stock Bank.) Roger Specke for his house in Bongayt 18*d*. (Wm. Milburn 1*s*. the 6*d*. was lost before 1683.) John Dickson for Belies house in Bongate, 3*d*. (F. Furness.) Tho. Wilson of Brafferton for his house in Norgayt 12*d*. (Edward Pease, formerly Nathan Robson.) John Harrison for house in Norgayt 3*s*. (J. H. Mowbray.) Wm. Stainsbye for his house in Norgayt 6*s*. 8*d*. (J. Kipling.) Mr. Skepper for a close at Cockerton bridge end 1*s*. (Skipper Close, Dr. Harper.) Vincent Hodgshon for his house 6*s*. 8*d*. Margery Budles for her house 3*d*.—Total 4*l*. 8*s*., reduced to 3*l*. 10*s*. 3*d*. in 1818, and now becoming gradually less.

† Certainly. Vide Eccl. Proceedings, Sur. Soc. p. 137. And in despite of both Cambridge and Oxford societies, I believe that the *sance* bell was quite distinct from the Sacringe bell, and for a different purpose.

> The *saint-bell* calls ; and, Julia, I must read
> The proper lessons for the saints now dead ;
> To grace which service, Julia, there shall be
> One holy collect said or sung for thee

"Are you sure the word is *revale?* (p. 205.) Can it not be *renale?* [*n* being hastily read *u.*] I have met with it before, but have never made it out. *Renale* might be the short 'polka,' so much in fashion, reaching only to the hips. Tissues of various mixed colours are often named in old times and *blac medle,* (p. 208.) I take it to be nothing more than our 'Oxford mixture,' or pepper and salt. Cloth *de Lyre (ib.)* I imagine to have been fabricated at Lira,* in the north of France. The cup *ad modum columbini* was in form of a columbine, and an exquisite standing cup it must have been. The flower was a favourite device : - - - I speak without any means of reference here."

P. 200.] In Jas. Allan's MSS., an office copy of Collen's account occurs. The last two sums of 25*s.* 4*d.* and 70*s.*, refer to a chantry at West Raineton, and another in Houghton-le-Spring church. In line 11 of this page for *chanters* read chantry.

P. 213.] The three churches of Darlington, and Blackwell Grange are conspicuous objects from Newtown Hill House, which stands near the centre of Newtown or Newton Ketton estate, and from which upwards of thirty churches and chapels are said to be seen with the naked eye, and even York Minster with a good glass.

P. 218.] It appears from the application of the money collected by the briefs of 1705, that the canted roofs of the church were lowered in pitch in 1707. The carpenters were "to take down all the wood roofes of the three high pitches, from the top to the bottoms thereof, and in re-building of the same, to lower the said roofes according to designe—to shirt the same, and every peice of shirting, above 2 inches broade, to drive or put in two nailes at every sparr—to lay the flooer, and plaine all the boards, on the upper side thirof—to make a gutter in every of the said pitches betwixt the severall roofes and the battlements—to sow and dres all rabters, dormans, and wall plates, and to put in what new dormans as shall be thought necessary—and to turne, dres, and order the old ones as they shall be directed—to sow. dres, and put in new sparrs where the old ones are wanting or decayed." The same style was therefore to be kept, and new wood only to be put in where wanted. The trustees to find timber, and the contractors, nails, and to have 50*l.* Battlements were to be built along the side, of freestone, from the quarry at Brussleton, "8 inches thick and 36 inches hie, lup and crese," for 24*l.*

P. 221.] In Elizabeth's time, much energy seems to have been exerted to Christianize the massss, by means of voluntary intinerant preachers, who were either dignitaries of the church or energetic incumbents. The custom continued for some time; and from Bishop Barnes's list of the preachers to be engaged, "from Michaolmes 1578, untill Michaellmes 1579, of their benevolent good wylls in assisting him in his greate cure and paroche, over and besides ther ordenarie *quarterlie* and *monethelye* sermones in their owne peculier cures and churches," I gather that, besides one preached by himself, a sermon was to be preached in Darlingetone by each of the following clergymen :—Mr. Leaver, (a prebendary), Mr. Archedeacone of Durham, Mr. Henry Nanton, (a prebendary), and Mr. Thomas Wheatone, (vicar of Coniscliffe.)

P. 222.] Kennet's Register mentions one Parish as an intruder here, in Cromwell's time; he conformed after the restoration, and had a living in Yorkshire, but was ejected. —*Jas. Allan's MSS.*

P. 223.] In 1661, Sir George Fletcher, bart., the then owner of the Deanery, presented George Bell to the "rectory," who waited on Bishop Cosin with the presentation, on the vacancy caused by the death of *Robert Hope, last* incumbent. The bishop denied the right of the impropriator, the written presentation was returned, and he presented

Dead when thou art, dear Julia, thou shalt have
A trental sung by virgins o'er thy grave ;
Meantime we two will sing the dirge of these,
Who, dead, deserve our best remembrances.
Herrick's Hesperides, no. 436.

† But if named from the style of manufacture as noted p. 208*, may it not be freely translated *Lute-string ?*

Bell himself, but Fletcher detained the churchyard from the new parson until he obtained a request for it. In 1693, Lord Barnard, purchaser from Fletcher, presented George Thomson. The bishop admitted him in compliment to his lordship, but denied the right of the latter to collate. On this occasion, George Bell, rector of Croft, voluntarily wrote to the Rev. Mr. Pickering, stating that his father was admitted to the curacy by Bishop Cosin, that the question raised "is matter of wonder to me that hath frequently heard that Mr. Grant, Mr. Hope, and Mr. Thomson, [Thomlinson ?] enjoyed and entered upon the abovesaid living by the same power before the rebellion against King Charles the first, that my father held it from 1661, nor did the impropriator of Darlington church ever collate any minister. - - - The present candidate for the place *Mr Hall*, [who succeeded Thomson], who officiates in the parish church, is a person whom I never saw; so that at the instance of a friend of mine, though I be a stranger to you, I shew my respect to justice."

In another letter he requests Thomson not to subpæna him to Durham, not being very capable of taking a journey, and ends:—"God grant me heaven, for this world is not a place for clergymen to live in with ease like other men." He states that his father accepted the living "by the report of a bill read twice in the House of Commons to make every market town - - - - - p. ann. which became frustrate."

Disappointed in the collation dispute, Lord Barnard in 1710 sued Thomson and wished to deprive him of his surplice fees, small as the living was. The action was defended by subscription, and failed. His lordship depended, *inter alia*, on his presentation, which was denied.

In 1712, Hall was presented by Lord Vane. *(Orig. Documents, Jas. Allan's MSS.)*

⁂ William Dunbar, one of the very best of the old Scottish poets, and who was an itinerant preaching churchman of the order of St. Francis, about 1480, in one of his pieces makes the devil appear to him in the likeness of his patron saint, with a religious dress, and advises him to renounce the world and be a friar; and the poet, hinting that he would go to heaven with more satisfaction if invested with a Bishop's robes, continues

"Gif evir my fortoun wes to be a freir,
The dait thairof is past full mony a yeir;
 For in to every lusty toun and place
 Off all Yngland, from Berwick to Kalice,
I haif into thy habeit maid gud cheir.

In freir's weid full fairly haif I fleichit;
In it haif I in pulpet gone and preichit
 In *Derntoun kirk*, and eik in Canterberry;
 In it I past at Dover owre the ferry
Throw Piccardy, and there the peple teichit."

†‡† 1581, Died James Forrest, of D., "parioche clerke: to be buryed in the parioche churche of Darlingtone neere to the stalls next vnto the quire doore: I desire the churchwardens and xxiiij of the sayd towne to be so good vnto Katherine my . . . . . grant her soome benefite of my sayd office for one yere after my decease toward her reliefe and bringinge vp of my children: I will that my wife paye vnto the colyar of Windlinton 3*s*. 4*d*.: rest to be divided betwene Katherine my wife and my two children Wm. Forrest and that other wherof she is not yet delivred and doe make theime [all three, unborn baby and all I suppose] joyntly executors." Inventory mentions the hall, the chamber by the hall, and the chamber beside the entrye, in which were *a par of claricords* (for practise in psalmody, no doubt), 5*s*.," and "ij paynted clothes, 3*s*." Parish clerks would never dream of burial in churches now, but at that time when learning was a prized jewel, being selected from the most highly educated inhabitants, as the beauty of the early registers, which they kept, testify, they sustained a much higher rank in society, and apparently exacted higher fees in proportion.

[*Old Toll Booth, &c., Darlington.*]

DIVISION IV.

DOMESTIC.

Darlington parish is composed of lands and burgages held under several tenures.

The whole of the copyhold portions belong to the episcopal Manor of Bondgate, in Darlington, for which two Halmot* Courts are held annually. Archdeacon-Newton is principally leasehold under the Archdeacon of Durham.† Other small territories in the parish are leasehold under the Bishop and the Dean and Chapter. The freehold is partly rent-free, but some portions pay small rents to the Bishop (see Blackwell manor), and a large proportion of that within the township of Darlington is in the *Borough of Darlington*,‡ which is a prescriptive episcopal one.§

The Borough constitutes a distinct episcopal freehold manor, for which

* Hallmot—the *mote* or assembly *met* in the customary *hall*.

† Lord Redesdale is the lessee of the principal portion.

‡ The borough includes the market-place and the greater part of the old *gates* or streets except Bondgate, with three farms called Brankin Moor, Geneva House, and the Dog and Gun. The boundaries are kept up in the highway assessments, and are sufficiently detailed in Surtees for the purposes of future antiquaries. The freehold, not comprised in the borough and Priestgate, is, with all the other tenures, in the township of Bondgate. The buildings on Bakehouse Hill are presented in 1741 as granted as copyholds and as "incroachments got from the freehold of the Burrow Streets," and the jury presented that the Lord could not grant any more waste there, it belonging to the common town street and king's highway.

§ Perhaps the freedom from toll of the burgesses at Darlington and *Auckland* markets, with other exemptions, were granted by Pudsey at the same period as he did the like good for Durham, which was also governed by a bailiff.

Courts Leet and Baron are held twice a year, though formerly the latter were held about every three weeks. There is the usual steward who jointly with the Bailiff* presides over the Court; indeed since about 1710 the two offices have been united in one person, appointed by the Bishop (Francis Mewburn, esq., present Bailiff and Steward). The Bailiff performs by his officers (the serjeants or constables) the duties of a greeve, but having the full management of the borough for the Bishop, is also clerk of the market,† and acts in summoning public meetings and permitting exhibitions in the public streets as a Mayor‡ does in an incorporated borough. Some obsolete powers will appear in the annals which follow. In the older records, a clerk of the court,§ two constables, four afferors|| and searchers of the markets, tasters of ale, bread, and butter, two searchers of black leather,¶ two ditto for red, two ditto for weights, two overseers of le Tubbewell, two ditto of Skinnergait well, and four grassmen and a hird-man for Brankin Moor appear as annual officers, and a common beadle,** and a cryer or bellman††

* Fee 100*s*. and the rent of a close of land (now "Bailiff's Close") at Dodmires, Bank Top, which was given by Edw. Backhouse, esq., in 1809 in lieu of "Court Close" in the Croft road.

The Bailiff was more connected with the Court Leet, the Court Baron was a mere manorial one, and often held by the steward alone.

The burgesses on every change in ownership, by death or otherwise, are to be admitted on the rolls and thereupon become free of toll, and are to appear to do suit twice a year at the Courts Leet.

† The bishops had power to create and rule markets. "1620, For that there haith beene at this courte greate complaint made of the negligence of borrowmen in giveing attendance to Mr. Bailiffe of this borrough for the ryding or walking the faires and markettes upon such cheiffe faire dayes as heretofore haith been accustomed for the proclaminge thereof in the Kings Mat's name and the Lord Bishopp of Durham the chiefe Lord of this Borrough, the same being a principall parte of theire service which they owe unto the said Lord Bishopp; And therefore in tyme may be a disparaigment to his lordships Roialties and services in this place. It is therefore thought meet and so ordered by this Courte that everye Borrowman within this Borrough of Darlington shall upon everye cheiffe and heade faire day from henceforth eyther himselfe or some other sufficyent man for him (*with some decent weapon in theire handes*, whereby they may be distinguished from other ordinarie merkett people) repaire unto the Tolboothe of Darlington by nyen of the clock in the forenoone of each of the said heade faire dayes to give theire attendaunce upon Mr. Bailiffe for the tyme being for the better grate and more orderlie and dewe execution of the said service."

The bishop had his own standard of weights and measures which he could alter at will. An established corn measure is mentioned in Pudsey's time [*Surtees*, *I*. 27]. In 1727 proper avoirdupoise weights were delivered to the Bailiff from His Majesty's exchequer for the use of the borough.

‡ The Bailiff of Darlington occurs in company with the Mayors of Stockton and Hartlepool in 1433 as swearing with the other magnates of the Liberty of Durham, before the bishop in the cathedral, to observe an article mentioned in certain royal letters to the prelate, who summoned his principal lieges.—*Surtees*, i. cxxxi.

§ Robert Hall, the first master of the Free School, signed as such in memorandums endorsed on deeds registered in the Borough Books.

|| To fix the amount of fines not expressly assessed by the jury.

¶ Shoes sold in the market of bad and insufficiently tanned leather were tryed by "six honest and expert tryers" on oath, and if found bad, forfeited, and the owner amerced.

** Garvan Whaller was amerced in 1624 "for beating the common beedle of the town."

†† It has been held by the bailiffs that persons exercising the vocation of bellman in opposition to the officer appointed by the bailiff cannot recover their charge in the borough court. Edward Coates, painter *et preco feralis* [a cryer of fairs or qu. of funerals?] bur. 1632. Margaret Longstaff, qondam *bell woman* of D., widow, bur. 1726-7. John Longstaff, town cryer [alias bellman], bur. 1731-2. The Longstaffes of Darlington were public men in their way. Have we not seen George Langstaffe's importance in the church accounts, whose relation, Thomas [salary 6*s*. 8*d*.], reigned in his sexton's stead. John L. was Thomas's understrapper. Wm. Longstaff, parish clerk, of liquid memory, d. 1825. The name is abundant in the vale of Tees, and begins with our register and continues down. A Longstaffe, of Darlington, should have been its historian, not a mere namesake of Westmoreland

whose offices were of longer term, occur. Many of these officers have disappeared.

Such is the constitution of the town. The rest of this division will consist of its domestic events in chronological order.

1170. Died Saint Godric, of Finchale, near Durham. Reginald (his cotemporary) in an account of his miracles gives us the sole evidence of a hospital at Baydale for lepers, which probably originated the free chapel that existed long after the cessation of the disease made the former establishment useless.* There is, says he, a vill in the bishopric called *Hailtune* [Haleton or Halughton, the ancient name of Haughton-le-Skerne] well known from all other towns in that region, in which dwelt a widow and her only daughter who was grievously tormented with a most loathsome leprosy. The mother remarried a man who soon began to view the poor girl with the greatest horror, and to torment and execrate her after the usual manner of a step-father. The mother yearned towards her offspring by another, and did all she could to screen her from her husband's persecution, yet could not admit her to any society not even her own family. She fled for aid to the priest of the vill, who, moved with compassion, procured by his entreaties the admission of the damsel to "*the hospital of Dernigntune*, which was almost three miles distant, and was called by name *Badele*,"† and accompanied by the mother and other poor friends, conducted her thither himself. In that "infirmary for those who by the secret judgment of God were stricken with the contagion of leprosy," she remained three years, but only grew worse daily. For a putrid scar, which never healed, completely crossed her face, and, with open sores of raw flesh here and there, running with gaping courses over the sound part in a poisonous stream, rendered her whole visage most horrible. A withered line marked the extremes of her lips all around, by reason of long sickness which had eaten the parts belonging them away to the bottom. These and other operations of her disease had so reduced her wasted frame, that all hope of any health at any period of life altogether seemed vain. At length with faith placed against the belief of all, having heard of the frequent miracles done at the sepulchre of the Saint, the mother led her afflicted offspring thither and earnestly entreated the compassion of the man of God. Once and twice, night and day, did her prayers seem lost and she returned home; but at her third approach Godric hearkened. Such a sudden pain darted into the head of the patient while at the tomb that she could scarcely bear so severe and sudden a feeling, for the clemency of the Saint was poured out, and he settled and removed the noxious humours. The sweat was so fervid that the mother led her to the water, washed her face, moistened her head, and returned to the tomb. She remained quiet for some time there, and drew the hood with the covering over it from her head, when her mother drawing nearer, and looking into her face, beheld it perfectly sound; all the sores of her former leprosy had disappeared, her lips were healthy and delicate, and her whole countenance clear as when a child. They returned home in joy, and never again did the disease return, but the patient lived long to extol the power given by God to his servant Godric. Of this miracle there were, continues the historian, as many true witnesses as there were men who frequented *Halietune* and the hospital of Badele, as

blood! In the Halmot books [the family being small copyholders at Blackwell] the name is *Langstreth*. In the registers it is chronologically Langstaff, Langstaffe, Langestaffe, Langstreffe, Langestraffe, Langstrafe, Langstraffe, Langstraff, Longstaffe, Lanckestafe, Langstaf, Longstaf, Longstaff. In 1624, none were to "let Richard Langstaffe a howse within the borroug of Darlington upon paine of 39*s*. 11*d*." In 1598, Wm. Hodgson, of Manor House, Lanchester, gives "To one John Longstaffe of Rabie yf he be living at the daye of my deathe and yf he be dead to his children, in considerac'on of his losses he sustayned by me in the layte rebellyon in the North in the sarvice of Charles the late Earl of Westmorland, 30*s*."

* Pudsey did much for this parish, and as he erected Sherburn hospital, it is probable he completed his good works here by a similar establishment. Possessed of royal sway in the palatinate, he had power to erect a free chapel and annex it.

† *Var.* Badela.

well as Ralph Haget, the sheriff [for Bishop Pudsey], who told the prior and convent that he had himself seen the girl both before and after it, and that although she was perfectly whole, the scars were marked by a slight redness, and that the extremes of her lips, which were surrounded by broken flesh, were round and full but rather elevated above the rest. Normanrus, the kind priest, asserted the same things, and exhibited his charge, wholly restored, in his church to the parishioners.

1197. The temporalities of the see, during a vacancy, being in the king's hands, the Borough of Derlinton' rendered account of 8*l.* : there was in the treasury 7*l.* 12*s* : owing 8*s*. The Bondmen 69*s*. 8*d*. : in the treasury 64*s*. 8*d*. : owing 5*s*.*

*** In the Treasury at Durham are a number of charters relating to the possessions of the Benets† and Walworths, the early *magnates* of the town, in which are many curious early names. Tho. Pannebrihite, Ric. *Cissor*, Walter s. David *Tinctor*,‡ Roger de Hundegate and William s. Hervice *le Raper* occur at the end of the 13th cent.: James ***Pelliparius*** (of ***Skinner***gate no doubt), William le *Mareschale*,§ Walter s. Duncan le ***Barker***,|| (elsewhere *Tannator*), William *called Redhode* of Derlingtone, &c., in the early part of the 14th.

* Pipe Rolls. NC. Soc. Ant. 1847, p. 201.

† Benedict de Derlingtone had a son William (called *Filius Benedicti* and *Benette*) liv. 1290, whose son John Benette m. Eustachia dr. Wm. de Mundeville who held much land about Burdon. She and her husband alienated *le Halleflat* at Derlingtone and numerous other properties at Burdon and Darlington to the Walworths. Bennet Hall and Bennet Field occur ages afterwards. I lose sight of the Walworths about 1360. A gleam surrounds the northern families of that name from the probability that the celebrated Lord Mayor of London, who turned the stream of Wat Tyler's rebellion, in 1381, was of their blood. In the same year he was executor to Bp. Hatfield. Thomas Walleworth, a canon of York, (cousin of Wm. Walleworth, rector of Haughton-le-Skerne, who died 1401,) bequeaths in 1409 to his sister Agnes, a gilt piece of plate, which formerly belonged to *his brother Sir Wm. Walleworth, knight, deceased*. The early charters have *Wallewrde* and *Wallewrthe*. The Benets seem to have originated as a local family in Benedict de Bermtone, to whom Ralph the Prior confirmed Bp. Marisco's gift of property in Derlingtone between 1217 and 1226.

‡ He sold a burgage in *Vrangelythe* in the field of Derlingtone. The antiquity of the Dyers as a craft in Darlington has been seen in Boldon Book. At the close of the 13th century the Walworths had transactions about property on *le Madergarthes*, evidently the place where the dye was grown, and which, in the 17th century, occurs as *Mathergarthes*, and was then split up into numerous burgages. "The time hath been," says Harrison, in 1577, "that wad and madder, have beene (next unto our tin and woolles) the chief commodities and merchaundize of this realme." *Vrange-lythe* is connected with Madder-garthes, the medieval name of the plant being *varantia*, quasi *verantia* the real, genuine dye.

§ Robert s. Guydo *Faber* occurs about the same time. Peter del Smethe held property here 8 Bury. Robert Rainert of *Smithie-hill* (Bakehouse-hill? where there was a forge) in Darlington, bur., 1623. A singular brass seal of Ralph, who calls himself the farrier of the *bishoprick*, (rather a large field for his labours,) was discovered near Darlington some years ago, and is now in the possession of Mrs. Todhunter, Harewood-hill. It is of the 14th century and reads (round the implements of the craft), "S[IGILLVM] RADVL[PHI] MARESCHAL [LI] D[E] L'EVECHIE D[E] DVREME." He was doubtless in a similar capacity here as the smith of Boldon Buke, who worked at the forge which, at Hatfield's survey the anti-monopolist tenants had got into their own hands, and L'EVECHIE is either an engraver's mistake for L'EVESQVE, or an evidence of a petty pride assimilating to that shown by our craftsmen "to the Queen" of the present day. The name of Marshall (akin to Smith, Faber, Farrer, Ferrar, &c,) has come to denote, not the primitive horse-shooer, but a governor or master of the horse, and eventually the highest military rank generally. The name ascended while the craft fell. A smith among the Britons was an ovate in the Bardic order, and a high personage among the Anglo-Saxons, and the progress of his descent in rank is curious. The smithery was evidently a feudal oppression, and we cannot feel surprised that the tenants of Darlington took it in the end into their own hands, as well as the mills, paying an annual rent. It seems clear from the way in which the ploughs of Little Haughton are mentioned in Boldon Buke (pp. 63, 65) that some of the agricultural implements were not private property, but lent out by the landlord from man to man. In every respect the episcopal surveys present most exact pictures of the mode of living before money-rents were fully introduced; which payments, as Mr. Surtees justly observes, coming in course of time to bear no proportion to the real value of the tenures, the modern wealthy farmer thus grew out of the ancient villain. As to the company of smiths, vide sub anno 1628.

|| There was a *Cecily le Barker* (probably Walter's mother) living at the same time, and

1302. After Beke's disgrace, he had to make peace with his vassals by the concession of several important privileges. One of them runs "And whereas no freeman ought by custom to be impleaded except in the free court of the bishop, yet the bishop's bailiffs compel them to be impleaded at the halemotes, and amerce them among villains, contrary to the common law of the realm ; The Bishop grants, that no freeman shall come unless he will come there to complain against a villain ; and if wrong is done him by any villain, and he will complain of it elsewhere, in the free court, a writ shall be granted him." He also granted that no carriage was to be taken, except in time of war, from the freemen, and that no sub-bailiff of the coroner should be mounted on horseback.*

The coroner of Darlington Ward was formerly chosen by the bishop, and was sometimes the bailiff and steward of Darlington also. There is a tale of *felo-de*-SEA connected with the coroneiship of George Ornsby, Esq., (1806-1816.) One Webster, a love-slighted swain, tossed his carcase into the Skerne, near Polam. The coroner being absent, old Attorney Arman reigned in his stead. The jury were about to return a verdict of *felo-de-se*, when one solid yeoman became alarmed at the deplorable ignorance of his compeers :—"*Nay, lads, nay, that wad nivver dee, everybody knew that he threw hi'sell int' t' Skeirne, folks wad all think us fules!*"

1311. Bishop Kellawe ordered that notice be given in Darlington church on Sundays and holydays that no person was to be molested in coming to the market and fairs which were of great usefulness.† It was a favourite mart of the religious houses.‡ There is

the name may either be a marital one or denote *the female tanner* who continued the business of her diseased spouse. Her daughter was *Alice Beeke;* and Walter *Bec*, perhaps the same as the Walter in the text granted land at Redmarshall to Adam the carpenter of Darlington. * Hutch. i. 248. † Kellawe's Reg.

‡ *Holy Island*. "1392-3. Expences of the Prior to the fair (*nundinas*) of Derlyngton." No cattle were sold by the priory this year to the mother house of Durham, and therefore the Prior's object must have been to lay in stock for the larder. Prior Aslakby, as his name implies, came from Aislaby, near Stockton, on the banks of the Tees. He would therefore meet his relations and friends at Darlington.—*Raine*.

Finchale Priory. In 1360-1, the cellarer was allowed his expenses at Derlington. In 1363, were paid "for the expenses of Sir John de Tykhill (the prior himself) going to Derlyngton fair, and 12 platters, 12 ditto to serve up meat in, and 12 saucers of copper, 1 brazen candlestick, with parchment bought, 18*s*.9*d*." Other journies to our fairs occur, and at that time Sir Ralph de Derlington was a brother. In 1458-9, the cellerar bought 21 twynters (cattle two winters old) here for 6*l*. 12*s*. 5*d*.

Durham Priory. In 1530-1, the Bursar's accounts contain items of "15 cows bought at Darnton by Americ Dande, the 21st of June, at different prices, together with the expences there, £7 13*s*. 6*d*.," and "2 cows bought at Darnton at 10*s*. 4*d*.,=20*s*. 8*d*. And expences at Hexham and Darnton, 3*s*. 8*d*. And expences at Darnton by Robert Best and comrade, 8*d*."

In 1531-2 are two items for driving cattle at Darnton, one on the fair after Whitsuntide, 6*d*., the other at Martinmas *(in die Martini)*, 9*d*.

In 1532-3 occur 18 cows bought at Darnton the fair after Whitsuntide by Americ Dande and comrade, 8*l*. 6*s*. 4*d*., and in 1533-4 at the same fair are bought by Americ Dande and Robert Best at Darnton, 31 cows, whereof 16 were at 10*s*. 8*d*. (8*l*. 10*s*. 8*d*.) and 15 at 10*s*. (7*l*. 10*s*)—16*l*. 0*s*. 8*d*. On the 23rd November in the same year Americ Dande bought 13 cows at Darnton at 12*s*. (7*l*. 16*s*.), his expenses there were 20*d*. He is styled "*Custos animalium*."

The times of holding fairs in these remote times has not altered.

Market and Fair Days.—Pay toll save where excepted.—Every Monday is a market-day ; also the day before Christmas-day. The first Monday in March, a show of horned cattle, sheep, &c. (pays no toll for cattle). Easter-Monday, for cattle and all goods and merchandize (pays no toll for cattle, save horses and pigs). Monday, before and after old May-day, a hiring day for servants. Whitsun-Monday [mentioned as a fair-day even by Harrison in 1577], for horned cattle, sheep, and all goods and merchandize. Great Monday, after Whitsuntide, which is always the Monday fortnight ; the same. Every Monday fortnight from Whitsun-Monday to Christmas is called a fortnight-day for horned cattle, sheep, &c. The 9th of November for horses, &c.; the 10th of November [Nought, i.e. Neat, Fair] for horned cattle, sheep, &c. ; the 13th of November for hogs and pigs. Monday, before and after old Martinmas-day, a hiring-day for servants. Nov. 22, Old Martinmas-day, for horned cattle, sheep, and all goods, &c. Great Monday, after Old Martinmas, which is always the Monday seven-night after Martinmas-day, except when Martinmas-day falls on a Monday, then Great-Monday fair will be that day fortnight, for horned cattle, and all other goods and merchandize. (From the Toll-table, by order of Chancery, in James Allan's time). Every Monday fortnight is now a "fortnight," or fair day.

a saying used as a gentle retort to one who is relating marvellously cheap purchases made at some distant fair :—" *Well, and what of that! I saw three stirks sell'd i'* DARNTON *market for five pounds a piece, as big as* CHURCHES ! "

1362. Margaret, wife of Robert de Orleyenes, died seized of a messuage and 15 acres, in Cockerton, held by the service of paying one penny farthing towards the reparation of the mill and the mill-cogs of Darlington mill, and one hen called a *wodehen* at the Nativity, leaving William her s. and h. (*Inq.* 17 *Hatf.*) See Hatfield's survey (p. 89) for wodsilver paid in hens.

Circa 1381. Died Alexander Surteys, chivaler, of Dinsdale, who according to the escheat after death (36 Hatfield) had enfeoffed trustees of a burgage and other small property at Darlington,* with Le Ryddin and Felling *in fraud and collusion*, to deprive the prince palatine of the wardship and marriage of the heir, an infant of twenty weeks'

* John de Murton (who had relinquished a paternal for a local name) gave lands in 1325 in *Murton on the Moor*, which he had by gift of his father William Surteys, to Ivo Bek of Derlyngtion. John was grand uncle to Goceline Surteys (younger brother of Sir Thomas Surteys of Dinsdale) who had (Inq. p m. 22 Hatfield) lands in Darlington and a host of other places of a very heterogeneous locality, which it is difficult to account for as possessions of a younger son except by supposing them purchases, indeed some at Nesham are expressly stated to be a mortgage. Dying *s. p.* these estates passed to his nephew Sir Thomas, the father of Alexander. Thomas Surtees dying childless in 1511, left a sister Catherine by the same mother and a brother Marmaduke by the same father but different mother, and although the latter was on every principle *of justice* the true heir, a barbarous *feudal* principle decreed that the most distant descendant of the whole blood might inherit before the nearest half blood. Marmaduke however was full of fire, tore the estates with the fangs of law, and forced the Places to assign him the manors of Over Middleton and Morton, &c.

This Marmaduke on one occasion beat a parson out and out. Some lands in Middleton-one-Rawe (of which Marmaduke is described as lord) had been granted by the family to his uncle John, who was incumbent of Dinsdale, for life and 20 years following, but after the lease had expired, the clergyman wished to consider it as part of the glebe. In 20 Eliz. John the only son of Marmaduke had a trial with the then parson about it, and John Hudson of Morton, grassman, aged 54, deposed that he was when " but a boy of a dozen or xiii years of age present at the buriall of John Sewerties [the parson] and then had a penny given him (the funeral dole)," that Marmaduke borrowing 10*s*. of Rowland Clerk (a succeeding parson) upon his signett, the latter within or about a month after requested to have his his money, when Marmaduke told him " that it was but a small thing that he the said Marmaduke had of him, and that therefore he thought that the said Rowland would not have bene so haistie with him. 'For,' quoth the said Marmaduke, 'if I would I could take the two oxganges of land which thoue occupiest here in this towne from the, which is a hundreth times better than than the money thow lent me.' 'Nay then,' quoth the said Rowland, 'that I thinck yow cannot do.' 'Yes,' quoth the said Marmaduke, 'that I can. But be thow good to me, and I will be good to thee.' 'Why, sir,' quoth the said Rowland, 'anything I have you shall comaunde.' 'And well then,' quoth the said Marmaduke, 'come hither to me againe such a day and I will show the good specialtie that the two oxganges is myne to do with what I list.' And so for that tyme the said Rowland departed." On their meeting the perplexed parson found that Surtees had right and had to compound for 4*l*. 10*s*. and the 10*s*. he had lent, for a life interest. He paid by instalments, and Archer another witness saw him come to Marmaduke at Darlington and say " Sir, now I have paide yow all my money according to our agrement, and therefore I pray yow now let me have assuraunce made for my life, that I be not any more troubled.' 'Marrie, parson,' quoth the said Marmaduke, 'that I will with good will. And come go with me to Mr. Hailes.' And so they went together to Mr. Hailes to have assuraunce made." At a later period, a parson of the adjoining parish of Middleton St. George was *cloked*. Wm. Killinghall, who held a moiety of the rectory, wanted Case the rector to join him in suing Francis Forster of Darlington for their joint tithes due from West Hartburn. The rector refused because by his daughter he had received at Darlington from Forster " 20*s*. *to buy a cloke*, 3 bushells of ry, and besides the said Francis Foster being a good friend unto him."—*Archives, R. H. A.*

The coheirs of Catharine Place, Blakiston, Brandling, and Wycliffe occur as burgesses, cotemporarily with some collateral Places (sans blood of Surtees) to whom they had alienated most of their mother's possessions in Dinsdale, &c. Sir Robert Brandling had no surviving issue by his heiress spouse, and her lands descended to his *coozen* William *the son of his brother* Thomas. This William was " born beyond the seas," and Sir Robert procured an act of *denesasion* for him. The knight had a younger brother Henry, who, in vain, attempted to set up some testamentary notes of Sir Robert *on papire* which he had been induced to make on " the unkynd dooings of William Branlynge, who was sodenly dep'ted into Flanders ;" as well as a forged settlement by him of the Darlington and other lands, which, after long suits, the Star Chamber on *violent presumpcions*, &c., decreed was forged. (*Star Chamber Record*, penes W.H.L.). William seems to have been a blustering, licentious man, from the Surtees Society's vol. of Ecclesiastical proceedings, pp. 72, 73.

22 First Ld. Alvanley _ 23. Shaw the Poet. 24. Cade the Antiquary. 1. 2. 3. Tokens of 17th Cent. _ Seals. 4. John de Derlyngton, Preb. of Lanchester 1380. 5. Grammar School before 1748. 6. Tho. Richborne 23 Hen. VI. 7. John Threlkeld of Denton 1433. 8. Used by various parties temp. Eliz. _ 9. John Middleton (IV) of Blackwell 1631 _ 10. Rob. Lambton of Stainton 1562. _ 11 12. Marg. and Alice Ellerker 1309. from York deeds. _ 13. Silver Coin, found on site of Prescott mans. at Blackwell. Autographs. 14. Tho. Blakiston Bailiff of Darlington 1669. _ 15. Emmerson the mathematician _ 16. G. Allan esq. of Blackwell Grange, d. 1744 _ 17. The Good Miss Allan _ 18. James Allan esq. father of 19. Allan the M.P. 20. Allan the Antiquary _ 21. Hutchinson the Historian.

This Plate is presented by

age, "the intention of the feoffment being that they should not disinherit the heir but that they should pay the debts of the said Alexander and should enfeoff the heir when he came to full age ;" a very virtuous disposition, as things *now* stand, in order to pay the dying man's debts and leave a little fund in friendly hands, to assist the heir somewhat beyond the strict allowance of a Court of Wards ; but *then* at the expense of the Bishop and his vested rights. Perhaps the Rydding (probably The Riding in Lanchester parish) paid the forfeit of the attempt, as it appears no more in the Surtees inquests.

1501. A most honest correspondence passed between Bishop Fox and Prior Castell. It seems that the system of farming the tolls, &c., of the boroughs, which from Boldon Buke appears to have been the plan adopted, even in the 12th cent , proved unsatisfactory, and that the usage of the dean and chapter confirming the appointment of bailiff has no remote origin. There is something extremely touching in the Prior's simple language.* "My especiallest good lord in my most humbly and due manner I recommend me unto your good lordship. And whereas your lordship wrote unto me lately for the confirmation of the bailiffwick of Derlyngton unto Wm. Betts ; my lord, there is one office passed afore unto master Hadoke of the office of Derlyngton ; and, my lord, I have made search within our records of the same office, and I can find no precedent thereof that ever your mitre was charged with any such fee. And, my lord, I have at your former commandment confirmed your grant both of Gatesheved and Aukland, whereas I can not perceive that ever any such grants was made aforetime, either by your records or ours. My lord, I am right well content to perform your commandment or pleasure in every behalf to the uttermost of my power, and yet, my lord, please it your good lordship to call unto your remembrance what your lordship would lay and say unto me, in case like, if I should charge your mitre with such fee as never was afore in your records nor in ours. Your lordship might be miscontent with all. My lord, how your successor will lay such matter unto my brethren's charge and mine, my lord, I know not ; but aye, my lord, I doubt the worst. And, my lord, secular people will say, that and if your bedemen, my brethren and I, confirm office or thing that your lordship or your successors is most content with ilk, then, my lord, the party will say that they will *assh* their fee of me and of my brethren, which is against all right and good conscience. My lord, I beseech your lordship to take with me no displeasure, *thof* I show your lordship my poor mind ; for, my lord, in time of need or cause of complaint, I have none other comfort of refuge and counsel but only in your good lordship. And I beseech the same so to use me and take me, and ever, my lord, to shew your good mind and lordship that will help in trouble or business in time of need. And thus to the blessed Trinity's keeping I ever commend your good lordship. From Duresme, the 14 day of August, with the hand of your humblest chaplain and orator, THOMAS PRIOUR OF DURESME "

The Bishop answers :—"Right entirely well beloved brother, as heartily as I can I commend me to you : and well I remember, that amongst other, I wrote unto you for the confirmation of Wm. Betts' patent of the bailiffwick of Derlyngton ; and by your last writing unto me I conceive ye make a difficulty therein for two causes ; one is that my servant Tho. Haidok hath one office of Dernton ; the second is that ye can not in your register find any grants of the said office with such a fee. Truth it is, Tho. Haidok hath a grant, but that is of the custody of the manor and not of the bailiffwick ; and where the boroughs have been commonly and for the most party before my time letten to farm, which was the occasion of evil justice and much extortion *et* hindrance of the lord's profits both at Derlyngton, Auckland, and Gateshead, I have in my time caused all the said boroughs to be occupied by way of approvement, and so I have granted this office of Derlyngton to Wm. Betts by way of improvement, which I make you sure hath been to me, and shall be to my successors, much more profitable than to let or put them to farm. Doubt you not, brother, I shall no thing desire you to do that

* The original orthography may be seen in the appendix to the Three Historians.—Surtees Soc.

shall be hurt or prejudice to the mitre of that my church, and therefore eftsoons I pray you, as heartily as I can, let the said William have my said grant of the office of Derlington confirmed - - - And thus heartily fare ye right, as I would do myself. At Richemount, the sixth day of Septembre, with the hand of your loving brother, RI. DURESME."

The prior, I presume, consented, as in 1514 Bishop Ruthall desires him to confirm unto his servants "Richard Waldgrave* th' office of baily of Derlyngton and Thomas Banks the crownership of Norton," which he did. In 1516, Ruthall's auditor delivered to the gaoler of Durham Castle the bodies of the collectors of Coundon and Redworth, Ric. Perkynson coroner of Derlyngton ward, and Thomas T . . . . bailiff of D . . . . . to be kept and subsist out of their own proper goods according to the statute, for their arrears due to the bishop on their Michaelmas accounts.

1511, Mar. 24. John Bulman, of Blakwell, begged sanctuary at Durham Cathedral, having in the house of one William Bulman, at Ripon, 13 *years before*, feloniously struck one N. Walley with a dagger in the breast *super le wythbone*, of which within two days he died.†

1526, July 30. Robert Holme, late of Darneton, co. Dunelm, pewterer, came to the sanctuary of St. John of Beverley for a debt only. And he was admitted and sworn. The men of the bishoprick often seem to have considered themselves safer at Beverley than under St. Cuthbert's privileges at Durham, and *vice versa.*

1558, Aug. 16. Will. of "Laurence Thornell baylyf of Darlington : my soule to Almyghtie God my maker and redemer and to our blessed ladye, &c. : to be buried in the churche yarde of Darlington at the Quere end : Francys Perkinson, 40*s.* ; and to Bryan P., Richarde P., and Dorathee P. everye of them 6*l.*, besydes theyre chyldes porc'ons [step-children] : Rychard Thornell my bastarde sonne 10*l.* : Sir Robert Wykinson [an unnoticed incumbent ?] 10*s.* : the heyghe alter 3*s.* 4*d.* : churcheworkes 20*s.* : every one of my men servaunttes at Darlington a lyveray coote and 5*s.* : my women servaunttes at D. an ewe or the price of an ewe : Marmaduke Fayrbarne and Mr. Halle and Wm. Tomson [p. 200], eyche 3*s.* 4*d.* : residue to Barbara my wyfe : Mr Henry Ducket my brother in lawe : brethren Nycholas T. and John T. : Francis Perkinson my wyfes sonne." A demise occurs, 4 Edw. VI. to Lawrence Thornell gent. of the Low Parke of Darlington and the Medowes on the Skerne. In Hartlepool chancel is a brazen effigy of a lady dressed in an open gown disclosing a richly embroidered petticoat, and most gallantly decked out with the hoop, ruff, hat and slashes of the period in which the maiden Queen held sway. A scroll from her mouth displays CASTA FIDES VICTRIX, and beneath is her name displayed. HERE VNDER THIS STONE LYETH BVRYED THE BODIE OF THE VERTVOVS GENTELLWOMAN IANE BELL, WHO DEP'TED TH'S LYFE THE vi DAYE OF IANVARIE, 1593, BEINGE THE DOWGHTER OF LAVERANCE THORNELL OF DARLINGTON. GENT. AND LATE WYFE TO PARSAVEL BELL NOWE MAIRE OF THIS TOWEN OF HARTINPOOELL MARCHANT. ÆTATIS SVÆ 40.

Whos vertues if thou wilt beholde
Peruse this tabel hanginge bye
Which will the same to the vnfold
by her good lyfe learne thou to die.

Arms. In a lozenge, Gules, 2 bars gemelles and a chief argent, on the latter a martlet for difference.—*Thornell* (of Yorkshire).‡

* In 1528-9 Wolsey appointed Wm. Wytham on Waldegrave's resignation.

† Sanct. Dunel. Sur. Soc.

‡ 44 Eliz. Thomas Singleton, D.D., and the scholars of King's Hall and College of Brasenose, Oxford, *v.* Percivall Bell.—Disputed claim to copyhold and freehold lands, viz. : Sadbury demesnes ; Darlington otherwise Darnton Court ; co. Durham.—*Catalogue of Pleadings in the duchy of Lancaster.*

1560, July 23. Will* of Richard Somersett of Oxnelfeyld : my brother Foreman 5*l*: and my buffe ledder coote : George Herrison my satten dublett : wife Margarett Somersett two of my best kyen.

1564. Michell Spence, of Derlinton, to my daughters Isabell, Barbara, Jayn and Cecill and to every of them 40 shepe, that is to saye 20 ewes and hoggs [sheep in their first year]: to Alyce Pacoke one hawket whye wiche I bought of my brother Willm. at Bedall and one ewe : Mr. Myghell Wandisforde and Mr. Bryane Palmes supervisors.

1565, Mar. 5. Will of Maude Wilson, of Darton. "I will that there be bestowed att my bringing forth 5*s*. : to my brother [in law] John Laynge and [my sister Agnes] his wife for the paynes that they have taken with me *or els I had died in the streats* one brasse potte the which my brother Xpofor Cottes and my sister [*Jennett*] his wife have in keapinge. Also the sayd Xpofor Cottes my brother in lawe hayth of myne in custodye and keaping 24*s*. 8*d*. the which I will shall be distributed as is above written [in small legacies]: to my curate Sir John Claxton 12*d*." A Christopher Cottes made his will 11 June, 1568. "Xpofor Cotts of Oxneldefelde, seke in body but holle of mynde : yf it shall please [God] for to tacke me unto his marcye at this present tyme I will that my body be buried in the Southe croft yle of the church with my mortuary dewe by the lawe : unto the poore mens boxe 12*d*. : unto church works 12*d*. : sonne Georg one quye of iijre yeares olde in full contentacion of his filiall porcion : sonne Nycholes one whyt reged cowe with one plaitt cotte : Jane Wate my dowghter one quye calfe, in full recompense of hir chylds porcion : sonne John one playt cotte one sword one dager one bukler one blacke spere one graye coulte stagg of iijre yeres owld : wyfe *Elizabeth* and dowghter Elizabeth all my houshold stufe : Xpofor Cots my god sone one quye caulfe : Xpofor Wate my good soune one gymmer : if anye of these named doith swarve and will not agre they shalbe utterley excluded and have nether part nor parsell of my goods but for to a byde the order of Lawrens Horseman Thomas Watson whom I do mack supervisors." (Lyen Tompson clerke, a witness).

1567. Mathew *Bland* of Darton : Esable *Gybson* my wife : To Sir John Clapham 12*d*. *to pray for me* [this was in Elizabeth's reign] : to the pore folks one bowll of wheat to be distrybuted in bread the day of my buriall (Anth. Coyngeres a witness). Mr. Edw. Parkinson owes me for wolle 13*s*. 4*d*. Mrs. Parkinson owes me in money that I did len her 20*s*. For meat and drynk the tyme that he [testator] laid and the day of his buriall 8*s*. 7*d*

1567. Cuth. Marshall, of Cockerton, to the heghe allter for my forgottin tythes 12*d*.: I will that al maner of arlowmes [heir-looms] the which my father left at his house remayne to Wm. my sonn that is to say, 1 stepe led [to steep the malt in] and one bruyne [brewing] lede, i. mask fatt and one wort stone and a flesh trowe, a brasing morter, a pestell, a great arke in the whet barne, and another in the chamber and a grett chist.

1568. Chr. Addison, of Darnton.—Inventory p. m. states his funeral expenses as 4*s*. and "for bred and drink and other vittalls to the [four] prasers 12*d*."

1569. Edw. Atkinson, of Darnton [lessee of the mills], to be buried in the churche earthe of D. : owing to me ; Sir John Clapon, to be paid of great Monday next 33*s*. 4*d*.. For bringing forth my husband 40*s*. : one cote of plaite, &c., 40*s*.

1570, Apr. 19. An inventorie of the goods and cattails off Cristopher Dayll† lait disseasied of the parisshe off Darlington, *inholder*.—*In the Hall :* Two silver peces weing

Thornell bur. 5 Sep. ; the wife of John Thornell 21 Sep., 1597 [both of plague]. *Chrisostome* Thornell and Margery Thaddie, m. 1 Jun., 1615. Cuthbert Thornell, gent., of Darlington, bur. Sep. 1615. *Darlington.*—Thos. s. Paterick Thornhill, of Darlington parish, bp. 23 Oct., 1642.—*Bp. Wearmouth.*

* The extracts from wills and inventories are given to illustrate costumes, manners, and rustic wealth. If any great and familiar names occur, they are noticed ; but for genealogical purposes the original documents must be searched.

† 29 Dec., 1570. Jenet Daill of Archdeacon Newton wedowe; to be buried in the parish churchyard of Darlinton ; Anthony Dale [a name in the Dales of Staindrop] my sonne the hole lease of my fermhold wherin I nowe dwell, James Dale his sonne, and his daughters ; Margaret Dale ; Alleson Stainsby my best gowne (to these two was left her household stuff) ; Chr. Stainsby five nobles that he doth owe me for a horse that I sold him ; his wife

16 unces at 4*s.* 4*d.* the ounce, 3*l.* 9*s.* 4*d.* : eight silver spoinnes 32*s.* : twelve pair of lyn sheits, four paire off harden sheits, twelve codwares 40*s.* : two cubbords, a long table, a counter, two formes, a longe settell, three old chares, 16*s.* : six puter platters, three latten bassons, a litle puter basyng, six latton candellsticks and ten old puter potts, 13*s.* 4*d.* : an iron chymnaye, a pairr of tongs, a por and a fyre shovell 10*s.* : summa 9*l.* 8*d.*—*The Parlour above the Hall:* One long table, one forme, one chare, one litle round table, a litle open cubard, 6*s.* 8*d.* : two standyng beddes, a trindell bed, furnished with bed and bolster, 40*s.* : a litle iron chymnay, a bason and ane ewer 2*s.* : putter candelsticks, three quysshons 7*s.*—*The Chamber over the Hall:* Two standyng beddes furnisshed with fether bedd and bolster and other furniture thereto belonging, two litle counters, one forme, 40*s.*—*The Newe Chamber:* Three standing bedes furnished, one trindell bed furnished, a litle table, a carpet, 26*s.* 8*d.*—*The Littell Chamber:* Two beddes furnished for men-servants, ane old chaire, a litle table, 10*s.*—*The loft benethe the doores:* Two beddes furnyshed for women servants 10*s.*—*The Buttrie:* One presse, two chists, one bord, a bread grate, 10*s.* : twenty peces of puter, ten sawcers, twelve puter plates, a litle brasen morter, 26*s.* 8*d.*—*The Kychen:* A capon cawell, two bords, 20*d.* : potthookes, a pair of cob yrons, two dripping pannes, three speets, 6*s.* 8*d.* : two cawdrons, six brasse potts, four pannes, 40*s.* : four tobes, a brewing lead, a masfat, a troughe stone, a latin laver, 26*s.* 8*d.* —*The Stable:* Haie one lode 6*s.* 8*d.* : six oxen, two kie, one horsse, 7*l.* : corne in the feild 10*l.* : one iron bound wayn, on long wayne, four yokes, two teames, one plowe and the plowe gere* belongynge, 40s.—sum of the goods 49*l.* 19*s.* 4*d.*

1570. An action was brought in the Durham Ecclesiastical Court by Isabella Walker against William Walker of Durham for restitution of conjugal rights. Thomas Whitfeilde of Durham, draper, said, "that as towchinge hir, the said Isabella Walker crowelness, or secking of his (William's) death, he knoweth nothing. Mary, he thinkith the said Isabell dyd not use hir selfe honestly to William Walker, hir husband, for, as it was commonly reportyd emongest hir neighbours, she went twyse frome hir husband, once in this towne, being then baliffe, and one other tyme to *Darlington.* And at hir going to Darlington she had hir husband s licenc to fett *money that she had borrowed of dyvers;* but one John Peirson, that caried hir thither, *culde not bring hir home with hym.* And yett afterward, at her home comyng, the said William Walker, by intrety of neighbours, was content to take hir again. He cannott tell for what cause she came into the contree. He thinks that William Walker is more lyke to bett Isabell his wyf, than she the said William." The fact was that when Isabell again left Walker, he took the matter very philosophically, and calmly married another woman, and altogether seems to have been an odd character. He was rather aged, but a witness thinks him "sufficiently able to curry [ruyll *interlined*] the said Isabell yf she were with hym."

1572. John Hope of Darnton, if we may judge from his inventory, might have carried his whole estate on his back. It only contains:—One dagger, 12*d.*; two Jerkins, 16*d.*; thre sherts, 12*d.*; one dublett, ij pare of hose, 2*s.*

1572. Nov. 19. Will of John Frankeleyne of Coken [and Archdeacon Newton] gent. He appears to have belonged to the Yorkshire family of Frankland, and mentions York kindred. He was third husband of Isabel, widow of Ralph Carr, of Cocken, esq. After a long and singular religious preamble he proceeds:—" My bodye as it most vyle Dunge slyme and earthe and by god creatid and made of the same, unto therthe therefore I will gyve and bequeath it agayne theire to remayne to the last daye wherin God by his potencyall power shall reigne in his glory as a most victorious conqueroure and as a most righteous juge shall geve sentence upon all humayne fleshe that ever were or

and children; Tho. Simpson's wife, Sissely her daughter a gret broad panne and every of her children besid, an ewe; Agnes Dobson my sister, a kerchif, a vaill, a smock, an apron, and all my workday rayment; Jenet Dobson a kerchif of my best lyne; the poure people of Darlington 20*d.*, and to my curate for his paines 2*s.*, and to the clarke 12*d.*

* A word used in all materials—woodgeare, waingere, &c.—the furniture of any thing.

shalbe from the begynnynge to the endynge ; and my goods lyke as I have by Gods highe provydence and goodness received of the worlde even so by Gods grace I will leave them to the worlde agayne, utterlye relynquysshynge and forsakynge the same for ever : My derelye belovyd wife Issabell Frankeleyne my parte of Archdeacon Newton which I presentlye do and hertofore have had and occupied durynge her lyf : after her death my brother Thomas Frankeleyn th' one halfe of the same duryinge my lease provyded that the said Thomas shall durynge the lease fynde his brother Harry Frankeleyn* a sufficient house to dwell in, the pasturage of two kye, and x shepe pastures wynter and somer, in suche sorte as he dothe fynde his owne without any rent, and gyve to the saide Harrye every weke durynge the lease one pecke of wheat and one pecke of masclechon [wheat and rye mixed]: to the said Harye two good mylk kye and ten good ewes : to my [brother] Thomas frankeleyne two drynkynge potts of sylver which was my uncles the dean of Wyndesore [William Frankling, dean from 1536 to 1553], my wyf to have the custodye of the same durynge her lyfe yf she please and then my brother Thomas. And th' other half of Archedecon Newton shalbe had by suche as my wyf shall apoynt it to as my promyse was as maye apeare by wryttyngs made betwene her and hyr childer and me: concernynge the two fermeholds that ar nowe in the tenure of Cuthbert Sotheron and Anthonye Dayle by lease, when these leases be expyred yf this wretched and wicked worlde do so longe contynew thaye or ther sequyles shall have the same agayne for reasonable *gressoms* [earnest money or fine on renewal] paynge to my said brother and his assignes for th' one half, and to the assignes of my said wif for th' other half, for one and twentye yeares a newe, and not to take above fortie marks for a fermholde, as they will answere at the great and terrible daye of Judgement for the contrary doynge : My brother Thomas and his assignes shall every yeare durynge my lease gyve in *Darnton Churche*, 20*s*. ; that is to say, the sondaye next before Christmas 5*s*., upon every Goode Frydaye 5*s*. upon the natyvyte of John baptyst comonlie called mydsommerdaye 5*s*., and upon Myghelmas daye other 5*s*., as he will answere at the dreadfull daye of Judgement ; And the same shalbe geven by th' advise counsell and knowleage of the Vickar or Curate the foure churche wardens and other substancyall of the parishe : Also I will desyre my wif upon Gods behalf and in the waye of charite that she will take order with those her childer that she shall leave the other half unto that they shall gyve other xx*s*. every yeare dureynge my lease : my cosyn Mr. Richard Frankeleyne of Yorke : my brother Thomas one rynge of golde with the letters of my name : my derelye beloved wif even upon Gods behalf to remembre Bartye Andersonne sonne of Mr. Bartyrem Anderson [of Neucastell] with some honest token, whensoever yt shall please God to take her to his mercye, bycause he was the nestlynge of all her doughters childre :—to Mr. Thomas Calverley and Issabell his wif two old angells and to my gods sonne xx*s*. to by hym books : cosyn frankeleyn of Amerston : to Mr. Barnarde Gylpyn p'son of Houghton one old angell [mentions before having previously given forti shyllyngs yerely to Master Gylpyns scole out of Cocken]: And because I will make all thyngs as playne as I canne so that nothinge be done vaynleye and that no blayme be laid to my wif for doynge les than some wolde thynke should be done for me I will and upon Gods behalf do charge and commande that no funerall pompe be done abowt my corpes at the tyme of my bureyall but that the same be laid in the churche or churche yeard whether they seme good without stone or anye other thynge vpon the same : but by cause my said wif haithe many frends childer and kynsfolks which peraventure wolde murmure yf nothynge were done for me I will therefore that my wif shall make a dynner for them and others such as she shall seme good to have, so that the poore in anye wise be not foregotten amonge which hir frends and myne which shall come to my buryall."

1575 or 1576. Margaree Wormeley sued Edmund Hodgson† of Cockerton, husband-

* Henry Franckland, gent., of Archdeacon Newton, bur. 1603.—John Franckland of Archdeacon Newton, bur. 6 Mar. 1607-8.

† The Hodgsons long swung between gentry and yeomanry at Fieldhouse, now the Nun-

man, aged about 40, for breach of promise of marriage, in the Ecclesiastical Court of Durham. He answered that about Michaelmas two years past, he being free from all former contracts had communication with her of marriage, on the backside of Thomas Hodgson's house at Darlington, before certain friends, viz., Thomas Hodgson, Richard Daniell, and Margerie's mother, but whether she was then free from all former contracts he did not know, for she was then in name with one Fra. Castell, Mr. Clarves (Clervaux's) man. There were never any tokens given between them, " no, not so moch as a handkeircher. Marye, this examinate gave the said Margarye an olde grote, upon frenshipe, but as no token." About a month after the communication, he, having newly set up husbandry, had an ox that *torfled* [had a dislocated joint], and upon " the friendship of said communication," he went to Croft to Margerie's father, and " made his moone" [moan] unto him to have some help. The father answered that he could not help him, and then Edward *required* the old man to borrow him sufficient money to buy an ox, who replied that he would not, he was not used to borrow any. The damsel was then moved with compassion and said, " Edmund Hodson, I am sory that my father will not help you, and yett I knowe he haith yt to helpe you ; never the less, for the good will that haith bein bitwex you and me, *I* will lend you 20*s*. unto Pentecost next, to help you to an ox." That sum he had not repaid. This savours of love, but the recreant added that his inamorata ever made small account of any communication that had been between them, and when he had charged her therewith, she said, " Take as good heid to your self as ye can ; I mynd to be *tytter* (sooner) provided for then ye wote, and will take both plight and perell of any thinge you can chard (charge) me withall."

1577. Jan. 11. There were " Articles concluded and agreed upon by the Burgesses and commonalitie of the Burrough Towne of Darlington to be observed and keept for the maintenance of the occupation of Cordwainyers and to continue from time to time for ever." None of the occupation were to take any *prentisse* under the term of seven years nor have above two apprentices at one time. Apprenticeships to be entered in the Register book, on a fee to the register of 6*d*. Any person of the occupation might set up on payment of a reasonable fine (part to the Bailiff of the town, and part to the maintenance of the occupation) and making a dinner according to his ability for the Masters of the occupation ; but any apprentice within the borough and town of Darlington should only make a dinner of a reasonable price to the wardens and masters of the whole occupation, and pay 12*d*. to the wardens, and the like to the registers. All of the occupation to assemble at nine of the clock before noon on 25th Oct., yearly, in the Tollbooth, and appoint amongst the said occupation and *fellowshipp* two wardens, who for the year might search all wares made by any of the occupation, and call a meeting of its members at any time at the Tollbooth. And if any misused the wardens in word or deed *the Head officer Mr. Bayliffe of the Burrough* should send his officers for the party and *commit him to Ward to have punishment according to his deserts*. None to offer any wares on Market-day in the market before the time appointed by the Jury of the Burrough, except on Christmas Even and Whitsunn Even when they might do so at all times ; nor dress any wares upon any Tollbooth days openly or secretly ; nor procure *inticke* (entice) and take any other man's servant to work except he be licenced first with the master he was hired withall. Every journeyman and hired man to pay 2*d*., yearly, to the wardens. And it was further ordained by the wardens and whole company of the trade that [and] *the currier for the time being*, whosoever should absent or

nery. Edmund could only sign by mark, and seems to have been of another branch.

13 June, 1560. Edmund Hodgeson of Derlingtone, merchaunt ; to be buried in the parishe church of Darlington so nighe the corps of my wyffe as maye be ; John Claxton of Hurworth my sonne in lawe ; doughter Eliz. Claxton ; to the right worshipfull Mr. Sergiant Menell my speciall good freind one olde ryall ; to the reparacons of the heigh waies of this towne 4*l*., and to the poore people that shal be at my buriall fower marke ; I forgyve my kynswoman Thomas Wardes wyffe all suche debts as she owith unto me to thintend she shall the better bring up hir childrein ; to every one of Marmaduke Fairbarnes childrein which is in numbre ix that he haith nowe with *this* wyff [how many was he to have by the next ?] Hewe Macames doughter 6*s*. 8*d*.

prolong himself by going abroad to work with any foreigners or have any foreign workman, without special licence of the wardens, should forfeit 6*s*. 8*d*.

These articles were confirmed at a free dinner by the Cordwainers and *a currier* in 1698, and again by all the Cordwainers and *one currier* in 1710, Richard Hilton and Math. Lamb respectively signing as Bailiffs. In 1737 it was agreed that all fees, fines, &c., should be added to the Company's stock instead of being paid to the Bailiff or Wardens own proper use, and that in disputes the Bailiff should have the casting vote.—In 1745, the Tanners promised to pay certain sums to the wardens or market-searchers and sealers of leather for the town and borough, for the providing a dinner for the Company of Cordwainers, and this seems to have been their annual custom till 1766. The stock of the Company was lent to its members in succession, and none were to transfer their right to it. In 1761, *three* apprentices were allowed to each member, and none were to employ any workmen or journeymen who should take any apprentices except the sons of such journeymen.*

1586. On a view of the Milldam, under an Episcopal commission, the boundary of Jennet Hodgshon's close is recognised. There was to be a bridge over the dam for carts, &c., at the North end of Norgate in the place accustomed, for the ease of the people, the landstaith whereof to be four yards wide, at the expence of the Bondgate tenants; the dam was to be cleansed of *willowes* and rubbish; Cuthbert Storie was to restore all stones and planks which he had taken from the said bridge, and no *webbs of cloath* were to be laid on the banks of the dam or nigh the same by seven yards.† Until 1757, when the Cockerton copyholders purchased freedom from such a service, the dam from the Mill holme‡ to the Mill was repaired by them, and "from Jennett Hodgson's hedge *where a stone is fixed in Cockerell Holme*" to the Mill Race Head by certain Bondgate copyholders, "from the said hedge to the Mill Holme." In 176 . . Rd. Stamper erected a new Leather Mill adjoining the Corn Mill, and the copyholders refused further payment, they being only liable to repair for the corn mill. In all leases of the Darlington and Blackwell Mills,§ the words "suke (or sock) and sucking" occur, meaning an absolute power of compelling both burgesses and copyholders of Darlington, Cockerton, and Blackwell to grind there.|| In 1650 Cuthbert Gray, occupier of Blackwell Milne, was ordered at the Halmot Court "to take upp the false clowe soe that the ouer flowing of water be taken away and soe as Will'm Corneforth be nott thereby damnifyed in his meadowe in not kepeing upp the said false clowe;" and Richard Johnson, a dyer who had newly set up a dyehouse near Darlington mill, to remove the rubbish near the said mills and make a descent for the water that came from his dyehouse, so that the water should be in no way noisome to the said mills.¶ After passing as leaseholds through

* Copies of original articles "sewed on a long screed of parchment" with the subsequent memoranda, admissions, &c.—penes R. H. A. † Mill papers penes R. H. Allan, esq.

‡ "1621, A paine of George Metcalfe of 10*s*. that he shall poule downe the howse wall in the mill home betwixt and lames next."—*Borough Bks.*

§ When the Darlington mill was enlarged in 181..., the labourers found, 8 feet below the surface, a portion of a pavement, a horse-shoe, and a spur with a large copper rowell.

|| On 3 Sep., 21 Jac. there was a Durham Chancery decree against Simon Jefford (p. 132), and in 1634 against Chr. Pyborne, an innkeeper and burgess of Darlington; the first for erecting a Horse Milne in his burgage, the last for grinding at Haughton Milne, another ancient episcopal mill, which he had farmed. There seems an oppressive monopoly in the nonsufferance of a man grinding his own grain in his own mill, but both defendants had been hawking for and obtaining malt, &c., to grind from other people, and thus disabling the farmers of the soke from paying their rent of 22*l*. for the *two* watermills at Darlington and that at Blackwell. *The* Horse-Mill *par eminence*, was *ultra Skerne*, in Clay Row, adjoining the Hermitage. It was demolished before 1760 and a shop erected on its site. In 1618 it is described as "a *house* called le Horsemill," and in 1713 "Darlington Horse-mill house." It was probably the scene of Gifford's discomfiture, as in 1683 it was occupied by more tenants than one, whom Mr. Lassells was ordered by the burgesses to *avoyde* or turn out.

¶ The new mill, built by John Kendrew in 1780, by a *Wear* across the mill-race threw much backwater on the old mill, and in 1803 an arbitrator decided that Mr. Jonathan Backhouse should carry away part of the Head or Wear, so as to leave the sole of the wheel case three inches above the water on the cessation of the wheel's motion.

many hands,* Darlington mills were enfranchised to Joseph and Edward Pease in 1829, and, being applied to manufacturing purposes, the soke is extinct. Blackwell Mill is still used for corn ; it is enfranchised, and the soke here also is lost, the mill having been at one time used for a manufacture.†

1587. Jane Nicholson of D. wedow, late wife of Cuthbert N. of D.: "to be buryed in good and christian manner: daughter Annes Dossy all my cotes except my wedding cote which I geve to Isabell Dossy daughter of Thomas Dossy and one red cote to my sister Margarett Wilkinson."

1587. Richard Glover of D., yeoman, by will mentions only one son Peter (see p. 150), and in the inventory p. m. 1587-8, are contained " 5 puder chargers, 20*s*.: 48 other puder dishes, 3*l*.: 28 salters and 8 pottingers, 13*s*. 4*d*.: 9 salts, 5*s*.: a paire of [chess ?] tables, 20*d*.: 18 chesses, 13*s*. 4*d*.: 20 salt fiches, 10*s*.:" 25 pair of sheets, 7 pair of blankets, 8 other blankets and 22 coverings or coverlets are enumerated.

1588. July 6. Died, Allison Chambers of Blackwell, a person of good discretion, who before her brother John was married, used to market for him, and take charge of his house as the *howswyff*. For divers days before her death, "she spoke somewhat idly and vainly by reason of the extremity of her sickness, and when asked by the folk that cam in how she did, she would answer somewhat vainly." Some of her neighbours asked her to whom she would give her goods, and whether she would give anything to her brother Leonard and sister Elizabeth Chambers, and she said that some time they should have somewhat. The sick woman was lying in the *foore house* or *hall howse* in John's house (being the general day room of the family), and on the day before she died, she sat up in her bed, where she lay by the fire side with her clothes on, and said to Henry Staveley, a labourer who had come in, (being of perfect mind and memory and of her own mind without any question asked), "Henrie, where is my brother John Chambers ?" John's wife Elizabeth and he answered that he was away in the field, and could not be gotten. Then she said, "I feele myself not right ; and if he cannot be gott, I pray you all [there being more than one neighbour present with Elizabeth, the good-wife of the house] to beare witness of my will, that their be no *comber* betwixt my brethren. I will *that I be honestlie brought forth like an honest man's barne*, and be laid in Darnton Church, as near besids my father as conveniently may be, and I'll give unto the poore of Darneton parish 20*s*. ; and all the rest of my goods I give to my brother John Chambers, and I make him executour of all." Then the said Elizabeth, being at that time about some occasions of her own in the chamber nigh the hall, said, "Lalle [diminutive of Allison], now, seing thou art so disposed to make thy will, thou might do well to sett in thy sister and brother as well as my husband ;" to which the sick woman answered that she would give them nothing, but give all to her brother John. And Henry Staveley asked her what she would give to him, and she said, "yea, marry, what gives thou me ? I will geve the nought, for thou never gave me any thinge."‡ She was of perfect memory at that time, and all the week before, save that sometimes by extremity of sickness, she would speak idle words.§

* Rd. Stamper in 1780 let "the Bishop's mill," the Mill Holme and the use of the grindstone adjoining the water wheel of the *Bark* Mill adjoining the Corn Mill, which was for grinding corn and malt and *sheeling* of oats. He sold his corn mill, *leather* mill and *bark* mill to Joseph Pease for 890*l*. the next year.

† The Moulter was 1-16th if the corn was conveyed by the miller, 1-32nd if by the owner. A boll of corn at Darlington is two bushells.

‡ Contrasts please. "Md. That Bryane Gule lait of Blackwell within the parishe of Darneton about the second or thirde weeke in lent last past then beinge sicke Butt of perfect mynde and memorie and being asked by one Thomas Addie to whome he would give his goods if he died the said Bryane answered and said That he would give all his goods if it weare more to Mrs. Garnett and Mr. Garnett meaning Mr. Bartholomew Garnett [lord of Blackwell Freehold Manor] and his wiffe and said *it was all to litle for them, for they had bene his and his wives succor in ther sicknes*: and about one or two dayes after he died then being present the said Thomas Addie nowe dead, Willin Wild, Thomas Kendall, Elizabethe Lyne and others.—Proved June 25, 1597.

§ Ecclesiastical Proc. Sur. Soc. 330. The testatrix was daughter of Stephen Chamber, yeoman, of Blackwell, who made his will 15 Oct., 1587, "to be buried on the North side of

1591. A postmaster occurs in Darlington, and in 1596 the *postshippe* is conveyed by deed (see p. 150). Such an ancient functionary attended to the forwarding of letters inscribed "Haste, haste, post haste!" and furnished horses which persons might ride till they dropped, as one of Sir Robert Carey's did when he rode the first to salute James I. as king. But no regular post at stated intervals was established till 1635, when a running post from London to Edinburgh was ordered. A letter from London to Glasgow before 1788 was five days on the road. The bags were carried by boys on horseback to the great profit of the highwayman.* The total want of safety in this system caused the first mail coach to leave London for Bristol in 1784. In 1841 the opening of the railway between Darlington and York effected a wondrous saving of time, and in 1847 the last mail coach from the North arrived in Newcastle decorated with a flag surmounted with crape.

1603. Wm. Thompson of this parish possessed at his death "on butterkette and sext stone of salt butter in it, 23*s*."†

1602. Mathewe Lambart‡ of Darnton, cordiner, "to be buried in the parish church of Darlington: to the mending of the carsaie going to the Armytage, 5*s*.: one brasse pott that was my fathers." Inventory mentions "the Hawle house, the buttrie, the East parlor, the shopp, the chamber, the West chamber, the kitchin, the stable."

1612. The Borough Books commence. The descriptions of debts in the borough Court are often interesting as showing ancient prices, e. g. "1612. For carriage of thre hors loads of fish to barn'dcastle, 3*s*.: Four lambs and flaxe, 15*s*.: Hire for malt making, 30*s*.: For losing of certaine work tooles, an each, a hand saw, a womble, a chezell, a persell bitt, with other things, 10*s*. - - - 1613, For detayning of a pare of scales for weighing of scpe to the value of 16*d*.: do. of a frame and iron spindles to the value of 3*s*. 4*d*.: For 140 loads of dunge, a waine stedd and plough stedd, and oxen stalls and longe setles with two window leaves, 39*s*. 11*d*.: William Boyes *v*. Margaret Welsh 25*s*. for rent for 4 years and for a *paire of bodies*,§ and for meat and drincke at severall times in the meane time - - - 1614, Cross action, same parties, 7*s*. 3*d*. for a waustcote of fustaine and wine and sugar and the makinge of a band and for sewing of a paire of sheets: For a loade of lyme 20*d*., and the laying it on 12*d*.: For one hogg sheep *which was found sturdie*, 4*s*. 6*d*.: In trespass, for dung, a ladder, a sadle, &c., and maungers and skeel, a shovell and halters, with a litle iron forke, damage 21*s*. - - - 1615, For a yard of linnen, 16*d*.: For want of five dozen cutts of yarne, damage 4*s*. 9*d*.: For unjust detention of xix'ene bords, three bowlls, a maze,|| and another mase, 26*s*. 9*d*.: Henry Oswold *v*. Tho. Rewe [an afferor] for a iron pynne and a stowpe of wood imployed

the font within the church of D.: sonne John a blacke stagge [young horse] with a whyte bridle starre in the forehead, &c.: toward the repairinge of Blackwell brige when the work goeth forward, 3*s*. 4*d*.: Hellenor Tod my wives daughter 20*s*. conditionaly that she shall not be hurtfull to my sayed children and if she be she shall have no part of the same: I forgive John Middleton the five nobles wich he oweth." The inventory was made only four days afterwards, on the 19th.

* 1763. John Boys Postmaster amerced 1*s*. 6*d*. for suffering his packett coart to stand in the wend or street leading from the Markett place into Skinnergate.—*Borough Records*.

1767. "I wrote to you lately, which the Darlington Postmaster tells me must come safe to hand, for he put it into the bag himself. Those Rascals the post-boys often receive the postage and destroy the letters, and put the postage in their own pockets."—*Toby Heyrick the epicurean Vicar of Gainford, to Mr Wood, Proctor of Durham.*

† Inventory p. m

‡ A much more recent Matthew Lambert possessed a little mustard garth at Brafferton, the produce of which was to be inspected by a Darlington seedsman. On the day fixed for the meeting Mat was engaged to work with a "mate" at some fences, and left his *cara sposa* Peggy with instructions to call him when the man of grains arrived. The day had far passed and no summons been heard, when a heron flew over the heads of the labourers on its passage from the Sand Holm, near Ketton, to Morden Carrs, crying *Crake! Crake!! Crake!!!* "Let me away, let me away," exclaimed Mat, "no doubt the mustard-man's come, for I hear Peggy calling on me at last." And therefore an heron is seldom known in that neighbourhood by any other name than One of Mat Lambert's mustardmen. Another version of this story lately appeared in the Literary Gazette in utter variance with tradition, but cooked for the sake of point.

§ The early appellation of a pair of stays, whence our *bodice*.—*Strutt*.

|| A bowl of wood, often maple.

to the *Duckstoole*, 5*s*.* - - - 1616, For a bushell of Moulter corne, 3*s*. 4*d*.: For want of delivery of x sacks of coales, 10*s*.: For v yards and a halfe lynnen and harden at 10*d*. the yarde, 4*s*. 7*d*. - - - 1617, For sharping of milne picks, 4*s*.: Wm. Thompson *v*. Thomas Gallon and Grace his wife 12*s*. for the tabling of the said Grace and needles: For ix sack of coales 7*s*., to be paid of Carter thorne coales: A paire of sparres, 12*d*. offered: For deteyning a doore, a locke, and a key, 6*s*. 8*d*. - - - 1620, A coverlet, 6*s*. - - - 1623, Rob. Robinson *v*. Will. Bulmer, for saying *thou art a theife*† *and stole my lofe* 39*s*. 11*d*. - - - 1624, 5 boords of fire 5*s*. - - - 1625, *una arca Anglice* one chiste, 10*d*. - - - 1630, A gunne, 8*s*. 10*d*."

"Orders and ancient paines maid and laid by the consent of the borrowmen and homigers to my Lord of Durham of the Borrow of Darlington the ixth of October Anno Regni Regis D'ni nostri Jacobi, &c. 19th, Scotiæ lvth, Anno D'ni 1621.

Paines. Imprimis, A paine that no man shall take into his howse within this borrow any servant but by the Consent of the Chefe officer and xij men of the said borrow, but such as are sufficient to maintaine themselves without charge to the town upon paine of 20*s*. Item, A paine that all have any under settles that they avoyde them before great moun-day after Martenmas next upon pane of 20*s*. Item, A paine that no malster or baker or any other persone doe buye any corne but in the open market and that at such time of the daye as hath bene accostomed upon paine of 6*s*. 8*d*.‡ Item, a paine that all those that dight or windowes corne or mault in the market place and all bread and groat sellers or other *that bringeth sward or stones for there ease to sit upon* shall imeadiately when they have done for that tyme or the next morning cary the same away upon paine of every default 12*d*. Item, A paine that every howseholder shall kepe and cause to be sweaped the street cleane before there doores and shall cause the myer and doung to be ccaryed away upon paine of 3*s*. 4*d*.§ Item, A paine further yf any affray or assault be in any howse or howses within the burrow and yf the owner of the same howses do not bring the parties before the Baliffe or his deputie to fynd surty for to kepe the peace within the burrow and the amerciament to my lord and his officer, he shall forfeit and pay 3*s*. 4*d*. Item, A paine that no tanner skinner nor glover shall take any neat skines shepe or calfe skines from any horse backe before the ouner of the same skines doe bring them into the market upon paine of 3*s*. 4*d*.|| Item, A paine that no smyth shall

* "1612, Marie, wife of Wm. Adamson, to be punished for *Scoldinge* according to law, viz. *ducked* upon the *Cuckstoole*, &c. 1614, Jane Willson and Rose Litle guiltie of an unseemelie assault and an open scoldinge betwixt them in the open marquet to be ducked three times either of them. 1619, Dorothy, wife of George Metcalf, a common scold to the common nuisance of the neighbours and against the peace of our Lord the King, &c., shalbe furthwith sett on the Cuckstoole and ducked according to the custom of the Borrowghe. 1620, Margaret Lumley, widow, and Isabella, wife of Roger Beecrofte the like. The wife of Henry Beecrofte, a common *Evisdropper* amerced 6*d*. The wife of Nicholas Hinde a common scold to be punished by ducking in water. The wife of Raignold Shawe and Katheren Shawe the like, and none within this borough shall harboure the said Katheren on pain of 39*s*. 11*d*." 1621, The wife of John Browne a common scould to be *cucked*. The wife of Nicholas Hinde the same." In 1624 some scolds were amerced, but the jury properly directed that the constable should "set upp the Duckingge Stoole within tenne dayes on on pain of 6*s*. 8*d*." The ducking system took place in Northgate, behind the shop of Mr. Robson (cabinet-maker) where the ducking pond was temporarily laid open a year or two ago, but was not always effective, as Metcalfe's wife was fined in 1622, for again being a scold, and making a savage attack on an afferror in the performance of his duty. The ducking stool or chair was at the end of a long pole which worked on an upright post.

† Yet what was this to Wm. Bullocke calling the Jury "*false scoundrels*," and Christopher Fawcett going to the length of telling them they were all "*mainsworne knaves*" in 1614.

‡ "1625, Noe townsmen shall receyve againe into theire howses any corne or grayne to be sett upp untill the next markett day which before haith been in the markett to be soulde."

§ In 1612 the butchers were commanded to collect all rams' horns by themselves in a place in the burrough for that purpose, and in 1629 Xpforer Sober and three other nasty men were amerced "for throwing intraills of beasts upon other mens fieshe." In 1720 Wm. Shaw was fined for emptying his "inmeats" in the public street.

|| "1621, Noe tanners shall bye any skins but upon the *Skynnehill* in the Markett Place."

suffer any horse or mare to be tyed att there shoppes on head fares and market dayes any longer then halfe a hoore after shooing upon paines of 12*d*.* ITEM, A paine that no man shall suffer there children or servants to put there horses or other cattell in the night into other mens grasse or groundes by there consent the masters or parentes of such children or servantes shall pay and forfeit 6*s*. 8*d*. ITEM, We lye a paine of 6*s*. 8*d*. to be levied of everye one that contrary to the borrow right shall fell whines and bring them of Branken moore without the consent of the Grasse men from this forward. ITEM, A paine none shall washe any clothes fyshe or scower any skeles tubbes or other vessels, but at or below the litle well at the tubwell upon paine of 3*s*. 4*d*. WE lye a dormant pane of 3*s*. 4*d*. that all forefrountes and backfrountes within this borrow shall according to neighborhood be maid upp by the owners att or before all Saintes day next ensewing.† ITEM, A paine that no person shall breake or open any ground in the borrow or street or market place before first licens thereof be granted by the baliffe or his deputie and the xii men of the Jury or the more part of them upon paine of 6*s*. 8*d*.‡ ITEM, A paine that if any within the borrow from hencforth harbor any foote person to them unknowne or knowne to be a wanderrer in the country or buy of any such any cloathes or other thinges before they or any of them do first make the persone knowne to the baliffe or his deputy or one of the Constables for every such default to forfit 20*s*. ITEM, A paine that every person shal be obedient to the commaundement of the officer in his majesties service and my Lord of Durham upon paine of 3*s*. 4*d*. ITEM, A paine that no person shall retaine harbor or kepe any woman suspected or defamed of whordome or any other notorious crimes or that have any base beggotten child or children to the charge of the towne and parish for every such default shall forfeit 20*s*.§ ITEM, We ly a paine that the searchers of aile taisters and fearors shall diligently execute their offices and that they shall search the markett every Mounday for th' assyze of bread and taiste ayle and beare every Moungth and that they present the offender that kepeth not the true assyse of ale and beare upon paine of every default 3*s*. 4*d*. ITEM, We ly a paine that noe inhaibiting within the jurisdiction of this borrow shall intertaine any inmates or undersetles, poor child or children, singlewoman, or any suspected persons, without first entring bond to the baliffe to discharge the towne of any charge that may come to the towne by them upon paine of every default 39*s*. 11*d*.|| ITEM, A paine that all these paines and forfa-

* In 1614, no buttermen nor colyers were to fodder their horses in the streets or against the towlboath.

† "1621, A paine of 6*s*. 8*d*. that the neighbours in Skinergait shall suffer men to passe over there frount steade with there draughts." Skinnergate road was bordered on each side with grass at no remote period.

In 1616, ordered "that every one make their severall fences betwene man and man," which are elsewhere called *side fronts*.

‡ In 1614, ordered "that no man either by licence of the baliffe or whomsoever shall digge or break upp any part of the marquett place for sand or gravell from th'east end of the Corne Causey to the West end of the tollboath and frome the strand or wayne way to the South end of the shambles, and that Mr. Baliffe shall not consent to the same." In 1616 two burgesses caused "a breach of such parts in the street as they did shortly fill upp and vest in Mr. Bailiff's *courtesy* being without compasse of the limited places forbidd." The sand-holes, by leave of the bailiff, were made in the market place as late as the 18th cent.

§ In 1614, there were "divers houses of evill note in Blackwellgait," viz. five, of which Richard Branson was first, and he was an old offender, for besides now harbouring "persons of ill liefe and lewde behaviour," in 1613 he "kept naughty woman and of badd behaviour in widow Clarkson's house." In 1618 the serjeant of the court himself, Wm. Tatton, unlawfully suffered suspicious people to be in his house at night and was ordered to have none such after nine at night. This Tatton was a knave, and in a case against his fellow-offender, Rd. Branson, if he did not serve execution in a fortnight, execution was to issue against himself. In 1621 and 1622 Edmond the Hatter was four times presented for keeping an "inwooman" and ordered to avoid her. He persisted in his sin, and poor creature, his pity was natural, for neither he nor any other burgess was to entertain her, as the sapient jury considered her as "a woman of a lewd and *suspicious* carriage." His fines were augmented, for his offence was "a great nuisance and evil example to his neighbours."

|| The rules against the poor were very harsh. They often lived in a "retrorsa domus, anglice backhouse," behind the wealthier burgess of the "frontispicium, anglice forepart." "1615, We lay a paine of Wm. Corker that he avoyd old Nell w'ch he keepeth upo' his

tures shall be presented to the jury of the next Borrow Court after the forfaiture maid upon the oath or oathes of the constables and sergantes or some of them upon paine of every omission or concealment by any of them 20*s*. ITEM, We do agree that all former paines and penalties as haith been heretofore used or any other paines concerning the well governing and using of the same shall continew and stand in force. ITEM, A paine whosever kepeth any swyne* unringed or mastereis unmusled within this borrow shall forfit 3*s*. 4*d*."

1621. The inhabitants of Richmond† and Durham petitioned the Bishop against some "upstart and new intended erection of fairs at Darlington." The former town had paid 40*l*. feefarm to the crown till Henry VI. reduced it to 19*l*. 13*s*. 4*d*. by reason of fairs being lately erected at Barnard-castle, Staindrop, Bedale, Middleham, and Masham; and this sum was chiefly raised by the tolls of the fortnight fairs from Palmson Even to Whitson Monday, "at which time the fairs beginning at Darlington, being but 7 miles distant, do so eclipse and dry up Richmond, that the 5 between are more worth than 15 after." The Richmond men stated that if his lordship "gave way to Mr. Pudsey's desires" they would have to ask his Majesty to abate still more of the rent, and "the poor town, wherein there are above 6000 living souls, utterly ruined and overthrown."‡ "So injurious and so unequal a request of him the said Mr. Pudsey," which was to prostrate old Richmond which had been long "specially supported by the concourse of the neighbours adjoining" was, I presume, that extra fortnight fairs should be established; an idea carried, *vi et armis*, into effect in 1664, when Cosin (incensed that his lieges should have "of their owne heads" erected a new market for the sale of all manner of cattle from the fortnight before Christmas to Whitson Monday, and with much violence resisted the opposers thereof by him appointed, "to the disgust of the people, and prejudice of other neighbouring faires and marketts") prohibited the same and ordered public proclamation by his sheriff or undersheriff to that effect in the market-place.§ The desideratum has nevertheless in the end been obtained.

1623, Sep. 14. "Thomas s. John Turner of Cleasbie bap., Sponsors *Thomas Salkeld*, Simon Giffard and Priscilla Tonstall." This entry occurs near others of recusants on the flyleaf of our register, and I suspect this Thomas Salkeld to be identical with him of Coniscliffe, of Westmoreland extraction, who in 1625 was esteemed a very dangerous Popish recusant. He obediently attended divers conferences with the vicar of Coniscliffe and curate of Gainford without success, and at a further conference, by order 13 July, 1626, the worthy couple did not yet perceive any conformity, "he being very peremptory in divers superstitious points." At length, says Surtees, "Mr. Salkeld's Catholic soul was wearied out of all patience by appearances and conferences, and 28 Sep., 1626,

backside." In 1620, John Crampton was either to *avoid* his tenant, or repair his chimney, which it seems was likely to set the whole borough in a blaze. If the poor had actually resided a year and thus gained a settlement, the orders were relaxed. As late as 1710 no stranger who might become chargeable to the town was allowed to remain more than three days under a burgess's roof.

* 1759, Joseph Dixon fined for suffering his swine to go at large in the *church-yard* and in the streets.

† In 1658, William Wetwange, a free burgess of Richmond, had a heifer seized in Darlington market and carried away for not paying toll, and at York assizes following obtained a verdict against Christopher Place of Darlington, the Bailiff, for the seizure. He proved that the men and tenants of the Honour of Richmond had time out of mind of man been free from payment of stallage, pickage, murage, &c. in every town and place in England; (a privilege confirmed by several charters under the Great Seal of England); that at Darlington, when any of the inhabitants of Richmond were arrested or molested any way for payment of tolls, upon giving satisfaction that they were burgesses of Richmond, they were dismissed without payment of anything; And that the carriers of Richmond being townsmen, who went constantly to London every month, were exempted from payment of toll on the whole road and at London.—The tenants of the Honour of Knaresbrough claimed similar exemption.—*(Pleadings Duc. Lancaster.*, 40 *Eliz.)*

‡ Clarkson's Richmond.

§ Bp. Chandler also in 1738-9, at the instance of Durham Corporation in a letter to the bailiff, James Allan, esq., forbid a sale of cattle on Monday, Mar. 12, and every fortnight till Easter, the town having no authority from the Bishop for such sale.—*Allan MSS. D. & C.*

the messenger reporteth 'that Mr. Salkeld is removed from his house, and that he cannot discover whither he is gone ; whereupon his recognizance is declared forfeited.' I am not sure that he did not die of vexation, and retreat into a stone coffin. 'At the West end of the stone before the Quire-doore, in the grave against the end of it, some halfe a yard from the stone's end, was found a stone coffin in the earth, in which Mr. Salkeld was laid.' This immediately follows an entry of 3 Nov. 1626, in the Coniscliffe Register."*

1624. Easter Hall, Wester Hall, and Halcland are mentioned as at Cockerton in the Halmot Books.

1628. The Burgesses and Commonalty of this Borough town agreed on Articles for the trades of *Smythes* of what kind soever. The regulations resemble those of the Company of Cordwainers in 1577, but the annual election of wardens in this case was on the 25 June. No wares to be sold in the markett before one in the afternoon, the time appointed by the homagers. The articles are in the Borough Books.

1631. Oswald Fawcett purchased of Cuthbert Hodgson "one fore shopp one back parlour and one lofte *overshooting* them both conteyning in length five yeards wanting fower inches and in breadth eight yeards two foote and fower inches with a stable on the back side."

1634. The author of "Certaine observations touching the estate of the Commonwealth, &c.," when talking about the waste of woods, says, "It is not much nedefull for mee to bringe in many examples (or waste time) to prove mine assertion, for our owne countrymen of Billinghame, Norton, Stockton, Seaton, Hartlepoole, and the inhabitants of Cleueland in Yorkshire (since Wharleton parke was cut downe) and of all the villages betweene Darneton (upon the riuer of Tease) and the sea-side, and from the sea-side vpon the Coast to Sunderland will generallie subscribe to mine opinion in this ; who (for the most part) are daily forced to buy their wooden instruments for tillage at other places, where they may be had, otherwise our Countie might of necessity want *that abundance of Corne which is daylie sold at* Durhame, Darlington, Auckland, and Barnard-castle which (for the most part) commeth from these places."

1634. "Three Southern commanders, in their places, and of themselves and their purses, a Captaine, a Lieutenant, and an Ancient, all voluntary members of the noble Military Company in Norwich, agreed at an opportune and vacant leysure, to take a view of the cities, castles, and chiefe scytuations in the Northerne and other counties of England : To that end and purpose, all businesse and excuses set apart, they had a parley, and met on Monday, the 11th of August, 1634, and mustering up their triple force from Norwich, with souldiers' journeying ammunition, two of them, (the Captain and the ensign) clad in green cloth like young foresters, and mounted on horses, they marcht that night to the maritime town of Lyn, and thence through Lincolnshire and Yorkshire." - - - "The nexte day we were to passe into another Kingdome, the Bishopricke of Durham ; for the Bishope is a Prince there. As soon as we left our Inn, at the end of the towne appeared to us a fayre and neat building, a Knights house (Sir Wm. Robinson's) most sweetly situated on the river Swale, and not far from thence another Knights seat (Sir Arthur Ingram's), and by dinner time we got to Darlington *where we were entertained with a hideous noyse of bag-pipes ; such a consort it was, as seemed strange to us, yitt we made them serve that small time we stayed there.* Two miles before we came thither, we crossed without or bridge the goodlie River Tees, which springs out of Stanemoore, and divides this large famous shire from that antient priviledged County Palatine of Durham, and there we left it, and hastned for the cittie of Durham."‡

* Joseph Salkeld of High Conescliffe, gentleman, and Mrs. Jane Green of Lanmouth, in Yorkshire. 3rd publication of banns 9 Nov., 1657.—Hannah Salkield of Darlington, widow, buried 26 Apr., 1764.—*Darlington Par. Reg.*

† MSS. Eccl. Dunelm. C III. 20, No. 3, p. 93. printed by Surtees and Raine in 1822.

‡ Landsdown MSS. Richardson's Imprints. John Fydeler de Derlyngtone occurs in a

1635. Sir William Brereton of Handford, Chesh., whese exploits as Parliamentary general are inseparable from English history, journeyed this year through the North. "From Caterigg Brigg to Peirs Brigg seven [twelve] miles, a straight way; thence to Bishoppe Auckland, seven mile. We lodged at Newton, two miles out of the road, and from Peirs Brig, with generous Mr. Henry Blackistone [of Archdeacon Newton, see p. 147] younger brother to Sir W. Blackstone of Gibsett, whose eldest son [Sir Wm. Blakiston of Archdeacon Newton, the gallant royalist] married my cousin [in reality, sister in law, the tourist's sister marrying this "cousin's" brother], Mary Eggert[on]. Here I was kindly and neatly entertained, and this gentleman brought me to Aukeland, [and] invited me to his brother's and his nephew Wren's, Mr. Linsley Wren, who married Sir Wm. Blackstone's [of Gibside] daughter [Barbara], a fine gentlewoman, very lively and of a free carriage, &c. [he afterwards calls her "a *mighty* gallant, a dainty fine gentlewoman, if she knew but how to value and prize the perfections God hath given her; whose husband hath impaired his estate in maintaining * * at so great height"]. Here he lodged all night, and (upon his return to Auckland next morn) staid with me until evening."*

1640. The following letter from Henry Clifford, 5th Earl of Cumberland, was omitted at p. 132. "My goode Lord—My heade hath so aked with rideing in the heate of the day, as I dare not adventure upon the night, itt beinge now 9 of the clock. Tomorrowe morninge I will attend you at 8 of the clock, desiringe your Lordship in the meane time to present my affectionate wishes to Mr. Justice Hutton.—My Lord, your Lordship's most affectionate frende and servant. H. CLIFFORD.—*Darneton this 20th day of Aug. at 9 in the Evening.* I gave notice this morninge to Mr. Mayor of Newcastell, and to all the Deputy Lieutenance of my intention to be at Newcastell tomorrowe before noone; soe have I likewise despatched a packett into Scotlande to my Lord of Montrose from whom I hope to heare within 48 hours."

1654. James Ward of Darlington, *danceing master*, occurs in the registers.†

1655. "*A Booke for Blackewell containeing what belongs the Towne and Greeve ther, with accompts for the highwaies*" commences. Throughout the book the rustic counsellors call their meetings "byelaws" or "bylaws of neighbours," a term now more applicable to the resolutions‡ made. It was ordered, in 1656, that every husbandman being constable was to find himself a horse at his own charge. I extract from the Constables' accounts. "1656, For going to Durham at the Assizes, 1*s.*: Passing the [Stapleton]

charter of 1404 (D. and C. 3369). In March 1561-2 the corporation of Newcastle "paid mor geven in rewarde to the wayttes of Darnton, 3*s*." The waits were public musicians who were hired to perform at marriage feasts and the like. The pipers of Darlington probably visited Newcastle during the Easter festivities, when the magistracy seem to have had great doings and to have bought up, or, at least drawn away, from the surrounding towns of Leeds, Thirsk, Darlington, Carlisle, Cockermouth, &c., all the musical talent they could muster, as well as the aid of Scotch and Irish minstrels.—Guilielmus fidlar sepultus 12 Nov. 1591. James Johnson of Darlington, Music professor, occurs 1619. Thomas Willson *vulgariter* called *bavet* of Darlington (elsewhere Tho. Bavie alias Wilson) occurs 1621 and subsequent years in company with a number of other pipers, the last entry of the sort being in 1673 of a piper of Blackwell. John Jackson of Blackwell, a blind fidler, aged 59, bur., 1812. Henry Wetherelt, *harper* (fidicen), bur. 1622-3.—1674, For drink and musick at the common dayes worke, 2*s*. 6*d*.—*(Bondgate Book)*.—One of the fields of Grange estate was named Fidler's close.—It was common for travellers to be victimized both in ear and purse with music at their various halts. The *Waits* were in their proper avocation *watches*, enlivening the night. The three waits at Durham played a tune and then called the hour.

* Richardson's Imprints.

† The Sword-dance (mentioned by Tacitus as common among our German ancestors) is sparingly kept up by fantastic groups at Christmas, but they do not perform the ancient drama, and the custom is lifeless. Hurworth is a great producer of sword-dancers.

‡ "The Towneship of Blackwell being fallen into divers inconveniences by reason of the neglect of certain ancient custömes, hath thought fit to revive them with a common consent, and to incerte them in their common booke, whereby their yong-men may have knowledg therof, and their inconveniences by that means may be taken away." "In testimony of which condicenc'on and agreement the neighbours" set their hands to the document, not in 1707, the date given, but, from some unaccountable delay, in 1718-19. The names of Cuth. Pepper and John Pemberton (the quondam lord of Aislaby) occur. The customs relate to the calling and proceedings at "by-laws," and have little interest.

boate twice with heu and cry, 2*d.* : Carring two cripples to Darneton, 4*d.*, given to either of them 2*d.* : To 5 poore and laime, with a horse, 6*d.* : For guarding a theefe over Tease, 4*d.* - - - 1657, To the booke keeper, 3*s.**: To a woman and a wench, 4*d.* : For passing the heu and crie warrant, 2*d.* : To two men with a passe from Colo. Wren, 4*d.* - - - 1658, For carriing two women to Darlington on horsebac, 4*d.*, given for being rid of them, 2*d*, : For setting Mason away and for apparrell for him as followeth ; a coat, 3*s.*, a dublitt, 3*s.*, a shirt, 1*s.* 6*d.*, a hatt, 1*s.*, a paire of showes, 1*s.* 6*d.*, a paire of stockings, 1*s.* 8*d.*, a paire of britches, 2*s.* 6*d.*, given him in mony 2*s.* 6*d.* : Three severall fowerpences, 1*s.* : For four horses to cripples, 8*d.* - - - 1659, My cherges to Durham staing all night, 2*s.* : For giveing a list at Durham what the alehouse keepers pay excise, 1*s.* : To two men which had been taken by pirates, 6*d.* - - - 1683, For carrying a criple to Croft and 4*d.* which was given to the same criple by Sir William's order, 1*s.* : Given to *eighteen* passengers together, 6*d.* - - - 1685, The accounts were seen and allowed according to the custome vizt. 1*d.* a passenger with a passe, 3*d.* or 4*d.* a lodger, 1*s.* to Awckland [petty sessions] and 2*s.* to Durham [sessions]. - - - 1687, Remainder [of constable's sess] 1*s.* 4½*d.* which was given to the constable in respect of his moderate charge. - - - 1691, A sesse gatherd at 18*s.* 4*d.*† p. li. for repairing the loss of Mr. Tillum's money taken from him in this ward of Darlington. - - - 1693, For paving 193 rood of cawsey, 5*l.* 4*s.*, for filling a sand-hole and scouring a stell at Hamper Carr,‡ and setting away the water at Towne end 1*s.* 6*d.*, for wood for the stoops and setting 2*s.* 6*d.* - - - 1694, To John Rudd for 92¼ roods of cawsey 4*l.* 12*s.* 6*d.*, spent when we bargained 1*s.* : For leading of 4 rood of stones 1*s.* : two women for carrying stones 1*s.* : Spent when wee paid the workemen 1*s.*§ - - - In 1678 Edw. Browne and wife agreed to keep and maintain Tho. Morgan son of Jo. Morgan with meat and drink convenient for him for *tenpence* per week. In 1696, Nought Bridge|| emerged from a construction of timber laid on stone piers to a stately erection of two brick arches, which were duly fashioned by Stellon the housewright and Hunter the mason for 20*l.*, and the timber and iron bolts of the old bridge. The 20*l.* "was laid at four times the book of rates," and was collected *by the contractors* "as much as would serve them," save 3*s.* paid by the surveyors. [The old stone piers were retained.]

1661. The following singular licence is transcribed from the original penes R. H. Allan, esq.:—"JOHN BY THE prouidence of God Bishop of Duresme To all Justices of peace Sheriffes Bailifes and other officers whatsoeuer within the County Palatine of Duresme and Sadberge Greeteing KNOWE YEE that whereas wee haue beene informed crediblely on behalfe of Henry Shaw yeeman that he is a free Boroughman of Darlington and that he and his ancesters haue solde grocerys and other wayres in Darlington as a Chapman there and that he hath noe other trade or calleing whereby he can maintaine his wife and many small children and familie haueing onely one small house in Darlington and haueing bene lately molested for vseing that trade as not haueing serued an apprentice therevnto by the space of seauen yeares contrary to the forme of the Statute in that case made and prouided and still greatly feareing to be troubled for the same

* Ordered the year before. 1*s.* had previously been paid. In 1687 5*s.* was paid.

† The heavy rates appearing in old township books lose their terrific appearance when the absurd smallness of the sums used as guides in the Book of Rates are considered. They merely fixed the proportions.

‡ One of the Grange enclosures, the green surface of which bears no resemblance to a watery carr now. The causey was evidently that extending from Blackwell to Prescott's stile on the way to Darlington. It is a substantial work still, bounded by vast outside stones ; and albeit the carrs have yielded to improvement, and the low road is no longer little better than a morass, the *magnum opus* of the "neighbourhood" of Blackwell in wet weather is a real comfort to this day, and may be calculated upon as fitted to last at least another century. A continuation may be dimly traced in the fields between Prescott's stile and Woodside, and who shall fix the age of the thorns which bound the whole work. The stell in Hamper Carr conveyed the water from the Blackwell road "at the town end" into Humblesyke till last year, when it was converted into a drain.

§ Every meeting, bylaw or otherwise, was the occasion of a "drink."

|| See p. 40. Called in one place this year *Nough Bride.*

Wee neuerthelesse heareing that the said Henry Shaw is of good name and faime amongst his neighbors and haueing consideration of his poore estate for diuerse causes vs moueing as much as in vs is are content to lycence tollerate and suffer the said Henry Shaw to vse and exercise the trade and occupation of a grocer or merchent or Chapman within the Towne of Darlington aforesaid or elsewhere within the said County Palatine of Duresme and Sadberdge not willing that he in or for exerciseing of the said Trade shall from hencefourth be impeached mollested fined sued or any way disquieted by vs or our successors or any Justices the Sheriffs or other Bailifes or officers within the County Palatine aforesaid for any fine forfiture or penaltie which by reason thereof or by force of the statute aforesaid to vs or our Successors shall bee due or appertaineing. Jn Wittnesse whereof wee haue hereunto set our hand and priuate seale Giuen at Durham this three and twentieth of September in the xiij th yeare of our Soueraigne Lord Charles 2d by the grace of God king of England Scotland France and Jreland defender of the faith &c. Anno Dom' 1661 and of our Consecration the first. Io : Duresme." Small Seal of Cosin. The document would prove the existence of a Merchants' Company at Darlington.

1665. The entries begin in " A Booke of remembrance, or an inrolment of memorable things belonging to Bondgate in Darlington," which the Greeve kept. The lists of officers however begin in 1630 and end 1722. There is mention of May Lands, Yowlands, " Towns land that payes Pinders oates, in all 33 oxg. 3 feet and 1-6th part ; these are lyable to scoure the pinders stell at the bridge proportionably," the Burrages, &c.* I extract a few items from the surveyors' accounts :—Jan. 22th : 1666 : Memorandum that it was agreed by the neighbours of the Burrough in Darlington at a Bylaw that an Assessment of 4*d.* per foote be collected of Brankin Moore according to the Auld stint which coms to 14 nobles, And alsoe an Assessment of all the Bourrough houses according to a 3 months sess, as is gathered for the Royall ayde which coms to 46*s.* & 3*d.* 3 farthings, be alsoe collected and gathered, for discharginge the said Inhabitants from 2 declarations which is com out of the Crowne office against them touching and concerning there highwayes : which said assesments was indevoured to be collected by severell of the Neighbours & was all gotten : except 12*s.* 7*d.* as by ther notes doth appere, so they received of Booth the assesments 06*l.* 07*s.* 00*d.* : Received more of Robert Ward Survaior 01*l.* 00*s.* 00*d.* : Received more Edward Pearson Cunstable 02*l.* 00*s.* 00*d.* : Received in all for this business 09*l.* 07*s.* 00*d.* Wm. Priscott. - - - February 11 th : 1666 : Paied to Mr. Rob. Coulthurst [see p. 256] uppon our a agrement with him for the cleareing of our towne from this sute and trouble, in mony as apperes by his acquittance 3*l.* 8*s.* : *but in truth he never did it*, and soe by his neclect we were put to more charge and forced to Imploy Mr. Tho : Gill of Barton, whoe did effect our work, unto whome we paid at severall times as apperes by his severell acquittances the sum of 6*l.* 3*s.* 4*d.* Paid 9*l.* 11*s.* 4*d.*, Recd. 9*l.* 7*s.* 0*d.* : soe there is disbursed more then received 4*s.* 4*d.* Wm. Priscott. - - - 1667. Spent at Widdow Surtisses, 3*d.* : Robert Cuthbert for his draught one day, 5*s.* : A man one day, 8*d.* : A cart and a man one day 2*s.* 8*d.* : two carts and seven men, 9*s.* 2*d.* : For drink bread and *tobacco* to them and the common dayes people, 3*s.* 7*d.* : To Peter Bowbank for bringing a stone from Sadbridge 6*d.* : For mending the *Hermitage cawsay* 6*s.* 3*d.* : For mending the *gantre* [for the drink to stand on] in Yarme lane 6*d.* : For mending Bondgate well, 1*s.* - - - 1668. To Jane Thompson for gathered stones, 4*s.* : For warning the out houses, 2*d.* : nine *woe*man at 3*d.* per day, and two woeman at 4*d.* per day, 2*s.* 11*d.* : To Jon. Wattson for paveing three days at 16*d.* per day, 4*s.* ; two servers for three days, 3*s.* : To Wiij† Waistle for ordering the small stones Moudon Laine, 4*d* : 2 journeys to

* Sir Jeremah Smisson occurs 1674 and 1676 in " arears which cannott be gotten tobe deducted," headed " *li. s. d. fa. bod.*" (bodles). He was an oddish character. " Anne, supposed daughter of Sir Jeremiah Smithson, fathered of the said Sir Jeremiah *in the church*, bap. 9 Ap. 1662."—*Forcett.*

† This extraordinary method of writing William is common in this year's account. The *m* is not so transmogrified in any other word.

Durham, 4*s.*: Paid att Tho. Parkinsons upon Jutis Carr view of the laine, 6*s.* 6*d*: The Clarke off peace 5*s.*, and the Cryer 6*d.*: Mending the horse brigge in Branking moore laine, 1*s.*: Returned to the new Surveyors a firme hack and an old *shuffle*. - - - 1675. 6 men for clencsing the *Scearne* one day 3*s.* 10*d.*: 3 burdens of whins 9*d.*: Matthew Taylorson for 21 cart load of brick, 5*s.* 3*d.*: Henry Wright for 2 carts half a day fo. Harmataig 2*s.* 9*d.*: Tho. Longstaff for mending the Church hack and iron layd on it, 9*d.*: To John Wright which he gave in earnege for the broken brick, 5*s.*: For a shovell 14*d.*: Lackenby boy for casting stones, ½*d.*: John Parkinson till 3 a'clock, 6*d.*: Ralph Elstob for a peceday 2*d.*: Mr. Hilton for drawing the bond from Tho. Phillips which we had from him for uphoulding the causeys he payved, 1*s.* - - - 1676. Allice Pilkington for 8 load of small stones, 2*s.* 8*d.*

1665. Feb. 20. "I John Warde of Darlington &c. Woollen draper *by the holy Inspirac'on of Almighty God* make this my will, &c.—to be buried where God shall call me out of this troublesome world, where my executor pleaseth—my father Rob. Ward of Dinsdale, co. Yorke—my two daughters Ann Ward and Eliz. Ward—my father shall have a reasonable thing for their educac'on out of their porcons."

1667. Edw. Elgie of Bishop Awckland, mason—to Dorothy my wife my best peece of silver plate which I *wonn* at Darlington and my houses in Darlington for life, then to Michael son of my bro. Anth. E. and if my bro. Anth. have another son, his name to be Edward and he to have the said houses: to the poore people in Darlington 5*li.*

1669. "The Bishop's attorney agreed with William Burleston, Gent. Coroner of Darlington Ward, for the payment of sixteen shillings yearly in lieu of twelve bushells of oats, called Coroner's oats, from the township of Blackwell." The Bordlands at Blackwell also paid *Board-Wheat,* perhaps for the maintenance of the Bishop's table [at Darlington Manor-house ?]

1672. Printed at Paris, the tour of Jorevin, a Frenchman, in England, in the 17th cent. It was copied into the Archæologia, vol. xvi, and the names of places are spelt in a manner scarcely warranted by the sound, even in a foreigner's ears :—" I came afterwards to Feril [Ferry-Hill], Actif [Aycliffe], Darlington on the river Nisen [Skerne] and the river Tees, which must be passed in a ferry-boat [at Neasham]. From thence to Smiton [Smeaton], Alverton, Sorsk [Thirsk] on the river [Codbeck], Lermbi [Thormanby ?]; a flat country, without hills to Esmond [Easingwold]. The high road lies by way of Darlington to Toklife [Topcliffe], but I left in on the left to go by Chip [?] and York."

1673. Died,* Richard Braithwaite, esq., a native of Warcop, in Westmoreland, the proven author of "Drunken Barnaby," in which, as he was a very wandering gentleman, he perhaps really gives some of his own tours, though in an exaggerated character. The Hurworth register contains the entry :—" Mr. Richard Braithwayte and Mrs. Frances Lawson married May 4th, 1617."

" Venit† Nasham Dei donum	" Thence to *Nesham*, now translated,
In cænobiarchæ domum.	Once a *nunnery* dedicated ‡
Uberem vallem, salubrem venam,	Valleys smiling, bottoms pleasing,
Cursu fluminis amænam,	Streaming rivers, never ceasing
Lætam sylvis et frondosam	Deck'd with tufted woods and shady,
Heræ vultu speciosam.	*Graced by a lovely lady.*

* See his epitaph in Catterick church, where it is stated that his only son Strafford Braithwait, knt., by his second wife, was slain in fight with the Moors, and was buried at Tangier.

† " Littora lentiscis, gemmarunt germina gemmis,
Murenulis conchæ, muricibusque comæ.
" Where shores yield lentisks, branches pearled gems,
There lamprels shells, their rocks soft mossy stems."

‡ Which the Lawsons then held.

"Veni *Darlington*, prope vicum,
Conjugem duxi peramicam ;
Nuptiis celebrantur festa,
Nulla admittuntur mæsta ;
Pocula noctis dant progressum,
Ac si nondum nuptus essem."

"Thence to *Darlington*, where I boused,
Till at length I was espoused ;
Marriage feast and all prepar'd,
Not a fig for th' world I cared :
All night long by th' pot I tarry'd,
As if I had not been marry'd."

After a few more peccadilloes, he bids a solemn farewell to all his follies, on his marriage and increasing years. He becomes a drover. From Northallerton fair

"Veni *Darlington*, servans leges
In custodiendo greges.

Thence to *Darlington* never swerving
From our drove laws worth observing."

And somewhat later is enchanted again with our lovely lawns of Tees :—

"Nunc ad Richmond, primo flore,
Nunc ad *Nesham* cum uxore,
Læto cursu properamus,
Et amamur et amamus :
Pollent floribus ambulacra,
Vera Veris simulachra."

Now to Richmond, when Spring's come on,
Now to *Nesham* with my woman ;
With free course we both approve it,
Where we love, and are beloved ;
Here fields flower with freshest creatures,
Representing Flora's features."

In after life he settled at Appleton near Catterick, upon what his biographer calls "an employment, or rather a second marriage." He wrote an epitaph on his first wife, whose mother was a Conyers.

"Teisis me genuit, sponsatam Westria cepit,
Corpus Candalium. Pectus Olympus habet."

"Near Darlington was my dear darling borne,
Of noble house which yet bears honor's forme,
Teese-seated Sockburn, where by long descent
Conyers was lord."

1679. I hope the almost exulting memorandum of the first recorded exciseman here had no real significance in its reiteration :—"Mr. Robert Cocks *an* exciseman was *buried* at Darl : *buried*." The language implies non-residence. "Mr. John Wood *the* exciseman" was buried in 1683-4.

1685. 29½ *Wood Hens* were paid in Blackwell. Mr. Whayre Fawcett (the heir, *jure uxoris*, of John Cornforth) paid the greatest number, viz. 6¼ hens.

1694. "At Darlington in the Bishoprick of Durham, on the 2nd of July 1694, about 3 of the Clock in the afternoon, a great dark cloud, arising from the West and by North, spread itself very wide over the compass of a great quantity of ground, when immediately a clap or two of thunder breaking from it with some flashes of lightning ere the travellers and such as were getting in their hay and about other rural affairs could get shelter, to which they hasted as fearing only a terrible wetting, great hailstones fell down to the bigness of pigeons eggs in great abundance, insomuch that divers people were sore hurt as also the smaller sort of cattle who stood piteously crying and blating in the fields and on the plains, the shepherds by the sudden surprize being forc'd to fly to shelter and leave them. The tiles and windows in some villages thereabouts were miserably shatter'd and broken, and divers starks crows and daws then upon the wing were beaten down, some dead and some wounded.

"The main force of this terrible storm continued scarce a quarter of an hour, but the oldest people declare they never saw any so fierce in all their time. The storm being over, divers of the stones were taken up and found to be 4, 5, and 6 inches in circumference and many in various forms, as swords, coronets, pears, peaches, plumbs, bearded ears of corn, roots and flowers, and divers others, which they really resembl'd or peoples fancy enclin'd them to."*

* From "God's Marvellous Wonders in England, containing divers strange and wonder-

1700. Sep. 10. Robert the son of Joseph Goodden [*qu.* an assumed name, being the exact pronunciation of *good one*] *Mountebank*, Darlington, bap. Some other notices of early performers occur, such as Mr. William Quelch of London, a comedian, 1747 ; Mr. Stephen Butcher, late of Coventry, a comedian, 1749 ; Henry White of a company of comedians now at D. 1758. William Bence, a stranger and puppet-shew-man, was buried 7 Jan. 1765.

1710. " We lay a pain of 6*s.* 8*d.* upon any Butcher that shall kill any Bull unbated and the like penalty upon the Bailiff for not finding a Rope"- - - 1723. The like order, adding " or shall sell its flesh within the Borough," penalty, 13*s.* 4*d.* (*Borough Books*). The idea was to throw blood into the flesh and thus shew it was bull-meat. The last bull-baiting here was about 60 years ago.* On that occasion Robin Gascoigne, a bird-catcher, came out of the Post House Weind in very gallant array ; the horns, tail, &c. of the valiant brute being profusely decorated with blue ribbons, which adorned Robin himself, who bestrode the back of the bull, which proved a very stupid obstinate animal, and " there was no fun." At a former baiting the bull broke loose, causing all youngsters to creep beneath the old shambles. He went against an inn door in which were quantities of women and children, it was however fortunately just shut against him in time. He then ran along the Skerne and surprised an old gentleman in his garden, who very composedly said " Stop a bit, man, till I get out of thy way," and, though infirm, darted past and shut his door. The bull eventually was taken by some butchers in a narrow yard. I have also heard of the enfuriated animal, on other occasions here, running down a cellar, breaking a regiment of pots kept there in all directions ; and playing a similar prank in the cellar of a tobacco manufactory, where it thrust its nose into a barrel of snuff ! The ring, to which the rope was fastened, still remains in the market place pavement where this inhuman sport was enacted, near the large lamp pillar.

1726. The bills of Darlington lawyers of this period are amusing. They frequently place a moderate or " about" sum, and add to the item a gentle hint that the client might give " what you please," or they leave the matter in total uncertainty, saying " 13*s.* 4*d.*, or 10*s.*, or 6*s.* 8*d.*," casting up with the least sum. The carriage of a box from London was little more than the present charge, being only 4*s.*†

1731. Bp. Chandler demises to Charles Moore, of the Inner Temple, esq., " The Burrough Bakehouse, the Toll booth, the shops *under the pillory,* all manner of Tolls whatsoever they be of and in the Burrough of Darlington, Affrayes, Amerciaments of the Burrough Court there, Suits of Court, Brew Farme, Leek Farme, of or in the same Burrough or Towne," for the lives of Daniell Moore William Moore and the said Charles Moore ; rent 16*l.* ; and appointed Thomas Wycliff, esq., and Thomas Langstaff, gent., his attorneys to deliver seisin.

1739. In a curious canvassing book at Streatlam, drawn up sometime previous to the election of Mr. George Bowes for Durham, 1741, — Cradock, esq., of Hartford, Yks., is stated to have " *pro. self at Darlington Races*, 1739."

John Conyers, a pauper, sworn before Hen. Forth, esq., at Darlington, stated " that upon his marriage with Dorothy his now wife (which was about 40 years ago) he became seized for his life of the manor or lordship of Wigington in the North Riding of the county of Yorke and also of a freehold estate in the township of Wigington aforesaid of 60*l.* a year and upwards, and was possessed of the said mannor and estate (and was assessed, &c., *and kept his court baron* for the said manor once in every year) for about 6 years, after which time he sold the same to one Mr. John Brown—hath not since gained any legall settlement elsewhere. John Conyers." (A good bold signature).

ful relations that have happened since the beginning of June, this present year. 12mo Printed for P. Brooksby at the Golden-ball in Pye-corner, 1694," a chapbook penes J. Orchard Halliwell, esq., to whom I am indebted for the passage in the text. The most marvellous wonders" are a shower of wheat in Wiltshire 27 June, and " sundry grass fields sprouting up with corn where none has been known to be sown for iv years past, near Maidstone in Kent, in the grounds of an honest farmer who was very charitable to the poor in these bad times." The capture of a whale, and discovery of two murders, come more to our present ideas.

* Inf. Edw. Pease, esq.

† Allan Archives, R. H. A.

1748. "A Gentleman" in his tour through Great Britain, after stating how Darlington excelled in *Huggabags* of ten quarters wide, which were made nowhere else in England, proceeds thus :—"A greater rarity, I may mention in this town, was our Landlord, at the Fleece Inn, by name Henry Lovell, who died in May, 1739, in the 93d year of his age, and had kept this inn ever since 1688. He was never known to have one hour's sickness, nor even the head-ach, tho' a free toper of ale, sometimes for days and nights successively, but had an aversion to drams of all kinds, and retained his hearing, sight, and memory, to his last moments. He never made use of spectacles, nor ever lost a tooth. He was esteemed in his life, and lamented at his death, being of a humane temper, and had the deportment of a gentleman.'

1749. An ingenious correspondent, who subscribes himself "Conyers," thus eulogizes Darlington in the Universal Magazine :—"In the middle is a spacious market-place upwards of 200 yards long, and 130 broad, well filled on *Mondays*, its market-days ; and a much greater every other *Monday* from the first of *March* to *Christmas* for cattle and sheep. *N. B.* There is also a small market on *Fridays* ; the shambles are well stocked with good meat always. I have seen a quarter of mutton there weigh 43 pounds weight. It is the chief town of the hundred of its own name, a post town, and the most noted place in the whole world for the linnen manufacture of that sort called *Huckabacks*, so much used for table-cloths and napkins, being made from half-ell to 3 yards wide, and the price from 7*d*. a yard to 18*s*. ; great quantities of which are sent yearly to *London*, the broad sort being made no where else in *England*. There is also fine plain linnen cloth made to 7*s*. 6*d*. per yard, and a large woollen manufactory carried on there ; at present it is a thriving place, and all sorts of necessaries of life are as cheap here as in any part of the country. It is also a good place for fire. *N. B.* Two lambs, bred this year (1748) were sold, the 10th of *October*, 1748, in this market for 7*l*. sterling."

The years 1749 and 1750 were memorable for a very fatal distemper among cattle in the Northern counties. The disease having spread from the South into the North Riding of Yorkshire, on Apr. 5, 1749, the general quarter sessions of Durham ordered that no live cattle, or their slaughtered carcases, wool, skins, or tallow, &c. should be suffered to pass or be brought over the Tees northward, till the court should order to the contrary. Notwithstanding, the disease appeared at Cleadon, near South Shields, in March 1749, and in May at *Darlington*, where one farmer lost five cows, another three, and a third, Mary Wardel, of Blackwell, lost twenty. The order for proclaiming the appearance of the distemper at Blackwell, in open Market at Darlington, every market day, addressed to the Bailiff, is dated May 12, 1749. On June, 1750, the orders were reversed, the plague being stayed. The favourite remedy of the country people, not only in the way of cure, but of prevention, was an odd one ; it was to smoke the cattle almost to suffocation, by kindling straw, litter, and other combustible matter about them. The effects of this are not stated, but the most singular part of it was that by which it was reported to have been discovered. An angel (says the legend) descended into Yorkshire, and there set a large tree on fire ; the strange appearance of which, or else the savour of the smoke, incited the cattle around (some of which were infected) to draw near the miracle, where they all either received an immediate cure or an absolute prevention of the disorder. It is not affirmed that the angel staid to speak to anybody, but only that he left a *written* direction for the neighbouring people to catch this supernatural fire, and to communicate it from one to another with all possible speed throughout the country ; and in case that, by any unhappy means, it should be extinguished and utterly lost, that then new fire, of equal virtue, might be obtained, not by any common method, but by rubbing two pieces of wood together till they ignited. Upon what foundation this story stood, is not exactly known, but it put the farmers actually into a hurry of communicating flame and smoke from one house to another with wonderful speed, making it run like wildfire over the country.*

* Newcastle Gen. Mag. The following notes by Mr. John Ord, of Newtown, upon the

1752. "June 6. Monday, the greatest market for wool ever known there [at Darlington], 1000*l.* laid out therein.*

1753. Sep. 30. Two young men went to the house of Mr. Moncaster, dyer, in Darlington, and after knocking at his door, asked Mr. Moncaster if his daughter was within, with other enquiries respecting her, and being denied admittance, they forced open the door, and went into the house, on which a scuffle ensued, in which Mr. Moncaster was so inhumanly used and bruised by strokes with their whips, &c., that he died within an hour after.†

1756. At Stockton-upon-Tees, on Sep. 14, and following days, a main of cocks were fought between the gentlemen of Darlington and Helmsley, which consisted of twenty-two battles, twelve won by the former and ten by the latter.‡ In 1773, the famous pit of the town was the Three Tuns' Pit, where, on May 12, there was a cock-fight "for the benefit of Oswald Robinson." Gargett's cockpit was in Priestgate. A cockpit existed in very recent times in Skinnergate, where the late Mr. Ord, of Newtown, leased a property for twenty-one years to one Thomas Claxton, who at the time vociferously exclaimed, "Depend upon it, Mr. Ord, if I take the premises, I'll soon make a perfect paradise of the place!" Three or four years afterwards the owner went to share the delights of paradise, and to his surprise and disgust found that Tommy's idea of it consisted in a cockpit!

1758. Founded, the society of "Gentlemen Archers of Darlington." Among the first subscribers are the names of Mr. James Allan, Rev. Mr. Nicholson, Wm. Chaytor, esq., Henry Chaytor, jun., esq., Thomas Peirse, jun., esq., Mr. George Allan, Mr. John Pease, Mr. Ralph Tunstall, John Wright, esq., William Moore, esq., Mr. Thomas Lee, &c. They purchased a silver medal, chain, and case, 11*l.*; a silver gorget, 2*l.* 2*s.*; and a "horn spoon and *tiping* with silver 1oz., 7*s.* 6*d.*" The medal is the captain's prize for the first gold. Obverse, an oval upon a group of quivers, bows and arrows, inscribed:— "*Instituted by the Gentlemen Archers of Darlington* 25 *March*, 1758;" and legend:— "*Hic honos erit quique levibus sagittis valet.*" Reverse, 3 archers at their pastime:—

early state of that place will prove interesting.—When I was young, the timber on the property was not very plentiful, and only to be found in hedge rows; it consisted chiefly of ash with a few sycamores, elms of bad quality, and common maple or dog-tree; almost every ash tree had formerly been lopped or the tops taken off, and many of them were much decayed and become hollow in their trunks, affording harbour and nests for owls, hawks, and other birds. Frequently in the summer season a swarm of bees has been discovered in the bowels of the decapitated logs, and the rich honey made a joyful feast to rural pilferers. I was informed that during some of the years between 1740 and 1750 a great famine prevailed in the vicinity of Newtown, and there being no provision or grass on the ground during July and August for the cattle, the farmers and their servants were for weeks employed every day in cutting off the tops and branches of all the ash trees, young and old, which grew on the property. They told me the cows, oxen, &c., no sooner heard the noise of the axe, than they ran lowing and bellowing to the place of destruction to procure sustenance. Many of the old tenants of the hedge row are yet standing and look very picturesque, showing their gigantic and decayed trunks amongst the thousands of fine healthy young trees lately planted.

In the year 1747 [1749?] a fatal disease called the plague or murrain prevailed in this county, and the farmers at Newtown lost most of their beasts. It happened during winter, and not an ox, cow, heifer or calf survived in the byers or folds at that place, to the great loss of the owners; and what caused the calamity to be of more serious consequence was, that in tilling the ground at that time more oxen were employed for draught than horses. The oxen were often kept to great ages. Fortunately to the farm-house where I reside there belonged, and still belong, two fold yards, at more than half a mile distance, where many of the horned cattle were then kept with hay and staw, and to which place the contagion did not reach. The reason assigned for their providential preservation was that my grandmother (then newly married) undertook their care and management, and for some months went with great regularity twice a day to administer their quota of provision, the snow being some times very deep, and the drifts far above the tops of the gates and fences. On these occasions she was very cautious on leaving and re-entering the house to change her garments, to prevent the infection from spreading. It was an arduous undertaking for a young female, but by care and perseverance she most assuredly saved the lives of all the animals in the two distant folds.

* Allan MSS. D. and C. † Newcastle Gen. Mag.

‡ Historical List of Horse-Matches, &c., in 1756, by *Reginald Heber!*

"*Ostende artem pariter arcumque sonantem.*" The gorget is the lieutenant's prize for the first red, and is inscribed :—"*Secundus hoc contentus abito.*" "Such persons who shall pierce, enter, or break the white circle, shall wear [in succession] in their hats or some other conspicuous place, a horn spoon." It is inscribed "*Risum teneatis amici.*" The original subscription district of four miles was extended to ten the same year, and the members determined with due pomp :—"And whereas we are of opinion that some Additions are still wanting which wou'd further add to the Dignity of this Society, We have therefore purchased a Silk Banner with this Company's Arms thereon, and have cloath'd a Poor Boy in Green." These arms appear in the book and articles of the society, which were written and illustrated by the elegant pen and pencil of Allan the antiquary. They are, Vert, 3 long bows proper. Crest, on a wreath, sable and or, a sheaf of six arrows saltierwise, or. In 1760, Richard Hodgson, the captain for the half year, proud in his integrity, refused to give the customary security for the medal ; it was ordered that the late captain should retain the same, and at the next meeting the gentlemen archers "absolutely refused to lett Richard Hodgson shoot that day ;" and next year the offender agreed to comply with the rules. The silk banner had been at first delivered to the lieutenant with the gorget, but was afterwards made an ensign's prize, for the first blue. In 1767, the colours being in pieces, the members present were "unanimous in *opinion* [*qu.* all saw with their own *eyes*] that the silver chain annexed to the medal is very cumbersome, and rather defaces the medal by being kept therewith ; and that the silver cup belonging to this society has several holes therein, and *consequently* [dear, what a phenomeon !] is of no use." They ordered cup and chain to be sold and a new cup bought for the lieutenant. In 1770, the half-yearly meetings were discontinued for yearly ones. About 1835 a silver bugle was made a prize for the captain of numbers. In 1847, a gold medal was purchased, design a Brunswick star with the colours of the target enamelled in the centre, a bow, and three arrows in gold being laid across it. This prize for the highest gross score was intended to be shot for once a month in the summer season.*

Mr. G. J. Wilson of this society won a prize for the greatest number of hits at eighty yards at the grand national meeting at York, in 1848, and a subscription salver for the best gold in 1838, at Dinsdale, where the archers of Darlington, Richmond, and Bishop-Auckland had assembled.

The "ancient silver arrow" of the Scorton archers has frequently been shot for at Darlington, the names of Robert Eden, esq., John Bowes, esq., and the Hon. Tho. Vane occurring among the earlier captains and lieutenants at the meetings here. The arrow is frequently termed the "golden arrow," and within the last few years bore traces of gilding. It is said to have been given by Hen. Calverley, esq., of Eryholme, in 1673 ; a statement probably arising from the circumstance of that gentleman winning it in that year in which the society was formed. However, the meetings were at first restricted to a district within six miles of Eryholme, a number afterwards enlarged to twenty ; and to suit modern enervation, the time of meeting has altered from eight to ten, a. m. The arrow appears from 1673 to have always been known as "ancient," and it is inferred that the shooting for it was only revived when the articles were formed. A horn spoon inscribed "Risum teneatis, amici," is said to be contemporary, and some other prizes have been added. Great bets ran between the Darlington and Durham gentlemen, when the Darlington champion, Thomas Watson, won the arrow at Ferryhill, 1765. The prize lists are crowded with Darlington names.

1767. April. "An account of the inhabitants of the Town of Darlington, householders, what they farm, their rent, and where their settlements are," was taken in districts, by three gentlemen to each. The result is as follows :†—

* See "Hargrove's Anecdotes of Archery" for the rules and an engraving of the silver medal. The costume is a green coat, with a club gilt button ; buff waistcoat ; white corded trousers ; green velvet cap, with loose top, and silver band ; a green leather belt and arrow pouch.

† Original, penes R. H. Allan, esq., and synopsis in Allan MSS. D. and C.

	Families.	Inhabitants.	No. Sett.
Church Row	29	91	28
Bakehouse Hill	13	56	15
Horse Market	42	183	10
Hungate	16	71	24
Blackwellgate	74	173	57
Head Row	60	240	39
Richardson's Yard	23	86	36
Post-house Wynd	17	79	21
Skinnergate	148	507	173
Bondgate	160	500	175
Northgate	135	510	91
Prebend Row	24	105	13
Priestgate...	25	115	31
Tubwell Row	80	287	71
Clay Row...	42	141	51
	888	3144	835

1770. Plans for a new Town house were made by Mr. Samuel Wilkinson,* of the King's Head Inn. This edifice was to have small cupolas at the corners, the N. and S. fronts to extend eighty-four feet, and the E. and W. seventy-two feet. In the centre from W. to E. the shambles were to extend, and to have a pump, the dungeon was to occupy the N. E. corner, while in the upper story of the West front was to be a large room, forty-eight by twenty-one feet, lighted by five windows. Style, Italian of course. Some rather rude copies of the plans and elevations are penes R. H. Allan, esq.

1772. May 22. The first number of "*The Darlington Pamphlet, or, County of Durham Intelligencer*, published weekly, price Two-pence," by J. Sadler, appeared. Each number contained eight pages of foolscap size. Advertisements "of a moderate length" were taken in at 3*s*. 6*d*. each. November following saw its exit, but it was immediately succeeded by "*The Darlington Mercury; or, Durham Advertiser*," also printed by Sadler, an eight-paged quarto, price Two-pence half-penny, being a less size at a higher price. The advertisement "of moderate length" for 3*s*. 6*d*. is defined as not exceeding thirty lines. As in modern papers, disgusting quack advertisements form a staple fund for the printer. There is, however, a sensible article copied from the "York Chronicle" on the subject, exposing a composition manure of Baron Von Haake, who declared that "by its magnetic quality it unites the powers of all the four elements; that 16 lb. of it are sufficient to manure a statute acre of land, if the soil be not very barren, and that this quantity shall last without further help for eight years." This splendid composition appears to have been nothing more nor less than common sea water evaporated and reduced to a solid form.

I have seen the Mercury to Aug. 6, 1773. At a recent sale in London of scarce books, and other antique relics of the "olden time," a full set of the Darlington newspapers, bound together, consisting of both series, in fine condition (now very rare to be met with), and including a Newcastle newspaper, in the obituary of which is recorded the death of "*Mr. Darlington Mercury*," sold for 7*l*. 10*s*.

* A clever artist, frequently employed in illustration by Allan. He was the draughtsman of Cade's view of the church in 1774, and of a large general view of the town from Park Lane in 1760, from which I have given the bridge and centre of a town in a plate. The subscription price was 4*s*., the size twenty-two by eighteen inches, and it was published in 1776 from the burin of Bailey. It is a fine spirited plate, with an inscription to the Earl of Darlington. Clay Row has a good line of trees, and the whole town is rich in old orchards and garths attached to the burgages. In the foreground is a burgess "with a decent weapon in his hand," and a shepherd piping to a milkmaid in the true Damon taste of the age. Wilkinson retired in 1772, died in 1803, and was buried in the church; a dole of five guineas being paid to the churchwardens for the poor by his executor Mr. Anthony Bower.

1772. June. Tremendous and fatal thunder storms pervaded the country. Wm. Chilton, a farmer, near this town, had a mare struck dead by the lightning; his wife and three children were within a few yards of her at the time, but fortunately received no harm.

Mr. Thomas Bates's company of comedians performed at the New Theatre in this town for the first time on Whitsun-Monday. Tickets were to be had, in 1773, at the inns and of Mr. Bates at Mr. Thomas Todd Hunter's in Northgate (afterwards Bondgate). At this time Cunningham* was one of the actors. He writes from Darlington, in June, 1772, to Ritson :—" I stumbled on a pair of stairs in an hurry going to rehearsal, and hurt my side pretty severely, but am better. Our business here does not answer entirely to the hopes we had encouraged, but 'tis likely 'twill mend.—There are carts come every day to our town with lead from Stockton, by that conveyance I shall hope to hear from you. Direct to Mrs. Dawson's, milliner, in the Market place, where the carts unload." James Cawdell was the nephew and successor of Bates, who was deservedly respected, not only as a caterer for the public entertainment, but also as a friend and almost a father to his performers, many of whom afterwards displayed talent at the metropolis. He never aspired to make a figure as a performer, his most lucky character being that of a clown in a pantomime; but Cawdell was an excellent performer and a great favourite from his talent in both public and private life, having a very happy facility in converting the popular topics of the day into songs. In the decline of his health his various theatres were purchased by Mr. Stephen Kemble. In 1785, Cawdell published Miscellaneous Poems, among which " Jephthah's Vow" is inscribed to Mrs. Allan, of Grange. There is also a poem on her benevolence. The Allans were great patronisers of the drama, and had a private theatre at Grange, but Darlington has now long forgotten Shakspere.

In 1772 there was residing at Darlington a famous oculist named Doctor de Bello. His cures were advertised from time to time in due form, after the most approved modern fashion. Ann Pierse, of Blackwell, aged 60, states that she was totally blind of her left eye, and the sight of her right eye very much decayed of that dismal disorder, a cataract, for two years, but that the Doctor restored her " to perfect sight in a Minutes Time." William Walker, formerly parish clerk of Haughton, aged 91, who had been totally blind of a cataract in each eye for three years tells the same tale, acknowledging that the cause of his cure was Providence, Dr. de Bello having accidentally seen him sitting at his door. De Bello stayed at one Mrs. Perkins's, and during his absence his son officiated. The rector and churchwarden of Hurworth certified that a little girl of Jarvis Robinson's there, who from Psorophthalmia had become blind for three months, had been restored to perfect sight in seven weeks time.

July. About this time there was an extraordinary antipathy among the people to taking Portugal gold, which was then in abundant circulation. This went to such a height that when a farm house near Gainford was robbed, the villains only took some ten guineas out of a purse holding about 14*l.*, the rest being Portugal gold, owing, as it was supposed, to the difficulty of passing it. The indiscriminate refusal of this gold

* John Cunningham, the pastoral poet, whose only vanity was when he thought he was an excellent actor and had attained " theatrical eminence," for which he had not a single requisite, performed at many of the provincial theatres of the North. On the 20th of June, 1773, (the year of his death) his benefit at *Darlington* was over; and he wrote Mrs. Slack, his kind protectress, that he was going with the company to Durham; but was so poorly that he resolved shortly to be in Newcastle. Alas! he was generous to a fault, and always poor. An anecdote is told of him by Burns, which I cannot omit. " A dignitary of the church coming past Cunningham one Sunday as the poor poet was busy plying a fishing-rod in the Wear at Durham, his reverence reprimanded Cunningham very severely for such an occupation on such a day. The poet, with that inoffensive gentleness of manner which was his peculiar characteristic, replied, that 'he hoped God and his reverence would forgive his seeming profanity of that sacred day, *as he had no dinner to eat, but what lay at the bottom of that pool.*'" He died 1773, Sep. 18, aged 44, but if we may judge from Bewick's portrait, he was more like 70 in appearance. Cunningham had been complimented by a considerable allowance from Bates's Company, which he lived but a short time to enjoy. Cawdell was one of his first and best friends.

caused such great inconvenience, that at a meeting at the Posthouse, on Sep. 22, the gentlemen and tradesmen of Darlington unanimously agreed to receive, as usual, all Portugal coin that was *good*. In Oct. Mr. J. Clement, of Darlington (banker), advertises to give in change for Portugal gold, guineas or London Drafts at one month. Another meeting was held in the Tollbooth on Feb. 26, following, and all good foreign gold agreed to be taken in payment, as usual. This encouragement of its circulation was, however, almost rendered abortive by the collectors of the revenue and the farmers in general refusing to take it, just as if a moidore of full weight was not as good as the light English gold then floating in currency.

1772. July 27. The wife of Thomas Brown, a woolcomber in this place, was delivered of two boys and a girl.

"A few days since was married, at Gretna-Green, Mr. Thomas Tweddle, of Cowton, to the beautiful Miss Flintoff of Slip-in, near this town, with a fortune of 1000*l*."—*Darlington Pamphlet, Aug* 7, 1772.

1773. Feb. 21. A young woman, of Sadberge, came to this town and bought a quantity of arsenic, which she took in some water, and expired soon after. She was to have been married the next day, but some difference with her intended husband, it was imagined, was the occasion of her committing this rash action.

March. One Robson, a weaver in Northgate, having taken a boy and girl as apprentices from some neighbouring parish, and received 10*l*. with them as a fee; the children were observed to pick raw fish guts out of the kennel [channel] and eat them with greediness. The neighbours acquainted the overseers of the poor, who immediately examined into the matter, when they found the poor children almost starved; they having had nothing to subsist on for some time, except bean-meal, and that only by stealth. The children were taken to the workhouse, and the master absconded.

A petition from this town was presented to the House of Commons, complaining of the great decay of the linen trade, and of the increased importation of foreign linens.

A subscription was entered into by several inhabitants to indict the owners of stallions, that shall let them be guilty of that indecent practice of covering mares in the streets, a nuisance that had been long complained of.

April. William Wildman, alias William Woods, was under sentence of death at York Castle for his old offence of horse-stealing, a fate he had narrowly escaped at the same place in 1768, under the name of Robert Johnson, alias William Smith, for stealing a chaise-horse from Mr. Eden of Darlington, by his Majesty's free pardon.

April 12. Monday. As a man, much concerned in liquor, was returning home through Blackwell, he rode over a woman with a child in her arms, the child was much hurt and the woman's life despaired of.

Apr. Committed to Coventry Gaol, by John Hewitt, esq., one Bryant Holland, a bookbinder, for robbing his master of a quantity of materials and tools; he appears to have belonged to a party of strolling players in the counties of York, Durham, &c., and to have been born at Ludlow, co. Salop; he was supposed to have robbed other booksellers where he had worked, as a considerable quantity of books, tools, leather, &c., were found in his apartments. He had formerly worked with Mr. Darnton, stationer, in this place.

May 21. Robert ——, a poor fisherman, who attended this market, was attacked as he was returning home, upon Burdon bridge, by three villains who beat him in a most cruel manner, and left him for dead; some people coming up soon after carried him to a house in Burdon, where he lay some time before he came to himself, but soon recovered.

May. A remarkable fat cow was killed in this place by Mr. Geo. Coats, butcher, of Haughton: her four quarters weighed 96*st*. 8*lb*., and the tallow 17*st*. 1*lb*.; she was seven years old, was bred by William Burdy, of Peirsbridge, and fed by Mr. Richard Thompson, Postmaster in this town. Many considerable wagers were depending on her weight: the knowing ones were greatly let in, it being their opinion that she would not exceed ninety stone.

1773. June. A salmon was caught in the river Tees, in the locks at Dinsdale, which measured 52*in.* in length, 22*in.* round, and weighed 47*lb.* 8*oz.*

July 6. As Mr. Thomas Mason, a very considerable merchant in Stockton, was returning from Cleasby to this town in the evening, and riding smartly down the lane from Blackwell, he fell from his horse, and was unfortunately killed on the spot. He left a disconsolate widow, and three small children.

July. "Married at Carlisle, Thomas Lowry, of Blackwell, esq., a gay batchelor of 60, and a fortune of 1000*l.* per ann., to his maid, a handsome accomplished girl of 25*l.*"

July 10. This evening a Jew from Poland was travelling through this town on his way to Birmingham, Sheffield, &c., to buy hardware, for which he had brought about 90*l.* with him. This fact being discovered by a set of desperate, idle young fellows, they attacked him in Skinnergate, and not content with robbing him of all the money he had about him, they beat and wounded him in a most cruel manner: after which they took him to a pump and pumped water upon him for a considerable time, and then threw him over a high wall into a field behind the town. "The poor creature," says the Darlington Mercury of the 16th, "has been delirious ever since, and is, at present, obliged to be confined in the workhouse. It would melt the most hardened heart to see him, sometimes tearing his cloaths to pieces, and in a manner raving mad; at other times making a most lamentable outcry for his money. Several of the offenders have been taken into custody, and two of them were carried before the rev. Dr. Vane, at Longnewton, who committed them to Durham gaol: one of them confessed he got part of the money, which, by his directions, was found hid in a field; they have informed against several of their companions who were concerned, and the constables are making diligent search for them, and it is to be hoped they will succeed in securing them, as they have long been a terror to such of the inhabitants of this place as had occasion to go along the streets at night. There is a person in this town who understands the Polish dialect, and has been very useful to the Justices in explaining what the poor Jew said on his examination, (he can speak very little English,) the above person being absent, and his son, a child, being playing in the street, some person (it is imagined some of the before-mentioned gang out of spite to the father) had beat and bruised him on different parts of his body, and he continued this morning in a very poor way."

On the 4th August Sir William Blackstone, Knt., and on the 5th Sir Henry Gould, knt., passed through this town on their road to Durham to hold the assizes, when John Coltman, Richard Preston, Matthew Vesey, and Francis Dixon, were to be tried for robbing a Jew, in Darlington, of 90 guineas. Matthew Vesey was executed for the offence at Durham on the 23rd.*

John Flounders, at Crathorne near Yarm, advertises his bleaching of linen, and says that cloth would be taken in by himself at his shops in Darlington, &c., and amongst other agents by "William Hall, *attorney at Law*, Barnardcastle."

1775. A committee and subscription formed for prosecution of felons. There are now prosperous associations at Darlington and Cockerton for the purpose.

May. Inconvenience having arisen to persons who sent corn to the windmill at Darlington from the uncertainty of the wind, the owner Richard Richardson expresses that he had often been uneasy at the disappointments of his kind neighbours, and states that he had taken the water corn mill at Haughton without moulter.†

1775. Nov. 27. As the harriers of John Burdon, of Hardwick, esq,, were running a hare, they chanced to unkennel a fox, which they ran and killed near *Darlington*, after a very smart chase of twenty-five miles, and crossed the Skerne: out of twenty-five horsemen, only two and the huntsman were in at the death.‡

In this year the book of Vestry resolutions begins. Thomas Williams in contracting

* Darlington Mercury.—Sykes. The events in 1772 and 1773 are chiefly from the Darlington newspapers and are given entire.

† Allan MSS. D. and C.

‡ Gillespy's Coll.

for the poor "agrees to find a proper person to execute the office of a *Beadle* for the township, who is to have a proper coat provided at the Towns Expence." In 1788 an Act of Parliament for the better regulation of the poor of this parish was ordered but not obtained. In 1790 the Overseers ordered to get William Robson, sonof Wm. Robson, Bricklayer, a lunatick *now confin'd in Durham Goal* released from the Gaol and put under the care of Dr. John Hall. 1791. April 26. Thirteen Gentlemen contract to keep the poor and perform all Township business at 1000*l.* per annum for six years. On 23 Nov. 1800, it was resolved that the Overseers should purchase Rye or any other kind of grain to be made into Meal and sold to the poor of the Township not higher than 2*s.* 3*d.* a stone. In 1805 the Act of 22 Geo. III. for the management of the poor was adopted. In 1819, "Resolved, That it is the oppinion of this meeting that the Free Grammar School is of little use to the Town and Parish, and that it might be made *escencially* so by some alterations in the present stat*ues.* (Written by a Grammar Scholar, *in margin*)". In 1824, the sapient vestry finding "that the evil was a growing one," ordered that *patres nothorum* should be shown up by their names being printed in the annual report with the amount of the weekly allowance they paid, a resolution qualified by an order in 1825 that the initials only of those who paid, but the full names of defaulters and the sums due, should be given.

1776. "Tell Story the NCastle papers miscarried the 2 last weeks and did not come here till Sunday morning, which was the reason he had not them in the usual course of post. Old Tom the Pacquet Man who brings them you know to be a sot."—*Geo. Allan to* . . . . . .

1779. The Southern district of the county and the vale of the Tees had long been remarkable for a breed of short-horned cattle of large weight, usually termed the *Tees-water-Breed*;* these are said to have been more than once crossed with the Dutch or Flemish stock. The weight to which some of these cattle attained (before any particular attention had been paid to their improvement by a judicious selection) was very great. On Dec. 17, in this year, was killed at Darlington, by Mr. Geo. Coates, an eminent butcher, the most remarkable, largest and fattest ox ever exhibited in the kingdom; rising six years old, bred and fed by Chris. Hill, esq., of Blackwell. His whole carcase was engaged to be cut up for the several gentlemen's families in the neighbourhood at 1*s.* the pound."† The total weight was 162*st.* 10*lb.* Mr. Hill's "Blackwell Bull" was an ancestor of the fine "Sockburn Short-horns," on which a singular tract was published by Mr. John Hutchinson in 1822. "The Durham Ox", bred by Mr. Charles Colling, at Ketton in 1796, was supposed to weigh 168*st.* when exhibited at a show in 1801, by Mr. Bulmer, who purchased him for 140*l.*, and in the same year sold him to John Day for 250*l.* This enormous animal (for which 2000*l.* was refused by Day) was exhibited for nearly six years in all parts of England and Scotland, and when slaughtered in Feb. 1807, he weighed 220*st.* In the spring of . . . . Mr. Basnett, of Darlington, purchased a cow, with a bull calf (the famous Hubback) at her foot, and putting her into a good pasture she got so fat that it induced him to dispose of her to a butcher in the August following, and the calf was sold to a farmer in the neighbourhood. At four years old he was purchased by Mr. Robert Colling and Mr. Waistell, of Alihill, who at that time did not keep a bull for any other purpose than serving their feeding cows; but Mr. Colling finding him have a great propensity to get fat, sold him to his brother Charles Colling, who was then beginning to breed, and anxious of selecting those with the best dispositions to fatten: for the same reasons and with the same view, he soon after purchased of Mr. Maynard, of Ayreholm, a cow and a heifer, her daughter. This bull and cow, selected with so much judgment, were the original stock from which the celebrated Durham Ox, and the justly acknowledged superior breeds in the

* "Beef to the heels, like a Durham heifer."

† Original Broadside. At the same time and place were killed three wether sheep, bred and fed by Mr. William Charge, of Cleasby, which weighed 47*lb.* a quarter.

possession of Mr. Charles Colling,* Mr. Robert Colling,† and Mr. Chr Mason descended. In 1808 Mr. Robert Colling sold in Darlington market a two-years-old ox for 22*l.*, supposed to weigh sixty-three stones: the price of fat stock at that time being 7*s.* per stone; and in 1810 Mr. Wetherill, of Field House, sold at the fair in Darlington, the first Monday in March, two oxen, under three-years-old, for 47*l.* 10*s.* each. The price of fat cattle at this fair was about 10*s.* a stone. At Mr. Charles Colling's sale in that year the bull "Comet" was sold for 1000 guineas. The "Teesdale Tupes" were of equal fame with the bulls of the district.‡

1780. A patent was granted to Thomas Proud for a turnip drill. He lived in Skinnergate and was on friendly terms with Dr. Peacock, who once asked him, "If our two names were put together what would they make?" He made agricultural implements to be delivered at Darlington and Horncastle, and in 1811 published at the former place an Essay on Drill Husbandry.

1780. Mr. Hutchinson computed his estimates of population by taking the baptisms, marriages, and burials for two periods of twenty years each, and multiplying the burials in 1780 by thirty, on the supposition that one-thirtieth of the inhabitants died yearly. This gave the population far too low, the multiplier ought to have been forty-four.§

Darlington Parish.	Bp.	Mr.	Br.
From 1660 to 1680	949	165	880
1760 to 1780	2858	715	2621

1780. Died, William Emerson, the deistical mathematician of Hurworth, and one of the many visitors to the famed fairs of Darlington. He was the son of Dudley Emerson, schoolmaster, Hurworth, and was born May 14, 1701. Cloddish as to learning in his youth he did not turn his attention to mathematics till when he was about twenty years of age. His wife was the niece of a Dr. Johnson, Rector of Hurworth, who had promised to give five hundred pounds with her, but when Emerson, some time after marriage, reminded him of this, he treated him with contempt, and chose to forget the circumstance. Emerson, stung to the quick, packed up his wife's clothes and sent them to the Doctor in a wheelbarrow, saying he would scorn to be beholden to such a fellow for a single rag, and swearing he would prove himself the better man of the two. He said truly, for in his first published work on Fluxions, in 1743, his forty-second year, he stepped forth like a giant in all his might. A set of his works is in the library of the Mechanics' Institute.‖ His person was robust, his diet low. His hats were few, and when he pur-

* He died at Monkend, near Croft, aged 85, in 1836.

† Robert Colling, of Barmpton, was worthily entitled "*The Prince of Skerne.*" The uncle to him and Charles was Ralph Colling, of Ricknal Grange, who by no means appears to so much advantage in popular diction, for an unaccountable order for some hammers has given rise to the simile "*Like Ralph Colling's hammers, all of a size and one bigger than another.*" All of one pattern was, perhaps, Ralph's meaning. I throw together one or two more Bishopric *likenesses*. An imaginary difficulty is to be "*as queer as Dick's hatband that went nine times round and still wouldn't tie;*" a washerwoman, when half frantic at the unreasonable heaps of work before her, declares herself "*as throng as Throp's wife when she hung herself with a dish-clout.*" "*Its like Timothy Spark, it's vast-lye clever,*" refers to an enterprising farmer of Dales House, who lost many a crop by copying what he termed "*vast-lye clever*" schemes of Bryan Harrison, of Barmpton, and other neighbours, without any consideration of their superior lands and advantages, and when nearly ruined by his folly exclaimed, "Lads, lads, wonkerins, but this is vast-lye bad wark." "*As great a liar as Jenny Byers*" is a memento of a masculine matron of Brafferton, of the last generation, who loved occupations of the dirtiest sort, generally pursued by the rougher sex, in preference to those of her own, and who was an inveterate teller of stories of a fictitious hue.

‡ "Mr. Francis Hunt, a considerable farmer in this neighbourhood, one evening last week selected from his large stocks into a convenient paddock, four of his ewes which seemed heaviest with young, which, the next morning, he found had produced him 13 lambs all strong and likely to do well."—*Darlington Mercury*, 1773, *Mar.* 26.

§ Bailey's Agricultural Survey.

‖ His fugitive pieces are often marked "Merones" (a transposition of the letters of his name), and "Philofluentimechanalgegeomastrolongo."

chased one it was of no consequence whether it was of the fashion of the day, or of half a century before. One of them, of immense superficies, in time lost its elasticity, and the brim began to droop, so as to prevent his being able to view the objects before him in a direct line. He therefore took a pair of sheers and cut it round close by the body of the hat, leaving a little to the front, which he dexterously rounded into the resemblance of the nib of a jockey's cap. His wigs were made of brown or a dirty flaxen coloured hair, which at first appeared bushy and tortuous behind, but which grew pendulous through age, till at length it became quite straight, having probably never undergone the operation of the comb : and either through the original mal-conformation of the wig, or from a custom of frequently inserting his hand beneath it, his hind-head and wig never came in very close contact. He commonly wore a drab waistcoat with sleeves only, sans coat. His linen was spun and bleached by his wife, for whom he made a spinning-wheel, shown in his "Mechanics," and woven at Hurworth ; and he frequently, in cold weather, wore his shirt with the wrong side before and buttoned behind his neck ; the reason being that he seldom buttoned more than two or three of the buttons of his waistcoat, one or two at the bottom, and sometimes one at the top ; leaving all the rest open : in wind, rain, or snow, therefore, he would have found the aperture at the breast inconvenient. In cold weather he wore, when he grew old, what he called *shin-covers*, which were made of old sacking, tied with a string above the knee, and depending before the shins down to the shoe ; they were useful in preserving his legs from being burnt when he sat too near the fire, which old people are apt to do.

Such was the Sanchotic figure of the great man who periodically appeared in Darlington market. When his stock grew low, on the Monday morning he took his *wallet*, which he slung obliquely across his shoulders, and set forward for the market ; always walking, for he seldom or never kept a horse, and had an aversion to riding. He would frequently lead the horse, when he had one, from market, by the halter, bearing the wallet stuffed with provisions. After having provided all the necessary articles, he did not always make directly home again, but, if he found good fair ale and company to his mind, he would sit himself down contentedly in some public house for the remainder of the day, and frequently during the night too ; some times he did not reach home till late on Tuesday, or even Wednesday : he remained talking, or disputing, on various topics, mechanics, politics, or religion, just as his company might be, and varying the scene sometimes with a beef-stake, mutton-chop, or a pan of cockles ; for it is remarkable that his ale did not injure, but rather improve his appetite ; and that he never felt the head ache, or any immediate ill effects afterwards. In these *durable* potations he would sometimes indulge, not only at Darlington, but in Hurworth, or some neighbouring village, and always in an ale-house, for he kept no stock of ale (his favourite beverage) at home ; and he was upon all occasions rigidly exact in apportioning each man's quota of the reckoning. His last excursion to Darlington with his wallet, was the only time, it is believed, he ever rode thither, and he was then mounted on a quadruped, whose intrinsic value, independent of the skin, might be fairly estimated at half a crown. Being preceded and led by a boy, hired for that purpose, he crawled in slow and solemn pomp, at the rate of a mile and a half in an hour, till in due time he arrived at Darlington, and was conducted in the same state, to the great entertainment of the spectators, through the streets to his inn. What idea Emmerson himself entertained of the velocity with which the animal could travel, appears from this, that when a neighbour of his from Hurworth asked him towards the evening if he wasgoing home, "D—n thee (said he), what dost thou want with my going home ?" "Only (said the man) because I should be glad of your company." "Thou fule, thou ! (replied the other) thou'lt be home long enough before me, man ! thou walks and I ride. Such expressions as "D—n thee," and "Thou fule," were mere expletives often with him, expressive neither of indignation nor contempt Indeed his style of conversation, always abrupt and blunt, was often vulgar and ungrammatical, and this induced some to say that his prefaces were not his own composition, or were *translated into English* by some other hand. At this he was very indignant, and exclaimed "A pack of fools! who could write my prefaces but myself?" They do in fact carry with them every mark of legitimacy, and his letters were well written. His hostility to riding was so marked that he used to say to Mr. Montagu, of Eryholme, when he asked him to get into a carriage, "D—n your whim-wham! I had rather walk."

His singularity caused him to be considered as a *wise* or *cunning man* by the ignorant, and they would tell how that by a magic spell he pinned a lad [the late Capt. Dryden] in the top of a tree where he had mounted to steal his fruit, and compelled him to sit there a whole Sunday's forenoon, in full view of the congregation going to and returning from church; the truth being that Emerson stood at the bottom with a hatchet, and swore that if he came down he would "hag (hew) his legs off."* An Irish woman came to know if her husband, who had been absent in the Indies for six years unheard of, was alive, she wishing to accept the proposals of another. Rising hastily from his tripod or three legged stool on which he usually sat, the prophet exclaimed "D—n thee for a b—h! thy husband's gone to hell: and thou may go after him." The woman went away quieted in her conscientious scruples. A young damsel met with a milder reception. She wanted to know if her fellow-servant had stolen some articles her mistress had lost. "Thou's a canny young lass," replied the smiling conjurer, "but thou's over late o'coming, I can do nought for thee." The poor girl mourned that she had not made her application sooner, supposing he meant that the mysterious moment was past.

The wisdom and probity of this world are folly before God, and Emerson seems to have been a sort of deist. He collected two small 4to. vols. of what he conceived to be contradictory passages of the Bible, and arranged them, like hostile troops confronting each other, on opposite pages; and as he by no means spoke of revelation or the church of England and its clergy with respect, he was an example to the vulgar not a little reprehensible. He did not wish to be admitted to the Royal Society, "because (he said) it was a d—d hard thing that a man should burn so many farthing candles as he had done, and then have to pay so much a year for the honor of F. R. S. after his name. D—n them and their F. R. S. too."

He was very fond of angling, and would stand up to his middle in water for several hours together, and when he was building a house on his small farm by the side of the Tees, he never hesitated to plunge into the water to gather stones from its bed. In fact, being somewhat effected then with gouty symptoms, he said that *wading* was serviceable to him because the water sucked the gout out of his legs. When he wrote his treatise on Navigation, he must needs make and fit up a small vessel; with this he and some young friends embarked on the the Tees that ran by his door, at Hurworth, but the whole crew got swamped frequently; when Emerson, smiling and alluding to his book said, "They must not do as I do, but as I say."

In the earlier part of his life he attempted to teach a few scholars, but made little progress and soon dropped. He never had a scholar that did him any credit, except Mr Richardson, of Darlington, who was always a great favorite with him, and of whom he used to say that he was the only boy who had a head in his school.†

* This tree feat was of great value. A lady lost her clothes in drying, and came to Emerson. "What, art thou sike a fule to believe in sike things?" said the conjuror, who proceeded to instruct her to give out that if the missing articles were not forthcoming by a certain day, he would cause the thief to mount a cherry-tree when the people were going to church. The clothes duly re-appeared one morning at the claimant's door.

† John Hunter, a common bricklayer, of Hurworth, became the pupil and the friend of Emerson, and acquired all the brusqueness of his master. Upon one occasion Emerson had been engaged in some abstruse mathematical calculation for twenty-four hours, and failing in the result, he carried his papers to John, who, glancing at the manuscript, thus addressed his master:—"Aye, but thou is a fule!—dis'nt thou see that thou's wrang at vary beginnin?" "D—n it, I *is* a fule!" was the response. One day as John was repairing the roof of Emerson's house, and the philosopher was serving him from below with mortar, a post chaise drew up, from which stepped out two gentlemen, who inquired if the great Mr. Emerson lived there? "Great or little, I am the man," was the answer. They stared a little, bowed, and informed him that they were a deputation from the Uni-

As he advanced in years he was much afflicted with the stone, and in agony he would crawl round the room on his hands and knees, sometimes praying and sometimes swearing, and devoutly wishing that the "soul might have shaken off its rags of mortality without such a *clitter-my-clatter*," as he called it. He died at last without much pain, 1782, May 21, aged 81, and was buried in Hurworth churchyard* at the West end of the church, where a Latin inscription commemorates him ("sepultum et *neglectum*") and his wife, who followed him in 1784. They had no children.

Emerson, with much persuasion, about a year before his decease, was prevailed on by his friend Dr. Cloudesley, of Darlington, to sit for his picture, which was taken by Sykes, and from which an engraving (now excessively scarce) was copied.

His telescope was formed of three or four cask staves, tied together; and his microscope was a small lens, set in the top of a spring window fastener. In 1781 he disposed of his mathematical library, which he valued at 40 or 50*l*., because, he said, he had none but a pack of fools to leave them to, and money would be of more value to them than books.† He was well skilled, by the way, in musical science, though he was himself a poor performer. He had (if the expression may be used) two first strings to his violin, which he said made the E more melodious, when they were drawn up to a perfect unison. His virginal he had cut and twisted into various shapes in the keys, by adding some occasional half-tones, to regulate the present scales and to rectify some fraction or discord that will always remain in the tuning; but he never could get it regulated to his mind. He had an odd instrument in the shape of a long handle with three strings and a quartern measure at its end, upon which he played.‡

1783. Sep. 15. Established at Darlington, the first agricultural society in the county, denominated the "Agricultural Society for the County of Durham." Each subscriber of 1*l*. 1*s*. was deemed a member, and at the first institution there were thirty-two subscribers of 2*l*. 2*s*., and twenty-three of 1*l*. 1*s*. each, making the whole subscription 91*l*. 7*s*.

versity of Cambridge, and had brought a difficult problem which they inquired if he could solve. Casting his eye upon it for a moment, he called his pupil, "John Hunter, come down, and do *thou* answer this." The mason descended, and after a few minutes of silent calculation, produced the answer, written with a piece of chalk upon the crown of his hat, which Emerson was about to hand, unlooked at, to the collegians; when, a little offended, they requested him at all events to revise it; on which he glanced at it for an instant, and then pronounced it "quite correct." The collegians not readily understanding Hunter's solution, Emerson testily told them to "take the hat home with them, and return it when they had discovered the explanation." It was reported, that he could call the stars from their spheres; and that he often *did* so. John Hunter was the accepted suitor to a village damsel who, upon Hunter informing her that *he* also could command the stars *as well* as his master, insisted upon ocular demonstration of the fact. Selecting that season of the autumn when falling or shooting stars are frequent, Hunter commenced his incantations, when a whole shower of meteors fell, and at the same time the northern lights shone with great splendour. His intended stared in amazement; but lo! she would have had them restored to their spheres; and what was to be done if he could not get them up again? Upon this the loving couple set off, the damsel in great agony of mind, to our philosopher, who professed to rebuke Hunter severely for his folly and presumption, and informed the trembling fair one "that it was most fortunate that he was in time to remedy the mischief, as otherwise all the inhabitants of the neighbourhood would have been consumed to ashes in their beds before morning." After this John left the stars to his master, but his wife always believed in her husband's power in that line.

* I have been told that Emerson's grave being opened for another interment some years afterwards, the body was found perfect, to the consternation of the grave-digger, but that it mouldered away.

† His first work did not procure encouragement, and probably his others would not have appeared in his lifetime if Edward Montague, esq., his great friend, had not procured him Nourse's patronage, who, himself learned in the more abstruse sciences, engaged Emerson to furnish a course of mathematics for students, and in 1763 Emerson went to London to fulfil his engagement. He treated every opponent of Sir Isaac Newton's philosophy as dull, blind, bigotted, prejudiced, or mad. Montague left him one hundred guineas, but the stern magician burst into tears and declared that "he would rather have seen Mr. Montague than his money."

‡ Compiled from his life by the Rev. W. Bowe, of Scorton: London: F. Wing, successor to Emerson's publisher, Mr. John Nourse, 1793; and touched up from Walker's Dinsdale and Croft; and original information.

They had four general meetings yearly; two at Durham and two at Darlington, when the premiums were adjudged by five of the members; but in 1794 and following years, the whole of the members present were the judges, and the society dwindled down till its ending in 1814.

1786. November. In the last desperate adventure of "Stoney Bowes" with his wife the Countess of Strathmore, it is well known that he bore her away from the protection of the Court of King's Bench to her mansion of Streatlam, and endeavoured by every threat to induce her to stay proceedings in the Ecclesiastical Court, and live with him as his wife. But crowds were round the house, and Bowes appeased them by procuring two disguised domestics to personate himself and the Countess at the windows, and thus persuade them she was safe;* in the meantime took her out by a back way, and dragged her, between ten and eleven o'clock, in the dark to a little cottage in the neighbourhood, where they spent the remainder of the night. There, finding threats in vain, he threw her on the bed and flogged her with rods. "On leaving the cottage in the morning, he had her set on horseback behind him, without a pillion, and took her over dismal heaths and trackless wilds, covered with snow, till they came to *Darlington*, to the house of his attorney, where she was shut up in a dark room, and where she was threatened (a red-hot poker being held to her breast) with a mad doctor and strait-waistcoat; but all in vain.†

"The hour of deliverance drew near. Hither they had been tracked, and here it was no longer safe for Bowes to continue, he therefore set out with her before day,‡ in the same manner that he brought her, taking her over hedges and ploughed fields, till being seen [near Neasham] by the husbandmen at work, he was so closely hemmed in, that an old countryman taking hold of his horse's bridle, and Bowes presenting his pistol to frighten him, he was knocked down by a constable [Chr. Smith] that was in pursuit of him, and felled to the ground with a large hedge-stake. Seeing him in that situation, her ladyship put herself under the protection of the peace-officer, and being on horseback, in a kind of womanish exultation bid him farewell, and mend his life, and so left him weltering in his blood; while she, with the whole country in her favour, made the best of her way to London, attended only by her deliverers, where she arrived safe.§"

* The sheriff's officers positively served the attachment on the wrong person.

† The tipstaffs from London were surrounding the house. It was where the Joint Stock Bank now stands.

‡ He skulked out the back way through the Sun Inn yard.

§ Such is the account in the Gentleman's Mag. for the day, from her ladyship's own statements, but Bowes swore that "after the service of the Habeas Corpus, he had, in compliance, proceeded to bring Lady Strathmore to town, but was unable to ford the river *Dee* with safety to her ladyship and himself. In consequence of which, he was returning by a nearer way, when he was met by the party who were sent to execute the attachment, by whom he was treated as has been already related." The manner of apprehending Bowes as told by his friends, also differs widely from that told by Lady Strathmore. They say nothing of the cottage; and that a few hours before the Habeas Corpus was served, apprehending an attachment, he took the Countess of Strathmore with him in a post-chaise and directed his route Northward. Being pursued by different parties, he was compelled to alter his course almost perpetually, and forsaking the coach road, to take his journey through the mountains, subject to all the inconveniences stated by her ladyship. Leaving the post-chaise, he took the Countess with him on a single horse, and instead of a pillion, was forced to substitute a blanket. At one period his pursuers were within a mile of him; being apprized of it, he changed his course, and travelled back seventeen miles of the way he had already passed, and proceeded towards Darlington. A few miles from that town he was met by two farmers, one of them declared his suspicion, but having no warrant, Bowes drew a pistol, and with violent menaces, threatened them if they interrupted him; a crowd coming up, the pistol was wrested from him and broken; he was pulled from his horse, and in his fall received two violent wounds on the back part of his head with the barrel, which, with the fall, deprived him of all power of further resistance. Bowes was then taken to the house of Mr. Thomas Bowes, at Darlington, where, notwithstanding his wounds, he knocked down the farmer that stopped him, and had him kicked out of the house. A posse of people, however, soon surrounded the house, and an express was sent to M'Manus, and other Bow-street people, then at Carlisle, who broke in upon him, executed the writ, and notwithstanding every stratagem to delay him, conducted him to London and produced him as before recited.—*(Foot's Life of Bowes and the Countess.* 133.*)* Bowes was sentenced to three years imprisonment, and to find a very heavy security to keep the peace, and a divorce was obtained.

The printed accounts of the transaction are so meagre that I am induced to add the substance of the affidavit of Mr. Christopher Smith, the constable of Neasham, contained in his memorandum book, which has been kindly lent me by his son, Mr. James Smith, of the High Row. "20th Novr. 1786. At half an hour past twelve o'clock at noon, an alarm was given by a man on horseback, that 'Bowes had killed his wife, and the country was in arms to take him.' I had seen a man ride past with a woman behind him, without a pillion, attended by another man on horseback, wanting a hat or any covering upon his head, and a bare sword by his side, and took them for pickpockets. Upon this I ran to the door, and said to my brother, 'Let us each get a stick, and we will go and take him.' We went after them, as did several of the village, about a mile, into Sockburn Lane. Upon our coming up, Mr. Bowes said, 'What do you all want?' I said, 'The country is alarmed with a bad report, and we are come to take you.' Mr. Bowes presented a pistol, and said he would blow out the first man's brains that dared to touch him. I said, if he would surrender, we would not hurt him. He again said he would shoot any one that came nigh him, and that he would pay any one who would take him to Northallerton. John Gunson said the Tees was too deep at Sockburn, he must go back to Neasham. I said he should not stir from the place till he was taken, and if he would not submit we would set upon him, and take him at all events; for he was a suspicious person, and had surely done something bad, or he need not ride through the country in the manner he did. Mr. Bowes turned about his horse, seeming to go away, when the woman slipped off from behind him, and, clasping her hands together, said, 'I am Lady Strathmore, for God's sake assist me.' I said, 'Are you indeed Lady Strathmore?' She said, 'I am, and am forced away contrary to my inclination by that man,' (turning to Mr. Bowes). I said, 'If you are Lady Strathmore, we will secure your person and take him,' and bade the men get sticks and we would set upon him, and take him at all events. Anthony Claxton put off his hat, and went near Bowes, which I perceiving bid him put on his hat and be upon his guard; and seeing Bowes rest the pistol upon the other in the belt, I rushed upon him, and seized them both, and called for assistance, when John Waiton came and took hold of the horse and led him past me. While Bowes struggled with me, one of the pistol handles broke in my hand, and by pulling them away, the guard of the trigger cut a piece out of the foremost finger of my right hand. I threw that pistol away, and with the other gave Bowes a blow upon the right side of his head which knocked him from the horse. Fearing he had more pistols about him, and that he might shoot some of us, I gave him another blow upon the back part of his head, and cut it about two inches. Lady Strathmore asked if he was killed, and desired we would not strike him again; and several times bade us search his pockets for pistols and take care he did not shoot some of us. Her Ladyship being then upon horse before Gabriel Thornton, bade us farewell. I sent John Gunson away for a surgeon to dress the wound, and took him to Eliza Stubbs's till Tho. Bowes, Mr. Turner, and Mr. Rudd's man came and dressed the wound, and then carried Bowes away to Tho. Bowes's house at Darlington. And on the Wednesday he was conducted to London by three men from Lord Mansfield's and Bow-street offices.' *

* The brave Smith died in 1797, leaving eight children, and a widow *enciente*. While lying in of her posthumous child (my informant James aforesaid) she received an anonymous letter containing five pounds. This was all his family received from the Strathmore race, notwithstanding all his bravery and losses, for he had borne his expenses of a journey to London himself.

Let me dip into his memoranda again.

"Decr. 23d. 1777. A remarkable fat wedder sheep, fed by Mr. Thos. Hutchinson of Smeaton, and killed by John Coates, which weighed 17st. 10lb. or 248lb. was shewn at Darlington. The Duke of Athol offered 2*s.* 6*d.* a pound for one quarter and could not have any, being all disposed of, but was presented with a neck by the hospitable Miss Allan, which graced his own table on New Year's day 1778."

"1789 was a very wet summer, it begun about the middle of April, and continued till the beginning of August. The rivers and brooks in all parts over-flowed their banks and sanded meadows and pastures. The corn did not suffer so much, and was succeeded with a most favourable winter."

1787. A number of Waxen Chatterers appeared about Darlington. These birds fed on haws, which were very plentiful that year. None have since appeared.*

1788. At this period there was a bowling green in James Allan's Pilkington Close.

1791. The pastoral "Hell-Kettles" of this date, mentioned in page 35, I have found to be the production of John Cade (vide 311 *post.*), from his letter to Allan, mentioning his intention to offer it to Miss Darnton. "The town (says he) is supposed to contain about 6000 persons.† - - - Of late years, horticulture has been brought to considerable perfection at Darlington, and agriculture pursued with avidity in the environs."

"Blackwell Races, Whitsun-Tuesday, 29th May, 1792.—1. A Hat and Gold Girdle to be run for, by any number of boys that will then start. 2. A Bridle and Whip to be run for by asses. 3. A Dozen of Pipes and a Roll of the best Tobacco under the sun, to be run for by any old women. 4. A match between two noted Shetland ponies, the winner to have the loosing horse. 5. A fine muslin Apron and Ribbon to be run for by girls not exceeding 15 years of age. 6. A new full trimmed Holland Smock, with a fashionable Cap, to be run for by any women that chuse to start. Many other diversions and prizes will be then given. ☞ The races to begin exactly at Two o'Clock." —*Original Handbill.*

1798. Mr. Frank, the attorney of Stockton, would appear to have thought of Darlington as a resting place, and in this year Ritson writes him thus :—"York, it seems, in case of a separation from Mr. Wolley, affords no prospect of a satisfactory establishment ; which you must, of course, look out for *in* some other place. Rowntree, no doubt, is a good judge of the superior advantages of Darlington, compared, that is, with the neighbouring country : but you might do well, in the mean time, to enquire into the state of Halifax, Wakefield, and other populous towns in Yorkshire, of which I have always had a much better opinion." Frank, as is well known, joined in partnership with Rowntree, for whom Ritson sketched a piece of pleasantry in coat armour after saying "I am convinced that your family stole into the world, nobody knows how or when. Though I can easily believe that when you yourself go out of it, your exit will be sufficiently notorious. Apropos ! there is one coat of arms which I should think you might adopt without offence to any, as it seems particularly appropriated to *gentlemen* of your honorable profession, representing at once the rewards you merit, and the means by which you attain them. Here it is." Then is sketched a regular coat, consisting of a man placed on the pillory, with two pens crossed over an ink-stand below, and a gibbet, in expectancy above him. Motto, "*Palma non sine pulvere.*"

1799. At the hour of nine p. m. the family at Newtown had just retired to bed, when there was heard a rap at the kitchen door, and on Mr. Ord asking who was there and what was wanted, a female entreated earnestly to be admitted and to have lodgings till the morning, as she had lost herself and was almost starved with cold. She said that she was the servant of Mr. John Atkinson, of Little Stainton, and after some further questions had been put to her, was suffered to remain till the next day. Very

"1795. Jany. 14th. Came on an intense frost and snow, which continued for 21 days, and after that time a succession of stormy weather, in all 7 weeks." [The Tees at the breaking up, was seven or eight inches higher than in the great flood in 1771. W.H.L.]

"1795. Mem. Corn advanced at the end of harvest, and got to the average of one guinea per bushel, owing to the vile speculators of the time, and other contraband dealers. The effects were, farms were advanced, taxes laid on, the public money sent to support the emperor of Germany and the king of Prussia, &c., till the Bank of England stopped payment.—1795, May the 25th. Corn was sold at Darlington at 9*s.* a bushell, continued advancing till it sold at one guinea a bushell, being engrossed and forestalled all the summer, till the 21st. of Septr. when new corn was produced."

"1796. Decr. 24th. Was the most intense frost ever known in England."

* Allan's MS. Cat. of the Grange Museum. "The Waxen Chatterer—Bombycivora garrula. *Temm.* Bohemian Chatterer Silktail. Plentiful in the Northern parts of this Island, annually visiting Edinburgh during winter."

† Gough, in 1789, mentions the dwellings as about 1200, and after stating the fame of the town for its manufactory of table-linen called huckabacks, and a great woollen manufactory, adds that the manufactory of small wares had been lately set at work.

soon after it transpired that the girl had purchased some arsenic at Darlington prior to this nocturnal visit, and had mixed it with flour, intending it for the destruction of her master, Mr. Atkinson, who was from home on the day the bad act was committed, but was expected to return in the afternoon. His mother, an old woman, made a pudding of the deleterious mixture, which was offered to her son on his return, but he refused to partake of it as he had got something to eat on his journey. The morning following, however, the frugal lady mixed the pudding with more flour and other ingredients, and transmogrified it into a large family cake for breakfast, which all eat of except the servant girl. In a short time the Atkinsons became exceedingly ill, and a medical man was hastily sent for ; he applied his remedies, and eventually all recovered save the mother, who lingered some weeks in great pain and then died. The family had no doubt of the girl's guilt, but discharged her from their service, and told her that if she never came near Little Stainton again, they would take no proceedings. The wretched being was an orphan named Mary Nicholson ; she was considered as of very weak intellect, and it was reported that her master had taken very great liberties with her, and treated her in a very cruel way. On being turned to the door and having no person to relieve her, she had wandered about the country for some days before she found a temporary rest at Newtown, and the day after her sojourn there, she once more returned to the house of the Atkinsons. She told them she could not rest day or night, and that they might send her to gaol, or treat her as they pleased. Accordingly she was sent to Durham, and tried at the Assizes following. She stood in court alone, without a friend, without a soul to speak in her behalf, and was condemned to die. On the 22 July, 1799, an immense concourse of spectators assembled to witness her end on Framwellgate Moor. After being launched from the cart, and remaining suspended for some little time, when still conscious, the rope broke in two and she fell to the ground. In a horrible state she actually remained half an hour, to the great distress of the lookers on, some of whom had come a great distance. At last another rope was procured, and so ended the butchery of poor unfortunate Mary Nicholson.

1800. Died, at Haughton-le-Skerne, Mr. John Kendrew. At one time nearly all the ground in Darlington upon which Albion-street is built, and extending Northward to beyond the new street, Kendrew-street, was cultivated as a market garden by a Mrs. Kendrew : and she and her son John were Friends. John, commonly called "Jackey Kendra," was brought up to weave "checked tammys," then woven by hand, in great numbers in this place, and pursued his daily labour without attracting any particular notice as a man of genius, although, like Arkwright, he employed his thoughts more on other matters than on those which belonged to his proper avocation. Optics composed his favourite study, and having formed a small machine for grinding and polishing both concave and convex glasses, for spectacles and optical instruments, he proceeded to the manufacture of the former, which, at the first, he hawked through the country occasionally, and subsequently, as his customers became more and more numerous, to the entire abandonment of the shuttle and the loom. Gough mentions his mill "for grinding optic glasses to the greatest perfection," yet the invention of this self-taught mechanic was of heavy and rude construction, though it was a great improvement upon the usual mode of performing the operation. Some readers will remember such a machine at work in an old gloomy little building, that stood a short distance East of the Bishop Blaize Inn ; but the business extended, and premises were built, and machines put to work, at what is termed the "Low Mill," now occupied by Messrs. Henry Pease and Co. Here spectacles were fit up in almost countless numbers, and sent to Birmingham, and other places. The cupidity of the Birmingham men suggested that they had better make themselves, than come to Darlington to buy. They pirated Kendrew's invention, and his trade died out. His mind, however, had a fresh subject before it ; for according to the old proverb, "as one door shuts, another opens." Itinerating into Lancashire, he there saw the jenny, which was then in use for spinning cotton, and at once took up the idea of applying the principle of that machine to the spinning of flax by machinery, turned by water power. On his return to Darlington, therefore, he enlisted a native of Barnard-castle, named Porteous or Porthouse (who had settled in Tubwell Row as a watchmaker, and had some money and mechanical skill, both useful to Kendrew), for his coadjutor; and two plodding men working together, as Arkwright and Kay had done before them, eventually, after many difficulties with the machine, and as many with the peculiar fibre they had to deal with, brought out a set of engines for preparing and spinning flax; for which, with the assistance of Mr. Backhouse, the banker, they obtained a royal patent in 1787, and spun a tolerable quantity for that day. "Mr. John Marshall, of Leeds," writes a native of the town in the Darlington and Stockton Times, "as I remember, (he would be the father of the gentleman now so well known and honoured in various walks of life, and one of whose rooms covers two acres, and has a field in the top), came over and bargained to give so much per spindle for the right to use the new plan. Marshall, however, ceased to pay Kendrew's charge, saying it was not the same thing, and the law refused Kendrew's claim for nine hundred pounds, a sum which I have been told, Marshall then said would have been of no use if the court had confirmed, for he had it not. How largely must his intelligence have subsequently remunerated!" When the partnership ceased, Porteous placed himself in the mill near Coatham Mundeville, and Kendrew in another (a great part of which he built) near Haughton; and there these two first English spinners of flax by machinery received line and tow from the hecklers in the neighbourhood, which they manufactured into yarns, at a charge of so much per bundle of sixty thousand yards. The machinery of Kendrew and Porteous, no doubt, was clumsy in its structure, but still these worthy men deserve no ordinary honour for giving a demonstration of the practicability of spinning flax by mechanical agency alone, and opening out an entirely new sphere for human industry and the acquirement of riches.* Their yarns, at the commencement, were no better than those which were spun with the common hand-wheel; but they were produced in greater abundance, and at less expense.†

1800. Tuke, in his "Agriculture of the North Riding," speaks very satisfactorily of the working of Proud's drill:—"Several farmers in the Vale (Cleveland) and also a few in Ryedale, have got a drill for sowing turnips made by T. Proud, of *Darlington*, which fixes to the plough-beam, consequently sowing and ploughing is performed by the same operation. This drill has some advantages beyond any I have seen: the seed is deposited in the fresh mould and upon the manure, whilst there is moisture in the soil (the land being manured immediately before ploughing), and if the soil is sandy, there is no need of harrowing: these circumstances have a great tendency towards insuring a crop." He mentions the "level land near the river Tees consisting of a rich gravelly loan" that the best short-horned cattle were bred near Darlington, Mr. Robert Colling having perhaps the best bull of the kind in the kingdom; and that the wool grown in Richmondshire was chiefly sold at Darlington, the stone there being 18*lbs.*

1801. The population of the parish according to the enumeration of March, 1801, was

	Blackwell.	Cockerton.	Darlington.	Archdeacon Newton.
Houses.				
Inhabited	54	88	864	11
Families	66	88	1111	13
Persons.				
Males	114	164	2158	40
Females	163	166	2512	32
Total of Persons	277	330	4670	72

* A woman was talking to a respectable tradesman of Darlington, not long ago, about machinery, and after expatiating thereupon, at last with much complacency concluded, "however, there *is* one thing they can't do with machinery after all, *they can't mak bairns!*"

† Ord's Cleveland, &c.

1804. "The cotton manufacture has lately been introduced and is at present in a flourishing state, under the direction of Mr. John Morrell, to whom the town is indebted for his exertions in favour of this establishment."*

1806. "JOHN CADE, of Gainford, gentleman (a batchelor), died Decr, 10th, buried Decr. 15th. Age 72 years." Such is the entry in our register of Cade the antiquary. He was born at Darlington in January, 1734, of humble but respectable parents ;† and after receiving the rudiments of such an education at the grammar-school as subsequently afforded him the pleasure of deciphering an inscription, was sent to the warehouse of a wholesale linen-draper in London ; in which, rising by honest industry from the lowest to the highest station, he obtained a share in a branch of the concern in Dublin. Having realized (principally by successful smuggling, I understand) a small fortune, he very wisely retired, about 1775, to Durham, from whence he removed to Gainford, for "individuals endowed with a literary turn, however limited their acquirements and however humble their pretensions, are seldom vassals to the demon of avarice." In 1784 he com-

* Beauties of England and Wales.

† GEORGE KADE or CADE of Darlington, *m.* Helener . . . . (bur. 15 Jan. 1691-2) and had issue

I. Matthew Kade or Cade, shoemaker, Darlington, bp. 13 May, 1688, br. 9 May, 1755, who had issue

- I. George, bp. 16 Apr., 1713 ; br. 25 Apr. 1729.
- II. Richard, bp. 26 Apr., 1715.
- III. Matthew, bp. 9 Oct. 1717.
- 1. Alice, bp. 15 Sep. 1719.
- 2. Elizabeth. bp. 19 Oct. 1725 ; br. as spinster, 21 Apr., 1797.
- 3. Eleanor, bp. 15 Sep., 1730.

II. George, bp. 20 May, 1691.

And probably also

III ? MARK KADE or CADE.

IV ? Anthony Cade, mentioned in the antiquary's draft will 1786. "To my uncle, Anthony Cade, of Richmond, an annuity of 20*l*. To my aunt, Julia Cade, the now wife of sd. Anthy. in case she survives her husband, an annuity of 10*l*."

1 ? Alice. "To my aunt Alice Dixon, of Moulton, in par. of Middleton Tyas, widow, an annuity of 15*l*."

MARK KADE or CADE, shoemaker, Darlington, b. about 1692 ; adm. to the Cordwainers' Company, Darlington, on making a free dinner and paying 5*s*. as a foreigner : will dated 7 June, 1751 ; d. 21, br. 22 June, 1751, ag. 59. He *m.* Elizabeth, dau. of Leonard Middleton, of Darlington, on 22 Nov. 1719 ; she d. 27 Aug. 1761, ag. 66, having had issue

I. Leonard, bp. 8 Sep. 1721 ; br. 23 May, 1722.

II. Mark Cade, surgeon, Darlington and Barnard Castle, bp. 5 Feb. 1724 : mentioned in the will of his father, who leaves him a shilling only, "having already bestowed a sufficient fortune upon him." By his wife Mary (bur. as of Darlington, widow, 6 Mar. 1792) he had a daughter

Dorothy, dau. of Mark C., formerly of D., apothecary, bp. 3 Jan., 1755.

but she had also issue

Robert, bp. 26 Feb. 1757, as "son of Mary C., wife of Mr. Mark Cade, surgeon, who has been upwards of a year on board his Majesty's ship the Monmouth ;" bur. 26 Aug., 1762, Mark Cade being styled "late of Bernard Castle, apothecary."

Matthew, bp. 11 Jan., 1767, as "son of Mary Cade, the wife of Mark Cade, apothecary, who has been absent from his wife these many years."

III. Leonard, bp. 24 Mar. 1731-2 : occ. 1754 as a member of the Cordwainers' Comp. : d. 14 June 1762, aged 30.

IV. JOHN CADE, THE ANTIQUARY, bp. 5 Jan. 1734.

V. William, bp. 5 Oct., 1737.

1. Mary, bp. 17 Apr., 1723.

2. Alice, bp. 27 June, 1727 : br. 9 Feb. 1732-3.

3. Elizabeth Cade, bp. 10 Mar. 1729-30 : (Qu. Mrs. Cade, Greentree, who received gloves at the funeral of John Killinghall, esq., in 1762, and Elizabeth Cade, an innkeeper, in 1769 ; see p. 262) residuary legatee and executrix of the antiquary in his draft will : d. 14, br. 17 Oct. 1812, aged 82, "singlewoman."

The family head-stone to the South of the walk leading to Darlington church is inscribed : —"Sacred to the memory of Mark Cade, who died the 21st of June 1751, aged 59 years. Also Elizabeth his wife, who died the 27th of Augt. aged 66 years. Also Leonard Cade their son, who died the 14th of June 1762, aged 30 years. Also John Cade their son who died 12th [an error for 10th] of Decr. 1806 aged 72 years. Also Elizabeth Cade their daughter, who died the 14th of Octr. 1812, aged 82 years."

plains of finding his name " dignified with the title of an *esquire* [in the list of subscribers to Charlton's Whitby]. Believe me," says he, " I ever wished to appear but what I really am, an honest *yeoman*, as I can have no pretensions to any other character. How the mistake happened I cannot say, but sincerely wish it had been otherwise, as it only serve the world to laugh at." He lived, I believe, on his own freehold at Gainford, and his yeoman estate did not prevent him using a book-plate. *Arms :*—Argent, between 3 lions passant guardant gules, each charged on the shoulder with a bezant ; a fesse azure, charged with a tower between two fleur de lis or. *Crest :*—A dexter arm in plate armour embowed, grasping a dagger. *Motto:*—VIRTUTE ET LABORE. " John Cade, *esq.*"

Mr. Cade's imperfect education and subsequent commercial pursuits, confined his attention to topographical antiquities, but he chose the most difficult, the undefined traces of roads and fortifications. He laid the Romans under contribution for almost every vestige he found of early work. Hutchinson certainly " took a pleasure in ruining poor Jack Cade's castles, and breaking up his roads," and in 1786, the latter bitterly writes : —" I think Mr. Hutchinson *illiberal* as well as *incorrect ;* the quotation from Hollinshed is *Duresme*, and not *Deiraham* as he has advanced. If he persists, I am determined to maintain the papers of mine published by the Society. I never desired to be an author. Dr. Kaye handed my letter to that literary body without my knowledge ; and I hope it will be the last time I shall have anything to do in that way, having some time ago refused his solicitations on that head. I cannot think why Mr. Hutchinson should desire my correspondence if he thinks me so incorrect." So indignant was Cade at what he apprehended to be unwarrantable liberties taken by Hutchinson with his letters on the Roman camps, that he with-held his plate of Darlington church from the history of Durham, and afterwards gave it to his friend Allan (p.219). A reduced copy was therefore made for Hutchinson's book.*

Cade's communications on Roman remains to Dr. Kaye, afterwards dean of Lincoln, and Mr. Gough, are in the Archæologia, vols. vii, ix, x. That he was not a member of the Society of Antiquaries arose from his peculiar diffidence and infirm health.† He traced two Roman roads, one from the æstuary of the Tees along the shore to Shields, the other from about Neasham by Stainton in the street, Mainsforth and Old Durham to Chester-le-Street and Gateshead ;‡ and probably but general correctness, " but every hill, natural or artificial, mound or earthwork near his line of march was to be Roman. The moated house of Bellasis, the mount at Bishopton, and the natural sand-hills at Mainsforth and Acley-heads were all declared stations." He sometimes indulged in Celtic fancies. He pitched upon Freeburgh Hill in Cleveland, the base of which occupies

* " I will get all the views I have done in the county of Durham printed off on thin paper, as you desire ; and shall take the first leisure hour to reduce the view of Darlington Church. At present I am fagging to fetch up the lost time during my peregrinations."—*Grose to Allan*, 1774.

† " I am now approaching my 57th year, and only *beginning to read*—with a confined education, owing to my own neglect, and other avocations in my juvenile days. Were I settled in the metropolis, and could benefit by the learned discourses read at the society, I should think it the greatest honour of my life to be a member of that distinguished body ; but alas ! various infirmities occasioned by repeated attacks of the gout and stone, have played with my faculties, and I find an irreparable loss of memory and conception. Having opened myself in this brief manner, I hope you will think it prudent in me not to display false colours. I cannot receive greater satisfaction than the learned society have already given me by their approbation and countenance ; and if my papers were entitled to merit, it was from the advantages I received from an attention to your publications and encouragement. These considerations must plead my excuse for not soliciting the honour you kindly proposed to me."—*Cade to Gough*, 1790.

‡ 1784. " I ventured upon an arduous undertaking, by endeavouring to trace the progress of the *Rycknild Street* from Monk's Bridge, Derbyshire, to Tinemouth in Northumberland."

1789. " Near Stainton in the Strata is a mansion styled the *Rycknild Grange ;* and at a little distance on the road I formerly described, a water mill on the Skerne, called the *Rycknild Mill*, in the oldest parish records where they were situated." [Now Ricknall, anciently Rickenhall.]

no less than six or seven hundred acres of land, and the height is four or five hundred feet, as "one of the greatest Celtic remains Britain can glory in." He remarks that it is constructed on the same model as Silbury, in Wiltshire, and that if Abury in the last county were a thousand years older than Stonehenge (as has been asserted); this place might surely claim an original nearly similar. The reader will be amused to learn that Freeburgh is a natural sandstone formation. After all, however, Cade brought many curious particulars to bear upon his theories, and many a shrewd comparison was the result.

Gothic architecture, then labouring to emerge from a thick cloud of urns and ovals, received more attention from Cade than from the majority of his cotemporaries; and, judging from his laments on the deplorable condition of our collegiate church, which has only grown more pitiful since his death, he viewed modern innovations with the true eye of taste. Camden and Bentham's Ely were his great favourites in literature, as were Stukeley, Gordon, &c., but his memory in respect of the English and Irish cathedrals was wonderful. He could describe every variation in these buildings with the most minute accuracy, and in correct terms of art; often, after descanting for some time, bringing or sending for a book of prints for his authority. His amusement with the Vitruvius Britannicus seemed to consist in pointing out defects in the buildings; and he always maintained that Keddlestone, in Derbyshire, was the only grand house in England, and that the present St. Paul's must be mean in comparison with the old one; an opinion in which I heartily concur. It had the finest choir in Europe.

His passion for illustrating books is said to have been so strong as to have led to the expansion of his copy of Dugdale's works to no less than a hundred volumes. "After quitting the city," says Mr. Geo. Allan, the M.P., "while he lived in the Temple, he amused himself in illustrating Bishop Gibson's edition of Camden's Britannia, with all the topographical engravings of every kind that had fallen into his hands; and though the selection was not formed with the taste the subject is capable of, nor included many prints which would have been worthy of it, it sold for a considerable sum. His illustrated Camden was a splendid and magnificent exhibition; and indeed all his books were valuable, not more from his extensive illustrating by prints, than by his own labour in blazoning arms, and, whenever there was an opportunity, imitating in colours, very minutely, the ancient illuminations of initials and title pages." He thus decorated several works for his friends, Allan and Tunstall; and in one of his letters, offers his services to Mr. Gough.* Allan's splendid illustrated copy of Camden is a monument of Cade's industry and skill in emblazoning.† In 1785 he complains of his want of Scotch and Irish arms, and that "when in London he found old magazines hard to get;" he therefore begs the refuse of Allan's mutilated numbers.‡ His numismatic knowledge was respectable.

He assisted Pennant, and in 1788 communicated to Gough several corrections by himself and Allan, for the counties of Durham and York, in the new edition of Camden; and after the publication of that work, which he told the editor he perused "with awful reverence," still continued to communicate for a future edition. In the same year his conjectures on the formation of peat mosses in the Northern counties were printed in the Gentleman's Magazine.

* 1789. [*To Gough.*] "I have coloured several volumes of Dugdale's Warwickshire, Drake's Eboracum, with Edmondson's Peerage, for my friend Mr. Tunstall, and others; which have met the approbation of Mr. Brooke, Somerset Herald. Should you, Sir, wish to have the latter six volumes blazoned, I have no doubt of giving you satisfaction, or in any work in that way you may please to honour me with."

† 1790. [*To Gough.*] "I seldom see or hear from Mr. Allan; he has been for some months past at the watering-places.—I have lately embellished his new edition of the 'Britannia' with about 3000 arms of Barons and Baronets, &c., mostly on the margins where they are mentioned; and others, dispersed in the most general order through the work, all properly blazoned, which has a good effect."

‡ Some of Mr. Cade's old magazines and other works are in the possession of Mr. H. Barber, of Catterick academy, near Richmond.

"About sixteen years before his death," continues Mr. Allan, "he had a paralytic stroke, which deprived him of the use of his legs, and he was confined to his bed ever after. During that period he was, nevertheless, always cheerful; and, frequently after dining below with his sister, I have enjoyed two or three hours of sociable conversation with him, over a bottle of wine, by his bed side. Some years before his death, I visited him, and he gave me Drayton's Polyolbion, Harding's Chronicle, Lord Clarendon's History of the Rebellion, and Knight's Life of Erasmus. He told he had sent all his illustrated books on antiquities, as a present to the son of his early benefactor, when in trade; who, he said, was a gentleman of property and education. I have heard of his name, but were I inclined to mention it, I must dip my pen in gall or vinegar, or at least in bitter black ink; for the unfeeling inelegant wretch sold the books in Mr. Cade's lifetime. After this my friend devoted himself entirely to reading sermons and theological tracts, of which he went through an immense mass before his death.* His conversation on this subject could not be learned or critical; but it was sensible, lively, and never gloomy. I believe, indeed, no man ever waited with firmer patience for his dissolution, or with a stronger reliance on christianity. He died at Gainford, December 10th, 1806, aged 72, and was buried at Darlington."

Mr. Allan appropriately concludes with a comfortable assurance that will apply to many others who have inclined to his pursuits, that "he was charitable, hospitable, cheerful, and as good a man as I could have wished to have been acquainted with when young, or as I can desire to form an intimacy with, as my age advances."

Among a selection of the professional papers of the elder Allan, in the possession of Sir Cuthbert Sharp, was the rough draft of a testamentary document, which that celebrated antiquary had prepared for Mr. Cade, so early as the year 1786. "To my dear Sister Elizabeth C., spinster, my freehold dwelling house in Gainford, with 3 pews or stalls in the parish Church.—my friend and old school-fellow, Wm. Robson of Darlington, son of Thos Robson, Butcher, deceased, an annuity of 2 guineas.—My two servants Mark Magennis and Jane Dixon, 50 (shillings?) a piece, provided they are in my service at my death.—Mark Magennis my wearing apparel.—Wilkinson Maxwell of Durham, gent.; Wm. Newcombe Geogehan, of the City of West Chester; and to Mrs. Mary Chamney of Dublin, 5 guineas each, to buy rings.—Geo. Fras. Tyson, Esq., son of my friend Edwd. Tyson, late of Queen Square, Ormond Street, London, deceased, "all my Library of books, with my diamond ring.—My godson, Richard Molineux, son of my dear friend George Molineux of Wolverhampton, Esq., the several collections I have made, as a supplement to, and further illustration of Camden's Britannia, and at this time laying unbound; the large picture of the Royal interview between the kings of England and France;† and also my profile drawn by Sykes.—Unto my dear friend George Allan, of Darlington, the Vellum pedigree of the family of Paston, late earls of Yarmouth; and also the copper-plate engraving of Darlington Church, which plate is now in his possession.—The Rev. R. Wilson, now Curate of Gainford, the three Vols. of Calmet's History of the Bible.—Mrs. Elizabeth Waugh of New Elvet Durham, widow, my silver cup and cover.—My god-daughter, Jane Adams of London, my large silver waiter.—Mr. Geo. Ashton of Old Elvet, Durham, my gold watch; and to Mr. John Adamson of Barnard-Castle, my large China Punch Bowl.—Sister, Elizabeth Cade, residuary legatee and executrix. My body to be carried to the church by six poor men, to have one guinea each."

Mr. Cade never married, but his maiden sister, here mentioned, resided with him, and died at Darlington 14 October, 1812; where she was buried by his side, in the church-

* "Enthusiasm or hypocrisy are here out of the question; Cade had none to deceive, and did not deceive himself. There is something magnanimous in thus giving up the serious toys which had amused the boy and man, and on the verge of eternity fixing his earnest and undivided attention on a future state of existence."—*Surtees.*

† This was, no doubt, the large print of "the Field of the Cloth of Gold," published by the Society of Antiquaries, and engraved after the original picture in Windsor Castle.

yard. By her desire, seven very elegant busts were sent to Geo. Allan, M.P., to add to his collections, and remain as a token of her brother's regard. There is a profile portrait of Cade at Crook Hall, doubtless that which he bequeathed to Mr. Molineux, and perhaps the only one which was ever sketched. It is in crayons, by Sykes—the same man who drew old Emerson ; and it represents a man of great mildness of countenance, with a sensible face, not devoid of character. It has a powdered head, with horizontal curls at the ears, a sky-blue coat, with a low turned down collar, and shirt frills of lace in profusion. It belonged to Mr. Ashton, Cade's friend and legatee, at whose sale Mr. Raine purchased it. "Ashton lived till nearly the age of ninety, and died only a few years ago. He always spoke of Cade with the deepest feelings of respect and attachment. There is abundance of proof that poor Cade, after he was dead, was little cared for by his representatives ; but Ashton was one of those that loved him, and had a respect for his memory ; and it is more than probable that he secured this profile of his friend, when he found that it was falling into the hands of those who could not appreciate it. At the death of Mr. Ashton, Mr. Cade's illustrated copies of Wallis's History of Northumberland, in two vols., and some other books which were in his possession at the time of his death, by gift or purchase, were presented to J. Ward, Esq., Solicitor, Durham."*

1808. April 13. The foundation stone of the present Town's Hall, in the Market Place, was laid by Geore Allan, esq., of Blackwell Grange; George Lewis Hollingsworth, esq., banker ; Richard Hodgson, esq., surgeon ; and Mr. William Kitching, ironfounder ; a great number of gentlemen being assembled. An earthern pot was placed underneath, in which was put six half-pennies, dated 1806, and one penny piece, dated 1798. It is an ordinary building of the Italian style. The appearance of its predecessor, the Toll Booth, may be gleaned from the cut at the head of this division, on page 271. The steps led to the Court-room, which occupied the whole length of the building. The ground floor was divided into shops, one of which, containing the projecting window in the view, was that of David Mackeown, the leading hardwareman of the town. Beneath was the town's dungeon or *kitty.* The migratory habits of rats are well known, and it is said that a curious instance occurred the night before this venerable building was pulled down. The enormous multitude of rats, which had completely undermined it, then left it in a body, and were met in army array at Broken Scarr, near Badle Beck. Ancient toll booths are generally of the rudest construction, and for sake of comparison, I annex a cut of that which formerly obstructed the fine market place of Thirsk.

* Memoir in Nichols' Literary Anecdotes, by Allan the M.P.—Surtees.—Ord's Cleveland. —Walbran's Gainford.—Darlington Par. Reg., &c.

1808. Oct. 25. The Darlington Dispensary, for the relief of the sick poor, was this day instituted, in commemoration of the fiftieth year of George III.'s reign.

The Duke of Cleveland, and the Lord Bishop of Durham are *patrons;* R. H. Allan, esq., and Edward Pease, esq., *presidents;* John C. Backhouse, esq., *treasurer;* John B. Pease, esq., and Edmund Backhouse, esq., *secretaries;* Beddoes Peacock, esq., M.D., *physician;* S. E. Piper, esq., *surgeon.* Fourteen gentlemen form a committee. During the year ending October, 1848, 682 patients had received the benefits of the institution. The funds are derived from subscriptions, and the interest of a donation from the late T. Backhouse, esq. Subscribers of half-a-guinea are entitled to four tickets for admission of objects, and others in proportion.

1810. Bailey speaks of Darlington as having "been long famous for its linen manufactures of huckaback, diapers, and sheeting, which employ about 500 looms. It has also a worsted manufactory of camblets, wildbores, bombazets, and tammies, or durants: the two latter are spun by hand; the former by machines: in these are employed about 300 looms, 100 combers, and 500 spinners by hand, besides a considerable quantity being sent into Scotland to spin. Mr. Pease alone has paid 800*l.* a-year for spinning in Scotland. It was here that the mills for spinning flax were first invented, by the ingenious Mr. John Kendry and Mr. Porthouse: of those mills there are four, and one for spinning worsted; here are also mills for dressing chamois leather, and for grinding and polishing spectacles. The former, a very worthy man, was the first that invented the mode of grinding optical glasses of a true spherical form, by machinery: he neglected to get a patent, and it was meanly stolen by some person of superior capital, near Sheffield, who engrossed nearly all the demand, by having riders to take in orders in every part of the kingdom. Barnard Castle, about 500 years since, and for many years before, had an extensive manufactory of worsted goods; but the manufacturers, in order to undersell each other, made their goods so very inferior, that in a few years they offended and lost their customers, and the workmen were obliged to go by degrees to Durham, Darlington, and other places, where the trade was under better regulations."

He speaks of the fortnight days as having for many years been continued through the year, and states that a pound of butter here is 22 oz., at Stockton 24.

1817. Feb. 2. A most destructive fire* occurred, by which the extensive woollen manufactory, belonging to Messrs. Edward and Joseph Pease, on the site of the Old Bishop's mill, and other property, valued at 30,000*l.* was destroyed, and five hundred people thrown out of employ.

Census 1821. Darlington Par. Chap.:—

	Darlington with Oxenhall or Oxneyfield.	Archdeacon Newton.	Blackwell.	Cockerton.
HOUSES.				
Inhabited	876	12	47	91
By how many families occupied	1,213	12	62	112
Building	2	1	...	...
Uninhabited	24	...	...	1
OCCUPATIONS.				
Families chiefly employed in agriculture	155	12	39	49
Families chiefly employed in Trade, Manufactures, or Handicraft	849	...	13	43
All other families not occupied in the two preceding classes	209	...	10	20

* "1667. For a fire at Darlington, May 1, 18*s.* 8*d.*"—*St. Nicholas' par. Durham.*

	Darlington with Oxenhall or Oxneyfield.	Archdeacon Newton.	Blackwell.	Cockerton.
PERSONS.				
Males	2,737	27	123	235
Females	3,013	37	145	234
Total of Persons	5,750	64	268	469
Increase since 1811	691	...	...	60
Decrease since 1811	...	7	13	...

The entire parish of Darlington contained 6,551 inhabitants.

1815. Dec. 30. At an early hour in the morning the wind rose to a perfect hurricane, but no particular damage was sustained, excepting to a large new building, erected by Messrs. Toulmin, Ianson, &c., for a spinning mill, of which nearly one half of one of the gable ends was blown down, and falling on the roof of an adjoining dwelling-house, broke through the same and the upper floor, which caused considerable damage. The inhabitants escaped without injury. The damage was estimated at upwards of 100*l.*

1817. May. A *Savings Bank* was established in Darlington, and a great number of persons availed themselves of that mode of investment. A panic however, owing to some real or alleged defalcations, broke the establishment up in 1833, but a new one was established in 1837. At the annual meeting of this institution in Dec. 1849, it appeared that there were 1092 open accounts. Payments to depositors during the year 5567*l.* 19*s.* 7*d.* receipts, 5867*l.* 9*s.* 3*d.*; whole deposits at present in the bank, 23,267*l.* 15*s.* 1*d.*

1822. Feb. 15. A young man, named John Gales, servant to Mr. John White, farmer, of Brankin Moor,* met an untimely death. White, who had lately exhibited symptoms

* The following ballad is given as it was furnished to me, from recitation, in this neighbourhood. It has scotticisms, and is probably a mere adaptation, but it may furnish variations useful to those, who, like Robert White, buried at Medomsley in 1681, and my friend Robert White, the minstrel Scottishman, now a resident in Newcastle, are to be registered as "famous for telling storeys" of faws and fairies, and unrequited love.

I.

Whea has not heard of a couple
That lived at Brankin-field;
Peggy was blythe and bonny.
For beauty each lassie would yield.
And she was betrothed to Willey
The lad with the golden hair,
The day was fix'd to be married,
It chanced on Martinmas fair.

II.

So in com our braw bride,
As she com dipping [dimpling] her [cheeks,
"Oh how can I be married,
I've nowther got blankets or sheets.
I've nowther got blankets or sheets,
I want a good coverlet too,
A bride who's to beg and to borrow,
Will find it right mickle to do."

III.

Then in com our bride's mother,
And sair she began to chide,
"I'd nivver a plack i' my pocket
The day that I was a bride.
My gown was linsey-wonsey,
I'd nivver a smock at a',
And she has gowns and buskins
More than yan or twa'."

IV.

In com our bride's father
As he com from the plew,
"Its hau'd your tongue, my doughter,
For ye'll hae dower enew.
Adzooks, I've a stirk i' the tether,
And a bonny grey meer i' the fau'd.
To bring corn hyam in harvest,
What wad ye be at, ye jade!"

V.

Then in com our bride's brother,
As he com from the kye,
"Willey wad hae nowt to do wi' her,
If he ken'd her as weel as I.
For she's baith proud and saucy,
Not fit for a poor man's wife,
And if I can't get a better
I'll nivver hae yan in my life."

VI.

"And what's the matter?" quoth Willey
"For we'll hae gear I vow,
We'll hire a lass of our awn,
And she'll spin claes enew,
And in the cau'd of winter
No danger that we'll freeze,
We'll lie the closer tegither
When leaves are off the trees."

VII.

So they all set off to Darnton,
The parson he buckled them there,
The clerk he cried "Amen,"
And seldom was seen sic a pair.

of derangement, the effects of *delirium tremens*, from excessive drinking; on the evening previous, was impressed with the idea that his house was infested by robbers, and would not retire to rest, but wandered about the house the whole night with a loaded gun, to shoot (he said) the robbers as they came in; fancying he heard and saw them at the windows. A young man, Bowser, from Darlington, who was with him all night, endeavoured, but without effect, to divert and dissuade him from his wild idea. Early in the morning White left Bowser alone in the kitchen, and again traversed the house with his gun. The deceased came down stairs about six o'clock, and proceeded to go out to his work, but finding the outer door fastened, he returned and went into the kitchen, where Bowser was standing by the fireside. White, at that time being in the passage, suddenly approached and fired, lodging the contents of his gun in the body of Gales, near the hip bone. He fell at Bowser's feet and expired in about two hours afterwards. A coroner's jury found that White was in a fit of mental derangement at the time, but the grandfather of his victim having appeared before a magistrate, and expressed himself dissatisfied, White was committed for trial at the assizes. The grandfather of Gales in the interim was *satisfied*, and White was discharged, the bill being *ignored*, by the grand jury, to the singular amazement of every individual acquainted with the circumstances of the case.

1822. Aug. 9. Robert Peat, aged 50, was executed in front of the County Court at Durham, for the murder of Robert Peat, aged 76, in Darlington. He was deeply affected and shed tears. The unhappy man being half cousin and heir-at-law to the deceased, had been left a legacy in a will of 1808, but having offended the testator, another will of 1815 left the whole property to testator's wife. He contrived to obtain the wills* and then gave the poison to obtain the property as heir-at-law. He lived at Ravensworth, near Richmond, and came to Darlington every market-day, always calling at the house of the deceased. On Monday, June 24, he called as usual, and the deceased's wife had put a piece of lamb in a quart of water on the fire, at ten o'clock, and gone out to market twice. The prisoner followed her the last time she returned and told her he had been in the house in her absence, and that her husband was then in an adjoining room. He then said that he had read in the papers that some persons had been poisoned by bad water, and asked her if she had heard of it; to which she replied that she knew nothing of it, and had something else to do than to read newspapers. He remained this time in the house but a few minutes and then went away. The deceased had gone into the yard and would not come in until the prisoner had gone. The deceased and his wife, after having partaken of the broth and lamb, which they remarked had a peculiar taste, vomited severely. The prisoner called again at four o'clock, and saw them vomiting; looked in at the window between six and seven, and visited them again at ten at night.† He had never before called more than once in a day. The deceased died at half-past twelve at night. Several neighbours to whom Mrs. Peat gave the lamb, and who tasted of it, sickened. The prosecutrix observed pieces of a broken phial on the hearth. The

* His visits were always unwelcome, but he persisted in coming, and that at a time when he knew prosecutrix would be at the market. He told a witness on the 10 June that he would watch the old woman going to market (who, he said, wanted to wrong him out of the "brass" he had), and go in and see the old man, and afterwards that he had got the will. On the day of the murder he took a bottle of laudanum out of his pocket and showed it to the same witness, saying, he wished the old woman had it, and that it would do her a trick. Indeed she was so ill that she was in bed from the Monday to the Friday, the day after that on which her husband was buried.

† Mary Bolam, who had been called in to assist, saw prisoner about half-past seven, and asked him to go for a doctor, but he refused, saying he did not want deceased's wife to know he was then in town. And yet on his visit at ten he wished to stay all night, but Bolam advised him to go home, which he did. Mrs. Peat was so penurious that no medical man was called in. The effects were so violent, and the meat became so dark coloured that it was surmised some other deadly poison had been mixed with the laudanum. Yet the faculty thought that at four weeks after burial an exhumation would lead to no result. Indeed the chemist and others were of opinion that the prisoner would after all have escaped punishment, had counsel been engaged for the defence. I am indebted to O. B. Wooler, esq., for the loan of the brief and depositions in the case.

prisoner had bought a phial of laudanum from Mr. John Smith, a chemist, on the morning of the murder, which he said was for ladies at Middleton, but which he told the chemist on July 22, after some suspicions were created, he had still in his possession.* Before he was sent off to prison, he wrote to his wife, in which he directed his son to give up the wills, and then added, "Think no more of me, my chance is very bad."† It is remarkable that the deceased had been buried four weeks before the prisoner was charged. A medical man gave laudanum to all who tasted of the lamb, and they recognized the same taste.

1823. March 24. An act was obtained for paving, lighting,‡ watching, and cleansing the town, under the powers of which it has been considerably improved by the commissioners appointed under it.

1825. The grand septennial festival, at Bradford, of wool-combers, comb-makers, dyers, &c., was held in honour of Blase, saint and bishop, who is said to have been the inventor of wool-combing. He was jumbled up in the procession with a motley crew, composed of a king, queen, Jason of the Golden Fleece and his fair Medea, guards, the bishop's chaplain, shepherds, &c., &c. The king was an old man named William Clough, of Darlington, who had filled the regal station at four previous celebrations. Many thousands were present, and Bradford was never before known to be so crowded with strangers. The saint, who was bishop of Sebaste, in Armenia, and now is the patron of wool-combers, was tormented with iron combs, and martyred under Licinius in 316. Ribadeneira, the Jesuit, gravely relates that St. Blase was scourged, and seven holy women anointed themselves with his blood; whereupon their flesh was combed with iron combs, but their wounds ran nothing but milk, their flesh was whiter than snow, angels came visibly and healed their wounds as they were made; that they were put into the fire, which would not consume them; after all which they were ordered to be beheaded, and beheaded accordingly. Then St. Blase was ordered to be drowned in the lake; but he walked on the water, sat down on it in the middle, and invited the infidels to a sitting. We are called to believe that *three score and eight tried the experiment*, and were drowned, and that St. Blase then quietly walked back to be beheaded.—Candles offered to the saint were good for the toothace, and for diseases of cattle; and that the Darlington wool-combers may lose none of the benefits to be derived from that immortal man, I give, from the same veritable Jesuit, a receipt for a stoppage in the throat:—"Hold the diseased party by the throat, and pronounce these words:—*Blase, the martyr and servant of Jesus Christ, commands thee to pass up or down!*" The bishop gives name to an Inn in Clay Row, a little beyond which, in Freemans Place, is the Wool-combers' Arms Inn.

A *Mechanics' Institute* was established in 1825, and at one time consisted of above one hundred and fifty members, who possessed a very valuable library. It, however, became extinct. In 1838 another Mechanics' Institute was formed, in which, at the close of the year ending 14 March, 1850, there were 341 members, but it has at times boasted of a far superior number. Volumes in the library, 1367. Lectures are given fortnightly in the winter months. President, Henry Pease, esq. Vice-Presidents, William Backhouse, esq.; Mr. Thomas Dixon. Treasurer, John Church Backhouse,

* He called on Smith, and asked if he recollected him, and then said that "he was blamed about Robert Peat," but that he had the laudanum at home.

† When prisoner was being conveyed to the committing magistrate, General Aylmer, of Walworth Castle, he desired his two sons to take notice of the road, in order to find their way home again, as he would not return with them. He also observed to the constable that the horse he was then riding, he had ridden many a hundred miles, but he thought that would be the last time.

‡ 1763. Thomas Robinson, carrier, amerced 17*s.* 6*d.* for suffering his cart and wood to stand and lye open in the streets, unless he do in one month put up in some convenient part of his dwelling-house a lamp, and keep the same constantly lighted in the night time for persons to see and avoid them.

esq. Hon. Secretary, Mr. Hugh Dunn. Auditors, Messrs. A. Common, G. Brigham, and W. H. Wise. Scrutineers, Messrs. Thomas Blyth, and George Shaw. Librarian, Mr. William Mossom.

In 1830 a Gas company was formed, and on Nov. 11 the town was first lighted with gas. The company was superseded, in 1846, by another, which bought the old works, and supplies gas on much more moderate terms. The latter was incorporated by Act of Parliament, 12 and 13 Vict. cap. 73, under the title of the Darlington Gas and Water Company, and supplies the town with water taken from the Tees near Baydale head.

By the census of 1831 the population of the parish stood at 8,574. The number of houses in 1831 amounted to 1,231; viz. 1,192 inhabited, and 39 uninhabited: and in 1841 (p. 323), an increase of 620 houses in ten years was shown. There was therefore an average of 6·1 persons to each house in 1831, and 5·95 in 1841. In 1849, the number of houses amounted to 2,790, or more than double that of 1831. A private enumeration made in 1849 gave the population as under 12,000.

The *Darlington Temperance Society* was instituted in 1831, and its first anniversary was held in the Wesleyan Chapel, Oct. 4, 1832, but being found inefficient it was broken up and a Total Abstinence Society founded, which has been of singular benefit.*

1834. July 29. Tuesday, Mr. Green, according to a promise he had made to the inhabitants of Darlington, in consequence of a failure in an attempt to ascend a few days before, commenced the process of inflating his balloon in a field, the use of which was granted for the occasion, adjoining Mr. Edward Pease's house. About a quarter before six o'clock, the balloon having received a supply of gas, the cords were slackened to allow it to clear itself. It was fastened on a cart with the car, in which Mr. Green and two females were seated, and then conducted up Northgate, preceded by a band playing some favourite airs. On reaching the market place, he made a splendid ascent, to the admiration of an immense multitude. He landed at Pillmoor house, near Croft, about four miles from Darlington.

In this year was published at Darlington, "A guide to Croft, Dinsdale, Middleton, Darlington, &c.," by J. Gordon, esq., solicitor, Richmond, who died at Durham in 1837. He was a native of Gilling, and was an able antiquarian and philologist. His book is tersely composed, and is adorned by four excellent sketches by Mr. W. R. Robinson.

1835. Mar. 2. A fire commenced in one of the lodging rooms of the Queen's Head Inn, owing to a person in a state of intoxication, who was stopping in the house, leaving his candle burning on retiring to rest, which by some means communicated with the bed clothes, which were speedily in flames: several beds were consumed, and it was with some difficulty the person himself was rescued.

1836. Dec. This month, as a family were removing from a village near Darlington, they observed a redbreast following them, which took their attention very much. On more closely noticing it, it was recognized as a bird which they had fed before they left the village. It continued its flight until it arrived at the place of their destination, a distance of about eighteen miles, and finally found its way into the very house the family were about to occupy.

1837. Aug. 12. Saturday, at night, about 12 o'clock, a fire was observed in the premises belonging to Messrs. Middleton and Sons, tanners and curriers. Although the alarm was soon given, and the fire-engines brought to play upon it, the fire spread rapidly, and great fear was entertained about the dwelling-house, but from the exertions of the firemen the fire next the house was got under, and the flames were confined to the workshops, which now assumed an awful appearance, and had it not been for the calmness of the night, the whole of the premises must have been burnt down. Two

* 1841. Apr. 12-13. The Teetotalers, Rechabites, Foresters, Odd Fellows, and other kindred associations of Alnwick, Blyth, Darlington, Chester-le-street, Corbridge, Hexham, Newcastle, Shields, &c., held processions and festivals.

engines were sent for to Stockton, but before they arrived, the fire was in a great measure extinguished. The fire got to a bark-house, in which was a great quantity of that material, which stopped the progress of the flames It was supposed that the fire originated in the engine-house. A great deal of thieving was carried on during the confusion. The damage was estimated at several thousands. A person of the name of Martin was much injured by the fall of the walls.

About 1838, there were published a plan and a sort of bird's eye view of some very grand arrangements for *South Darlington*, to occupy Bank Close, since purchased by R. H. Allan, esq., and Edmund Backhouse, esq., at the angle of the Blackwell Lane, in the Grange Road, and then stated as belonging to Mr. Wm. Falkous. The front houses were to have gardens before them, and altogether it must be confessed that the plan, if executed, would have had a very imposing effect. But the matter completely fell through.

1839. Jan. 7. "Windy Monday." The shop shutters were closed, and a vast amount of damage done to walls, chimnies, &c. Another tremendous gale happened on Friday, Feb. 3, 1843.

1840. Apr. 28. About half-past ten o'clock at night, a fire broke out in a detached part of the premises of Messrs. Miller, Cradock, and Co., rope-makers; supposed to originate from one of the workmen carelessly fixing a candle to part of the building for his convenience. As the men had not left work, the fire engine was speedily procured, which soon extinguished the flames. It is curious that there were fires at Benton North Farm, and Gateshead Park on the same day.

July 30. Mr. J. Walker, the landlord of the Railway Tavern, having lost a valuable young sow in farrowing, and wishing to save the breed if possible, kept the young ones to bring up with pan and spoon; singular to say, a bull bitch took charge of two young grunters, and suckled them regularly.

October 1. Five lads, named John Preston, Frederick Hindle, James Hindle, Alfred Hindle, and John Watson, all of Darlington, were fined five shillings each for attaching a fiery rope to a cat's tail, and thereby causing it to play divers pranks in the stable-yard of Warren Maude, esq., of Green Bank. Had it got into the hay chamber, the consequence might have been serious.

October 19. A fire broke out in the workshop of Mr. Michael Windle, builder, (during the absence of the workmen at breakfast), by some sparks from the stove setting fire to the shavings. With the aid of the town's engine, the fire was soon extinguished.

November. In the list of new patents for this month, is one to Charles Parker, of Darlington, flax-spinner, for improvements in looms for weaving linens and other fabrick, to be worked by hand, steam, or any other motive power.

1841. The census of this year gives the parish as follows:—

WARD.	Area	Houses.			Persons.			Ages.				Persons born.	
NAMES. Darlington Ward. South Eastern Division.	English Statute Acres.	Inhabited.	Uninhabited	Building.	Males.	Females.	Total.	Under 20 Years. Males.	Under 20 Years. Females.	20 Years and upwards. Males.	20 Years and upwards. Females.	In this County.	Elsewhere.
Darlington Par.													
Archd. Newton, Tsp.	910	11	1	...	27	36	63	16	19	11	17	54	9
Blackwell......... Tsp.	1670	65	1	...	135	164	299	55	77	80	87	211	88
Cockerton......... Tsp.	1580	116	...	...	246	236	482	119	95	127	141	400	82
Darlington ...... Tsp. Oxneyfield......Ham.	3470	1783	52	16	5257	5776	11,033	2543	2617	2714	3159	7275	3758

"The entire parish of *Darlington*, including 101 persons in the Union Workhouse, situated in the township of Darlington, contains 11,877 inhabitants, and 7630 acres. The hamlet of *Oxneyfield* contains twenty-five inhabitants."

1841. Nov. 5. Friday, being the anniversary of the "Powder Plot," the town was the scene of one of those acts which had long disgraced it, and which ended in the partial demolition of the town-hall windows, about thirty squares of glass being broken. In anticipation of the accustomed display on this day, the borough bailiff (Thos. Bowes, esq.) caused a notice to be printed and circulated, cautioning any person from throwing any squib, cracker, &c., which had only the effect of rendering the excitement greater. As early as five o'clock, a bonfire was lighted in the market place. In a very short time, all descriptions of fireworks were exploded ; and for four hours or upwards every moveable combustible was in danger of being taken and burnt by a set of thieves, throwing defiance in the teeth of the police—the interference of whom was the signal for attack on the town-hall—they flying in every direction, chased by fifty or a hundred boys, yelling and whooping like so many denizens of the woods.

1842. Jan. 26. The weather at this period was extremely severe, with heavy falls of snow, and a tremendous wind blowing from the South. During the whole of the above day, Wednesday, most of the shops were closed, and several of them sustained injury. Many of the coaches and carriers were unable to proceed to their respective places, on account of the great depth of snow.

March 28. Monday evening, a violent attack was made upon the police whilst apprehending Walter M'Lauchan, for disorderly and drunken conduct in a public house in Bondgate. The party belonging to the accused, and many of the lower orders, followed the policemen whilst taking M'Lauchan to the lock-up house, pelting them with stones and dirt, and because they could not accomplish their object in the prisoner's rescue, they smashed the town-hall windows.

Aug. 10. A tremendous thunder storm took place in the evening of this day (Wednesday). The electric fluid descended into the workshops of Messrs. Coates and Farmer, printers, about a quarter past nine o'clock, and set fire to them, but being immediately discovered, the fire was extinguished without the aid of the engines. It also descended the chimney of the adjoining house, occupied by Mr. Dobbinson, who, with his family, was sitting beside the fire. The fire-grate was forced out of its place, but all escaped unhurt. The offices of Mr. Peacock, solicitor, were also struck by the fluid, and a speaking pipe was completely severed by the heat. Fortunately he was absent.

1843. May 25. Christopher Wetherell, esq., solicitor, aged 38, was found dead in his bed, and an inquest returned a verdict of apoplexy. Mr. Wetherell was the most bulky person in the north of England, and at the age of 30 he weighed 33 stones.

1844. Oct. About twilight, one evening, a brace of partridges alighted in an arched passage, near the offices of Joseph Pease, esq., one of which was secured by the hostler at the King's Head Inn.

December 23. The Duke of Cleveland's stag hounds met at Manfield village, in a grass field, near to which a stag was uncarted. He went off in gallant style, in the direction of Barton for half a mile, then driving away by Howden Hill and Cleasby village, to the river Tees, crossing to the Durham side near Tees Cottage. He then went straight for Blackwell, where he twice crossed the river. From Blackwell, he took the road to Darlington, *passing through the town*, and crossed the river Skerne to the Great North of England Railway Station, taking the line of railway to Croft. He then passed Pilmore House, crossed the Tees again to the Yorkshire side, near Dalton, and went direct to Eryholme. Leaving the latter place, he went away for Entercommon, and thence for Birkby. Turning short of that place, he was run up to near the Cowton station of the Great North of England Railway, having run upwards of 20 miles in two hours and ten minutes. The stag died of his wounds before the arrival of the van to convey him to Raby Castle. From Eryholme to the finish the pace was very fast, an at almost every fence the strength of some gallant steed failed, and the rider reluctantly compelled to cry—enough ; not however, in many cases, until thrown to the ground by the falling of the horse. On the 24th March, 1848, the same brilliant pack found a fox at Selaby, under the huge antlered oaks which erst had seen old Brakenbury's stalwart race, when, after making a " pretty considerable " *detour* in search of the picturesque, away went the " artful dodger " at so tremendous a pace, that " bellows to mend " soon became the order of the day. Without a check—without a turn—and as swift as the wind, on flew the bristling pack, " frantic for blood," until the " varmint," after having led the field a merry dance, of little short of 20 miles, was finally run into, and died game, on the lawn in front of Blackwell Hall, the seat of R. H. Allan, esq. Out of a numerous field, many of whom were " tailed off," and were " no where," the noble and gallant duke was the first to clear the sunk-fence, followed by the huntsman, T. M. Maude, esq., Major Healey, Robert Lambton Surtees, esq., and a few others.

1845. Feb. 1. This night (Saturday) the servants of Mrs. Chisman, Queen's Head Inn, Darlington, became alarmed at hearing a saw in motion in the Odd-Fellows' Lodge Room. They gave immediate alarm, and on going to the room they found the door fast inside and some person at work sawing. On trying to break the door open, the parties inside made their escape by jumping out of the room window into the street. On the door being forced open, it was discovered that the large chest belonging to the Odd-Fellows was nearly sawn in two. In another minute or so the thieves would have been in possession of its contents, amounting to a considerable sum.

1846. Apr. 14. A young man of respectable appearance, named Percival, supposed to be a native of Appleby, who had recently come from London, retired to one of the upper rooms of the Black Bull, and desperately cut his throat, dying in half an hour afterwards.

May 15. The first exhibition of the Darlington Horticultural Society was held in the Assembly Room, Sun Inn. This society was preceeded by another with the same objects, but which proved a failure. Patronesses: Her Grace the Duchess of Cleveland, Her Grace the Duchess of Northumberland, the most noble the Marchioness of Londonderry, the right honorable Viscountess Seaham, Lady Musgrave, Lady Eden, Mrs. Williamson, and Mrs. Aylmer. President: the lord Bishop of Durham. Vice-Presidents: Lord Harry Vane, M.P. ; James Farrer, esq., M.P. ; Sir George Musgrave, bart. ; Sir William Eden, bart. ; Rev. R. H. Williamson ; John Bowes, esq ; Robert H. Allan, esq. ; Joseph Pease, esq. ; John C. Hopkins, esq. ; G. H. Williamson, esq. ; right Rev. Dr. Hogarth. Treasurer: William Backhouse, esq. Secretaries: Mr. Joseph W. Pease, Mr. Bousfield, Mr. William Robinson. There is a committee of Darlington gentlemen, and a country committee containing representatives for district places.

The shows have been eminently successful, and the productions of cottage gardeners in particular created great emulation. At the show of Sep. 23, 1848, there were present the Duke of Cleveland, the Marquis and Marchioness of Londonderry, Lord and Lady Seaham, Viscount Hardinge, the honorable Miss Hardinge, Sir W. F. Middleton (whose Italian gardens are the finest in the kingdom), Mr. Disraeli, M.P., Lord Robert Clinton, the hon. Mr. Duncombe, Lord Alfred Churchill, Lady and Miss Foulis, &c. &c. A fine remark fell from the lips of the elegant author of Coningsby on the occasion :—" The palace is not safe where the cottage is not happy, and no home can be happy where the presence of woman is not felt." The shows are at sometimes held in the Central Hall, and at others in the well-cultivated grounds of the Friends. There is a soiree each winter.

Aug. 24. The magistrates of the South-Eastern division of Darlington ward held their first sitting in a new station house in the Grange Road. They had previously met in the Town Hall. John Sheilds Peacock, esq., is their clerk. The new building presents an unpretending but very chaste front of stone, and contains every accommodation for magistrates, policemen, and prisoners. The cells are of great strength ; and the superintendent of police, Mr. Anthony Robson, resides on the premises, which were built partly out of the county rate, and partly by subscription. The new County Courts are also held every month here. Henry Stapylton, esq., judge ; John Edwin Marshall, esq., (of Durham) chief clerk ; George Taylor, esq. (of Durham), high bailiff; Mr. Ralph Chambers, assistant clerk ; Mr. Wm. Oliver, assistant bailiff.

In the summer of this year, a very violent diarrhœa was extremely prevalent and fatal in Darlington. It roused an old and widely spread superstition that bread made on a Good Friday is an infallible remedy for many complaints. The older the bread is the better, and a most surprising cure was stated to be effected by some Good Friday bread, which had been carefully preserved for three or four years.*

This year " The Darlington Quoit Club " was established. At the anniversary meetings a silver quoit is contended for, as the captain's prize, and a white flag, the gift of the ladies of Darlington, at the second anniversary, as the lieutenant's.

Dec. The whole of the bankers and merchants, with the principal of the railway offices, agreed to close their offices at one o'clock. Some of the solicitors did the same, others commenced to close an hour earlier each evening.

Dec. 11. Friday. A most severe snow storm commenced. Darlington was the southern point of its most heavy fall, Edinburgh the north. The railway was so stopped that no mail reached Durham from the south between Tuesday evening and Thursday afternoon, when the bags were brought from Darlington by a chaise and six. The trains were also much impeded further north. The storm commenced early on the Friday morning, some lighter snow having taken place previously, and during the evening of that day there were some very brilliant flashes of lightning. The snow fell with little intermission throughout that night and the whole of Saturday. On Sunday morning the majority of roads were impassable, the wind was strong, and enormous drifts were formed : after this an intense frost set in.

1847. June 2. The public buildings in the Bull Wynd, in the Italian style, were

* An odder cure was effected at High Coniscliffe in 1848. A poor man of the name of Dickinson, was buried there in the hope of restoring the use of the left side of his body, which for seven years had been rendered nearly useless by paralysis. Dickinson was an inhabitant of Shields, and happening to meet in the street with an elderly gentleman, who stated that he was a physician of Edinburgh, was advised by him to undergo this strange operation. The soil with which he was to be covered, was to be that of his native place, and accordingly, Dickinson, strong in faith and nothing doubting, set off on foot, and resolutely dragged his half paralysed body to High Coniscliffe, the village of his birth, a distance of about forty miles. A man engaged in embanking by the Tees side, was the grave-digger: he made a hole in which the patient lay with his shoulders slightly elevated, and he then heaped soil upon him to the depth of about two feet. The burial was to last four hours ; at the expiration of about a quarter of an hour, the patient broke out into a profuse perspiration, and continued in a perfect lather the rest of the time. Shortly afterwards a violent pain came into the paralysed knee, extending from thence to the hip, ascending to the back and thence descending to the loins. The pain in this part was so intense, that the patient feared he should faint, and nothing but the encouragement of two or three friends, who now and then came to him, enabled him to persevere, which he did till within a quarter of an hour of the prescribed four. When taken out, the paralysed side is described as having had the white and wrinkled appearance of a washerwoman's arms after a hard day's wash. The man was dressed with the soil attached to him, and walked away from his grave with a step more nimble than he walked to it. This was evident to every one. In the evening of the operation, he declared he felt very much better, and expressed great thankfulness in consequence. He stated, however, that the pain he had suffered was so severe, in a side, by the bye, that had not known feeling for many years, that he would hardly undergo the operation again to save his life. The man who buried him too, says, that when he saw him turn as he did, " black in the face as soot," he repented having buried him, and was obliged to take off a portion of the soil, fearing lest he should die. On the subject of this cure, a correspondent in the Durham Advertiser writes, that he remembered seeing in Prior's Voyages, a plate shewing Dampier, labouring under illness, buried to the chin on the shore of an East India Island. A gentleman of Darlington also informed him that a Maltese physician was, some forty years since, on a visit to his (informant's) father, who said, as to the treatment of the plague, in his broken English, " We do take the peoples that are seized, and do bury them in the ground till they do SWEAR." " Swear, doctor ? swear, did you say ? What can swearing have to do with their cure ? you probably mean SWEAT instead of *swear*." " Oh ! yes, sweat, that is the word ; we do bury them in the ground till they do sweat."

A few ancient spirits still enquire of druggists in Darlington for a penny puke. The word is classical, and is used by Vanbrugh. " Only Doll puked a little with riding backward, so they hoisted her into the coach-box—and then her stomach was easy."

opened by a tea-party and soiree in connection with the Mechanics' Institute. The hall is eighty-two feet long by forty-four feet wide ; there is a platform at one end, and a gallery capable of holding two hundred persons at the other : the light is obtained from the roof. Architect, John Middleton, esq. Total cost, including purchase of land, about 8000*l*. The chair was occupied by Lord Harry Vane, M.P., and addresses were delivered by several gentlemen. A very handsome rosewood desk was, on the same occasion, presented by the institution to their honorary secretary, Mr. Hugh Dunn.

The public buildings comprise the great "Central Hall,"* lecture room, committee room, and various private offices. Kitchens are attached. The Mechanics' Institute has a large library and class room on the basement storey. The old buildings adjoining and fronting into the market place are also fitted up as rooms for the Subscription Library and offices.

June. A doe-rabbit at Darlington was stolen, leaving a family of young ones unprovided for. About the same time, a cat lost all her kittens save one. It struck the mind of somebody that she might possibly prove a mother to the rabbits, and, upon trial, she took to them, and suckled both them and the kitten. They seemed to flourish under this discipline for some time, but at last died.

Oct. 2. Commenced at Barnard-castle by Messrs. George Brown, Henry Atkinson, and other shareholders, a liberal journal, price three-pence half-penny, entitled "The Darlington and Stockton Times, and Barnard-castle, Richmond, Auckland, Middlesbrough, Hartlepool, Teesdale, and Swaledale Journal. A newspaper for Durham county, Richmondshire, and Cleveland." In Feb., 1848, the publishing of the paper was removed to Darlington, under the auspices of Mr. Robert Thompson, who had joined the concern. It was soon found that, to keep pace with the requirements of the day, the size must be enlarged, and the price increased to four-pence. To these changes Mr. Thompson's allies being averse, and declining investing any extra capital, in Feb., 1849, he became sole proprietor, and effected the change. The paper has an extensive circulation, which is steadily increasing.

1848. March. A full grown lamb was born at Harewood Hill, on the estate of John C. Hopkins, esq., with two distinct heads and necks joined at the breasts, also two back bones parallel to each other, and joined at the middle of the back, one bone alone continuing from thence to the tail; it died soon after birth. On dissection two hearts were discovered, but only one liver.

1848. March. A remarkable case was brought before R. H. Allan, Esq., in which two servant girls were complainants. Two women had called on them, one acting as soothsayer, the other as recommender. After some conversation a bargain was struck, and the soothsayer was to tell these silly girls "who their chaps were," but this she could not do unless she had their clothes to divine from. The girls were accordingly persuaded by her to lend all their best clothes to her, which they did. The women decamped, sold the articles to a dealer in second-hand apparel, and were no more seen by the dupes. The woman, however, had been pursuing the same system of tricking at Richmond, and after being released, they were captured for the present offence. The charge being clearly proved, they were committed to Durham for two months at hard labour, and the clothes given up to the owners, on their paying half the cost of the second-hand dealer, Mr. Allan thinking it only right that they should be punished a little for their credulity.

There certainly is a strange amount of curious superstition floating in the neighbourhood. Soothsaying by old women is still patronised even by parties in the higher ranks of life. When a corpse does not stiffen immediately, another death in the family is very speedily to take place. "Wise men" still are considered better than policemen, but

* A countryman was overheard one day directing a woman's attention to the "Celestial Hall." The same week, at the hirings, two servants met, and thus ran their chat, "Weel Mary, how is ta, where dost ta live now ?" "Why I's weel enew—but I *don't live*, I's getten wed."

their efforts are unsuccessful if the thief has passed a running stream. "*The Skerne water-witch*," of old most notorious near Darlington, has been succeeded in the present day, in close neighbourhood, by an aged crone, who was a plaintiff at the magistrates' meeting in 1849, she having been most villainously assaulted and beaten by a termagant neighbour, no doubt excited by prevailing complaints of the old woman. For, horrible to relate, it seems that she goes "blazing about the house all night," and a year or two ago was very audacious in killing cattle of an adjoining farmer,* being seen at midnight "in nought but her petticoat and smock sleeves," neither walking nor running, but gliding or *fleecing* along the road to his farmstead. Nor was he unmolested until he summoned courage to procure a beast's heart, stick it full of pins, and roast it. "I assure you, sir, she's a very uncanny woman, and a very dangerous one to have for a neighbour." Poor soul, she seemed indeed more sinned against than sinning.

Ghosts are also in full play, to the great depreciation of property. At one house are melancholy footsteps heard of a person in silks, who amuses himself or herself by breaking spiritual sticks or trailing chains along the floor, emerging from under beds, but only showing half a man's head; jumping into bed in the shape of a child beside a person, or with a clay-cold hand raising him half out of his resting-place. The ghost has been seen in the shape of a well-dressed man coming out of the Skerne, setting his back against the house door and vanishing. Tenant after tenant has left, the reason given being that the tenement is hopelessly afflicted by the sprite of a man said to have been murdered in that locality some twenty years ago. Whenever a person comes unfairly by his death, his unhouselled soul lingers round its ancient haunts. A white figure, headless, has been seen *in open daylight* (!) come out of the door of an embattled cow-house behind Polam, walk leisurely round it, and disappear past its corner. It is said that a man hung himself there. White rabbits, and nondescript animals with "eyes as big as saucers," find ready credence still. They run about the town, and occasionally personate the souls of those who have sold themselves to Satan.

Some twenty or thirty years ago a woman came in great tribulation to Edwd. Pease, esq. She stated that she could not work at all; a ghost sat on her wheel-head and prevented her spinning; and that she would very soon starve. She knew he could *lay* the ghost and begged him to do so. He saw through the phantasy, and said at once that he *could* lay it. So he took a bit of paper, adorned it with some large B's and red wafers, held it to the fire, and put it on the wheel-head. The woman soon acknowledged with joy that the ghost had vanished.

April 18. About two o'clock, a.m., the fire bell rang, and fire was discovered raging in the house formerly the Allan residence, and now the property of Messrs. R. and W. Thompson. About six o'clock the fire was subdued by the great exertion of the inhabitants, but the amount of damage was 500*l*. or 600*l*.

* Darlington market has been unlucky to the farmers of Hawsley (near Great Stainton). One of them (named Boazman) had promised the daughter of Sarah Close, of Aycliffe, marriage; but, like many other people, failed to perform his intentions. The old lady (who had a suspected cat, and in passing whose door school-lads, some sixty years ago, always ejaculated, FOUR FINGERS AND A THUMB, WITCH! I DEFY THEE!! accompanying the conjuration by the action of placing the thumb on the middle of the palm, and the four fingers upon it) had her revenge. The faithless swain soon began to lose all his flocks and herds, either by murrain or witchcraft; their bodies were thrown into a ditch near Newton Ketton, and were pointed out to my informant by his father years after, and so frightful was the visitation, that he is known to have come in tears to say that he had not one horse left to take away the dead bodies out of the foldyard. For some time even the cattle, given or sold very cheap to him by the pitying neighbours, died also; but at last he began to prosper. In returning from market, one Monday evening, "half seas over," he fell from his horse, and was suffocated in a dirty pool of water near *Patie's Nook*; in fact, where the new bridge has lately been built, and produced such angry litigation among the good folks of Burdon. About forty years afterwards, the witch-bound farmer's nephew met his death on a similar journey from market, in the same state of intoxication, at the same place, and in exactly the same manner. The two succeeding occupiers of Hawsley also suffered violent deaths; the first by jumping from a train near Stillington when tipsy, the second by a corve of coals running over a staith and crushing him when standing beneath.

The modern characteristics of Darlington shall be shortly summed up. In doing so I desire that Mr. Ranger's excellent report on the township of Darlington, presented to the General Board of Health in 1850, may be read with mine.

Up to that period the town was improved and kept in order under the powers of the somewhat obsolete and half-yearly Borough and Halmot Courts, and of the Local Act of 1823. The Commissioners named in the Local Act for carrying out its provisions were 127. Vacancies were to be filled up by surviving Commissioners: they were therefore self-elected. There was great difficulty in obtaining a proper attendance of Commissioners, even of 5, the required quorum. Many of the Commissioners named in the Act did not even reside in the town, and had never been qualified. A sanitary committee was appointed by the Commissioners in 1847 as a step in the right direction. In 1848 notices were given of an intended application to Parliament for a new Local Act. The idea fell through. In 1849, on the petition of one tenth in number of the ratepayers, the General Board of Health by their superintending Inspector, William Ranger, esq., held an enquiry which led to the application of the Public Health Act in 1850. Mr. Ranger's report abounds in curious detail, much of it indeed is unsuitable to a work for general readers, but it forms the basis of many of the following remarks.

Darlington is seated near the junction of the upper new red sandstone with the magnesian limestone. The former crops out in the bed of the Tees at Croft, three miles south of the town; at Middleton, five miles to the east; at Coniscliffe, four miles to the west; and at Aycliffe, five miles to the north. The level stratification of superficial accumulations of sand, gravel, and clay (the latter in some places passing into marle) seem to be formed of the debris of the magnesian limestone: the clays, which belong to the red marle series, contain no dull and decomposing matter of magnesian lime.

The town occupies an area of about 140 acres. According to the census return of 1851 the population of Darlington parish was—males, 5,728; females, 6,724; total, 12,452.

Violent contrasts occur in Mr. Ranger's report. Out of every 100 children born in one part of the town, 28 died under 1 year, in the country only 5. A table of the deaths per 1000 of the population appears in the report, but to reprint it very numerous qualifications and explanations would be necessary, the character and age of the people being so diverse in different districts, I therefore omit it, only observing that the average number of deaths in 1000 persons was about 22 during 7 years, and that Grange Road, Northumberland Street, Paradise Row, Paradise Terrace, Mount Pleasant, Harewood Hill, Harewood Grove, West Terrace, and High Terrace, appear to be the best conditioned places, the average of deaths there was only 9.34 in 1000, the average age varied from 44 in the worst to 56 in the best conditions of those places. But after all, little is proved by this, taking into consideration the superior class and cleanliness of the inhabitants in such localities, and the fact that so many of them have passed the crisis of life. Generally where the average of deaths, was high the average age at

The Boazmans were relations to Squire Boazman of Stainton, whose daughter marrying a carrier of Darlington in opposition to a resident at Wackerfield, out came the stanza from the squire:

Off goes the waggon wheel, down comes the pack,
Maxom of Darlington's beat Wackerfield Jack.

Two other rhymes are remembered from his pen:

Stainton-le-Street stands on clay,
By it to Stockton there is a way;
There is a church without a steeple,
A blind parson, and few good people:
The clerk he sings alone by hissel,
The reason why, I cannot tell.

Maclaren of Stainton has no corn,
Jordison hasn't a shaff,
Jack Boazman has got plenty,
And that makes him to laugh.

death was low, but in some places the number of deaths was low, yet they were confessedly dirty, and the average age at death was low also, infants could not be reared. The caution necessary before coming to conclusions from returns will be apparent. For in some streets where the average deaths were from 25 to 35 per 1000, the average age was 16 to 39 ; other streets shewed an average of 17 to 20 per 1000, yet the average age was only 12 to 22, and only in one instance 48.

The greatest number of deaths were from consumption of the lungs. Then came scarlatina, fever, and small pox. The lower parts of the town are much subject to fever. In former days the intermittent fevers and agues were the prevailing ailments, but the Skerne has been damned in and these have nearly ceased. I have heard it remarked in various places by old men how in their young days such diseases prevailed, and how time has wrought a change. It arises simply from improvement of the land.

The atmosphere of Darlington is mild and relaxing. Strangers on arriving feel its influence. It may not lessen the amount of health,* but it tends to induce the low subacute character of the diseases which do occur, and has its general effects both physically and mentally. The prevailing diseases are adynamic or athelic, neither admitting nor requiring the vigorous active treatment that can be pursued in colder and more hilly districts, or where the air is stimulating and invigorating.†

The Skerne is a fertile source of disease, improved though it be. The gravelly rapid stream at Aycliffe meanders through the alluvial holmes from Haughton to Darlington with scarce a ripple, and when at the town what small descent it had has been for centuries nullified by the damming requisite for ancient mills, no wonder if in summer its surface should be green and its smell offensive. And then all the drainage of the town is to boot. The Bishops could not conceive the river to be the natural sewer of their borough when they plotted out their mill, though I believe after all, that if that were the only mill, the whole drainage might be taken into the Skerne below it. Until the application of the Public Health Act the sewerage of the town depended on the surveyors of the highways, who were not justified in forming it.

The miserable condition of many dwellings, ventilation and overcrowding, and the thousand and one nuisances of Darlington are those (and in many cases in far worse degree) of every town in England. The surveyors of the obsolete districts of Borough Bondgate and Priestgate used to repair the streets. The commissioners under the local act cleansed them ; both parties being irresponsible for joint action. The borough had less length of road to repair, yet having no country district, paid double the rate of Bondgate in the pound. About six feet of paving which had been taken up to insert a drain, remained unfinished for years in consequence of a dispute between the authorities of Bondgate and the Borough. Priestgate having only one street to repair, was exempt from rate for years together. The new Board of Health during their first year, notwithstanding the expenses of the elections, stationery, rents, and extra offices, did not levy more than the aggregate amount raised by the three sets of surveyors and the old Commissioners, and were content with a shilling rate. Yet in that year heavy expenses were incurred to place the working of the scheme on a proper basis. Thus crippled in means, from a disinclination to increase rates, various improvements have been postponed, but much has been done, and that in a substantial and permanent manner. Catterick's Yard, where fever, measles, and small pox reigned triumphant, has been drained, and not a single case has been reported since. Instead of a man and boy with a horse and cart to do the scavenging, four men and a stone mason are constantly employed, and these with the stonebreakers repair the roads and cleanse the streets. The improvement is immense all through the consolidation and efficiency of officers. It should be added that Mr. Geo. Mason the surveyor, and Mr. Piper the officer of health, have every local advantage, and have made good use of their facilities.

The cattle fairs in the centre of the town are an intolerable nuisance. In 1851 they were made weekly instead of fortnightly. It appeared in evidence before Mr. Ranger that the cattle slaughtered in the town were chiefly forwarded to the London market, while those for town consumption were slaughtered in the country ; and that a practice prevailed to a considerable extent of driving *diseased* cattle into the town during the *night* for the purpose of slaughtering and transmission to London. I have been *told*

* Many instances of Darlington longevity have been given in p. 235. The following, I believe, refers to cheerful Mr. Watkin. "There is now living in Darlington, a gentleman upwards of eighty years of age, who one day last week walked from that place to Newcastle.. It was his custom, when resident in Richmond, and carrying on the business of a draper there, always to walk to Manchester, a distance of ninety-three miles, to purchase his goods ; and should any good Samaritan perchance offer him a ride in his vehicle, he would never accept it. During his absence, having no assistant in his shop, it was his custom to put a card on the door, bearing the inscription, 'Gone to market.' "

† Mr. Fothergill, Ranger's Report.

that about the year 1826 there was a dreadful mortality in the feline tribe, and kittens were brought to Darlington market and sold at from 8*d.* to 18*d.* a head according to age and beauty.

The degrees of hardness in the springs of Darlington vary from 38 to 70. Of the water in the rivulets, the following report from Mr. Mason to the Board of Health gives the most intelligible idea. "Dr. Playfair has stated that ten gallons of water of fourteen degrees of hardness requires three ounces of soap to make it detergent or of a cleansing quality; whereas the softest public pump water in Darlington is thirty-eight degrees, or nearly three times harder. Skerne water contains about eighteen degrees, Cockerbeck twelve degrees, and Tees water three and a half degrees; so that for every ten gallons of water used for washing, pump water will require eight ounces of soap, Skerne three and three quarters ounces, Cockerbeck two and a half ounces, and, *Tees water three quarters of an ounce;* or in money value, with soap 6*d.* per lb., the cost for soap for ten gallons would be with pump water 3*d.*, Skerne 1¼*d.*, Cockerbeck nearly 1*d.*, *and Tees little more than a farthing.*" Infusions of tea, brewing, &c., have given similar results.

The spring water of the town is pleasant to the palate; but the public pumps are insufficient. Soft water cannot be obtained in any large quantity. The Darlington gas and water company obtained an act, 12 *and* 13 *Vict.*, *c.* 73, under which they supply water from the Tees. They take it from near the head of Baydales. Their engine will lift 500 gallons per minute. Their service reservoir is situate in the Hill Close House estate, and will hold 800,000 gallons.* Another company, formed in 1851, take water hence along the Darlington and Yarm road, and the railway, and supply Yarm, Stockton, and Middlesbrough. They have a second reservoir at Fighting Cocks.

Many veterans shook their heads at the Tees water when its introduction was mooted. They said that cattle became diseased in the lungs after grazing by the side of the Tees; that cattle imported from Middleton in Teesdale, and the ripe of Swale were a bad speculation, for they became "belloned," or short winded; that the water was frequently charged with lead by the practice of hushing, and killed the fish; and now were men also to be diseased in the lungs, and belloned, and poisoned. Therefore foot-races would be known only by report of more favoured parishes, and by Strutt's Sports and Pastimes; the gush of melody would be no more heard from the sweet voices of men; but after being a bad speculation to their neighbours, the majestic bipeds would, like the fish, turn upon their backs and perish with uplifted and distorted eye. Others reported that they would be happier and cleaner and healthier: that the beer would be better, and the tea stronger: the fishermen *near* the lead never saw their joy damped, nor were the cattle belloned so long as they kept at Middleton Teesdale: and mysterious analysts, Professor *Playfair* among them, found no lead in the inkiest water. They thought the people might still delight in the brisk water from the springs as far as their throats were concerned; and although it is not right for a man to be all white without and corrupt within, there seemed to be no reason why he was to be white within and corrupt without. There seemed no valid objection to fires being extinguished at Darlington, the people were not all fatalists, nor was it clear that an absence of water cleansed the streets.† And at last opinion began to grow favourable to the Tees water, and another idea arose, that small houses were not quite the places to disport in the water. More room and more Tees water would be better. So with a subscribed capital of 630*l.*, and various munificent donations,‡ some 1,000*l.* was gained, no bad beginning for a convenient array of *Public Baths.* There is another step in the ladder, men of Darlington! there are institutions called *Public Washhouses.*

The gas works are about a mile north of the market place, close to the station of the Stockton and Darlington railway.

One of the most pressing wants of the town is that of a public cemetery. Burials in the old church are exceedingly rare: the churchyard attached to it contains 2 acres and 38 perches, and this quantity includes an addition. When it is considered that this graveyard, to a recent period, was the *only* one, except that belonging to the Society of Friends, its state need not be insisted on. The area of the cemetery attached to Trinity church is 1 acre and 8 perches. It is of course impossible to transfer the town sepulture to such a space even for a limited period. The ground belonging to the

* The office is in the Central Buildings. Secretary, Mr. H. Robinson,

† The Local Board of Health have contracted with the company for a supply of water for both purposes.

‡ Robert Henry Allan, esq., 100*l.*; the Duke of Cleveland, 50*l.*; J. C. Backhouse, esq., 50*l.*; Mrs. Barclay, 50*l.*; Miss E. Pease, 50*l.*; Edmund Backhouse, esq., 30*l.*; William Backhouse, esq., 30*l.*; Lord Harry Vane, M.P., 25*l.*; James Farrer, esq., M.P., 10*l.* 10*s.* The baths are in Kendrew street.

Friends contains 1 rood and 20½ perches ; the depth of the graves is very great, and the annual burials amount to an average of four only.

The number of public houses and beershops (about eighty) is much too great for the town. The circumstance of magistrates having no voice as to the increase of beershops is very pernicious to morals; and as the extent of income lowers so does the stake and respectability of the householders.

"The gentry to the King's Head," as Heywood has it in his Signs of 1608, is still true in Darlington, though the "Sun" shines very brightly opposite.* Some of the older signs, such as the Talbot, have already been noticed in this work. Many significant ones still occur, such as the Pack Horse, the Fleece,† the *Dun Cow*,‡ the Hole in the Wall,§ the Boot and Shoe,|| Red Lion, Three Blue Bells, Royal Oak, Hat and Feather, Bull's Head,¶ Dolphin, Rose and Crown, Black Swan, Half Moon,** and the Black Bull. These houses may not all be ancient, though the signs assumed are so. In the old view of Darlingtin, in the possession of Mrs. Bowes, the royal badge of a stag couchant appears in Prebend Row. There were two "Rising Stags," one near Dr. Peacock's house in Skinnergate, the other in Tubwell Row. In 1720 we have the messuage in the Head Row lately called the White Horse Inn. In 1730 the Cross Keys occur in Tubwell Row.††

In addition to the chronological notices already given of the companies and progress

* Thomas Turner, chieftain of the King's Head Inn, is the namesake of a very respectable family in Darlington, who delighted in affording a Thomas Turner in 1650. But, while Thomas Turner of 1650 basked in "Sun Row," Thomas Turner of 1850 is diametrically opposite to his rival the Wright-son of the Sun ; and probably instead of supporting the son of rectitude in front, would, if he is a prudent tradesman, sincerely wish to see his neighbour to the right about. We generally, I think, find the best inns of a place clustering together as if the culinery art can only flourish where the cold air is kept out by other fires fuming and browning and frowning and reeking.

† Said, I know not why, to have been the town residence of the Prescotts. I think it only belonged to them. A very ancient door studded, and adorned with a cruciform knockerplate and fleurdelis, guards the yard entrance to the street. It is an old and substantial hostelry re-edified. It occurs as the "*Old* Fleece Inn."

‡ A house in Post House Wynd is styled the *Old* Dun Cow Inn. It is in truth behind what was the Dun Cow Inn, namely the house at the south-east angle of the Wynd. The other Dun Cow, in the Horse Market, is of recent date. The Durham legend is of course alluded to—a legend in no way original, and almost exactly similar to stories about Salisbury cathedral, and Finchale abbey. Nor at Durham is it even ancient ; it occurs in none of our sufficiently credulous early writers, and it may have arisen from a sculpture as much as a sculpture from it.

§ The inns of this sign were not uncommon, and are considered as so named from being snug *par eminence*, and, but in a better sense, like the chamber mentioned in Ezekiel, viii., 7, as approached by a hole in the wall. But, though in general they were named from being good *skulking* holes for those who loved drinking better than work, "in summer shady, and in winter warm," where in this season the beer was brought up, and in that kept down, to a proper state ; the Darlington example is said to arise in a far-fetched pun upon one Hollywell or Halliwell who kept it.

|| In an agreement of 1762 the inn in Tubwell Row now called the Golden Cock is described as "formerly the Blue Boar, now the sign of the Boot and Shoe, in Tubwelrow," In all the title deeds no sign is mentioned, the house being merely described as a burgage. I cannot therefore say anything about the antiquity of the former appellation. The Blue Boar was followed by the Three Jolly Travellers ; and Mrs. Edmondson has the signboard, excellently painted. On the reverse is the subsequent Boot and Shoe. It is now the Golden Cock.

¶ The Neville Crest.

** The Percy badge. "The half moon shining all so fair."

†† 1615. We finde Tho. Branso' to keep one undersettle and find him not fitt to keep any alehouse.—1617. Noe keepers of Tiplinge howses within the iurisdiccon of this Borough of Darlington shall from henceforth take or receyve into theire howse or howses any forreyners or straungers to them unknowne to lodge or entertaine by the space of one hoore together without firste makinge the head officer therewith acquainted upon paine of forfeitinge toties quoties 39*s*. 11*d*. ob.—1741. Every Innkeeper Brewer or Retailer of Ale and Beer within the said town and burrow of Darlington (for time beyond the memory of man) have always paid and ought to pay yearly and every year at the feast of Easter the sum of 2*d*. to the Lord Bishop of Durham's Lessees of the tolls for the time being of the said town and Burrough for their lycence and brew-farm for leave to sell ale and beer within the same town and burrough according to the ancient usage and custom of the said town and burrough.—1723. Ordered that all Innkeepers move *their sign-posts* upon or before 1 August. Borough Books.

of trade, the registers afford some data. A challonweaver* occurs 1626; fuller and ropemaker, 1652; chandlemaker, 1653; feltmonger, 1654; loriman,† 1655; silkweaver, 1657; Robert Coarson, tobackoman,‡ 1658 (called merchant in 1667); Tho. *Bill*, proctor, 1665; coverlid worker, 1666; Wm. Fledge, of Norridge, stapler, was buried in Darlington, 1681; mettleman, [a copper smith or tinman], firkinmaker, 1683; scepper [basket-maker], of Cockerton, 1698; Jersey comber, 1698; ale draper, of Blackwell, 1702; wood heal maker, 1704; ho-boy, 1704; wauker,§ 1708; Mr. Wm. Middleton, of Blackwell, watchmaker [an odd place for such a craft], 1716; bucklemaker, 1746; rough-rider, 1754; peruke maker, 1757; china-mender, 1784; spectacle-frame maker, 1789;‖ James Mc Kenn, quack doctor,¶ a stranger, bur. 1797.**

At one time upwards of 1500 looms were employed in Darlington and the neighbourhood.†† Steam has changed the tune. Darlington and its colonies, however, are still no dwarfs in manufactures. In the great exposition of 1851, the material of the flags which from the exterior of the crystal palace fluttered a welcome to all, was made here by Messrs. Pease and Co.; the very iron was smelted by Pease's coke; Mr. Pease's fire-bricks gained a prize; patent fuel made at Middlesbrough, a council medal; and the Coburg cloth, manufactured here by Henry Pease and Co., carried away a prize against Halifax competitors and numerous old houses who had considered themselves unapproachable. Mr. Charge exhibited a hunting saddle, which, though the prize was borne away by a case containing *three* saddles, was considered quite equal to them.

The largest manufacturing establishments at Darlington are those of H. Pease and Co., two large mills for woollen goods, and another for cotton; Overend and Co., flax; J. and F. Kipling, carpets; Kipling and Teasdale, M. Middleton, J. H. Bowman, and W. and R. Child, leather.

About 184.., Mr. Heslegrave, land surveyor, Darlington, patented a very superior atmospheric spring for railway carriages which was soon in constant operation on the Stockton and Darlington line. In 1848 also, Mr. W. Froude, of Darlington obtained a patent for a valve to cover the longitudinal opening of an atmospheric railway tube. Mr. Stephen Carlton, coachmaker, Northgate, is proprietor of a very simple and comfortable carriage-spring, which is registered.

In the matter of signs, the following is perhaps our most vigorous effort:—

"Richard Bolam is my well known name,
For sweeping chimneys extoll'd by fame;
From a cottage to a castle, I will attend
The shortest notice, from each friend.
With my machine and attendant by my side,
I'll sweep your chimneys either strait or wide."

* John Glover, of Darlington, *chalen wever*, aged 44, a witness in the ecclesiastical court, 1595.

† A manufacturer of small works in iron.

‡ The following tradesmen's tokens struck at Darlington before 1672, (when their circulation was stopped, and government copper issued,) occur. 1, "ROBERT COARSON," (king's head to the left) rev. "* IN DARLINGTON," 1666" (a roll of tobacco). 2, "RICHARD SCAIFE" (king's head to the left), rev. "*IN DARLINGTON, 1666," (grocers' arms, Scaife being of that calling, and a recusant). 3, R . . . . . . B . . . . [Branson?] effaced. 4, Michael Middleton, (king's head, looking left). 5, Michael Middleton, a variety and much larger coin; "MICHAEL MIDDLETON, OF," rev. a crown. "DARLINGTON, HIS HALF-PENNY."

§ Walk-mill-nook is the name of two fields on the Skerne between Blackwell mill and Snipe bridge. A walker was a fuller of cloth. A century ago there were two walk-mills at Piersebridge.

‖ A craft consequent on Kendrew's discoveries. Vide sub. anno. 1800.

¶ Francis Bainbrigge of Darlington, *barbar surgion*, and Robert Raynere *medicus*, occur 1626. Robert Ward, of D., *trance latter*, 1663. Mary Bullock, of Blackwell, *mide*wife, bur. 1708.

** I have mislaid the dates of "Whitesmith alias *malman*," and "*higler*," i. e. huckster or pedlar.

†† When I was a little girl, about seven years old,
I hadn't got a petticoat, to cover me from the cold;
So I went into Darlington, that pretty little town,
And there I bought a petticoat, a cloak, and a gown.
I went into the woods and built me a kirk,
And all the birds of the air, they helped me to work;
The hawk with his long claws, pulled down the stones,
The dove, with her rough bill, brought me them home:
The parrot was the clergyman, the peacock was the clerk,
The bullfinch played the organ, and we made merry work.
Halliwell's Nursery Rhymes.

But the stanza is altered to suit many towns.

This production went further. It was transplanted with slight variation into a card with a brilliant border, and heading, which gave additional information that Mr. Bolam was also a "smoke-jack cleaner." A rival sweep was all on fire. He came to a friend of mine to request that he would compose him a "poem," also, but I fear that the errand was fruitless. I don't know that I can excel the above ensign. There was another amusing one, I remember. "R. Noble—Taxiderdmist—Warranted."

The tradesmen of Darlington have a "Marine Insurance Association," to provide for risks in the transit of goods. It took the place and in fact is a continuation of "The Darlington Commercial Mutual Insurance Company," established in 1782. Mr. O. B. Wooler is the solicitor.

The supposed origin of the benefit clubs in the ancient guilds or trade companies, seems to me a fanciful theory. The two have their coincidences as far as the risk are concerned, but there the similitude ends. The guilds were the organs of the burghal monopoly. The restriction of modern societies to trade is the exception. I have seen tickets of contribution to the charity stock of the "Darlington Old Society," dated the last century From their *illustrations*—a ram, the church, and "Bishop Blaise,"—I assume this was a restrictive club: "liberty, property, no deceit," was their heading. There are several flourishing benefit societies in Darlington; among them are courts of the well known and "ancient order of Foresters," and the ancient order of Shepherds,* Grand United Order of Odd Fellows, and the Manchester Unity of the Order of Odd Fellows, have their lodges. These societies number near 1000 members at Darlington. There are also two or three Free Gift associations, promoting prudence in expenditure, they divide their funds annually, and make no provision for sickness. The Wesleyans have a benefit society. The Christian Visiting Society employ a town mission to search out cases of sickness and poverty in order to their relief.† The average allowance in these prudent institutions amounts to about 7*s*. weekly for sickness, and 2*s*. 6*d*. per member per annumn for medical attendance. The aggregate yearly expenditure of the enumerated societies, including funeral donations for members and their wives, is near 500*l*., making a total expenditure (including the Dispensary and Wesleyan Benevolent Society, see p. 253) of some 670*l*.

The poor rates at Darlington are low, about 3*s*. 2*d*. per annum. Able-bodied paupers are scarce; but vagrancy is a heavy burden, Darlington being a stage on the great north road.‡

Since the account of the charities of Darlington was written (p. 262) the fields in the township of Blackwell, called Poor Howdens, belonging to the Bellasses charity, have been appropriated for the purpose of a public park, or place of sports and recreation. A new bridge over the Skerne connects with the road (bought in 1841) and so with the Croft turnpike.

A Savings Bank in the town has proved a very great boon to the industrious.§ (See

* They also are Foresters, in the second degree of Forestry, and their court is called "a Sanctuary of Ancient Shepherds."

† Mr. H. Spencer furnished an excellent summary of all these societies to Mr. Ranger, on his Inquiry. It is in his Report.

‡ The Act of 22 Geo. III., relating to the poor, was adopted for Darlington township. Under this act the palace was enlarged in 1809. There were no particular regulations with respect to clothing. Such of the poor in the house as were able to work, were mostly employed in the manufactories of the town, such as spinning mills, weaving, &c. Their earnings were brought weekly to the credit of the township. The annual amount raised by the poor rate, for the five years preceding 1810, amounted to 1750*l*. During that period houses paid 3*s*. in the pound, and land 4*s*. 6*d*. This act continued in force until the New Poor Law included Darlington, which was then made the centre of a Union which comprises several parishes in both counties, and is sufficiently laid down as respects Durham in Hobson's map of that county. Carlbury however, an extra-parochial portion of Coniscliffe, is independent. The workhouse is a pattern of cleanliness, and is rarely equalled, I should suppose, in comfort. One old woman has been in the house almost all her life, for only two out of her seventy years has she been absent. There is a relieving or vagrant house for the vagrants in Bowes street, containing two rooms furnished with seats, and each room is capable of holding about six persons, who may squat on the floors or sit on the few forms which are there provided for them. The two sexes divide for the night, into the two rooms: and no wonder that vagrants beg for alms, openly detailing the horrors of this Black Hole of Darlington, when some thirty persons occasionally sleep (?) in a room fitted for six in the day, and less at night. The elysium begged for by the poor creatures will be one of the lodging houses so abundant in Skinnergate, few of which have less than ten beds, and in some of them there are as many as nine beds in one room. Space is purchasable sometimes at all events, threepence being the price of a bed. At this price three, two, or one may constitute the number of its occupants. On the most moderate calculation, at least 22,000 wanderers pass in the half year through Darlington.

§ The following are the other banks in the town. Backhouse and Co., who have branch banks from Thirsk to Sunderland, draw on Barclay and Co.: this old bank was established

p. 319). The Mechanics' Institute,* (p. 321), the Subscription Library, a News Room, and various other little etceteras give considerable facilities and comforts to our agricultural town. Debating and cricket clubs have been of much use, and a Christian young men's society promises favourably. Libraries are attached to the Church Sunday School, and to most of the dissenting chapels.

The old terms of 13 May and 23 November are the usual ones in Darlington, but there are still many houses called "*Great Monday Houses*," taken from the Great Monday after Whitsuntide (see p. 275), the ancient and accustomed day of quitting houses in this town.†

I had intended to construct a map of the ancient parish of Darlington. But I find myself miserably deficient in much of the identification necessary for such a purpose, and all I can do is to hope that the evidences amassed in this volume may at least be no unacceptable addition to those necessary for the full investigation of the extinct topography of the parish. Its general situation has been already detailed (pp. 1, 9), and its form is readily ascertained in the county maps, and the maps appended to Rawlinson's Report. My index will bring all my scattered details into one focus. A few extra particulars may here be added.

The fine market place contains 1,700 square yards. The building are generally good, and very different from the time when the corner house was thatched and panelled.‡ A number of incongruous buildings obstruct the noble square ; and as the shambles have been renovated and improved, reformation seems hopeless. The value of the property in the centre of Bondgate has hitherto also prevented width and improvement in that street. Let it not, however, be understood that the streets of Darlington are narrow. As compared with those of thickly populated old towns, they are of princely width, but in the country one expects expanse.§ An isolated tree near the Green Tree Inn, in Skinnergate, has a very happy effect. The old cottages opposite the house of Edward Pease, esq., in Northgate, close to the great boulder stone, were known as "Darlington House,"|| ending the town to the north. Now in that and all directions, handsome villas and spreading gardens extend themselves, stretching from Bondgate to Northgate, and from Northgate to Haughton road : a belt of countrified farm land intervenes : but near the church they again begin, covering the Skerne's¶ deep holmes, and insinuating themselves to its bank tops. The Polam (anciently Polinpole) district is of great area on both sides of the river. Crossing the Croft road,

in 1774. The Darlington District Banking Company also draw on Barclay and Co. A branch of the National Provincial Bank of England is represented by Hanburys and Co., and by the London and Westminster bank. A very handsome front was lately erected by this bank on the High Row, in the style of some of the Italian palaces.

* 1850, May 22. The thirteenth annual meeting of the Yorkshire Union of Mechanics' Institutes (which includes those of Stockton and Darlington) was held in Darlington. Forty delegates from twenty-nine institutes met at twelve o'clock, in the lecture room, Central Buildings, Edward Baines, esq., of Leeds, chairman. It was stated that in 1845, the Union contained 20 institutes, it now comprised 109, with 18,516 members, and had been the means of obtaining paid lectures to 31 institutes at a considerable saving when compared with the funds required for isolated engagements. A paid lecturer was now on constant service. The exertions of Mr. G. Linnæus Banks, of Harrogate, Mr. Norman, Mr. Wilkinson, &c., were highly applauded. Twenty-seven new institutes were then admitted. The Darlington institute had adopted a book committee who examined the proposal book before it was submitted to the general committee, and at a recent committee meeting out of twenty-eight books proposed twenty-four were rejected as not desirable for the library of the institute. The president of the Union, Edward Baines, esq., was re-elected. The annual dinner took place at the Sun Inn, assembly room, Francis Mewburn, esq., the borough bailiff, in the chair. A soiree was afterwards held in the Central Hall, at which some 400 persons were present. The Dean of Ripon occupied the chair. Among other resolutions, the continued prosperity of the Darlington institute was desired, it having a larger number of members, considering the population of the town, than almost any institution with which the proposer (John Hope Shaw, esq., of Leeds) was acquainted. It was universally thought that the meeting was of great advantage to our institute, in suggesting means of improvement and exhibiting the experience of other towns.

† Letter from James Allan, esq., to General John Lambton, 1786, copy penes R. H. A.

‡ Inf. Edward Pease, esq.

§ About 100 years ago Skinnergate was merely a back lane, as an outlet to the houses on the High Row, with here and there an old thatched cottage on the west side. *(Inf. Fra. Mewburn, esq.)* New thatching over the bridge and in Bondgate occur in the Allan rent rolls for 1761 and 1774.

|| John, son of Anthony Fryer, late of Darlington House, carpenter, deceased. Apprenticed 1690. (Newcastle Masters' and Mariners' Books.)

¶ Can Skerne have ought to do with *sker*, to slide swiftly, to skate. In some parts the verb would not be inapplicable.

Woodside, and the pleasant houses of Harewood, attract us. These stretch almost to Coniscliffe Lane, bounding Southend (formerly Borrowses) the seat of Joseph Pease, esq., our quondam M. P. In Coniscliffe Lane we have the Chief Bailiff's residence (Larchfield), and the Vicarage. Cockerton road again is lined on each side—the house of Pierremont exhibiting an ornate Gothic style, windows stained with the "b's" of Botcherby and other decorations. It would be invidious generally to descriminate the status of a villa as distinguished from a house, much more so to usurp the office of a directory and give the owners of the various domiciles favoured by the title. To give the stranger an idea of the society of Darlington, it is sufficient to say that *generally* the out-residences are filled by Friends, who excel greatly in horticulture. Their grounds are enviable places of solace and retirement, where they allow the Horticultural Society's meetings to be held. The only but unavoidable drawbacks to the beauty which the approaches to Darlington assume from the snug homes of its magnates, are the long ranges of wall bounding the road. These are bald enough, but, near a town, what could be done?

The Bishop's Park was on the east side of the Skerne; it is now divided into fields, chiefly held by lease under the see. Depressions have been filled up with bark and rubbish and on this decaying substructure streets have been built, the perpetual abode of fever and disease.

The lands about St. John's Church constitute a district called Dodmires, once a rough miry place enough, no doubt, and probably harbouring some awkward hobgoblin or dudman, as the portion lately bought by the Freehold Land Society was anciently called Dodman's closes. But whether he was covered with *duds* and was a nasty ragged sprite, like the household ghosts of the north, or was a shifting Will-of-the-whisp, *dodging** poor unfortunates, I really am not spiritual enough to discern.†

Cockerton and Archdeacon Newton call for small remark. The latter is a purely agricultural township, with scattered dwellings. The former is a long, miserable village, with an ancient well, and a dead-alive November aspect. There is a ballad on "the lass of Cockerton," sadly belying the title of Ritson's Bishopric Garland to its claim as "a choice collection of *excellent* songs."

The name of Rice Carr, or Riscar, no doubt takes its name from some carrs or low grounds supplying abundance of saplings to form the interwoven fences of "rice and stake."‡

Blackwell has figured before in this volume. The village was once much more extensive. R. H. Allan, esq., had great difficulty in draining Prescott's field, in consequence of foundations of houses. The Tees has done its work of destruction, and the late John Allan, esq., pulled down several wretched tenements of mud. At present Blackwell is a very ancestral looking place, with its Allan halls, and wooded domains. J. C. Backhouse, esq., and Mrs. Milbank, have pleasant residences here. A few more houses and white cottages with rich little gardens in front compose the habitable area. Mr. R. H. Allan, who added these little gardens and otherwise much improved the village, gives annual prizes for the best horticulture, and great are the struggles of the patriarchs. There is in Blackwell, by the way, a very old door studded with iron in a framework marked with a cross. It hung at the entrance of Prescotts' old mansion, in the precincts of which a Flemish coin, the size and style of our silver pennies of Edward I., and struck at Alost, was found.§ A small circle of lead, ornamented with pellets, and perforated, was also found in the grounds attached to Blackwell hall, and is there preserved.

A more minute description of the neighbourhood of Darlington will not be interesting to strangers, and the inhabitants will not care about it.

Some remarks on manners and customs may be expected. Of these one of the most remarkable was that of *Riding the Stang*, an exposure to infamy of offenders in matrimonial or domestic affairs generally. Adultery, corporal chastisement of the fair sex, and over-reachings in trade, all were properly revenged. If persons worked on holidays, or when there was a strike, or if boys offended against the juvenile bye-laws of a school. they were stanged. Eric, king of Norway, had to fly from the hatred of his people for inflicting this stigma on a celebrated Islandic bard. It was then of the most tremendous character. The Goths erected a nidstaeng or pole of infamy, with the most dire imprecations agai nst the guilty party, who was called *Niding*, or the infamous, and disqualified from giving evidence.

* Daddyke, *Belg.*, wavering.

† The root of the name is abundant all over England, and by enthusiastic antiquaries is hunted up to Thoth of Egypt, Tot of Ethiopia, Teut of Germany, Taute of Phœnicia, Zeus, Deus, Dieu, Deity.

‡ Pennant's Tour through South Wales.

§ Penes R. H. Allan esq.

The proper mode of enacting the stang is by bearing the offender mounted backwards upon the stang, or pole. On this fickle and painful seat he was treated with huzzas and missiles from the children. Latterly, the culprit has been represented by a sort of Richard Roe, who proclaimed that he was thus treated by the populace (his John Doe) on account of another person, and narrated the offence, which was slyly represented as being performed through the instrumentality of some article which bespoke the offender's trade, and at once marked him.

This practice is parallel to the "riding Skimmington" in other parts of the country. I have witnessed the custom in the parish of Darlington once, but it ended in such increased cruelty to the poor victim revenged, that I verily believe she died from grief, and I apprehend it will never be transacted again. It had then become so obsolete that one great, and to the ridiculed man insulting, characteristic was forgotten, the demanding fourpence for degrading him! At Stockton the custom lingers lifelessly. The stang itself is pretty much dispensed with all over. To atchieve the necessary pain, however, at Norton when the stang was ridden the reciter was put into a donkey cart. This was furiously pushed along at a great velocity, and brought to a sudden and jolting stop, and then the harangue was commenced. In Yorkshire it continues in full pomp. At Thirsk a succession of ridings may occupy a week, but then each case needed three ridings on successive nights. The *poetry* was changed each night by the leader of the stang-band, an important officer of the town indeed; and the last night an effigy was burnt before the offender's door, and the spokesman then proceeded to him for the groat, which was usually paid under the influence of fear or custom. Formerly the spokesman there was carried on a ladder on men's shoulders, but is now drawn in a cart. An old shoemaker once accompanied the fourpence with a treat of ale, which the stangrider drank greedily. It was dozed heavily with jalap. The magistrates decline to interfere with the old custom as long as no property is damaged, and in the absence of rural police they scarcely have the power to do otherwise. If damage did occur the spokesman was to be liable. I remember a tradesman losing a cause at the County Court. A powerful party of the poor were so delighted that they rode the stang for him.

I have been unable to obtain a South Durham version of the stang rhymes from any authority I can depend on to furnish a truly popular and *unenlarged* copy, but the following *morceau* recited for a druggist at Thirsk, some twenty years ago, was obtained from its *author* the retained stangrider aforesaid :—

Hey Derry! Hey Derry! Hey Derry Dan!
It's neither for your cause, nor my cause
That I ride the stang.
But it is for t' Peg Doctor for banging his deary,
If you'll stay a few minutes I'll tell you all clearly.
One night he came home with a very red face—
I suppose he was drunk as is often the case,
Be that as it may; but—when he got in,
He knocked down his wife with a new rolling pin.
She jumped up again, and knocked off his hat,
And he up with the pestle, and felled her quite flat.
She ran out to the yard and shouted for life,
And he swore he would kill her with a great gully knife.
So all you good people that lives in this raw (row),
I'd have you take warning, for this is our law;
And if any of your husbands you wives do bang,
Come to me and my congregation, and we'll *Ride the Stang!*

The poet modestly adds "The language used by the generality of those who have acted as spokesmen on different occasions has been such low and unmeaning stuff that it is not worth repeating. I by no means wish you to understand by this that I am an egotist, as I consider my own productions in this line, generally speaking, unpoetical, being usually composed on the spur of the moment, something fresh every night for three nights." No doubt the above is a choice specimen in its way, though it gives a good notion of what I used to hear, which had the addition of some truly "low stuff," a general chorus, I believe, to stang rhymes, and which I am glad indeed to consign to oblivion, as far as in *me* lies. The obscurity of the last line but one of the above verses is a masterpiece of sybillic application to either sex.

Skepping used to be a favourite punishment among the wool combers. They would tear any offending brother from his wife and home, put him into a cart, cover him with one of their skeps or large baskets, carry him round the town with fife and drum, and then duck him in the Skerne right soundly.

In the "Entertaining Repository," an old collection of 1810 or so, one Blazius communicates an epistle from a Devonshire man giving an account of the northern treat of "a Scadding of Peas" he witnessed at Darlington.

"When peas begin to change their colour,
And some are green, and some are yellow,

. . . .

You see a big—a waling pot,
Well crammed with peas—all smoking hot;
Peas—swads and all—

. . . .

Swift to the purport of my story,
To sing O DARLINGTON thy Glory.
The peas at length being done enough,
That is, some tender, numbers tough,
Into a Dish of course they pour 'em,
While all stand ready to devour 'em;
And 'bout the centre of the dish
Round which these amorous gluttons fish,
Two saucers commonly are plac'd,
And one of them with Butter's grac'd,
The other doth some salt contain,
When all fall *too* with might and main.
First into those they dip their swads
Then draw them through their filthy gabs,
When Peas and Mauks all sink together,
One serves to qualify the other."

Stangs and Scaddings are however usual enough, and really Darlington possesses few peculiarities of custom which may not be found and enlarged upon in Brockett's Glossary as common to various parts of the north country. I scarcely dare say much about them. They tempt long annotation, shewing how sword-dancing is mentioned by Tacitus, and whip-top by Persius and Ovid. Hurworth was the great nursery of the Christmas sword-dancers. Yule is still observed decently and in order, with its cakes, candles, and goose pies, which in truth have many good birds more than geese in their composition. The old rhymes "God rest you merry gentlemen," &c., greet one a little before this jocund time, and Christmas Eve provokes its "frumenty." Creed wheat is however a singularly great favourite here nearly all the year round. Shrill cries of "Creed wheat cakes!" awake the scholar from his sleep, albeit required since the midnight oil. Then too we have birth-day cakes, and funeral cakes; pagan carlings for the Sunday but one before, and veal for Easter itself; Collop Monday, and Pancake Tuesday, all gloriously accomplished before Ash Wednesday; and a host of knead cakes and spice wigs to tea which frighten "false southrons" from our groaning boards. We firmly feel that men are "cooking animals" and are glad to make the most of any excuse to confirm the characteristic. A "covering in supper" on building, or a "welcome supper" on changing, or a "farewell supper" on leaving, are all excellent things. A man cannot go out of the world with his friends fasting; a Richmond testator plainly expressed his determination to "depart with meat and drink;" and certainly he cannot come in so, for he floats in smoothly and comfortably, and you will hear many a joyful proclamation of "I am going to so and so's *to wash a bairn's head* to night." All the old superstitions of times and seasons, of first-foots on New-year's day and so forth, and the fire-works and bone-fires of the fifth of November, are kept on foot. Our houses are not thatched, and our minds are not cold. Their elder faiths are not idolatrous, and they do not hate the parliament, so keep we our customs and feastings and fires. "We are not made of wood or stone, and the things which connect themselves with our hearts and habits, cannot, like bark or lichen, be sent away without our missing them."*

The Durham pronunciation has been described as "soft, but monotonous and drawling." A plague-smitten native, I am prejudiced, but I think the observation is correct. The Darlington dialect partakes more of the peculiarities of Yorkshire and its English than of Northumberland and its Scotch or perhaps rather Danish dialect. But many things are in common. Broth, for instance, is always plural. "Will you have some broth?—I will take a few, if they are good." Some one has observed, that we have here the Scotch *broes*, taken as in the plural.

I now come to arts and literature—to notices of the few whose memories will live when the tombstone is broken and their friends departed. If in this respect, we have not giants, still we have in numbers and fair merit above the average of a country town's productions.

Henry Heavisides will be perhaps associated with Stockton; but he was born at Darlington in 1791. He there received a tolerable education, and was apprenticed to his father, who was for many years a respectable printer and bookseller here. The latter was however unfortunate in trade, and was obliged, from ill health and a dis-

* *Guy Mannering.*

position totally unfit to battle with his difficulties, to retire from it altogether. Henry had nearly finished his term, and was left to make his way as a journeyman printer. He wandered about and at last settled in Stockton, where he still resides, the honoured author of the "Pleasures of Home and other Poems," published in 1837. They are graceful earnest efforts, the production of the evening hours of a laborious printer. His gifted son, EDWARD MARSH HEAVISIDES, produced under similar avocations in 1845, his "Songs of the heart." These and very abundant and graphic sketches in prose and verse gave great promise of future excellence; but he died in 1849, at the early age of 28. His works were collected into a posthumous volume for the benefit of his family.

THOMAS EASTOE ABBOTT is another of our local bards. Born at East Dereham, in Norfolk, he passed the best of his days in the inland revenue department, and having been ten years an officer, and nearly twenty in the rank of supervisor, retired to repose for the evening of life. In the soft glades of Skerne, among those garden bowers, he pitched his snug tent and named it Rose Villa.

Of the following his principal works, all save the two last were written in Yorkshire, and that they were favourably received may be gathered from the fact that to the "Soldier's Friend" there were about 400 subscribers, comprising several noblemen, together with many of the clergy and magistracy of Yorkshire. By the way, this is a desirable book to have were it but for its beautiful miniature of the Duke of York commemorated therein, and its valuable notes and illustrations communicated to the author by Sir Herbert Taylor, the Rev. Dr. Dakins, and others. A large paper copy of this work was presented to His Majesty George IV. by the present Bishop of Winchester. Mr. Abbott's poems are written with great simplicity of language, full of genuine patriotism and Christianity; some of them much resembling in style that of Wordsworth. The principal works alluded to were these. "Peace" a lyric poem dedicated to the mayor of Hull, London, 1814. "Resignation," a poem on the death of H. R. H. the Princess Charlotte of Wales, Hull, 1817. "The Triumph of Christianity, a missionary poem; Commerce; and other Poems," dedicated to William Wilberforce, esq., M.P., London, 1819. "The Soldier's Friend," a poem to the memory of H. R. H. the late Duke of York, dedicated to Major General the late Lord Macdonald, London, 1828. "Lines on Education and Religion," printed at Darlington for Trinity Church Bazaar, 1839.

Mr. Abbott has published other smaller poems. He had moreover printed a very useful tract (Durham, 1845), containing the "Charter of the Royal Free Grammar School," with notes and an address to the inhabitants, for gratuitous circulation. This I have found of considerable service. It is levelled at that detestable abuse in the free grammar schools of England, the restriction of the word "grammar" to the meaning "dead languages." The word "free" is now, I believe, often omitted in the style employed in the title of the Darlington school, contrarily to the charter. Mr. Abbott was one of the wardens who removed Mr. Wray (see p. 259), and, for several years after that removal, the scholars were freely admitted to general instruction. For this and various other public duties Mr. Abbott has deserved well of his adopted town.

THOMAS WATSON is a southron by birth, the son of an auctioneer, himself an auctioneer of renown at Darlington, who lightens each dull hand-bill with scientific and romantic allusions. He was born in London, and removed in childhood to the New Forest, where he remained some years and nearly up to the time of his entering business. He came to Darlington about 1832, and in 1835 or 1836 he published a poem of about thirty stanzas entitled "The Mameluke." I believe he was a grocer at Darlington, but when he published his "Ruin and other Poems" (1840), he had become a commercial traveller. "The Ruin" is written in those too facile eights, and slides smoothly away. All Mr. Watson's poems are musical in excess, very pleasant to such as the writer, who reads poetry for its lightsomeness, as a change from arid lore. They may lack reflection and weighty moral, they may not have all their ornaments in keeping, and their luxuriousness of description may exceed bounds, and be as the leaves of summer to the feathered burstings of spring; but never mind, they are very sweet: and Tom Watson is a true man, attending to his own business, save when he helps some goodly cause or greets a well known friend.

Then there is a lady who has employed the Darlington press, MISS E. COLLING, of Hurworth, who printed at Mr. G. Harrison's press a few years ago, "The Rival Sisters," "Ode to Care," "Ode to The Elements," &c. These are dead-weight subjects to choose, but I have been told, (for I never saw the books, which are privately circulated), that they possess considerable delicacy and nervous boldness of composition.

JOSEPH SAMS of this town, is an eminent bookseller, possessing probably one of the most extensive collections of Biblical, classical and other scarce, and important works in this country. Amongst them are many valuable *editiones principes* of the classics, which my readers will scarcely need to be reminded, rank next to MSS. as evidences of unadulterated text and readings. As alterations creep into later editions, these firstlings of the press are naturally much sought after, and bring high prices.

This gentleman is a remarkable character; and has not only visited the chief countries and cities of Europe, but has also travelled extensively in eastern climes, as in Egypt, Arabia, Syria, Palestine, Asia Minor, &c. His journies, in different years, were undertaken partly from the general motives which induce men to examine foreign countries and as promotive of health, and partly to amass Biblical and classical manuscripts, and rare early printed books. So successful was the search, that when the late Duke of Sussex was in the north, he bought of Mr Sams, at one purchase, to the value of upwards of 400*l*., and from a catalogue, two years after, he ordered above 100*l*. worth. I one heard in a call I made, that the pecuniary preparations for these journies in foreign lands, was the circular 20*l*. notes of Herries and Co, of St. James's Street, London, of use only to the taker who has signed a letter which he carries with him. As one changed is about 25 gold Napoleons, it was hazardous to have so much on the the person in dangerous parts, such as Spain; so a screw ferrule was contrived at the bottom of a walking stick, to contain the 25 pieces. This mode did not answer in the east, Napoleons being scarcely known there. Mr S. traversed Egypt from end to end, visited the pyramids, and was above the great Cataracts of the Nile, in Nubia, the Ethiopia of the Scriptures. He afterwards traced much of the route of the Israelites in their way from Egypt to Canaan, visiting Mounts Horeb and Sinai, and surveying Jerusalem.

The traveller was in the habit of taking on these occasions, to endeavour to circulate, religious tracts and books. He supplied himself at Malta with volumes of Holy Scripture. Of tracts he was partial to "Allen's Importance of Religion," and took out copies in Italian, and in Arabic, the vernacular language of Palestine, Egypt,* &c. He was presented at Alexandria to the noted Mohammed Ali, by our consul-general. Previously to the presentation, he communicated to the consul his wish to request the Pasha's acceptance of one of the volumes of Scripture. This the consul rather discouraged, fearing, as did several German missionaries, sent by the London Missionary Society, that the gift would not be well received, and might tend to block up their way. However, Mr S. still wishing to take the book, said that if he saw the way open, he would present it, but if not, he would bring it away, with this the consul was satisfied. The Pasha was sitting, crosslegged, on rich cushions that went round the beautiful eastern room, smoking his chibouk. The great officers of state stood around. The strangers were received with kindness, and requested to sit, which they did, near to the Pasha, who after refreshment had been handed, entered into conversation with, and asked questions of Mr S. about England, &c., and told him his own native place was near to Salonica, the ancient Thessalonica, and became cordial and familiar. Mr S. thought the way was open, and producing the volume (which he had taken care to have in a superior binding) requested the acceptance of it as a collection of sacred books. The Pasha accepted it with great complacency, read in it a while, and thanked the donor for his attention.

The missionaries, who were in an outer room, seemed delighted, and welcomed the stranger by warm shakes of the hand and congratulations. Mr Sams was afterwards applied to by an officer, who it is thought was present, and who begged to know if he could kindly supply *him* with a copy of what he had presented to his highness Thus was another copy, it appeared, well placed. Mr S. took some copies also to the Egyptian Thebes, and he gave two to the ancient convent at the foot of Mount Sinai. These perhaps were the first printed copies of Scripture placed thus in Egypt and at Sinai.

A journal was kept by Mr Sams but has not been published. His publication is confined at present to a folio volume of accurate plates, finely coloured, with short descriptions, entitled "Objects of Antiquity, forming part of the extensive and rich collections from Ancient Egypt, brought to England by J. Sams." This beautiful work, issued in 1843, is however of a very limited impression, and will always be very rare. The Egyptian collections of its author are singularly extensive, and considered amongst the most important that have entered England. I shall briefly enumerate a few of the objects. Two massive ear-rings of gold, circular, but broad and fluted, each weighing nearly half an ounce. An extraordinary signet, wholly of gold; it turns on a swivel, and contains in a royal cartouche, the name of one of the most ancient Pharaohs, under whom according to some historians, Joseph governed. Mr Sams has refused 100*l*. for this relic several times, not wishing to separate any important object. A signet of another Pharoah was found some five or six years ago, for which a physician resident in Egypt, is asking 300*l*. In the collections are two other gold seals set with engraved stones. A sarcophagus of marble, smaller than Belzoni's, but having its cover, and a

* Turkish is the *court* language of Egypt.

mummy in fine tact. Belzoni's wanted the cover. A table of oriental alabaster *with its stand turned* out of one solid block. An inkstand with chain to attach a case, all of bronze; the case still retaining an ancient pen of reed, for writing on papyrus. Double vases, attached like the Siamese twins. A vase of glass, variegated in several colours. Adjuncts for the lady's toilette, with several divisions, to contain different powders for painting the person, and a style for laying them on. An entire chain of gold. We read that Pharaoh, particularly to honour Joseph, besides using other adornment, "put a chain of gold about his neck." A collection of ten MSS. *on fine linen of Egypt*. A *book* of papyrus, written in the ancient Coptic, and a number of papyri in the hieroglyphic, and other languages. The collection consists of upwards of 2,200 objects, many of which are judged to be unique. There is a much larger enumeration of these highly interesting collections (illustrated with plates) in the Gentleman's Magazine for April, 1833. I say nothing of their age; it is no doubt extreme; but I never dived deeply into the abyss of dynasties. These collections, as well as large series of ancient Greek and Etruscan vases, and Roman and Greek medals, and coins, and a very splendid mass of ancient biblical and illuminated MSS., Mr. Sams preserves in London, (56, Great Queen Street, Lincoln's Inn Fields.)

At Darlington, however, the establishment well merits a visit. The stock of books is not in so exact order since a removal from Prospect Place; but its extent and rarity are very striking. Some idea of its contents will be derived from the proprietor's large catalogue, which in three parts extends to 720 octavo pages. These, and some later catalogues, possess a permanent interest, in the valuable notes, abundant in them, and for the scarcity of the items, which include many of the earliest and rarest editions of the Holy Scriptures and some Caxtons.

Mr. Sams's home is Darlington; but he is necessitated to be often, and for some time, in the metropolis.

The air of Darlington has not been favourable to the fine arts; and as far as numbers go, the list of painters is miserable enough. The ban extends to importations, for when the south side of Messrs. Pease's mill was accessible, and Carmichael had planted himself near the wheel to take a sketch of church and bridge, down came a torrent of anything but simple water on his head through the *artless* device of the mill girls. The artist eschewed Darlington for ever; and when he wanted a view from the Bank Top, for publication, he got Mr. Bewick to make it.

Samuel Wilkinson, our early draughtsman, is mentioned in page 299. In later times James Atkinson, a young house-painter, the son of a woolcomber, painted portraits, *strong* likenesses, and at London published a series of letters on art, addressed to Barry. A gentleman found him the means to become a surgeon, and secured him a post in India, where by the aid of his taste for the higher accomplishments in life he pushed his fortune, and sent over to his aged parents 200*l.* a year for their lives.

Edward Robson, the amiable and accomplished botanist, was fond of landscape painting, in both oil and water-colours, and used to rise by four o'clock to gratify his taste, which was, as we shall see in Bewick's case, much repressed at the time, as a *useless* acquisition to the business of life.

I might perhaps mention George Mark, who, besides being a sign-painter, bookbinder, bird-stuffer, herbalist, engraver, historian, and antiquary, painted landscapes and transparencies. He possessed a *smattering* of Latin, Greek, Hebrew, and French; which with a thorough knowledge of his own language was of ample use to him in his profession of politician—on the side of liberty and freedom of course. His "studio" was unique, and might lead to the impression that he was an astrologer, and in full pursuit of the philosopher's stone, to boot.

We come to more certain ground in Bewick.

William Bewick.

William Bewick, son of William and Jane Bewick, was born at Darlington, Oct. 20, 1795. His grandfather, William Bewick, a native of Hedley-fell-house, par. Ryton, co. of Durham, engraved large figures on wood; and his cut of a Highlander, 10 inches long, is said to have displayed considerable skill. Thomas Bewick, *the* wood-engraver, arose at Cherryburn, in the same neighbourhood; and the numerous races of the name scattered in that country are understood to be of one stock. If we may believe a dolorous ballad, in Scott's Border Minstrelsy, wherein Sir Robert Bewick and the Laird of Graham having quarrelled about the merits of their sons, hurried the young men to an untimely end, a *buke* would have been as good a pun a *buck** for the Bewick crest, for old Bewick urges in argument:—"Nay, were thy son as good as mine, and of some books he could but read—they *might* have been called two bold brethren," &c. At the Eglinton tournament our artist was sitting close to his friends Sir Wm. Allan, and Franklin (of Chevy chase eminence). To the great amusement of the company, the jester on recognising him stopped his horse, pointed his bauble, and menacingly quoted the old ballad just mentioned:—

"O hauld thy tongue now, Billie Bewick,
And of thy talking let me be!
But if thou'rt a man, as I'm sure thou art,
Come o'er the dyke, and fight wi' me.

The youth of William Bewick was similar to that of many men of talent. He was of delicate health and tender affections. At a local school, kept by a quaker, he preferred the concocting of a camera obscura, a profile machine, a machine which had perpetual motion for a few days, and such trifles; while a lump of chalk, and afterwards a pencil, were equally busy in their own line.

* I use the word in its Saxon sense. *Bucca*, a he-goat.

He followed his father's business (an upholsterer) until the age of nearly 20; but his artistic aspirations were high, he wrote of "the horror he had for portrait painting—for the drudgery and prostitution of his noble art to the gratification of personal vanity, and the sordid gain of money to the artist." He grew very unhappy, he longed for the means of studying historical art, and with 20*l.*, raised by the sale of some of his drawings, left home for London. Some felt sympathy with his views; but many persuaded his father that they were visionary and frivolous, and thus created a prejudice which prevented any paternal communication for nine months after his arrival in the metropolis.

By chance he met an exhibitor of statues in the King's Mews, who could give a ticket to draw from the Elgin marbles then at Burlington House. Pleased with Bewick's oil paintings, he presented him with the ticket. The lonely and nervous stranger took his seat in the shed containing the sculptures, before practised eyes and eminent professors. But he was noticed by Haydon, then the rising star, who invited him to his house. A sympathy was sprung, Bewick became Haydon's avowed pupil. The master soon finding his scholar's real position—that he was all but a runaway, and that his means were indeed scanty, wrote letters of conciliation to the father, and endeavoured to continue the interest of Bewick's early patrons. To Lady Chaytor and her mother Mrs. Carter, he did not appeal in vain. They made great exertions in his favour, and substantial assistance was rendered. The Royal Academy and Sir Charles Bell's dissecting rooms soon received Bewick. But his incessant labour from six in the morning to twelve at night, accompanied by severe privations, soon brought him down to his native air, and his friends now received him with joy and approbation. His anatomical efforts were here confined to the dissection of smaller animals, but falling in with a donkey of extraordinary beauty, his study of it was transferred to Haydon's picture of Christ riding into Jerusalem. The Elgin marbles were now removed to the museum, and on Bewick's return to London he executed some full-sized studies. On the exhibition of these in the museum, West came and delivered an address to the students present, eulogizing the drawings and course of study. They indeed excited much interest, and were purchased by Wm. Hamilton, esq.

In the midst of heavy expenses and pecuniary shortcomings, an eminent painter visited Bewick, kindly encouraged him, and on hurriedly parting had passed a crushed piece of paper into the young artist's hand—a bank note. At Haydon's house where he attended every evening to read and write for his master, whose eyes were affected for two or three years, he met Sir David Wilkie, Hazlitt, Keats, Horace Smith, John Scott, Wordsworth, Miss Mitford, Belzoni, Sir William Allan, Hugo Foscolo, Sir Charles Bell, &c. The most spirited conversations on art were between Wilkie, Haydon, and Hazlitt, the latter urging on an argument, for he used to say to Bewick that he never or rarely could get Haydon to *talk* about art. I have been told by Mr. Bewick that Wilkie was hesitating and obstinate, with a strong smack of the Scotch accent when excited, and dry and cautious: Haydon was fluent, powerful, and firm, with gentlemanly deference and attention to every opinion, trying to convince by illustrated facts: whilst Hazlitt kept the ball rolling by excited appeals and invective. His was a spontaneous eloquence, as extraordinary as it was nervous and to the point. He would lead Haydon off to indulge him with imitations of the conversations on art by Fuzeli and Northcote, giving Fuzeli's foreign and Northcote's Devonshire peculiarities. Hazlitt enjoyed the home of Haydon, his enthusiasm, his hearty laugh, and open manner. There he would read his rough drafts and observe their impression. Sometimes he tried the effect before committing to paper. Rising from his seat, he would pour out a flood of impassioned language, with streams of indignation, sympathy, or tenderness, that equally affected his sensitive hearers. With this effect he was satisfied, and "went to press." Bewick used to visit Hazlitt when he resided at Milton's house in Westminster. In an ancient wainscotted room the two looked out between two large trees that crossed the windows into some ornamental ground with fine old trees in it. Hazlitt would point to an old gentleman often walking there, of rather eccentric appearance, and loose habiliments, and would say, "That, sir, is the famous Jeremy Bentham."*

Bewick now, by order through the German consul, executed a large cartoon of some of the figures in the Elgin marbles for the poet Goethe, to give the German men of taste an idea of the sculptures. The poet expressed their approval, and stated that his sovereign, to whom he had presented the work, had ordered it to be placed in the Royal Academy of Arts, and would be pleased to know whenever the artist should visit his

* "On leaving Whitehall, in 1652, Milton removed to a house in Petty France (now Queen Square Place, Westminster) the very same that Jeremy Bentham lived in for so many years, and at his death left to his friend and executor Dr. Bowring. A friend of ours who had occasion when a boy to see Bentham in his garden, remembers the enthusiasm with which the philosopher spoke of the poet's walking in the same place."—*Knight in "Old England."* An error. Bentham let Milton's *house.*

kingdom that attention might be paid to him. In company with his friends the Landseers he next made full-sized drawings from Raphael's cartoons which were publicly exhibited with great success. He also commenced painting from life. An original composition from the "Faery Queen" was painted for Sir John Leicester. And now a friendship was contracted with James Bandinell, esq., of the foreign office, which subsisted up to Mr. Bandinell's melancholy decease at the Salisbury meeting of the Archæological Institute in 1849. He had procured a head painted by Mr. Bewick at Darlington, and both Wilkie and Calcott mistook it for a Murillo!

Again worn health compelled repair to the country, but a picture was there painted of the kyloe heifer for Mr. Hilton Middleton, of Archdeacon Newton, ("High-priced Hilton,") which was engraved by Turner, A. R. A. "Jacob meeting Rachel," 10 feet by 7, was painted and exhibited at London on the artist's return, and afterwards in an exhibition of his works at Darlington, in 1822, the first attempt of the kind here. Haydon spoke very highly of the picture just alluded to, and of that of Una (the one purchased by Sir J. Leicester). His opinions were printed in what is now a rare and curious descriptive catalogue of this exhibition.* The figure of Rachel comprehended one of those evanescent expressions which belong to unripened innocence, so difficult to portray, and both pictures bore out Keat's opinion that Bewick "would do some of the tenderest things in art." A subscription was commenced to commission Bewick to paint an altar piece for Darlington church, and one subscription was a "fatted ox," which was proposed to be brought to Darlington market decorated with ribbons and attended by music, and sold whole or in joints at a high price. The resident curate, Mr. Atkinson, considered the picture to come under the description of "*a picture or image to excite idolatrous worship*," and notwithstanding the arguments of the Rev. James Thornhill, who came expressly from Raby to reason with him, he succeeded in bottling the scheme.

Another subject from scripture exhausted the young painter's resources midway. He retreated to the country to renew them by undertaking small orders or portraits, but on arriving at Darlington, a professed *friend* advised the completion of his great work, and promised the loan of 200*l.* for the purpose. Some weeks passed over in London in anticipation of the advent of this sum. Haydon was overwhelmed by calamities: and his pupil was again compelled to leave his great work then far advanced to completion, by the last suffering—the deprivation of the common necessaries of life, not to mention the despair of mind occasioned by the lack of the promised sum or any part of it. Not even an explanation of its nonarrival was ever conceded. A trifle borrowed from a friend secured a passage to Edinburgh, where Bewick was received in the most handsome manner by Sir William Allan, (who had seen "Jacob and Rachel" on the easel,) Nasmyth, Williams, Thompson of Duddington, Simson, and Andrew Wilson, and he found himself moving among the first artists and most distinguished society. Bewick formed at Edinburgh an anatomical drawing class, and there Liston studied for the purpose of obtaining that precision of hand in operations for which he became so distinguished. Our artist also began his very valuable life-sized memorials of the eminent men he has met with. Captain Basil Hall, with Sir James Hall, his father; Lord Eldin, Sir John Sinclair, Sir David Brewster, Lord Jeffrey, Dr. Greville, Professor Wilson (author of the Isle of Palms, &c.), Geo. Thomson (the friend and correspondent of Burns), Mrs. Grant of Laggan, Allison (the author of the "Essay on Taste"), Dr. Jamieson the lexicographer, Mackenzie ("Man of Feeling"), Combe the phrenologist, M'c Culloch the political economist, Liston the surgeon, Williams, Nasmyth, Wilson, and Allan, the artists, were among the number. I am particular in my enumeration of these heads, because it is desirable to know the locality of portraits. At Glasgow he made an exhibition of his works, and obtained the heads of Hooker the botanist, Professor Thompson the chemist, M'c Cree the biographer of Knox, Lord A. Hamilton, James Sheridan Knowles, &c. He had once painted a portrait of Birkbeck, the founder of mechanics' institutions, for his first institution, that of Glasgow, and now the artist having been requested to be present at one of its meetings, the deputation that had waited upon him in London, introduced him, when the whole mass of heads rose and cheered the painter who was lifted off his feet upon the lecture-table that all might see, and the names of Bewick and Birkbeck resounded through the hall.

Dublin next received the Darlington runaway. Here he again frequently met with Knowles; and at the table of Sir Arthur Clarke, Curran, like the artist, had an invitation whenever disengaged. Bewick added to his portfolio the portraits of Lady Olivia Clarke, her sister Lady Morgan, Chief Justice Bushe, the facetious Lord Norbury the "hanging judge," O'Connell, Curran, Shiel, Carmichael the eminent military surgeon, &c. At the appointed hour for drawing Maturin, he found him pacing his drawing-

* See Newcastle Magazine, 1822.

room, in full dress costume; with new black curled wig, stiff cravat and collar up to his eyes; his pale cheeks rouged to excess; and an elegantly bound book, placed upon a cambric pocket handkerchief, edged with lace, and strongly perfumed, resting on both hands. And this was the caricature of that "extraordinary creature," who should have been in his dark and gloomy study lighted by its skylight of a single pane, the walls dingy and *black*, with the wafer stuck on his forehead as a sign that no sound might interrupt his wild strain of terrors, and he writing "Melmoth." The painter, alive to the man, of course threw aside all the dress-toilet and rouge, and so succeeded that Sir Walter Scott, when he first saw this portrait of his unseen correspondent, exclaimed, "Bless me! the very man I had pictured in my imagination!" and begged a copy, which he acknowledged as being *very acceptable*. A higher compliment was a letter received during a stay at Abbotsford:—

"York Street, Dublin, Nov. 14, 1824.

"My dear sir.—I have a request to make which under existing circumstances I am sure you will not refuse. When you were last in Dublin, you took the most striking likeness of Mr. Maturin I ever beheld. As the original then lived, I had no desire for the copy; but now that he is in the grave, I will esteem it an everlasting favour if you will let me have it, and if this is not convenient, a copy. I would not so far trespass on you, but that I know not any one except yourself who ever took a *faithful* likeness of Mr. Maturin. Believe me, my dear sir, most sincerely yours, HENRIETTA MATURIN. To ——— Bewick, esq."

This letter was handed to Sir Walter Scott, at breakfast, who said with inexpressible tenderness, the tears coming to his eyes: "Poor Mr. Maturin then is no more! Well, sir, what do you say?—you can do no less than send a copy of your beautiful drawing, although it is not expected you can part with the original?" The copy was recently noticed in Jerrold's Magazine as in the possession of the family, and as possessing extraordinary character.

On the occasion of Hazlitt's marriage, he came to Melrose, and Knowles and Bewick met him there. Then it was that the latter made the drawing which has been engraved in Hazlitt's Remains, and called forth the following sonnet by Knowles.

"Thus HAZLITT looked! There's life in every line!
Soul—language—fire that colours could not give;
See! on that brow how pale-robed thought divine
In an embodied radiance seems to live!
Ah! in the gaze of that entranced eye,
Humid, yet burning, there beams passion's flame,
Lighting the cheek, and quivering through the frame;
While, on the lips, the odour of a sigh
Yet hovers fondly, and its shadow sits
Beneath the channel of the glowing thought
And fire-clothed eloquence, which comes in fits
Like Pythiac inspiration!—Bewick, taught
By thee, in vain doth slander's venom'd dart
Do its foul work 'gainst *him*. This head *must* own a heart."

Bewick then visited Sir Walter Scott at Abbotsford for a few days, and made a copy of the head of Mary Queen of Scots, painted by Anias Cawood at Fotheringay, which represents the head of the Queen in a silver salver covered with black crape. Sir Walter Scott told Mr. Bewick that the body of the Queen was locked up in a room at Fotheringay for three days after the execution, and it was supposed that the painter made the picture during that time. The following correspondence throws some further mystery into the subject:—

"39, Castle Street, 16 May, 1824.—Dear sir.—I have pleasure in affording you all the information I possess concerning the picture, but it is not much. Mr. Bullock, the naturalist, brought me a message from a gentleman then going abroad, and disposing of a collection of pictures, expressing a wish that I should be possessed of this one, either by gift or purchase, naming a moderate price, (10*l*., I think, but am not certain,) if I preferred the latter arrangement. He stated that the gentleman who had so kindly thought upon me had received the picture in a present from a friend in Prussia, and therefore did not wish to expose it to public sale. This is all I know of it. I have forgotten even the name of the former proprietor, but I have it written down somewhere. I am happy to have had an opportunity of gratifying your curiosity, which will not however be altogether gratis, for I am afraid the ladies will hold you but a perjured person unless you favour them with a copy of the sketch of Abbotsford which you had the goodness to promise them, and which will find us here if sent by any of the coaches. I will be happy to see you if you will call as you pass through Edinburgh; being, dear sir, your most obdt. servant, WALTER SCOTT. To Mr. Bewick, 110, George Street, Glasgow."

"Durham, Sept. 12, 1832.—Dear sir,— I received from the hands of Mr. Balmer (the painter) your elegant drawing of Queen Mary's head. It will be interesting to you to read the following extract of a letter from Miss Scott of Abbotsford, in reference to the painting from which your first drawing was made. The letter is addressed to Mrs. Surtees of Mainsforth, who was so good as to write to Miss Scott, to inquire the history of the painting.—' You ask me about Mary Queen of Scots' picture. It was copied by Mr. Bewick, and is thought an original. It was bought in Germany, not by papa, but by a very strange old man, who wished to give it to papa, thinking it of great value. This papa refused. He then offered to sell it, and named forty or fifty guineas, as he always said no one else should have it but him. All the artists admire the picture very much. This is all I remember about it.'—Letter written in Sir W. Scott's room darkened on account of his illness, and during attendance upon him. Your faithful humble servant, Edwd. Shipperdson.—To W. Bewick, esq."

At a second and more lengthened visit to Abbotsford, Wilkie, Lockhart, Sir John Malcolm, Lord Minto, and other distinguished guests were also there. Sir Walter Scott sat to Wilkie and Bewick at the same time, the former commencing a painting, the latter a drawing of him. The portfolio also received a finished drawing of Sir John Malcolm. Malcolm used to tell original and long Persian stories, divided into "miles." So many miles occupied an evening until bed time. The company gathered from all parts of the house to hear these Persian Nights Entertainments. *The* story-teller sat as a listener, absorbed in the plot, anticipating the denouement—nudging and laughing and rubbing his hands in the fullness of glee. Sir John had his own ideas of his auditor. He told Mr. Bewick that he had contrived to be in every room—there was every kind of book, but not a Waverley Novel in the house. This fact had satisfied his mind as to who was the "great unknown."

Hogg treated Bewick with the sport of spearing salmon, in the Yarrow; and the latter drew the poet in his plaid. Hogg wrote his autograph at the foot and presented the artist with the first draft of his "Camerons Welcome Hame."

Bewick was soon the guest of Mr. Graham among the lakes at Gartmore, and made a copy of a Rembrandt (purchased for 4,000*l*). The person who had sold the original obtained a loan of the copy, but an application for its return produced the cool information that "he would never see it again, for he (the borrower) had always regretted parting with the original, and this copy was the only reconciliation to its loss, for it was as nearly equal as possible." Bewick was requested to name his price, and he got it there and then; but never saw his picture again.

The success of this copy reached Glasgow before Bewick, and he was there requested on account of a wager, to make a facsimile of the sketch in the College of the University, the dispute being about the *vehicle* that Rembrandt used. Bewick used, as he was requested to do, one simple material for the purpose. Having progressed nearly to completion he placed his copy in the frame, and the original upon his easel, to compare the effect the frame made. Whilst contemplating the two, some of the Professors of the college stopped to see "how he was getting on with his copy," and, taking the original for it, they thought it "exceedingly well, and very like the original." The anecdote passed to the disputants, and settled the wager. The copy afterwards deceived a great judge of Rembrandt's works in London, who offered to purchase it as genuine, but the artist assured him it was only a copy.

Scotland, at a crisis, had been a great boon to Bewick; but there his income barely covered his expenditure; and he returned to Darlington and painted several landscapes for different parties, to enable him to see the works of the Italian schools. Sir Thomas Lawrence became aware of his intention, and offered him 100 guineas for a large copy of Michael Angelo's Delphic Sybil in the Sistine chapel. He bounded to the realisation of early hopes, waited on Lawrence, and increased his commissions. At Florence, he met with Walter Savage Landor, and made a highly finished drawing of him. Gibson, Eastlake, Severn, Wyatt, and Campbell, who had heard of his London exhibitions, received him gladly at Rome. He erected a scaffolding 60 feet high in the Sistine chapel, and at great risk to his health, and chance of being overpowered by malaria and falling from the top, he commenced his work. Close to the original, he first made a careful study of detail, half size, in chalk and colour, producing the exact effect of the fresco, and made use of this for the minutiæ of the large copy, which was executed on an easel on the floor of the chapel. Sir Thomas next wanted a copy of "Jeremiah lamenting the Destruction of Jerusalem," in the same chapel, which was in like manner finished. The two subjects were highly approved by their owner and the artists on their arrival in England, and an order was sent by Lawrence for the whole series of prophets and sybils in the chapel. These he intended as a present to the academy as a pendant to Raphael's Cartoons, and as a memento of his presidency.

Four large copies in oil, and the whole of the studies of detail, were completed when Lawrence suddenly died. Mr. Bewick had to return to look after his interests, and came to an arrangement with the President's executor. He then came to the north, painted portraits and fancy pictures by the hundred, and with ready pencil but wasted health he soon was enabled to retire from the *profession* of painting. And he now lives at Haughton-le-Skerne, his house and gallery being full of examples of the noble art to which he was devoted. In concluding this memoir, I have to thank him for being at the trouble to copy a mass of correspondence* at my request, for the purpose of filling up the gaps I found in the notices by the periodicals of the day. Still more for suffering much *viva voce* inquisition. Curious are the vicissitudes of such a life. One time Bewick was in London, literally without a crust of bread and studying night and day; at another, as when at Abbotsford, Edinburgh, and Dublin, cheek by jowl with the first of the land—again, in Rome, sipping his tea with the elegant Queen Hortense, the most accomplished woman in Europe, and Prince Louis Napoleon her son, at her select evenings, not to speak of all the fashionable society of the eternal city.

I must in parting from my subject express my best acknowledgment for the handsome manner in which Mrs. Bewick has gratified my wish to preserve the early appearance of her husband, by presenting the admirable engraving which stands at the head of this memoir. It was executed by Smyth, from a spirited crayon sketch thrown from the gifted hand of Charles Landseer, Esq., and now in the possession of J. C. Quelch, Esq.

There are at the present time two landscape painters resident in Darlington—James Peel, and Thomas Thorpe, (a pupil of Carmichael)—both clever artists. The only *native* of the town now pursuing the arts, I think, is Mr. Dobbing, who served his time with Mr. Spencer as a cabinet-maker. He draws in water colour, and exhibits and teaches drawing in London. Clement Burlison, of Durham, whose works have been much noticed, is connected with the town by apprenticeship, and here his taste for art was first manifested in a practical way. Among his works, two of the most publicly known are portraits. One of Sir Robert Peel, painted as a memorial to that great man, and now in the New Town Hall, Durham. The other of that learned and accomplished scholar and antiquary, the Rev. James Raine, M.A., Rector of Meldon. Excellent, because it is faithful; it appears from the burin of W. Walker, London, in the highest finish, at the expence of R. H. Allan, Esq., prefixed to Mr. Raine's admirable History of North Durham. All these aspirants will doubtless some day have passed through that romance of art which distinguishes the memories of painters from those of ordinary men.

It may be expected that I should not leave this division withot taking notice of my pioneers, but really they are very scanty. First comes George Allan's commencement of "Historical Collections relating to the Town of Darlington," of which he tired after he had printed a few pages.† Then Cade's tract mentioned in p. 35, the description of Darlington in which is good as far as it goes. Next paces in the uncompromising Hutchinson who had undertaken the arduous task of compressing Allan's collections into three library quartos. It is such a comfortable reflection that his noble

* The following remarks by Lawrence must be interesting:—"What can I say to you respecting the wishes of the Queen Hortense; and the opinion which she has done me the honour to request from me? The government—the directors of the National Gallery acting under its influence, have for the present ceas'd to purchase pictures, and I know of no private collector who would go to great extent of price for even a known fine picture. With regard *particularly* to Corregio, there is no purchasing works, stated to be by him, but after actual inspection. Testimonials—attestations—seals of academies, are often nothing, the moment the work is seen. A very early production actually by Corregio, may, from its exceeding incorrectness, be very indifferent; and his later pictures may, as you know from his finished style, be very skilfully copied. A true picture from the Marischalchi collection, was a year or two since sold to Mr. Baring, but still it was so unpleasing a work that I could not have recommended it. You must then, with my humble respects to the Queen, state these difficulties, which in honour I feel myself bound to mention, and pray make what apologies you can for my too long silence on the subject. The English character is well received abroad when it is well represented, and I have been pleased to hear that you are noticed in society by the accomplished, the fascinating, and the great. On firm minds, there can be only favourable influence from such association, and those of higher rank than ourselves feel always justified in their attentions when they see that they do not interfere with the independent pursuit of our profession, that earnest of future *permanent* comfort"—*Addressed to Bewick.*

† See p. xvi., hereafter.

book which still stands unrivalled in its collections of the legal and Roman antiquities of the county, should fairly proceed from this parish that I make no apology for adding to my remarks in pp. xvi and xx, hereafter, what Mr. Raine has, in his edition of the Life of Surtees, since said. "The point is settled by Mr. Allan's affidavit in Mr. Hutchinson's 'Apology,' prefixed to his third vol., that the book was composed and written by the latter from materials chiefly supplied by the former. Mr. Allan's rough copy of the sheets, as they belonged to the late Sir Cuthbert Sharp, and are now the property of the dean and chapter of Durham, by the gift of the bishop, proves that as far as those sheets go, they were all submitted to Mr. Allan's revision, and corrected; and they further prove that Mr. Allan was the sole author of the Introduction prefixed to the first vol., and extending to p. xxxvi., the whole of which, with its various corrections and alterations is in his handwriting."* Of Surtees and other writers, good, bad, and indifferent, who have treated on the whole county, I need not speak; their merits and demerits are obvious, and they are not especially connected with Darlington in any way. In 1834 (see p. 322) Gordon's very excellent guide was published for the neighbourhood. Dr. Peacock, the late eminent physician of Darlington, had previously published an acute summary on the Dinsdale Spa. The first part of a new guide on Dinsdale, Croft, and the neighbourhood, was published at Darlington by T. D. Walker, esq., surgeon, Hurworth, in 1849; but does not, I think, profess to include Darlington. So that I really have the ground in a tolerably virgin state, and consequently have to give all my evidences in a lengthy form; but I hope to see them of use to more popular writers.

* "I am near 58 years of age, and may hope to retain my strength of mind for some years. All the grief that I have had in my station here, was from not having a quarter part of the business my industry sketched out wishes for; and thence to supply the hours of leisure I pursued those moderate avocations, I hope, few men can blame."—*(Hutchinson to Allan, in a letter dated Barnard Castle, 12 Dec., 1790, penes R. H. A.)*

DIVISION V.

TRANSIT AND AGRICULTURE.

I. TRANSIT.

THE origin of most of our great lines of road will probably never be proved. The Romans might either find them or form them. The Saxons could only view them when made, and in astonishment ascribe them to the labours of their own demigods.

Little has been done for their history. The old-fashioned antiquary preferred to ascertain their exact route, however unimportant, to the more thoughtful and laborious task of viewing them in their great generalities. How much of interest lies in their mere names? How few in reading my account of Catkill Lonning in p 127, and the absurd legend engrafted upon it, would detect the word *Cat* in it, a little syllable so common to British roads and places of fight, or draw the conclusion that Ketton took its name from it?* And who in traversing our Forth Moor reflects that its appellation may have reference to the ancient horsetrack through it?†

At one time the poet Dyer contemplated a general review of England's features. His notes on Roman roads are perhaps founded on southern experiences, but they are worth consideration. "In the Roman roads are seen, flint-stones, chalk, hard gravel, hard clay, laid in layers. Qu. 1st, a hard binding clay, then flint-stones, then chalk, on the chalk gravel, all about six or eight feet thick. Chalk and gravel bind—flint and pebbles endure. Next to navigable rivers, good roads deserve the public regard; although our attempts to make them are few and weak: not like those of the Romans, and other ancient nations, whose great men (taking a pride in being any way serviceable to the public) were successively the surveyors of them. But our customs are different; and these toils are left to the inferior sort, who, after the pattern of their little minds, construct our public roads, where the manufacturer often sees his carriages half buried, even at the entrances of public and trading towns. Yet, upon such accidents, the

* Ketton is *Cattun* in its earliest appearance. I believe I am not far wrong in stating that at Newton Ketton, there have been more flint celts found, than in all the rest of the county put together. Indeed the immense quantity of these, (for bronze celts are unknown at that place) and the numerous beads and other early remains gathering together by Mr. John Ord, an antiquarian farmer of his own soil there, have sometimes led me really to give way to an impression that there had been a manufactory of such weapons upon his land. St. Cuthbert's beads are found in equal abundance.

† See p. 26, for the "Forth versus Aclemore quod ducit a Windleston usque Derlyngton." Forth or ford is a British word for a road, but perhaps in its application in England it had rather the same signification as when applied to an assart or place cleared for cultivation, cut forth and out of the waste, like the Forth in Newcastle and the Friths among woods. I am not sure that "road" has not a similar import. *Roda* or *Rode-land* are terms for assarts. The adjuncts *royd* and *rod* in names of Lancashire and Yorkshire villages are reduced to them, and in Durham seem to be represented by *forth* and *worth*. This is not the book for a long discussion on the subject, else I could lay before the reader a wonderful array of evidences upon it.

laborious inhabitants reflect but little; their arm is busy with the loom or the hammer. Their eye is intent on the thing they fashion. It is the man at large, the man of fortune, who, on this, ought to exert a spirit. But he is quite ignorant of what happens, he, and all his peers. They live at a great distance from their old hereditary acres, and the neglected avenues to them, and from all that is country. The great town and her luxuries possess them wholly, and devour up their virtues.'"

The roads generally laid down as Roman may have been British ones, and even as connected with the Romans give no correct idea of all the lines of communication adopted by them. Many others may be traced by the names on their routes; and we do not sufficiently remember that there would be a distinction between their military and ordinary roads. We have innumerable old ways of unknown antiquity, often strongly marked for long distances, but more generally broken by their disuse and the increase of culture around them. An old rustic once told me that his father said that roads originally followed the course which water ran.

I have sometimes stumbled upon an old causeway or horsetrack in the centre of a modern farm, the commencement and termination of which were only problematical. Such roads are generally accompanied by a goodly portion of sward, which in former times was common to the tenants, or reserved to the lord of the manor. They would almost seem to have been left for agricultural use in summer only, the leading of the harvests, and are probably the remnants of those rough roads called balks between each man's occupancy upon a common. The Medomsley freeholders in 1609 ordered "that none pass out of the way on the balke in the Innfield called the kirk-balke into the corn riggs there"—a very proper resolution, for in 1596, Roger Hopper, an iniquitous person who went "gadding abroad in the night at unlawful hours, did mak common ways with his cattle through the corn fields and meadows contrary to conscience." In part of the old horsetrack, from Entercommon in Yorkshire to Sedgefield in Durham, called Lingfield Lane, which occurs in the parish of Haughton-le-Skerne immediately after leaving *Forth* Moor, the horsetrack crosses the sward from hedge to hedge more than once. When I traversed it, it was in reference to the repair of the lane, the township disclaiming anything more than the horsetrack, the remainder having formerly been crossed by gates, let out for eatage, and altogther treated as private property. The owner was beaten on a technical flaw in the indictment. As the road has since been repaired, the appearances I have mentioned may to some extent have disappeared. In Forth Moor Farm, which evidently takes name from the road, the latter has lost its hedges and been thrown open to the fields

The extreme narrowness of the ancient ways would almost lead to the impression that sidings for the passing of vehicles would be required. There is a small lane leading from Gainford to the Tees the queer nooks of which have been supposed to have answered the same purpose. Popular tradition places a sentry in each in rebellion time. I confess these assumed sidings were not of the width I expected, yet in so contracted a lane the smallest advantage would be of service.

The subject of horseroads reminds me of a picturesque but singular custom existing in the Auckland district at a very late period, to which my attention has been drawn by Mr. Fenwick. At a funeral, the neighbours used to mount the corpse upon a horse, a living wight jumped on behind to keep his cold companion steady; and thus, at a slow and solemn pace the procession moved on to the churchyard. Coffins were a rarity in all places, but the usual mode of conveying the body after packing it in a winding sheet, was by means of a rude parish bier. Whitaker states that before interments began to take place at Muker in Richmondshire, the bodies of the dead were conveyed on men's shoulders upwards of twelve miles to the parish church of Grinton, not in coffins but in rude wicker baskets.*

We have no reason to believe that the Romans often followed the plan of having bridges with arches of stone. A stake which once helped to support the crossing of Watling-

* The inhabitants of Harewood, a small vale of the Tees, are proverbially fools, at least with their neighbours of Weardale, who tell an absurd story (which is localized in many another place) of a stray cuckoo (a rara avis there) wandering to that obscure glen. The astonished natives banded together to capture the unusual visitant, which, being no less astonished than themselves, allowed them to *build a wall* with loose stones round his temporary residence, and they declared they would have succeeded had not one of their leading shepherd's cur dogs dashed into the enclosure and proved to the confiding bird that there were dogs even at Harewood. At that time there was no regular road into Harewood, and on the completion of one, some time afterwards, a surveyor drove up to inspect the new work. He was seated in a four wheeled carriage, which was a fresh object of wonderment to the clan of ninnies. The whole population ran after it, declaring to each other "*Carra*, lad, d'girt wheil's gaun t'owertak t'little un." These tales are so well known in Weardale and confessed in Teesdale that on any feud they are at once bandied, and the words "Did ter help te catch t'cuckow?" or "Dost ter think t'girt wheil will ivver owertak t'little un?" will at once raise the blood.

street, at Piercebridge, remained in very recent times, as well as some black oaken timbers at the presumed course of the Roman road over a beck or burn near Streatlam. At Ebchester we have the sort of bridge, adopted, as it is believed, by the Romans, wood upon stone piers ;* and near Newton Ketton, a late but singular instance of a footpath, carried across amphibious fields, on minute arches, covered with flags.

On the subject of such bridges, I may mention that in 1299, Edward I. marched northwards. On the 25th Nov. he was at Beverley; and on the 28th mass was celebrated in his presence in his chapel at Apelton.† On the 2nd December, Sir Peter de Donewick was summoned to the court at Darlington, and remained with the court, by precept of the king, 148 days. On the 4th, the king had arrived at Durham. The beginning of the same month, the king's alms of 45*s.* 2*d.* were bestowed on *Adam de Sutton, bailiff of Darlington, for the repair of a bridge in his town, where the king's treasure and various carriages had to pass.* Wood and nails were the materials, and we may assume a wooden platform, on stone piers, as the likely appearance of the structure, whether over the Skerne or Cockerbeck, the customary planking being doubtless all too weak for the intended load.‡

In 1274, the Prior of Durham had conveyed Robert de Insula, prior of Finchale, to London. The latter had just been elected bishop of Durham, and the train in attendance, upon so important an occasion, as when an elected prelate and a prior, who stood in the capacity of dean in his cathedral church, journeyed to seek confirmation of the appointment by the king, must have been very considerable. Their rate of motion cannot be taken as a fair criterion of the ordinary speed of travelling, as every convenience and aid would be specially supplied. They reached London on the 15th day after leaving Durham. Two kinds of carriages are mentioned, *carectæ* and *bigæ*. The former were four-wheeled carriages, the latter two-wheeled. The road pursued was by Northallerton, Boroughbridge, and Pomfret to Doncaster; and the first night was passed at Ketton, where the Monastery possessed a grange. The party did not pay by meal but by what was actually consumed, for they had prepared a stock of provisions to be carried in their carts, and a stock of herrings was despatched from Northallerton to Doncaster against their arrival at that town. At Ketton they paid for kitchen stuff, drink and bread, all other accommodation being ready and gratis. Further on, charges occur for forerunners, oats, hay, and litter for their horses, beer and wine. There must have been an inn at Ketton where the beer and wine were purchased, the expression being "in taberna ibidem." The whole journey *up* cost 75*l.* 15*s.* 5*d.* The return was more rapid. The party reached Ketton by a ten days travel.

In the Exchequer calendars, 18 Edw. I., we find mention of receipt, by Richard Knut, of 10,000 marks out of the king's treasury at York, by the hands of the merchants of Luca, to be carried at Knut's own risk and peril from York to Newcastle.

In 1304, £4,000 was transmitted from York to Scotland; five carters were engaged for the transit, twelve archers accompanied them, six men to watch the carriage. Besides, John le Convers and Walter de Gilling had the general oversight of the transaction. The money was pached in eight barrels, made with all proper economy out of three empty casks. The first day they reached Easingwold, the next night Darlington, the next Chester-le-Street, and during this stage six esquires on horseback were added to the escort, at the cost of 6*s.* for their services. The next stage was Chester to Morpeth.

In 7 Edw. II. a royal messenger passed through Darlington from London to Berwick. Nine days completed the transit.

In the beginning of December, 12 Edw. III. £200 was carried from York to Newcastle in three days. It laid in panniers on a horse's back, and two men-at-arms and four archers guarded it. £2000 was brought from London to Berwick under charge of ten men, in the depth of winter, and in fourteen days. Fifteen days took £600 from London to Dunbar, and this in the same season. In March 2 Edw. III, the bishop of Lincoln and Sir Geoffrey le Scrope passed from York to a parliament at Edinburgh. The bishop reached Northallerton the first night. *Sedgefield* the next, and Newcastle the next, perhaps taking the old track by Lingfield Lane. Scrope came by Thirsk, Darlington, and Durham, and returned circuitously by Newcastle, Durham, Auckland,

* In Feb., 1644, the Scots army 'marched to the water of Darwent, and with difficulty got their foot files over a *tree-bridge* at Ebchester, half over night, and the rest next day; so that they all passed that night on the field.'

† He had a sort of portable chapel. Appleton-upon-Wiske seems to be meant, tending to the old pass of Pountey's Bridge. In Henry I.'s reign Robert de Brus gave to St. Mary's Abbey, York, his Lordships of Appilton and Hornby, and all the lands lying betwixt the same, and the great road leading from York to Durham, being part of his Lordship of Middleton.—(*Collins.*)

‡ Wardrobe accounts, pub. by Soc. Ant.

Winston, Witton, to Clifton in Richmondshire, and so to York. The bishop returned by Newcastle, a grange *near* Durham, Nesham, Topcliffe, and so to the King at Stamford. The bishop of Norwich came to the same parliament from York by Allerton Maleverer, Brimiston, Dornyngton (Darlington), Durham, and Newcastle; and returned by Darlington, Birmiston, Miton, &c. William le Zouch went by Thirsk, *Lasingby*, *Sedgefield*, Durham, and Newcastle; and returned by Newcastle, Auckland, Lesyngby, Shubton, Pontefract, &c. to Stamford like his fellows. The various routes suggest the comparative absence of the chief roads of modern times, and probably one causeway was nearly as good as another.

In 48 Edw. III. John Fenwick, sheriff of Northumberland, conveyed the ransom of of King David from Berwick to York, himself having a guard of seventeen men-at-arms and nineteen archers. He set out on June 23 or 24, and did not arrive at York till July 4.*

The "Raid of the Bishop," *ad vadum Cirporum inter Fery et Wodom*, or Rushyford, when Gilbert stole the bishop, and the chattels of his cardinals, points to the present north road, as in use at the time, for the unlettered prelate had received timely warning of danger at Darlington.† In the march of Edward III. after the Scots, he reached Durham the same day he had left Topcliffe and in 1333, Queen Philippa made the journey from Knaresbrough to Durham in one day, a distance of fifty miles and upwards.

On the march to Flodden Field the Earl of Surrey "wyth hys fyve hundred menne came to Yorke, and the xxvi day he went toward Newcastell, and notwythstandynge that he had the fowleste daye and nyght that could be, and the ways so depe, in so muche that hys guyde was almoste drowned before hym, yet he never ceased, but kept on his joiney to geve example to them that shoulde folowe. He beynge at Durham was advertysed &c. All that that nyghte the wynde blewe coragiously. * * * * The earle harde masse and appoynted wyth the Prior for saincte Cutberde's banner, and so that daye beynge the thyrty daye of August, he came to Newcastell."‡

Croft bridge was then "the most directe and sure way and passage for the Kinge our Sovraigne Lorde's armye and ordynance to resort and passe over into the North parties and marshes, over the which bridge suche armys and ordynances hathe hertofor always bene accustomyd to goo and passe: and as yt is thought by dyverse wyse and experte men, yt wes veray difficil and herd to fynd any other way over the said ryver commodius and at all tymes redy and easfull for the said caryages and passages."§

These and other scanty notices we possess of early travelling before the 16th century, prove nothing, as far as regards ordinary conveyance. The marches and progresses of kings and prelates have nothing in common with the movements of their subjects. But now came regular postmasters bound to furnish horses for the irregular news-carrier who was to ride for his life. Their office was called a *postship*, and was so far a monopoly as to be regularly conveyed as a freehold.¶

By 1577, the comfort to be prepared for travellers had become a science. Harrison speaks rapturously of the linen used at table being washed daily; and each comer having clean sheets. He mentions something of the price of a bed. If the traveller had a horse, an animal which has always been a source of iniquities innumerable, his bed cost him nothing, but if he was on foot, his bed was sure to cost him a penny. Hideous concerts of bagpipes greeted new comers in the northern towns; the constables expected their shilling for the safe custody I suppose of the strangers' chattels, and another shilling was spent upon two guides from one place to another, especially, one would think, over commons. The cost of ten post-horses was 15*d*. or 16*d*. the modern posting mile.||

The diary of Thomas Chaytor, of Butterby (1612 to 1617), contains some interesting possages illustrative of conveyance. At his time the roads between Durham and Newcastle seem to have been in a most deplorable state, so much so that notwithstanding articles of consumption were to be obtained in greater plenty and at cheaper rates by

* Rev. Jos. Hunter in York Volume of the Archæological Institute.

† Graystanes, p. 17. But Whessoe Lane was probably the route to Aycliffe.

‡ Hall's Chronicle. Sub Flodden fight.

§ Surtees iii. 408, in a brief requesting Christian people to repair the bridge. 10th July 33 Hen. viii.

¶ In 1596, George Bainbridge, of Darneton, gent., conveyed his *postshippe* of Darneton to Peter Glover, whose relative John Glover was long postmaster and master of the old posting house now the Talbot Inn.

|| "For 10 post horses from Allerton to Derington [16 miles] 20*s*.: to two guides, 12*d*.: to the constables at Allerton, 12*d*. For the like from Darinton to Durraham [18 miles] 23*s*. 4*d*.: to two guides, 12*d*.: to the constables at Darinton, 12*d*." These from the posting charges of William Davision, esq., sent by Elizabeth on special message to James of Scotland, in December, 1582. (*Gent. Mag*., June, 1840).

coming to Newcastle; he solemnly affirms, May 1612, "I think it more profit to buy in Durhm market than to send to Newcastle, all things weighed." One of these things was however the inferior quality of rye at Newcastle. It was principally, if not wholly imported, and before the passage I have just quoted he says, "Rye at Newcastle 8*s*. 6*d*. the bowll. I bought eight bowells, which beinge dressed was not more than six pecks and a half to the bowell and little more. Mine own rye lasted till the last of June." He does not seem to have had any difficulty in riding to Croft and back in one day. On one occasion of his being there, 17 June, he writes, "It was the cruellest day for wet and rain that ever I rode in, and notwithstanding I came again of one day." This speaks well for the roads to the south of him. Indeed on one occasion in March his speed appears to have been marvellous. "15th: to Sadbury, my wife and I. 16: to see my neice Willey [at Houghton-le-Side] and returned home that night in two hours." On the 15th May following he rode to Rippon in one day. In Jan., 1615, he rode to Esh, was a godfather there and came back to dinner. The next month he set his brothers-in-law, Bertram Bulmer and Thomas Tempest, on their road to London. "The snow was so great in wreaths in the loaninge at Ferie Hill that, the ways being unbroken, they passed with great difficulty in very many places and for a long quantity of ground, the snow being higher than the height of their horses." In October he again had reason to lament at the journey to Newcastle. "Rob. Denny in going to Newcastle with my cousin W. Chaytor's man to help to sell his horse, did fritidge my mare that was worth 10*l*."

Sir Bertram Bulmer appears from the diary often to have taken a trip to the great city. On the 3rd of April, 1616, he set off with 6*l*. of Thomas Chaytor's to furnish him with some things which he thought Bertram could manage nicely for him; and returned the 2nd of May, a short journey enough at the time. On the 12th of May, 1617, poor bishop James died of vexation at Auckland from king James's scolding, and the news was carried to the king at Berwick, by post, and reached him the same day. The next day, the 13th, the king took progress from Berwick northwards, and on that same day the report reached Durham that Dr. Neile was to be the new bishop. During the whole of this century the prevailing fashion was to take long journeys on horseback. At its close we find Henry Chaytor taking horse from London for Croft accompanied by Sir Wm. Hustler. His sister on another occasion came by coach. The carriage of a vial of dropsy water and a pint of gripe water from his father in London to York for the same Henry in his last illness, by coach cost 3*s* 6*d*.

When our good bishop Cosin was growing grey, gouty, and crabbed, a journey seems to have been a terrific bugbear to him. An original letter of 1670, from him in London to Mr. Stapylton at Durham Castle, in the collections of the late John Brough Taylor, contains the following very significant sentences:—"You do not say clearly whether you sent my letter to archdeacon Greensyte to Sedgfield or no, but tell me of his mad journey to Yorke and of his intention to come with his wife to London, *I suppose in a hackney coach, which is able to distemper her for a year after*, though truly I think he is more distempered than she is."—"You fright me with your own fears about my journey. I think the motion of a litter will shake me and trouble me as much or more than a coach will do upon plain ground. I shall therefore incline rather to have a sedan carried along with me upon a horse, which may be taken down to carry and ease me by Ned the footman and the groom wheresoever I come to a stony and rugged way: and this is the advice of Sir Alexander Fraser my chief physitian. Through God's help I hope to get well to you, and meet you about Wetherby before I get to Brafferton.*—I have spoken this day with my coachman. He saith the driver of the carioll and a groom, if you can get a good one, must be sent up with the horses, which are either at Auckland or at Brafferton after they have been taken up there from feeding on the ground abroad, and put into the stable for a week's time to make them fit for travaile. This will take up the whole next week, and the week after will bring them hither to town where they will remain a week before I begin my journey. If you cannot provide me a good groom to look to the horses and to go along with the carioll and lead the horse that carries my sedan by it, and be able also to carry me in the sedan (he and Ned the footman together) when I go thorough stony towns and rugged way, you must give us notice of it time enough so that we may the better provide such a groom here in town. My coachman tells me that he thinks all my horses are at Brafferton whither you sent them to eat up my hay there for want of hay at Auckland. If this be so must write to John Abbey and give him those directions that I have given to you. The post is loaden this time so that I cannot send any Acts of Parliament to you."

The roads in the southern division were long famous for their miserable condition. The road between Darlington and Croft through the marshy pastures of Oxenlefield was

* Upon Swale in Yorkshire.

denounced by the Duke of Cumberland in 1746, as the worst he had travelled upon. An attempt, however, was now made to remedy this sad state of affairs. Turnpike roads were first made in the county in 1742. In the act of 1745* for repairing the high road from Boroughbridge through Northallerton to Croftbridge, and through Darlington to Durham, the preamble states that "by reason of the *deepness of the soil*, and many heavy carriages passing through the same, many parts were become very ruinous and much out of repair, and in the winter season were so bad, that coaches, waggons, and other carriages could not pass without great danger." Yet, in 1810, Bailey complains that the great north road from Darlington to Newcastle was very ill kept. "On the authority of the great Will Roughhead, for so long a time guard of the Telegraph coach, in 1800, and for one or two years ofterwards, the road from Rushyford to Durham was so bad, that he, as guard, was in winter provided with a flambeau, and used to walk for several miles before the coach, calling out to the driver to put his horses to the right or left according as the holes were more or less deep. The late Mr Hoult, of Rushyford, has been known to state that in the winter of 1811 he lost no less than seven horses, whose legs were broken on the rough road between Durham and Darlington! Nor were other roads any better; for, before the Stockton and Darlington Railway was made, the *turnpike* between these two towns was repaired by throwing trees into the ruts, the trustees having no funds for doing the work better. Before the building of Winston Bridge, towards the latter end of the eighteenth century, the coal carriers from the north riding of Yorkshire, when coming into the county of Durham, always provided themselves with axes in order to be prepared to render the roads passable by mending them after the primitive fashion now pursued on the corduroy roads in the backwoods of America."

The morasses, however, might have been endured had they been unfrequented. But every sound in the ears of the nervous traveller was the harbinger of the highwayman. Even towns were not safe. Thomas Chaytor in 1615 says:—"John Constable's man of Biddick came out of a house in Gateside at the end of the bridge and with his sword gave a grevous and mortall wound to my servaunt. The said Craw by a warrant was apprehended and by a mittimus sent to the gaol at Durham quousque q." It is possible, however, that in this case there might have been some private feud before.

The especial retreat of rogues and road pads was Darnton in its dirt. "To take Darnton Trod," or "Darnton Road," is to adopt desperate measures, in order to avoid immediate consequences—to fly the country for debt or crime. "This is," says Brockett, who gives the phrase to Yorkshire, "I suppose the London road." But other roads, such as the footpath from Newton Ketton to Darlington, are termed Darnton Trod, and the saying is most common in Westmoreland and Cumberland. At schools in Teesdale, if a boy has done mischief, a friendly voice will warn him to "tak Darnton Trod," that he may get out of the way and escape chastisement. I am inclined to think, as we never hear of any sanctuary privileges at Darlington, that the saying refers to a junction with the lawless marauders of the place temporarily, or, if the of the offender liked their line of life, for ever. The "black troops" of modern times give one but a very faint idea of the power possessed by the earlier reprobates. In Cosin's time, Barwick, Middleton, and Copperthwaite were the Adam Bell, Clim-of-the-Clough, and William of Cloudeslie who infested Darlington and Neasham for the new and old roads, and filled passengers with terror.†

The roadside hostelry of Baydlebeck is famous in tradition as the chosen palliard for a celebrated clatch of thieves called *Catton's gang*, as well as for "Sir William Browne," knight of the order of St. Nicholas, and his retainers. A rhyme is handed down as

* Act for the Stockton and Barnard Castle road 1747; for road from Darlington to Railey Fell and Piercebridge to Royal Oak, 1751; for road from Cockerton to Staindrop, 1795.

† "At my returne to Durham I met with the noise of a crewe of highway robbers, (Barwick, they say, the ringleader), who have beene so bold as to attempt sundry houses, as that of Mr. Peacock's neare Durham, Mr. Barker neere Pearce Bridge, and Mr. Pearceson minister of Great Stainton. Thence being removed hither to Eaglesclifte (to reside with my family for a time,) on Saturday last three of us had a meeting, at Sir George Vane's, where was Mr. Ra. Davison, where we resolved to send to the justices of those wards, to whom it properly belongs, to order watches, &c., about the places of their haunts, which, if neglected, wee will take the best course we can. Meanwhile we have bound to the good behaviour and to the next sessions two notorious harbourers of those leude persons, (one Buttrick and another John Ward by name, of Haughton neere Darlington,) and by them wee have made some discoveries: one Orde, a notorious mate of those robbers, I found in the Gaole of Durham, to be one of my auditours there on Sunday was a fourtennight."—Dr. Basire to Cosin, 8 Nov., 1669.

addressed by him to Mr Bowes who was sitting in front of his old mansion, Thornton Hall :—

Who knows, but Mr. Bowes,
In his old days, will mend his ways.*

This desperate king of modern mosstroopers received sentence of death in 1743 at Newcastle for returning from transportation. After sentence was passed, he begged earnestly to be transported again ; but the judge giving no ear to him, Sir William broke out into all the opprobrious language he could think of, against both the judge and the whole court, and wished that God Almighty might d—— all their souls to h——. He was executed at the Westgate, Newcastle. To the vicar, who attended him, he expressed great concern for his past wicked life, and seemed very penitent. Two companies of soldiers, quartered in the town, guarded him from the castle, and were drawn up at the place of execution, for fear of his being rescued by his band.

Baydalebeck hostelry is built of cobble stones of very small size, and has been an inn for time immemorial, but gained so bad a name from its thievish frequenters that the landlord some 20 or 30 years ago let it for 8*l.*, and agreed to keep a cow for the tenant in the bargain. The cow's keep would now exceed the 8*l.* The house (which was haunted, by the way) with 20 acres of land, was bought afterwards for some 500*l.* only. In its palmy days none durst come near after nightfall. At present, it a very favourite resort of the sprigs of Darlington, who rejoice in the capital oat cake and whiskey prepared by the worthy landlady, Mrs. Naisbitt.

In 1773, the postboy going between Durham and Darlington was attacked at Chilton Lane end, by two persons on foot, of 9*s.* and his whip. The very frequent robberies of the same kind at last caused the transfer of the bags to coaches. The first mail from Newcastle to the south conveyed by the royal mail coach was transmitted on Nov, 22, 1786. It is said that no one at first would take the mail in at Darlington,† but James Trenholme, of the Red Lion, in Blackwellgate,‡ at last consented. Coaches depending on private support had been running some time before. In 1764, and long after, a stage coach ran from Newcastle to York. The termination of the first day's journey was Darlington, of the second Thirsk, and at the close of the third day it reached its destination, returning again at the same rate. But the whole distance from Newcastle soon occupied but three days, by means of a "machine," as a coach was then termed.

The *Darlington Pamphlet* contains the following announcement :—" NEWCASTLE POST COACH, *Darlington, May* 22, 1772. Began to run Three Days a Week, on *Monday* the 29th of *January*, 1770, and continues setting out from the *George* and *Blue Boar* Inn, *Holborn*, LONDON, every *Monday*, *Wednesday*, and *Friday ;* and from the *Bull* and *Post Boy*, in NEWCASTLE, on the same Days : will go from LONDON to NEW-

* I once wished that a gentleman whose opportunities and collections for an assemblage of our popular rhymes and proverbs were very extensive, wonld publish them. Since then a collection professing to contain them has appeared. But, alas ! it has all the characteristics of that dishonest school of imitation antiquaries, who suppose that evidences and their illustrations are wanted ; not for the purpose of ascertaining the manners, customs, and language of our fathers ; but to make readable stories, which are generally far exceeded by those of Joe Miller and Charles Dickens. The collection I am compelled to allude to by way of appropriate caution oddly enough appeared in a newspaper under some significant initials, at the very time another correspondent was employed in exposing the inaccuracies of Hagar's Directory. Its contents are too much like the coins of the notorious John White who constructed a penny of bishop Sherwood by altering the mint mark of one of bishop Fordham, *i. e.*, several " either never existed, or were altered by his ingenuity to suit his fancy and impose upon collectors. These falsifications have destroyed all confidence in the work, which cannot be referred to as a proof of any rare peculiarity." I have to give this explanation here, to account for my not adding that Sir William Brown passed Thornton Hall early one morning, returning with his companion from some highway robbery in the west, that the road was very bad, that his horse was tired and sunk to his knees in mire every step, that it fell at Thornton and flung the knight, to flounder in the mud and soused head and foot to arise, when he saw Mr. Bowes. I am as fearful of transplanting such details from such a source as Mr. Hawkins is of John White's plates ; I tell the tale in the text as it is told to me ; and I am most credibly assured that I there tell all that remains of it. Traditions and oral rhymes are too inaccurate to begin with, to allow of further alteration or addition ; and popular user must say that an individual's dictum has sufficient pith, utility, or wit to be perpetuated as a saying or proverb.

Seminat in vulgus nugas, auditaque lingua
Auget, et ex humili tumulo producit olympum.

† At first coaches were declared vey effeminate, and afterwards very murderous, vehicles. Scarcely half a century has elapsed since stage coaches were charged with proceeding at a fatal pace—several passengers having died of apoplexy.

‡ About 50 years ago, a gentleman who was lodging at Trenholme's, and was somewhat deranged, drowned himself in the smallest of the Hell Kettles.

castle in Three Days, and from Newcastle to London in the same Time (provided no material Accident happens) to carry six inside Passengers, each to pay Three Pence *per* Mile; to be allowed 14 lb. of luggage; all above to pay Four-Pence Halfpenny *per* Pound, or in proportion to the Miles they go, No Livery Servants will be carried, except such Servant's Master or Mistress is in the Coach at the same Time. *** The Proprietors of this Machine beg leave to acquaint the Public, that they are determined not to carry Money, Plate, Jewels, or Watches, upon any Consideration whatever: And that the said Proprietors do hereby give Notice, they will not be answerable for any such Articles, sent by the said Machine after the Date hereof. SAM. WILKINSON, Clerk. N.B. The above Coach goes through Darlington for the South, at Ten o'Clock in the Forenoon, and for the North at One o'Clock in the Afternoon, every *Monday*, *Wednesday*, and *Friday*." A subsequent advertisement of the August following informs us that the machine ran every day during the summer season, "and in order to make this machine more agreeable to those Ladies and Gentlemen who choose to travel in it," the proprietors would not carry any outside passengers or livery servants in the inside, except the latter under the regulations given in the former notice; nor carry any children under two years of age, and all above that age to pay full price; nor carry any dogs within or without the coach upon any consideration. The coaches in and about 1774 were termed *flies*, or *fly coaches*. Allan, the antiquary, mentions in that year the coach to Durham by such names.

Mr. Wm. Davison, of Alnwick, very lately fixed and perhaps still fixes an old or copy of an old woodcut to his yards of songs, which presents a very odd machine, drawn by four horses, and of unusual length. There seem no outside conveniences, but the interior has two compartments somewhat after the fashion of a modern railway carriage.

In the days of *machinery* however, the *magnates* generally travelled to London by other means. One mode was the procession of nine or ten days in all the solemn state of lonely grandeur; the other by obtaining a partner in the lighter expense of a chaise.* "Wanted," says a *Darlington Mercury* of 1773, "a partner in a post chaise to London, on Sunday, Monday, or Tuesday next. ☞ Enquire of the Post Master in Darlington." The very great cost of the former plan may be gathered from an account of Miss Ann Allan's expenses of a journey to and from London in 1762, extracted from her household book.

The worthy spinster's journey up consumed nine days. Six coach-horses, a coachman and postillion, came from York for her, and in the service were occupied fifteen days, for which they were charged *26l. 5s. 0d.*, besides coachman and postillion's fees. The coach and six horses down again cost 28*l.* 14*s.* 0*d.*; and the road expenses down, 51*l.* 6*s.* 3½*d.* The total cost of the journey up and down was 150*l.*†; and some 700*l.* were spent by the lady in town. In the Ettrick Diary there is a curious and painful account of a journey to London, performed by the squire and his lady on horseback; of their misery and consternation when their horse "Dragon' fell lame; and of the frightful expenses of the journey, which are partly accounted for by the dolorous husband, "because his wife would have all her own way."

In days of old, there was a discreet decree among travellers on horseback, and even by stage coach,‡ that when Sunday came, it should be a day of rest for both man and beast in the slow progress on the road. The custom gives occasion to one of Scott's

* About 80 years ago, there was but one post chaise in Darlington, and it had only three wheels. When another innkeeper set up an opposition chaise to it, the rival hosts adopted the practice which prevailed up to a recent period at bathing places, of watching the approach of chaises into the town, and handing cards to the travellers, soliciting their favours. *(Inf. Fra. Mewburn, esq.)*

† "1762, Jan. 29. Paid bill at Darlington for chaises and horses, 1*l.* 2*s.* 7*d.*: at Northallerton, 2*l.* 1*s.* 0½*d.*: Boroughbridge, all night, 2*l.* 3*s.* 5*d.*. Wetherby, breakfast, 10*s.* 7*d.*: Aberforth, dinner, 1*l.* 5*s.* 0*d.*: Ferrybridge, all night, 3*l.* 1*s.* 1*d.*: Doncaster, dinner, 1*l.* 13*s.* 5*d.*: Barnbymoer, all night, 2*l.* 14*s.* 1½*d.*: Tuxford, breakfast, 6*s.*: Carleton, dinner, 1*l.* 9*s.* 8*d.*: Newark, all night, 2*l.* 18*s.* 7½*d.*: Grantham, dinner, 1*l.* 13*s.* 5½*d.*: Cotesworth, all night, 2*l.* 14*s.* 0½*d.*: Stamford, dinner, 2*l.* 10*s.* 8*d.*: Stilton, all night, 2*l.* 16*s.* 1*d.*: Bugden, dinner, 2*l.* 6*s.* 5½*d.*: Biggleswade, all night, 3*l.* 2*s.* 4*d.*: Stevenage, breakfast, 1*l.* 1*s.* 9*d.*: Hatfield, dinner, 1*l.* 18*s.* 5*d.*: Barnett, all night, 3*l.* 4*s.* 9*d.*: fifteen days hire of six coach horses, coachman, and postillion, from York to Darlington and from thence to London, and return to York, at 1*l.* 15*s.* 0*d.* a day, 26. 5*s.* 0*d.*: said coachman, extra present, 2*l.* 2*s.* 0*d.*: paid postillion do., 1*l.* 1*s.* 0*d.*: May 17, coach and six horses, from London to Grange, 28*l.* 14*s.* 0*d.*: road expenses from London to Grange, 51*l.* 6*s.* 3½*d.* Total cost of journey, 150*l.* 1*s.* 9½*d.*

‡ Diary of George Grey, esq., of Southwick. 1702. "Returned to London in the stage coach with Sir William Bowes, Thomas Harrison, of Copgrave, esq., and others; we staid all Sunday at Stamford."

happiest scenes in "Rob Roy," laid at the jolly landlord's sign of the Black Bear in Darlington, and filling chapter iv.

The tolls taken at the turnpike gates from Boroughbridge to the city of Durham, from 1 May, 1745, to 1 May, 1746, amounted to only 811*l*. 6*s*. 9¼*d*. ! ! ! The tolls taken on the same roads from the 1 Jan., 1835, to 1 Jan., 1836, (before the introduction of the York, Newcastle, and Berwick railway,) amounted to 7054*l*. 11*s*. 10*d*.—shewing a wonderful increase in the traffic of the country. And the tolls taken on the same roads (since the establishment of the railway) from 1 Jan., 1849, to 1 Jan., 1850, amount to 1707*l*. 15*s*. 2*d*.

The accidents on roads were of course innumerable.

In Oct., 1789, the Rev. Mr. Bainbridge, of Kirk Merrington, was unfortunately killed on the high road near that place, by a post chaise driving violently against him, which the heavy fall of snow prevented his seeing in time to avoid it. His horse was staked, and both it and its driver were killed on the spot. The month before, the musical world sustained the loss of Samuel Ellis, esq., of Great Surrey Street, Blackfriars Road, who in his 41st year was killed by a fall from his horse near Darlington. To the study of the classics he had added a knowledge of the modern polite languages, and he had attained to such excellence in music, that Salomons, Cramor, Parke, and many other professors and amateurs of the art, frequently attended the concerts which he gave every Wednesday morning at his own house. On the 1st of May preceding he had given up his business to a young man who had lived with him some years; and hoped to spend the remainder of his days in comfort and in contributing to the happiness of those round about him.

It was, no doubt, a gallant age when the Mail, the Telegraph, the True Briton, the High-flyer, &c., daily rattled along the orderly turnpike and unmacadamised streets amid the joyful winding of horns. Yet altogether, the danger, cost, loss of time, little ease, inevitable night-exposure, and the thousand ills attendant on horse traction, fully prepared the nation to receive as a boon of no little consideration the introduction of a totally new principle, albeit at the expense of a mighty amount of road romance. For if a journey to the metropolis was a fearful thing by the stage coach, what must it have been for those luckless third-class travellers who adopted the stage-wagon, drawn as it was by eight or ten heavy-looking horses at the majestic pace of two miles an hour!

Many middle-aged people of Darlington remember the time when there was but one coach from Stockton. It ran three times a week only, passing through Darlington to Barnard Castle, and yet, notwithstanding the extent of its district, it was fairly starved off the road. The times have changed. The country between Darlington and Stockton was the first which saw a passenger-carriage drawn on a principle which has worked results in society generally of so startling a nature that they scarcely can be viewed as yet in any calm and philosophical manner.

It rose from the coal trade. In the earliest times, Durham was an inexhaustible supplier of fuel to her extensive sister on the south. In Leland's age there was "in Swaledale little corn and much grass, no wood but ling and some nut trees. The wood that the inhabitants burnt their lead with was brought out of other part of the shire, and out of Dirhamshir." And again, there were "no coal pits in Richemont; yet the easterly parts of Richemontshire burnt much sea coals brought out of Dyrhamshire." The roads leading from the pits were called "Coal Streets," and were always the most important and best repaired of the district. One of these proceeds from Auckland and separates at Burtree gate into two branches, one runs through Cockerton and Blackwell to Croft (and by a branch to Darlington), the other joins the Darlington and Stockton road between Haughton and Burdon. In 1489, the bishop attempted a negociation with Sir John Paston, of Norfolk, for an exchange of coal for corn, wine, and wax. "whereby our familiarity and friendship may be increased. There was always a sort of small coasting trade, but the use of coals was so little known to our ancestors that a bill was introduced temp. Elizabeth to prohibit their use, at least during the session of parliament, because the air was filled with unwholesome smoke and vapours to the great prejudice of the health of the inhabitants, especially those who had lately come from the country. Harrison in the same year laments the decay of timber, attributing it to the greater state of houses. "In times past men were contented to dwell in houses buylded of Sallow, Willow, Plummetree, Hardebeame, and Elme. . . . Yet see the chaunge, for when our houses were buylded of Willowe then had we Oken men, but nowe that our houses are come to be made of Oke, our men are not only become Willow, but a great many altogither of Straw, which is a sore alteration. . . . Nowe have we manye chimnyes and yet our tenderlinges complaine of rewines, catarres, and poses, then had we none but reredosses, and our heades did never ake. For as the smoke in those dayes was supposed to be a sufficient hardning for the timber of the house, so it was reputed a farre better *medicine (!)* to keepe the goodman and his family from the quacke or pose, wherewith as then very few were acquainted." He fears that sea coal, whins, &c., would be good merchandise even in the city of London, where some of them had already taken up their inns in the greatest merchants' parlours.*

Provisions for working of coal occur at a very early date, and my lord prior of Durham and other ecclesiastics seem to have been the principal colliers. Arrangements for pits, and drifts or trenches (thus the term *aqueductum sive treneheam subterraneam* occurs), for carrying off the water and winning the coal are found.

The Chaytor house at Butterby seems to have burnt coal continually, and Thomas Chaytor evidently disliked wood as fuel. In Dec., 1614, he was forced to furnish his house with coals by his own horses, for the Wear kept so high for eight or nine weeks that he could not pass over with his wain. Feb. 13, 1615, was, says he, "the most outragious day for wind and snow that ever did blow. Neither horse nor man able to pass from this house to Durham. I had no coals, nor could send to the pits with horses or wains, and was forced to send for four horses load to my house at Durham the 10, and they lasted till the 13, and then we could pass for no more but was forced to make use of wooden fires.' From his account there never was so long and deep a storm of snow as existed all over England at that season. In August, 1616, the following entry occurs. "Mr. John Fowler came of purpose from London to me the 27 of this, and took infinite pains in setting up my father's monument, and took journey towards Newcastle 13 of September following. I satisfied him for all disbursements at London, and gave him 40*s*., and *five chalder of coals*, which cost me 3*li*. 10*s*." From the diary of Sir William Chaytor at the close of the 17th century while in the Fleet liberties, we gather that he paid 7*s*. for six bushels of coals.

Up to 1600, it appears that coals were conveyed from the collieries in carts on common roads, and in some cases in baskets on the backs of horses, like the sacks on the trains of asses in our own day. A grant of wayleave occurs from bishop Ruthall in 1530, for "carriages by wayne, cowpe, or horses, from the coal mines and pits now opened or which shall be opened in Ravensall and Eighton, through all the grounds, waists, and moors of the said Rev. Father' for 21 years, at 5*s*. rent.

Grey, in his Chorographia of 1649, mentions the fame of the north parts for the coal trade, which he says began not past four-score years before, in consequence of the decay of woods in southern England. In those days the owners of collieries were frequently beggared, and the employed seem to have had the best time of it, many thousand persons being engaged. Many men, says he, lived by conveying the coals in waggons and wains to the Tyne. Among various southern gentlemen who came to hazard their money, "Master Beamont, a gentleman of great ingenuity and rare parts, adventured into our mines with his 30,000*l*., who brought with him many rare engines not known then in these parts; as the art to bore with iron rods to try the deepness and thickness of the coal; rare engines to draw water out of the pits; *waggons with one horse to carry down coals from the pits to the stathes, to the river*, &c. Within a few years, he consumed all his money, and rode home upon his light horse."

Roger North thus describes the northern roads in 1676:—"When men have pieces of ground between the colliery and the river, they sell *leave* to lead coals over their ground, and so dear, that the owner of a rood of ground will expect 20*l*. per annum for this leave. The manner of the carriage is by laying rails of timber from the colliery down to the river exactly straight and parallel, and bulky carts are made with four rowlets fitting these rails, whereby the carriage is so easy, that one horse will draw down four or five chaldrons of coals, and is an immense benefit to the coal-merchants.'

In the rude and early waggon-ways the rails were about six or seven inches in breadth, and were joined to the transverse sleepers by pins. They were soon worn away by the attrition of the wheels, and the holes in the sleepers became too large for the pins after these had been once or twice displaced in order to renew the rails, while the sleepers themselves were seriously deteriorated by the horses' feet. The "double railway" was then contrived. In this, other pieces of wood were laid upon and fastened to the first rails by pins so that they could be renewed without touching the sleepers, and the superior height thus gained allowed the sleepers to be covered and secured from injury in the centre of the road. The regular load of a horse and cart on the common road

* Of Cole mines we have such plentie in the North, and Westerne partes of our islande as may suffice for all the realme of Englande. *And so must they doe hereafter in deede, if woode be not better cherished than it is at this present*, and to say the truth, notwithstanding that very many of them are caryed *into other countryes of the maine*, yet theyr greatest trade beginneth to growe from the forge into the kitchin and hall as may appeare already in most cities and townes that lye about the cost, where they have little other fewell, except it be turfe, and hassock. I marveyle not a little that there is no trade of these into Sussex and Southampton shire, for want whereof the Smithes doe worke theyr yron with charre coale. I think that farre carriage be the only cause, which is but a slender excuse to inforce us to carye them unto the mayne from hence." (*Harrison*, 1577.)

was 17 cwt., on a railroad 42 cwt. In curves or acclivities, thin pieces iron of were nailed over those parts of the rail which opposed resistance to the wheels.

The middle of the last century is generally stated to have witnessed the first adoption of the ordinary tramroad in which iron was substituted for wood, and the extension of the iron-works of Shropshire and Staffordshire is stated as the reason. About 1767, iron plates were first laid down upon wooden rails in Shropshire. This is no evidence on their use in the north ; but one can scarcely doubt that in this district they were introduced long before. Rails wholly of iron are said to have been unsuccessfully tried at Whitehaven in 1738. Randall, who lived until 1774, says expressly in his annotated copy of Bourne's Newcastle :—" Waggon ways are reported in the neighbourhood of the collieries to have been first used on the River Were, soon after the revolution, by Mr. Allan, of Flatts, and on the Tyne by Charles Montague, esq., at Stella." The date indicated by these two names would be about 1690. Allan is said by Hutchinson to have been the first introducer, indeed he is still remembered as Lord Newark, a soubriquet acquired from the universal question " Hev ye been te see Allan's *new wark?*" We can scarceley imagine any modification of the early wooden trams (which notoriously were in use long before) sufficiently striking to deserve these statements.*

The first iron tramroads were formed of the plate rail, consisting of cast iron rails about four feet long, having a flange or upright ledge three inches high, to keep the wheel upon the horizontal part, which was about four inches wide and an inch thick, and another flange at the other side projecting downwards to strengthen the rail. The friction on such rails was very great, compared with that on the later edge rail, in which the flange is on the wheel and does not require to be more than one inch in depth. The introduction into the country of cast iron wheels is said to have taken place about 1754, and the adoption of the wheel flange in 1789.

Notwithstanding all the improvements by enterprising men, wooden tramways still continued to be used on the score of temporary cheapness, to almost our own day. They were on the edge rail principle, and anecdotes of the miseries consequent on the breaking of the wooden flanges off the wheels are still rife among the peasantry. When iron was used, the old plate rail was still in very constant vogue, as requiring much less weight of metal.

Before the success of Stephenson there were railways. There were indeed locomotive steam engines, with rack-wheels, and roughened wheels, chains. and even with legs, feet, and shoes!† But the railways were small, the mode of progression miserably slow, and the engines so encumbered and troublesome from the contrivances to overcome an ideal obstacle, the want of sufficient adhesion in the wheels, that horse-labour was preferable. In 1813, things took a turn. Mr. Blackett by a series of experiments on the Wylam waggonway found that wheels and rails required neither racking nor roughening, and George Stephenson made his first locomotive at Killingworth Colliery. " Yes! Lord Ravensworth and Co. were the first parties that intrusted me with money to make a locomotive engine. That engine was made thirty-two years ago, and we called it *My Lord.*"‡ It would cary about thirty tons at the rate of four miles an hour. Up to the time of the Stockton and Darlington railway, steam progression, *non obstante* the confessed superiority of the 1814 engine, was still for general purposes, a dead letter.

In 1767, a navigable canal had been projected, to lead from Stockton by Darlington to Winston, with side cuts from Darlington to Croft, from Thornton to Piersebridge, and from Cotham Stob to Yarm, Length, 33½ miles: fall, 328 feet. At a meeting held at the Post-house, in Darlington, Nov. 9, a subscription was commenced to defray the cost of a survey which was made by Brindley and Whitworth,§ who estimated the cost of carrying the design into effect at 63,722*l*. It was proposed to derive the water from Staindrop beck and Sutburn beck, buying Alwent mill. The reports and map were published at Newcastle, in 1770, and in an improved map of that year, branches

* It must, however, be confessed that in the letters of William Scott, Lord Eldon's father, published in Richardson's Imprints and Reprints, and reaching from 1745, to 1748, nothing occurs save rails and wheels of various woods. These are rather detailed in the correspondence. The southrons, thinking the demand inexhaustible, overstocked the market with these wooden articles.

† Ritchie gives a cut of this absurd machine. It was to travel 2½ miles an hour.

‡ Speech of G. Stephenson, 1844. The progressive improvements in rails and engines effected by this gentleman and others do not affect my *locale*. They are very sufficiently detailed in Ritchie's little book on railways. Malleable edge-rails were first tried about 1803, at the Wallbottle colliery. The cast iron ones would have been unsuitable for high rates of speed.

§ Leather states that Mr. Rob. Whitworth received his instructions on the 19 Sept. only, and he had finished his survey, plan, and report, on the 24 Oct.

are laid down to Cockfield Fell, Etherley, &c. The primary object was the same as that of the present railway, to bring lead and coal to the Tees. In surveying and trying to forward the canal, George Dixon, of Cockfield took an active part. He was an extensive coal-owner, &c.* His grandson,, John Dixon, was George Stephenson's first assistant in making the Stockton and Darlington railway, and is now the chief engineer on that line.

The following curious statistics, as arguing for the probable success of the scheme, are contained in Hutchinson ;—

		Tons.
Coals won at the coaleries at Etherley. West Auckland, Cockfield, Norwood, Butterknowle, Eldon, and Bishop Auckland, in one year		101,700
Lead shipped at Stockton—foreign	1506	
" " " coastwise	1574	
		3,080
Allum do. do. foreign	154	
" " " coastwise	724	
		878
Lime from the kilns		7,000
Slates and flags from Brignal, &c.		1,000
Coals to supply Stockton (town's use)		4,500
The adjacent country		9,500
Coals brought into Darlington (town's use)		5,300
" passed over Croft bridge		12,000
" " Piersebridge		18,000
" " Winston bridge		15,000
" consumed at the lime kilns		5,000
" " in the county, west of Darlington		5,000
Coals and cinders passed Yarm bridge in 1769		12,018
Coals imported coastwise at Stockton		3,075
Lime do. do.		2,369

The Stockton items are the mean of the years 1766, 1767, 1768. In 1770, 4096¼ chaldrons and 65 tons were landed at Stockton ; in 1780, and 1790, the number had sunk to about 220 chaldrons. At the first period coals were brought into the port for the Yorkshire alum-works, but owing to the high duty after that time, the works were supplied by land-sale coal at cheaper rates.

In Tuke's "Agriculture of the North Riding" is inserted a letter from M. G. Steele, esq., urging strongly that a navigation from the Swale up the Wiske to the Tees between Croft and Yarm should be formed to communicate by an aqueduct over the Tees with a canal to be brought from the Durham coal pits. By this was to be conveyed lead, coal, lime, and blue slate, from this county and Westmoreland into Yorkshire, while the butter, cheese, and barley, were to return by Darlington and Barnard Castle, into the dales and western country.

In 1810, Bailey thought it feasible that a canal for the conveyance of coals might favourably be made by taking the deep dene called Thristleden Dene, a little east of Ferryhill, as the highest point, and proceeding westward on a level through the coal district. A conveyance from the dene to Morden carrs would be easily obtained by two or three locks, through which carrs a level line might be taken to the turnpike road near Sedgefield, and another to near Rickneld mill, and thence by a few locks to Darlington.

In the same year, after the dinner to celebrate the opening of the new cut at Stockton, (Sept. 18,) there was a general meeting, at which a committee was appointed to enquire into the practicability and advantage of a railway or canal from Stockton by Darlington to Winston. The committee reported on the 17 Jan., 1812, to "a meeting of gentlemen, merchants, and others," held in Darlington, (George Allan, esq., of the Grange, being in the chair,) and Mr. Rennie was appointed to make a survey and report on the comparative advantages of the two measures. Another committee was formed. George Allan, esq., Grange ; John Allan, esq., Blackwell ; Mr. Jonathan Backhouse, jun. ; Mr. Robert Botcherby ; George Lewis Hollingsworth, esq. ; Mr. William Kitching ; Mr. Edward Pease : Mr. Joseph Pease ; Mr. Bright Wass, all of Darlington ; William Chaytor, esq., Croft ; &c., were the gentlemen from this neighbourhood in the list, which is spread over a wide tract of country.

In 1812, or 1813, a survey was accordingly again made for a canal from Darlington to Stockton, by Renie, which was to cost 95,600*l*. Some commercial disasters in the county of Durham rendered the execution of the great engineer's plans hopeless. He at last thought a tramroad preferable to the canal. In 1816, an iron railway from Darlington to Winston was conceived, to cost 45,860*l*.

* See Bailey's Durham.

All these lines included Darlington *en route*. In 1818, Christopher Tennant, esq., of Stockton, engaged Mr. Leather to make a survey for a canal from the Tees near Portrack to the Gaunless near Evenwood Bridge, by the Billingham beck, and Rushyford. Length, 29½ miles: rise, 442 feet: locks, 50. The Skerne was to be conveyed under the canal by an inverted siphon. Estimated cost, 205,283*l*. A drainage clause for Morden carrs was proposed. The required land it was thought might be bought at 40*l*. an acre! A branch was talked of to run from Bradbury to near the Wear at Tudhoe, for the city of Durham, 9 miles 6 furlongs in length, 25 feet rise, and taking land at 35*l*. per acre, to cost 35,812*l*. 4*s*. At a public meeting in Stockton, 9 July, 1818, Mr. Tennant propounded the scheme and read the engineer's report. The meeting was delighted; it testified approbation of Mr. Tennant's disinterested motives in procuring a survey at his own expense and bringing forward the measure; and appointed a committee to print the report and convene a general meeting on July 31. On that committee were "E. Pease, Jona. Backhouse."*

At this meeting (the Earl of Strathmore in the chair) it was resolved that application should be made so parliament for an act authorising a company to make the canal from Portrack to Evenwood Bridge, if two-thirds of the estimated cost was subscribed before 1 Jan. 1819. In November, a deputation (Messrs. Cartwright, Crowe, and Tennant,) attended a meeting in London for promoting the measure, but were unsuccessful in raising the necessary subscription. The scheme, therefore, fell to the ground,† and fortunate it was so, for a more disastrous scheme could not have been devised. At a subsequent period Mr. Tennant suggested a line of railway in room of this canal, for which an act was obtained in 1828, called the Clarence railway.

The advocates for the Darlington route awoke. By their opposition the canal project fell through; but it had determined the hesitation to improve transit. In the course of enquiry for a canal to Darlington Rennie's plan had again been brought forward, and an anonymous writer, supposed to have been Mr. R. Miles of Yarm, kindly "ventured to submit" whether a railroad might not be preferable. The notion soon became general.‡

A meeting was held in Darlington, Sept. 4, which directed estimates to be made for a line from Stockton by Darlington to the collieries, with branches to Yarm, Croft, and Piersebridge, as well by the joint mode of having a canal and railway as by railway the whole distance.§ The committee the same year, 1818, published a report and afterwards some observations on the new plan. At that time they considered that coals could not be shipped on the Tees on so low terms as on the Tyne and Wear, and that no increase of revenue could be expected from exportation.‖ Mr. Geo. Overton, of South Wales, and Mr. David Davis, made the surveys. The estimated expense was 82,000*l*. The line led from Stockton *via* Darlington, Summerhouse, Ingleton, and Hilton, to the West Auckland coal field, and the company went to parliament in 1819, but were defeated in the Commons through the influence of the landowners, headed by the Earl of Darlington, by a majority of 13, the numbers being 106 and 93. Overton then altered his track, and planned a line by School Aycliffe, Middridge Grange, and Shildon, to West Auckland and the collieries; but when this bill was before parliament, George III. died (1820), and the measure was postponed till 1821, when the first act was passed. George Stephenson was then called in, projected great improvements, and was

* Printed report.

† A second report by Mr. Leather had been ordered by the committee on the Stockton and Auckland canal, and they engaged Messrs. Buddle, Fenwick, and Steel, great coal-viewers near Newcastle, to examine the Auckland coals. The statements of these gentlemen were published in the closing part of the year 1818. Mr. Leather thought it was not *an extravagant* supposition that 100,000 tons, or one 28th part of their export from the Tyne and Wear, would be exported from the Tees. The highest price in London for Newcastle coal (Russell's, and the various Wallsend coals) per chaldron, free on board, was then 34*s*. In the field then surveyed, the coal-viewers thought 28*s*. the highest price, free on board, in the Tyne and Wear, and the coals to bring that price were from the old engine pit, (Eden Main Colliery,) and Norwood. Those from Blackboy (afterwards Tees Wallsend) were put down at 23*s*., and they shewed the little value of the viewers' opinion, for they afterwards brought the second price in London.

‡ Gateshead Observer, 11 Sep. 1852.

§ A rival scheme was sprung in Stockton, on the abandonment of the canal project, of Dec. 15; and a committee appointed to enquire into the expediency of a railway on the most direct road to the collieries. This Stockton and Auckland Railway was abandoned, 14 Dec. 1819, on the Darlington committee making some concessions advantageous to the public.

‖ Estimated home consumption in tons, Darlington, 40,794; Yarm, 13,000; Stockton, 29,000. Total, 82,794 tons, to be despatched annually from the collieries. Out of the allowance to Stockton, it was presumed 14,500 tons would go into Cleveland.

appointed engineer to execute the entire work. His alterations were sanctioned by an act of 1823.

The act then passed in 1821. It was "for making and maintaining a railway or tramroad, from the river Tees at Stockton to Witton Park colliery, with several branches therefrom, all in the county of Durham." The first rail was laid by Thomas Meynell, esq., of Yarm, near St. John's well, Stockton, where the depot for coal was afterwards erected, 23 May, 1822, with public ceremony and rejoicing. George Stephenson was retained. He had got leave to go from Killingworth to lay down a railway at Hetton, and now he came to Darlington. The works were rapidly completed. In 1824, in parnership with his son Robert, Messrs. Pease, of Darlington, and Mr. Michael Longridge, Mr. Stephenson founded that famous engine-building establishment at Newcastle, which has had so long a run of prosperity; and on Sept. 27, 1825, the railway was to be opened, and a locomotive engine was to be the instrument. The work was then a single line of rails, 25 miles in length. It extended from Witton Park and Etherley, near West Auckland, to Stockton-upon-Tees, with branches to Darlington, Yarm, &c., and was chiefly composed of malleable iron rails. At the western extremity of the line a deep ravine occurred at the river Gaundless; on the summit of the hills on each side of which a permanent steam-engine was fixed. The engine on the western side of the vale was called the Etherley engine, and that on the eastern side the Brusselton engine. The latter, in addition to conveying the goods up from West Auckland, continued the transit down the eastern side of the ridge: below this, to the east, the conveyance was performed by locomotive engines. The proprietors were to assemble at the permanent steam-engine below Brusselton Tower, about nine miles west of Darlington, at eight o'clock. Accordingly, the committee, after inspecting the Etherley engine plane, assembled at the bottom of Brusselton engine plane, near West Auckland, and the carriages, loaded with coals and merchandise, were drawn up the eastern ridge by the Brusselton engine, a distance of 1960 yards, in seven and a half minutes, and then lowered down the plane on the east side of the hill 880 yards in five minutes. At the foot of the plane the locomotive engine was ready to received the carriages; and here the novelty of the scene had attracted an immense concourse of spectators—the fields on each side of the railway being literally covered with ladies and gentlemen on horseback, and pedestrians of all kinds. The train of carriages was then attached to Stephenson's locomotive engine, in the following order:—Locomotive engine, with the Engineer (Mr Stephenson) and assistants. Tender, with coal and water. Six waggons loaded with coals and flour. A covered coach, with the committee and proprietors.* Twenty-one waggons, fitted up for passengers; and last by six waggons loaded with coals,—making a train of thirty-eight carriages, exclusive of the engine and tender. Tickets were distributed to the number of near 300, for those whom it was intended should occupy the coach and waggons; but both loaded and empty carriages were instantly filled with passagers. The engine started off and the scene became most interesting—the horsemen galloping across the fields to accompany the engine, and the people on foot endeavouring in vain to keep up with the cavalcade. On this descending part of the Railway it was wished to ascertain at what rate of speed the engine could travel with safety. The speed was frequently twelve, and for a short distance near Darlington, fifteen miles per hour; and at that time the number of passengers was counted to 450, which, together with the coals, merchandize, and carriages, would amount to near ninety tons. The train arrived at Darlington, a distance of eight miles and three quarters, in sixty-five minutes, exclusive of stops, averaging, about eight miles an hour. Six carriages of coals, for Darlington, were left; and after obtaining fresh water, and accommodating a band of music and passengers from Darlington, the engine set off again. The Railway from Darlington to Stockton in one place is quite level; and as in the upper part, it was intended to try the speed of the engine; in this part it was proposed to prove its powers of draught. The engine arrived at Stockton in three hours and seven minutes after leaving Darlington, including stops, the distance being nearly twelve miles, and upon the level part of the Railway, the number of passengers in the waggons was counted about 550, and several more clung to the carriages on each side, so that the whole number could not be less than 600, which, with the other load, would amount to about eighty tons. The fields, lanes, and bridges, were covered with spectators. The procession was not joined by many horses and carriages, until it approached within a few miles of Stockton. Here, the situation of the Railway, which runs parallel and close to the Turnpike-road, gave a fine opportunity of viewing the procession. Numerous horses and vehicles travelled with the train, in some places within a few yards, without the horses seeming frightened; and the passengers by the engine had the pleasure of cheering their brother passengers by the stage-coach, which passed alongside, and of observing the contrast between the engine with her six hundred

* A table ran down its centre.

passengers and load, and the coach with four horses, and only sixteen passengers. Part of the workmen were entertained at Stockton, and part at Yarm, and there was a dinner for the proprietors and their more distinguished guests at the Town Hall, in Stockton. Mr Meynell was in the chair, and the Mayor of the town acted as vice-president.

The railway cost about 125,000*l*. It was the property of sixty shareholders.

The great starting point of steam locomotion on public railways is the opening of the Stockton and Darlington line, yet men did not grasp the invention or pay extraordinary attention to it at *that* time. The locomotives were worked by vertical cylinders, and the motion was communicated to the wheels by an endless chain. Their power was not one-tenth of some of the present locomotives, and their greatest speed was some eight miles an hour. A directory of 1827 mentions that several coaches drawn by horses, travelled daily, at the rate of seven to nine miles an hour on this rail-road, from Darlington to Stockton; while six locomotives engines were employed in the transit of goods. The reason for not employing steam-power to passenger traffic was, I presume, of a financial complexion. My readers will remember what a long time elapsed before the Clarence Railway had anything more than a horse-coach to its northern terminus, although, it had become the ordinary route from Stockton to Newcastle. A *train* of coaches was a speculation of unheard of risk in the early days of the Stockton and Darlington. Passengers were not courted; almost they came uncalled for if they came at all. An old stage coach, mounted upon a strong frame of railway wheels, with no springs, was the only accommodation conceded. The distinction of outside and inside passengers was retained. Road stations were unknown, for the coach conveniently stopped where you would.

"The coach had no springs of any kind, and yet the motion was *fully as easy as in any coach on the road.* A very slight jolt is felt, accompanied with a click or rattle, every time the wheels pass over the joints of the several rails and also at the breaks which occur at the different passing places, and then, if anything, *feel harsher than in a coach.* . . . At any bends of the road, or other places where the view is obstructed, the coachman blows a horn to give warning of his approach, to any waggons or vehicles that may be coming or going on the way. . . . Some parts of the way were laid with rails of cast-iron, joined at every four feet, and in coming upon these, the jerks and jolts were more frequent, more audible, and more sensible, resembling exactly, as the coachman justly observed to us, the clinking of a mill hopper." The journey from Darlington to Stockton occupied about an hour and a quarter.

The processional engine mentioned above, the first employed on a public railway, and the first employed for the transport of passengers, is, I believe, in existence still.

In 1846, it was brought out to head the procession at the opening of the Middlesbrough and Redcar Railway. I have myself seen another of Stephenson's early engines (1826, I was told was its date) in active and ordinary employment on the Springwell and Jarrow colliery line,* an ugly square and comical object enough; and I understood that a still more ancient engine was in use on the same line.

All kinds of rails and chairs have been used on this line; and some very antiquated specimens may yet be seen in use upon some of the sidings or branches where the traffic is not great. The original rails were for a few miles of cast iron, in lengths of about 4 to 5 feet, weighing 56 lbs. per yard. The remainder were of malleable iron, of the fish-belly pattern, or Birkinshaw's patent, made at Bedlington, and costing £12 10s. per ton. They weighed 28 lbs. per yard. Those now in use weigh 75 lbs., and cost £5 10s. per ton. On the York and Berwick and other new lines 80 lb. rails are becoming general.

On 27 Oct., 1829, the Croft branch was opened with an interesting procession. It consisted of numerous coaches, each drawn by one horse, crowded with from 30 to 50 passengers, and supplied with banners. These were followed by a train of waggons, laden with coals from every different mine, for the supply of the North Riding. The company gave a cold collation at the Croft Spa Hotel. Mr. Mewburn, their solicitor, was in the chair, and in one of his speeches on the occasion he ventured to prophesy that in a few years a railway would be made from Darlington to London, and so quick would be the travelling that passengers would leave the former place in the morning, arrive in London in time to go to the opera, and return home next day! This prophecy was received with shouts of laughter.

On May 1, 1830, the Haggar Leazes branch was opened. It extended from West Auckland to Cockfield Fell, and thence in the direction of Butterknowl Colliery, in all a distance of five miles, and was finally completed and opened for full traffic on Oct. 30 following.

On Jan. 1, 1831, a suspension bridge, erected by Captain Brown, R.N., over the Tees

* It conveyed the members of the Archæological Institute from Jarrow, in August, 1852.

at Stockton, was cómpleted for the passage of the railway. Great things were anticipated from this unfortunate bridge, but where completed it was found not to be strong enough even for twenty waggons, the number then stipulated for. The first trial was made with sixteen, upon which the bridge gave way ; *i. e.* as the sixteen carriages advanced upon the platform, the latter, yielding at first to their weight, became elevated in the middle, so as by degrees to form an apex, which was no sooner surmounted by half the number than the couplings broke asunder, and eight carriages rolled one way, and eight another—the one set onward on their way, and the other back again. In consequence of this misadventure, the co struction was necessarily altered, the platform remaining suspended as before, but being fortified underneath by four starlings, upon which it was supported.* The bridge then received an indefinite number of waggons. It was 274 feet long, 25 broad, and 60 high.

The truth was, that the same parties who took the warmest interest in the line had founded a new capital of the port of Tees. Its history belongs to Cleveland, but must be briefly glanced at here. The far sighted Friends found that Stockton like Newcastle was more suitable for the trade of ancient days — when ships were multitudinous at York!—than it was for their purposes; that the water was deeper, and the facilities for shipping was better lower down the river, at a decayed vill of some three or four farm-houses. They had vast facilities of diverting trade to the new town, therefore the proprietorship of the site must be profitable; and Stockton should not complain, as it had not been an export place for coals. Accordingly in 1829, a company purchased the Middleburgh (or as, from some unaccountable and tasteless whim, it was now written, Middle*s*brough) Estate, some 500 acres. In 1830, coal was first shipped from Middlesbrough. An immense entire coal, weighing upwards of two tons, was sent down by the railway from the Black Boy Colliery, calculated when broken to make two London chaldrons.

Middlesbrough of course prospered. Building sites sold from 20s. to 30s. the square yard. The coals were shipped by staithes, or drops, which were a great attraction to the curious. The waggons were lifted on a platform 20 feet high, and lowered to the ship's deck.† A commodious dock succeeded this arrangement in 1842, contain-

* Head's Home Tour, 1836.

† See Head's Home Tour for a full account.

ing an area of nine acres. A branch railway terminates in ten threefold lines leading to ten drops on the dock. The triangle covered by these diverging lines affords standing room for 3,000 loaded waggons, or more than 9,000 tons of coal.

The old farm-house in the town lasted long after its solitude had departed. When it was pulled down, the walls of the desecrated chapel of the ancient vill were discovered. It was in the perpendicular style (I annex a drawing of one of the windows) ; earlier mouldings were however tossing about, one or two zigzagged ones carrying us to the Norman period, when Robert de Brus gave the edifice to Whitby Abbey as a cell.

From 1801 to 1841, the populatiou of Middlesbrough had risen from 25 to 5,809 ; and in 1851 amounted to about 9,000. Its permanency in importance seems fixed by the splendid discovery of surface ironstone all around it. Bolckow and Vaughan have enormous ironworks here.

While all these things were going on, the rival railway, which kept the northerly route, something on the plan of Tennant's exploded canal, had sprung up, called the Clarence Railway. The plan was unsuccessful, more from mismanagement, I am told, than from lack of good levels or line. The Company guiding it tried to rival Middlesbrough by a "Port Clarence," or more popularly and antiquely "Samphire Batts,' just opposite the creation of the Friends. It never attracted much notice or trade, and is an unsalubrious and mean place. The Clarence Railway was afterwards leased to the Stockton and Hartlepool Company, and is an important part of the route from Leeds to Ferry Hill, since the Leeds Northern Company completed their line from Leeds to Stockton.

We must now recede in the order of time and look at the changes which had taken place in the mode of giving motion to the merchandise which thus raised towns at command. We have seen the comparative slow pace of George Stephenson's early engines. Their maker knew that their speed might be accelerated, but he *dared* not do so. The people interested would not hear of it, becase they were afraid that others would consider them in the light of *demented* folk. Every one knows how Stephenson had to submit to the *suppressio veri* process in connexion with the Liverpool and Manchester railway, in order not to put a "cross on the concern." He had attained a glimmering idea of great attainable speed. "It was not, ' says he, "an easy task for me to keep the engine down to ten miles an hour ; but it must be done, and I did my best." The parliamentary committees still, however, thought him mad. The memory of the days when the enormous speed of stage coaches was blamed for the apoplexy of some of their passengers had not passed entirely away.

Although the Stockton and Darlington railway commenced with two locomotive engines, the traffic in coals soon exceeded their capabilities and a great amount of traffic was hauled by horse power.

The coal field being situated fully 320 feet above the level of the tidal river where the coals are put on board ship necessarily gives a descending line of railway, and for several miles the inclination is such that the laden waggons will run of themselves, or, more scientifically speaking, by the force of gravitation. But although the laden waggons require no power on such parts to take the coals to the place of shipment, the empty wagons must be hauled back, and, for this purpose, the horses had to trot down to be ready to begin their work, and inasmuch as the laden wagons were suffered to run down at a rate of six or eight miles an hour, heavy work-horses were soon fatigued by the down journey. Some one ingeniously suggested that it would be a great saving of horse-labour to let them ride down those portions of the line where the descending gradient was sufficient to make the waggons run without any dragging or hauling. For each horse a homely waggon, with low wheels, railed on all sides but at one end, ironically called a dandy cart, was constructed ; and although the poor brute might question why he was through coaxing and whipping made to mount himself into such a novel situation, yet such is the sagacity of the horse that the species very soon discovered that it was easier and more pleasant to ride than to walk, and in some instances became very expert in getting into the dandy carriages even when in motion, having been taught that if they did not display some alacrity in mounting that they would have to run on foot several miles. There was in 1836 an old horse employed in this "cart before the horse" fashion upon the Stockton and Darlington line. On being unhitched, he invariably first allowed the carriages to pass him, and then trotting after the train leaped on to the low dandy of his own accord ; and he performed the feat not only without urging, but on the contrary, with so much eagerness as to render it difficult to keep him off, although the carriage was two feet from the ground, and the progressive rate nearly five miles an hour. A basket of hay was suspended on the dandy, and therefore the only wonderful part of the ceremony was its performance.*

* Head's Home Tour.

In 1842 the Shildon tunnel, near Bishop Auckland, was opened with great rejoicings. Before that time the coals had been conveyed along two inclines, called the Black Boy and the Brusselton inclines. This operation was frequently found to be attended with great delay; and to be injurious likewise to the waggons and coals. To obviate these inconveniences and loss, a company projected the formation of a tunnel beneath the hilly ground on which New Shildon stands; and after making the necessary preparations, the work was commenced on the 23rd of April, 1839; twenty-one months only being occupied in its construction. It is 1,300 yards long, or nearly three quarters of a mile. Its height is 23 feet 4 inches, and its breadth 21 feet at the point whence the arch springs. The greatest depth from the surface is about 20 fathoms. The tunnel is constructed for two lines of railway; and, during its formation, was worked by seven shafts from the surface.

Another alteration was effected in 1844, by the removal of the old suspension bridge and its mass of wooden supports. A flat iron bridge on stone pillars was substituted; and, to the great amusement of the Stocktonians, some of whom regretted the loss of the picturesque failure on the suspension principle, supports of wood were speedily annexed to the new bridge, in consequence of the failure of one in a Cheshire railway on the same plan having been attended by loss of life.

The Stockton and Darlington railway had now received adjuncts in the shape of the Wear Valley railway at one end, and the Middlesbro' and Redcar railway at the other. These with the branches made the length of the line under the control of the company 90 miles, nearly 40 miles belonging to the Stockton and Darlington railway proper.*

The Company paid £8,200 per annum to the Tees Navigation Company, under a lease (dated 1845) of the tolls on the river. This they did to make the river free, as far as regarded coals shipped from their works, or by arrangement with them. The dues arising at Port Clarence consequently fell from £4,000 to about £7 per annum, the coal-owners on the north side refusing to pay the sum towards the rent that those on the south did. In 1821, when the lease was nearly expiring, the Company wished to obtain a Tees Conservancy Act, paying off the Tees Navigation Company, and taking the management of the river upon themselves. This scheme has been set aside by the Tees Navigation Company promoting a Bill of their own for a River Commission. The happy scite of Hartlepool, and the circumstance of the Leeds Northern Railway favouring both it and the port of Tees, render it the effect of all the exertions made by various parties very uncertain. Whatever may be the tendency of the coal trade, the Tees has one great element of success, the iron of Cleveland—that immense tract of surface ore which has slept unheeded for centuries, and now is revolutionizing the aboriginal society it lies among. The Middlesbrough and Guisbrough Railway will branch from the old father Stockton and Darlington, along which the ore is conveyed to the furnaces in the west part of Durham County, where the iron mines are discontinued for the more easily wrought wealth of Cleveland.

There is much room for thought in all this. I leave my readers to their own reflections. Darlington and its Friends have set in motion a vast motive power, and what shall the end be?

"From what small causes do great matters spring!"

The success of the Stockton and Darlington experiment was instantly apparent in its results—a host of similar experiments. In 1823, an anonymous pamphlet appeared in town, proposing a railway from London to Edinburgh, with branches to all the principal towns. In November, 1825, a plan was concocted at York for making a railway from Selby, *via* York to Newcastle and Sunderland, shortening the distance between the north and south limits twelve miles, and to carry goods at 3*d.* per ton, per mile, at *six* miles per hour. In 1827, some observations were published at Ripon, on the "advantages of the continuation of the Stockton and Darlington Railway from Croft Bridge to the City of York," which had been proposed in the York Herald in December, 1826.

This scheme assumed a tangible form by an Act passed in 1836, which incorporated the Great North of England Railway Company. The Company intended a thorough line from Newcastle to York, with a branch from Woodend, near Thirsk, to Leeds; and Mr. Thomas Storey, C.E., planned the route accordingly. The act enabled them to make the most difficult portion. that from Croft to Newcastle, that being surveyed first, in order to allow more time for its proper execution. It was an excellent line, passing close east of Durham, west of Chester-le-Street, and arriving at the Tyne by the course known as that of the Team Valley. The circumstance of the railway forming part of the great line of communication from London to Edinburgh, coupled with pecuniary

* The traffic on this line in 1851 is said to have been, at least, 1,500,000 tons.

motives, altered the intention of the promoters to make the north section first. They resolved to bring up the railway convenience from London to Darlington by the construction of the longer but cheaper section to the south, and an act was obtained for the line from York to Darlington. This straight and beautiful road was opened first for coal, and afterwards for passengers in 1841, and Yorkshire received the rich Auckland diamonds. The passenger train at the opening went the distance 44½ miles in little more than three hours, including rather long stoppages. Then came the halcyon days of the King's Head, where passengers arrived from London, and stayed all night at Darlington for the ordinary coaches in the morning.

The Croft branch of the Stockton and Darlington Company was partially occupied by the Great North of England Company, who purchased it.

The formation of the line from York to Darlington, comparatively facile as it was, had infringed so much on the means of the company, that they relinquished the idea of completing their line to Newcastle: and a separate body, the Newcastle and Darlington Junction Railway Company, arose for the purpose of purchasing such lines as were tolerably *en route*, and completing the chain of communication. The minutiæ of this undertaking do not enter into my jurisdiction. The line was opened in 1844, by a train arriving in Gateshead from London in 9½ hours only* (303 miles). Branches were thrown from the Great North of England line to Richmond, Bedale, and Boroughbridge. An arrangement was then entered into for the lease and eventual sale of that line to the Newcastle and Darlington Junction Company, who assumed the style first of the York and Newcastle Railway Company, and afterwards by another annexation that of the York, Newcastle, and Berwick Railway Company.†

Thus Darlington has had much to associate it with that wondrous system which threatens to annihilate time and space. The Stockton and Darlington has grown from a little line into a vast one; it commences in a mountain 1,600 feet above the level of the sea, and terminates on the sea shore. The first passenger railway coach, omnibus fashion, with a table running down the middle, "the Experiment," is succeeded by a set of far more handsome and *clean* carriages than are to be met with on the majority of more ostentatious railways. "The Active," No. 1 engine; which in a distance of four miles, in 1825, beat the road coach by 100 yards only and in 1846, at the opening of the Redcar railway, occupied 35 minutes in traversing 8 miles, although only one passenger carriage and two trucks were attached; was accompanied on the same occasion by the celebrated "A" which ran against the broad guage engine and won the day for the ancient width. The express runs the 45 miles between York and Darlington in 40 minutes! And all this springs from GEORGE STEPHENSON and THE STOCKTON AND DARLINGTON RAILWAY.

Hence traffic flowed—the flag of truce unfurled,
And, with new pinions, commerce skimmed the world,
As meteor-like her fiery engines flew,
O'erleaped the bourn or pierced the mountain through.
Let nobles fight—let monarchs war for fame,
The world resounds our great mechanic's name!
We claim for Darlington the railway meed,
She formed the nucleus, she foretold the speed
In after years, by competition gained
As science rose, and peace her palm attained.

* The ordinary expresses now do the distance in nine hours.

† Much romance is attached to the blocking up of the line from Darlington to Newcastle by snow, in Dec. 1846, but the varied fates of the trains and exploratory engines belong rather to the history of Gateshead. It may, however, be mentioned that the express train from the South being blocked at Washington, on Tuesday evening, and deserted by all the passengers, the last ones departing under the guidance of the engine-drivers at noon on Wednesday; William Donaldson, of Darlington, the guard, stayed true to his duty till Thursday afternoon, never leaving the train till it was reached by the excavators and conducted to Gateshead, thus faring the inclemency of two nights and nearly two days. The mail-bags from Newcastle to Darlington were despatched at two o'clock, on Wednesday morning, by post-chaise, and were eighteen hours on the road. An attempt by the same mode from Darlington, at eleven the same morning, failed a mile north of Aycliffe. On Thursday morning, a chaise with the mails again started at ten, and arrived in Newcastle at six in the evening. The next mails from Newcastle were sent to Carlisle, where they met the west mail going south. The principal cause of failure both in the ordinary trains and the exploratory ones was the destruction of friction. Successive layers of snow drifts are compressed by each engine, until all adhesion is destoyed, and the steam is exhausted in merely turning round the driving wheels without progress. At Washington, on stoppage, the snow gathered round the engines and soon extinguished the fires.

And now the olive's waving in the breeze,
The electric chord connects the distant seas !
Transmits its embassies as lightning flies,
With power invisible our wants supplies :
Whilst soft vibrations sweep the extensive wire,
And harmonize the world's Æolian lyre.

T. E. Abbott.

II. AGRICULTURE.

On the agriculture of this district, the multitudinous publications of the present day render unnecessary any lengthened observations. These writings, the numerous meetings of the agricultural societies, and, above all, the introduction of railways, have assimilated the practice of farming more than was formerly the case.

The soil here is various, the vallies of the Tees and Skerne consisting of very fine deep alluvial soil ; while to the eastward and running for some miles is a tract of thin clay of exceeding poverty. It is difficult to conceive how much of it can pay for cultivation. Lands of this description, and the better kinds of strong clay, are divided into farms generally of from 100 to 200 acres. That quantity is fully as much as the farmer's family, having but little external assistance, except at harvest, can manage. The farm-buildings are poor, and the tenants are too often in a similar predicament. Fallow, wheat, and oats constituted for ages the rotation ; no help being afforded by artificial manures. These, indeed, are of recent introduction, and have given a very strong impetus to agriculture ; but bones do not particularly suit undrained clays, as, in becoming pasted over, their proper decomposition is thereby prevented. Thorough draining is gradually improving the system ; but, as there is a strong and perhaps well-founded opinion that turnips cannot be cultivated with profit, the progress is comparatively slow. There is the usual controversy in the neighbourhood as to the merits of deep and shallow draining ; four feet being called deep, and two feet shallow. Deep drains at thirty feet or more apart, where the soil is of a porous nature, are generally approved ; but, on strong pasty clays, it is thought that drains two and a half feet deep, and fourteen feet or so apart, are much more effectual. It is certain that this is almost the universal view of the labourers who dig the drains ; and, when the strong chemical affinity that clay has for water is taken into account, it seems impossible to get the water off the land too fast. When all is done, it cannot be so dry as naturally dry land. If turnips are grown upon it, they cannot be fed off with sheep advantageously, for, not only is the condition of the land injured by treading, but it is too cold a bed for the animals to lie upon, and so greatly injures their progress in feeding. This very important consideration, which may make all the difference between profit and loss, seems scarcely to have received the attention it deserves. Many of these clays are of a nature which, except perhaps in the extent of their fertility, has been most accurately described by Baron Leibig:—" Finally, there are certain kinds of soil, which ought, from their chemical composition, to be very fertile ; but which, on the contrary, are sterile for many kinds of plants. Such soils are those that consist of clay mixed with a large quantity of very fine sand. Such a soil converts itself into a kind of mud after a heavy fall of rain ; and this prevents all accesses of air, and it dries without much contraction."* On the deep alluvial soils, the rotation generally commences with turnips, led off and partially consumed upon the old grass, by sheep and cattle, but mainly by cattle in stalls, loose boxes, or straw yards ; as it is not firm enough for sheep, which sink deep in wet weather. Barley or eats succeed, with seeds and spring wheat—the introduction of spring-sown wheat having taken place about one hundred and twenty years ago, and been chiefly promoted by the imposition of the malt tax. After the seeds comes winter wheat, or oats, as the case may be. This is called a four-course shift or rotation, which is varied occasionally with potatoes and beans.

* Chemistry in its Applications to Agriculture. 3rd edit. : folio 137.

The rotations on the clays are more difficult of management. A bare fallow is the usual and most effectual mode of extirpating weeds, and producing such a good mechanical state and disintegration of particles, by atmospheric exposure, as will last for four or more years, when it should again be renewed. This period may be prolonged by good drainage. Turnips are, to a small extent, cultivated with doubtful success; after which the land should be twice ploughed for oats or barley, if the condition is good, and seeds sown. These may be pastured with sheep the following summer, and sometimes to the second spring, and then fallowed for winter wheat. Green crops, as tares, &c. may be fed off in summer where the land is dry, but in no other season with advantage. On these lands lime has been for ages nearly the only manure led, and the consequence has been their gradual but certain deterioration. A better system is now beginning to prevail, and manures that accumulate, as it were, riches in the soil, are more used: whereas lime is a stimulant and exhauster, promoting good crops for a time, but in each crop making the land poorer. Lime however, as a necessary ingredient in all crops should never be wanting, and it often improves the quality, when it does not add to the quantity, of the crop.

Corn, on the good land, is sown with the drill, but the hand or broadcast sowing is almost universal on the strong soils, and is perhaps as good as any other method, where the quantity of seed used cannot be so nicely regulated as on dry land.

In the immediate neighbourhood of the town of Darlington is a great quantity of very fine old grass, which is well manured and mown for hay, and the after grass depastured. A traveller between Edinburgh and London, more than one hundred years ago, noticed, that "the land about Darlington was rich," and that "they practised a method of feeding in sheds," at that time very rare indeed; proving, in this respect, that they were rather in advance of the age than otherwise. The fame of the district must now rest upon former honours, for in a science where all are striving so assiduously for advancement, none can hope long to enjoy any peculiar pre-eminence.

There was once a very large breed of sheep, in the southern part of the County of Durham, called Tees-water sheep. They often weighed from fifty to sixty lbs. the quarter, and bore very heavy fleeces, but the improved breed of Leicesters has nearly superseded them, coming earlier to maturity, and therefore more profitable; whilst the public taste for large and intensely fat meat has sensibly declined. What are called half-bred sheep are now the fashion, being a cross between the black-faced moor sheep and the Leicester race; the pure Leicester even being deemed too large and fat, and selling for less money per lb. in the market. The Tees-water sheep may be said to be numbered with the things that were, but improved Durham short-horned cattle stand at the head of all other breeds for symmetry, beauty, and excellent qualities of feeding and milking, and supply almost entirely the large dairies of London and other towns. They will yield sometimes from twenty to thirty quarts of milk per day; they will bear to be almost constantly tied up, and eat almost any kind of food. They can be made fit for the butcher so early, as in less than two years old, and in that time have reached as far as 65 stones of 14 lbs. The breed is said to have been originally from Holland, or, if indigenous, crossed repeatedly with a Dutch stock, as well as with the Scotch cattle, but, whatever the source, they have been extremely altered by a judicious selection in breeding, and very careful attention. The Messrs. Collings were amongst the earliest and most celebrated breeders of this stock, for which they realised enormous prices; 1000 guineas being given for the bull Comet, and 2000*l.* refused by the owner for the celebrated Durham ox.* The Collings were assisted and followed by several breeders of great celebrity, and, of late years, herds have been established all over the kingdom, and great numbers have been exported,† to almost all parts of the world, at very high prices.‡

This, I think, is the proper place to introduce some lists of the local fauna and flora. Darlington, an old place of residence of the Friends, has, almost as a matter of course,

* See page 303.

† The Emersons of Eryholme, and Mr Thornton of Stapleton may especially be mentioned as chief breeders of fine cattle near Darlington at this day. The Belgian government has made large purchases at Darlington. On one occasion in 1846, Mr Thornton presented the King of Belgians with a splendid four years old ox, bred by himself. He excited much attention abroad, as many as 200 agriculturalists coming in a day to see it. When slaughtered it weighed 160 st. 10 lbs., and was presented by the king to the hospital of the aged poor people of Brussels. In 1849, a gold medal and letter was received by Mr. Thornton from his majesty as a mark of his remembrance and high satisfaction.

‡ I have to express my acknowledgments to Henry Chaytor, esq., for the very sufficient summary, in the text, on a subject I have no knowledge of myself.

had a sequence of naturalists. Stephen Robson, the second son of Thomas Robson, and Mary (formerly Hedley), his wife, of Darlington, and born 24 June, 1741, was the author of a useful British Botany. The title is "The *British Flora*, containing the select names, characters, places of growth, durations, and time of flowering, of the plants growing wild in Great Britain. To which are prefixed, the Principles of Botany, by Stephen Robson.—York, 1777." He married Ann Awmack in 1771, and had issue, Thomas Robson, living at Sunderland. His nephew, Edward Robson, the son of Thomas Robson, by his wife, Margaret (formerly Pease), was born at Darlington 17 October, 1763, married Elizabeth Dearman in 1788, and died 1813, leaving issue Dearman Robson, &c. Edward Robson was also an accomplished botanist and draughtsman. The lists of plants in Brewster's Stockton and Hutchinson's Durham are his. It would be invidious to attempt discrimination of living talent in such walks.

I have acknowledged my debts in p. xciv of the division on families. I have not a late list of rarities in the Darlington flora, but I suspect they are so sorely extirpated, by necessary improvements in the soil, that the older lists will be thought more interesting every day, as hints of what straggling survivors of the ancient stocks may be expected.

I. FAUNA.

Mammalia.

Pipistrelle Bat (common).
Reddish grey Bat (Vespertilio Nattereri).
Long-eared Bat (common).
Water Shrew.
Common Shrew.
Hedgehog.
Polecat (rare).
Stoat.
Weasel.
Fox.
Otter (now rare).
The usual *Rats* and *Mice*.
Mole.
Hare.
Rabbit.

Birds.

Eagle. An eagle alighted in the grounds at Southend some years ago.
Kestrel Hawk (common).
Sparrow Hawk (do.)
Barn Owl—bred for some years in a dove-cot in Northgate.
Brown Owl (now very rare).
Spotted Flycatcher (in summer).
Missel Thrush (common).
Song Thrush (do.).
Blackbird (do.)
Fieldfare (common in winter).
Redwing (do.)
Wheatear (occasionally seen).
Whinchat (common).
Redbreast (common).
Redstart (frequent).
Grasshopper Warbler (very rare).
Sedge Warbler (Salicaria Phragmitis—not uncommon).
Nightingale—a pair appeared many years ago at West Lodge, and were taken by a bird-catcher.
Blackcap Warbler (common).
Garden Warbler (do.)
Whitethroat (do.)
Lesser Whitethroat (not uncommon).
Yellow Willow Wren (not uncommon).
Willow Wren, Gold Crest, Greater Tit, Blue Tit, Cole Tit, Marsh Tit, Longtailed Tit, Hedge Sparrow } common.

Pied Wagtail.—Common. Very few remain here during winter.

Grey Wagtail. A few in winter. Breed in the higher parts of the county.

Yellow Wagtail.—Common in summer.

Tree Pipit.—Common.

Meadow Pipit.—Common.

Skylark.—Common.

Greater Bunting.—Common.

Blackheaded Bunting.—Common.

Yellowhammer.—Common.

Snow Bunting.—Appears in severe winters.

Common Sparrow.

Tree Sparrow.—Not uncommon.

Chaffinch.—Common.

Mountain Finch.—In severe winters often abundant.

Siskin.—Rare.

Goldfinch.—Not common.

Linnet.—Common.

Lesser Redpole.—Common.

Mealy Redpole.—Occasionally.

Hawfinch.—Very Rare.

Greenfinch.—Common.

Crossbill.—Rare.

Bullfinch.—Common.

Starling, Crow, Rook } Common.

Hooded Crow.—Only occurs so far inland in very severe weather.

Jackdaw.—Common.

Magpie. do.

Jay.—Occasionally.

Green Woodpecker.—Very rare here.

Waxen Chatterer.—A number appeared about Darlington in 1787, and fed on haws, which were plentiful that year. None have since appeared. (*Geo. Allan.* **Fox's** Synopsis, p. 204).

Wryneck.—Occasionally.

Nuthatch.—Rare.

Creeper.—Common.

Wren. do.

Cuckoo. do.

Nightjar.—Very rare here.

Swift.—Common.

Swallow, Martin, Sandmartin. } Common.

Kingfisher.—Not uncommon.

Ring Dove.—Common.

Pheasant.—Not often seen here.

Partridge.—Common.

Heron.—Not often seen.

Bittern.—Now very rare. Formerly inhabited the Four Riggs bog.

Green Sandpiper.—Rare.

Common Sandpiper.—Occasionally.

Woodcock, Snipe, Jacksnipe } Now much less common than formerly.

Water Rail.—In very severe winters.

Corn Crake, Water Hen, Peewit. } Common.

Golden Plover.—Occasionally.

Wild Duck. do.

Teal. do.

Golden Eye Duck.—Rare.

Goosander.—Formerly used to come up the Tees and Skerne.

Little Grebe.—Occasionally.

Black throated Diver.—One was got in the Skerne, near the town.

Mollusca.

Limax maximus.—Common in gardens.

  agrestis. do.

Arion ater. do.

  hortensis. do.

Vitrina pellucida.—In moist woods.

Helix aspersa.—Common in gardens.
arbustorum.—Common in hedges.
nemoralis. do. do.
hortensis. do do.
pulchella.— Rare under stones.
fulva.—Among moss.
granulata.—Grass in moist places.
hispida.—Nettles.
concinna. do.
rufescens. do.
rotundata.—Under stones.
pygmæa.—Among old leaves.
Zonites cellarius.—Outhouses.
nitidulus.—Moss in woods.
lucidus.—Moss in bogs.
crystallinus.—Among grass and leaves.
Vertigo palustris.—Moss in bogs.
Clausilia bidens.—Beech trees in woods.
rugosa.—Woods.
Zua lubrica.—Moss in woods.
Azeca tridens.— do.
Carychium minimum.—Old leaves in woods.
Succinea putris.—Grass near water.
Planorbis corneus.—In a pond near the town.
albus.—In a pond near Baydales.
marginatus.—Common in ponds.
imbricatus.—Ponds.
spirorbis.— do.
contortus.—Ditches at Polam.
Physa fontinalis.—Common in ponds.
hypnorum.—Sometimes in ponds.
Limneus auricularis.— Polam pond ; fine.
pereger.—Common in ponds and streams.
" var. lacustris.—Skerne at Polam.
stagnalis.—Ditches at Polam.
palustris.— do.
Ancylus fluviatilis.—Cockerbeck.
Cyclas corneus.—Common in ponds.
Pisidium amnicum.—Cockerbeck.
pulchellum.—Cattle ponds sometimes.
pusillum.—Ditches in bogs.
nitidum.—Cattle ponds sometimes.
obtusale.— do.
Anodon Cygneus.—In ponds and rivers, varying in size according to the locality.
var. anatina.— do.

II. FLORA.

1. *Extracted from Hutchinson's Durham. The names are partially modernized for convenience of reference.*

Hippuris vulgaris.—In the Skerne at Darlington.
Veronica scutellata.—In Hill-close-carr, near Darlington, but scarce.
Veronica montana.—In Dinsdale wood, near Darlington.
Cladium Mariscus.—In Hell Kettles, near Darlington.
Eriophorum vaginatum.—In Birch-carr, near Darlington.
Galium boreale.—Near Darlington, but scarce.
Potamogeton natans, perfoliatus, lucens, crispus, densus, compressus, gramineus, marinus. } In the Skerne, near Darlington.
Lysimachia vulgaris —By the Skerne, near Darlington, but scarce.
Samolus Valerandi.—Sparingly by the Skerne, near Darlington.
Atropa Belladonna.—Near Piersbridge.
Ribes nigrum, rubrum } By the Skerne, and the latter by the Tees in many places.
spicatum.—By the Tees, between Piersbridge and Gainford. Vide the paper and figure presented to the society.

Vinca minor.—Near Blackwell, but probably the outcast of a garden.
Smyrnium Olusatrum.—By the Tees, near Hurworth.
Parnassia palustris.—In wet places, common about Darlington.
Linum perenne.—In Baydales, near Darlington.
Drosera rotundifolia.—In Birch-carr, near Darlington.
Myosurus minimus.—Near Darlington, in one place only.
Galanthus nivalis.—On the banks of the Tees, about Blackwell and Coniscliffe, in situations which do not admit of its being the outcast of gardens.
Narcissus Pseudo-narcissus.—Near Piersbridge.
Allium oleraceum.—Baydales, near Darlington.
Ornithogalum luteum.—By the Tees, near Piersbridge.
Colchicum autumnale.—Near Darlington.
Alisma ranunculoides.—In Hill-close-carr, near Darlington.
Vaccinium Oxycoccos.—On *Gilly-gate, near Darlington.* [Durham ?]
Butomus umbellatus.—In the Skerne, near Darlington.
Pyrola rotundifolia.—In Birch-carr, near Darlington.
Chrysosplenium alternifolium.—In Baydales, near Darlington, but a rare plant.
Saponaria officinalis.—Near Croft bridge, and plentifully in the wood near Middleton-one-row.
Stellaria nemorum.—In Baydales, near Darlington.
Cistus Helianthemum.—By the roadside between Conniscliffe and Piersbridge.
Nuphar lutea.—In the Skerne, near Darlington, plentifully.
Aquilegia vulgaris.—In Baydales near Darlington.
Ranunculus Lingua.—In moist places. Hell Kettles, near Darlington.
Turritis hirsuta.—In Baydales, near Darlington.
Geranium phæum.—Near Darlington.
rotundifolium.—By hedges, about Darlington.
lucidum.—Near Darlington.
Astragalus glycyphyllos.—In Baydales near Darlington.
Senecio erucifolius.—In Baydales, near Darlington, and many other places.
Anthemis tinctoria.—Which was found by Ray in a bank near Sockburn, and considered as peculiar to this county, has of late years been frequently sought for, but without success.
[Ophrys muscifera.—In Dinsdale wood and Middleton-one-row.—S. Robson, 1777.]
Ophrys apifera.—In Baydales, near Darlington.
Serapias longifolia.—In several marshy places near Darlington.
Chara tomentosa.—In Hell Kettles.
Carex dioica. } In Polam, near Darlington.
pulicaris. }
pendula.—By the Tees, near Croft.
Salix pentandra.—In many places about Darlington.
Helix.—By the Tees, common.
repens.—Birch-carr, near Darlington.
Bryonia dioica.—By hedges about Darlington, very common.
Equisetum fluviatile.—In many places about Darlington.
Sphagnum palustre.—In bogs on heaths. Birch carr, near Darlington.
Fontinalis minor.—By the Tees near Piersbridge.
Splachnum ampullaceum.—On cow's dung; near Darlington; very rare.
Mnium palustre.—In marshes, near Darlington.
Bryum extinctorium.—On rocks and hedge banks, not common. Baydales, near Darlington.
Hypnum aduncum.—In wet places about Darlington, not unfrequent.
riparium.—On stones in the Tees near Dinsdale.
dendroides.—In a moist pasture by Rice carr, near Darlington, plentifully.
Jungermannia purpurea.—In Birch carr, near Darlington.
Lichen Parellus.—On stones near Walworth.
Agaricus ostreatus (Curtis).—On decayed ash; frequent about Darlington.
lateralis (Huds). } On decayed stumps of trees, but rare. In Baydales, near
pectinatus (Huds). } Darlington.
substrictus (Bolton).—Near Darlington, but very rare.
suberosus (Bolt. 162).—Common on willows about Darlington; has a sweet smell. I suspect it to be the *Boletus suaveolens*, LINN.
confragosus (Bolt. 160).—On some willows near Darlington.
Peziza coccinea (Bolt. 104).—On rotten sticks in woods. In Baydales, near Darlington.
Clavaria muscoides.—In Baydales wood, near Darlington.
Lycoperdon stellatum.—On a hedgeback near Darlington.*
Sphæria fraxinea (Huds). S. concentrica (Bolt.).—On decayed stumps of ash; near Darlington, but scarce.

"The author was indebted to the ingenious Mr. Edward Robson, of Darlington, for permission to publish this list, he having presented it to the Darlington society, established 'For promoting the study of General and Natural History, Antiquities, &c.' "

* There is a drawing of a very curious and square fungus, probably the Lycoperdon stellatum of Linnæus, or the L. fornicatum of Hudson, which grew within a quarter of a mile of Darlington, in the Gent. Mag. for Feb., 1792, furnished by E. R[obson.]

2. *Additions observed about* 30 *years ago.* (*J. B.*)

Thalictrum majus.—Near Low Coniscliffe.
Trollius europæus.—Bartrams Bottoms, by the Skerne.
Turritis glabra.—Between High Coniscliffe and Gainford.
Hypericum Androsæmum.—Near Middleton-one-Row.
Linum perenne.—Baydales.
Rhamnus catharticus.—Lowson's Slack, &c.
Rosa Sabini —Baydales.*
Ribes rubrum, *b*, petræum.—Baydale Beck.
Chrysosplenium alternifolium.—Monkend Wood.
Campanula latifolia.—Blackwell.
Pyrola rotundifolia.—Birch Car, near Middleton-one-Row, and Halnaby.
Pulmonaria officinalis.—Cliffe Wood. Probably an outcast from the garden.
Myosotis sylvatica.—Baydales.
Myosotis collina.—Darlington. On dry hedge banks.
Primula farinosa.—Cockerbeck.
Lysimachia vulgaris? This plant possibly L. punctata. By the Skerne above the Stockton and Darlington Station.†
Samolus Valerandi.—Baydales.
Paris quadrifolia.—Monkend Wood.
Ruscus aculeatus.—Cockerton, on the West Auckland Road.
Schœnus nigricans.—Birch Car.
Blysmus compressus.—Tees Side.

* The plant figured as Rosa villosa in Sowerby's English Botany was from a bush of R. Sabini in Baydales, and the fruit figured along with the rose was from a garden plant of Rosa pomifera; so little were Rosæ understood at that time.

† In the herbarium of the late Wm. Backhouse, esq., both species occur from the locality, the L. punctata with the date 1803; and in Winch's Flora (in the Trans. Nat. Hist. Soc. NC., 1802) the place is described by Mr. B. as both above and below the railway bridge. The specimens gathered there subsequently by Mr. Ward are pronounced by Mr. Winch as starved examples of L. vulgaris. A specimen having been sent of L. vulgaris, as supposed, from Mr. Sewell's grounds in Heaton Dene near Newcastle, to Mr. Watson, by Mr. John Storey, of Newcastle, and turning out to belong to L. punctata, it is hinted in Watson's Cybele Britannica, 1852, that both species may exist in the same habitat. Mr. Storey informs me that he has since, on Aug. 10th, 1852, found both species in Heaton Dene intermingled, the rarer L. punctata being the more plentiful, and in full flower, whilst the flowers of L. vulgaris were not generally expanded.

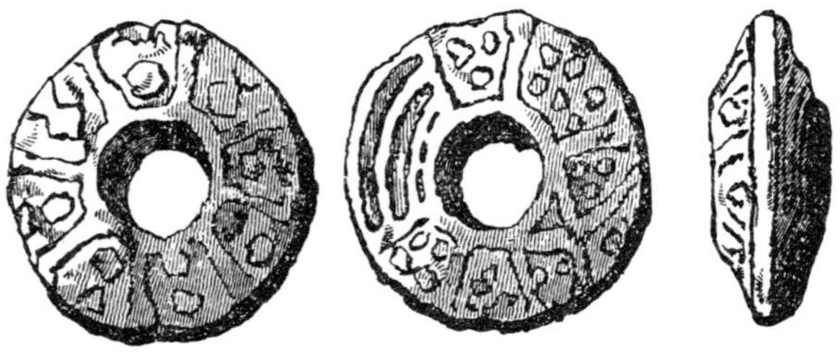

[*Circle of Lead found near Blackwell Hall. See p.* 336.]

TABULAR PEDIGREES,

TO ILLUSTRATE

DIVISION VI.

Royal Descent of the Lords of Blackwell Freehold Manor.

Margaret, daur. of Philip III., king of France, 'the Hardy,' m. 1299. *2nd wife.* = Edward I., king of England, b. 1239, d 1307. = Eleanor, daur. of Ferdinand, king of Castile and Leon, d. 1290. *1st wife.*

Thomas Plantagenet, eldest son of the second marriage, 'de Brotherton,' earl of Norfolk, created earl-marshall of England, 1385-6. = Alice, dr. of sir Roger Halys, kt., of Harwich.

Lady Margaret Plantagenet, eventually sole heiress, created duchess of Norfolk, d. 1399. = John, lord Segrav d. 1353.

Elizabeth, d. and h. A charge against Norfolk and Surrey, her descendants in Henry VIII.'s time, was that they placed the royal arms in their first quarter, *without due difference of their ancestry.* The charge was well founded. Several letters of Norfolk remain, sealed with the three lions passant. The charge about wearing Edward the Confessor's arms was also for not differencing them.—*See State Papers*, i. 891. = John, lord Mowbray, of Axholme d. 1360. The badges of his family were lions and mulberry trees the ancient name being Molbray.

Hugh, 2nd earl of Stafford, K. G. 1386. = Lady Philippa Beauchamp, dr. of Thomas 3rd earl of Warwick, K.G.

"That brave and god-like brood of Beauchamps, which so long
Them earls of Warwick held; so hardy, great, and strong,
That after of that name it to an adage grew,
If any man himself adventurous happ'd to shew,
Bold Beauchamp men him termed, if none so bold as he.
With those our Beauchamps may our Bourchers reckoned be."

Drayton.

Princess Joan Plantagenet, 'd'Acre,' d. 1307. = Gilbert Clare, 3rd earl of Gloucester, and 7th of Hereford, d. 1295. *1st husband.*

Lady Margaret, countess of Gloucester, dr. and coh. = Hugh, lord Audley, d. 1347.

Lady Margaret, d. and h. = Ralph, 1st earl of Stafford, K.G., d. 1372.

John, Lord Neville of Raby, K G., filled the highest offices of the State, died 1389, *seised of a mess. and 9 acr.* at *Blackwell, by fealty only*, bur. in Durham abbey. (*Arms*, Gules, a saltire argent. The seal given above apparently belongs to Geoffrey Neville, temp. Hen. III., who retained his paternal arms of Fitz-Meldred, but assumed the name of his mother, Isabel, the heiress of Neville. Mr. Surtees sent the drawing in 1827 to R. H. Allan, esq., as being unpublished.) = Maude, daur. of Henry, lord Percy, br. in Durham abbey. *1st wife.*

'The name of PERCIES and NEVILLES have long been honourable and well-beloved.'—*Thomas Norton's Address to the Northern Rebels in* 1569, *deterring them from the Rising.*

Edward II., king of England; murdered 1327. = Isabel, 'She-wolf of France,' dr. of Philip, king of France.

Edward III., king of England, d. 1371. = Philippa, dr. of William, earl Hainault.

*** "I am informed the said sir William Gascoigne doth intend to bear my lord of Westmerlande's armys, pretending title to the earldom of Westmerland. If he so do, it will turn to great business amongst ourselves; for the other will not suffer him so to do; nor no more will none other do, that were able to resist the same; nor, as I believe, he ought not to bear them, considering that my lord of Westmerland and his father, grant father, and many others, *hath enjoyed the land without interruption;* and no man may bear the armys of his antecessors without difference, *unless he be possessed of the inheritance.* I beseech your grace to speak with the heralds in this matter, and to write unto sir William Gascoigne for the reformation therein; that I have no business to do therein, when it shall be time to look upon our enemies. He hath, or now attempted to have borne the armys, but, the earl of Westmerlande's father not being content with the same, he hath laid down the same."

Surrey to Wolsey from Newcastell, 3 *Oct.* 1523.—*State Papers*, iv. 43.

The Gascoignes were certainly entitled to the whole arms, if heirship general of blood were the criterion; but lights are continually breaking in upon the influence of property on heraldic right.

John of Gaunt, 3rd son, duke of Lancaster, king of Castile and Leon, K.G., d. 1399. = Catherine, d. of Le Payn Roet, and relict of sir Otho de Swinford, kt. d. 1403.

Lionel Plantagenet, 2nd son of Antwerp, duke of Clarence, earl of Ulster, etc., K. G., 2nd don, d. 1368. = Elizabeth de Burgh, dr. and h. of William earl of Ulster, by Maude Plantagenet, granddr. of Edmund, earl of Lancaster, 2d son of k. Henry III. *1st wife*, m. 1352, d. 1363.

Lady Philippa Plantagenet, only child and heiress, born 1355. = Edmund Mortimer, earl of March, d. 1381, lineally derived from the marriage of Ralph Lord Mortimer of Wigmore, with the Princess Gwyladys, dr. of Llewelyn ap Jorwerth, prince of North Wales, by the daughter of king John.

No. ii.—Allan of Allan's Flatts, etc.

George Allan, of Yarm, esq., bur. 1674 = ... Clifton.

George Allan, esq., of Blackwell Grange. *See* No. 1.

Thomas Allan, 'lord Newark,' eldest son, bap. at Yarm, 5 Feb. 1651, of Newcastle, 1698, engaged as a coal-owner and vender; by which as *unfree* of the Hostmen's company, he excited the wrath of that fraternity, and more than once had his coals seized by them under the strict and absurd laws of the time, the seizors obtaining part of the spoil. In 1702 and 1703, he was in partnership with Colville as a large trafficker in cattle, and the latter (who probably in his freedom also *coloured* his connection's *coals*) was fined for his audacity in cotrading with a foreigner against the privileges of the 'Free Butchers and Hostmen.' However, in spite of the brethren, Allan raised an immense fortune out of cattle and collieries, and of later years was squire of Allan's Flatts, a seat near Chester-le-Street, where he was bur. 6 May, 1717. = Susanna, daur. of ...... Bailey, bur. at Chester-le-Street 5 May, 1716.

Adam Colville, of Boldon, co. pal., gent. = ...

1*st*. Anne Ladler, m. 25 June, 1682, br. 14 Oct. 1686. She had only two children by her husband 1. Anthony, bap. 1 July, 1683, bur. 19 Apr. 1685. 2. Anne, bap. 22 Mar., bur. 16 Dec. 1684. = Edward Colville, of Newcastle-upon-Tyne, butcher and hostman, who realized what was then thought a large fortune, and retired to Whitehouse, on Gateshead Fell, in comfortable squirearchy; d. 13 June, 1750, *aged* 105; br. in All Saints' church, Newc: in the burial place belonging the family. N.B. Colville's chare leads from the Butcher-bank to the Quayside, Newc: The family had it appears, property there. = 2*nd*. Sarah, daur of .... br. 25 June 1713.

I. John Allan, d. unmar.

II. George Allan, d. at Worcester 5 Oct. 1729, and bur. there. = Anna Lambert.

I. Thomas Allan, d. inf.
II. Lionel, died young.
1. Anne, mar. William Hicks, surgeon of Chatham Hospital, by whom an only son, George Hicks, esq., M.D., of Stable-yard, St James.
2. Catherine, m. Rd. Pidgeon.
3. Susanna, died unmarried at Greenwich, 13 Sep. 1781
4. Rachael, d. unm. at Greenw.
5. Caroline, mar. John Dumarsque, captain, R.N., and d. s. p. 13 Feb. 1783.

IV. Thomas Allan, of Allan's Flatts, esq. (*secundus*), a grand juror 1725, and a justice of the peace for the county of Durham; admitted free as hostman of Newcastle 1704-5, and like his father, one of the principal coa'owners on the Wear; died 21, bur. 26 Dec. 1740, aged 52, in a vault near the pulpit in Chester-le-Street church. On the death of his only son in 1745, his widow and daughters succeeded to his estates and collieries. = Margaret, dr. of ...... Hardwick, d. 19 Nov. 1752, aged 62, buried in Chester-le-Street church, near her husband. In the vend of coals on the river Wear for the half-year ending December, 1747, 'Mrs. Allan and daughters'' collieries produced 16,018 chaldrons; John Tempest, esq., 10,359; Henry Lambton, esq., 8,937; and sir Richard Hylton, bart., and Ralph Milbank, esq., 8,622 chaldrons. These, in addition to some smaller collieries, made the entire vend amount to 76,884 chaldrons; whilst that for the half-year ending December, 1847, amounted to the enormous quantity of 611,752½ chaldrons: a wonderful increase indeed in little more than one hundred years.

III. Lionel Allan, an eminent merchant at Rotterdam, died there. = 2. Susanna Colville, bap. 21 Dec. 1690; died at Rotterdam 11 Jan. 1783, ag. 92, having outlived her husband, ten brothers and sisters, and buried ten children.

I. Edward, bap. 30 July, 1700, bur. Aug. 4, 1703.
II. Robert, bap. 17 April, 1705.
III. John Colville, bap 20 July, 1708, sometime of West Boldon, esq., and afterwards of Whitehouse; a grand juror for the county of Durham 1746; d. s. p. 31 Oct. 1781, aged 73, M. I. Boldon (Charles Allan, son and heir of Lionel Allan, Charles 3rd earl of Tankerville, and Jacob Pearson, son of Roger Pearson, being his heirs-at-law.) He married Joan, daughter of William Fawcett, of West Bolden, gent., and left her his estate in fee. She died 20 Feb. 1785, aged 74, M.I. Boldon.
1. Elizabeth, bap. 20 Jan. 1688-9.
3. Ann, bap. 2 May, 1693; m 6 July, 1710, to Wm. Hanby, of Newcastle.
4. Sarah, bap. with Ann.
5. Rosamond, bap. 14 Nov. 1695, mar. Roger Pearson, of Tritlington, co. North'd, esq.
6. Camilla Colville, bap. 8 Mar. 1697-8, sometime lady of the bedchamber to queen Caroline, ma: Charlet Bennet, 2nd earl of Tankerville, who died 14 March, 1753, of an apoplectic fit, at the Green Man, on Epping Forest, as he was travelling to London. She died 8 Oct. 1775, aged 77.
7. Catherine, bap. 11 December, 1701.
8. Jane, bap. 2 March, 1702-3; by will, 26 March. 1746, names sisters Susanna and Rosamond and their husbands, as then living; married 1*st*. Charles Clarke, junior, of Gray's Inn, attorney-at-law; 2*nd*. Robert Fenwick, of Lemington, co. Northumberland, esq., but d.s p.

Thomas Allan, of Allan's Flatts, esq. (*tertius et ultimus*), one of the principal coal-owners on the Wear, bap. at Chester-le-Street 20 Sep. 1719, d. at Durham, and bur. at Chester-le-Street 5 May, 1745. Will dated 29 April previous, and proved at Durham.

1. Susannah, coheiress of her brother, mar. at St. Oswald's, Durham, 10 Dec. 1751, to Ralph Jennison, of Walworth Castle, co. pal. esq.; M.P. for Northumberland 1722-27-34, and Master of the Stag-hounds to George II. She had an only son, Ralph Jennison, who d. inf., and d. 10 April, 1782, bur. in Chester-le-Street church.
2. Margaret, 'Miss Peggy Allan,' coh.; mar. 24 Nov. 1750, to Jennison Shafto, of Wratting Park, co. Cambridge, esq., M.P. for Leominster, 1750; and d.s.p. 20 March, 1766, bur. at St. George's, Hanover-square, co. Middlesex.
3. Dorothy, 'Miss Dolly Allan,' coh., mar. to James Garland, of Michael Stow Hall, co. Essex, esq.
4. Camilla, coh. to her brother (portion 20,000*l*), bap. at Chester-le-Street, 30 Sep. 1728; mar. at St. Oswald's, Durham, 14 April, 1752, to Robert Shafto, of Benwell, North'd, and of Wratting Park, Camb., esq.; high sheriff for North'd 1754. She was bur. at St. John's, Newc: 19 July, 1782, leaving a dau. Camilla, h. to her brother, who married Hugh *alias* William Adair, esq., father of the present sir Robert Shafto Adair, bart., at St John's, Newcastle, 23 Sept. 1784.

*** These dates scarcely bear out the remark of George Allan, esq., M.P., in *Nichols' Literary Anecdotes*—"Those ladies (the *five* daughters of Thomas Allan, *secundus*), considering themselves to be old maids, the youngest being then 45 [in reality 23], they adopted my father as their heir, and for some years he resided with them during his vacations from school. They, however, changed their minds afterwards, and married into the families of Shafto and Jennison, and the whole of the property was divided and dissipated in horse-racing." I have only accounted for *four* daughters, but who was the '*Miss Allan, of Allan's Flatts*,' buried at Chester-le-Street, in the midst of bridal preparations, 24 Feb. 1752.

Mr. Jennison Shafto performed one of the most extraordinary feats reported in the sporting annals, namely, that of riding 100 miles a day on Newmarket heath for 29 successive days. The match was, that he should be provided with a fresh horse every day, and ride that same horse one hundred miles. On the fifteenth day a horse named Quidnunc, which he had mounted, tired at the end of the sixtieth mile; he then got upon a black mare, belonging to Mr. Major, and rode her one hundred miles—making one hundred and sixty miles the same day. The same mare he rode on three several days during the performance. The whole distance ridden by him in twenty-nine successive days was 2,960 miles.

II. Charles Allan, of Rotterdam, afterwards of Norwich city, esq., joined in the Stannington tithe conveyance, 1775, living 1783. = Hannah, dr. of ...... Brown.

I. John Allan, d. s. p., killed by a fall from his horse.
1. Sarah, mar. Wm. Rogers, and d. 1781; in 1775, described as a widow, and a party with her aunt the countess of Tankerville, and several others to a deed of conveyance of tithes at Stannington, North'd. sold to Mathew White Ridley, esq., of Blagdon.
2. ...., m. Mr. .... Davison, of Red Lion-square
Other issue.

1. Susannah Allan, dr. and coh., m to Mr. Littledale. 2. ...... dr. and coh., m. to Mr. Jarkas, of Holland.

Issue of George Allan and Ann Nicholson.

I. George Allan, of Blackwell Grange, esq., M.A., F.S.A.; M.P. for Durham city 1813; a deputy lieutenant for the co. of Durham, and foreman of the grand jury of the county 1815; succeeded to the entailed estates; b. 8, bp. 31 July, 1767; d. s. p. at St. Omers, in France, 21 July, bur in the Grange vault 13 Aug. 1828. Will dated 4 Feb. 1815, codicil 27 May 1822. Portraits at Blackwell Grange and Blackwell Hall. He mar. Prudence, daur. of Wm. Williams, gent., in Sept. 1796. She gave 50*l.* for a bell for Trinity church, Darlington, and d. 31 Mar. 1844.

II. James, bp. 22 Feb. 1772; capt. in 29 Reg. Foot; d. in the isle of Grenada 28 May, 1795, unm. ag. 23, of the yellow fever, at the point of obtaining at that early period the rank of major.

1. Anne, bp. 24 June, 1768; bur. 24 Mar. 1797, in the Grange vault; m. 4 Sep. 1786, to John Wright, esq., of Bolton-on-Swale, Yorkshire, captain in lord Darlington's Princess of Wales' Dragoons. They had issue, I. James Allan Wright, of Darlington, a captain in the Durham Militia, d. unm. 4, bur. 8 Jan. 1834, in the Grange vault, ag. 44; II. John Allan Wright, a lieutenant, R N., died unm. 29 Apr. 1844, ag. 51, bur. in the Grange vault: 1. Ann, m. William Jones, of Cambridge, and had issue: 2. Elizabeth, d. 14, bur. 18 Oct. 1795, in the Grange vault: 3. Catherine.

2. Elizabeth, bp. 15 June, 1769, d. 24 Nov. 1794, ag. 24, bur. in the Grange vault; m. Nov. 1791, to Seymour Hodgson, of Richmond, Yorkshire. They had a son and a daughter, who both died unmarried.

3. Hannah, bp. 28 Nov. 1770, d. inf.

4. Dorothy, d. unm. at Blackwell Grange, 18 Sep. 1821, bur. in Grange vault.

Issue of Robert Allan and Eliz. Harrison.

I. Robert Allan, of Newbottle, co. pal., esq., first remainder man in tail under Miss Ann Allan's will to the Allan or Grange estates, b. 10 Apr., bp. at Stockton-upon-Tees, 7 June, 1769; died 27 Dec. 1813, bur. in Bishop-Wearmouth church 2 Jan. 1814, ag. 44. In 1811 he joined his cousin, George Allan, esq., in suffering recoveries of the entailed estates; and after the same were made chargeable with the sum of 83,000*l.* as portions for younger children, and for other purposes, he resettled the same upon his eldest son, William Allan, for life, with divers remainders over. Will dated 15 Feb. 1809, codicil 4 May, 1812, republished 2 and 22 June, *id. ann.* proved at Canterbury 13 May, 1814, by John Allan and George Allan, esqs. Under the above arrangement, the manor of Nether otherwise Low Worsall, was sold to E. G. Waldy, of Barmpton, co. pal., esq.; the manor of Appleton-upon-Wiske to Benjamin Dunn, of Hurworth, esq., who resold it to R. H. Allan, esq., in 1847; and divers lands and burgages in and about Darlington, to various parties.

= Hannah, daur. of Wm. Havelock, of Sunderland-near-the-Sea, esq., and sister to Wm. Havelock, of Ingress Park, co. Kent. (father of the late lamented lieutenant-colonel William Havelock, K.H., of the 14th Light Dragoons, who bravely fell in battle 1848; and of lieutenant-colonel Henry Havelock, C. B., deputy adjt.-general of the Queen's forces at Bombay, the author of a *Hist. of the Burmese War*, and of a *Hist. of the War in Affghanistan in* 1838-9); bp. 9 Feb. 1767; m. 20 Dec. 1792; d. 9, bur. in Bishop-Wearmouth church 14 Jan. 1837, ag. 70. Will dated 10 May, codicil 8 June, 1833, proved at Durham 15 Mar. 1837, by John Allan, of Blackwell, esq.

II. John Allan, of Blackwell Hall and Barton, esq., M.A., J.P. for co. Durham and Yks. N.R., nominated for high sheriff co. Durham (*Gazette*, 13 Nov. 1843;) bn. 29 Aug. 1778; d. in London 4, bur 9 Sept. 1844, in the Grange vault, ag. 66. Devised his estates to his nephew, Robert Henry Allan, esq. Will dated 17 Aug. 1841, codicil 7 Oct. 1843, pr. at York 15 Oct. and at Cant. 18 Dec. 1844, by R. H. Allan, sole executor.

III. James, } d. inf.
IV. Sober, }

1. Elizabeth, b. 19 Dec. 1770, m. to John Maling, of Hylton, co. pal., esq. (cousin to admiral Maling), d.s.p. 5 Oct. 1810, bur. in Bishop-Wearmouth ch.

2. Ann, b. 5 Nov. 1772, d. unm. 30 May, 1807, br. in in Bishop-Wearmouth church.

3. Catherine, b. 17 Nov. 1776, d. unmar. 13 May, 1796, bur. in Bishop-Wearmouth church.

4. Mary, b. 27 Oct. 1782; m. 13 June, 1802, to John Henry Johnson, capt. in North York Militia, (son of Owen Johnson, of Waterford), who died 1 Aug. 1825, and had an only son, Henry Robert Allan Johnson, b. 25 Mar. 1803, named in the will of John Allan, esq., of Blackwell Hall.

II. William Allan, of Blackwell Grange, esq., eldest surviving son and heir, a J. P. for the county of Durham, b. 21 May, 1796, and bp. at Bishop-Wearmouth 17 June following; succeeded, as heir-at-law to his brother John, to a moiety of the manor or lordship of Dalton-upon-Tees, purchased by George Allan, esq., in 1710, and is tenant for life of an estate called Stressholmes, tsp. Blackwell, under the will of his uncle, John Allan, of Blackwell, esq., living unmarried 1851.

III. Robert Henry Allan, of Blackwell Hall and Barton, esq. F.S.A. lord of the manors of Appleton-upon-Wiske, Barton Grange, Wandesford otherwise Wilkinson's manor, and Ward's formerly Ingleby's manor, co. York; and owner of estates called Blackwell, Polam Hill Farm, Far Howdens, the Baydales, (Blackwell manor, formerly the Nevilles',) Nordykes, Hill Top Farm, and Nessfield, co. Durham; b. 22 Jan., bap. 10 Feb. 1802, at Bp.-Wearmouth; a justice of the peace for co. of Durham and co. York, N.R. High sheriff co. Durham 1851.

= Elizabeth, dr. of John Gregson, of Durham city, and Burdon, co. pal., esq., by Elizabeth his wife, daughter and heiress of Lancelot Allgood, esq.; mar. 14 July 1841, at Bishop-Wearmouth.

Robert Killinghall Allan, b. 25 Dec. 1842; d. 25, bur. 28 Sep. 1843, in Bishop-Wearmouth church.

6. Caroline Jane, mar. 28 Sep. 1831. She married 2ndly on the 23 Oct. 1845 John Murray, esquire (whose first wife was Caroline Jemima, dr. of sir Jno. Leslie, bart.) & d. in London 30 Nov., being bur. 8 Dec. 1849, ag 37, in Bish.-Wearmouth ch. next her 1st husband

= William Hunter Burne, esq., a capt. in the Durham militia [grandson of Charles Burne, of Sunderland-near-the-Sea, by Philadelphia, dr. and coh. of Tho. Lambton, of Hardwick, co. pal. esq., great-grandson of sir William Lambton, knt. slain at Marston Moor 2 July 1664, and ancestor of the present earl of Durham.] He was sometime owner *(jure uxoris)* of lands in Northgate, Darlington, and of Bowlby's Lands [on which Pierremont stands]; d. 8, bur. 15 July, 1844, in Bishop-Wearmouth church.

Freville Lambton Burne, bn. 20 Dec. 1835.

Caroline Jane Burne, d. 10 Oct. 1837, bur. in Bishop-Wearmouth church.

I. James Allan, b. 16 Oct. 1793; d. 22 April, 1794, bur. in Bishop-Wearmouth church.

IV. John Allan, of Dalton-upon-Tees, Yorkshire, esq., b. 25 June, 1803; mar. Elizabeth, daur. of Mr. Jeffries; d. s. p. Dalton, 18, bur. in Bishop-Wearmouth church, 25 March, 1844, aged 40.

V. George Thomas Allan, esq., owner of estates at Eryholme, Yorkshire, and a deputy-lieutenant for the county of Durham; bn. 11, Oct. 1804; mar. at Brampton, Cumberland, 11 Oct. 1843, to Maria, dau. of the Rev. Thomas Ramshay, vicar of Brampton.

VI. James Allan, b. 2 Dec. 1807; d. 26 Mar., bur. in Bishop-wearmouth church 2 Apr. 1833, unm. Will dated 24 Mar. 1833. Letters of administration with the will annexed, granted at York to George Thomas Allan, 21 Jan. 1836.

1. Elizabeth Ann, mar. 21 May, 1832, to Benjamin Dunn, of Hurworth, co. pal., esq.

2. Catherine Mary, d. 18 June, 1799, bur. in Bishop-Wearmouth ch.

3. Ann Allan, of Harewood Grove, Darlington, the owner of Hill Close House estate, tsp. Darlington, purchased by George Allan, esq., of Robert Richardson, gent., in 1725.

4. Joanna Mary, m. at Bishop-Wearmouth 22 Sep. 1836, to Edw. Haygarth Maling, of that place. esq. They have one son and one daughter.

5. Mary Emma, m. 10 July, 1837, to Wm. Wheatley, esq., of London. He died 30 Sep. 1850, s.p.

5 Aug. 1753. The pall was supported by the duke of Cleveland, lord Barnard, the hon. Thos. Vane, Capt. Edw. Milbanke, Mr. Carr, Mr. Bendlowes, Mr. Bland, and Mr. Whitley, who all were to have rings. The corpse was to be taken out of the hearse at the town end, and all persons had glasses of white and red wine as usual.—*Funeral Papers*. Portrait at Grange.

of Blackwell, esq. (*See* No. III.) bp. 13 Feb. 1692, married 13 Aug. 1717, and bur. 11 June, 1731.

Yarm, bur. at Middleton St. George; will dated 23 Dec. 1741, appoints his 'father, George Allan, esq., executor.') They had issue John Killinghall, of Middleton St. George, esq., bp. 27 Feb. 1726-7, d. 20 and bur. 23 June, 1762, when the ancient and wealthy family of Killinghall became extinct (*See* No. IV.) He devised to his aunt, Hannah Eden (late Hannah Allan), his sole executrix, the manors or lordships of Barton-Grange, Wandesford otherwise Wilkinson's manor, and Ward's, formerly Ingleby's manor, both at Barton, by will dated 19 June, 1762. There are portraits of Mr. and Mrs. Killinghall and their son John at Grange.

2. Dorothy, bp. 29 Nov. 1693, bur. 18 Feb. 1694-5, in the church, her *liare stall* costing 1*s*. 8*d*.

3. Ann bp. 18 Nov. 1696, d. unm., br. 16 Nov. 1737. Portrait at Grange.

4. Hannah, bp. 14 Sep. 1698, mar. 13 Dec. 1743, to Farrow Eden, of Darlington, gent, steward of the borough court 1721, deputy steward of same 1733, under Cha. Moor, esq., who was bur. 21 Feb. 1744-5. She was lady of the two manors at Barton, devised to her by her nephew John Killinghall; will dated 12 Sep. 1778, pr. at York 20 Mar. 1779, by her niece Ann Allan, sole executrix; bur. 23 Dec. 1778, in the nave of Darlington church, where are brasses inscribed 'Hannah Eden, died 15 Dec. 1778, æt 80,' 'Farrow Eden, died 18 Feb. 1744.' Her funeral expenses were 486*l*. 2*s*. 6*d*., including 85*l*. 6*s*. 9*d*. 'distributed as a dole to the poor at Darlington,' 16*s*. 6*d*. 'to Quakers' poor, who refused to receive it publickly,' and 2*s*. to 'Christopher Watson, for *paving* near Mr. Holmes,' where dole given.' Pall-bearers, Mr. Vane, sir John, Eden, col. Milbanke, Mr. Arderne, Mr. Alexander, Mr. Neasham, Mr. Robinson, and Mr. Raisbeck, who, with thirty-four other persons, were presented with rings.—(*Funeral Papers*.) Portrait at Grange.

Ward's, formerly Ingleby's manor; and owner of estates at Eryholme, Yarm, Stainton, and Maltby, and of a moiety of the manor or lordship of Dalton-upon-Tees, in the North Riding of Yorkshire; and of estates at Blackwell Grange, Blackwell, Darlington, Polam Hill Farm, Hill Close House, Ingleton, and Nessfield, etc., co. Durham; b. at Staindrop 23 Oct. 1712; d. at Blackwell Grange 19 Jan. 1790, ag. 77; bur. in the south transept of Darlington church 24 *eod. mensis;* will dated 30 May 1789, pr. at York 2 and at Canterbury 25 Feb. 179 , by his two sons, James Allan and Robert Allan, to whom he left 28,500*l*. three-per-cent. consols. He settled the two Barton manors, and property at Yarm, Maltby, Stainton, Ingleton, Darlington, and Nessfield, on his son Robert. Portrait at Blackwell Hall.

ton, gent. by Elizabeth, dr. of John Killinghall, of Middleton St. George, esq., b 12 July 1710, mar. at Great Aycliffe, co. pal. 18 Nov. 1734, d. 25 and b. 28 June 1756, in the south transept of Darlington church.

III. Robert, bp. 6 June, 1699, bur 12 Aug. 1699.
IV. George, d. inf.
V. Sober Allan, of Stockton-upon-Tees, born 8 Nov. 1703, d. unm. 9 Apr. 1773, ag. 70. Will dated 20 Sep. 1766, pr. at York 17 Sep. 1773.
VI. Thomas, } Born at
VII. Lionel, } Staindrop,
VIII. Nicholas, } and died
IX. Henry, } inf.
1. Elizabeth, bp. 5 Oct. 1694, br. 9 Mar. 1694-5, in the church, her *lairestall* costing 1*s*. 8*d*.
2. Dorothy, bp. 24 Feb. 1697, died inf.
3. Elizabeth, bp. 20 May, 1700, died unm. [cart.'
4. Dorothy, 'killed by a
5. Jane, died unm.

George Allan, bp. 13, bur. 17 Apr. 1721.

1. Dorothy, 'Miss Dolly Allan,' bp. 14 Mar. 1712-3, d. at Grange, unm. and intestate, 26 Oct., bur. 1 Nov. 1760, in a new vault in the north transept of Darlington church, usually styled the 'Grange vault.' Pall-bearers, lord Darlington, sir Ralph Milbanke, Mr. Shafto, Mr. Chaytor, the hon. Fred. Vane, capt. Milbanke, Mr. Bland, and Mr. Bendowes.
2. Ann Allan, 'the good Miss Allan,' of Blackwell Grange, at length sole heiress of her father; lady of the manors or lordships of Nether Worsall, otherwise Low Worsall, Appleton-upon-Wiske (which she purchased), the two Barton manors derived from her aunt Hannah Eden, and owner of estates at Eryholme, and of a moiety of the manor or lordship of Dalton-upon-Tees, co. York, N.R., and of several estates co. Durham; bp. 21 Apr. 1718; d. unm. 16, bur. in the Grange vault 25 Oct. 1785. Pall-bearers, John Arden, of Pepper Hall, Yorkshire, esq., and Richard Pepper Arden, esq., afterwards baron Alvanley (her two cousins and legatees), the hon Mr. Vane, sir John Eden, sir Henry Vane, Mr. Tempest, Mr. Robinson, and Mr. Nesham, who together with lord Darlington, lady Darlington, the bishop of Durham, the bishop's lady, and sixty-two other ladies and gentlemen, were presented with rings. She entailed the Allan or Grange estates upon her cousin, James Allan, esq., for life, with divers remainders over. Will dated 28 Jan. 1783, pr. at York 8 Nov., at Canterbury 19 Dec. 1785, by James Allan, sole executor.
3. Catherine, 'Miss Kitty Allan,' bp. 19 June, 1719, d. unm., and bur. 'with great funeral pomp' at the west entrance of Darlington church, 10 June, 1753. Pall-bearers, sir Robert Eden and sir Ralph Milbanke, barts.; the hon Fred. Vane, the hon. Thomas Vane; Wingate Pulleine, Robert Shaftoe, Edward Milbanke, and James Bland, esquires.

1*st*. Ann, only daur. and hs. of James Colling Nicholson, of Scruton, Yorkshire, gen., b. 21 Dec. 1741; m. at Scruton, 18 Sep. 1766; d. 5, bur. 8 Dec. 1787, in the Grange vault, ag. 45. Mr. Colling, her father, took the additional name of Nicholson by direction of his uncle the rev. Thomas Nicholson, rector of Stainton-in-the Street, co. pal. He resided at Grange with his son-in-law, and d. 8, bur. 12 Feb. 1794. ag. 85. His wife d. at Darlington of the small pox 19, bur. in the church 21 Sep. 1772.

= I. George Allan, of Blackwell Grange, esq., F.S.A., 'the antiquary,' succeeded to entail'd estates; bn. 7 bap. 9 June 1736, d. at the Grange, 17, bur. in the Grange vault 24 May 1800, ag. 64. Will dat. 15 May, pr. at Durham 21 June, 1800, by his wife, Mary, and d. Dorothy Allan. There are portraits of him, his 1st wife, and her father at Blackwell Hall.

=2*nd*. Mary, dr of John Pallister, of Archdeacon Newton, m. about 1798. The only issue of this mar. were, 1. James, b. at Harrogate, Yrks., d. at Burdon, co. pal. 26, bur. in Darlington church, 30 Jan. 1804, ag. 6, being called, by mistake in the register, *George*, and his mother *Elizabeth*; 2. Elizabeth, b. at Grange 11, d. 15, & b. 18 Feb. 1800, in Darlington church.

III. Robert Allan, of Sunniside, par. of Bishop-Wearmouth, co. pal. and of Barton, co. York, esq.; b. 12 Sept., bp. 24 Oct. 1740, d. 27 Mar. bur. in Bishop-Wearmouth ch. 1 1 Apr. 1806, aged 65. Will dated 23 Dec. 1803, codicil 6 Feb. 1806, pr. at Cant. 8, at York 10 Apr. 1806, by his son John Allan, esq., sole executor, to whom he devised his landed estates. He bequeathed to his son Robert Allan, and daurs. Elizabeth, Ann, and Mary 39,500*l*. 3-per-cent. consols, and 11,000*l*. 4-per-cent. consols.

= Elizabeth, dr. and coh. (with her sisters, Ann, wife of John Maling, of Bishop-Wearmouth Grange, esq. and Mary, wife of William Russell, of Brancepeth Castle, co. pal., esq., 'one of the richest commoners in England', and grandfather of the late William Russell, esq., sometime M.P. for the co. of Durham, and of Emma Maria Russell, now (1850) of Brancepeth Castle, m. to the hon. Gustavus Frederick Hamilton, only son of viscount Boyne) of Robert Harrison, of Sunderland-near-the-Sea, esq., m. there 23 Feb. 1767; d. 31 Dec. 1808, bur. in Bishop-Wearm. ch. Will dated 3. Feb. 1808, pr. at Cant. 3 June, 1809, by her son John Allan, esq.

II. James Allan, of Darlington, esq., a deputy lieutenant for the co. of Durham; b. 21 Oct., bp. 1 Dec. 1738; d. unm. 26, bur. in Darlington church 29 Sep. 1800, ag. 61. He devised his estates to his brother, Robert Allan. Will da. 19 Dec. 1799, pr. at Durham 26 July, 1802. He was a freeman of Newcastle-upon-Tyne.
1. Elizabeth, b. 6 Nov., bp. 16 Dec. 1743, bur. Mar. 17 5-6.
2. Hannah, b. 29 Sep. 1746, m. 20 July, 1765, to Jeremiah Rudd, of Darlington, surgeon; d. 12 Nov. 1767 人.
3. Ann, b. 19 Mar., bp. 18 Apr. 1749; d. unm. 28 Aug. 1767.
4. Susannah, b. 27 Nov. 1751, bp. 9 Jan. 1752; m. 12 Dec. 1770, to Bristowe Pease, of Darlington. She died 29 Sep. 1814, bur. in the south transept of Darlington church. 'Both my uncles,' remarks Geo. Allan, esq. M.P. in *Nichols' Lit. Anec.*, 'died after the father in very opulent circumstances, but a very respected aunt, now living in Darlington, has derived but a scanty provision either from her father or her rich brothers, one of whom died a bachelor.'

*** The Register dates in this Pedigree are from Darlington, except where otherwise stated.

Henry Allan, esq., lord of the manor of Buckenhall, co. Stafford, in 1290, from whom, according to Wood, descended the learned Thomas Allan, through six generations. ╤ ....

I. Ralph Allan, of Milrich, co. Staff.

IV. Robert Allan.

II. John Allan, of Brockhouse, co. Staff., esq., *jure uxoris*, in 1330. ╤ Alice, daur. and hs. of Thomas de Maschon, of Brockhouse; temp. Edw. III. and Rich. II.

III. Thomas Allan, of Garringshall; from whom descended Thomas Allen, M.A., born 21 Dec. 1542, died at Gloucester Hall, Oxford, 1632, where he had been bred. Erdeswick says that he derived his original from "Alanus de Buckenhall, lord of Buckenhall, temp. Edw. II.," and that he was born at Bucknall, Newcastle-under-Line; but Fuller, Wood, and Camden (who calls him "*plurimis optimisque artibus ornamentissimus*,") give his birth-honor to Uttoxeter. He was a most excellent mathematician, and left many MSS., which are frequently quoted by other authors, and mentioned as having been deposited in the *Bibliotheca Alleniana*. Fuller laments their being latent with private possessors.

John Allan, temp. Henry IV. ╤ Agnes, daur. of ....

Ralph Allan, esq., temp. Henry VI., d. 1452. ╤ ....

I. John Allan, d.s.p.

II. Thomas Allan, esq., temp. Edw. IV. and V. ╤ ...... daur of ...... Walkenden.

III. William Allan, whose father gave him lands in Longmoor and Raskton-Spencer.

Ralph Allan, esq., temp. Ric. III. and Hen. VII. ╤ Elizabeth, daur of John Allan, of Rosalton, Lancashire.

William Allan, d.s.p. = Margaret, daur. of John Collier, of Darlaston, Staff..

John Allan, esq., of Brockhouse, temp. Henry VIII., Edw. VI., and Mary. ╤ Elizabeth, daur. of .... Robinson, of Drayton Basset.

1st. Eleanor, daur. of John Coyney, esq., of Weston-Coyney, co. Staff. ╤ William Allan, esq., of Brockhouse, d. 2 July, 1589. = 2nd. Helen, dr. of ...... Macken, of Buckenhall.

I. William Allan, of Brockhouse, d. 5. Oct. 1607. = Jane, daur. of Humphrey Nicolas, and wid. of John Philips, d. 5 Jan. 1608.

II. George Allan 'went to settle in the co. palatine of Durham.'—(*Visit. Staffordsh.*) ╤ ......

III. John = Joan, daur. of John Rowley.
IV. Thomas = ... daur. of William Kell.
1. Susanna = John Malpas.

I. George Allan, esq.: liv. 1630: of Yarm, co. York, 1651, bur. at Yarm 4 Dec. 1674. ╤ .... daur. of ...... Clifton.

II. John Allan, who m. and had an only daur. and hs. m. to Mr. Swainston, of Stockton-upon-Tees, by whom she had a son, Nicholas Swainston, and a daur. mar. to Mr. Richard Bowlby, who was father to Thomas Bowlby, gent. The lands in the township of Darlington, called '*Bowlby's Lands*,' [on which is Pierremont, the estate of Henry Pease, esq.,] belonged to this family, and were sold by the above Thomas Bowlby to George Allan, esq. in 1726.

I. Thomas Allan, of Allan's Flatts. *See* No. II.

II. John, bp. at Yarm 18 June, 1653.

III. Henry Allan (of whom there is a portrait at Grange), bp. at Yarm 6 Nov. 1655, died at London. By his first wife ...... he had issue Dorothy, bp. 2 Apr. 1689, at Yarm, who m. Capt. Mewse 人; and by his second, Dorothy, daur. of ...... Grainge, of Stockton-on-Tees, he had issue Margaret, who m. William Francis, a surgeon of London 人.

IV. George, bp. at Yarm 22 Jan. 1660-1, bur. there 2 Oct. 1662.

VI. Mr. Robert Allan, bp. at Yarm 18 July 1666, of Darlington 1695, d. at Antigua. He mar. and had issue:—1. Dollack, bp. 7 Feb. 1693, and d. unm.; and 2. Elizabeth, bp. 18 June, 1695, m. to John Burke, esq. They had an only daur. and h. Elizabeth, m. to Martin Blake, esq., and who d. 3 Jan. 1771, leaving a son, John Blake, an annuitant under Miss Ann Allan's will, and four daurs., of whom Margaret Blake m. John Thomlinson, esq., M.P., and left a daur. Mary (who d. 1818), the wife of Edward Beeston Long, esq., of Hampton Lodge, co. Surrey, who dying in 1825, left a son, Henry Lawes Long, esq., who m. 25 July, 1822, the lady Catherine Walpole, youngest daur. of the late and sister of the present earl of Orford.

VIII. Joshua, bp. at Yarm 3 Jan. 1670, d. inf.

1. Dorothy, bp. at Yarm 9 Mar. 1657, bur. there 15 Feb. 1660.

V. George Allan, esq. of Darlington and of Blackwell Grange, bp. at Yarm 9 Aug. 1663; d. 24 Mar. 1743-4, bur. in the west entrance of Darlington church. He purchased the manor of Nether Worsall, otherwise Low Worsall, estates at Eryholme, and a moiety of the manor or lordship of Dalton-upon-Tees, in the North Riding of co. York, and several estates in co. Durham, and built or re-edified Blackwell Grange in 1710, adding the south wing in 1717. Will da. 2) Nov. 1743, pr. at York, 31 May, 1744. He gave Blackwell Grange (where his portrait remains), and a moiety of his estates to his son in his lifetime ╤ Ann, dr. of Mr. James Grundy; d.7, bur. 9 Feb. 1709-10. [Mr. Jas. Grundy bur. at Yarm 19 August, 1696.]

VII. Nicholas Allan, of Darlington and Staindrop, co. pal., merchant, bp. at Yarm 12 May 1668, mar. 7 March, 1691. 'Mr. Nicholas Allan and Elizabeth Sober at Cockerton.' d. 4 Mar. 1716, a. 49, br at Staindrop. ╤ Elizabeth, only daur. of William Sober, of Cockerton, (son of Rob. Sober, of Nessfield, par. Darlington); b. 20 Sep. 1676. and bur. in the south transept of Darlington church 30 Aug. 1755, ag. 78. Her grandson, the antiquary, used to quarter '*Ermine, on a chief vert three garbs or*, in her right.

IV. George Allan, of Blackwell Grange, esq., J.P., bp. 30 Jan. 1694, d. 'universally respected,' 31 July, br. in the family vault in the west entrance of Darlington church, ╤ Thomasine daughter and co-heiress of Arthur Prescott,

I. James, bp. at Yarm 15 Aug. 1686, bur. 17 Dec. 1713.
II. George, bp 4 July, 1688, bur. 23 Mar. 1693.
III. Thomas, bp. 6 Dec. 1690, bur. 15 Aug. 1695.
1. Jane, bp. 20 July, 1692, bur. at Middleton St. George 1 Mar. 1726; mar. set. dated 3 Sep. 1719; mar. 10 Oct. 1719, to Robert Killinghall. of Middleton St. George, esq. (d. 13 Feb. 1758, ag. 76, at

X. James Allan, of Blackwell Grange and Barton, co. York, esq., lord of the manors of Nether-Worsall, otherwise Low Worsall, Appleton-upon-Wiske, Barton Grange, Wandesford, otherwise Wilkinson's manor, and ╤ Elizabeth, daur. of William Pemberton, of Darling-

I. John, bp. 18 Feb. 1695, bur. at Darlington ch. 6 Mar. 1763, unm. Will dated 10 Sep. 1762.
II. William, bp. 6 Feb. 1696, bur. 2 Apr. 1697.

William Pemberton, of Darlington, died 1730. = Elizabeth Killinghall, died 1745, whose descendants were eventually heirs of her ancient house.

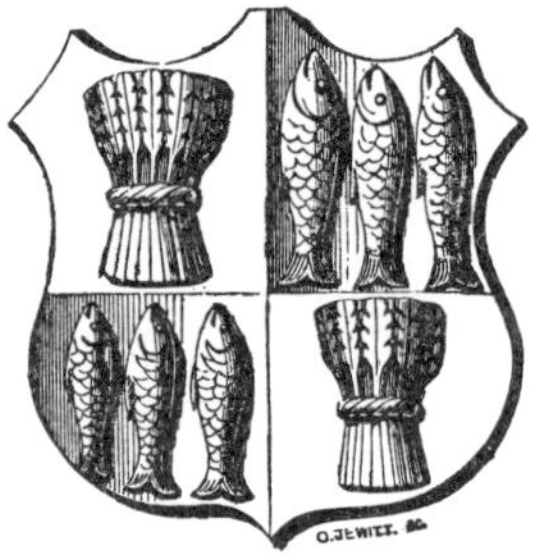

VIII. KILLINGHALL (formerly WALLEWORTH, of Darlington adopted as the coat of Killinghall, evidently by heirship of blood and lands)—*Gules, a bend raguly argent, between two or three garbs or, banded vert*, reduced sometimes to one, without the bend, as in an ancient coloured boss, penes R. H. Allan, esq., given in the margin.

IX. KILLINGHALL, ancient.—*Sable, a chevron or, between three kelyngs or cod-fish argent.—(Illuminated Ped. of Clervaux, temp. Eliz.)* In the boss the chevron is omitted, and the field is azure. A single kelyng was probably used as a badge, as in the seal of John Killinghall, who died about 1574; used by his son Henr in 1586.

*** The arms of the famous sir William Walworth, knight, were 'Gules, a bend raguly argent, between two garbs or.' The same occur in the cloisters of Durham, and are identical with the bearings of the Killinghalls, who increased the garbs to three, and at last ousted their paternal *keylings* altogether. Now the Killinghalls had acquired the ancient possessions of the Walleworthes, in Hundon and Nesse and the presumption is, by marriage with the heiress of the Walleworthes. The main lands of the Darlington Walleworthes lay at Burdon and elsewhere, in the parish of Haughton-le-Skerne; and their influence had obtained the rich living of Haughton for a William Walleworthe, who was buried in York Cathedral. He was apparently the brother of Thomas, of Darlington, who was found son and heir of Olive, widow of William de Walleworthe, in 1359, as by his will of 1401, he leaves '*Johanni filio Thomæ fratris mei mutulato*' 20 marks. Another Thomas, a canon residentiary of York, whom he calls his cousin, is also affectionately remembered. The cousin Thomas the canon died in 1409, and leaves as a very precious relic to Agnes his sister 'one gilt piece *which formerly belonged to Sir William Walleworthe, Knight*, his deceased *brother*. Sir William was chosen executor of the will of Bishop Hatfield, in 1381, the year of his struggle with Wat Tyler. His craft was that of monger of stock-fish, which were imported in large quantities from Iceland to Newcastle and other northern ports, from whence he probably transferred them to his warehouses in London. The garbs have no punning allusion to the name of Walleworthe. In early times a rich family of Benet, descended from Benedict of Darlington, resided at that locality, giving name to Bennet-hall and Bennet-field. John Benet occurs during the first twenty years of the 14th century in a great number of grants to (seemingly) more than one person named William de Walleworthe. They appear to have been friendly conveyances rather than sales, and as eventually nearly all the Benet possessions vested in William de Walleworthe and Olive before mentioned, Surtees's hint that she may have been an heiress of Benet will properly be adopted. We find garbs to have been a favourite bearing of persons with the syllable *Ben* in their names. The arms given for Bennette are sable, between three garbs, or, two shepherds' crooks in saltire of the second. The Darlington Benets would probably wear them with a little difference, and the staff is the acknowledged origin of bends and other raguly ensigns. Hundon, and lands in Nesse were both Benet estates, and thus both fields and shields continued in one blood for some hundreds of years.

James Allan, esq., of Blackwell Grange, died 1790. = Elizabeth Pemberton, whose descendants were eventually heirs of her ancient house.

I. ALLAN.—*Sable a cross potent quarter pierced or, charged with four guttes de sang, in chief two lions' heads erased of the second, all within a bordure engrailed erminois.*

II. PEMBERTON.—*Argent, a chevron ermines, between three griffins' heads couped sable.*

a quo all the present male representatives of Allan.

The whole coat will therefore be quarterly of eighteen:—1. ALLAN; 2. PEMBERTON; 3. HINDMARSH; 4. GREY; 5. COMYN; 6. HETON; 7. GREY of Horton; 8. KILLINGHALL; 9 KILLINGHALL (ancient); 10. HERDEWYKE; 11. LAYTON; 12. GOWER; 13. LINLEY; 14. LAMBTON; 15. BARNES; 16. SANDERSON; 17. DODSWORTH; 18. As the first.
Crest and *Motto* as in the registered bearings.

Issue of John de Kyllynghall.

Issue of Thomas Layton.

Issue of John Barnes.

SirRalph Grey, of Werke, etc., knt *Inq. p. m.* 1443. = Elizabeth, daur. of Henry lord Fitzhugh, of Ravensworth, Richmondshire, by Elizabeth, daur. and heiress of Sir Robert Grey, lord Marmion, of West Tanfield, in Richmondshire, by his wife Lora, 2nd dau. and coh. of Herbert St. Quintin.

Azure, three chevronels interlaced in base or, and a chief of the last, for FITZHUGH, *and vairy, a fess gules, for* MARMION, are given to the Greys in sir Edw. Walker's *Nobility*, temp. Car. I., in Coll. Arm. fo. 158., *after* their quartering of Grey of Horton. And in the arms allowed by the Coll. Her. to Dorothy, d. and coh. of sir William Fenwick, of Meldon, who married Isabella, d. and h. of sir Arthur Grey, of Spindleston, knt. Harl. M.S. 6821, they occur in the same way. It may be enough to state, that the Fitzhughs did not run into female descent for two generations after the match given above, and that the representation never could by any possibility vest in Grey. Consequently these two quarterings are not admitted on the present occasion.

Henry Killinghall, of Middleton St. George, esq., died 1620. = Ann Layton, dau and coh. of Robert Layton, esq., of Sproxton, and Skutterskelfe, probably the Robt. Layton buried at Hutton Rudby 8 Oct. 1595.

The arms of Layton, with their quarterings of Gower and Linley, are entered in Her. Coll., c. 13, fo. 135.

XI. LAYTON.—*Argent, a fess between six cross crosslets sable: a crescent for difference.*

William Lambton, esquire, of Great Stainton, co. pal., descended from Richard Lambton (son of Robert de Lambton, by Alice, dau. and sole heir of John de Kelloe, of Kelloe), who was held at the baptismal font by Richard Neville, earl of Salisbury, Thos. Langley (cardinal) bishop of Durham and Joan, countess of Westmorland, sister of Henry 4, and was slain on the part of Lancaster at Towtonfield, 1461 = Margaret, dau. and coh. of John Barnes LL.D. (Chancellor of Durham ?) and brother of Richard Barnes, bishop of Durham.

XV. BARNES. *Quarterly, or and vert, on a fess sable, three estoiles or*

These arms are given quarterly with Sanderson on the bishop's seal, and on his brother John's seal as below.

EARLY QUARTERINGS OF THE GREYS.

V. COMYN.—*Or, three garbs gules.*

VI. HETON.—*Vert, a lion rampant within a bordure engrailed argent.*

Richard Pemberton, of Stanhope Will pr. 1563. = Alice Hindmarsh, dau. and coh. of John Hindmarsh

III. HINDMARSH *Gules, in a marsh a hind lodged proper.*

Sir Ralph Grey, of Chillingham, knt d. 1565. = Isabel, d. and coh. of sir Ralph Grey, of Horton, knt.

VII. GREY of Horton.—*Barry of six argent and azure, on a bend gules a besant*, as shewn in the funeral certificate of sir Thos. Grey of Horton who d. 1590. I. v. f. 179 b.

John Killinghall, esq., of Middleton St. George, died Jan. 1651. = Margaret Lambton dau. and coh. died 1691.

XIV. LAMBTON *Sable, a fess between three lambs passant argent, a trefoil gules on the fess for difference.*

John Pemberton, esq. of Aislaby, co. pal. mar. 8 June, 1612. = Isabel Grey, dau. and eventual coheiress of Henry Grey, esq., fourth son.

IV. GREY.—*Gules, a lion rampant within a bordure engrailed argent: a mullet for difference.*

John Killinghall, esq., of Middleton St. George, buried 30 June, 1682. = Mary Dodsworth, dau. and coheiress of Robert Dodsworth, of Barton, co. York, esq. Her bro. Thomas, who d. s. p. 1680, names in his will his 'cozen John Dodsworth, of Wattlasse, esq.'

XVII. DODSWORTH.—*Argent, a chevron sable charged with three bezants between three bugle-horns stringed, of the second.*

Pedigree of Allan, of Buckenhall and Brockhouse in Staffordshire, Darlington and Blackwell in Durham, and Barton in Yorkshire.

Arms.—Quarterly of eight (as exemplified and confirmed in the Herald's College, London). 1. Sable, a cross potent quarter pierced or, charged with four guttes de sang, in chief two lions' heads erased of the second all within a bordure ingrailed erminois, for ALLAN. 2. Argent, a chevron ermine inter three griffins' heads couped sable, for PEMBERTON. 3. Gules, in a marsh, a hind lodged proper, for HINDMARSH. 4. Gules, a bend raguly argent inter three garbs or, for KILLINGHALL. 5. Or, a maunch sable, inter three martlets gules, for HERDEWYK. 6. Sable, a fess inter three lambs passant argent, a trefoil gules on the fess, for difference, for LAMBTON. 7. Argent, a chevron sable, charged with three bezants inter three bugle horns stringed of the second, for DODSWORTH. 8. As the first.

Crest.—On a wreath a demi lion rampant argent ducally crowned gules, holding in the dexter paw a cross potent or, and supporting with the sinister paw a rudder also gules.

Motto.—Fortiter gerit crucem.

The above insignia are those registered in the Heralds' College, but recent researches have shown that a number of other quarterings also vest in the ALLANS, which will be most conveniently shewn in the following tabular form:—

General Table, showing the representation in blood and right to sixteen quarterings vested in the family of Allan.

*** The mark ⋎ appended to that of marriage =, denotes that more descents intervened between that couple and their descendants next given in the Table. The numbers prefixed to the descriptions of arms, shew their rank in the ALLAN shield.

Thomas Layton, of Sexhowe, in Cleveland, 9 Hen. VI., of an ancient family, seated at East Layton, in Cleveland, which removed to Sexhowe early in the reign of Richard II. = ⋎ Elizabeth Gower, daur. and heiress of ...... Gower of Sexhowe, 9 Hen. VI. Her family was evidently an early branch of Gower of Stainsby, in Cleveland (or perhaps the main line), as Thomas Gower of Stainsby, by will dated in 1548, makes Christopher Laton a supervisor. John Gower, of Sexhowe, by charter of 46 Edw. III., settles lands at Thormodby on his son Nicholas, John Gower of Stanesby being a witness.

XII. GOWER.—*Azure, a cheveron, between three talbot dogs passant argent.*

John de Kyllynghall, esq., a justice itinerant, seised of Nether Middleton manor before 1400. = ⋎ Agnes de Herdewyke, dau. and heiress of John de Herdewyke.

X. HERDEWYKE.—*Or, a maunch sable, between three martlets* (hirundines ?) *gules.*

Thomas Layton, of Sexhowe, esq. died 12 January 1524. (*Hutton Rudby Obituary.*) = ⋎ Muriel Linley, dau. and coh. of Thomas Linley, of Scutterskelf. His will is dated 1529: 'to be buried in choir of Hutton Rudby before the parish clerk's seat.'

XIII. LINLEY.—*Argent, on a chief sable three griffins' heads erased of the first.*

John Barnes, of the co. of Lancashire, of the same family as the lords Barnes or Berners, who merged into Bouchier. = ⋎ Agnes, dau. and h. or coh. of Henry Sanderson, of Ditton, of the family of the Bolds.

XVI. SANDERSON.—*Az. a bend argent charged with a bear passant sable; on a chief of the second three roses gules, irradiated with rays of the sun proper.*

Issue of Robert Helton.

William de Helton, held the manor of Burton of Thomas Clifford, 31 Henry VI *a quo forsan* HILTON OF BURTON. No. II.

Thomas Helton. lord of a moiety of the manor of Helton Bacon, 31 Henry VI. (Rd. Ristwald the other owner): coroner for Westmoreland, 33 Hen. VI. *Qu.* the Thomas Hilton, bailiff of Rouen, present with the duke of Somerset at the winning of Harfleur, in 1437?

John Helton, witness to an agreement, 1518, between the croporation of Appleby, and the chaplain of St. Mary's chantry in St. Lawrence, Appleby. Helton Bacon is in the par. of St. Michael, Bondgate, Appleby.

Roger Hylton, mayor of Appleby, temp. Henry VIII.

*** 1526. Sir Wm. Hilton, knt., (Baron Hilton) settles his estate on himself and sons, rem. Cuthbert s. Tho. Hilton, late of Hedworth, gent., rem. *Roger*, s. George Hilton, late of Wylome, gent., rem, Wm. his bro., remr. to the Hiltons of London, and Parke, in Lancashire.—Cuthbert was ancestor to the Hiltons of Usworth; he seals his will with *three saltires*.

In another entail of 1561, Cuthbert is omitted, Roger and his brother Wm. stand first after the baronial stock, then come the Lancashire and London people, and last *Thomas Hilton of Burton, co Westm.* (*See* No. II.) rem. Henry Hilton of Wynston.

Robert Hilton, lord of Helton Bacon, (*i.e.* that moiety containing the old manor-house, the other, or Ristwald portion, passed to the Hiltons of Burton No. II.): called out by sir Thomas Wharton for the border service in 1543, as 'Robert Hilton, 2 horse.' = ... dr. of Tho. Blenkinsop, of Helbeck, esq.

Issue of John de Helton.

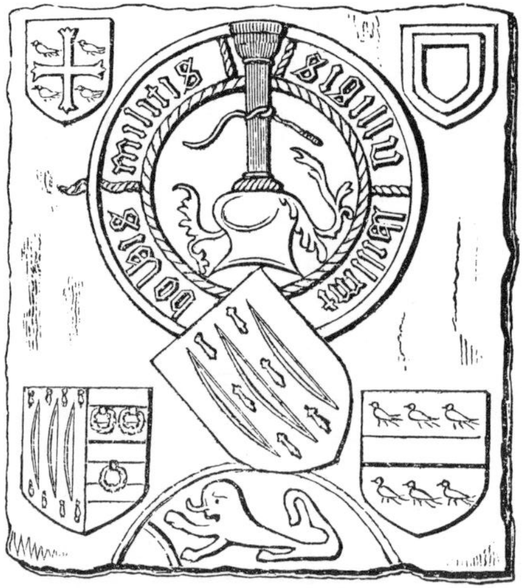

Issue of Sir Robert Bowes.

'Old Sir William Bowes,' lost his young wife in the first year of their marriage, 'and thereon he toke moche thoght and passed into France,' where he mingled in warfare, was a principal favourite of Bedford, and was knighted at Vernoyle in 1424. After 20 years he returned and built Streatlam *a fundamentis* from a French model. He never remarried, and died in 1465, aged at least 86. = Jane, d. Ralph lord Greystock (who d. 1417), who died under 20 years of age, and for whose sake her husband continued a widower 50 years. Her mother was Catharine dr. of Roger lord Clifford, who attended Wm. Graystock's funeral 1359. Through the Cliffords the Hyltons descended from their old feudal masters the Veteripontes, and through Clifford, Beauchamp, and Mortimer, from Ralph de Mortimer, who m. the princess Gwyladys, dr. of Llewelyn ap Jorwerth, prince of Wales, by Joan dr. of king John of England.

Sir William Bowes, knt., warden of the middle marches, and sheriff of Northumberland for the house of York, had livery 18 Oct. 1466, ag. 30 and upwards. = Maude, daughter of lord Fitzhugh of Ravensworth.

Anne Bowes, whose sister Margery m. sir William Hilton of Hilton Castle, knight. = Ralph Wycliffe, esq., lord of Wycliffe-on-Tees, son of Robert Wycliffe by Margaret, dr. sir Chr. Conyers of Hornby, knt.

Anne Wycliffe, daughter and co-heiress. = Anthony Brackenbury of Sellaby, esq., grand-nephew of sir Rob. Brackenbury, the lieutenant of the Tower.

II. Anthony, died unmarried.

III. John Hilton, of Gainford, co. pal., gent.

I. Thomas Hilton, of Helton Bacon, lord of that manor in 1 and 2 Philip and Mary; occ. as husband of Cath. Brackenbury in Vis. Dur. 1575. = Catharine Brackenbury seems to have returned to her own county, probably living with her son Lancelot; bur. as 'Catheran hilton widdowe,' at Gainford 23 Sep. 1587. Her bro. Henry, by will 1601, gives 'unto my nephewe Lancelot Hilton fortie shillings in money.'

I. Thomas Hilton, of Helton Bacon and Murton Hall (which he bought 11 Jas. I.) par. Appleby; bur. 10 May 1629, at St. Michaels. *See* No. II. = Jane, d. and coh. of Reginald Hartley, of Appleby.

1*st*. Catherine, eldest d. and coh. of Ralph Alwent, of Dyons, par. Gainford, esq.; ag. 4, 27 Oct. 1575; m. 23 May, 1587 at Gainford; had livery 1592; bur. 14 Apr. 1602, at Gainford; brought Dyons and property at Killerby to her husband, and in the Visit. 1615, her arms, 'Gu. on a bend ar. cotised or, three martlets of the first, a mullet for difference,' are entered for her husband. *See* No. IV. = II. Lancelot Hylton, of Gainford 1595, of Dyons, gent., 1615, a trustee with his cousin, Francis Brackenbury in a settlement of Anthony Hutton, esq., of Hunwick, (whose son Christr. married Anne the sister of Francis) 11 Dec. 47 Eliz. (*Inq. p. m. Anth. Hutton*, 1 *James*); bur. 16 Dec. 1625, at Gainford where his children were all baptized. = 2*nd*. Elizabeth, d. Leonard Smelt, of Kirkby Fleetham, Yks., wid. of Rd. Cork or Cockfield; m. 17 Oct. 1603, at Gainford.

III. Nicholas, vicar of Sockburn, 1579, rector of Hurworth 1589, d. there 18 Dec. 1616. *See* No. III.

III. Lancelot Hilton, of Durham city, and of Hilton, in Staindropshire, attorney-at-law, bp. 1 May, 1608; a collector of ship-money in Crossgate Constablery 1635-6; under-sheriff during the Usurpation, 1652; of Hilton 1658; ag. 58, 27 Aug. 1666; died 28, buried 29 May, 1685, at Bow church, Durham. = 1*st*. Mary, sister of *Abraham* and daur. of Tho. Colmore, of Durham city, (son of Clement Colmore, LL.D., spiritual chanc., on whose wife's death in childbed in 1592, dean Matthew preached from *Gen.* xxxv. 16, 21,) by Eleanor, d. Nicholas Fulthorpe, of Tunstall; and through the Lumleys, descended from the Saxon earls of Northumbria. Her children bap. at Bow ch., Durham. = 2*nd*. Dorothy, d. Wm. Wright, of .... co. Cumb. and widow of John Cradock, of Gainford, (son of vicar Cradock): bur. 4 July, 1675, in Durham Abbey yard. *See* No. VI. = 3*rd*. Anne, d. Ralph Salkeld, of Berwick-upon-Tweed, widow of William Hilton, apothecary, par. All Saints, Newcastle-upon-Tyne (grandson to Nicholas above. *See* No. III.) whose will is dated 1 Apr. 1676. *She remarried* 8 *June following*, at Long Benton, in the county of Northumberland.

I. Leonard, bur. 28 Feb. 1605-6.

II. Francis Hilton, of Killerby, bap. 2 Mar. 1605-6. *See* No. V.

1. Ann, bap. 28 July, 1610, liv. 1618.

John de Helton witnesses several Westmoreland transactions with all the chivalry of the county, temp. Hen. III. and Edw. I.; a juror in a Westmoreland question 21 Edw. I. (*Placita de quo warranto.*) Had (*cum uxore*) a grant from Robert de Beacon and Magota his wife, of lands in Hilton, etc. 17 Edw. I., and (alone) another from John s. John de Sandford, of lands in Sandford, par. Warcop, 18 Edw. I. (Thomas de Helton witn.) Had (*cum uxore*) the wardship of Johan, daur. and h. of Wm. de Sulleby, soon after 25 Edw. I., rendering a reasonable rent during her minority to the exors. of Isabella de Clifford. ═ Agnes, .. (Bacon ?) grantee with her husband from Rob. de Bacon.

Stephen de Boughes. ═ ..

Master Johannes de Boughes, pres. rector of Kirklevington, Cumb., by bp. John Halton, held property in Stretford in Richmondshire, and in Kirklevington, Blencarne, and Ulnesbye, co. Cumb., also 1½ acr. *in Hilton, co. Westm.* Wm. s. Stephen de Bowes, his elder bro. and h., his heir. Inq. p. m. at Richmond, Yks. 5 Edw. II. (1311-12.)

Adam de Boughes, manens in Maugneby, (near Kirkby Wiske, in Richmondshire,) grants to Nicholas, s. of Stephen de Boughes, his late brother, all his lands in Maugneby, Kirkeby Wyske, and Thyrnetoft.

Thomas de Helton, a grantee of lands at Ormeshead from [his bro.] William by deed dated at Burton 20 Edward I. ═ ..

William de Hilton, lord of Burton Manor (wardship worth 10*l.* cornage 13*s.* 4*d.* a year) in 8 Edw. II. (*Inq. p. m. Rob. Clifford:*) d. s. p., and *qu.* the Wm. de Helton, rector of Wiggeton 1317, who was dead before 1332 ?

John de Hilton. ═ ..

William de Boughes, s. and h., aged 30 and upwards 1311-2; bailiff of Richmond, Yks. in 1304; gives property near the bridge of Thoresgil to Eggleston Abbey 1329, dating from Startford.

Nicholas, grantee of all his lands in Maugneby, Kirkeby Wiske, and Thyrnetoft, from Adam de Boughes his uncle, to whom he gave a rent of 38*s.* out of them.

Robert de Boughes, grantee from his bro. Nich. of all the lands acquired from Adam de Boughes, their uncle. He sold Thirnetoft to Wm. Clervaux, of Croft, in 1323, on the cartulary of whose family these early Bowes descents are principally founded.

Adam de Bowes, knt., son of Stephen de Bowes (*Durham Visit.* 1575,) bailiff of Richmond 1310; sheriff of Durham 1314 seneschal for bp. Kellaw; chief justice of the Common Pleas 1331; lord of Streatlam, co. pal. jure uxoris; liv. 1347 and 1356. Arms on his seal, *On a fess three crosses between as many cross-crosslets.* ═ Alice, dr. and h. of sir John Trayne (who d. 1310) and lady of Streatlam.

William de Helton, held the hamlet of Burton, 43 Edw. III. (apparently in trust for John de Hilton); M.P. for Appleby 50 Edw. III. ═ ..

John de Hilton, son of John de Hilton, of Burton, by deed dated at that place, 2 Ric. II., settles lands, tenements, rents, and services in the vills of Sandford and Hilton Bacon, upon Agnes de Hilton, his daughter, as it seemeth, and the heirs of her body, rem. Thomas s. John de Hilton and his heirs of his body, with remainders over. ═ ..

Thomas de Hilton, s. John de Hilton, heir in remainder to Agnes de Hilton. ═ ..

*** Walter de Helton, between whom and the abbot of St. Mary's, York, there was a cause in King's Bench, 36 Edw. III., concerning a mess. in Colby, par. St. Lawrence, Appleby.

*** Adam de Bowes bailiff of Richmond, 1332, 1334

1*st.* .... ═ Robert Bowes. ═ 2*nd.* Elizabeth, daur. of sir John Lilburne, of Lilburne, Northumberland, knt.

Catherine, daur. of Wm. Hilton, esq., mar. to William Thornburgh, of Selside, co. Westmoreland. ⅄

William de Helton, seized of the hamlet of Burton, *jure Agnetis uxoris* 15 Richd. II. (*Inq. p.m. Rog. Clifford.*) He also held it in 10 Henry V., by homage, fealty, and 13*s.* 4*d.* cornage. (*Inq. p. m. John de Clifford.* ═ Agnes de Hilton, heiress of Burton.

John de Helton, 18 Rich. II.; of Helton-Bacon 6 Hen. IV. M.P. for Appleby 20 Rich. II. and 12 Hen. IV. ═ ...., daur and heiress of Andrew Ellerton, 6 Hen. IV. Ellerton is in some copies Ellerker, an evident error. It may be remarked, that Ellerton (Argent, on a chevron sable three bucks' heads cabossed of the field) is a quartering of Wycliffe, and thence of Brackenbury. The most distant cousinships were kept up in former days, and the marriage between Thomas Hylton and Catherine Brackenbury, whose mother Wycliffe brought the Ellerton quartering, is accounted for. I do not detect the relationship of the Wycliffe Ellertons with the Hylton family of that name yet.

*** John Helton. M.P. for Carlisle, 20 Richard II. 1 Hen. IV., and 6 Hen. VI.

Robert Bowes, son and heir, by several deeds in 1356, released to his father's executors his interest in Hilton, in Staindropshire, except certain lands, etc.; allowed that rents in Hilton, etc., should descend to the issue of Elizabeth, his step-mother, rem. to himself, and granted the reversion of lands in Hilton, once Alan Nevils', [Menil's ?] to his bro. Tho., rem. to his bro. Willm.; d. s. p.

Thomas grantee of lands in Hilton, in Staindropshire, from his brother Robert, d. s. p. Inq. p.m. 35 Hatf. held of *John Heron* and Eliz. *ux.* 60 acres in Hilton, rendering a rose.—*Hutchinson.*

Sir William Bowes, of Streatlam, created knt-banneret at Poictiers, 1356. ═ Maude, dau. and heiress of Robert de Dalden, lord of Dalden, etc. Will 1420. 'Willielms de Bowes *chl'r* filio Roberti de Bowes i. pece de argento cum opertorio habentem *in le frounte caput sagittæ*—Vicario de Dalton linthiamina *quæ sunt circa corpus* meum cum sex coverchiefs die sepulturæ meæ, ut habeat me in memoriam suam ad terminum vitæ suæ—Matildi filiæ Baronis de Hilton filiolæ meo i. *romance boke is called ye gospelles.*' Inq p.m. 28 Apr. 15 Langley. Held in dower a 3rd of the vill of Hilton, under Ralph earl of Westmoreland, who held Hilton, with the other members of Raby by one stag and 100*s.* to the prior.

Robert Helton, made a settlement, 15 Hen. VI. of certain lands at Ormeshead and Great Ashby, son and heir of Wm. H., s. and h. of Wm. H., s. and h. of Thomas H., bro. and h. of Wm. Helton. ═ ....

John de Helton, lord of a moiety of the manor of Helton Bacon, 10 Hen. V. (Rich. Ristwald holding the other half); M.P. for Appleby 1 Hen. VI. ═ ....

Sir Robert Bowes, created knight-banneret at Rouen siege 1419; slain with Thomas, duke of Clarence, at Baugy Bridge 1421. ═ Joan, d. sir Robert Conyers of Ormesby, in Cleveland, by Aline, widow of William de Dalden, uncle of Maude de Dalden aforesaid.

Pedigrees of the Heltons, Hyltons, or Hiltons, of Helton-Bacon, Burton, and Ormside in the county of Westmoreland, Hilton-in-Stain-dropshire, Stranton and Darlington in the county palatine.

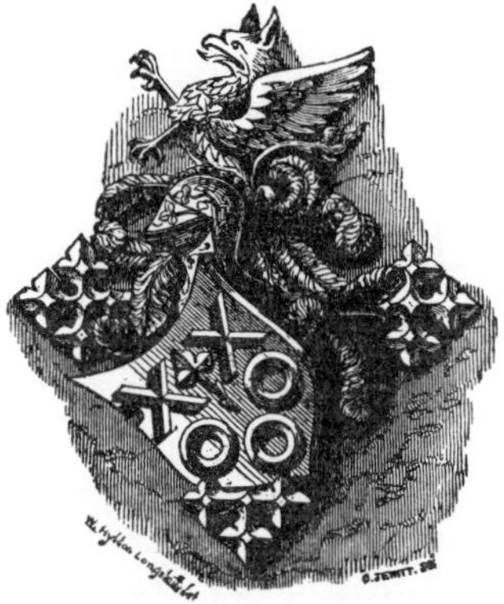

No. i.—Helton, Hylton, or Hilton, of Helton-Bacon, Hilton-in-Staindropshire, Stranton, and Darlington.

Arms.—Sable, three annulets and in chief two saltires argent. *Crest.*—A demi-griffin argent.—*Dugd. Visit.*

The heralds have added in recent times, a gold trefoil to the arms, and a sable one to the crest for the South Durham branches. The descendants of Dr. Hylton have given the trefoil in the shield argent, and I am inclined to venture, for convenient distinction, to make it gules in the crest.

The foundations of the early descents are from Nicholson and Burn, and the Heralds' Coll. pedigree, but they are very imperfect. A few wills would give a very different face to the skeleton.

A very brief abstract of title to the manor of Helton Bacon shall help to explain the early descents. In 14 Edw. 1. Thomas de Hellerton and Robert de Bacon are mentioned as the owners. Thomas de Hellerton granted to his cousin Andrew. In 8 Edw. II. Robert Bacon and the heirs of Andrew de Hellerton held the manor. The latter were infants, or another Andrew intervened before 43 Edw. III. when we find the Hellerton moiety in the hands of William L'Engleys and John de Appleby (evidently another name for John de Helton of Appelby parish, who married a daur. and h. of Andrew Hellerton), and Adam Bacon holding the other half. In 4 Hen IV. William Whapelote in right of his wife Ellen (perhaps the widow of L'Engleys) and Adam Bacon held (where is the other coheir of Hellerton in this record, and what record is it?) After this Bacon is lost sight of, and Restwold and Helton are owners for some time. All this from Nicholson and Burn. From the same authors (i. 511, and ii. 444,) we find that Julian, the heiress of L'Engleys, married William Restwold, and Restwold of the Yatch, quartered by Bunny of the Bishoprick, gave Engleys as a quartering. We therefore have the Hellerton moiety represented by Restwold and Helton We also have traditional and strong presumptive evidence in gifts by Robert Bacon to John de Helton *and his wife*, that Helton at all events married into Bacon. Is it not most likely therefore that Hellerton descended from another daughter of Bacon, and that on the extinction of the Bacons male, their moiety fell back into the heirs general, who already represented Hellerton ?

Romanus de Helton, knight of Helton, held three knight's fees in the co. pal., *de veteri feoffamento*, 1166.=------

Alexander de Helton, expressly named as one of the barons of the bishoprick *in pleno placito apud Dunelm*, in a charter of Roger de Kebblisworth 1180. = ...

William de Hilton, baron of the bishoprick, died before 1208; mar. to Beneta, daur. and h. of Germanus Tyson: *a quo* barons Hylton, of Hylton Castle. Their arms were, Argent, two bars azure.

Robert de Helton, stated in an old family roll pedigree of the barons, copied by Geo. Allan, to have been brother to the husband of Beneta Tyson, and to have married the 'daur. and heiress of Rd. Bacon, esq., of Westmoreland (whose arms were, Sable, three annulets, in chief two saltires argent),' and so originated the name of Helton Bacon. That seat was a later acquisition, but Robert de Helton appears witnessing Thorphin and Robert's grant of lands at Warcop and Bleatarn to Byland Abbey, with other witnesses of the period of Robert de Veteriponte I., who died 12 Hen. III. (1227-8.) Burton is in the parish of Warcop; it appears as the oldest seat of the Hiltons in Westmoreland, 'probably,' say Nicholson and Burn, 'by marriage of the heiress of Burton, whose arms were, Argent, a bend wavy, sable.' John de Veteriponte, who died 26 Hen. III., freed the lords of Warcop, Sandford. Burton, and Helton, from the pulture of the foresters, but on the condition that they should find *witnesman* to the foresters in cases of trespass, etc. = *Qy.* the heiress of Burton.

Gerard de Boughes, grantee from Adam de Puntayse [*i. e.* upon-Tees] of lands in Thirnetoft. par. Ainderby-Steeple, in Richmondshire, which he and his wife Avice had purchased. The name Adam hints the possibility of this being a friendly grant to a son-in-law. = ...

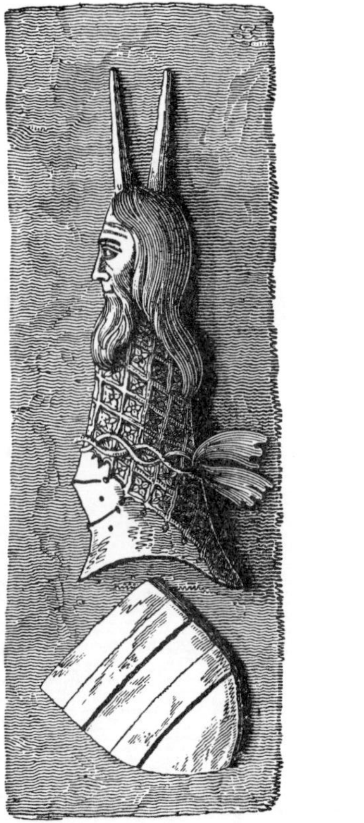

1. William Prescott, *ultimus suorum*, bap. 29 July, 1687, died unm. 27 Apr. 1706, when his father's lands at Darlington, Blackwell, and Eppleby, passed to his two sisters Thomasine and Sarah.

II. Arthur, bp. 3 June, 1703, d. 18 Dec. 1705.

1. Katherine, d. inf.

2. Sarah Prescott, coh. bap. 20 June, 1689; mar. 6 May, 1708; living a widow at Darlington 21 June, 1727. Her moiety of the Blackwell estate of Prescott was sold in 1830, by her great-grandson, Richard Pepper Arden, baron Alvanley. *2nd wife.* = Cuthbert Pepper, of Moulton, par. Middleton Tyas, and of South Cowton, Yks., esq., of an ancient family of the name and locality, which dates at least from temp. Henry VIII. 'Pepper of East Cowton, bears for his coate armor, gules, on a chevron between three demy lioncells rampant, or, as many grains of *long pepper proper*.'—*Whitaker's Richmondsh.* = Margaret, daur. of William Killinghall, of Middleton St. George, co. pal. esq.; settlements dated 5 May, 1705. She died at Moulton, and was buried at Barton 5 Mar. 1705-6, s. p. *1st wife.*

3. Thomasine [a Brass name] Prescott, co-heiress, of whom there is a portrait at Grange, bap. 13 Feb. 1692-3, mar. 13 Aug. 1717, to George Allan, of Blackwell Grange, esq. Her moiety of the Blackwell property of Prescott, is now (1851) vested in R. H. Allan, esq., of Blackwell Hall. ⅄

Prescott Pepper, esq., of Pepper Hall, which he built; d. s. p. 3 Feb. 1742. There are portraits of this gentleman at Grange.

Sarah Pepper, her brother's heiress: will dated 3 Mar. 1742, codicil 12 May, 1753; died in that year. = John Arden, of Stockport, Cheshire, esq. (grandson of sir John Arden, of Arden, knt.; will dated 19 Oct. 1781, codicils 2 June, 1783, and 23 Nov. 1786, (proved at Canterbury and York by his son John; died 3 Dec. 1786.

IV. Richard Pepper Arden, b. 1755; an eminent lawyer; Solicitor-General 1782; Attorney-General 1784; Master of the Rolls 1788; Chief Justice of the Common Pleas 1801; created Baron Alvanley of Alvanley, Cheshire, 22 May, 1801: named in Miss Ann Allan's will: died 19 Mar. 1804. "When Mr. Pitt proposed to Pepper Arden the office of Master of the Rolls, Pepper handsomely wished to decline it, saying that he was sure it would be disagreeable to lord Thurlow. Pitt replied, 'Pepper, you *shall* be Master of the Rolls; and as to Thurlow, I may just as well quarrel on that as on any other subject with him.' Thurlow on hearing of the appointment, said that his time would be spent in reversing that fellow's decrees."—*Twiss' Life of Lord Eldon*, i. 188. In a letter 29 April, 1801, George III. propounds to lord Eldon the query, 'How soon will the shins of Pepper permit him to take the coif.'—*Twiss' Life of Lord Eldon*, i. 372. = Anne Dorothea, eldest dr. of Richd. Wilbraham Bootle, esq., and sister to Ed. Bootle, lord Skelmersdale, married 1784, died 17 Jan. 1825.

I. John Arden, esq., of Pepper Hall, Yorkshire, and Harden, Cheshire; named in Miss Allan's will: will dated 11 Sep. 1820, (proved at Canterbury and York by the right hon. Edw. Bootle, lord Skelmersdale, and Wilbraham Egerton, esq.): died unmarried 18 July, 1823.

II. Leigh Arden, died unmarried 1766.

III. Crew Arden, rector of Tarporley, Cheshire; named in Miss Ann Allan's will; died unmarried; admin. of his estate granted to his brother, Richard Pepper Arden, 1 Sep. 1787.

1. Lætitia Arden; will dated 3 Mar. 1806 (proved by Randle Wilbraham at Canterbury 12 June, 1806); d. 4 May, 1806, aged 60; mar. Rev. Edw. Rudd, rector of Haughton-le-Skerne, who died 4 Sep. 1782, bur. at Haughton. They had an only daughter, Lætitia, married to Randle Wilbraham, esq., of Rode, Cheshire.

2. Sarah Arden; will dated 18 July, 1807, proved at York by her sisters and devisees, Anna Maria and Frances, 20 Dec. 1813.

3. Margaret Arden, died unmarried 1793.

4. Frances Arden; will dated 10 June, 1814, proved at York by her sister Anna Maria, 19 June, 1822.

5. Anna Maria Arden, died unmarried 28 Apr. 1831, aged 92. She and all her sisters are named in Miss Ann Allan's will.

II. William Arden, 2nd baron Alvanley, b. at the Rolls 8 Jan., bp. 20 Feb. 1789, at St. Dunstan's, Fleet-street, d. unm. 9 Nov. 1849. He was distinguished in the *beau monde* as one of the wits and *bons vivans* of the day, and it is told of him, that the epitaph he suggested for a noted gambler, now deceased, was—'Here lies .... awaiting the last *trump*.'

III. Richard Pepper Arden, of Pepper Hall, bn. 8 Dec. 1792; a lieutenant-colonel in the army, succeeded his brother as 3rd Baron Alvanley 9 Nov. 1849; late owner of a moiety of the Prescott estate, which he sold in 1830, and part of which was purchased by John Allan, esq., of Blackwell Hall, and devised by him to his nephew, Wm. Allan, esq. of Blackwell Grange for life, rem. to R. H. Allan, esq., in fee. = Lady Arabella Vane, youngest daur. of Wm. Harry, duke of Cleveland, by Catherine, daur. of the last duke of Bolton; mar. at St. James', Westminster, 25 Apr. 1831.

I. John Arden, died 24 Apr. 1787.

1. Sarah Arden, bn. 1787.

2. Mariannne Arden, died 1791.

3. Frances Henrietta Arden, b. 9 Apr. 1791, m. at St. James', 25 June, 1831, to John Warrender, esq., who on the death of his only brother, the right hon. sir John Warrender, bart., succeeded to the baronetage, 21 Feb. 1849.

4. Catherine Emma Arden.

Pedigree of Prescott of Darlington and Blackwell.

Arms borne by the Family.—Sable, a chevron, between three owls argent.—Prescot is a place in Lancashire, and as a family of the name of Glover was settled there (*Surtees*, iii. 207), it is possible that the Glovers of Darlington emigrated in company with the Prescotts.—The registers in this Pedigree are from Darlington.

Richard Priscot, yeoman, Darlington, surrendered in 31 Eliz. a messuage at Blackwell, and pasture for one cow and five sheep upon le common moore called le Brakinmoore, to Wm. Cornforth; di d before 2 Aug. 5 Jac. = ...

Elizabeth Priscott, mar. 13 July, 1608, to Anthony Sotheron.

Bulmer or Bowmer Priscott, merchant, Darlington, bap. 1 Nov. 1590, apprenticed to Robert Lawson merchant-adventurer and boothman, of Newcastle-upon-Tyne for ten years, 2 Aug. 5 Jac.; sued Nic. Hinde for 7*s*. 3*d*. for iron delivered in 1618; purchased of Chr. Hodgson two burgages, with the Kilne-garth, in Hungait, near the Deanery, 1626; received of the churchwardens 8*s*. for wine, 1639; bur. 31 Aug. 1644. = Margaret ...., paid St. Paul's rent for Kilnegarth, 1646; br. 25 Feb. 1648-9.

Helenor, bur. 3 Dec. 1594.

Jane, bur. 8 July, 1595.

1*st*. Jane Marshall, married 2 May, bur. 2 June, 1637, after scarcely a month's wedlock, in the church, her lairestall costing 6*s*. 8*d*. = I. William Priscott, merchant, Darlington, bap. 11 April, 1615, a stout parliamentarian; bought Beckfield and Ellyhill of Geo. Rickatson, a recusant, in 1642; paid in 1646, 20*l*. owing by his father to Thos. Barnes and William his son, to the parliament committee, they being delinquents; signed a bold congratulatory address to Oliver Cromwell, 28 April, 1653. Will dated 20 July, 1682: 'to be buried in Darlington churchvarde as nigh my relations as conveniently may be; grandchilde Willyam Pemberton 400*l*. out of Beckfieldes, alias Elly-hill; Elizabeth Priscott 10*l*.; George P. and Addam P. 5*s*. a piece; Arthur P., now apprentice att Newcastle, 4*l*., to be paid so soon as he is out of aprenticeship, if he happen to die before, to my sonn Arthur Priscott; Ann Parkinson, my maid-servant, 3*l*.; residue to sonn Arthur.' Died 16 Aug. 1682. 'Darlington—Hic reposita sunt corpora Gulielmi Priscott de Darlington generosi et ejus uxoris Sarah Prescott: obijt ille decimo sexto die Augusti Anno Dom'i 1682. Ipsq' vitam hanc peregit vicessimo septimo die Martii Anno Dom. 1673. Vita nobis mors est, morsq' nobis vita est nova.—Prescott's arms, owls.'—(*Randall's MS. Copies of Monuments.*) = 2*nd* Sarah, ..., died 27, buried 28 Mar. 1672-3. Perhaps a Turner, as in that year her husband paid for 'Mrs. Turner's lairestall 6*s*. 8*d*.'

II. George Prescott, woollen draper or clothier, Darlington, bap. 17 Nov. 1622; had the two burgages and the Kilnegarth, and another burgage in Hungaite (bought of Grace Tollerton, spinster), settled on him by his father, 1644; bur. 9 Dec. 1665. = Dorothy .... paid St. Paul's rent for Kilnegarth, in 1667; buried 26 Oct. 1680.

III. Richard, buried 26 Apr. 1642.

1. Elizabeth, bap. 14 Jan. 1616-7, married 28 Nov. 1637, to Ralph Wilson.

2. Bridget, bap. 21 June, 1625, buried 4 Dec. 1628.

3. Jane, bap. 27 July, 1628, buried 30 June, 1638.

III. Arthur Prescott, of Darlington and Blackwell, esq. (so titled in grand jury lists), bap. 1 Oct. 1646, s. and h. of his father 1682. Will dated 2 Feb. 1705-6, 'of Darlington, gent.; the interest of 40*l*., one moyetie to the poore widdows of Darlington, the other to the poor of the town of Blackwell; coz. Francis Bell, for coz. Eliz. Horsman and children; cozen and nephew Wm. Pemberton; brother Brass; servant and cozen Margt. Shipperd; Katterin now wife 80*l*. p. ann. in case my son Wm. die in her lifetime, and my lands descend and come to my daus. then 100*l*. p. ann.; das. Sarah and Thomasin 800*l*. each, and annuities of 20*l*. each, charged on freehold lands at Darlington and Eppleby; Mary Mawer one half broad peece of gould [11*s*. 9*d*., *Note to copy will*]; wife and drs. all household goods, except the choysest of one of my silver tankards to my sonn Wm.; friend Rob. Bowes, esq., and my well-beloved cozens Tho. Thursby, Tho. Swainston, and Fra. Bell; sonn Wm. the mare he usually rides on:" d. 9 Feb. following. There are portraits of him at Grange, and another at Blackwell Hall. = Katherine, d. of Wm. Brass, of Flass and Broome, co. pal., gent. executrix to her husband 1705, living in 1713.

I. Bulmer, bap. 3 Nov. 1639, br. 14 June, 1642.

II. William, bap. Mar. 1641-2, br. 6 July, 1642.

IV. William, bur. 10 Feb. 1651-2.

1. Margaret bap 21 Mar. 1640-1.

2. Sarah Prescott, bap. 8 Jan. 1650-1, mar. 19 Sep. 1678, to John Pemberton, sheriff of York city (2nd son of Michael P. of Aislaby, esq.), whose son Wm. released Beckfields alias Elly-hill from the legacy left him by his grandfather, William Priscott, in 1700. The representatives of this marriage are the present Allan family of Blackwell. ⅄

I. Bulmer Prescott, bap. 12 Mar. 1650-1, appr. to Hen. Kirkhouse, master and mariner, of Newcastle-upon-Tyne, 1667.

II. William, bap. 22 Sep. 1652, bur. 4 July, 1677.

III. George, mariner, Darlington, bap. 22 June. 1654; appr. to Thomas Richardson, master and mariner, of Newcastle-upon-Tyne, 1668; sold two burgages, and two garths called Kilnegarths, with a maltkiln thereon, in Hundgate to Geo. Allan, esq., 10 Dec. 1697.

IV. Richard, bap. 1 May, 1656, bur. 17 Feb. 1659-60.

V. Adam, bap. 13 Sep. 1660, living 1682.

VI. Arthur, bap. 15 July, 1663, appr. to a shipwright of Newcastle-upon-Tyne, 4 Apr. 1679, admitted free 25 June 1688, died just before 17 Dec. 1699.

1. Margaret, bap. 19 Dec. 1649, bur. 27 July, 1651.

2. Elizabeth, bap. 13 Sep. 1660, living 1682. *Qu*. 'Cozen Elizabeth Horsman and children,' mentioned in her cousin Arthur's will?

I. John Pemberton, of Gockshill, co. Linc., bap. 10 Dec. 1702, mar .... daur. of .... Hillyard, of co. Linc., died before 1750, s. p.

1. Mary, bap. 16 Feb. 1698, bur 20 Aug. 1718, at Darlington, unm.

2. Anne, bap. 6 June, 1700, bur. in Darlington church 1 Feb. 1758, unmarried.

3. Margaret, bap. 29 Nov. 1711, bur. 28 Aug. 1756, unm. She and Anne lived at Blackwell, and conveyed a pew as sisters and coh. of John, in 1750.

I. William Pemberton, b. 8 Jan. 1718, a surgeon of Plymouth, whose son, William Pemberton, esq., succeeded by devise of his cousin, John Killinghall, esq., to the manor or lordship of Middleton St. George, which had continued to be the estate and chief residence of the Killinghalls from a period anterior to the year 1400. He was succeeded by his son, William Pemberton, esq., of Middleton St. George, who died 11 March, 1801, s. p., when the representation in blood of Pemberton and Killinghall devolved on the Allans. This last William Pemberton devised the Killinghall estates to his maternal aunts of the family of Cocks, of Plymouth, to the prejudice of his cousin and heir-at-law, George Allan, esq. M.P., who with a view to invalidate the will, had a trial at law at the Durham assizes in 1806, when a verdict passed in favour of the parties claiming under the will, and the Cocks family have since remained in enjoyment of the estate.

3. Elizabeth Pemberton, bp. 12 July, 1710, m. at Great Aycliffe 18th Nov. 1733, died 25th June, 1756. = James Allan, esq. of Darlington, and Blackwell Grange, co. pal. and Barton, co. Yk. born 1712, d. 1790, buried with his wife in the Pemberton bur. place in the south transept of Darlington ch.

1. Sarah, born 23 Oct. 1704, d. s. p. July, 1781, the wife of George Pinkney, of Dalton-upon-Tees.

2. Mary, bap. 9 May, 1706, died unmarried July, 1750.

4. Anne, bap. 1 May, 1712, died unmarried.

5. Catherine, bap. 7 July, 1714, married Robert Brown, of London, merchant; 'disagreed and parted.' She d. s. p.

6. Margaret, bap. 6 Sep. 1716, died unmarried, buried near her parents. 'Margaret, the daughter of William and Elizabeth Pemberton deceased, died the 28th X'br, 1745.'—*M. I.*

George Allan, esq., of Blackwell Grange, F.S.A., 'the antiquary,' died 1800. = Anne, daur. of James Colling Nicholson, esq.

Robert Allan, of Sunniside, par. Bishop-Wearmouth, and of Barton, esq., died 1806. = Elizabeth, daur. and co-heiress of Robert Harrison, esq.

George Allan, esq., M.P., of Blackwell Grange, *bought the Blackwell Freeholds* of the Hills in 1803, d. s. p. 1828.

Robert Allan, of Newbottle, co. pal. esq. d. 1813. = Hannah, dr. of W. Havelock, esq.

John Allan, of Blackwell Hall and Barton, esq., M.A., J.P., died 1844. *He purchased Blackwell Hall, the Home-garth, and Castle-hill, in* 1808, *from his cousin George, and the remainder of the Blackwell Freeholds in* 1833 *from his representatives.* His purchases (including this estate) in the township of Blackwell amounted to 34,300*l*.

William Allan, of Blackwell Grange, esq., a justice of the peace, living unmar. 1851.

Robert Henry Allan, esq., J.P., F.S.A., of Blackwell Hall and Barton, high sheriff of Durham, 1851, *devisee of the whole of the Blackwell Freeholds, composing the ancient manor formerly the estate of his ancestor, Ralph Neville, first earl of Westmoreland,* under the will of his uncle John Allan, esq. = Elizabeth, daur. of John Gregson, esq., of Durham and Burdon.

Issue of Hen. Neville. *Issue of Hen. Grey.*

Charles Neville, 6th and last earl of Westmoreland of the great and noble house of the Nevilles of Raby, 'the most potent, both from their possessions, and from the character of the men, that has ever appeared in England.'—*Hume.* He was attainted 1571, and his estates forfeited, *at which period he held lands in Blackwell.* He died at Newport, in Flanders 1601, aged about 58, leaving by his wife, the daughter of the accomplished Surrey, 3 co-heiresses.

*** In writing a note above, with the same mark, I was under the impression, from Leland's language, that the heiress wife of sir Wm. Gascoigne was the daur. of John Neville, only son of the 2nd earl of Westmoreland; but she seems to have been daur. of John Neville, of Althorp, son of Ralph Neville, of Oversley, *second* son of the 1*st* earl. I cannot, therefore, at present explain the claim, on the death of t'e 2nd earl, by his *uncle's* descendants, seeing the earl had brothers. Leland's words are, 'This Neville lakkid heires male, wherapon a great concertation rose betwixt the next heire male and one of the Gascoynes.' The representation of Gascoigne fell into the unfortunate earl of Strafford, whose title of baron Raby was conferred upon him in honour of his heirship of Neville. In the Gascoigne memorials at Harewood, the bearing of Neville is given by Whitaker as undifferenced.

1. Isabella Grey, eventual coheiress mar. at Grindon, co. pal. 8 June, 1612, to whom her father in law, Michael Pemberton, of Aislabie, gent. in 1624, bequeaths 'one piece of gould, xxij. shillings.' = John Pemberton, of Aislaby, co. pal. esq. had livery 1626, (descended from John Pemberton, seated at Stanhope, co. pal. in 1400.) His sister Mary mar. Anthony Garnett, lord of Egglescliffe. His father left him in 1624, 'all my armure and furniture, and all my books and implements in my study.' (Appr'd at 3*l.* 6*s.* 8*d.*)

2. Mary Grey, eventual coh., mar. 31 Jan. 1613, at Grindon. *Had an annuity of* 50*l. settled on her out of Blackwell.* = Toby Ewbanke, of Staindrop and Eggleston, co. pal., esq., *acquired the freehold manor of Blackwell from Geo Parkinson, of Haghouse,* & settled 70*l.* annuity thereout on himself by deed 6 Nov. 1668

I. Thomas Gray.

II. Edward Grey, of Staindrop. Will dated 2 Nov. 1658, 'aged and infirm'; proved 1673; mentions his nephews George Errington, of Newcastle-upon-Tyne, and Leonard Scott of Hull, merchants (which latter in 1658 obtained a judgment against Toby Ewbank for 600*l.* debt and 21*s.* costs. *In* 29 *Cha. II. a mess., garden, orchard, and four closes called Longdraught, Broadfield or Lambflatt, Castle-hill, and Castlebancke, were extended as a moiety of Ewbank's possessions in Blackwell, and delivered to Scott till payment.*

III. IV. Robert and another son.

I. Michael Pemberton of Aislaby, a major in the service of Charles I, baptized 1615, executor to his father 1648. = Alice, daur. of Chr. Place of Dinsdale, esq. (great-great-grandson of Rowland Place, esq., by Anne daur. of sir Edward Radcliffe, knt., of Cartington, Nd., warden of the east marches.) She remar. Jno. Garnett, esq., son of Anthony G. [by Mary Pemberton,] a captain of horse in the service of royalty, who sold Egglescliffe, and retired to Darlington. She was buried there in 1685, having survived her 2nd cavalier husband 10 yrs.

II. Henry Pemberton, bap. 1620, a captain in the service of Charles I., in which service he was slain.

III. John Pemberton, a captain in the service of Charles I., and probably in colonel John Hilton's corps. Evidently the same John Pemberton as he of Hilton, who was agent or steward to John Hilton, of Hilton Castle, (son of the colonel,) who had himself been a royalist captain, and who in his will, 1668, calls Pemberton his 'true friend,' and advises his executors to be guided by him. His son Michael, of Bainbridge Holme, gent., mar. Ann Holmes, of Darlington, and was ancestor of the Pembertons, of Barnes, of which family Ralph Stephen Pemberton, esq., was high sheriff for the county palatine of Durham in 1845.

I. Henry Ewbanke, of Windsor, esq., an officer in the army, *sold Blackwell Freehold, with the 'Court Leet and Court Baron,' etc., to William Richardson, esq. in* 1684. *Seals to Blackwell title deeds,* penes *R. H. Allan, esq., dated* 14 *Nov.* 1668, 30 Aug. 1670, and 13 Nov. 1675, *with Ewbanke and Grey quarterly.*

II. Tobye, *had* 10*l. annuity settled on him out of Blackwell.*

Mary, married 1660, at Middleton-in-Teasdale, to Roger Bainbrigg, gent., *who had* 20*l. annuity settted on him out of Blackwell.*

Michael Pemberton, of Aislaby, esq., bap. 1644, afterwards of Northallerton, where he was bur. 1685-6. = Ann, daur. of George Metcalfe, of Thornbrough, Yorkshire.

Sarah, daur. of William Prescott, of Darlington, gent., bap. 8 Jan. 1650-1, there; mar. 19 Sep. 1678 1*st* wife. = II. John Pemberton, bap. 5 Sep. 1648, sheriff of York city 1684, and afterwards of Hurworth; d. at Koningsberg, in Denmark. = Mary, d. and coh. of Robert Dodsworth, of Barton; Yorks., esq. (and wid. of John Killinghall, esq.) m. at Hurworth, 18 Dec. 1683, br. 2 Feb. 1730, there. *2nd wife.*

John Pemberton, gent., sold the manor of Aislaby, and resided at Blackwell, where he held lands called Linnholm; d. 18, bur. 21 May, 1729, at Darlington. = Mary, dau. and h. of Christopher Place, of Darlington, gen., mar. 13 June, 1697, died 14, buried 16 April, 1755, at Darlington.

William Pemberton, of Darlington, merchant, bur. in the south transept there 27 Oct. 1730, under a flag inscribed 'Here lyeth the body of Mr. William Pemberton, who departed this life the 25 day of October, An'o Do: 1730, aged 51.' By the second marriage of his father, he and his wife became brother and sister-in-law. = Elizabeth, daur. of John Killinghall, of Middleton St. George, esq.; bur. 16 June, 1745, near her husband, under a flag inscribed 'Elizabeth Pemberton, died 14 Iune, 1745.' On the death, in 1762, of her nephew, John Killinghall, esq., *ultimus suorum,* her descendants became representatives of her ancient and wealthy house.

Catherine Mowbray. = Sir Thomas Grey, 'with the crockett foott'—(*Visit. Northd.*, 1575)—of Heton, co. Northumberland, knt., ag. 10, 1369.

Lady Margaret, d. 1370, br. at Brancepeth. *1st wife.* = Ralph, Lord Neville, of Raby, K.G. 'the great earl,' created earl of Westmoreland 1397, served at Agincourt, elevated the house of Raby to its utmost splendour, and died 1426, *seized of the manor of Blackwell*; bur. at Staindrop. = Joan de Beaufort, half sister of Henry IV. *2nd* wife.

The Lady Elizabeth Mortimer. = Henry Percy, the renowned Hotspur, slain at Shrewsbury 1403.

Sir John Neville, s. and h. died *in vita patris* in the wars of France 1423, bur. at the Grey Friars, London. = Elizabeth, sister and coh. of Tho. Holland, earl of Kent and duke of Surry.

Lady Alice Neville, whose father bequeathed her, by the name of 'my daughter, my Gray,' one gilt goblet. = Sir Thomas Grey, of Heton, knt., beheaded 5 Aug. 2 Hen. V.

Lady Eleanor Neville. = Henry Percy, 2nd earl of Northumberland, b. 1393, in exile in Scotland, the hero of the 'Hermit of Warkworth,' called back to England by Hen. V. 1415, and remained a faithful adherent of the Lancaster line, and fell at St. Albans 1455. In 1436 he encountered earl Wm. Douglas at Pepperden, near the Cheviot Hills, and is supposed to be the earl Percy of 'Chevy Chase.'

Sir John Neville, knt., 2nd s. slain at Towton-field, 1461, for the red rose. *2nd husband.* = Anne, dr. of John duke of Exeter, widow of John, lord Neville, her second husband's nephew.

Sir Ralph Grey, of Werke, Heton, and Chillingham, knt. (*Inq. p. m.* 1443), 'died in France,' (*Visit.* 1575.) = Elizabeth daur. of Henry, Lord Fitzhugh, of Ravensworth Castle, in Richmondshire, by Elizabeth, d. and h. of sir Robert Grey, knt., (who was bro. and h. of John Grey, lord Marmion, one of the sons of John lord Grey, of Rotherfield,) by Lora, second dau. and coh. of Herbert St. Quintin. Her mother lady Fitzhugh, in 1427, leaves her 'a chaplet of perle, with dooble rooses.'

Sir Ralph Percy, knt., seventh son, bn. 1425, died at Hedgley Moor for the red rose, when his partizans had fled, exclaiming, 'I have saved the bird within my bosom,' 1464. On the spot where he fell is a cross marked with the Percy fusils, lucies, and crescents. = Eleanor, only dr. and h. of Laurence Acton, esq., living 1498.

Ralph, lord Neville, succeeded his uncle Ralph as 3rd earl of Westmoreland; died of much thought on his son's death; buried at Hornby 1523. = Matilda, daur. of sir Roger Booth, of Barton, Lancash., knt. bur. at Brancepeth.

Sir Ralph Grey, of Werke, Heton, and Chillingham knt., beheaded at Doncaster 4 Edw. IV. = Jacquetta, ...

Sir Henry Percy, knt., held various distinguished offices on the Borders under the earl his cousin and the crown; died 1486. = ... [Middilton? d. or sister of sir John Myddylton, knt.? who was liv. 1498, as her son John enjoyed his lands near Bamburgh.]

> "For Wetharryngton my heart was woe,
> That ever he slain should be,
> For when his legs were hewn in two,
> Yet he kneeled and fought on his knee."

Ralph, lord Neville, died before his father; buried at Brancepeth. = Edith, daur. of sir Wm. Sandys, of the Vine, co. Hants, died 1529.

Sir Edward Grey, of Werke, Heton, and Chillingham, knt., died 1533. = Elizabeth, dr. of sir John Clifford.

Margery Percy. (See *Collins's Peerage*, ii. 364) = Sir Henry Widdrington, of Widdrington, knt., probably married about Jan. 1492, when an indenture was made between his father and his wife's mother and step-father, sir Wm. Evers, knt.; d. 26 Aug. 1518.

Ralph Neville, 4th earl of Westmoreland, K.G., d. 1549-50. = Catherine, daughter of Edward Stafford, duke of Buckingham.

Sir Ralph Grey, of Chillingham, knt., d. 1565. *A quo* the earls of Tankerville, and the earls Grey of Howick. = Isabel dr. and coh. of sir Ralph Grey, of Horton, kt: by Dorothy daugh. of Ralph lord Ogle.

Sir John Widdrington, of Widdrington knt. M.P. for co. Northumberland 1552, warden of the middle marches. = Agnes, dr. of sir Edw. Gower, knt. *2nd wife.*

Edward Perkinson, of Beaumond Hill, near Darlington, gent., died 1567, *seized of property in Blackwell, acquired from the fifth earl of Westmoreland.* Will 2 July, 1567; '6*l.* 13*s.* 4*d.* to be geven and distributed amonge the most poore and nedie people within the parishe of Howghton, the parishes of Heighinton, Aycliffe, and Derlington, immediatelye and so sone after my deathe as convenientlye it maie be done; Henry P., my son, my best silver salte, and xiij. silver spones whiche haithe the image of Christ and the xij. appostels upon them, etc.; suster Killinghall for a token of remembrance, my silver beeds.' = Anne, dr. of Ralph Hedworth of Harraton, co. pal. esq. liv. 1567.

Henry Neville, 5th earl of Westmoreland, K.G., died 1564, bur. at Staindrop; *sold lands at Blackwell* in 1563 *to Edw. Perkinson.* He was instrumental in founding the Free Grammar School at Darlington. = Anne, dr. of Thos. Manners, earl of Rutland.

Henry Grey, esq. of Newminster Abbey, in the county of Northumberland, fourth son, buried in the chancel of Morpeth church 10 May 1597. = Mary Widdrington. Her half-brother, sir John Widdrington, knt., sheriff of Northumberland in 1579, and governor of Berwick, was (*with John Claxton*), *in* 1617, *examiner into a claim made by Anthony Nevell, a gentleman of Blackwell* (*whose son and heir was named Charles*), *upon the property sold by her sister Margerie to George Parkinson.* Her sister Barbara married John Ewbanke, probably a relation of Tobye, in the next generation, as another sister, Rebecca, lived at Staindrop, a spinster. A third sister married—1. Thomas Sandford, esq., of Askham, co. Westmoreland, whose widow she was in 1625; and 2. .... Hilton. A brother Isaac bap. a son James at Darlington in 1592.

> ". . . A beateous maid, as fair as fair might be,
> The dewdrop on the lily's cheek was not so fair as she.
> Fair Widdrington the maiden's name . . . . .
> Her sire an old Northumbrian chief."

Margerie Widdrington, *who in her widowhood,* 1615, *sold property* (*for* 800*l.*) *at Blackwell to G. Parkinson, of Haghouse, gen. who also bought in* 1638 *the Garnett property, formerly Perkinson's,* held by knight's service, and 24*s.* 10*d.* rent. = Henry Perkinson, gen. s. and h., called one of the 'principall rebels' of 1569, and reported 'to have saved the earl in the rebellion time;' sold Beaumond Hill 2 June 30 Eliz.

Cuthbert Perkinson, second son, *devisee of the Blackwell estates of his father for life.*

II. Abraham Hilton, of Durham and Hilton, attorney at law, bap. 10 Jan. 1637-8; purchased the manor of Hilton from the Marleys; ag. 31, 27 Aug. 1666: will da. 28 Aug. 1771, codicil 25 Oct. 1718; buried 29 Oct. 1718, aged 88, at Staindrop.
= 1*st*. Eleanor, d. Henry Marley, of Hilton in Staindropshire, gent., bur. 29 Mar. 1694, at Staindrop. She had one child, Mary Hilton, ag. 11 mos. 27 Aug. 1666; bap. 10 July, 1665, bur. 21 Mar. 1666-7, in Staindrop church.
= 2*nd*. Eleanor, d. Thomas Mossock, of Headlam, co. pal. mar. at Staindrop 14 August, 1699: mar. set. dated day *following;* residuary legatee in her husb. Hilton's will; mar. 2*nd* at Cockfield, 4 Sep. 1723, to Samuel Burton, of Keverston, gent.; bur. 14 December. 1736, at Staindrop.

N.B. A moiety of the vill of Hilton appears in the Inquisitions of the Nevilles. The Bowes family are stated to have held under them. It was, I presume, through the forfeiture of the Neville lands, that James I. in 1616 granted the manors of Bradbury and Hilton to Thomas Emerson, esq., for one thousand years under the yearly rent of 550*l*. Passing through the Mannings, Henry Marley purchased Hilton of them, and then Hilton was charged with 160*l*. as its portion of the rent.

III. Richard Hilton, of Darlington, atty. at law, bap. 26 Nov. 1642; occurs as bailiff of Darlington 1698; bur. there 11 Sep. 1715. On his admission to the temporal courts of Durham, the oath of allegiance only (supremacy *struck out*) was directed to be administered to him, and it is stated that he had served his brother Abraham. Children bap. at Darlington.
= Anne.... bur. at Darlington, 24 July, 1723; liv. a widow 1718. Her husb. often sealed with a pointed elliptic seal, with a lozenge, a chevron between 3 fleurs - de - lis. *Qu.* her arms?

IV. Cuthbert Hilton, of Durham city, attorney - at - law, bap. 26 Nov. 1642, died and buried in the night, 28 April, 1686, as near his father as possible.
= Jane, d. Robert Newhouse, atty, and registrar of the Consistory Court, mar. before 18 Sep. 1668, died 5 Dec. 1732, buried in Durham Abbey yard.

V. Robert Hilton, of Durham city, gent. liv. 1666, d. before 1717.
= Rebecca .. mentd in her bro. in law Abraham's will 1717.

I. Lancelot, bap. 12 Aug. 1635, bur. 25 Apr. 1637, at Bow.

1. Eleanor, bap. 12 Feb. 1639; mar. 3 Feb. 1667-8, at Durham Abbey to John Yapp, bailiff to the Dean and Chapter. ⅄

I. Abraham Hilton, of Blackwell, and of Darlington in 1712, esq., bp. 17 Nov. 1681; will dated 21 Aug. 1713; d. 15, bur. 18 Sep. 1713, at Darlington.
= Martha Shadforth, sister of the Rev. Tho. S. minister of St. Andrews', Newc: and curate of Brancepeth, liv. 5 Nov. 1724, when her bro.'s will proved

II. Richard, bap. 22 May 1684, bur. 4 May, 1690, at Darlington.

1. Catherine, bap. 17 Jan. 1670.

2. Mary, bap. 17 Dec. 1674, mar. Henry Forth, esq., J.P. of Darlington, son of Mr. Henry Forth, alderman of London, and of Albinia, posthumous daur. of sir Henry Vane, of Raby. She died 18 Dec. 1728, bur. in the entrance of Darlington church.

3. Jane (*Gane* in reg.), bap. 15 Mar. 1676-7, bur 16 July, 1703, at Darlington.

I. Robert Hilton, of Bishop-Auckland attorney-at-law, registrary to the see 1708; bn. 29 June, bp. 1 July 1668, at Bow: buried 8 Sep. 1728, at St. Andrew's, Auckland; will
= Elizabeth, d. and coh. of Geo. Crozier, of Newbiggin, gent., ag. 4 1666; mar. at Heighington 8 July, 1693-4; br. 23 Mar. 1723, at St. Andrew's, Auckland.

1. Barbara, bap. 27 Oct. 1670, at Bow, br. 3 Dec. 1718; m. 27 Dec. 1694, at Bow, to Jeffry Shaw, of Barnard-Castle. ⅄ In 1744 Hilton Shaw was mayor of Durham.

2. Jane, mar. 25 Feb. 1706, at Bow, to James Smith, of Auckland, merchant, both living in 1717.

3. Elizabeth, living 1717.

4. Maria, bur. 23 Mar. 1675-6, at Durham Abbey.

2*nd*. Jane, eldest daughter and coheiress of Isaac Surtees, of Miers Flatt, parish of Haughton-le - Skerne. ['Isaac Surtes of Darlington' buried 3 Jan. 1711 - 2, at Haughton] by his wife Ann, dr. of William Hewgill, of Smeaton, esq., who had been mar. to .... Robson, of Stapleton, and had issue Ralph Robson, bailiff of Darlington, bur. 8 Mar. 1737-8, at Darlington. Will da. 1711. The children of this match. bap. at Darlington.
= I. Robert Hylton, or Hilton (signs both ways), of Darlington, surgeon, commonly called 'Dr. Hilton,' bap. 2 Oct. 1690, at Bow, as 'son of Mrs. Rebecca Hilton;' named in his uncle's will 1717, as 3rd in rem. to the Hilton estates; b. 13 June, 1746; bur. at Monk Hesilden; will da. 28 Jan. 1742 pr. in Lon. 1747. I have a book inscribed 'Abraham Hilton, 1725. Ex dono suo ad Georgium Lowthian, *Silic' a Geo: Lowthian Rob'to Hilton patruo suo 28th Mar:* 1744,' the part in italics being in the doctor's writing. After his third marriage, he lived in Stranton Manor-house. = 1*st* Hannah, daughter of Richard Hilton, his cousin; married 8 May, 1714, at Staindrop, in the county palatine; buried 1 Feb. 1719-20, s. p. at Darlington.
= 3*rd*. Mary ('Madame Hilton') d. Robert Weemes, gent., of Little Ryle, co, North'd., and Stranton by his 1st wife Jane, only dr. and h. of John Kitchin, of Yarm, gent., by the heiress of Gibson of Stranton; lady of one-third of the manor of Stranton, one-fourth of the manor of Seaton, and owner of lands in those places, Brereton, North Hart (in her own right, being sole heiress of her mother, and co-heiress of her father), and Hesilden and Monk Hesilden (the two last estates being devised by her 1st husband, and disposed of by her); mar. to Hilton at Stranton, 20 July, 1741; of Hartlepool 1751; of Durham city 1766. Will dated 1 Feb. 1766; bur. at Durham same year. She had m. 1*st*, George Bromley, of Monk Hesilden & Stranton, gent., who di d 1737, and whose issue is now extinct.

1. 2. Elizabeth and Anne, both living 1717. One of them m. .... Rawlin-
3. Rebecca; will da. 5 Mar. 1756, pr. 1758. 'Mrs. Rebecca Hilton, of Darlington, single woman, bur. in the ch. 23 Apr. 1758.
4. Alice, br. 29 Nov. 1761, at Darlington, as of that place, = 1*st*, Chr. Blackett, of Newham, Nd. gen. = 2*nd*, Fran. Smart, of Snotterton, gen. uncle to the poet. = 3*rd*. Thos. Bellasyse, of Haughton-le-Skerne esq. d. 27 Aug. 1751. leaving a d. & h. Martha Maria, b. 8 Mar. 1721, & m. to Rd. Bowes, esq. of Darlington, ⅄ *Qu.* Elenor d. Rob. Hilton, br. 10 Jan. 1685, Dur. Abbey.

I. Captain Abraham Hilton, of Haughton-le-Skerne, esq., bap. 11 Mar. 1711; brought up an attorney; d. s. p. 11 April, 1778, ag. 57; monumental inscription at Haughton; mar. Elizabeth, daur. of ...... Smith, died 28 Dec. 1788, ag. 70; mon. inscrip. at Haughton.

Mary Hylton, or Hilton, only child of the 3rd venter, (except a son d. inf.). whose descend-
= Rev. William Longstaffe, son of George Longstaffe, gent., of Soulby, Westmoreland, 'a favourite estate, which his an-

Issue of Abraham Hilton.

4. Elizabeth, bap. 3 April, 1679, mar. 1 June, 1708, at Cockfield, to Capt. Anth. Smith, whom she survived. 'At the foot of this tablet lies the body of Mrs. Elizabeth Smith, the widow of Capt. Anthony Smith, and daughter of Richard Hilton, gent. After having fulfilled the severe duties of a good wife, a good friend, a good neighbour, and, to compleat the character, of a good Christian, she exchanged this life, we trust, for a better, on the 28th day of November, in the 51st year of her age, of our Lord 1729. It will be hard to exceed her; but if thou art a woman, go and do like her.'—*Wooden tablet in the entrance of Darlington Church.*

5. Hannah, bap. 15 June, 1686, mar. her cousin, Dr. Hylton.

I. Abraham Hilton, of Cockerton and Hilton, gen., lord of Hilton, by devise from his grand-uncle; bap. 30 April, 1706, at Staindrop, buried 9 Nov. 1748, at Darlington. Will dated 5 Nov. 1748, at Cockerton, never proved. = Margaret, younger dr. and coh. of Isaac Surtees, of Miers Flatt, gen. sister of Dr. Hilton's wife; had an annuity of 20*l.* out of Hilton estate, died 16 Novem. 1789, ag. 86. Monumental inscription at Haughton.

II. Richard, bap. 1 July, 1708, at Darlington, living in 1718.

III. Shadforth, bap. 18 Mar. 1709-10, at Staindrop, bur. 9 Jan. 1710-11, there.

1. Ann, bap. 30 May, 1712, at Darlington, living in 1718.

II. Abraham Hilton, of London, one of the six clerks of chancery and afterwards of Hilton, esq. bn. at Darlington; bap. 23 Apr. 1731; died 22 Decem. 1789; bur. in Darlington church; sold Hilton manor. = Ann, daur. of James Close, of Richmond, Yorkshire, gent.; mar. there 29 Aug. 1765: died a widow, of consumption, at Barnard Castle, 27 June, 1799, ag. 65; bur. 30, in Darlington ch.; will 28 May 1799.

I. Henry Hilton, of Hilton, esq., bap. 5 Sep. 1729, at Darlington; mar. Margaret dr. of Henry Hewgill, of Smeaton, in Richmondshire, 17 Jan. 1753, at Middleton St. George (she died a widow 13 Feb. 1806, ag. about 72, and was bur. at Darlington); d. s. p. 20, bur. 23 Jan. 1759, at Darlington.

1. Mary, only dau. bap. at Stockton 4 Aug. 1723, d. unm. 7. Feb. 1807, at Darlington. M. I. Haughton.

Issue of Robert Hilton and Elizabeth Crozier.

dated 22 August, proved 25 Sep. 1728

5. Margaret, bap. 1 Jan. 1677, at Durham Abbey, living unm. 1717.

6. Martha, bap. 23 July, 1679, d. inf.

I. Cuthbert Hilton, of the North Bailey, Durham city, and of Bishop-Auckland, bap. 30 April, 1695, bur. at Durham Abbey 8th Sep. 1724, *in vita patris.* Will dated 29 July, 1724, pr. same year at Durham. He mar. 3 June, 1718, Mrs. Jane Hodgson, widow (bur. 2 Dec. 1722, at Durham Abbey), and had a dau. Ann Hilton, to whom he left five guineas, and liv. 1728.

1. Jane, living 1728, mar. Ellis Veryard, of Boxhill, Wiltshire, and Sunderland-by-the-Sea, gent.

2. Eleanor, died Aug. 1734, bur. at St. Andrew's, Auckland; mar. 4 Sep. 1722, at Bishop-Auckland, to Sir William Richardson, of Bishop-Auckland, and Kelso, in Scotland, baronet of of Nova Scotia.

3. Elizabeth, bap. 11 Aug 1702, mar. 6 Aug. 1725, Thomas Beckwith, of Berwick-upon-Tweed, gent., living 1729.

4. Ann, bap. 27 Mar. 1705, bur. 5 July, 1706, at St. Andrew's, Auckland.

Issue of Robert Hilton and Jane Surtees.

II. Isaac, bap. 13 April, bur. 7, May, 1723, at Darlington.

III. Robert, bap. 16 Aug. 1732; a midshipman, R.N.; died coming from the East Indies. His widow Ann was living a widow at Gosport in 1758, s. p.

1. Anne, bap, 8 July, 1724, bur. 25 May, 1730.

2. Jane, bap. 12 June, bur. 17 Aug. 1726.

3. Margaret, bap. 31 Aug. 1727.

4. Jane, bap. 29 Aug. 1729, bur. 12 July, 1732.

5. Hannah, bap. 24 Nov. 1731; living 1758; mar. Cornforth Gelson, of Edinburgh, musician, and had issue Robert Hilton Gelson, under 21, 1778.

6. Rebecca, bap. 19 Feb. 1734-5; living unmarried with her aunt Rebecca in Darlington, 1758; mar. ...... Trow, a silk dyer in London, and had issue Abraham Hilton Trow, living 1794, 'formerly of Bermondsey-street, par. St. Mary Magd., Bermondsey, scowerer, but now of Old-street-road, par. St. Luke's,' resid. legatee of his uncle Abraham.

Issue of Rev. William Longstaffe.

ants became sole heirs of her mother and coheirs of her father, bap. 4 Aug. 1743, at Stranton; marriage settlement, by which Stranton entail was barred, 13 Jan. 1767; m. 26 Feb. 1767, then of Durham. Will 28 Septem. 1767, Stranton to her husband for life, remainder to her children equally; died 9 Mar. 1778; in Sedgefield Rectory house, after a marriage of 'Eleven years and eleven days.'

cestors had long and comfortably enjoyed,' who died of a broken heart, and was buried at Kirkby-Stephen about 1750, by Ann Hawden; born at Soulby; educated under Yates at Appleby; adm. Magd. Coll. 1754; curate of Sedgfield and Elmdon 1758; vicar of Kelloe 1771; deputy lieutenant of militia 1785; chaplain to the earl of Aboyne 1796; will 30 Dec. 1804, proved at Canterbury 6 Feb. 1807; d. 1 Dec. 1806, at Kelloe, ag. 73. He was a tolerable poet, and resided partly at Stranton manor-house, *jure uxoris.* All his children were bap. at Sedgefield.

Arms.—Azure, a chevron, between three quarter-staffs arg. *Crest.*—A demi-lion rampant proper, bearing a quarter-staff arg.—(*Old seals, etc.*)

III. William Longstaff, of Newcastle-upon-Tyne and Stockton, surgeon, born in the Rectory House, Sedgefield, 20 Feb., bap. 2 March, 1770; died at Newcastle-upon-Tyne 13, bur. among the Cornforths at St. Oswald's, Durham, 17 Apr. 1795. Portrait, *penes auct.*, shewing a strong likeness to the Lees. = Anne, 2nd d. of William Cornforth, of Newcastle and Stockton, gent. by his wife Elizabeth Hylton, (mar. at Kelloe by lic. from the Spir. Court of Durham, 23 Mar. 1754, 'both of this parish,' born about 1721. "Here lieth interr'd the body of Elizabeth the wife of William Cornforth, who died the 28th Day of April, 1783, aged 62 years. 'On tombs enconiums are but vainly spent—a virtuous life is the best monument.' And also the remains of the much valued William Cornforth, her husband, who departed this life Dec. 17th, 1805, in the 74th year of his age."—*M. I. St. Oswald's*): bur. among the Cornforths at St. Oswald's. 'In memory of Ann, daughter of William Cornforth, and widow of the late Wm. Longstaff, surgeon, obt. 2nd Jany. 1821 æt. 53." Portrait *penes* me. Died intestate.

I. Abraham, d. 7 Oct. 1767.

II. Robert, d. 5 Oct. 1767.

Twins, born 3 Oct., immediately bp. bur. 8 at Sedgefield.

IV. George Hilton, b. 23, bap. 24 Dec. 1774; d. 10, bur. 11 Jan. 1775, at Sedgefield.

A dead child, born Sept. 1771 (*Lowth's Letters*). Two other children, who d. inf. were probably born in 1772 and 1773.

1 Mary, born. 2, bap. 8 Dec. 1768; d. 2, bur. 4 Aug., 1769, at Sedgefield.

2. Mary Hilton Longstaff, born 17, bap. 26 July, 1776; took half of Stranton estate; d. 4 Apr 1839, bur. at Stranton; m. Wm Lynn, of Stranton, gent. d. 8 Aug. 1840. ag. 73, br at Stranton.

William Hilton Longstaff, esq., only child, of Norton, near Stockton, co. pal., M.R.C.S., born 14 Nov. 1792; educated at Appleby; a pupil of William Ingham, esq., surgeon, Newcastle-upon-Tyne; admitted surgeon 1816; sold his moiety of Stranton estate; a herald and genealogist; died 1, bur. 5 Nov. 1842, at Norton, aged 49. Portrait *penes* me. = Elizabeth Dyer Franks, b. 26 Nov. 1802, bap. 5 Mar. 1803, at St. Giles'-in-the-Fields, mar. 22 Apr. 1824, at St. John's, Newcastle. She is eldest d. and coh. of Samuel Franks, esq., of Clapham, co. Surrey, by

I. Abraham Hilton, esq. b. in London 5 Oct. 1766, atty. at law, and one of the 6 clerks of chancery, d.unm. 1, bur. 5 Oct. 1792 in Darlington church.

II. Ralph, bp. 27 Sep. 1767, at Staindrop, d. inf.

III. Henry Hilton, of Barnard-Castle, spirit-merchant, *ultimus suorum*, b. in Lond., 25 Oct. 1768, *ob. cœlebs* 19 Sep. 1843.

IV. James Surtees Hilton, esq., lieut. 62 Reg. Foot, capt. 16 Light Horse, ; b. at Hilton 17 Nov. 1772 : died unm. at Darlington 30 Oct. 1796, ag. 22, after his return from the West Indies : bur. there 'of Barnard-Castle.'

V. William Freeman Hilton, esq. b. at Hilton 6 Mar. 1775, sometime cornet 27 Light Dragoons ; d. unm. in May, 1798, on board the *Earl Spencer* East Indiaman, in the Bay of Bengal, in his passage homewards.

2. Mary Ann Hilton, b. at Hilton 16 Jan. 1778, died unm. of consumption 5, bur. 8 May, 1803, in Darlington church.

Margaret Hilton, b. 16 Aug. 1770, at Hilton, bp. at St. Andrew's, Holborn, London, mar. 13 June, 17 3, at Darlington ; d. 14 Sep. 1830, at that place, br. at Haughton-le-Skerne, M.I. = Harrington Lee, of Darlington, woollen-draper, son of Robert Lee (bn. at Easingwold, afterwards of Darlington), by Mabel Rencher (born and mar. at Droghada, in King's County ; d. 1, bur. 6 April, 1822, at Haughton-le-Skerne, ag. 77), born 11 April, 1767, at Holbeck, near Leeds ; died 25, bur. 29 Dec. 1824, at Haughton. He acquired some property by devise from John Lee, esq. of London, who d. 12 Feb. 1814, ag. 48, & was no relation.

I. William Lee, b. 8 Nov. 1796, bap. at Darlington 11 Mar. 1797, *obiit cœlebs* at Caen, on or about 15 Nov. 1823, aged 27.

II. Harrington Lee, b. 30 Jan. 1802, bap. at Darlington same year, died there 25 Oct. aged 8, bur. at Haughton 26 Oct. 1810.

III. Hilton Lee, b. 23 June, 1803, bap. at Darlington 27 Aug. same year ; a surgeon at Stokesley ; died very suddenly there 11 Jan. 1831, aged 27, unmar., bur. 15, at Haughton.

IV. Surtees Lee, spirit-merchant, Hungate, Darlington, b. 4 Nov. 1805, bap. June, 1806, at Darlington, died there 15 Jan. 1812, aged 36, unmar., bur. 18, at Haughton.

2. Mary Lee, b. 25 Jan. 1800, bap. at Darlington 1 April same year, died at Newcastle-upon-Tyne, 27 Nov. 1834, buried at Haughton.

1. Margaret Lee, b. 4 May, 1795, bap. at Darlington in July following, mar. 14 June, 1814, at Darlington, died at Burdon 21 April, 1831, aged 35, buried at Haughton, 26. M. I. Portrait by W. Bewick, *penes* W. W. R. = William Robson, of Stockton and Great Burdon, co. pal., gent., died 18 Aug. 1838, aged 47, buried at Haughton. M. I. Portrait *penes* W. W. P.

I. William Wastell Robson, of Great Burdon, gen., b. 2 July, 1815.

II. John Robson, b. 4 Mar. 1817.

III. Edwin Robson, b. 24 Nov. 1827.

IV. Frederick Robson, b. 28 Feb. 1829.

V. Alfred Robson, b. 27 Apr. 1831, died inf.

1. Elizabeth Robson, b. 18 July, 1819, d. 25 Apr. 1837.

2. Margaret Robson, b. 5 Jan. 1822.

3. Mary Ann Robson, b. 15 Jan. 1824.

4. Emma Robson, b 31 May, 1826, mar. Geo. Brumwell Simpson, of Earby, near Greta Bridge, farmer.

Elizabeth Dyer, only child of the Rev. John Gaunt, D.D., Rector of Higham-on-the-Hill, and author of six sermons against the Methodists, by Elizabeth Dyer, eldest daughter and coh of the Rev. John Dyer, the gentle poet, whose portrait and MSS. are before me, by Sarah, eldest daughter and coh. of James Ensor, of Wilncote, par. Tamworth, gent., by Sary, daughter and heiress of George Strong, of Sutton-by-Broughton, Leic., gent. 'My wife's name,' says Dyer, 'was Ensor, whose grandmother was a Shakspear, decended from a brother of everybody's Shakspear.' James Ensor's mother was 'Grace,' who is believed on armorial evidence at Wilncote, to have been a Symmes. George Strong's wife was probably the Shakspear. Dyer's mother was Catherine, daughter and co-heiress of John Cocks, of Comins Worc., by Elizabeth, daughter and heiress of Edmond Bennet, of Mapleton, Hertfordshire, gent., by whom he quartered the arms of Webbs of Gillingham, in Kent, through 'the daughter of Charles Webbs, the son of John Webbs, who was burnt in Queen Mary's days. [See *Fox's Martyrs*.] She was an heiress, and married Dr. John Bennet, who was [*MS. decayed*] to prince Henry, and lost the pelf in search of the philosopher's stone.' Dyer also states a descent through Fisher and Williams from Bishop Robert Farrer or Ferrars, who was burnt at Carmarthen in 1555. And so much for the blood of 'a Dyer, such as dyed without a stayne,' and one whom Wordsworth thought it meet to praise.

*** The descendants of this match may I believe fairly wear the following coats if they choose :—1. *Longstaffe*, as borne by their Westmoreland ancestry. 2. *Hylton*, with the trefoil argent. 3. *Weemes*. Or, a lion rampant gu'es. 4. *Glen* of Inchmarlin, arg., a lion rampant sa. armed and langued gules. (These coats appear on a seal of Sir Davy of the Weems, 1423, and are quartered with Hylton on an old map of Stranton.) 5. *Franks*, az., a fess or charged with 3 tortauxes between 6 bezants (so borne by Samuel Franks). 6. *Gaunt*. Barry of 6. or and az., a bend gules, (so worn by Dr. Gaunt and all his relatives.) 7. *Dyer*. Gules, 3 eagles displayed argent.—(Dyer's MSS.) 8. *Cocks*. Sa. a chevron between 3 stags' attires fixed to the scalp arg.—(Ibid.) 9. *Bennet*. Gu., a bezant between 3 demi-lions arg.—(Ibid.) 10. *Pierry* of Nicholson, co. Heref. Arg., on a bend sinister sa. 3 pears or.—(Ibid.) 11. *Webbes* or Webb. Gu., a fesse between 3 owls or.—(Ibid. and Cook's Grants, fo. 4.) 12. Or, a fesse between 3 lozenges az. 13. 6 ermine spots, 3, 2, 1. 14. Arg., a fess gules between 3 estoiles sa.—(Quarterings of *Webbes*, in Dyer's MSS. and Burke's Armory.) 15. *Ensor*. Arg., a fess (in Dyer's MSS. and some of the Wilncote seals a chevron) gules between 3 horseshoes sa.—(Visit. Staff. 1583.) 16. *Hopwas* of Hopwas. Ermine, on a bend....3 plates —(Seal 39 Edw. III. allowed to Ensor 1583) 17. *Comberford* of Comberford, Gules, a talbot passant arg. (allowed to Ensor 1583.) 18. *Strong*. Quarterly, or and gules, in the first quarter an eagle displayed (gu.?—Old book plate.) The motto '*Steddy*' has been worn by Dyer and Franks successively, in right of Strong. The motto of the clan of Hylton was *Tant que je puis*.

I. William Hylton Longstaffe, of Gateshead, co. pal., born at Norton 2 Sep. 1826, bap. next day, christened 22 Jan. 1829; of Thirsk from 1842 to 1845, of Darlington 1845-1850, *crudus auctor*.

II. John Henry L., born 14 Mar. 1834.

III. Edward James L., born 25 Oct. 1837.

IV. Samuel Francis L., born 16 Nov. 1839.

V. Charles Robert L., born 4 Aug. 1842, bap. 5 Nov. 1842, being the day of his father's burial.

} Of Norton 1851.

1. Emma Franks L., of Gateshead, born 24, bap. 25 May, 1828, at Norton, christened 22 Jan. 1829.

2. Elizabeth Dyer L., born 2 Sep. 1830, at Norton.

3. Mary Anne L., born 14 June, 1832.

4. Eleanor Frances L., born 20 June, 1836.

} Of Norton 1851.

*** Since this Pedigree was set up, I have found Madame Hilton's baptismal register at Stranton, 'Maria filia Roberti Weemes generosi de Stranton, bap. 17 Jan. 1698.'

No. ii. The later Hyltons of Westmorland.

*** I have drawn this Pedigree with care, but from imperfect materials. I believe that it is generally correct. The baptisms and burials are, in the Burton branch, from Warcop; in the Helton Bacon one, from St. Michael's, Appleby, except where otherwise stated. The arms on Helton gate mentioned below are given for Helton in a MS. Ordinary *penes* the Rev. James Raine; the annulets are argent on sable the three saltires sable on an argent chief. Many small variations occur.

THE BURTON BRANCH.—

Christopher Helton, of Burton, esq. temp. Edw. IV. = Margaret, daur. of Thomas Marshall, of Kirk Oswald.

Robert Helton, or Hilton, esq., lord of Burton 18 Hen. VIII.; lord of a moiety of Helton Bacon, by grant of his brother Edward, 19 Hen. VIII.; died before 29 Hen. VIII. = ... Hartley.

Richard Helton, or Hilton, of of Burton, esq., died before 29 Hen. VIII. = Isabel, daur. of John Barton, of Ormshead, co. Westmorland, esq., and sister and co-heiress of Robert Barton, esq., of the same place; living 29 Hen. VIII.

Edward Hilton, clerk, rector of Bleachyngdon (pres. 1507), and Charleton-on-Otmore, Oxon., 1535; bought half of the Helton Bacon manor of Richard Restwolde. Will 26 Feb. 1526; founds an obit in Warcop Church 15 July; 2nd will 6 Oct. 1533, founds an obit in Queen's College, Ox. on the same 15 July, confirming the Warcop one.

Sisters mentd. in Edward Hilton's will.

Sir Ambrose Hilton, Oxford, clerk, a trustee mentd. in Edw. Hilton's will 1526; liv. 1535, as perp. vicar of Newbold, co. Warwick, (appr. to Queen's College, Ox.)

Thomas Helton or Hilton, esq., lord of Burton 29 Hen. VIII. and 1 and 2 Philip and Mary; mentioned in the entail made by Thomas baron Hylton, of Hylton Castle, 1561. = Anne Wharton, of Kirby Thore, co. Westm. Gilbert, second son of Henry Wharton, of Wharton Hall, d. 1436, having by his wife Joan, d. and h. of Kirkby, of Kirkby Thore, originated the Whartons of that place.

Andrew Helton, of Burton, esq., temp. Elizabeth, called by Dugdale the son of Richard; by Fleming the son of Thomas. = Alice, daur. of John Aglionby, of Carlisle.

I. John Hilton, esq., s. and h., d. about 1630. In 1675, this coat, put up in 1622, was remaining on the outside of Burton Hall. = Mary Saxton, daur. and coh. of .... Saxton, of Byham Hall, co. Essex.

1. Winifred, = Leonard Musgrave, of Johnby, Cumberland.

2. Julian. = 1*st.* An Irish lord. 2*nd* A sea captain.

H.

I. M.

I. Cyprian Hilton, of Burton, esq., s. and h., had the manor of Ormshead, *jure uxoris*, died 22 Dec. 1652. Brass in north aisle, Ormside. (2*nd* husband.) 'The hall of Ormside is an ancient *tower - house.* There is a well that springs under the kitchen.'—(*Nich. and B.*) = Frances, illeg. but only child and heir of sir Chr. Pickering, of Ormeshead, by his milkmaid at Threlkeld, whose name was Todhunter. She had been previously mar. to John Dudley, of Dufton, a lawyer, and in 1689 a brass vessel was found in the Eden at Ormside, marked F. D.

II. George Hilton, of Burton, gent. bap. 1608. = Jane, d. of .... Fletcher, of Dovenby, co. Cumb.

John, buried 1611.

Johan, d. unm. buried 1648.

I. Christopher Hilton, of Burton, and Ormside, esq., aged 36 in 1664. = Barbara, dr. of George Braithwaite esq., of Warcop, by Winifred, daur. of sir Rd. Fletcher of Hutton, co. Cumb. mar. 1660.

II. John Hilton, of Stanemore, mar. Isabel, daur. of John Farer, of Warcop Tower. (Mary wife of John Hilton, bur. 1667, at Warcop.) There are still Hiltons at Stanemore, and still the name of Cyprian occurs.

III. Andrew, d. s. p.

1. Mary, mar. William Farer, of Warcop Tower.

George Hilton, apprenticed to Robert Jennyson, sen., merchant adventurer and boothman, of Newcastle-upon-Tyne, 1 June, 1660, crossed out of the Merchants' books by mutual consent 1 July, 1664.—*G. B. R.*

THE HELTON BACON BRANCH.

Robert Hilton, lord of Helton Bacon, called to the Marches 1543. = ... dr. of Thomas Blenkinsop of Helbeck, esq.

I. Thomas Hilton, of Helton Bacon, lord of that manor 1 and 2 Philip and Mary. = Catherine Brackenbury, of Sellaby, d. a widow 1587. *Vide* No. I.

II. Anthony, died unmar.

III. John Hilton, of Gainford, co. pal. gen. (*Dugd.*) = ...

Robart, sonn of John Hilton, bur. 5 Nov. 1598, at St. Michael's, Appleby, being one of 'such as died upon the plague.'

Ann, daur. of John Hilton, of Hilton, in Westmorland. = Leonard Robinson, of St. Ninians, near Richmond.

Their son John, mar. Syth, dau. of Leonard Smelt of Kirkby Fleetham, and *sister to Lancelot Hylton's second wife.* (*See* No. I. and *Clarkson's Richmond*, 436.)

Thomas Hilton, esq., lord of Helton Bacon, bought Murton Hall; bur. 10 May, 1629. = Jane, daughter and co-heiress, of Reginald Hartley, of Appleby.

Lancelot Hylton, *a quo Hylton of Darlington*, etc. *Vide* No. I.

Nicholas Hylton. *Vide* No. III.

II. Thomas Hilton, esq., lord of Helton Bacon, bap. 1 May, 1584; died on Ascension day, 1645. Arms, over the chimney-piece at Helton Bacon Hall, the usual coat impaling Sandford; and over a washhouse door. Hilton with a bordure and T. H. = Elizabeth, daur. of Tho. Sandford, of Askham, Westmoreland, esq., by Martha, daughter of sir John Widdrington, of Widdrington (he died 1593), and mentioned by Hodgson as having married, after Sandford, 2, ... Hilton of .... On her grandfather's buildings at Askham Hall, is the inscription—

> Thomas Sandford esquyr
> For thys paid meat and hyr;
> The year of oure Savioure
> xv. hundrethe seventy foure.

I. George, died unm.

1. Katherine, mar. Brian Garnet, of Kendal.

I. Robert Hilton, of Murton, esq., lord of Helton Bacon, J. P. b. 1619; a trustee of the estate appointed by Ann countess of Pembroke to keep the tombs of her family in repair; governor of Appleby school; enfranchised various tenements in Brackinber, Helton Bacon, Ellerholme, and Bondgate; retired to Durham College, and died very suddenly 8, bur. 9 Jan. 1683, at Durham Abbey. Over the gate or entrance into the court of Helton Bacon Hall—Hilton (three annulets, *on a chief three* saltires) impaling Hylton, of Hylton Castle, a bordure running round both coats. He was aged 45 in 1664, at Visit. Dugdale, who gives him the usual coat mentioned in No. I. = Mary, daur. of John Hylton, baron Hylton of Hylton Castle; mar. in Hylton Chapel 2 Nov. 1647; bur. 28 Feb. 1684, at Durham Abbey.

II. Thomas.

III. George, bp. 6 Jan. 1621; d. inf.

IV. George of Bondgate, Appleby, bap 23 Jan. 1624.

1. Martha, mar. Robert Collingwood, of Hetton, co. pal.

I. Cyprian Hilton, of Burton and Ormside, esq., with his wife, enfranchised divers customary tenements in Helton Bacon, 1684; died 27 Dec. 1693, aged 34; brass at Ormside. Copy of the arms on an old tankard in the hands of Mr. Christopher Hall, corn merchant, Liverpool, and said to have belonged to the last Cyprian Hilton, of Burton, gives Hilton impaling Wharton, in marvellous corruption, and some other coat. The Saltires (joined into a sort of fret) and the annulets are azure, the fess gules, the field argent. The crest is a stag's head erased. = Abigail Wharton, only child of Hugh Wharton, esquire, 'of a younger branch of the Whartons, of Wharton Hall, he being called their relative in an inquisition of 1693; she survived her husbaud.

Winifrede, bap. 1662.

II. Thomas Hilton, esq., of Murton, lord of Helton Bacon, bap. 14 Apr. 1651; son and heir-appar. 28 Chas. II. Built a fair house near the scite of Betham Rectory. The manor of Helton Bacon was alienated 1696. On the door top at Helton Hall—

E.
T. H.
1682.

= Elizabeth, daur. of Charles Walker, of Workington, and widow of James Duckett, of Grayrigg, par Kendal, esq. from whom she had a portion of Betham Rectory.

I. John, bap. 5 Nov. 1648, died s. p.

III. Robert, probably of Durham (Elenor, d. Robert Hilton, bur. 10 Jan. 1685-6, and Mrs. Mary Hilton, bur. 20 May, 1712, both at Durham Abbey), bur. 15 Sep. 1713, as Robert Hilton, gent., at Kirby Hill, in Richmondshire, to which Gayles is closely situate.

1. Elizabeth, bp. 14 Jan. 1650 N.S.; mar. John Wycliffe, of Thorp, co. Ebor. Their son and heir Soloman, *of Gayles* and Thorpe, esq., was born 19 July, 1675, at Murton, and d. s. p.
2. Alice, bap. 26 May, 1654.
3. Mary, m. Tho. Butler, of Old Acres, co. pal. esq., settlement on the issue of this marriage 1683.

I. Christopher Hilton, esq., of Burton = Mary, daur. of John Pattinson, of Penrith, gen.

II. George.

III. Mr. Hugh Hilton, of Warcop. = ..

1. Margaret.
2. Barbara.
3. Elizabeth.
4. Mary.
5. Abigail.

IV. John Hilton. This seal belonged to him, descended to Miss Robinson, his grand-daur., and is now in possession of the Rev. Geo. Thompson.

= .. George Hilton, esq., s. and h., of Betham, a papist, rose in 1715 fled, and after the act of grace lived privately at Betham in a house he built at the south end of Betham Park. The Rev. Wm. Hutton, (vicar of Betham in 1762, who made a collection of curious matters concerning his parish, and lodged the same in his vestry for the information of posterity desiring the same might never be removed, with vacant pages to be filled up as materials should occur to his successors), takes notice that some few years ago there was found in an old chest a journal of George Hilton's life, which unfortunately afterwards became lost or mislaid. It appeared to have been taken by himself every night, or sometimes at the end of the week. An extraordinary account of his broken vows, and carnal and carnivorous failings in Lent, is extracted from the diary by Nicholson and Burn, in their History of Westmorland and Cumberland, *sub tit.* Betham.

Several sons died young, and six other daughters.

Mary, eldest daughter. = Daniel Robinson, esq., under sheriff of the county of Westmoreland; a good antiquary, and assistant of Burn in his History of Westmoreland.

I briefly express my acknowledgements to one of the numerous desendants of this match, the Rev. George Thompson, of Wisbeach, a truly enthusiastic member of the clan of Hilton; to John Hill, esq., of Appleby; and to the Rev. Thomas Bellas, of the same place, for their ready co-operation in the attempt to weave a pedigree of the distracted house of Hilton.

I. Cyprian.

1. Abigail, both d. inf.

1. Mary Hilton, only daur. and h. had 'twice one, and twenty children;' m. 1713. = Thomas Wyberg, of Clifton Hall, co. of Westmorland.

a quo
the Wybergs of Clifton Hall, representatives of Hilton, of Burton.

Theodosia, bap. 1713, bur. 1728.

*** *The following Darlington people may have been stray scions of the house of Burton.*

Christopher Hilton, of Darlington, bur. 19 Mar. 1636-7. = ...

William Hilton, of Darlington, tailor, adm. burgess to a burgage, in le Sowth rawe in le Burragh of Darlington, *jure uxoris* 1619; Oct. 5, sells (with his wife) a copyhold mess. in Bondgate, 2 Cha. I. = Elizabeth d. and h. of Michael Jefferson (lately dead Oct. 5, 1619, when his son-in-law was adm. to the burgage), of Darlington; bur. 4 Sep. 1644.

Isabella Hilton, mar. 2 Nov. 1628, Tho. Busby, at Darlington.

I. Richard, bap. 24 Sep, 1622, bur. 6 Dec.

II. Christofer, bap. 4 Nov. 1627, bur. 25 Feb. 1653-4.

III. Ralph Hilton, of Darlington, glover, bap 20 Mar. 1633-4; bur. 24 Sep. 1673. Will 11 Sep. 1673.

1. Mary, bap. 25 Mar. 1624-5, mentioned in bro. Ralph's will; mar. 7 Oct. 1652, William Witheraw, of Darlington, dead 1673.

2. Suzanna, bap. 20 June, 1630, probably the Susan Foster of her bro. Ralph's will.

3. Elizabeth, bap. 15 May, 1636, bur. 12 Apr, 1640.

4. Jane, bap. 2 Oct. 1638. (*Qu.* Jona Hilton, of Darlington par., and Peter Plainer, of Catterick par., mar. 28 May, 1667.)

5. Alice, bur. 29 Aug. 1641.

6. Meriol, bap. and bur. 10 Apr. 1643.

*** Simon Hilton, par, Dighton, mar. 5 Nov. 1667, Maria Brewer, par. Darlington.

No. iii.—Descendants of Nicholas Hilton.

Nicholas Hilton (brother of Lancelot, the settler in Durham), A.M., pres. Vicar of Sockburne 20 Sep. 1579 (*Allan's Sherburn Hosp*); res. 1604, = ... rector of Hurworth, appointed so 22 July, 1589, occurs as such 1591; died 18 Dec. 1616, at Hurworth.

1. Jane, bap. 17 Nov. 1591, at Hurworth. (*Qu.* Twin with Samuel?)
2. Mary, bap. 1597, at Hurworth.
3. Jane, bap. 6 Aug. 1598, at Hurworth.

I. Samuel, bap. 17 Nov. 1591, at Hurworth.

III. Thomas, bap. 23 Sep. 1599, at Hurworth.

II. William Hilton, bap. 10 Mar. 1592, at Hurworth; a merchant at York; adm. to his father 1616-7, Mar. 16. = Anne, daur. of James Rand, prebendary of Durham (*Surtees*, iii. 417); mar. 7 Nov. 1620, at Norton, where her father was vicar. The latter in his will, 1621 (he was buried that year at Norton) mentions 'daughter Mrs. Anne Hilton; To my sonne-in-law William Hilton his daughter, an ewe and lamb.'

1. A daughter, living 1621.

I. William Hilton, apothecary, par. All Saints, Newcastle, claimed 320*l.* from the Corporation of Newcastle, as due to his uncle, Dr. Samuel Rand, physician to the town. The freedom of the corporation was conferred upon him in 1657. 17 Jan. 1658, Wm. Hilton, of Newcastle, appoticary, bound to the stewards of the goldsmiths, plumbers, pewterers, and glaziers of Newcastle, in 100*l.*, he having been admitted to the fraternity simply to enable him legally to carry on business, and also to obtain the aid of the members thereof in repelling the attempts of the unfree of his particular trade; the company require him to enter into this bond, in order to prevent his occupying in any way any of the branches of trade which the company professed—also providing that he shall take no apprentices with the intent of making them free of the corporation, or of employing journeymen in any of the above trades. Seal *dim*, being in paper and wafer, but apparently the head of a bird, or possibly the demigriffin of Helton Bacon, for as Hilton was in a good position, it is probable he had his own seal. (*G.B.R.*) Will 1 Apr. 1676. = Anne, daur. of Ralph Salkeld, of Berwick-upon-Tweed, banns pub. Oct. at All Saints' Newcastle, mar. 2 Nov. 1654, at Berwick. Will 2 April, 1695. Mar. 2nd, Lancelot Hilton, of Durham, *Vide* Ped. No. I.

I. Samuel, bap. 3 Oct. 1658, bur. 3 Sep. 1659, at All Saints', Newc.

II John, bap. 6 May, 1660, at All Saints'.

III. James, bur. 20 Sep. 1661, at All Saints'.

1. Anne, bap. 7 Aug. 1655, bur. 9 Aug. 1656, at All Saints'.

2. Mary, bap. 16 Nov. 1656, bur. 11 May, 1657. at All Saints'.

3. Sarah, bur. 20 Aug. 1676, at All Saints'.

*** Nicholas Rand, of Newcastle, gen., and Susan Hilton, mar. lic. 2 Sep. 1718.—(His relationship to the main stock of Rands not shown.)
Eliz. dau. Tho. Hilton and Susannah *ux.* bap. 3 Aug. 1704.
Susanna Hilton, a surety 5 Feb. 1711. *Reg. St. Nich. Newc.*

No. iv.—Hilton of Dyons, Stockton etc., co-heirs of Alwent.

Arms.—The two saltires and three annulets, without a trefoil, gules on an argent field. *Crest.*—A demigriffin gules.—*Seal of Robert Hilton and book-plate of David his son.*

Lancelot Hilton, of Dyons, par. Gainford, *jure ux.* d. 1625. (Dates of children from Gainford,) = Catherine, eldest dau. and coh. of Ra. Alwent, of Dyons, esq., mar. 1587, d. 1602.

1. Katherine, bp. 3 Aug. 1590, br. 9 Sep. 1591.
2. Alice, bap. 3 June, 1595, mar. lic. dat. 17 Aug. 1616, mar. 20 Aug. 1616, Humphrey Elstob, of Foxton, co. Dur.
3. Margaret, bap. 24 Dec. 1598, ment. 1615. 'Margaret Hilton,' bur. 8 Sep. 1615. Gfd.
4. Merial, bap. 25 July, 1601.

I. Thomas, bap. 2 July, 1592.

III. Christopher, bap. 27 Aug. 1597, buried 20 Nov. 1620, s. p.

IV. John, bap. 13 July, 1600, d. s. p. before 1666.

1*st.* Grace, dau. of John King, of Durham, coroner and notary pub-public, bur. 18 Feb. 1633, at St. Mary le Bow, Durham. = II. James Hilton, of Dyons, bap. 28 Apr. 1594; James Hilton, a common-councillor of Newcastle 1617; living at Dyons 1636; subscribed 6*l.* 13*s.* 4*d.* to the re-edification of St. Mary le Bow, Durham, 1637; 'Anthon. Theobalds, gen. coronat. Warde de Easington. Practicavit medicinam et tabernam tenuit in Owengate prope Gaolam, quam domum vendidit *Jacobo Hilton, gen.*;' bur, 6 July, 1638, at Durham Abbey. Will 29 June, 1638, pr. 1642 at Durham; bequeathes a ballast shore at South Sheels, subject to any right of Christopher Mickleton and Mary, *ux.* (d. and h. of Thomas King) therein. = 2*nd.* Barbara, wid. Thomas King, jun., of Shields, gent. living 1638, 1646.

I. John Hilton, apprentice to a draper taillor 1630, shortly after 'turned to another.'

III. James, adm. of Gray's Inn, 4 May, 1638.

IV. John, *secundus*, bap. 14 Feb. 1633, bur. 26 Nov. 1634, at Bow.

An infant of James Hilton's bur. 21 May, 1616, at Gainford.

1. Barbara, bap. 6 Mar. 1618 at Gainford; m. 28 Sep. 1637, at Houghton le Spring, Hen. Moorcroft, of Durham city, gen. (*See* ped. of Moorcroft, *Surtees*, iii. 415.)

3. Alice, living 1638.

4. Elizabeth, bap. 15 Sep. 1626, as *Besse* Hilton.

5. Jane, bap. 19 June, 1631, at St. Mary le Bow, bur. 13 Nov. 1634.

2. Jeronyma, bap. 8 June, 1623, at Gainford, as '*Joanna Ananias*,' bur. 10 Mar. 1704 (Stockton), as 'Mrs. Hieronyma Moorcroft,' mar. 3 Sep. 1639, at St. Giles', Durham, Edward Moorcroft, A.M. (2nd son of George Moorcroft, of Kingham, Oxon., and preb. of 9th stall in Dur. Cath.) vicar of Hesilden, and rector of Redmarshall, co. pal.; apparently nephew of Hen. Moorcroft *ante*; bur. at Redmarshall 18 Oct. 1694.

1*st.* Mary, daur. of .... buried 23 Aug. 1652, at Heighington. 'Mrs Mary wife of Mr Lancelot Hilton.' = II. Lancelot Hilton, son and h., of Durham, gen. bap. 9 June, 1622, at Gainford; apprentice to John Cosin, of Newcastle-upon-Tyne, draper. = 2*nd.* Bridget, daughter of .... bur. 19 Feb. 1654, Bow.

Mary, bap. 27 Nov. 1647, at Denton.

Robert Hilton, bap. 1652, of Stockton, attorney-at-law, died 17 May, 1727, ag. 75, bur. at Stockton. M. I. Adm. of the draper tailors' company 29 Dec 1699, as of Stockton, and son of Lancelot, of Durham, gent. Will 27 Nov. 1725, ' cousins *Anne*, Thomas, John, and Edward Rudd, and cousins *Ann* Stainsby and Esther Raisbeck; my cousin John Moorcroft his children; cousin Alderson, deceased;' proved at York 19 Nov. 1729; acquired one-fourth of the manor of Hurworth in 1702, from John Marley, gen. = Esther, daur. of Thomas Watson, alderman of Stockton, bap. 27 June, 1659, mar. lic. 29 Nov. 1680, mar. 21 Dec. 1680, at Stockton; bur. 13 Aug. 1723, ag. 64, at Stockton. Her sister Alice mar. the Rev. Thomas Rudd, vicar of Norton, and had issue, *Thomas* (a clergyman and schoolmaster, whose dau. Catherine mar. the Rev. Wm. Sisson, another Norton vicar, M.I. Darlington), *John (the compiler of Rudd's MSS.* solr. genl. to the bp., and afterwards of Winyard, esq.), *Edward*, *Mary* mar. to *Robt. Stainsby*, a surgeon at Stockton), and *Esther*, mar to Wm. *Raisbeck*, of Stockton, gen.

James, bap. 5 April, 1654, at Bow, bur. 25 Oct. 1659, St. Nich, NC.

I. James, bap. 25 July, 1682, died 28 July, 1689, Stockton.

II. William, bap. 27 April, 1687, bur. 18 Sep. 1689, Stockton.

III. Thomas, bap. 18 April, 1689, bur. 12 Sep. 1689, Stockton.

IV. Robert, bap. 20 Oct. 1690, bur. 31 July, 1696, Stockton.

VI. John, bap. 14 Apr. 1696, bur. 14 Sep. 1696, Stockton.

VII. George (twin with John), bap. 14 Apr. bur. 19 Aug. 1696, Stockton.

VIII. Robert Hilton, of New Elvet, Durham, attorney at law, bap. 28 Apr. 1698, bur. at St. Oswald's 12 Nov. 1764. = Ursula, dau. of H. Sedgwick, of Tudhoe, b. 7 Dec. 1701, mar. 29 Sep. 1726, bur. 7 Nov. 1792, at St. Oswald's.

1. Meriol, bap. 7 Dec. 1684, bur. 27 Jan. 1686, Stockton.
2. Esther, bap. 16, bur, 19 Feb, 1692, Stockton.

2nd. Silence, ..., bur. 1 Mar. 1732. = V. Lancelot Hylton, of Stockton and Brancepath, attor-at-law, b. 16, bap. 19 Aug. 1694, died 16 Oct. 1757. M. I. Stockton; appointed seneschal for life by bishop Crewe 1715. = 1st. Ellen Conset, m. 13 Aug. 1719, at York cathedral; buried 21 Jan. 1729, at Stockton. M. I.

1. Margaret, bp. 29 Jul. 1725, bur. 29 May, 1727, Bow.

2. Elizabeth, bp. 29 July, 1725, bur. 2 Jan. 1725-6, Bow.

1st. Sarah, ..., bur. 16 Aug. 1725, Bow. = IX. David Hilton, of Durham, barrister at law (Middle Temple), (apparently twin with Robert), bap. 28 Apr. 1698; joins 2nd wife, Mary Morland, etc., in selling Graystones and Nesbett, otherwise Humbleton, to George Surtees, in 1744, for 4,400*l*. He was seneschal to bishops Crewe (appointed for life 1719), Talbot, Chandler, Butler, Trevor, and Egerton; recorder of Hartlepool in 1749. = 2nd. Catherine, d. and coh. of John Morland, of Windleston, mar. lic. 25 June, 1731, m. at St. Oswald's; living in 1773, a widow at Bath.

1. Elizabeth, bap. 29 Sep. 1732, bur. 22 Aug. 1737, Bow.
2. Esther, bap. 2 Aug. 1734. Bow, d. s. p. 1804; mar. .... Davis, of Bath.
3. Mary, bap. 19 June, 1736, Bow; mar. .... Andrews, esq., of Wells, and had issue Rev. Robert Andrews, who d. s. p. 1820.
4. Catherine, bap. 23, bur. 28 Oct. 1741, Bow.

I. Robert Hilton, b. 11, bap. 12 Jan. 1737, Bow; fellow of Trinity Coll., Cam.; A.B. 1760, A.M. 1763; prebendary of Llandaff cathedral. He was sometime of Renton, co. Camb. and Durham city, and died at Bath, of a repeated stroke of palsy, 12 Mar. 1804, s. p., ag. 67.

II. John, bap. 13 July, 1740, bur, 24 Sep. 1741, Bow.

Elizabeth, bap. 19 Aug. 1729, at St. Oswald's; mar. 25 June, 1752, at Yarm, John Hopper, esq., of Shincliffe, who by her had issue Robert Hopper, esq., who marrying the heiress of Williamson, assumed that name, and was the ancestor of Williamson, of Hurworth. (*See* Burke's *Landed Gentry.*) Robert was recorder of Newcastle, and chancellor of Durham. ⅄

III. William Hilton, the poet, a mercer of Gateshead, bap. 4 May, 1727, at Stockton; riding officer in the customs at Sunderland from 5 April, 1781, to 13 May 1787; died Apr. 1798, at Gateshead. = Anne, daur. of Richard Dobson, of Redheugh, near Gateshead, staithman, mar. at Gateshead 15 Feb. 1756, died 9 Dec. 1822, at Windmill Hills, Gateshead.

I. Robert Hilton, of Elvet, Durham, esq., an officer of infantry. bap. 1720, at Stockton; died 8, buried 10 Apr. 1770, at St. Oswald's. = Margaret, dau. of Rev. Robert Blakiston, vicar of Merrington, co. Durham, by Margaret, dau. Wm. Tempest, esq., of Old Durham, mar. lic. 5, mar. 6 July, 1745, at Houghton le Spring; d. 4 Mar., bur, ' from Newcastle,' at St. Oswald's 7 Mar. 1791.

II. Edmund, free of drapers' company, 13 Feb. 1750.

1. Elizabeth, bap. 27 Feb. 1721, bur. 4 Nov. 1722, Stockton.

2 Esther, bap. 19 July, 1725, at Stockton, died 18 June, 1795 ag. 69. M. I. Hitchin; mar. Rev. John Pilkington Morgan, of Houghton le Spring, vicar of Hitchin, co. Hereford, 1755; fellow of Trinity College, Cambridge; died 16 July, 1788. M. I. Hitchin. ⅄

3. Isabel, bap. 7 Apr. 1765, bur. 21 May, 1767, Gateshead.

4. Ellen, bap. 17 Dec. 1766, Gateshead, died 1846, aged 80. M. I. Gateshead.

5. Anne, bap. 7 Aug. 1768, Gateshead, d. 1794.

6. Esther Margaret, bap. 15 Oct. 1770, living at Gateshead 1833, died at the Windmill Hills 1844, aged 74. M. I. Gateshead.

I. A son, b. June, 1760, (*Hilton's Poems*, i. 136.)

II. Richard, bap. 24 July, 1769, Gateshead, a sailor, and was drowned.

III. Spencer William, bap. 12 Jan. 1772, Gateshead, d. 6 Mar. 1789 (*Walbran*, 1799, *Surtees.*)

1. Isabel Ellen, b. 1756, bap. 6 Jan. 1557, Gateshead, bur. 28 Mar. 1759, Gateshead.

2. Catherine, b. 24 June, 1758 (*Poems*), bap, 19 July, 1758, Gateshead, died unm.

I. Robert, bap. 7 Jan. 1757, St. Oswald's, bur. there 29 Apr. 1760.

II. William Hilton, of Collier Row, Durham, master mariner, bap. 28 Oct. 1759, St. Oswald's, liv. 1833, s. p.; mar. Rosamond, daur. of Robert Horn, of Frampton, co. Lincoln, 1 Feb. 1791.

1. Elenor, bap. 18 Jan. 1755, St. Oswald's. died 5 Feb. 1829, bur. St. Oswald's; mar. Robert Scott, of Newcastle-upon-Tyne, silversmith, d. Mar. 1793, bur. St. Oswald's, Of this match there was issue, Margaret Scott, living in Newcastle 1829, unmar., and the Rev. Robert Hilton Scott, sometime lecturer of St. John's and St. Andrew's churches, Newcastle, afterwards of Plymouth, and in 1847 of Bedford Street, Bedford Square, London, who has a numerous family.

No. v.—Hilton of Killerby.

The dates are from Heighington, except where otherwise stated.

Francis Hilton, of Killerby, par. Heighington, son of Lancelot Hilton by Elizabeth Smelt, bap. 2 Mar. 1605, at Gainford, bur. 13 Nov. 1680, at Heighington. = Elizabeth, daur. of ...... Raine, sister to John Raine, bur. 29 Dec. 1638.

I. Lancelot Hilton, of Killerby, bap. 26 Oct. 1634, bur. 20 June, 1675, in Heighington choir. M.I. = Margaret Atkinson, mar. lic. 3 June, 1663, bur. 25 Aug. 1697, in Heighington choir. M. I.

II. Henry Hilton, bap. 19 Mar. 1636, of Midderidge Grange 1664, of Denton 1676, of Somerhouse, par. Gainford, 1686, gent., bur. 26 July, 1712, at Gainford. = Margaret ...., bur. 14 April, 1705, at Denton. *Qu.* if 'Mrs. Anne Hilton, Somerhous,' bur. 27 Aug. 1722, at Gainford, was not his 2nd wife ?

1. Jane, bap. 24 April, 1632.

I. George Hilton, of Killerby, gent., born 4, bap. 10 Apr. 1666; will 8 Aug. 1721; bur. 11 May, 1723, in Heighington choir. M. I. = Lydia, daur. of John, only son of William Douthwaite, of Staindrop, d. 4 Nov. 1745, ag. 77, M.I. Heighington. 'Mrs. Hilton, of Gainford, bur. 7 Nov. 1745,' at Gainford.

II. Thomas Hilton, of Elswick, co. Northumberland, gent., b. 7, bap. 7 Mar. 1671; ag. about 41, 1713; bur. 17 Mar. 1714-5, at St John's, Newcastle. = ..

1. Margaret, bap. 14 Feb. 1663-4.
2. Elizabeth, born 26 Dec. 1668, bap. 2 Jan. 1668-9. *Qu.* E.... Hilton de Killerby, bur. 19 Jan. 1681, at Denton.
3. Mary, bap. 8 Oct. 1674, died unm. 25 Aug. 1697.

Florence, bap. 17 Jan. 1665, at Denton, bur. 15 Feb. 1666, at same place.

Henry, bap. 6 Sep. 1668, at Denton, liv. 1676.

II. Francis, bap. 11 Apr. 1700, living 1713.

III. Thomas, bap. 21 Apr. 1702, Denton, as Tho. s. Geo. Hilton, a *Kitsworbie*, bur. 26 Apr. 1718. M.I. Heighington, 'son of Mr. George Hilton.'

IV. Henry, bap. 16 Nov. 1703, bur. 23 Jan. 1723-4.

V. Alexander, bap. 13 Nov. 1705, d. 20, bur. 26 Mar. 1732. M I. Heighington.

1. ...... a dau. bur. 10 Apr. 1690.

2. 3. Margaret and Lydia, twins? bap. 6 Oct. 1693.

4. Deborah, bap. 4 July, 1695.

5. Tamar, bap. 27 Oct. 1696.

6? A daughter, bur. 23 .... 1724.

I. Lancelot Hilton, bap. 14 June, 1698, sometime of Cowclose, par. Bowes, Yorks. (1722-4) and of Mirekeld 1726. = Jane Bayles, of Bowes, mar. 3 May, 1721, at Richmond, Yorkshire.

I. John, bap. 9 Jan. 1706, St. John's, Newcastle-upon-Tyne.

II. Thomas, bap. 4 Sep. 1711, St. John's, Newcastle.

2. Dorothy, bap. 25 June, 1724, Bowes.

3. Deborah, bap. 19 June, 1726, Bowes.

1. Lydia, bap. June, 1722, Bowes: mar. 24 Mar. 1739-40, bur. 24 Feb. 1781, Barnard-Castle. = John Hilton, of B. C., bur. 12 Apr. 1789; (possibly the above John, bap. 1706)

I. Lancelot, bap. 22 Feb. 1740-1, B. C.

III. John, bap. 5 Feb. 1764. B. C.

II. Alexander, bap. 24 Feb. 1742, B. C. = Jane Carr, m. 5 Jan. 1769, B.C.

1. Mary, bap. 5 Nov. 1749, B. C.

2. Ann, bap. 25 Dec. 1751, B.C., mar. Tho. Peacock, 8 Apr. 1779, B.C.

3. Debora, bap. 14 Sep. 1755, B.C., mar. Robt. Heaton 16 Sep. 1773. B.C.

4. Penelope, bap. 28 Mar. 1758, B.C.

5. Lydia, bap. 1 Feb. 1761, B.C., mar. Jacob Prest, 15 Aug, 1782, B.C.

I. Thomas, bap. 9 Mar. 1770, B.C.

II. James, bap. 16 Aug. 1771, B.C.

III. Alexander, bap. 30 Aug. 1778, B.C.

1. Jane, bap. 2 July, 1773, B.C.

2. Mary, bap. 10 Dec. 1775, B.C.

3. Dorothy, bap. 11 Mar. 1781, B.C.

*** John Dent and *Martha* Hilton (a true Bowes name), of Barnard Castle, mar. there 10 Feb. 1727-8.

No. vi.—Hilton of Denton.

Lancelot Hilton, of Durham, gen.; d. 1685. = Dorothy, d. Wm. Wright, wid. John Cradock, d. 1675.

1. Dorothy, bap. 13 May, 1651, at Heighington. Ralph Wilkinson and Dorothy Hilton, mr. 2 Dec. 1697, Abbey.

2. Ann, b. 29 May, bap. 9 June, 1657, at Staindrop, mar. 8 Feb. 1678, at the Abbey, John Geldart.

II. ......, a son bap. 20 Jan. 1654, at Heighington.

III. Francis, bap. June, 1653, at Heighington, bur. in the chancel of Staindrop church 8 Oct. 1658.

3. Elizabeth, b. 9, bap. 17 Jan. 1658 at Staindrop. *Qu.* Peter Burrell, and Mrs. Elizabeth Hilton, mar. 12 Oct. 1686, St. Giles', Durham.

I. Alexander Hilton, bap. 10 Sep. 1654, at Heighington, curate of Denton 1674 to 1682. He resigned the curacy of Denton for the rectory of Romaldkirk (patrons Abraham and Henry Hilton) 14 Oct. 1682, and died there the same year before 16 Dec. = ... liv. 1682.

No. ii. Chaytor.

"TO ALL AND SINGULER, aswell nobles and gentils as others, etc. William Flower, esquire, *alias* Norroy Kinge of Armes of the east, west, and north partes of England, from the ryver of Trent, northward, Sendith greetinge, etc. FOR AS MUCHE, as auncientiy from the beginninge, the valiaunt and vertuouse ac'es of excellent persones have ben commended to the worlde and posterity with sondrey monumentes and remembrances of their goode deseartes; Emongest the which the chiefest and most usuall hath ben the bearinge of signes in shieldes called Armes, beinge none other thinge then evidences and demonstracions of prowesse and valoir diversly distributed accordinge to the qualytes and deseartes of the persones meryt-inge the same; To the entent that such as by their vertues do adde to the advancement of the common weale the shyne of their goode lyfe and conversation, may therfore receyve due honor in their lyves, and also deryve and contynew the same successively in their posteryty for ever. EMONGEST the which nombre *Christopher Cheytor, of Butterbee, in the countie of Durham, esquire*, beinge one who of longe tyme hath used him self so vertuously and discreetly that he well deserveth and meriteth to be in all places of honor admitted, reputed, and taken in the fellowship, nombre, and company of other gentils. IN CONSIDERATION whereof, and for a further declaration of the worthynesse of the sayde Christopher Cheytor, and at his instant request, I the sayd Norroy Kinge of Armes, by power, etc., have assigned, etc., unto the sayd Christopher Cheytor these arms and creast followinge: That is to say; *the field party per bende endented argent and asure, three cinque foyles counterchanged: Upon a heaulme on a torce argent and asure a bucke's hedde, lozengy of the torce and therof horned*, videlicet: *one horne argent and the other asure: Mantelled gueules; doubled argent;* as more playnely may appeere depicted in this margent. WHICH arms, etc., I, etc., ratify, etc. IN WITNESSE wherof, I, etc., have signed these presentes with my hande, and sette therto the seale of myne armes and of myne office the xxvjth day of Octobre, in the yere of our Lord God a thousand five hundred seventy and one. And of the reigne, etc.—*p' moy Wyllam flower, alias Norrey Roy darmes*." (Seals of Flower and the King of Arms in the north parts. The grant contains Flower's portrait in heraldic dress on the initial letter, and the Tudor rose, with an illuminated running scroll.)—Either the grant merely confirms a coat worn before (and from its simplicity, this was probably the case), or the descendants of other Newcastle Chaytors sheltered themselves under it. The Sandersons of Newcastle and Brancepeth quartered such arms by right of Eleanor, daughter and heiress of Piers Chaytor, of Newcastle. She was living at the death of her husband in 1549. A reduced facsimile of the illuminated arms on this grant is exhibited in the left cut.

There also occurs "a patent to William Chaytor, of Croft Hall, in the co. of York, living Ao. 1614, the sonne of Anthony, the sonne of Christopher Chater, of Butterby, in the bishoprick of Durham, which Christopher married Elizabeth, daughter and heir of William Clarvaulx, of Croft Hall, in co. Ebor.," by R. St. George, Norroy, 12 July, 1612. ARMS.—Azure, a chevron erminois, inter three annulets argent, on a chief or three martlets gules, *Chaytor*, quartering, Sable, a saltire or, *Clarvaux*. CREST.—On a wreath, a crane proper, capped gules.—(*Cooke's Dockets, W. Radcliffe*, and *Chaytor MSS.*) This conceit of the knight does not appear to have had any extended time of grace, and I have not detected the new coat on any one document. The crane was of course the crest of Clervaux borrowed for the nonce. The cut shews the crane at rest, as in a rough sketch of the new arms in the Chaytor MSS., but the heralds ascribe a heron statant proper as a second crest of Chaytor.

In the Visit. 1615, Chaytor, of Butterby, has no mark of difference assigned, but the metal in the shield is *or* instead of *argent*.

A third grant was made to the present baronetical family:—Party per bend dancettèe argent and azure four quatrefoils counterchanged. CREST.—A stag's head, erased, lozengy argent and sable, armed or. in the mouth a trefoil slipped, vert. MOTTO.—(from Clervaux), *Fortune le veut*.

*** ......Clarvaux. ╤ ......

Richard Clarvaux, of Stockmier, par. Croft, yeoman. Probably set up a claim as heir male to the Croft estate, as in 1598, with a good signature, for 40*li.* he quitclaims to Anthony Chaytor all actions, demands, etc. from the beginning of the world.

Cuthbert Clarvaux. 'Richard Clarvaux and Cuthbert Clarvaux shall enjoy their terme of eighte yeares from the feast of Philipp and Jacobb next, paying the rent of 3*l.* 6*s.* 8*d.* either of them yearly according to my graunte.' (*Richard Clervaux's will* 1586.) = ... Clarvax, wife of Cuthbert Clarvax, bur. 8 Nov. 1617, at St. Oswald's, Durham, evidently through the Chaytor settlement at Butterby.

Robert Clarvasse, of Darlington, buried 24 Feb. 1598-9, at Darlington. ╤ Margaret Clarvax, widow, bur. 3 May 1606, at Darlington.

Margaret Clervax, married 5 Jun. 1607, Rowland Willson, *alias* Eglesfeild, at Darlington.

Anna Clarvisse, of Darlington, spinster, aged about 28, a witness in Eccl. Court proc., 1594-5. — Anna Clarvax, of Darlington, spinster bur. 14 March, 1628-9.

Richard Clarvasse. ╤ *Qu.* Jenet Watson, mar. to Ric. Clervause, at Romaldkirk ...... 1592.

A son, bap. at Darlington 22 Nov. 1592.

Tobias Clerveux, a plaintiff at Darlington Borough Court, 1623. [Isabella (incerti parentis vulgo) filia Tobiæ Clarvis bapt. 16 Martii 1619; spons: Henricus Haswhittle, Isabella Runthwait et —— Newton.—*Denton Reg.*]

Thomas Clarvasse, of Darlington, a freeholder, bur. there 14 Apr. 1631. 'Thomas Clarvis, of Darlington, pedler, ag. about 38,' a witness in Eccl. Court proc. 1594-5. The registers of his descendants are from Darlington. ╤ ..

Mary, bp. 21 Feb. 1597-8 = 3 Dec. 1626, Cuthbert Grainger.

A daughter, buried 15 Dec. 1599.

Thomas Clervax, or Clarvaise, bap. 30 Dec. 1600, of Skinnergate, 1653. 'To Tho. Clarvis, being sick att severall times, 2*s.* 1*d.*, 1661' 'To Mr. Bell, for burying Tho. Clarfax, 11*d.*, 1671. ╤....

Agneta, bap. 19 Jan. 1602-3 *Qu.* Anne Clervax, who mar. 22 Jan, 1626-7, Peter Fleming.

William Clervax, bp. 21 Apr. 1622.

Elizabeth, bp. 29 Jan. 1625-6.

Agnes, bp. 28 Apr. 1629.

George, bap. 21 July, 1631, buried 22 Feb. 1632-3.

Margaret, bp. 21 Apr. 1652.

Elizabeth, bp. 7 Feb. 1653-4, buried 30 Sep. 1660.

William Clervas, bap. 21 Apr. 1656. 'To Will. Bellwood, with young Clarfax, 1*l.* 5*s.*, 1670.' Bur. 10 Mar. 1676-7, 'William Clervax wynding sheet, 1*s.* 6*d*' 1676.

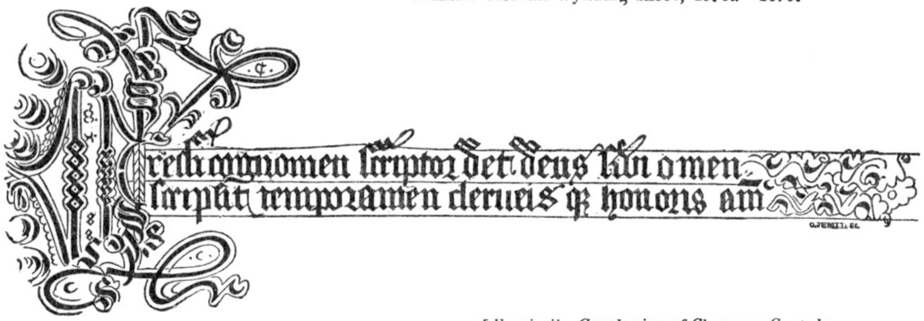

[*Facsimile Conclusion of Clervaux Cartulary.*

Issue of Sir Richard Clervaux.

John Clervaux, of Croft, esq. died sans issue male. = Jane, dau. of John Hussey, of Sleeford, co. Linc.

Marmaduke Clervaux, esq., succeeded his bro. at Croft; died 14 Hen. VII. (1498 or 9.) To be bur. before Croft high altar. He erected the tomb of his father. = Eizabeth, daur. of sir James Strangwayes, of Harlsey Castle, Allertonshire, knt.

Robert. *Qu.* Robert Clarvaux, arm. Serviens Episcopi, bailiff of Whickham for life, with a fee of 2*d*. per diem, 12 May 3 Sinews (about 1505), No. 86.

Henry, died young. (*Glover.*)

Elizabeth, mar. 1. William Fitz-Henry; mar. 2. Wm. Clarjenet. [The De Clerjonets, of Richmunde, are often previously mentioned in the Clervaux Cartulary.]

Margare', mar. Tho. Laton, of Saxhowe, in Cleveland, esq., de:cribed in the ind. of mar. 12 Jan. 1458, as eldest s. and h. of Robert Laton, of Melsonby.

Joan, mar. Chr. Aske.

Beatrix, a nun at Syningthwaite.

Isabell, mr. Wm. Conyers, esq. of Wynyard, co pal., s. and h. of sir Roger Conyers, kt. 4th son of Chr. Conyers, of Horneby.

Margery. = John Fitz-William, of Sprotburgh and Haddlesey, esq., whose descendants became heirs male of the *vetusta equestris familia Gulielmiadum* (as Camden has it), on the el er line of Sprotborough running into females. His daughter Margaret married John Cranmer, elder brother to the Reformer. This John "continued ever faithful to the house of York, as his father did, and was a captain under Richard duke of Gloucester, who, after the fall of his master, withdrew himself from the court, and lived contentedly."—(*See Hunter's South Yorkshire*, i. 339.)

John Clervaux, of Croft, esq., son and heir, died 5 Hen. VIII. (1513 or 14.) = Margaret, daur. of Richard Hansard, esq., of Walworth, by Elizabeth, d. Tho. Blount, 2nd bro. of Walter 1st lord Mountjoy.

John Clarvis then was 'nexed near,
With Stapylton of stomach stern;
Next whom Fitz-William forth did fare,
Who martial feats was not to learn.
Old Poem of Flodden-field.

William Clervaux esq., of Croft, heir to his niece the baroness of Hylton. = Isabella, or Elizabeth, daur. of Tho. Bellasis, of Henknowle, co. pal. esq., by Margaret, d. sir Lancelot Thirkeld, knt.

Elizabeth, mar. Percival Lambton esq., of Bellasis, par. Billingham, in which church there was a brass plate in 1794, inscribed:—"Hic jacet P'civallus Lambton d' Bellases armiger & Elizab'th uxor ejus una filiarum Marmaduci Clervaux d' Croft qui q'd'm P'civallus obiit sexto die Novembris Ao. D'ni Mo Do p'mo et dicta Elizab'th obiit xiiio die Augusti Ao. D'ni Mo Do xxiijo quor. A'i'ab's p'pici. deus."

Eleanor, mentioned in her father's will.

John Clervaux, d.s.p. (*Roll.*)

Elizabeth Clervaux, sole heir, d. s. p., = Sir Thomas Hylton, baron Hylton, of Hylton Castle, in the bishoprick.

John Clervaux, esquire of the body of king Henry VIII., d.s.p. 'This man was an unthrift.'

*** Thomas Bowes, 2nd son of sir Wm. B. and Maude de Dalden, died before 1421; mar. Agnes ...... *widow of John Clervaux, of Croft*, on whose marriage the Bowes manor of Luttryngton was settled.—George Bowes, their son, liv. ag. 22, 1421.

Henry Bowes, great grand-nephew of said Thomas; executor to his brother sir Ralph B. 1482; mar. 1. .... widow of ...... Clarvaux, of Crofte. (*Visit. Durham*, 1575.)

1. Margery, dr. of Robert Killinghall, esq., whose brother John Killinghall, by will 1572, names 'his brother, Mr. Richard Clarvax.' Had issue, which died. She was widow of Rowland Place, of Halnaby, esq. whose son Anthony Place, by will 1570, names his father-in-law, Mr. Clarvaux. = Richard Clervaux, of Croft, esq. Will 24 Feb. 1586-7, pr. May, 1587, at Richmond. Inq. p. m. 13 June, 1587. He died 26 Feb. previous. = 2. Margery, dau. of Mr. Rob. Place.

Elizabeth, Clervaux sole heiress of her ancient house, br. 14 Dec. 1584, at St. Oswald's, Durham, 'a vertuous & a good gentlewoman.' (*Parish Reg.*) = Christopher Chaytor, esq., of Butterby.

Richard Clervaux, of Croft, esq. son and heir, born 13 May, 1585; ag. 1 year 8 months 13 June, 1587; died 21 Jan. 1590-1. Inq. 12 Mar. following. 'Anthonie Chater, sonne and next heire of Elizabeth Chater, coosen and next heyre.'

A daughter, d. inf.

CHAYTOR, OF CROFT AND BUTTERBY,

See Ped. II.

†‡† 17 Edw. IV. Escaet. No. 18. Margareta Clervaux, widow, d. and h. of Gerard Salvayn, knt., Sandall near Howden manor, Houeden manor, Brunby, Ayton, part of Wilton manor, Thorpe Parva, the suit of court of Thorpe Parva manor, all in Yorkshire.

Ralph Clervaux, of par. Blacktoft, Howdenshire, mar. lic. 20 May, 1618. = 18 May, 1618, at Darlington, Elizabeth Bower, of the Oxenlefield family.

John Clervaux, of Croft, esquire, son and heir; executor 1390; living 1416. On his marriage, his father settled all his property in Stapilton, Joleby, in Croft, which the tenants of Jolby farmed, and in York, on the young couple. = Isabella, daur. of Richard de Richmond, by Elizabeth, daughter and heiress of William Burgh. The brother of Isabella took the maternal surname, and originated the Burghs, of Burgh Hall, par. Catterick. The arms of Clervaux occur in Catterick Church.

Thomas Clervaux, said to have married Isabella [or Agnes, as Thoresby has it], d. and coh. of Hngh Thoresby, esq., of Thoresby, co. York [he was living 25 Edw. III], and to have had by her Thomas and John. She is said to have remar. 2, Tho. Dodsworth, and 3, John Aston.

Richard Clervaux, to whom his father, in 1390, left a house in Guthrumgate, York, for life, d.s.p.

Agnes, mar. ...... Studdowe. (*Glover.*)

Robert. (*Glover.*)

William Clervaux, executor and resid. legatee 1390)

Margaret, daur. of Sir Ralph Lumley, knt, by Eleanor Neville, sister of Ralph, the great earl of Westmoreland; executrix to her husband 1443. = Sir John Clervaux, knt. Will 13 July, 1443; to be buried in Croft Church. M. I. there, in the Clervaux aisle. He was high sheriff of Yorkshire 1430.

Sir Richard Clervaux, of Croft, son and heir, 1442 'Dominus de Croft;' escheator of Yorkshire in 1447; esquire of the body to king Henry VI.; knighted by Henry VII.; died 1490. M. I. in the Clervaux aisle in Croft ch. In his time the Clervaux cartulary was formed. = Elizabeth, daughter of sir Henry Vavasour, knt. of Haselwood, high sheriff of Yorkshire 10 Edw. IV., by Joan, dau. of sir William Gascoigne, kt. and widow of Richard Goldsborough, esq, of Goldsborough.

The roll mentions a brother John, who married, and d. s. p.

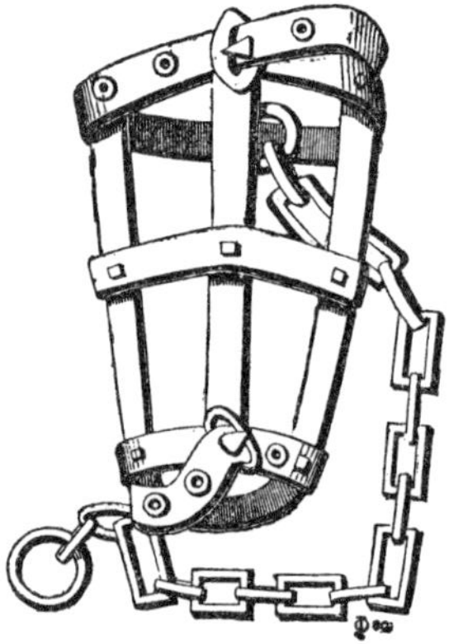

Thomas Clervaux, to whom his wife's father in 1431 bequeathed a purse, a pair of gloves, and a ring; a legatee of his bro. in 1443. = Isabel, dr. of Robert Conyers, of Sockburn, esq. who in 1431 bequeathed to her a purse, with his ring.

Robert Clervaux, d.s.p. (*Glover.*)

Alice, mar. John Faunt, of Wyston, Leicestersh. (*Glover.*)

Elizabeth, mar. William de Levesham, citizen and merchant, of York, on whom and his wife, her father settled lands in Munkegate, York, from Munk barr to the fosse, and in default of issue, the heirs or assigns of said William to enjoy for 40 years after his death, then to revert; d.s.p.

Beatrix Clervaux, = John Killinghall, esq. of Nether Middleton, son of John Killinghall, esq. one of the bishop's justices itinerant, by Agnes, daughter and heiress of John de Herdewyk; died 21 Feb. 1442. ⅄ The representatives of this marriage are the Allans, of Blackwell. (*See No. III., Royal Descent.*)

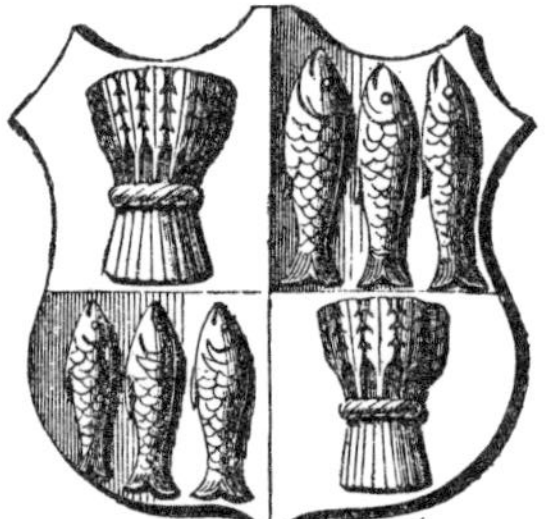

O. JEWITT. SC.

Margaret, mar. William Vincent of Great Smeaton, esq.; (an executor 1443); on whom and his intended wife her father settled in free marriage his property in Great Smetheton in 1416. William Vincent, in 1450, enfeoffed trustees of property in Atelaucouton and Southekylvyngton, for his son William; Berningham, Shetesby, Whitewell, Great Cowton, for son Roger; manor of Great Smetheton for said Roger and heirs, rem. Ric. Clarevaux and the heirs of his body; residue of Smeton for said Roger; Brompton juxta Allverton, for said Roger and heirs, rem. right heirs of John Synflete; Carleton juxta Forset, and Richemound, for Wm. Vynsent, jun.

Agnes, mar. John Headlam, of Stainton in the Carrs; he died 1461.

Johan, mar. Henry Taylboys, of Hurworth, esq; an executor to her brother 1443; on whom and his wife, her father settled his lands in Hurworth.

The roll mentions another son, Henry Clervaux, who d. s. p.

John Clervas, or Clervaus, of Croft, '*senior*,' to whom as s. and h. *with John his brother*, Master Stephen de Welber, clerk, granted property at Croft. Occurs with his brother John in various instruments, and granted to the latter all the vill of Walmyr, in 1349. (*See seal.*) Occurs 1338-1368 Grants to his brother Robert 43*s.* rents in York and suburbs, 1354. ═ Eleanor, dr. of sir Alexander Percy [*Glover*], for whom the impalement with Clervaux, Or, 5 lozenges conjoined in a fess sable, in a window in the old Clervaux mansion at Croft in 1666, was intended. In 1364, John Clervaux, of Croft, granted to William de Newport, parson of *Spofford*, and *Henry de Percy*, valet, a mess. and six oxg. of land in Irton, juxta Semore. Dated at Spofford. (*Ex Cartulario, penes Carolum Fairfax*, 74. *Dodsworth*, 19.)

John Fyton confirmed the manor of Est Couton to John, s. Will. Clervaus, of Croft, in 1324, and in 1345 it was found by inquisition, that John Clervaux *and Isabella his wife* held the manor of Temple Couton, as it is then called, and that Cecily, widow of John Fyton, had dower, which the sheriff was ordered by the king to see that said John and Isabella paid. In temp. Ric. II. these possessions are mentioned as being held by John Clervaux, and anciently by Conan, son of Elias. Conan was living temp. Stephen, and gave the church to Bridlington Priory. The Fytons held them as early as 1240, when they had a free chantry in the chapel of St. James. The picture of the Castle of Richmond [*Harl. MS.* 4219·2] said to be of the time of Edw. I., gives 'Sable, a saltire or,' as the standard at the station of Conan, son of Elias, near the court of the tower, on the east part, at the outside of the wall. As the former arms of Clervaux were a lion rampant, the saltire probably went along with the estate, as '*feudal arms*,' or 'arms of succession.'

John Clervaus, '*junior*,' grants Irton juxta Semer, and Walmyr, in 1349, for $4\frac{1}{2}$ years, to his elder brother John, the reversion to be to John, s. John Clervaus, senior, and Beatrix, his wife, and their heirs; rem. John C., senior, aud heirs. *Qu. Sir John de Clervaus, chaplain*, to whom Wm., s. Arnald de Croft, granted all his property in Croft. [*See* Robert below.]

Thomas Clervaus, to whom, with John his uncle, Beatrix, widow of Wm. Walche, of Croft, granted property at Kyrkegat, Croft, in his father's lifetime.

Robert de Clervaus, to whom John Walmir, of Croft, gave 8*d.* rent from lands which his *dau. Beatricea had of his feoffment in free marriage*; gave to *John Clervaus, rector of Wikliff*, all the property in Croft he had by grant of John Walmyr. [John de Walmyr, a burgess of Darlington, remaining at Croft, was living 1317-28, and was grantee from John, s. Gilbert, of lands adjoining those of *Gilbert Clervaus*.]

Alice Clervaux, enfeoffed of all her father's lands in Jolby 3 May, 1328, by his attornment to 'Johem filium meum minorem,' to give seisin. John Clervaux, of Croft, and Alice his sister, demise four acres there in 1331. In 1353 and 1351, as the widow of Edmund de Denum, she granted property in York to Robert Clervaux, her brother, dating from Stamford, and in 1356 [from York, as dame Alice, etc.] to John Clervaux de Croft, all her property in Jolby and Stapilton.

John Clervaux, citizen and apothecary of York. Will 1357, to be bur. in cemetery of All Saints' on the Pavement, York, near the monuments of my parents; rents from property in Skeldergate, North-strete, the house of John de Guthrum, in North-strete, called le Bakhous, Nessegate, Thurselane, Conyngstret in the par. of St. Wilfrid; other property in same parish, of which *Nicholas Clervaux* feoffed Wm. de Burgh, in Carnificio, Gotherumgate, without the bar in Munkegate, and in merk in Hundegate, all in York, to wife Marjory for life; rem. Wm. s. and h., rem. son John, rem. Thomas his bro., rem. son Robert, rem. daur. Katerine; son Wm. *the reversion of a hall*, with houses which John Rose inhabits, *when they fall in at the death of Agnes de Salby*. ═ Margery, executrix to her husband in 1357, formerly wife to Hugh le Tallour, of Castlegate; to whom, with her husband Clervaux, Christiana, widow of John de Ellerker, of York, confirms all claim on ny property the said John and Margery had in York. [*Clerv. Cart. sub tit. Pons Castri.*]

Alice Clervaus, liv. 1344.

Ma garet Clervaus, liv. 1344.

Sir John Clervaux of Croft, knight of the chamber of Richard II. Will dated 1390, to be buried in Croft Church; on whom, with Beatrix his wife, his father granted all his property in Darlington, Catherton juxta Bylburgh, Hunttyngdon juxta York, Walmyr in Richemondeshir, and in York city. ═ Beatrix, dr. of sir John de Maulevever (*Glover*), residuary legatee and executrix of her husband, 1390.

Robert Clervaux joins his father and bro. John, in letting St. Saviourgate property, 1360. (Said to have mar. ...... dau. of 'Mr. Colvell, esquier,' and d. s. p).

Nicholas Clervaux, d.s.p. (*Glover.*)

Thomas Clervaux, on whom his father settled thirty acres in Croft, the property in Stapilton, Warlauby, Solbery, and Thirnetofte, for life.

1. Joan, mr. John Sothill. (*Glover.*)
2. Margaret, a nun. (*Glover.*)
3. Anastasia, mr. Tho. Fitz Henry, knt. (*Glover. Christopher* Fee Henri, knt. was witn. to her brother's will.)
4. Alice, mar. sir Thomas Colvell, knt. (*Glover*), who was executor to h r bro. John.

William Clervaux, son and heir. John. Thomas. Robert. Katherine. } All mentioned in their father's will 1357, and then under age.

The roll pedigree gives another daughter Agnes, who mar. Thomas Firthine, and it makes Margaret marry a certain unknown Wm. Boynton, of Sadburie, esq. I keep to Glover and the cartulary.

before 1246. Acquired rent of 2*s.* out of property *in marisco* in York, from John Godshere, of Tresk; part of *la grene extra muros*, which he granted to Henry de Sexdecim Vallibus or Sessewaus; and other property in that city. From another source. I find the English 'alias' of the last surname was Thixendale. He held in Athow Cowton, otherwise Est Cowton, two parts of the tythes formerly of Wymar Dapifer, and which in 1276-7, had descended to John de Clarisvallibus.—(*Kirkby's Inquest.* 5 Ed. I.)

Thomas. 1294.

William Fayrfax, of York, granted the recovered lands to William de Clervaus and Margaret, dau. Tho. Stodelay in free marriage—if no heirs, to revert. Granted property in Carnificio, Ebor., to Alice, who was the wife of Thomas de Stodlay, and to master Tho. de Stodlay, and the latter granted to Wm. de Clarisvallibus, of Croft.—Gilbert de Sherman granted Wm. Fayfox, of York, a house in Saynt Saviregate, apparently afterwards belonging to Clervaux.

John Fairfax quitclaimed to William Clervaus and Margaret his wife, his brother William's grant. Granted property in Usegate, at York, 1314. *Qu.* same as John Fairfax, of Walton, who granted property in Mikelgate to William de Banewell, who granted to William Clervaus, of Croft, in 1318. =

Thomas, s. John Fayrfax, quitclaimed p'pty in York and Huntyngdon, which Wm. Clervaus, of Croft, had by feoffment of Tho. de Stodlay.

Sir Thomas de Clerevaus, knt., to whom sir Hugh Gubyun in 1268 granted 10*l.* rent paid by Yedingham Convent; which he granted to his bro. Simon, to keep a chaplain in All Saints' Church, for the souls of his father and mother. Granted all Croft, reserving 10*l.* rent, to his brother John, and in 1297-8 granted same rent to Nicholas his brother (dating at Kyrkham), and having received it back, released it to his nephew William, who was paying it. Also granted all his lands *in maresco in villa Ebor.* to his brother John. Acquired lands in Joleby (near Croft) = Constance [said in the roll to be dau. of lord Grey of Codnor, co. Derbie], dau. of sir Hugh Gobyon.—*Glover.*

*** Sir Richard Gubyun =

Sir Hugh Gubyun, knt., for my 'soul, and the souls of Roger de Merlay my uncle, William de Merlay his brother, Richard Gubyon my brother, and my ancestors,' gave his land in Yedingham to the convent there, save 10*ll.* rent to him and heirs, granted it to his son Hugh, and confirmed the latter's grant to Clervaus. =

Sir Hugh Gubyun, knt., son of Hugh G., son of Ric. G. grants the Yedingham rent of 10*li.* to sir Thomas de Clervaus, knt., in 1268, and released all claim he had or could have in 10*li.* which Will. s. John de Clervaus paid to sir Tho. de Clervaus for his lands.

Katherine de Clervaus, quitclaims, 1 Apr. 1269, to her uncle John de Clervaus, the stone house in York, in par. Sci Salvatoris *in maresco*, which he had of the grant of sir Thomas her father; mar. but d.s.p.

Christiana de Croft, to whom John de Clerevaus left half a mark in 1283. — John de Clarevaus, Clervaus, Clerevals, or Claris Vallibus, of Croft, & citizen of York, to whom Roald, s. Roald, confirmed all his father was grantee of in Croft. Gave his 'legitimate son John' property his mother Eve had given him in villa Ebor. in Mikelgate; in default of issue, to revert. Grantee in 1274 (with his brother Simon) of the whole town of Doncastre, with its mills and those of Hesthorp, from Peter de Malo lacu secundus (save the rents and tenements given to Peter his son and Nichola his wife in marriage) with power of cutting wood in his wood of Sandal for the sustentation of the mills, for their lives. Will 1283: to be bur. in cemetery of All Saints', York, if he died there or at Stineton; and at Croft, if he died there: mortuary to St. Saviour's York. = Matilda, dau. of Adam (not Robert) le Cerf; whose bro. Thomas granted property in Usegate, York, to his sister Matilda de Clervaus. William le Cerf was executor to her husband. Will 1297, proved same year at Gilling; to be bur. in Croft Church.

Thomas, a legatee of 20*s.* 1283.

Elen, a legatee of 5 marks, 1283.

Joan, a legatee of 20*s.* 1283.

Robert, to whom his father left five marks for all actions, demands, and debts, if in any such he was held to him, and if he should claim any debt from the executors, he should not receive the legacy.

Sir Nicholas de Clervaus, citizen of York, to whom his bro. Tho. in 1297-8, granted 10*li.* out of Croft p. ann. which rent he granted back. M.P. for York city 26 Edw. I. = Helwise [de Seleby?] Will 1282; to be bur. in St. Dennis' church yard, York. Husband and Thomas de Seleby her brother, executors.

Master Simon de Claris Vallibus or Clervaus, to whom, with the executors of his brother John, Peter de Malolacu was bound in 1288, in 24*s.* arrears of rent due from him, and to be received from mills in Doncastre. Rector of Lithe and official of Cleveland 1274-5.

William de Claris Vallibus [said to be parson of Croft], grants a rent in Walmegate, York, to William, s. John de Claris Vallibus, and Agnes widow of Roger de Bychehill and Robert her son, quitclaim.

Peter de Clervaus, to whom his brother Thomas confirms his father Robert's legacies, except the house of Robert his brother.—[*Sub tit. Glovergail, Ebor. in Clervaux cart.*]

Robert de Clerevaus, attorney for his brothers Simon and Thomas in 1295 and 1297-8.

William de Clarisvallibus or Clervaus, of Croft, under age 1283. Acquired various properties at Croft from Arnold, s. John de Croft, etc. (1299 to 1325), Jolby (1315-1328), Colyergate, and Marketskyr, York (1322-6), Aldwerk juxta pontem Castri, Ebor. from Alice, called Aligod de Ellerker, & Margaret her sister, sisters of Master Nicholas de Ellerker, clerk, deceased, and John de Ellerker, *cissor*, his cousin confirms, Stapleton (1321), Nesham (1324), Smetheton, Warlauby (1322), Solbergh (1324), Thirnetoft (1323), and Yrton, *juxta Semer.* = Margaret (not Anne), dau. of Tho. de Stodelay, of Jubyri, and Alice his wife (apparently connected with the Fairfaxes), who settle property in Walmegate, Jubretgate, Dynnyndyk in vico de Mersk, near the cemetery of St. Saviour in marisco, etc., in York, on the marriage, and their son and heir Thomas confirms in 1316. She had also a sister Alice, married 1st, to John del Poll, and 2nd, to Ric. de Wodehull, living 1325; and another brother John, living 1316.

John Clervaus, residuary legatee under the wills of 1283 and 1297, with his sister Matilda; manens in Croft 1309; of Croft 1316: held lands in Jolby which he acquired in 1277, and several parcels in Croft, which he acquired in 1315, etc.

Thomas de Clerevaus, executor of his mother's will, 1297.

Katherine de Clerevaus, mentioned as having received her share from her father in his lifetime, 1283.

Matilda de Clerevaus, mentioned 1283 and 1297, to whom, with her brother William, John de Breton mortgaged the whole vill of Walmyr in 1322, and afterwards released it to them. Purchased property in Usegate, York. Apparently d. s. p.

Constance de Clerevaus, a legatee of 20*s.* in her mother's will, 1297.

Isabella, 1st wife of sir Wm. de Crathorne, knt. who was living 1332, called 'dr. of sir John Clervaux, kt.' in the Crathorne pedigrees.

Elen Clervaus, a legatee of her mother, 1282.

Peter Clervaus, the same.

John Clervaux, citizen of York. Will 1344; to be buried in All Saints' church, in Ousegate, York; son John and wife executors. = Agnes, executrix to her husband

Pedigrees of the Clervaux of York city; and Croft and Cowton in Richmondshire, and Darlington, co. pal.; and of their representatives the Chaytors of Croft and Butterby.

No. i.—Clervaux.

Where not otherwise stated, this pedigree is on the authority of the Clervaux Cartulary at Clervaux Castle, and J. Brough Taylor's Copy f Glover's Visitation of Yorkshire.

Arms.—A lion rampant. Seal, 1349.

Sable, a saltire or. Worn by the later Clervaux, and probably in right of Cowton, this being the coat on the standard of Conan son of Elias, a former owner, at his station on Richmond Castle. In Glover's Ordinary (*J. B. Taylor's copy*) the tinctures are reversed, for 'Clarvaux de Ebor.—of Croft;" and in another shield of 'Clervalx' they are as usual, with the addition of a black rose in the centre. A radically distinct coat, argent, two bars sable, in chief three mullets pierced of the last, is in the same collection ascribed to 'Clarvaux, Clarwas,' and with the mullets not pierced, for 'Claravallis.' In the Heraldic Dictionaries, the usual coat with a silver mullet in chief occurs for Clarevaulx of Yorkshire.

Crests.—A demi-eagle displayed. Croft Hall, 15th cent.

A heron or crane in two positions. In the illuminated family roll it is azure, beaked or, combed gules; a facsimile of this example is given in the margin. Of the following seals, the first is that of Henry Chaytor, brother to the baronet, in 1675, the other two were used by Henry Chaytor, the baronet's son, 1713. The last has evidently belonged to one of the later Clervaux, and perhaps is the signet of the ring alluded to by the loyal baronet in his distress. "Mr. Brockly lent me a guinea, 1*l.* 1*s.* 6*d.* I gave in pawn my wedding ring *and old Clarvaux ring*, to pay the guinea in fourteen days. I gave my son Harry of it 15*s.* 6*d.*"

Motto.—FORTUNE LE VEIT. (*Tomb of Ric. Clervaux, Croft.*) Did the golden ring of slender form, just meted for a lady's use, and found in the moat of Butterby, 1827, belong to Elizabeth Clervaux, and refer to the motto of her house? It was chased on the exterior, and, within, it bore—'*No foe to fortune.*'

Badge.—A muzzle.—(*Richard Clervaux's tomb in Croft Church.*)

Robert de Clervall, mentioned in the regal charter to his son.—Glover begins with him, and calls him 'knight.' The earlier fictions appear first in the illuminated roll, temp. Eliz., and were either unknown or rejected by Glover in 1584. = ...

Robert de Claris-vallibus, Clervall, Clerevaus, or Clervasse, citizen of York, son of Robert de Clervall; to whom Peter de Maulay leased his manor of Rosington, Yorks. W.R. (except the patronage of the church of the said manor, and the mill,) for eight years, which transaction Henry III. confirmed 8 Sep. 1254. A grantee of various lands, mills, etc., in Croft, Yorks', = Eve, daur. of Wm. Fairfax (*Glover*), [said in the old roll to be daur. of sir Wm. Fairfax, of Gilling, knt., who I believe does not occur in the Fairfax pedigrees], gave land in Mekelgate, York, to her son John. Settled lands in la Grene, York, on her son Simon for eleemosynary purposes, which were recovered against him by Agnes Fayrfax.

⁂ Thomas Fairfax and Agnes *ux.* had from Henry de Sexdecim Vallibus certain property extra civitate Ebor juxta Mykkelgate (distinct from that given by Robert de Clervaus to said Henry). = Agnes, granted seven acres in la Grene, recovered from Clervaus, to her sons Tho. and Wm. in 1294.

I. William Hilton, b. 10, bap. 18 Dec. 1677, 'was bred an attorney, and went mad.' *Qu.* 'Mr. Wm. Hilton, bur. 3 May, 1724,' Heighington.

II. Lancelot Hilton, b. 13, bap. 22 May, 1679, at Denton, living 1682. 'Lancelot Hilton, who died at Bolam 14 Dec. 1711, bur.' Denton.

II. Cuthbert Hilton, b. 3, bp. 11 Jan. 1680-1, at Denton, *Pontifex Maximus*, bur. 7 Jan. 1755, at Barnard C. = ...

I. Abraham Hilton, bound apprentice to a draper tailor 17 Aug. 1719, bur. 20 Nov 1780, at St. Oswald's, Durham, as 'Ab. Hilton, tailor' mar. 19 Oct. 1728, at St. Nich., Durham, Anne, dau. of ...... Lampson. = 2 Sep. 1730, at Gateshead, Lucy, daur. ...... Ord. bur. St. Oswald's, Durham. M.I.—(*J. B. Taylor and Sur.*) = 10 Feb. 1742, at St. Giles', Durham, Dorothy, daur. .... Watson, of Newbottle, Durham, widow of ...... Gibson, br. 1 Mar. 1781, at St. Oswald's.

** Who was 'Jane, w. to Abraham Hilton,' bur. 3 May, 1741, St. Andrew's, Newcastle?

III. Solomon, served his time with his bro. Abraham, died in the East Indies, in Admiral Hawke's fleet; bap. 18 July, 1720, Barnard Castle. = Jane Fletcher, of London, m. at St. Clements Danes.

III. Job. bap. 13 Nov. 1718, B.C. of Barnard Castle, carpet weaver.

V. Cuthbert, a player = ..

IV. David, bap. 17 Feb. 1721, BC.

VI. Alexander Hilton. 'Elizabeth bd. daughter of *Alexander Hilton of Durham* and Rachel Watson of Darlington, bp. 26 Mar. 1729.—Mary, bastard dau. of Rachel Watson, keeper of the bakehouse in Black-wellgate, and of one *Alexander Hilton*, a stranger, bur. 3 Nov. 1736. (*Darlington Reg.*)

I. Isaac, bap. 14 Dec. 1734, St. Nich. Dur., bur. 25 July, 1736, *ib.*

II. Jacob, bap. 23, br. 25 July, 1736, St. Nich. Dur.

III. Abraham, bp. 1 Oct. 1737, St. Nich., adm. of the draper-tailors' co., Dur. 30 Sep. 1760, bur. 8 May, 1776, St. Nicholas', Durham.

IV. Jacob, bap. 24, bur. 29 Dec. 1739, St. Nich.

V. Alexander, bap. 1 Oct. 1737, St. Nich. bur. 24 Jan. 1740-1, *ib.*

1. Elizabeth, bap. 18 July, 1731, St. Nich., bur. 27 Dec. 1732, *ib.*

2. Sarah, bap. 15 Jan. 1733, d. 8, bur. 10 June, 1734, at St. Oswald's. M.I.

II. Jacob Hilton, of Cockermouth, apothecary, bap. at St. Giles', Durham, 8 *Jan.* 1743-4. ('twin with John, twice married.'—*Surtees.*) = Mary Hixon, of Durham, mar. 1767.

I. John Hilton, bap. 8 Jan. 1743-4, at St. Giles; adm. of draper-tailors' co. 24 June, 1765; mar, and had issue John and 3 others.

1. Dorothy, bap. 28 Apr. 1745, St. Giles', mar. 10 Oct. 1763, at St. Mary le Bow, David Le Royd. 人

3 Jane Hilton, married Ralph Smith, and died at Battlebridge. 人

III. David Hilton, of Sadler-street, Durham, hair-dresser, and most worthy citizen, admitted of draper-tailors' company 10 Jun. 1784. Will dated 26 June, 1822. = Mary Usher, of Hexham, Northumberland.

2. Mary, bp. 10 Jan. 1748, bur. 10 Apr 1749, S. Nich. Dur.

I. William Hilton, of South Shields, 1818, b. 1744, bp. St. Clements Danes, London. = Mary Linton, mar. at St. Margaret's ch. Durham.

II. David, b. 1759, living at So. Shields 183..

1. Sarah. *Qu.* Joseph Heslop and Sarah Hilton, of Barnard Castle, married 9 Dec. 1795. Witn. John H.

2. Anne, died young.

3. Jane.

1. Cuthbert, bap. 21 Dec. 1748, St. Nicholas', Durham.

II. Robert, bap. 5, bur. 23 Aug. 1750, St. Nicholas'.

III. Ralph, bap. 3 Sep. 1751.

IV. William, bap. 4 July, 1755.

I. William, bap. 10 July, 1784, married Dec. 1817, Anne Hilton, of Durham.

II. David, b. 18 July, 17.0.

1. A daughter.

I. John bap. 19 Oct. 1768, St. Nicholas', Durham.

II. Thomas Nettleton H., bap. 16 May, 1773, at Crossgate church, Durham.

1. Ann, bap. 10 Nov. 1771, St. Nich., Durham.

I. David Hilton, of No. 8, Penton-street, Pentonville, Middlesex, bookseller, newsman, and stationer, bap. 21 May, 1779, St. Nich., Durham, admitted of the draper-tailors' company 13 July, 1802, d. 24 April, 1835, aged 55, bur. at St. James, Clerkenwell. = Sarah, daur. of George Newcote, of Gray's Inn Lane, London, widow of John Brookes, of Gray's Inn Lane, died 14 Feb, 1842.

I. Elizabeth, born 3 Mar. 1771, St. Nich., Durham, mar. Tho. Thomson, of...... hairdresser.

2. Anne, bap. 17 Apr. 1774, d. inf.

3. Jane, bap. 1 April, 1781, St. Nicholas', Durham.

II. George Hilton, b. at Durham 23 Jan. 1808, of No, 11. Half-moon Crescent, Islington. = Sarah Brown.

I. David Hilton, b. at Durham, 18 April, 1805, of 8, Penton-street, Pentonville, bookseller, etc. voted for Durham city, 1830.

III. Henry Hilton, bn. at Durham 11 July, 1813, mar. Caroline Trotter.

1. Mary Ann, b. at London 31 Dec. 1804.

I. George Frederick Hilton, b. 28 Oct. 1838.

1. Mary Ann Hilton, b. 25 Feb. 1840.

** Compare the following evidences with the dates of the *Pontifex Maximus* and his son Cuthbert:—

Cuthbert Hilton. = 6 May, 1697, at St. Giles', Eliz. Moor. *Qu.* Eliz. Hylton, bur. 16 Jan. 1759, St. Giles'.

Thomas, s. Cuth. Hilton, *glaser*, bur. 20 Oct. 1702, St. Giles,

Cuthbert Hilton. *Qu.* Cuth. Hilton, bur. 1 Jan. 1768. = Mary Cooper, mar. 4 Oct. 1742, at St. Margaret's.

William, s. Cuth. and Mary Hilton, bur. 21 Feb. 1744, at St. Margaret's, Durham.

Will. s. Cuth. H., bur. 30 Oct. 1757, St. Giles.

†‡† 'Sacred to the memory of Ann Hilton, who for many years conducted the principal boarding-school for young ladies in this city; she died 22nd of February, 1832, in the 86th year of her age, deeply lamented by her surviving pupils and an extensive circle of relations and friends, to whom she had endeared herself by the kindness of her disposition and the genuine goodness of her heart.'

St. Giles' Churchyard. Durham.

Issue of John, lord Clifford.

Thomas lord Clifford, b. 1415, d. 1454. = Joan, dau. of Thomas lord Dacre, of the North.

John, lord Clifford, the 'Black Clifford,' or 'the Butcher,' b. 8 Apr. 13 Hn. VI., slain 1461. = Margaret Bromflete, baroness Vescy in her own right.

Henry, lord Clifford, 'the Shepherd Lord,' born 1454, died 1523. = 1. Anne, only dr. of sir John St. John, of Bletso, 'one of the first that caused tapestry hangings to be made, at that time a rarity in England.'

Elizabeth Clifford, sister to the 1st earl of Cumberland. = Sir Ralph Bowes, of Streatlam, etc., knt., high sheriff of Durham under five bishops, & for 30 years, d. 1516.

Margery Bowes, = Sir Ralph de Eure, slain at Panyerhaugh, *in vita patris*.

Frances Eure. = Robert Lambton, esq., of Lambton, co. pal.

Isabella Lambton, = Sir Nicholas Tempest, of Stella, made a baronet 1622.

Jane Tempest, known in the Chaytor family as '*The Star of Stella*.

'Lambton erat matris,
Stella domusque patris.'

= Thomas Chaytor, of Butterby, esq. 2nd son.

a quo
THE SECOND LINE
OF
CHAYTOR OF CROFT.

Issue of Henry Percy.

Henry Percy, 3rd earl of Northumberland, fell for the red rose at Towton, *die dominica in ramis palmarum*. = Eleanor, d. and h. of sir Richard Poynings.

Joan Clifford. = Sir Richard Musgrave, of Musgrave, co. Westm.

Sir Edward Musgrave, of Edenhall, co. Cumb. = Joan, d. & coh. of sir Chr. Ward, of Grindale, co. Ebor.

'God prosper long from being broke
The luck of Edenhall.'

Sir Simon Musgrave, of Edenhall. = Julian, d. William Ellerker, of Ellerker, co. Ebor.

Anne Musgrave. = Sir Nicholas Curwen, of Workington.

Elizabeth Clervaux, sole heiress of her ancient house. = Christopher Chaytor, esq., of Croft and Butterby, co. pal.

Anthony Chaytor, of Croft, esq. son and heir = ...

Sir William Chaytor, of Croft, knight, = Frances Bellingham.

a quo
THE FIRST LINE
OF
CHAYTOR OF CROFT.

Sir Henry Curwen, of Workington. = Catherine, d. of sir John Dalston, of Dalston, co. Cumberland.

Agnes Curwen. = Sir James Bellingham, of Lewins, co. Westmoreland.

Issue of Richard Neville.

Alice Neville. = Henry, lord Fitzhugh, of Ravensworth

Margaret Percy. = Sir William Gascoigne, of Gawthorpe, Ebor.

Anne Gascoigne. = Sir Thomas Fairfax, of Walton, co. Ebor.

Sir Nicholas Fairfax, of Walton. = Joan, d. of sir Guy Palmes, of Naburn, Ebor.

Mary Fairfax. = Sir Henry Curwen, of Workington.

Elizabeth Fitzhugh. = Sir William Parr, of Kendal, K.G.

Agnes Parr. = Sir Thomas Strickland, of Sizergh, co. Westm.

Walter Strickland, of Sizergh. = Elizabeth, dr. .... Salkeld

Sir Walter Strickland, of Sizergh. = Catherine, d. and co. of sir Ralph Neville, of Thornton Briggs, Ebor.

Agnes Strickland. = Sir Thomas Curwen, of Workington.

Issue of Richard Plantagenet.

Edward IV. and Richard III. kings of England.

Issue of Sir John Clervaux.

Sir Richard Clervaux, said on his tomb to be related in the third degree to Edward IV. and Richard III. = Elizabeth Vavasour.

Marmaduke Clervaux, esq. of Croft, Ebor. = ..

William Clervaux, esq., of Croft. = ...

Issue of J. Kelynghall.

John Killinghall, esq. Inq. p. m. 1486. = ...

Robert Killinghall, esq. represented by ALLAN of BLACKWELL.

Joan had dower 1483. = Thomas Blakeston, of Blakeston esq., d. 1483, mentions his brother Robt. Killinghall in a settlement of 1482.

William Blakeston, of Blakeston, esq. = Anne, d. of sir Roger Conyers of Wynyard, (4th son of Chr. Conyers, of Hornby, in Richmondshire,) and sister to Wm. Conyers, who mar. Isabel Clervaux.

Sir William Blakiston, of Coxhoe, esq. Will 1561. = ..

Mary Blakiston. = Christopher Fulthorpe, of Tunstall, esq.

Nicholas Fulthorpe, esq., 1615. = Margery, d. of .... Heyfield, and niece of sir Robert Brandling, knight.

Helen, bap. 1584-5, at Stranton, m. 1605, at same place. = Thomas Colmore, of Durham city, gent.

Mary Colmore. = Lancelot Hylton, of Durham and Hilton, d. 1685.

a quo
HYLTON OF DARLINGTON.

Issue of W. Fulthorpe.

Thomas Fulthorpe, of Hurworth, par. Kelloe, esq. d. 1468. = ..

Philippa Fulthorpe, coh. = Richard Booth, esqr., nephew to bishop Booth of Durham, and great-grandson to sir Thomas Booth, of Barton, co. Lancaster, called 'Tomalin of the Boothes.'

Ralph Booth, esq. = Elizabeth, d. of .... Swinnow,

Anne, d. and coh. = Thomas Fulthorpe, esq., descended from a brother of the chief justice. He was son of Chr. Fulthorpe, esq., of Hipswell, in Richmondshire, by Agnes, d. of sir James Metcalfe, of Nappa, and grandson of Alan F., constable of Middleham castle, by Catherine, d. of Wm. Burgh, esq., of Burgh, par. Catterick.

Henry, lord Percy, present at the glories of Cressy; died 1368. = Lady Mary Plantagenet, daughter of Henry, of Lancaster, 2nd son of Henry III.

Maud Percy. = John, lord Neville, of Raby, K.G., buried in Durham Abbey.

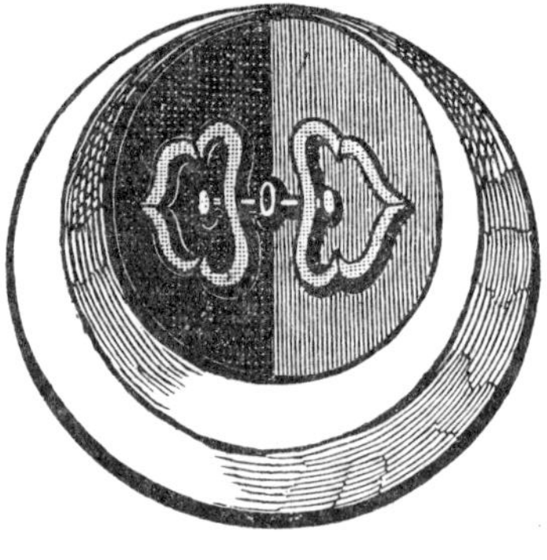

EDWARD III., king of England, 8th in descent from WILLIAM THE CONQUEROR, of England, and 4th from ST. LOUIS, of France; and also grandson of PHILIP LE BEL, king of France. = Philippa of Hainault.

Prince Lionel of Antwerp. =

Prince John of Gaunt. = Catherine Roet, daughter and coh. of sir Payn Roet, widow of sir Otho de Swinford, and sister-in-law of Chaucer.

Ici gist dame Katherine, duchesse de Lancastre, jadys femme de la tres noble et tres gracious prince John duc de Lancastre; fils a tres noble roy Edward le Tierce. La quelle Katherine moreult le x jour de May, l'an de grace mil. cccc. tierz. De quelle almes Dieu eyt mercy et pitee, Amen.—*Lincoln Cath.*
Peck.

Henry Percy, 1st earl of Northumberland, married secondly the heiress of Lucy, who stipulated that the Percys should quarter her arms for ever. He fell at Bramham Moor, 1407-8. = Margaret Neville, sister to Ralph, the great earl of Westmoreland, and cousin to her husband

Lady Philippa Plantagenet. = Edward Mortimer, earl of March.

Joan Beaufort, second wife. = Ralph Neville, the 'great earl' of Westmoreland.

Filia Lancastr. ducis inclyta, sponsa *Johannis*
Westmerland primi subjacet hic comitis
Desine, scriba, suas virtutes promere, nulla
Vox valeat merita vix reboare sua.
Stirpe, decore, fide, tum fama, spe, prece, prole,
Actibus et vita polluit immo sua
Natio tota dolet pro morte. Deus tulit ipsam.
In Bricii festo, C. quater M. quater x.
(Lincoln Cath.)
Peck.

Eleanor, to whom her father left two banerett beddis de Norfolk, cum curtinis. = Ralph lord Lumley, died in battle against Henry IV., at Cirencester.

Isabel Lumley. = Sir William Filthorpe, knt., of Tunstall, co. pal. (son of sir Roger F. the attainted chief justice of Ireland for Richard II.

Henry 'HOTSPUR,' = Lady Elizabeth Mortimer.
'Amongst a grove the very streightest plant.'

Roger Fulthorpe esq. = ...

Elizabeth Percy. = John, lord Clifford, b. about 1389.

Henry Percy, 2nd earl of Northumberland, the hero of bishop Percy's 'Hermit of Warkworth,' and supposed to be the earl Percy of Chevy Chase. He shared in the fame of Agincourt, and fell for the Red Rose 1455. = Lady Eleanor Neville.

Richard Neville, earl of Salisbury, = Alice, d. and h. of Tho. Montague, earl of Salisbury.

'Cecily of Raby, Never so good a lady,' popularly termed 'The Rose of Raby,' possibly in allusion to the red rose of Beaufort, the badge of some members of her father's house. = Richard Plantagenet, duke of York.

Margaret, niece to Ralph Neville, 1st earl of Westmoreland. = Sir John Clervaux of Croft, knt. died 1443.

Beatrix Clervaux. = John Kelynghall, of Nether Middleton, esq., died 1442.

William Fulthorpe esq. = ..

Issue of Charles, duke of Lorrain.

Gerberga, d. and h. = Lambert Barbatus, cont de Brabant and Lovaine, killed 1015, brother of Regnier IV., of Hainault.

Lambert II., 'Baldric,' count of Brabant and Lovaine, died 1054. =

Henry, earl of Brabant and Lovaine, d. 1068. =

Godfrey Barbatus, 1st duke of Lower Lorraine, d. 1139. =

Issue of Regnier IV.

Regnier V, died 1033. =

Richildis, heiress of Hainault, Brabant, Mons, and Valenciennes. = Baldwin VI. earl of Flanders (de Mons), d. 1070, whose sister Maud married William the Conqueror.

Gilbert de Gaunt, came into England with the Conqueror, and received 130 lordships in Lincolnshire alone; resided chiefly at Folkingham; buried at Bardney Abbey. =

Emma, only daughter. = Alan de Percy le Meschin, 'the Great Alan,' bur. at Whitby.

William de Percy, living 1168. =

Josceline de Louvaine, brother of Adeliza, queen of Henry I. = Agnes de Percy, eventually sole heiress of her house, on the death of her sister; covenanted that her husband should bear the arms of Percy, and omit his own, or continue those of Louvaine, and take the name of Percy. He adopted the latter alternative.

Henry de Percy, d. in vita matris. Had a brother Richard, who usurped the paternal estates to the grievance of his nephew William, who eventually recovered them. Richard had a grandson, *Alexander de Percy*, liv. at Settel in 1303, who afterwards had a grant of lands at Aton, in Yks. = Isabel. dr. of Adam and sister of Peter de Brus, of Skelton.

William de Percy, d. 29 Hen. III. = Elen de Baliol, dau. of Ingelram de Baliol, who had Dalton Piercy, co. pal., to her dower, which passed successively to her younger sons Ingelram, William, and Walter lord of Kildale, ancestor of *Sir Alexander de Percy*, of Ormesby, in Cleveland, lord of Sneaton, living 1354.

Henry, lord Percy, gave 900*l* in 33 Hen. III. (1248-9), for livery, and that he might marry whom he pleased; died 1272. = Eleanor, dr. of John Plantagenet, earl of Warren and Surrey, descended from Hameline Plantagenet, base son of Geoffrey Plantagenet, and half brother to king Hen. II.

Henry, lord Percy, youngest son, purchased Alnwick, died 8 Edw. II. = Eleanor, d. Rd. Fitz Alan, earl of Arundel.

Henry lord Percy, present at the battle of Neville's Cross, died 1351-2. = Imania (*Test. Ebor.* 57), dau. of Robert, lord Clifford.

Issue of Robert, king of France.

Alice, or Adela, widow of Richard III., duc de Normandie, =

Issue of Baldwin IV.

= Baldwin V., earl of Flanders, 'the Gentle,' died 1067.

Issue of Ethelred the Unready.

Edmund Ironside, king of England, murdered 1016. =

Edward the Outlaw, d. 1057. =

Duncan, prince of Cumberland and king of Scotland, 1033, slain by Macbeth in 1039. He descended from Achaius, who is said to have wreathed the lilies of his friend Charlemagne round his own rampant lion. Few characters are so well immortalized as Duncan, Macbeth, and Syward. = ..., sister of the famous Syward, earl of Northumbria.

Margaret, died of grief at the deaths of her husband and son, 1093. = Malcolm III. Canmore, king of Scotland slain at Alnwick 1093.

David I. king of Scotland, died 1153, aged 73. = Maud, widow of Simon de St. Liz, earl of Huntingdon, dr. of Waltheof, earl of Northumberland, by Judith, dau. of a sister of William the Conq:

Henry, prince of Scotland and earl of Northumberland, died 1152. = Ada or Adama, or Adeline, daur. of William earl of Warren, 2nd earl of Surrey (by Elizabeth, daur. of Hugh the Great, earl of Vermandois, in Switzerland), and granddaughter of William de Warren, earl of Surrey, by Gundreda.

WILLIAM THE LION, king of Scotland, died 1214. = ... dau. of Robert de Avenel.

Isabella, alleged by her descendant, William de Ros, a candidate for the Scotch crown at the memorable crisis of 1291, to have been legitimated. = Robert de Ros, lord of Hamlake, great grandson of Peter de Ros, by Adeline, sister and coh. to the famous Walter Espec, baron of Helmsley or Hamlake. Became a templar, and was buried in the Temple church 11 Hen. III.

Sir Robert de Ros, of Werke and Ingmanthorp, had two sons, Robert of Werke, and William of Igmanthorpe, both summoned to parl't 22 Edw. I. = Margaret, sister and coh. of Peter, the last Brus, baron of Skelton, gave the castle of Kendale, in right of her mother or grandmother, Helewise de Lancaster, to her son William, who died 3 Edw. II.

Isabella. = Marmaduke de Twenge, lord of Kilton, had summons to parl't. 35 Edw. I to 16 Edw. II. His mother was Lucy, another sister and coh. of Peter de Brus, lord of Skelton, Kilton, etc.

Lucy, dr. and coh., who took Kilton lordship into the family of Lumley. = Sir Robert Lumley, knt., descended from Liulph, who married Aldgitha, dr. of Aldred, earl of Northumberland, and was murdered at Gateshead, temp. Wm. I.; died 1338.

Sir Marmaduke Lumley, of full age 1339, said to be prior of the military order of St. John of Jerusalem, at Kilmainham, in Ireland. = Margaret Holland.

iii. Royal Descent of Clervaux, etc.

Through Percy, Neville, and Lumley.

CHARLEMAGNE, emperor of the West, died 814. = Hildegarde of Swabia.

Louis le Debonnair, emperor, died 840, = Judith, dau. of Guelph I.

Charles the Bald, king of France, died 878. = Hermentrude, dau. of Vodon, earl of Orleans.

Louis the Stammerer, died 879. = Osberga, dau of Oslac, the king's cup-bearer. *1st wife.* = Ethelwulph, king of Wessex, mar. to Judith 856, died 858. = Judith, d. 880. = Baldwin, 'the Arm of Iron,' forester of Arden, made 1st earl of Flanders by his wife's father.

ALFRED THE GREAT, king of Wessex, etc., died 26 Oct. 900 or 901, aged 52. = Ealswitha, dau. of Eadburh, of the royal family of Mercia, and sister of Athulf; an ealdorman; died 905.

.... *1st wife.* = Edward the Elder, king of Wessex, died 924. = Ædgifu, dau. of earl of Sigelina (?) died 953.

Alfritha, Elfrida, or Elstreth, or Ethelswida. = Baldwin II., 'le Chauvre,' count of Flanders, died 918.

Charles the Simple, king of France, died 929. = Edgiva.

Ethilda. = Hugh Magnus, count of Paris, 950.

Edmund the Elder, king of England, 941. æt. 18; murdered 946. =

Arnolf I., earl of Flanders, died 965. =

Baldwin III., 'le Jeune,' count of Flanders, died in vita patris, 961. =

Arnolf II., count of Flanders, died 988. =

Baldwin IV., earl of Flanders, 'le Barbu,' died 1036. =

Louis IV., 'Outremer,' king of France, died 954. =

HUGH CAPET, king of France 987. = ...

Edgar, king of England, died 875, aged 32. = Elfrida, dau. of Ordgar, earl of Devon, and widow of Athelwold, a Saxon earl, murdered by order of Edgar.

Charles, duke of Lorrain. died in prison at Orleans 991, being set aside by Hugh Capet. =

Hadwige. = Regnier IV., count of Hainault.

Robert, king of France. = ...

Ethelred the Unready, king of England, d. 1016. =

Issue of Edward Fenwick. *Issue of Benjamin Sorsbie.* *Issue of William Peat.* *Issue of George Brown.* *Issue of Henry Gunter.* *Issue of William Scott.*

Edward Fenwick, born at Hexham, 16 Sep. 1758; mar. at St. Andrew's, Newcastle, 1781; died 27 July, 1839, buried at Westgate Hill Cemetery, Newcastle. M.I. in Hexham Abbey church. = Mary, dau. of John Shield, of Catton, in Allendale, b. 2. Feb. 1758; died at Belle Vue, Gateshead Fell, Aug. 1831, and buried at Westgate Hill Cemetery, Newcastle. 'The name of Shield is of old standing above Hexham, as appears by Bishop Nicholson's Border Laws.'

Robert Fenwick, unm. 1815.

John Fenwick, son and heir, of Newcastle-upon-Tyne, attorney-at-law, and sometime alderman of that town; bn. at Hexham 14 April, 1787; mar. at Alnwick 9 June, 1814. = Ann, youngest daughter of Abram Rumney, master of the Grammar School of Alnwick.

Edward Fenwick, b. 7 Feb 1792, d. s. p. 8 April, 1838, bur. at the Westgate Hill Cemetery, Newcastle. = Hannah, dau. of Ralph Elrington, of Lintz Hall, co. pal.

John Fenwick, born 3 Sep. 1784; bap. 1 May, 1785, at Hexham; died 12, buried 13 Dec. 1786, at Hexham.

Henry George Liddell Fenwick, born 10 Aug., bap. 14 Oct. 1789, at Hexham; died June, 1815, unmarried; buried at St. John's, Newcastle.

Robert Fenwick, born 23 April, 1794; died 1 May, 1800, buried at St. John's Newcastle.

Edward Fenwick, b. 22 Sep. bp. 3 Nov. 1782, at Hexham, died 30 Nov., br. 2 Dec., 1790, at Hexham.

1. John Clerevaulx Fenwick, of Newcastle-upon-Tyne, attorney at law, b. 1 Nov. 1825.

II. Edward Ambrose Fenwick, b. 27 June, 1827, d. 13 Aug. 1833, bur. at the Westgate Hill Cemetery, Newc.

2. Mary Fenwick, b. 10 Novem. 1816, mar. 24 June 1847, the Rev. Henry Christopherson, of Bowdon, co. Chester.

3. Jane Fenwick, born 10 June, 1818, d. 18 June 1844, bur. at St. Stephen's, Rochdale. = Robert Schofield, of Rochdale, esq., m. 23 May, 1837.

1. Ann, b. 11 May 1815, d. 11 April 1839, bur. at the Westgate Hill Cemetery, Newc.

4. Hannah Eliza, b. 13 Mar. 1820, d. 15 Mar. 1844, bur. at the Westgate Hill Cemetery, Newcastle.

5. Elizabeth, b. 11 Mar. 1822, d. 8 May, 1823, bur. at St. John's, Newcastle.

6. Maria Rumney Fenwick, b. 29 Oct. 1823.

John Fenwick Schofield, b. 17 Mar. 1842.

Agnes Percy Schofield, b. 7 June, 1844.

Malin Sorsbie, a merchant in Newcastle, died 1817 or 1818. = Elizabeth Potts.

1. Clara Bernard, d. s. p. = Benjamin Sorsbie, esq., alderman of Newcastle, and twice mayor of that town (1814, 1827), d. 1849 = 2. Catherine, d. of Tho. Robertson, merchant, by his wife Catherine Paine, and widow of Wm. Fox, esq., R. N., mar. at St. Hilda's, South Shields, May, 1809: died 1848.

Malin Sorsbie, died 1848.

Thomas Robertson Sorbie, d. inf.

Catherine Sorsbie, liv. 1852.

Mary Sorsbie, liv. 1852.

Jonathan Sorsbie, died under age.

Robert Sorsbie, clerk, M. A., curate at Whickham, 1851.

Mary Elizabeth, b. 20 Aug. 1805, married 1828. = Joseph Hawks, of Gateshead, and now (1852) of Newcastle, esq.

Mary Susannah married 6 July, 1852, at St. Andrew's, Newcastle. = Captain Richard Clement Moody, Royal Engineers.

Juliana Hawks.

Emily Hawks.

Juliana Peat, only child. = William Boyd.

Mary = .. Lubbren.

Elizabeth, d. unmarried.

Anne, mar. to John Bernard, living his widow 1851, s. p.

William Boyd, of Newcastle, & now (1852) of Burfield Priory, esq. bn. October 1773. = Esther Locke, mr. 21 Aug. 1802.

Fenwick Boyd, died 1825. = Dinah, d. of .. Stephenson, of Newcastle, mar. about 1809 or 1810, d. 1830.

Juliana, d. 1836.

Fenwick Boyd, liv. 1852.

William Boyd, b. 21 April, 1809, married 1836. = Isabella, dr. of Geo. Twining, of the Strand, London

William Boyd.

Charles Boyd.

Robert Boyd.

Edwd. Fenwick Boyd, b. 30 Aug., 1810, mar. 1841. = Ann, 4th daughter of Thos and Ann Anderson, of Newcastle.

William Fenwick Boyd.

Charles Fenwick Boyd.

Ann Boyd.

All died in Feb. 1848.

Juliana Boyd,

Edward Fenwick Boyd. died Mar. 1848.

George Fenwick Boyd.

Robert Fenwick Boyd.

Juliana, b. 31 Aug. 1803.

Robert Boyd, of Newcastle-upon-Tyne, b. 27 Aug. 1804, died at Carthagena, in Spain, Dec. 1844, unmar.

Elizabeth, b. 22 Oct. 1807, d. 21. Jan. 1808.

Charles Boyd, b. 17 Dec. 1811, died in the Straits of Malacca on board the E. I. C. ship *General Kyd*. 26 Aug. 1829, unm.

Matthew Boyd, b. 30 July, 1815, died at Tynemouth 15 Sept. 1815, unm.

Edward Brown, died 25 Mar. 1744, aged 7 hours, buried with his mother, 'close to her side.' M. I. Kirkwhelp.

Henry Gunter, captain, R.N. commanded the Nautilus sloop of war.

Walter Scott, M.D. of Stamfordham, a J. P. for Northd.; and sometime Head Master of Stamfordham Free School; mar. 1. Eleanor Walker, d. s. p. = 2. Mary Bell.

Mary Mandall d. of Tho. Mason, esq., of Doncaster, solicitor. = William Robson Scott, of St. Leonard's, Exeter.

Walter John Scott, liv. unmar. 1852.

Martha Jane, mar. William Forster: s. p. 1852.

Walter Scott.

Mabel Fenwick Scott.

Mary Mason Scott.

William Henry Scott.

Elizabeth, bp. 3 Feb., 1655, br. 5 Aug. 1656, at Bambrough.

Francis, bap. 31 Decem. 1656, at Bambrough, 'esq., eldest son and heir, died in the life-time of his father.' (*Tocker ped.*) = 'His wife, Mrs. Smith.' (*Tocker ped.*)

Isabel, bap. 24 April, 1658, bur. 26 June, 1660, at Bambro'.

Agnes, bap. 30 Nov. 1659, br. 10 Aug. 1661.

Catherine, bap. Dec. 1664.

Mary, bap. 30 Sep. 1666, bur. 5 Aug. 1667, at Whalton.

Susanha, bap. 5 Nov. 1667, at Whalton.

William, bap. 27 Oct. 1668, bur. 5 July, 1675, at Whalton.

John, bap. 14 Dec. 1669, at Whalton, bur. at Stamfordham 29 Sep. 1700. 'Mr. John Liddall, son of *Sir* Francis Liddale, was buried in the quire, 29 Sep. 1700.' (*Par. reg.*) 'John Liddel, 2nd son, died after his brother Francis, without issue.' (*Tocker pedigree.*)

Nicholas, bap. 29 Feb. 1671, bur. 27 Nov. 1673, at Whalton.

Agnes, bap. 19 Mar. 1673, bur. 15 May, 1674, at Whalton.

Mary Liddell, spinster, mar. lic. 1 May, 1685. 'One of the daughters married to the Rev. Mr. Fenwick: The other daughter married to Mr Herring, of .... in the county of ....' (*Tocker pedigree.*) = Rev. Edward Fenwick, descended from Ambrose Fenwick, brother of sir Wm. Fenwick, of Meldon, whose 2nd daughter Catherine mar. Francis Radclyffe, esq., afterwards created earl of Derwentwater; curate of Whalton at the time of his marriage; vicar of Stamfordham, in Northumberland, to which he succeeded, about 1685, on the death of Ralph Fenwick, who was presented to that living by Charles II. in 1662. Had Redheugh, in com pal. *jure uxoris*, and exchanged it for the advowson of Simonburn, Northd', with his cousin Francis earl of Derwentwater, under the cloak, it is believed, of a mortgage, the mortgagees conveying to the earl, who devised to the hon. Thomas Radcliffe and lady Mary Radcliffe. In 1748, lady Mary Radcliffe conveyed to Adam Askew, of Newcastle, M.D. Mr. Fenwick died pending suits with government respecting Simonburn advowson, or restitution of Redheugh, the exchange having been asserted to be simoniacal, and the advowson included in the confiscation of the Derwentwater estates. These suits were instituted at the instance of Dorothy Forster's episcopal husband, lord Crewe. At the time of the exchange, the incumbent is stated to have been above 90 years old, but he survived the Ratcliffe attainder. Henry Wastel was presented by Government in 1723. 'Edw. Fenwick, Vicar of Stamfordham, buried in the Quire, 11 Dec. 1730.—(*Stamfordham Reg.*) He is however stated to have resigned that living in favour of his son Ambrose, in 1719. The register at Whalton—'Ambrose Fenwicke, of Whalton, bur. 8 Sep. 1662,' probably refers to his father. Mr. Fenwick mar. 2, Mrs. Robison, of Black Heddon, co. Northumberland, by whom he had no issue.

Frances, dau. and sole heir, = Francis Gatonby, of Howdon Pans, co. Northumberland.

Mary, dau. and sole heir. = Walter Tocker, eldest son of John Tocker, of Gwyiner, co. Cornwall.

Francis Liddell Tocker, eldest son, died an infant.

William Burford Tocker, 2nd son, an infant, living 1724, in which year an engraved pedigree of Tocker was privately struck off. From this pedigree the foregoing descents are derived. *Arms*—the usual coat of Tocker, having Gatonby on an escutcheon of pretence, and also impaling the quartered coats of Gatonby and Liddell.

Frances, filia Edwardi Fenwicke, bap. 20 Sep. 1686 (*sic*), bur. 18 Aug. 1686 (*sic*), at Whalton.

Margaret, filia Edwardi Fenwicke, bap. 4 Aug. 1687, at Whalton.

Rev. Ambrose Fenwick, vicar of Stamfordham, on the resignation of his father, 1719; d. 1, buried in Gateshead church. 3 Feb. 1731-2. M. I. s. p. = Elizabeth, d. and h. .... Bradley, esq., of Gateshead, atty. at law, died June, 1738; buried in Gateshead ch.

Rev. Edward Fenwick, vicar of Kirkwhelpington, Northumberland, inducted 1720; died of a broken heart, occasioned by his suits with the Crown; buried at Stamfordham, 24 July, 1734. He is said to have had a decree in Chancery for Simonburn advowson, but these transactions are confusedly told, and cannot be satisfactorily unravelled with present evidence. The Derwentwater family, though Romanists, always owned him as a relative, and befriended his family. Even Ralph Spearman says that he 'was a most exemplary clergyman, and universally respected.' Spearman told a strange story in corroboration of this, that the parishioners of Kirkwhelpington reaped their fields on the Sunday after the vicar's death, in order that the widow might have the benefit of the tithe. The baptisms of his children are from Kirkwhelpington. = Ann, d. Thomas Newton, esq. of Hawkwell, Northumberland, of an ancient family of the branch of Newton by the Sea. 'They hold to the old heraldic story of Newton killing a Moorish king of Spain, to which the southern Newtons' crest refers.'—(*Spearman of Eachwick.*) From another daughter descended the Woodmans of Morpeth and the Fenwicks of Netherton; from a third, the Surtees' of Mainsforth, and the Culleys of Northumberland; and from a fourth the Greenwells of Ford, co. pal.

Edward Fenwick, eldest son and heir, bap. at Stamfordham 14 Feb. 1729-30; mar. at Hexham, 29 Decem. 1757; d. at Gunamaco 4 Nov. 1762. = Mary, d. of Robert Wilson, of Hexham; d. there.

II. Newton Fenwick, b. 31 Mar., bp. 3 Apr. 1734, d. unmar.

1. Elizabeth. = Benjamin Sorsbie, M.A., youngest son of Malin Sorsbie, D.D., rector of Ryton, co. pal. His father was lord of the manor of Owlerton Hall, co. York.

2. Mary, bn. and bap. 23 Feb. 1720. = William Peat.

3. Catherine bap. 21 Oct. 1722, d. 30 Mar. br. at Kirkwhelpington 1 Apr. 1744, ag. 22. M.I. = George Brown, of Cambo, par. Hartburn, co. North'd. bro. of lord Burlington's Brown, better known as 'Capability Brown.'

4. Anne, bap. July, 1724. = Henry Gunter.

5. Margaret, b. and bp. 1 July, 1726, died unmar.

6. Isabell b. and bp. 29 Mar. 1728, d.s.p.=Wm. Yarrow.

7. Martha, bn and bp. 18 Jan. 1731-2. = William Scott, M.D., of a truly old family of Toderick, in Scotland; by his mother, of the family of Robson, of Tollestone, owner of North Stokoe, Shelburn Haugh, etc.

W. Hylton. L. del — C. Jewitt sc

No. iii. Descendants of Agnes Chaytor, heiress of the first line of Chaytor of Croft.

Richard Tonge, of Ekylsall, co. York. ╤ Isabel, dau. of Rob. Hedworth, of Harraton, co. pal.

William Tonge, of Ekylsall, ╤ Elizabeth, dau. of Henry lord Clifford, sister of Henry 1st earl of Cumberland, relict of sir Ralph Bowes, of Streatlam, co. pal., knt.

George Tonge, of Eklysall, and of West Thickley, co. pal., esq., d. 1593 ╤ Helen, dau. of John Lambton, of Lambton, co. pal., esq. d. 1611.

Henry Tonge, of Thickley and Denton, esq., d. 1615. ╤ ...... Watson, of the Bishoprick.

Sir George Tonge, of Thickley and Denton, knighted 1617, d. 1639 ╤ Elizabeth, dau. of Thomas Blakiston, of Newton Hall, near Durham, esq., mar. 1609-10.

2. Mr. Dawson, of Ripon. ╤ 1. Nicholas Forster, of Bambrough and Blanchland, co. Northumberland, esq., aged 13, 1 Chas. I. (1625); died 10 Dec. 1636 or 7. ╤ Agnes Chaytor, only daughter, and eventually heiress of sir William Chaytor of Croft, bart. (*See* No. II.), born 27 Apr. 1615; died at Croft January, 1669. Her brother, Henry Chaytor, married *widow Dodsworth, of Barton*, for subsistence.—(*Chaytor MSS.*) She married thrice. ╤ 3. Sir Francis Liddell, knt., second son of sir Thomas Liddell, bart. 'of Ravensholme Castle,' co. pal.; bap. 8 Jan. 1606-7, at Lamesley; mayor of Newcastle 1664; d. circ. 1680. ╤ Elizabeth Tonge, ag. 3, 1615; m. at Denton 30 Aug. 1632; br. 10 Aug. 1648. Her arms, a bend (omitting the cotises) between six martlets; impaled by her husband's, Liddell, with a fret, instead of fretty, are on the Gateshead stalls. The crest a lion rampant. Motto, *Fama semper vivit.*

Issue of Mr. Dawson: Agnes, married to Mr. Bateman (*Sir Wm. Chaytor's MSS. about* 1700.)

Issue of Nicholas Forster and Agnes Chaytor:

Sir William Forster, of Bambrough, knt., ag. 30, 1666; bur. 12 Nov. 1674, at Bambrough. His sons all died issueless, as also his daughter Dorothy, wife to bishop Crewe of Durham. The representation of Agnes Chaytor then vested solely in the descendants of her sister Frances, who married Thomas Forster, esq., of Etherstone, and had a large family. Of these, Ferdinando, the second son, was stabbed by Mr. John Fenwick of Rock, in Newcastle. The eldest son, Thomas, by joining the rebellion of 1715, forfeited Bambrough, which bishop Crewe purchased, and devoted to charitable purposes. Joseph Forster, of Buston, was only prevented from joining 'his cousin of Bambrough' by his wife's throwing the contents of a silver kettle over him, and scalding his legs! On the death of the above Thomas Forster in exile 1738, the representation was transmitted to his brother John and his issue, who dying out, it descended to the Bacons of Staward Peel, they representing Margaret, sister of the above named Thomas, Ferdinand, and John.

Mary, married to .... Moore, liv. 1674.

Frances, bur. 30 May, 1675, at Whalton co. N'd. as Francisca, wife of Francis Liddell, of Ogle, esq. ╤ I. Francis Liddell, born 1633, of Redheugh, afterwards of Ogle Castle, esq. He is called *Sir* Francis in the Tucker pedigree, and so also in the burial registers of himself and his son John. He died at his son-in-law Fenwick's house, at Stamfordham. 'Sir Francis Liddle, of Stannerton, bur. in the Quire 11 Oct. 1702.'—(*Stamfordham Reg.*) Tradition reports him to have been a large muscular man, wearing a gold chain in many folds round his neck, which, when extended, reached the length of the vicarage kitchen. The 'vicar's tomb' was opened some years ago, and some bones of large size were found, which there was reason to suppose were those of sir Francis Liddell. His will has been abstracted from the Registry at York.

Issue of Frances and Francis Liddell: John, bur. 17 Nov. 1659, at AllSaints, Newc.

Issue of Sir Francis Liddell and Elizabeth Tonge:

II. William, s. p.

III. Robert. s. p.

IV. Henry, bap. 1 Feb. 1635, at Gateshead.

Elizabeth, bap. 27 July, 1637, at Gateshead. *Qu. John Dodsworth and Eliz. Lyddall* married at St. Cuthbert's, Barton, 13 July, 1669.

Isabel, bap. 18 Oct. 1638, at Gateshead.

Anne, bap. 18 June, 1640, at Gateshead, bur. March, 1640-1, at Lamesley.

V. Thomas, bp. 18 Oct. 1641, at Gateshead.

VI. Ralph, bap. 22 Dec. 1643, at St. Nicholas' Newcastle.

Mary, bur. at Whickham 14 May, 1647.

North Riding; born at Gilling 11 Jan. 1732; died May, 1819. He drew up an elaborate pedigree of his family.

camp in Germany.

V. John, b. 8 Sep. 1751; d. young, of the small pox, at Croft, and buried under the Clervaux tomb.

Croft, to Caleb Redshaw, afterwards Morley, esq., of Richmond and of Beamsley, in Craven, who died 1797, and was buried at Richmond.

Betty Chaytor, bn. at Croft 23 July 1763; mr. Geo. Pearson, esq. of Harperley Park, co. pal. and had an only child, Elizabeth Jane Pearson, who married George Hutton Wilkinson, esq., recorder of Newcastle-upon-Tyne, and judge of the Northumberland circuit of county courts, 1852.

I. Henry Chaytor, esq., a lieut. col. in the 1st Regiment of Foot Guards; born at Kirkby Stephen 12 Nov. 1765; d. 10 May, 1824. = Jane, daur. of William Marriott, esq.: m. 6 Feb. 1797; died 24 Aug. 1809, bur. at Meals, co. Salop.

1. Hannah Jane, b. at Kirkby Stephen, 20 Feb. 1767 · died in Lower Grosvenor Street, London. 12 Dec. 1825.

3. Mary, b. 20 Sep. 1769; d. 21 Dec. 1830.

4. Isabella, b. 1 Aug. 1771, d. 12 Oct. 1843.

5. Juliana, b. 6 Aug. 1773, d. 1 Nov. 1849.

6. Charlotte, b. 6 Sep. d. 3 Dec. 1774.

7. Harriet, b. 5 Dec. 1778, d. 16 Jan. 1841.

8. Maria, b. bap. & d. 6 July, 1782.

I. Sir William Chaytor, of Witton Castle and Croft; b. 29 April 1771; created a baronet 30 Sep. 1831; M. P. for Sunderland in the first Reform Parliament; a justice of the peace for co. Durham and the North Riding. He was one of the first promoters and chairman of the Stockton and Darlington Railway, and after building Clervaux Castle on his manor of Croft, died 28 Jan. 1847, and was buried under the Clervaux tomb. = Isabella, dr. and coh. of John Carter, esq. of Tunstall and Richmond; married 18 Aug. 1803; liv. 1852, at Clervaux Castle.

III. John Clervaux Chaytor, esq., of Spennithorne Hall, Yks.; bn. 9 June 1782; a J.P. for the North Riding; died 1839. = Anne, eldest daur. and coh. of John Carter, esq., of Tunstall & Richmond; mar. 16 Jan. 1810

II. Matthew, d. 1825.

1. Jane, d. unm. 1811.

2. Mary, b. 1772; liv. 1852.

3. Charlotte, d. unm. 1792.

4. Elizabeth, mar. 12 Dec. 1804, to Tim. Hutton, esq., of Clifton Castle and Marske Hall, Yorks.

5. Harriet, died unm. 1798.

II. William, b. 30 Aug., d. 15 Sep. 1770.

III. Charles, b. 11 Jan. 1776, d. 11 Aug. 1816.

2. Anne, b. at Kirkby Stephen, 13 Apr. 1768, d. 30 Mar. 1830.

Annie, daur. of Mr. Lacy, of Easingwold; mar. Sep. 1836; died Sep. 1837. = I. Sir William Richard Carter Chaytor, of Croft, bart.; b. 7 Feb. 1805; M. P. for Durham city, 1831 to 1834; a J.P. for co. Durham, and for the North Riding. = 2. Mary, 4th dau. of John Whitney Smith, of Northallerton, esquire, married there 16 March, 1852.

William Chaytor, b. 8 Sep. 1837.

II. John Clervaux Chaytor, esq., of Croft, b. 8 Sept. 1806. = Lydia Frances, eldest dau. of Thomas Brown, esq. of New Grove, Middlesex, mar. 30 Jan. 1834.

IV. Henry Chaytor, of Croft, esq b. 14 Sep. 1812.

III. Matthew Hutton Chaytor esq., of London, born 31 Dec, 1807. = Elizabeth, daughter of Nathan Horn, esq. of Bishop Wearmouth, justice of the peace for co. Durham.

V. Nicholas Smith Chaytor, d. young.

1. Mary Ann, died young.

2. Isabella, = Thomas Drewett Brown, esq., of Jarrow, co. pal., and has issue one son, Drewett Ormonde Brown.

3. Jane.

4. Harriet.

I. John Clervaux, b. 28 July, 1836.
II. Walter, b. 19 Apr. 1838.
III. Edward, b. 30 Dec. 1840.
IV. Arthur, b. 27 July, 1843.
V. Henry, d. young.
VI. Brian Tunstall, b. July, 1847.
VII. Charles, b. 16 Apr. 1849.
VIII. Francis.
1. Fanny, b. 6 Nov. 1834.

Claud, d. young.

D'Arcy.

Hugh.

Alfred.

I. Christopher William Carter Chaytor, esq. = Arabella Sophia, d. of Henry Darley, of Aldby Park, Yks. esq.

II. Matthew John Carter Chaytor, died young.

1. Charlotte, = Fra. Morley, of Marrick Park, Yks., esq.

2. Anne, = Alexander John Ellis, esq., of Brooklands, Hunts.

1. Clervaux Darley, b. 28 Apr. 1844.
II. Henry, b. 1 Sep. 1847.
III. Alfred William, d. inf.
1. Adeline Sophia, d. inf.
2. Matilda, b. 4 Dec. 1842.
3. Mary Anne, b. 12 Jan. 1846.
4 Arabella, b. 21 Jan. 1849.

3 Elizabeth, mar. Alfred Horatio Darley, esq.

4. Mary, mr. Willoughby Wood, esq. of South Thoresby, co. Linc.

III. John Chaytor, esquire, captain in the Royal Engineers, born 28 January, 1802. = Annie Martha, only dr. of Tho. Greatorex, of Upper Norton Street, Portland Place, esq. dec. m. Sep. 1836.

I. Henry John Chaytor,
II. William.
III. Edward Clervaux.
IV. Robert.
1. Mary.
2. Alice.
(All living 1851.)
Two other daughters, died infants.

I. Rev. Henry Chaytor, of Sunderland Bridge, co. pal.; b. 16 Jan. 1799, = Sarah Stamper.

II. William Charles Chaytor, of Durham city, esq., b. 23 Oct. 1800; living unmar. 1852.

IV. Gustavus Adolphus Chaytor, esq., M. D.; died 1 June, 1844.

1. Ann Jane, b. 4 Dec. 1797.

2. Mary, b. 10 July, 1804, died 13 Aug. 1834.

Issue of Thomas Chaytor. *Col. Henry Chaytor.* *Margaret Hebburne.* *Agnes Chaytor.* *Issue of Nicholas Chaytor.*

the maternal home, where the grandmother might teach her own experience in nursing and bringing up); d. 25, bur. 29 Mar. 1641, at Croft.

Hunter's South Yorkshire.) Settlement after marriage 5 May, 1635, dead before the 27th of July, 1638.

estates upon his cousins, the sons of Nicholas Chaytor, in tail male; will dated 20 Jan. 1663-4; died sans issue, and bur. at Croft. 'The buriall of my noble friend Coll. Chaytor was the 25th Oct. 64.' *(St. Cuthbert's, Barton Reg.* formerly *penes* Tho. Gyll, esq.)

duced to 30*l.* in 1699, and parcelled out the remainder upon the sons and daughters of sir William Chaytor; will dated 25 Sep. 1703, d. 24 Feb. following, ag. 105 yrs. 'The burial of Mrs. Margarett Chaytor the 26th of Feb. 1703, ag. 100 years & odd.' (*St. Cuthbert's, Barton.*)

Croft, which had been entailed by her brother on his cousins; died at Croft, and was bur. in Jan. 1669, 'under the pew' in Clervaux aisle. For her husbands and descendants, *See* Ped. No. III.

John Chaytor, esq. of Croft, b. 15 Dec. 1635; settled Croft on his son Thomas, rem. to wife Eliz. for life, rem. to his heirs charged with 200*l.* annuity to his grandmother Frances; d. 1659 or 1660. = 1. Sarah, daur. of sir William Allanson, of York, knt., unmarried at date of her father's will, 11 June, 1656. = 2. Elizabeth, dr. sir Tho. Davison, of Blakeston, co. pal. Set. after mar. 26 Sep. 1659, by which it appears she was then with child. She remar. the hon. Nic. Fairfax, Walton, Yks., who became entitled to his wife's life-interest in Croft, & sold it to Hen. Chaytor. the heir, for 150*l.* annuity.

A daughter, d. inf.

Thomas Chaytor, died Jan. 1660, aged about one year and a half.

II. Sir William Chaytor, of Croft, b. 24 July, bap. 5 Aug. 1639; created a baronet 28 June, 1671; appointed colonel of the Richmondshire reg. of militia by Tho. lord Falconbridge, 1689; succeeded to all the loyalty and misfortunes of his family, and to the estate of Croft on the extinction of the main line in the male blood; alienated the whole of the *Chaytor* estates under a private act of 1695, for payment of debts and for making provision for younger children; but even these being insufficient, he was committed to the Fleet, where he lived seventeen years, and died in Jan. 1720, aged 79. The registers of his children are from Croft. = Perigrina, d. of sir Jos. Cradock knight, of Richmond, Yorksh. (who in 1660, built Cradock Hall, in that town); mar. set. 17, mar. 21 Aug. 1675; died 16, buri d 19 June, 1704, at Kensington.

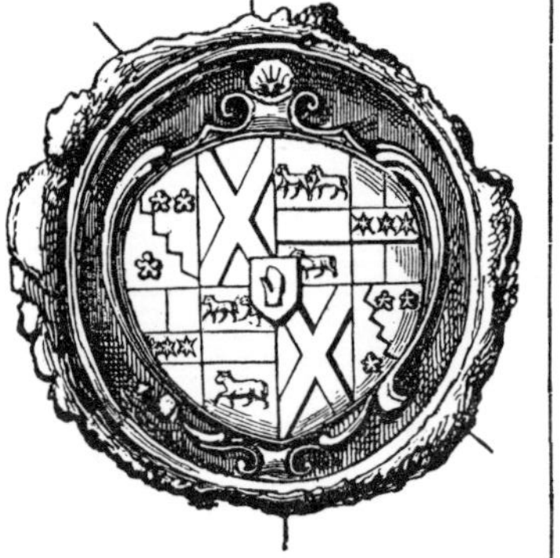

III. Henry Chaytor, of Hurworth, co. pal., gen.; bp. 2 May 1648; of the Middle Temple, 1671; d. 4 May 1719. = Isabel, d. and coh. of Cuthbert Marley of Ingleton, co. pal. & rector of Winston.

I. Thomas b. on Good Friday, bap. 23 May 1637, buried 9 May 1647.

IV. Nicholas, bp. 23 Jan. 1643, at Croft, d. inf.

V. Walter, bap. 27 May, 1650, 'of Croft, merchant;' died at Rotterdam, unmar. 1678.

1. Anne, b. 10 Jan. 1636, will 12 Mar. 1716; d. 1728; = Thomas Ogle, par. St. Andrew Holborn, and Blackburn, in Lanc., esq., d.s.p. before 1714, seised of half the manor of Great St inton, which he purchased from the Killinghalls.

2. Isabel, bap. 9 Nov. 1640, at Haughton le Skerne, bur. 13 Aug. 1642.

3. Jeronima, bur. 8 Feb. 1643-4, at Haughton.

I. William, b. 26 June, bp. 5 July 1681; br. 1 June 1689.

II. Joseph, b. 5, bp. 15 Aug. 1682; br. 11 Mar. 1682-3.

III. Henry Chaytor, b. at Croft 5 Apr. bp. 2 May, 1686, a major in the army, who served four campaigns under the great Marlbrough; d. 17 Oct. 1717, at York, of a dropsy: bur. at Croft.

IV. Thomas, b. 24 June, bp. 23 July, 1688; adm. of Trin. Hall. Camb., and went to sea; v. p. and s. p.

V. Clervaux, b. 2, bp. 23 Apr. 1690; br. 29 May 1693.

VI. Walter, b. 8 Jan. bp. 11 Feb. 1691; br. 19 May 1693.

VII. Nicholas, b 3, bp. 8 Mar. 1695-6, br. Apr. 1697.

VIII. Clervaux, d. 18 Jan. 1715-6.

1. Jane, br. 14 July, 1677.

2. Anne, b. at Croft 11, bp. 24 Jan. 1676-7; d. unmar. 15 May, 1708.

3. Peregrine, b. 21 Apr. bp. 15 May 1684; br. 6 June 1687.

4. Jane, b. 22 Aug., bp. 21 Sep., br. 2 Oct. 1695.

5. Peregrina.

Henry Chaytor, esq., of Croft, born at Hurworth 1689; succeeded his uncle sir William in the Croft estate; died at Croft 9 Feb. 1774, bur. under the Clervaux tomb. He obtained an act 2 Geo. II., to enable him to limit a jointure to a wife, and to let leases for twenty-one years. = Jane, only d. and h. (on the death of her brothers) of Matthew Smales, esq., of Gilling, in Yorkshire, by Alice Alderson, his first wife; d. at Croft 24 May, 1760, ag. 53, buried under the Clervaux tomb 27 May 1760.

Isabella, only dau. married Samuel Hobbins, esq., of London; d. s. p. a widow at Croft; buried under the Clervaux tomb.

I. William Chaytor, esq. of Croft and Spennithorne, in Wensleydale; M.P. for Hedon; barrister at law; recorder of Richmond; vice lieutenant and J.P. for the = Jane Lee, d. 20 Jan. 1825.

III. Matthew, b. at Croft 22 Aug. 1739, d. inf.

IV. Matthew, b. at Croft 21 Apr. 1742; an ensign in the 1st Regiment of Foot Guards; d. unm. 23 Oct. 1762, of a fever, at his

1. Jane, b. at Croft 11 Mar. 1737; liv. 1787; mar. at Croft 1764, to John Trotter, esq., M.D., of Darlington, who d. 8 Feb. 1784, ag. 53.

2. Alice Mary, b. at Croft 4 Aug. 1744; d. 5 July, 1833; mar. at

1. Betty, d. and h. of Christopher Gregson, esq., of Bondgate, in Appleby, co. Westmorland; mar. 22 May 1760; died of small pox, in childbed, at Croft 25 July 1763. = II. Rev. Henry Chaytor, LL.D., rector of Croft, and vicar of Catterick; prebendary of Durham etc.; born at Croft 14 Nov. 1734; died there 9 June 1789, and buried 'under the pew,' in the church. = 2. Ann, daughter of Charles Robinson, esq., of Appleby; married there, 5 Feb. 1765; died at the same place 16 June 1790, buried under the pew in Croft church.

John Cheytor, merchant-adventurer, of Newcastle-upon-Tyne. = ……

Christopher Chaytor, of Butterby, esq., youngest son, but eventually heir to his father, born 1494, in the par. of St. Andrew's, Newcastle; surveyor-general for Elizabeth of Durham and Northumberland, 1575, registrar of the Consistory Court of Durham, and justice of the peace; purchased Butterby from the Lumleys: died 17, bur. at St. Oswald's, Durham, 18 Apr. 1592, 'unto whom God send a joyful resurection.' (*Reg. St. Oswald's.*) Will 13 April previous. 'To Mrs. Colpton, one old ryall, to *his* daughter *my wif* Allice one angell, Mr. John Clopton, of Sledwish, supervisor.'—'my daughter Thornton.' = Elizabeth, the heiress of Clervaux. (*See* Pedigree I.) Bur. 1584.

1. Margaret daur. John Witham, esq. of Cliffe, Yorkshire; mar. set. 27 Feb. 1582-3, d. s. p. at Cliffe. = I. Anthony Chaytor, of Croft, esq. aged 28, 1575, heir to Richard Clervaux, 1590-1; will 1605; d. 13, bur. 14 May 1612, in the vault under the Clervaux tomb at Croft. = 2. Margaret, daughter of William Thorneton, esq. of East Newton, or White-house, Yks. marriage settlement 24 May 1591, died 4 Sep. 1613.

II. Hugh, of London, gen., 'quirrie' to queen Eliz., d. unmar. 10 Jan. 1593, at London.

III. Christopher, d. s. p. br. 8 Jan. 1632 at S. Oswald's, Durham.

1. Eleanor daur. of …… Thornell, of East Newton, in Rydale Yks. esq; d. s. p. br. at St. Oswald's, 22 July, 1603. = IV. Thomas Chaytor, esq. of Butterby (by gift of his father); b. 1554; succeeded his father as surveyor-general of Durham and Northumberland under Elizabeth and James, and registrar of the Consistory Court. Will 6 July, 1614; to be buried in St. Oswald's church, as near his beloved parents as conveniently might be, if he departed this life near thereunto. Died July, 1618. = 2. Jane, dau. sir Nicholas Tempest, bt. of Stella, by Isabella Lambton, whose royal descent is shown in Ped. IV. She d. an aged widow in Aug., and was br. 1 Sep. 1666, at St. Oswald's' Durham.

1. Margaret, = Tho. Backesworth, of Thormanby. (*Glover's Visit.* 1584.)

2. Jane, =. Ralph Willey, of Houghton le Side, co. pal., gen., before 1575. ⅄ = 2. William Frankland, of Houghton le Side, gen. He was a trustee of the settlement of Butterby on Tho. Chaytor, and was dead in 1592, when his widow is mentioned. Her son Richard Frankland living 1615. = 3. Richard Tancred, younger son of Ralph Tancred, esq., of Arden, before 1614. (*See* Walbran's Gainford, 123.)

3. Elizabeth, = …… Staveley before 1592. *Qu.* Wm. Staveley, of Thormondby, Yks., gen., who lent 105*l.* in 1615 to Margaret Lambton, of Haughton Field, widow. (*Arms.*—Argent, on a chevron between three lozenges sable, three harts' heads of the first.

4. Beatrix. *Qu.* 'my daughter Whitfield,' 1592. (Robert Whitfield was trustee of Butterby under Christopher's settlement on Thos. Chaytor.)

5. Helen, unmarried 1592.

I. Sir William Chaytor, kt., b. at Croft 2 Aug. 1592; attained age 2 Aug. 1613; settled his estates in tail male, charged with 1000*l.* for his daur. Agnes's portion; died 30 Mar., bur. 1 Apr. 1640, at Croft. = Frances, d. sir James Bellingham knt. of Helsington & Levinz, in Westmoreland, by Agnes, daughter of sir Henry Curwen; mar. 9 Jun 1614; br. 19 Nov. 1669, at Croft.

II. Richard, liv. 1617, at Croft, d. s. p.

III. Thomas, liv. 1605, d.s.p.

1. Isabel, = at Croft, 13 April, 1613, to Chr. Richmond, of Highhead Castle, in Cumberland (mar. set. 18 Mar. before), d. s. p. 10 Sep. 1613.

2. Margaret, under age 1617, = Ralph Hutton, esq. A. B., Mainsforth, who d. 1638-9.

3. Mary, under age 1617, = Charles Hutton, of Berwick-on-Tweed, notary publique (bro. to Ralph), who received her portion 4 Feb. 1624, and d. 1638.

*** 1662. The 6th day of October, a very sad accedent befell Mr. Henrie Chaiter of Gaineford, as he was coming from Darlington, in soe much that he fell from his horse, and was suddenly slaine, from which Good Lord deliver us, and was buried nobly by his friends and neighbours the 8th day of the aforesaid mounth, together with his funeral sermon, the subject of which was the 22 of Revelations, and the 12th verse.—Et ecce venio cito: et merces mea mecum est; etc. etc. (*Gainford Reg.*)

I. Henry Chaytor, esq., of Butterby, aged 8, 1615, d. unmar. 'Mr. Henrie Chaitor, esq., son and heire of the Rt. Worshipfull Thomas Chaitor, of Butterbie, esq., bur. 1 May 1629, æt. 20,' at S Oswalds.

II. Nicholas Chaytor of Butterby and Haughton Field, esq. *jure uxoris;* bp. 6 Dec. 1608; lieutenant colonel under the marquis of Newcastle, & suffered deeply for his loyalty; will 8, d. 10 Feb. 1665, at Croft. = Ann, d. and coh. (with her sister Margaret, wife of John Killinghall, esq. of Middleton St. George) of William Lambton, esquire, of Haughton-field, co. pal. by Ann his wife, daur. and coh. of the Rev. Jno. Barnes LL.D. rector of Haughton le Skerne, and niece of Richard Barnes, bishop of Durham; b. 22 July, 1584, at Haughton le Skerne; mar. 19 Jan. 1635; bur. 2 Aug. 1664, at Haughton le Skerne.

III. Thomas, b. 6 June, 1615, bap. at home same day; d.s.p.; bur. 27 June, 1631, at St. Oswald's.

IV. George, b. 26 Aug. 1616, bap. same day; of Whessoe, co. pal., gen.; bur. 18 Nov. 1678, at Haughton le Skerne, s. p.; 'and fiftie shillings forfeited to the poore of the parish of Haughton, because he was not buryed in woollen onlye, w'h money was paid to the overseer of the poore of Haughton, and accordingly distributed to the poore of Haughton parish.,

V. Robert, bur. 6 June. 1629, at St. Oswald's, s. p.

1. Jeronima, liv. 1636, = Tho. Swinburne. esq., of Barmton, co. pal., liv. with his s. and h. John of full age, 1664.

2. Isabel, d. s. p. = James Bela sis, of Owton, co. pal., (being his second wife), the donor of Poor Howden's Charity, Darlington.

3. Margaret, = Ralph Bates, esq., of Halliwell, North'd.

4. Troth, b. at Butterby 20, bap. 26 May, 1612, at Croxdale (her aunt Troth Tempest a godmother); bur. 27 Feb. 1631, St. Oswald's, s. p.

5. Mary, b. at Butterby 28 July, bap. at Croxdale 3 Aug. 1613; bur. at St. Oswald's 8 Sep. 1631, s. p.

1. Thomas Chaytor, esq. of Croft, b. 8 Feb. 1616, bap. at Levinz (and for obvious reasons, we find first children generally born at = Mary, daughter of Thomas Lewis, esq. of Marr, in Yorkshire, of the Ledstone family. (*See*

II. Colonel Henry Chaytor, of Croft, *ultimus suorum*, bn. at Croft, bap. June, 1617, the brave defender of Bolton Castle, for the royal cause; 'his picture in armour, with red hair, is at Croft'; settled his = Margaret, d. Arthur Hebburne, esq., of Hebburne, North'd. widow of Robt. Dodsworth, of Barton, esq. (ancestor of the Allans, and who died in 1651); had 90*l.* annuity out of Croft, which she re-

Agnes Chaytor b. 27 April, 1615, bap. the last Sunday in the same month, at Croft; made a vain attempt to recover her inheritance of

DIVISION VI.

FAMILIES.

I. ALLAN.

The Allans have long occupied a distinguished position in the county of Durham, and held the foremost place among the *magnates* of the neighbourhood of Darlington, not so much for their territorial influence, as that, in the words of Ord, the elegant historian of Cleveland, they are "a family illustrious, not only in antiquity and honourable descent, but also in science, literature, and the achievements of the intellect; without which the glittering coronet is but an empty bauble, and the pomp of heraldry a ridiculous burlesque."

That pageantry, the rise and zenith of family wealth, names and dates, and all that constitute reality, and truth in genealogy, are sufficiently detailed in the careful pedigrees appended to this memoir. It remains but to give a succinct idea of family worth and talent. And in doing so, it will be well to commence with the Durham advent of the race, as Thomas Allan, the mathematician, who throws a gleam of sunshine over the storyless Staffordshire descents, is a man sufficiently known through the medium of general biographies. In Wood's Athenæ Oxonienses, he is called the "father of all learning and virtuous industry, an unfeigned lover and furtherer of all good arts and sciences, and an eminent antiquary and philosopher. His sufficiency in the mathematic science being generally noted, he was thereupon accounted another Roger Bacon, which was the reason why he became terrible to the vulgar, especially those of Oxon, who took him to be a perfect conjurer. He was a great collector of scattered MSS. of whatsoever faculty, especially those of history, antiquity, &c., sparing neither cost nor labour to procure them." Robert the *Elizabethan* Earl of Leicester, consulted him in matters of moment, and confided with the greatest attachment in his talents and secrecy, so much so, that the author of "Leicester Commonwealth" openly accused him of using the art of figuring to further his patron's schemes to bring about a match with the Queen.*

Of the eventual fate of the branches which lingered round their ancient homes in Staffordshire, I am profoundly ignorant. Whatever destiny conspired to the disruption of his house, or whatever cause, whether political or otherwise, led to the entry of the herald itinerant that "Geo: Allan went into Com: Dunelm:" one thing is certain, that he departed not from his father-land, but with a well filled purse. His grandsons at once, through a

* William Herbert, Earl of Pembroke, the W. H. of Shakspere's sonnets, according to Wood, died suddenly in Baynard's Castle, London, his residence, in 1630, according to the calculation of his nativity, made several years before by Mr. Tho. Allen, of Gloucester Hall. Allen lived to see the death of the subject or perchance victim of his calculation, and followed, two years after, at the great age of ninety. Judicial astrology is said to have been his "favourite and first pursuit," and he left a MS. commentary upon the second and third books of Ptolemy *de astrorum judiciis*, which fell into the hands of William Lilly. Allen was closely associated with Dee, but in truth was "deemed in those days the father of all learning." Clarendon tells a story of a party of gentlemen drinking Pembroke's health at Maidenhead, and one of them remarking "That he believed his Lord was at that time very merry, for he had now *outlived* the day which *his tutor Sandford* had prognosticated upon his nativity he would not out-live; but he had done it now, for that was his birth-day, which had completed his age to fifty years." The next morning they heard of his death. Unless Sandford is a mistake for Allen, it follows that two astrologers concurred in their interpretations of the horoscope.—*Gent. Mag.*, Oct., 1832.

vast command of capital for that day, struck deep root on the banks of the Tees and the Wear, and took the front rank amongst the squirearchy of the palatinate.

Of these grandsons, THOMAS ALLAN, esq., born in 1651, speedily became one of the largest, if not the largest, coal owner on the Wear, purchased estates, and settled at Allan's Flatts, near Chester-le-street. He is singularly connected with modern Durham enterprise, by having been the *first introducer** of waggon-ways or tramways on the Wear, which, even in their infancy—in their rude unimproved state—saved an immense amount of horse labour. The novelty was so exciting to the boors, that the universal salutation on meeting was "Hev ye been te see Allan's *new wark?*" and this fact became so notorious, that at last his usual *soubriquet* was "Lord *Newark!*" This was about 1690.†

* "Waggon-ways are reported in the neighbourhood of the collieries to have been first used on the river Were, soon after the revolution, by Mr. Allan of Flatts, and on the Tyne by Charles Montague, esq., at Stella."—*(Randall's note in his copy of Bourne's Newcastle)*. Waggons themselves were used at Team staith as early as 1671, for the carriage of coals, but even in our days asses were employed in the Auckland district and various parts for their conveyance in pokes.

† One of his sons, LIONEL ALLAN, was an eminent merchant at Rotterdam, and marrying Susanna Colville, became connected with a curious tradition of the county of Durham. In the early part of the last century, Edward Colville, who had realised a handsome fortune as a wholesale butcher and extensive grazier, resided in a mansion called the White House, which may still be seen in the vicinity of Gateshead. The respectability of his character, and the style in which he lived, were such as to admit of his daughter Camilla attending the assize balls in Newcastle; and gifted by nature with an elegant person, and with some advantages of education, Camilla was a young lady eminently qualified to grace those assemblages; at one of which she had the good fortune to attract the attention of a young nobleman, Lord Ossulston, the eldest son of the Earl of Tankerville. It occasioned no small flutter in the room, when this nobleman, after the proper formalities, requested of Miss Colville the honour of being allowed to walk a minuet with her. She blushingly consented, and rarely had the ball-room of Newcastle exhibited a more striking display of graceful movement than what was displayed while this stately dance was in the course of being performed. Lord Ossulston was charmed beyond all measure by the beauty of his partner, and the next day beheld the heir of the house of Tankerville, at an hour which would now be considered preposterously early, calling at the White House to pay his respects to its fair tenant. Next day, and the next again, he renewed his visits; and the young lady's father, from being simply flattered, began to fear that feelings might arise between the parties which would only lead to disappointment. Perhaps he had even graver fears, which any one acquainted with the maxims of the gentlemen of that age will not deem to have been at all unreasonable, especially as Camilla would not be aged more than sweet sixteen.

He therefore made some efforts to keep Lord Ossulston out of the company of his daughter; but, denied admittance to the house, the young nobleman still could beset her when she went abroad, seat himself near her at church, and get insinuated into any little social party where she was expected. Mr. Colville at length saw it to be necessary to take very decided measures, and he resolved to place the young lady for some time in a new and distant home, where her sister, who was eight years older, might be a proper guardian.

Mr. Lionel Allan, his son in law, had settled as a merchant in Holland, and he had also a friend who conducted a vessel of his own regularly between South Shields and the ports of Holland and the North of France. It may here be remarked, that the ship-owners, who in those days navigated their own vessels from South Shields, were a highly respectable class of men, generally possessing good education and manners, and living, when at home, in a style of considerable dignity. Amongst the descendants of more than one of them, might be found members of both houses of parliament. They took the name of Captain, and had, we believe, some solid grounds for doing so, as trading beyond certain latitudes and longitudes specified by Queen Elizabeth, gave masters of merchant vessels a modified permission to assume that title. Captain Aubane, (of the family of Aubane of Great Yarmouth, not Aubone of Newcastle) readily entered into the views of his friend Colville, and undertook to convey the young lady to her relative in Rotterdam. She was, accordingly, conducted in the most private manner to South Shields, and put on board his vessel; for if, as is likely, she regarded her lover with affection, and deemed the voyage a compulsory exile, the authority of parents was in those days too awful and inflexible to admit of her making any thing like effectual remonstrance.

The voyage passed in safety, and Camilla was consigned to Mr. Lionel Allan. If Mr. Colville, however, believed that Lord Ossulston had been "thrown out," he was mistaken; for, before many weeks had elapsed, his lordship made his appearance in Rotterdam, and became as troublesome to Mr. Allan's family, who had charge of his mistress, as he had formerly been to her father. The Linden Walks lent their shade to meetings of the lovers, and, when such were denied, his lordship made signals from the street, which Camilla could furtively read in the friendly mirror projecting from the parlour window. Mr. Allan

THOMAS ALLAN, esq., the youngest son, and brother of Lionel Allan, succeeded to the bulk of his father's property. His death is thus recorded: "On Sunday, 21st December, 1740, died at his house at Flatts, THOMAS ALLAN, Esq., one of the principal coal-owners on the river Wear. He was a gentleman whose integrity and worth placed him in the highest estimation, and whose good nature and generosity endeared him to all his acquaintance. He was earnest in promoting the good of his country, and particularly that great support of it, its trade; in the cause of which he embarked his fortune, and applied a most laudable industry; manifesting in his affairs an uncommon elegance and propriety; and as his life was adorned with every virtue that dignifies human nature, so his death is universally a most melancholy occasion of sorrow."*

The failure of the Flatts branch (which was, in fact, the elder line) in co-heiresses merging in the baronetical family of Shafto Adair, is shown in the pedigree, and I now proceed to the Blackwell families, the principal object of this memoir.

GEORGE ALLAN, esq., born in 1663, another grandson of the settler, pitched his tent at Darlington as a general merchant, and being very fortunate in a contract to furnish government with a large quantity of salt, it has been generally reported that he bought South Sea stock to a great amount, which, being let into the secret, he sold before the bubble burst, and pur-

now became more distressingly alarmed than even the father had been, and resolved to get quit of his perilous charge. Captain Aubane, ere long, returned to Rotterdam for another cargo, and Camilla was once more put on board. The Dutch coast had for a day been lost in the blue distance, and honest Aubane was congratulating himself on the prospect of soon committing Miss Colville in safety to her father's keeping, when, descending into the cabin, how was he astonished to behold, kneeling at her feet, that very Lord Ossulston whom he supposed to have been left lamenting on the quay of Rotterdam! He soon learned that the lover had contrived, by the connivance of a sailor, and, doubtless, with the concurrence of his mistress, to secrete himself on board the vessel, in a cask, a little before it sailed. It was too late to think of returning to the Dutch harbour to put Lord Ossulston ashore; but he commanded him to withdraw from the cabin, and not to appear there again, unless in his company, and by his express permission. He also stipulated that, while he was himself on deck upon duty, Lord Ossulston should remain beside him, at whatever time of day or night, and under whatever circumstances of weather. The lover found himself compelled to submit to all these restrictions; but the privilege of seeing his mistress once a-day, even in the presence of a third party, served in no small degree to reconcile him to their strictness.

In the course of the voyage, which was not a short one, the heir of Tankerville made a more favourable impression on the mind of Aubane, who became convinced that, however frivolous or otherwise objectionable might have been the feelings with which he at first regarded Camilla, he was now inspired by an honourable affection. He was also induced to believe the young man when he protested, in the most earnest manner, that the future happiness of his life depended on his obtaining the hand of Miss Colville. The South Shields ship-owner did not, indeed, like the idea of encouraging a young nobleman in an object which must be regarded with dislike by his father and other relations; but on this point also his scruples were at length overcome, doubtless by persuasives strictly honourable. On arriving at South Shields, he allowed Lord Ossulston to become an inmate of his house, in company with Camilla, until the consent of her father was obtained, and the necessary preparations were made for their marriage. The union of the pair took place at Jarrow church, the ancient seat of the Venerable Bede; a place of worship which, from some local prepossession, has been for ages the resort of young couples seeking to enter the bonds of wedlock without the consent of parents. They resided with the lady's father at White House for some years. At length the death of his father made Lord Ossulston Earl of Tankerville, the second of the title; and Camilla Colville, as Countess, became entitled to the chief seat in the splendid halls of Chillingham Castle. Our heroine was afterwards one of the ladies of the bed-chamber to Queen Caroline, the consort of George II. She played her part as a peeress with a due portion of dignity and spirit, and continued, long after being the mother of three children (one of whom, George, was godson to his namesake the king), to be one of the most beautiful women at the English court. She survived her husband in a long dowagerhood, and died in 1775, not indeed at the age of 105, as has been repeatedly stated in grave works of authority, but of 77. Her father however reached the former age, and her sister Susanna Allan outlived her whole generation, her husband, ten brothers and sisters, and ten children, dying at the age of 92.—*Chambers's Edinburgh Journal . . . p. 375; and family traditions and papers of the Allans.*

* Hutch. Hist. Durham II., p. 401.—Surtees II., p. 191.

chased estates. This must be a mistake, as the South Sea scheme did not take place until 1719, nine years after, and he bought estates in one year alone, namely 1710, which in 1814 let for five thousand pounds per annum. It is possible, however, as he purchased afterwards a variety of small farms and parcels of ground near Darlington, that he might have been a lucky proprietor of South Sea stock. He built, or perhaps re-edified Blackwell Grange, the subsequent calm and lovely seat of his family, in 1710, but it is probable, if we may judge from fire-places, &c., of an apparently more ancient form, that the *vestigia* of an earlier mansion are incorporated with the present spacious structure.* In 1717, his son, George, took unto himself a wife in Thomasine, the wealthy co-heiress of Prescott, with "*acres* of charms," and the delighted senior in the exuberance of his joy, whilst his son and daughter in law were absent on their bridal excursion, added the noble south wing to Grange as an agreeable surprise to them on their return. On the leaden spouts of that period are their initials, disposed as in the margin. The father in fact gave the Grange, with a moiety of his estates, to his son in his lifetime, and died in 1743-4, full of years and wealth.† His amiable wife had died thirty-four years previously, and was commemorated in the papers of the day by an effusion of no common elegance.‡

T
G 1717 A

The younger George Allan died in 1753, "universally respected," leaving two daughters and co-heiresses, of whom the younger sister, Ann Allan, is well remembered as "the good Miss Allan," for her benevolence and extensive charities. A bowl of pence was given out every morning for the relief of every distressed person who might call at the accustomed fount of kindness, and meat and drink were plentifully supplied. The worthy lady, in spinster state, had a great penchant for cats, of which animals she had a very fine and large breed; and as she would not suffer any of their numerous progeny to be immolated, a number became wild, and infested the neighbourhood, to the distress of her nearer friends. For the extravagant company at Grange itself, a large provision had to be made, and a man at Hurworth was retained as feline fisherman in ordinary. As to their patroness, a variety of

* The hearths in the old portion were on the floor, with capacious seats around.

† Beautiful was his hand-writing, and the characteristic has never been wanting in the family of Allan. Painfully exact was the caligraphy of the antiquary, and that of old James his father was the more sprightly, and bold.

‡ "On Tuesday, the 8th instant [8th Feb., 1709-10], died, greatly regretted by her family and friends, the wife of George Allan, esq., of Darlington. A most affectionate wife and a most tender mother, ever assiduous in searching for and relieving distress. She was of 'every friendless name the friend.'"

"*On the death of Mrs. Allan, of Darlington.*

The voice of grief, the unavailing sigh,
  Can reason's cold indifference restrain,
When she who wiped the tear from every eye
  Expires, the victim of relentless pain?

Her mind with no illusive image teemed
  To no fastidious taste did she pretend;
Careful to act, content to be esteemed
  As daughter, mother, neighbour, wife, and friend.

Be this her praise, with no factitious grace,
  Domestic tenderness and virtue mild,
The social smile, serenity of face,
  That looks on fortune as a froward child.

Ye youthful pledges of a mother's care,
  A father in his anguish soothe and save;
O be whate'er inspires a mother's prayer,
  And keep at least one parent from the grave!"

her costly habiliments, which were bequeathed to her servants, were floating for some time in Darlington. The following articles bought by Miss Allan in her father's lifetime, for herself and two sisters then living, of Swann and Buck, "mercers at the Wheat-sheaf in King Street, Covent Garden" (whose bill-head is duly garnished with their sign, like that of a modern innkeeper), will show the prices our ancestresses paid for their superb dresses.

			£	s.	d.
1748.					
Jan. 14.	19 yds. white, gold, and coloured brocade	29*s.*	27	11	0
Miss Kitty.	18 yds. white, silver, and coloured do............	28*s.*	25	4	0
	12 yds. white ground, bordered blues	17*s.*	10	4	0
Miss Dorothy.	17½ yds. white, silver, and coloured blue str.	26*s.*	22	15	0
	40 yds. white taffety Persian	2*s.*	4	0	0
			89	14	0*

The loss of this "worthy lady of Grange" was sincerely lamented by all. "Her household, always at unity in itself, not so much from the command of the mistress, as from the influence of a persuasive example, exhibited an instructive lesson of virtue and piety. Possessed of an ample fortune, she dispensed blessings to all around her. Pope's Man of Ross built a church and an alms-house. Miss Allan's charities were more extensive; many of them were public and open; more secret and silent; nor were they confined to sect or party, or to her own neighbourhood. Wherever she heard of misery and distress, though at some hundred miles distance, her heart and hand were open to alleviate them; and in such numberless instances, that it may be truly said of her, that she fed the hungry, cloathed the naked, and caused the widow's heart to sing for joy."† She died in 1785, and after the custom observed at the Allan funerals, was buried in the Grange vault in Darlington church, with great pomp, the affair costing not less than 1000*l.* But that was nothing to the tears of the poor. The last members of the solemn procession had not left the Grange precincts as the first were entering the churchyard. A dole was on the occasion given to between nine thousand and ten thousand people. The town of Darlington itself, twenty years before, only contained some three thousand one hundred persons; the parties who received the dole must, therefore, have come from all the country round. The adults received one shilling each, and the small fry six-pence; and as the crowds compelled the simultaneous distribution at various stations in the town, the desideratum was to pass quickly from one doler to another and thus obtain the charity twice over.

Her cousin, the antiquary, shortly afterwards writes to Gough:—"What will Mr. Bartolozzi expect for a portrait in the chalk style, to print in colors, the size of the Bishop of Durham enclosed? [probably the plate in Hutchinson's Durham]. Pray enquire. I have some thoughts of having the late worthy lady of Grange done. Collyer had ten guineas for this head of bishop Egerton." The print was nevertheless engraved by Mr. Joseph Collyer, and

* In addition, it would appear from the following expensive items in a bill (amongst many others) of How and Masterman, of London, dated Feb. 19, 1762, that Miss Allan, like the rest of her sex, was by no means unmindful of "the foreign aid of ornament."

	£	s.	d.
"162 fine rose diamonds added to a pr. of 3 Drop'd Earings and makeing a pair Double cluster 3 Drop'd Rose Diamond Earings with large rich knotts containing 294 stones	50	18	6
A large fine Rose Diamond Necklace of a great length, very neatly sett in Flowers and Sprigs, &c., containing 225 large and small Rose Diamonds and 6 Brilliants that *was* taken from a pair of old earings...	157	10	0"

† Gent. Mag. of the day.

the memory of its subject was so much and deservedly revered at Darlington, that a copy long hung over the chimney-piece of every respectable parlour in the place. It is mentioned by Geo. Allan, the M.P., as having been taken from a wax model in his possession. An impression was sold, in 1812, at Miss Cade's sale for twelve shillings. Under this portrait is inscribed: "Ann Allan, of Blackwell Grange, near Darlington, died 16th Octr., 1785, æt. 68. In gratitude to her memory, this plate is inscribed, by Geo. Allan, 1787." It represents the good lady sitting, with a book in her hand, the countenance strongly defined, but quiet and benevolent. There is an original portrait, slightly differing from the print, at Blackwell Hall. In this picture, Miss Allan is represented as possessing a milder and altogether a very agreeable cast of countenance. She deliberates on the answer to be given from a well filled purse in her hand, to "The humble petition of a poor old man," lying open before her on the sill of a window, which is margined with the ancient vines of Grange, and discovers the soaring spire of St. Cuthbert's collegiate church.

With Miss Allan the first Grange line of the family had completely worked out, and the Flatts branch had merged into females. The only male descendant of the settler from Staffordshire was a youngest child, a tenth son, who had survived his fourteen brothers and sisters, and was the only one of his family that married. This was James Allan, the son of Nicholas Allan, brother of George, the first of Grange, who, like his brother, had made his pelf by being a merchant at Darlington and Staindrop, and who married a Sober, of a race occurring in the former parish at least as early as temp. Elizabeth, and found, in 1605, at Nessfield (now the property of their descendant, Robert Henry Allan, esq.), where they lived on their own inheritance, until their extinction in the male line carried their representation of blood and compact lands to the Allans. "Elizabeth *Sober, an old maid,*" was buried 1 Feb., 1739.

James Allan, "Mr. Allan's nephew," had been appointed Borough Bailiff in 1738 by the bishop, through the influence of his wealthy relative of Grange, and he long exercised the profession of the law with great success at Darlington. He was, as might have been expected, called to the possession of the estates of his family, by the grand-daughter of his early patron, who could hardly have suspected that his youngest nephew would, by the strange mortality which occurred, ever have succeeded to the right of the first-born. The family estate, augmented with the possessions of Sober and Killinghall, was now at the zenith of extent. In 1812, the rental of the estates enjoyed by his two grandsons, George Allan, esq., and John Allan, esq., amounted to rather better than 10,000*l.* per annum.*

To "Auld Jem Allan," as he is popularly called (like the "Old Sir William" of the Bowes family, or "Auld Will Lambton, alias Old True Blue"), the founder of the second race of Grange, Mr. Hutchinson, in his History of Durham, tenders his acknowledgments, "for his compendious collection of extracts from public records, as well those of the acts of the crown, as parliamentary and provincial, references to authorities compiled in an ex-

* 1812.	Annual rental of the old Allan or Grange estate	£6,348
	Of Baydales (Blackwell Manor), afterwards purchased by John Allan, esq.; and Blackwell Holme, afterwards purchased by Major Bower, and J. C. Backhouse, esq.	1,054
	Of the estates of John Allan, esq., chiefly derived from Sober, and Killinghall	2,700
		£10,102

tensive train of reading, and other valuable materials." He was a good lawyer, and a very accurate antiquary; particularly skilled in the old court hands, and his grandson thought that of the two, he could read an ancient charter with even more facility than his son "the antiquary." He was very fond of old records, and was a great index maker. His dress, which he never varied, and his manners, were of the old school; but he possessed a fund of lively anecdote, was generous and convivial, and one of the most agreeable men anywhere, but in his own family. At home, except when he had company, he was peevish and austere to an excess; and "I believe," says his grandson the M.P., "I am the only one of his family that ever presumed to enter into any unrestrained familiar conversation with him. Indeed, my father often acknowledged, that he never could get the better of a sort of timidity, bordering on fear, when in his presence, during the whole of his life. - - - My grandfather and my father, though of congenial pursuits, were nevertheless at variance during almost the whole of the life of the former, from causes which it would be uninteresting to relate; but no reconciliation ever took place."*

The withering sarcasm and severity of James Allan was of such note, that I have been told in Darlington he was the crossest and sternest man that ever lived, and that he stretched the balival authority to the utmost bound of prerogative. But he was a great man, such as is produced in a family only once in five or six generations. He had prudence, confidence, and talent; and the fortune he had obtained with his wife, (the eventual heiress of Killinghall and Pemberton), the meed of a long period of laborious professional labour, and the ample estate of his departed relatives, raised him to a high pitch of worldly affluence. He died at Grange the 19th of Jan., 1790; a day rendered memorable in the annals of the parish, in consequence of a terrific storm, which tore up trees by their roots, and shook Grange and Darlington to their foundations.

GEORGE ALLAN, THE ANTIQUARY (honoured name!), succeeded to the entailed estates, comprising the old Allan patrimony, only. The Killinghall estates of Barton, together with the unentailed Durham property, a portion of which now belongs to R. H. Allan, esq.; and the immense personal estate of his father, were left to his other children, from reasons partaking, probably, more of common consideration and affection, than of any virulent hatred to his son and heir. "My father," says the M.P., "was a good man, a man of almost uncommon generosity and hospitality; but he had faults—and who is without them? He was warm in his affections but very keen in resentment, and though, I believe, as temperate a man as ever existed, he was extremely irritable during the latter years of his life. I have no doubt but the distribution of my grandfather's large property, and particularly the Killinghall estates, to the youngest son, now possessed by a cousin of mine

* In 1789, Dr. Carr, of Hertford, writes to this George the younger: "As you say nothing of the present state of your father's health, I hope it is better than some time ago. So generous and ingenious, so honest and friendly a man, is worthy of all that fortune can bestow, and I have often grieved to think of the peevishness and jealousy of old age standing in the way of his prospects. With regard to your brother, I own myself somewhat mortified at his keeping his resolution so profound a secret, because I had concluded that he was sensible of my best wishes." This last paragraph refers to the antiquary's youngest son James, who was educated by Dr. Carr, entered of Trinity, and for whom very ample preferment was intended in the church. But, according to a popular truism, "THERE NEVER WAS AN ALLAN A PARSON." He chose a military life, and his career was short indeed. He was a Captain in the 29th regiment of foot, and at the point of gaining, at an early period, the rank of Major, when he died of the yellow fever at the island of Grenada, in 1795, aged 23, lamented by every one who knew him.

[John Allan, esq.], was the cause of it." Where is content to be found? Not even in well-portioned antiquaries.

The Antiquary was born on the 7th of June, 1736, and his passion for transcribing soon developed itself. When a boy at school he had his Horace interleaved; and he copied the whole of Francis's translation in the neatest hand-writing. Not a blot or correction is to be seen throughout the whole. The octavo edition of "Clarke's Homer's Iliad," he also embellished with Pope's translation. "I have," says Mr. George Allan, jun., "a few of his school exercises, which are not more extraordinary than such things generally are; but they, and indeed his whole life exhibit a rare instance of continued labour, and attentive industry. I conceive from the variety of transcripts I possess, that he must have been in the habit, when a young man, of borrowing books he could not afford to buy; such, for instance, as Dugdale's Monasticon, from which he made voluminous extracts, though I remember it to have been in his library as long as I can recollect."

His strong and active mind enabled him to pay very great attention to antiquities and genealogical researches. In heraldry especially, he had acquired so very extraordinary a degree of skill, that in 1763 he had serious thoughts of publishing an elaborate copper-plate Peerage, for which he actually circulated proposals; but after engraving at least one large plate, partly deterred by the prospect of the hazard and expence, and partly from two similar works having been about the same time entered into by Mr. Jacob and Mr. Edmondson (appointed Mowbray herald extraordinary, 1764), he declined the undertaking, which was to be executed in a large degree with copper-plates, the pedigrees being in a tabular form.*

From a congeniality of pursuits, he soon became acquainted with Ralph Bigland, esq., (at that time Somerset Herald and Registrar, afterwards Garter King at Arms), and with Isaac Heard, esq. (then Lancaster Herald, afterwards Sir Isaac Heard), who assisted, as Garter King at Arms, at the ceremony of the coronation of king George IV., in 1820. His correspondence with these gentlemen was on all sides mutually communicative and instructive; and in 1764,† on a vacancy of the office of Richmond Herald, Mr. Allan was very handsomely invited to accept it; an offer which he as handsomely declined, his connexions in life rendering his acceptance "as improper as it was unnecessary."‡

* He however before finally giving up, attempted a different mode of publication:—"Mr. Allan's compliments to Lord Lincoln, and has taken the freedom to wait on his Lordship to return thanks for his encouragement to his Peerage; but, as the expence of engraving amounted to such a large sum a 3000*l*. at least, he could not possibly think of carrying it on in the manner proposed, unless assured of 200 subscribers. He has been desired to print it at the letter-press, in which he will have an opportunity to make many more curious and valuable remarks than he could have done by the means of copper-plates; notwithstanding which, numbers of the plates, and all the arms, &c., will still be inserted in the course of the work; and the price of the whole peerage will not now exceed 10 guineas. Should his lordship approve of this last scheme, when he has seen the proposals, Mr. Allan still hopes for his Lordship's encouragement." The modern antiquary, accustomed to the compact and voluminous pedigrees printed by Nichols, and the Hodgsons and Richardsons of Newcastle, can have little idea of the heavy clog upon his predecessors, arising from the rude letter-press of the day. They were driven to the expensive copper-plate. It must be owned that Edmondson's plates, arranged after the modern fashion, are much more close and intelligible than the circles of Allan, connected by creeping stems and love-knots. An extremely beautiful pedigree, on vellum, of his family, in the same style, rich in gold and blazonry from the pencil of the latter gentlemen, is in the possession of R. H. Allan, esq.

† 1764. "If it could conveniently be done (not else) that you could procure, or employ a proper person to take copies of the inscriptions on the monuments or gravestones in the church or churchyard of Darlington, such as you think may be useful as pertaining to good or creditable families, I shall gladly pay the expense.—R. B." Allan copied them himself. "I have hardly an hour to devote to my favourite study. I am daily, however, transcribing them."

‡ With Mr. Edmondson he was an occasional correspondent; though, from the offer

He was now in correspondence with the Countess Dowager of Stafford, by whom he was highly esteemed, and who kindly interested herself in reconciling him to his father, and for the time satisfactorily. He compiled a careful pedigree of the Stafford race. She writes Jan. 15, 1765:—"I am exceeding glad you are so happily settled with your family; and only wish, if you employ your *four hours*, which is but a short recess from business, which requires so much application of the mind, as the study of the law, and you make that of an antiquary your amusement, though you do it with so much more ease than any one else could; yet I should think your health must suffer, unless you allow yourself some time for exercise, and to quite unbend your mind."* But Allan scoffed at such advice. He never read but with a pen in his hand; and if the expression may be used as to heraldry, antiquities, and natural history, as well as classics, his *adversaria* are numerous and valuable. Considering his extensive professional business before he retired, and his constant labour in writing, it is believed he wrote almost a quire for every day he lived.† His habits were very regular and temperate; but, nevertheless, he did not preserve a healthy regimen, and was constantly ailing. He rose at half-past seven, ate a hearty breakfast at eight, very seldom took any exercise, and scarce ate any animal food at all; about three glasses of wine were his allowance after dinner. He drank tea, but seldom ate supper, and, although constantly employed, the conversation of others never appeared to interrupt him, and yet he heard all that passed. In consequence of this faculty he never stopped work for callers, but went pot-hooking on, quite unconcernedly. It was generally two o'clock before he retired to his room; and he always read the newspapers in bed by a reflecting lamp, which burnt all night.

On the 24 Sep., 1766,‡ Mr. Allan added considerably to his comforts and

which had been made to Mr. Allan, the young Herald (who had enjoyed his appointment only two months) conceived an unaccountable jealousy. They continued, however, their friendly correspondence, as appears by a letter dated Jan., 1765, wherein Mr. Edmondson says,

"I have looked among my MSS. but can find nothing worth sending you; I have now by me the finest visitation of Yorkshire in this kingdom, as it is full of deeds, charters, records, domesday, &c., which I should be glad you should see; but I do not know how it can be done, as the book is only lent me, and also valued at £21. I have one favour to beg of you. I am informed by different hands that, when the last vacancy was in the Heralds' office, Messrs. Heard and Bigland sent you a letter, that, if you would come to town, they could get you the vacancy. The truth of this assertion I beg to know, as it will be of infinite service to me, therefore I hope you will oblige yours, &c. J.E."

"What Mr. Edmondson means by this enquiry," says Mr. Allan to Mr. Bigland, "I cannot tell. What you and Mr. Heard were so obliging as to write to me on that head, I never mentioned to any person except my friend Mr. Stevens, and that no more than saying, that both of you were so kind as to send me an account of a vacancy, if I had any inclination to apply for it." Mr. Bigland remarks in a letter, 15 Jan., 1765, "The extract of Mr. Edmondson's letter we do not think so extraordinary, having experienced many disagreeable proofs of his behaviour. As to the visitation of Yorkshire, worth £21, I imagine it is one that I saw (which he then called his own) some years ago at his house, which he then boasted much of. We have, I dare say, the selfsame thing in every particular, besides many others for the county of York."

* "The first vacant day, you say, Mrs. Allan and you will dine with us. Is it not as difficult to calculate when you will have a vacant day, as it is the return of the great comet?"—*Rev. D. Watson, of Middleton Tyas, to Allan*, 1783.

† It is said of Master Prynne, that he wrote a sheet for every day he lived; but it must be remembered that his was composition.

‡ "Darlington, Nov. 17, 1766.—Proposals for an Assembly for Six Months to be held once every Thursday month, the first assembly on Thursday the 27 instant. Every subscriber to pay 7*s.* 6*d.*; every nonsubscriber to pay 2*s.* each night; to begin each night *exactly at* 7 *o'clock*. N.B.—Tickets Transferrable. *Gentlemen.* Geo: Allan, Newy. Lowson, Willm. Dent, James Allan, Junr., Hen: Ornsby, H. Thornhill, Young Lowson, Thos. Constable, Thos. Hill, Junr., Wm. Turner. *Ladies.* Miss Bowes, Mrs. Allan, Miss Tukey, Mrs. Rudd, Miss Lowis, Miss N. Lowis, Miss J. Lowson."

to his property, by a marriage with Anne (than whom, says her son, "a better woman never breathed"), the only daughter and heiress of James Colling Nicholson, of Scruton, Yorkshire. This gentleman lived for the last twenty years of his life with his son in law. A portrait of him is inscribed "JAMES COLLING NICHOLSON, died Feb. 8th, 1794, aged 85. Sibi et Amicis D.D.D., G.A."*

The marriage also added in after years to his antiquarian treasures. He and his son were at Scruton where Mr. Nicholson then lived, when Mr. Gale lent him the volumes of his grandfather's MSS. He could not be prevailed upon to prolong his visit a single day, because no proper paper could be procured in the village, and therefore instantly returned home and began his labours. "Last week," writes he to Gough ("the Camden of modern times"), "I accidentally called to see an old school-fellow, Mr. Henry Gale, the grandson of Roger Gale, the antiquary. This gave me an opportunity of enquiring after that gentleman's books and papers; when I had the pleasure to hear him say, there were two or three MSS. left in the house, which he was so obliging as to shew me. You cannot imagine how my heart leaped for joy when I looked over their contents, and found them all fairly wrote with his own hand, and containing such valuable papers. To double my joy, my friend permitted me to take them home with me, and make what use I pleased of them. Inclosed, I send you a catalogue of what is contained in the first volume; and in a few posts you shall have the contents of the other. You will be surprised when I tell you, that I am determined to make a true transcript of all the volumes; and hope, before winter is over, to say *Exegi opus*, having within these few days done forty pages."†

In 1768 he entered his pedigree (which was in a great measure adopted by Surtees) in the Register 6th D 14, fo. 22, 23, but I imagine that he and old James were not on terms at the time, as it is extraordinarily incorrect on points regarding which his father could at once have put him right. A plate of the Heralds' College and the officers' seals, &c., gave him the idea of having a plate engraven of the episcopal and corporate seals of the county, but he found that the price of the former plate was 48*l*., and he abandoned the design. "Inclosed," says he to Bigland, "I send you a specimen of our present bishop's seal (which will not bear the examination of an engraver); it is the first attempt. The middle parts are my own etching; but it is an art I have no inclination to proceed in. You will be surprised when I tell you I have turned printer, and have got a little press, and a small font of letters to amuse an idle hour.

Thus originated the famous Allan or Grange tracts. They began with the tract containing the charter and other documents relating to the Free Grammar School at Darlington. A list was published by the late John Trotter Brockett, esq., of Newcastle. A more copious catalogue, accompanied with a life of Mr. Allan, was edited by R. H. Allan, esq., in 1829, of which

* He assumed the name of Nicholson by the direction of a uncle of that name (Rector of Great Stainton). He was one of the most affectionate and best of men, though not the least of a literary turn. It is believed on the contrary, that the Bible, Moore's Almanack, and the provincial newspapers, were the full extent of his reading. In his younger days he kept a small pack of fox hounds, and amused himself with a farm of his own of 150 acres.

† The manuscript which is entitled "Reliquiæ Galeanæ, &c., is written in his usually clear and distinct hand, with very clever drawings, in pen and ink, of tombstones, monumental tablets, and antiquities. On the title is an autograph note by Mr. Allan, in which he states "The Society of Antiquaries had these volumes a long time, and from thence were selected the quarto volume, published under the title, and direction of Richard Gough, esq."

fifty copies were printed for private distribution only; but probably the best is in Martin's "Catalogue of Privately printed Books," published in 1834. There are, however, an immensity of broadsides inserted in his illustrated Camden, which do not appear in any catalogue. At Mr. Brockett's sale in 1823 his collection of the tracts was sold to the late Earl of Durham for 52*l*.10*s*. They consist almost wholly of documents illustrating the history of Durham, the most important being collections relating to Gateshead Hospital* (1769), Greatham Hospital (n.d.), and Sherburn Hospital (1771, a number of the records seen by Allan having been mislaid or lost), the life of bishop Trevor (1776), Hegge's Legend of Saint Cuthbert (1777), and the origin and succession of the Bishops of Durham (1779, a beautiful tract). "Of Gateshead Hospital," writes his son George, "there were but fifty copies printed; and that was when I was too young to have made any observation. I can only add, from what I have been told, that a great part of it was executed by a small folding press; but a regular printer having set up business in the town during the progress of it, a frame was made to hold four quarto pages (the previous part having been performed by a page only at a time), which were composed at home, and sent, with the paper damped, to be worked off by the printer. The tracts relating to Greatham and Sherburn Hospitals, were printed in the same manner; and it is curious to observe, that an intimate acquaintance of my father's, now living, asserts that the proofs scarce ever stood in need of correction, he being himself not only the compositor, but the distributor of the types, when the form was broken up. I remember the folding press very well, and the arrival of that from London, with which he worked, even within the last year of his life; nay, so fond was he of the office or employment, he had undertaken, but a few months before his last illness, to print for me a translation I had attempted of a small German novel, in which the philosophy of Professor Kant is particularly satirized; and actually corresponded with me respecting the number of pages it would run to, and in what manner I wished it to be executed. - - - Independent of the antiquarian tracts, and the little performances for his friend, a great variety of fugitive satirical pieces were printed, particularly election squibs, but whether by design or accident, I have not a copy of any one. He printed also, copies of the family wills; and I once heard him say, he would transcribe and print all the title deeds of his estate, which would certainly have been a labour of little use or profit. His last intention was to have printed a catalogue of his museum; which, by his MS. preparations for it, I think would have been very amusing; and I lament he did not execute it. After his death the press and materials were sold to a printer in the town, without my knowledge.† I should otherwise have been tempted to have kept them

* This, I believe, is the first tract on which he printed his favorite motto :—"Gather up the Fragments that remain.—6 John v. 12."

† An eye witness "well remembers, when a mere child, being taken in a van or spring cart for a ride to Grange. It was a dismally dark dank night, and the men, who had a lantern, remarked on nearing Glassensikes, that its light would prevent their seeing the ghost. On passing the sombre but noble avenue of stately limes, the ancient abode of squirrels, rooks, bats, and owls, he arrived at Grange, and by some mischance was left in a spacious apartment trembling and alone! His courage which had become 'small by degrees and beautifully less,' had now fairly oozed out, and he screamed aloud in mortal fear. Awful sounds and distant echoes, as of the voice of haunted chambers, reverberated through the passages of the ghostly halls, and the vaulted sepulchres of the dead could not have been more appalling to his infantile imagination. He was soon, however, conducted from this 'chamber of horrors' to another room where a number of men were busily engaged in taking to pieces and packing up the printing press, type, &c., with which the Allan Tracts had been struck off. These printing materials had been purchased by a young aspirant to historic fame, John Rountree, a printer, of Darlington, who, it is said,

as a memorial of past times, and present pleasing recollections rather than for any use I could have made of them. During a vacation from college, he once prevailed on me to become a compositor; and I made a tolerable proficiency in the art; but I was not very enthusiastically fond of the employment. - - - Having occasion, a few years ago, to shew my title to a particular estate, to a very eminent attorney in London, to whom I was not personally known, I left a printed copy of a will at his chambers, the authenticity of which he might have explored at Doctors' Commons, yet this circumstance appeared to him so strange, that he took it to be an imposition, and it was necessary for me to explain, through my own attorney, that my father had had a private press, under the impression of which almost every matter he was interested in, fairly went; and that I had left the printed copy of the will required merely to save time."

Among his other *good customers*, for he printed *gratis*, was Thomas Pennant, esq., F.R.S., the celebrated naturalist and traveller, who in his Tour from Alston Moor to Harrogate, p. 114, says "I had here the good fortune to make acquaintance with George Allan, esq., of Darlington, a gentleman of the law, but since possessed of a large fortune in that neighbourhood." Allan and he on that occasion made a careful excursion to Brimham Craggs. The introduction was through the medium of Bishop Egerton. The tracts "printed by the friendship of George Allan, esq., at his private press at Darlington,"* for Pennant, are the rarest of all the series, thirty copies only having been struck off.†

In 1774 Mr. Allan became possessed of the Rev. Thomas Randall's MSS. An intimacy had subsisted for many years, and Mr. Randall always promised Allan his MSS.‡ in case of death, which by will, 1774, he bequeathed to him.

had made some collections towards the history of the county. His career might happily have been marked with usefulness, had he not been cut off, an early victim to his humorous and social qualities, which attracted 'jolly companions every one' from all parts of the country. In their selfish amusements they led him on to ruin and the grave. The Allan press was then purchased by William Appleton, another printer and bookseller of the place."

In those days, the rising generation—the dashing blades of Darlington, were too prone in exercising their talents in practical jokes, which were indulged in to a serious extent even by many of the most respectable people of the town, and this young man too was drawn into the vortex of their heartless follies. In making a sham freemason, he penned the cabalistic paper which was to induct the party to all the mysteries of the fraternity, and when it was necessary to translate the document before the magistrates, the writer could explain no further than that he supposed *hocus* meant hoax, and *pocus* the poker.

* 1779. "I doubt not before this you have expected a return of the proof sheets of your Zoology. One reason of the delay was, I was obliged to discharge my Devil for ingratitude; and the small letter did not arrive till about a week ago. I have none now to assist me; but notwithstanding that, can manage myself any future sheets you may want, which I beg you will not be nice in sending. Pray return these as soon as you can, that they may be wrought off, and say how many copies you will have. I can print 4 pages at once, as well as two." And again. "I am happy to find the printed sheets please. My ink is too white. Let me intreat more work; I will not be so long about them as the last."

† Before the printing of these, in 1777, Pennant had a notion of commencing amateur printer himself, but Allan's experience terrified him. "It is a pretty amusement; but without a proper person to direct you at first starting [and Pennant never could get one], you will, I am afraid, throw it aside in a pet; patience is a most necessary virtue to be endowed with. Did I not send you an advertisement for a portable press? On what construction that was, I cannot say; for, to print 4 pages in 4to, will require about 180 pounds of Pica letter, Roman and Italic. - - - There are many, very many other requisites besides types - - - I have lately got a complete screw-press from London, made by the best hand there, which cost me 16 guineas. Upon the whole, I do suppose my workshop in this Art has cost me 70*l.*; but then I have three different sorts of letter, that would set up 14 close quarto pages or more."

‡ Randall was master of the free school at Durham, and had free access to the libraries and public offices. His MSS. consisted of about twenty vols. in 4to. and several others in a cruder state, but they were all extremely minute and careful. He pasted these words on their covers in his lifetime, "*The gift of the Reverend Mr. Thomas Randall of Durham,*

This induced him to turn his thoughts towards a *History of the County Palatine of Durham*, for which he circulated his "Address and Queries to the Public, relative to the compiling a complete Civil and Ecclesiastical History of the ancient and present state of the County Palatine of Durham;"* but soon relinquished his plan in favour of Mr. Hutchinson, to whom he became a most assiduous and very excellent assistant and patron. Mr. Allan, in a letter to Dr. Henry, of Edinburgh, says, "This gives me an opportunity of inclosing you the proposals for a laborious work, a virgin county. If your interest amongst the curious can procure a few names as subscribers, it will be remembered with the utmost gratitude. It is chiefly my collections and ground-work;† but neither having leisure nor health to finish the work, have consigned every paper to my industrious friend, Mr. Hutchinson, who will usher it into the world, I flatter myself, with credit to himself." Both Hutchinson and Surtees gratefully acknowledge their debts to Mr. Allan, whose library contained, besides his own collection (including a vast mass of charters, transcripts of visitations, and legal and genealogical documents), the greater part of Randall's MSS., and a large portion of those of Gyll, Hunter, Mann, Hodgson, and Swainston;‡ and it is no discredit to Hutch-

to George Allan, of Darlington;" evidently the composition of the latter. A number of printed books were included. The MSS. were sold with the Allan MSS., in 1823, to the Dean and Chapter of Durham for 150*l*. A valuable copy of Bourne's Newcastle, extensively annotated by Randall, is at Blackwell Hall.

* In the title page he says:—"Antiquitates seu Historiarum reliquiæ sunt tanquam tabulæ naufragii, quas homines industrii et sagaces a temporis diluvio eripiunt et conservant." And in a letter to the Rev. *Mark Noble*, (who was indebted to Allan in his *Coins* of Durham), in 1780. "The public has been long amused with Dr. Gower's Chester, but I despair now of seeing it, it will bear some affinity to the sister palatinate. My collections for this county would astonish you. I will send you in my next a small address I drew up for another work, a few years ago, and distributed to every clergyman and gentleman in the county, to solicit assistance; but, alas! few communications were made. Let us despise all those snarling dogs in the manger. Send the essay you mention. I will print it with pleasure, and send you as many copies as you please."

† In 1788, Mr. R. Marshall Hutchinson writes to James Allan "to send the several printed sheets you intend for my father to me, as your son has all the MSS. by him, and sole direction of the work before any part thereof goes to the press, and both are now at a stand. The printed sheets wanted are to save trouble of transcribing." "I have to lament," says Hutchinson, in a letter in the Gentleman's Magazine, for March, 1793, "that an involuntary and unfortunate delay has happened in the publication of the remaining part of my History of Durham. The MS., when completed, was, with the consent of the editor, placed in the hands of a literary gentleman, for his revisal and correction; but, by his family engagements, in consequence of a great increase of fortune, and by his necessary journeys to Bath and Bristol, on account of his health, he withheld the MS. and prevented its going to the press, unwilling that the conclusion of the work should appear less perfect than the former parts, which he had regularly attended to, even in the laborious exercise of correcting the press."—Hutchinson's address and proposals were printed at the Allan press.

‡ Mr. Allan also possessed the MSS. of Thomas Wright, F.R.S., the eminent mathematician, with whom he appears to have been on intimate terms, as among these manuscripts was a small portfolio, containing scraps by George Allan, Cuthbert Shaw, and Thomas Wright. Regarding Wright's manuscripts, the Rev. Professor Chevallier, of the University of Durham, addresses the following remarks to R. H. Allan, esq.:—

"The attention of the scientific world has been recently directed to the works of a remarkable man—Thomas Wright—who lived at Byers Green, and died about 60 ago. It appears that he anticipated many speculations of much later date: and such writers as Arago and Sturm are engaged in vindicating Wright's literary and scientific claims. From an account of Thomas Wright in the Gentleman's Magazine, for 1793, I find that Mr. Allan of the Grange, near Darlington, was then in possession of various writings and plates which had belonged to Mr. Wright, and might probably contain some matters of importance to science......I perceive Humbolt refers to Wright, in his Cosmos."

He died at Byers Green—the place of his birth, and was interred at the Church of St. Andrew, Auckland, on the 25th of February, 1786. "Several plates have been rescued from the copper-smith, by falling into the hands of George Allan, esq,, of Darlington, who purchased his collection of prints, mathematical instruments, and other valuable articles."—(*Gent. Mag., for Jan.*, 1793.)—The bulk of the "various writings" referred to by the learned professor, were sold by Sotheby, in December, 1844.

inson's industry to say that his elaborate work proceeded under the guidance of Mr. Allan's judgment. "Mr. Allan's indefatigable labour," says Hutchinson, "has accumulated most of the materials from which this work is compiled, and from whose unexampled bounty and generosity they are submitted to the author's arrangement for the public use." "It is pleasant indeed," says Mr. George Taylor, in his admirable life of Surtees, "to observe the cordial respect and gratitude with which both Hutchinson and Surtees speak of his indefatigable industry in collecting, and liberality in the unreserved communication of his stores. And the same spirit seems to have descended on his son, and to have conciliated the respect and affection of Mr. Surtees." Allan began to print "Historical Collections relating to the Town of Darlington," in good earnest. After a few pages* he tired, and left the virgin soil alone to the author of this memoir. *Sequiturque patrem non passibus æquis.*

In 1776 he acknowledges Pennant's compliment in expressing himself "*superlatively* indebted to Mr. George Allan, of Darlington," in his "Tour to Scotland," and mentions having had so severe an inflammation that his life was despaired of, and all business habits suspended. Old James, *malgre* his irascibility, rushed to the rescue. "A good old father reassumed his pen, and managed for me."

About the same period (1774) Mr. Allan commenced a correspondence with that eminent antiquary, Francis Grose, esq., by whose particular recommendation he was elected F.S.A.† on the 15th December, 1774, which led to an intimacy with Mr. Gough, at that time director of the society, and the celebrated author of "British Topography." He was a valuable aid in the compilation of the new edition of Camden, by Gough, who must indeed have been flattered by Allan's use of it. In 1779, he writes to Pennant, "I am hard at work with Camden, and have already got about 2000 prints placed in it. It swells to *seven volumes.*" In 1798 he writes to Nichols, "I have received your favour, and think myself highly obliged by your kind offer to furnish me with the several plates you name, which will be a grand acquisition to the illustration of the 'Britannia.' I therefore beg you will send *the whole* of the plates to the magazine, from 1782 down to the present time, as also all belonging to the 'Bibliotheca Topographica Britannica.'" He got all his literary friends to strike him off extra plates; Cade was his illuminator of marginal and other arms; and in so costly and splendid a manner was the work illustrated with plates and extra letterpress and notes (many being printed for the purpose at his own press and others in his own caligraphy), that it finally extended to twenty-nine volumes, containing upwards of 6500 portraits, views, maps, plates of antiquities, original drawings, coloured coats of arms, &c.; the whole forming an extensive and elaborate assemblage of the topography of Britain. These volumes were sold by Sotheby in Dec., 1844, and were purchased by Robert Henry Allan, esq., F.S.A. There were

* He adds to the title—

"Si qua videbuntur chartis tibi lector in istis,
Sive obscura nimis, sive Latina parum,
Non meus est error."

A vast hoard of collections for the purpose remain, but they are mostly dry bones, full copies of legal documents, &c. The spirit who could have clothed them has departed, and I could not follow his intended track. One volume, 400 pages, in the D. & C. lib. is wholly devoted to Darlington.

† In 1800, he presented to the society 26 4to vols. of MSS. relating chiefly to the University of Oxford, collected by Wm. Smith, formerly fellow of Univ. Coll. and rector of Melsonby, near Darlington.

some five copies of Hutchinson's Durham struck off on very large 4to, which were so contrived, by printing the letter-press somewhat in a corner, as to leave very wide outer and bottom margins for illustration. One of these was split by Allan into nine volumes, and extensively pictured, especially with original drawings. It was also purchased at the sale by Sotheby in Dec., 1844, and now lodges near Camden.

Mr. Bailey (Hutchinson's draughtsman and engraver) and Samuel Wilkinson, of the King's Head Inn, Darlington, were frequently in his employ, copying drawings and making original ones.*

He was a kind friend to his correspondent John Wallis, the historian of Northumberland, who never attained to anything better than a curacy of 30*l.* per annum :† and, amongst other eminent literary characters,‡ Mr. Allan also corresponded with that redoubted champion of ancient lore, and anti-Wartonian critic, Joseph Ritson, who was making collections (now in the possession of R. H. Allan, esq.) for a history of Stockton. "I have a book," says he to Mr. Allan, "which contains every scrap I could pick up relative to this place, and am only in want of the key of an old chest in the Town-house, which I have not yet got through the ignorance and ill nature of the Steward (who has often promised me), and the folly of the Mayor, to complete my collections."§ "My father (says Mr. George Allan, jun.) gave him an introduction to the British Museum, in which his labour commenced. I have lived in the same house with him two or three days at a time, at Mr. Harrison's, in Durham ; and, to do him justice, he was very good company ; but it may be accounted for, as he considered his host as his infallible oracle in black-letter research. I met him once at a gentleman's table in London ; and, being for that year steward for the charity instituted in Durham, for the benefit of widows and orphans of the clergy, I ventured to ask him for a benefaction, as I knew he had property in the county. He snarled furiously, and I was afraid he would have bit too ; but he answered, with less wit and acrimony than I expected, 'The drones in the Cathedral at Durham ought to maintain their own brats !'"

* 1778. "Mr. Bailey has left Darlington, and is now mathematical master at a school above Auckland."

† In 1779, he thanks Pennant "as much as if it were for himself," for his kind hint of Wallis to the Dishop of Durham, who, however, had to reply that from the size of his list of persons for promotion and his bad health, his good will would never be of service. Wallis had been curate, *pro tempore*, of Haughton-le-Skerne, in 1775, he then removed to the curacy of Billingham, which increasing infirmaties compelled him to resign and remove to Norton, where he died, with all the consciousness of a well-spent life, in 1793, aged 79. Bishop Barrington allowed him, in the most feeling manner, an annual pension, after his resignation of his curacy.

‡ Mr. Beckwith, in his edition of Blount's Tenures, 1784, offers his acknowledgments to Allan for many tenures in the bishoprick, and the notes marked A. One of these was the following:—"About seven years ago, a white hare was found in the grounds near Great Aycliffe, in the county of Durham, which for upwards of two years had been several times hunted by many dogs, and as often beat them, for which reason the hare was reputed a witch, by the vulgar. At last she was killed. Mr. Allan, of Darlington, got the skin, had it stuffed, and hung up as a curiosity for above two years, till it decayed, and was thrown away. It was not of a very white fur, but rather a grey."

§ "Stockton, April 19th, 1775.—Sir,—As I am informed, a history of the county palatine is shortly to be expected from you; and as your collection of materials equals, I doubt not, the grandeur of your design, you will most probably have several papers relative to the History and Antiquities of Stockton. If it be so, and you would be pleased to permit me to inspect them, either at Darlington or here, I shall ever retain a grateful sense of the favour. In return, if my service, in procuring you any information you may want in this place or its neighbourhood, would be worth your acceptance; I shall with the greatest pleasure receive your commands on the occasion. I am already possessed of several papers relating to this town, but the principal sources of intelligence (which I conjecture to be at Durham), I could have no access to. I wish you all the success in the undertaking you can desire; and am, &c., J. Ritson."

In 1776, he was busily searching for Allan in the London records.

In 1790, on the death of his father, Mr. Allan declined business; but with unremitted ardour continued his antiquarian and other scientific amusements, and made a very considerable addition to his stock of curiosities (of which he had always been a collector), by the purchase (at the splendid price of 700*l.*) of the entire museum of his departed friend *Marmaduke Tunstall*, esq., F.R.S., and S.A.,* of Wycliffe Hall, co. York, in which the collection of birds alone is said to have cost 5,000*l.*† An interesting memoir of Tunstall, who was considered an able Zoologist of his day, is prefixed to the "Synopsis, 1827," of the Allan museum by the late George Townshend Fox, of Durham, esq., F.L.S. Mr. Allan named the subjects scientifically in a very masterly manner, the labels were in the neatest and most beautiful writing, with the common and scientific names of the specimens, and references to authors. Of this museum, the birds alone filled a catalogue of *two* volumes. His accounts of the animals were drawn up in a remarkably well compressed form, containing oftentimes original notices, though, principally perhaps, selected from the works of authors he referred to.‡ A *third* volume of the catalogue comprised "A Collection of Curiosities brought by Captain Cook from Otaheite, &c.—a collection of Indian Armour inlaid with gold, consisting of Sabres, Bows, and Arrows;—a small collection of Shells and Fossils; some Reptiles, and a variety of specimens of Roman sculpture in Brass; some Insects; some Coins, a few rare ones—but the bulk chiefly of the Lower Empire; a pretty numerous collection of provincial Half-pennies; some specimens of Roman Pottery, and Chinese Curiosities." He had many Roman antiquities, querns, altars, crosses,§ seals, coins, and Roman pottery, with several fibulæ from Piersebridge, &c.

The museum was removed from Wycliffe to Mr. Allan's residence at Grange, where it occupied two large rooms on the North side of the house. The greater room was principally filled with the birds, the cases of which were so placed in partitions, back to back, as to form the room into three smaller apartments, through which you passed by two arches in the centre:—On the first, "*These are thy glorious Works, Parent of Good:*" and on the second, "*O Lord, how manifold are thy Works—in wisdom thou hast made them all: the earth is full of thy wisdom.*" On the entrance to the museum was hung

* Author of a Synopsis of British Birds, folio. See Lit. Anecdotes, iii. 688.

† "Mr. G. A. has been with me to spend a day at Mr. Tunstall's. I wish you had been with us. Such a collection of books, manuscripts, paintings, prints, coins, gems, &c., is not every day to be seen. I have good authority for saying they cost him above 20,000*l.* Indeed, this account came from his brother, who has still a much larger collection. For Mr. Constable's house is a palace, and the gallery a vatican; but he can well afford it, having the best fortune of any Roman Catholic commoner in the kingdom.

"The latest news from Durham is, that Liddell has won a wager by having a wolf to sleep with him all night, on or in the same bed, I know not which."—*Rev. Daniel Watson to Harrison.*

‡ Fox. Preface to Synopsis.

¶ At the Allan Museum was the crosier of Abbot Seabroke, of Gloucester, who d. 1457, and the head of a very early one of Easby in ivory, which are both figured in Fox's Synopsis, tiles from Fountains' high altar pavement, the supposed font of Easby with the arms of Roaldus? (or Aske?), Scrope of Masham, Neville, Fitzhugh, Mowbray (Percy?), Earls of Digby? Az. a bend of the limb of a tree reguled and truncked, and surmounted by a rose or a wheel or (Query a rebus) and Sa. a rose and stem or. Mr. Allan coloured them as above, but see a full disquisition on them and a cut in Fox, who doubts whether it was a font, for its having no pedestal and no perforation. The font however at Thornton Steward is quite as low in design. There was too an old painting of Christ's head, on wood, inscribed, "This present figure is the similitude of our Lord Jesus oure Savior imprinted in Amyruld by the predecessors of the Greate Turke and sent to the Pope Innocent the VIII. at the cost of the Greate Turke for a token for this cawse to redeme his brother that was takeyn presonor." Innocent VIII. was Pope 1484-1492. All these were taken to Newcastle as also a "seal of *Lord Darlington, in yellow wax. Antient*," and a silver seal, found in a grave in Croft churchyard, 1787, inscribed, "S. ANDREE PISTORIS."

a label with these words, "*Quid hic? Intueri naturam.*" "To many of the departments," says Mr. Surtees, iii. p. 371, "Mr. Allan made considerable additions. Paintings were not forgotten; these filled every pannel, gradually insinuated themselves along the passages, and clothed the walls of the great staircase." Of the portraits, some of the most remarkable were, Anna Boleyn, by Holbein; Lord Fairfax, three quarters' length, by Sir Peter Lely (sold to G. Hartley, esq., for 37*l.* 16*s.*); Sir Henry Wotton, by the same (sold to G. Hartley, esq., for 22*l.* 1*s.*); Lady Castlemaine, by the same (bought in, and still at Grange); William, Earl of Pembroke, and his lady, by Jansen (bought in); Margaret, sister to Henry VIII, when young,* by Mauberge (sold for 11*l.* 11*s.* to Messrs. Todd, of York); Polly Jones, in crayons, by Cotes (bought in, and still at Grange; see Walpole's anecdotes, iv., 127); Companion of Lady Seaforth, in crayons, by Gainsborough (5*l*). There were also several admirable crayon-drawings, by Francis Place, of the Dinsdale family; *inter alia*:—Philip Woolrych, esq.† (2*l.* 6*s.*); a fine head of Charles II.; and William Penn and his wife (sold to Surtees, resold to the late John Allan, esq., at the Surtees sale, and now at Blackwell Hall). Mr. Surtees also bought an original sketch of Henry VIII. Then there were a lion-hunt, by old Wyke (sold to G. Hartley, esq., for 22*l.* 1*s.*); a landscape, by Teniers (sold to Capt. Watts, R.N., for 6*l.* 6*s.*); and the head of a corpse "horribly expressive," by Caracci (sold to Rev. J. Robson for 10*l.* 10*s.*).

The museum was first opened *(gratis)* for public inspection in June, 1792;‡ and from that time to January, 1796 (three years and a half), it had been viewed by 7,327 persons, as we are informed by a printed label of Mr. Allan's, now at Grange.

This noble collection was sold under Mr. Allan's will, and was bought of the executors in 1801 by his son, remaining at the Grange till 1822, when, under the auspices of G. Townshend Fox, esq.; John Adamson, esq., of Newcastle; and John Trotter Brockett, esq., of the same place, the museum articles were purchased by the Literary and Philosophical Society of Newcastle-upon-Tyne, for 400*l.*

The celebrated Thomas Bewick drew many of his birds from this collection; indeed the Wycliffe museum was the origin and occasion of his work. Allan had patronized him at least as early as 1779, when he inclosed Gough "a specimen of engraving on wood by a young man at Newcastle." Bewick was then busily employed on his "Quadrupeds."

In 1791 Mr. Allan offered to copy pedigrees from the Leicestershire Visitation of 1619, for that "veteran in the field of topography," John Nichols, esq., F.S.A. "It has ever," said he, "been a pleasure to me to lend every assistance in my power to forward any literary work."§

* She visited Darlington Manor House, in 1502, on her journey to meet her royal spouse in Scotland.

† He married Anne, dr. of John Killinghall, of Middleton St. George, esq., by his wife Margaret, dr. and coh. of Wm. Lambton, of Great Stainton, esq. Mrs. Woolrych died at Darlington, in 1723, aged 91.

‡ "A society has lately been instituted at Darlington, for the promotion of the knowledge of natural history, antiquities, &c., which, from the public characters of several of its members, we have every reason to believe will flourish. It is intended to consist of corresponding as well as ordinary members. George Allan, esq., F.A.S., has opened his museum for the use of the society."—*Gent. Mag. for Nov.* 1793.

§ Sir John Prestwick, in his "Respublica," which contains a copious account of the name and arms of Allan, thanks Mr. Allan for "his politeness when he made the tour of the northern parts of Britain," and designates him as an "esteemed friend,"—a "learned, studious, and careful preserver of English antiquities, and a favourer of literature."

A few years before his death, he borrowed a MS. Visitation of Yorkshire, by Dugdale, which he accurately copied in two volumes folio, and emblazoned the arms in a very beautiful manner. Sir M. M. Sykes purchased the original (which was, however, in fact only a copy itself), but Allan's copy was preferable. It is now in the Durham library, and has a portrait of Sir William Dugdale, from Dallaway's Heraldic Inquiries. In the same collection is a copy of Flower's Visitation, 1575, with St. George's, 1615, incorporated, and some additions by Allan, as well as a volume containing sixty-five pedigrees of Durham families, with upwards of two hundred richly emblazoned shields, and numerous monuments, registers, grants of arms, &c., "collected by George Allan, Darlington, F.A.S."

Whilst thus usefully and pleasantly employing his fortune and his leisure, he was interrupted by a warning thus described in a letter to the Rev. Daniel Watson, rector of Middleton-Tyas in Yorks., Aug. 3, 1797. "On Tuesday week, at Grange, I was suddenly seized with a paralytic stroke, which deprived me of all reason and sight for near two hours. I was writing, when seized, and fell off my chair. Till Tuesday last, I continued very poorly; however, I thought a stir from home, with more exercise, might relieve me; and accordingly I arrived here last night, and I have the pleasure to say, I am daily grown better, and hope to God I shall soon recover, though my eyes and head are still much affected."

He again, however, rallied; and resuming his former occupations, survived till May 17, 1800, when he died at his seat at Grange, aged 64. "George Allan, of Blackwell Grange, in this Parish, Esquire, died May 17th, Buried May 24th, Age 64 years."—(*Darlington Par. Reg.*) He was buried in the Grange vault in the North transept of the church.

Mr. Allan had portraits of himself and Mr. Hutchinson engraved in one plate. The two are seated in council, Hutchinson engaged in writing his history under the guidance of Allan, who holds a charter of Pudsey, and has before him a pedigree of Neville.* Durham cathedral appears (through a window) in the distance. The plate was sent by Mr. G. Allan, jun., to Nichols, who inserted it in the eighth volume of his Literary Anecdotes.† "The portraits (says the donor) were painted by an itinerant artist [J. Hay], and engraved by Collyer. Both have done ample justice to the subject, as better likenesses never were exhibited. It was intended by my father as frontispiece to the first volume of the History of Durham; but he changed his mind in consequence of the trial at Newcastle, between the printer and Mr. Hutchinson. On that occasion Mr. (now Sir Alan) Chambre led the cause on the part of the printer; and among other matters of sarcasm, he held up the print in his hand, and said, 'This is the representation of Mr. Allan and his amanuensis Mr. Hutchinson; and there is a dog placed between them. What is the dog intended to represent?—but my client who has been used like a dog!' Sir Alan Chambre is now (1814) a Judge of the Common Pleas: but my father considered he had been under professional obligations to him at a former period, and did not expect him to be witty at his expence. I believe he never forgot it; nor would he, when the last volume of the

* A tomb of Neville, charged with the saltire, in a ruin, also appears in Allan's book-plate, engraved by Bailey. The descent from that noble race may be hinted at. The same insignia occur in his portrait at Blackwell Hall.

† Some of the earlier copies of the plate are coloured. It is said by Brockett to be sometimes prefixed to the collections relating to Sherburn Hospital, but the remark must apply in a very limited sense, as the plate was engraved some years after that private publication.

Blackwell Grange.

This Plate is presented by William Allan Esq.r J.P.

T.L.Busby pinx.[t] 1815. T.A.Dean. sculp.[t] 1833.

GEORGE ALLAN, ESQ. M.A. F.S.A. M.P.

of Blackwell Grange, near Darlington,

Died 21st July 1828, Æt. 61.

This Plate is inscribed to his Memory by

Rob: Henry Allan

History was published, permit the print to be applied as originally intended. He was particularly fond of dogs, and animals of all descriptions; though I have heard him say, he never saw a partridge shot, or a hare taken, in his life. I was present when he was sitting for the portrait, and a very old favourite placed his feet on his knees; which being observed by the painter, he said, 'Pray let them stay there, it will assist the drawing.'"

The late John Trotter Brockett, esq., F.S.A., who purchased the plate of Nichols, had prepared a life of Mr. Allan, which, it is probable, will be published by his son, William E. Brockett, esq.

The antiquary was succeeded at Grange by his son, another GEORGE ALLAN (born July 8, 1767,) generally known as "ALLAN THE MEMBER," with whom, after the fashion of his father James, he had been on only indifferent terms. "It was *my* misfortune also," says the son, "to differ with my father for a period of three or four years, which I chiefly spent on the continent; but it is an heartfelt satisfaction to me to recollect we were reconciled some years before his death. I was not at his house when the event took place; but my sister informed me that her father executed a very short will only an hour before his death, on which occasion he said, 'I always promised my books and prints to George; but, as I leave little, and he will have enough, he must buy them, but you will not drive a hard bargain.' The late Mr. Todd, a very respectable bookseller, of York, was sent for; his valuation was satisfactory to all parties, and I am possessed of what I esteem more than if I had had a considerable legacy in money."

The younger George "was not more distinguished for his literary talents than for an elegant, accomplished, and generous mind, and the most bland and conciliatory manners and demeanour." The Rev. Daniel Watson, rector of Middleton-Tyas, had, while curate of Muggleswick, the tuition of Dr. John Carr* (a native of that place), who afterwards repaid the service by treating young Dan, the eldest son† of his preceptor, along with young George Allan,

* Carr's correspondence is full of "punctual pleasantry." "I think," says he to Allan, senior, "Mr. Hutchinson should be at the expense of purchasing from the Heralds' College, in London, all the Durham families recorded there. Such of his subscribers as have had fathers and grandfathers, would, no doubt, be glad to see themselves in the midst of so much good company as it is in Mr. Hutchinson's power easily to assemble. The Heralds' visitation comes down to about 1660 or 1666, but it would not be difficult (except, perhaps, for such poor devils as J. C.) to fill up the succeeding years with a suitable number of knights and esquires, all in their best apparel. If I were this moment in the church of St. Helen's Auckland, I should look about, before it went out of my mind, for a brazen ancestor, with an *e* to his name, *Carre*. Prior's 'Son of Adam and Eve' is a very good translation of *Atavis editus*, two words which I have adopted as my motto, conveying, as I think, no bad satire on family pride. However, after all, *good blood is a good thing*."

Carr was also chosen for young James Allan's tuition, and often had to acknowledge the receipt of salmon and goodly goose-pies, bearing evident marks of Darlington. When young George was at Chelmsford with the Durham militia, only a few months before his master's death, he wrote to him, and in a postscript added that Mrs. Allan's poor favourite Tom was dead, and that she despaired of getting a poet in the whole garrison to sound his praise. Tom was a cat that had often visited the doctor with them, and had travelled on the continent and elsewhere, constantly on their carriage. The old man once more took up pen and returned a poetical answer, full of good nature and playful humour. He died in 1807. He had a brother Joseph, who never attained any preferment higher than a curacy in Northumberland, and who died at Allendale, in 1806.

After old Allan's death, Carr had some correspondence with Gough, as to parting with the museum, which had been directed to be sold for the benefit of those to whom the personal estate was left, but the price offered by Mr. Fothergill, of York, not exceeding what young George himself, who was reluctant at parting with his father's collections, was inclined to give, he bought them all, and for a time they continued at Grange.

† He unfortunately died in 1783. His father writes in the beginning of that year to Allan, the antiquarian:—"I return George's exercises; very good ones. Dr. Carr takes great pains in grounding him in Greek. A hive of bees! Some Linnæus and Aldrovandus, or, perhaps, a Pennant, must be found for Dan; for the old trade of poring in hedges and ditches for weeds and insects still goes on. George is more usefully employed, and will

at Hertford school in the most affectionate manner. It may be mentioned to Mr. Watson's honour, that he resigned his vicarage of Leek on his appointment to Middleton-Tyas, from noble and conscientious scruples, and it is remarkable that the venerable Dr. Thomas Zouch, who stated this fact on his departed friend's monument in Bath cathedral, himself afterwards refused a bishoprick. Watson was the author of a very superior "Historical Catechism on the progress of revealed religion, &c.," of which thousands have been distributed in all parts of the world, and was intimate with all the head churchmen of his day. His correspondence was truly delightful. He died in 1804, at Bath, aged 86.

Young Allan took the degree of M.A. at Trinity Hall, Cambridge, after a brilliant curriculum in collegiate acquirements.*

In 1797, he proceeded on a continental excursion with his wife. His reasons are best given in his own words. "Some time previous to the year 1796, I had meditated a tour through the whole Russian dominions—to see at once society in its progress from a rude state to refinement, and to have it in my power to contemplate on the spot as well the splendid grandeur of a court, as the efficient means by which a government can extend its influence over such a vast and boundless empire. I had beyond this a strong inclination to look into the mysteries of the Greek church, and by attending to the general laws, commerce, manners and customs of such a distant people, I flattered myself I might have returned with some little addition to the knowledge I set out with."

Unfortunately at Memel he received letters of family importance, which precipitated a hasty return to England, through Prussia and Pomerania to Stettin. But the result was a charming MS. volume entitled "Travels and miscellaneous observations in a series of familiar letters written in the year 1797."† His elegant language glides on in one unruffled stream, and depth of thought is everywhere mingled with extreme beauty of expression.‡ In

soon be up to him. But *trahit sua quemqua voluptas;* and one man has as much pleasure in making mouse-traps as another has in calculating the return of the great comet."

"Dr. Carr has endangered his veracity by boasting of the improvements of his native country. It is our business to assist him. His words are, 'what do you think one of those very large sheep in the county of Durham, called *Mugs*, would weigh, put into the scales alive, with his fleece on his back? Talking on this subject lately, I endangered my credit, I am afraid, and wish for chapter and verse.' Get me well-authenticated intelligence as soon as you can, but without the trouble of weighing, from some of your most respectable gentleman farmers. A wager, at Lewes, in Sussex, once occasioned the late Billy Hodgson, in Bishop Trevor's service, to order a leg of mutton to be bought in Darlington market, and sent to Lewes; which convinced the infidels in Sussex, how much our sheep exceeded theirs in size."—*Watson to Geo. Allan, sen.*

* "Dear Sir,—A letter, not from your grandson, whose modesty prevented him writing himself, but from one of his friends, has given me so much satisfaction, that I cannot resist the pleasure I have in communicating it to you.

When he appeared in the soph's school, out of 16 arguments advanced against his question, he took off 12. And the moderator dismissed the combatants with these words:—

Domini opponentes, satis et optime disputastis: Tu autem; Domine Respondens, non sine magno acumine ingenii satis et optime disputasti, et in hoc tuo certamine, ut primus ordinis, tantum exemplum industriæ prebuisti, ut non solum de me, sed de tota academia tandem maximam mereris.

He being the first fellow commoner that ever appeared in the schools, occasioned a most astonishing audience, above 200. The compliment is equally great and just, and does him honour that will not soon be forgotten. I sincerely give you joy of it, and am, dear sir, your much obliged humble servant, D. Watson. Middleton Tyas, March 11th, 1788. To James Allan, esq., Grange."

The severe James must have greatly delighted, for whatever might be the state of feeling between father and son, that between grandfather and grandson was of a very pleasant description.

† Now possessed by R. H. Allan, esq.

‡ The translation into English by A. Anderson Feldborg, of the "Great and good deeds of Danes, Norwegians, and Holsteinians, collected by Ove Malling," is thus dedicated:—

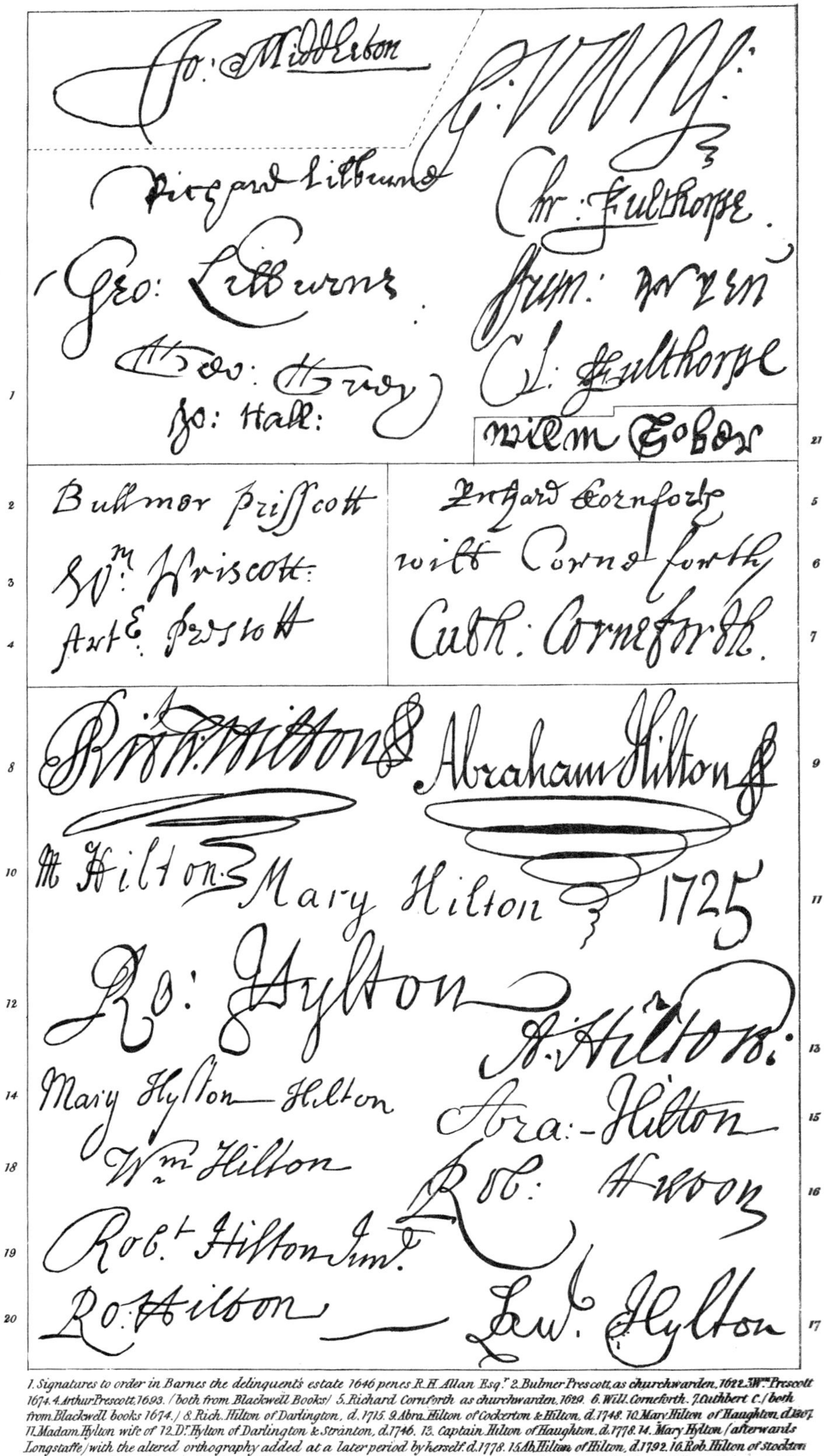

1. Signatures to order in Barnes the delinquent's estate 1646 penes R.H. Allan Esqr 2. Bulmer Prescott, as churchwarden, 1622. 3. Wm Prescott 1674. 4. Arthur Prescott, 1693. (both from Blackwell Books) 5. Richard Cornforth as churchwarden, 1629. 6. Will. Corneforth. 7. Cuthbert C. (both from Blackwell books 1674.) 8. Rich. Hilton of Darlington, d. 1715. 9. Abra. Hilton of Cockerton & Hilton, d. 1748. 10. Mary Hilton of Haughton, d. 1807. 11. Madam Hylton wife of 12. Dr Hylton of Darlington & Stranton, d. 1746. 13. Captain Hilton of Haughton, d. 1778. 14. Mary Hylton (afterwards Longstaffe) with the altered orthography added at a later period by herself. d. 1778. 15. Ab. Hilton of Hilton, d. 1792. 16. Rob. Hilton of Stockton d. 1727. 17. Lanc. Hylton his son, d. 1757. 18. Hilton the poet, d. 1798. 19. Rob Hilton of Durham, d. 1764. 20. Rob Hilton of Hilton Beacon, d. 1683. Nearly all these from originals penes W.H.L. 21. Wm. Sober of Nessfield, from an exhibit on a deed, 24 Eliz. penes R.H. Allan Esqr

after years he chose Nichols's Literary Anecdotes (vol. viii) as a repository of most amusing memoirs of his father, and Carr, Cade, Harrison, Watson, Noble,* and Heyrick, which were "freely and lightly sketched by his gentlemanly pen." "His light and elegant manner," indeed, as Surtees truly remarks, "adorned whatever it touched."†

Mr. Surtees says that he "is indebted to the kindness of many valued friends, for a large portion of the MS. collections already in existence relative to the county. Under this head his first acknowledgments are due to George Allan, of Grange, esq., M.P., for the whole of his late father's collections, enriched by the MSS. of Randall, and a large portion of those of Gyll and Hunter."

For the "unreserved communication of this invaluable collection," Sir Cuthbert Sharp, in his "History of Hartlepool," acknowledges his obligations to the antiquary's worthy son, to whom that able work is thus dedicated:—"To George Allan, esq., M.A., F.S.A., Member of Parliament for the City of Durham; this attempt to delineate the ancient and modern history of Hartlepool, is dedicated with every sentiment of esteem and friendship."

Mr. Robert Harrison, one of Allan's memoralized literary heroes, was Master of Trinity School (where he had the honour to number the illustrious brothers Lords Eldon and Stowell among his pupils), in Newcastle, and a fellow tourist of the older Allan; and afterwards lived in quiet competency at Durham. His dress at dinner was neat, a dark blue coat without a collar, but not exactly a century old in fashion. When he walked out he wore a triangular hat, and carried a cane with a large amber head to it. During his last stay at Grange (June, 1802, he died the November following, aged 88‡) a gentleman who had seen much of the world, and who had been introduced to Harrison, on getting into his carriage said, "Mr. Allan, when I was first introduced, I thought you possessed one of the most extraordinary pieces of library furniture I could have imagined, either of ancient or modern times; but, since dinner, I find in Mr. Harrison, if it were permanent, you would possess an ample library, if you had not a single book in the house."

He wore his beard in fashion exactly like that portrayed by Carlo Dolci in his famous *Ecce Homo* at Burleigh, and it was erroneously said that he let his beard grow out of respect to the memory of the Saviour, but the real fact, says Mr. Allan, was this—"He had been accustomed to shave himself: and that operation he performed, after having lathered his face, as he walked up and down his book room, with a book in one hand and a razor in the other, seldom looking at a glass. About the age of 78 his hand began to shake, and he employed a barber. This fellow often interrupted him when busy

"To George Allan, of Blackwell Grange, in the county of Durham, esq., Sir,—To your liberal patronage the following pages, principally, are indebted for their existence, and I cannot usher them into the world unaccompanied by my most grateful acknowledgements. But public testimonials, sir, are feebly expressive of private feelings;—my proud attachment lives in my heart, and will cherish every opportunity of displaying the zeal and fidelity with which I have the honor to be, most respectfully, sir, your most obedient, and most humble servant, A. Anderson Feldborg. London, June 4, 1807."

* The Rev. John Noble, master of Scorton, to whom a handsome monument was erected by his quondam scholars in Bolton-on-Swale parochial chapel. The idea seems to have originated with Mr. Allan, sen.

† I am indebted at almost every turn of this memoir to the brilliant effusions of his "gentlemanly pen."

‡ Anne Harrison, of the city of Durham, late Hett, of Darlington, wife of Rob. Harrison, gent., late master of the Trinity House, Newcastle-upon-Tyne, d. 8 bur. 10 June, 1799, aged 82. Robert Harrison, of the city of Durham, gent., a widower, d. 29 Oct., bur. 2 Nov., 1802, aged 85.—*Darlington Reg.*

with his books, and often for two or three days together did not attend at all. I was with him one morning when he was anxious to walk with me to Bp. Cosin's library in Durham; and his patience in waiting for the tonsor being exhausted, he said suddenly, 'Let us walk, and my beard may grow on.' He permitted his beard to grow after that time, and often exulted in the comfort he said he had experienced in having dismissed the shaver."*

He constantly wore a close coif of black silk on his head, such as the serjeants formerly wore, and his profile strongly resembled that of Oliver Cromwell, and though generally known as *Philosopher Harrison*, and esteemed by the vulgar as a Magician and Atheist, he was a sound Christian, and the day before his death corrected a young lady who, by accident, was reading to him the wrong lesson for the day. His knowledge was astonishing, especially as a linguist and mathematician, and in alluding to any passage he could direct to any particular edition, and even to the page.

His historian concludes, "It is to me a proud recollection, that I enjoyed, as a young man, the familiar friendship of three such men as Dr. Carr, Mr. Cade, and Mr. Harrison."

The Rev. John Warcopp, sometime of St. Andrew Auckland and Coniscliffe, was one of the scholars intimate with the two Allans and Harrison. An unaccountable *Bibliomania* seized him after he was unable to read. Allan sen., once wrote to Harrison to say, as to some promised books for Warcopp; "It will make no difference whether you send a Latin Bible or the Pilgrim's Progress." On the cover of his will, deposited with the antiquary of Grange, was written in his own hand, "Where the tree falls, there let it lie;" and in obedience to the precept he was buried at Heighington, where he died in 1786.

In 1809 Bishop Barrington omitted the names of the Rev. Robert Spencer and Mr. Curry from the peace commission for some unintentional illegality in granting a publican's licence at Auckland. Much angry correspondence ensued, and Allan, remembering former days, rose as a lion. There is much fine offended feeling, conscious of equality in his manifesto. It reminds one of an emperor's diction:—

"My lord, he who presumes to address your lordship is George Allan, of Blackwell Grange, in the county of Durham, Esquire, one of his Majesty's Deputy Lieutenants, a Barrister-at-Law of the Honourable Society of the Middle Temple of London, and Master of Arts of Trinity Hall, in the University of Cambridge. He is the representative of an old and respectable family of the same name; and, as is known to your Lordship, he inherits ample possessions on either side of the river that divides the two counties of York and Durham.† It may nevertheless be a matter of surprise to many, though

* Harrison's propensities are whimsically hinted at by Allan, the M.P., in a letter to him from Memel. "18 Dec., 1797,—I could have made you a present of a *pipe*, as well as book, of which there is a wonderful variety in this part, but I recollect you have no contemptible collection at home. Here it is an article of most expensive luxury, and the exchange of a horse for a pipe is most common among intimate and sworn friends. I have myself smoked with a pipe highly ornamented and at least three yards in length. I could tell you something about *beards* also, but that perhaps will come with better effect when I get among the Jews in Poland."

† "Mr. A. thought proper to commence his address in the above manner (though it may appear quaint or affected) both that he might avoid egotism, and that he might have an opportunity to inform his lordship in a note, that by a statute unrepealed, justices of the peace are to be made of the most sufficient knights, esquires, and gentlemen of the law within the county. He by no means wishes to insinuate that the present bench at Durham is not as respectable as that of any county in the kingdom. On the contrary, he knows the justices to be *boni et habiles*, honourable men, and fully capable of the administration of their office. He has the modesty too to believe, they have not experienced any loss, in the want of his assistance, during the years his name has been omited in the commission. Whether the proceedings in his lordship's court of common pleas are conducted with the same decorum as those of the quarter sessions, he cannot tell. He remembers to have

perhaps none to your Lordship, that he who for some years past has devoted himself altogether to a literary retirement, should obtrude himself either on your notice or that of the public. But your Lordship's illegal (he will not say, as some have done, unchristian-like) conduct towards two of the magistrates of the county, has called to his recollection his own case with your Lordship, and he is induced at once to offer his opinion, and to add his decisive condemnation of the measures your Lordship has adopted. He pledges himself further, as soon as he can obtain a copy, to endeavour a refutation of every sentence contained in your Lordship's letter addressed to the very worthy chairman of the Quarter Sessions, which he has read, through the communication of a magistrate in the neighbourhood, but not with that strength of memory that would authorize the immediate attempt. If arrogance, or vanity, should be attributed to him on account of this address to your Lordship, he will only add, that those who know him will absolve him. By speaking of himself on this occasion, he intends to put his character in antithesis, as a private gentleman, with that of your Lordship. He claims indeed no merit from his descent, it would be foolish if he did; nor does he vaunt of any other attainment than the character of being an honest religious man, which he trusts he is entitled to in common with your Lordship. It can be at this time but of little moment that his father was a laborious antiquary, or that your Lordship's father was a presbyterian statesman. He claims however the merit of an education equal to that of your Lordship in every respect; and setting that aside, his rank as a barrister, who had attended the courts at Westminster sedulously for ten years, his fortune and residence in the county, and the circumstance of your Lordship having found his name in the peace and other commissions, on your coming to the see, and having continued it for some years afterwards, he humbly thinks altogether ought to have produced a more conciliating or probably a more gentlemanlike answer than the following, to a query, why the name of George Allan had been left out of the peace commission in the year 1802?

To George Allan, esq., Abingdon Street.

Sir,—How your name was omitted in the last Durham Peace Commission, I cannot say, certainly not by any direction of mine; but being a stranger, you will excuse me if I do not replace it, till I know whether the gentlemen in the neighbourhood want your assistance.

I am with regard, S. Dunelm.

To such a letter nothing short of a severe reply could be returned. If it was intemperate, it must be attributed to the common infirmity of our nature. We are not equal to all times, but he who has the honour to address your lordship, trusts he has borne the affront with Christian patience, and but for recent circumstances, the matter would have been forgot equally by your lordship and himself."

Mr. Allan then went on to the subject in question, and in conclusion says, "it may be proper for you to make a suitable atonement to the offended gentry of the county; for gentlemen of condition and independence will not gratuitously subject themselves to unmerited and capricious castigations."

In another letter Mr. Allan announces himself as then prepared for the controversy, and says, "if any satellite of the Bishop of Durham will venture to undertake in his own name a general defence of his Lordship's secular character (as a regular ecclesiastic no one admires him more than I do) I pledge myself again to crush him with a giant's strength." A long anonymous letter from "a Landlord on one side of the Tees," then appeared, ridiculing Mr. Allan's manifesto in no small degree. Mr. Allan replied to this "miserable wretch" in a tone of supreme contempt, ending with, "I will at once give him the attribute due to impotent insolence and malignity, and pronounce him a fool, a liar, and a coward."

Sir John Eden, bart., the chairman of the quarter sessions, in a letter dated Dec. 15, 1809, thus wrote to Mr. Allan:—"I honour you for your labours in defence of the constitution, for I am decidedly of opinion that the Bishop's proceeding against Mr. Spence and Mr. Curry was not constitutional;"

witnessed the late Mr. Ambler making a motion to the court, and *then stepping on to the bench to grant it;* a circumstance which struck him at that time, though young, as monstrously indecent."

and Michael Angelo Taylor, esq., M.P., requested his name to be erased from the commission of the peace in consequence of the Bishop's irregular proceedings as Custos Rotulorum.

On the vacation of Mr. Lambton's seat in 1813, by his accepting the Chiltern Hundreds, a severe and expensive contest for Durham city ensued. It was of nine days duration,—the longest on record in the electioneering annals of Durham, and the candidates "bled" profusely, but on its termination on the 10 Dec., Mr. Allan, who was a very popular man, was returned by a large majority; and during the period that he sat in parliament his votes were consistent, and marked with the strict sense of independence.* During his parliamentary career he had a curious repository in his London residence which he termed Chaos. A room was divided by a high partition, on one side of which were thrown all his letters, notes, and waste papers in hopeless masses. What a scene for an autograph gatherer!

He was a candidate at the next election of 1818, but the Grange estates were now deeply sinned against, and two days before the election he took leave of the freemen. His farewell address, replete with eloquence, excited a powerful sensation at the time. "The constancy of my friends in London," says he, "my canvass in your city, and the general support of the distant voters, would have secured my return beyond a doubt; but I have to repeat my inability to command such pecuniary resources as would be necessary to secure my election. If, however, at any future time I should be deemed worthy of your attention, you may rest assured I shall be ready to serve you; and in thus taking my leave, if I said reluctantly, I should but ill express the anguish of my feelings, when a retrospect to the day of my election calls to my view the proudest period of my life, and the present the most painful moment of my existence."†

Mr. Allan, immediately after this election, retired to France, and lived at St. Omers, greatly respected, for several years "with limited means, yet without repining, and devoting his leisure to the pursuits of literature." There he died childless, after a short but severe illness, in 1828, his hearse being followed out of that town by the principal English gentlemen resident there, and the corpse brought to England. It was interred with his relations in the Grange vaults.

The beautiful portrait‡ of this gentleman, which by the kindness of R. H.

* The other candidate was George Baker, of Elemore, in the county of Durham, esq., grandson of George Baker, esq., who represented the city in 1714. Regarding Mr. Allan's competitor for parliamentary honours, Mr. George Taylor, in his Life of Surtees, spiritedly enunciated the following observations:—"Persons who had never, probably, looked into a topographical history, till their attention was called to scenes and characters in which themselves and their families were immediately interested, felt astonished at the expenditure of money, labour, time, and talent manifested in Mr. Surtees's work. This feeling was characteristically expressed by the late Mr. Baker, better known by his own designation of himself, as "the last George Baker, of Elemore:" the genuine representative of the hunting and cock-fighting 'squires of the last century.—"I wonder, Mr. Surtees, why you spend so much money and time over a History of Durham."—"I wonder, Mr. Baker," (was the reply), "why you spend so much money and time in following a pack of hounds after a poor hare."—Books were the pointers that indicated, and hunters that enabled Surtees to pursue, higher game than was ever dreamed of in the imaginations of these men. By his profound researches he unearthed the forgotten wisdom and ennobling virtues, the deterrent vices and the fancy-stirring traditions of our ancestors; teaching the men of present and future times not to narrow their minds by concentrated attention on what is now; but to enlarge their view and comprehension of that, by reflection on what has been."

† In a letter to a friend dated Aug. 9, 1818, he says, "I tell you candidly and honestly, as an old and good friend, that, had I not resigned a *single day too soon*, I should have been re-elected for Durham to a certainty."

‡ Quite that of an Allan. A remarkable family likeness runs from the earliest portraits at Grange.

Allan, esq., adorns this brief memoir, was originally presented by him to Surtees's Durham; and no worthier tribute to the memory of the departed may be given than the lamented historian's own letter. "Mainsforth, Dec. 27, 1833.—Dear Sir, I am very much obliged to you for the proofs. According to my recollection, the likeness is admirable. It has been hit off in a happy moment, and fully expresses the character, a sort of mild educated countenance. I shall be very glad to grace my last volume with poor George's portrait; *for, with all his foibles, there were few men whom I loved better, or from whom I received more constant kindness.** Believe me, yrs. most truly, R. SURTEES.—To Robert Henry Allan, Esqre."

The male line on the death of George Allan, the member, was again interrupted, and we must return to the issue of James Allan. ROBERT ALLAN, esq, the brother of the antiquary, had prospered so abundantly under the tender care of his good old father that he was enabled to bequeath to his son Robert, and daughters Elizabeth, Ann, and Mary, no less than 50,500*l.* in the Consols, besides leaving large landed estates, and a considerable amount on mortgages and bonds to his son John. By his wife, Elizabeth Harrison (whose sister Mary married William Russell, esq., of Brancepeth Castle†), he had two sons, Robert Allan, and John Allan. The eldest, ROBERT ALLAN of Newbottle, co. pal., esq., married Hannah Havelock (the aunt of those gallant soldiers in India of the name‡), and in 1811 joined his cousin George

* Surtees had the run of all the valuable MSS. at Grange as long as they were there, and delighted in his visits to that elegant and hospitable retreat. Sir Cuthbert Sharp had a *carte blanche*, and took many away, and then almost the whole in volumes were sold to the Dean and Chapter of Durham, an account of which may be seen in *MSS. Ecclesiæ Dunelm. Catalogus*, printed in 1825. A few were disposed of by Sotheby, in December, 1844.

† "One of the richest commoners in England," and grandfather of the late Wm. Russell, esq., sometime M.P. for the county of Durham, (who died Jan. 30, 1850, aged 51), and of Emma Maria Russell, now (1850) of Brancepeth Castle, married to the Hon. Gustavus Frederick Hamilton, only son of Viscount Boyne, who has assumed by royal licence the name of Russell. The two brothers-in-law, Allan and Russell, carried on a bank in Sunderland together in partnership, during the period of which they continued sinking the famous Wallsend Colliery, which had originally been commenced by a Mr. Chapman, though, before it was finally won, Allan withdrew from the concern, being alarmed at the increasing engineering difficulties. But Russell, possessing more nerve and less money to risk, persevered, and eventually won one of the best collieries ever known in the north, which afterwards brought him in prodigious wealth, and enabled him to purchase some of the finest estates in the county of Durham, which are now inherited by his descendant and heiress, the Hon. Mrs. Hamilton Russell. The coals of this colliery were afterwards known by the name of Russell's Wallsend. A good mining speculation was not at all distasteful even to old James Allan, who it appears actually took a lease from the Killinghalls of the *copper mines at Barton*, when, after much serious deliberation, prudence stepped in the way, and suggested to him the propriety of not engaging in operations of such a hazardous complexion. It may perhaps be proper to remark that this was almost a century ago, and that the engineering difficulties which then existed, would now, of course, be readily surmounted by the aid of the steam engine, and other improved modern mechanical appliances.

‡ 1848. Nov. 22. Killed in action at the head of his regiment, the 14th Light Dragoons, (in their desperate but successful charge, unsupported by either a single gun or bayonet, on the Sikh army, which was driven from the left bank of the Chenab, near the ford of Ramnuggar), Lieut. Col. Wm. Havelock, eldest son of Wm. Havelock, of Ford Hall, near Sunderland, and Ingress Park, co. Kent, esq., (who *d.* 1836, aged 82). He was born in 1795, and was created a knight of the Royal Hanoverian Guelphic Order, for his services at Waterloo.

"A more fearful sight," says a correspondent of the Agra Messenger, "was perhaps never witnessed on a field of battle, for the British army stood drawn up, both artillery and infantry, silent spectators of the bloody conflict of 450 sabres against an army amounting to more than 15,000 men, with heavy canon." Havelock, cheering, led on his 1st and 2nd squadrons down to the bank, then into the Nullah; crossed it at a gallop, and coming to close quarters with the Sikhs, charged through and through their ranks, and sabred hundreds of the enemy under the most frightful shower of missiles from their cannon and matchlocks. They then retired a short distance, formed up, were joined by the remainder of the corps, and the 5th Cavalry, and again they went to their work. Then, amidst a terrific cannonade from the enemy's artillery, which swept away both men and horses, and

Allan, esq., M.P., in suffering recoveries of the entailed estates of Allan, and after the same were made chargeable with 83,000*l.* as portions for younger children and for other purposes, he resettled the same upon his eldest son, Wm. Allan, esq., for life, with various remainders over. Whilst the sales and apportionments, caused by this arrangement which was followed by two heavy Chancery suits, almost decimated the good old family estate; they emancipated Darlington from the operation of an entail of many year's duration, which had contributed in no small degree to retard building and other improvements in the town and the neighbourhood. The second son, JOHN ALLAN, of Blackwell Hall, and Barton, esq., expended 34,300*l.* in purchases at Blackwell, and founded, in conjunction with the Killinghall and Sober lands, quite a distinct Allan estate. He was offered a Baronetcy in 1831, which he declined, and died before he could fulfil the office of High Sheriff of his native county to which he had been nominated, universally respected.*

a shower of bullets which fell among the troops like hail, the gallant Havelock, in the front of his regiment, charged amidst the undiverted fire from the batteries of the enemy and met his death. He had his right arm severely wounded and his left leg and left arm nearly cut off, and was left dead upon the field; eleven of his men fell fighting by his side, and their bodies were found a fortnight after the fight, decapitated, when they were buried.

This chivalrous sabreur had been engaged in all the glorious victories of the Peninsula, and was wounded at Waterloo, where he was Aide-de-Camp to Baron Alten, and received the cross of the Hanoverian order. The following singular act of heroism is recorded of him in Napier's Peninsular War:—

"There, however, he (Giron) was arrested by a strong line of abbatis, from behind which two French regiments poured a heavy fire. The Spaniards stopped, and though the adventurer Downie, now a Spanish general, encouraged them with his voice, and they kept their ranks, they seemed irresolute, and did not advance. There happened to be present an officer of the 43rd regiment, named Havelock, who being attached to General Alten's staff, was sent to ascertain Giron's progress. His fiery temper could not brook the check. He took off his hat, called upon the Spaniards to follow him, and putting spurs to his horse, at one bound cleared the abbatis, and went headlong amongst the enemy. Then the soldiers, shouting for "El chico blanco," (the fair boy,"—so they called him; for he was very young and had light hair); with one shock broke through the French; and this at the very moment when their centre was flying under the fire of Kemp's skirmishers from the "Puerto de Vera."—*(Gent. Mag. Obituary.)*

Another brother, Lieut. Col. Henry Havelock, C.B., deputy adjt. gen. of the Queen's forces at Bombay, is the author of a "History of the Burmese War," and of a "Narrative of the War in Affghanistan, in 1838-9." This latter officer commanded the right column of the handful of brave men (not exceeding 1700) under the gallant General Sale, when a glorious victory was obtained over Akhbar Khan's numerous army at Jellahabad, on the 7th of April, 1842. He was appointed a companion of the most hon. military order of the Bath, for the important services which he rendered on that occasion. This officer has since been honourably mentioned for his services at the battles of Tezeen, Istaliff, and Ferozepore, at which latter engagement his conduct "commanded the esteem and admiration" of the late gallant Sir John M'Caskill. At the sanguinary and decisive conflict at Sobraon, he assisted in conveying the commander-in-chief's orders to various points, "in the thickest of the fight, and the hottest of the fire." A third brother, Major C. F. Havelock, late captain in the 16th Lancers, "was present," says Lord Gough, "in the field at Sobraon, but unable from the effects of a wound, [received at Aliwal], to discharge the duties of his office." He then held the appointment of Dep. Assist. Quarter-Master-General of Cavalry. The youngest brother, Thomas Havelock, was killed in the Spanish service.

* "1844. (Sept. 4). Died, at Limmer's Hotel, London, after a short but severe illness, aged 66, John Allan, of Blackwell Hall, in the county of Durham, esq., a justice of the peace for the county of Durham, and North Riding of the county of York. This mournful event has cast a deep gloom, more particularly over that part of the county, and the North Riding of Yorkshire, where he was universally esteemed and respected. To a mind imbued with the keenest sense of right and wrong, was added a suavity of manners and an unostentatious liberality, which won golden opinions from all ranks of society. For many years, even to the last of his valuable life, he was most assiduous in his duties as a magistrate, presiding at the petty sessions in the town of Darlington. Having a natural taste for the study of the laws of his country, the quickness of his perception and the soundness of his judgment were felt and appreciated, both by his brethren on the bench and the public. Connected with these acquirements, he possessed a vigour of intellect, a cheerfulness of disposition, and quickness of fancy, which gave a zest to his hospitality. Had his life been prolonged, he would have succeeded in the ensuing year to the important office of high sheriff for his native county. He could boast of a phalanx of friends. Few, if any, were to be found his enemies. To the poor he was always accessible—to whose appeals of distress his heart and hand were open as the day. His mortal remains were consigned to the

Robert·Henry·Allan·Esq·of·Blackwell·Hall·&·Barton·
FORTITER GERIT CRUCEM

In politics Mr. Allan, who spoke with fluency and much elegance, was a whig of the old school. At the elections in 1828 and 1831, he nominated his cousin, William Russell, esq., of Brancepeth castle, as a candidate for the representation of the county of Durham. In 1832 he acted as chairman of Mr. Robert Duncombe Shafto's committee, and in 1841, he nominated Lord Harry Vane for the Southern division of the county of Durham.

WILLIAM ALLAN, esq., had succeeded to the Grange with but the skeleton of its ancient estates; and his uncle, John Allan, being childless, left him a portion of his estates, but the bulk was devised to another nephew, the second son of Robert Allan and Hannah Havelock, ROBERT HENRY ALLAN, esq., F.S.A., now of Blackwell Hall, and Barton. This gentleman was one of the chief promoters of, and is the principal proprietor* in that important and successful work, the Hartlepool Dock and Railway; an undertaking which has so much tended to advance the mining, commercial, and maritime interests of this county. He has also distinguished himself by the improvements he has effected in the large landed estates to which he has succeeded, and by his unwearied exertions as a justice of the peace, ever at his post.† He was the friend and correspondent of the late Robert Surtees, of Mainsforth, esq., the historian of the palatinate, and in 1824 arranged for Mr. Thomas Hoggett, bookseller, Durham, a useful little work, entitled "An historical and descriptive view of the city of Durham and its environs; to which is added a reprint of Hegge's Legend of St. Cuthbert, from the edition of the late George Allan, esq., F.S.A." This publication, which "is neatly got up, and elegantly edited,"‡ has since been republished, with additions, by George Procter, bookseller, Durham. In 1829, Mr. Allan printed, *sibi et amicis*, a "Life of the late George Allan, esq., F.S.A., to which is added a catalogue of books and tracts printed at his private press at Blackwell Grange, in the county of Durham." Since this period Mr. Allan has devoted much time and labour in promoting the publication of various works connected with history, topography, and genealogy, the value of whose assistance is best evinced by the cordial acknowledgments of their several authors.§

family vault in Darlington church, on the 9th instant. The assembled numbers, and the long train of friends who followed him to the tomb, were a tribute to the memory of one whose life had been characterised by kindness, charity, and good will to all men:

Quis desiderio sit pudor aut modus,
Tam cari capitis?"

—*Local Papers of* 13 *Sept.*, 1844.

"I had the pleasure of being acquainted with Mr. John Allan for a very great number of years, and I can assure you there is no one for whom I entertained a higher regard and esteem."—*Duke of Cleveland to R. H. Allan, esq., March* 4, 1845.

* In July 1850, the three principal proprietors in this undertaking held the following shares, viz., R. H. Allan, esq., 163; Henry Hill, esq., 142; and Mrs. Webb, 106.

† "The Mayor of Durham (R. H. Allan, esq.,) entertained the Leet Jury of this city, to dinner, at the City Tavern, on Tuesday last; and as the worthy gentleman is about to remove from this city, to take up his residence on the estate left to him by the will of his late uncle, John Allan, esq., of Blackwell, he paid the members of the Town Council the compliment of including them in the invitation. Nearly forty gentlemen assembled on the occasion; by whom the festivities of the evening were maintained until an advanced hour. The healths of the mayor and his lady were drank with the warmest enthusiasm; and while all present felt regret at their separation from a gentleman who, during his long residence in the city, has won universal esteem and confidence, and who, in the office of mayor, has shown himself an able and upright magistrate, all rejoiced in his accession to the ample fortune of which he has become the possessor, which places him in the foremost rank amongst the gentlemen of the county, and will enable him to exercise his talents and virtues in a more extended sphere than has hitherto been afforded for their development." —(*Durham Chronicle*, 25 *Oct.*, 1844.)

‡ See review in Gentleman's Magazine, Nov., 1824.

§ Among those may be enumerated the following:—The late John Burke, esq., the eminent and accomplished genealogist and author of the well-known "Peerage," handsomely

The Allan garb of literature wears wonderfully. The voice of honest praise applied to cotemporaries is by many scarcely distinguished from flattery; and the intimacy, of which I am justly proud, existing between Mr. Allan and myself is a further drawback to my placing on paper, feelings which are the growth of neither vanity, nor altogether of a sense of patronage, the most generous and undeserved. But this I may say, that even to corrections and additions at the very moment of going to press, Mr. Allan (in addition to allowing boundless access to documents which have been used in almost every page of my "Darlington") has been a most faithful and obliging pioneer. It will indeed have been observed that this is the characteristic of the family. They have zealously assisted others rather than by any *magnum opus* secured the fame of authorship for themselves. Mr. Allan has also encouraged the arts by munificent donations of plates to various works;* stained glass to the church of St. Mary's the less, Durham, and to the new Town's Hall of Durham; and communion plate to St. John's, Darlington: as well as by the insertion of an extremely handsome Gothic monument† in the north side of the choir of St. Cuthbert's church, Darlington, from a design by Hopper, of London, which does great credit to the sculptor, Mr. John Day, of Bishopwearmouth, and forms a singular contrast to the stately classic tablet on the opposite wall, erected by George Allan, the antiquary.‡

Blackwell Grange,§ with its noble avenue of ancient limes filled with rooks;

acknowledges the assistance he received from Mr. Allan, in the compilation of his elaborate and important work, the "History of the Commoners," the first edition of which was published in 1833. The late Mr. John Sykes, in his "Local Records," 1833, makes his acknowledgments "to Robert Henry Allan, of Durham, esq., F.S.A., for his unsolicited favours in kindly communicating many valuable particulars, and also for his interest in obtaining for him several subscribers, he owes a deep sense of gratitude." The editor of Mackenzie and Ross's "History of the County Palatine of Durham," 1834, "tenders his thanks for many interesting communications, to Robert Henry Allan, esq., F.S.A., of Durham, the value of whose favours is enhanced by the manner in which they are conferred." John Walker Ord, esq., the historian of Cleveland, 1846, "is deeply grateful to Robert Henry Allan, esq., for much valuable information." The third volume of the "Patrician," 1847, edited by the late John Burke, esq., has the following dedication: "To Robert Henry Allan, esq., F.S.A., of Blackwell Hall, co. Durham, the earliest and most constant promoter of the genealogical pursuits of the editor, this volume of the Patrician is inscribed with feelings of sincere esteem."

* E. g. Surtees's Durham; Robson's British Herald; Burke's Heraldic Illustrations; Brockett's intended Life of George Allan; Longstaffe's Darlington, &c.

† It is of the perpendicular style, beautifully enriched. Along the basement are carved in the panelings seven shields of the armorial bearings of the families of Allan, Pemberton, Hindmarsh, Killinghall, Herdewyke, Lambton, and Dodsworth. The following is the inscription:—"In this church are deposited the remains of George Allan, of Darlington, and Blackwell Grange, in the county of Durham, Esquire, (sixth son of George Allan, of Yarm, in the county of York, Esq.), born in 1663, and died 24th March, 1744, aged 80 years. Also of his son George Allan, of Blackwell Grange, Esquire, born in 1694, and died 31st July, 1753, aged 58 years. Also of James Allan, of Blackwell Grange, and of Barton, in the county of York, Esquire, born in 1712, and died 19th January, 1790, aged 77 years. Also of his son George Allan, of Blackwell Grange, Esquire., F.S.A., the eminent antiquary and collector, born in 1736, and died 17th May, 1800, aged 63 years. Also of George Allan, of Blackwell Grange, Esquire, M.A., F.S.A., sometime M.P. for the city of Durham, (son of the last named George Allan), born in 1767, and died 21st July, 1828, aged 61 years. Also of John Allan, of Blackwell Hall, in this county, and of Barton, Esquire, M.A., a justice of the peace for the county of Durham, and North Riding of the county of York, (grandson of the above named James Allan), born in 1778, and died 4th September, 1844, aged 66 years. In testimony of his respect and affection for their memories, Robert Henry Allan, of Blackwell Hall, and Barton, Esquire, F.S.A., caused this monument to be erected, A. D. 1845."

‡ "Choro cœlesti beatarum Virginum accessere, Dorothea et Anna Georgii Allan, de Blackwell Grange, arm. filiæ; illa, anno 1760, æt 38; fœminarum dulce decus, et invidia major; hæc, anno 1775, æt 66, pauperum Solamen, omnium deliciæ, utraque Christianis virtutibus eximia; has erga, et in memoriam Annæ suæ conjugis charissimæ, anno 1787, æt. 46, abreptæ, hoc grati animi pignus posuit Geo. Allan, de Darlington."

§ "In the way from Darlington to Blackwell, you pass the Grange, on an elevated situation, with a S. E. aspect, long eminently distinguished as the seat of benevolence and the virtues; ostentatious ornaments are not displayed here; rural beauties and simplicity are maintained as the chief graces of this pleasant place."—*Hutch. Hist. Durham, III. p.* 193.

its laurelled walks, and choice accompaniments of every kind, is indeed a lovely retreat; close to the town of Darlington, and yet with scarce a wall; so bounded by pleasant plantations and verdant grass, that it loses not a charm of rural beauty. A delightful vista terminated by the tower of the church of St. John on the one hand, and a magnificent champaigne view ending in the Yorkshire hills on the other, constitute it the very spot for the man of refined and educated ideas. At the entrance of this elegant and spacious mansion lies a fragment of a coped tombstone, said to have come from Hartlepool, sculptured with foliage. The interior of the Grange is rich in paint ings, owing to the fine taste of its present owner, Wm. Allan, esq. Among these are the following,—ascribed to the masters annexed:—Cattle, by Morland; two Game pieces, by Schnyder; two Moonlight scenes, by Mespether; Landscape, by Poussin, formerly in the Lambton mansion of Biddick; portrait of a lady from Lumley Castle, said to be of a favourite of Prince Charlie, and inscribed "Wm. Verelst pinxit 1736;" Adam and Eve driven from Paradise, by Coypel; a long and very minute prospect of Naples; Groop of Cavalry, by Wooverman; Landscape, by Both; Zenobia at the tent of Aurelia, by Bassano; Embarkment, by Murillo; Satyrs and Bacchantes, by Berchet; Cattle, by Rosa da Tivoli; Head of Carravaggio, by himself; and many others, some of which are mentioned in page xix, as having been bought in at the Grange sale.*

The state chamber, where the family lie in the solemn pomp of death (of course a haunted spot), exhibits in its bedstead, mantlepiece, and panelling, some deeply undercut and fine specimens of carving. There is a very long and grand suite of rooms in Grange, extending through the Southern wing; and a number of old portraits of the Allans, all bearing a striking resemblance to each other, look grimly down, and fill up the ideas of the stranger as to the long-continued residence and wealth of the inmates.

Blackwell Hall, the elegant seat of Robert Henry Allan, esq., is also rich in pictures and prints. Robson's chef d' œuvre in water colours, the celebrated view of Durham Cathedral, painted for Bishop Van Mildert, and which was purchased by its present possessor on his lordship's death, has found its way from Auckland castle to the stately dining-room (which has dined two hundred persons), built by the late John Allan, esq. This place has long rejoiced in a famous breed of terriers, two of which, "Pincher," and "Chivers," have been immortalized in a capital picture by H. B. Chalon, an engraving of which, by Duncan, appears in the "New Sporting Magazine" for April, 1834. The views from the hall, over the Neville manor of Blackwell, through which the silvery Tees winds in a radiant line of light, or dashes down in darkness and in thunder, are extensive, rich, and exceedingly beautiful. The varied grounds contain fine specimens of the cypress, cedar of Lebanon (one of the finest examples in the North), and the singular tulip-tree.

Here the vast collections of documents, title deeds, correspondences, and MSS. formed by James Allan and his son the antiquary (but principally

* W. Harker, esq., of Theakstone Villa, near Bedale, possesses two fine paintings, formerly at Grange. One presents the head of St. John the baptist, held by his female foe in the charger, and by a convenient anachronism the circumstances which led to the wondrous grace of Herod. The other a not unusual design, "J. Hus, Bulinger, Zanchi, Cnox, Zuingle, Martin, Bucer, Prague, Perkins, Melanchton, Luther, Calvin, Beza, Whiclif," and another reformer round a table, on which a candle is triumphant over the fierce blowings of the Devil, the Pope, a cardinal, and a monk. This picture was, according to Allan the M.P.'s statement in a letter to the owner from St. Omers, sent in 1722, to the then George Allan, of Grange, by Lionel Allan, his wealthy cousin in Holland. There are several engravings from other variorum copies, some bearing the exclamation, "We cannot blow it out!"

the former), from which many new facts and conclusions have been, by the kindness of their custodier, dragged to light, are deposited. Yet many strongholds are yet unexamined. The rich and early series relating to Barton, and Appleton-upon-Wiske, I have never had time to examine. But if it please God to permit me, in future years, to complete a cherished scheme of elaborating and publishing these family memoirs in a more extended form, I trust that I may still be permitted to revel among those, to me, joyous hoards, and to publish many curious and novel *excerpta*. Whatever James Allan took in hand was finished in a most extraordinarily minute and careful manner; and his MSS. are, to my fancy, quite as interesting as those of his son. On one occasion, after being out at dinner, he expressed his supreme disgust and indignation at an impudent fellow* who had never taken his eyes off him. Whenever James had lifted up his head and glanced at the man, he invariably found him staring with all his might and main; and the dinner passed away without relish. The result was a most capital profile in wax of the victim, who had an insurmountable objection to gratifying his family by sitting for his portrait. This memento is now at Blackwell Hall.

And now I leave this honoured race. Few families of present wealth can boast of having been richer one hundred years ago than they are now. But the Allans can do this, and they can do much more. The Allan garb of literature has worn most bravely and enduringly.†

* Qu. The Rev. John Jones Thornhill, afterwards vicar of Staindrop, who had the faculty of modelling minute portraits in wax under a table, unobserved. My friend, Mr. Bewick, had an instance of it performed for his gratification at dinner, at the late Sir Wm. Chaytor's, Bart. The object was Bishop Barrington.

† While Geo. Allan, esq., was M.P., he moved the house for a renewal of the visitations of the Heralds, which was opposed by Mr. (afterwards Baron) Graham, and was rejected by a majority. Mr. Allan expressed, on writing to a friend in reference to the matter, his disappointment at the failure in carrying out this favourite scheme, and said that his legal opponent knew as little of pedigree as he did of sound law.

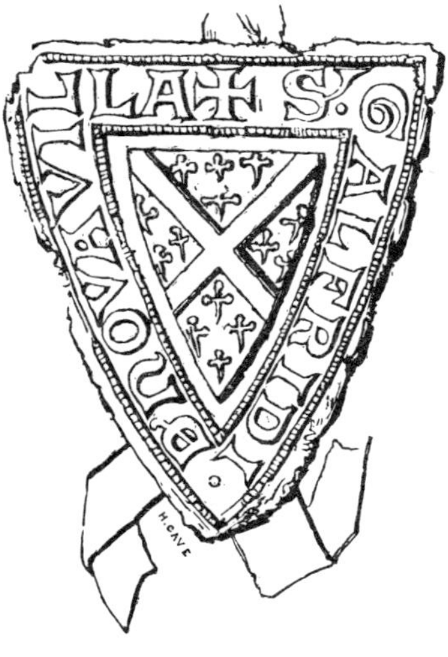

II. HYLTON.

PERHAPS no feeling of clanship ever animated any race in a stronger degree than that which characterized the Hyltons* in the North. The line of pedigree might be utterly lost, a long track of country intervene, but still every man of the name looked up to the Baron of Hylton as his kinsman and natural protector, however humble his station and remote his claim. The idea at the present day has in no way altered, though the Barons have passed away. Universal tradition,† similarity of arms to those of undoubted scions of the parent stock,‡ acknowledgment by the Barons,§ and the never failing characteristic of the blue eye and fair flowing hair of the Saxon, have led the Hyltons of Westmoreland and South Durham in all ages to look back to the green manors on the Wear as their fatherland, to remember their Saxon parentage, and their origin in one of Odin's ravens and a mild maiden of the Bishoprick; in fine, to look upon the towers and traditions of the Barons as their own.

* The name, both in the Durham and Westmoreland families, in the most ancient documents relating to them, is uniformly Helton, which may mean the town in the hole or by water, as Hylton Castle stands. Helton Bacon, (now Hilton Beacon), in Westmoreland, is under or at the foot of a hill, and Hilton, near Staindropshire, which also occurs as Helton, is really what its present name implies, standing high, and commanding a most extensive view over some of the finest parts of Durham and Yorkshire. The spelling Hilton is perhaps the most usual, but the later barons employed Hylton, and as it is adopted by their heirs, the Jolliffes, and is found, more or less, in all other races of the name, I am inclined to adopt it for its associations. But I shall follow the taste of the parties I treat of. After all, is not the name from the Saxon *Healle*, a hall, palace or great mansion? The Haltons, of Halton, in Craven, bore the same arms as the Barons Hylton; and what is more to the point, as regards our Westmoreland people, the arms, "Sable, 3 saltorels argent," are ascribed in the General Armory to *Holton.* And in the Durham Pipe Rolls, the Baron of *Holton* is mentioned in 1197, and Robert de *Hyolton* in 1211.

† Some of the descendants of the Helton Bacon family, have actually "been bold enough to lay claim to the estate of Hilton castle, which, in their opinion, is in want of an owner, with no better title than the name they bear."

‡ Cuthbert Hilton, of Great Usworth, co. Durham, gent., the next in entail to the baron's own two sons, by a long settlement of 1526, seals his will, which was proved in 1576 (Sir Wm. Hilton being the supervisor), with 3 saltires. (*Sir C. Sharp's MSS.*) I am not prepared to say that Roger, son of George Hilton, of Wylome, co. York [Northumberland ?], the next in entail to Cuthbert, was in any way connected with the Helton Bacon family, or with the cotemporary Roger, mayor of Appleby, but the additional annulets in the Westmoreland coat of saltires and annulets are easily accounted for by the general custom of the Veteriponte subfeudatories adopting that bearing of their lords. "His [John de Veteriponte's] seal bore on a knight's shield and on his horse's trapping, annulets, the proper arms of the Veteripontes, hence the gentry under the family generally also bore annulets differing in colour and number from theirs."—(*Pemb. MS. p.* 9, 11.) The barons indeed actually granted arms, differing in small degree from their own, as William, baron of Graystock, did by regular deed to Adam de Blencowe in 1357.

§ Thomas Hilton, of Burton, co. Westmoreland, and Henry Hilton, of Wynston, are called into a baronial entail of 1558, though long after the Roger of the last note, who again occurs. In the family rolls, however fabulous, the connection was allowed in the old heralds' own way, and the arms of the barons differenced assigned them, with the saltires and annulets as those of the heiress of Bacon only. This may all be fictitious, but it shows the feeling of the head of the clan; and the marriage of Robert Hilton, of Helton Bacon, in the 17th century, with Baron Hylton's daughter is also to the point. The "saltire-bearing Hiltons," of Usworth, gradually sunk into the estate of yeomen and tenants to their baronial cousins at Usworth and Biddick, and a century after their ancestor Cuthbert, "claimed a sort of kindly right, a half-asserted tie of consanguinity," by "beseching their worshippfull freend and landlord Sir Willyam Hilton, or Henry Hilton, esq., to be supervisor of their wills, and to be good maister to their children."

It shall not be mine to check such a feeling. If some have forgotten the bright and minute path of honour—if worldly wealth has in them blighted and deadened every affection—they have paid for the error in bitterness and sorrow; but to those who have emulated the virtues which endeared the long line of the barons to their people, and stuck to their candour and chivalry, in ever so small degree, God has been very gracious.

A trace of the name occurs among the Darlington landowners in the 14th century,* but for the ancestors of those Hyltons who sought sepulchre in St. Cuthbert's church, we must seek the quiet vales of Westmoreland. There they occur at the commencement of the 13th century, in gentle state under the Veteripontes. ROBERT HELTON, their *homo præpositus*, occurs at the very period when the roll pedigrees of the barons state their kinsman of that name to have migrated, and married a Westmoreland heiress. That the Heltons or Hyltons of Westmoreland (for their name underwent the same change as that of their chiefs of Durham) did not take appellation from Helton Bacon,† their subsequent seat, seems all but certain from the fact that their first seat was Burton, and that the settlement in Helton Bacon was only achieved by degrees. The feeling which prompted it was in all probability the same with that which caused the settlers in South Durham to cling to Hilton, near Staindrop, as a home, that they, too, might be styled "the Hiltons of Hilton."

The Heltons occur in early charters as witnesses in company with the very best families of Westmoreland, and divided into two great branches; one settled at Burton, the other at Helton Bacon. Both occur in the lists of parliament as furnishing members to the lower house.

The BURTON line (pedigree No. II.) furnished a rich ecclesiastic in the time of Henry VIII., who purchased a moiety of the manor of Helton Bacon, which had never been acquired by his kindred of that place. His will makes numerous proper provisions for an imposing obit in Warcop church, for his own soul's health and that of all his fore-elders, successors, friends and benefactors, and all Christian souls, not forgetting a decent sum at that time for the officiating priests "to have to drynke among theym," and bread and ale for the poor. On his tomb a hearse was perpetually to stand, and five tapers be burnt thereon.‡ The ancient faith evidently lingered in his race.

* 1309. Robert s. Guydo Faber, of Derlington, to Wm. de Hilton and Matilda his wife, an acre in Derlington. 1320. John Benet of Derlingtone and Eustachia his wife, to William de Heltone and Matilda his wife, property in Great Burdone. About the same time Will. Hiltone alienated to Wm. de Walleworde and Olive his wife, 2 burgages in Derlingtone.—*Charters in Treasury, Durham.*

† In the parish of St Michael, Bondgate, Appleby. In the north aisle of the parish church is a large vault, the ancient burying place of the Heltons, of Helton. There was formerly a chapel about ¼ mile from Hilton Beacon (as the name now stands) long since demolished. Some very extensive lead mines, which yield a considerable quantity of silver, are worked here. It is observable that some early owners of half the manor of Helton were named Hellerton.

‡ 20 Feb., 1526. Edward Hilton, clerke, parson of Blechesdon, in the counte of Oxfordeshyre—My cotage meys or tenement in Helton Baken and all thynges pertenynge, to the vicar off Warcope and on off the churchemen or churchewardens off Warcope, and an other churcheman or churchewarden off Burton—to finde observe and keppe an annyversary or obit yerly for evermore the xv. day of July with placebo and dirige over evyne and v. masses to be songe or seyde the forseyde xv. day of July, one de quinque vulneribus, another de Nativitate Johannis, another de Sancta Trinitate, another de Annunciatione beatæ Mariæ, with a collect, secret, and post communion at every masse ut in die annyversario, and the hye masse of Requiem in die annyversario to be songe or seyde in Seynt John's porche [the north aisle of Warcop Church which belongs Burton Hall] at the altar of Seynt John within the parysshe churche of Seynt Combe [Columb] of Warcope—for the soulls off the sayd Edward Hilton, hys father Christopher Hilton and his mother Margaret wyffe of the sayde Christopher, and for the sowlls of hys bretheryne and sisters, hys fryndds and benefactors and for the sowlls of all the predecessors and successors of the forsaid

Andrew and John Hilton were respectively assessed annually upon the stated amount of 100*l.* for the county of Northumberland, as recusants in the strict reign of Elizabeth. In the seventeenth century the manor of Ormeshead was acquired through marriage with the natural daughter of Sir Christopher Pickering by his milkmaid, at Threlkeld; and the heiress of the family, Mary Hilton, a prolific lady who bore her delighted spouse "twice one, and twenty children," originated the Wyberghs, of Clifton Hall, the present representatives of her ancient house. Her cousin, Mary Hilton, married Daniel Robinson, esq., the Westmoreland antiquary, and assistant of Nicholson and Burn in their history of that county; whose descendant, the Rev. George Thompson, of Wisbeach, informs me that the fine hair and blue eyes were peculiarly characteristics of her family.

"Thomas Hilton, bailife of Roane," figures in the chronicles as accompanying the English noblesse and the Duke of Somerset, when that nobleman won Harfleur (lately before gotten by the French), to his high praise and glory, which vanished with his rise, for when he was regent he lost not only Harfleur and Rouen, but also the whole duchy of Normandy, which now as a deputy only he conquered. As there was no other Thomas Hilton of any eminence at that period, I am inclined to identify the bailiff with Thomas Helton, of HELTON BACON, coroner of Westmoreland in the reign of Henry VI.

"Robert Hilton, 2 horse," was called out for the border service in 1543. He married a daughter of Thomas Blenkinsop, esq., and two of his sons became intimately connected with the county of Durham. John settled at Gainford, and his elder brother, of Helton Bacon, matched with a daughter of the gallant house of Brackenbury. From this marriage nearly all the Hyltons of South Durham derive. Thomas, the heir, purchased Murton Hall, in the parish of Appleby, and removed from the seat of his fathers to his new acquisition, which was "a good old house, and convenient, a spring of water running through it." There was a chapel there. His grandson, Robert, married a daughter of the Baron of Hylton, in the chapel of Hylton castle,* and thus united in a true lovers' knot the long slackened cords of relationship between the two houses. He sinned deeply, however, against his paternal acres, and died at Durham. "Robert Hilton, esq., Justice of the Peace for Westmoreland, came to Durham, and lived in the coledg; dep. this life the 8th day of Jan., being Thursday, this year 1683; he died very suddenly, having been out to supper the night before, &c."† His son

Christopher Hilton, and for all crysten sowlls—Rents shall be dysposede as followethe—the vycar of Warcope beynge present to have viii *d.* and every en of the other iiii prysts to have vi *d.* and to have to drynke among them viii *d.*; paryshe clerk for syngyng and ministeryng at the alters and helpyng at masses ii *d.*; to ather churcheman or churchwarden on of Warcoppe and another of Burton beyng present at the seyd masses ii *d.*; v. childrynge helping at the seyd masses v *d.*; v. poyr neydfull pepyll v *d.*; and for breyd and hale to be spent within the forseyd porche of Seynte John, after the dirige v *d.*—that v *d.* be offeryde i.e. after the offertory of each mass i *d.*; to the vycar or his curete to pray for the sowlls before rehersyde upon Sondays iiii *d.*; and v *d.* for v. tapers to stande uppon the herse in tyme of dirige and masses recedew to poyr pepyll of the paryshe of Warcoppe—That thys wyll be regestraytt in the regesture of my lord bushape off Karlyll that iff anny lett this my wyll they shall be called afor my sayd lorde or his officers, to be chargt by corporal hothe or other censure off churche that they shall not thensforthe lett this my wyll nor wythedraw anny dewte to the forseyde cotage &c. pertenynge, and in case any dewty wythedrawn that they shall restore it agayne under the payn of cursyng, or off other censurs off the churche—Robert Hilton of Burton and his heirs for evermore supervisors and overseers.

* Mr. Robert Hilton and Mrs. Mary Hilton mar. in ye chapell of Hilton, 2 Nov. 1647.—(*Boldon Reg.*)

† Jacob Bee's diary.

continued to live at Helton Bacon, but in 1696 the manor was sold to Sir John Lowther.* He married the widow of James Duckett, esq., of Grayrigg, under whose will she possessed part of Betham Rectory. Her second spouse built a fair house nigh to the place where the old rectory house stood, which was improved and rendered more commodious by his son George Hilton, who was a Roman Catholic, and joined the rebels in 1715. He made his escape ,and was pardoned amongst the rest of his companions, by the act of grace in the year following. He ever afterwards lived private, and built a house at the South end of Betham park, unto which he retired.

I now come to the Durham branches of the family. From the marriage with Catherine Brackenbury proceeded two younger sons, Lancelot and NICHOLAS HILTON. The latter was parson of Sockburn and Hurworth. His son William, a merchant of York, married Anne Rand, daughter of a Norton vicar.† Her sister Ruth married Samuel Liveley, of Pilgrim-street, Newcastle, who by will 1649 says, "My chesnut mare I bequeath to my brother in law, Dr. Rand; *protesting a dislike to have her used as his Greatham horses;* however, I shall not be troubled at it, being gone of the earth." The will of John Rand, a skinner of Newcastle (1610), who seems to have married a namesake, is also curious for its affectionate language. "To the care of my loving brother in law, Dr. Rand, her brother, and Tho. Milburn, I commend the care of my wife *that can never be too much cared for.*" The descendants of Wm. Hilton settled at Newcastle.—*(see ped. III.)*

LANCELOT HYLTON, the other settler, originated a great many distinct branches, and before drawing the direct line of Hylton, of Hilton and Darlington, I shall make way for it by noticing the various twigs branching out at different periods from the widely spreading tree. Lancelot, the patriarch, married first, the heiress of Alwent, and lived upon his wife's inheritance at Dyons (now a single modern farmhouse, to the North of Cock-lane, near Gainford)‡.

The line of Hilton, in which the blood of ALWENT flowed, settled at DURHAM and STOCKTON, and produced some extremely eminent lawyers. One of the ladies of the family, of the formidable name of Hieronyma, was registered

* "The Lowthers buy, but never sell,
The family of Lowther of Lowther castell."

† They had a son, William Hilton, an important apothecary of Newcastle. In 1655 Anthony Bullock and Thomas Shevill informed the company of smiths there that a profane brother "Thomas Hall's man did sett 2 shewes of Will. Hilton's horse upon St. Cloyd day," for which he was fined 6*s*. 8*d*.; and in 1659, Thomas Hall was fined 3*s*. 4*d*. for saying "he would shoe Mr. Hilton's horse in spite of Thomas Woodhave's teeth." The brawny fraternity seems to have contained some most outrageously riotous members, whose egotistic and angry speeches often called down the anger of their conclave. One irate brother, Wm. Thompson, was hard upon poor Wouldhave, and asserted that he was "a botching fellow, and that he knew no more what belonged to his trade than the sole of his foot," took away a horse from his stall, interrupted "Mistris Shaftoe's horse that was goeing to Thomas Wouldhave's shopp," and called him a botching rogue. Another, Alexander Hall, said his apprentice was as honest a man as Thos. Wouldhave. And a third, Maltland, was fined for "making debate and teareing Robert Woodifield's scutcheon at Tho. Wouldhave's wife's burial." Wouldhave himself was quite as bad. He called Henry Horsley "a w—masterly fellow," and what was far worse, was guilty of "throwing a cabbish stock in at the window and spoyling the bookes and the orders" of his company. As to Thomas Hall, the wicked scorner of Bishop Clodulphus; George Trunbull was fined for saying he would have cured Mr. Lanckasters mare three times sooner than Thomas Hall.—*(Extracts from the Smiths' books, N.C. by G. Bouchier Richardson.)*

‡ There are traces of a village in a garth to the West. The place is called Deindes in 1207. It is remarkable that in the entry of Lancelot Hylton in the Durham Heraldic Visitation of 1615, the arms of Alwent are entered for him. The informant has been so little versed *in re Hilton* that he blanks the name of Lancelot's second wife who must have been still living. It is probable that he may have been some one of the blood of Alwent, who wished the representatives of the main line to be thus marshalled in gentle array.

at Gainford in 1623, by the strange baptismal prænomen of *Joanna Ananias.* The broad lands of Alwent soon *all went,* and the family settled at Durham and Stockton. Old ROBERT HILTON, of Stockton, "attornatus, magna in rebus forensibus experientia, nec minori fide,"* who lived to the good age of 75, by his wife Esther Watson, "femina pia et prudens, ejusque in conjugio fidelis per annos supra 40 socia," had three sons, heirs to his fame. The heiress of ROBERT HILTON, of Durham, the eldest, married John Hopper, esq., and was the mother of Robert Hopper Williamson, esq., the chancellor of Durham, and father of the Rev. R. H. Williamson of Hurworth. LANCELOT HYLTON, the second son, of Mont Pelyer Row, Stockton,† and Brancepeth (for attornies and barristers in olden time received their clients in remote villages; e.g., the Hiltons, of Hilton, in Staindropshire, and the Gills and Dodsworths, of Barton); "qui probitate animi et suavitate morum insignis omnibus sese prestitit dilectum," was seneschal under Bishop Crewe, and was succeeded on his resignation, in 1719, by his brother DAVID HILTON, a barrister, who continued in office under six bishops—Crewe, Talbot, Chandler, Butler, Trevor, and Egerton. With the other officers of Talbot he fell in for Spearman's lash in 1729. "All the law offices being in the bishop's gift," says that bitter writer, "are either sold or given to his servants. Mr. Hilton the present cursitor, paid between 6 and 700*l.* for his office of cursitor." He had a corrupt clerk of the halmots, Mr. Mowbray, who actually refused to enroll the admittance of Sir John Eden to his father's lands, which his principal, Mr. Hilton, had himself granted, and declared both to Hilton and Lady Eden, on Sir John's death, when the former was desired to admit Sir Robert his son, and was very willing to do so, "that he had orders to the contrary, and upon her ladyship's asking him if he was ordered to do an unjust thing, would he do it? his answer was, He was the bishop's officer and must obey directions." However, the threat of filing a bill against the bishop and his officers forced Mowbray to enroll both admittances. In another part of his book, Spearman speaks of Hilton as the prelate's "steward, whom the bishop calls *Old Buff,* other *Volpone;* he (to have the greater influence in affairs) presides in court and cabals here, and lately presumed to close up with rails (made with the bishop's timber) one end of the most ancient street in the city, called the King's street, thereby obstructing the passage of either coach, carriage or horse, to the great nusance and prejudice of the subject; and took down an ancient gateway and gate in another street called Bow-lane; and another gate going from the palace green to the Broken-walls; both which gates used to be locked up at nights in winter time by the constable of the parish of St. Mary-le-Bowe, and was of great security to that part of the city from pilfering thieves, and did this in an *arbitrary manner,* and without legal authority, or consulting the neighbours, and applied the frames of timber, gates, hinges, bolts, and stones to the Bishop's or his own use,

* "Hic sepulti sunt Robertus Hilton, attornatus, magna in rebus forensibus experientia, nec minori fide, Obiit Maii die 17, A.D. 1727, ætatis 75. Et Esthera Hilton, Femina pia et prudens, ejusque in conjugio fidelis per annos supra 40 socia. Obiit Augusti die 13, A.D. 1723, ætat 64. Juxta etiam conditur quod mortale fuit Lanceloti Hilton, attornati, Qui probitate animi et suavitate morum insignis omnibus sese prestitit dilectum, natus 16 Augusti 1694, obiit 16 Octobris, 1757."—*(Low altar tomb, Stockton churchyard.)* The attornies of Stockton always ran in long sequences and cliques. I presume the Hylton dynasty would be succeeded by their relations, the Raisbecks, now represented in the law by Messrs. Wilson and Faber. The connection of Hylton and Raisbeck was by the blood of Watson, Mrs. Hylton's sister marrying the Rev. Tho. Rudd, whose daughter, Esther, married Wm. Raisbeck, gent.

† "Lant. Hylton de Mont Pelyer Row, Stockton, gentleman, Epiphany 1732, Laus Deo in Eternum, Amen.—E Libris Wm. Hilton given him by his Father Anno 1745."

although belonging to and provided by the parishioners." Verily, the master seems to have been little better in his own way than the man, though the gates in our days would be scarcely suffered by the night-wandering scions of gentry. ROBERT HILTON, David's son, of Trinity Coll., Cambridge, was a favourite member of the True Blue, where he first grew into an intimacy with Lord Torrington, who, on leaving college, appointed him his domestic chaplain; and he, as it were, followed the fortunes of that generous nobleman. When his lordship was charge d' affaires at Brussels, he accompanied him, and was there introduced to the Duke of Portland, who distinguished him by particular marks of friendship, and on his appointment to the Lord Lieutenancy of Ireland, offered him a bishopric then vacant, which, by some inconceivable misunderstanding, Mr. Hilton did not accept. About 1800, the Bishop of Llandaff presented him to a prebend in his cathedral; and within six weeks before his death, in 1804, the Duke of Portland obtained him the living of Bothal, value 1000*l.* yearly, but a paralytic affection of two years' duration had rendered him past the enjoyment of, and death, from a repeated stroke, prevented even the possession of his good fortune.

This clergyman had a cousin William (son of Lancelot, the good attorney of Stockton), known as "HILTON THE POET," a native of Stockton and a mercer of Gateshead. He lived and had a shop on Old Tyne bridge, which was swept away by the great flood in 1771; and was one of the trustees under the act for building a temporary bridge and completing a new one. He was in the habit of giving copies of a long letter of the best advice to his apprentices in the cloth trade, in which he praises the church of England, notwithstanding its defects; and attributes the frequent bankruptcies to the high living of the period. Poor fellow! in 1772 he (with his partner and relation Wm. Raisbeck of the Stockton family) was bankrupt himself, doubtless from the effects of the flood. In 1775 and 1776, "from motives of *real* exigency," he published his poems at Newcastle, in two volumes, consisting of tragedies and minor effusions, which if not entitled to high praise as poetry, are full of character and feeling. He calls them "a sort of collective salvage narrowly saved from an unavoidable wreck in fortune, and ever since carefully preserved through a long disagreeable series of unmerited persecution." His talents, integrity, and manly resignation to accumulated misfortunes won him a good subscription list, but to the disgrace of his numerous and wealthy relations, his cousin the clergyman (six copies) is the only individual of the blood of Hylton that occurs. From 1781 to 1787 he was riding officer in the Sunderland customs, and in the former year, being then resident at Whitburn, he wrote memoirs of the life and writings of his "dear bosom friend," John Spencer, gent.; a bard of Newcastle, whose poem "Hermas, or the Arcadian shepherds," he had published in two vols. He died in 1798 at Gateshead. Of his brother, Captain Robert Hilton, who, he says, was "crossed in youth, when coming fortune smiled, and to his latest hour with flattering hopes beguiled," I only know so much that in 1753 he paid George Bowes, of Gibside, 350*l.* to be handed to Major Clayton, of Carlisle, on his procuring him the commission of Town Major of that city in exchange for his half-pay as Lieutenant of foot. Richard Hilton, the poet's son, was a sailor, and was drowned, and the male blood of these Hyltons seems extinct.

The second wife of Lancelot the settler was a Smelt, of Kirkby Fleetham, and from this marriage originated a family settled at KILLERBY (another estate of the Alwents), and buried in the choir of Heighington church under an ancient blue stone;* but with all its Lydias, Deborahs, Tamars, and Penelopes, the line is possessed of little interest.

A second Lancelot, son of the first, was ancestor of the Hilton and Darlington people, and by a second wife, the widow of a "crafty Cradock," commenced a race whose pedigree (No. 6.) is ominously headed by Surtees;†—"This page may be called the decline of all the Cuthbertine or BARBER*ini* branch of the Hiltons, for poor Jacob *Abramides, fra. David,* perished in Allan and Baker's contested election, without benefit of clergy, a proper retribution for the scandal of his great ancestor the pontifex of Barnard-Castle." Alexander, son of Lancelot, was curate of Denton, and rector of Romaldkirk, and died in 1682, leaving two sons; William, who "was bred an attorney and went mad," and, I believe, was the Hilton of Denton who carried about a brief describing himself as mad, and praying for means to put himself into prison; and CUTHBERT HILTON, who having taken orders in no church, but having been trained as bible clerk under his father, is thus described by a quaint writer:—"Cuthbert Hilton, who used to entangle certain sons and daughters of iniquity in an illegal tie upon Barnard-Castle bridge, in the middle of the river, between the county palatine of Durham and Yorkshire, where the Lord Bishop's writ does not run."‡ He resided at one time at Cleasby, and the Darlington registers, in 1750, witness his delinquencies. The issue of the parties "who continue to live under a marriage of Cuthbert Hilton's of Barnard Castle, a layman," are entered as illegitimate. He died at Barnard Castle in 1755. This pontifex maximus left issue *Abraham, Job, Solomon, David,* Alexander, and Cuthbert. Solomon died in the East Indies in Admiral Hawkes's fleet; Cuthbert was a player; Alexander is connected in the Darlington register with one Rachel Watson, keeper of the bakehouse in Blackwellgate; Job was remarkable for his industry and ingenuity as a carpet weaver in Barnard Castle, and he and some of his brothers were the first artizans in that town who practised the art of dying cloth of various colours; and Abraham, a tailor of Durham, had issue *Abraham, Sarah,*§ *Isaac, three Jacobs in succession,* DAVID, and other children; one of whom, Dorothy, married David-le-Roy; one of whose descendants I remember having some ultra notions about an origin from the kings of France!

DAVID HILTON, on whom many a *barber*-ous joke was played, is immortalized by Ritson:—

> Hilton my hair did dress, who beats
> The world, you know, in shaving feats.

He was "a man of special grave remark," and a most worthy citizen of Durham. His shop in Saddler-street was the lounge of all the literati of the city; for David, albeit joked, could wink at the fun, and enjoy to pass a

* Which is robbed of its more ancient brasses. "Lydie, the wife of Mr. George Hilton; died Nov. 4th, 1745, aged 77. Sub hoc marmore *jacet corpus* Lance. Marg. et Thomæ Hilton: L. sepult. Jun. 20. 1675., M. Aug. 25, 1697, T. Apr. 26, 1718. Et corpus Georgii Hilton de Killerby, sepult. undecimo die Maii, Anno Domini, 1723. Alexander Hilton, died March 20th, 1732."

† J. B. Taylor's MSS.

‡ "Cuthbertus Hilton qui solebat quosdam et quasdam filios et filias iniquitatis illicita copula irretire super pontem Castri Bernardi, nempe in medio flumine inter com. pal. Dunelm. et Ebor. ubi breve domini episcopi non currit."

§ "Here lies the body of Sarah Hilton, daughter of Abraham and Lucy Hilton, died June 8, [1734] aged . . . ." [some few months].—*Headstone, St. Oswald's churchyard, Durham.*

joke himself. On one occasion he was sent for to go to an hotel and shave a gentleman who had just arrived. The knight of the bason was well known to all the grandees of the palatinate, and possessed numberless anecdotes of their families. Such a standing had given him a tacit privilege to become very inquisitive as to the whole pedigree of every new comer. He, according to his wont, began to pump. The stranger was not easily accessible, but, at last, wearied with David's curiosity, said, "Well—if you *must* know—I believe myself entitled to the Barony of Hylton, and have come down to see about it." "Oh, but you know," said David, with a smirk, "that's all nonsense, because if any one ought to be Baron of Hylton, it's myself!"

Of course such a distinguished character was entitled to a coat of arms *with a difference.* The saltires gave way to two razors in saltire proper, on a field azure, and the shield was completed by a chief gules charged with a comb argent. Crest, upon a barber's block in profile, a wig proper. "It is our intenc'on," saith the witty Surtees thereupon, "speedily to assigne A Coate of Armes and creaste to master Davide Hilton, of d'resme, gent., within our jurisdicc'on as depicted inffra."* There was, however, no reason why the saltires of the younger line should not wholly give way to the bars of the barons, so another design was concocted by the same fertile brain; three bars each charged with a razor; and duly inserted in an old ordinary of arms.† The crest was the same as in the former insignia, but affrontee to correspond with the Moses' head used by the Lords of Hylton, and under all was inscribed:—"Maister Davyde Hylton de Duresme barber chyrourgeon, MDCCCXVII ut per cartam Abrah'i p'ris sui," which charter is believed to have been his father's handbill. David, like Blynd Lambton,‡ was easily led by the heralds. Surtees and a friend had one day been listening to his account of his great ancestor Cuthbert's delinquencies, and on coming away, remarked, "Well, you know, the fellow must have had a marriage service, let us make him one." An old witching rhyme, of very frequent occurrence, was at hand. Cuthbert was made, after causing the parties to leap over a broomstick, to say,

My blessing on your pates,
  Your groats in my purse;
You are never the better,
  I am never the worse.

And this doggrel was recited to the barber. "Was that what he said to them, David?" "The very thing, Sir," was the reply. Away went the rhyme to Sir Cuthbert, down into his History of Hartlepool and Bishoprick Garland it found its way, and there it stands as a grave tradition "still remembered in the neighbourhood."

His successor, DAVID, *Barberides*, an eminent bookseller and newsman at Pentonville, was particularly instrumental in procuring the abolition of the monopoly of the post-office clerks, in regard to the sale of newspapers. This monopoly was an extreme hardship upon the independent tradesman, and it was principally through the active exertion and the judicious conduct of Mr. Hilton, that an end was put to so nefarious a traffic. The respectable body of newsvenders in the metropolis, at, it is believed, his suggestion, formed themselves into a society, for their mutual protection against the schemes

* J. Brough Taylor's MSS. † Penes Rev. J. Raine.

‡ Who furnished a *blind* pedigree in 1575, and omitted his own father!

and manœuvres of Dicas and others; of which society Mr. Hilton was the honorary secretary, and discharged his duties with exemplary assiduity and fidelity, under circumstances which imposed on him no ordinary responsibility. Several prosecutions and convictions took place, while he held this situation, among which was that of Mr. Onwhyn, the respectable bookseller, of Catherine Street, Strand, for selling the *Satirist* newspaper. On the occasion of these vindictive proceedings against the news trade, a subscription was entered into by the persons principally interested; but though nearly all the trouble fell on Mr. Hilton, it is almost certain that so far from his deriving any advantage from it, he was a considerable loser both of time and money. Mr. Hilton was enlightened, liberal, philanthropic, and benevolent beyond his means.

Hylton, of Hilton in Staindropshire, Darlington, and Stranton.

It cannot be doubted that the match of THOMAS HILTON OF HELTON BACON, paved the way for the immediate admittance of his younger son, Lancelot, into the ranks of squirarchy in the county palatine.* Catherine

* "The Pedigree of the ancient family of Hilton, of the County Palatine of Durham, compiled from the records in the College of Arms, London, by William Radcliffe, Rouge Croix, Pursuivant of arms, 1809," which was procured by Mr. Surtees for the late Henry Hilton, of Barnard-castle, being merely taken from the imperfect records of the Heralds' College, misses out two or three generations, and being unaware of the Brackenbury match, although given in the Durham visitation of 1575, Radcliffe has with some show of probability supposed Lancelot Hylton to have been son of John Hilton, of Gainford, who was in truth his uncle. I am not certain whether Lancelot's grandmother was daughter of Thomas Blenkinsop, who died about 1546, and who was married about 1532, or of his father, Thomas Blenkinsop, esq., who died about 1522, by Eleanor Leigh. Radcliffe says the former, I incline to think the latter; but as from the early marriages then prevalent, his theory is *possible*, I will (in order to escape any family reflections for being too severe a herald, and downright disturber of cherished honours) here briefly give the royal descent, disclosed by accepting the line adopted in the Heralds' College pedigree.

KING EDWARD III., by his queen Phillippa of Hainault, had a second son,

LIONEL DUKE OF CLARENCE, who, by his wife Lady Elizabeth de Burgh, had an only daughter and heiress,

PHILIPPA, who married Edmund Mortimer Earl of March, and had issue

ELIZABETH MORTIMER, who married Sir Henry Percy, knt., the gallant Hotspur, and by him bore

ELIZABETH PERCY, who by her first husband, John de Clifford (slain at Meaux, 10 Hen. V.), had a son

THOMAS DE CLIFFORD, slain at St. Albans, for the red rose, 1455, having had issue by his wife Joan, daughter of Thomas Lord Dacre of Gilsland, by Philippa, daughter of Ralph Neville, the great Earl of Westmoreland, a daughter

JOAN DE CLIFFORD, who by her husband, Sir Richard Musgrave, of Eden Hall, knt., (he died in 1491) was mother of

SIR EDWARD MUSGRAVE, of Harclay, knt., who married Joan, dau. and coh. of Sir Chr. Ward, of Grindall, co. York, and had a fifth daughter named

MAGDALENE MUSGRAVE, who, about 24 Hen. VIII. (1532-3, her marriage articles being dated that year) wedded Thomas Blenkinsop, esq., of Helbeck (will dated 37 Hen. VIII., 1545-6), and with various other daughters, is said to have had the one mentioned in Dugdale's visitation, 1666, as

. . . ., daughter of Thomas Blenkinsop, of Helbeck, who married [say about 1549] ROBERT HILTON, esq., of Helton Bacon, whose eldest son

THOMAS HILTON, of Hilton Bacon, married [say about 1566] Catherine Brackenbury, eldest daughter of Anthony Brackenbury, of Selaby, gent. (Inq. p.m. 8 Aug. 1556). Her brother, Cuthbert, married about 1528, and her brother Henry was born about 1529. She seems to have returned with her son, Lancelot, to her own country and friends, and was buried at Gainford in 1587, having had issue

THOMAS HILTON, whose eldest son was born in 1584, and LANCELOT HYLTON, who married Catherine Alwent (aged 16), in 1587, and originated the South Durham Hyltons.

This accepted plan requires each head of the last three generations, on the average, to marry at the age of 16 or 17.

Mr. Walbran obliged me by a copy of the Hylton pedigree, printed for the second part of his History of Gainford. Surtees, Radcliffe, and he differ in some minute points and dates. When I have not been able to refer to the original register, I have given the month or year only, and not the day in dispute, so as to be right as far as I go.

Brackenbury* was great grand niece of Sir Robert Brackenbury, the celebrated lieutenant of the Tower, whose character has been so variously represented; and through her the Hiltons acquired a tinge of blood from each of the great families of Wycliffe, Bowes, Greystock, Audley, Fitz-Hugh, Scrope, Marmion, St. Quintin, Grey of Rotherfield, Willoughby of Eresby, "bold Beauchamp," Mortimer, (through whom a descent from king John and earl Strongbow), and, not to multiply fine names by the dozen, from the Veteripontes, the ancient lords of Westmoreland, in honour of whom they wore their constant annulets. So distinguished was this latter family that the Barons of Hylton, who had heired the blood of a younger branch by the Stapletons, always quartered Veteriponte, whatever other quarterings they might omit or insert.† Lancelot Hilton occurs in the family transactions of the Brackenburies, and in 1601, Henry Brackenbury leaves "unto my nephewe, Lancelot Hilton, fortie shillings in money."‡ By his wife Elizabeth Smelt,§ he had a younger son, Lancelot, who settled at Durham; and left to his own resources, turned out an eminent attorney, though perhaps rather a shifting one, as we find him collector of the obnoxious ship-money in Crossgate constablery, in 1635-6; and yet sufficiently in favour with the succeeding powers as to be appointed under-sheriff for this county during the usurpation, in 1652. His first marriage with Mary Colmore was as glorious for his family as his grandfather's. It brought in descent from Fulthorpe, Crathorne, Burgh, Metcalfe of Nappa, Lumley, Swinnow, Booth, Blakiston, Conyers, Lisle, Langton. Clervaux, Killinghall, Herdewyke, &c., and in compliment to the lady's brother, Abraham, that patriarchal name. Her grandmother died in childbed in 1592, and dean Matthew preached her funeral sermon (as we learn from his diary) from Genesis xxxv, 19 and 21.|| Hilton's second wife, the ancestress of the Barberini branch, was buried 4 July, 1675. Before a year had elapsed he found himself sufficiently composed in mind to marry a third spouse, a lady whose former husband (William Hilton, of Newcastle, descended from Nicholas Hilton, before mentioned) had died not two months before. He occurs of Hilton, near Staindrop, in 1658. It was an ancient manor of the Bowes family; and in those days when the most distant consanguinities were carefully remembered, it is possible that his own descent from Bowes through Wycliffe and Hilton had place in directing his feelings. His son,

* "The black lion under the oken tree
Made the Normans to fight and the Saxons to flee."

Var. "The black lion under the tree
Made the Normans to fight and the Saxons to flee."

Var. "The Brackenbury under the tree
Made the Normans to conquer and the Saxons to flee."

The first of these well describes the crest of Brackenbury. It is said to have been written on the tomb of Perse Brakenbury, who is reported to have accompanied the Conqueror from Brakenbury in Neustria!

† The full bearing was Gules 6 annulets, 3, 2, and 1, or; but the Hylton Barons often wore them as only 2 and 1. An instance of this practice occurs in a window in Croft church, in the chantry of the Clervaux, the heiress of whom married Thomas Baron of Hylton, where the annulets are gules on a field of or.

‡ "Lanc. Hilton" is also witness to the will. 44 Eliz. Eliz. Dei. Gra., &c., Will'o Bowes mil. *Nic'o Hilton* et Mich'i Walker cl'icis s. Cu' Henr. Brakenburie de Osmondcroft in co. D. arm' et senio confectus, &c. (Randal's MS. Book of Pedigrees, *not* in the D. and C. Lib., sub tit. Bowes.)

§ Of a highly respectable visitation family, of Kirkby Fleetham, in Richmondshire. Her father was seneschal and secretary to Emanuel Lord Scroope, of Bolton, and her grandmother Ann, dau. of . . . . Conyers, of Hutton Bonville. Her brother, Thomas of Hornby, gent., was admitted to a burgage in Blackwellgate, Darlington, 1627, under her father's will, but he sold it the following year.

|| Hutchinson's Durham, ii., 212. *Sed qu.* if not 16 *to* 21 meant.

Abraham, married a daughter of Marley, of Hilton, and purchased the manor of Hilton of her family. Lancelot, after seeing his sons in the best worldly weal, died, aged 77, and was interred in the Abbey yard at Durham, in great honour with his friends.* Cuthbert, his fourth son, also an attorney, succeeded at Durham for a very brief span, dying the next year, and was buried the same day that he died, in the night, as near to his father as possible.† His descendants were in the law at Auckland, and one of the females married Sir William Richardson, of Bishop-Auckland and Kelso, bart.

ABRAHAM HILTON of HILTON, esq., the eldest son, married two Eleanors, but his only child, Mary Hilton, died under two years of age. He attained a high position‡ in his profession of the law; and he, Sir Robert Eden, bart., and John Spearman, gent., were the trustees to whom James Mickleton, the eminent Durham antiquary, in 1693 left his MSS. for four years, and afterwards, as to certain of those papers, to the same persons or their nominee, till they were printed. The childless old lawyer lived to the great age of 88, having survived all his younger brethren, and called in the descendants of his next brother Richard to the succession. RICHARD HILTON was an attorney of Darlington, of which borough he was sometime bailiff, and in the most extensive practice of the day. Scarcely a title in Darlington exists without the gallant signature of old Richard as attesting witness. He seems to have been in great goodwill with his clients, the churchwardens; indeed, he once filled that office himself, but I suspect that he was deeply tinged with puritanism, as a commission is awarded out of the Durham Court of Chancery, in 1666, to administer to Mr. Richard Hilton (who had served his brother, Mr. Abraham, as a clerk for seven years) "the oath of [supremacy, *struck out*] allegiance, and the usuall oath of an attorney." I also suspect that his brother Cuthbert's night burial was in consequence of some recusancy, *non obstante* his intimacy with the Bow parson. Both father and sons seem to have played their religious cards admirably.

One of Richard Hilton's daughters, Mary, married Henry Forth, esq., an active magistrate of Darlington, the son of Albinia, youngest and posthumous daughter of the great Sir Harry Vane.§ Another wedded Captain Anthony

* "Mr. Lancelot Hilton, my very kind, much esteemed, and honoured friend, departed 28 May, buried near his brother [in the law] Christopher Mickleton, in the Cathedral churchyard, 29 May, 1685."—*St. Mary-le-Bow Par. Reg., Durham.* He had been a subscriber to the rebuilding of that fabric in 1637.

† "Mr Cuthbert Hilton, son of the said Lancelot, my like friend in all respects, departed this life the 28th day of April, 1686, and was interred in the night, in a grave adjoininge and as neare his father as possible."—(*Bow Reg.*) "Cuthbertus Hilton, Gen. ad Legem Attornatus, obiit et sepultus fuit xxviii die Aprilis Anno Dni MDCLXXXVI . . . . . ."—(*Monumental slab, Abbey yard.*)

NIGHT FUNERALS.—In 1631, Edm. Bolton (an heraldic writer) complains to Sir William Segar of nocturnal funerals "now so frequent, but well deserving (in my poor opinion) together with the first devisers (sonns of night and of the earth) to bee buried in the darknesse and dust of oblivion." Those who bear arms, he says, "ought to have solemnitie in rule." "My good freind (of immortal memorie) William Camden late Clarenceux king of arms, did both by word of mowth, and in a special leter, occasionallie complain unto mee, against these blanck nocturnal funerals, which to mee doe seem to resemble somewhat infernal, or mask as it were of lucifugian ghosts and furies. Certainly (in my poor opinion, as I have alreadie said) they are unfit for the noble, who have ensignes and markes of honor to display, and should so have spent theyr time, that theyr luciflorian deeds should not need, after theyr deceases, to fear either speech or light." The funerals in question were it seems "a bane to the heralds' rightfull benefit, and of the principal meanes of theyr laudable maintenance."

‡ "Those that have been the most eminent practisers (now living) [of Durham] are, Mr. John Spearman, Mr. Ra. Gowland, Mr. Fra. Mascall, R. Spearman, Joseph Hall, Abraham Hilton."—(*Gutch's Coll. Curiosa*, ii., 108.)

§ "Mr. Forth used often to say that his mother Albina was begot in the Tower of Lon-

Smith, of the army, and was deservedly esteemed for her many virtues. Their father died aged 73, and the two succeeding generations of Abrahams formed an exception to the previous longevity of the family. ABRAHAM HILTON, of Blackwell and Darlington, died in his father's lifetime, and his son, ABRAHAM HILTON, of Cockerton and Hilton, the legatee of his grand-uncle Abraham primus, lived only to the age of 42. He married a coheiress of Surtees, of Myers Flatt, par. Haughton, whose mother was a Hewgill, of Smeaton, in Richmondshire. After her husband's death, she lived, to the age of 86, with one faithful domestic in the snug house in Hungate, which long after was the home of her daughter Mary Hilton,* an ancient maiden lady of 74, and her representatives the Lees. Both mother and daughter rest in the Surtees' burial ground at Haughton le-Skerne, a sunny, comfortable, high, dry bed.†

HENRY HILTON, esq., of Hilton, son of the Surtees match, greatly delighted in horse races, and married a relation, a Miss Hewgill, of Smeaton. He died, aged 29, childless, and the only male descendant of old Richard Hilton the wealthy lawyer was his brother ABRAHAM HILTON, who succeeded to the Hilton estates and spent them. He had been one of the six clerks of Chancery, and the character of this member of his "fine talented family, who had minds far above the common run" (according to a sturdy veteran of Darlington's definition of this branch of Hilton), was that of a witty, flashy, extravagant, reckless, kind-hearted squire of the toping school. At London he was the constant and good-natured butt of the gallants in Gray's Inn coffee-house, and his clever answers generally set the table in a roar. Some military sprigs were one night holding a grave dissertation on martial matters, and on a sudden stopped, saying, that after all it was little use their talking over matters which could be of no interest to a lawyer, who they didn't suppose knew what fortifications meant at all. "You are mistaken," said Abraham, drily, "*forti-fications* are *twice-twenty-fications*." At Hilton he was the rhymster for all the neighbourhood. The famous blacksmith epitaph, "My sledge and hammer lie reclined," &c., in Gainford churchyard, is traditionally his, but if so, it could only be a mere application of a composition as old as the hills. A sign for a Killerby publican rests on a better foundation.‡ Being "far too good for this world," he was compelled to sell Hilton manor for 10,040*l.* to the Earl of Darlington in 1789, but he died at his ancient seat the same year, and was buried in Darlington church, under a rhyming layerstone which remains in the Westernmost bay of the North aisle.§

don the night before Sir Henry Vane, her father, was beheaded."—(*Geo. Allan, in Hutchinson's Durham.*) "Here lieth the body of Mary, the wife of Henry Forth, esquire, who departed this life the 18th Dec., 1728. Henry Forth, esquire, died June 17, 1746, aged 72." —(*Flag in Western bay of Darlington Church.*) At his death, a dole was given by "The Honorable Hen. Vane, esqr." to the poor, which was distributed in Blackwell along with Buck's dole the January following.

* Her brother Abraham *ultimus*, of Hilton, and Ann his wife conveyed to her, in 1772, five mess. and garden on the South side of Houndgate, in the tenancy of James Allan, Margaret Hilton and others.

† "In memory of Margaret Hilton, widow of Abraham Hilton, who died 16th of Novr. 1789, aged 86. Also of Mary Hilton their daughter, who died 7th of Feb., 1807, aged 72."—(*Headstone, Haughton.*) The descendants of Richard Hilton were generally buried in Darlington church.

‡ "At Killerby Charles Hogg does dwell,
And he has got good ale to sell;—
The ale is good, be not in haste;
Pray, gentlemen, walk in and taste.—
Also bread, the staff of life,
Sold by Mary, Charles Hogg's wife."

§ "To the memory of Abraham Hilton of Hilton, who departed this life December the 22d. 1789, aged 55 [should be 58, as he was baptized in 1731.]

Of his sons, ABRAHAM, a lawyer, and one of the six clerks in Chancery* who had been brought up an attorney at Darlington, died in 1792, aged 25, being succeeded by his brother HENRY HILTON, *ultimus suorum*, who was a well-known spirit merchant at Barnard-castle. He had the fair blue eyes of his ancestors, and will be long remembered as the cultivator of an enormous patriarchal beard, and as bathing every morning, winter and summer, in *Hilton's Hole*, as that part of the Tees is now called from the circumstance. Even when the ice was thickly spread on his accustomed haunt, he would break it and courageously leap into the cold, comfortless stream. A younger brother WILLIAM FREEMAN HILTON, who was in the army, and was drowned at the age of 23, on board an East Indiaman, in the Bay of Bengal, on his passage homeward, was a remarkably handsome young man, and at Denton school was famed for his delicate flaxen hair, which hung down his back in long and small crisp ringlets, after the manner of one of the wigs of Charles II.'s time. "I never saw such hair before or since," said one of his school-fellows to me; and when he recalled the memory of Freeman to an elder of Gainford, "And was'nt he a fine fellow?" the other exclaimed in exstacy, "Why, bless ye, they can't mak sike now!" Another star of light at the rustic academy was MARY ANN HILTON, his sister, full of life, and joy, and mischief, and well remembered for her pious frauds in promising apricots, and peaches, and rare fruits (which excited the imagination of her boyish comrades in no small degree, but of which the gardens at Hilton are stated to have been very innocent in their country riches of good old plums and substantial apples) in order to have her sums worked for her; for I believe persons of light and airy temperament are rarely very grave arithmeticians. She died of consumption at the age of 25, and was buried in Darlington church. JAMES SURTEES HILTON, another of this last generation of the Hiltons of Hilton, an officer in the army, died aged only 22, soon after his return from the West Indies. And thus they passed away, and the representation of their branch ran into the issue of the only one who married, MARGARET HILTON. She was the wife of Mr. Harrington Lee, an eminent mercer of Darlington, who built Polam Hall and Tees Cottage, both near that town, where he successively resided. He was injured by his thrashing machine at the latter place, which crushed him against a wall, and he lived only a week after. His wife died of apoplexy brought on by an attack of tic doloreux. Of their children, William Lee, the eldest, died at Caen in 1823,

Here whilst his soul ascends its native skies
The dust of much lamented Hilton lies,
O'er which each feeling heart must sure bestow
The genuine tear of unaffected woe;
For in his character not only blend
The tender husband, parent, gen'rous friend,—
The social virtues of his boundless mind
Prov'd him the general friend of all mankind."

Arms: Three annulets, in chief a trefoil between two saltires. *Crest:* A demigriffin charged with a trefoil. The wife of the jolly squire thus commemorated, was a Close, of Richmond Of all the families of Richmond, "none ranked during the last century before the Closes. They were a house of lawyers, and appear to have risen and flourished in the law. They were Town Clerks of Richmond continuously for about a century." John Close, esq., clerk of assize for the Northern district resided a short time at Scorton, and intending to reside at Easby Hall, furnished it accordingly, but died very suddenly the night before he intended entering it, 4 April, 1772. Some genealogical account of the Closes may be seen from the able pen of W. D'Oyly Bayley, esq., in the Topographer and Genealogist, i., 559; but the husband of Mrs. Hilton, who is there made the cousin of John named above, is wrongly styled Benjamin. She died at Barnard-castle, aged 65, "of consumption," but was buried near her spouse.

* "Lately, at Darlington, Abraham Hilton, esq., one of the *sixty* clerks in the court of Chancery."—*Gent. Mag., October*, 1792. *Obituary.*

aged 27, and was buried by the English Consul in our national burial ground there, and a monument was afterwards erected to his memory by his father. The night this young man died in a strange land, his mother asserted that she distinctly saw his figure on going into the room where he had usually slept. She ran down stairs, exclaiming, "Oh! I am sure something has happened my poor boy," and became so ill that she was confined to her room for some weeks afterwards, though the news of her son's death did not arrive till after some time had elapsed. Harrington Lee, the second son, died young. Hilton Lee, the third, a surgeon at Stokesley, died there very suddenly, aged 27. He felt as it were a pain in his finger, this increased in extent till it reached his head, and he died in two hours.

After the sudden deaths of Mrs. Lee and Hilton Lee, Surtees Lee—"the last leaf on the blasted tree"—grew exceedingly nervous and fearful of a like fate. To such an extent did this feeling go that he would not sleep alone. His will excluded his own relations from the executorship, and the testator dying insolvent, and his estate being greatly wasted by the excesses of his boon companions, who came, as he said himself, "merely for what there was to drink," his treasured trifles—things which even in a bankrupt's case are held sacred—the splendid brocade dresses of the Hyltons, the visiting-dresses, bonnets and caps of his sister Mary, all the articles to which privacy attaches; nay, the very gown in which Mrs. Lee had been seized with her death-stroke, were brought to the hammer.* A burst of indignation attended so shameless an exhibition, and the scene was as unnatural as it was startling. The hardly suppressed feelings of the more educated part of the community were ever and anon offended by the brutal laughter of the mob at the ancient make of some of the habiliments brought out. The chrism-cloth of crimson, silver and golden threads, in which the members of the family of Hylton had for long been baptized, was purchased by Mr. Abraham Hilton, of Barnard-castle.†

Richard Hilton, the balival lawyer of Darlington, and founder of the stock last traced, had a brother ROBERT HILTON, of Durham, gent., whose descendants adopted the orthography Hylton, rather than Hilton. His daughter Alice, married for her third husband Thomas Bellasyse, esq., of Haughton-le-Skerne, and had by him an only child, Martha Maria Bellasyse, who married Richard Bowes, esq., and originated the family of Bowes, of Darlington.‡ ROBERT HYLTON, esq., the brother of Mrs. Bellasyse, commonly styled DR. HYLTON, an eminent surgeon, of Darlington, in 1727 bought Polam Hill, alias Glasensikes, for 600*l.*, and sold it in 1728 for 605*l.* to Lawrence Brockett, of Hilton, esq. He married first, his cousin Hannah Hilton, the bailiff's daughter, who died childless; second, Jane, coheiress of Isaac Surtees, of Myers Flatt, whose sister had married her husband's

* She was washing herself at the time, and the pin with which she had hastily fastened her tucked-up sleeve was still remaining in the gown when it was thus exposed.

† A gothic turreted headstone of some pretence, but very meagre execution, was erected in Haughton-le-Skerne churchyard. It presents an adumbration to the arms of Hylton, giving the field *purpure* and omitting the trefoil; and for a crest, a *wingless* griffin. "The family burial place of Harrington and Margt. Lee, of Darlington. Harrington died 28 Decr. 1824, aged 57 years. Margt. his wife died 13 Septr., 1830, aged 58 years. Hilton, their son, died 11 Jany., 1831, aged 27 years. Mary, their daughter, died 26 Novr., 1834, aged 35 years. Surtees, their son, died 14 Jany., 1842, aged 36 years." On an altar-tomb, S.E. of the church, is another child commemorated. "In memory of William Robson of Great Burdon, grandson of Wm. Wastell of the same place, who departed this life the 23rd of Decr., 1828, aged 78 years. Also Mary his wife, who died May the 26th, 1822, aged 69 years. Also on the 21st of April, 1831, aged 35 years *Margaret* [Lee] wife of their son William Robson of Stockton, who departed this life August 18th, 1838, aged 47 years.

‡ See pedigree of the descendants of Alice Hylton at the end of this memoir.

cousin, Abraham Hilton, by which matches the Hyltons became connected with the Robsons of Darlington.* By Jane Surtees Dr. Hylton had a son, Captain Abraham Hilton, brought up an attorney, who lived in the old-fashioned looking house at the East end of Haughton-le-Skerne, now occupied by the Miss Wrightsons, and was probably tinged with eccentricity. His constant perambulations on his front have perpetuated the name of "Captain Hilton's walk" to the distance between his house and what is now the "Black Lion Inn;" and in 1760 he joined the Quakers in returning gloves at Miss Dolly Allan's funeral. In 1753 he had received a scarf for the funeral of George Allan, esq., of Grange, but his rude conduct evidently caused his omission in the lists for that of John Killinghall, esq., in 1762. The altar-tomb to his memory existed in Surtees's time, to the West of the church of Haughton.† As it has totally disappeared, it was probably in that part of the churchyard now devoted to the formation of cottage gardens. His brother Robert Hilton, a midshipman, R.N., died in coming from the East Indies. Both were childless, and the male blood of their line ceased.

Dr. Hylton (who died in 1746) took unto himself a third spouse in Mary, the daughter and coheiress of Robert Weemes,‡ gent., the heiress of a manor at Stranton, and other lands, formerly belonging to her ancestors the Gibsons of Stranton, who is well remembered in tradition, in connection with divers heavy potations of old ale doled out in Christmas time at the manor-house of Stranton, where her husband resided after the marriage. She died in 1766.§

The only child of this marriage, Mary Hylton, or, as she afterwards spelt it, Hilton, the coheiress of her father, and whose family (on the extinction of the issue of George Bromley, the first husband of her mother "Madame Hylton," in Frances Pewterer, the wife of William Bacon Forster, esq., of Newton cap, and of William Bentham, of Lincoln's Inn, esq., F.A.S., and L.S.) became sole heirs of her mother, married the Rev. William Longstaffe, of a Westmoreland family,‖ curate of Sedgefield, under the learned Bishop

* See pedigrees of the Robsons and Peases, after the last pedigree.

† "Abraham Hilton, ob. 11th April 1778, ætat. 57. Elizabeth Hilton, ob. 28th Dec., 1788, ætat. 70."

‡ Originally of Little Ryle, in Northumberland, and connected with the Sheraton family of Weemes, represented by the Richmonds of Stockton. We have a tradition that the Weemes races of Durham came joyously out of Scotland on the heels of king Jamie, and certainly my great grandame quartered Weemes of Bogie, co. Fife. John Weemes, A.M., minister of Laythaker, in Scotland, was a learned writer on divinity, and in 1634, at the special recommendation of Chas. I., was inducted prebendary of the second stall at Durham. In 1644, there was a warrant to sequester two parts of the property of Robert Weemes, a papist at Trimdon. I am inclined to trace a line of the name at Darlington to him. Robert Weames of Darlington, shoemaker, a papist, bur. 23 May, 1724, mar. Susanna (bur. 31 Jan., 1714-5) and had a son Jo'n, a papist, bur. 8 Apr., 1718. Robert, s. Widow Weemes of Darlington, bur. 16 Nov., 1727. Thomas Weemes, a papist of Darlington, taylor, bur. 23 March, 1759.

§ "Mrs. Hylton of Hartlepool" gave 20*l.* to the Newcastle Infirmary in 1751. By will, 1766, Mary Hilton, then of the city of Durham, widow, gave to the poor of Stranton, Hart, and Monk-Heselton, 20*l.* each; and of Hartlepool, 40*l.* to be distributed in sums of not more than 1*l.*, nor less than 10*s.*, to each oldest housekeeper or poor family, and to the ministers of the same places 1*l.* 1*s.* each for their trouble.

‖ "The traveller was born at Soulby. Alas! his poor father felt the heavy hand of oppression; a favourite estate, which his ancestors had long and comfortably enjoyed, was wrested from him: this misfortune preyed upon his spirits a few years; he at length sunk under it, died of a broken heart, and his family was turned adrift upon the wide world. The memory of these particulars occasioned reflections bitter as wormwood; and were not a little aggravated from beholding the house that first covered me in a most inclement season converted into a barn." Family tradition states that this woeful passage in the vicar's MSS. for 1785, alludes to the circumstance that George Longstaffe his father owned an estate at one side of the stream which runs through Soulby; his neighbour on the opposite brink went to law with him about a petty matter which five shillings would have

Lowth,* where he resided some years after he was made vicar of Kelloe. He was appointed a Deputy Lieut. of the county of Durham in 1785, and chaplain to the Earl of Aboyne in 1796; was a tolerable poet, possessing a keen perception of the beauties of nature; and his sketches of his rural and topographical excursions, in which he much delighted, are drawn with a true and graphic hand. He was a remarkably short man, and very plain withal, and it is added that his talents must have been the only reason for Miss Hylton's preference. He occasionally resided in the Hylton manor-house at Stranton, and after his wife's death† had a cross old housekeeper there who made her puddings so heavy that they would, my father always said, roll down Roseberry Topping without breaking, under the pretext that "it was nae use making things that warn't substantial." He died in 1806, aged 73, having survived all his children save his daughter Mary Hilton, who married Mr. William Lynn, and whose descendants still preserve a portion of the Stranton estate.

His son William Longstaff, esq., a surgeon, had died in 1795, "aged 25 years, one month, 3 weeks, and 3 days." His wife was Ann Cornforth‡ who brought in another vein of Hylton blood. Her mother, Elizabeth Hylton, is said to have been daughter of a squire, a retired *Captain* in the army, who resided in an old hall house in Cumberland or Westmoreland, and to have lived at one time with a maternal uncle, a rich merchant in London, who, kind soul, had as he thought provided her a proper spouse in a wealthy old comrade of that city. It has not been a prevailing characteristic in the Hylton damsels to allow themselves to be bought and sold like cattle, by

rectified; they fought on, and both were ruined. The father retired to Sunderland; and William, his eldest son, under the patronage of honest old Yates, of birching memory at Appleby, was admitted at Magdalene College, Cambridge, in 1754.

* I possess a long friendly correspondence between rector and curate. In one place the latter had been assaulted by a parishioner, and obliged to take him before a justice, when he declined to prosecute, and showed all proper lenity. In another (1764), Louth, then a prebendary at Durham, writes, "Robinson, the clerk's son, has been just now with me to let me know that his father is going to marry Ann Gelson, and to desire me to put a stop to his design, if I can. He says that he has this day been here, and has actually got a licence. If the fool is capable of listening to any remonstrance, pray represent to him the scandal and inevitable ruin that will come upon him; and tell him from me, that I will take care, *that his marriage shall be immediately celebrated by his spouse's doing penance in the most public manner*, and that *he* shall officiate at the ceremony; and further, that *I will never rest till I have got him turned out of his place*: for if I cannot do it myself, I will complain of him to the bishop, as a scandal and offence to the parish. In short, I beg you to use all legal methods of preventing the execution of his purpose."

† "Heu! uxorem omnis curæ casusque levamen,
Amitto Mariam:—

"March the 9th 1778. At eight o'clock, in the morning of this dismal day, died my dear wife Mary Longstaff in the Rectory House at Sedgefield, after we had lived happily together in the married state *Eleven years and Eleven days*: and after she had born to me nine children—two of whom now survive her (viz.) William Longstaff and Mary Hilton Longstaff. May it please God to preserve and keep them!"—*Family Bible.*

‡ Mrs. Longstaff's eldest sister, Mary Cornforth, married Jonathan Midgley, esq., of Newcastle-upon-Tyne, descended from the famous Rev. George Hickes, D.D. Of their numerous family, two only survive, the Rev. Edward James Midgley, the perpetual curate of Medomsley, aud Mrs. Mary Elizabeth Taylor, of Cleadon, the widow of the lamented John Brough Taylor, esq., F.S.A., of Bishopwearmouth, one of the first collectors of his day; his ample mind grasping genealogy, numismatics, antiquities in general, botany, mineralogy, and his surgical profession, which would be happily relieved by skilful playing at chess or whist. He was indeed one of those happy individuals who could be delightful in any society. His own publications were confined to the reprinting of Hegge's Legend of Saint Cuthbert, from the Freville Lambton copy (now in his widow's possession), and the joint editorship (with Sir Cuthbert Sharp) of the Durham Heraldic Visitation of 1615, but he contemplated a minute survey of the geological strata on our Eastern coast. He was one of Mr. Surtees's main props, having an enormous collection of genealogical data, copies made by himself of voluminous visitations and ordinaries, &c.; and his assistance is warmly acknowledged in the work itself, but the reader will in vain search for his name among the Mainsforth guests in the life prefixed to the posthumous volume.

parents, guardians, or any body else; or to give their hands without their hearts, and Lizzie Hylton's fire in an instant rose. She fled; and some earlier connection with the Seaforth family induced her to attach herself to them, and take charge of the daughters of Lord Fortrose, who seems to have resided occasionally at Coxhoe, the estate of his mother the heiress of Kennet, who had died in exile at Paris in 1739, although pardon had been granted to her husband, the fifth Earl of Seaforth, in 1726. Miss Hylton is described as having been a very fine woman, and in every way calculated for her charge. Richard Cornforth was steward for the estate of the titular Lord Seaforth, and his son William married the fair runaway in 1754.* "None but the brave deserve the fair," and in proper obedience to the precept conveyed, the highminded girl had pitched on a man of no small prowess. William Cornforth was born at Manfield near Darlington, and was descended from a sturdy race of yeomanly gentry seated at Blackwell (where they were the largest copyholders) from the fourteenth century.† They had however broken up there at the close of the seventeenth century, and were dispersed into the country adjoining; keeping up, with a faithful memory of their Darlington origin, an inveterate fondness for their ancient names of Richard, William, and John. "Squire Cornforth, whom Yorkshire and Bishopric own for breeding and hunting's exceeded by none," lived at Barford on Tees, and was famed as the owner of the Barford red bull,‡ the sire of the celebrated Raby ox, which weighed when alive 240*st*. About 1772 he frequently occurs in the Northern race lists as owner of horses, one of which won the 50*l*. plate at Wakefield in that year. But I have heard a tradition in my family that the whole race was desperately addicted to horse racing and hunting, and that near Darlington is a place called "Cornforth's leap," a locality I have never pitched upon. Indeed, Elizabeth Hylton's spouse had such a liking for that sort of thing, that he had a race horse which was only prevented from winning at Stockton races by the saddle-band having dishonestly been cut nearly through, by which means it at last snapped and the jockey rolled off. He was a supervisor of excise, and possessing all the hardihood and daring of his Nimrodian ancestry, was the terror of the smugglers far and near. One of his most dangerous districts was Weardale, into which he penetrated fully armed with sword and pistols, and where, not being able to procure corn for such a purpose, he had to feed his charger with bread and beer. The deadly revenge of the smugglers proved the death of his son Richard, who was in the same service. Richard was on a

* It is traditionally said that the younger Seaforth followed the rash example of his father, (who d. 1740,) and was involved in the affairs of 1745, and in vain attempted to persuade Miss Hylton to accompany his family abroad. But I am in a "Scotch mist" in the matter, all I know being that Coxhoe was sold before 1749, that the titular earl died in 1762, and that William Cornforth could not be engaged to Elizabeth Hylton in 1745 (as tradition says to account for her love for English soil) since he was then aged about 13 only. His uncle John Cornforth is described as of Coxhoe Hall. What induced Lizzie to remain in the country from 1745 or 1749 to 1754, I know not. Her family had a Seaforth cradle, but it is now destroyed.

Aberdeen, Mar. 14, 1746. "All the advantages the rebels will have gained by taking fort George and fort Augustus; and the retreat of Lord Loudoun, will be drawing the seat of the war amongst the hills; and protracting it a little time; and the only junction they have gained there, is some few of the Mackenzies, headed by the *lady Seaforth*, but the lord of that name is with Lord Loudoun, as is Mr. Mackintosh, whose wife is likewise in the rebellion." [*If this be a contrivance, it may save or lose their heads, according as the word* WIFE *is understood.*]—*London Gazette, Mar.* 22, *quoted by Gentleman's Magazine of the day.*

† See pedigree annexed to this memoir. The bulk of the Cornforth lands in Blackwell subsequently passed by purchase to the Prescotts and Allans.

‡ Bought of Esquire Milbank, of Barningham.

fine full-blood mare in the Whitby district, and whilst he was off it, some wretches played the same trick as I have mentioned was done on the Stockton race course. But here the end was fatal. The young man dashed into a creek near Skinningrave. The water was high, and in its centre the girth gave way. The rider was plunged into the current and rose no more.

Some portraits and the locket of John Scott Hylton, esq., of Lapal House near Hales Owen, and agreeable letters from Shenstone to that gentleman (who was his friend and neighbour) have descended to the issue of Elizabeth Hylton.* He was an elegant scholar, a clever rhymster, and a large collector of coins. His relative, William Hilton Longstaff, esq., was also a minute amateur etcher, collector, and illuminator of coins, shields, book-plates, and seals.†

I would that the good and eloquent Surtees had lived to write the memoir to attach to his pedigree of the Hyltons ot Hilton and Darlington. *My* pen may be guided, and my opinions coloured by affection. Yet I have endeavoured to be impartial in my story, to hide no fault. I have no more earnest wish than that the landless heirs of Hylton may ever have a proper pride, a deep respect for the memory of the departed just, which will keep those who view their pedigree as a "great moral," from any tinge of meanness, rapacity, or dishonour. Their genealogy is besprinkled with the evil, but sparingly; and the beneficent Being who showered his blessing on their virtuous forefathers, will not cease to provide for them, if they do "that which is right in the sight of the Lord, according to all that their fathers have done." Let them never stoop to be busy flatterers, slaves of gold, and (if they rise again in temporal riches) forgetful of the claims of relatives who may not stand so high in earthly honour; but be they chivalrous, independent, and kind. There is a benefit in family history, which the irreligious, the miserable souls that despise it, cannot derive; and though, by the extravagance of those who "have spirted as do fountains through the air," the nourishing soil of more than one goodly branch of the

* He wore the arms of Hylton of Hylton Castle, but I scarcely know the connection, unless he was a Hylton of the Staffordshire family settled at Reahall. Among his papers is a letter from J. Hilton, Birmingham, 4 Oct., 1736, to "my dear sister" Mrs. Hilton at Mr. Fransisco's, in Plumb Tree street, St. Giles's, London, on the death of his father, on 29 Sept., who was bur. in Yardley church by desire. He mentions another sister and his mother who designed to be buried beside her husband at Yardley.—"*Capt.* Edmund Scott Hylton, manager for Ed. Garthwaite, to get a coat of arms 1748, and make out a pedigree."—*(Sir Cuth. Sharp's MSS.)*—Oddly enough, John Scott Hylton was an intimate friend and correspondent of my maternal ancestor, the Rev. Dr. Gaunt (a sort of crusader against early Methodism) and was witness to my grandmother's baptism. Dr. Gaunt had procured some of his memorials, which with his correspondence with him have now joined the papers &c. which came by my father's line. He settled at Lapal House, in 1753. He also corresponded and was on very friendly terms with the vivacious Lady Luxborough, and dying in 1793, aged 68, was buried in Hales Owen Church, under a stone which described him as "a safe companion, and an easy friend." Mrs. Cornforth d. in 1783, aged 62.

† I regret very much that I have neither blue eyes nor Saxon hair, and I very much doubt whether any antiquarian taste descends from their possessors to me. So that it is probable that old Dyer and I with our little brown peepers among the ruins of Rome would have been a much more companionable pair, than any one of my paternal namesakes with me. Still I have a fond clinging to my blue-eyed friends, and I would not have the memory of my sire wholly pass away. The grass grows green on his unrecorded grave, and some may only name him as the vendor of ancient family possessions. But I knew him as a man so full of curious information that we never walked without my returning struck with something new and attractive. I have his delicate armories, and limnings of flowers, and careful anatomical etchings. Many facts have, to my extreme mortification, died with him, and rendered the memoir of the Hyltons less ample than it might have been, for it must be owned that a very tithe of his genealogical knowledge was committed to paper. An arrangement for his admittance into the Heralds College fell through, but his collection of some 1200 bookplates, mostly original from old books, but many gorgeously illuminated designs from his own pencil, form a volume of no ordinary beauty, and prove him to have been most fitted for such an office.

stately cedar has utterly passed away, there is no real ground for repining. Some natural tears of sorrow may not be foregone, but yet

"We bide our time."

*** The old High-street passing over Pounteys Bridge, near Dinsdale, became gradually deserted, for that across Croft Bridge, in some measure it is said from the ferquent robberies in the wet hollow pass of County's Lane, and this tradition receives confirmation from a letter of Bp. Cosin. His lordship, be it premised, was anxious to secure the carriage of some gold into Yorkshire, to pay for the purchase of Brafferton. "Agree by private letters between Mr. Ralph Rymer and your selfe how the money shall be safely conveyed unto him according to the former agreement, which was, that hee should send two men to you to Durham, who might help to guard it with your own company to Brafferton [near Boroughbridge]; unto which company Dr. Gilbert will give order to two of his family at Greatham Hospitall, that upon your sending for them, they shall come provided to goe along with you from Durham; for *Mr. Hilton's sonne*, who brought your letter hither, tells us that he was in great danger to be robbed about *Darnton and Neesum* by thieves and highwaymen that lay upon the street there, to set upon passengers who they thought carried any money with them; and he named Barwick for one, a famous thiefe, with others in his company, besides one Middleton, and one Coperthwaite, who layd at Neesum for their prey, and that he was putt to ride full speed for four miles together to escape them in their pursuit of him. Therefore I shall pray you to be well appointed when you carry the money, and to let it get no wind before you take the journey for that purpose; and to give warning to Mr. Rymer, that the two men whom he intends to send to you shall not know or make it known to any person for what end they come to goe along with you. And so have you all the punctuall directions that I can give you herein: ouly you are to pay Mr. Rymer allowance of interest for two months after Michaelmas."—The road from Pounteys proceeds "with a truly Roman pertinacity," as Surtees remarks, to Sadberge, and thence to Stainton-*in-the-Street*.

Pedigree of Cornforth of Blackwell.

(See p. xlix.)

AGNES CORNFORTHE (probably the relict of JOHN CORNFORTH who held copyhold property at Cockerton at the date of Hatfield's survey, about 1380) having a widow's right surrendered in 30 Langley (1436-7) to her son

WILLIAM CORNFORTH, 2 mes. and 4 oxg. in Blackwell, to which his widow *Jane* was adm., 2 Sherwood (1487). In 11 Booth (1468-9) he surrendered 1 mes. ½ oxg. at Blackwell to his son

JOHN CORNEFORTH, who died about 1509, and had issue

JOHN CORNEFORTHE, called junior in 1506-7 when Robert s. John Hudson surr. to him half of 8 oxg. of Burdland at Blackwell: adm. s. and h. of John C., cousin (*consanguineus*, next of kin) and h. of Agnes C. to 2 mes. 1½ oxg. and 2 mes. 4 oxg. in 1 Ruthall, 1510. Mar. *Catherine*, d. and h. of *Richard Wolfehill*, who brought Topcliffclose at Blackwell to the Cornforths, and had issue

RICHARD CORNEFORTH, s. and h. to his mother, adm. as h. of his father to the 2 mes. 4 oxg., and to 1 oxg. of Burdland, 3 Wolsey, 1525. Mar. *Elen*, adm. as his widow to the 2 mes. 4 oxg. and the Bordland, 11 Tunstall, 1541, and had iseue

WILLIAM CORNEFORTH, adm. as s. and h. to the 2 mes. 1½ oxg., and the 2 mes. 4 oxg., 19 Tunstall, 1549, and had issue

ROBERT CORNEFORTH, on the authority of the admittance in 37 Eliz. to Topcliffclose (in which the whole descent from Catherine Wolfehill is stated) of his son William. On Jan. 1, 1569-70, *John Corneforth*, concerned in the Rising of the North, was received into the protection of the Earl of Warwick and the Lord Admiral.

William Cornefurthe, yeoman, Blackwell, acquired property in Towneland, Brakinmoore, Malande, and Stickbitchlande in 10 and 31 Eliz.: adm. to Topcliffclose, 37 Eliz.: bur. at Darlington 21 Dec., 1604: inq. p. m. 4 May 3 Jas. (held 9 acr. near Glasensike). He had issue

Cuthbert.
? Frances Cornfoorth, mar., 1591, to *Anthony Branson.* In 1642, Frances Branson held halfe of Stickbitch.
? Elizabeth Cornforth, bur. 1596-7.
? Margaret Cornforth, bur. 1597.

Cuthbert Cornfoorthe, of Blackwell, s. and h. aged 40, 4 May. 3 Jas. (1606) acquired half of Adamponds lands in 37 Eliz.: bur. 27 Apr., 1616. Mar. *Jane,* adm. 15 Jas. as widow to Adamponds lands, &c., and bur. 9 Sep., 1657, her son William paying 10*s.* for "his mother's layrestall" in the church. At the division of Blackwell commons she obtained 167 acr. 20 p. in Little Ings, Milne feild, North feild, Snipe, Horseclose and Brankinmoor (by her own request), and 31 acr. on Brankinmoor abutting on France Dike on the N. and Darneton Moor on the E. The commissioners usually set out for every original oxgang 19 acr. in the Townefeilds, and 1 acr. on Brankinmoor. Cuthbert and his wife had issue

i. William, bp. 1600, br. 1601.
ii. Richard, of Blackwell, adm. as s. and h. to his father's Blackwell lands, 22 Cha. I.: bp. 1601-2, held the largest copyhold in Blackwell, 1642, having with other towneland, boordland, coterights, &c., Stickbitche flatt, France, and half of Stickbitch: bur. 25 Jan., 1655-6, in the church. In 1636 he was collector of the obnoxious ship-money in the Darlington division. In 1653 there was letten by the Darlington wardens to John Ratcliffe and his wife two seates in the backer of souther most stall that was Richard Cornforth, and to Raphe Wilson one seat for himselfe in the same stall. In 1655 to Wm. C. that stall which was his brother Richard's, and in 1658 to the same, tow seats in his owne stalle for tow of his children which was John Rattlefes and his wife's seats, received 2*s.*
iii. William, bp. 1605, owned in 1642 (when the Cornforths were the largest copyholders in Blackwell) property in towneland, the noutebrigg loning being 9 acr. town land (Snipe lane), a midding stead *nowe belonging to Branson howse*, the fower bankes and a threshwood stead: held Nordykes (now the property of R. H. Allan, esq.): liv. 1675: "1636, Received of Willm. Corneforth of Blackwell, for one seat in the stall that joynes of Mr. Hopes pue where he reades common prayer on the West side (elsewhere called "of the West side of the pulpit and next to it")." Mar. *Susannah,* bur. in the church, 19 Mar. 1676-7, and had issue

i. Francis, bp. 1656.
ii. Cuthbert, bp. and bur. 1644, in the church.
iii. William, bp. 1647-8. *Qu.* William Cornforth, of Darlington, shoemaker, Roman-catholic, bur. 8 Mar., 1727-8, who by his wife Mary, liv. a widow, Rom. Cath. in 1728 he had issue *Mary,* bur. 30 May, 1728, R. C., and probably also *William Cornforth,* a cutler, papist, Darlington, bur. 1761.
? iv Cuthbert C., junior (in distinction to his cousin Mr. Cuthbert), of Blackwell, occurs as such at least till 1685, had a son by Elizabeth Younge *Robert Cornforth alias Younge* bp. 24 Nov., 1666, and by his wife Elizabeth [Younge?] (bur. 25 Dec., 1680, as wife of Chuthbert C. of B.) a son Thomas, bp. 3 July., 1679.

*** 1680. "Cuth. Cornforth in right of his father the tow seats fore in that pew which his father had commonly called by the name of *Cornforth seates* on the South alley adjoyning upon Mr. Middleton pew on the North being built at the charge of his predecessesers."

1. Elinor, bp. 1639.
2. Suzanna, bp. 1641.

iv. Thomas.
v. John, of Blackwell, bp. 1614-5, bur. 20 Apr. 1659, in the church. He had issue

i. Mr. John Cornforth, of Blackwell, bp. 18 June, 1644; a collector for the poor, 1667; Will 1 Mar., 1675, by which he left 40*l.* to the poor of Blackwell, the profit to be distributed yearly,—nieces, Elizabeth and Mary Fawcett (under 18)—nephew, Whayre Fawcett (under 15)—if my brother Fawcett dye without issue begotten of my sister, reall estate to Cuthbert Cornforth—brother Edward Burbeck, brother Richard Burbeck and sister Jane Burbeck, cossen Christopher Hodgson and Anthony Elgye, Michael Hodgson and John Elgye their sons, uncle William Cornforth and cosen Cuthbert Cornforth 20*s.* a piece to buye them rings—Robert Swainston 40*s.* to make amendment for his bargain—Phillis which was the servant of Roger Fowler 40*s.* for her wage. Bur. in Darlington church, 4 Mar., 1675-6. Mar., in 1671, Bridget, dau. of Edward Birkbeck, esq., of Hornby, liv, 1685. d. s. p.
1. Jane, mar. to Whayre Fawcett, and had issue. "1676, For Mr. Fawcett child larestall—for laying stone over Mr. Fawcett child—1680, Mr. Fawcet mother larestall—for Mr. Fawcett chyld grave stone—1684, for Mr. Whayre Fawcet child leyre-stall."

1. Margaret, bp. 1598, mar. in 1621, *Timothy Hutton* of Blackwell, and had issue, Elenor, bp. 1622; Anne, 1623-4 (bur. 1634); Christofer, 1629; and Robert, 1634.
2. Jane, bp. 1600, bur. 1601.

Qu. Elizabeth Cornforth, of Blackwell, bur. 29 Jan., 1674-5.

THOMAS CORNFORTH, of Blackwell, bp. 1612, possessed, *inter alia*, in 1642, 14 acr.' in Stickbitch nooke, quondam Geo. Garnett's, and the howse quondam Mr. Place's, bur. 2 Mar., 1668-9. Mar. 22 Dec., 1638, *Anne Taylor*, bur. 2 Feb., 1661-2, by whom he had issue

i. William, bp. and bur. 1661.
ii. CUTHBERT.
iii. John, bp. 1659.
1. Margaret, bp. 1642, bur. 1642-3, in the church.
2. Jane, bp. 1645-6.
3. Frances, bp. 1653-4.
4. Frances, bp. 1655.

MR. CUTHBERT CORNFORTH, of Blackwell, of Tollthorpe, co. York, gent., 1674 (when he sold part of the present Woodside property); of Darlington, 1681, bp. 21 Jan., 1640-1; bur. 20 Nov., 1711, at Darlington; adm. in right of his father Thomas to 2 seats or places described in 1688 as on the North side of the middle alley adjoyning to pew belonging to a certain house in Darlington called the White horse. Mar. *Mary*, bur. 13 May, 1715, as of Darlington, widow, by whom he had issue

i. Francis, bp. 1666-7. *Qu.* Francis Cornforth, of Durham, who mar. Mary Simson, of Darlington, 4 Dec., 1709, and was mayor of Durham 1711, 1716, 1723.
ii. Charles, bp. 1668.
1. Elizabeth, bp. 1670.
2. Ann, bp. 1676, bur. 27 Sep., 1781, in the church.
3. Mary, bp. 1679.

*** Crispin Viewly, shoemaker, and Grace Cornforth, both of Darlington, m. 19 Nov., 1749.

Descendants of Alice Hylton. (Bowes of Darlington).

THE family of Bowes of Darlington claims origin from the great house of Streatlam, and there is little doubt of the correctness of this family tradition, which is supported by long continued usage of arms.* There is direct evidence of descent through Hylton, Brackenbury, and Wycliffe. They have also the honour of representing the Durham branch of the ancient family of Bellasis. I have not a tittle of new matter to add to the excellent pedigree of this latter eminent house given by Mr. Surtees. Sir William Bellasis of Newborough Abbey, co. York, eldest son of Richard Bellasis, of Murton, par. Houghton-le-Spring, had issue Sir Henry, the ancestor of the Earls of Fauconberg; Bryan, from whom descended the houses of Owton, par. Stranton, Brancepeth Castle, and Murton House; and James, of Owton, par. Stranton, the donor of the Howdens charity to the parish of Darlington, who died childless. In after times the families of Owton and Brancepeth Castle became extinct by the deaths of Henry Bellasyse (the eldest representative of the Owton branch) who was living in Cheshire in 1794, aged 84, s. p. and of Bridget Bellasyse last descendant of the Brancepeth family, in 1774, unm. when the representation devolved on Thomas Bowes, Esq. of Darlington, the grandson of Thomas Bellasis, of Haughton-le-Skerne, the last heir male of Bellasis, of Murton House.

The following letters may amuse my readers before they plunge into the cold bath of pedigree. The first is from the Harleian MSS., the second in

* The customary bearings of Bowes and Bellasis are given quarterly.

the possession of Thomas Bowes, esq., and is addressed to his ancestor Col. William Belasys, son of the sheriff mentioned in the earlier epistle.

"Salutem in Christo.—Sir,—Nowe I knowe to whome I am beholding for twoe younge roebucke pyes, and I thanke you heartily for them. They came not as you intended, but I will take leave to tell you how they came. The twoe pyes came to me a little before Christmas, as moldye as if they had been sent from a farre countrye. No direction at all came with them, but only that they came from Duresme; soe I thought they had been my lord bishop's kindnes, and either I did give him thankes for them, or intended to doe. Nowe in the midle of May came your letters, by which I understand the pyes came from you, and truly I thanke you as heartily as if they had come to me in very good case, for soe I knowe you intended them. And with these thankes I leave you to the grace of God and rest,—Your loveing freinde,—W. Cant.—Lambeth, June 3, 1634.—To my very loveing freind, Sir William Bellasys, sheriff of the bishopricke of Durham, these." [This "W. Cant." was the celebrated Archbishop Laud.]

"Brusselles, 18 March, 1660.—This bearer hath informed me of the greate affection and zeale you haue for my service, and of the opportunity and interest you haue to advance it, which I doute not you will use with all the dexterity you can: It is not possible for me in these greate changes and variety of accidents which euery day fall out, to giue you any instructions for the carrying on my seruice; nor can I dislike the methode the bearer tells me you intende to obserue, but you will best iudge with the aduice of my frindes who are upon the place with you, what is most proper and seasonable to be done, towards the atteyning the good end you ayme at; and I hope God will blesse your ioynte endeavours for the peace and happynesse of the Nation: You will easily beleeue I haue the sence I ought to haue of your care and kindnesse, of which, if God blesse me, you shall finde the effects; and that I am, Your very affectionate frinde,—Charles R."—*Seal—France and England; quartering Scotland and Ireland.—C.R.*

The letter is *Stuartish* to the backbone, the loyalty and losses of the sheriff's sons, which nearly occasioned the utter ruin of the family passed unrewarded amidst the crowd of suffering loyalists, and Murton seems to have been sold soon after the colonel's death.

Mr. Bowes has also a handsome miniature set in gold of a Sir William who is said to have perished at Naseby. He is a puzzling personage, though doubtless some scion of the Murton race, for the sheriff, the only *Sir* William, died in 1641, at the very commencement of the civil broils, and his gallant son William, the receiver of the letter, lived till 1678. The case is inscribed on the back:—"DULCE EST PRO REGE ET PATRIA MORI." Then the Belasis arms (a chevion inter 3 fleurdelis) and their motto. "BON. ET. BELLE. ASSEZ." Around:—*Effigies Gul. Bellassis Eqs. Aur'ti qui tempore Caroli primi in Bellis Civilibs. Angl. fortiter cecidit.*"

Alice, daughter of Robert Hylton, gent., named by Abraham Hilton, of Hilton, esq., as his niece, bur. 29 Nov., 1761, at Darlington, as "Alice Bellasis of Darlington, widow." Mar., first, Christopher Blacket, of Newham, co. Northd., gent. (son of John Blackett, of Hoppyland, esq.), who d. 13 Sep., 1712, ag. 27. M. I. Staindrop South aisle, by whom she had issue

i. Charles, d. inf.
ii. Another, d. inf.

She mar., second, Francis Smart, of Snotterton, gent., bp., 29 July, 1684, bur. 22 July, 1718, at Staindrop, and uncle to the unfortunate poet of the name, by whom she bore

Elizabeth, bp. 29 Sep., 1716, at Staindrop, d. unm. 1776.

And third, Thomas Bellasyse, of Haughton-le-Skerne, esq., who d. 27 Aug., 1751, having had issue

Martha Maria Bellasyse, only surviving child of Alice Hylton, b. 8 March, 1721, bur. 14 July, 1767. Mar. Richard Bowes. esq., surgeon, Darlington, son of Richard Bowes, who formerly held the manors of Boythorpe and Bugthorpe in Yorkshire. He d. 1757, having had issue

i. Charles, bp. 22 June, 1742, d. 12 July, 1746.

II. THOMAS.
III. Belasyse, bp. 22 Mar., 1750, bur. 16 Mar., 1752.
1. Martha Timothea, bp. 23 Nov. 1743, mar. 15 Nov. 1767 (signing "Marthatymothea Bowes") to *James Atkinson*, lieutenant upon half-pay in the 51st regiment of foot, and then of Darlington, gent.
2. Margaret, bp. 26 Apr., 1745, mar. 18 Sep., 1764, to *William Turner*, surgeon, Darlington. She was living a widow at Selby, Yks.
3. Ann, bp. 29 May, 1747, d. 14 Feb., 1749.
4. Frances, bp. 22 Feb., 1748, mar. 19 May, 1771, to *Thomas Meslen Browne*, of Selby, surgeon.

THOMAS BOWES, esq., an attorney, Darlington, bp. 15 Aug., 1753, bur. 16 Apr., 1806. Mar. *Dorothy Stephenson*, of Huntingdon, 8 Feb., 1776, at Darlington, and by her (who was bur. 23 Apr., 1812) had issue

I. THOMAS.
II. Richard, bp. 20 Aug., 1780, d. 3 Jan., 1781.
III. William, bp. 1789.

1. Isabella, bp. 9 Apr., 1778, d. 1785.
2. Martha Maria, bp. 1779, d. 26 July, 1797.
3. Anne, bp. and bur. 1782.
4. Mary Eleanor, bp. 11 Nov., 1784, mar. 1 Aug., 1804, *James Agnew*, of Howledge, co. pal., esq., captain in 8th foot.
5. Isabella, mar. the *Rev. John Topham*, of Droitwich.

THOMAS BOWES, esq., attorney at law, Darlington, and Borough Bailiff of that town 1816—1846, bp. 23 Feb., 1777, d. 3 Oct., 1846. At his funeral the shops were closed and a muffled peal was rung. Mar. *Elizabeth*, d. of David *Crawfurd*, of Howledge, co. pal. They had issue

I. THOMAS.
II. Richard, of Havre-de-Grace, b. 14 Mar., bp. 10 Apr., 1818, mar. *Hester*, second daughter of *Mons. le Forestier*, of Havre de Grace.
III. Charles Belasyse, bp. 20 Nov., 1819, bur. 3 Mar., 1820.
IV. Charles Belasyse (II.), bp. 18 Oct., 1820, bur. 7 Mar., 1821.
V. George, b. 1 July, bp. 23 July, 1824.

1. Dorothy.
2. Catherine.
3. Martha Maria, d. 27 Sep., 1829.
4. Elizabeth, mar., July, 1840, *John Hull Fell*, esq., of Belmont, Uxbridge, co. Middlesex.

THOMAS BOWES, esq., attorney at law, Darlington, the present representative of the family, b. 14 Apr. bp. 8 May, 1813.

*** The dates are from Darlington.

††† 10 Oct., 1636. James Bellasses of Owton in the Countye Pallatyne of Durham Esquire of sound bodie—to be buried in the Parish Church of Stranton neare vnto my late wife Mary of famous memory deceased, and doe bequeath one hundred markes to be bestowed of a Tombe to be erected in the memory of her and me, and for the fartherance hereof I desire that Isabell my now lovinge wife will joyne with us in that good worke and be an adiutant herein—xx[li] for a stocke for the poore of the parish of Stranton,—and for the true performance therof I desire the aide and assistance of my worthie frends as namely Mr. Fulthorpe, Mr. Dodsworth, Mr. Allen, and the rest of my good neighbors—(devise of burgage at Darnton to place workemen for a Lyninge or a Woollenge trade as shalbe most needfull for the townes of Blackwell and Darnton and the countrey next adjoyninge)—And for the poore people of Blackwell my will is that fortye shillings in money shalbe distributed to the poorest sort of people in that towne as my faithful freind Mr. John Middleton and my honest ancient servant Thomas Wilkinson shall seecme most needfull; and for the good and honest service made by my said servant Thomas Wilkinson I will and bequeath vnto him one cow to give him milke, one horse to ride on, and ten sheepe towards the cloathinge of him and his children, and fower pounds in money for a stocke—40*s.* towards the mendinge and repairinge of the high way leadinge from Whitland gate stead to the towne of Darnton—40*s.* for the mendinge of the highway betwixt Haughton and Darnton—40*s.* for the mendinge and repairinge of Coxhy Bridge and the Causey thereunto adjoyninge desireinge Mr. William Kennett that he will see the same so performed and be an adjutant thereunto with his benevolence—With my lovinge remembrance unto my honorable Lord Faulconbridge wishinge all good blessings honor and happiness to him and his house, unto his hopefull sonne my nephew John Bellasses a geldinge to the value of tenn pounds which I desire may be as acceptably taken as it is thankfully given—My noble and much honored nephew Sir Conyers Darcy kt. and to his much honored and my most lovinge neece the Lady Dorothie Darcy his wife a gould ringe in remembrance of my love to her—god sonne

James Darcy—nephew Henry Darcey 10*ll.* and all honor and happiness to him and all his familye—I also commend my best love and remembrance unto my nephew Thomas Harrison of the cittie of Yorke Esquire and to my neece his wife a gold ringe in remembrance of my love to her—My nephew Sir Thomas Metham kt. one of my best browed mares with a loving remembrance unto my nephew Jordan Metham and to his eldest sonne to buy him bookes with all the summe of tenn pounds hopeinge he will prove a worthy and famous scholler—My nephew Sr. William Bellasses kt. one peace of plate left me by my uncle called the nutt which I desire may be an heireloome to his house—(devise of land in Howden and Blackwell to the same uses as his burgage in Darnton)—in bounden thankefullnes of our worthie uncle of famous memory Richard Bellasis Esquire deceased and for a tombe to be erected in his memory in Houghton church I will and bequeath the summe of fortye markes so that my Lord Falconbridge and my said nephew S. William Bellasis they their heires and assignes doe joyne in this good worke for severill proportions in charges therof they havinge reseived so great meanes and bountie from him as well deserveth the same—with my love and dutie welbeloved mother in lawe Mres Jane Chayter of Butterbey one of my best paiseing mares—with my loving remembrance unto the noble kt. Sr. Thomas Tempest of Stelley one ox—the Lady Troath Tempest his wife and my much esteemed mistris a gould ringe—my lovinge brother in lawe Mr Nicholas Chayter one of my geldings—my best love and remembrance unto my loving brother in lawe Thomas Swinburne Esquire, unto him one of my best horses, and to my worthie and loving sister Jeronima his wife a gould ringe—my lovinge brother Mr. George Chayter a parte of my bookes with a great desire that he will read and make use of them—my God daughter Isabell Swinburne and *Pretty John* her brother either of them (*blank*)—my loving sister in lawe Mris. Margarett Chayter whose care and love in my health and sicknes I have much approved and one whom of her vertues is worthelye esteemed one hundred markes and three hundred pounds more which my mother standeth indebted unto my wife's porc'on which out of the true profession of her religion and for the payment of a due debt I hope she will thankfully pay being given for the preferment of her owne deare daughter—And farther in testification of my thankefulnes unto Almightie God that hath given and indued me with many his blessings parte of which in thankefullness I ought to bestow on such of my servants and well-willers who in their love and service have beene obedient and deserved—first for my ancient servant Xpopher Leigh 10*l.*—my ancient servant John Emmerson two kuy to the valewe of 7*l.* and 5*l.* in money—(four other legacies to servants)—my honest servant Roberte Morton and for his faithfull service to me done one horse to ride on, one cow to give him milke, and five sheepe for cloathinge on him and 20*s.* in money or gold—to nowe Baliffe Wm. Thompson and to my clerke Wm. Killington—maid Maudlin Fairlasse—my worthie and lovinge freind Mr. John Middleton whom I have alwayes found his love and freindship a free grant of what in me lyes of the farme in Skelton in Cleaveland, and a horse to the valew of 10*l.* or money—my old servant Richard Halleman 5*l.* intreating him that he will be a faithfull servant to my wife in such occasions as she shall have neede to imploy him in—my ancient servant Anne Hull of Eassington 10*l.* and a cowe to give her milke—40 labourers 20 men and 20 women each of them 5*s.* a peice to helpe to carry me to the church and buriall—executors Sr. Thomas Tempest Barronett and Tho. Swinburne Esquire haveing in them a true affieance of their fidelitye faith and due respect to my wife and to performe the true respect of trust which I repose in them for her of whom I bestowe two of my best horses—my welbeloved Sr. Raiphe Conyers kt. and my faithfull freind Mr. John Middleton supervisors—Subscribed 10 April 1637—my said supervisor Sir Raiphe Conyers one of my brood mares—James Bellasses.

Robson of Stapleton and Darlington.

(See p. xlvii)

Ann Hewgill, of Smeaton, dau. of Wm. Hewgill, of Smeaton, esq., unm. in 1711 when her father's will was made, interred in the Surtees' burial place at Haughton-le-Skerne, M. I.; mar., first, Isaac Surtees, of Myers Flatt, par. Haughton, gent. (whose will is dated 15 Dec., 1711, proved at Durham 1712. "Isaac Suretes of Darlington," bur. 3 Jan., 1711-12, at Haughton-le-Skerne), by whom she had issue

1. Jane Surtees, 2nd wife of *Robert Hylton*, esq., "Dr. Hylton," of Darlington:
2. Margaret Surtees, wife of *Abraham Hilton*, esq., of Cockerton and Hilton; a quo the Lees of Darlington.

And second, Ralph Robson, of Stapleton, by whom she had issue

- i. Ralph.
- ii. Henry Robson, mar. . . . . . *Kelsoe*, and had issue.
- 1. Anne, d. unmar.

Ralph Robson, esq., an eminent attorney at law, Darlington, and a most zealous Borough Bailiff of that town from 1753 to 1774 ; d. 9 Mar., 1774, aged 59, and was bur. at Darlington. He kept a racing mare that once ran at Doncaster, and the Darlington folks were of course on the tiptoe of expectation. The first word received was that she was " a second," but the voice of *Io triumphe* was sadly toned down when a fuller intelligence proved her to have been " the twenty-second." This mettled bailiff mar. *Susannah Haigh*, bur. 29 Aug., 1769, and had issue

- i. Ralph.
- ii. James, bp. 1746, bur. 1748.
- iii. Haigh Robson, of Darlington and Middleton, esq., attorney at law, b. 18 July, bp. 21 Aug., 1752, mar. *Eliz. Richardson*, of Middleton, co. pal. He was a great hunter, and on one occasion, after a hard day's work, plunged all bespattered in most filthy wise into a company of worthless young fellows, who, not content with gambling all Shrove Tuesday evening, had ventured into the holy bounds of Lent, which was "enough," their ancient crone of a hostess exclaimed, " to bring the deevil amang them." Immediately Nimrod entered, she turned as white as a sheet, and could only ejaculate in monosyllables, "Oh ! dear, dear ! I told you how it would be, I knew he would come." In Haigh Robson's time the heron was still considered game, and he was the *primum mobile* of great "heron sue feasts" at the Chopping knife (now the Cleaver) Inn, in Skinnergate, Darlington ; its hostess, Mrs. Tully, being the happy, and only person, that could please the palates of the connoiseurs of heron meat to a hair.
- iv. James, bp. 26 July, 1754.
- v. Francis, bp. 23 July, 1758.
- 1. Susannah, bp. 3 Feb., 1743-4, bur. 1749.
- 2. Anne, " a most accomplished young lady with a large fortune," bp. 20 Jan., 1747-8, mar. 4 Aug., 1772, the *Rev. Wm. Addison*, rector of Dinsdale, and was mother to *Robert Addison, esq.*, of Heighington, and *Joseph Addison, esq.*, the eminent barrister at law.
- 3. Mary, bp. 18 Aug., 1749, mar. 3 Nov., 1767, Wm. Dent of Darlington, grocer.
- 4. Martha, bp. 8 Feb., 1750, mar. 9 June, 1773, the *Rev. Jos. Watkins*, M.A., sub-curate of Darlington.
- 5. Susanna, bp. 15 June, 1755, d. unmar. 1774.

Lieut. Ralph Robson, of the 23rd reg., bp. 5 Mar., 1741-2, bur. 22 July, 1766, mar. at Whitby, *Isabel*, dau. of *John Pease* of that town, grocer (see that pedigree), and had issue an only and posthumous child

Susannah Robson, b. 14 Sep., 1766, mar. *Wm. Harle Nichols*, esq., surgeon, of Whitby, and died at Darlington, 1850. s. p.

Pease of Whitby and Darlington.

John Pease, owned a goodly family bible set with bosses, &c. " This Booke Bought att Rott^{r}dam p' me Jno. Pease in West Auckland Octob^{r} 1700 p' Edwrd Ward." d. 22 bur. 24 Feb. (" Shrove Sunday"), 1722-3, aged 52 on 9 Jan., 1703-4, mar., on 6 Aug., 1691, *Mary* d. Wm. *Ward*, who d. 14 June, " aboute ye same hour she was delive'd ye Thursday sennet before," (i.e. six in the evening), by whom he had issue

- i. " A Sonne whoe was Borne a Liue butt dyed imediately being nott at full Time."
- ii. John.
- 1. Margarett, b. 14, christ. 26 Oct., 1693, d. 17, bur. 19 Feb., 1727-8, at Thornaby Chapel, nigh Stockton, mar. 11 May, 1727, *Iohn Bennet*.

And second on the 31 Aug., 1698, *Dorothy* d. John *Ward*, b. 31 Mar., 1661, ag. 43, d. 14 May, 1731, by whom he had issue

- i. William, b. 3 Aug., 1705, " Witnesses, *Mr. Abraham Hilton*, and Madam Richmond."
- 1. Susanna, b. 29 Oct., christ. 17 Nov., 1700, d. 6 June, 1710.
- 2. Priscilla, b. 14 Apr., bp, 12 May, 1702.

John Pease, of Whitby, b. 4, bp. 13 June, 1696, "Witness Sir Robert Eden, Esqr. Whitfeild and Madam Rea," a grocer at Whitby, d. 7 July, 1770, ag. 74, having had 21 children born alive, though *only* 17 are mentioned in the Bible. Mar. on 31 July, 1726, *Elizabeth Bateman* d. Robert and Margaret Bateman b. 7 Nov., 1703, mar. at Lyth church by her uncle Ralph Bateman, d. 25 Feb., 1782, aged 78. She had a brother John, b. 27 July. 1706, and sister Margaret, b. 18 Feb., 1702. They had issue

i. John.
ii. Robert, b. 9 Aug., 1728, lived three hours, "being not at full time," but was bp.
iii. William, b. 13, d. 15 May, 1729, "not at full time," was bap.
iv. Ralph, b. 23 Feb., 1729-30, lived about two hours, "not at full time," was bp.
v. Robert, b. 29 Oct., 1732, lived twenty-four hours, bur. 1 Nov.
vi. Edward, b. 25 May, 1737, bur. 8 June following.
vii. George, b. 10 Mar., 1740-1, certif. at Whitby 8 Apr., 1741, d. 10 *March* following.
viii. William, b. 2 June, certif. at Whitby church, 1 July, 1742, d. young
ix. Robert, b. 16 Dec., 1744, certif. at Whitby church, 25 Jan., "brother John Bennet, sister Margt. Bateman," sponsors, d. of small pox 12, bur. 14 Apr., 1747.
x. James Pease, b. 23 Apr., certd. in Whitby church . . . . d. unmar., aged 32.
xi. Bristowe Pease, b. 14 Aug., 1748, certified in Whitby ch. 18 Oct., "Mr. Richard Bristowe" a godfather: d. 18, bur. 22 Jan., 1824, in Darlington church, aged 75. He was a merchant at Darlington. Mar. 12 Dec., 1770, *Susannah*, d. of James *Allan*, of Darlington and Blackwell Grange, esq., b. 27 Nov., 1751, bp. 9 Jan., 1752, d. 29 Sep., bur. as of Hungate, 2 Oct., 1814, in Darlington church, aged 62. They had issue

1. Elizabeth Pease, d. 1837, mar. 13 Nov., 1793, at Darlington, *Moses Harrison*, raff-merchant, Darlington. Wit. to mar., Bristowe Pease, Catherine Pease, Dorothy Allan, and Margaret Pease.
2. Catherine, b. 1 Mar., 1773, of Darlington, d. unm. 2 Aug., 1848, aged 75. Bur. Trinity.
3. Margaret, d. young.
4. Isabella, bur. 22 Aug., 1792, at Darlington.

1. Mary, b. 28 July, 1731, certified at Whitby church 8 Sep., d. 8, bur. 11 Feb., 1731.
2. Elizabeth, b. 30 Oct., 1733, certified at Whitby church 4 Dec., d. 19 June, 1737, of small pox.
3. Mary, b. 6 Dec., 1735, certified in Whitby church, 11 Jan., d. 19 June, 1737, of small pox, and was bur. in the same coffin with her sister Eliz.
4. Margaret, b. 21 Sep., bp. 6 Oct., 1738, d. of small pox 15, bur. 17 Apr., 1747.
5. Isabella, b. 24 Feb., 1739-40, certified in Whitby church 8 Apr., d. 10 Nov., 1811. Mar., first, at Whitby, Lieutenant *Ralph Robson* (*see foregoing pedigree*), and second *James Benson*, of Aislaby, co. pal., by whom she had issue

i. James Benson, d. inf.
ii. John Benson, esq., b. 7 Dec., 1780, of Seaton, 1848: mar., *Isabella Brewster*, dau. of Thos. B. of Newcastle, the brother of the Stockton historian.
1. Grace, b. 21 July, 1777, liv. at York 1848, mar. *Marmaduke Nelson*, of Brantingham, near Hull. Their only child, Ann, mar. *William Richardson*, esq., solicitor, York.

6. Dorothea, b. 19 Nov., 1743, certified 18 Jan., d. 5, bur. 7 Feb. following at Whitby.

John Pease, b. 13 May, bap. 11 June, 1727, at Whitby, settled at Darlington as grocer, d. 29, bur. 31 Dec., 1794, at Kirby Ravensworth.—"1758, William Robson, senior, of Darlington, bricklayer, George Waters, of Darlington, carpenter, both kill'd by the fall of an arch in building a cellar for Mr. John Pease."—*Darlington Reg.*

About 1760 he bought the whole courtyard and premises formerly the burgage called *le Bull*, at one side of the Bull Wynd, and adorned with the Bulmer crest, down to Hungate, and brought the purchase money, 400 guineas, on a pillion from Whitby. The venerable gentleman who furnished this interesting information, has also been told of an heiress's fortune, 10,000*l.*, being brought, a short time before, from Hull to Whitby in a waggon heaped over with straw, accompanied by two stout fellows at the side, who were accoutred with flails, and pretended that they had been thrashing. Mar. 29 Dec., 1757, at Darlington, by lic. *Hannah Haigh*, who d., 10 Jan., 1766, bur. at Darlington. Witnesses to mar., Ra. Robson, Isabella Pease, *Mary Hilton*. They had issue

i. John Pease, b. 20 Feb., 1760, left England in 1785, and has not since been heard of, but is believed to have died in the East Indies.
ii. James, b. between 1761 and 1765, d. when a fortnight old.
1. Elizabeth, b. 19 Nov., 1758, d. 1844, mar. 21 Feb., 1797, *Cornelius Stovin*, of Hirst Priory, Lincolnshire, who d. before 1848. Their only child, *Cornelius Hartshorne Stovin*, d. May, 1845.
2. Hannah, b. 14 Mar., 1761, d. 25 Sep., 1799, bur. at Warmsworth in the Friends' burying ground.
3. Mary Pease, b. 10 Mar., 1765, d. unm. at Darlington, 7 Apr., 1848, intestate, aged 83, bur. Trinity. M. I.

III. CLERVAUX.

At every step the genealogist meets with lessons the most mortifying to his own fancied security, and humiliating to the pride of man in general. If there is one instance more to the very point than another, the family of Clervaux presents it. The race for generations slept in happy ignorance of the real glories of their ancestors; heralds contented themselves with a tall, worm-like, miserable adumbration to a pedigree, in which a long file of misty warriors peeped from the gossamer webs of fraud in which the heralds had enveloped it. Yet the Clervaux gave the most extended and knightly state of any of the families on the Tees. Surtees, and Baliol, Aslakby, and Conyers, after a brilliant but transient succession of important representatives, departed like the thin shades of morning; but from the time of Henry III. to the present day the heritage of Croft has passed in only two names, and in but one blood.

It has been my privilege, and I feel it to be a proud one, to be the first man who has dared to sweep away the brilliant but false covering from the history of Clervaux. If I have knocked off two centuries from the dull list of dateless names, I have, I trust, given an interest of a more abiding and of a much more important character to the subject. It has been my luck to be favoured with a lengthened use of a fine cartulary, containing copies of every document in existence at the period of Henry VI. which referred to the title of the widened estates of Clervaux at that time:* and by the aid of the splendid array of evidences contained in that beautiful volume, and a huge selection of other family records, the wretched skeleton is now being clothed with healthy sinews.

The Clervaux cartulary measures 12 by 15 inches, contains one hundred and sixty-six leaves closely written on both sides, and comprises fair copies of no less than nine hundred and forty-nine documents, arranged under the several estates to which they refer. The marriage feoffments and wills are principally kept together, and at the end of the book are various instruments referring to Richard Clervaux, who lived in the troublous days of the Rosy wars, but nevertheless found time to look after its compilation.†

A fine illuminated pedigree, drawn up in the time of Elizabeth, and the generally received genealogies, commence the line with "Sir Hammon Clervaux came into England with William the Conqueror, who gave him certaine landes without Bothome juxta Yorke." All ancient families commence in a sort of mythic state, and though it would be absurd to fight against the

* I have never made my acknowledgments of aid with greater pleasure than when I return my most sincere thanks to Henry Chaytor, Esq., of Croft, for the constant kindness and courtesy I have experienced at his hands, during my prolonged researches *in re Clervaux*.

† The book has been written before binding, and the leaves are signed with letters and figures at the foot in octavo divisions, as in a printed book.

very name (both Clerewaus and Chayters occurring in the roll of Battle Abbey) and deny that a Clerevaux did arrive from Normandy and maintain his foreign surname through several generations, till his descendants in the time of Henry III., by their riches, acquired broad lands on the Tees;* yet, it would be equally wrong to attribute any more weight to the airy knights of Croft, than as a very misty adumbration to the truth.† Like many other most ancient families who doted upon a descent from Brutus of Troy, the Clervaux, who bore the blood of Alfred, Charlemagne, and William the Lion, little needed any assistance not strictly verified.

Robert de Clervaux (son of Robert) the first man on record in the cartulary, was a rich citizen of York, and though his fathers are unknown, they had probably been no mean carles, for when Sir Thomas releases to his brother Peter all the lands and rents (in York) which his father Robert had left him by will, he adds, "which legacies the said Robert had of hereditary right or by his own industry acquired to himself." No title is shown to certain parcels held in York; but they were not in Bootham, where the family had no property. The money of Robert reared the family on a most substantial basis. He advanced thirty marks to Roald son of Roald son of Alan the Constable of Richmond, "in his great necessity," and forty marks to his brother Henry, son of Roald, in the same strait. Roald had the whole vill of Croft in grant from his father Roald.‡ The wealthy citizen soon bought

* The saltire of Clervaux occurs among the banners held behind Alan Rufus on his receiving the grant of the Honor of Richmond from the Conqueror, in a MS. illustration to Coll. MSS. Faustina, B. 7. The scribe gave arms to the companions of Earl Alan as they occurred long after in the subfeudatories of Richmond, and see the pedigree as to whether the saltire was not a coat attached to Cowton estate.

† The descent may properly be given as a note.

Sir Hammon Clervaux, &c., (*Arms*, Sable, a Saltire or) had issue

Albon Clervaux, *m.* . . . . . d. Sir Lambert Bashee (*Arms*, Argent, 3 bars Sable) and had issue

Jordeyne Clervaux, *m.* Ancareta d. Lord Nevell of Horneby in the countie of Lancaster (*Arms*, Argent, a saltire gules), and had issue

John Clervaux *of Croft* esquier, *m.* Oswolda d. Sir Adam Bruce (*Arms*, Gules a saltire or, a chief divided per fess dancette gules and or,), and had issue

Thomas Clervaux of Croft esquier, *m.* Tymothee d. John Gascoigne, esq. (*Arms*, Argent on a pale sable, a demi lucy erect, couped, or,), and had issue

Robert Clervaux of Croft esquier, *m.* Anne d. Edward Anlatheby, esquier (*Arms*, Argent, three chess-rooks sable), and had issue

Sir John Clervaux of Croft, knt., *m.* Herodea d. Lorde Marmean (*Arms*, Vaire, a fess gules), and had issue

Henrie Clervaux esquier, *m.* Johnathey d. John Nesome, esquier (*Arms*, Barry of eight, ermine and sable), and had issue

Robert Clervaux of Croft [with whom the proven pedigree begins, and who was in truth the son of another Robert]; John and William, who both d. s. p.

So far the illuminated pedigree. From Robert any errors are of small extent, and will be pointed out in the pedigree hereafter.

‡ Omnibus, &c. Roaldus filius Alani Constablar' Richem'd, salutem. Sciatis me dedisse et concessisse, et hanc presenti carta mea confirmasse, Roaldo filio meo, pro humagio et servicio suo quod mei fecit, totam villam de Croft, cum omnibus pertinenciis suis, infra villa et extra, sine ullo retinemento. Habenda et tenenda predicto Roaldo et heredibus suis, de me et heredibus meis, in feodo et hereditate, libere et quiete et honorifice, faciendo mei, et heredibus meis, forinsecum servicium quantum pertinet ad octo carukatas terre in feodo, unde duodecim carukate terre faciunt feodum unius militis. Ego vero et heredes mei warantizabimus, &c.

In 1260 Sir Roald, son of Roald, with Dame Matilda de Marra his wife, granted the whole vill of Croft to Roald, son of Alan his nephew, and mentions among the tenants, Thomas de Clervaux for a tenement and two mills and two holmes.

In 1255 John de Clerewaus having been impleaded by Sir Groceline Daulle and Sarra his wife, the widow of Roald son of Alan, for her thirds of his property, had brought forward Roald son of Roald, who warranted, and the inquisition was expunged.

It will be useless to note all the small buyings up by the Clervaux family in successive generations. There are no very peculiar tenures. The rent of a rose was always to be paid "in the time of roses." But the strong dislike of the early owners to part absolutely with their small patches of cultivated ground is striking. They almost always reserve a up from him a firm holding in the place. First went the "*ploghswayn oxganges*," the toft and croft *Helle*, and many an oxgang more (in all thirteen, with tofts and crofts)—then all the mills of Croft, a splendid acquisition in those days, with the holms of that vill, and all that meadow between the meadow which was John's the son of the dean, and the wath of Stapylton—forty-two oxgangs more and thirty-one acres *ad incrementum*—confirmation of all these at rent of 18*d*., after the kind payment of the thirty marks—licence to impark his animals—small properties at Helmekeldenge and near Clowbec, and beginning at Stapilton Wahde—and leave to pasture twenty-six cattle in his cultured demesnes. Then, to keep him in good humour, Clervaux gives Roald an easement for his demesne animals, with his own, in the holmes he had acquired, as long as his father Sir Roald lived; and Roald the son, in 1246, obliges himself to grind the winter corn consumed in his household, to the thirtieth bowl (vas), and his malt without multure at Croft mill, but would take none belonging to the men or tenants of Clervaux. All Roald's grants were confirmed by his brother Henry, who for the forty marks above mentioned, granted two oxgangs, &c. The father of these young men, Roald son of Alan the Constable, confirmed the seventeen and a-half oxgangs and thirty-one acres, and eight acres of meadow, and all mills, and suits of the same vill of Croft, which his son Roald had given.*

In York he was acquiring property the same way. He gave John Godshere, of Tresk, money "in his great necessity," and received a rent of 2*s*. out of property *in marisco*. He also acquired land from Hugh Scyrloc, of Croft, and his son John, 1242, for money so paid to the latter, and was a grantor of part of "la grene extra muros juxta Mykkelgate," in York, to Henry *de sexdecim vallibus* or *Sessewaus*, another citizen of that city.

His widow Eve granted property in Aldwerk, York, to a carpenter his heirs and assigns, *except religious men and Jews*, at the rent of 4*s*., in default of payment, to revert; and if after building any erections thereon he wished to sell, he was not to remove them; and the same caution against religious men and Jews occurs in another of her grants. But she gave property in la grene to her son Master Simon for life, and then to John his brother on his making yearly two commemorations of the faithful, and paying certain sums, and allowing certain pasturage to four houses of Friars,† and one "pitaunce" of 5*s*. to the Monks of St. Clement for the soul of her mother and predecessors. Unfortunately the Fairfax family claimed and recovered the land from Master Simon, yet they settled it on the donor's grandson William, on his marriage with a Stodelay, of York. Simon still however held some other York property of his mother's gift, which he granted to his nephew William, to make the same alms to the friars preachers and minors, as he had made. He was rector of Lithe and official of Cleveland.‡

rent of some kind; often a rose was to be paid for so many years, and then a heavier class of payments commence. We find at Croft, "le Breeches," Gyllesikesmarch, the waynebrigge, *Askhouwe* (a draconic hill we fear), Cranberymyre, *le brynepole*, Barton dikes, Brakenberysik, Hemyngcrosse, le Harestane, Askowker, and Hammondebuttes. Often a grantee had to have the alienated lands for life at a small rent.

* "Quieta et libera ab ommodis forinsecis serviciis et sectis curie mee."

Another confirmation occurs of 13 oxgangs "which I gave to Roald my son for the annual rent of 13*l*. received every year from the vill of Taneshoner."

† Fratres minores Ebor'—fratres predicatores—fratres de Monte Carmeli—fratres de sacas.

‡ Rot. Hund. 1274-5. Radclyffe's ped. in Whitaker's Richmondshire from the Heralds' Records makes this pious parson marry, and have two sons William and Henry! 6 Kal. Apr., 1301, Henry, abbot, and the convent of Ryevalle in public chapter—established three monks of their house to celebrate three masses for ever for the health and prosperity

The citizen's son was a knight. SIR THOMAS DE CLERVAUX acquired from the Gobyuns (whose proved descents in the pedigree will be a serviceable addition to Hodgson's Northumberland, ii, 452) the rent of 10*l.* reserved from lands in Yedingham to the monastery at which place the lands had been granted.* This rent he granted to his brother Simon the ecclesiastic and his heirs *in descendendo,* and assigns, to sustain for ever one chaplain in York to celebrate mass for the souls of Robert de Clerwaus, and Eve his mother, and all the faithful, in the church of All Saints in Usegate, at the altar of Blessed Peter the apostle; and offer every year on the vigils of the assumption of Blessed Virgin Mary, one wax candle weighing one pound, before the greater altar in the church of Yedingham; and in default to pay five marks farm to himself and heirs. Simon, in 1295, granted the rent on the same trusts, and reserving a rent of 100*s.* to himself for life, to his nephew William, who in 1324 granted half of it to the Prioress and convent of nuns of Yedyngham. He had a house in Husegate, York, on the stone wall of which he gave leave to Sir Thomas Baudewyn, knt., to establish a shed (pentiem) *ultra cellarium dicti Dni Thome Baudewyn,* but not to make a claim, and also a stone "place" in the marsh† in St. Saviourgate, which is long mentioned by his brother John's descendants. He acquired property in Jolby from Henry de Joleby, and held it by the rent of a pair of white gloves.

His brother, JOHN DE CLERVAUX, citizen of York, had obtained from him a grant of Croft; and Roald, son of Roald, confirmed to him 18 oxgangs, and all that Robert his father had of his gift. Roald son of Alan de Rychmund, also confirmed the grants of Roald son of Roald, his uncle, and gave leave that he might enclose nine acres in his own proper land wherever he liked, with a wall or dike *(fossato).* This Roald also confirmed lands in Jolby, which John de Clervaux had acquired, and gave another toft in exchange for Helle. John bought a number of other small parcels at Croft; amongst others from Brother Thomas, Abbot of Jorevall and his convent in 1259, property they had of the gift of Roald son of Alan, in perpetual lease of 24*s,* which was reduced to 4*s,* by Clervaux giving 20*s,* yearly *in elymosina.* He resided at Stiveton, York and Croft, and died

of life of their beloved in Christ Master Simon de Clervaux, rector of Lith church from that date, at three altars in their church, viz., at the altar of S. Matthew where a mass of the Blessed Virgin is celebrated, the altar of S. Martin the bishop, where one for all the faithful departed is daily celebrated, and at the altar of the blessed Thomas the martyr a mass. So that the three monks at the three altars while Master Simon lived should say a collect for his special health, viz., *Deus qui caritatis dona, &c.*, in a convenient place, and at a mass at St. Martin's altar aforesaid to be daily celebrated for the health of the soul of Sir Thomas de Clervaux his brother, a special collect in like manner daily should be said, viz., *Deus cui p'p'iu est, &c.*, in the second place or other convenient place; but when Master Simon, whose prosperous life might the Highest prolong, should die, at the three masses celebrated at the three altars a collect, viz., *Deus cui p'p'iu est* for the health of both of the souls aforesaid.

* Sir Hugh Gubyun, knt., son of Ric. Gubyun, for the health of my soul; and the souls of Roger de Merlay my uncle, Wm. de Merlay his brother, Richard Gubyun my brother, and the souls of my ancestors—to God and the church of Blessed Mary of Yedingham and the nuns there serving God, all my land in Yedingham—which I held of Roger de Merlay—rendering yearly to me and my heirs 10*l.* for all service, &c.—the said monks shall find one priest to celebrate the mass of the Blessed Virgin in the monastery of Yedingham every day for ever, as it may most conveniently be done according to the use of the said house for the health of the said souls—if mass be not said, during cessation the nuns to pay five marks to my heirs—and when my heirs are in ward to pay to my lord Roger de Merlay and his heirs. This would be Roger de Merlay the 3rd, lord of Morpeth.

† Or rather "in vico de Mersk", where Tho. de Stodleye had a grant to enclose a waste piece called Dinnyngdyk for the enlargement of his mansion, in 31 Edw. I., but not to the nuisance of Wm. de Claris Vallibus, who had a right of road over it, but who consented to the grant. The Stodelay property lay between Clervaux's house and the cemetry of St. Saviour in Marisco, and was granted to Clervausc and his wife Margaret Stodelay.

about 1283.* His wife Matilda lived till 1297.† His brother, Sir Nicholas, a citizen of York, when returning a rent out of Croft to Sir Thomas his eldest brother the grantor, "because his seal was not well known, procured the seal of the Prior of Kyrkeham to be affixed" to the instrument.‡ Nicholas was, I believe, the ancestor of a race of wealthy tradesmen at York.§

WILLIAM DE CLERVAUX, the next owner of Croft, followed his grandfather's example and by giving Alexander Scyrloc and his wife Alice, the successors of his ancestor's victims, money "in their great necessity,"

* In the name of the Father, Son, and Holy Ghost, Amen. I, John de Clarevaus, sick in body and sound in mind, on Monday, next after the feast of St. Martin, in winter, A.D. 1283—my body to ecclesiastical burial in the cemetery of the church of All Saints, in Usegate, if I die at York or Stivetun, but if at Croft, then to be buried there—all my movable goods to be divided in three equal parts, one part in (*sic*) another part to Matilda my wife, and a third part to my legitimate children; except my heir, whom I wish to be content with his heritage in unmovables; and except Katherine my daughter, who sufficiently received her part in my lifetime and to the full—to the Church of St. Saviour *in marisco* at York, one mark in place of a mortuary—to the Church of All Saints in Usegate at York 10s—to the expenses of my funeral, 10 marks—to the Friars preachers of York, one mark—the Friars minor of York, one mark—the Friars of the Order of St. Augustine and of Mount Carmel, and the Friars of the sack, one mark—the Nuns of Munncketunn, one mark—every recluse of York 12d—wife Matilda all house utensils in cups whatsoever, silver spoons, gold rings, firmacles, brasen vessels, skins, vats, tubs, leads, and in all manner of household stuff—whatever shall remain in my house after the day of my burial in flesh, fish, fuel, and all belonging to the provision of the house shall wholly and peaceably belong to my wife and children—Thomas, my servant, half a mark, &c.—to every servant of mine not named, 6d—three marks of silver to bny linen and woollen, and shoes, to be distributed among the poor of Stivetun and Croft, by the counsel and advice of my wife—my wife may have my stone house *in marisco* at York, which I gave her at the door of the church in dowry with her thirds. In witness, &c., my executors have placed their seals with my seal hanging and placed above. Given at Stivetun. (Firmacles were brooches or fibulæ.)

† Matilda de Clerevaus—Sunday on the feast of the Holy Innocents; A.D. 1297, before William and John, my sons, and Roger de Cunesclif, this hearing and seeing—to be buried in the church of blessed Peter of Croft, and with my corpse my best beast—for wax and the exequies about my body on the day of my burial, 3 marks—to the church of St. Saviour in *merske* at York half a mark—the Friars preachers of Yarm, 4 marks—Adam de Beleassis, 2*s*—Elizabeth and Matilda, daughters of Peter de la Haye, each a mark—son Thomas, one silver cup and a gilt piece of 3½ marks—son William, one silver cup and a gilt piece of 30*s*, and a white cup of maser (*macereum*)—son John a silver cup, and a gilt piece of 30*s*—daughter Matilda, one cup with a foot of silver, and a gilt piece of 20*s*, and one zone of silk, and a maser cup—my (sic) Cicily one cup and one zone of silk—Matilda Rose, one cow—to this testament I have placed my seal along with the seals of my executors. Proved at Gilling before our official of Richmond, ij. id. Febri. 1297.

‡ Helwis, wife of Nicholas Clervaus, on Monday after the feast of St. Martin, 1282: to be buried in the cemetery of St. Denis—for my corpse-present my cloke *de marlet*—Elen, my daughter, my robe of green and my cloke *de murret*, my robe *de mearlet*—Alice, daughter of Cecily Nayrum, one supertunic *de murret'*—Alice de Mikelegate one cloke of green—Elen de Hoser, my cape *de p'so*—Sibilla de Holthe, my supertunic of scarlet—*mat'c' mee Agneti*, my supertunic of red and tunic *de murret'*—*p'cose churhill* my cloke *de plu'bet'*—Agnes de Acaster my cloke of scarlet—Enota, my servant, my supertunic of green—Elen Darel, a supertunic *de murret*, and my tunic *de viridi havice*—to the son of Paulmer the goldsmith, a supertunic of red—to the wife of Paulmer the goldsmith, my cloke *de Burnet'*—Matilda de Houedonschir, my tunic of saye—sister Elen *unum tressur'*—daughter Elen, all my linen cloths, one gold firmacle—son Peter, 20 gold rings. Executors, Sir Nich. Clervaus, my husband, Thomas de Seleby, my brother.

§ John Clervaux, citizen of York, 13 Apr. 1344—to be buried in the church of All Saints, in Ousegate, York, and with my corpse my better robe in the name of a mortuary—for wax to be burned round my body at the time of my exequies, 20 lb. of wax—son John, my psalter, with my greatest gold ring, with one better silver foot—wife Agnes, one other lesser silver foot with a cup thereto annexed—son John, one silver cup—son, my better gold firmacle—wife Agnes, my other gold firmacle—to be expended about my funeral, 40*s*.

Sunday, before Palm Sunday (*diem d'nicam Ramis Palmarum*) 1357. John Clervaux, citizen and apothecary of York—to be buried in the cemetery of the church of All Saints', on the Pavement at York, near the monuments of my parents—to the Rector of the church of Saint Crux, at Fossegate ende, for my mortuary my better robe—for my forgotten tithes, 2*s*—in wax to be burned round my body the day of my burial 8 lbs. of wax—the chaplain of the parish of St. Crux aforesaid, 18*d*—the clerk of the same parish, 12*d*—the sub-clerk of the same, 4*d*—for the expenses of my funeral to be made the day of my burial, 4 pounds of silver.

acquired their property with that of many others, and obtained power from Luke Tylbys (Tailbois) knt. and Robert, son of Robert de Hephale, the possessors of the lordship of Hurworth, to fix the pond of a water-mill in the water of These, upon their waste of Hurthwith ; and Richard de Havigdone Vicar of Derlington, William son of Peter, and John Bruis of Derlington, were bound to him in 8 marks for a fourth of the tithe of sheaves of Blacwelle, for the year 1321, to be paid to him at Derlington. He acquired the manor of East or Temple Couton by mortgage for 34*l.* soon followed by a full grant from John Fyton its lord in 1324,* properties in York in the same way, the mortgage monies having to be paid on St. John Baptist's and St. Andrew's days, in the greater church of St. Peter at York, and other property at Stapilton,† and (with his sister Matilda) the lordship of Walmire in 1322, by mortgage and subsequent release from John le Breton, son and heir of Sir Philip le Breton, and from other parties; also property at Hurworth, in 1324, by mortgage and release from John de Kendal, servant of the Rector of Hurtheworth,‡ and the same year by the same means, property in Solbergh,§ pledged for 12*l.* from Hugh Breton, and in Thirnetoft from the early Bowes's, whose names from the cartulary will be a valuable prefix to Surtees's pedigree of Bowes of Streatlam.‖ He gave to the Prioress and Nuns of Yedyngham

* Long after this, the 15 Juyn, 3 Edw. IV. Richard Clervaux of Croft, squier, and Thomas Fyton of Cawrwyn, co. Chestr., gentilman, met at the seat of the former's father-in-law, Sir James Strangwayes, to adjust a long variance about 100*s* rent Fyton claimed out of the manors of Croft and Est Cowton, which Clervaux "denyed to pay by cause of certeyn evydence that he had a writeng under old seles which he thought was sufficient in the lawe to discharge hym." The rent was bought out for 40*l.* There certainly is no reservation of the rent in the Fyton grants, but an inquisition in 1344 found John and Isabella Clervaux to hold the manor of Temple Couton, charged with .... rent to the Fyton heir. It was, I believe, in right of Cowton, that the banner of Clervaux waved on the quondam station of Conan son of Elias, at Richmond Castle, near the court of the tower on the east side, at the outside of the wall. Robertus Clarevaux tenet in Athow Cowton aliter East Coulton duas partes decimarum de Dominicis quondam Wymari Dapiferi,—*Gale.* Wardæ Castri Richmund Temp. Ric. II. De Conano filio Eliæ pro i feodo in magna Cowton red. pro ward. dim. marc Johannes Clerevaux modo tenet.

† In the documents relating to Stapleton, we have "Stephen, called Milesman, of Stapeltone," 1315, and his widow Alice, formerly wife of Stephen Milisman of Stapelton, and elsewhere, plainly out—"of Stephen the servant of Sir Miles de Stapilton, knt." We find the knights of Stapylton then still holding property at their ancient home. There is mention Sir Miles, and Sir Nicholas Stapylton, knt. his b. and h. (1322 and 1342). And now, as to names, in the Clervaux evidences of Walmegate property in York, we have an ecclesiastic significantly named "William called *Fox*, clerk, of York," and afterwards plain "William Fox."

‡ Inter alia, a rood at the cross of Nesham (probably the boundary between Nesham and Hurworth townships) Anneysheng, &c. The latter under the name of *Dameagneysheng*, with other lands, had been granted to Kendal by Richard son Geoffrey de Nesham, (Wm. Taylboys a bounding owner) and grants from Adam, son of Thomas de Nesham also occur to him.

§ Juxta Warlaby in Richemondshire.

‖ Villa de Tirnetofte [par. Ainderby Steeple]. Thomas Baingnard of Tirntoft to Adam de Puntayse and Avice ux. all his land there for twenty years—Adam de Puntayce to Gerard de Boghes, the oxgangs and 3 tofts there he bought of one Henry—Adam, son of Gerard de Boughes, remaining in Maugneby, to Nicholas, son of Stephen de Boughes, my late brother, all his lands in Maugneby, Kirkeby Wysk, and Thyrnetoft—Nicholas, son of Stephen de Boughes to Adam de Boughes his uncle remaining in Maugneby, a rent of 38*s* out of his lands at those three places—Same Nicholas to Robert de Boughes his brother, all his lands in the same places he had had of the grant of his uncle—Robert de Boughes to William de Clervaux; if said Clervaux should pay to Bowes 6 marks *die sabati prius quindenam sci Hylarii* at Rychemund, in the church of Holy Trinity, 1323, two oxgangs and 4 tofts and crofts in Thirnetoft should remain to said Clervaux; if he failed they should not; and if Bowes paid to Clervaux 6 marks on the said day and place, the feoffment and seisin should be void. Here was a mortgage in anticipation of a regular purchase, a way William Clervaux was much addicted to.—Same to same: the property in Thirnetoft he had from his brother Nicholas, in consummation of the last document. With regard to Trayne, of Streatlam, who married an heiress of Ralph De la Haye, of Stainton, to whose relation Peter del Haye, her husband John Trayne granted in that lucky year half the rent of 10*l.* they paid him under the Gobyun grant.*

This William had two sons of the name of JOHN, one of whom, *senior*, (II) he who succeeded to Croft, was one of the knights or esquires of the North Riding from whom twenty men at arms were to be chosen against Scotland† in 1338. He was probably trammelled by serving in the wars of the time, as we find him mortgaging to Sir Michael de la Pole, knt., at Colthorp, in 1368, the Solbergh lands his father had obtained by lending, until he should pay 20*l.* The property passed by grant to his younger son Thomas for life and back from him to John de Clerevaux his cosyn [nephew] and heir, the grandson of the mortgagor, and still it was fettered, so difficult was it in those days to redeem a mortgaged estate.‡ John Clervaux, *senior*, wedded a Percy and thus commenced a connection with the great house of Northumberland which was continued, and was succeeded by a son of the same name.

JOHN CLERVAUX (III) was a commissioner of array for the North Riding against Scotland in 1388. In 1389 referees of note determined that Sir William Lescrop should for his transgressions and misprisions in the Bishop of Durham's franchise, by way of penance offer a jewel at St Cuthbert's shrine. The worth of the jewel being left to king Richard II. to determine, his beloved and trusty *knights of his chamber* John Clarvowe and Nicholas de Sharnefeld waited on him at his manor of Havenyng for his determination, when he decreed that the jewel should be worth 500*l.* at least.§ In a document of 1386 this John is called "Johannes Clarvaux super Tesee,"‖ and died in 1390.¶ His son JOHN (IV) was followed by a knight** SIR JOHN CLERVAUX (V) who matched with the lordly house of

Streatlam in 1310—take notice that Peter de la or del Haye granted property at Yrton juxta Semer to William de Clervaus and his son John, and that Matilda de Clervaus, William's mother, in 1297 left a mark each to Elizabeth and Matilda daughters of Peter de la Haye.

* JUBERY, EBOR.—Edward I., at York, 4 Apr. A.R. 19. granted to Rob. del Neweland [a skinner] of York, and Alice his wife, "the place in which the Jews of York were buried, with the houses and tenements to that place contiguous, which were the residences of the same Jews in the suburb of the said city, by the exile of those Jews from our realm hitherto escheated to us and in our hands remaining, by the rent of a penny." Alice de Gysburne, Robert's widow, alienated to the Stodlays who granted Jubyri to their kinsman Wm. de Clervaus.

† Rot. Scotiæ.

‡ The last document I find relating to it was of the 24 Nov., 1392, between Esmond de la Pole Chivaler, Rob. de Bolton clerk and Robert de Garton clerk, and John de Clerevaux cosyn and heir of Thomas de Clerevaux, "tesmoigne q' come le dit Thomas uncle a dit John dona et q'unta a mons' Mich' de la Pole iadys Conte de Suff," &c.—Clervaux to pay 20*l.*—

Henry Stele—have given to Sir Ac'is [Akaris] de Halnaby, John de Clervaus, and John Freman, together and not separately, goods to the fabric of the chapel of B. Mary Magdalene in the vill of Wallemyr and for a chantry in the same, if at a future period they be able to extend the same goods, viz. goods to be left by other husbandmen to the said fabric to the amount of goods I have given to God, viz. 4 horses and 2 oxen for the plough, 3 cows, 1 stotte, and 2 stirks, and 2 calves, 40 sheep, and 20 lambs, 12 acres of wheat and 12 acres of somir falow with one tenement which owes yearly 12*s.* to the lord. —(if one trustee die, the other two to choose another)—Given on the feast of B. Mary Magdalene, A. D. 1341.

§ Raine's St. Cuthbert, 134.

‖ Clervaux Cart. fo. 86.

¶ Friday after the feast of the assumption of B. Mary 1390.—John Clervaux of Croft infirm in body—to be buried in the parish church of St. Peter of Croft—to the patron of the church of Croft 10*s.* [the convent of St. Mary's, York, were patrons at the time]—the friars minor of Richmond 6*s.* 8*d.*—the friars of Yarum 6*s.* 8*d.*—the friars of Allerton 6*s.* 8*d.*—son John 8 oxen for one plough, silver cup with a cover after the death of my wife Beatrix, and one whole best bed but one—friar John de Yngelby 6*s.* 8*d.* to celebrate for my soul—Robert de Rokeby chaplain 6*s.* 8*d.*—son John 12 silver spoons after decease of my wife Beatrix.

** Thes endenture made betwix John Clervaux Sqwyer of the to partie and John Hexham of York carpenter of the tothir partie Wittenes that the forsaid John Hexham sal mak thre new tenementz wyth thre chaumbres opon the grounde of the forsaid John Cler-

Lumley, his wife's mother being Eleanor daughter of John Lord Neville by Maud daughter of Henry Percy.

This splendid match which brought in the royal descent and connections shown in the pedigree, was always carefully paraded by the Clervaux race. Sir John, who had played his cards so well, died in 1443, and was honoured by his son Richard with an altar tomb in the South or Clervaux Aisle of Croft, but "the tomb is broken, the shields displaced—and the words for pews may scarce be traced."*

RICHARD CLERVAUX found himself, through his mother, in a most goodly company of relations,† and stands conspicuous as the "magnus" of his race.

vaux in Peseholm in York als it lys be twix the tenement of Piers Bukey of the to partie and a staun place of the forsaid John Clervaux of the tothir partie the quylk tenementz sall be made in the bred beforsaid and in the lenkth of lij fute and the forsaid John Hexham sall fynd all maner of tymber except lattes and louers And allso he sall fynd all maner of wryghtnote with dures wyndowes nayles bynkes (covered seats in front of houses) and durebands. The quylk tenementz sall be wele and wermanly made and perfournysshed in all maner of thynges beforsaid be the fest of Saynt Martyn in wynter next for to com efter the date of this presence. For the quylk tymber wryghtnote wyth all othir thyngs beforsaid wele and werkmanly to be made the forsaide John Clervaux sall pay to the forsaid John Hexham or his certayn attorne wele and treuly xviij marces of sterlinges that is to say vj marc befor the fest of Saynt Elyn next for to com And als touchyng the xij marc the sam John Hexham sall have the forsaid thre tenementz when thai er made and othir iiij tenements in Peseholm beforsaide of the forsaid John Clervaux to hald and to have the forsaid tenementz unto the sam John Hexham and to his assignes unto the tyme that he have takyn and resavyd the forsaid xij marc of the tenementz beforsaid and the same John Hexham sall have all the ald tymber and all othir appurtenancez of the forsaid iij tenementz to his awne propre use and spence In to the wittenes of quylk thynges the parties beforsaid ther seals to the parties of this endentures sonderly has set to. Made at York the v day of marce In the zher of King Herry the fyft efter the conquest the fyft. [1417-8]

* Top and sides are all flat under pews. Whitaker discerned ". . . . . Joh'es Clervaux . . . . . mccccxliii. et D'na Margareta uxor ejus filia Radulphi . . . . , Militis . . . . .," but in 1846, the part of the legend presenting itself to me was ". . . . et Joh'es Clarvaux m . . . . Et nepos Rado neuil p'o Co'iti Westm'l'nd q' ob't A'd'ni m cccc li." At the visitation 1666, it appeared thus :

> Hic jacet Joh'es Clervaux miles qui obiit xiiii Aug' ti A'o D'ni M'o CCCC'o XLIII'o. Et D'na Margareta uxor ejus, filia Radulphi Lumley militis Et Nepos Rad'o Nevill p'o Comiti Westmerlaundie; que obiit vicesimo Die Decembris [a' d'ni m cccc li ?] Rich. ejus filius hanc Tumbam fieri fecit.

On the dexter side the arms of Clervaux, on the sinister those of Lumley. The side containing those of Lumley is still visible under a thick matting. 13 July 1443. John Clervaux, knight—to be buried in the church of St. Peter the Apostle at Croft—to every parson and beneficed vicar being at my exequies and burial 20*d.*, and to every chaplain at the same 12*d.*, and every clerk 6*d.*—friars of Yarum 6*s.* 8*d.*—of Northallerton 6*s.* 8*d.*—of Richmond 13*s.* 4*d.*—the friars carmelite of York 20*s.*—residue to Margaret my wife and she shall find for me and her good estate one chaplain to perform divine offices in her presence for her whole life and that such chaplain have 100*s.* for one year's celebrating for me in the church of Croft—said Margaret my capital messuage in Sant Savorgate, York; also 4 of my better mares—son Richard 3 covered cups and two without covers with 12 spoons and half of my vessels of brass and pewdyr and a hanging (*doser*) with a tostor of arrase for the hall and one bed with curtyns and tostors in the new chamber and 5 other beds without curtyns and tostors; all my draught animals, &c.; 24 oxen and cows with a bull, 8 calves at Croft and half of my mares not bequeathed; and one silver salt without a cover—Wm. Gybson chaplain 20*s.* beyond his salary due to him—Margaret Clerionet 10 marks of silver, 3 cows, 4 bullocks, and 3 styrk—Henry Taylboys [his brother-in-law] one covered cup—Wm. Vincent [the same] one covered cup—Ric. Mason a draught fily, a cow, an acre of wheat, and part of my vestments, viz. a hayk of skarlatt and a hood—Wm. Cabery a draught fily—every servant of mine a vestment—Wm. Leds a draught fily or a stage [a young horse] and a dublet—Tho. Blakman a cow and a mark of silver.

† The settlement of his uncle (in law) William Vincent of Great Smeaton in 1450, presents a splendid array of names. He enfeoffs "my most noble lords Richard [Neville] Earl of Salisbury, Henry [Percy] Earl of Northumberland, and Henry Percy Lord de Ponynges, Thomas Percy Lord de Egremound, Ralph Percy knight, Richard Clarevaux and John Vyncent," whom he humbly supplicated that notwithstanding the feoffment they would hold his estates upon the conditions he named in trust for his children. The witnesses to the transaction were James Strangways and Ralph Pudsey knights, Christofer Conyers, Robert Playce, and others.

For him was compiled the splendid family cartulary which contains minute evidences of his doings. In 1442 his father John Clervaux chivalier and Henry Vavasour esquier entered into a proper agreement on his marriage with the latter's daughter Elizabeth,* and the next year the good old man died and the bridegroom reigned in his stead. He was "esquier to the bodye of kinge Henrye the sixt," and in 1443-4 received permission to trade to Iceland to barter for Stokefycsh.† On Feb. 14, 1446-7, he received a full general pardon from the king as "Richard Clervax of Crofte co. York esq. otherwise called Richard Clervax esquier of our household" for all transgressions, misprisions, murders, rebellions, felonies, conspiracies, &c., and all offences whatever as well against the reigning monarch as his dearest father deceased, including a remission of all fines, causes of fine, &c., before the 1 Sep. 1441. The singular proviso occurs that this instrument was not to avail or in any way to extend to Eleanor Cobenham, daughter of Reginald Cobenham, knight, John Bolton of Bolton co. Lancaster, bladsmith, William Wyghill late keeper of Nottingham, nor to the felony of the death of Christopher Talbot, knt., feloniously slain, lately perpetrated, nor to offences against the Staple, nor to certain treasurers and other high officers of the king in trust. In the year 1441 mentioned, Dame Eleanor Cobham, Duchess of Gloucester, had been accused of treason for sorcery against the king and condemned to perpetual imprisonment, and the duke her husband was murdered the 28th Feb. 1446-7, fourteen days after Clervaux's pardon, which is dated at Bury St. Edmund's, where a parliament was then assembled, on the second day of which the duke was arrrested. It would seem as if some of the king's household were apprehensive of being connected or were really named as having been friends to the duke or his treasons. I suspect Clervaux's pardon was only a precaution, as on the 24th of the same month he was appointed (at pleasure) to observe whether any fleeces, hides or skins produced in Yorkshire were carried across the water of Tese or any part thereof towards Newcastle-upon-Tyne to be shipped in that port to foreign parts against the statute and such to seize, and to have the fees accustomed. In Nov. 1447 he was appointed Escheator in Yorkshire, an office one would imagine to have brought him in prodigious wealth.

He was in high favour with his neighbours, the Nevilles, for in 1445‡ Bishop Robert Neville of Durham "for the good and laudable service which our beloved cousin Ric. Clervax to us and our church of Durham has done and shall do" granted him an annual rent of 100*s.*, to be paid him by the coroner of Derlyngton Ward, and in 1447-8 "Ralph Earl of Westmoreland and Lord de Nevill" in his own princely style gave to "*our* beloved and trusty cousin Ric. Clervax, esq.," for his past and future services, a rent of 6*l.* 13*s.* 4*d.* from "our manor of Oxenhale juxta Derlyngton," for life.§ In

* The Indenture is dated 15 May. Another succeeds four days after. "This Indenture beris witnes that Sir John Clarvax knyght hais resaveyd of Henri Vavasour squyer c mark the xix day of May the yer of kyng Henri the sext after the conquest xx and yf it be so that oght bot good os god forbyd com to Richard or Elizabeth befor the day of mariage then the said John his herres or hys executors to make repayment in whylk wyttnes the said Sir John & Henri has set to ther selis."

† Henry &c.—we have granted *dilecto scutifero nostro Ricardo Clervaux* that he by himself his deputies or attornies may freight two ships of whatever burden they may be, in any port or ports in our realm of England wheresoever it please him together or separately with any merchandise except merchandise of the staple, and convey the same ships *ad terram Islandie* and return with fish called Stokefycsh there bought and provided together or separately as often as he the said Richard during 7 years may think fit—Test. apud Westm. xiiij Feb. A. R. xxii.

‡ 20 Apr. 7 Pont.

§ "Fermes payed of Oxnel. Memorand be the cummundment of the Tressurer Willm Claxtun I payed wn to Harre Deanem of Stayndrop in the Town of Rayby x*li.* and witness

In 1447,* the king having granted to Wm. Grymesby, treasurer of his chamber 200*l.* for the expenses of his chamber out of the temporalities of the then vacant see of Durham, and William having represented that he could not get it, he appointed Thomas Nevyll of Brancepeth, knt. (nephew of Bp. Neville) and our squire Richard to levy it better.

In 1449, William Cabery, an old family servant remembered in his father's will, had become worn out in the service and was affectionately provided for by Richard, as to clothes and food, which were it seems, expected to amount to one pennyworth per day.†

Like his own willows in the holmes of Croft, Clervaux prudently bent to every storm and was always a loyal subject to whatever king was uppermost at that day. He shook off the badge of the ruby rose and placidly basked in the ray of the *Rose en Soleil* on its first rise.‡ He concentrated his possessions in 1464-5 by exchanging all his property in Stapylton, Cleseby, Jolby and in "the grenes withoutyn Mekillyth in the suburbes of York" for all that in Croft of John Lord Scrope who held the manor by purchase from the descendants of Roald, but Scrope still reserved the wardships marriages, and reliefs.§ After this transaction, Richard styled himself Lord

ther of John Clarvaux of Rewas and Harre Chyne and Willm Adesun.—Also after that I content and payed wn to Ric Deaynem of Darntun in Willm Zodsun hus x*li.* wetnes ther of master Graistock for a payrt that tym the sayd Rie Denem a lowed me for Master Graystok.—Also after that I content and payed to Ric. Denem of Darnton in the perlleur at Kroft x*li.* wetnes ther of a man of Willm Claxtun and Thomas Laytun esqweer.—Allso after that at Rayby To Willm Claxtun in the Cunteng hus x*li.* And that tym Willm Foster telld the sellver wetnes wher off Jhon Clarvaux of Raffais and Pelkengtun that is with my lord Nevell and Thomas Cundun."

* 16 Aug., 25 Hen. VI. *sic in cartul.* Yet Robert Neville was bishop from 1438 to 1457. There is also a grant of the custody of the manor or lordship of Dyghton, Yks., then in the king's hand, for 12 years, rendering 14*l.* 3*s.* 4*d.*, dated 13 May 1450.

† "This Indentur beris wittnes that Richard Clervaux of Croft skwier has graunttyd to Will'm Cabery of Croft his yhoman for his gude servys that he has don to his Elldirs and hym mete and drynk and clothyng when he gevysse chechyng to his yhomen and in the same forme as thay have for terme of the lyve of the forsaid Will'm and the forsaid Will'm sall com into his place and sit with his yhomen at the mete and far as thy do als lang as he may cum to his mete and yf he have seknes that he maynatt cum to his mete and his drynk it sall be sentt to him resnabely and he send for hit and yf it so fall that the forsaid Richard ses of his lyve or will dwell in other plas whar hym lykys better he and his ayrise sal gyff to the forsaid Will'm for terem of his lyve evere day a pene In wittnes herof ayther part enterchangeabill puttis to thar sealles Writtyn at Croft on Pallme Sonday the zer of our lord Kyng Henry the sext efter the conquest of Yngland twenti and sevyne."

‡ "R. E. Edward by the grace of God Kyng of England and of France and lord of Irland To oure welbeloved Richard Clarvaux squier Gretyng For so much as we been enformed by oure ryght trusty and entierly biloved cosyn of Warrewyke that ye be vexed with such infirmite and disease that ye ne bee of any power to labure withoute grete jeoperdie we of oure grace especial in concideracon of your sayde impotencie and at thinstance of our sayde cosyn have perdonned you and holde fully excused of any attendance upon us or other by us hereafter to be assigned and comitted to laboure at any Ridinges or Journeyis within this oure reame licencing you by auctorite and warant of these oure lettres to abide at youre awne place or any other to youre ease from this day furth any commissione or other comandment from us hereafter to bee directed for assemble of our subgettes natwithstandyng Provided always that your servantes and tenantes at all such tymes as by our comandment ye and thai have warnyng to attende upon us or such as we wol assigne thame un to for the defence of oure landis ye arredie and sende tham in competent nombr to the same entent accordyng with youre degre as other gentylmen of the cuntre about you of like reputacon shall doo We therefore straitly charge all oure officers ministres liegemen and subigettes that thai ner noon of tham attempe or suffre to be atempted contrary to this our licence and perdonne upon the peyn that may there of ensue at thair peril Yevnen under our signet at Meddelham the xvij day of Januari The secunde yere of our reigne". (1462-3)

§ 11 Jan. 4, Edward IV. Indentor betwex John Lord Scrop, and Richard Clarvaux of Croft, Esquier—Richard shall have the chefe mese of the same lord in Croft, with all the demayn landes, &c., with mores, marras, watyr banks, meres, &c., (and all his property in Croft)—reserved the homage fealte escuage rent and suite of Richard, &c., for the lands, &c., he haldeth of same John by knyght service in Croft, with the warde marriage and releve of the heires of the same Ric.—and the fealtie and the rent with doubileng of the same by of Croft. An elaborate full pardon from Edward IV. on Nov. 5, 1472, to him by six or seven styles,* up to the 30 Sep. 1471 was perhaps rendered necessary by his having supported or been named in conjunction with Warwick, his relation and old advocate, in his restoration of Henry VI., a rebellion totally quenched in blood during the latter year. This matter settled, in 1473 he gave all his lands in Jolby (except Saint Nicholas' land charged with 13*s.* 4*d.* yearly to St. Nicholas' Hospital beside Richmond) to Rowland Playce esq. of Halnaby for all his in Croft, and in 1476 partitioned a moor between himself and Mr. John Pakenham treasurer of the cathedral kyrke of York and perpetual farmer of Dalton.† In 1477-8, (Feb. 26.) Edward IV. granted Clervaux free warren in the lordships of Croft, Walmyre and Escowton, and elsewhere in Yorkshire, but alas, the liberty led him in less than a month after into sad quarrels with his neighbour Place about their game, &c.‡ Their good will would scarcely be

the way of releve after the course of the lawe and for the landes &c. same Ric. haldeth of same John Lord Scrop in the town of Croft in Socage—and of all other tenantez that haldeth of same John as of the maner and seynorye of Croft—if this dede indentyd be not formall ne sufficiaunte in lawe for the exchange &c. this same writeng shal be reformed and amendyd by Gy Fairfax serjant of the law aftir the trew intent of the same. As the exchanges occur in full latin the same date, Guy the conveyancer was probably called in. From a statement afterwards in the cartulary, it appears that Henry Lord Scrope in 1305 let his "lyvelod" in the lordship to Will. Clarvaux for xii *li.* rent for a term. In June 1402, the tenantes paid Sir Richard lord Scrop 9*l.* 10*s.* 8*d.*, and on the date of the exchange to John the lord Scrop, 7*l.* 15*s.* 2*d.* The lands Scrop had then in Croft came to 240*a.* 1*r.* ; and those Clervaux gave him in Stapilton and Clesby to "xiij oxganges and xlvi acre *evere oxgang contenyng viij acre*", and in "the *sowle* of Jolby" 109*a.*, and in the grenys withowtyn Mikyllyth bare 20*a.*, total, 280*a.* [279]. These "lyvelod'" of Clervaux appeared in his rental at 12*l.* 3*s.*—"Allso it is to Ramamer that Ric. Clarvaux haldis all the lordship of Croft of John the lord Scrop in Socage be the sums of xviij*d.* payng in the yere all maner of suttes and servis ward and mariagis only except to mes ix scor iiij acre and a rode and a halffe of land as is in the featur of the said lordes Scrops mor playnly specyfyed the land that the sayd Ric' had of the sayd lorde Scrop in exchange the sayd Ric' aw nozt then for nowder sute ne servys warde ne mariage be the vertu and strenth of the sayd exchange Item the sayde Ric' haldis of the sayde lorde Scrop in the towne and lordship of Crofte thes places and landes vndyr wryttyn be knyghtes servys which amountes to the fyve meses and ix score iiij acre of land a rode and a halff as is be fore wryttyn the whiche places and land is thes at is specyfyed folowyng after this the whyche is all the places and land that the sayd Ric' haldes of the sayd lorde Scrop within the lordship of Croft be knyghtes servys where by the sayd Scrop and his heres may chalang or clame be ryght of the sayde Ric' or his heres ony sute or servys warde or mariage. [Here follow free tenants to the tune of 6*s.* 8*d.* of whom Thomas Clarvaux held a mess. and 60 acr. called Marchallandes for life, rev. John Clervaux and heirs, by 14*d.* and a barbed arrow, and Richard Clarvaux junior 1 mess. and 30 acres late called Schollande and then Detlande, for life with same reversion by 4½*d.*] Item the sayde Ric' and his Ancesters has payd to the sayd John lord Scrop and his ancestres of tyme that no myndc is for sute of cowrte for all the lyvelod that he haldes of hym be knyght servyce in the yere vjd."

* "Ric Clervaux of Crofte near Northallerton, co. York, esq., alias Ric. Clervaux of Crofte in Richemondshyre, co. York, esq., alias Ric. Clervaux of Crofte near Northallaron, co. York, esq., alias Ric. Clarvaux of Crofte esq., alias Ric. Clervaux of Crofte, co. York, esq., alias *Ric. Clarvaux, esq.*, alias *Ric. Clarvaux esq.*"

† The solemnity of this document about an old hedge is striking. Clervaux agreed to make and uphold a partition dyke, hedged above with "whyte wode of whyte thorne and breres." "Furthermore, if it so befalle that the dyke and heege be noght thrughtly mayde and performyd accordyng to the boundes and poyntimentz above wryttn, or els so performyd then aftir thrught laagges *displesaunce* or *self-wyll* or any other cause that casuelly may spryng in tyme to come *which god forbede* on the be halve of the sayde Richard esqwyer any of his heyres or assignes the dike and heedge be not suffeciauntly mayntenyd" after ¾ of a year 10*l.* forfeit to the Dean and Chapter and ¼ after that the D. and C. to enter upon their common over the whole moor.

‡"Richard Duc of Gloucestr gret Chamblayn Constabyll and Admirall of England—where Richard Clarvaux squier and Roland Playce squier by obligacions bearing date the xxth day of Marche the xviij yere of the Reigne of kyng Edward the iiijth (1477-8) stand bounder in c*li.* upon condicon that if they fro hensfurth be of gude bering and fullfyll our doome &c. We tendirryng the peas and welle of the contre where the said parties inhabite and also gladly willyng gode concorde Reste and frendly suite to be hadde &c." (they) shall sufficiently fence with dike qwykfalle pale or heege the boundes of there grounds—if cattle &c.

augmented by the scowling looks that would naturally glance from their opposite seats in the chancel in which Richard "the Bloody Boar of York," their arbitrator, ordered them to continue.* Clervaux pleased the Boar on his elevation to the throne in the same happy manner as he had done his predecessors, insomuch that in 1484 he ordered "his beloved servant Richard Clervaux esquire" for life a tun of wine out of his prize wines in the port of Hull. This would gladden the old boy's heart, but his amiable conduct on once more changing won him the golden spurs which all his previous manœuvring had failed to acquire, and when Henry VII. at Durham, confirmed his predecessor's grant for life of one tun of the red wine of Vascon, on Aug. 10. 1487† it was to "our beloved and trusty Richard Clervaux *knight*." The last royal grant to him in 1489 was of still more importance. It freed him in his old age of being placed or impanelled on any assizes juries or inquisitions whatsoever, of being a Justice of the Peace or trying any felonies or delivering gaols, of being a commissioner, admiral, mayor,

trespasse shall not take amendes for the hurte but easely dryve thame of hys grounde"—shall not "breke the *peas* of the kyng"—shall be content with the former exchange. Also we "deme that the sayd Rich Clarvaux and hys wyffe from hensforth shall hold thame content to sitt in there parishe churche chaunsell on the south side in such places as he and hys ancestres and their wyffys hertofor have always used to sitte and none other wysse attene to make their syttynge within the said church or chaunsell." Place and his wife similarly to "holde tham contentent to sitt in the sayde parish church chaunsell on the north syde in such places as he and hys ancestres" &c. and none otherwise, &c Ric' "in no wyse shall *beleve* take to his service or reteigne to do hym service any servaunt or tenaunt belonging to Rouland or dwellyng upon the ground of Rouland [*and vice versa*]. Ric' in no wyse shall hunt hawke fische or foule the severell groundes of Rowland beyng warren without his wylle and licence [*and vice versa*]—if any of the hundes of Ric to be caste of or let reune within hys awne grounde to any game and come into the groundes of Rowland Ric' shall not passe hys awne grounde in folowyng hys hundes but strake and blow for thame enlesse licenced by Rowland and if Rouland fynde the hundes of Ric' so folowynge the game upon his grounde he shall *rebuke* thame and no oder hurt ne damage do thame [*and vice versa*]—if hereafter unkyndnes happyn to fall betwene the parties we wolle that the parte so grevyd shewe hys greffe to Thomas Mountfert William Burghe squiers Sir Willm. Pudsey parson of Bolton and Thomas Franke squier—and if the sayde greffe be of such weight that thai in no wysse can appeasse the same than thai to show unto vs the cause why thay ne so can. These premisses to be obsERVyd upon payne of forfaitur of thair sayde obligacons—we have set our seale and signe manuell Ycvyn at our Castell of Meddelham xij Apr xviij Edw iijj. (1478)." In a subsequent quarrel in 1480, about "Awykfalle dyke," the parties very sensibly took the "discrete advice and concell" of Moundferd, Burghe, Pudsay (parsone of Grysmyre and of Bowlton in Bowland), and Franke. Place was to "have the holow of the dyk and the wode growynge thereapon toward Halnathby feld and the cam and the hight of the dyk to the backsyde of the wykfalle and as myche space at the backesyde of the wykfalle in ward in to Crofte feld as he may juste to the wykfall set a fensable heege." Clervaux licenced him "to brynge tynsell for the fence of the dyke and to stand upon the grounde of Ric' for the tyme of makyng the fence or heege so that the servants of Rowland nether grasse turffe dike ne delffe ne no swarth breke bot onely at the careage brynyng the tynsell moste of verray necessiti and dryssyng of the stakys of the heege." Parties bound in 20*l*. to obey.

* This chancel is covered by a flattish but fine florid roof, with delicately enriched bosses, among which occurs the shield of Clervaux. The tower is oddly added upon the West end of the South aisle, and on the S. side displays Place impaling Halnaby "R. P." and Clervaux, "R. C." There are also other sculptured stones irregularly built in, amongst them is the monogram "*ihc*," and close to it a small figure bearing the Clervaux shield.

† *Sic in Cartul*, "*anno regni secundo*," and the notice to the Chief Butler is dated at Richmond 22nd Aug. A.R. 3, the years of that reign commencing on Aug. 22. The recital of the following document is therefore clerically wrong by a year. "John Fortescue knyght Cheiff Butelar of our sowyng lorde the kynge of this realme of England to my deputie or deputiez in the porte of our sowyng lorde the kynge of his town of Kyngeston uppon Hull —where our said sowayn lorde by his lres patents, werof the date er the xth day of August the iijde of his noble regn hath giffen and graunted to his trusty and welbelouyd Richard Clarevaux knyght a ton of wyne of Gascoyn to be taken and pceyved yerly durynge the lyfe of the said Richarde of our said sowayn lorde prise wynes in the said porte coming or growyng at the feast of Saynt Mtyne in Wynter by the handes of the Cheff Boteler of Englund or his deputie in the said porte. I wille and in the name of our said sowayn lorde the kynge charge you that zhe from hensforth yerelie during the lyfe of the said Richard delyvir unto the same Richard at the same fest the said tun of wyne of Gascoyn of the said first priese wynes." x Nov. v. Hen. vii.(1489).

sheriff, escheator, or in fact of being in any official position whatever high or low. The sandglass ran out, the next year he died. The man who conciliated all dynasties and changes of advisers in six reigns of the roses, and still more, one whose veins flowed with the blood of the turbulent Nevilles and rash Percys, must have been a very extraordinary character. And in all his troublous and chequered life he found time to have a voluminous cartulary prepared for the honour of Clervaux, to square and complete his domains on the sweeping Tees, and to leave the estates wider and better than he found them.* His arms surmounted the portal of his (probably re-edified) mese at Croft, a long series of proud escutcheons marking Neville, Percy, Lumley, and Plantagenet, gleamed to his glory from its traceried lights,† and as if to complete his magnificent state, even in death

* He acquired estates at "Eryome *A Pountesse*," Crofte from Isabella and Margaret *Makeadoo* daughters of John M., and at Derlington *in vico fori* between the burgages of Roger Thornton and Thomas Surteese (1470) from Wm. Pudsay, knt. and Jakes Pudsay confirmed (4 Nov. 5 Hen. 7). He was seised of diverse lands in the soyle towne and felde of Derlyngton, two burrowages the tone on the borowraw between those longynge to the colage kyrke of Darl. and to Rob. Emeryson of Wardalle, and the toder in Skynnergate, and enfeoffed Tho. Alderson of Derlyngton, smeth, with xxxij landes lyenge in Granow Bodome *by a Rose garlande* on the nativite of Sancte John Baptiste if askyd. To show the enormous extent of the Clervaux possessions, I may mention that the cartulary contains evidences as to those in the following localities, besides mention of many more York properties in the wills as appurtenant to the potic arian branch. Croft ; Joleby hamlot' dominii de Croft ; dominium de Walemire ; dominium de Est Couton ; strata de Walmegate in suburbio civitatis Ebor., Fosgate, Colyergate, Saynt Saviregate, Dynnyngdyk, Goodromegate, Aldwerk, Mungkgate, Jubery, Hunttyngton, Jubritegate, Carnificium, Glovergail, Feskergat, Pons Castri, Ussegate, Mekilsgate, Mykylgate Gryne, Marketskyre, omn. in civ. Ebor.; Stapilton ; Derlington (21 pages); Hurtheworthe ; villa de Smetheton; villa de Warlauby, Stokeslay ; Solbergh ; villa de Tirnetofte ; Yedingham ; Donecastre ; Yrton juxta Semer ; Eryome ; Cleseby ; Hoton Longlers ; Magna Hoton juxta Wyclyffe ; Dalton.

† At the visitation 1666, were the following arms in the old house of the Clervaux family, I copy from Whitaker ; for the additions in ( ) I am responsible.

IN QUANDAM FENESTRA TRICLINII.

1. *Neville*, Marquis of Montacute, 1. and 4. *Montague* quartering *Monthermer ;* 2. and 3. *Neville* with a label compone, or and azure.
2. *France* and *England* encircled with a garter and surmounted by a ducal coronet.
3. (*Bishop Neville* of Durham). Gules, a saltire argent, charged with 2 annulets conjoined, of the first, and azure ; surmounted by a mitre, through which is a crozier, whose staff goes out at the back of the shield.
4. (*Clifford*). Checquey, or and az., a fess gu.
5. *Lumley*. Ar. a fess gu. between 3 popinjays vert, with a mitre and crozier as No. 3. (Marmaduke Lumley, Bishop of Carlisle, brother to Richard Clervaux's mother.)
6. *Neville*.
7. *Percy* quartering *Lucy*.
8. *Neville*.
9. *Lumley* impaling *Neville*.
10. *Neville* (*Clervaux ?*) impaling Or, a chevron erm., betw., 3 lions' heads erased sa. (This coat occurs in the illuminated pedigree temp. Eliz. with the lions' heads *gu.* as the coat of *Stodelay* of York. See the pedigree.)
11. *Clervaux* impaling *Gascoigne*, Arg. on a pale sa. a demiluce or. (The name of Gascoigne occurs in the early fabulous portion of the pedigree. I am inclined to think that a marriage did take place with that family, but where to put it, I know not.)
12. *Clervaux* impaling (*Sir Alexander Percy's arms ?*) Or, 5 lozenges conjoined in fess sa. (In the illuminated pedigree the usual tinctures of Percy are given.)
13. *Clervaux* impaling Vert ; a stag argent, horned or, and a chief of the last. (*Cerf*, according to the illum. ped. This impalement was in the Allan Museum in coloured glass, doubtless the same.)
14. *Clervaux*.
15. (*Vavasour*) Or a fess dancette sa. impaling Barry of six arg. and gu., in chief a greyhound courant, sa.
16. *Clervaux* impaling *Lumley*.
17. *Chatour*, Party per bend, indented, arg. and az., 3 cinquefoils, 2 in chief and 1 in base counterchanged. Crest : a stag's head erased, lozengey, argent and az., the dexter horn of the first, the sinister of the second.
18. *Chatour* quartering *Clervaux*.
19. *Chatour* quartering *Clervaux*, impaling quarterly 1 and 4. (*Bellingham*). Arg. 3 bugle horns sa. stringed gu. ; 2 and 3 . . . . . .

he lay west of his father, cancelled with a rich parclose screen,* under a tomb of the most marvellous hugeness, chastity, and grace.†

The estate of Croft on the decease of JOHN CLERVAUX, (VI) esq., son of Richard, fell to his younger brother MARMADUKE CLERVAUX, esq., who in a curious undated draft will in the cartulary makes provision to be buried not in his own paternal aisle, but on the steps before the high altar in Croft church, under a blue marble slab inlaid with the effigies of himself and wife Elizabeth Strangwayes.‡ This has disappeared unless it be one of the slabs

SCULPTA IN MURO EXTRA TRICLINIUM SUPER FENESTRAM.

20. (*Clervaux*) a saltire ; 21. (*Vavasour*) a fess dancette , 22. (*Clervaux*) ; 23. (*Vavasour*) ; 24. (*Clervaux.*)
25. *Lumley.*
26. (*Clervaux*) ; 27. (*Vavasour*) ; 28. *Clervaux.*
29. *France* and *England*, surmounted by an imperial crown.
30. (*Vavasour.*)

SCULPTA SUPRA PORTAM.

31. (*Clervaux.*)
32. *Clervaux*, with a knight's helmet and mantling. Crest : a demi-eagle displayed. On each side the letters " R. C." (I believe these to be the identical insignia now in 2 pieces and in the Clervaux porch of the church.)
33. (*Vavasour.*)

IN QUADAM FENESTRA MAGNÆ CAMARÆ.

34. *Scrope* quartering *Tibetot*, encircled by a garter.
35. *Clervaux* encircled by a collar of SS. (*Ric Clervaux.*)

* He also had a private chapel in his mansion. "1453 [1473 ?], Mar. 14. Licencia per Dominum Vicarium Generalem Ricardo Clairvaux, armigero, *Domino Dominii de Croft*, archidiaconatus Richæ. ut posset facere celebrari missas, voce submissa, per capellanum idoneum in capella sive oratorio, infra mansum suum apud Croft, per unum annum."—*Clarkson's Richmond*, 66. The parclose screen in the church is of oak, perpendicular, and still retains the saltire of Clervaux.

† This vast tomb of grey marble measures 11 by nearly 5 feet. On the east and west ends are the arms of Clervaux and Vavasour impaled, surrounded by a label wrapping about a rod, and inscribed with the motto "*Fortune. le. veit*," repeated in blackletter. On each of the other two sides is the muzzle badge of Clervaux four times repeated : on the north is the fess dancette of Vavasour, on the south the saltire of Clervaux, each surrounded by a gorgeous SS. collar. The whole tomb is so perfect, so incorruptibly hard, so crisply wrought, and withal so plain in its elegance, that it forms the most extraordinary feature of the whole church, and is indeed a singular contrast to the pompous overloaded tomb of a Milbank in the north aisle, surmounted by a batch of imitation armour and tattered banner, and on which the impaled shield is exemplified by two cherubs, the *baron et feme*, kissing in heaven. The chamfer round Clervaux's tomb contains the following verses :

Cleruaux ricardus Jacet Hic sub marmore clausus, Crofte quondam d'n's Huic miserere deus, Armig' Henrici regis et pro corpore sexti, Quem deus exelsi duxit ad astra poli, Sanguinis edwardi quarti terni que ricardi Gradib' in ternis alter vtriq' fuit Qui obijt A'o d'i M'o cccclxxxx.	Richard Clervaux lies beneath this marble buried, God have mercy on him. Of Croft he once was lord ; a squire of the body of King Henry VI., whom God raised to the stars of the lofty pole; and of the blood of Edward IV. and Richard III., in the third degree the one to the other. Who died A. D. 1490.

‡ In *die* nomine Amen. Be it knowen un to God and all the world that I Marmaduk Clarvaux In gud hell and prospirate And with myn own hond writen with owt mewefeng temppeng or stereng of one creatore bot god only Be the geft and the grac gefen of god almyghty for to mak my well and testment . . . . world that Is to sai and I dy at Kroft my bons to be bered at Croft Kerk in the wher emong the grecis befor the blesed sacrament and my sowll be the grac of ih'u ffor to be had with angelles in to the hegh heven in the seght of the blesed tranite In lyk wyes and I dy at Zork for to be bered my bones in the menster a ffor sant xpor and lykwys and I dy at Lundun my bones ffor to be bered Powll menster A for owr layde of grac in the bode in the cherch and this is my well That my younger sun that is to say Will'am Clarvaux hayf for the term of his lyf the holl lordshipp of Walmyr that is to say with the lowg' and the fesseng the chapell and the chapell garth and the mawr of Kroft that pertenes to the sayd Wallmyr as the olld dyk makes mensun that was of Bretuns land and also xx *li.* of the best plaiet of myn and also iij c shep of the best taken owt of Stolkmyr park [in Croft, granted by the Scyrlocs as Stockemyreflat] and Oxnell and also this my well Also be the seght and gud adwys of my lady Wells of Reppley that my doghter Elenor for to hayff of my gud that is to

peeping from under the pews in the choir. His son, JOHN CLERVAUX, (VII) esq., of Croft, engaged in the battle of Flodden Field, and is mentioned in the poem of that name, leaving an only child an heiress who was the first spouse of Sir Thomas the four-wived Baron of Hylton. The Baron changed with all creeds and like Richard Clervaux ruled himself with such prudence that he was a welcome subject of both popish and protestant monarchs. His arms form the only remnant of the stained glass in the Clervaux Aisle of Croft church.

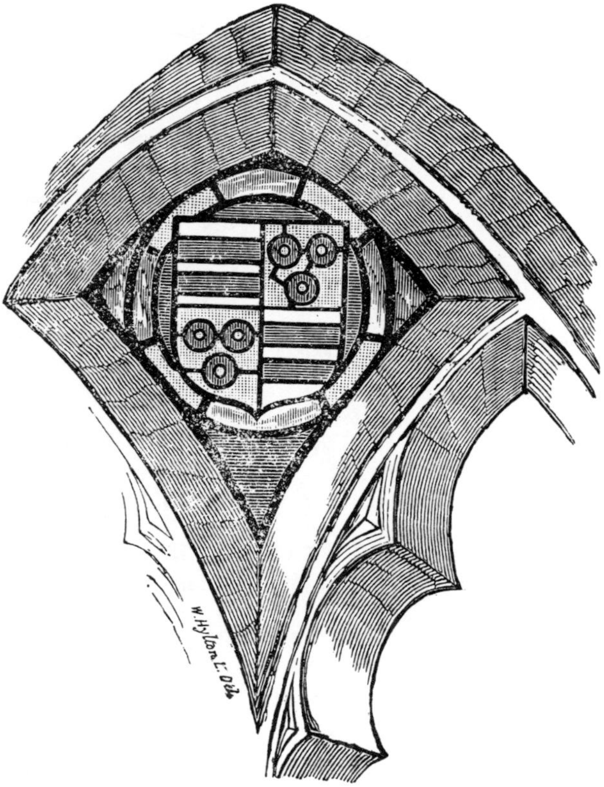

saye of pene and peneworth iiij schore pundes and the sayd iiij schore pundes for to be at the rewell of my sayd lady Wells upon the be huf of my sayd doghter Elenor Clarvaux and at my sayd doghter for to be that . . . . . well . . . . . . or marrag and gyden' of my said lade un to the tym that my said doghter be put wn to gud . . . . ffor my doghter well and & wirchipe this is my well Also that sun Will'am Clarvaux that he hayf and rewys all the land that I haif purchest or bogth that is to say the landes in Cowton that was Xpor Woufane that is to say the strif oxgang with an toft and an croft perteneng therto and also an . . . . . klos in Dalton apon tays of Ruger Stertfurd inneng of the knos of the gret plac' in the said Daltun the wech lies to me ffor an sun of sellver Also if kays be that offeises of seknes or besenis or one odar leteng that I may not provyd no get an marbell ston that is to say ffor be laied in the greces at the hegh alter befor the blessed sacrament in Kroft kerk wher than is my said well that my sekturs that is to say my lade Wells of Repplleday and Thomas Surteys of Dinsell and my zownger sun Will'am Clarvaux that thai provid an marbell ston in the said plas ffor to be laid and ij imag of latyn t'on a man in his armes and an woman in my kot armor on hir mantell and on hir serkot with Strangways armys on hir and an skoceon with myn armys on the onn syd and Strangways on the toder syd the wech salle for my wyffe and me And also that Sir Georg haif owt of Mekillmr groyng ffor vij zers after my desses to seng for me that is to say evere zer to is fowd or wages iiij *li.* xij *s.* and iiij *d.* ffor that ffermald is exempt it the ded of mareng ffor the term of xl zers to ffulfyl such detes or dewtes as is ffor my well or wells and after the said termys of xl zers than the said landes of Mekillmire to remayn to the stok and ayer a zayn And also that evere husold serviand or oder servand that is to sey that weres my leveray kletheng for to haif xx *s.* in silvor or in pene worght the full valer ther of.

There was no issue of the match, and Croft went to his lady's uncle WILLIAM CLERVAUX, esq., whose sons JOHN (VIII) and RICHARD both d.s.p. The former was "sworne esq. to the bodye of Kinge Henrie theight, died without issue. *This man was an unthrift.*"* The statement may be fully believed, for it cannot be doubted that the Chaytors inherited but little of the princely inheritance of Clervaux from his sister. And here ends the male line of Clervaux. A humble race of cadets occur at Darlington long after the broad lands of their parent tree had passed into another name, and they seem to have gradually sunk into utter pauperism.† The pedigree will shew them to have been nearly related to the main branch, as the Chaytors had to buy out any claim they had.

About 1541, Lord Scroope laid a deep scheme. He induced the unthrifty Clervaux to enfeoff John Uvedale, esq., of Marrick, in his manors, to the use of himself and heirs, remainder to Uvedale. "The consideration of this feoffment was at the motion of the Lord Scroope for that John Clerveax, being much giving to dicing, carding, and riotous gaming, ahould not lewdly play away his land, and consume it in riot, at which time Lord Scroope was minded to have married John Clerveax afterwards to one of his own kinswomen, hoping thereby to have issue of their bodies to inherit."‡ Uvedale was perhaps in trust for the right heirs, for the unthrift's propensities for parting with his emerald pastures became so alarming, that his relatives obtained from him a series of instruments confirming what was left to his own kin.§ The first of these was a lease of a messuage, fourtye shillynges close, Cotwellfeyld, the Lyon close, the welclose, *&c.* in Croft to his brother Richard for 21 years at a rent of 20 marks if John did not pay 80*l.* at lammas next. The mortgagee was to find to the borrower "one habyll man well furnyshed bothe with hors and harnes to serve the Kings majestie in his marshall (martial) affayres." This was in 1548, and in the following year John was bound to settle Croft and Walmire in exact heirship on trustees. A grant, however, soon after occurs to Richard of Walmyer and demeynes of Croft and Croft moor. In 1570, for the appeasing of variances between the brothers, and "for the stay of thinheritance of the said Richard," John was to make estate to trustees of the reversion of the manor-house and parks, holms, *&c.* of Crofte and Warleybie. Part was to be Richard's for life of John—then to John's heirs male (which Richard was doubtless well aware would never exist) and then to Richard and heirs, and afterwards the Chaytors. The manor house, and a proper portion of park was to be Richard's till John married, then for him and the new wife for life, and then for their heirs as before. Richard was to pay 20 marks and 20 nobles to John; and out of the whole arrangement were excepted the following bachelor's lodgings for the rake;—"the great parlour and the inner parlour, the kytchynge, the paistry, a rowme betwene the paistrie and inner parlour, and thre chambers directlie over the said two parlours and paistrie, and the orcharde and pounde garth." The estate was doomed to be rifled

* *Ped. temp. Eliz.*

† 1661, To Tho Clarvis being sick att severall times, 2*s.* 1*d.* 1670, To Will. Bellwood with young Clarfax 1*l.* 5*s.* 1671, To Mr. Bell for burying Tho. Clarfax 11*d.* 1676, Wm. Clervax wynding sheet 1*s.* 6*d.*

‡ Nichols' Collect. Top. part xix.

§ Sir Wm. Chaytor, writing in 1704, says, "He being quirrie to King Henry the eight, and living a profuse court life, though born to great estate, had spent the greatest part of it, whereupon his brother William (Richard) and Chr. Chaytor prevailed with him to settle Croft and some other small estate to be preserved in the name and blood of his family."

by reckless heirs, for Richard himself seems in his dotage to have enacted some odd transactions. Somehow setting aside John's settlement, he made what Anthony Chaytor the eventual heir endorses it, "a false forsworne lease" of Croft and Walmire to the use of "Christopher Place of Dinsdale and Tonnstell parson of Croft, who callid his name Rauffe Tunnstell which lease he causid to be maid in his sonne Thomas Tunstell [of Cotham] name" for 20 years or until his son Richard Clervaulx came of age, to such uses as he himself should declare by *will.* The same day (24 Feb. 1586-7) he had given 4*l.* annuity out of Lynggie Feilde in Walmyer manor to Wm. Place one of the sons of Mr. Roberte Place of Dinsdale "for the better maintenance and augmentation of lyvinge." The inspection of the signatures to

these deeds will satisfy the reader that the Tunstall document was written after copious potations with his uxorial friends the pleasing Places. After all Anthony Chaytor's irascibility, there is nothing very objectionable in the will founded on the lease, unless there were some comfortable pickings in the way of fabricated debts and executorship in general.* In 1587, however, the trustees granted 20*l.* yearly to Hugh Chaytor, who was equerry to Queen Elizabeth, during the life of their ward little Clervaux, by what power does not appear.

*24 Feb. 1586. "Richard Clarvaux of Crofte esquire—*advisedlymyndinge* to bestowe &c. —to be buried whythin my parishe churche of Crofte—(recites lease to his 'verye trustie freinds' Christopher Place of Dinsdale and Tho. Tonstall of Cothum of manors of Crofte and Walmyre to the uses of his will and charges them with his debts and legacies: for that purpose a sum of Two thousand marks was to be raised the surplus of which was to be paid to the heir.)– my worshippefull cosens and welbeloved frends Sir Willm Bellesis knighte, Raulphe Tailboyes, and Richard Bellesis esquires to everie one of theme one old anngell—my servants fof their travell and paynes taken with me as also certayne that have watched with me 20*l*—the poore inhabitants next adjoyninge this my parishe with my poore parishioners 20*l*—towards the repayringe of the towe bridges of Crofte and Sunbecke with some repayringe of Dalton lonynge 20*l.*—Marye Place the yongest doughter of Mr. Robert Place my father in lawe 10*l.*—Richard Clarvaux and Cuthbert Clarvaux (evidently poor relations on the estate, the latter liv. 1591) shall enjoy their terme of eighte yeares from the feast of Philipp and *Jacobb* next payinge the rent of 3*l.* 6*s.* 8*d.* ether of theme yearlye according to my graunte—(provides that other tenants should remain during his son's minority at their accustomed rents, &c.)—Mr. Raulphe Tonstill a whyte gray colt, nowe goinge in the demaynes which said Rauphe I make my executor of truste—reste to Richard my sonn"—Proved May 1587 at Richmond—Richard Clarvaulx sonne and heire aged 1 year and 8 months when extent taken 13 June 1587 and his wardship and marriage granted by the queen (of whom, as of her castle of Richmond, 3 *carues* of land at Croft were held by the 4th part of a knight's fee) to Place and Tonstall 24 May 1588 when rental stated at 11*l.* 5*s.* 4*d.*, a *carue* of lande in Walmere houlden of Henrye lorde Scrope of Bolton by the 12th parte of a knyght's fee to his fee of Realde, letting above all chardges for 35*s.* 4*d.* The remainder of the rental was from Croft. The trustees had in 1587-8 a grant of Crofte and Walmyer from Henry Lord Scrope, on paying him 40*l.* a year thereout

There is much difficulty in deciding upon the fatherland of the Chaytors. The father of old Christopher was a merchant of Newcastle, and was cotemporary with Peter Chaytor, another Newcastle merchant. The family tradition is that the family came from Cheshire to the banks of the Tyne. If this be the case, they doubtless halted in the luring haughs of Richmondshire, and made an early match with Smales; for I find among the family archives copies of the register of *Anthony* son of *Thomas* Chaiter in 1606, and several later Chaiters or *Chatters* from Wensley; in company with *Anthony* and *Christopher* Smales baptized in 1575 and 1601. The cousinship of the poorer Chaytors of Newcastle was for some time claimed and recognized. Oswald Chaitor, an honest linen-weaver was solemnly appointed parish clerk of St. John's in that town in 1582, *ad legendum, cantandum, respondendum, et in divinis officiis deserviendum.* He died in 1623, and it was, I may assume, his son Oswald who in 1646, being sick in body, wished to be buried in St. John's church among his predecessors, and distributed his trifles as tokens. Uncle Thomas was honoured with his best hat; brother Thomas his black gaiters; brother Cuthbert his cloak and a vice which he already had; and daughter Jane his silver beaker.

Christopher Chaytor, who had wedded the eventual heiress of Clervaux, sat quietly down in the aguish land of Butterby, having purchased its ancient moated manor-house from the Lumleys in 1566. There can be no doubt but that the wealthy lawyer was well fitted to *purchase* the lady of the then rather decadent house of Clervaux, the sister of John the "unthrift." There was ample chance of the issue of her younger brother preventing her being heiress of even what graceless Jack had left. In 1827, in cleaning the moat at Butterby, a slender gold ring was found, just large enough for a lady's finger. It was chased on the exterior, and would be a very proper one for Elizabeth Clervaux to have worn, for it was inscribed within, "*No foe to fortune.*" Chaytor in his youth had been a servant or retainer in the family of Jane Seymour's brother, the ambitious Somerset, and came with the first into the principles of the Reformation. The duke

(he having right to the wardship of the heir who held of him by knight's service) "at the porche dorre of the Southe syde of the perishe churche of Crofte." In 1548, Christopher Chaytor had given a bond to Clervaux the unthrift that if the latter paid 130*l.* he should enjoy Flatt (Fat) hill and Crossefield in Croft again. This deed is endorsed by Anthony the grumbler thus "For Fathill—an obligation. Fy of false. False brether. God blese my childer, this obligatione is if ned requier to have as God for byd." The conclusion jumped at is not very obvious, as any obligation consequent upon the mortgage would appear to have been cancelled by a full grant from Clervaux to Chaytor two years afterwards. In 1573, old Christopher settled 40*l.* a year out of the Fatt hill on his "welbeloved sonne Anthony," and in 1577-8 10*l.* annuity on his son Thomas out of Crosfield, and in 1583 settles both on Anthony and his issue by Margaret Wytham. There was no such issue, but in 1588, the father granted the lands to Anthony and his heirs for ever, in addition to the estate he had. A month or two after Robert Wytham the brother-in-law of Anthony had empowered the latter to sue his father Christopher Chaytor on the marriage settlement. The "false brether" certainly included Thomas, to whom his father "nowe growing aged and infirm, for his more ease and quietnes sett over all his goods and cattels movable and unmovable" in 1586 on condition that he should be found "all such necessarye and competent provision as from hencforth shall be requisite for the findinge and mainteyninge of the houskepinge and familie of the said Christofer Chaytor after such rate and value and in such sorte and order as yt is nowe and heartofore hath bene kept and mainteyned" and pay the old squire 80*l.* a year at his house at Butterby. Thomas somehow walked over both father and grant, for the old man after leaving his heir his signet of gold with his arms engraven (by which appellation he elsewhere designates the crest his will is sealed with), beseeching God to bless him and make him loving and kind to his brethren and sisters, and stating moreover that he was not natural unto his brethren and sisters nor obedient unto him his father and made him not privy to his last marriage nor of the assurance of his lands made to his wife ("god forgive him and I pray God to bless him"); entailed by his will Fathill and Crossfield in tail male on his sons Hugh and Thomas before the wretch Anthony, who in 1600, had to buy them up.

at his death gave him a gold ring set with a turquoise, which was bequeathed to his daughter Helen Chaytor. He bore many legal offices under the crown and bishop palatine, and at the age of 98, full of riches and honour, seems to have broken his neck by tumbling through the roof of his house at Butterby.* His descendants tell us with becoming solemnity that he was 2 years younger than Henry VIII. How differing the length—the character of their lives! It is remarkable that his will was made only four days before his death, and in that document he speaks of the uncertainty of death "as we dalie see by other neighbors."

William Chaytor who succeeded his father Anthony at Croft is said to have been knighted by James I. in his progress to assume the English crown, but at that time he was only 11 years of age and his father living. His second son Henry Chaytor, the last heir male of this line, after serving under the celebrated George Monk in Ireland till the latter was taken prisoner, escaped himself, and became colonel and governor of Bolton Castle in Wensleydale, by the commission of Prince Rupert. He defended it till his little band was reduced to the necessity of eating horseflesh, and then marched to Pontefract, continuing in the royal service during the whole of those unhappy wars. The estate of Croft from the effect of jointures was in no very happy condition but he nevertheless purchased it from a dowager who had a life interest in it, and settled a heavy rent-charge on her. His loyalty had confirmed his poverty, and he "was forced to marry widow Dodsworth of Barton for maintenance." This lady who was an ancestress of the present family of Allan of Blackwell had the good fortune to see three centuries, being born in 1598 and dying in 1704, aged 105.

On Henry's death, his sister Agnes, would have succeeded to the inheritance of Clervaux, but the colonel had been assisted in his purchase by his cousin Nicholas Chaytor, (as gallant and suffering a loyalist as himself) on the promise of a settlement, and this he performed by suffering a recovery and by will, "which he desired should be very surely done, for that he knew very well that his sister Liddell would, if she should survive him, make very much to do about his estate and make his will void if it were possible and therefore charged William Place to make it strong enough, for that she should never have it, and that he had rather it were in the sea than that she should have it." The deed of settlement had stated that he wished the better continuance of his estates," for so long time as it should please God, in his name, kindred and blood."

* In golden capitals, on a square blue stone, fixed to the Eastern wall of the North aisle of St. Oswald's church, Durham, is the following singular inscription :—

" In obitum Christoferi Chaiter de Buttrobie, Armigeri, qui obiit 17 Aprilis, Anno D'ni 1592, anno ætatis suæ 98.

Aspice quam subito volvuntur singula casu ;
Occidit heu inopum fautor p' tecta Butrobi,
A Christo nomenq. ferens cognomine Chaiters ;
Hic custos pacis, custos fuit ille registri :
Hic viduæ causas egit, causasq ; pupilli ;
Hic Regius terram signavit limite mensor ;
Fidus erat fidis, nullusq ; in pectore fucus ;
Omnibus et mitis, dictis fuit ille facetus.
Terra tegit cineres, mens vivit in æthere summo.
En, gnatus natu minimus, nunc p'manet hæres
Condigni patris, nec non suæ mun'a prestans.
Hæc tibi devinctus, scripsit monumenta Dethiceus."

Arms and crest as in the grant of 1571. "August, 1616 : Mr. John Fowler cam of purpose from London to me the 27th of this and took infinitt paines in settinge upp my father's moniment, and tooke jorney towardes Newcastle 13th of September followinge. I satisfied him for all disbursments att London, and gave him 40*s.*, and 5 chalder of coales, which cost me 3*li.* 10*s.*"—(*Thomas Chaytor's Diary.*)

When Sir William, the son of Nicholas, came to his estate, he found four dowagers claiming their allowances, the incumbrances exceeding the rents, and very awkward foes in Sir Francis Liddell and Agnes his heiress lady. They procured all sorts of delays to the granting probate of the colonel's will, and with half a score colliers from Newcastle Sir Francis entered Croft hall during Sir William's absence at Darlington. On returning, Sir William and a party found Liddell in possession of old Nicholas's chamber, wherein stood a desk with the will and proceedings on which it was grounded. The invaders were ejected, and had not the power to convey these away, which Chaytor very properly observes, was to him "a great providence." It happened after this, that, Agnes's mother being in possession of part of the house, she was prevailed upon to let Lady Liddell come and remain with her, which, says Sir William, "was a great grievance to me, she always studying ways to torment me. At last, pretending to be friends, she prevailed with widow Chaytor [the colonel's relict who had another part of the mansion and who, in consideration of the kindness of her husband Chaytor to her children the Dodsworths, settled her annuity out of Croft upon his legatees] and her steward to let her a piece of ground (the stinking pits) to keep her coach horses in, promising to pay me a rent, but instead thereof, kept possession in the name of the whole estate, which forced me to bring ejectments and we had a trial at York assizes, where I obtained a verdict to my great charge of above 60 *li.*, and I enjoyed the estate peaceably afterwards."

The descendants therefore of Agnes, this spirited representative of the first line of the heirs of Clervaux,—who had to be content with a fortune of 1000*l.* settled upon her by her father,—have gained nothing further than "men's opinions, and their living blood." Of these, the Forsters of Bambrough belong to general history The world of letters has a property in John Fenwick, Esq., of Newcastle-upon-Tyne, whom, I may safely style my most worthy and faithful kinsman and friend It is unnecessary to panegyrize a man who by his honour and talents has won so largely the esteem of his literary companions, and the affectionate respect of those who benefit by his experience and view him as one of the last of all his cotemporary chivalry. His various tracts bear with elegance of touch, the most valuable legal authority, and a far more important character, a stern uncompromising reflection of the modest religion of their author.*

The new possessor of Croft was the grandson of Thomas Chaytor the darling son of old Christopher the patriarch of the race who succeeded his father in his appointments, and left behind him a singular chronicle composed of prayers, annals of racing, floods, funerals, and feastings, his "agieuish dreams and sloomes all night," his "marvellous coughs," wooings and winnings, wheatsheaves and wants, and a curious account of King James's progress to Scotland in 1617. Through the whole of the entries a deep tone of piety, resignation, and sole trust in providence is very patent, and his mention of his brother Anthony and his children by no means countenances the illnatured remark that he was a false brother. Sir William Chaytor also left many curious autobiographies. Nothing better than an empty baronetcy was the reward for the continued loyalty of his family. After passing his time from "1666 to 1675 with indifferency as to matri-

* They are privately printed. One of Mr. Fenwick's most valuable essays, a profound mastering of the great principle of the Revolution, blushes as a modest preface to a short genealogy of the Radclyffes, in allegiance to whom at the crisis of 1715 the star of Fenwick waned.

mony, making his observation of the general unagreeableness of married people, where he was conversant," he wedded a Cradock, of that crafty race to whom he had had an utter aversion. In consideration of great advancement in lands and money, which his father-in-law only promised, he so settled his estates that he could not traffick with them. Heavy incumbrances, the debts of his loyal father, and accumulated interest pressed him to the ground, and the sole resource was an Act of Parliament allowing the sale of the Chaytor estates for the payment of debts and furnishing of portions for younger children, reserving those of Clervaux for his heirs. It was all insufficient. For 17 years he dragged out a miserable existence in the liberties of the Fleet prison, reduced to absolute penury,* and sharing his last shilling with two or three scamps of sons; one of whom in drunken dotage, by the cleverness of an attorney, who in a recovery had given him the reversion in fee and who had not a drop of Chaytor blood flowing in his veins, was induced to sign a will giving Croft to this sharp practitioner in trust for his heirs, with remainder to the lawyer himself. Sir William, in utter despondency, died childless.

The scene brightens. After long attempts by the broken-hearted baronet and his heirs to set aside the will, the attorney was induced to sell his interest, which although a prospective and doubtful one, was of extreme inconvenience in locking up the estate and preventing the heirs making proper marriages by reason of not allowing settlements. And then a season of continued exertion brought up the family from a depth of trouble to which many a gallant cavalier had hurried his children, and from whence but few of them ever emerged at all.

* He was continually pawning an old ring, which he calls "Old Clervaux," and which doubtless gave the impressions on comparatively late Chaytor documents of the insignia of Clervaux only.

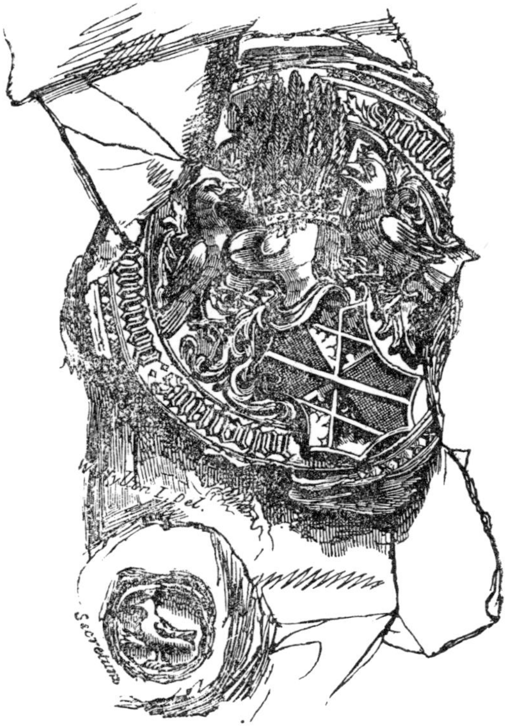

The Seal of John Lord Scrope of Bolton, in 1465, from his exchange of Croft with Richard Clervaux. The curious seals on the last page are those of Alan Menel of Ingleton and his wife Johanna, in 1357, from the Clervaux archives.

IV. BARNES.

THIS may truly be termed the Balival family of Darlington. It produced, either of the name or relationship, at least seven bailiffs of the Borough. The early part of the pedigree, prior to the grandfather of the Bishop, is principally from an illuminated pedigree drawn up in the Bishop's lifetime, in the possession of the late Sir Wm. Chaytor, checked by Collins's account of the family. HUGH DE BERNERS occurs in Domesday as holding Evresdone in Cambridgesh.

WILLIAM BÆRNES*, knt., d. 14 Ric. I. (arms, afterwards quartered by Bourchier, Quarterly, or and vert.) [The Barnes or Barney family of Bercheston, Worc., according to Visit. 1569, bore these arms with a cinquefoil in the centre, and a *barn*acle goose proper for a crest.] He had

RALPH BÆRNES, knt., d. 8 John†, who had

RALPH BÆRNES, knt., 46 Hen. III., took part with the Barons in 49 Hen. III., was sheriff of Berkshire 13-14 Edw. I. and died 25 Edw. I. seized of the manors of Iseldon (vulgo Islington) com. Midd.; West-Horslegh in Surrey, of the inheritance of his wife Christiana d. and h. of Hugh Fitz-Other; Ikelingham in Suffolk, and *Bernestone*, Rothings and Berwyke in Essex. He had

EDMUND BÆRNES, knt., 31 Edw. I. ag. 26, and in Gascony on his father's death, who by Alice his wife had‡

Sir JOHN BÆRNES, knt., of Berneston in Essex, 5 Edw. III. d. 35 Edw. III. and had by Nichola his wife

I. James Bærnes, knt., of Berners and Roding in Essex, a great favourite of Richard II. In the 11th year of the reign, when the great lords were prevalent, he and other reputed enemies to the public were arrested of treason, and committed to Bristol Castle. In the middle of May he was condemned in Parliament and beheaded (being "a lusty young man") on Tower hill, with Sir John Beauchamp. By his wife Anne§, (d. 4 Hen. IV., 1402-3,) he had

I. Richard Bærnes, of West Horsley, "*Lord and Baron of Bærnes*," d. 5 Hen. V. Mar. Philippa d. Thomas Knolles, citizen and alderman of London¶. She died 9 Hen. V. leaving issue

Margaret, heiress, who married first John Feriby, esq.; second John Burchier, knt., "who in her right was made Lord of Bærnes", and by her had issue the Bourchiers, barons of Berners or Barnes.

II. Thomas, of Writtle, Essex, whose grandchild John Berners, esq., in days when "Richard that sweet lovely rose" and his followers were once more in favour, was gentleman usher to the destined queen of Henry VII., and sewer to her brother Edward V.

III. William, ancestor of Berners of Finchingfield in Essex.

II. EDMUND.

III. John, of Amerden-hall, Essex, whose son Nicholas left a d. and h. Catherine m. to Sir Thomas Findern.

EDMUND BÆRNES, knt. "This Edmund with his sons having espoused the part of King Richard II., whose marshall he was, was proscribed by Henry IV. of Lancaster and had his estate confiscated. His sons following various courses with varying

* So the roll. In 6 Ric. I. *Robert* de Berners gave 200 marks for obtaining the king's favour and restitution of his lands.

† Qu. if not an error for 8 Hen. III. in which year the king enjoined the Sheriff of Sussex to make livery to the Bishop of Ely of all the goods and chattels of Ralphe de Berners in his manors of Bromfield, Black Nuttelegh, and Newenton, to distribute for the health of his soul.

‡ Another Sir Ralph is interposed by Collins from a MS. in Bibl. Joh. Anstis. as living temp. Edw. II.

§ *Alice*, according to the same MS. who remarried to Sir Roger Clarendon knt. base son to Edward Prince of Wales, and died in 1408.

¶ Philippa, d. of Edmund Dalingrug. *Ibid.*

fortune, at length settled in divers parts, whence the orign of the Barnes's now existing." He had

I. Oliver.
II. James, "*dictus Surreius*."
III. Ralph, lived in the county of York.

Oliver, "*dictus Sudovelgius*" resided in the province of Lancaster. (Arms:—*Quarterly or and vert, on a fess sable, 3 estoiles of the first).* Mar. Eleanor, d. John Gerrard of Ince in Lancashire, esq., (azure, a lion rampant ermine, ducally crowned). They had issue

Edmund Bærnes of Lancashire, gentleman. Mar. Elizabeth d. John Ashton of Penketh, esq. (arg. a chevron between 3 mascles gu.) and had

Edwin Bærnes of Lancashire, gentleman. Mar. Emma d. John Dichfeild of Ditton, esq. (az. 3 pine apples arg.) and had

James Bærnes of Lancashire, gent. Mar. Alice d. Henry Lancaster of Rainhill, co., Lanc., esq. (ar. 2 bars gules; on a canton of the second a lion passant of the first) and had

Edward Bærnes of Lancashire, gent. Mar. Jane d. . . . . . Bold of Bold*, co. Lanc., (arg. a griffin segreant sable, beaked and legged gules) and had

John Bærnes of Bold in Lancashire, gent. "Mr. John Barnes father to my Lord of Durham," bur. 29 June, 1584, at St. Andrew's Auckland. Mar. Agnes, d. Henry Sanderson of Dytton *quæ et ipsa de familia Boldorum*, (azure, a bend argent charged with a bear passant sable; on a chief of the second three roses gules radiated with rays of the sun proper). They had

I. Richard Bærnes, or Barnes, the bishop of Durham, 1577, b. at Bold, called by some youngest son, but by a pedigree in Coll. Arms, the eldest. In the illuminated pedigree already mentioned he is placed in the centre, the compiler's mode of expressing seniority. The arms also are not differenced. The time of his birth coincides with the latter statement, he d. 24 Aug., 1587, ag. 55, and therefore 52 years elapsed between his birth and his father's death in 1584. Upon his promotion to the see of Carlisle, he had (13 Eliz.) a new grant of arms which were composed of those of Sanderson, with the addition of a Barnes estoile argent at each side of the bend, and a naked child upon the latter, which the bear is ready to devour. These probably refer to the history of Elisha commanding a bear to devour the *bairns*, as a foolish pun upon the bishop's name. On the accession to the see of Durham he continued to use them, and his chancery seal dated 1571 gives a noble *rose en soliel* as in the arms, in which his shield (on which the said monstrosity is impaled with the cross flory and the lions of the see) is most sweetly nestled. Above are two arms descending from the clouds, containing the book of doctrine and scourge of discipline. In later years the prelate eschewed the pun, and his later episcopal seal gives the old arms (which were confirmed to him in 1580) quarterly with Sanderson. These, with a bear passant, sable on a wreath of or and vert., both differenced with a lable, appear in the illuminated pedigree for his son Emanuel, besides whom he left issue, several sons and daughters.

II. Henry Barnes, said in the Visit., 1615, to be brother to the bishop and "eldest sonne," probably an error for "second sonne," as the arms entered are those worn by Barnes of Lancashire in 1584, and by the bishop, with the crescent of a second son for difference, though this might be occasioned by William of Bedborne, his son being a second son. He is not named by Strype.

III. John Barnes, L.L.D., rector of Haughton-le-Skerne, 1578, and justice itinerant to the Queen within the co. pal., 1584, bur. at Haughton, 17 Apr., 1591. He bought up several parcels in Haughton Field and Darlington, including Hundon Closes, from the Pudsays and Killinghalls; some of them are described in 1582 as being on the south of the King's-street, leading frem Halghton town to Darnton town, called *Innell-lonyng*, or Halghton-lane. "This dede was executed signed sealed and delivered upon the ground within specifyed &c." His seal presents Barnes and Sanderson quarterly, with the bear crest, as in the illuminated pedigree, which, as it alone mentions him of all the bishop's brothers and is in the possession of his descendants, was probably a copy made for his use. By his wife Mary . . . . .† he had

* Bold is in the parish of Prescot. The Prescots of Darlington bore arms similar to those of their Lancashire namesakes. I have also seen mention of Glover of Prescot, as well as Glover of Darlington. Did a whole *posse comitatus* follow the steps of Bishop Barnes?

† In Sep. 1617, Thomas Chaytor was a commissioner in a cause "betwixt Mr John Featherstonhalgh, and Mr Topsall and his wife laite the wife of Doctor Barnes and they both wer maid his executors, but flinched from yt."

I. Richard, bp. 27 Dec., 1585, bur. 28 Oct., 1586, at Haughton.
1. Fredismonda, bp. 12 Oct., 1582, bur. 15 Jan. following. Haughton.
2. Anne, daughter and co-heiress, bp. 22 July, 1584, at Haughton, d. s. p. 1599. Inq. p. m. 30 June, 1599, Anne Place, late wife of William Place, gen. deceased, who died seized of ½ the manor of Little Haughton, or Haughton Field, Freth Moore, &c., &c., all held of the bishop in capite by one pair of shoes, or 6d., and worth beyond reprises, 6*l.* per ann.
3. Elizabeth, bp. 13 Feb. 1586, bur. 1May 1588, at Haughton.
4. Margaret, daughter and co-heiress, bp. 5 Jan., 1588, at Haughton, and heiress to her sister, 1599. She was the wife of William Lambton, of Great Staynton, Esq., and died 1631. Her two daughters and co-heiresses, Margaret and Anne, are represented by the Allans and Chaytors, as will be seen on reference to the pedigrees of those families.

III. IV. V. Oliver, Edmund, Edwin.
VI. James, "Jacobus Barnes, sep. 27 July 1593." (St. Mary le Bow, Durham.)
VII. Edward.
} All married according to Stripe, ii. 484.
Elizabeth, liv. 1590, wife to Francis Bold of Cranshaw co. Lanc.

HENRY BARNES, second son, mar. . . . . d. of . . . . Gifford, probably a near relation of the bishop's first wife Fridesmunda d. Ralph Giffard of Buckinghamshire, esq., or one of the kindred race of the name at Darlington. They had

I. John, liv. 1605.
II. WILLIAM.
III. Richard, liv. 1605.
IV. James, liv. 1605.

WILLIAM BARNES, of Bedborne Park, gent., of Darlington in 1604, *Bailiff of Darlington*, and Coroner of Darlington Ward: Will 26 Sep. 1591, names *cousin John Barnes of Durham* (who would be the Bishop's son, and clerk of the Peace; bur. 1613, at Bow Church, Durham): bur. 17 Oct. 1605, at Darlington. Mar. Barbara, d. Thos. Turner of Darlington, bur. in the church (as "Barbary Lisle of D. widow") 19 July, 1630, her son Thomas paying 6*s.* 8*d.* for the layer stalle of his mother. Barnes is said to have been her first husband. Ralph Evers of Edgenole, esq., her second. The order should perhaps be reversed; for her third, John Lisle of Darlington and Bedborne, was *Bailiff of Darlington* in 1606. He was some time of Durham City, and was brother of James Lisle of Barmston and Durham (father of Talbot Lisle the loyalist of Biddick) being grandson of Percival Lisley of Hart (Philpot II. 154) the second son of Sir Humphrey Lisle of Felton, by Margaret Bowes of the palatinate. He died s. p. before 2 May, 1623, when his will was proved by the lady who now was widow for the third time. Barnes and his wife had

I. Emanuel, bur. 23 Jan. 1590 (probably named after the Bishop's son Dr. Emanuel Barnes).
II. Christopher Barnes, of Darlington, gent., s. and h. bp. 19 Nov., 1590; ag. 24, 1615, when he attests the pedigree: *Bailiff of Darlington* 1625, p. m. Lisle, and Coroner of Darlington Ward: d. s. p. seised of a burgage in Skinnergate and of lands called Glassensikes and Windmill Hill: bur. 5 Mar., 1630-1, in Darlington church.
III. THOMAS.
IV. Henry, under age, 1605. [Mr. Hen. Barnes, clarke of Bradley Burne forge, 1631. —Henry Barnes, of Witton-le-Wear, gent., compounded for his estate in the civil wars for *l*20.—Henry Barnes, gent., Bailiff and keeper of the Castle of Stockton.—Hen. Barnes, of Dalton Piercy, gent., a referee in the Stockton Commons Division, 1658.—Mr. Henry Barnes, of Dalton Piercy, a worthe gentleman, was buried in the body of the parish church of Hart, before his own seat or pew, ob. 19 Nov., 1703. (*Hart.*)]
V. William, bp. 30 Apr., 1597, under age, 1605.
1. Bridget, *m.* Bryan Belte, gent., of Escombe, and afterwards of Darlington, who was bur. in Darlington church 5 May, 1634, Mr. Thos. Barnes paying his layrestall.
2. Anne, bp. 30 June, 1594, *m.* Rich. Heron, esq., Brockenfield, co. Nd.
3. Margaret, bp. 27 Oct., 1595, liv. 1605.
4. Elizabeth, liv. unm. 1642.
5. Jane, *m.* 9 May, 1626, at Darlington, to Robert Place of Hurworth. Their eldest son Wm., mentd. by his uncle Thos. Barnes in 1642. [Who was Jane Barnes that married Robert Parkinson, at Darlington, in 1605.]
6. Dorothy, liv. 1605.
7. Mary, bp. 20 Nov., 1604, bur. 9 Feb., 1604-5, at Darlington.

THOMAS BARNES, of Darlington, gent., a royalist delinquent bp. 22 Nov., 1591, heir to his brother Christopher, and adm. as such to a copyhold field called *Polam* (Glassensikes) parcel of the office of punder of Darlington: steward of Darlington

Borough 1615 and 1616: bought Huntington's close of John Lisle 1618: *Bailiff of Darlington*, 1625, p. res. Chr. Barnes: will 17 Nov. 1642; "brother-in-law Rauff Pudsey, esq.; brother-in-law Anthony Watson; the poor of Darlington 10*l.* for a stock; Rowland Place of Dinsdale, esq., and Nicholas Chaytor of Haughton Field, esq., supervisors: bur. 25 following at St. Helen's Auckland. These dates agree with the strange circumstances narrated in the following extracts. "Did they (the Scots, &c.) not rob and plunder sundry of his majestie's leige people at Dornton, in such cruell manner, *that the prime officer of the toune died of greife within three or foure days?* Did they not give an assault upon Piers-bridge to their losse?" *(Answer of Earl of Newcastle to Fairfax's aspersions, Lond.* 1642.*)* "For this plundering at Darnton, as you say of the Romish Communion, so say I, perhaps the souldier might reach forth his hand further than his commander gave him leave as is usuall in times of Warre, and scarce preventable. And for the losse at Piercebrig, we know little, but a losse of powder and shot on our parts, and a losse of a Howard, Colonell, and others on yours." (*Observations* on the above answer, 1643.) The Piersbridge fray took place on Dec. 2. Barnes married Margaret . . . . who was bur. 1625-6, at Darlington, and had issue

I. WILLIAM.
II. Thomas, bp. the day of his mother's burial at Darlington: called an apprentice in London, in his father's will, 1642.

WILLIAM BARNES, of Darlington, and afterwards of Low Coniscliffe, gent., a staunch royalist delinquent; will 10 Mar. 1666, "*to be buried at Croft church, in the place where my former relations were buried;* friend Leonard Pilkington one 22*s.* piece of gould, to buy him a ring with; Rob. Cuthbert, of D., one 22*s.* piece of gould, and to his sonn Wm. my little Galloway mare; *kinsman Wm. Chaitor, of Croft, esq.*, five angells of gould; the same to friend Mr. Ralph Willy of Cockerton; kinsman Wm. Place, of Darlington, gent., my lease of the tolls of Darlington Burrow [which had been held by his grandfather Wm. Barnes and Barbary ux. and his uncle Chr. in 43 Eliz.]; Mr Chr. Place and Anne Place, bro. and sister to the said Wm.: my friend Edw. Dunwell of D. my great gray gelding and my best Spanish suite trimmed with red ribbins; Wm. Smith of Stappleton and Joane Trotter 20*s.* each in gould; witness Eliz. Tunstell; Wm. Place and Wm. Chaytor supervisors." By his first wife Elizabeth d. John Calverly, of Eryholme, Yks., knt., who was bur. in Darlington church, 19 Nov., 1655, her layrestall remaining unpaid for till 1657 (a wedding probably putting the funeral six months before out of the memory of her tearless spouse). He had

William, br. 11 Dec. 1647, at Brancepeth.
A Child, bur. in Darlington church about 1650, when the layrestall was paid for.

And by his second wife Elizabeth, d. John Buck, esq., of Sadberge (last publication of banns at Darlington 11 May, 1656), his widow 26 Mar. 1666, he had

Layton Barnes, bp. 14 Oct., 1659, bur. 21 Oct. 1664, at Darlington.
DOROTHY.

DOROTHY BARNES, sole heiress, named as under age in her father's will, in Sadberge Reg. as "The Hon. Lady Brown, who was baptized in this chappel 7 August, 1670 [some error]; in memory whereof she gave a pulpit-cloath and cushion of red shagg in the year 1725": built the market cross of Darlington, which is inscribed "This Cross: Erected: By: Dame: Dorothy: Brown 1727." Mortgaged the Town-end fields, Dickon-Kists and Thorney Beck closes in Darlington tsp. to George Buck of D. gent., for 400*l.*, 1686: Married first at Norton, 16 Sep., 1674, Michael Blackett, gent., an alderman (sheriff 1676) of Newcastle-on-Tyne; and son of Sir Wm. Blackett bart., b. 5 bp. 10 Aug. 1652: *Bailiff of Darlington* by patent 1680: entered 1674 *jure uxoris* the d. and h. of Mr. Wm. Barnes dec. in those two stalls in Darlington church "which was her father's and built by her predecessors:" d. 26, bur. 29 Apr., 1683 (M. I. St. Nic. N. C.); and had

Elizabeth, only child, bp. 1 Feb. 1676: d. 12 Jan. 1677. (M. I. St. Nic. N. C.)

Second Sir Richard Brown of London, bart. (art. before mar. 30 Sep., 1688), d. bef. 17 Aug. 1691; and third John Moore, D. D., Bishop of Ely, who d. 1714, having had

I. Daniel Moore, of par. S. Andrew, Holborn, esq.: *Bailiff of Darlington* by patent 1710: d. s. p.
II. William Moore, esq., d. s. p.
III. Charles Moore, of the Inner Temple, esq.; steward of Darlington 1733: *Bailiff of Darlington* by patent 1736: took a lease of Darlington tolls 1731. He *m.* Elizabeth. . . . . . admix. to her husband Feb. 1738.

V. BOWER OF OXENLEFIELD.

Arms. Gu. a human leg, couped at the thigh or, vulned and transfixed by a spear broken chevronwise; the point downwards to the sinister ppr.: on a canton az. surmounted by the dexter half of the spear, the arch of a bridge embattled of the third, thereon a castle triple-towered of the second.—*Surtees.* [In the cut given in Sharp and Taylor's edition of the Visit. 1615, the arch is nothing more than the door of the castle, and the spear does not surmount the canton.]

Crest. On a wreath, a human leg, couped at the thigh ppr. charged above the knee with a plate, and distilling therefrom drops of blood.

The Bowers of Bridlington, Welham, Scorton, Killerby Hall and Tickhill in Yorksh. bore similar arms with a change of tincture.

William Bower of Latham, Lancash. m. Jane dau. of . . . . . Brickwell, and had issue

I. William Bower, or Bore, of Oxenlefield, gent., in 1615, having bought that manor of Thomas Brickwell (probably a relation) in 1602. He settled one third of his hamlet or grange of Oxnetfield on Francis Anderson and Roger Anderson (see his dau. Jane) to uses, and by indenture 22 Dec. 16 Jac. another third on Sir Robert Jackson, knt., and Wm. Bore, jun., to which latter he granted a burgage on Head Raw in 1618. The adm. took place in 1622, after the grantor was dead. In 1621 he gave to Bulmer Prescote of Darlington, marchant, and Wm. Rotheram of Blackwell, yeo., his burgage on the Heade Rawe bounded by the King's street on the S. and E. to the use of himself and his bro. Richard for their lives, rem. Wm. Bower, junior, who in 1625 possessed the right of the said Richard for his life and was adm. Bur. as Guilielmus Bower senior de Oxenetfielde, 20 May 1622. He m. Elizabeth, dr. Capt. Robert Carre (Sharp and Taylor; Gam, Surtees.) of Berwick upon Tweed, bur. 24 July 1611, having had issue

1. Margaret, d. and coh., bp. 30 Oct. 1591; m. Stephen Jackson of Berwick upon Tweed, by whom she had issue Robert (the Sir Robert Jackson, knt., of 16 Jas.?)
2. Jane, d. and coh., bp. 25 Mar. 1593, m. 20 Jan. 1613-4 to Roger Anderson of Newcastle upon Tyne. As there was no other Roger contemporaneously marriageable, this marriage upsets Surtees's statement that Roger's first wife Anne Jackson was "the wife of Roger Anderson," bur. 19 Nov. 1620, at St. Nicholas. From the baptism of his d. Dorothy she was clearly Jane Bower, and I think it worth while to give this new genealogy in a note.*

* Francis Anderson, of NC., merchant and sheriff 1595, mayor 1601, 1612, br. 26 Apr., 1623, *m.* Barbara Nicholson 13 Dec., 1581, and had issue (besides a number of other children not to my purpose)

Dorothy, bp. 28 Mar., 1584, probably she who *m.* Simon Giffard in 1637-8, (see p. 131).
Roger.

Roger Anderson, of NC., merchant, afterwards of Jesmond, gent., sheriff 1612, bp. 5 Dec., 1585, br. 1 Sep. 1622, will 28 Aug., *id. an. m.* 1. Anne dr. Wm. Jackson, of NC., 14 Apr. 1612; 2, Jane Bower, at Darlington 20 Jan. 1613-4, bur. 19 Nov. 1620, by whom he had issue

1. Francis, afterwards Sir Francis Anderson, of Bradley, knt., and a noted loyalist, who by Jane Dent of Barnard-Castle originated the Andersons of Bradley, par. Ryton. This worthy, who was bp. 21 Dec., 1614, is called by Surtees the son of Anne Jackson, but in the visit, 1615, he is expressly given as one of the coheirs of Wm. Bower through his dr. Jane.
2. Dorothy, bp. 26 Dec., 1615, sureties *John Wilkinson, gent.*, [her uncle, who mar. Jane Bower's sister Elizabeth] Lady Margaret Selby and Mrs. Jane Burrell, at St. Andrews.
3. Barbara, liv. 1622.
4. Anne, bp. 21 Feb., 1618, liv. 1622., bur. 30 Aug., 1626, at St. John's.
5. Elizabeth, bp. 9 Nov., 1620, d. an infant [her mother probably died in childbed.]

He *m.* 3. Adeline, dr. George Brabant of Brancepeth East Park, named after Adeline Neville, widow of Tho. Lawson of Cramlington esq.; she rem. for her 3rd husband James Cholmley of Brancepeth and Durham, gent.

Henry, bp. Feb. 1621, at St. Andrews, was of this marriage.

The dates are from St. Nicholas.

3. Elizabeth, d. and coh., bp. 1 Apr. 1594, bur. 30 Mar., 1622, at Merrington, *m.* John Wilkinson, of Ferry Hill, and Oxenlefield, *(jure uxoris)* gent., dead in 1647. (See Surtees, ii. 349). Of this marriage sprung Mary and Elizabeth, (both living in 1615,) Philadelphia bp. 30 July, 1619, Catherine 1 Nov., 1620, both at Merrington, and Cuthbert, who as s. John Wilkinson, late of Oxenfield, co. Dur., gent., deceased, was apprenticed to Thomas Maddison, merchant and boothman, of NC., 1 Sep., 1647, "committed fornication within tearme and confessed it to Mr Governor, 1655."
4. Robert, bp. 11 Apr., 1595, bur. 15 Sep. following.
5. An infant daughter, bur. 16 Mar. 1596.
6. Tobias, bp. 12 June, 1597, br. 10 Jan. following.
7. Catherine, bp. 11 Feb., 1598-9, br, 8 June following.

II. THOMAS.
III. Richard, *m* 29 Sep., 1625, to Agnes Branson. Richard Bower of Bondgate in Darlington, bur. 4 Apr. 1628. Anne Bower, widow, of Darlington, br. 20 May, 1629.
QU. 4. Dorothy Bower, *m.* Peter Moore, 6 Mar. 1603.

THOMAS BOWER, held copyhold property in Blackwell, and was dead in 1619, when his son William was adm. to it and demised the same to Elizabeth Clervaux, wife wife of Ralph Clarvaux, probably his sister. She was *m.* 21 May, 1618. The mar. lic. being between Ra. Clarvaux par. Blacktoft, Howdenshire, and Elizabeth Bore par. Darlington. This

WILLIAM BOWER, the *junior* named by his uncle, was of Blackwell in 1623, of Oxneltfeilde in 1631, yeoman. Acquired a burgage on le Head Rawe from John Wickliffe of Thorp, Yorks., in 1622-3, and sold a burgage to Anthony Eastgait in 1628. Churchwarden in 1632, and signed the registers by a mark. Will 8 Aug., 1646, of Darneton, yeoman—*to be buried in the churche in my uncles grave,* [1633, Recd. of Wm. Bower for the litle seate in the south side of the stall whereon his unckle Bower did sit 12*d.*]—son William 160*l.*—son Robert 100*l.*—dau. Elizabeth 140*l.*—son Cuthbert and dau. Elizabeth executors. Witness, William, Thomas, and John Cornforth. Guilielmus Boer de Darlington, sepultus 18 Aug., 1646. He *m.* Anne . . . . . . bur. 3 Dec., 1665, (will 2 May previous, mentions grandchild Tho. Emerson) and had issue

I. William Bower, bp. 15 July, 1623 ; adm. as Will. Boore, alias Bower, son and heir to his father's Blackwell property, bur. 16 Oct., 1651, "of Darlington, Batch'lour."
II. Robert, a legatee of 1646.
III. CUTHBERT.
4. Elizabeth bp. 15 Oct., 1635. Thomas Emerson, of Hilclose House, and Elizabeth Bower, of Darlington, published 3rd time 25 June, 1654.

"CUTHBERT BOWER alias BOARE," or *Boer*, bp. 12 Dec., 1631, (the entry is in his own writing, and an insertion, as I found by comparison with his signature,) of Darlington, butcher, in 1656, of Skippbriggs, par. Hurworth in 1673 and 1685, in which former year he sold part of 2 burgages in Blackwellgate which he heired by his father's will (the houses at the corner of the High Row, settled on his father by Wm. Bower, senior, in 1621) and in the latter was still a freeholder here. Bur. 1 Aug. 1689.

He *m.*, 1655-6, Thomasine dr. Lawrence Stainsby, of Cockerton, who was bur. 13 Apr., 1681, having borne him issue

1. Anne, bap. 11 Dec., 1656.
2. Elizabeth, bp. 10 Feb., 1657-8.
3. Jane, bp. 21 July, 1664.
4. Dorothy, bp. 3 Feb. 1666-7.

I suspect that the two following Williams might be son and grandson of Cuthbert.

WILLIAM BORE, of Darlington, "poor," bur. 13 Oct., 1727, as William Bover of D. gardiner. His dau. Hannah, was bp. 12 Apr., 1698, br. 14 June, 1704.

WILLIAM BORE, called *jun.*, in 1726, which he had ceased in Nov., 1727, of D., labourer. His dau. Anne was bp. 1726, br. 28 Nov., 1727.

There was a BRIAN BOOW, of Darlington, who had a son Wm., bp. 30 Sep., 1690.

The whole family presents a pitiable declension from good to worse and worse. "Gentleman—yeoman—butcher—poor gardener—labourer."

VI. ILE.

This family evidently derives its name from the old *del Ile*, and the visitation pedigree of 1666, entered by Robert Ile of Newcastle, begins with "Robert Ile of Darnton, acknowledged by Lisle* of Felton [Northumberland] to be a descendant of that family." It was, however, respited for proof of arms. I believe John Lisle the bailiff (see p. lxxxiii) to have had no *immediate* connection with the present line. At a later period one Mark Lisle was a dissenting minister here. "Shaftoe dau. of Mark Lisle, formerly Dissenting Teacher at Darlington, bur. 8 Mar., 1728-9." He had lived at Startforth, near Barnard Castle, "Lyonel, son of Mr. Lisle, a dissenting teacher, born 19 June, 1720" appearing in Startforth Register.

. . . . Isle, of Darlington, *m.* . . . . a sister of George Fennye of Darlington, (see p. 130,) and had issue

I. Christopher Ile, Isle, or Ilee, of Newcastle-upon-Tyne, (whither his Fennye connections would naturally lead him,) apothecary, mentioned in his uncle George Fennye's will "to nephew Christopher Ilee, 4*l.* per ann. out of Clarybutts." Will dated 30 April, 1614, naming *his daughters Barbara, Elinor, Alice, and Elizabeth, all then living ; his cousin Clement Ile ; his aunt, wife of Mr. Robert Surtees, of Durham ; and his kinsmen Sir Peter Ridell and Mr. Robert Shafto.*" He *m.* at St Nicholas, Newcastle, (where the whole of the succeeding baptisms, &c., in this pedigree took place, except where otherwise expressed), Alice Carr, 10 Dec., 1593. She was probably a dau. of Oswald Carr, of NC., merchant, and if so was *bap.* 5 Feb., 1575. Became administratrix to her husband 7 Feb.. 1614, and was *bur.* 23 May, 1632. Mr. Robert Anderson, Mr. Nicholas Tempest, and *Mrs. Alice Ile* sureties at the bap. of Robert s. Mr. More, *physissioner*, (whose prescriptions were probably made up by Christopher Ile, and the intimacy readily arise,) at St. John's, NC., 8 Mar. 1614-15. Nicholas Tempest, gent., Mrs. Elinor Clavering, and *Mrs. Alice Ile*, sureties at the bap. of Elinor d. Anthony Swinborne, gent., at the same place, 27 Nov., 1615. Alice Lyll surety at the baptisms of Thomas s. Robert Maltland, 5 Dec., 1614, and Anna d. John Reasley, 12 Nov., 1615, also at St. John's, being accompanied on the latter occasion by Oswald Chaytor, par. clerk of St. John's, and Anna Ogle. By her Chr. Ile had issue

1. Robert, *bp.* 30 Mar., 1595, *br.* 16 Jan., 1599.
2. Jane, *bp.* 20 June, 1596, *br.* 23 Mar., 1618-19, having *m.* Cuthbert Ellison of Newcastle, merchant adventurer, the ancestor of Ellison of Hebburne.
3. Barbara, *bp.* 25 Apr. 1598, *m.* 19 June, 1615, to Anthony Errington.
4. Eleanor, *bp.* 6 Sep., 1599, liv. 1614, *m.* 14 Feb., 1620-1, to William Anderson. *Ellinor Ile*, sponsor at a bap. at St. Andrews, NC., 1619.
5. Alice *bp.* 14 Apr., 1601, *m.* 4 Feb., 1618-19, to Henry Shadforth, as *Alles Ile.*
6. Elizabeth, *bp.* 6 July, 1603, liv. 1614.
7. Mary, *bp.* 21 Apr., 1605, *br.* 10 Mar., 1605 6.

II. Robert Ile, of whom presently.

III. ? Thomas Ile, or Iley, of Cockerton, *m.* Margaret Rickby, 14 July, 1597, at Darlington, where she was bur. 3 May, 1607. Thomas Leighley a defendant in the Borough Court in 1618, and goods attached.

IV. ? "Elliner Ile" bur. 28 June, 1610, at St. Nicholas, belonged I suspect to this generation, as her name occurs in the families of her brother Christopher and nephew Bulmer.

Robert Ile, Ilee, or Iley, of Darlington, witness to and legatee under his uncle Geo. Fennye's will of a house in Darlington. Overseer of the Tubbwell in 1612. Br. 8 Feb., 1632-3, at Darlington, his son Bulmer administering to his effects 12 June, 1633. He *m.* Jane . . . ., br. 19 Apr., 1630, at Darlington, having issue

I. Bulmer.
[Willi Iley and Janne Birkbeck were *m.* 6 Aug., 1626, at Gainford.†]

Bulmer or Bowlmer, Ile or Iyle, of Newcastle-upon Tyne, merchant and apothecary, bur. 25 Nov., 1644. His will dated 22 Jan., 1638-9, will require a few notes. *Bulmer Ile of Newcastle, merchant, to be buried in the south porch, lately builded of*

* In the List of St. Paul's Rents, 1667, we have Mr. Robert *Lisle.*

† Anne, d. Geo. Ile, of Killerby, bp. 21 Apr., 1680. *Denton.*

St. Nicholas Church, under my own blew stone which I bought from a quarry at the Heugh in Northumberland; 40s. to the poore of St. Nicholas parish, and 4l. to the church worke; 4l. to the church worke at Darlington [probably alluding to the Jacobean stall work in the north transept]; *wife Anne a burgage in the side, son Robert one silver beare* [beer] *bowle, a booke called Jerrard's Herball* [he succeeding to the apothecary's business and of course in want of the guide to the virtue of simples] *and one gunn called Harquebus de Crack.* This important weapon had probably figured in the defence of Newcastle in 1644. Its owner had been assessed 19 Jan., 1642-3, at 6*l.*, and his son Robert at 2*l.*, towards the loan required by Sir John Mearlay for the payment of the garrison (more than three fourths of the townsmen being assessed in sums under 5*l.* only) and on the 3 Feb., the Merchant's Company ordered that all the brethren were to join in a note of what arms they had, to Thomas Davison.

Son James, Turner's Herbal [he was a mercer, but still might be in want of such a book] *and a burgage in the side and closes called Darlington Waistes which I had from Mr. William Warmouth, Alderman.* Thereby hangs a tale. Wearmouth who from some undefined reason was the purchaser of various properties in Darlington Parish, surrendered a copyhold messuage and land here in 6 Cha. 1. to Ile, who, in his governorship of the merchant's company, was admitted to the freedom of the merchants by redemption, he paying a large fine for obtaining freedom without any right of patrimony or service but simply by favour. Well, some years afterwards at a court of the company held in 1672 to decide whether Richard Baites apothecary should be admitted to personal freedom, the secretary was about to read the petition, when "Mr John Dobson immediately stood up, and handed in (before it could be read) a paper, and said it was the apprentices' petition in opposition to the former; and some other brethren seeming very zealous in asserting the privilegee of the company, which they were jealous might be intrenched on by such actions, were told that the matter had already beene under the consideration of the governor and assistants, whose judgement it was, and that upon such grounds (though not fitt to be published) as (they conceived) would give any unbiazed person satisfaction. But his admission upon a considerable fine would be noe disadvantage to the company, nor any weakening or deminution of their priviledges, of which there divers former presidents, and one especially in the case of *Mr. Bulmer Ile*, a person of the same profession, admitted whilst Mr. William Warmouth (a grave and judicious magistrate) was governor and one as well versed in the law as their priviledges, and that to the satisfaction of the company at the fine one hundred markes; though Mr Dobson was not ashamed most falsely to affirme it in the face of the company, *that Mr. Ile was admitted upon the consideration of advancing the price of some landes was to be sould to him by the same Mr. Warmouth*, which was so evilly resented by the cheife of the company, that they judged it fitt he should withdraw, and deserved deeply to be fined for such scandalous aspersions upon soe worthy a person and benefactor, but was till another opportunity suspended." Baites was admitted on agreeing to pay 100*l.*, and at the ensuing meeting Dobscn "upon his submissive and ingenious acknowledgment that his aspersions were in his passion, indiscreetly and unadvisedly spoken (for which he was troubled) the company were pleased in hope of his future moderation to pass by the same."

To daughter Anne a wine-bowle with the Sarrazain's head upon it; the Bull Inne in Darlington, and a garth on Brankyn-more. In 1613 Elizabeth Barton lately the wife of Ambrose Waller and then the wife of Ralph Coatsworth wos fined at the Borough Court for not doing service for the burgage called *le Bull* and in 1624 John Smith of Oswoldkirke co. Ebor. yeo. and Mary ux. one coheir of Ambrose Waller late of Stanck co. Ebor. gent. deceased conveyed to Ile their messuage &c. occupied by Helen Bradley upon le South Rawe in Darlington in le markett place commonly called *le Bull.* Bulmer now became a burgess and paid his relief. Yet although he bought from the Wallers, the house was formerly the Bulmers'. On the East side of the house at the N. W. corner of the Bull Wynd are two ancient stones let in. One is the Bulmer Crest, being a long brute of a bull with a tail exactly like a fire-shovel, the other (which is near the ground) has in rude Roman capitals the inscription ANTHONE BVLMER AND MARIE LASINBIE. These persons might be brother and sister, man and wife, or father and daughter, and it may be worthy of remark first as regards Ile that Rowland Lassingby accompanies Bulmer Ile's father Robert as witness not only to George Fennyes will, but to other signatures of the same man about 24 Eliz., and second as to Lasinbie that Bowmer or Bulmer Lasonby of Darlington had issue Gascoigne Lasonby bp. 15 Apr., 1592, Bowmer Lazanby bp. 10 Mar., 1592-3, Mary bur. 4 Mar., 1595-6, and Helenora bp. 1 Feb., 1595-6. In these cases, the prænomen Bulmer probably actually arose from relationship or connection, but I will not assert that Bowmer or Bulmer Priscott bap. 1590 (who also had a grandson Bulmer) Bulmer s. Mat. Smart, (by Jane Branson his wife) bp. 1613, Bullmer s. Tho. Lumbley, bp 1616, Bulmer s. Tho. Allonson of Oxenetfeild bp. 1623, Bulmer s. Richard Boyes of

Darlington bp. 1632, Bullmer s. Tho. Teward of Darlington bp. 1632, Bulmer s. George Car of D. bp. 1636 and Bulmer s. Francis Oswolde of D. br. 1644-5 were *all* named for that reason. For the great Bulmers of Tursdale, and Ketton were powerful in Bulmer's Landes at Aycliffe and different properties in the neighbourhood and as in the case of Tempest Raine the son of a yeoman of Stella, territorial juxta position and feudal respect often influenced names as well compliments to the sponsors. Nevertheless there were Bulmers of Darlington who might have a hand in the matter. Robert Robinson sued William Bulmer in 1623 upon a case for saying *thou art a theife and stole my lofe*, damage 39*s*. 11*d*. This William Bowmer or Bulmer was bur. Jan. 1646-7. His wife Jenet was br. 6 Aug. 1621, he waited a couple of months and *m.* a second wife Agnes Gibson on the 21 Oct. following, she bore him Ann bp. 14 Sep. 1623 (bur. 2 Mar. 1644-5) and was bur. 13 Sep. 1623. His children Christopher br. 1643, and Mary br. 1640 were I suppose by his former wife. Alice wife of Mark Bulmire of Sunderland by sea, sailor, bur. 1 June 1711.

Besides, Bulmer Ile bought of Tho. Wilson in 1625 a capital messuage on le Churchrawe with four pasturegates on Brankinmoor, yielding thence to the churchwardens *on the feast of the Conversion of St. Paul* 6*s*. 8*d*.* yearly, and in 1629 two other burgages in le Church Rawe of Anthony Raynarde and Thomas Lumley s. of John Lumley of D. deceased. In 5 Cha. I. he was adm. at Nesbett, par. Haughton to lands in Low Mylne Holme and Ashefeild, and in 13 Cha. he purchased from Chr. Hearon a close at Cockerton called Mussey Wray, to which his widow Anne was adm. 22 Cha. I. *Halmot Bks.*

Mention is made in the will of *his daughter Marie ; father in law Mr. Lawrence Pollard ; brothers John Lunn and John Smith ; Anthony Normane, Scrivener ; wife Ann and son James executors.*

Bulmer Ile *m.* 1. Agnes Cock on the 26 Jan. 1611-12 sur. at the bap. of Mary d. Tho. Rutter 29 Mar. 1614 at St. Johns bur. 7 Dec. 1614, which was apparently the day she died, perhaps owing to some pestilent epidemic. Her tombstone in 1817 was inspected by Sir C. Sharp in the nave of St. Nicholas and at that time it presented several inscriptions of other persons not connected with Ile and at the foot a coat given by Surtees as "Arms . . . . a fess between three escallop shells . . . . . a mullet for difference, *Ile*, impaling Ermine on a cross engrailed . . . . a mullet *Pollard:* Crest, a demi lion rampant holding between his paws an escallop shell"; yet however remarkable the last coincidence with Ile's second wife may be, the original coat consists of Semee of cloves, a chevron, for the Company of Grocers and Spicers, impaling 2 coats one above another, the top one was much mutilated but seems to have been a plate between three cocks for Cock, the lower one is barry of 4 . . . . . . and ermine, each of the former divisions charged with 4 trees *(Pollards?)* "Bulmer Ile Apothecarie and Grocer of this Towne and *Anne* his Wife She Departed to the Mercie of God the 7 December 1614." It will be observed that Bulmer did not adopt the Lisle Lion Rampant, and he merely gives the company's crest, a dromedary, which I suppose would convey the spices from India. The stone appears to have been laid after the death of the 1st wife and posterior to the marriage with the second one, who was Anne Pollard dau. of Lawrence P. of Newlathes, Yorks., gent., *m.* 9 Jan. 1614-15 (a brief month after Agnes Cocks's death. What funny old fellows our benedicts were formerly !) as "Ann *Pullet*" bur. 2 June, 1669, as "Mrs. Anne Ile widow" having born to Bulmer

1. Elizabeth, bap. 26 Feb., 1615-16.
2. Ellinor, bap. 17 Apr., 1618, Qu. Elliner Ile bur. 22 Feb., 1632-3.
3. Elizabeth bp. 29 Nov., 1619.
iv. Robert.
5. Anne bp. 1 Dec., 1623, *m.* Feb., 1641-2, to Robert Jenison of Newcastle merchant, and had, *inter alios*, a son *Bulmer* Jenison bur. 31 Mar., 1657.
vi. James, bp. 31 July, 1626, apprenticed 20 Dec., 1644, to Robert Ellison of NC. merchant adventurer and mercer, d. 20, bur. 21 Apr., 1653. He held his father's burgage in Ratton Rawe and paid the Paul's Rent for it in 1648, and sold it to Richard Harrison just before his death.
7. Jane, bp. 19 Jan., 1628-9.
viii. Henry, bp. 18 July, 1631.
ix. Bulmer, bp. 20 Jan. 1632-3.
10. Mary, bp. 8 Oct., 1636, *m.* 15 Dec., 1656, to Lancelot Westgarth of Newcastle, merchant and apothecary, who had been apprentice to Robert Jenison and was set over to Robert Ile to serve the remainder of his term and —— run sweet upon his sister. In 1675 Mrs. Mary Westgarth, relict of Mr. Lancelot West-

* 1630. St. Paules Day, of Mr. Bulmer Ile for his houses in Ratton Rawe, 6*s*. 8*d*. of Robert Ile for his doore into the Church yeard. 1633, Rec. of Mr. Bullmer Iley 10*s*. [evidently a considerate gift to the poor.]

garth, humbly petitioned the company of merchants "for theire brotherly and Christian charity towards the releife of hirself and small children; beeing in a very sad and deplorable condition. The company taking hir petition into theire serious consideration, and beeing satisfied that hir husband had paid a considerable sume to them for impositions in the managing a trade, not greatly advantageous to himselfe; and judging it expedient to supply hir with such a sume of money for a stock whereby she might be enabled to follow a petty trade in some commoditys by way of rettaile, and to prevent any petition for reliefe for the future, were gratiously pleased to graunt to hir the sume of ten pounds. And it was ordered that it should be paid by the wardens to Mr. Robert Ellison whose care was desired that it might be imploied accordingly." Ellison was the master of Mary's brother and trustee for her neice Ann, and would appear to have been the friend and adviser of the family.

ROBERT ILE,* of Newcastle, merchant and apothecary, bp. 15 Oct. 1620. On 17 Jan. 1641-2 he petitioned the merchants for admission into their fraternity and requested that in fixing the fine for his admission (as he could not claim by either service or patrimony) they would take into consideration "the great fyne his father had paid" the which "in greate favour to him they were pleased to doe," and soe he was admitted on paying 10*l*.† In 1666-7, in consideration of his natural affection for his daughter Ann he releases unto Robert Ellison and Wm. Grey, of Newcastle, merchants, a house in the Side, NC., adjoining that in which he himself lived, as also a messuage or tenement in Darlington, in the market place there, late in the possession of John Middleton, draper, his tenants, &c., boundering upon a messuage then or late in the possession of John Turner, yeoman, on the west part, the winde or lane called *Bull Winde* on the east, the King's street on the north, and a street called Hungate on the south; and 7 beastgates or pasturegates in Brankinmoore, to the use of himself for life, rem. Ann. It would appear as if he had purchased this property from his aunt Ann Jennison, to whom his father left it. The house has long been rebuilt, but still retains the court-yard and semblance of an hostelry. From the nicely fitted flags of the pavement in Mr. Mewburn's offices, it has evidently formed part of a very superior domicile in its day.

Robert (24 Jan. 1641) m. 1. DEBORAH, d. of CUTHBERT GRAY of Newcastle, merchant, bur. 29 Dec. 1666, and erroneously registered as "*Rebecca*, wife of Robert Ile, pothecary and grosser," which must be a clerical mistake, as all her children are baptized up to the period as those of Robert Ile and *Deborah* his wife. They were

A. Robert, bp. Nov. 1643, d. young.
B. Cuthbert, bp. 26 Apr. 1644, d. young.
C. BULMER.
D. Elizabeth, bp. 18 Sep 1645, d. young.
E. Robert, bp. 23 Nov. 1647, bur. 27 Feb. 1647-8.
F. John, b. 16, bp. 22 Jan. 1649, d. young.
G. Deborah, bur. 12 Nov. 1655.
H. Ann, b. 4 May 1654, unm. in 1666, when her father settled the Bull Inn upon her.
I. Robert, b. 27, bp. 28 May 1657, d. young.

Ile m. 2. on 14 Nov. 1667, ANN BRIGGES who was bur. 5 Oct 1675, having had issue

J. Robert, bp. 15 Oct. 1668.
K. William, bp. 23 June 1670.
L. Charles, bp. 1 Jan. 1671.
M. John, 31 July 1673, bur. 29 Mar. 1676.
N. George (a Brigges name, George Brigges, merchant, was possibly Ann Brigges's father) infant son of Robert Ile, merchant, bp. 29 Sep. 1674 (St. John's, N.C.), bur. 22 Jan. 1675-6.

Robert Ile does not appear to occur as holding any office in the merchants' company after 1676 or therefore nor has his burial register turned up at Newcastle, circumstances which may be explained by the marriage of Mr. Robert Ille with Mrs. ELIZABETH WILLIAMSON at St. Helen's Auckland 28 Sep. 1676, and the return of the bridegroom to his ancestral parish. "Mr. Robert Ile of Cockerton" was bur. 6 Oct. 1679,‡ and

* 1645. Let on seate to Robt. Ile which his father bult. *Ch. Acc.*

† NC. Merchant's Bks., per G. B. R.

‡ Consequently, the Bank Close at the junction of the Croft and Blackwell roads in the manor of Bondgate, is properly described in 34 Cha. 2., as being bounded on the W. and S. by lands *late* of Robert Ile. Notwithstanding the list of freeholders in Bondgate, Darlington, for 1685, given in Surtees, includes the name of "Robert Ile, gent., at Newcastle." 1679, Recd. for Mr. Ile laire stall, 6*s*. 8*d*.—*Darlington ch. acc.*

"Elizabeth Isle of Cockerton, widow," 17 Nov. 1725, both at Darlington. From this marriage sprung

o. Thomas, "son of Mr. Robert Ile of Cockerton," bp. 4 Mar., 1678-9, and bur. 28 Sep., 1681, at Darlington.
p. William Iley, "son of Mrs. Iley of Cockerton," bur. 13 Mar., 1683-4, at Darlington.*
Who was Isabel Iley, of Darlington, widow, bur. 5 Jan., 1727-8?

Bulmer Isle or Ile, son of Deborah Gray, was aged 21, 25 Aug. 1666, and then the only son living, was apprenticed to Mr. Robert Ellison *(the family friend)*, merchant adventurer and mercer, on 11 Nov. 1658, and adm. to his freedom 18 Nov. 1668. "Bulmer Isle, merchant," bur. 7 Feb. 1685-6.

BOWES.

One family of the name is noticed under the head of Hylton. A number of struggling members of this wide spreading race occur as living here. Thomas Bowes bur. 1597. Elizabeth Wall alias Bowes, illeg. d. of Margaret Wall and Robert Bowes, bp. 1539-40, bur. 1641. Robert Bowes, gent., a freeholder 1617, was probably identical with

Robert Bowes of Bondgate, who m. Margaret Gregorie, 1641, and had issue

Thomas, bap. 1642 Thomas Bowes, of Darlington, bur. 15 Aug. 1699.
Robert, most likely the same as

Robert Bowes, a weaver of Cockerton, bur. 29 Apr. 1677, whose wife was bur. 4 June 1680, as "Elizabeth Bowes of Cockerton, widow." He had issue

Margaret, bap. 1655.
Robert, bap. 1659. "Robert Bowes, a young man of Cockerton, bur. 28 May, 1684."
John.

John Bowes of Cockerton, bp. 1665-6, m. Eleanor Lazenby of Cockerton, 22 May 1699, and had issue
John, bap. 6 Oct. 1700.

William Bowes sold a burgage in 1614.—Susan Bowes, d. of Mary Bowes of Darlington, bur. 12 Apr. 1664.—George Algood and Jane Bowes, both of Darlington parish, m. 25 Nov. 1684.—Edward Bowes, one that came from Brantum to Darlington, bur. 1688.—Magdalene, d. of Wm. Bowes of Darlington, innkeeper, bp. 1726.

William Bowes of Blackwell, yeoman, (his wife probably "Elizabeth Bowes of Blackwell, widow," bur. 1 June 1729) had issue

Thomas Bowes of Darlington, butcher, who as s. and h. of Wm. Bowes late of Blackwell, yeoman, deceased, with Anne Aire of Blackwell, widow of Robert Aire, late of Blackwell, yeoman, deceased, sold a messuage with "the forefront or *sheppens*," in le Well Row in 1731.

Peggy Stow Stowell late Bowes of Darlington, wife of William Stow Stowell, farmer, aged 43, d. 8 Jan. 1811.

* 1683, Recd. of Mrs. Isle for her child laire stall, 6*s*. 8*d*.—*Darlington ch. acc.*

EMERSON.

The Emersons lived at Hill Close House for centuries. Thomas Emerson of Darneton was a disclaimer in 1615. Henery Emmerson a stranger of Brough was buried in 1698-9. The estate afterwards belonged to the Richardsons, and in 1725 Robert Richardson, gent., sold it to Geo. Allan, Esq.

Hill Close House is now the property of Miss Allan, and though shorn of half its extent, has survived all its cotemporaries, and still asserts itself the only Tudor house of stone in the parish. Enormous thickness of wall, deep-splayed mullioned windows and picturesque gables are there, and the ancient pond close by is oddly placed on the top of the hill. The situation is passing beautiful. A glorious view of the west imparts to the mind's eye the impressions produced by the charming peeps in some Yorkshire dales. The sturdy owners perhaps scarcely appreciated all this, and their comforts may seem strange when I remark that within a recent period one of the room floors was *paved with blue flints*. Part of the estate is called *Bottle Hull* or *Hall*, and I have heard a tradition of some very extensive foundations being found there, which were considered to be the remains of another old manorhouse or hall. Bottle is a Saxon name for a mansion. Robert Emmerson of *Hoole House* was buried at Darlington 11 Oct., 1603.

DAYKINS.

Thomas Daykins, son of Arthur Daykins, gent., of Darlington, bur., 13 Apr., 1631.

Arthur Dakins was probably a member of the Linton (East Riding) branch of the name. It is even possible that Arthur the heir of that race, aged 8 in 1612, was for some reason holding a *temporary* residence here, for the name occurs no more. An elder line of Dakyns, Dakeyne, Ducking, Dakyn, Deakinne, Daking, Dakeny, De Akeny, D'Elking, De Okeny, &c., was settled at Biggin Grange, in Derbyshire, and one of its members married Katherine, dau. of Patric Schange or Strange, of Edinburgh, gent., naturalized 37 Eliz., having been a favourite maid of honour to Mary Queen of Scots, and reputed to have attended her to the scaffold. This may be queried, since she was married before that event, in fact her son John was born in the same year. Her luckless mistress left her 400 francs by her draft will made at Sheffield, but as this sum does not appear in her last testament it was probably given to Catherine on her marriage. The descendants of her eldest son John are the families of Deakin or Dakeyne, late of Bagthorpe House, co. Notts, represented by my indefatigable correspondent and fellow-worker in gentle genealogy, Henry Charles Dakeyne, Esq., of 34, Hamilton Terrace, St. John's Wood, London, and of the Old Hall, East Bridgeford, Notts.

The motto **Strike, Dakyns, the Devil's in the Hempe,** was granted to General Arthur Dakyns, of Linton, in 1563, and if generals then commanded on the water as well as on the land, it may allude to some most gallant hacking at the enemy's hempen cords. It certainly is a maritime motto, for the crest presents an arm brandishing a battle axe out of a naval crown. The main branch assumed it in 1610.*

* See further in my tract containing "Observations on Martial Mottos."

MISCELLANEA.

A number of families are noticed in the body of this work. Many houses of good name occur in the registers, such as Lumley, Brand, Carr, Lowther, Tunstall, Catherick, Addison, Teasdale, Bainbrig, Pepper, Denton, Vaux and Clifford—but they are storyless—their remote descent from ancient families rendered more remote by forgetfulness of their fathers.

The name of Bee has become classical since the publication of Jacob Bee's Diary by Sir C. Sharp. Ralph Bee and Jane Armstrong were married at Darlington, 22 Aug., 1631. The names of Bellamie and Bowbank are of very frequent occurrence. Peter Bowbank was a wealthy man of the parish about 1640. A family of Crathorne, scions of the great Cleveland race of the name, occurs from the commencement of the registers to the present day. An Allan Craythorne now resides at Cockerton. John *Dakers*, of Darlington, *labouring man*, died in 1709. The Gregorys were a numerous class of yeomen. It was customary to notice departures from the parish church in any rite: therefore John Gregory is expressly stated in 1695 to have been baptized in Haughton church. Church registers were then kept on a much better footing than now. For any purpose the present statutory form is almost worthless, and we are driven to the civil registers.

A gentlemanly family of Turner resided here in the sixteenth and seventeenth centuries —so also of Ward. The grandmother of Mr. John Arrowsmith Storey, the present clerk of the church, was a Conyers, related to the Bakers of Elemore. (See Surtees; 125.) A mercantile and very respectable race of Raines flows in a gentlemanly stream from the sixteenth century downwards, connected with the Raines who occur all up and down Teesdale, and some of whom were merchants in the then metropolis of monopoly —Newcastle.

BACKHOUSE.

The Backhouses as bankers, stern and steady, have long been respected throughout the North, besides being active and devoted in support of Bible Societies, Public Schools, and other charitable institutions. Their Bank was established at Darlington in 1774. Thomas Backhouse, esq., of West Lodge, Darlington, was for many years chairman of Lloyd's, and was presented by the body with a silver urn bearing an appropriate inscription, on his resigning the chair. He will live in story as the benevolent provider of a life-boat at Seaton Carew, at his own expense, when he saw how much time elapsed before the Redcar and Hartlepool ones could reach ships in distress on the north side of the Tees. Arts and agriculture have often owed debts to the plain Quakers. On 25 May, 1813, the Society of Arts presented a gold medal to William Backhouse, esq., of Darlington, for planting 300,000 larches and 50,000 other timber trees on waste ground at Shull and Wolsingham; and a silver one to Jonathan Backhouse, jun., esq., of Darlington, for planting 271,000 larches, at the same time that the lesser silver medal was given to Thomas White, esq., of Woodlands in this county, for his application of larch bark to answer all the purposes of oak bark in tanning leather: and on 31 May, 1814, the same society presented a gold medal to Mr. Edward Backhouse, of Darlington, for planting 363,000 larches on waste land.

Jonathan Backhouse, esq., of Polam Hall, head of the firm, died 7 Oct., 1842. He was a man of active benevolence, and had been one of the chief promoters of the formation of the Stockton and Darlington Railway.

A striking dispensation of Providence occurred on 9 June, 1844, being Sunday. William Backhouse, esq., banker, a much respected partner in the old banking house, of the age of 65, attended the evening meeting as usual, when during service (probably feeling unwell) he stood up, and instantly afterwards fell and expired. Mr. Backhouse had arranged to go out with his nephew by the Manchester steamer to Hamburgh on the voyage in which she was lost. It was his intention to proceed from Hamburgh to Norway on a missionary tour. There is every reason to believe that his sudden death was the means of saving his nephew as well as himself from the melancholy end of those who perished with that unfortunate vessel. He was an eminent botanist, and his tastes have descended, for his son the present William Backhouse, esq., of Darlington, is a sound zoologist. James Backhouse, esq., of York, is also a noted botanist, and is better known as "the Australian Traveller," and by his work on our Polynesian Empire. The whole family is indeed fond of the works of nature.

This is perhaps the best place to acknowledge my obligations to the above William and James Backhouse, esquires, who have furnished the local fauna and flora. John Church Backhouse, esq., of Blackwell, has also courteously handed me divers MSS. for the purposes of this work.

Arms: per saltire az. and or, a saltire ermine. Crest: Upon a snake embowed, nowed at the tail, an eagle displayed. Motto: Confido in deo.

PEASE.

The name of Pease is indissolubly connected with popular progress and the rise of railways. It has indeed become one of the main associations of Darlington, and strangers generally link the Peases and Backhouses with the place. As far as I can gather the traditions of the family together, they briefly state that the Peases of Darlington descend from the highly respectable West-Riding family of the name settled near Wakefield, where an old house remains called Pease Hall: that they and the Peases bankers at Hull, are of that common stock: that the said Darlington branch particularly trace from an austere father who considered himself qualified to think for his children as well as himself, and turned the Darlington ancestry from house and home for becoming Quakers, somewhere of course on this side of the civil wars: and that thereupon the rejected ones very sensibly making the best of their decadence in caste, rushed into manufactures and trade, and have created more money and noise in the world than ever did their inheriting fathers. The grandfather of Edward Pease, esq., the present patriarch of the family, another Edward, married Elizabeth d. and coh. of Michael Coates of that Lynesack race which binds so many of the heads of the Durham Friends in one common descent. The late John Coates, esq., had a strangely diverging genealogy, very accurately prepared I believe, but without a single date in it! Joseph Pease, esq., of Southend, our quondam M. P., married one of the race of Gurney, whose participation in the murder of Edward II. has been fully redeemed in our own time; and, oddly enough, the late Joseph Pease, esq., of Feethams, married a Bradshaw, of the family so well known in consequence of the trial of Charles I.

ORNSBY.

The Ornsbys of Darlington spring from a family long seated at Lanchester. Christopher Ormsby of that place, in temp. Hen. VIII., married Matilda, daughter and coheir of John Lille.

HENRY ORNSBY, of Lanchester, in co. pal. gent., bap. 12 Nov., 1706, bur. at Lanchester 19 Jan., 1747. He married, 4 Oct., 1735, Mary dau. and coh. of Thomas Rippon of Patrick's Close, par. Lanchester, gent., and by her (who remarried Mr. Thomas Wilkinson of Lanchester) had issue

I. George Ornsby, of Lanchester, esq., a captain in H. M. Royal Marines, b. 12 Oct., 1736; d. at Gateshead, bur. at Lanchester, 12 Aug., 1809, s. p. "On the 11th inst., at Gateshead, in his 72nd year, George Ornsby of Lanchester, esq., captain in H. M. Royal Marines. The greater part of his life was spent in the service of his country; he was engaged in the siege of the Havannah; and greatly distinguished himself in the naval engagement with the Dutch off the Dogger Bank, under Admiral Parker." (*Newcastle Courant of Aug.* 19, 1809.) He mar. Mary dau. of Edward Searle, esq., of Overton, Hants. "March 15, 1812, died at Overton, Mrs. Ornsby, an amiable woman, relict of the late Captain Ornsby, (who fought in the memorable action off the Dogger Bank, Aug. 4, 1781, and died Aug. 11, 1809,) and only daughter of the late Edward Searle, esq., of Overton, Hants, who died March 6, 1809." (*Gent. Mag.* lxxxii. part i., p. 668.)
II. HENRY.
III. Thomas, d. young.
1. Ann, mar. Alan Greenwell, of Greenwell Ford, in co. pal., esq., and left issue.
2. Mary, d. young.

HENRY ORNSBY, of Darlington, in co. pal., solicitor, bailiff and steward of the Borough of Darlington, and coroner of Darlington Ward, b. 27 Mar. 1739, died 6 Aug., 1806, bur. at Darlington. He mar., 6 Feb., 1769, Ann dau. of Christopher Dent, of Darlington, gent., and widow of Mr. John York, and by her (who was bur. at Darlington 12 Sept., 1775) had issue

I. GEORGE.
II. Henry, died young.
1. Ann, b. 10 Dec. 1769, d. 30 June, 1785, bur. at Darlington.
2. Mary, died young.

GEORGE ORNSBY, sometime of Darlington, solicitor, bailiff and steward of the Borough of Darlington, and coroner of Darlington Ward; afterwards of Lanchester Lodge, esq., a J. P. and deputy lieutenant for the County of Durham; b. at Darlington, 6 Oct., 1772; d. 8 Aug., 1823, bur. at Lanchester. He mar. at Ripon, 5 May, 1808, Margaret third dau. of William Askwith, esq., Alderman of Ripon; now (1852) living a widow at Darlington; and by her had issue

I. GEORGE.
II. Henry William Ornsby, of Darlington, solicitor; b. 6 Sep., 1815. He mar. at Trinity Church, Darlington, 31 Dec., 1846, Elizabeth, eldest dau. of John Robinson, esq., of Cockerton, and by her has issue

I. Henry Ornsby, b. 7 Aug., 1849.
1. Margaret, b. 9 Oct. 1847.

III. Robert Ornsby, M. A., and late Fellow of Trinity College, Oxford; b. 26 Apr., 1820. He mar. 9 Sep., 1846, Elizabeth, eldest dau. of William Dalgairns, esq., of the Rosaire, in the island of Guernsey, by whom he has issue

1. Harriet Lowe Ornsby, b. 16 Nov, 1847.

1. Ann, b. 24 Apr., 1813, d. at Durham, 28 Oct., 1828, bur. at Lanchester.

GEORGE ORNSBY, in holy orders, now (1852) vicar of Fishlake, co. Ebor.; and author of "Sketches of Durham," published 1846; b. 9 March, 1809. He mar. at St. Mary's in the South Bailey, Durham, 1 May, 1843, Anne eldest dau. of John Wilson, esq., of The Hill, in the par. of Brigham, co. Cumb., and by her has issue

I. George Radcliffe Ornsby, b. at Whickham, co. pal., 20 July, 1849.
II. John Arthur Ornsby, b. at Whickham, 1 Sep., 1850.
1. Frances Gertrude, b. in Durham, 22 Feb., 1845.
2. Anne, b. at Whickham, 22 Dec., 1847.

MEWBURN.

There was a very respectable family of this name in the last century at Blackwell and Darlington (see p. 244) connected with the Cleveland race. Thomas Mewburn (dead before 1760) had three sons. Thomas, a gentleman of Blackwell; John, an attorney at Darlington; and James, who lived at Monkend, in right of his wife, Miss Aislaby. Thomas and James left sons; but the male representation died out presently. Mr Henry Mewburn, surgeon at Newcastle in 1790, was of this family.

The name,* I have sometimes thought, may have reference to the idea that by placing mews, mows, or piles of corn by the sides of burns or rivulets, the grain dries more quickly and can be housed earlier from the effects of the current of air following the channel. Mow-burnt corn is a phrase too well known.† The Cleveland family occur in the registers at their outset.‡ They have acquired some interest by their connection with the Bowyers, the great printers, through a common descent from the Prudoms of Danby. Thomas Bowyer *ultimus suorum* died in 1783, leaving his Danby estates to his second cousin Francis Mewburn, the son of James Mewburn, the son of John Mewburn, by Elizabeth Prudom, half sister to Thomas Prudom, of Danby and London, whose daughter Anne married William Bowyer, the second printer. See some curious matters about the Bowyers extracted from MSS. lent by the present Francis Mewburn, esq., borough bailiff of Darlington, in Ord's Cleveland, p. 339.

William Mewburn, of Eston, of this Prudom blood, married Joanna Consett of Ormesby, whose mother was a Pennyman. He left many curious remarks in MS.; having been much engaged in agricultural experiments and improvements. I have given a few extracts in a note which may be interesting, having been entrusted with some of the MSS. by their possessor, our said episcopal ruler.§ Mewburn was a bearer at the funeral of Sir James Pennyman in 1808, when he was 71 years of age. He died in 1811. His son William (" baptised over a bowl of punch") had emigrated to America in 1788.

From his long and extensive practice in the law, joined to a literary turn of mind, Mr. Mewburn, of Darlington, has amassed large collections of local memoranda and evidences. His assistance is especially noted in the last edition of Brockett's Glossary of North Country Words, in Ord's Cleveland, and repeatedly in the diadem of Northumbrian literature, the princely History of Durham by Mr. Surtees. I have to add that my

* Mewburn in Westmoreland " was often anciently written Medburn; which seemeth to indicate that it received this name from the burn or rivulet (of Lyvennet) running all along down the middle of the vale." (Nicholson and Burn, i. 502.) In Northumberland (and I may add partially in Durham too) the Mewburns are called Meburns. In Lincolnshire, where part of the family are located, the name is spelled Meaburn.

† See Tusser sub August.

‡ Nicholas Mewburn, of Stokesley, weaver, was *excommunicated* in 1745 for refusing to pay his Easter offering to the minister.

§ Memorandum the 6th of August, 1767, Eston. Last week was killed at Gisbro' by Messrs. Dales and Corney a milch cow (called Cheezey) the property of Mr. Wm. Mewburn, of Eston, whose four quarters weighed 75 st. 10 lb. Tallow, 11 st. 1 lb. Head, &c., 13 st. 3 lb. In all, 100 st. at 14 lb. per stone; which reduced to London weight, is 175 st. The publick are desired to take notice that this cow was never fed or in the least intended to be fatted, having never eat any kind of corn, turnips, or oil cake, nor anything but hay, straw, and grass; and what is more remarkable, she was a whey calf, and offered to sale for 30*s*. She was milked twice a day, untill she was killed. Price 20 guineas. Her fellow the same age, viz., gone six years old, who has had the same usage and now a milk cow, is supposed by the best of judges to weigh at present 10 st. more; and for which Mr. Mewburn has been offered 30 guineas. N. B.—Mr. Mewburn has this clipped from a ram sheep 21 lbs. of clean washed wool. The above is a copy of what was in the newspapers, &c., &c. Cheeses sold in 1766 to John Elgie . . . . Sep. 17, delivered at Cargo Fleet, 44 cheeses, first of that sort ever made at Eston; weight 5 ct. 0 qr. 1 lb. Two ewe cheese sent to Mrs. Hustler, in London. Cattle bought in 1769.—April 25, a cow of *my coz'n at Croft.* [James Mewburn of Monkend] read and white 10*l.* 10*s*. Cattle sold in 1770.—Jan. 31, at Stockton, *being the first fair ever their*, a bay mare rising five, 12*l*. Memorandum of all the Doctors by me [circa 1790 or 1800] W. Mewburn, P. Physicians, &c., (i. a.) of Stockton, 7.—Doctor Nicholson, P. Doctor Horseley, P. and S.—Mr. Kirton, Mr. Weiar, Mr. Walker, Mr. Wray, Mr. Fall. Darlington, 1—Mr. Pratt. Sir Charles Turner, bart., born 28 January, 1773, *the same day of the month his father was born*.

obligations to him in constructing this parochial topography have also been very great. I should be guilty of serious laches as a chronicler of the part Darlington has had in the early promotion of steam land-transit were I not to describe Mr. Mewburn as one of the solicitors to the Stockton and Darlington, to the Auckland and Weardale, the Wear Valley, the Middlesbro' and Redcar, the Great North of England, and the Middlesbrough and Guisbrough Railway Companies. Such a connexion with the first passenger railway in the kingdom and its succeeding locomotive peers in South Durham is something unique to look back upon.

Arms worn by Fra. Mewburn, esq., of Darlington.—Arg. 3 lions, 2 and 1, rampant gules.—Impaling Smales. Crest: a demigriffin. Motto: Festina lente.

HILL.

The Hills have been mentioned in connexion with Blackwell and the improvement of cattle. They held the Blackwell estate for three generations. Thomas Hill, of Manfield took it by marriage with the heiress of Denton (see p. 117), and died in 1773. He had three sons—Christopher, of Blackwell, who died in 1795, s. p., Thomas, who died in the lifetime of his father, and Robert, who died in 1786. The latter left numerous children; the eldest, Thomas William Hill, esq., of Blackwell, sold the estate in 1803 to the Allans. One of the daughters, Elizabeth, married John Douthwaite Nesham, esq., of Houghton-le-Spring, at Darlington, 5 May, and again at Houghton, in consequence of an error in the marriage license, on 5 July, 1801. One of their sons, David Nesham, esq., resides between Darlington and Haughton-le-Skerne. Thomas William Hill died at Startforth, 1833, and all his brothers are dead, save William Hill, esq., of Ryhope, who is still the owner of some tythes in the township of Blackwell.

LOWSON.

The Lowsons at one time possessed considerable property near Darlington. Edmund Lowson married Jane Emmerson at Darlington, in 1705, and died in 1729. His son Francis, an attorney at law here, married Mary Young, of Tofthill, and died 1765, leaving numerous issue. The eldest son Francis married Elizabeth, daughter of John Wardell of Ketton, and died 1768, leaving no surviving issue. Two other sons, Young Lowson and Newby Lowson, each left a family. Newby Lowson, esq., of Witton-le-Wear, represents the latter.

[*Brass frame of one of the pouches or gipcieres commonly worn appended to the girdle in mediæval times. Found near Yarm in forming the Leeds Northern Railway.*]

ADDENDA ET CORRIGENDA.

The ordinary typographical errors are not noticed.

P. 5. *Vasey of Coniscliffe.* The High and Low Coniscliffe estate passed to Marshall Vesey, of Darlington, and afterwards of Newcastle (1783), bookseller. He married Margaret Sanderson, daughter of Patrick Sanderson, the well known stationer, of New Elvet, Durham. The Low Coniscliffe estate included a close called *Gallow-hill*, doubtless the site of Lord Greystock's Gallows, (see p. 48), as it was held under the Howards. The estate containing 238 acres was alienated to Francis Holmes by Marshall Vesey, before the previous tenant for life died, for £2,600, and was sold under the Holmes assignment for £1,950 to Mr John Shepherd. The tenant then paid £110 rent, and £5 to the Howards, free rent. The vendors assumed £122 19s. 4d. a fair rental, being at the rate of 10s. 4d. per acre. Twenty years' purchase at £110 gave £2,200. The purchaser however had to buy out a possible annuity of £50, settled on Margaret Vesey, in case she survived her husband Marshall. The Gallow hill was then High and Low Galley hill.—*Allan MSS., in the possession of R H. Allan, esq.*

The lands near Darlington, in this important Holmes sale, were estimated at from £1 5s. 6d. to £3 p. acre, according to quality and situation. Mr. Holmes total debts were £16,261, his credits about £13,900. His purchases of property, £10,792, ranged 1754-1780; his bonds 1752-1782. His valuation of his property was £11,949, and it sold for £11,689. He was baptized 1722, and declined business in 1749, his father Francis having died 1747. He had a large summer house with a nursery of trees, in his Low Park estate, concerning which George Allan, very unintentionally, has this significant description:—"Folly in own hand." "Kendrew for Glass mill" is another item.—(*Annotated Sale list, penes F. Mewburn, esq.*)

P. 6. *Darlington Surname.* Mr. Darlington, of Ince Hall, Lancashire, is one of the most extensive proprietors and viewers of coal in that county, and has used the steam jet to admiration.

P. 14. *Prescott Superstitions.* The ghost of the old deserted mansion of the Prescotts, of Blackwell, is called "Old Pinkney," and wears a red nightcap. A well under the house is "Pink-e-ney's well," and when used was never disturbed after nightfall.

P. 20. *Flood of* 1822.—"From Piersbridge to Croft, bankings and trees were forced down. The battlement of Croft Bridge was forced down. At Yarm, by the overflowing of the Tees, the water was seven feet deep in the main street. No lives, however, were lost there, and but little damage sustained in property." *Newcastle Mag.* The authority I quoted from must be incorrect; the reader will therefore substitute *Yarm* for *Stockton.*

P. 21. *Note* ‡—Read "To it."

P. 26, line 2. *Skerne.*—After Holmeslaw add, "Stotfald per petras ex parte orientali dicti Stotfald et a dicto Stotfald usque Holmeslawe"

P. 29. *Ellestantoftes.*—Halliwell has a Northumberland word *Beck-stans,* which he says means *the strand of a rapid river.*

P. 29. *Helle.*—1418. There is a survey of Bishop Langley in the auditor's office of this date. Polam is *Polumpole.* Ralph Eure held 3 acres called *le Helle.* The Punder's half acre at Ellyngmedowe in Hatfield s survey is described at *de Ellyng.*

P. 35. *Hellkettles.*—There are some dozen of similar pits in the range of red sandstone banks on the east side of the Ure in Yorkshire, commencing at Hutton Conyers and extending to Bishop Monkton. They are generally circular, about 30 feet in diameter. Some are nearly filled up by the sides crumbling in, and present a semicircular or angular section. Some are deep and dry, and others full of water. One is full *to the top,* never higher in winter or lower in summer, like the Hellkettles, or the little mountain lake of Gormire near Thirsk. This is at Littlethorpe, and fell 56 years ago. Mr. Milburn, of Sowerby, near Thirsk, to whom I am indebted for these particulars, has heard read a letter from the clergyman residing at Littlethorpe at the time. The circumstance occurred about three o clock a.m. There was a loud thundering noise and shaking, and in the morning the hole, which gradually afterwards filled with water, made its appearance. Another of these pits was formed in Bishop Monkton about 26 years ago. The men present came running in to their master, Mr. Charnock, saying, the stackyard was being swallowed up. He went and found the land gradually dropping down into an abyss of an unknown depth, and was indeed swallowing his stacks. He immediately sent men to cart away those nearest to it, and the ground kept sinking in circularly till it had swallowed up the sites of those also. It filled with water, or nearly so, and so it remains. This is the only pit which seems to have sunk *gradually*. It is 20 yards in diameter.

The water is not more peculiar than as being cold and hard and brilliantly clear. From the appearance of some of the old pits, Mr. Milburn considers that they must have fallen at intervals of one or two centuries each.

The lake of Gormire, seated in an amphitheatre of the Hambleton rocks, has always been considered to owe its origin to some vast convulsion. It has no perceptible inlet or outlet, and is accompanied with the usual tradition of the sinking of a wicked city, and the appearance ever and anon of its turrets and chimnies beneath the sullen water.

Mr. Raine once mentioned to me a tradition about the Hellkettles. The farmer there would work on St. Barnaby's day, and on being remonstrated with, said:—

"I'll hae my cart load of hay
Whether God will or nay."

Whereupon the Hellkettles swallowed him his carts and horses, and *when* you can see the bottom of Hellkettles, *then* you can see the agricultural denizens also.*

Leland in giving the extract from the *Tynemouth Chronicle* about the Oxenhall earthquake at Christmas, 1178, says, "*Vidi ibidem aliquot puteos, quos vulgusHelketels appellat.*"

P. 40. *Humble-Sykes.*—Humble-Sykes occurs as *Hummersom-Sykes* in 1796.

P. 91. *Bishop Booth.*—1474-5. Clerk of the works. Paid 14*s.* 3*d.* for the meat of divers tenants of my lord riding with my Lord from Auckland to Allerton, as well for food for horse as men, attending upon George Lumley in Derlynton for keeping the peace on the market day.

Bishop Dudley.—1478. Expenses by my lord of Duresme's counseyll at Derlyngton. A quarter and half of pease, 7*s.* 6*d.* Half a quarter of haver, 16*d.* For baking of horse brede to the baxster, 12*d.* For half a quarter of branne, 4*d.* For eight threffe of stray to litter, 12*d.* For making of hekks and mayngors, 18*d.* Payd to Richard Denom, for a swall to the maynger, 4*d.* To a wryght, be the commandment of John Raket, 3*s.*—*Raine's Auckland.*

P. 92. *Contents of an Oxgang.*—Fifteen acres composed an oxgang in Darlington, according to the old and new measurements of the Nestfield Copyholds, and George Allan calls this the "General computation." At Langley's survey, this was the contents of an oxgang in Cockerton. At Blackwell, twenty acres went to an oxgang, (p. 7.)

Hopton in his Baculum Geodæticum 1614, says that Fabian, writing of the Conqueror, sets down a measure very necessary for all men to understand—Four akers, (saith he,) make a yard of land, five yards a hide, and eight hides make a knight's fee, which by his conjecture is so much as one plough can well till in a year; in Yorkshire and other counties they a hide an *oxe-skinne.*

P. 94. *Richard III.*—Line 9 of text, for "his" read "the Tudor's."

P. 96. *Princess Margaret.*—I have come to the conclusion that the Fiancels were in 1503, and that "hys day of installcyon" in the record does not mean "the anniversary of his (Fox's) installation," as Hutchinson has it, but the actual installation of Bishop Sever. Indeed in 1502 the See was vacant. Sir Wm. Bulmer was not appointed sheriff till 16 Jan., 1502-3. Sir Ralph Bowes was sheriff to Fox until the latter was translated to Winchester, 6 Oct., 1501.

W. Robinson, of *Darthelington*, was appointed in 1501, apparitor in the city and archdeaconry of Durham, *sede vacante.* (Barnes proc. S. S. app. ii.)

P. 98. *Wolsey's Episcopacy.*—1524. The Duke of Norfolk in office on the marches, writes to Wolsey from Dernton:—"I have remayned in this your Grace's town and nere thereaboutes, doing dyvers pylgrimages thies 5 or 6 dayes, loking every houre to have herd of th'Ambassadours commyng; and tomorrowe, with Godes grace, I shall comme forewardes towardes the Kinges Highnes and your Grace; ye maye be assured, with a right good will."—(State papers.)

P. 101. *Bp. Tunstall.* 1543-4.—Clerk of Works. Payd the Smyth of Darlington, for 5 lodis for my Lorde by the hands of Mr Chaunseler, 5s. 8d.—*Raine's Auckland.*

* A correspondent of the *Durham Advertiser* says, that they may be seen on a fine day and clear water "*floating midway*, many fathoms deep."

P. 108 Note †. I had quite forgotten Surtees's own accounts of the ballad of Langleydale. "I have only just heard, a few hours ago, the first stanza of this, 'evidently founded on Plumpton Park:' can recover no more of the original than the two lines, which I suppose were the burden. I have filled it up as a kind of cent from such ideas and passages as occur to me at this present writing. I would give ten pounds for the original Lament." Life, by G. Taylor, 43.

P. 114. *Manor of Blackwell.* In Langley's survey, 1418, Cecily Blackwell is stated to hold 1 mess. and 5 oxgangs by foreign service, and multure of one-sixteenth, *et cooperiet molendinum super le louthre*, and renders yearly 23s. 8d. (Cecily Blackwell was very likely the wife of John Middleton, mentioned in Hatfield's survey). Robert Hurworth, *jure uxoris* held 3 acres at *Spynkbit* formerly Emma Moriall's. In another paper in the Auditor's office I find under Blackwell, a farm rent of 6s. 8d., of a pasture called *Batell* demised to the tenants there; another of 16s. of a pasture called *Langdraught* demised to the tenants of the vill there with their husband-lands; and another of 18d. increased rent of a croft there. (See p. 114.)

P. 117. "Doctor Isaac Basire" in the text was son of Dr. Isaac Basire the prebendary mentioned in the note.

P. 118. John Church Backhouse, Esq., whose estate at Blackwell adjoins that of R. H. Allan, Esq., and is affected by the sudden curvature of the river, was at half the cost of the stone jetty in the Tees.

P. 119. *Garnett*—1626. Offic, against Anne Garnett, of Blackwell, par. Darneton, detected for intertaining Popish Preists, for taking upon her unlawfully to christen children, and suspected to live incontinently with one who liveth in her house. (Raine MSS.)

P. 128. *Parish Books.*—The extracts on this page are nearly all imperfect and orthographically inaccurate, being taken from Surtees before I had the original book. The differences are not so material to history as to need enumeration, but the entry "To ringers at my Ld. Bpp's going out of the country, 2s. 7d.," occurs in 1631, not 1632. The book was found in Sir C. Sharp's MSS., and returned.

P. 129. *Parish Books.*—In the extract from the parish books of 1650, read "To *two* companyes of Irish travellers."

P. 129. *Hermitage.*—1545-6. The Bishop's dues mention, firepence—Somerlace *alias Heremitag'*—waste called *baronland*. 1169-70.—The Bishop's dues mention the fishery of the water of Skyrne extending from Burdon to Oxhenhall—the rent of *a hermitage* demised to Thomas Fryth; this is afterwards called a piece of land named *Swynhirdplace, alias le Hermitage.*—See pp. 283, 292. In 1782, a freehold house and garth at the foot of the Hermitage Bank in Darlington (rent £8) was sold with the property of Francis Holmes, Esq. It is elsewhere called Bank-top house. It was conveyed by Holmes's assignees, as "all that mess. ten. or dwelling house, stable, garth, and appurtenances called the Hermitage, in or near Darlington, boundering on the Post Road from Darlington to Northallerton on the E. and S., the mess. or ten. of Edw. Selby on the W., and lands of Miss Allan on the N." In 1731 the mess. or ten. called the Hermitage had been lately rebuilt and converted into dwelling houses: a horse-mill and orchard adjoined. In 20 Geo. II. (1746-7) a fine was levied of the "parcel whereon a horse-mill lately stood, containing 12 yards in length by 8 yds in breadth at a place called Hermitage." The Hermitage was in fact the larger portion of the isolated portion of the borough in Clay Row.

P. 130. *Forster.*—1570-1.—12 March, 13 Eliz. Elizabeth dau. of Christopher Place of Halnaby, Esq., was wife of Francis Forster of Halnaby.

P. 132. *Civil War.*—1640.—Immediately after the victory of Newburn, the Scots planted their ordnance at Gateshead. Newcastle yielded the next day. The inhabitants would not have their houses battered down, and the officers, as report went, deserted the soldiers, who marched out of the town westward, crossed Newburn ford (where the Scots had passed) and "soe to the King's forces at Darneton, some 12 miles on this side Durham, where the randevous now is, and hoped on the King's part there are at this tyme or will be within two days 30,000. Soe a battayle is suddenly likely to be. God blesse his Ma'ty army with success." (Letter from London, Sep. 4, printed in J. G. Bell's Tracts, sub. tit. Great Newes from Newcastle.)

P. 134. *Piercebridge Skirmish.*—There is a monument to Sir Thomas Howard of Thursdale, co. pal. knt., the 7th son of Belted Will, in Wetheral Church, Cumberland. It says he "died valiently fighting in the cause of his king and country at Piercebridge, Dec. 2d 1642." He was buried at Coniscliffe. (Hodgson's Northd.)

P. 135. *Civil War.*—1644. "The Enemy marching to Durham, it was resolved our army should go to Easington, where wee might intercept the Enemies provisions from Hartlepoole, enlarge our own Quarters, and strengthen [straighten? W. H. L.] theirs; where wee stayed till April 8, (having kept a Fast the day before) and on that day marched to Quarendon hill near Durham, intending to force the Enemy either to fight or flee, which fell out accordingly; for having little forrage for his horses, and little store of provisions; after he had sent for some forces from Lumley castle and Newcastle to strengthen his foot, upon the 13 of April, hee marched away early in the morning in great haste, leaving behinde him severall provisions; our horse was at forrage, but having notice of their flight, marched after them with all the expedition could bee, and came on the Lords day to *Darnton*. The next day the enemy having some advantage in the way, directed his march to York; the Generall fearing lest he should have surprised the Lord Fairfax his forces, and either given them a defeat or driven them to a corner, and so get occasion to encrease his forces, sent severall advertisements to them, and so hasted our march, that some of our forces over-took some of the enemies reare, killed and took about 80 of them."—*(Letter from Wetherby by one of Leslie's folks. Richardson's reprints, sub tit.—The taking of the fort at South Shields.)*

P. 136. *Hutton.*—1551. Ralph Hutton, of Walworth (p. 136), was younger brother to William Hutton, of Hunwick. John Hutton, of Hunwick, his nephew and supervisor, by will 1565, mentions "Marye Biggins, his uncle Raufe Hooton's daughter."—*(Randall's Pedigrees and Wills,* not in the D. and C. Lib.)

P. 136. *Rickatson.*—Geo. Rickatson's seat in the stall next the Belles, was let to Francis Bainsbrigg in 1630. In 1641, Jennet, his wife, took a seat, and in 1650, Rickatson was buried in the church, as was his wife in 1659.

P. 139. *Middleton.*—1651. John Middleton, esq., and Member of the Committee of Militia, in the co. of Durham, by authority of Parliament, was one of the parties to whom John Headworth, of Harraton. addressed his "oppressed mans out-cry" in 1651.

P. 139. *King's Arms.*—1660. "To John Deniss for the drawinge the King's Armes, and for the wreete and Masons, and Cooles, and Smith and other cherges, 1*l.* 18*s.* 6*d.*" The entry in p. 139 is faulty. I had not the original then.

P. 148. *Mrs. Gerrard.*—10 Jan, 1665-6. To Mrs. Gerrard, (Mary Cosin, afterwards Lady Gerrard,) to give Symon Armestrong, a poore old man in Darlington, by my Lord's order, 1s.

14 Mar. Given Mr. Gerrard's man that brought a great pike as a present 2s. 6d.

6 Apr., 1666. Given Mr. Gerrard's man that brought some pikes and tench 1s.

23 Aug. To Darlington footpost that brought letters about the Quakers 2s.

In 1667, Lady Gerrard and little Mr. Gilbert and children appear resident at Auckland.—*Raine's Auckland*

P. 151. *Charles Husband.*—1626. *John* Husband was the lawyer. Charles, the husband of Dorothy Glover, sold candles in 1634.

P. 152. *Parish Books.*—1684. Read "To Mr. Bell, *for* a letter from London with the names of the Royal family, 6*d.*"

P. 155. *Postmaster's Daughter.*—1733. Feb. 2nd, died, Mr. Clement, postmaster of Durham. *(Gent. Mag.)*

P. 168. *Elections.*—"The only occasion upon which Mr. Surtees is known to have spoken in public was at the election for the southern division of Durham, at Darlington, in 1832, when he proposed Mr. Bowes, of Streatlam Castle, in a speech in which judgment and brevity were happily united. At the dinner which followed upon the election, at Darlington, Mr. Surtees was present, and an amusing scene occurred in which he acted a part. He was sitting at table near a gentleman with whom he was intimately acquainted, and from that gentleman an apology was required for a hasty expression in the course of the evening. "Gentlemen," said the apologist, with great good-nature, "I beg your pardon: I did not, if you'll believe me, mean to say what I did, but I've had the misfortune, you see, to lose some of my front teeth, and words get out every now and then without my knowing a word abont it." The speaker was proceeding when Surtees laid hold of him by the tail of his coat, and placed him gently upon his seat. "Sit down," said he, "and don't say one word more. Never was there so perfect an apology. If you add one word more you'll spoil it most completely.' —*Raine.*

P. 170. Another election for the southern division took place at Darlington on July 15, 1852, when Lord Harry Vane and Mr. Farrer were again returned without opposition. The former was nominated by Joseph Pease, esq., and Robert Henry Allan, esq., in able and eloquent addresses; the latter by Marshall Fowler, esq., and H. Stobart, esq. John Bowes, esq., the High Sheriff, attended, and his feelings in that arena where in former days he had been the successful candidate, and expended some 30,000*l.*, must have been of no ordinary character. Lord Harry Vane, after being girt with a sword as a Knight of the Shire, was drawn through the town in his carriage; but Mr. Farrer, who was escorted by a posse of the county constables to the King's Head Inn, reluctantly refrained from any procession by advice of the town authorities and some of the magistrates, in consequence of the disorderly disturbances manifested against him at the hustings A parcel of 30 or 40 dirty young urchins had styled themselves "The Juvenile Band of Hope," in connection with the Temperance Society, and brought a banner inscribed "The Working Classes demand Political Rights—Free

Trade for ever—there's nothing like Teetotal!" On one of the poles of the banner was a loaf and red herring, on the other a cat-o'-nine-tails. In front of this stood a young man without his hat, who ever and anon pointed to the banner, waved his hand in a mystical manner above his head, and led the Band of Hope into astounding hisses and frantic yells, which effectually prevented between 3,000 and 4,000 men from hearing a word from Mr. Farrer and his party. It was by some considered that the leader was of weak intellect; and a deputation from the Temperance Society waited on Mr. Farrer, and explained to his satisfaction their annoyance, that such disgraceful proceedings had for a moment been coupled with their name.

P. 183. *Raby Vane.*—In mentioning Raby Vane, I thought it only proper to give the strange entry which passed through the periodicals of the day about a marriage with Miss Eyres, daughter to the late *Bishop Eyres*, on 17 April, 1768. It is seldom that such notices are altogether incorrect, and not finding a date ascribed to the match with Miss Sayer, daughter of Dean Sayer, I printed the entry, fearing that a second match might have escaped writers. Since that time Randal's pedigree of Vane, full of curious remarks, has passed through my hands, and I find the same date ascribed to the wedding of Miss Sayer, which shews that a strange misunderstanding was afloat about her at the time. I can only attribute it (and even then it exceeds proper bounds of variation) to the circumstancs that her mother was a daughter of *Archbishop* Potter of Canterbury.

P. 188. *Manor House.*—There are a number of accounts for repairs of Darlington Manor House in the auditor's office. The lime came from Cornforth, it (including carriage) was 3*s*. 4*d*. per fodder, the slates (sclatstanez) from Racwodd-hyll; six loads and carriage came to 22*s*. For working six dayes in hewynge of blowinge tymber in the parke and in hewyng sawynge and framyng of tymber for one roof for *a jaykes in my lordis chalmer* at 8*d*. the daye for one 7*d*. for on other and 6*d*. eyther of thoder —for an hundrethe lattis 8d.—for caryage of iiij or foder of tymber firth of the perke into my lordis maner at iiij*d*. the loyd 16*d*."

P. 190. *Royal Visits.*—Another Royal visit took place on the 29th August, 1850, at 20 minutes to 12, a.m., when a second portion of this book, emblazoned by the author, was graciously received by Her Majesty from the hands of the Borough Bailiff.

On Thursday, 28 Aug., 1851, at 11 a.m., a Royal train again passed through the Darlington station, on the same route as before, when the High Sheriff of the county (Robert Henry Allan, esq.), and the Borough Bailiff, and between 300 and 400 ladies and gentlemen were on the platform to pay their respects to Her Majesty. The High Sheriff had the honour of offering to Her Majesty a beautiful bouquet from the gardens of Blackwell Hall, which she was graciously pleased to accept.

At a quarter-past 12 on Tuesday, the 30th August, 1852, much the same preparations were made, and at that hour the Royal cortege arrived from the south, and it so happened that the Queen's carriage halted opposite the unreserved portion of the platform, and a great number of persons were unexpectedly gratified by their close proximity to Majesty. A basket of fruit from the conservatories of the Duke of Northumberland, at Stanwick Park, was presented to Her Majesty; as was also a beautiful bouquet, culled from Mr. Harrison's gardens.

On all these occasions, dense multitudes naturally lined the sides of the line outside the station, and their loyal and respectful feeling required neither restraint nor spur.

P. 129. *Brankin Moor.*—1674. The freeholders of the borough had sold their cattlegates on Brankin Moor, the purchasers agreeing to pay half the county rates that the borough houses were charged with, and to maintain the common high road over the same. In this year a dispute arose, and the arrangement was confirmed by quarter sessions. Under the act 12 Geo. .. ... the owners on the moor again refused payment and demanded an equal pound rate over the whole constabulary.—(*Allan's MSS.*)

P. 194. *Taxation of* 1292.—The vicar's portion should be £6 13s 4d.

P. 195. *Feethams.*—This property was part of Mr. Holmes's estate, and sold by his assignees in 1782 to Miss Lumley,* who resided there, and was a creditor to the tune of £4674. The land was on lease of lives from the Bishop: three dwelling-houses from Lord Vane, for 999 years from 1694: and there was a piece of ground on the front of the house and then part of the garden, 55 ft. N. to S. by 20 ft. E. W. "formerly the Tyth Barn, of which a lease was granted by Lord Vane, in 1757, to Mr Holmes, for 21 years, renewed 1778. The garden on the S. side of the churchyard was part of the property comprised in the in the grand lease by the Vanes.

P. 201. *Deanery.*—The Deanery did not pass direct from the Nevilles to the Vanes, —See p. 269.

P. 210. *Spiritual Court.*—Isabel Dowker alias Denton, wife of one Denton of Dar-

* She was, I believe, some relation to Holmes. Mr Thomas Lumley died 1758.

lington, hath stood excommunicate in the court at Richmond 5 or 6 years, and dwelleth at Darlington, and hath brought forth 2 children in fornication.—*Richard Gregson subtraxit feoda Judicis Registrarii et apparitoris.*

P. 224. *Incumbents.*—Cornelius Harrison, Dr Johnson's cousin, lived in the Prescott house, in Hungate, afterwards the residence of the Allans, and occupied the Kilnegarth and Ninnefield or Ninneyfield.

P. 242. *Communion.*—1579. Darneton. Brian Todie, Robert Crofton, and Thomas Heughe did not receive [communion] at Easter. To do penance in their parish church in their usual dress, having a sheet above the same, to receive, and to certify.

P. 245. *Epitaphs.*—1761. There was a noted stone-cutter, named Hodgson, in Darlington. His nephew tried to follow his steps, and a memorial in the churchyard to his predecessor was the result.

"Here lieth the Body of John Hudson, who departed this life
the 15 day of May, 1761 In the 51st year of his age.

Aflickshons sore long time he bor e
Physicians were in v ain
tell death did sezes
As god did please
And eased him of his pan e ."

Allan's copies of Epitaphs in Sharp's MSS.

P. 249. *St. John's Church.*—The cost of this church was eventually about 4,000*l.*

P. 257. *Grammar School.*—1783. Died the Rev. Thomas Cooke, master of the Grammar School at Darlington in 1748, and discharged 1750. The following is compressed from the account in the *Newcastle Courant* of the day, which James Allan has kindly preserved in his Darlington collections. "The Rev. Thomas Cooke was the son of a shoemaker at Hexham, and born in 1719. He was King's scholar, at Durham school, and took the degree of M.A. in Queen's College, Oxford. While he was curate of Embleton, in Northumberland, a turn for mysteries led him to study mystic writers; he caught the same enthusiastic flame which warned them, and was looked on as a second Jacob Behmen, though he had some notions peculiar to himself. For here he publicly maintained, that the Christian dispensation did not abrogate the Mosaic institutions, and actually supported his doctrine of the necessity of circumcision by practising it upon himself. On this occasion he assumed the names of Adam, Moses, Emanuel, and ever after constantly signed himself A. M. E. Cooke; even when he became more cool and temperate. While he was curate here, he also made an attempt to follow the example of Christ in fasting 40 days, and fasted 17 days without a taste of any thing whatever, and for 12 days more allowed himself, each day, only a trifling crust of bread, and a draught of water. So strange were his notions and so extravagant his behaviour, that he incurred the reprehensions of his superiors, and was by them soon discharged from his curacy. On this our *Jewish Christian*, in his canonicals, and with a long beard, the growth of which he had for some time encouraged, went to London, where he published many pieces of unintelligible jargon in politics, divinity, &c., two plays, and many whimsical projects, among others, one for collecting all the markets into a grand subterraneous one, under Fleet Street. Here he first signalised himself by street-preaching, which he afterwards very frequently practised, wherever he went, particularly in this town, and in Oxford, where, after hearing the University sermon in St. Mary's, he used to give the text a *second* discussion in the street, in which he generally took excessive liberties with the *first;* and strange as his sentiments and his expressions were, larded with long, though faithful, extracts fiom the classics and the Hebrew Bible, he had always, in the latter place, a numerous, respectable, and attentive audience. When in London, he conceived that all the good things of this world should be common. He would go into a coffee-house in a morning, and take the first muffin and pot of coffee he saw. The strangeness of his appearance, or the knowledge of his character, used to screen him from expostulation on the part of the gentleman for whom the breakfast was intended; nor did he meet with interruption from the waiters, till he had finished, and, after saying a short grace, was going towards the door without discharging the reckoning. The coffee-house master would expostulate, while he would prove, by *mode and figure*, that the good things of this world were common; the bucks would then form a ring for the disputants, till the one would be obliged to give up the contest, unable to make objections to arguments, brought from the *Talmudists* and from Hebrew, Greek and Latin authors. After he had gone on for some time in this eccentric manner in London, the charity of some clergymen got him sent to Bedlam, where he staid two or three years. When discharged, he travelled over the greatest part of Scotland on foot, without a farthing in his pocket; subsisting, as he informs us in a pamphlet, by the contributions of the well disposed. After travelling over most of Ireland, also on foot, he went to Dublin in 1760, where he was kindlo entertained, for some time, by the Society of Trinity College. When he returned to England he visited Oxford, where much notice was taken of him by some gentlemen of distinction, particularly by the head of one of the colleges, with whom he lodged. He, about this time, proposed visiting the interior parts of America; a project, which, till within these few years, he has wished to put in execution, but never could from the state of his finances. After living in London many years, he came down into this country, and within these last two years has subsisted on a pension, allowed him by the "Society of the Sons of the Clergy;" amusing himself with writing odes, letters, epigrams, strictures of one kind or other, and, which was his last undertaking, a plan for the alteration of St. Nicholas' Church, and a project for making, what he called, a grand universal church upon true evangelical principles."

P. 266. *Churchwardens.*—1507. With reference to the term "*masters (magistri)* of the fabric" Halliwell has the word ***Kirk-master*** as a Northumbrian expression in the same sense.

P. 270. *Patronage of the Church.*—The Clavis Ecclesiastica of Bishop Barnes says that Darlington Collegiate Church is " dissolved and in the Quene's handes, but was of the patronaige and giefte of the Bishop of Durham." At a later date the words " Donatives of the Q. giefte" opposite the Vicarages of Darlington and Staindroppe are struck out, and opposite the former stands " Sir Geo. Fletcher," and the latter " Dns. Vaine."

P. 282. *Hodgson.*—1591-2, February 18. Charles Hodgson *v.* Jane Marshall.—Robert Branson, of Darlington, yeoman, aged 56, says, "that about thre or fower daies next before the death of John Marshall, the said John lying sick in his owne house in Darlington, did say that his ant Hodgeson (meaning the said Charles Hodgeson's wife) should have his daughter Elizabeth to bring up and xx li. with hir, saying further that he wey......... [weysted ?] not xx li. for that his ant would bring up his daughter well and in the feare of God."—*Eccl. Proc. Dunelm.*

P. 304. *Mr. Mason.*—" Surtees would often tell with much glee a " passage," as he called it, between his former butler, John Hall, and Mason, the agriculturist. To John, upon his leaving service, his master had let a small farm, and it had in consequence become necessary that he should now and then attend the weekly market at Darlington. Thither John was trudging one morning on foot, when he was overtaken by Mr. Mason, who had a spare seat in his gig. ' Get up, John,' said the latter, in his plain hearty way, ' and I'll give thee a ride.' John expressed his obligation, and accepted the offer. ' Now, John,' said Mason, as they were jogging along, ' does thou think that two honester men than thou and me'll enter Darnton market this day ?' ' Answer for yoursell, Mr. Mason,' said John, ' I can only speak for one.' Mason the very next day, told the story to Surtees in raptures, and it was never forgotten."—*Raine.*

Mr. Colling.—" Upon another occasion, we (Raine and Surtees) met, by appointment, at Darlington, on an expedition to York. We had as companions in the coach, a lady rather above the middle age, and a drab-coated farmer, evidently a man of substance in his way, from Barmpton or its neighbourhood. The latter amused us exceedingly for some time with ghost stories, and especially with a true and particular amount of how Mr Colling, of Barmpton, the great breeder of short-horns, who had died a-while before, might be seen every morning through the window of his room, sitting and shaving himself after his fashion when alive. I know not that I ever saw Surtees in higher glee. Every word that fell from his mouth was fun and frolic, and the farmer, to whom he talked in his own plain way, was enraptured with the old-world stories which he heard in return." [As to shaving, " here is a Bishopric idea more horrible. He cannot rest, sir, he cannot live in t' house. Old —— 's ghost comes and stands beside him every morning as his shavin himsel."]

P. 306. *Emerson.*—1773. Previous to Dr. Charles Hutton's going to London to stand examination for the Professorship of Mathematics, in the Woolwich Royal Military Academy, he at the suggestion of his friend, Mr. George Anderson, consulted the celebrated Emerson, at Hurworth. The necromancer having examined him in mathematics encouraged him to proceed, and gave him a letter to the examiners. The result is well known in its triumphs. Emerson was so interested in it that he wrote to Mr. R. Harrison, then living in the Flesh Market, Newcastle, to ask Hutton to send him particulars of the ordeal, and tell him who were his partners in the Critical Review. ' I am glad" says he, ' he has met with such success, and that he has got his revenge on Clarke, who is a very silly fellow, pretending to what he knows little about. He revised my third edition of mechanics, but durst alter nothing, because I remonstrated against it, but he has left several faults uncorrected.'—***Bruce's Memoir of Charles Hutton***, 1823.

P. 310. *Population.*—In 1789 Cade mentions Darlington as having doubled its inhabitants in half a century, and as enjoying a temperate wholesome air, at that time there being a man, his wife, and sister, inhabitants of one house, whose ages together amounted to near 270 years. Consumption was less pregnant there than in any of the adjacent market towns.—*Archæologia.*

P. 310. *Mary Nicholson.*—Read 1798 at the commencement of the paragraph. The trial took place in August of that year, "for the murder of Elizabeth Atkinson, of Little Staynton, and for mixing poison with pudding meat from the eating of which four persons now lie dangerously ill.—Guilty, but her case referred to the twelve judges." —(*Newcastle Chronicle of that date*). The next assizes, July, 1799, are reported in the same paper:—"The following prisoners in Durham gaol have been tried, and have received the following sentences; (i. a.) Mary Nicholson, charged with the murder of Elizabeth Atkinson, by mixing a quantity of poison with some pudding meat.—Guilty, death." The same years at York City assizes, the trial of Ellen Kipling was postponed till the next assizes. The *Chronicle* in narrating Mary Nicholson's execution, says that upwards of an hour elapsed before another rope was procured after the first had broken. "In the interim she recovered her faculties, and conversed with her unhappy relatives till a rope was brought, when she was launched into eternity amidst the shrieks and distressful cries of the surrounding spectators."

P. 317. *Tollbooth.*—3. Tho. (1512?) Darlington Rents—"v. shoparum ex parte australi domus Theolonei, qualibet shopa ad v.s.—unius shope subtus pilloriam—(other shops at the sides of the Tollbooth occur)—domus granorum infra idem Theoloneum—26*s.* 8*d.* de firma *custume tinctorie* voc' *Littferm* hoc anno solvend' pro tinctoria burgi—12*s.* 8*d.* de divers' personis pro stallag' et (*blank*) in foro ib'm."

1543-4.—Clerk of the Works' account "Derlyngton. Plumbers for mendynge of the leddes over the porche of the tollebooyth."

Pedigree of Allan of Allan's Flatts.—Charles, *fourth* Earl of Tankerville, was John Colville's heir at law. Charles Allan, another co-heir was living as "only son and heir of Lionel," at Norwich, in 1800. Jacob Pearson, of Tritlington, the 3rd co-heir was also living in that year, and was "only son and heir at law."—*Halmot Rolls, Boldons.*

Pedigree of Prescott.—George Allan, in the Sharp MSS., mentions the Prescott tomb as of blue marble, close to the west door of the church, and roughly figures the arms, which are the usual coat of Prescott, impaling, between 3 fleur-de-lis a chevron charged with 3 mullets.

For 1755 the date of baptism of the first Lord Alvanley, read 1745.

Pedigree of Hylton.—In the enumeration of quarterings, in No. 14, for "fess" read chevron.

P. xxviii. *Allan Estate.*—1833, Oct. 15, 16, and 17.—A portion of the Allan, or Blackwell Grange estates in and near the town of Darlington, was sold by public auction at the King's Head Hotel, Darlington. The three days sale produced the sum of £29,340. The outlying estates were disposed of at subsequent periods, and the entirety of such of the property as was sold under two separate decrees of the Court of Chancery fetched about one hundred thousand pounds.

P. xxxvi in Family History. In †, "St. Cloyd" must be an error for "St. Eloyd," or "St. Loy," the patron of blacksmiths—See *Surtees*, iv. ii. 34..

P. li. *Pedigree of Cornforth.* In Langley's survey, 1418, *Thomas* Cornford held the 2 mess. and 2 oxgangs "each oxgang containing 15 acres," *formerly held by John Corneford.*

P. lxxxii. *Barnes.*—1580. Darneton, *Mungo Barnes*, being a slanderer and a brawler with his neighbours, did, the 5th July, draw his dagger, and almost killed John Appelby the younger, but that two women did resist his purpose; and then the constables took him, but did not punish him. Yet forthwith he came again, and set upon the constables with a drawn sword, bragging that, if they durst set him in the stocks. After that the constables did make hue and cry in the Queen's name, but he did take a house and did defend him from punishmect. Does not appear.

1595. To Wm. Barnes, for the diet of the Judges at Darlington, 40s.—*Raine's Auckland.*

P. 98. *Darlington unfit for receiving Henry VIII. with credit.*—1536, April 25. Lord Howard writes to Henry VIII. that he had told the Scotch in answer to their proposition that Newcastle should be the place of meeting between the two kings, that "your Majesty could not be furnished to your honour, neither with sufficient carriage, nor with victuals, nor lodging betwixt York and Newcastle."

Sessions of the Council of the North at Darlington.—1536, December 8. "Please it your Majesty to be advertised, that on the last day of September last past we began to sit at Darneton, in your county of Duresme, for th' administration of justice unto all your subjects in those north parts that would complain; and there continued daily for that purpose by the space of one whole month, where we were very well assisted by the presence of my Lord of Westmorelande, and also by Sir William Eure, knight, most part of all the same time; setting then in good stay and order divers and many causes between a great number of your subjects in those parts. And considering that there were no prisoners within the gaol at Duresme, and also that the plague then reigned sore in sundry places of your counties of Northumbrelande and Duresme, we thought it expedient not to call or make any assembly of your subjects together in any one place thereabouts (having no prisoners there to deliver) but have deferred the same until our next return into those parts after Easter next coming. . . . . At our being at Darneton, calling thither before us the Deputy Wardens of your west, east, and middle marches foranenst Scotlande, we in your Grace's name, with as good and sore monitions as we could devise, admonished them and every of them severally to look more surely and diligently unto their duties and charges on your borders than they have done in times past, and to spare no manner of person, but to do take and render justice to all subjects of both sides without respect of persons, as they and every of them would answer unto your Highness at their uttermost perils: which they plainly affirmed and promised to do." One of these deputy wardens says that at Darnton the Council "*dreadly* commanded" him to proceed to Scotlande foranent his charge.

Scotch Lords at Darlington.—In 1543, a special consultation with the Scotch lords was going on at Darneton. "My Lord Lieutenant" was also residing here in May of that yeare. In September a number of great personages are found here consulting on an invasion of 10,000 men to be made into Scotland, "for annoyance as they trust to God shall be done to Scotlande this winter by the West Marchers of Ynglande." They advised a frightful course of action in their "opinions."

It would be tedious to sum up all the business done at Darlington concerning the Borders. Yet it may be well to enumerate some of the noble and gentle personages then frequenting the place, and filling up the picture of departed pomp and circumstance. Foremost stands the bishop, the gentle Tunstal, who frequently occurs as residing at Darneton, in company oftentime with Charles Suffolk. The two in July, 1543, assure the king that the peace with Scotland on agreement for the match between the young Queen of Scots and Prince Edward of England should be proclaimed in this town "upon Monday," (the market day). Suffolk seems to have sometimes resided here by himself. We have also William Parr joining the Bishop and Suffolk; and the Bishop, Shrewsbury, and Sir Ralph Sadler. "We have (write the three latter in 1545), by proclamation and otherwise, stirred up all the bishopric here, and put them in such readiness for the better resistance of the Scots' malice, as they may set forth towards the Borders with all possible haste, as the case may require." And again—"The whole power of the bishopric here is preparing with all possible diligence to repair unto the Borders to minister a further aid and strength unto the wardens if the case shall so require." The same year Shrewsbury says, in reference to the victuals for an intended aid of foreigners to assist on the Borders, "as for all parts by north of Yorkshire, there can nothing be had to serve for this purpose, for I, th' Erle of Shrewsbury, cannot find in this country furniture sufficient for mine own household here." Shrewsbury was succeeded as Lieutenant General in the north by the Earl of Hertford, who is found here in the same year, 1545, with the Bishop and Ralph Sadler.

P. 231. *Plague.*—Hertford removed from Darlington to Newcastle, and in October, 1545, gives a characteristic notion of the former place. "The plague reigneth in many parts of Northumberland, and continueth yet still at Berwick, whereas most part of the people of the town are dead of the same, and now beginneth in this town of Newcastell; wherefore after I have discharged hence the strangers to London, which are to be 'cassyde', and taken order for th' establishing of the garrisons, which shall continue, and dispatched the rest; having tarried here in this town longer than I would have done for any gain, but only in respect of my duty for th' order and accomplishment of these things, I do intend to remove hence to Dernton, and so to Yorke; for at Dernton we cannot remain conveniently, as well for that *the sickness hath been there of late, and not yet ceased,* as also for that no kind of honest furniture or provision is to be had there, for ourselves nor for our horses, by reason that *all these three years past the Lieutenant and Council wiih their trains have lien there almost continually*, and also the strangers, now and heretofore passing through the town, and also lying there, have made all victuals, both horsemeat and man's meat, so scarce and dear thereabouts, that no convenient provision is to be made there for our furniture any time, ne yet do I know any other place meet or convenient for us to remove unto at this present in these north 'parties' nearer than Yorke."

*** Since printing p. 327, steps have been taken to erect a separate building for the purposes of the Darlington Mechanics' Institution. The foundation stone was laid on the 12th of May, 1853, by Miss Pease of Feethams. The estimated cost is upwards of £2,000; and it is gratifying to observe that no less than £700 of this sum has been subscribed by *two* ladies:—Miss Pease contributing £400, and Mrs. Barclay £300. The site is in Skinnergate, and has been purchased of the Earl of Beverley. The style of the building necessarily assumes nothing beyond the merit of plain Palladian usefulness. Mr. Joseph Sparkes of Darlington is the architect, and has contrived a Lecture Hall capable of holding six hundred persons, with a suitable Reading Room, Library, Class Rooms, Committee Room, and Residence for an attendant.

LITTLE HAUGHTON, OR REDHALL.

This manor is so much mixed with the territorial history of Darlington, and so contiguous as a seat, that I am induced to trace its descent with some minuteness.

It first appears as a leasehold for years under the Bishop. "In Little Halghton [var. Halughton]," says Boldon Book, "are five men, who hold 8 acres conjointly, and each a toft and croft, and they render 5*s.* 6*d.*, and in another part they render for 40 acres a mark. Adam de Selby holds to farm the demesne of the same place, with a stock of 2 ploughs and 2 harrows, and with the sown acres, as is contained in the chirograph,* with *the grange and enclosed court*, and he renders 8 marks, and he shall find at Derlyngton a litter for the Lord Bishop in his journies; and moreover he keeps at his own charge the houses and the court-house of the Lord Bishop at Derlyngton, and whatever is brought thither, in return for a certain parcel of tillage *(cultura)* called Hacdale, which he holds in the field of Derlyngton, opposite the hall on the east side across the water. The pasture with the sheep is in the hand of the Bishop, but Adam, if he shall choose, shall be able to have in the same pasture 100 sheep, but only so long as he shall hold the said farm."

Here is a manor. The demesne or lord's part leased out. The sheep-walk retained. Within the demesne is the grange; and around it the *curia clausa*, or yard, enclosed with a wall or hedge, and no doubt here, as in many other places, with a ditch. Within it was every convenience for the inhabitants of the farm, their animals, implements and produce. The arrangement is very perfect at Wardley near Jarrow, where the Prior had a grange, the moat remaining deep and fine. At little Haughton it is much decayed, but the great square of mound and moat is still very visible in the field adjacent to the present farm house of Redhall. And to the east and south smaller enclosures appear, perhaps the tofts of the other tenants, who would naturally cluster round the means of safety. At the north east corner of the main square is a hollow. Loads of material have been led to it, but they always settle down after a season. It is said to make the entrance to a passage which leads northward to a tumulus standing in the next field close to the Skerne, and at the side of which, next to the river, was a well.

According to some copies of Boldon Book, the smith of Darlington provided the ironwork for the ploughs of Little 'Halton;' but the passage seems an addition.

* Here an indenture of lease.

Between 1183 and 1194, Bishop Pudsey, who was nephew to King Stephen, granted to William-fitz-William-fitz-Stephen the king, Little Halcton with all its appurtenances, to hold by free service of fifth part of a knight's fee, honourably, &c., as *any other of his barons* held other land in his bishoprick. All freeholders in capite were originally termed barons.

In the list of knights present at the battle of Lewes, in 1264, added to the auditor's copy of Boldon Buke, we have "Rauff de Middleton a Petit Halghton." The later corrupt copy, said to be found in Lord Conyers' study, agrees in substance:—"Sir Ralph Middleton de Halton."

In 1403, Sir Richard le Scrop, 1st Lord Scrope of Bolton, died. He was the hero of the Scrope and Grosvenor controversy, and at Hatfield's survey held Little Halghton by 6*d*, or a pair of spurs, on St. Cuthbert's day in September. His grandson, Lord Richard, died young, about 1420, seised of the manor of Little Haughton, which contained 30 oxgangs, *each of* 15 *acres*, and each worth 9*s*. 9½*d*. per annum, by knights' service, suit of court once a fortnight, and a pair of spurs on the nativity of St. John Baptist, or 3*s*. 4*d*. His son, Lord Henry, died in 1459, possessed of Little Haughton, *alias* Haughton field juxta Derlyngton,* and leaving Lord John le Scrope of Bolton his heir, and, amongst other children, Robert le Scrope. Between 1476 and 1483, Alexander Cressener (who must have been trustee under some family arrangement) enfeoffs (by license of Bishop Dudley) the manors of Little Halghton and Highley Hall,† (the latter held of the Earl of Westmoreland as of the manor of Raby) with some smaller Durham properties, on Robert le Scrope and Catherine [Zouch] his wife, and Robert's issue male, remainder to John le Scroope, knt., of Bolton. Catherine survived, and on her death in 1515 an inquisition found that the manor of Little Halghton was held of the Bishop by fealty and a pair of spurs or 6*d*., that it was worth per annum beyond reprizes 13*l*. 6*s*. 8*d*.; and that it descended (Robert dying sans issue male) to Henry le Scroope, knt., Lord le Scroope of Bolton, as cousin [grandson] of John named in the feoffment.‡ Robert being seised in fee tail but Catherine only as free tenant, the manor is mentioned in the inquisition on Henry, the father of Henry last named, in 1509,§ Robert then being dead. The Henry who regained possession had a son, John Lord Scrope, who by will, 1548, leaves property in Little Houghton, Heghlie, Winston, &c., (he had possessions in 55 places), to his heir Henry le Scrope. This Henry had a sister Elizabeth, who took 300 marks by her father's will.‖ She married Thomas Pudsey, of Bolton and Bardford, esq., and to him the manor seems to have been alienated. He died in 1568.

The Pudseys made several small grants, which were partially, at all events, purchased up by succeeding owners. In 1582, William Pudsey, esq., of Bolton, Barford, and Mortham, in Yorkshire, (son of Thomas) granted to George Pudsey, of Walworth, gent., (a younger son, if I recollect the pedigree rightly) his messuage of Haughton field. In 1587 George, then of Stapleton, granted his chief messuage in Haughton field to John Barnes, L.L.D., Rector of Haughton, who had purchased the adjoin-

* Surtees.

† Heighley Hall, par. Winston, belonged to Scrope *of Masham*. Robert's mother was a daughter but not an heiress of that house, and I assume that Heighley was her marriage portion.

‡ Clervaux archives. § Surtees. ‖ Fryar MSS., G. B. R.

ing estate of Hundon closes, in Bondgate manor, of the Killinghalls.* Hundon closes, in some family disputes, after the Rector's death, in 1590, were conceded to his nephew Timothy Barnes, who alienated to the Forsters. But the manor under consideration fell to his two daughters Anne and Margaret, to whom, in 1591, there was a pardon for purchasing from their father the manor of Little Haughton or Haughton fields. Anne, the eldest, married William Place, gent., and the inquisition of 1599, after her death, contains half of the manor, and of Freth moore, &c., parcel of the manor, all held of the bishop in capite by a pair of spurs, or 6*d.*, and worth yearly beyond reprizes, 6*l.* Her sister Margaret, the wife of William Lambton, esq., of Stainton and Haughton field, was her heir, and her inquisition post mortem of 1630 gives the same closes in entirety. Of this Mrs Lambton, of *Red House*, Charles I. required 15*l.* in 1625. At that time he demanded of his richest subjects a loan, "doubting not but that, this being the first time he had required anything in this kind, he should receive such a testimony of good affection with such alacrity and readiness as might make the same so much the more acceptable, seeing he required but that of some, which few men would deny a friend, and had a mind resolved to expose all his earthly fortune for preservation of the general."† Of course the lady had to pay, for after Henry VIII.'s time such demands were considered imperative. They were badly or not at all repaid, and were one great cause of raising the kingdom to the ferment which ended in the destruction of royalty.

There were again two heiresses of the estate, and of the same names as before. Anne married Nicholas Chaytor, esq., of Croft, who re-annexed Hundon closes by purchase from the Forsters, and otherwise consolidated the estate. He lived at Haughton field. Margaret married John Killinghall, esq., of Middleton St. George. About 1666 the open fields were enclosed, and a partition took place then or sometime after 1657. The manor seems to have included the whole of that part of Haughton township south of the Skerne. Red House fell to the Chaytors; Forth Moor to the Killinghalls. The former, I apprehend, was so named from being formed of bright red brick in distinction to stone or post-and-pan-work Thus we have the Redhouse or New-hall, mentioned at Middleton in 1596; and what is more to the point, Redhall in Leeds, so called because it was the first such mansion that was built of brick, in 1628. From the same circumstance arises the saying —"As red as Rotherham College." There is indeed very fine clay on the Redhall estate, and a place is pointed out from whence it is said bricks were made. As to Forth Moor, I have very little doubt but that its name refers to the old causeway from Neasham through it (see p. 350). The causeway, passing along Lingfield Lane, crossed Haughton Bridge, which the old arch shews to have been only suited for horse traffic, and went west of the church through the piece of churchyard formerly quarried for sand and gravel. When a portion of that waste was given as a school-garden in 1814, the paved way was discovered at 18 inches below the surface, and 5 cart loads of its stones were sold to repair the highways. The road is visible in many places between Haughton and Ketton, and thence passed to Sedgefield.

* He also purchased of the same George half (for the Dycons of Haughton somehow had the other half) of le *Lyngefyelde* or Westefyelde parcel of the lands or tenements of the *Grange* called Halgheton feilde, *alias* Little Halgheton, containing 360 acres, or thereabouts.

† Clervaux archives.

Whenever the gravel was taken away, bones fell with the undermined soil.* In 1816, Mr Scotson measured one skeleton, and found it to be 6 feet 4 inches from the crown of the skull to the heel. These skeletons are connected by tradition with a direful struggle to prevent an enemy crossing the ford where the bridge now stands, and weapons of war are said to have been found. An unbeliever would see nothing more than an evidence of the cemetery having been a very early one.

In 1675, Sir William Chaytor, bart., (son of Nicholas) settles on his marriage Redhouse *alias* Halghton fields, and by the same description it was included in the Act of 1694, or 1695,† licensing a sale of the Chaytor estates, and sold in 1697-8 to Mr Robert Colling of Long Newton. In 1693, William Killinghall, esq., mortgaged Fourth Moore farm, parcel of the farm-hold belonging unto Haughton field house, otherwise the Riddhall, and in 1697, conveyed to Mr Colling. His son, Robert Colling, of Hurworth, mentions in his will (1744) Haughton Fields and Forth Moore. Forth Moor went to Leonard Colling, his younger son,‡ but eventually devolved upon Robert Colling, of Hurworth, at whose decease, in 1824, it was sold to Mr Hodgson, of Bishop Auckland. Redhall has descended from its purchaser Robert through a line of Robert Collings to the present owner, Robert Colling, esq., of Redhall.

The farm house of Redhall is just west of the moated enclosure previously noticed. It has a good old oak staircase. The handsome stone mansion near it, with its gables, was built in 1830, from the designs of P. W. Wyatt, esq., of London. With a picturesque outline, it combines interior comfort of arrangement, without elaboration of ornament; solid, but not heavy. Mr Wyatt's genius prompted a plan upon the spot, and on the spur of the moment.

* Inf. Mr Scotson. † Clervaux archives.

‡ Abstract of Forth Moor Title. Allan archives. R. H. A.

+SIGILLVM:COMMVNE:DE DERNINGTVN

LIST OF ILLUSTRATIONS.

PLATES, &c.

TABULAR PEDIGREES.

WOODCUTS.

IN DIVISION VI. AND ADDENDA.

IN THE PEDIGREES OF ALLAN, &c.

IN THE PEDIGREES OF HILTON.

IN THE PEDIGREES OF CLERVAUX, &c.

	Drawn by	*Engraved by*	*Presented by*
Clervaux Crest	The Author	Cave & Son ..	J. Fenwick, Esq.
Seals of Clervaux and Chaytor	The Author	Jewitt	J. Fenwick, Esq.
Seal of John Clervaux	The Author	Jewitt	J. Fenwick, Esq.
Arms of Sir Richard Clervaux, formerly on his Mansion at Croft, and now in Croft Church	The Author	Cave & Son ..	J. Fenwick, Esq.
Clervaux Badge	The Author	Jewitt	R. H. Allan, Esq.
Autograph of Sir Richard Clervaux	The Author	Richardson ..	J. Fenwick, Esq.
Boss of Arms of Killinghall ..	The Author	Jewitt	R. H. Allan, Esq.
Hylton Arms, on Hylton Chapel	Sir C. Sharp		W. H. Brockett, Esq.
Autograph of John Clervaux ..	The Author	Richardson ..	J. Fenwick, -Esq.
Seal of same	The Author	Jewitt	J. Fenwick, Esq.
Conclusion of Clervaux Cartulary	The Author	Jewitt	J. Fenwick, Esq.
Chaytor Arms on grant of them	The Author	Jewitt	J. Fenwick, Esq.
New Arms granted to Chaytor	J. Storey..	Utting	J. Fenwick, Esq.
Seal (double size) of Sir William Chaytor	The Author	Cave & Son ..	J. Fenwick, Esq.
Arms of John Fenwick, Esq., and Shields, and allied families ..	The Author	Jewitt	Mrs. Fenwick.
Seal of Henry Percy, Earl of Northumberland	Blore (in Surtees) .	Jewitt	J. Fenwick, Esq.
Seal of Ralph Neville, the first and great Earl of Westmorland	Blore (in Surtees).	Jewitt	J. Fenwick, Esq.
Percy Badge of the Crescent ..		Cave & Son ..	J. Fenwick, Esq.
Neville Badge of *b. b.* (Bertram Bulmer)	The Author	Jewitt	J. Fenwick, Esq.
Neville Badge of the Dun Bull from Raby	G. Ornsby (in Sharp's memorials)	Jewitt	J. Fenwick. Esq.
Fenwick Arms			J. Fenwick, Esq.

GENERAL INDEX.

FINIS.

DARLINGTON :
PRINTED AT THE "TIMES" OFFICE,
CENTRAL BUILDINGS.